D1523146

SPANISH AMERICAN WOMEN WRITERS

SPANISH AMERICAN WOMEN WRITERS

A Bio-Bibliographical Source Book

Edited by DIANE E. MARTING

GREENWOOD PRESS
NEW YORK
WESTPORT, CONNECTICUT
LONDON

Library of Congress Cataloging-in-Publication Data

Spanish American women writers : a bio-bibliographical source book /
  edited by Diane E. Marting.
     p. cm.
  Includes bibliographical references.
  ISBN 0–313–25194–0 (lib. bdg. : alk. paper)
    1. Spanish American literature—Women authors—Bio-bibliography.
  I. Marting, Diane E.
  Z1609.L7S6   1990
  [PQ7081]
  016.8609′9287—dc20   89–27283

British Library Cataloguing in Publication Data is available.

Library of Congress Catalog Card Number: 89–27283
ISBN: 0–313–25194–0

First published in 1990

Greenwood Press, 88 Post Road West, Westport, Connecticut 06881
An imprint of Greenwood Publishing Group, Inc.

Printed in the United States of America

The paper used in this book complies with the
Permanent Paper Standard issued by the National
Information Standards Organization (Z39.48–1984).

10 9 8 7 6 5 4 3 2 1

CONTENTS

Preface   ix

Acknowledgments   xi

Introduction   xv

Delmira Agustini (Uruguay)
by Ivette López Jiménez   1

Claribel Alegría (Nicaragua, El Salvador)
by Nancy Saporta Sternbach   9

Isabel Allende (Chile)
by Linda Gould Levine   20

Albalucía Angel (Colombia)
by Raymond Leslie Williams   31

María Luisa Bombal (Chile)
by Lucía Guerra Cunningham   41

Marta Brunet (Chile)
by Mary G. Berg   53

Fanny Buitrago (Colombia)
by Teresa R. Arrington   64

Silvina Bullrich (Argentina)
by Erica Frouman-Smith   72

Julia de Burgos (Puerto Rico)
by Diana Vélez   85

Mercedes Cabello de Carbonera (Peru)
by Mercedes Mazquiarán de Rodríguez   94

Lydia Cabrera (Cuba)
by Ada Ortúzar-Young   105

Nellie Campobello (Mexico)
by Catherine Nickel   117

Julieta Campos (Cuba, Mexico)
by María-Inés Lagos-Pope   128

Rosario Castellanos (Mexico)
by Maureen Ahern   140

Madre Castillo (Colombia)
by Stacey Schlau   156

Rosario Ferré (Puerto Rico)
by Margarite Fernández Olmos   165

Sara Gallardo (Argentina)
by Norma Beatriz Grasso   176

Griselda Gambaro (Argentina)
by Sandra Messinger Cypess   186

Elena Garro (Mexico)
by Anita Stoll   199

Gertrudis Gómez de Avellaneda (Cuba)
by Hugh A. Harter   210

Juana Manuela Gorriti (Argentina)
by Mary G. Berg   226

Luisa Josefina Hernández (Mexico)
by María Elena de Valdés   241

Sara de Ibáñez (Uruguay)
by Monique J. Lemaître León   254

Juana de Ibarbourou (Uruguay)
by Evelyn Uhrhan Irving   261

Sor Juana Inés de la Cruz (Mexico)
by Julie Greer Johnson   272

Claudia Lars (El Salvador)
by Amanda Plumlee   282

Marta Lynch (Argentina)
by Birgitta Vance   292

Clorinda Matto de Turner (Peru)
by Mary G. Berg   303

María Luisa Mendoza (Mexico)
by Magdalena Maiz and Luis H. Peña   316

Gabriela Mistral (Chile)
by Carmelo Virgillo   330

Nancy Morejón (Cuba)
by Yvonne Captain-Hidalgo   341

Carmen Naranjo (Costa Rica)
by Patricia Rubio   350

Silvina Ocampo (Argentina)
by Melvin S. Arrington, Jr.   360

Victoria Ocampo (Argentina)
by Doris Meyer   371

Eunice Odio (Costa Rica)
by Rima de Vallbona   382

Yolanda Oreamuno (Costa Rica)
by Arlene Schrade   394

Olga Orozco (Argentina)
by Elba Torres de Peralta   407

Teresa de la Parra (Venezuela)
by Gabriella Ibieta   415

Violeta Parra (Chile)
by Marjorie Agosín   427

Cristina Peri Rossi (Uruguay)
by Gabriela Mora   436

Alejandra Pizarnik (Argentina)
by Ana María Fagundo   446

Josefina Plá (Paraguay)
by Linda Britt   453

Syria Poletti (Argentina)
by Susana Hernández-Araico   461

Elena Poniatowska (Mexico)
by Beth E. Jörgensen   472

Magda Portal (Peru)
  by Daniel R. Reedy   483

Armonía Somers (Uruguay)
  by Nora Erro-Orthmann   493

Alfonsina Storni (Argentina)
  by María A. Salgado   501

Marta Traba (Argentina, Colombia)
  by Celia Correas de Zapata   513

Salomé Ureña de Henríquez (Dominican Republic)
  by Lizabeth Paravisini-Gebert   522

Luisa Valenzuela (Argentina)
  by Sharon Magnarelli   532

Indian Women Writers of Spanish America
  by Nancy Gray Díaz   546

Latina Writers in the United States
  by Norma Alarcón   557

The Latin American Woman Writer: A Bibliography of
Bibliographies and General Criticism   569

Appendix A: List of Authors by Birth Date   577

Appendix B: List of Authors by Country   581

Appendix C: List of Authors by Genre   585

Title Index   591

Subject Index   625

About the Editor, Contributors, and Translators   635

PREFACE

This volume, which was enormously complex to develop, requiring contributions from over one hundred scholars of Spanish American literature who served as contributors of the entries, translators, and readers or commenters on manuscript drafts—often in more than one such capacity—is rather simply described. It consists of analytical and bibliographical studies of fifty of the most important women writers of Latin America from the seventeenth century to the present, representing most Spanish-speaking American nations and a variety of literary genres. Each entry provides biographical and career information, discusses the major themes in the body of work, and surveys criticism, ending with a detailed bibliography of works by the writer, works available in translation if applicable, and works about the writer. In many cases, the bibliographies are selected listings rather than complete ones. Two general chapters complete the volume: One examines the "oral testimony" of contemporary Indian women outside of the literary tradition, whose words have been recorded by others. The other surveys Latina writers in the United States, an area not otherwise encompassed in the scope of this volume. Also included is a bibliography of reference works and general criticism on the Latin American woman writer and title and subject indexes. Appendixes classify the writers in the main body of the work by birth date, country, and genre.

The introduction to this book was one of the more difficult things I have ever had to write because I wanted to say something new and different about Spanish American women writers since finishing *Women Writers of Spanish America* (Greenwood, 1987). Yet many of the facts remain the same as they were ten years ago: lack of materials, lack of information, lack of translations, even lack of original texts—but no lack of talent among the writers. Furthermore, the art of introduction-writing is not particularly conducive to originality. Nevertheless,

I have experimented a bit with the form of parts of the introduction in the hope of communicating more completely my ideas.

The first part of the Introduction, "The Passion: A Prose Poem," freely associates themes and images with/about/for this literature. The section "From Annotations to Essays" explains the history and process of this collaborative effort, my conflicts regarding this type of book, and the problems surmounted by its many excellent contributors. Next, "Sisters of the Word: A Survey of Themes and Issues" traces some feminist concerns that recur in this book, providing commentary, analysis, suggestions for further research, and hypotheses to be tested.

A Note on Titles. Spanish words and titles are translated if they are not immediately obvious to someone unfamiliar with the Spanish language. A translated title does not indicate that the work actually has been translated into English unless that work appears in the appended bibliography in the section on writings available in English translation.

Asterisks following proper names in the entries indicate that that person appears as a separate entry in this work. Spanish American women writers' names are alphabetized in this book in the same way that they can be found in the Library of Congress (or libraries that use similar systems). This system follows general rules from Hispanic usage, alphabetizing under the first last name, whether or not the last names are hyphenated. Other names are usually to be found under the final last name, unless hyphenated, as is usual in the United States.

ACKNOWLEDGMENTS

The joy of a cooperative venture such as this one lies in the contacts with others who have the same goals and common motives, but different information and opinions. Trying to express this joyful experience, however, is frustrating for the writer because the acknowledgment is never enough to truly thank the people involved and frustrating for the reader because it results in lists of names that are not very pleasurable to read. My only hope is that the reader will become aware that this book is not the result of just one person's work, nor of one person with the contributors whose names appear with the entries; but of myself, the contributors, the translators, the readers, my friends, the contributors' friends, bibliographers, Marilyn Brownstein, my editor at Greenwood Press, who suggested the idea for the book, and others.

The first stage in which a large number of people influenced the final shape of this book was in the selection of the fifty authors to be treated. Over fifty people answered my queries and voted for certain authors over others from a basic list I had suggested. Naomi Lindstrom was particularly helpful for her suggestion of the two general chapters, "Indian Women Writers of Spanish America" and "Latina Writers in the United States." The list of fifty authors went through a few minor modifications in the process of finding contributors but was basically set at this point. During the final stages of editing, the help of Mary G. Berg was crucial. Not only did she contribute three entries herself, but she also constantly provided me with bibliographical details unavailable to the contributors while I was abroad.

The following list names seventy-eight readers who commented on the entries in a cooperative spirit of help and reinforcement rather than one of mere acceptance or rejection. All of us are extremely grateful for their careful and time-consuming work. The number in parentheses refers to the number of entries read when more than one.

Marlene Acarón Ramírez, University of Puerto Rico at Mayagüez

Hugo Achugar, Northwestern University (Illinois)

Marjorie Agosín, Wellesley College (Massachusetts)

Raysa Amador, Adelphi University (New York)

Electa Arenal (2), University of Delaware, Newark

Melvin S. Arrington, Jr. (2), University of Mississippi

Teresa R. Arrington, University of Mississippi

Efraín Barradas, University of Massachusetts

Mary G. Berg (3), Harvard University Center for Literary and Cultural Studies

Linda Britt, University of Maine at Farmington

Yvonne Captain-Hidalgo, George Washington University (District of Columbia)

Dale Carter, California State University, Los Angeles

Cida S. Chase, Oklahoma State University

Daisy Cocco de Filippis, York College, CUNY

Sandra Cypess, University of Tennessee—Memphis

Gisela Dardón, California State University, Stanislaus

Inés Dölz-Blackburn, University of Colorado at Colorado Springs

Michael Scott Doyle, San Diego State University

Keith Ellis, University of Toronto

Nora Erro-Orthmann, Florida Atlantic University

Ana María Fagundo, University of California at Riverside

David William Foster, Arizona State University

Lucía Fox-Lockert, Michigan State University

Martha Paley Francescato (2), George Mason University (Virginia)

Marta Gallo, University of California, Santa Barbara

Delia Galván, John Carroll University (Ohio)

Elizabeth Garrels (2), Massachusetts Institute of Technology

Rita Geada, Southern Connecticut State University

Marlene Gottlieb, Lehman College, CUNY

Norma Beatriz Grasso (2), Stockton State College, Pomona (New Jersey)

Lucía Guerra Cunningham (2), University of California at Irvine

Gleider Hernández, Université du Quèbec à Chicoutimi (Canada)

Rosario Hiriart, writer, Scarsdale (New York)

Leo J. Hoar, Jr., Fordham University (New York)

Evelyn Uhrhan Irving, Tennessee Technological University

ACKNOWLEDGMENTS

Tom Irving, Tennessee Technological University
Mary-Garland Jackson, Central Michigan University
Elena de Jongh, Florida International University
Amy Kaminsky (2), University of Minnesota
Patricia Klingenberg, Illinois Wesleyan University
Efraín Kristal, Harvard University
María-Inés Lagos-Pope, Washington University (Missouri)
Marvin A. Lewis, *Afro-Hispanic Review* (Missouri)
Naomi Lindstrom, University of Texas at Austin
Ivette López Jiménez, University of Puerto Rico at Bayamón
Ellen McCracken, University of Massachusetts at Amherst
Magdalena Maíz, Davidson College (North Carolina)
Z. Nelly Martínez, McGill University (Canada)
Irene Matthews, University of California at Davis
Adriana Méndez Rodenas, University of Iowa
Doris Meyer, Connecticut College
Hebe Beatriz Molina, Universidad Nacional de Cuyo (Argentina)
Gabriela Mora, Rutgers University, New Brunswick (New Jersey)
Mary Patricia Mosier, University of Houston (Texas)
Michèle Muncy, Rutgers University, Camden (New Jersey)
Graciela P. de Nemes, University of Maryland, College Park
Estrella B. Ogden, Villanova University (Pennsylvania)
Julian Palley, University of California, Irvine
Lisa Paravisini-Gebert, Lehman College, CUNY
Luis Peña, Davidson College (North Carolina)
Julieta Pinto, Universidad Nacional de Costa Rica
Ileana Renfrew, Northern Michigan University
Eliana S. Rivero, University of Arizona-Tucson
Asela Rodríguez de Laguna, Rutgers University, Newark (New Jersey)
Lorraine Elena Rosas (2), Wellesley College (Massachusetts)
Patricia Rubio, Skidmore College (New York)
María Salgado, University of North Carolina at Chapel Hill
Flora Schiminovich, Barnard College (New York)
Stacey Schlau, West Chester University (Pennsylvania)
Arlene Schrade, University of Mississippi
Elizabeth Starćevič, City College, CUNY
Jonathan Tittler, Cornell University (New York)
Luz María Umpierre (2), Rutgers University, New Brunswick (New Jersey)

L. Teresa Valdivieso, Arizona State University
Jeanne Vaughn, San José State University (California)
María Mercedes de Velasco (2), Fitchburg State College (Massachusetts)
Gloria Waldman, York College, CUNY
Hensley C. Woodbridge, Southern Illinois University

INTRODUCTION

The Passion

Women writing, writing it all. Writing because, writing in spite of, writing self.
   Writing over living, emotions over reasons.
Expectations, infectations, permutations, invitations, reception.
Translating the differences, transcending the commonalities, transferring the blame,
   transcoding the message, transplanting the hope.
Creativity, the nativity of. Clarice, Castellanos, Ana Cristina César,* Isabel Allende.
Diamond tongues speak to the *sea and you*. God, goddesses. Angst, frank, tanks,
   lanky soldiers.
Foremothers, rejections, encouragement. Mothers and fathers, brothers and sisters.
   Pessimism, optimism. Woman human female. Poet poetess. Judgment, fair, female,
   feminist.
Coinciding, co-inciting, coinhibiting, correlated, corrected.
Denounce, pronounce, announce. Political prisoners, masculine impunity, abuse of
   authority, taking back the word, slogans and seeing anew. Silence . . . speaking out,
   speaking in tongues, seeding.
Centered, marginal, centering, de-centering. Privilege, underprivileged. First world,
   third world, their world, my world.
Political, sabbatical, rabbinical, habitual, restrict-ual, breaking through, topical,
   mythical, *ensimismitical*.
Naming, listing, pointing the finger. Raising the question, suggesting the opposite, deconstructing the sign, constructing a monument to.
Asserting the female, manifesting a radical, mirroring an inner, recognizing an
   inevitable.

---

*Ana Cristina César is a young Brazilian poet who recently committed suicide.

Solitude, solicitous, solipsistic, solar, so far so good.
Lunar, the moon, lunátic, the attic, Jane Eyre, clean air, the Amazon, amazonian,
    ama-zone, love zone.
Difference, inference, infra rays, in how many ways.
Risk, frisk, tisk-tisk! frittering away at your, tittering at the brink, evaluating the
    literature, titillating abysm.
Participation, emancipation, collaboration.

Documenting the freedom of others to create
without creating oneself
is like taking a picture of wild horses running free
and hanging the photograph in a gallery

                                                                    Diane E. Marting

FROM ANNOTATIONS TO ESSAYS

The differences between this book and *Women Writers of Spanish America: An
Annotated Bio-Bibliography* (1987), its predecessor, is the desire here to produce
a work that goes more profoundly into the subject and thereby functions as more
than lists and brief reviews. The 1987 bibliography should be consulted for more
details about works themselves by Spanish American writers, whereas the present
volume gives more information about their biographies, themes and, for the first
time, about the criticism of their works.

   In the earlier bibliographic volume, the problem of selecting which writers to
include was one that I managed to avoid because the idea was to be as inclusive
as possible. I would have preferred to have had that option once again, but
practical limitations forbade such openness for this book from the start. To begin,
I chose a preliminary list of fifty writers, trying to avoid a monopoly of those
from the Southern Cone and Mexico, and attempting to include a mixture of
those who are well known and often studied in Spanish Departments with those
who are relatively unknown but have a great deal to contribute to the study of
feminism in literature. This early list was shared with contributors to the bibliography volume and other scholars who had published on Spanish American
women writers. Their suggestions enabled many modifications, including a better
ethnic balance among the chosen authors and a more historic picture of women's
writing in Spanish America as a whole. Of necessity, the result is still an imperfect
picture of the rich panorama, but I believe the project has in part fulfilled its
goal of selecting for treatment here from among the more prominent, more
accessible, and more feminist writers.

   The audience for *Spanish American Women Writers* differs slightly from that
of *Women Writers of Spanish America* in that the reader for the present book is
presumed to read some Spanish, although those who do not are not neglected
entirely. Extensive translations of titles and quotations as well as a listing of

published translations in each entry's bibliography were included with the monolingual in mind. By attempting to deal with the needs of the student, translator, and general reader in addition to the scholar, the entries respond to a lack of general reference works in the area of Spanish American literature.

The over fifty writers treated here (fifty in individual entries and others in the two collective articles) have had quite varied histories of reception, creating different exigencies for each contributor who needed to furnish a minimum standard of biographical and bibliographical information. For instance, when writing about the most famous authors, such as Sor Juana Inés de la Cruz (Mexico), Gertrudis Gómez de Avellaneda (Cuba), or Gabriela Mistral (Chile), the contributors needed to sort through a deluge of criticism. With writers previously famous but basically lost to the present generation of readers, such as Juana Manuela Gorriti (Argentina) or Sara de Ibáñez (Uruguay), sorting through the criticism and recovering texts often took on certain aspects of an archaeological dig. Other writers, such as Josefina Plá (Paraguay), have never received a global treatment of their work in English before, or extensive feminist analysis in English, such as Griselda Gambaro (Argentina), or a complete, chronological bibliography, such as Rosario Castellanos (Mexico). Whereas the rather rigid format of the entries has reduced their virtuoso nature, the ease with which the book can be consulted should compensate somewhat for the loss. In addition, the consistency attained in this way should make more readily apparent the areas in which the critical soil has been previously tilled versus those areas where there remains much untilled land.

SISTERS OF THE WORD: A PERSONAL SURVEY OF POLITICAL THEMES AND ISSUES

Introductions usually describe the critical essays contained in the book being introduced, but as editor of *Spanish American Women Writers* (*SAWW*), I feel I have already seen incorporated, either implicitly or explicitly, many of my own opinions and judgments. Even though I do not agree with every statement made in this book, if I were to comment on the entries again, it would be to praise unendingly the contributors for their research skills, writing, patience, and intellectual openness. So rather than providing a kind of second, prose table of contents, in which I would look back and comment on the entries themselves, I would like to look forward and contribute my own sketchy, idiosyncratic overview of the lives and works of the Spanish American writers studied. The entries in this book treat individually fifty Spanish American women writers, and others in the group entries on Indian and U.S. writers. Even if I do not mention all the writers/entries or give them each equal time, I hope that this personal survey will be helpful to the users of this book, before, during, and after they have consulted the entries of interest to them.

Biography

A good place to begin is with those writers who address the experiences of the woman writer. Sor Juana Inés de la Cruz (Mexico), in her famous autobiographical "Respuesta a Sor Filotea de la Cruz" ("Reply to Sor Filotea de la Cruz"), subtly shows the determination and defiance required of a girl or woman who wanted to read, write, and compose verses in seventeenth-century New Spain. Twentieth-century writers, like the Argentinean Victoria Ocampo in her multivolume work *Testimonios* (1935–1977; Testimonies) and in the editing of her journal *Sur*, and Rosario Castellanos (Mexico) in *Sobre cultura femenina* (1950; About female culture) and *Mujer que sabe latín . . .* (1973; A woman who knows Latin . . .), thoughtfully evoke their literary foremothers and the matrix of issues that those women represented. In Castellanos's farcical play, *El eterno femenino* (1975; *The Eternal Feminine*), she treats Western society's sexism humorously, ridiculing stereotyped figures, even those of the typical woman writer and woman reader/dilettante.

Most recently, the Puerto Rican writer Rosario Ferré has written about the connections between women artists' lives and works in an essay called "La autenticidad de la mujer en el arte" (The authenticity of the women artist, *Sitio a Eros*, 1980). She asserts that the outer, material problems of women artists are "en camino de resolverse" (on the way to being resolved) in comparison with the past; the exercise of the woman artist's inner freedom thus acquires a new priority in today's world. Ferré's premise should be questioned because Latin American women writers, like the men, are suffering from the hyperinflation, entrenched class differences, and economic stagnation afflicting their countries. But whether or not one discards Ferré's assumption, her concern with the imaginative freedom of women artists is a consideration of the utmost importance. Clearly, much work remains to be done to remove the inner barriers keeping some writers from producing their best works. For even when one is fighting for survival or against government censorship, it pays to explore one's own internal censors.

Yet Ferré argues in her essay that sexism still prevents women from having "coherent personalities" and that this prohibition has inevitably had a discernible, detrimental effect on the writings that women produce in comparison to men. In this, Ferré has forgotten that sexism distorts men's as well as women's writings. Although men and women are affected in different ways by sexism, it produces its effects strongly in both. If women were affected more negatively than men, as Ferré argues, then her measuring stick must be one skewed toward male values rather than female values. Women's lack of "integration," if it indeed exists, may be positive when measured on a different scale. There is some reason to believe that women's cultural differences from men may provide a key to avoiding some of the consequences of humanity's destruction of the environment, overregulation and excessive institutionalization, bellicose attitudes, and other elements of patriarchy's legacy. For instance, one study in the bibliography of general criticism at the end of *Spanish American Women Writers* which treats thematic differences between women's and men's writings is Francine Masiello's interesting article on the 1920s avant-garde novel. Masiello finds that the women's novels deny the legitimacy of the patriarchal family as a model for values and virtues, and demonstrate a search for "lateral relations," of equality in brothers, sisters, friends, and lovers. Yet the differences Masiello found between men and women novelists may not be biologically determined by the artists' sex; they result from historical tendencies, conscious choices, and unconscious intertextualities that divide the works produced by men and women. The truly creative moment, whether experienced by women or men, is the act of exercising one's inner freedom. Therefore, it is also the act of going beyond the limits of sexism and racism, even beyond the limits of the individual self.

In their writings on women writers, Sor Juana, Castellanos, Ocampo, and Ferré have fought against the prejudices that have weighed them down. Their weaponry has consisted of an international, sophisticated sense of culture and of sexual justice, and their imagination, qualities and faculties they share with many other writers. The Peruvians Clorinda Matto de Turner and Magda Portal have also written nonfiction about women, but in more general terms than as writers or intellectuals. They emphasize women as political individuals, thinkers, voters, and citizens. The ideas of Albalucía Angel (Colombia), Julia de Burgos (Puerto Rico), Julieta Campos (Cuba-Mexico), and Alfonsina Storni (Argentina), to mention only four names, cannot be fully understood without divining the nature of their critique of men, sexism, and patriarchal society, because these are the themes featured in many of their literary creations. In a certain general way, of course, all fifty-plus writers studied in *SAWW* are contributing to the debate about women writers simply by producing their literature.

One of the questions frequently asked in the United States about the lives of Spanish American writers is whether or not they are feminists. Many of those studied in *SAWW* were indeed committed in their lives and works to changing gender structures and ideologies in their times. But classifying an individual as 'feminist' is complicated by the differences between Latin American and North American feminist movements and between twentieth-century and earlier ways of thinking. It is not an exaggeration to say that the location of the line that defines feminism from other beliefs varies in each of the countries of Spanish America. As a result, only in the broadest sense—as a consciousness of injustice based on gender and sexual identity—can one speak accurately and meaningfully to North American readers of these writers' feminisms. But whether identified as feminists or not, Spanish American women writers have tended more and more over the last twenty years to recognize themselves as part of a women's community, probably for reasons of emotional and spiritual survival.

Since Spanish American literary magazines are few in number and books are expensive luxuries for the well-to-do, income from writing them has been available to only a limited number of writers. The difficulties that all Latin American writers face in living from their writing, and the additional obstacles faced by women in earning a living, may explain some similarities in *SAWW*'s biographies. The profession that many women writers have chosen as an alternative, if this volume is an indication, is newspaper journalism. Among the twentieth-century writers studied in *SAWW*, the following have practiced journalism for long periods or sporadically throughout their careers: Isabel Allende (Chile); Silvina Bullrich (Argentina); Julia de Burgos (Puerto Rico); Rosario Ferré (Puerto Rico); María Luisa Mendoza (Mexico); Nancy Morejón (Cuba); Yolanda Oreamuno (Costa Rica); Alejandra Pizarnik (Argentina); Elena Poniatowska (Mexico); Alfonsina Storni (Argentina); and Luisa Valenzuela (Argentina). The teaching profession has also been a favorite, as well as a tradition that began well before this century. The Nobel Prize-winning poet Chilean poet Gabriela Mistral taught before beginning her diplomatic career, and the Argentinean poet Alfonsina Storni kept poverty at bay for a period through this means. Some writers have worked also or instead with arts other than literature. Storni, a journalist and a teacher, performed as an actress and a singer when young. Violeta Parra (Chile) gained fame as a performer of her own songs, and Albalucía Angel (Colombia) has performed as a singer. Nellie Campobello (Mexico) was also a dancer; Marta Traba (Argentina-Colombia) is most famous as a critic of painting and sculpture.

Exile, both voluntary and imposed, has occurred frequently in the lives of writers from the region up until the present day. Among the women writers examined in *SAWW*, temporary, voluntary exile is only slightly more common than permanent, involuntary expatriation. María Luisa Bombal (Chile), Lydia Cabrera (Cuba), and Luisa Valenzuela (Argentina), in addition to many of those listed in the chapter on Latina writers, were born in Spanish America but have lived or live in the United States. Claribel Alegría, Eunice Odio, and Yolanda Oreamuno are twentieth-century Central Americans who have lived in various countries within the Central American region. Two European-born writers included here emigrated to Latin America: Josefina Plá (Spain-Paraguay) and Syria Poletti (Italy-Argentina). The following count among those Latin Americans who make or made their homes in Europe: Albalucía Angel (Colombia); Fanny Buitrago (Colombia); Elena Garro (Mexico); Gertrudis Gómez de Avellaneda (Cuba); and Cristina Peri Rossi (Uruguay). Juana Manuela Gorriti and Marta Traba, both from Argentina, lived as virtual gypsies in many South American countries.

Themes

Thematic similarities abound in the works of the writers studied here. Not surprisingly, certain areas affected by the condition of being female frequently crop up as *topoi*. For instance, women in general are poorer than men within the family unit and in most professions, and occupations in which women predominate tend to pay poorly. Although some writers were independently wealthy women who did not have to worry about earning a living, poverty, either relative or absolute, has been a repeated theme in a large number of women's works. In poetry, Julia de Burgos (Puerto Rico), Eunice Odio (Costa Rica), and Gabriela Mistral (Chile), and in prose, Elena Poniatowska (Mexico), Magda Portal (Peru), and the Indian writers Domitila Barrios (Bolivia) and Rigoberta Menchú (Guatemala), among others, have exposed with dignity, sensitivity, and at times with outrage, the economic plight and physical suffering caused by the lack of financial resources sufficient to feed one's family or to acquire an education.

The general topic of relations among women occurs in many short stories, poems, and novels by the authors studied here; the rich theme is beginning to be charted in criticism, as will be seen in some entries in *SAWW*. Homages to literary foremothers and poems of sisterly sentiment by the poorly named postmodernist poets (Storni, Agustini, Ibarbourou, et al.), for instance, would not have been appropriate to pursue very far here but have not been studied extensively elsewhere either. Sexual relations between women are treated sporadically by many writers, such as Armonía Somers (Uruguay), Luisa Valenzuela (Argentina), and Albalucía Angel (Colombia), and figure predominantly in the works of Alejandra Pizarnik (Argentina) and Cristina Peri Rossi (Uruguay). Female heterosexuality as a theme reigns in the early works of María Luisa Bombal (Chile) and Juana de Ibarbourou (Uruguay), and is sprinkled liberally throughout the opuses of Delmira Agustini (Uruguay), Julieta Campos (Mexico), Rosario Ferré (Puerto Rico), María Luisa Mendoza (Mexico), Eunice Odio (Costa Rica), Armonía Somers (Uruguay), and Luisa Valenzuela (Argentina).

Another repeated theme that can be seen from studying the entries in *Spanish American Women Writers* is that of family relationships, which vary in these writers' works with all the variety of the human family. Mothers and mothering is one important subdivision of the theme. Both Eunice Odio (Costa Rica) and Gabriela Mistral (Chile) wrote of wishing to be mothers, and in Mistral an almost divine aspect is attributed to maternity. The Mexican Nellie Campobello's 1937 *Las manos de Mamá*, recently published in English (*Cartucho and My Mother's Hands*, 1988), intimately portrays a mother in the midst of the Mexican Revolution. The title of *Mothers and Shadows* (1986), a posthumous translation of Marta Traba's first novel, *Conversación al sur* (1966), also places in relief the mother figure. The mother-daughter relationship is the featured theme in *Muerte por agua* (1965; Death by water), a novel by Julieta Campos (Cuba-Mexico).

Perhaps the most famous Spanish American woman poet to treat children as a topic was Chilean Gabriela Mistral. Claudia Lars (El Salvador) and Rosario Castellanos (Mexico) both wrote poetry using the names of their own children. In Spanish American women's fiction, the child narrator has been used for the most diverse literary purposes, from representing the innocent eye and the uncorrupted possibilities of humanity to incorporating cruelty and egoism in their pure form, as yet unadulterated by mature, civilizing sentiments. In Castellanos's early novel *Balún-Canán* (1957, translated as *The Nine Guardians*, 1958, 1959), the child narrator criticizes white racism against Indians and sexism within her family.

Child narrators in Argentinean Silvina Ocampo's fantastic and gothic stories offer a shocking means of mapping the unreal. The Argentinean Syria Poletti's portrait of female intergenerational communication and harmony provides an unusual image of women and girls that subverts the ageism that would pit the generations against one other. Gabriela Mora shows in her entry how Cristina Peri Rossi (Uruguay) attacks capitalism in her late prose by means of her characterization of poor street children. Fanny Buitrago (Colombia) portrays many orphans and abandoned children as characters in her works. (For a list of writers who wrote *for* children, see List of Authors by Genre in the Appendix.)

Indianist and indigenist themes appear in Spanish American literature from the time of the earliest writers of the colonial period, including Sor Juana Inés de la Cruz (Mexico). The bitter political confrontation between cultures that has been an unavoidable part of Latin America's multicultural richness has occupied many women's works. Rosario Castellanos (Mexico), in *Oficio de tinieblas* (1962; The practice of darkness), and Clorinda Matto de Turner (Peru), in *Aves sin nido* (1889; *Birds Without a Nest*, 1904) and other works, have contributed to the region's literary search for justice for its oppressed native peoples. Nancy Diaz' discussion of various Indian women ''writers'' contains contemporary oral accounts of today's realities. Domitila Barrios (Bolivia), Rigoberta Menchú (Guatemala), Basilia, Facundina and others have described their struggles for survival and for dignity to reporters, writers, and anthropologists in order to make known the governmental and police violence they have suffered or the way in which they experience their culture at the present moment. Despite their poverty and lack of formal education, these women articulate the forces that are mutilating their lives, at times at risk to themselves or at the cost of exile or imprisonment.

Literary treatment of blacks in Latin America began slightly later than that of Indians for obvious historical reasons, yet a strong body of work, with much written by women, has accumulated over the centuries. Among the women writers who can be found in bibliographies of black literature, Nancy Morejón (Cuba) and Julia de Burgos, a Puerto Rican mulatto, have complete entries devoted to them here. Among other studied writers who have written on black themes, two writers from Cuba, Lydia Cabrera in the twentieth century and Gertrudis Gómez de Avellaneda in the nineteenth century, stand out. Gómez de Avellaneda's novel *Sab* (1841) was banned in Cuba in its time because of the aggressiveness with which antislavery sentiments and Romantic ideas of justice were pursued.

Repressive regimes in the Southern Cone have motivated the exile of many Chilean, Argentinean, and Uruguayan writers and have spawned many literary accounts of torture and disappearances in the last twenty years. Much of Luisa Valenzuela's career, for example, from her early surreal stories to *Cola de lagartija* (1983; *The Lizard's Tail*, 1983), portrays terror in Argentina. Griselda Gambaro's plays often articulate the dilemma of those confronted with institutional violence, and although most of her works have universalized and dramatized texts and contexts, they were created against the backdrop of her experiences in Argentina. Isabel Allende (Chile) and Cristina Peri Rossi (Uruguay) also figure prominently among those who treat this subject. Like Avellaneda's *Sab*, Allende's international bestseller *La casa de los espíritus* (1982; *The House of the Spirits*, 1985) was banned and only available in Chile clandestinely for several years after its publication.

In several countries of Spanish America, violence against those participating in the revolts of 1968 became the subject of major novels. Two Mexican novels treat this theme: Elena Poniatowska's *La noche de Tlatelolco* (1971; translated as *Massacre in Mexico*, 1975) and María Luisa Mendoza's *Con él, conmigo, con nosotros tres* (1973; With him, with me, with us three). The Colombian Albalucía Angel's *Estaba la pájara pinta sentada en el verde limón* (1975; The painted bird sitting in the lime tree) shows the convergence, for a whole generation of Colombian young people and intellectuals, of the student movement with La Violencia, an historical period of violence in Colombia often interpreted as lasting up to the present. Experimentation in style and form has characterized treatments of this theme.

Revolution or organized rebellion has appeared as a positive element primarily, but not exclusively, in Cuban and Mexican works. The mother, the daughter, or the lover who had witnessed men fighting for a cause in these works sometimes picks up a gun herself, sometimes leads the men to fight, sometimes takes over in order to end a battle. For example, Nancy Morejón stands firm as an ally of post-Revolutionary Cuba and an unabashed critic of the United States in her poetry. Among Mexicans, Nellie Campobello has fictionalized her experiences during the Mexican Revolution that began when she was a child. Elena Poniatowska's testimonial novel *Hasta no verte, Jesús mío* (1969; *Until We Meet Again*, 1987), offers an account of the life of Jesusa Palancares, a woman whose life story traverses the Revolutionary period. Elena Garro's famous first novel, *Los recuerdos del porvenir* (1963; *Recollections of Things to Come*, 1969, 1986), plays with the nature of time against the historical background of the Cristero Rebellion in post-Revolutionary Mexico.

Nevertheless, a vision of peace has become associated more closely with women's literature around the world than one of rebellions and revolutions. According to this view, women's literature tends to see war not as differentiating "between the men and the boys," that is, not as a spiritual testing ground, but more a time and a place that kills both men and boys indiscriminately. The prolific prose writer, Juana Manuela Gorriti, a nineteenth-century Argentinean activist in politics and an outspoken leader, wrote about the devastating effects of war on individuals and communities. The Uruguayan Sara de Ibáñez pleads in hermetic verses for reason before a nuclear holocaust ends the world. Gabriela Mistral (Chile) not only wrote of orphans and war refugees, universalizing them in her poems, but in her life she also donated money and time to help the victims of the Spanish Civil War. The contemporary poet Claribel Alegría mourns for those massacred and those surviving in war-torn El Salvador.

Religious feelings and devotion have inspired poetry on metaphysical themes by Gertrudis Gómez de Avellaneda (Cuba), Juana de Ibarbourou (Uruguay), and

Gabriela Mistral (Chile), among others, whereas not quite as orthodox a treatment of metaphysics can be found in the verses of Eunice Odio (Costa Rica) and Olga Orozco (Argentina). Religious writings within traditional Catholicism can be seen in the works of Madre Castillo (Colombia) and Sor Juana Inés de la Cruz (Mexico), both of whom lived in convents for extended periods of time. The nineteenth-century Peruvian feminist Clorinda Matto de Turner has dramatized the need for clerical reform in *Aves sin nido* (1889) and *Indole* (1891). Religion in its syncretic Afro-Cuban forms has been the repeated subject of Cuban Lydia Cabrera's fiction and nonfiction. On the other hand, the Costa Rican prose writer Carmen Naranjo is roundly antireligious in her stories and novels; Armonía Somers (Uruguay), Claribel Alegría (Nicaragua-El Salvador), and Luisa Valenzuela (Argentina) have shocked more than a few readers with their unorthodox use of religious symbols.

Contemporary North American feminism is involved in changing attitudes not only about sexism, but a myriad of other issues that unfairly discriminate between or that harm people. Feminists in general combat poverty and war and are exploring spirituality in nontraditional ways, for example, three themes discussed above. Some of the prejudices being fought by feminists are well known such as those against lesbians and homosexuals (heterosexism), blacks, Indians, and other people of color (racism), and the poor and underprivileged (classism). Feminism is famous for its concern with the structure of the family unit. As we have seen, these issues and attitudes have often been themes in the literature of Spanish American women writers as well. Others of feminism's efforts have been less recognized, however, such as its recent work to diminish the prejudice against and fear of the handicapped (able-bodyism) and the sick. Yet these issues, too, have appeared in some Spanish American women writers' works.

The Mexican novelist Elena Poniatowska, for instance, wrote a work of testimonial literature, *Gaby Brimmer* (1979), in conjunction with Gaby Brimmer herself, a victim of cerebral palsy. For the critic Amy Kaminsky, Poniatowska's and Brimmer's book has explored in new ways the concepts of the body-mind division, sexuality, and dependence/independence for women. (See the Poniatowska bibliography for this and other articles on her works.) Susana Hernández-Araico describes the thematic importance of the social experiences of women and girls who have minor physical impairments or slight deformities in Argentinean Syria Poletti's works (including some for children).

Criticism and Other Tools

In general, Spanish American women writers are becoming known in the United States for the first time, particularly with the popularity of writers such as Isabel Allende (Chile), Luisa Valenzuela (Argentina), and Elena Poniatowska (Mexico) in the late 1980s. Within Spanish America, the distribution of women's works has frequently been limited to within their countries of origin, as has been the case with all but a few exceptional men's works as well. Yet with women writers, there is an additional problem of little public recognition and general knowledge of their works, since most Spanish American countries have not yet experienced the publishing boom in women's books that the United States has. The availability of most literature in Latin American bookstores specializing in the humanities is surprisingly haphazard, except for the fact that women writers' works seem more neglected than most.

The so-called Boom in Latin American letters has recently seen the creation of an international market within the region as well as greatly increased speed and frequency with which works are translated and published in other languages. The number of writers, both men and women, who have benefited as yet from this situation is quite limited but seems to be improving. As of 1989, the only woman writer to have published a best seller both within Latin America and abroad is Isabel Allende (Chile). But such historic firsts as Allende's publishing success may have a positive effect not only on the availability of her works in the future but also on that of other women's works. Until the time comes when there will be equal consideration for writers of equal talent regardless of gender, however, one may still find it hard to find many of the original works and the books and articles of criticism mentioned in the bibliographies of *Spanish American Women Writers*, except in research libraries and private collections.

Many scholarly, critical, and bibliographical tasks remain to be accomplished, even related to the best known writers in this collection. Only recently has feminist criticism of canonized authors begun to surface; more often than not, pioneering articles have served to indicate how much still remains undiscovered about the issues of gender and power in well-known literary works. Another example of the kind of endeavors needed is the prose and journalism of poets Alfonsina Storni (Argentina) and Julia de Burgos (Puerto Rico), which need to be collected and made available to scholars of their poetry, instead of languishing in the original periodicals until lost forever. Certain historical periods and countries have tended to monopolize the pages of critical journals in the United States; studies of Spanish American women writers from the eighteenth century are hard to find, for example. From this period, only Madre Castillo (Colombia) has an entry devoted to her here. In terms of themes, sexual identification, colonialism/imperialism, women's suffrage, abortion, the democratization of power, and the nature of utopian visions number among those that could be pursued to continue the efforts that *SAWW* and other books of feminist criticism have begun.

Classic novels, like those of Teresa de la Parra (Venezuela) and Gertrudis Gómez de Avellaneda (Cuba), should not wait any longer to be translated. Like Avellaneda's *Sab*, Cuban Lydia Cabrera's short stories and Puerto Rican Julia de Burgos's poetry await translation into English and publication in book form. With short fiction in translation, the recent practice (which I hope will continue) has been to publish anthologies of stories by various authors. However, there is a paucity of complete volumes in English by single authors. Enough twentieth-century story writers come easily to mind just from among those studied in

Spanish American Women Writers that an entire series of brief volumes could be published by an enterprising publishing house: Albalucía Angel (Colombia); Marta Brunet (Chile); Fanny Buitrago (Colombia); Silvina Bullrich (Argentina); Rosario Ferré (Puerto Rico); Cristina Peri Rossi (Uruguay); and Armonía Somers (Uruguay). Similarly, the poetry of Olga Orozco (Argentina), Julia de Burgos (Puerto Rico), and Juana de Ibarbourou (Uruguay) has never appeared in English in book form, nor are reprints in Spanish as frequent or as easy to obtain as they should be. The icon of the lives of certain writers, such as Delmira Agustini (Uruguay), Magda Portal (Peru), or Violeta Parra (Chile), has so overshadowed the literature itself that the texts are in need of reprinting, translating, and close textual studies. Most of the dramatists in *SAWW* have not just one but several unpublished plays listed in the bibliographies. (See the List of Authors by Genre for a complete list of playwrights.) A volume of plays by women on feminist themes would be welcome in English and/or Spanish.

In terms of bibliography, one need only mention the dramatic case of feminist literary magazines to point up the need for more published research. In the last decade, many small magazines have appeared in Latin American capitals and major cities, and quite a few of them have disappeared again before the material published in them could be recorded or made more widely available for the future. Each of us with contacts in Latin America should make sure that copies of quality magazines are given to MLA bibliographers to be indexed, and to feminist centers of documentation or to the Library of Congress for future consultation. At the end of this volume, I have appended a bibliography of articles and books either of a general nature or about groups of Spanish American women writers. Yet few titles listed there are from feminist magazines from the region because of the difficulty of accessing those works.

In 1978 Celia Correas de Zapata, one of the pioneering critics in the area of Spanish American women writers, published an essay for which she counted articles and bibliographical entries to document the lack of material on Spanish American women writers in libraries in Argentina, Paraguay, and Washington, D.C. A decade later, the situation has improved greatly. My hope is that today research has proliferated to such an extent that a project such as hers could only be thinkable with a computer and a vast team of researchers. I will leave to the users of this collection the task of locating the stories, novels, poems, and plays on the topics that touch them most. This book is dedicated to all those who, with pleasure and with passion, create or are touched by the creations of Spanish American women writers.

DELMIRA AGUSTINI
(1886–1914)
Uruguay

Ivette López Jiménez
Translated by Dwight García

BIOGRAPHY

Agustini was born in Montevideo, Uruguay, in 1886, the daughter of an Uruguayan family of the upper bourgeoisie. Her education was one becoming a woman of her class and her time; playing the piano and writing verses were the prized adornments. In this milieu, she grew protected by her mother's possessive love, reading the Romantic and *fin de siècle* French poets and, even more importantly, the well-known Spanish American *modernistas* such as Rubén Darío (Nicaragua), Julio Herrera y Reissig (Uruguay), and Leopoldo Lugones (Argentina).

A conflictive duality defines Delmira Agustini's life. She first considered poetry a mere adornment of her social self, but it soon became a passion, a constant dedication. She met and knew many of the literary figures of early twentieth-century Uruguay, and actively participated in activities with them. In 1907 she published her first book, *El libro blanco* (The white book); three years later she published *Cantos de la mañana* (Morning songs). Under the literary name "Joujou," she wrote about women intellectuals and women artists of her time. During the same years, her double life, her game of masks, began. She was a divided woman: at times a bourgeois girl, at times a poet of ardent verses, at times a woman who passionately loved. Her letters, gathered under the title of *Correspondencia íntima* (Intimate letters), reveal this conflict: Occasionally, the writer of erotic verses assumes a child's mask and writes to her mother or to her fiancé using that guise.

The official literary world promoted these dual images of Agustini. The author of the prologue to *El libro blanco* calls her "a candid girl," even though she was already a young woman at the time. "A beautiful girl" are the words used by Darío to describe her in the prologue to *Los cálices vacíos* (1913; "The empty chalices"); Agustini was twenty-seven years old. She was also "a sorceress of pantheism," "a disciple of Pan," according to the critics of her time who promoted the adult mask. Occasionally, she consciously assumed these conflicting images.

In 1913 she married and two months later she left her husband. She kept meeting him, however; their strange relationship eventually led to her death, when in 1914 her husband killed her and then committed suicide after one of their many furtive encounters in a rented room. They were both buried the same day; her death and funeral made the front pages of Uruguay's newspapers. Her violent death was another item that has contributed to the creation of a literary personality for Agustini and to her being read as a character in a love story with a morbid ending, more than as a poet. Numerous studies of her life and work have been written taking her life as their starting point. As has been the case with many women poets, these extraliterary considerations have weighed on the interpretation of her works, obscuring many of its important aspects.

MAJOR THEMES

Rubén Darío's Modernist love poetry, with his pan-erotic vision of the world, his direct erotic language (leaving aside spiritual love poetry), and his symbolic representation of sexuality, opened the way to the new sexual rhetoric. Quite a few writers in Latin America at the beginning of the twentieth century employed this new language. Among them, Delmira Agustini is the first woman to break with the language and the conventions expected of women by making sexual love and her own body the center of her poetry.

It is revealing to observe the way in which Agustini absorbs the Modernist's new attitude toward the erotic, and how this attitude differs in her poetry from that in her models. In her work one can find a movement the inverse of Darío's, representing a different mode of eroticism. Whereas in the Nicaraguan's work the body signifies the outer world, in Agustini's poetry the body points first toward itself and then inward, toward the subjective world. The text turns upon itself; the code acts as a verbal boomerang. Hence, the delirium of desire that marks her writing is born, and sexual love devours itself.

Despite Romantic remnants and Oriental themes which she soon leaves behind, *El libro blanco* (1907) already contains the axis that supports much of her later work. To a large extent, Agustini's first book is marked by a search for a rhetoric, by her attempt to define her own writing. The titles of the poems are signs of this search: "El arte" (Art), "La musa" (The Muse), "El poeta y la diosa" (The poet and the goddess), and "Mi musa triste" (My sad Muse). The volume is divided into two sections, "Frágil" (Fragile) and "Orla Rosa" (Pink fringe). A constant dialogue with other texts of her time characterizes the first section, which ultimately consists of poetic encounters with poetry, with the Muse. The book's opening poem, "Levando el ancla" (Weighing anchor), defines the first section with its command in one of its verses: " ¡Partamos, musa mía!" (Let us go, my Muse).

The second section represents, as its title "Orla Rosa" suggests, a border or a fringe. Its few poems are marginal in relation to the rest of the book but are important when the reader considers the totality of Agustini's poetry. Its referents are malevolent longings, abysses, flowers opening, a sea of madness. Its images differ from those of the poems of the previous section. As one of the poems, "Amor" (Love), states, this section is written in the "lenguaje del torrente" (language of the torrent), a passionate rhetoric expressing erotic passion.

Goblet, vase, flower: These are the images, only occasionally present in the last section of *El libro blanco*, which are later repeatedly associated with a female "I" and which acquire their full meaning as part of a poetic system in later books. A representative symbol of women in *fin de siècle* literature, the sphinx already has some of the meanings that will become increasingly important in her poetry. The sphinx is associated with a mysterious, menacing world, containing "abismos sin fin" (abysses without end), which represent a descent to the furor of sexual passion, to pain and to death. Sexual passion is less veiled in her second book, *Cantos de la mañana* (1910), and is transparent in *Los cálices vacíos* (1913), her last book published during her lifetime.

In Agustini's third and posthumous books, where evil is one of the dominant elements, the erotic self-analysis consists of the body reading the body. Corporality in these poems is expressed as an abyss and anguish. A rhetoric of tensions focusing on the body is constructed. In *Cantos*, the poems are repeatedly structured around dualities: Heaven/Hell, light/shadow, lily/mud. The poem borders on that dark world that soon will be identified with sexual passion. In this book, passion is defined as a "raíz nutrida en la entraña del cielo y del averno" (*Poesías completas*, ed. M. Alvar, p. 163, root nurtured in the womb of heaven and hell). The world of desire is viewed here as an abyss in which violence is identified with a "sed maldita" (cursed thirst) devouring the poetic self. In poems like "El vampiro" (p. 160, The vampire), the erotic language points to death, wounds, and daggers: The poetic speaker identifies herself with the vampire and with a "nameless evil" driven by a thirst that wounds the heart. The duality presented in this poem, the dilemma of being a vampire or a pure lily, is related to the confinement of desire within her own body.

The topic of the erotic encounter is extensively elaborated by "Supremo idilio" (p. 161–64, Supreme idyll), a poem in which a female speaker, identified at the beginning of the text as a "figura blanca" (white figure), dialogues with a male character represented as a "cuerpo tenebroso" (gloomy body) and a black cross. The white/black opposition is inscribed within the larger duality of good/evil. The allegory of the encounter is constructed, as in Darío, through the profanation of Christian referents. The female speaker yields to the dark figure, opening her "great chalice of snow" and stretching her "eucharistic arms" to embrace the black cross. But whereas in Darío's poems sexuality is associated with plenitude, in Agustini's text it is viewed as the loss of purity, as a fall into evil and death. A serpent, a sinister spell, a devouring abyss, and a cross are its images.

"Primavera" (spring), one of the last poems of *Cantos de la mañana*, deals precisely with this theme of sexuality in Agustini's writing; the poetic subject, identified as the poet, describes the "awakening" of her lyre, now "transfigured, powerful, free." The lyre's symbolic awakening is also the opening of a bud (a sexual referent and a metaphor for the lyre) and, as in "Supremo Idilio," the opening of a body waiting for an embrace in which low and dark things will merge with others more "brilliant and lofty." Those "low and dark things" will become clear in *Los cálices vacíos* and *El Rosario* de *Eros*, books that treat female sexuality openly.

The title of the third section of *Los cálices vacíos*, "De fuego, de sangre y de sombra" (On fire, on blood and on shadow), defines the turbulent world and the tumultuous process represented by the book's metaphors. The prologue by Rubén Darío, considered the "master" among the Latin American and Spanish poets of his time, recognizes that Agustini's poetry says new things, exquisite things that had never been said before. He obliquely refers to things never written down by women in Latin America's literary tradition, words considered forbidden.

Cálices' opening poem, "Ofrendando el libro, a Eros" (Dedicating the book, to Eros), proposes eroticism as a union of opposites: "El lazo / esencial de los troncos discordantes / del placer y el dolor, plantas gigantes" (p. 199, The essential / bond of the discordant trunks / of love and pleasure, gigantic plants). The joining of pleasure and pain, Eros and death, is represented through metaphors like Hell and Paradise, refulgent soul and dark shadow, innocence and vice. The joining of opposites had also been present in earlier poems such as "Supremo Idilio."

In another poem of *Cantos de la mañana*, the speaker, defined in terms of the *fin de siècle* image of the exotic and sinful Salomé, relates love and death to one another as she holds in her hand the head of her dead lover. But in *Los cálices vacíos*, love's relationship to death becomes constant and defined. Love, turned toward her own body, finds no exit; the tension generated by this movement leads to the void, to death. In "Ofrendando el libro," love (Eros) is presented as a human figure in whose hands rests the lily of death. In "Inextinguible" (p. 275, Inextinguishable), the lover is sleeping so deeply that he cannot awake and his pupils resemble "a tomb." In "Visión" (pp. 210–11, Vision), the relationship between Eros and death constitutes the structuring nucleus of the poem. The lover becomes a "hongo gigante, muerto y vivo" (huge mushroom, dead and alive); his body is seen as devoid of movement. A statue of lilies and a reverent swan are two of the metaphors that represent him. Facing that mirror of desire which is the lover's body, the poetic subject contemplates and represents herself as a snake moving toward the dark, in the middle of a bedroom "de soledad y miedo'' (of solitude and fear). The poem is a vision of a sexual encounter that ends in darkness and shadows.

At the end of *Los cálices vacíos*, Agustini mentioned a forthcoming book, *Los astros del abismo* (Stars of the abyss). After her death her editors published two books: *El Rosario de Eros* and *Los astros del abismo* (1924). The first five poems of *El Rosario de Eros* are meant to be beads in a sexual rosary. The somber love constructed by the texts is said to resemble death. The poetic speaker assumes the emblems with which *fin de siècle* poetry represented women: the abyss, the poisonous fountain, the beast, the snake. In the corpus of images of the last books, the poet is also the repository of Eros. The swan, which in Symbolism and Modernism was a sign for male sexuality, is identified with the female poetic speaker: ''Yo soy el cisne errante de los sangrientos rastros'' (in ''Nocturno'' [Nocturne], *Los cálices vacíos*, p. 229, I am the wandering swan of bloody trails). In other poems, the swan retains its Modernist meaning as a male lover ''de pico de fuego'' (with a beak of fire) to whom the female speaker offers the ''vase'' of her body (''El cisne,'' pp. 230–31, The swan). Once again, the chalice (vase, goblet, body of love) becomes a metaphor for female void, a ''dark chasm'' with which the female body is identified throughout the text. The transition from the ''vaso sellado'' (sealed vase) of *El libro blanco* to the empty chalice of both *Los cálices vacíos* and *El Rosario de Eros* is a movement from a love obscurely sexual to a desire concentrated in the body. Only absolute terms can represent the tension produced by this desire—thus the many metaphors for pain and pleasure in her last books.

The center of Agustini's erotic vision is the relationship between Eros and death, as a desire inscribed in the body. Her best poetry treats the encounter with the erotic, in which anguish, her horror of herself, and the abyss of her own body are joined together. In this sense her work departs in another way from Darío's approach to the erotic. In her poetry the relationship between Eros and death is intensified; the erotic is not viewed as harmony; death is at its center. Agustini's eroticism is circular; the body is subject and object in which many struggles and tensions are concentrated: ''A veces ¡toda! soy alma; / Y a veces ¡toda! soy cuerpo'' (p. 231; at times, all of me!, I am a soul / and at times, all of me!, I am a body).

Agustini is the first woman in Hispanic poetry to represent the female body and to engage it directly in her writing, in a search for a language that can express it. The anguish produced by the conflict between her acceptance of desire and the code of sexual behavior imposed on women at the time (both in social reality and in literary discourse) is the price she paid. This conflict is constantly present in her work; the poetic anguish is caused by the attempt to assume a code that cannot be fully assumed.

By incorporating her own sexuality into her text, Agustini surprised social and literary tradition in Latin America. Poetry written by women was perceived as an elegant adornment; erotic conflict and its expression in literature was far from the accepted female code of behavior. Before her poetry, woman's body and the rhetoric of the erotic had been expressed in terms of male desire. Delmira Agustini inscribes female desire in the text. In this sense, her poetry marks a beginning. Her discourse, in various ways, was imitated by other Spanish American women poets. Agustini's female discourse about the female body was the beginning of woman's recuperation of female sexuality in her poetry, and even though the female body still is often seen as a sexual object, it was perceived as women's own.

SURVEY OF CRITICISM

Much of the criticism written about Agustini deals with her biography. The voluminous book by Ofelia Machado, *Delmira Agustini* (1944), which examines Delmira's manuscripts, stands out among biographical criticism. Also important is Clara Silva's *Genio y figura de Delmira Agustini* (1944). One could include among this type the poet's own *Correspondencia íntima*, a collection of letters edited by Arturo Sergio Visca (1969). These three books provide information on Agustini's social persona: her personality, the conflict between her life as a bourgeois young lady and the ardent, "unladylike" images of her poetry; the secluded way in which Agustini was brought up, never going to school and being educated by her own mother and private teachers; the domineering affection of her mother, which prolonged some childish attitudes. Also frequently treated by her biographers are her friendship with intellectuals and writers of her time and her dedication to literary work; the manuscripts found show the poet corrected the original works many times, contrary to the image she gave of depending on a single moment of inspiration, which many critics had taken as true.

In Uruguay, Alberto Zum Felde was one of the first writers to speak about her work, in his now classic *Proceso intelectual del Uruguay y crítica de su literatura* (1930). In 1944 Zum Felde edited and wrote the preliminary study of Agustini's *Obras completas* (Complete works). He establishes the basis for much of the criticism of her work by stating that the erotic provides this poetry with a transcendent quality and that texts do not refer directly to sexuality. This is the view assumed by Sarah Bollo in her *Delmira Agustini: espíritu de su obra y su significación* (1963) and by Doris Stephens in *Delmira Agustini and the Quest for Transcendence* (1975).

Other writers have studied the poet's relationship with *modernismo*. The most detailed of these studies is Manual Alvar's *La poesía de Delmira Agustini* (1958), which served as the basis for his Introduction to the *Poesías completas* (Complete poetry), a 1971 edition that excluded the books published after Delmira's death. Alvar analyzes the *modernista* themes (exoticism and dreams, among others), oppositions, stylistic innovations like rhythm, and the constant images in her poetry: night, statues, serpents. He points to Agustini's contribution in these areas and states that in her poetry, innovation is closely related to the expression of things that had been suppressed, themes considered forbidden in a woman writer. Agustini's relationship to *modernismo* is also studied by Sarah Bollo in *El Modernismo en el Uruguay. Ensayo estilístico* (1957). A more recent study by Silvia Molloy, "Dos lecturas del cisne: Rubén Darío y Delmira Agustini" (1984), offers a novel reading of the dialogue between Darío's and Agustini's texts, and of the way in which the Uruguayan poet answers the Nicaraguan.

Some critical works have studied the national context of Delmira Agustini's poetry. Among these, *La literatura uruguaya del 900* by S. Cabrera places the poet in a generational context. Emir Rodríguez Monegal in *Sexo y poesía en el 900 uruguayo* emphasizes the importance of sexuality in Delmira's life and works. In this sense his study constitutes a departure from the prior critical boycott of this subject.

The myths constructed around Agustini, particularly that of the subordination of the erotic to the spiritual and the contrasting images of the poet, have been studied by A. Visca in his introduction to *Correspondencia íntima* and by D. García in "Las 'poetisas' ante la crítica: el caso de Delmira Agustini," an article that analyzes how the critics received Agustini's poetry and how dominant ideology and sexism influenced their perspective. Recent research on Agustini has been continuing in Uruguay; bibliography concerning the most recent publications has been provided by Marlene Acarón, who has also informed this writer about Agustini's impact on contemporary Uruguayan culture. A ballet under the name *Delmira* was presented in Montevideo (Teatro Solís, February 1987) by the choreographer Alberto Alonso, and a play inspired by her life and works (*Delmira y otras rupturas* by Milton Schinca) was published in 1977. Despite all this activity, there are still many aspects of Agustini's works to be considered, and her work awaits new readings.

BIBLIOGRAPHY

Works by Delmira Agustini

El libro blanco. Montevideo: O. M. Bertani, 1907.
Cantos de la mañana. Montevideo: O. M. Bertani, 1910.
Los cálices vacíos. Montevideo: O. M. Bertani, 1913.
Obras completas de Delmira Agustini. Vol. 1: *El Rosario de Eros*. Vol. 2: *Los astros del abismo*. Montevideo: M. García, 1924.
Correspondencia íntima. Ed. Arturo Sergio Visca. Montevideo: Biblioteca Nacional, 1969.
Poesías completas. Ed. Manuel Alvar. Barcelona: Labor, 1971.
Delmira Agustini, Antología. Ed. Esther de Cáceres. Biblioteca Artigas Vol. 69. Montevideo: Ministerio de Educacion y Cultura, 1986.

Works about Delmira Agustini

Alvar, Manuel. *La poesía de Delmira Agustini*. Sevilla: Publicaciones de la Escuela de Estudios Hispanoamericanos, 1958.

Bollo, Sarah. *Delmira Agustini: espíritu de su obra y su significación*. Montevideo: Corón, 1963.

———. *El modernismo en el Uruguay: ensayo estílistico*. 2d ed. Montevideo: Universidad de la República, 1976.

East, Linda Kay Davis. "The Imaginary Voyage: Evolution of the Poetry of Delmira Agustini." Ph.D. diss., Stanford University, 1981. (DAI 41 [May 1981]: 4728A–4729A.)

García, Dwight. "Las 'poetisas' ante la crítica: el caso de Delmira Agustini." *Plural* 1, 2 (July–Dec. 1982):144–51.

Gatell, Angelina. "Delmira Agustini y Alfonsina Storni: dos destinos trágicos." *Cuadernos Hispanoamericanos* 68 (1964):583–94.

Loureiro de Renfrew, Ileana. *La imaginación en la obra de Delmira Agustini*. Montevideo: Letras Femeninas, 1987.

Machado, Ofelia. *Delmira Agustini*. Montevideo: Ceibo, 1944.

Molloy, Silvia. "Dos lecturas del cisne: Rubén Darío y Delmira Agustini." *La sartén por el mango*. Eds. Patricia E. González and Eliana Ortega. Río Piedras: Huracán, 1984, p. 57.

Pedemonte, Hugo. "Delmira Agustini." *Cuadernos Hispanoamericanos* 92 (1961):161–87.

Perricone, Catherine. "A Bibliographic Approach to the Study of Latin American Women Poets: Delmira Agustini." *Hispania* 71, 2 (May 1988):276–77.

Rodríguez Monegal, Emir. *Sexo y poesía en el 900 uruguayo*. Montevideo: Alfa, 1969.

Rosenbaum, Carmen Sidonia. "Delmira Agustini y Albert Samain." *Revista Iberoamericana* (July–Oct. 1946):273–78.

———. "Sobre Delmira Agustini." *Revista Hispánica Moderna* 11 (1946):57–58.

———. "Vida y obra de Delmira." *Revista Nacional de Cultura* (Caracas) 23 (1960): 88–110.

Schinca, Milton. *Delmira y otras rupturas*. Montevideo: Ediciones de la Banda Oriental, 1977.

Silva, Clara. *Genio y figura de Delmira Agustini*. Montevideo: Ceibo, 1944.

Simonet, Madelaine. "Delmira Agustini." *Hispania* (Stanford) 39 (1956):397–402.

Stephens, Doris. *Delmira Agustini and the Quest for Transcendence*. Montevideo: Geminis, 1975.

Valenti, Jeanette. "Delmira Agustini, A Reinterpretation of Her Poetry." Ph.D. diss., Cornell University, 1971. (DAI 32 [1971]:460A.)

Vilariño, Idea. "Delmira Agustini: una amorosa." *Brecha* (Montevideo) 12 (Sept. 1986): 29–30.

———. "Ecos de la poesía de Delmira Agustini." *Brecha* (Montevideo) 12 (Sept. 1986): 29–30.

Vitale, Ida. "Los cien años de Delmira Agustini." *Vuelta* (Mexico) 2 (Sept. 1986):17–19.

Zambrano, David. "Presencia de Baudelaire en la poesía hispanoamericana: Darío, Lugones, Delmira Agustini." *Cuadernos Americanos* 18, 3 (May–June 1958):217–35.

Zum Felde, Alberto. "Delmira Agustini." *Proceso intelectual del Uruguay y crítica de su literatura*. Montevideo: Imp. Nacional Colorada, 1930. pp. 316–29.

CLARIBEL ALEGRÍA
(b. 1924)
Nicaragua, El Salvador

Nancy Saporta Sternbach

BIOGRAPHY

The life of Claribel Alegría, one of the major contemporary voices of Central America, is itself a testimony to the very issues about which she writes. Although she was born in Nicaragua, Alegría moved with her family to El Salvador at the age of one year where she lived until the late 1940s. Living across the street from the headquarters of the National Guard when she was still a small child, Alegría witnessed the 1932 "Matanza" (The massacre) of thirty thousand Salvadoran peasants, an event that would later appear as a regular motif in her literature in the writer's attempts to contextualize and exorcise this early trauma. After attending college in Washington, D.C., Alegría lived in Argentina, Mexico, and other Latin American countries, a true woman of the Americas. Her current place of residence is Nicaragua, although she also tries to spend some part of each year in Mallorca, Spain, her home for many years.

Alegría also collaborates on many projects with her husband, U.S.-born journalist, Darwin Flakoll (Bud). Their joint projects tend to be testimonial or historical (*No me agarran viva: La mujer salvadoreña en lucha* [1983; *They Won't Take Me Alive*, 1984], *Para romper el silencio: Resistencia y lucha en las cárceles salvadoreñas* [1987, Breaking the silence: resistance and struggle in Salvadoran jails]), although one of their first efforts was the novel *Cenizas de Izalco* (1966; *Ashes of Izalco*, 1988). In her poetry and short fiction, however, Alegría works alone. Nevertheless, their collaboration in these works tends to manifest itself in translations: Flakoll is also one of Alegría's best translators. This fact explains the apparent anomaly of certain texts, such as *Luisa in Realityland* (1987; *Luisa en el país de la realidad*; 1987), appearing in English before Spanish.

Known as an indefatigable worker for human rights and freedom in El Salvador and a defender of Nicaragua's right to self-determination, Alegría frequently travels in order to participate in symposia about the Central American situation. She calls this activity her contribution to the struggle, her own "Letras de emergencia" (emergency letters), a response to the crisis situation through speaking (out) and writing. It is this response, either directly or allegorically, that characterizes all of Alegría's work.

MAJOR THEMES

Claribel Alegría is well known and highly respected in Latin America for her poetry, in part because she won the prestigious and coveted Casa de Las Américas poetry award for *Sobrevivo* ("I survive") in 1978. Although the Central American theme appears in her work as early as 1966 with the publication of her and Flakoll's novel, *Cenizas de Izalco*, it was not until the 1980 assassination of Archbishop Oscar Romero that she resolved to take up her pen in the cause of human rights in Central America. It was then that she and Flakoll left their residence in Mallorca and moved to Nicaragua. In an interview, she cites Romero's assassination as a decisive moment in her literary trajectory as a political writer. Yet, many of her works which appeared before Romero's death had also begun to examine the Central American theme. In her collection, *Sobrevivo* (the volume from which many poems of *Flowers from the Volcano* are taken), for example, her poems "Flores del Volcán" ("Flowers from the Volcano"), "Sorrow" (original title in English), and "Tamalitos de Cambray" ("Cambray Tamales") attempt to portray an historic, yet personal, account of the conflagration, the class struggle, and the ingredients that comprise the principal features of the "emergency" in Central America. Such a commitment has also led her to produce new kinds of literature (testimony, poetic prose) both in conjunction with and beyond her poetry.

Still, in spite of her prolific list of publications (more than two dozen titles), she is yet to be "discovered" by more than a handful of critics in the United States; yet to be read with the fervor that the North American public has reserved for either the writers of the Boom or the testimonies of Central American revolutionaries or *campesinos* (people of the land). Nevertheless, the recent appearance of her new works in English (*Luisa* and *They Won't Take Me Alive*) may change that dynamic in the coming years. At the time of this writing, *Ashes of Izalco* and a new volume of poetry are also in press.

Since 1980, in addition to poetry, Alegría has cultivated the novel, the novella, testimony, the essay, and a series of short vignettes in poetry and prose characteristic of new Latina writing in the United States, which can best be described as "woman as storyteller" (*Luisa in Realityland*). As much as Alegría is a poet, she is also a proponent and practitioner of weaving and creating stories, with both humor and compassion. In *Luisa*, billed as a novel but really a series of short, short stories interspersed with poetry, the narrator informs us that many of Luisa's family were "fabulous liars," including "of course, Luisa" (p. 53).

While the creation of fiction always constitutes "lying," Alegría is instead the terrible truth-teller of contemporary Central America. In contrast to narrators who claim to be reliable, but who are not, Alegría claims to be lying while actually telling the truth. Such is the case in *Album familiar* (1984; *Family Album*, 1989), which chronicles the marriage of a Central American woman to a man from the industrialized world, who continually struggles with trying to make her husband understand both her and her "women's" stories. In this version, Marcel, the meticulous French husband, is bored by his wife's story-telling, never suspecting that the continuation and repetition of those stories, their weaving and intermingling with each other, are his wife's lifeblood. As we will see, the inability of the elegant, work-oriented, organized, First World husband to comprehend his storytelling Central American wife not only eloquently characterizes female-male relations, but also chronicles and parodies Third World–First World relations and, thus, is repeated regularly in Alegría's fiction.

Clearly, Alegría is a writer with a political message. "I have no *fusil* (rifle)," she tells Carolyn Forché (*Flores del volcán*, p. xi) but she does use the word as her weapon in her ceaseless struggle for equality and the elimination of exploitation and injustice. For this reason, she situates herself in the large family of Latin American "political" writers who have experienced loss, exile, absence, and the disappearance of loved ones. In Alegría's litanies, the names of her fellow travelers include Roque Dalton (El Salvador) and Julio Cortázar (Argentina); Mario Benedetti (Uruguay) had compiled an edition of her poetry; the life of Víctor Jara (Chile) and the verses of Pablo Neruda (Chile) punctuate her own poem, "Sorrow." She is a woman writer who has managed to be recognized by the male writers of her generation. Although she does not share their fame, she has expressed her feeling of a kindred spirit with them and considers them her literary family. While we may assert that she has had literary forefathers, and, indeed, we may wonder which women writers inspired her, there is no absence of women in her works. On the contrary, women of all ages and stages of growth and personal evolution populate her work. Whether Alegría is writing testimony or fiction, poetry or essay, the voice, the heart, the mind of women— Latin American women—are central and omnipresent. From an early age, Alegría has defined herself as a feminist, as her work amply demonstrates.

One theme for which she shows great predilection, in fact, is precisely the intersection of a feminist and political consciousness in her female protagonists. Speakers in the poems and protagonists in her fiction are often Central American women who have chosen a comfortable, bourgeois life outside their country. Furthermore, these women are not in a state of political exile, but rather are complacently content with their washing machines and other technological comforts (*Cenizas de Izalco, Albúm familiar, Despierta, mi bien, despierta* [1986; Wake up, my love, wake up]). A sudden change in the woman's life (a return trip home, a visit from a politically active cousin, a love affair with a revolutionary) literally shakes the woman's life from the ground up. For this reason,

perhaps, Alegría so frequently employs the metaphor of an exploding volcano
to represent both the awakening of a woman's consciousness that explodes the
earth around her, and the "eruption" of a political consciousness in any of its
citizens. Alegría is at her happiest when these two coincide. Also evident is her
strategy to dismantle and undermine upper class values by dialectically situating
the oligarchy that locks itself up in its walled mansions drinking itself into
oblivion (*Flowers from the Volcano*), with a middle or upper middle class capable
of hearing the message of the revolution. In this way, Alegría demonstrates the
social components of the revolution: those who have most to lose juxtaposed
with those fighting for their lives.

The narrators of these works, especially in her most recent, *Luisa in Realityland*, lead us to believe that when women are still children, there is more
freedom both to envision a free life and to speak about it; this is especially the
case for well-to-do children such as Luisa. The child Luisa, in this sense, has
the conviction and courage to rebel against socially assigned gender roles when
she asks for a baby: "I don't want to be married; I don't like the way men treat
women . . . So . . . as soon as I have my baby . . . let my husband die" (p. 39),
she prays. In *Despierta, mi bien, despierta*, a novella that takes its title from a
well-known popular song, the idea of waking up, both politically and sexually,
again establishes what may be called Alegría's Sleeping Beauty metaphor. The
protagonist, Lorena, muses to herself, "No debe ser privilegio de los hombres
tener amantes jóvenes. Detesto el machismo" (p. 31, It shouldn't just be men's
privilege to have younger lovers. I hate machismo). In *Cenizas de Izalco*, Carmen
returns to a fictive Santa Ana (Alegría's home town and the site of nearly all
her fictional works) for her mother's funeral, and while visiting is presented with
a diary, not written by Carmen's mother herself, but rather by her mother's
lover. Such a presentation foreshadows Alegría's later use of the idea developed
in *Luisa in Realityland* that a woman's legacy or testament is her word, as
exhibited in Luisa's complex relationship with the illiterate Gypsy. The Gypsy,
while inspiring the young Luisa to pursue her own creativity, simultaneously
dictates love poems to her young protegée, which were then recorded "in a
special notebook she kept by her bedside" (p. 17).

Both techniques—Alegría's narrator as the recorder of another woman's history through conversation, and the appearance of small family possessions such
as diaries and photo albums—have become symbolic in Alegría's works and
anticipate the use that Alegría and Flakoll will later make of them in testimonial
literature. In the fiction, however, such objects tend to take on a life of their
own, metamorphosed by the circumstances. When, for example, the face of her
cousin becomes erased from the album of family photos in *Album familiar*,
Ximena not only knows that he has died, but also that it is now her responsibility
to replace him in the struggle against the Somoza dictatorship. Such a representation, the faceless photograph serving as a metonymic symbol, is a departure
and evolution from Alegría's early poems in which the speaker is also confronted

by the death of loved ones, but is incapable of any response but anger, frustration, and sadness.

In fact, the entire trajectory and use of death images marks significant transformations and stages in Alegría's continually changing outlook. Clearly, hers is a literature in which death is no stranger. The reader of her work is assailed by the death of children, the rape of the landscape, the assassination of poets, the genocide of peasants, the atrocities of military regimes, and the cruel, torturous, and grotesque deaths of political activists. Such litanies not only comprise plots and eulogies in her work, but also serve to filter the effect of these deaths on the living, and the immense toll their loss takes on those left behind to struggle. Although the expected result is sorrow, and, indeed, this theme has predominated in *Flores del volcán* and *Sobrevivo*, in more recent works, through communication with her dead and their ghosts, the speaker comes to acknowledge their presence in her life. In so doing, they provide her with humor, conversation, sustenance, and the motivation to continue to live and struggle for the dead *and* the living.

In her poetry, the images of Alegría's "own" dead repeatedly "populate" the text as well as haunt and inspire the speaker. In "Sorrow," for example, Alegría invokes dead poets who also fought against military regimes, as if the poem itself were part of the collective struggle that it symbolizes, written from within prison walls, exile, or even from beyond the grave. One of her translators, Carolyn Forché has written, "Alegría is comfortable with her deceased." Indeed, they "wait" for her at the corner, "smile" at her, they "rise up," "stand watch," and "send signals" from the southern depths of Chile to her own Salvadoran Izalco ("Eramos tres" ["We Were Three"], *Flowers*); and her writing serves as a way to answer them. The girl child of *Luisa*, we learn later, was taught that "the dead need to be remembered and to be named so they don't fall into limbo" (p. 13). Indeed, they appear in all her work: poems dedicated to dead friends, stories of loss, of disappearance, of death, either through "natural" causes, or the most bizarre and grotesque ones. However, it is not only the dead who need to be remembered to keep them from falling into limbo; throughout Alegría's work, the images, symbols, and signs of the dead also keep the *living* from falling into limbo. What is clear from Alegría's evocative imagery is that the living, in order to nourish their struggle, turn to the dead for support, strength and, not least of all, inspiration, demonstrated in such poems as "Untimeliness," "Erosion," and "Where Was Your Childhood Lost" (*Luisa in Realityland*).

In the twenty-year span that separates *Cenizas de Izalco* from *Luisa in Realityland*, with the important appearance of *Sobrevivo* almost exactly between them chronologically, Claribel Alegría not only has learned to live with her dead, but also has herself evolved emotionally about their significance. While in the early works the sense of trauma and horror pervaded Alegría's writing to create sad, pessimistic texts, her recent writing confirms the fact that literature, that "esoteric'' and "elite'' form of communication, can personally assist the writer in exorcising her own dead. What is more significant, however, is that this same writing has a much more far-reaching effect than merely comforting the writer: the dead will not have died in vain if their struggle is known, if the outrage is made public and international, if the world knows the atrocities committed in that small corner of the earth known as El Salvador. For this reason, then, Alegría continually names her dead in her poetry, and by so doing, she keeps them and their struggle alive. Similarly, by naming El Salvador's dead in her testimonial texts, she enables their ideals to live on beyond their physical bodies. For her, this is one of the primary tasks of a writer.

Both in her poetry and in interviews, Claribel Alegría has called herself a "cementerio apátrida" (a cemetery without a country in "Eramos tres," *Flores*, 54). In another poem, the speaker states: "I begin counting the names / my rosary of names" ("Sorrow" in *Flores*) of the loss. These "transient guests" allow the speaker in Alegría's poetry to recuperate the lost voices of poets all across the Americas for " [t]heir persecuted voices are one voice," one collective voice that reiterates the same message. But their bodies, the bodies of the dead, are "too many to bury" ("Eramos tres"). In this sense, Alegría's dead become friendly ghosts who guide her through the pain of their collective struggle. Thus, while Alegría is *un*burying the dead, broadcasting their voices and their message, she conceives of herself as a root, delving further into the earth to attain truth, while at the same time creating the "lies" we call fiction or the images we call poetry.

Yet it is not only Alegría's "own" dead who concern her, but rather others who have died in El Salvador's struggle for liberation. When death and violence are seen as the only political solution, as expressed in the poem, "Because I Want Peace" (*Luisa*), or in the testimony, *They Won't Take Me Alive*, the task of the writer is not only to name the dead, but also to ensure that they will be remembered with all the dignity of their struggle. Thus, the testimonial literature that Alegría and Flakoll produce often derives from interviews with survivors, family and friends of the dead, whose experiences uncannily mirror their own.

Just as Alegría has called herself a cemetery, she is also the earth in which the dead are buried, and, hence, in which ideas sprout—the exact opposite of the gruesome image of burial and death so often conveyed in her works. This is to say that Alegría likens herself to a Mother Earth symbol in reverse. While the traditional archetype both gives and takes life, here Alegría supplants the image of suffering motherhood with a new motherly image, one that gathers all her dead children and converts their struggles and stories into words. It is by means of what Alegría calls her *semillero* (seedbed, "The Cartography of Memory," *Luisa in Realityland*, p. 151), the earth in which poems and stories germinate, that this dynamic process occurs. Furthermore, Alegría keeps a "notebook of ideas" which she also calls her "seedbed," a place where she nourishes poems and stories until they reach maturity. Thus, her poetry substitutes her dead, now "too numerous to be buried." In this way, the poem, or the writing process in general, allows the poet to root herself dialectically into Mother Earth to bury her sorrow, to germinate creatively, and to nourish growth in the face of the death around her. For this reason, perhaps, Alegría is so intensely preoccupied with the intersection of motherhood and revolution, their interlocking and bonding goals, as portrayed in *No me agarran viva*.

Just as the inverted imagery of Mother Earth plays a central role in Alegría's works generally, more specifically, the evocative landscape of her "native" El Salvador, especially its rivers and volcanos, holds a preeminent position. Similarly, the erupting volcano that figures prominently in *Cenizas de Izalco* and *Flowers from the Volcano* also suggests that the eruption of conscience is an event no less remarkable with just as far-reaching implications, even in the absence of actual volcanos. Often, Alegría situates her protagonists (almost all women) in a hazy mist that might be called "before the volcano." In their situations of the easy life of the bourgeoisie, a confrontation with political events requires them to take a stand in which they simultaneously recognize their previous ignorance and acknowledge the liberation struggles of their people. The ensuing class war in Alegría's fiction, then, often occurs within the confines of the family, the female protagonist's newfound political consciousness, at war with her father, brother, or husband. Such is the case in her novella, *Despierta, mi bien, despierta*. In this process, the protagonist often discovers that her own liberation as a woman is inextricably linked to the liberation of her country. By freeing herself of her sexist husband, for example, she also discovers his role in the carnage of innocent people, a revelation that leads to her further alienation from him and, thus, motivates her to become actively involved in the liberation struggle. That such consciousness-raising is often framed by yet another story (a love story—either past or present, the appearance of ghosts, the magical quality of life) further links the personal to the political, a quality of almost all of Alegría's fiction.

In *Cenizas de Izalco*, an early work that anticipates all Alegría's subsequent writing, the narrator juxtaposes both spatially and temporally the eruption of the political situation with the eruption of the volcano. Alegría's childhood trauma as a witness of the 1932 "Matanza" is now enacted in literary terms as the narrator herself attempts to grapple with her memory and the ways in which it haunts her. Nowhere is this more evident than in the problematized relation between mother and daughter in this novel, when the protagonist, Carmen, a Salvadoran woman residing in Washington, D.C., returns home for her mother's funeral. Through the medium of a diary, her mother's only legacy to her, Carmen begins to unravel her mother's past, a story that bears uncanny resemblances to her own. In this testament, the written word, and the mother's exalted respect for it, empower her daughter. Writing becomes the powerful emblem that enables Carmen to question her own life. In their town, while everything appears to be normal, just beneath the surface (again expressed in volcanic metaphors) another revolution is brewing: A woman is taking charge of her destiny. Thus, the silences that have characterized relations within the family are merely gaps in which no one is speaking, but not indicators that they have nothing to say. While cultural constraints have dictated the mother's silence about her love affair years earlier, the diary of the man who was her lover serves as a bridge between the cultural, social revolution (the political sphere) and the private, intimate one (the personal) of one woman's life. The political constraints, on the other hand, have imposed another type of silence. Thus, the diary emblematizes the silence imposed by the authoritarian regimes to keep their bloody story out of world view and opinion.

Yet, like much of Alegría's work, the novel can also be read as a political allegory: Carmen represents the Central American country struggling for liberation while her "gringo" husband, Paul, enacts the (im)position of cultural and political imperialism that characterizes U.S.-Salvadoran relations (Schwartz, p. 1). This early novel, then, contains the elements of what we later find in all Alegría's work: a woman's political and sexual awakening; a condemnation of the oligarchy, its ways and repressive regimes, whether these are North American or Latin American; the use of family documents as a means to bring about consciousness-raising; the use of the epistolary mode; the role of memory, especially woman's memory, in reconstructing her own and her country's history.

Alegría employs a similar tactic and recurring metaphor in her novella, *El detén* (1977; The medallion), the story of an adolescent girl of Central American heritage, residing in a Catholic boarding school somewhere in California. As the story unfolds, the reader learns that the girl, like so many of Alegría's protagonists, maintains a lively and active relationship with her "ghosts" who visit her regularly at the school and comment on her relationship with the nuns, whom the girl, Karen, takes great delight in scandalizing, by recounting her sexual-sensual experience with her mother's lover. Alegría's point here is not merely the issue of imperialism, or treating a woman metaphorically as a colony, as mentioned above, but rather to expose the nuns' fascination and complicity with the story, and the teenager's keen awareness of her spellbinding tale. Here, Alegría plays, as she often does, with the social *mores* that permit hypocrisy, provided it is private. The narrator's point, then, is to expose hypocrisy, to condemn "stepfathers" who sexually abuse their stepdaughters, as is the case here, or to condemn husbands from whom wives must beg money, to condemn the wives who tolerate it, and to disclose the private world of middle-class matrons whose only life is the monotonous, gossipy world of the Salvadoran upper class, and whose main interest in life is dissecting others' business.

In short, more than any other aspect of Alegría's writing, the role and function of memory, especially that of female protagonists in fiction or speakers in poetry, serves as a powerful tool for self-realization, recognition, and determination, or as one critic (Basilia Papastamatiu, 1978) has put it, constitutes a "poetic bridge" between the word and those who fight for the liberation of Latin America. Although Alegría's works are suffused with images of exile, absence, and even the impossibility of return to her native El Salvador, the written word—Alegría's poetry—is the antidote to the death, farewells, and adioses everywhere else.

Against the backdrop of military regimes that turn into people-snatching monsters, and the constant disappearance of loved ones, it is the experience of writing, with a musicality and rhythm that parallel a heartbeat, that exorcises Alegría's dead. As in all Alegría's work, the truth of the story lies smoldering under the surface, like the volcano on the verge of eruption, the bloodpulse of a people.

SURVEY OF CRITICISM

Until the early 1980s, with the bilingual publication of *Flowers from the Volcano/ Flores del volcán*, Claribel Alegría was virtually unknown outside Latin America. Even though she has been considered part of the literary world there and has published dozens of titles, only recently have we begun to see any critical works whatsoever devoted to her work. Yet these are few and are clearly written with the same sense of political and feminist commitment that Alegría's works are. With practically one new title, or new translation each year, it is possible that in the next few years, we will see more critical attention paid to her. The majority of the attention she now receives is in the form of reviews that have, by and large, been very favorable.

BIBLIOGRAPHY

Works by Claribel Alegría

Anillo de silencio. Mexico City: Ediciones Botas, 1948.
Suite de amor, angustia y soledad. San Rafael (Mendoza): n.p., 1951.
Vigilias. Mexico City: Ediciones Poesía de América, 1953.
Acuario. Santiago de Chile: n.p., 1955.
Tres cuentos. San Salvador: Ministerio de Cultura, Departamento Editorial,1958.
Huésped de mi tiempo. Buenos Aires: Americalee, 1961.
Vía única. Montevideo: Editorial Alfa, 1965.
Aprendizaje. San Salvador: Editorial Universitaria de El Salvador, 1970.
Pagaré a cobrar y otros poemas. Barcelona: Editorial Llibres de Sinera, 1973.
El detén. Barcelona: Editorial Lumen, 1977.
Sobrevivo. La Habana: Casa de las Américas, 1978.
Homenaje a El Salvador. Madrid: Visor, 1981.
Suma y sigue. Antología. Madrid: Visor, 1981.
"Literatura y liberación nacional en El Salvador." *Casa de las Américas* 21, 126 (May-
    June 1981):12–16.
Flowers from the Volcano/Flores del volcán. Pittsburgh: University of Pittsburgh Press,
    1982.
Poesía viva. London: Black Roads Press, 1983.
Album familiar. 2d ed. San José, Costa Rica: Editorial Universitaria Centroamericana
    (UCA), 1984.
Pueblo de Dios y de Mandinga. Mexico City: Ediciones Era, 1985.
Despierta, mi bien, despierta. San Salvador: UCA (Universidad Centroamericana Edi-
    tores), 1986.

Pueblo de Dios y de Mandinga. Barcelona: Lumen, 1986.

Luisa en el país de la realidad. Mexico City: Joan Boldó i Climent, Editores, Universidad Autónoma de Zacatecas, 1987.

Y este poema-río. Managua: Editorial Nueva Nicaragua, 1988.

Works Published with Darwin Flakoll

Cenizas de Izalco. Barcelona: Seix Barral, 1966. 2d ed. San José: Editorial Universitaria Centroamericana, 1982.

La encrucijada salvadoreña. Barcelona: Dossier Cidob, Centre d'Informació i Documentació, 1980.

Nicaragua: La revolución sandinista. Mexico City: Ediciones Era, 1983.

No me agarran viva: La mujer salvadoreña en lucha. Mexico City: Ediciones Era, 1983.

Para romper el silencio: Resistencia y lucha en las cárceles salvadoreñas. Mexico City: Ediciones Era, 1984.

Works Complied and Translated with Darwin Flakoll

New Voices of Hispanic America. Boston: Beacon Press, 1962.

Translations of Claribel Alegría

Alegría, Claribel, trans. "The Two Cultures of El Salvador." *Massachusetts Review*. Special Issue entitled *Latin America* 27, 3–4 (Fall-Winter 1986):493–502.

Flakoll, Darwin, trans. *Ashes of Izalco*. With Darwin Flakoll. Willimantic, Conn.: Curbstone Press, 1988.

———. *Luisa in Realityland*. Willamantic, Conn.: Curbstone Press, 1987.

———. *Woman of the River*. Pittsburgh: University of Pittsburgh Press, 1988.

Forché, Carolyn, trans. *Flowers from the Volcano*. Pittsburgh: University of Pittsburgh Press, 1982.

Hopkinson, Amanda, trans. *Family Album*. London: Women's Press, 1989. (Contains the novellas *Album familiar*, *El detén*, and *Pueblo de Dios y de Mandinga*.)

———. *They Won't Take Me Alive*. London: Women's Press, 1987.

"The Politics of Exile." *You Can't Drown the Fire: Latin American Women Writing in Exile*. Ed. Alicia Partnoy. Pittsburgh and San Francisco: Cleis Press, 1988. Pp. 171–77.

"The Writer's Commitment." *Lives on the Line: The Testimony of Contemporary Latin American Authors*. Ed. Doris Meyer. Berkeley: University of California Press, 1988. Pp. 306–11.

Works about Claribel Alegría

Arenal, Electa. "Two Poets of the Sandinista Struggle." *Feminist Studies* 7, 1 (Spring 1981): 19–27.

Benedetti, Mario. "Introduction." *Suma y sigue. Antología*. Madrid: Visor, 1981. Pp. 9–16.

Forché, Carolyn. "Interview with Claribel Alegría." *Index on Censorship* 13, 2 (Apr. 1984):11–14.

———. "Preface: With Tears, Fingernails and Coal." *Flores del Volcán*. Pittsburgh: University of Pittsburgh Press, 1982. Pp. xi–xiv.

Papastamatiu, Basilia. "La sobrevida poética de Claribel Alegría." *Casa de Las Américas* (Havana) 110 (Sept.-Oct. 1978):148–50.

Peri Rossi, Cristina. "Cuatro poetas latinoamericanas." *Hora de Poesía* (Barcelona) 8 (Mar.-Apr. 1980).

Saporta Sternbach, Nancy. "Re-Membering the Dead: Latin American Women's 'Testimonial' Discourse." Forthcoming in *Latin American Perspectives*.

Schwartz, Rachel. "Cenizas de Izalco." Unpublished manuscript.

Yúdice, George. "Letras de Emergencia: Claribel Alegría." *Revista Iberoamericana* 51 (July-Dec. 1985):953–64.

———. "Recuperating the Voice of the People: Central American Testimonial Literature." "Politics and Culture in Central America." MIT Symposium. Cambridge, Massachusetts, Apr. 24, 1986.

ISABEL ALLENDE
(b. 1942)
Chile

Linda Gould Levine

BIOGRAPHY

Literary critics have pondered for years the complex issue of the relationship between a writer's life and work, neatly establishing the boundaries of both in some cases or deftly erasing them in others. The phenomenon of Isabel Allende gives new meaning to this exercise and alluringly invites the critic to view art and reality once again as a unified whole. She was born in Chile in 1942 to a family that includes among its members her father's first cousin, Salvador Allende, and a series of eccentric figures on her maternal side. Her childhood resembles that of her character Alba in *La casa de los espíritus* (1982; *The House of the Spirits*, 1985). Following the sudden disappearance of her father when she was very young, Isabel and her brothers moved into her mother's parents' house. Her grandmother was an "extraordinary" woman who practiced spiritism. Her grandfather was a "reactionary" but "tender" patriarch whose domineering manner caused his wife to retreat into silence (Coddou, "Para leer," 1987, p. 132). The house itself was an unusual one, filled with countless books and a basement containing old love letters, photos, and a skeleton from a relative's medical career.

The years Allende lived there represented a period of intense intellectual and creative development. She read everything from Shakespeare to Freud to the Marquis de Sade; she rebelled against her religious education and declared her desire to be a writer "Agatha Christie" style. Most significantly, she formed a close and insoluble bond with her mother and grandparents. Today she still guards in her pocketbook a photo of her grandmother Isabel as a talisman of good fortune.

These rich experiences and loving cast of characters are summoned from the past some thirty years later in *La casa de los espíritus*, Allende's personal rendition of her family saga in the style of Latin American magical realism. The deeply political content of this novel and her subsequent one, *De amor y de sombra* (1984; *Of Love and Shadows*, 1987), are a product, however, of her adult years. Following her travels through Europe, Bolivia, and the Middle East with her mother and stepfather in her early adolescence, Allende returned to Chile at fifteen. She promptly finished high school and took a job as a secretary in the Department of Information of the United Nations Food and Agriculture Organization. At one point, she was placed in charge of a fifteen-minute television program on hunger. Her success was so great that she was offered a weekly slot on Chile's first television network. For many years she also wrote a column called "Impertinentes" in the woman's magazine, *Paula*. It was known for its humorous satire of such Chilean "vices" as *machismo*.

On September 11, 1973, a military coup led to the assassination of President Salvador Allende and transformed overnight the political climate of Chile. Isabel Allende joined the efforts of Church-sponsored programs which responded to the crisis by providing food and aid to the needy. She spent hours gathering testimonies of families of the disappeared. She transported the persecuted to safe asylums and documented events that would subsequently be integrated into *La casa de los espíritus*. Allende's subsequent dismissal from her job at *Paula* and her decision to move with her family to Venezuela in 1975 marked a difficult period in her life. Eventually, she renewed her career as a journalist, worked in a primary school in Caracas, and initiated the silent process of weaving together the threads of her first novel, originally begun as a letter to her one-hundred-year-old grandfather who was dying in Chile.

Allende has often spoken about this period of her life and its relationship to the genesis of *La casa de los espíritus*. She tells us:

When I left Chile after the military coup, I lost in one instant my family, my past, my home. . . . If there had been no exile, no pain, no rage built up over all those years far from my country, most likely I would not have written this book, but another. (Agosín Interview, p. 53)

Upon completing her novel, Allende faced numerous difficulties in having it published. No publishing house wanted to read it; it was very long, and in addition it was written by an unknown author who happened to be a woman. Finally accepted by Plaza & Janés of Barcelona and published in 1982, it became an instant success and cast Allende into the role of one of the most widely read women writers in Latin America. It has also enabled her to fulfill her childhood dream of devoting herself entirely to literature. Initially censored in her native country, copies of the book were smuggled into Chile and clandestinely xeroxed and circulated until its publication was finally authorized by the government. It immediately became a best seller there and has been translated into fifteen languages.

Allende's second novel, *De amor y de sombra*, continues her testimony of Chilean repression. It is based on the disappearance of fifteen peasants in the region of Lonquén. Allende brings to bear her many years of work as journalist in her portrayal of the novel's protagonist, the young reporter, Irene Beltrán, who is forced to come to terms with the political horror of her country. Allende has stated that journalism taught her to "search for truth and to try to be objective, how to capture the reader and hold him firmly and not let him escape" (Agosín Interview, p. 56). This technique explains part of the mastery of *De amor y de sombra*, a gripping political novel.

Despite the incredibly painful and difficult material that Allende writes about, neither she nor her novels are filled with a sense of pessimism or despair. Allende has often said in her public lectures that such emotions are paralyzing. She believes profoundly in the ability of the human spirit to endure. It is perhaps for this reason that her novels are ultimately so uplifting as well as entertaining. A born storyteller, Allende renders tribute to this gift in her most recent work, *Eva Luna* (1987; whose title is the protagonist's name), a modern picaresque novel about a twentieth-century Scheherazade who spins tales to survive in a politically unstable Latin American society.

It is difficult for one who has met Isabel Allende not to immediately find pieces of her in all her female characters. They share her sharp intelligence, playful sense of humor, force of decision, love of words, romantic temperament, desire to live life as if it were a novel, and healthy sense of female identity. Allende is a dynamic and exuberant public speaker who attracts packed audiences wherever she speaks. Her lectures are much like her novels themselves: a thoughtful blend of the personal and the political, a call for bearing witness, and a strong statement on the power of women and their ability to create a new morality in times of violence. Allende has recently posed for herself in public forums the difficult questions: "For whom do I write? Why do I write?" If her answers are as complex as the questions themselves, they nonetheless can be synthesized in the following words: "I feel that writing is an act of hope, a sort of communion with our fellow men, a tiny bit of light. I certainly write for myself, but mainly for others. For those who have no voice and for those who are kept in silence. I write for you. I write so that people will love each other more" (Montclair State College, Feb. 1988).

MAJOR THEMES

La casa de los espíritus has been aptly compared to that great line of novelistic sagas which includes Thomas Mann's *Buddenbrooks*, Leon Uris's *Trinity*, and Gabriel García Márquez's *Cien años de soledad*. It is the story of four generations of the Trueba-del-Valle lineage set against the backdrop of Chilean politics from the beginning of the century to the military coup of Augusto Pinochet in 1973. Allende skillfully weaves together fiction and history as she creates a text that is a "kaleidoscope of jumbled mirrors where everything and anything could happen" (*The House of the Spirits*, p. 72), including the unusual merging of the real and the magical, the fictitious and the historical, the spoken and the written, the politically exigent and the Utopian possibility, the male and the female.

Allende's concept of female characterization is of prime importance in the novel. She presents a rich universe of women who are strong, creative, and able to resist the powers of patriarchy and convention through acts of will. Consider the diverse models of luminescence that Allende suggests through the names of her characters: Nívea, the suffragist who fights for women's rights at the turn of the century; Clara, the spiritist who initiates the family tradition of writing; Blanca, Trueba's daughter, who lives a passionate love affair and forges new realities out of clay; Alba, the youngest member of the line, who combines her great-grandmother's political activism with her grandmother's love of writing and her mother's passion in love.

Allende highlights the political content of her novel by joining together in a macabre scenario the two grandchildren of Esteban Trueba: his legal heir and granddaughter, the political activist, Alba, and the dispossessed descendent of his first rape victim, Esteban García. García's intense jealousy of Alba, combined with his rise in the military hierarchy following the coup, gives way to his vengeful persecution of her and subsequent act of rape. Allende brings to bear all her skills as journalist and chronicler of her country's history when she describes Alba's descent into the underworld of the Chilean torture chambers. She unites Alba's story with the stories of other women, equally brutalized and tortured in the makeshift jails and concentration camps of the country.

Allende has stated that "in Latin America . . . in situations of extreme danger the people who take the greatest risks are often women. They are capable of total selflessness, total courage" (Engelbert and Levine Interview, p. 8). The final chapters of her novel are a tribute to those women whose presence and inspiration save Alba from immersion in total despair: Ana Díaz, the student activist who urges her to write down her story as a means of therapy; the unknown woman who shelters her after curfew and helps her to return home following her release from jail; her grandmother, Clara, whose message of creativity and hope encourages her to bear witness and survive. Alba's testimony itself—a mirror reflection of Allende's novel—is one that underlines the major principles of life her author believes in: the need to remember and continue onward.

In the final pages of the novel, Alba awaits the birth of her child, without knowing if the father is her lover, Miguel, or her rapist, García. As she waits, she records the testimony of her torture, together with other events of her family history written down in Clara's journals. She is joined in this task by her grandfather, Esteban Trueba, whose first-person narration of determination and despair provides a counterpoint to her own. The first sentence of Alba's text coincides with the beginning of Allende's novel, a familiar literary device designed to reinforce the veracity of the tale.

Allende has indicated in many interviews that the conclusion of the novel suggests the capacity of the human spirit to endure and regenerate life in a continuum of hope that is never totally extinguished. She has also stated that her belief in love, justice, and generosity is so strong that she has no qualms about being called sentimental for purporting such values in her works. Nowhere do these principles seem more apparent than in her second novel, *De amor y de sombra*, a work that chronologically follows the course of Chilean history begun in *La casa de los espíritus*. Nowhere else is her fusion of fiction and testimony more striking than in this novelistic account of real events that took place near the village of Lonquén in 1978 and that were subsequently documented by Máximo Pacheco Gómez in his 1980 book, *Lonquén*.

Allende's research for *De amor y de sombra* centered around Pacheco's account of the discovery of fifteen bodies in an abandoned mine by a group consisting of three high Church officials, two lawyers, and two journalists under instructions from the archbishop of Santiago (Moody, p. 40). She transformed this political testimony into a suspenseful novel centering around a young journalist, Irene Beltrán, and her companion, Francisco Leal. The two unwittingly become party to related political events that lead to their discovery of the bodies and to their attempt to publicize the atrocities sanctioned by the Chilean government.

Allende skillfully weaves together the love story of Irene and Francisco with the protagonist's own awakening to political realities. If Irene may be viewed as Alba Trueba's spiritual sister because of similarity in social class and commitment to truth, Allende has nonetheless provided this character with the opportunity of interacting with women of other socioeconomic classes whose courage and honesty radically change her own life. Most significant in this regard is Digna Ranquileo, the mother of the young girl, Evangelina, who is seized by Lieutenant Ramírez and never seen again. Recognizing that, despite class differences, a sense of female kinship unites her to Irene, Digna seeks her help in deciphering the crime. Also important is Evangelina Flores, the sister and daughter of the five Flores men whose bodies appear in the mine and who takes upon herself the mission of denouncing their deaths to the tribunals of the world.

As with *La casa de los espíritus*, Allende does not allow history to destroy her characters. Although Irene's life is gravely endangered by the bullets she receives from her enemies, she recovers and escapes into exile with Francisco Leal. There she not only joins Blanca and Pedro Tercero García from *La casa de los espíritus*, but also the immense wave of fellow countrymen whose exodus from Latin America is characteristic of our times.

While *De amor y de sombra* lacks the rich imaginative flights of fantasy of *La casa de los espíritus*, it contains a continual air of tension unmitigated by anecdotal events or even by the love story itself. Allende has succeeded in re-creating an important chapter on Chilean history sinisterly closed by the government's pardon of the criminals and the dynamiting of the mine, two events faithfully transcribed in her novel.

Allende's interest in capturing the complexities of Latin American politics takes a different twist in her most recent novel, *Eva Luna*. Here she focuses on the left-wing guerrilla movement in an unnamed country in the tropics which appears to be her adopted land, Venezuela. Once again, Allende has based aspects of her novel on extensive research done in library archives: The sacking of the presidential mansion described in the novel is a direct account of the sacking of the Somoza estate in Nicaragua; the portrayal of Professor Jones who discovers the secret of embalming also had appeared in newspaper reports, as did the birth of a child with two heads, similarly described in the novel (Levine interview). That Allende has exaggerated and dramatized these events in her work is no surprise for her readers. Testimony combined with imagination are the trademark of her narrative structures.

Whereas in her previous novels the balance between fiction and history is integrally preserved, *Eva Luna* gives the appearance of tilting the scales in favor of imagination and invention, despite the documented evidence of many events. It is the tale of a young woman born without the trappings of privilege of her sisters Alba Trueba and Irene Beltrán. Orphaned at an early age, Eva learns to survive through her wits and incomparable skills in telling stories. Befriended by people of different walks of life, from the future *guerrillero*, Huberto Naranjo, to the Turkish merchant, Riad Halabí, to the transsexual Mimí and the grand-motherly Elvira, she slowly comes of age and realizes her destiny of becoming a writer.

If Alba's mission is to record her personal history and the history of her country in a novelistic form, if Irene Beltrán's is to publicize a political crime in her journalistic accounts, Eva Luna's is to use television as a medium for introducing to the public such unusual concepts as guerrilla warfare, transsexuality, Indian heritage, and passionate love—the very fibers of her own life— set to the best of the mass media. Allende has stated her belief that "all means are legitimate for the writer—songs, radio, journalism. They are all forms of writing and ways of reaching the public. All means are valid if we intend to communicate" (Montclair State College, 1988). Her final portrayal of Eva Luna as a writer for a television serial program who revolutionizes the media is an excellent example of this theory set to practice in her own works.

Less political in focus than her two preceding novels, *Eva Luna* is an entertaining book that sweeps the reader along in a sort of picaresque journey through different spheres of society. As in her other novels, Allende has individualized her many characters and endowed each one with uniquely human and unforgettable qualities endearing them to her readers. Allende has indicated that Eva Luna's life is not only a tribute to her own love of storytelling, but also an example of a kind of femininity and womanhood naturally achieved, without despair, doubt, or self-interrogation (Levine Interview 1988). Eva looks in the mirror and decides that she is pretty because she wants to be and after that never gives the matter another thought. At the end of the novel, she falls in love with Rolf Carlé, the filmmaker. That she is able to love and maintain her creativity at the same time is a further homage to the models of artistry and passion that Allende continually offers her readers as possibilities for women's lives in Latin America.

SURVEY OF CRITICISM

At the present time, much of the published criticism on Isabel Allende centers necessarily on her first novel, *La casa de los espíritus*. Only two articles, written by Michael Moody and Gabriela Mora, have treated *De amor y de sombra*. The publication of *Eva Luna* a few months prior to the writing of this entry precludes the possibility of gathering meaningful criticism on this work. Despite this paucity of critical sources in general, *La casa de los espíritus* has provided critics of Latin American literature with countless opportunities for analysis.

It is difficult to find any serious article on this work that does not devote a significant amount of space to comparing it to García Márquez's masterpiece, *Cien años de soledad*. The relationship between the Buendía family saga and the Trueba-del-Valle lineage, the concept of magical realism and circularity, the similarities between Remedios la Bella in the Colombian novel and Rosa in Allende's, as well as between Pilar Ternera and la Nana and such events as the flood in *Cien años* versus the earthquake in *La casa de los espíritus*, have been scrutinized by the critics with an eye worthy of Cervantes's priest and barber.

Marcelo Coddou suggests that the "obsessive preoccupation" of some critics in comparing these two novels is in reality an attempt to "discredit the originality and validity of *La casa de los espíritus*" and thus "turn the attention away from those aspects of the novel which endanger the discourse of power." Coddou cites as examples a substantial list of articles published in Chile by representatives of the official line of thought ("Las ficciones," p. 12).

Other critics have devoted their attention to the question of what differentiates these two works and makes Allende's novel an original and compelling piece of literature. Insightful articles in this respect have been written by Marjorie Agosín, René Campos, Marcelo Coddou, Linda Gould Levine, Teresa Méndez-Faith, Juan Manuel Marcos, and Mario Rojas. This group of critics has been adept in underlining one of the essential differences between Allende's novel and García Márquez' text: the concept of female characterization. Juan Manuel Marcos states that, while the Colombian author provides an "apology of the so-called metaphysical virtues of housewives," Allende "subjects to a profound critical and dialectical revision the condition of women in Latin American society" ("Isabel viendo llover," p. 131). Marcos and Méndez-Faith add that Allende presents an array of female characters, the majority of whom break "all forms of patriarchal stereotypes" ("Multiplicidad," p. 67).

Rojas, Agosín, Campos, and Coddou have used current theories of feminist literary criticism to underline Allende's female-centered orientation. Levine suggests that Allende rereads or rewrites García Márquez's concept of male authorship and creativity. As opposed to the lineage of Aurelianos who enclose themselves in "a room of their own," in order to decipher Melquíades's manuscripts, Allende's new generation of women, symbolized by Alba (Dawn), rehabilitate Virginia Woolf's concept of "a room of her own" and reconstruct and complete Clara's writings ("A Passage").

Another aspect of Allende's novel fiercely debated by the critics concerns the conclusion of the work. Gabriela Mora has written one of the most interesting articles on this topic. Mora states that the political message is diminished through Allende's circular structure and Alba's act of waiting for "better times." For Mora, such an ending can be interpreted "as an acceptance of the conservative position that injustice and crime are inevitable" because it evokes the image of the "resigned passive female of other times" ("Ruptura," p. 78). Marcelo Coddou focuses the question of the novel's conclusion from a different point of view. He suggests that Alba's written testimony consolidates Allende's message of solidarity and denunciation. Levine adds that Alba's integration of her pen and womb (writing and gestation) at the end of the work reinforces Allende's continual fusion of traditional male and female symbols. Rojas has similarly studied the concept of androgyny and Allende's creation of characters who "transcend generic stereotypes" and "absorb both feminine and masculine positive qualities" ("Un caleidoscopio," p. 923).

The critics have also sought to situate Allende's writings within the context of contemporary Latin American literature. For Juan Manuel Marcos and Teresa Méndez-Faith, Allende's novel coincides with the writings of such authors of the post-Boom as Antonio Skármeta, Mempo Giardinelli, Luisa Valenzuela,* Osvaldo Soriano, and Saúl Ibargoyen. Quoting Angel Rama, Marcos and Méndez-Faith consider these writers "refuters of power" who reject "all forms of power which are manifested in different levels of social life" (linguistic, sexual, economic, etc.), and seek to "reintegrate History into fiction in a dialectical and questioning way designed at comprehending . . . the present conflictive reality" ("Multiplicidad," p. 62). Marcos further suggests that, in contrast to the works of García Márquez "in which the historical references acquire a vague and abstract substance," in *La casa de los espíritus* "characters and situations which are mythical and hallucinating coexist and appear together with those which are strictly real." These include "Pablo Neruda, Salvador Allende, the popular demonstration in favor of the new socialist government, Agrarian Reform and the expropriation of funds, . . . the military coup, the bombardment of the Moneda Palace, curfew, the massive refuge of those seeking asylums in the embassies of the country, Pinochet," etc. ("Isabel viendo llover," pp. 133–134).

Gabriela Mora also acknowledges Allende's skill in disseminating "under the guise of fiction many of the most unfortunate deeds of the last decades of Chilean life." She states, nonetheless, that in both *La casa de los espíritus* and *De amor y de sombra* many of the main characters are "incapable of transcending the personal terms of their own drama" to include the "collective drama of the Chilean tragedy" ("Las novelas," p. 55). Mora cites as examples of this kind of "individual egotism" and trivialization of history Esteban Trueba's "lucid and happy" last moments, Francisco Leal's sense of male pride at being alone with a "vulnerable" Irene at the abandoned mine where the bodies are buried, and Pedro Tercero García's tranquil experience of love and exile ("Las novelas," pp. 56–59).

Mora's reasoning is provocative and intelligent. She has acutely pointed out "stereotyped clichés" present in "the ideology of even the most educated and progressive" of Allende's characters ("Las novelas," p. 58). Her arguments seem to minimize, however, the balance that Allende creates between her characters' political consciousness and their own sense of self, which at times is detached from the "collective drama" and which also gives her novels their profoundly human quality. Mora has also situated Allende in the context of such Latin American women authors as Cristina Peri Rossi,* Luisa Valenzuela,* and Albalucía Angel,* in whose works politics and the family are also central focuses and who similarly use humor and sexual freedom as prime components of their writings.

Marcelo Coddou and Mario Rojas offer two convincing opinions for the tremendous success of *La casa de los espíritus*. For Coddou, it is due to the extraordinary fusion of personal history and collective history and to the presence of "fantasy . . . put to the service of a scrutiny of reality in the best Latin American tradition" ("Introducción," p. 9). For Rojas, the success of the novel is not only due to Allende's "extraordinary narrative ability," but precisely to those "popular elements of the novel" that are accessible "to the great mass of readers who have been neglected for so long" ("Una aproximación," p. 99).

Although Allende herself believes that the true measure of her success will not be known until the future, it is unlikely that her novels will be forgotten. As in the best Cervantine tradition, she entertains and instructs at the same time that she continually reminds us of our moral obligations as human beings. It is no wonder that she has become one of the most widely read Chilean writers of all time.

BIBLIOGRAPHY

Works by Isabel Allende

La casa de los espíritus. Barcelona: Plaza & Janés, 1982.
De amor y de sombra. Barcelona: Plaza and Janés, 1984.
"Testimonio de Isabel Allende." *Discurso Literario* 2, 1 (1984):67–71.
Eva Luna. Barcelona: Plaza and Janés, 1987.
"La magia de las palabras." *Revista Iberoamericana* 132–33 (July-Dec. 1985):447–52.

"Los libros tienen sus propios espíritus." *Los libros tienen sus propios espíritus*. Ed. Marcelo Coddou. Mexico: Universidad Veracruzana, 1986. Pp. 15–20.

Translations of Isabel Allende

Bogin, Magda, trans. *The House of the Spirits*. New York: Alfred A. Knopf, 1985.
Engelbert, Jo Anne. "The Spirits Were Willing." *Lives on the Line: The Testimony of Contemporary Latin American Authors*. Ed. Doris Meyer. Berkeley, Calif.: University of California, 1988, Pp. 235–42.
Peden, Margaret S., trans. *Of Love and Shadows*. New York: Alfred A. Knopf, 1987.

Works about Isabel Allende

Agosín, Marjorie. "Entrevista a Isabel Allende/Interview with Isabel Allende." Trans. Cola Franzen. *Imagine* 1, 2 (Winter 1984):42–56.
———. "Isabel Allende: *La casa de los espíritus*." *Revista Interamericana de Bibliografía/Inter-American Review of Bibliography* 35 (1985):448–58.
Bautista Schwartz, Gloria. "De *Cien años de soledad* a *La casa de los espíritus*: Del realismo mágico al post-boom." Ph.D. diss., State University of New York at Albany, 1988. (DAI 48, 8 [1988]:2072A.).
Campos, René. "*La casa de los espíritus*: mirada, espacio, discurso de la otra historia." *Los libros tienen sus propios espíritus*. Ed. Marcelo Coddou. Mexico: Universidad Veracruzana, 1986. Pp. 21–28.
Coddou, Marcelo. "Introducción. *La casa de los espíritus*: de la historia a la Historia." *Los libros*. Pp. 7–14.
———. "Las ficciones de Isabel Allende." *Ediciones de la Frontera* 39 (Winter 1987): 11–12.
———. "Para leer a Isabel Allende. Su vida en su obra." *Araucaria de Chile* 38 (1987): 125–36.
Engelbert, Jo Anne, and Linda Gould Levine. "The World Is Full of Stories/Interview with Isabel Allende." *Review: Latin American Literature and Arts* 34 (Jan.-June 1985):18–20.
Gazarian Gautier, Marie-Lise. "Isabel Allende." *Interviews with Latin American Writers*. Elmwood Park, Ill.: Dalkey Archive Press, 1989, 5–24.
Hart, Patricia. "Narrative Magic in the Fiction of Isabel Allende." Ph.D. diss., University of North Carolina at Chapel Hill, 1987 (DAI 48, 7 [1988]: 1785A).
Levine, Linda Gould. Interview with Isabel Allende. New York, Feb. 3, 1988.
———. "A Passage to Androgyny: Isabel Allende's *La casa de los espíritus*." Ed. Carol Maier and Noël Valis. *In the Feminine Mode: Essays on Hispanic Women Writers*. Lewisburg, Pa.: Bucknell University Press, 1990.
Marcos, Juan Manuel. "Isabel viendo llover en Barataria." *Revista de Estudios Hispánicos* 19, 2 (May 1985):129–37.
Marcos, Juan Manuel, and Teresa Méndez-Faith. "Multiplicidad, dialéctica y reconciliación del discurso en *La casa de los espíritus*." *Los libros*. Pp. 61–70.
Moody, Michael. "Isabel Allende and the Testimonial Novel." *Confluencia* 2, 1 (Fall 1986): 39–43.
Mora, Gabriela. "Las novelas de Isabel Allende y el papel de la mujer como ciudadana." *Ideologies and Literature* 2, 1 (Spring 1987):53–61.

————. "Ruptura y perseverancia de estereotipos en *La casa de los espíritus.*" *Los libros.* Pp. 71–78.

Rojas, Mario, "*La casa de los espíritus*: una aproximación sociolingüística." *Los libros.* Pp. 91–99.

————. "*La casa de los espíritus* de Isabel Allende: un caleidoscopio de espejos desordenados." *Revista Iberoamericana* 132–133 (July-Dec. 1985):917–25.

ALBALUCÍA ANGEL
(b. 1939)
Colombia

Raymond Leslie Williams

BIOGRAPHY

Born in Pereira, Colombia, in 1939, Albalucía Angel came from an upper middle-class family background in Colombia's wealthy coffee-producing Department of Quindío. She went to Bogotá to pursue the study of literature and art at the major private university of Colombia's elite, the Universidad de los Andes. Angel continued her study of the history of art in Paris and Rome. In the 1960s she earned her living as a folk singer in Europe, and in the late 1960s she began writing. During the 1970s, she lived in both Europe and Colombia. Angel returned to Colombia for several months in 1975 and received the Vivencias National Novel Prize. During the 1980s she has lived in Great Britain and lectured at international literary conferences, particularly on feminist topics. She was married to the Chilean writer Mauricio Wacquez for several years, and later they separated.

Angel's early work reflects her experience in Europe. The novels *Los girasoles en invierno* (1970; Sunflowers in the winter) and *Dos veces Alicia* (1972; Alice twice) represent settings in the Europe with which she had just become acquainted. The setting for *Los girasoles en invierno* takes place in the cafés and streets of Paris and *Dos veces Alicia* in London in the 1960s. In *Estaba la pájara pinta sentada en el verde limón* (1975; The painted bird was sitting in the green lemon tree), she returns to the experience of her youth in Colombia during the period of La Violencia (1947–1958). This novel recounts the crude and stark realities of an extraordinarily violent period that left an indelible mark on all of Angel's generation. Her experience with Colombia remains a central preoccupation in the short stories *¡Oh gloria inmarcesible!* (1979; Oh unfading glory!). Angel's personal and professional interest in feminism during the 1980s is reflected in the two novels *Misiá Señora* (1982; The missus) and *Las andariegas* (1984; The travelers).

MAJOR THEMES

Angel's thematic concerns have developed throughout three basic periods of her total work. During the first period (1970–1972), her initial experimentation with fiction, she explored the relationship between reality and fiction. In the second period (1973–1979), she investigated the reality and consequences of Colombian history and culture for individuals. In the third period (1980–1984), her major themes were essentially feminist and related to postmodern issues.

The novels of her first period of initial experimentation were *Los girasoles en invierno* and *Dos veces Alicia*. *Los girasoles en invierno* consists of brief narrative segments (usually one to four pages in length) narrated by a female voice who reacts to her immediate circumstance (in Paris) and relates memories of a very recent past in traveling around Europe. An indication of Angel's experimentation is evident in the handling of the plot: There is no consistently developed plot—only a sketchy story line that deals with the relationship the narrator has with a novice painter. This novel also has an innovative structure with two types of chapters, which encompass, in turn, the novel's two basic spaces. The odd-numbered chapters are interiorizations of the protagonist which reveal her thoughts and feelings while she is seated in a café in Paris. The even-numbered chapters take place in other parts of Europe, and an omniscient narrator describes the protagonist and her group of friends as they travel throughout Europe. The odd chapters feature a play with language as a type of intellectual game, although this manipulation of language is not very consequential. The travel chapters are a 1960s version of the familiar story of the Latin American discovering Europe for the first time. The most notable aspect of this first novel is the invention based on pure language play, although Angel's use of language is occasionally amateurish. For example, she sometimes proceeds by simply name-dropping: "Miró el pueblecito que parecía más bien un dibujo de Klee" (she looked at the little town that looked more like a Klee drawing).

Angel's second experiment with fiction, *Dos veces Alicia*, is vastly more sophisticated than *Los girasoles en invierno* and considerably more successful. It consists of twenty-two narrative segments, set in Great Britain, which relate the relationships the female protagonist has with a series of real and imagined friends. Significantly enough, the novel's epigraph, "let's pretend," is from Lewis Carroll's *Alice Through the Looking Glass*. The book's title also relates it to Carroll's *Alice in Wonderland*, and Angel has emphasized the importance of this book in her writing. *Dos veces Alicia* contains many illogical elements, which perhaps have their roots in Angel's experience in England: "Lewis Carroll was a master of logic, and the escapism of Alice to the world of the illogical, the world of the mirror, was a totally real reflection for me" (Williams, 1977, p. 156).

Rather than narrating a linear plot, *Dos veces Alicia* is developed according to a series of associations. The only unifying element for these disperse associations is the presence of the narrator. She insists on freely practicing the right of invention and invites the reader to imagine with her. For example, at the end of one chapter, the narrator decides to leave the remainder of the anecdote to the reader's imagination: "El resto voy a dejarlo a la imaginación de cada cual" (p. 91, I'm going to leave the rest to the imagination of each).

The narrator in *Dos veces Alicia* presents the text in the act of creation, offering numerous observations about the story in the process of becoming. The narrator claims on the first page, for example, that she suffers from "pereza mental" (mental laziness), and then proceeds to explain how she must concentrate and be disciplined to relate the story: "Si me concentro entonces de seguro que la historia resulta" (p. 11, If I concentrate then surely the story will work out). This type of interruption on the narrator's part throughout this novel makes it an experiment in self-conscious fiction.

In the second period (1973–1979), Angel addresses issues directly related to Colombian reality. The representative works of this period are the novel *Estaba la pájara pinta sentada en el verde limón* and the volume of stories *¡Oh gloria inmarcesible!* The political and historical context of *Estaba la pájara pinta sentada en el verde limón* is La Violencia, the period of civil war that was particularly intense from 1948 to 1958, but that many scholars have dated from the 1930s to the present. Different accounts of this conflict have set the number of deaths between 1947 to 1958 at 150,000 to 300,000. Incited by the assassination of Liberal presidential candidate Jorge Eliécer Gaitán in 1948, La Violencia took the form of murder, terrorism and the destruction of property. Social scientists have attributed numerous political and social tensions to this phenomenon, including partisan politics, economic deprivation, personal vindictiveness, and anticommunism. The effects of La Violencia were profound, and many of its actions and consequences appear in the abundant literature on this subject. Among the most renowned novels to deal with this topic were Eduardo Caballero Calderón's *El cristo de espaldas* (1952; Christ on his back), Daniel Caicedo's *Viento seco* (1954; Dry wind), Gabriel García Márquez's *La mala hora* (1962; In evil hour), Manuel Mejía Vallejo's *El día señalado* (1964; The appointed day), and Gustavo Alvarez Gardeazábal's *Cóndores no entierran todos los días* (1972; Condors aren't buried every day). Within this historical and novelistic context one can speak of Angel's contribution to Colombia's growing literature of La Violencia and insert her novel *Estaba la pájara pinta sentada en el verde limón*.

Estaba la pájara pinta sentada en el verde limón begins with a quotation from a politician who refers to "este laberinto de hechos, hombres y juicios" (p. 5, This labyrinth of facts, people and opinions). "Labyrinth" is indeed an appropriate description of the reader's experience. The labyrinth consists of twenty-seven unnumbered and untitled segments. The first sentence intercalates a historical narration—minute by minute—of the events that preceded the assassination of Gaitán into the characters' subjective perceptions of these events. The assassination of Gaitán is the point of departure for a chaotic situation that becomes progressively worse with the passing of time, developed on the basis of two narrative lines. The odd-numbered chapters are the most extensive (twenty to twenty-five pages) and narrate the disorder that begins as mere vandalism, becomes a more organized rural violence, and then turns into a student problem and a chaos with ideological roots. This development, of course, represents an interpretation of La Violencia. The initial chapters of the novel are briefer (five to eight pages) and deal with a boarding school for girls. Some of these girls will participate in the political chaos. Later, these chapters, which describe the childhoods of Ana, Tina, and Julieta, are more varied: We see a journalist who writes some brief notes while he is in jail; we observe the guerrilla leader Teófilo Rojas who writes his diary also in jail; we follow the fortunes of the state's enemies.

The effect of the novel's circular structure depends on establishing in its narrative segment themes that will be developed later. The first segment begins with a narrator who is in bed and contemplates images from the past. The images are vague, but the reader notes her preoccupation with the past: "Yo no me creo la historia que ellos cuentan, que se la traguen los pendejos" (p. 7, I don't believe the story they tell, let the fools buy it). Consequently, the narrator's examination relates to the search for the authentic history (not the one in which the "fools" believe). It has certain sexual connotations from the beginning: "otra vez mi sexo descubierto y penetrará en él, como buscando" (p. 8, once again my sex discovered and it will penetrate in it, searching). What is she searching for? The search goes back chronologically to the past in order to "terminar de una vez con este cosmos inflamado de imágenes sin lógica" (p. 8, to end for once and all this cosmos inflamed with images without logic). At the end of the novel, the innocent girl of the beginning is with the revolutionary Lorenzo, and once again the imagery ties the search for an authentic past with creation and the sexual act. These images do not suggest hope or rebirth, but impotence. Impotence is also a constant theme in the anecdote in general.

Estaba la pájara pinta sentada en el verde limón represents what Mikhail M. Bakhtin would identify as a text of "heteroglossia," that is, a many-languaged text. Angel uses the language of other texts to confront the Colombian reality of La Violencia. For example, at the beginning of the novel, she incorporates a fragment from the book *El 9 de abril en palacio* (1948) by Joaquín Estrada Monsalve. The multiple languages of this novel are also based on other historical texts dealing with La Violencia, and these texts can be identified directly or indirectly.

Angel's use of historical and sociological documents also makes *Estaba la pájara pinta sentada en el verde limón* a testimonial/documentary novel. By fusing documentary materials and fiction, the novel questions the very process of creating "the facts." It also inquires into the censorship of these facts. As a documentary novel, *Pájara pinta* explores the relationship between the role of the writer and artistic creation in contemporary society. A product of Angel's documentary creation and a revelation of heretofore unknown facets of Colombian history, *Estaba la pájara pinta sentada en el verde limón* represents her most profound confrontation with Colombian reality.

Angel continued exploring Colombian reality in the volume of short fiction *¡Oh gloria inmarcesible!* The volume consists of thirty-five short fictions divided into eight parts. They present a vast panoramic overview of Colombia set in its different geographic regions. They are vignettes that capture the essence of different aspects of Colombia's rich and heterogeneous cultural traditions and that vary enormously according to region.

The first part, "Turistiando en el Valle" (Touring in the valley), entails two brief narratives set in the western valley of Colombia, the Valle del Cauca. This region, like the Caribbean coast, is triethnic (Spanish, Indian, and Afro-American) and culturally heterogeneous. The two narratives set in this region feature aspects of this cultural heterogeneity, such as its unique colloquial language.

The second part, "Souvenir de San Andrés" (Souvenir from San Andrés), contains six narratives set in the Caribbean island of San Andrés. Even though the island belongs to Colombia, it also participates in a special Caribbean culture that includes the English heritage. The heterogeneous cultural and historical heritage of San Andrés has been communicated from generation to generation by means of legends and oral tradition. Angel captures the sense of this legend in stories such as "Por la vereda tropical" (On the tropical path), an account of the initial images and impressions of a woman who arrives in San Andrés for the first time. The conflict between the traditional culture of San Andrés and modernity is also a thematic concern in these stories, particularly in the story "El Polaris II."

Angel's social conscience is evidenced in the third section of this volume, "Paisajes del Otún" (Passages from Otún). The contradictions of Colombia's hierarchical class structure are presented in this section. The poverty of Colombia's lower classes and lumpenproletariat is portrayed in "La Doctora Lyuba" (Dr. Lyuba). The author's solidarity with Colombia's disenfranchised is indirectly communicated in "Paisajes del Otún" and "Un Plano Americano" (An American map). A character's efforts to survive in an unjust society are the focus of "Campirana" (A churlish woman).

The section "Postales de Boyacá y una fotico en Santa Fe" (Post cards from Boyacá and a little picture of Santa Fe) presents a variety of settings in Colombia's highland region and in the area of Bogotá. Working-class individuals and everyday situations are the focus of these fictions, which have both urban and rural settings.

Class conflict rather than regional society or culture is the focus of the fifth part of this book, "Estampas de la Guerrilla" (Scenes from the guerrilla war). The three stories in this part portray dissident guerrillas in three different situations. In each case, guerrilla warfare is combined with a male-female relationship.

The remaining three parts of this volume are brief portraits of cultural encounters in the region of Chocó and the Caribbean coast, both of which contain
a strong Afro-American component. Several of these vignettes re-create the
colloquial spoken language of Afro-Americans in these regions. The title story,
"¡Oh Gloria Inmarcesible!" employs not oral language, but a heterogeneously
written discourse: a collage of newspaper articles.

The major themes of Angel's third period are essentially feminist and related
postmodern issues. The two novels of this period, *Misiá Señora* and *Las andariegas*, are also her most hermetic works. The protagonist of *Misiá Señora*,
Mariana, is reared by a family of the landed aristocracy in the coffee-growing
region of Colombia. She eventually finds herself caught between the expectations
a traditional society holds for young women—marriage and motherhood—and
a less conventional but more potentially meaningful existence. The nontraditional
lifestyle is stimulated through her friendships with Yosmina and Anais.

The structure of *Misiá Señora*, divided into three parts, relates three chronological stages of Mariana's life. These three parts are formally identified as
"*Imágenes*" (Images). The first of these *Imágenes*, entitled "Tengo una muñeca
vestida de azul" (I have a doll dressed in blue), deals with Mariana's childhood
and adolescence. The second, "Antigua sin sombra" (Ancient one without
shade), relates her courtship, marriage, her two children's births, and her weak-
ening mental state, which results in a stay in a mental institution. The third
Imagen, "Los sueños del silencio" (Dreams of silence), relates a series of drama-
like visions that often relate to her mother and grandmother.

Gender differences are the central theme in *Misiá Señora*. Much of the first
Imagen deals with different aspects of female sexuality. Mariana's childhood
involves sexual harassment, initial experiences with *machismo*, and the gradual
discovery of her own sexuality. Sexual harassment is a vague and incomprehensible experience for Mariana as a child, and yet one of the significant "images" that will be remembered in adulthood. The expression of *machismo*
involves a variety of experiences, including the expression of the male role
model as the ideal.

Gender issues are also associated with the doctrine of the Catholic Church
and with class structure in *Misiá Señora*. The protagonist's experience with the
Catholic Church involves her indoctrination as a child that the body represents
sin. For example, she learns that "mirar a alguien desnudo era pecado" (looking
at someone nude was a sin) and that touching her own body was also a sin. She
lives the female legends of sexuality and sin as related to her by traditional adult
females. Later, as an adult, she will struggle to overcome the mental barriers
of this indoctrination in order to express herself sexually. When she loses her
virginity, she thinks of all that the priests and monks had taught her as a child,
and she feels the need to liberate herself from this past with the Church. Social
class also relates to this novel's presentation of gender issues to the extent that
Mariana had been destined to become a passive "niña linda" (pretty girl) of
provincial aristocracy.

Misiá Señora is a novel of images and imagination, as defined by its tripartite structure divided into three *Imágenes*. The protagonist, who occasionally assumes the role of writer, demonstrates a rampant imagination and proposes a search for a new female consciousness. As a child, Mariana's reaction to her identity crisis is to take refuge in her imagination. She imagines herself flying: "volar volar como Nils Olgerson cuando viajaba" (p. 74, Fly fly like Nils Olgerson when he traveled). As an adult, Mariana often interprets the concrete reality around her on the basis of her imagination. Consequently, in *Misiá Señora* the reader is presented a fictional world in which the line between reality and imagination is tenuous. One aspect of this highly imaginative experience is the creation of a new language as part of Angel's feminist project.

Las andariegas is explicitly presented as a feminist project and is Angel's most radical experiment in fiction to date. It can be viewed as a search on two levels. On the one hand, it is a search for a female language; on the other, it is an evocation of a female sense of courage. *Las andariegas* is also a postmodern project in the sense that it is a self-conscious attempt at fictionalizing postmodern feminist theory into a novel. It begins with two epigraphs, a statement by the author that sets forth the feminist project, and a third epigraph. The first epigraph is from *Les guérrillères* by Monique Wittig. The context of this epigraph refers to females breaking the existing order and to their need, above all, for strength and courage. The second epigraph is from *Las nuevas cartas portuguesas* by Maria Isabel Barreno, Maria Teresa Horta, and Maria Velho da Costa, and refers to women as firm and committed warriors. These two epigraphs are explained by the author's page-long statement, the third prefatory section to appear before the narrative. Angel explains that her reading of Wittig's *Les guérrillères* inspired her to undertake this project with female warriors who advance "desde ninguna región hacia la historia" (from nowhere to history). She used as a guide images from stories from her childhood, transformed into fables and cryptic visions. The final product of her search, according to Angel, is the hope that women have held throughout time. The third epigraph is from the mythologies of a Colombian indigenous group—the Kogui—and emphasizes the role of the female figure in creation.

The sixty-two brief anecdotes of this novel present a view of women who have been censored from history rather than a plot line. They represent parables that heretofore have been denied a female voice. These brief anecdotes relate the experiences of "viajeras" (traveling women) in an affirmative way.

Language is the most innovative aspect of *Las andariegas*. Much of the narrative consists of brief phrases, often with unconventional punctuation. Rather than developing a consistent plot, these phrases often contain an image. The use of verbal imagery is supported by visual images—a set of twelve drawings of the female in the novel. Angel also experiments with the physical space of language in the text, in a manner similar to concrete poetry. The four pages of this type feature a variety of circular and semicircular arrangements of the names of women famous in history. The presence of these four pages universalizes the story of these constantly traveling women.

Las andariegas ends with a type of epilogue: another quotation from Monique

Wittig, consisting of four brief sentences that call for precisely the project that is the essence of Angel's last two novels: a new language, a new beginning, and a new history for women. The author expresses optimism for this new beginning with the final sentence: "Ellas dicen que el sol va a salir" (They [female] say that the sun is going to come out).

SURVEY OF CRITICISM

Angel's work has been the subject of relatively little scholarly work compared to other Latin American writers of her generation. Her work has been frequently ignored in histories of Spanish American literature. In recent years her name has been appearing progressively more often in the Colombian press and in international academic journals. This brief survey of the criticism will be divided into three parts: (1) a chronological survey; (2) comments on her work in studies on Colombian literature; and (3) scholarly articles on her fiction.

Critical reaction to Angel's work was generally superficial until the 1980s. The critics mainly ignored her first two novels; only a few journalistic notes appeared in Colombia. The national novel prize brought Angel into the limelight in Colombia during the mid-1970s and resulted in numerous interviews and reviews in Colombian newspapers and cultural magazines. She was introduced to the English-speaking world by means of an interview published in English translation in 1977: "An Interview with Women Writers in Colombia" (Williams). During the 1980s scholars outside Colombia—academics in the Hispanic world and in the United States—began to take greater note of her work. By the mid-1980s Angel's fiction had drawn the attention of feminist critics of Hispanic literature.

Angel is mentioned in some general studies on contemporary Colombian literature. In a book-length study of Colombian literature of the 1960s and 1970s, Colombian critic Isaías Peña Gutiérrez (1982) discusses Angel's novels *Los girasoles en invierno* and *Dos veces Alicia*. He notes the circular structure of each and considers *Dos veces Alicia* the more successful of the two. Peña concludes that *Dos veces Alicia* does not show any influence of Angel's compatriot Gabriel García Márquez. In Raymond L. Williams's book-length study (1981) of the Colombian novel of the 1970s, Angel's first three novels are placed within the context of the 1970s.

Recent scholarly articles have been close readings of individual novels. Sharon Keefe Ugalde (1986) has published a reading of *Misiá Señora* using Wolfgang Iser's concepts of readers finding themselves "halfway between a 'in longer' and a 'not yet'." Keefe Ugalde concludes that the reader is left to innovate and to paint a portrait of woman to replace the familiar one the novel negates. In a study of *Estaba la pájara pinta sentada en el verde limón*, Dick Gerdes (1987) approaches this novel as a testimonial and documentary work. He concludes that one objective of the work is to demonstrate a virtually unknown version of history. Despite the confusion of reality, according to Gerdes, this documentary novel proposes to explain it by means of the artistic juxtaposition of the details selected.

BIBLIOGRAPHY

Works by Albalucía Angel

Los girasoles en invierno. Bogotá: Bolívar, 1970.
Dos veces Alicia. Barcelona: Seix-Barral, 1972.
Estaba la pájara pinta sentada en el verde limón. Bogotá: Instituto Colombiano de Cultura, 1975.
¡Oh gloria inmarcesible! Bogotá: Instituto Colombiano de Cultura, 1979.
Misiá Señora. Barcelona: Argos Vergara, 1982.
Las andariegas. Barcelona: Argos Vergara, 1984.

Works about Albalucía Angel

Aguilera Garramuño, Marco Tulio. "La pájara pinta, Albalucía Angel." *Seminario Cultural, El Pueblo* (Cali) (July 3, 1977):5.
Alvarado Tenorio, Harold. "De la razón a la soledad." *Seminario Cultural, El Pueblo* (Cali) (July 3, 1977):5.
Araújo, Helena. "Ejemplos de la 'niña impúdica' en Silvina Ocampo y Alba Lucía [sic] Angel." *Hispamérica* 38 (1984):27–35. Also, *La Scherezada criolla*. Bogotá: Universidad Nacional de Colombia, 1989. Pp. 99–106.
Estrada Monsalve, Joaquín. *El 9 de abril en palacio*. Bogotá: Editorial Cahur, 1948.
Filer, Malva E. "Autorrescate e invención en *Las andariegas* de Albalucía Angel." *Revista Iberoamericana* 51, 132–133 (July-Dec. 1985):649–55.
Gerdes, Dick. "*Estaba la pájara pinta sentada en el verde limón*: novela testimonial/documental de 'la violencia' en Colombia." *Revista de Estudios Colombianos* 2 (1987):21–26.
Keefe Ugalde, Sharon. "Between 'in longer' and 'not yet': Woman's Space in *Misiá Señora*." *Revista de Estudios Colombianos* 1 (1986):23–28.
———. "El discurso femenino en *Misiá Señora*: ¿Un lenguaje nuevo o acceso al lenguaje?" *Discurso Literario* 4, 1 (Autumn 1986):117–26.
López Pulecio, Oscar. "*La pájara pinta*: un libro de la violencia." *Magazín Dominical, El Espectador* (Bogotá) (Dec. 21, 1975):9.
Mora, Gabriela. "*El Bildungsroman* y la experiencia latinoamericana: *La pájara pinta* de Albalucía Angel." *La sartén por el mango*. Eds. Patricia Elena González and Eliana Ortega. Río Piedras, Puerto Rico: Ediciones Huracán, 1985. Pp. 71–81.
———. "Lectura de Albalucía Angel." *Hispamérica* 9, 27 (1980):109–112.
Peña Gutiérrez, Isaías. "Dos veces Albalucía Angel." *La narrativa del frente nacional*. Bogotá: Fundación Universidad Central, 1982. Pp. 214–16.
Peña Gutiérrez, Joaquín. "Los críticos oyeron cantar a la pájara." *Seminario Cultural, El Pueblo* (Cali) (July 25, 1976):12–13.
Williams, Raymond Leslie. "An Interview with Women Writers in Colombia." *Latin American Women Writers: Yesterday and Today*. Eds. Yvette Miller and Charles

M. Tatum. Pittsburgh: Latin American Literary Review Press, 1977. Pp. 155–61.

———. *Una década de la novela colombiana: la experiencia de los setenta*. Bogotá: Plaza and Janés, 1981. Pp. 41–42.

MARÍA LUISA BOMBAL
(1910–1980)
Chile

Lucía Guerra Cunningham

BIOGRAPHY

María Luisa Bombal was born in Viña del Mar, Chile, on June 8, 1910. At the age of twelve she journeyed to Paris, where she lived until 1931. She received most of her formal education in France: first entering Nôtre Dame de L'Assomption, then La Brùyere, and finally enrolling at La Sorbonne where she earned her degree in French literature. The fact that she spent the decisive years of her youth in France had a significant influence on her artistic and intellectual development. The period 1924 to 1931 was not only one of the most effervescent periods in French art, but also crucial years during which the avant-garde movement was born. In this period Bombal attended lectures given by Paul Valèry; studied violin with Jacques Thibaud; performed at L'Atelier, the famous acting school directed by Charles Dullin; and joined Fortunat Strowsky's literary workshop, where she won her first prize as an author with a short story written in French.

Although French seemed destined to be the language in which she would make her way as a writer, she nonetheless continued reading and writing in Spanish, as "a secret love, a natural impulse I cultivated in private." Among the books she treasured in her youth were Goethe's *The Sorrows of Young Werther*, Knut Hamsun's *Victory*, and the novels of Selma Lagerlöff, along with *María* by the Colombian Jorge Isaacs and the works of the Argentinian, Ricardo Güiraldes.

In 1933, following a two-year sojourn in Chile, Bombal moved to Buenos Aires. There, amid the city's glittering cosmopolitan society, she soon joined the ranks of a group of writers gathered around Victoria Ocampo,* founder and director of the magazine *Sur*. Hence, she became a charter member of one of Latin American literature's most illustrious workshops, one composed of such

celebrated figures as Pablo Neruda, Jorge Luis Borges, Oliverio Girondo, Federico García Lorca, Amado Alonso, and José Ortega y Gasset.

In 1934 Bombal wrote her first *nouvelle*, entitled *La última niebla* (The Final
Mist, 1982), while sharing the kitchen table with Pablo Neruda, who at the time
was composing *Residence on Earth*, a book that would revolutionize the lyrical
genre. But, as Amado Alonso (1936) has pointed out, *La última niebla* was an
equally significant landmark for Latin American prose. Published during a period
in which the predominant literary trend was *criollismo*, a nativistic depiction of
Latin American prototypes and their peculiar geographic environment rendered
through the aesthetic mode of realism and naturalism, *La última niebla* presented
an avant-garde vision of reality expressed through new literary techniques. The
book quickly became an outstanding example of the emerging avant-garde in
Latin American writing, as well as a precursor of the Latin American novel of
the 1960s. In a moving testimony to the influence of her innovations, Carlos
Fuentes once stated that "María Luisa Bombal is the mother of us all" (in
Cunningham, 1982).

With the exception of "La maja y el ruiseñor," an evocation of her childhood
published in 1960, Bombal stopped publishing in 1946, although she wrote two
plays, *The Foreign Minister* and *Dolly and Jeckill and Miss Hyde*, both in English
in the original and as yet unpublished. In spite of the outstanding quality of her
work, she was repeatedly denied the Chilean National Prize of Literature because
her production was not deemed sufficiently prolific.

Nevertheless, her voice remains unique in Latin American letters. She was a
pioneer, a daring innovator who took chances in exploring the possibilities of
language, the complex potential of structure, and the multiplicity of narrative
modes. After a brief illness she died in Chile on May 6, 1980, leaving a novel
unfinished. The fact that today in Chile, where she spent her last few years in
near poverty, there is a $10,000 prize named the María Luisa Bombal Award
stands as an ironic epitaph, and yet one befitting so fine an artist.

MAJOR THEMES

In Bombal's literary production, reality is conceived as a complex conglomerate
in which the concrete, the oneiric, and the marvelous are simultaneously fused.
Her short story entitled "Lo secreto" (1941; "The Unknown," 1982) is undoubtedly the epitome of her fantastic elaboration of reality. Following the format
of a typical pirate's tale, the author presents her characters in a marvelous realm
under the sea inhabited by shiny sea horses, velvety flowers, and enigmatic
mermaids. After being sent by a storm to the bottom of the sea, the pirates land
in an uncanny desert where silence and darkness prevail as malign forces that
represent the irrevocable loss of God.

The creation of a reality where the concrete and the marvelous coexist not
only reveals Bombal's confluence with the avant-garde movement, but it also
expresses her view of women as individuals of an intuitive nature who are able

to grasp the mysterious irradiations of the universe. If the author's works were defined as the presentation of feminine experiences through a feminine perspective, one would be omitting its enriching complexity that lies in the opposition between both sexes. The defining core of Bombal's works lies inserted in the dialectic of the sexes, and the two sexes are conceived as irreconcilable forces doomed to incommunication and sterility.

The most important contribution of *La última niebla* is a new concept of reality representing a rejection of Positivism. In contrast with the realist world-view that assumes reality to be a concrete and tangible phenomenon objectively grasped through methods based on the individual's rational powers, *La última niebla* conceives reality as a mysterious and polyfaceted conglomerate in which there are no distinguishable limits between factual events and dreams. Similar to its avant-garde predecessors in Europe, subjectivity (and its complex relationship with exterior reality) is the fundamental source from which the novel flows, thus configurating the structure of the narrator, the narrative mode, the disposition of events, and the elaboration of motifs. This highly subjective apprehension of reality, an ambiguous entity oscillating between the concrete-objective and the oneiric-supernatural, creates a lyrical narrative mode. The narrator expresses her feelings and sensations in a first-person account of events structured in the immediate present, in this way annulling the distance between act and actor which is so typical of the objective point of view in the realist tradition. The reader is therefore faced with a fragmented reality, a subjective microcosmos.

Ambiguity arises from two main phenomena observed in the text: the absence of specific objectivity regarding exterior reality and chronological time, and the elimination of exact and rational limits between oneiric experiences, daydreams, and concrete reality. The protagonist of *La última niebla* is a married woman who seeks fulfilling love; details of concrete reality are therefore important only in terms of her agony and her hidden wishes. Thus, the rain and the cold on her wedding night, for instance, symbolize her husband's indifference to love. The temporal element is also measured in the context of the feminine experience of approaching old age, an old age that represents a constant and ever-increasing anxiety that the opportunity for love is inexorably moving beyond her reach. Her encounter with a man who makes love to her in a mysterious house is tinged with ambiguity, arising from the convergence of common details (such as the cretone curtains) as well as her lover's supernatural qualities: his silence, the halo of light surrounding his body, his mysterious appearance as if an apparition in the wee hours of a misty night. The ellipsis of a clean transition between the love scene and the moment the protagonist finds herself in bed beside her husband leaves the reader in doubt as to whether the lover really existed or was part of a dream. Furthermore, this doubt is never resolved: From that moment on, the reader enters a three-dimensional world whose landscape is, simultaneously, concrete, oneiric, and supernatural. The leitmotif of mist reinforces the ambiguity, producing strange mirages and creating a disquieting uncertainty.

La última niebla is also a powerful statement about the social predicament of

Latin American women in a world dominated by masculine values. This basic conflict is illustrated by an unresolved dilemma between the protagonist's intimate desires and social conventions that prevent her from attaining love. Social values have forced her into marriage with a man she does not love in order to escape the stigma of spinsterhood in a society that made marriage women's only goal in life. Burdened by spiritual dissatisfaction and erotic frustration, she is forced into an anguished search for love. A typical problematic heroine as defined by Georg Lukács, she undergoes a spiritual adventure that leads her to a profound and shattering understanding of the inconsistency between feminine aspirations and the moral conventions of society. The opposition between light and darkness, silence and sound, coldness and fire, the enclosed space of the house versus open nature, death symbolized in the mist leitmotif set against passion represented by Regina, all serve to illustrate the static and repressing quality of marriage versus a wild desire for love that transgresses moral conventions. Eroticism in *La última niebla* is a synonym for subversion. Under the strict moral code that demands virginity and monogamy for women, the erotic instinct is sublimated through a sensual contact with nature and the cherished longing for a lover whose very existence is doubtful.

The lover motif creates a metaphor of vitality: His body radiates luminosity and warmth; his embrace evokes the vital movement of the sea. The real or imaginary fulfillment of repressed instincts is, in essence, an attempt to reaffirm life and to overcome the moral restrictions of marriage, defined in the novel as "life in death." Social conventions symbolically represented by the enclosed space of the bourgeois house are, according to the world-view in *La última niebla*, regulations that annul the natural essence of the feminine. For Bombal, women are primordial human beings intimately united to the cosmic forces of nature, sharing an ancestral bond that has been undermined by patriarchal society. The recurrent sensual contact with trees and water (traditional symbols of fertility and cosmic regeneration) is an ancestral instinct to recapture the essence of femininity. Sublimation, however, becomes meaningless and insufficient, the power of social conventions being inescapable and the elusiveness of the long-remembered lover grown so unbearable that the protagonist must face an ordeal that admits no escape. The final mist underscores the tragic fate of female existence irrevocably condemned to life in death by a social system that regulates and represses women's essential instincts.

In *La amortajada* (1938; *The Shrouded Woman*, 1948), Bombal explores another mysterious facet of reality: the unknown and supernatural realm of death. The plot of the novel departs from a static event easily recognized as part of empirical reality. Ana María lies dead and is surrounded by those who once had a relationship with her. This situation, however, evinces supernatural dimensions that go beyond objective reality. Although she is dead, Ana María can still hear and see those who are mourning her. She recapitulates her past life while simultaneously undergoing an archetypal journey into death. The ambivalence between past and present, the factual and the marvelous, the visible and the invisible, is elaborated in the novel through the techniques of counterpoint, perspectivism, and montage.

At an immediate and concrete level, the reader grasps Ana María's highly sensorial experiences as she lies dead in her casket. Simultaneously, she is led into the past as the protagonist recalls significant events in her life, and she enters the supernatural realm of death inhabited by mysterious voices, uncanny landscapes, and strange insects and flowers. Such a montage in counterpoint captures the coexistence of elements of reality traditionally conceived as separate entities. The past binds to the present, both merging into one single instant; consciousness survives beyond physical death; and concrete objective reality fuses with the mysterious zone of death.

On the other hand, the highly complex elaboration of different perspectives reinforces the vision of reality as a relative and multifaceted conglomerate. The distance of the omniscient narrator, for instance, frequently changes, in the manner of a cinematic camera fluctuating between panoramic views and closeups with the intention of presenting reality in all its dimensions. This attempt to attain objectivity strongly contrasts with the narrator's close identification with the protagonist, which, in turn, produces in the discourse a highly emotional mood tinged with compassion, surprise, and wonder.

Besides the basic narrator, several other narrators give their testimony on Ana María, in this way adding conflicting views and interpretations to the story of her life. Thus, Ana María becomes a multifaceted character: a passionate lover, a selfish woman, a naive girl, a strict mother, a loving sister, an intuitive human being with mystical doubts about God. In *La amortajada*, fragmentation and perspectivism, two basic characteristics of avant-garde art, express the painful desire to capture a reality whose complexity is intangible for human beings and their limited cognitive power.

As in *La última niebla*, love in *La amortajada* is conceived as the only gratification for women, a concept Simone de Beauvoir has defined in *The Second Sex* in terms of the subordinate relation of women (the other) to men (the Absolute). The protagonist, a prototype of Latin American women in the 1930s, has no active participation in history, and her restrictive role of wife and mother compels her to search for love. Her relations with Ricardo, Antonio, and Fernando reveal three crucial stages in her life: sexual initiation, the passive acceptance of social conventions symbolized by marriage, and erotic sublimation in unconsummated adultery.

Ana María's love experiences with Ricardo are tinged with sensuality nurtured by sensations equated with nature. Ricardo's adolescent body is compared to the vitality of the wild forest and the indomitable strength of a stallion. Ana María ignores the social regulations that demand virginity and gives in to instincts deeply rooted in nature. Thus, when she becomes pregnant, she feels completely identified with budding trees, the graceful flight of doves, and the sounds surrounding her. Ricardo's abandonment and her miscarriage destroy this natural and harmonious relationship with nature. She encloses herself in a room and passively accepts Antonio's marriage proposal.

Married life is described as empty and unfulfilling. In spite of her frustration, Ana María pretends happiness, keeping up with appearances, although she is conscious of the unfair situation regarding men and women. As years go by, Ana María withdraws within herself, becoming narrow and petty. She encourages Fernando to court her in a selfish act that gratifies her vanity, but she never allows him to kiss her, thus protecting herself from moral transgression in committing real adultery. Moreover, her relationship with Fernando is marked by selfishness and cruelty. Although she is not in love with him, it is significant that her life is still dependent on a relation with a man.

Ana María's trajectory must be defined in terms of this existential subordination to men who are characterized in the novel as symbols of power. In this sense, the lover motif is highly significant: domination and physical strength in Ricardo, pride and power in Antonio, selfishness and rationality in Fernando. Ana María represents a tragic view of women and their place in society. As though screened in by a shroud, the protagonist ends up alienated by being forced into a passive acceptance of the status quo. Ironically, the solution to this dilemma lies not in changing her historical role but rather in the supernatural realm of death.

Death is seen as a process of immersion in the primordial cosmos. A mysterious voice invites her to abandon her coffin and explore a magical zone that belongs to the unknown. Light and darkness, life and death merge as in the primordial stage of biblical genesis. She descends to the origins of the universe, going down into the earth where she encounters flowers of bone and marvelously intact human skeletons with their knees drawn up as if once again inside the womb. Immersed in the ancient flow of life and death, she now feels new islands emerge; far off mountains of sand tumble down to give rise to other forms of life in a cyclic movement of death and regeneration. Ana María's return to this ancestral realm is also, according to the world-view presented in the novel, a return to the essence of the feminine closely united to primordial matter.

Implicit in *La última niebla* and *La amortajada* is a vision of women as human beings who reject a logical and scientific approach to reality, relying instead on intuition, emotion, and sensations. This rejection of scientific concepts and rational norms opposes the dominant ideology for the sake of a suprareality that is intangible, supernatural, and incomprehensible. In "El árbol" (1939; "The Tree," 1982), the frame of the short story—a concert—evinces from the beginning this sensual and intuitive approach to reality. While sitting in a concert theater, Brígida ignores the technical aspects of music and gives herself to the sensorial evocations and various moods produced by Mozart, Beethoven, and Chopin. The three musical pieces denote different stages in Brígida's life: playfulness and innocence in Mozart, unfulfilled passion in Beethoven, and the triumph of love in Chopin. At the stylistic level, language skillfully reproduces the tone, rhythm, and mood inherent in the composers' music, assuming musical qualities that reinforce the main thematic units in the text. On the other hand, the alternation between light and darkness has an important function in terms of the character's development. Darkness in the concert hall prefigures, at Brígida's existential level, unawareness of the deep meaning of her impulsive actions; light, on the other hand, symbolizes the profound understanding of her predicament in life.

In her next three works ("Las islas nuevas," "Trenzas," and "La historia de María Griselda"), one may observe a significant change both in the worldview presented and in Bombal's methods of artistic elaboration. Instead of presenting a central conflict based on the opposition between marriage and feminine aspirations, Bombal now omits the specifically Latin American social context, expanding it to a more universal level. On the other hand, more emphasis is given to the archetypal essence of the feminine, a thematic core that is established through the use of more traditional literary formats such as the fairy tale or the legend.

In her works Bombal presents the female archetype as observed in matriarchal societies, but she makes an important modification in the ancestral myth by presenting these positive qualities as essential women's attributes, annulled by the triumph of reason, science, and technology in the modern world. This concept is evident in one of her short poetic essays entitled "Mar, cielo, y tierra" (Sea, heaven, and earth), published in the magazine *Saber Vivir* in 1940. In this piece, women emerge as possessors of the ancestral mysteries of water and earth, two realms inhabited by magical and supernatural beings described in a highly poetic language. Heaven, on the other hand, is the domain of masculine consciousness, a fragment of the universe subject to mathematical speculation and scientific theories. This conflict between primitive intuition, which perceives the latent mysteries of the cosmos, and rational speculation, which attempts to define and classify the phenomena of the universe for the sake of utilitarianism, lies at the core of Bombal's later works.

"Las islas nuevas" (1939; "New Islands," 1982) is constructed on two conflicting planes: the realistic which describes the visit of Juan Manuel, a lawyer from Buenos Aires, to a large farm in the Argentinian pampa; and the supernatural denoted by Yolanda, a woman on the hacienda who has an aura of strangeness about her. Her slim body and her voice possess an extraordinary resemblance to those of a seagull, and on her left shoulder a small wing grows that she tries to conceal. The juxtaposition of the real and the supernatural creates an uncertainty on the part of the reader whose interpretation constantly fluctuates between concrete reality and the impossible. As Tzvetan Todorov has indicated in his structural analysis of the fantastic, such a fluctuation creates in the receptor a constant doubt that constitutes the very essence of the fantastic genre.

The fantastic in "Las islas nuevas" is, at bottom, a subversion of the real as it is traditionally conceived. By presenting the impossible as the possible, Bombal denounces the logical limits attributed to reality when apprehended exclusively from a rational and scientific perspective. Mimetic representation included in the realistic elements of the text functions as an axis that refracts in a paraxial area composed of supernatural events. The tension created by such conflicting elements is, in itself, an oxymoron that violates reality.

At a mythical level, the fantastic attributes of Yolanda come from the feminine archetype of Mother Earth. Yolanda's physical features resemble those of wild and free animals such as the snake and the seagull; thus, by extension, she is part of indomitable and primordial nature. This significant bond is reinforced at the structural level by the juxtaposition of Yolanda and the mysterious emergence of new islands in the pampa. Furthermore, the mysterious emergence and disappearance of the new islands implicitly symbolize the eternal cycle of death and regeneration in the cosmos. As a symbol of Mother Earth, however, Yolanda cannot actively participate in the natural process of Eternal Return. In a modern world where the ancestral mysteries of nature have been suppressed by the civilizing enterprises of Man, Yolanda's primitive attributes become a bizarre impediment that prevent her from either marrying Silvestre or establishing a love relationship with Juan Manuel. Her once-positive qualities are now a stigma condemning her to loneliness and sterility. If in ancient mythologies winged-supernatural beings represented spiritual values, wisdom, and mystical transcendence, Yolanda, in a world where the sacred has been degraded, has become a bizarre deformity, a horrifying human being who is doomed to unhappiness. Juan Manuel's confrontation with the supernatural could have become a transcendental experience at the mythical level of the archetypical hero; his rejection of Yolanda symbolizes the overt triumph of Positivist science in the modern world.

The emphasis on the dehumanizing effect of science and technology seems to become accentuated in Bombal's world-view by her new experiences in the United States, a country where she lived from 1940 to 1973. Her poetic essay entitled ''Washington, ciudad de las ardillas'' (1943; Washington, city of squirrels) is highly revealing. In this piece, she describes Washington as a place governed by ''The Big World's Machine,'' a feverish monster that demands to be fed by constant labor, bureaucratic files, and political affairs. As a way to reaffirm fantasy and imagination in a pragmatic society, Bombal focuses her description on the squirrels, wild little animals who are a testimony to innocence and natural life.

Aware of the overwhelming power of the civilizing forces in modern society, Bombal instills in her later works a tragic overtone of defeat. In ''Trenzas'' (1976; ''Braids,'' 1982), such a vision of the modern world is presented through two contrasting formats: the essay, a form that traditionally exposes an intellectual premise, and the legend, a fictitious tale rooted in a remote past. From a structural point of view, ''Trenzas'' is organized into three parts: a thesis, a demonstration, and a conclusion. The thesis does not present a concept to be analyzed through intellectual methods. On the contrary, it reverts to the primordial myth of Paradise Lost embedded in the collective unconsciousness. The narrator states that modern women have lost their ancestral bond with the cosmic forces because they have been subdued by Positivism. Therefore, they now ignore the fact that their hair is vestigial matter closely united to the depths of the earth where life has its origins. The narrator then proceeds to demonstrate the mythical and magical power of long hair by offering legendary examples that function as paradigms. The stories of Isolde, Melisande, and Ann Boleyn illustrate the concept that braided long hair is a magic source of immortal love, that it is a living echo of the sound of deep waters springing from the heart of the earth.

On the other hand, women who have cut their hair have symbolically capitulated to the pragmatic masculine order in an act of self-mutilation that has led them to degrade their feminine essence. The sadness of a once magical tide, the weakness of those images that were vivid in the past, and now prosaic dreams underline the irrevocable loss of a forceful union with transcendental nature and the degradation of the feminine in modern society.

A similarly pessimistic view is presented in "La historia de María Griselda" (1946; The story of María Griselda). Although the protagonist encompasses all the positive qualities of Mother Earth intimately united to wild nature, fertile water, and telluric energy, she is a source of unhappiness in a world dominated by jealousy, ambition, and passion. María Griselda is characterized as a personification of perfect beauty. Her harmonious relation with wild nature makes her resemble the Goddess of Vegetation, and, as this mythical figure, her perfect beauty ascends to a pantheist natural order. María Griselda's characterization is one typical of a fairy tale: She exhibits the exceptional qualities of beauty and kindness; like Cinderella, doves follow her and fireflies come to rest gracefully on her shoulders. On the other hand, the motif of the frog who is in love with her befits the wondrous nature of such a tale. This traditional format, however, undergoes a radical modification as the story approaches its tragic denouement. María Griselda's beauty and kindness are doomed to produce unhappiness in those who surround her. Her husband Alberto is prey to jealousy, and in his desperation to possess her, he has become an alcoholic. Anita envies her; and Sylvia kills herself upon realizing that Fred is in love with her. What André Jolles has defined as the essence of the fairy tale—the triumph of good over evil—is tragically reversed in "La historia de María Griselda," a tragic account of modern society defined as a microcosmos where kindness and natural beauty are no longer valued as transcendental qualities.

SURVEY OF CRITICISM

Within the context of Latin American literary criticism and public reception, Bombal's texts stand out as an exceptional case. Although the writings of women authors have traditionally been ignored and devalued by a male-dominated critical discourse, her novels and short stories have consistently been acclaimed. Undoubtedly Amado Alonso's article "Aparición de una novelista" (1936, Appearance of a novelist) is, to some extent, a factor that contributed to the recognition of her work as a peculiar expression of feminine experience. He was the first to point out the avant-garde qualities of *La última niebla*, the symbolic function of space, and what he at the time defines as "the feminine mode of writing a novel" demonstrating that Bombal radically departs from *criollismo*, the dominant literary trend in the Chilean novel of the 1930s.

Since then, literary studies on her texts have evolved from a formalistic approach to a feminist reevaluation. Cedomil Goič (1968) expands on Amado Alonso's critical hypothesis, focusing mainly on the structure of the narrator, the leitmotif of the mist, and the surreal elements of *La última niebla*. From a similar perspective, Margaret V. Campbell (1961) studies the juxtaposition of dream and reality, while Andrew Debicki analyzes structure and imagery in "El árbol" (1971). Saúl Sosnowski (1973) and Arthur A. Natella (1977) are the first studies that establish significant relationships between imagery and the author's concept of the feminine as a prolongation of nature and cosmic cycles.

The first book devoted entirely to Bombal's work is *María Luisa Bombal: La feminidad enajenada* (1976) by Hernán Vidal, who analyzes her novels and short stories in terms of psychoanalytic theories to demonstrate that the feminine condition represented in her work is a state of alienation from historical and political circumstances.

Mercedes Valdivieso (1976) marks the beginning of a new critical approach that attempts to study Bombal's texts from a feminist perspective. Valdivieso emphasizes the protagonist's predicament within the historical context of women in Latin America. Within this new critical framework, Lucía Guerra Cunningham (1980) analyzes her entire literary work. The conflict between masculine power and feminine marginality is studied both in terms of patriarchal structure and the elaboration of the feminine archetype as a literary representation of the defeat of the feminine in a dominant phallocentric order. Marjorie Agosín (1983) focuses on the development of the feminine characters, taking into account similar critical paradigms.

Apart from these studies, one must mention "Lectura interpretativa de 'Las trenzas' de María Luisa Bombal" (1974) by Julia S. Hermosilla as the first essay that centers on the seminal importance of this short story within Bombal's ideology. On the other hand, Kemy Oyarzún (1986) is the first critic to interpret Bombal's novel from a Lacanian perspective, shedding light on the meaning and function of feminine desire within the masculine symbolic order.

BIBLIOGRAPHY

Works by María Luisa Bombal

La última niebla. Buenos Aires: Colombo, 1935.
La amortajada. Buenos Aires: Sur, 1938.
"Las islas nuevas." *Sur* 53 (Feb. 1939):13–34.
"El árbol." *Sur* 60 (Sept. 1939):20–30.
"Mar, cielo, y tierra." *Saber Vivir* (Buenos Aires) 2 (1940):36–37.

"Trenzas." *Saber Vivir* (Buenos Aires) 2 (1940):36–37.
"Lo secreto." *La última niebla.* Santiago de Chile: Nascimento, 1941.
"Washington, ciudad de las ardillas." *Sur* 106 (Sept. 1943):28–35.
"La historia de María Griselda." *Norte* 10 (Aug. 1946):34–35, 48–54.
"La maja y el ruiseñor." *Revista Viña del Mar* 7 (Jan. 1960):8–12.
La historia de María Griselda. Quillota, Chile: Ed. 'El Observador,' 1976. Includes
    "Trenzas."

Translations of María Luisa Bombal

Bombal, María Luisa, trans. *House of Mist.* New York: Farrar, Straus & Co., 1947.
———. trans. *The Shrouded Woman.* New York: Farrar, Straus & Giroux, 1948.
Cunningham, Lucía Guerra, trans. *New Islands.* New York: Farrar, Straus & Co.,
    1982. (Includes "The Final Mist," "The Tree," "New Islands," "Braids," and
    "The Unknown.")

Works about María Luisa Bombal

Adams, M. Ian. *Three Authors of Alienation.* Austin: University of Texas Press, 1975.
    Pp. 15–35.
Agosín, Marjorie. *Las desterradas del paraíso, protagonistas en la narrativa de María
    Luisa Bombal.* New York: Senda Nueva de Ediciones, 1983.
Allen, Martha E. "Dos estilos de novela: Marta Brunet y María Luisa Bombal." *Revista
    Iberoamericana* 18, 35 (Feb.-Dec. 1952):63–91.
Alonso, Amado. "Aparición de una novelista." *Nosotros,* 3 (June 1936):241–56.
Baker, Armand F. "El tiempo y el proceso de individuación en *La última niebla.*"
    Revista Iberoamericana 135–36, (Apr.-Sept. 1986):393–415.
Bente, Thomas O. "María Luisa Bombal's Heroines: Poetic Neuroses and Artistic Sym-
    bolism." *Hispanófila* 28, 1 (Sept. 1984):103–13.
Campbell, Margaret V. "The Vaporous World of María Luisa Bombal." *Hispania* 44,
    3 (Sept. 1961):415–19.
Cunningham, Lucía Guerra. *La narrativa de María Luisa Bombal: Una visión de la
    existencia femenina.* Madrid: Playor, 1980.
Debicki, Andrew P. "Structure, Imagery and Experience in María Luisa Bombal's The
    Tree." *Studies in Short Fiction* (Winter 1971):123–29.
Fernández, Franco. "Análisis de *La última niebla,* de la escritora chilena María Luisa
    Bombal." *Repertorio Americano* 3, 5 (Oct. 1976):53–59.
Gligo, Agata. *María Luisa* (biography). Santiago, Chile: Andrés Bello, 1983.
Goič, Cedomil. "*La última niebla.*" *La novela chilena: Los mitos degradados.* Santiago,
    Chile: Universitaria, 1968. Pp. 144–62.
Gutiérrez-Vega, Zenaide. "Aproximaciones a *La última niebla* de María Luisa Bombal."
    Annali Istituto Universitario Orientale, Napoli, Sezione Romanza 23, 2 (July
    1981):607–14.
Hermosilla S., Julia. "Lectura interpretativa de 'Las trenzas' de María Luisa Bombal."
    Estudios Filológicos (Valdivia) 10 (1974):81–92.
Levine, Linda Gould. "María Luisa Bombal from a Feminist Perspective." *Revista/
    Review Interamericana* 4, 2 (Summer 1974):148–61.
Levine, Suzanne Jill. "El espejo de agua." *Revista de la Universidad de México* 39,
    Nueva época, 26 (June 1983):36–39.

Natella, Arthur A. "El mundo literario de María Luisa Bombal." *Cinco aproximaciones a la narrativa hispanoamericana.* Madrid: Playor, 1977. Pp. 133–59.

Nelson, Esther W. "The Space of Longing: *La última niebla.*" *The American Hispanist* 3, 21 (Nov. 1977):7–11.

Oyarzún, Kemy. "Ecolalia e intertextualidad en *La última niebla.*" *Discurso Literario* 4, 1 (1986): 163–83.

Peña Muñoz, Manuel. "La presencia del mar en el cuento 'Lo secreto.' " *Nueva Revista del Pacífico* 4 (Dec. 1976):128–31.

Rábago, Alberto. "Elementos surrealistas en *La última niebla* de María Luisa Bombal." *Hispania* 64, 1 (Mar. 1981):31–40.

Sosnowski, Saúl. "El agua, motivo primordial de *La última niebla.*" *Cuadernos Hispanoamericanos* 277–78 (July-Aug. 1973):365–74.

Torres-Rioseco, Arturo. "El nuevo estilo en la novela." *Revista Iberoamericana* III, 5 (Feb.-May 1941):75–83.

Turek, Rosa. "El escapismo: Dos perspectivas del mismo tema en *La última niebla* de María Luisa Bombal." *Norte* (Mexico) series 3, 275 (1976–1977):59–62.

Urza, Carmelo. "Alienation and Symbol in Mariotti's 'No Fundo, Fundo' and María Luisa Bombal's *La última niebla.*" *Luso-Brazilian Review* 21, 1 (Summer 1984):89–98.

Valdivieso, Mercedes. "Social Denunciation in the Language of 'The Tree' by María Luisa Bombal." *Latin American Literary Review* 9 (1976):70–76.

Vidal, Hernán. *María Luisa Bombal: La feminidad enajenada.* Barcelona: Hijos de José Bosch, 1976.

Williams, Lorna Valeria. "*The Shrouded Woman*: Marriage and Its Constraints in the Fiction of María Luisa Bombal." *Latin American Literary Review* 10, 20 (Spring-Summer 1982):21–30.

MARTA BRUNET
(1897–1967)
Chile

Mary G. Berg

BIOGRAPHY

Marta Brunet was born in Chillán, Chile, on August 9, 1897. She was the only child of Ambrosio Brunet and his Spanish wife, María Presentación Cáraves de Cossío. Brunet's mother was a chronic invalid and needed more care than was available in the country. Thus although her father owned an estate in Pailahueque, most of Marta Brunet's childhood was spent in the small town of Victoria. Because there was no school for girls there, Brunet studied at home with various tutors. She was an early and avid reader of every book within reach, and this precocious passion for reading was encouraged by her teachers and parents. She began to write at a very early age. She was fascinated by the country life around her, by details of natural beauty and landscape, and especially by the lives of country people: their ways of speech, their legends and folklore, and their reactions to daily events.

When she was fourteen, Brunet traveled through Western Europe with her parents for three years, returning to Chile in 1914 by way of Argentina, Uruguay, and Brazil. She would later speak of the importance to her of authors encountered at that time: Proust, Unamuno, Pirandello, Giroudoux, Gorki, Ortega y Gasset, Morand, Azorín, Joyce, Claudel, and others. By 1919 the family was back in Chillán. Brunet was part of an active literary group and began to publish poems and stories in a local newspaper, *La Discusión*. She sent some of her poems to a well-known critic in Santiago, Hernán Díaz Arrieta (''Alone''); he did not care for her poems but liked her prose, and subsequently arranged for the immediate publication of her short novel with a rural setting, *Montaña adentro* (1923; Back country), which was greeted enthusiastically by critics, who marveled at how a ''young lady writer'' could portray country customs and speech so realistically.

In 1925 Brunet moved to Santiago, where she worked as a journalist and immersed herself in literary life, publishing literary notes and short stories in a variety of magazines and newspapers. Her first collection of short stories, *Don Florisondo* (Don Florisondo), appeared in 1926, as did a second short novel, *Bestia dañina* (Treacherous beast). A third short novel with a rural setting and peasant protagonists, *María Rosa, Flor del Quillén* (María Rosa, flower of the Quillén), appeared in 1927, and in 1929 Brunet won her first major literary prize, first place in a short story contest sponsored by *El Mercurio* of Santiago, awarded for "Tierra bravía" (Wild land). A fourth rural novel, *Bienvenido* (Welcome), was published in 1929, and a short story collection, *Reloj de sol* (Sundial), in 1930. Although the countryside is important as setting in these two books, Brunet's increasing interest in portraying more sophisticated, more self-analytical, urban-educated characters may be seen.

Brunet won the Premio de Novela of the prestigious Sociedad de Escritores de Chile in 1933. In 1934 she wrote her first book for small children, *Cuentos para Mari-Sol* (Stories for Mari-Sol), and she became the editor of the magazine *Familia*, published by Zig-Zag Publishers in Santiago. She remained editor until 1939, when she was appointed by the government to a consular position in Buenos Aires. She was warmly welcomed in literary circles in Buenos Aires and by 1940 was publishing extensively in such periodicals as *La Nación* of Buenos Aires, and the magazine *Sur*. A new short story collection, *Aguas abajo* (Downstream), appeared in 1943 and won the Atenea Prize of the University of Concepción for the major literary work of the year. She advanced in rank at the Chilean Consulate in Buenos Aires and continued to participate actively in literary affairs.

Humo hacia el sur (Smoke on the southern horizon), considered by many to be Brunet's most important novel, was published in 1946 and very widely reviewed, as was a short novel, *La mampara* (The outer door), which appeared later that same year. These novels mark the completed transition of Brunet's focus of interest from southern rural life to the psychological and sociological dynamics of urban living. Brunet was designated third secretary of the Chilean Embassy in Buenos Aires in 1948. In charge of cultural affairs and cultural relations, she did a great deal to expand Argentine awareness of Chilean literature and culture. Her short story collection, *Raíz del sueño* (Root of the dream), appeared in 1949, and was highly praised by critics. Brunet was promoted to second secretary of the Chilean Embassy in 1950 but was asked to resign in 1952 by the government of Carlos Ibáñez. Extensive protest appeared in Argentine periodicals but Brunet was not reinstated, and she returned to Santiago in 1953. She was invited to lecture and to give short courses on Chilean and Spanish American literature in programs established by the University of Chile. She continued to do this for many years, lecturing in Santiago, Valparaíso, Arica, Antofagasta, Chillán, Valdivia, Constitución, and Punta Arenas. She also lectured on other topics, such as children's literature and the craft of writing.

María Nadie (Mary nobody), the most popular of Brunet's novels during her lifetime, was published in 1957.

A volume of stories in verse for small children, *Aleluyas para los más chiquitos* (Hallelujahs for the smallest ones), appeared in 1960, and that year, Brunet traveled to Spain for an eye operation at a clinic in Barcelona. She traveled extensively in Western Europe in 1961, and during her absence from Chile, was awarded the major Chilean literary prize, the Premio Nacional de Literatura. She returned to Santiago in November 1961 to the many literary and cultural activities in which she participated actively, as president or director of the Institute of Journalists, of the Sociedad de Escritores de Chile, of the Pen Club, of the Zonta Club, and as a member of many other committees.

In 1962, the most controversial of Marta Brunet's novels, *Amasijo* (Lump of dough), was published, and she was designated cultural attaché of the Chilean Embassy in Rio de Janeiro, Brazil. In 1963, she was transferred to Montevideo, Uruguay. Her *Obras completas* (Complete works), including much hitherto unpublished material, was published in 1963 with a prologue by her old friend, Hernán Díaz Arrieta. She was still in Montevideo as cultural attaché, and in the middle of a lecture at the Uruguayan Academy of Letters, when she died suddenly of a cerebral hemorrhage on August 9, 1967, at the age of seventy.

MAJOR THEMES

Marta Brunet's eight novels and over sixty short stories all have as a major theme individual human identity and its realization (or lack of realization) within the context of the individual's life circumstances. Although individual definition and destiny are always paramount, all of Brunet's fiction reveals an interest in how whole communities function: rural ranch and village groups in the early novels, larger towns in the later fiction. She is particularly interested in women's identity problems and in how women are affected by their social roles.

Brunet's early fiction (1923–1927) describes rural settings and powerful natural forces that barely allow individual yearnings to be defined, let alone fulfilled. Within a few years of Brunet's move from southern Chile to Santiago, her fiction (1929–1943) reflects a greater interest in educated, articulate protagonists, although rural settings still affect the ways in which their inhabitants can determine their freedom. Brunet's later fiction (1946–1963) is set in towns: claustrophobic small towns in *Humo hacia el sur* and *María Nadie* and disorienting big cities in *María Nadie*, *La mampara*, *Amasijo*, and many stories. The emphasis of the later works is a gradual psychological unfolding of what motivates the characters, what paralyzes them, and what enables them to function in their families, jobs, and towns. The most interesting characters of Brunet's later fiction are small children and women. The protagonist of Brunet's last novel, *Amasijo*, is a man, but he is so warped by his experiences with strong women (his mother, his housekeeper, his only friend) that he is dysfunctional, as are the main male

characters of *Humo hacia el sur*. Brunet portrays small children with extraordinary skill. The childhood worlds of Solita in *Humo hacia el sur* and *Solita
Sola* and of the two young boys, Cacho and Conejo, in *María Nadie* are convincingly and vividly presented. They are splendid and memorable achievements,
all the more effective because the children are presented as children rather than
serving primarily as novelistic devices to show us aspects of adult worlds,
although they accomplish that as well.

Brunet's first three novels (*Montaña adentro*, *Bestia dañina*, and *María Rosa,
Flor del Quillén*) and many early stories are set in the primitive countryside of
southern Chile, the area near Victoria that Brunet knew well in childhood. These
novels are usually described as being within the *criollista* tradition of emphasis
on specific local description, local customs, and local color. Natural settings are
described in great detail: the rough magnificence of forests and mountainside
terrain, simple farmhouses and outbuildings, pastures and fields bursting with
life, and the rigorous extremes of climate. The inhabitants of this inclement but
beautiful land are rough country people, engaged in a constant struggle for
survival, of simple and direct speech, and of elemental, often brutal, passions.
Montaña adentro is the story of a young woman, Cata, who is a cook for a
ranching enterprise. Pregnant by a man who has left her, proudly insistent on
her own self-reliance, Cata comes to care for a kind and fair man, Juan Oses,
but he is killed by her jealous first lover before they can marry. Strength of will
and a fatalistic acceptance of injustice and adversity allow Cata to endure.

Bestia dañina and *María Rosa, Flor del Quillén* are also stories of passion,
sensuality, and pride. *Bestia dañina* chronicles the reactions of the daughters of
Santos Flores to their father's remarriage (because he yearns for a son) to a
younger woman who wants an easy life while she carries on with a young lover.
Meche, the middle daughter, runs off with a lover rather than be party to her
father's humiliation, and the unity of the family is destroyed; in the end, Don
Santos kills his adulterous wife in bitter grief that she has caused his daughters
to suffer. *María Rosa, Flor del Quillén* portrays the sexual tensions and loneliness
inherent in the marriage of a young girl to a much older man; María Rosa is
proud of her resistance to the attentions of young suitors, although the truth is
that they have not engaged her interest in any way. Her self-image is defined
by the community recognition of her rectitude and of her lonely status as the
Flower of Quillén. When she succumbs to the wooing of a local Don Juan only
to find out that he had made a bet that he could seduce her, she attacks him
furiously, and the community believes that she is once again defending her honor
from assault. María Rosa is the first of a series of Brunet protagonists to deal
extensively with the disparity between individual private feelings and a perception
of how she is viewed publicly by those around her; this lack of equivalency
becomes a central theme of later novels such as *La mampara*, *María Nadie*, and
Amasijo.

Although the southern countryside still serves as setting in *Bienvenido* and
many of the stories of *Reloj de sol*, the primary focus is on urban-educated

protagonists who view themselves as distinct from the country folk among whom they live. The country landscape is extensively described but is no longer a necessarily integral part of the human emotions and actions depicted. This distance between inner self and physical environment produces a new loneliness which in its turn occasions certain behavior. This alienation becomes central in Brunet's later novels, but in *Bienvenido* it is one of many factors that cause Juan Ramírez, a young agricultural engineer in charge of an isolated ranch, to feel as ambivalent as he does about the two women in his life: his submissive, traditional wife and Marcela, the overtly sensuous siren from the big city. Juan wants them both and, in other ways, rejects them both. He would be incapable of resisting the flashy promises of immediate sexual excitement were it not for the fortuitous announcement of his wife's pregnancy. The baby is welcome (the "bienvenido" of the title) as an excuse to reject the temptation that so troubles Juan, but the novel ends without real resolution.

Aguas abajo is a trilogy of powerful tales of country life: two stories of mothers and daughters who confront bitter realities, and "Soledad de la sangre" (Solitude of blood), Brunet's most anthologized story, which tells of the loneliness of an educated, sensitive woman isolated on a ranch in a loveless marriage. She escapes into daydreams and nostalgia, but when her phonograph, the symbol of her freedom of imagination, is smashed, the crisis forces her to reevaluate the worth of her life.

Humo hacia el sur, Brunet's most ambitious novel, and the one most often referred to as her masterpiece, is a complex anatomy of life in a lumbermill town in 1905, which enjoys booming prosperity owing to the circumstance of being for a time the southernmost station on the new railroad line. Most importantly, it is the story of the women who live in this town: Batilde de la Riestra, the power- and money-hungry dynamo who has built up the town; María Soledad, who represents traditional ladylike virtues, and her remarkable daughter, Solita, an outspoken child who resists society's many layers of hypocrisy; La Moraima, a shrewd businesswoman and compassionate whorehouse madam; foreigners such as Mademoiselle, Solita's governess, and the mysterious Smiths; the middle-class women who compete for social ascendancy and apparent respectability; and the poorer women of the town, wives of lumbermill workers, and servants. The novel includes the complete social spectrum of the town. The women are the strong and interesting figures; although power is nominally in the hands of men, they are shown as hollow tormented puppets of their own compulsions and weaknesses. Batilde's angry energy has pushed her husband into political prominence; María Soledad's passivity allows her husband to dominate their household even as he is being devoured by sexual obsessions that make his public life a sham; Pedro Molina, the only other man of intelligence and initiative in the town, is spending his life literally in prison, trapped also by frustrated sexuality and anger.

The differences between socially defined "good women" and "bad women" are a recurring theme in Brunet's fiction, although it is seen quite differently in

each book. In *Montaña adentro*, Cata's sense of self-sufficiency and her declaration that she can provide for her baby by herself are contrasted with her
mother's more traditional wish that her daughter should marry and her worry
that Cata's illegitimate child will mark her as a "bad woman" who flouts
conventional *mores*. *Bienvenido* approaches the issue from the point of view of
the man who has purposely married a traditional, unassertive woman, yet is
attracted to the sexually available city sophisticate who is his wife's opposite.
In *Humo hacia el sur*, aggressive, domineering Batilde is contrasted with dec-
orative, passive María Soledad. Both are respectable society matrons, so it is
no longer a question of a contrast between a dutiful meek wife and a partygoing
playgirl, but rather part of a consideration (which runs through many novels) of
what qualities serve women best and how and why they are developed. Both
Batilde and María Soledad are trapped in small-town life in marriages that affect
their behavior: Batilde becomes domineering, amasses property, and tyrannizes
over her husband and servants in an unconstrained greed for more and more
control over her environment; María Soledad becomes childlike, slipping into a
role as pretty doll, playing with her small daughter as though they were the same
age.

La mampara provides a similar contrasting pair of women, and it, too, examines closely how women are formed and changed by their circumstances. In
La mampara, two sisters confront their family's poverty very differently: Ig-
nacia Teresa becomes the "good" daughter, drudging at a dull secretarial job
to support her mother and social butterfly sister, Carmen, who manages to
cling precariously to a partygoing existence in wealthy society. The lives of the
two sisters and of their mother are recounted and considered from within the
consciousness of each woman. The insensitivity of their immediate communities as to who they really are and what they need and want is dramatized, as
are their dreams and aspirations. The superficial, often hypocritical values of
the upper class social world Carmen inhabits are particularly criticized, but the
major theme is again the painful disparities between how society views people,
how they define themselves, and how they would like to be regarded by others.

These latter dreams and hopes are central in Brunet's next collection of stories,
Raíz del sueño. All of the stories of *Raíz del sueño* describe women in anguish
and solitude, women with powerful fantasy lives, women whose daydreams can
become nightmares, women who nearly all become increasingly isolated and
alienated from the families and towns that suffocate them. Insanity and death
lurk at the edges of their imaginations; often, they are unable to find any sat-
isfactory balance between self-image and social environment, and they are tipped
into a self-destruction they are unable to restrain. Only in "Un trapo de piso"
(A floor rag) is the protagonist enabled by her imagination to understand and
finally to accept the rigidity and bossiness of her mother-in-law.

In *María Nadie*, a setting of southern Chilean mountain and forest terrain is
again of great importance. The first part of the novel provides a description of

the physical and social environment, of the bare but beautiful mountainsides and the small company-built town of Colloco. As in *Humo hacia el sur*, the town is seen primarily through its sets of contrasting women: Ernestina, a traditional conscientious wife and mother, and Petaca, founder and mainstay of the town's store and restaurant; and Melecia and Liduvina, the busybody sisters who run the mail and telegraph services. Two male pairs complete the village panorama: Ernestina and Petaca's two young sons, Cacho and Conejo, and the fathers of these two boys, Reinaldo and Lindor, both embittered and tormented men, obsessed by dreams of success that are quite out of touch with reality, men whose frustration has made them viciously destructive of their own and others' happiness. María López, who has recently arrived in town as the operator of the new telephone system, is seen first through these various perspectives of the town, and then through her own consciousness in the second part of the book. Her aspirations and frustrations, her life story, and her final sense of exclusion from any possible place in this small town are vividly told. For this town and possibly for any human community, she is "María Nadie," unable to reach out of her inwardness and connect with others, trapped and isolated within her own emotional turmoil.

Amasijo is also the story of a solitary, agonized human being who is unable to find a place for himself in conventional society. Like *María Nadie, Amasijo* is an analysis of the psychological history that leads implacably to this extreme distress. Both María López and Julián García of *Amasijo* are shown to have family backgrounds that eventually cripple them emotionally. The novels are thus bitter analyses of social tolerance of situations that corrode a basic human ability to function, and psychological investigations of the life histories and pathologies of the victims. As in Brunet's other fiction, sexual behavior serves as the primary indicator of an individual's ability to relate to others. María López is devastated by an abortion she did not choose to have and by her lover's nonchalance, his lack of commitment to their relationship. Julián García, permanently warped by being his sick mother's plaything as a young child, is unable to free himself of sexual inhibition in either homosexual or heterosexual relationships. Nor is he able to liberate himself by writing, although he is a successful playwright. He suffers from desperate loneliness and isolation, qualities seen to some extent in all of Marta Brunet's major characters.

Brunet's fiction for and about children is altogether different, less often shadowed by the desperation and frustration that afflict her adult characters. Children figure as major protagonists in *Bestia dañina*, *Humo hacia el sur*, *María Nadie*, and in many of the best stories of *Reloj de sol* and *Raíz del sueño*. *Solita Sola* includes a series of stories about the child of *Humo hacia el sur*, the little girl Brunet referred to as her favorite fictional character of all those she created. *Cuentos para Mari-Sol*, *Aleluyas para los más chiquitos*, and *Las historias de Mamá Tolita* (Mama Tolita's stories) are collections written for children. They are magical, lyrical tales of fantasy worlds full of personified animals and elements of Chilean folklore.

SURVEY OF CRITICISM

All of Marta Brunet's books were widely reviewed when they were published. *Montaña adentro* startled critics in 1923; although most of them were enthusiastic about Brunet's talent, many did express shock and amazement at her realistic depictions of crude rustic behavior. How could a well-brought-up young woman know so much about life on primitive southern farms, they wondered. Her later novels often horrified her critics with their forthright discussions of abortion, homosexuality, sexual aberrations, suicide, and pathological behavior. Can these be appropriate topics for a lady novelist, wondered many who wrote of her work. These questions may have diverted readers from appreciating the complexity and excellence of Brunet's writing. Although her novels and collections of stories were reprinted and republished in many editions, and although Marta Brunet won major literary prizes, including the Chilean National Prize for Literature in 1961, and although she was recognized during her lifetime as a major twentieth-century Chilean writer, she has received little critical attention in recent years.

The individual reviews of each of Brunet's books provide some discussion of prominent aspects of each work as it was perceived when it appeared. Particularly interesting reviews include those by Fernando García Oldini and Emilio Vaïsse on *Montaña adentro*; César Rosales on *Humo hacia el sur*; Homero Castillo, Raúl Silva Castro, and Víctor Valenzuela on *María Nadie*: and Guillermo de Torre on *Raíz del sueño*. The following more general articles about Marta Brunet were among those published early in her career: Julieta Carrera (1939), Hernán Díaz Arrieta (1931), Januario Espinoza (1930), and Julia García Games (1930).

General articles on Brunet published during the latter part of her lifetime include essays by María Carolina Geel (1949), Julio Durán Cerda (1961), Nicómedes Guzmán (1961), Luis Merino Reyes (1955), Angel Rama (1967), Emir Rodríguez Monegal (1962), Milton Rossel (1961), Raúl Silva Castro (1961), Guillermo de Torre (1963), John F. Tull (1966), and Víctor Valenzuela (1956). Roger Peel's unpublished Yale Ph.D. dissertation of 1966, "The Narrative Prose of Marta Brunet," is a perceptive overview of all of Brunet's fiction and includes a more extensive analysis of *Humo hacia el sur*.

Since Brunet's death in 1967, one book-length study of her fiction has been published: Esther Melón de Díaz' comprehensive *La narrativa de Marta Brunet* (1975), which discusses each of Brunet's books and analyzes her fiction in terms of themes, characterization, and narrative techniques. Melón de Díaz concludes with a study of Brunet's use of language, and the book provides a helpful, though incomplete, bibliography. Both Peel and Melón de Díaz divide Brunet's fiction into two periods: that of the early, realistic descriptions of the countryside and rural customs, and that of the later stories and novels that focus more on individuals and portray their loneliness and insecurity, frustration and despair. Among the many articles about Brunet's work published since her death are the following: Hugo Montes Brunet (1974, 1978, 1982), Sonia Riquelme (1987), Milton Rossel (1967), Dora Isella Russell (1968), and Víctor Valenzuela (1974).

Studies of specific Brunet works include Gabriela Mora (1984) and Charles Param (1968) on "Soledad de la sangre"; and Lucía Fox-Lockert (1979) on *María Nadie*. Comparisons of Brunet's fiction to works by other writers include the following: Marjorie Agosín (1985) on Brunet and Ana María Matute; Martha E. Allen (1952) and Marjorie Agosín (1984) on Brunet and María Luisa Bombal*; Edna Coll (1968) on Brunet, Teresa de la Parra,* and Magdalena Mondragón; and María-Inés Lagos-Pope (1985) on Brunet and Rosario Ferré.*

BIBLIOGRAPHY

Major Works by Marta Brunet

Montaña adentro. Santiago: Nascimento, 1923. Other editions: 2d ed. 1933; 3d ed. Prol. Guillermo de Torre. Buenos Aires: Losada, 1953; 4th ed. 1965 same as 3d; 5th ed. Prol. Hugo Montes Brunet. Santiago: Editorial Andrés Bello, 1978.
Bestia dañina. Santiago: Nascimento, 1926. Other editions: 2d ed. Prol. Guillermo de Torre. Buenos Aires: Losada, 1953; 3d. ed. 1965 same as 2d.
Don Florisondo. Santiago: Lectura Selecta No.15, 1926. Included in *Reloj de sol*. Santiago: Nascimento, 1929. "Don Florisondo" and "Doña Santitos" republished in many anthologies.
"María Rosa, Flor del Quillén." *Atenea* 2 (1927):119–43 and 3 (1927):217–40. Other editions: 2d ed. Santiago: La Novela Nueva, Vol. 4, Dec. 1929; 3d ed. Santiago: Nascimento, 1929; 4th ed. Prol. Guillermo de Torre. Buenos Aires: Losada, 1953; 5th ed. 1965 same as 4th.
Bienvenido. Santiago: Nascimento, 1929.
Reloj de sol. Santiago: Nascimento, 1930.
"Americanismo también es obra femenina." *Repertorio Americano* 36 (1939):279–85.
Cuentos para Mari-Sol. Santiago: Zig-Zag, n.d. [1941?]. Many subsequent editions.
Aguas abajo. Santiago: Cruz del Sur, 1943.
Humo hacia el sur. Buenos Aires: Losada, 1946. Other editions: 2d ed. 1967.
La mampara. Buenos Aires: Emecé, 1946.
Raíz del sueño. Santiago: Zig-Zag, 1949.
María Nadie. Santiago: Zig-Zag, 1957. Other editions: 2d ed. 1961; 3d ed. 1962; 4th ed. 1962; 5th ed. 1965.
"El mundo mágico del niño." *Atenea* 130–32 (1958):265–76.
Aleluyas para los más chiquitos. Santiago: Editorial Universitaria, 1960.
Amasijo. Santiago: Zig-Zag, 1962.
Antología de cuentos. Prol. and biobibliography by Nicómedes Guzmán. Santiago: Zig-Zag, 1962.
Obras completas de Marta Brunet. Prol. and biobibliography by Alone (Hernán Díaz Arrieta). Santiago: Zig-Zag, 1963. Includes all of the novels and stories listed above as well as additional material, including *Solita Sola* and *Las historias de Mamá Tolita*.

Translations of Works by Marta Brunet

Bauman, Marilyn, trans. "Francina." *Spanish American Literature in Translation*. Ed. Willis Knapp Jones. New York: Frederick Ungar, 1963. II:289–94.
"Doña Santitos." *Andean Monthly* 2, 1 (1939):49–52.

Works about Marta Brunet

Agosín, Marjorie. "La anomalía del ensueño: los niños en Marta Brunet y Ana María Matute." *Alba de América* 3, 4–5 (1985):31–38.

―――. "*La casa iluminada* en la penumbra: un cuento de Marta Brunet." *Silencio e imaginación*. Mexico City: Editorial Katún, 1986. Pp. 49–60.

―――. "La mimesis de la interioridad: 'Soledad de la sangre' de Marta Brunet y 'El árbol' de María Luisa Bombal." *Neophilologus* 68, 3 (1984): 380–88.

―――. "Marta Brunet: A Literary Biography." *Revista Interamericana de Bibliografía* 36, 4 (1986):452–59.

Allen, Martha E. "Dos estilos de novela: Marta Brunet y María Luisa Bombal." *Revista Iberoamericana* 18, 35 (1952):63–91.

Berg, Mary G. "The Short Stories of Marta Brunet," *Monographic Review/Revista Monográfica* 4 (1988):195–206.

Carrera, Julieta. "Marta Brunet." *América* 1, 4 (1939):45–47.

Castillo, Homero. "Marta Brunet, *María Nadie.*" *Revista Iberoamericana* 45 (1958):182–86.

Coll, Edna. "Teresa de la Parra, Marta Brunet y Magdalena Mondragón: abresurcos en la novelística hispanoamericana." *La novela iberoamericana contemporánea; XIII° Congreso Internacional de Literatura Iberoamericana*. Caracas: Universidad Central de Venezuela, 1968. Pp. 187–95.

Díaz Arrieta, Hernán ("Alone"). "Marta Brunet." *Panorama de la literatura chilena durante el siglo XX*. Santiago: Nascimento, 1931. Pp. 147–48.

―――. "Prólogo." *Obras completas de Marta Brunet*. Santiago: Zig-Zag, 1963. Pp. 11–16.

Durán Cerda, Julio. "Marta Brunet, puente de plata hacia el sur." *Anales de la Universidad de Chile* 119, 124 (1961):89–94.

Espinosa, Januario. "Rural Life in Chile Finds a New Portrayer." *Chile* 8, 46 (1930):68 and 95.

Fox-Lockert, Lucía. "Marta Brunet: *María Nadie.*" *Women Novelists of Spain and Spanish America*. Metuchen, N.J.: Scarecrow Press, 1979. Pp. 195–201.

García Games, Julia. "Marta Brunet." *Como los he visto yo*. Santiago: Nascimento, 1930. Pp. 159–67.

García Oldini, Fernando. "*Montaña adentro.*" *Doce escritores*. Santiago: Nascimento, 1929. Pp. 97–108.

Geel, María Carolina. "Marta Brunet." *Siete escritoras chilenas*. Santiago: Editorial "Rapa Nui," 1949. Pp. 47–61.

Guzmán, Nicómedes. "La escritora Marta Brunet en las letras chilenas." *Antología de cuentos*. By Marta Brunet. Santiago: Zig-Zag, 1961. Pp. 7–16.

Lagos-Pope, María-Inés. "Sumisión y rebeldía: el doble o la representación de la alienación femenina en narraciones de Marta Brunet y Rosario Ferré." *Revista Iberoamericana* 132–33 (1985):731–49.

Melón de Díaz, Esther. *La narrativa de Marta Brunet*. Río Piedras: University of Puerto Rico, 1975.

Merino Reyes, Luis. "El criollismo de Marta Brunet." *Atenea* 363–64 (1955):338–41.

Montes Brunet, Hugo. "Marta Brunet." *Historia de la literatura chilena*. Santiago: Editorial del Pacífico, 1974. Pp. 269–73.

―――. "Poesía de Marta Brunet." *Revista Chilena de Literatura* 20 (1982):41–62.

―――. "Prólogo." Marta Brunet. *Montaña adentro*. Santiago: Editorial Andrés Bello, 1978. Pp. 7–15.

Mora, Gabriela. "Una lectura de 'Soledad de la sangre' de Marta Brunet." *Estudios Filológicos* 19 (1984):81–90.

Param, Charles. " 'Soledad de la sangre:' A Study in Symmetry." *Hispania* 51, 2 (1968):252–58.

Peel, Roger Martin. "The Narrative Prose of Marta Brunet." Ph.D. diss. Yale University, 1966. (DAI 27 [1967]:2541A.)

Rama, Angel. "La condición humana de la mujer." *Soledad de la sangre*. By Marta Brunet. Montevideo: Arca, 1967. Pp. 7–14.

Riquelme, Sonia. "Notas sobre el criollismo chileno y el personaje femenino en la narrativa de Marta Brunet." *Discurso Literario* 4, 2 (1987):613–21.

Rodríquez Monegal, Emir. "Marta Brunet en su ficción y en la realidad." *Narradores de esta América*. Montevideo: Alfa, 1962. Pp. 139–46.

Rosales, César. "Marta Brunet: *Humo hacia el Sur*." *Sur* 138 (1946):99–103.

Rossel, Milton. "Marta Brunet." *Atenea* 418 (1967):157–63.

―――. "Reencuentro con Marta Brunet." *Atenea* 394 (1961):3–13.

Russell, Dora Isella. "Marta Brunet." *Cultura Universitaria* (Caracas) 98–99 (1968):20–24.

Silva Castro, Raúl. "*María Nadie*, novela, de Marta Brunet." *Atenea* 378 (1957):258–62.

―――. *Panorama literario de Chile*. Santiago: Editorial Universitaria, 1961. Pp. 306–11.

Torre, Guillermo de. "Marta Brunet: *Raíz del sueño*." *Sur* 176 (1949):81–82.

―――. "Marta Brunet y su narrativa chilena." *Tres conceptos de la literatura hispanoamericana*. Buenos Aires: Losada, 1963. Pp. 199–204.

Tull, John F. "El desarrollo de la novela de Marta Brunet." *Duquesne Hispanic Review* 5, 2 (1966):57–62.

Vaïsse, Emilio. "Marta Brunet: *Montaña adentro*." *Estudios críticos de literatura chilena*. Vol. I. Santiago: Nascimento, 1940. Pp. 65–69.

Valenzuela, Víctor M. "El fatalismo en la obra de Marta Brunet." *La Nueva Democracia* 26, 4 (1956):24–27.

―――. "Marta Brunet: *María Nadie*." *La Nueva Democracia* 38, 2 (1958):105.

―――. "Marta Brunet." *Grandes escritoras hispanoamericanas*. Bethlehem, Pa.: Lehigh University, 1974. Pp. 83–97.

FANNY BUITRAGO
(b. 1940)
Colombia

Teresa R. Arrington

BIOGRAPHY

Although born in Barranquilla, Colombia, Fanny Buitrago considers Cali, Colombia, her literary birthplace, since she won her first literary prize there in 1964 for her only published play, *El hombre de paja* (Scarecrow). Buitrago spent her childhood at boarding school where she cultivated her imagination to escape from the tedium of her environment and of her schoolmates. Classic works of children's literature, especially Lewis Carroll's *Alice in Wonderland*, helped Buitrago pass her free time at school and continued to stimulate her imagination into her adult life.

Buitrago took to writing at an early age. Prior to the publication of her first novel in 1963, Buitrago's work appeared in newspapers and magazines such as *Zona Franca, El Nacional,* and *Papeles* (all of Caracas, Venezuela) and *Cuadernos del Viento* and *El Cuerno Emplumado* (of Mexico). She stunned the Colombian literary world with her first novel, supposedly written at age eighteen, *El hostigante verano de los dioses* (1963; The harassing summer of the gods). Subsequent editions, a rare event in Latin American publishing, appeared in 1977 and 1984. In this novel, we see her portrait of Colombian youth overcome by an apathy that even sexual promiscuity cannot conquer, a situation that scandalized Buitrago's reading public.

In May of the following year (1964), her ballet *La garza sucia* ("The Dirty Heron," 1965), based on one of her own short stories, premiered at the Teatro San Martín in Buenos Aires, Argentina, under the direction of Roberto Trinchero. This ballet received the Summer Season Prize in Buenos Aires in 1965. Buitrago's other 1964 publication, *El hombre de paja,* won the National Theater Prize at the IV Cali Theater Festival the year it was published. Against the backdrop of revolution in a nearby town, the play portrays the actions of Jafet, a writer, in response to an unnamed girl, a refugee from the nearby town. For all his attempts to stimulate others to action or compassion, Jafet, at the end of the play, is seen hanging from a tree, as powerless as the scarecrow of the title. This play was published in a double volume with a collection of six short stories entitled *Las distancias doradas* (Golden Spaces). These stories rely more on mood and atmosphere than Buitrago's later works, but deal with some of the same themes that even permeate her recent writing: betrayal and death; love and sanity/insanity; the relationship between parent and child.

Since 1970 Buitrago's record of major publications has been fairly constant, with a new work appearing approximately every three years. Her tripartite novel, *Cola de zorro* (Foxtail) appeared in 1970 and was a finalist in the Seix Barral Literary Contest in 1968. Utilizing a blend of flashforwards, flashbacks, and time-line plot developments, Buitrago's story deals with Ana, Emmanuel, and Malinda, who are all interconnected through the mythically disappearing and reappearing character Benito. *La otra gente: cuentos* (Other people: stories) is a collection published in 1973 of fourteen short stories dealing with ghosts, family curses, the bad luck of abused and abandoned children, and the often tortured relationships of husbands and wives. In 1974 Buitrago won prizes awarded by *El Tiempo* (Bogotá), *El Nacional* (Caracas), and the *Revue de Deux Mondes* (Paris) for her story "Pasajeros de la noche" (Night passengers), which was later published in the collection *Bahía Sonora, relatos de la isla* (Sonora Bay, Tales of the Island; hereafter referred to as *Bahía Sonora*) in 1976. The story ends with a twist worthy of Alfred Hitchcock as the first-person narrator reveals his identity to his sister's murderer as well as his intended revenge.

In this same year, Buitrago won the Children's Literature Prize sponsored by Seguros Médicos Voluntarios with her version of "La princesa chibcha" (The Chibcha [Indian] princess). In the stories in *Bahía Sonora*, Buitrago has created the marvelous world of a coastal island just off the shore of an unnamed Caribbean country, peopled with an infinite variety of characters who reflect her obsession with love/betrayal, parents/children, and reality/dreams. Buitrago's first full-length contribution to children's literature, *La casa del abuelo* (Grandfather's house), won second prize in the First Latin American Children's Literature Festival sponsored by Unesco and the Editorial Voluntad de Literatura Infantil in 1979. This lighthearted book tells the story of Falsy, Elsy, and Luisito through charming vignettes of a loving, happy childhood, in sharp contrast to Buitrago's view of childhood in her works for adults. Her novel *Los pañamanes* (The Pañamanes), set in the same locale as the stories of *Bahía Sonora*, also appeared in 1979. Buitrago artfully fleshes out the problems inherent in a culture based on rape and pillage by the archetypical Spanish colonial conqueror, the *pañamán* (Spanish man) referred to in the novel's title.

In 1982 Buitrago presented a paper at the Congress of Spanish Language Writers held in Caracas, Venezuela. Her presentation, "En busca del lector perdido" (In search of the lost reader), concerned the threat to literature from radio, television, and the nonprint media. That same year Buitrago was invited to Germany for the Berlin Artists Program (DAAD), where she presented her paper "Débiles y poderosos de la literatura colombiana" (The weak and the powerful in Colombian literature) at the Horizon Festival. A collection of four short stories and a novelette were published under the title *Los amores de Afrodita* (The loves of Aphrodite) in 1983. All these stories deal with different aspects of love that is betrayed for money or power. In that same year, her story "Camino de los búhos" (Road of the owls) was scripted for television and was later presented at the Second Latin American Festival of University Teleducation in Lima, Peru. In 1985 a short film was made of this same story-script under the direction of Mónica Silva. In March 1984 Buitrago received the Villa de Avilés Prize in Asturias, Spain, for "Tiquete a la pasión" (Ticket to passion). From September to December 1984, Buitrago resided in Iowa as a participant in the International Writing Program at the University of Iowa. In her most recent work, a juvenile novel, *La casa del arco iris* (1986; Rainbow house), she continues the story of the characters presented in *La casa del abuelo* with another vacation visit to Grandfather's house in the country. At the present time (1988), Fanny Buitrago resides in Stockholm, Sweden.

MAJOR THEMES

Fanny Buitrago shares many of the concerns of her fellow Latin American writers: love, death, family honor, the search for personal fulfillment and acceptance, the influence of genetic or racial memory, superstitious beliefs, and so on. She also writes about topics of interest to many female writers: rape, or the threat of rape; unwanted pregnancy or its converse, a pregnancy desired in the face of infertility; a woman's place in a male-dominated society; a woman's relation to her child(ren) or spouse. Although there are both male and female characters in Buitrago's writings, most of her protagonists and narrators are female. In fact, the world in Buitrago's writings is a woman's world, centered on the eternal triangle of man + woman + child. This triangle is usually seen from one of its sides: man + woman; woman + child; child + man. Although these interrelations are sometimes buried under layers of social convention and seemingly irrelevant plot developments, nonetheless they form the basis of Buitrago's world-view.

Many themes are present in Buitrago's work, yet they can be reduced to a single dichotomy: absence/presence, which can also be expressed as lack/fulfillment. For example, the theme of the abandoned child runs throughout her work, from her award-winning play to her novels and short stories. The absence of the biological parent(s) may or may not be resolved in each work, and sometimes a substitute or pseudoparent is involved, so that this dichotomy can appear skewed in its realization within her work. Yet the underlying structure is one of an unfulfilled natural pair (parent/child) with one member of the pair missing. In other instances, an infertile woman or single man adopts a child, either legally or de facto, in order to complete this natural relationship, which is seen as basic to the culture that Buitrago describes and creates in her works.

Jafet's attempts to find a suitable caregiver for the unnamed girl in *El hombre de paja* is an excellent example of this situation. Although the focus in *El hostigante verano de los dioses* is on the young adult characters, one member of the group, Esteban, has a retarded foster child, Edna, toward whom all the others feel protective and parental, regardless of their marital or real parental status. Two stories in *Las distancias doradas* deal specifically with relationships between child and family. In "Víspera de boda" (On the eve of the wedding) the illegitimate daughter Leda usurps her mother's new husband on their wedding night. The husband (who had married the mother for her money, only to receive none) becomes Leda's source of vindication in her view of the world, which had been warped by her illegitimate status. Like Edna in *El hostigante verano de los dioses*, the protagonist in the story "Años de miel" (Years of honey) is another young retarded girl.

The abandoned child in *Cola de zorro* is Benito (also known as Bernabé), who was orphaned at birth and raised by no one in particular, yet seemingly by the entire town. Ana, who is sterile, attempts to adopt Benito, but is foiled by Claudia who could have had children of her own. When he is an adult, Benito is responsible for several illegitimate pregnancies, as if he were destined to re-create the circumstances of his own unknown paternity and mysterious birth, in an almost mythic way. Many of the selections in *La otra gente* could be classified as horror stories, some of which involve children. In "Los espectros de la Calle de Cantarana" (The ghosts of Cantarana Street), a mother sees ghosts everywhere and eventually comes to view her own daughter as a demon child intruding on her unstable marriage. The mother eventually attacks both husband and child with a knife, although he is able to escape. This story illustrates that the abandoned child theme is but a corollary to Buitrago's overall philosophy: that the traditional family pattern of husband + wife + child is, in itself, an unbalanced relationship, and that either the marriage or the parent/child relation must fail. In "Un baile en Punta de Oro" (A dance in Punta de Oro), from the same collection, the abandoned child Lilí Fresa is taken in by Georgina Camargo and forced, when grown, into an arranged marriage, which brings Lilí four children and material well-being, but not satisfaction. When Lilí dies at a ball she had been promised by her husband, her true love Federico forces the guests at gunpoint to dance in front of her dead body. This scene completes the picture of social vindication by which she had sought to compensate for her classless origins. Once again, the traditional trappings and arrangements of society have brought neither personal satisfaction nor true love.

Two stories in particular in *Bahía Sonora* deal with parents and children. In "Paternidad" (Paternity), a man wants to bestow his name legally on the ille- gitimate child of his live-in guest. He does not realize, however, that the gift of his name, while it would bring legitimacy to the child, would also involve his full responsibility for the child's welfare. Again, Buitrago has set very strict limits on parent/child relationships beyond the merely biological relation of natural parent/natural child. Likewise, in "En la playa" (At the beach), Dr. Castro feels tremendous love for his wife, almost as if he were bewitched. Yet, when a storm breaks while the family is out swimming, he consciously saves only his children, not his wife. Here again, Buitrago shows that the complete family triad (husband/wife/child) is somehow not natural, that it is overbalanced, and that only one side of the triangle can be preserved.

Even Buitrago's lighthearted children's books deal symbolically with the abandoned child theme. In *La casa del abuelo*, the three children visit their grandfather's house because their father is away on an extended business trip. Although he returns unexpectedly at the end of the story for a Christmas visit, it is made obvious that this is only a temporary change in the children's fatherless state. Likewise in *La casa del arco iris*, which deals with the same three children when they are a few years older, Father is again absent when the children visit.

The foundation of the island culture presented in *Los pañamanes* is based on the legendary cry of women giving birth, "*pañamán*," the "Spanish man," an allusion to the metaphorical rape of the island historically being repeated when illegitimate children are born. The expression then becomes a deep cultural obscenity, abhorrent to all members of the culture, yet the very basis of all their relationships, even generations after the original "rape" of the island. Characters in the novel include the illegitimate Nicasio Beltrán, also known as Nick-boy, who kills an albatross and is cursed with thirty years' bad luck, and the woman he wants to marry, Sabina Galende, who later trades Nick-Boy's soul for a television set while they are living together. Sabina is later stolen away by Nicasio's legitimate half-brother, and then Nicasio's own legitimacy is recognized by his father, Jerónimo Beltrán. Just as Nicasio achieves success with a soup he creates that has aphrodisiac powers, Buitrago introduces another abandoned child into the plot. Etilio Beltrán, who had stolen Sabina, returns to town as a beggar, with a young female child tied to his waist. Sabina had abandoned them both in a foreign country. The Gang of Young Boys (drug addicts/alcoholics who run the island's underground activities) is given custody of the girl. Eventually the girl's natural grandmother, Celmira Galende, gets custody of the child, but her father dies, leaving her cut off again from a natural parental bond. Stability in family relations is never quite achieved in Buitrago's works.

Another major theme in Buitrago's work is the nature of love, of male-female interrelations. There are many couples in her writings. However, the ones who are shown as truly in love are usually not married, at least not to each other.

For example, the collection *Los amores de Afrodita* consists of four short stories and one novelette dealing with various aspects of love. Unfortunately, this love is often betrayed for power and money. In the story "¡Anhelante, oh anhelante!" (Yearning, oh, yearning!), a mother addresses her son whom she feels is about to marry someone inappropriate. When he divorces his first wife Yiri to pursue his political ambitions with Maclovia Aranda (the unsuitable one), he soon discovers that her political ambitions are even greater than his and that

she has no real feelings for him. In the end he becomes involved with revolutionaries and is forced to flee the country. From Switzerland he calls home for
Yiri, since Maclovia has asked for an annulment. Buitrago seems to be saying
that passionate love and a successful marriage are not always synonymous.

In "Rosas de Saron" (Roses of Sharon), Lisabeth is proud of her adopted
daughter, Saskia (the child of a couple murdered by Mafia drug traffickers). As
a professional seamstress who makes her living copying designer originals,
Lisabeth feels that her own family is a copy of the model family. In the end,
however, Saskia runs off with Lisabeth's husband and life's savings. Again, the
unnatural child (adopted, not born into the family) causes a break between the
other members of the family triad, demonstrating Buitrago's contention that
children can destroy male-female love relationships.

An extreme example of Buitrago's vision of the incompatibility of marriage
and love occurs in "Mammy deja el oficio" [Mammy leaves the trade] from *La
otra gente*. In this story, a woman with a decent upbringing marries well and
has children. Unfortunately, she has abominable taste in clothes and dresses like
a prostitute, at least according to her neighbors. In the end she gives in to
pressure from her social peers and becomes what people think she is, a prostitute,
with her husband as her client. In Buitrago's world-view, legal marriage means
a nonlove relationship. Since these two people truly love each other, the marriage
must dissolve, and a relation built purely on passion and not on legal contracts
is established in its place. The actions of the partners in the relation have not
changed; only the status of the legal document. Yet that status change engenders
a distortion in the reader's perception of the relation between the man and the
woman, since the reader usually shares the same societal constraints as those
symbolized by the now defunct marriage certificate.

In *El hostigante verano de los dioses*, likewise everything is a matter of
appearance over substance, even for people who call themselves "gods," as if
they were in control. Society continues to function as it has for centuries—there
are weddings, balls, funerals—but it is all for show. People who are not in love
with each other marry, while maintaining affairs with those they truly love.
Elaborate funerals are held for people who are socially prominent, yet universally
despised. The structures of society remain in place, yet Buitrago shows us that
they are hollow, with no real foundation in fact. Stable relationships are not
built on paper but on lived physical commitment, on a day-to-day basis.

Buitrago never states explicitly that she is against marriage or traditional family
structures, but all her characters demonstrate that the fictional world she has
created is violently opposed to these kinds of relationships. Natural disasters
(floods, storms), unconquerable forces (disease, revolution, war)—all seek to
destroy these structures. Just as the world of her coastal island was created out
of rape and violence, so too those who inhabit that island in later generations
confront the constant threat of rape, murder, and violence. Except for her contributions to juvenile literature, Buitrago's humor tends to be on the dark side
and brings little relief to this world formed from chaos and still chaotic beneath

its façade of normalcy. Fulfillment can only be found in unconstrained love, love given freely and openly without legal stricture, as in the natural bonds of parent and child or between two lovers.

Whether Buitrago's writings are deliberately set on her coastal island or in other fictitious Colombian towns, the action involves the same basic themes of abandonment, marital incompatibility, and social constraints versus personal freedom that form her world-view. In each case there is a fictive realization of the basic dichotomy that informs her works: absence-presence. This may take the form of absent parent(s) and abandoned child(ren), or infertile or unmarried parent(s) seeking to adopt; a man or woman in love seeking the supposed stability of formal marriage when satisfaction may only be gained from its opposite, an open nonmarital relationship. In each case an absence is seen or a lack felt, and a presence or fulfillment is sought in order to achieve wholeness. In Buitrago's world-view, however, wholeness can be realized in a very limited number of ways. Although her characters fight against the constraints of society in their searches for personal fulfillment, the world in which they have been created imposes its own constraints on that fulfillment.

SURVEY OF CRITICISM

To date, no book-length study of the life or works of Fanny Buitrago has been published in the United States, nor has one been listed as published elsewhere in standard reference sources such as the *MLA International Bibliography*. The only study readily available in the United States is a chapter in an unpublished dissertation by Nancy McCarty (1986). The articles by María Salgado (1987), Antonio Benítez Rojo (1982), and Raymond Williams were unavailable to this author.

The dearth of critical material in the United States on Fanny Buitrago is difficult to understand, since her work has earned her so many literary prizes abroad over the years. The fact that her landmark first novel has been republished twice in a region of the world not known for major printing runs should be evidence of the significance of that novel, yet no one has undertaken a critical study of *El hostigante verano de los dioses*.

BIBLIOGRAPHY

Works by Fanny Buitrago

El hostigante verano de los dioses. Bogotá: Tercer Mundo, 1963. (Subsequent editions
    in Bogotá: Plaza & Janés, 1977, and Oveja Negra, 1984.)
La garza sucia. 1964 [Ballet]. Unpublished in Spanish.
El hombre de paja y Las distancias doradas. Bogotá: Espiral, 1964.
Cola de zorro. Bogotá: Monolito, 1970.
La otra gente: cuentos. Bogotá: Instituto Colombiano de Cultura, 1973.

Bahía sonora, relatos de la isla. Bogotá: Almanaques Supremo, 1976.
La casa del abuelo. Illus. Mario Duarte. Bogotá: Voluntad Unesco, 1979.
Los pañamanes. Barcelona: Plaza and Janés, 1979.
Los amores de Afrodita. Bogotá: Plaza and Janés, 1983.
La casa del arco iris. Illus. Yezid Vergara. Bogotá: Carlos Valencia Editores, 1986.
Cartas del Palomar. Bogotá: Carlos Valencia, 1988. Children's story.

Translations of Fanny Buitrago (by the author)

"The Dirty Heron." *Américas* 17, 3 (Mar. 1965):31–32.
"The West Side of the Island." *Américas* 18, 4 (Apr. 1966):36–38.

Works about Fanny Buitrago

Benítez Rojo, Antonio. "*Los pañamanes*: Mito y realidad en el Caribe." *Prismal/Cabral* 7–8 (Spring 1982):5–20.
McCarty, Nancy Jane. "The Colombian Novel of the Atlantic Coast." Ph.D. diss. University of California-Irvine, 1986.(DAI 47,3 (1986)):923A.
Salgado, María. "Temas y técnicas en *Los amores de Afrodita* de Fanny Buitrago." *Revista de la Universidad Central* (Bogotá) 8, 28 (Mar. 1987):174–84.
Williams, Raymond L. "An Interview with Woman Writers in Colombia." *Latin American Women Writers: Yesterday and Today*. Eds. Yvette E. Miller and Charles M. Tatum. [Pittsburgh, Pa.]: Latin American Literary Review, 1977. Pp. 155–61.
———. "Fanny Buitrago." *Una década de la novela colombiana: La experiencia de los sesenta*. Bogotá: Plaza and Janés, 1980. Pp. 27–38.

SILVINA BULLRICH
(b. 1915)
Argentina

Erica Frouman-Smith

BIOGRAPHY

Silvina Bullrich was the second of three daughters, born on October 4, 1915, to Dr. Rafael Augusto Bullrich and María Laura Meyrelles in Buenos Aires, Argentina. Dr. Bullrich was a distinguished cardiologist and professor of medicine who came from a family of German descent. Since his father was a diplomat in France, Dr. Bullrich received most of his education in that country and did not arrive in Argentina until he was eighteen. Silvina Bullrich's father was shaped by three passions throughout his life: love for French culture, devotion to his career, and the acquisition of an important art collection. The author remembers him as an aloof man whom she loved and respected but also whose traditional concept of women caused him to belittle his daughter's efforts at a writing career. His influence on her was apparent in her lifelong love affair with anything and everything that was French.

Bullrich's mother, of Portuguese descent, was a traditional woman in her devotion to her daughters and to her husband, despite his series of extramarital affairs. She was especially close to her middle child, Silvina, whom she regarded as her favorite. The author recalls her as an affectionate, loving mother whose protective attitude toward her daughters stemmed from a history of tragedies and suicides on her side of the family. She considered her inability to produce a son a major disappointment in her life, something she never allowed her daughters to forget.

Bullrich remembers her childhood as a period of great happiness where intimacy, love, and warmth freely flourished and life centered around intellectual and cultural pursuits. She felt extremely close to her sisters but especially so to her eldest sister, Laura. The two girls, with their younger sister, Marta, grew up in an affluent environment, surrounded by uniformed, white-gloved servants, and objects of art and culture. The three attended school in the morning and spent the afternoons studying French with a private tutor. Bullrich admits to being a poor student in any subject other than French or literature. She was able to satisfy her intellectual curiosity through her father's excellent collection of French and Russian literature. All three sisters would dream constantly of France, a place they eventually got to know during late adolescence. Paris became the city Bullrich would constantly return to throughout her life.

Although Bullrich regards this period as an extremely idyllic one during which she was surrounded by her loving family in a home filled with discussions of art, literature, and music, she complains bitterly about one issue. Her parents, despite being cultured people, maintained a traditional attitude toward the education of women. As a result, the young girls received a formal education only through the sixth grade. This illogical view on the part of parents who obviously loved their daughters was typical of a period in which women were expected to follow only two careers: marriage and motherhood. Bullrich's lament throughout her life that she was not properly educated for anything beyond the two vocations in which she never succeeded, becomes an important theme in her work.

Notwithstanding her parents' lack of support and guidance, Bullrich began her writing career during adolescence, eventually paying to publish a book of poems, *Vibraciones* (1935; Vibrations). She knew then that she wanted to dedicate her life to writing, even though it was difficult for women of her era to do so. She resented the idea that women were not expected to pursue serious goals or ambitions but were instead forced to wait passively until they were chosen in marriage. In addition to writing poetry for the journal, *Atlántida*, Bullrich fulfilled her strong desire to work by becoming her father's secretary.

In December 1936, at the age of twenty-one, Bullrich married Arturo Palenque Carrera, a man with similar intellectual interests, who, at the time, was studying to be a lawyer. Very early in the marriage the author realized that, in spite of their mutual physical attraction and common interests, the relationship was doomed to fail. Ten months after they married, Bullrich's one and only child, Daniel, was born. This was a difficult period for Bullrich. Confined to a small apartment, she missed her family and the spacious home. The lack of fulfillment she felt in the role of wife and mother coupled with serious financial problems further added to her unhappiness. She resented her father both for allowing her to marry a man who could not properly take care of her and for not helping them out. She did receive assistance from her sister Laura, who married very well, and from her husband's aunt. As a realistic writer, Bullrich faithfully documents the changes in her life in her fiction. Most of her early works deal with the lifestyles of upper class women who encounter difficulties with love, marriage, and money.

From the early 1940s through the mid-1950s, Silvina Bullrich faced a steady stream of personal misfortunes. One by one she witnessed her loving family disappear before her eyes. She lost her beloved paternal grandmother in 1942.

Two years later her father, the famous cardiologist, died of a heart attack. Bullrich's older sister Laura succumbed to breast cancer at the age of thirty-one in July 1945. That same year, Bullrich and her husband separated, and they became officially divorced in December 1946, exactly ten years after they married. In 1947 Bullrich discovered she had tuberculosis and was forced to send her son away. She was lucky enough to be cured soon afterward because of the fortuitous introduction of antibiotics. Years later, looking back on this difficult time when her writing served as an important emotional and practical support, Bullrich rationalized that her own escape from death was further evidence that she was destined to serve as a model to other Argentine women writers. Unfortunately, the solitude she has always felt is a condition she has escaped only temporarily.

The early 1940s saw the outpouring of Spanish intellectuals fleeing the civil war in Spain. Bullrich participated in weekly discussions in Buenos Aires with Spanish and Latin American writers who were significant influences in her literary growth. Ricardo Baeza, José Ortega y Gasset, María de Maeztu, Margarita Sarfatti, along with Argentines Jorge Luis Borges and José Bianco, joined with these and other authors in making the city the cultural center of the Spanish-speaking world. Being with them affirmed in Bullrich's mind the appropriateness of her chosen vocation. The writers echoed her own sentiments about writing and its significance. Jorge Luis Borges and Eduardo Mallea were most directly helpful. Borges corrected Bullrich's manuscripts, and Mallea provided an entrée into the prestigious *Sunday Literary Supplement* of *La Nación*. Bullrich regarded Mallea's *Historia de una pasión argentina* (The history of an Argentine passion) as her Bible. It helped to shape her lifelong concern: the development and growth of Argentina as a nation politically, economically, and spiritually.

In 1944, Bullrich received the Municipal Prize of Buenos Aires for *La redoma del primer ángel* (The first angel's vial), her third novel. In 1951, *Bodas de cristal* (Crystal wedding anniversary), her fifth novel, was her first big commercial success. In addition to being translated into several languages, it was published in paperback in France, which made Bullrich particularly happy.

During the 1950s, owing to the loss of much of her family, Bullrich turned more and more to writing. She became well established in the rhythm and pattern of a highly successful writing career that centered principally around novels but that also included short stories, essays, articles for the major journals and newspapers of Buenos Aires, literary and film criticism, and the translation of major French writers like Simone de Beauvoir, François Mauriac, Prosper Mérimée, George Sand, and Guy de Maupassant. From the age of twenty-three to the present, Bullrich has maintained an important relationship with *La Nación*, where she still makes regular contributions and does occasional film criticism.

In 1951 Bullrich met and later married Marcelo Dupont, the man who reaffirmed her view that life is complete only when two people devotedly share their love. Although Bullrich divorced her first husband in 1946 during the short time when divorce was legal in Argentina, her second marriage was recognized neither by the Argentine government nor by her mother, a devout Catholic. Nonetheless, Bullrich considered Marcelo, a man thirteen years her senior and well versed in French culture, the perfect mate. Together they embodied the author's conception of the ideal *pareja* (couple)—two people joined by strong physical attraction as well as similar background, values, and goals. During this time Bullrich stopped writing so she could luxuriate in this newfound happiness. But Marcelo urged her to continue writing, and in 1954, in order to please him, she published *Teléfono ocupado* (Busy signal). It was her only novel written while they were together.

The year 1955 marked the start of a new phase of life for both Bullrich and her country. The Perón government fell and Bullrich's remaining sister, Marta, perished in a plane crash along with her daughter. The following year, Marcelo died of cancer in spite of his wife's intense efforts to save him by seeking additional medical help abroad. Although she believed the force of her love would sustain him, it did not. Once again she was alone. In *Mientras los demás viven* (1958; While others live), the author tried to console herself by writing about her grief. But not pleased with the results, Bullrich made a second attempt with *Los pasajeros del jardín* (1971; The passengers in the garden), which was a truer-to-life version. It was enthusiastically received by the public and by critics who responded well to the tragic story of a "perfect couple."

Several years after Marcelo's death, Bullrich experienced a passionate but destructive relationship that she re-created in *Un momento muy largo* (1961; A very long moment). This event led the author to decide she was too old to make any more compromises on her career because of her relationship with a man. It was also around this time that Bullrich unsuccessfully tried to reestablish her life in Paris. But once there she realized that she was meant to live in Argentina where she felt she belonged and where she could fulfill her mission as a writer: by serving as an inspiration to other women writers and by giving testimony to her times.

From the 1960s to the present, Bullrich has continued to chronicle the problematic situation of upper class Argentine women. In addition, she more completely devotes herself to her ever bleaker vision of the Argentine nation, eventually forming a trilogy that began with her most critically successful novel, *Los burgueses* (1964; The bourgeoisie). Since then her life has settled into a pattern of spending part of the year writing in Buenos Aires. During the summers she vacations in the popular resort town of Punta del Este, Uruguay, a place that fulfills her lifelong desire to live peacefully in the countryside, away from the commotion and complexities of city life. Bullrich also devotes significant time to traveling abroad either on her own or as a guest of foreign governments and, indeed, has made the rounds of very exotic places. Such travels have been the subject of a book of essays, *El mundo que yo vi* (1969; The world that I saw), and continue to serve as material for her regular contributions to *La Nación*. These trips reaffirm her need to return to Argentina where she feels wanted, needed, and appreciated by her readers and by the many younger Argentine

women writers for whom she is a model and to whom she dedicates her autobiography, *Mis memorias* (1980; My memoirs).

MAJOR THEMES

Silvina Bullrich is an essentially realistic writer whose novels reflect the chronology of her life. Her body of work may be divided into three periods: an early
one from 1939 to 1949; a second, which can be characterized as sentimental
narratives, from 1951 to 1961; and a third period from 1964 to the present. What
they share is Bullrich's commitment to two major themes: women's problems
in a patriarchal society and her concern for Argentina and its ability to develop
as a nation well outside the shadow of Europe. (The second theme reflects the
influence of Argentine essayists, particularly Manuel Gálvez and Eduardo Mallea.) These two principal preoccupations later will often merge in her vision of
the *pareja* since it symbolizes two people who, united by profound spiritual and
physical love, will be able to work for the good of the nation.

During her early period, Bullrich wrote six novels, one novella, and a biography of the French writer, George Sand. Her first novel, *Calles de Buenos Aires*
(1939; The streets of Buenos Aires), is a fictional re-creation of the author's life
during the unhappy early years of her first marriage, a time of loneliness and disillusionment, since her relationship lacked the warmth and affection of childhood.
The emptiness and lack of purpose Bullrich felt are seen in the lives of wealthy,
upper class women of the affluent Barrio Norte section of Buenos Aires. Bullrich
focuses on a circle of women friends who remain essentially flat figures. Their
main purpose is to voice the lack of fulfillment for individuals and the nation, the
conflict between love and career, and the materialism of upper class *porteños* (residents of Buenos Aires) who are deficient in moral values and use adultery as a
solution to marital conflicts. *Calles* is significant for the following reasons. First,
for the criticism Bullrich, as one of very few women writers of the period, boldly
levels against her own social class. In doing so she anticipates many of the concerns Simone de Beauvoir will voice ten years later in *The Second Sex*. It is interesting to note that Bullrich translated several of Simone de Beauvoir's novels into
Spanish and regards her as one of the greatest novelists of the twentieth century.
Second, for representing, through her female characters, the essential problems
of women of her generation: They are educated only to be wives and mothers
without taking into account other options. Third, for setting a thematic tone that
indicates the direction that later works will follow.

Bullrich's second phase began auspiciously with *Bodas de cristal* (1951). The
number of novels produced during this ten-year period (five) was limited by the
author's marriage to Marcelo Dupont. Through these works Bullrich demonstrates her ability to capture the essence of the Argentine woman's reality regarding love and marriage within the upper middle class. *Bodas* is significant
for attracting the attention of the public and establishing an important relationship
between Bullrich and her readers that has continued through the present. It is

also important for certain formal innovations. In fact, it is in this novel that Bullrich uses the principal female character as the first-person narrator, which will become the hallmark of her most successful works. Expressed in very lyrical language, the first-person narration of the Wife alternates with a third-person omniscient narrator who introduces the other principal characters: the Wife's husband, Luis, and his three mistresses. In addition to the principal theme expressed in the title of the book, that is, that marriage is a fragile state, are the themes of the contrasting temperaments and perspectives of men and women on matters of the heart, adultery, and the status of women.

On the morning of their wedding anniversary, the Wife evokes fifteen years of marriage characterized by Luis's endless series of extramarital affairs. He is the stereotypical Latin male who devotes his life to the sexual conquest of women. Together they embody a typical Argentine couple, outstanding only in their mediocrity. The Wife has the status of the ''other'' as her world is perceived in terms of her husband. The three mistresses add further reinforcement to this theme. As is typical of Bullrich's works, irony plays a large part. We realize that each of the women is superior to Luis in many ways, but all live with the ingrained notion that they must share their lives with men.

Bullrich's third phase has been a very productive one. In addition to a large quantity of novels, sixteen as of 1987, Bullrich has produced one collection of short stories, a novella, one biography, seven books of essays, and her memoirs. Hardly a year goes by without a new publication. During this phase her two major concerns, the evolving drama of the Argentine woman and the problematic situation of the Argentine nation, often merge. Her fiction continues to reflect the evolution of her life and her growing disillusionment with the future of the country.

The publication of *Los burgueses* (1964)—the first in a trilogy on the status of Argentina (it is formed by *Los salvadores de la patria* [1965; The saviors of the nation] and *Los monstruos sagrados* [1971; The sacred monsters])—brought both satisfaction and disappointment. Although *Los burgueses* is her most well-received novel, the longed-for fame and recognition to which she aspired has not accompanied it. The novel is a successful combination of traditional and innovative novelistic techniques skillfully used to portray the intertwined story of four generations of the once aristocratic Barros-Inglebaard family. The story is seen through the eyes of a narrator whose identity the author tries to make ambiguous but whom most readers regard as the father of Loreley. His scornful, pessimistic tone underscores the theme of the spiritual decline of Argentina as seen in the four generations of the family as well as in Loreley. The once promising young girl has now become a middle-class wife and mother leading an uninspired, monotonous life. Outwardly, the family pretends to celebrate both the ninetieth birthday of the patriarch as well as the couple's sixtieth wedding anniversary. In reality, their only concern is how much they will inherit from the grandparents. Thus, they are the petty bourgeoisie of the title: people of mean aspirations lacking imagination, ambition, and leadership who sadly seem to symbolize the future predicament of Argentina.

In addition to examining the development of the nation, Bullrich's voyage of self-discovery continues in her ironic and lyrical novel, *Mañana digo basta* (1968; Tomorrow I will say, enough). It is a first-person narration, in diary form, of the crisis of a middle-aged Latin American woman who, as a widow and mother of three grown-up daughters, no longer feels indispensable to anyone. She comes to an out-of-the-way setting, the resort town of La Paloma, Uruguay, to confront her solitude head on, hoping to find peace. During this inward journey, Alejandra contemplates such issues as growing old, the conflicts of motherhood, her new independence, and her rediscovered sexuality. Ironically, her attempts to deal with her solitude are thwarted by an uninterrupted stream of visitors, particularly her three daughters. They are portrayed as self-centered and materialistic, thus embodying many of the author's complaints regarding the younger generation. In following the trajectory of the author's life, *Mañana* presents the problem, still central in many countries, of being a woman alone in a society that values women only in a subordinate relation to men. Alejandra must deal constantly with prejudice on the basis of her sex. She realizes that unfortunately not much has changed for the women of her generation. Yet, we must note that, through her, Bullrich creates a protagonist whose self-image is no longer based on traditional values. Her crisis is not confined to her role as a wife and mother but is set within the larger framework of an individual striving for internal peace in spite of her loneliness. The result is more universal in its perspective.

In *La Bicicleta* (1986; The bicycle), Bullrich presents us with her latest view of the current status of Argentina. The portrait, somewhat similar in tone and technique to *Reunión de directorio* (1977; The board of directors' meeting), is one of utter despair. It again shows the author's talent at irony, satire, and black humor. Argentina, here called La Bicicleta, is a grotesque parody of all Latin American nations which lack order, stability, and international significance. The nation is so inconsequential that it cannot be seen on a map, and its very existence is constantly in doubt.

The term *bicicletear* is used by the natives of La Bicicleta to mean to speculate or to gamble. On another level the verb refers to the idea of a country constantly having to move forward without aim or direction, for to stop would mean falling down. This happens as a result of its lack of roots and foundation. The natives are obsessive materialists who are always gambling to make more money. Serious work is to be avoided as a means to earning one's living. But their efforts are continually frustrated since the national currency is so unstable that its value is more like monopoly money. (One of the main characters is a banker who carries his money only in American dollars.) Here life is a constant game, and politics is the biggest game of all. The prevailing philosophy is to live for today for you never know if tomorrow will exist. The profound love shared by the two main characters has no chance in such an unstable world.

This work is an important culmination of the concepts and themes expressed throughout Bullrich's writings. The idea of the couple who through love for one another will in turn work for the good of the country is no longer a possibility.

The hope expressed in early works regarding the future of Argentina is nowhere to be seen. Like the optimism of Roque and Alegría in the early chapters, it has come to a crashing halt. Significantly, however, Bullrich continues to pursue her view of the writer's function by giving her latest testimony on Argentina, no matter how bleak it may be.

SURVEY OF CRITICISM

In a continent where only a handful of writers do well enough to devote themselves full time to writing, Bullrich is part of that select group. She is a national institution in Argentina where her books are seen everywhere. Yet, despite her popularity, there are no major critical works about her other than the reviews of her fiction and nonfiction and the essays by her ardent admirer, Nicolás Cócaro. In the United States, several doctoral dissertations study her alone or as part of a group of either Argentine or Latin American women writers. More scholarly articles have emerged over the last fifteen years owing to the rise of the women's movement and the surge of interest in Latin American literature.

In 1968 Diane Birkemoe's doctoral dissertation, "Contemporary Women Novelists of Argentina (1945–67)" studied eight writers and included Bullrich along with Estela Canto and Beatriz Guido as forerunners of the generation of the 1960s. Birkemoe includes twelve of Silvina Bullrich's novels from *Su vida y yo* (1941; His life and mine), through *La creciente* (1967; The flood). She praises Bullrich for the great diversity of her work and her understanding of human behavior. She admires the later political-sociological commentaries on Argentina (in *Los burgueses, Los salvadores*, and *La creciente*) and considers her earlier production as principally entertaining novels.

In 1972 Bobs Tusa wrote one of two doctoral dissertations that deal solely with Silvina Bullrich, "The Works of Silvina Bullrich." It is an original and exhaustive study that examines the author's works in the light of twentieth-century definitions of interpretations and criticism as presented by E. D. Hirsch in his article, "Objective Interpretation" (*PMLA* 80 [Sept. 1960]:463–79). The study includes fiction published through 1969. Tusa regards Bullrich with the utmost respect and seriousness. Even though she recognizes the flaws in certain works, she attributes the same serious intent to some of her more obviously commercial fiction. Tusa includes a detailed biography based on the limited information available before the publication of Bullrich's autobiography. She notes that the same ideology regarding self-realization is present throughout the author's works, and she recognizes the significance of the author's concept of the couple as a way of achieving fulfillment (p. 283).

Bradley M. Class in "Treatment of Politics by Argentine Female Novelists" (1974), like Birkemoe, also deals with eight women writers. He analyzes two novels considered by Birkemoe, *Los salvadores* and *La creciente*. He is concerned with Bullrich's statement on Argentina but analyzes her technique and her own comments on her lack of political views in the light of accusations made by her critics. His close analysis of both works leads him to a positive evaluation of the author's technical skills. In *Los salvadores*, he praises Bullrich's "brilliant application of irony" (p. 176).

Anna C. Tavenner, in "Aspectos de conflicto y enajenamiento de la mujer en las novelas de Silvina Bullrich, Beatriz Guido y Clarice Lispector" (1977), is the first to regard seriously Bullrich's contribution in depicting women. She focuses on Bullrich's novels through 1974. She notes that Bullrich is not a feminist but that her works reflect Argentine reality and the problem of women's lack of education for careers. She concludes that the author sees the solution for individuals and the nation in the *pareja*. She indicates that the author's female characters fight hard to be men's equals and therefore are not the kind of women who fit a traditional mold. Tavenner believes Bullrich fulfills her own conception of the importance of feminist literature through her sincerity and realism.

My own dissertation, "Female Roles in the Fiction of Silvina Bullrich" (1979), is the second doctoral dissertation to focus solely on Bullrich. It studies her works from 1939 through 1977. In addition to analyzing the author's portrayal of women, it looks at the kinds of female roles that reappear throughout her works—Wife, Mother, Mistress/Lover, and Independent Woman. It also studies the author's use of novelistic technique and notes Bullrich's development of an appropriate mode to express her female characters' innermost thoughts. The results link her to leading women writers everywhere. That her female characters embody male-female traits fulfills the need for an androgynous ideal as expressed by writers such as Simone de Beauvoir, Colette, and Doris Lessing.

Nicolás Cócaro, an Argentine poet, short story writer, critic, and journalist, has often reviewed Bullrich's novels for *La Nación*. An enthusiastic admirer of her works, he wrote the introductory essays for two similar collections of works: *Silvina Bullrich* (1979) and *Páginas de Silvina Bullrich seleccionadas por la autora* (1983; Pages from the works of Silvina Bullrich selected by the author). The first contains excerpts from her novels (through *Reunión*), essays in addition to articles, an autobiographical sketch, and a bibliography. The second contains excerpts from her novels through *Después del escándalo* (1981; After the scandal), her essays, many articles, a chronology of her life, a bibliography of and about the author, and excerpts of reviews of her works. The first essay, "La pequeña comedia humana en la obra de Silvina Bullrich" (The small human comedy in the works of Silvina Bullrich), deals with the themes of her fiction, her criticism of her own social class for their lack of values, her concerns about Argentina, the importance of her travels, and her narrative abilities. He concludes that Bullrich has been successful with her proposal to write a "modest, human, Argentine comedy" (p. 23).

In the second, more interesting essay, Cócaro reviews Bullrich's background and her literary influences, and notes the change from her passion for the French to her passion for Argentina. Her novels, he believes, are a rich mosaic of many human types but are always directly tied to reality. He notes that her style is very personal and uncompromising. He believes her popularity has much to do with the personal attacks on her life and her literary production. He values the author's lack of compromise in the face of difficulties she encountered being a working woman in a world not yet ready to accept such a novelty. According to Cócaro, Bullrich defies bourgeois convention and is therefore a rebel in a society that denies women the same rights as men. Despite this he notes that she does not consider herself a feminist: "I am not a feminist because, after many years of working and roaming about through life, I have noticed that the sense of responsibility is greater in men than in women" (p. 20).

In my article, "The Paradoxes of Silvina Bullrich" (1983), I discuss Bullrich's biography and the three phases of her work. I point out that Bullrich's self-conception as a writer is connected to being Argentine and giving testimony of her times. The novelist's views on feminism as reflected in her essays on women and in her links to Simone de Beauvoir are also presented. Finally, I indicate some interesting paradoxes regarding Bullrich's commercialism versus her need to be taken seriously.

Naomi Lindstrom's article, "Literary Convention and Sex-Role Analysis: Silvina Bullrich's 'Abnegation' " (1982), is important for detailing many of the negative aspects noted by other critics who do not look well on Bullrich's commercial success. Nevertheless, she notes that the story conveys the message of the importance of language in perpetuating female stereotypes.

Despite Bullrich's contribution to the world of Argentine letters for nearly fifty years, relatively few critical studies of her work have appeared. Those that do exist give an overview or focus on her portrait of women. What is lacking is an assessment of her work as a social critic of Argentina from the start of her career and an examination of how her vision has changed. Finally, her influence on the succeeding generation of Argentine women writers is another area worth studying.

BIBLIOGRAPHY

Major Works by Silvina Bullrich

Vibraciones. Buenos Aires. By the Author, 1935. Poetry.
Calles de Buenos Aires: Barrio Norte. Buenos Aires: Ediciones Dos Mundos, 1939. In *Entre mis veinte y treinta años*. Buenos Aires: Emecé Editores, 1970. Pp. 11–123. Novel.
"La inquietud de Buenos Aires en la literatura argentina contemporánea." *Nosotros* 4 (Aug. 1939):341–57. Essay.
Saloma. Buenos Aires: Talleres Gráficos de A. Contreras, 1940. In *Entre mis veinte y treinta anos*. Pp. 127–227. Novel.
Su vida y yo. Buenos Aires: Espasa-Calpe Argentina, 1941. Novel.
La redoma del primer ángel. Escritores Argentinos. Buenos Aires: Emecé Editores, 1943. Buenos Aires: Santiago Rueda Editor, 1967. In *Entre mis veinte y treinta años*. Pp. 229–347. Novel.

La tercera versión. Novelistas Argentinos Contemporáneos. Buenos Aires: Emecé Editores, 1944. In *Entre mis veinte y treinta años*. Pp. 349–420. Novel.

George Sand. Buenos Aires: Emecé Editores, 1946. In *Entre mis veinte y treinta años*. Pp. 421–522. Biography.

"Hágase justicia" (written in Buenos Aires, 1949). First publ. in *Entre mis veinte y treinta años*, 1970. Pp. 555–608. Novel.

Historia de un silencio. Buenos Aires: Medina del Río, 1949. Caracas: Monte Avila, 1976. In *Entre mis veinte y treinta años*. 525–54. Novella.

Bodas de cristal. 1st ed. Buenos Aires: Editorial Sudamericana, 1951. In *Tres novelas: Bodas de cristal, Mientras los demás viven, Un momento muy largo*. Buenos Aires: Editorial Sudamericana, 1966. Novel.

Teléfono ocupado. 1st ed. Buenos Aires: Editorial Goyanarte, 1954. Buenos Aires: Emecé Editores, 1971. Novel.

Mientras los demás viven. Colección Novelistas Hispanoamericanos. Buenos Aires: Editorial Sudamericana, 1958. In *Tres novelas*. Novel.

El hechicero. Colección Tiempos Modernos. Buenos Aires: Editorial Goyanarte, 1961. Novel.

Un momento muy largo. Colección El Espejo. 1st ed. Buenos Aires: Editorial Sudamericana, 1961. In *Tres novelas*. Novel.

"La primera piedra." *Ficción* 33–34 (Sept.-Dec. 1961):6–19. Short Story.

Los burgueses. 1st ed. Buenos Aires: Editorial Sudamericana, 1964. Novel.

Historias inmorales. 1st ed. Buenos Aires: Editorial Sudamericana, 1965. Short stories.

La creciente. Colección El Espejo. Buenos Aires: Editorial Sudamericana, 1965. Novel.

Los salvadores de la patria. 1st ed. Buenos Aires: Editorial Sudamericana, 1965. Novel.

"Nosotros fuimos 'los iracundos.' " *La Estafeta Literaria* [Madrid], Sept. 23–Oct. 7 1967:16–18. Essay.

"Prólogo." *La redoma del primer ángel*. Buenos Aires: Santiago Rueda Editor, 1967. Essay.

Mañana digo basta. 1st ed. Buenos Aires: Editorial Sudamericana, 1968. Novel.

Carta abierta a los hijos. Buenos Aires: Emecé Editores, 1969. Essay.

El calor humano. Colección Tiempos Modernos. 1st ed. Buenos Aires: Editorial Merlín, 1969. Novel.

El mundo que yo vi. Buenos Aires: Editorial Merlín, 1969. Travel essays.

La aventura interior. Buenos Aires: Editorial Merlín, 1970. Literary criticism.

"La mujer, eterna postergada. ¿Por qué?" *La Nación* (Buenos Aires), Nov. 3, 1970. Essay.

"Nota autobiográfica." *Entre mis veinte y treinta años*. Buenos Aires: Emecé Editores, 1970. Pp. 609–20. Autobiographical essay.

Carta a un joven cuentista. Buenos Aires: Santiago Rueda Editor, 1971. Essay.

Los monstruos sagrados. Colección El Espejo. 1st ed. Buenos Aires: Editorial Sudamericana, 1971. Novel.

Los pasajeros del jardín. Novelistas Argentinos Contemporáneos. 1st ed. Buenos Aires: Emecé Editores, 1971. Novel.

"La mujer argentina en la literatura." Buenos Aires: Centro Nacional de Documentación Educativa, 1972. N. p. Essay.

Mal don. Novelistas Contemporáneos. Buenos Aires: Emecé Editores, 1973. Novel.

Un hombre con historia. Colección Tiempos Modernos. Buenos Aires: Editorial Merlín, 1973. Short stories.

Su Excelencia envió el informe. Novelistas Contemporáneos. 1st ed. Buenos Aires: Emecé
    Editores, 1974. Novel.
Te acordarás de Taormina. Novelistas Contemporáneos. 1st ed. Buenos Aires: Emecé
    Editores, 1975.
Reunión de directorio. Escritores Argentinos. 1st ed. Buenos Aires: Editorial Sudamer-
    icana, 1977. Novel.
Los despiadados. Escritores Argentinos. Buenos Aires: Emecé Editores, 1978. Novel.
Silvina Bullrich. Ed. Nicolás Cócaro. Buenos Aires: Ediciones Culturales Argentinas,
    1979. Collection of excerpts of fiction and nonfiction.
Mis memorias. Buenos Aires: Emecé Editores, 1980. Autobiography.
Después del escándalo. Escritores Argentinos. Buenos Aires: Emecé Editores, 1981.
    Novel.
Escándalo bancario. Escritores Argentinos. Buenos Aires: Emecé Editores, 1982. Novel.
Flora Tristán, la visionaria. Buenos Aires: Río Inmóvil Ediciones, 1982. Biography.
La mujer postergada. Buenos Aires: Editorial Sudamericana, 1982. Essay.
Cuento cruel. Colección Cuentorregalo. Buenos Aires: Editorial Abril, 1983. Short story,
    essays.
Páginas de Silvina Bullrich seleccionadas por la autora. Ed. Jorge Cruz. Colección
    Escritores Argentinos de Hoy. Buenos Aires: Editorial Celtia, 1983. Collection
    of excerpts of fiction and nonfiction.
¿A qué hora murió el enfermo? Escritores Argentinos. Buenos Aires: Emecé Editores,
    1986. Novel.
La Argentina contradictoria. Buenos Aires: Emecé Editores, 1986. Essays.
La Bicicleta. Escritores Argentinos. Buenos Aires: Emecé Editores, 1986. Novel.
Cuando cae el telón. Buenos Aires: Emecé Editores, 1987. Essays.

Translations of Silvina Bullrich

Frouman-Smith, Erica, trans. "The Divorce." *Contemporary Women Authors of Latin
    America: New Translations.* Eds. Doris Meyer and Margarite Fernández Olmos.
    New York: Brooklyn College Press, 1983. Pp. 141–46.
Lewald, H. Ernest, trans. "The Lover." "Self-Denial." *The Web: Stories by Argentine
    Women.* Ed. H. Ernest Lewald. Washington, D.C.: Three Continents Press, 1983.
    Pp. 37–47.

Works about Silvina Bullrich

Birkemoe, Diane. "Contemporary Women Novelists of Argentina (1945–67)." Ph.D.
    diss. University of Illinois, 1968. (DAI 29 [1968]:2249A.)
Blanco Amor, José. "Por siempre best-seller." *Cuadernos Americanos* 181 (1972):213–
    20.
Class, Bradley M. "Treatment of Politics by Argentine Female Novelists." Ph.D. diss.
    University of New Mexico, 1974. (DAI 35 [1974]:6132A.)
Cócaro, Nicolás. "Estudio preliminar." *Páginas de Silvina Bullrich seleccionadas por
    la autora.* Buenos Aires: Editorial Celtia, 1983. Pp. 11–22.
———. "La pequeña comedia humana en la obra de Silvina Bullrich." *Silvina Bullrich.*
    By Silvina Bullrich. Ed. Nicolás Cócaro. Buenos Aires: Ediciones Culturales
    Argentinas, 1979. Pp. 11–23.
Frouman-Smith, Erica. "Entrevista con Silvina Bullrich." *Chasqui* 7 (Feb. 1979):37–
    46.

————. "Female Roles in the Fiction of Silvina Bullrich." Ph.D. diss. University of New Mexico, 1979. (DAI 40 [1979]:4617A.)

————. "The Paradoxes of Silvina Bullrich." *Contemporary Women Authors of Latin America: Introductory Essays*. Eds. Doris Meyer and Margarite Fernández Olmos. New York: Brooklyn College Press, 1983. I:58–71.

————. "*Reunión de directorio* by Silvina Bullrich." *Latin American Literary Review* 7 (Spring-Summer 1979):76–78.

Lewald, H. Ernest. "Aspects of the Modern Argentine Woman." *Chasqui* 3 (May 1976):19–26.

Lindstrom, Naomi. "Literary Convention and Sex-Role Analysis: Silvina Bullrich's 'Abnegation.' " *Denver Quarterly* 17 (Summer 1982):98–104.

Mathieu, Corina S. "Argentine Women in the Novels of Silvina Bullrich." *Latin American Women Writers: Yesterday and Today*. Eds. Yvette E. Miller and Charles M. Tatum. Pittsburgh: Carnegie-Mellon University, 1977. Pp. 68–74.

Muniz, Enrique. "Silvina Bullrich: una úlcera en el pedestal." *Siete Días Ilustrados* (July 1971):5–11.

Tavenner, Anna C. "Aspectos de conflicto y enajenamiento de la mujer en las novelas de Silvina Bullrich, Beatriz Guido y Clarice Lispector." Ph.D. diss. Texas Tech University, 1977. (DAI 38 [1977]:3537.)

Tusa, Bobs M. "The Works of Silvina Bullrich." Ph.D. diss. Tulane University, 1972. (DAI 33 [1972]:6132A.)

JULIA DE BURGOS
(1914–1953)
Puerto Rico

Diana Vélez

BIOGRAPHY

Born into a large family—twelve siblings—in the rural neighborhood of Santa Cruz, Carolina, Puerto Rico, Julia de Burgos attended rural public schools and graduated with honors. Her family was extremely poor, and six of her siblings died in infancy because of poor nutrition and other conditions related to poverty. Before she was fifteen years old, her parents lost their subsistence farm and were forced to move to a slum in Río Piedras. Her parents struggled to provide Burgos with an education, applying for small grants so that she could attend her local high school. There are still people alive who remember her worn clothing and her thinness. But she was a superior student, and, in 1933, she took her degree at the University of Puerto Rico's normal school and began teaching.

By 1933 Puerto Rico, along with the rest of the world, was suffering through the Great Depression, with the average Puerto Rican family's income being reduced to two-thirds of what it had been in 1929. In 1934 Burgos married Rubén Rodríguez Beauchamp, a journalist. The marriage would only last three years. She worked briefly distributing free breakfasts to children through the Puerto Rico Economic Rehabilitation Agency (PRERA), part of the New Deal program. While working for PRERA, she met some of the most respected and talented Puerto Rican poets of the period: Luis Palés Matos, Luis Lloréns Torres, and Evaristo Ribera Chevremont. When the agency ceased functioning in 1935, Julia de Burgos went to work in a rural school.

She was at times the victim of red-baiting and discrimination because of her open commitment to the cause of Puerto Rican independence. She was a member of the Nationalist party and frequently addressed large gatherings from the same podium as Pedro Albizu Campos, Puerto Rico's indefatigable nationalist leader.

During this same period, when Spain was engaged in its own resistance, Julia de Burgos wrote several poems in support of the Spanish Republic. Because of her political activism, she was fired from her job on a radio program, as she was considered unfit to disseminate information because of her political beliefs. During this early period she went through some very difficult financial times, always contributing her meager salary to the support of her family. But her passion was writing and she always managed to find time for it, even after a day's work. During her entire lifetime she never managed to escape poverty.

Unfortunately, there are no known copies of the typescript of Julia's first collection of poems, *Poemas exactos a mí misma* (1937; Poems exactly like me), which was never formally published.

Her mother, Doña Paula García de Burgos, was diagnosed as having cancer in 1935, so when Julia's second collection of poetry, *Poema en veinte surcos* (Poem in five furrowed time), was published in 1938, Julia traveled throughout the island in *carros públicos* (zone taxis) selling the book herself in order to help pay for her mother's treatments and operations. Burgos went heavily into debt to provide whatever support she could to her ailing mother. Despite all of Julia's efforts and the medical care provided, Doña Paula succumbed to the illness in 1939.

That same year, Julia de Burgos met Dr. Juan Isidro Jiménez Grullón, a prominent public figure from the Dominican Republic and the man who was to inspire some of her best love poetry. That year, too, the Puerto Rican Atheneum celebrated a poetry recital in her honor. In December 1939, she published *Canción de la verdad sencilla* (Song of the unadorned truth), which received the prize of the Instituto de Literatura Puertorriqueña.

The following year Burgos traveled briefly to New York, where her work was well received. Newspaper interviews and poetry recitals publicized her presence in the city, and her work was widely read. That same year she traveled to Cuba, to join her lover, Jiménez Grullón. When they moved to Havana in 1949, she enrolled in courses at the university, making the acquaintance of writers and intellectuals such as Juan Marinello, Juan Bosch, Raúl Roa, and Manuel Luna. She participated in public seminars on Puerto Rican independence and worked on her fourth collection of poetry, *El mar y tú* (The ocean and you), which was published only posthumously in 1954. In 1942 she met Pablo Neruda, who, impressed with her poetry, promised to write a prologue to the collection.

Between March and June, relations between Burgos and Jiménez Grullón, an upper class man and public figure, deteriorated, partly because of his unwillingness to go against his family's wishes by marrying a *mulata*. They had told him that marrying her would be equivalent to committing suicide. In her letters to her sister Consuelo, the poet describes her life in Cuba as being one of boredom, as she was forced to spend many hours engaged in traditionally feminine activities such as crocheting with the other women while Jiménez Grullón would not publicly acknowledge their relationship, introducing her as "a friend" to his acquaintances whenever they were seen together on the street. Finally, either she cut off relations with him or he with her; versions vary.

In any case, she then left Cuba for New York, where she worked at various jobs: optical inspector, laboratory assistant, lamp saleswoman, editor, office worker, garment worker. She was never able to make a living there either in journalism or teaching, her two professional fields, and it is generally acknowledged that she was the victim of ethnic and racial discrimination. Once, when she filled out the admission form for a hospital, entering the words "writer, journalist and translator" under the heading for "occupation," some functionary crossed out those words and replaced them with the word "amnesiac." This was a sign of his or her unwillingness to allow Burgos, an impoverished Puerto Rican, to claim her rightful definition of self. She was forced to move frequently from apartment to apartment as her jobs were often temporary and ill paid.

In 1943 she married Armando Marín and moved to Washington, D.C., a city she disliked, calling it "the capital of silence." While there, she worked in the office of the Coordinator of Inter-American Affairs. In 1945 she and Marín returned to New York, which she considered her second home, especially the Puerto Rican neighborhood known as El Barrio. While in New York, she was again the object of public acclaim, having received the Instituto de Literatura Puertorriqueña's journalism prize for her 1945 essay "Ser o no ser es la divisa" (The emblem is whether or not to be).

At this time she began to put on weight and suffer from bouts of serious depression. She became more isolated from her friends and her alcoholism began to worsen, resulting in a series of hospital internments. These included an extended stay at Goldwater Memorial Hospital, a hospital for the terminally ill on the then nearly deserted Welfare Island (now Roosevelt Island). While there, she wrote two anguished poems in English, a language she loved, as well as numerous letters to her sister Consuelo. These letters record her struggle to maintain her dignity and composure before undeniable evidence of declining health. Diagnosed as having cirrhosis of the liver as well as polyps on her vocal chords, she slid into a state of deep depression.

Although some of this depression can correctly be presumed to have been caused by her ill health, there were other contributing factors. For example, her sister, Consuelo, had been unsuccessful in finding a publisher for Julia's latest collection of poems, El mar y tú. In addition, the independentista's (Puerto Rican independence movement's) armed insurrection of 1950 had been brutally crushed by the United States, and prospects for Puerto Rican independence—a cause to which she was deeply committed—seemed ever more remote. In the United States, the McCarthy period had begun, and in Puerto Rico, the infamous "Law of the Muzzle," the equivalent of the Smith Act, was put into effect, with thousands of independentistas and sympathizers rounded up and jailed without trial, often for extended periods.

Burgos had been obsessed with death for some time and had written numerous poems whose major theme was her own death. Some of these poems have become well known, especially the anguished "Poema para mi muerte" (Poem for my death) and "Dadme mi número" (Give me my number). In June 1953, a week before her death, she wrote the last of a series of letters to her sister Consuelo, who still lived in Puerto Rico. The letter is evidence of a spirited woman valiantly trying to cope with a painful personal and political situation. On August 4, 1953, she was found unconscious on 105th Street and Fifth Avenue in New York. Since she was carrying no identification and was dead of pneumonia on arrival at Harlem Hospital, the authorities buried her in Potter's Field, the city's common grave for indigents. A month later her family identified her through a picture taken at the morgue. Her body was exhumed and buried in Puerto Rico, near the Río Grande de Loíza, which she had immortalized with her poem by the same name. Members of the *Ateneo Puertorriqueño* rendered posthumous homage to this great poet, considered by many critics to be on a par with her compatriot Luis Palés Matos.

MAJOR THEMES

Much of Julia de Burgos's poetry and prose remains dispersed in newspapers and magazines in Cuba, Puerto Rico, and New York. Moreover, her first collection of poems—never published but merely reproduced in mimeographed form—has been lost. Some of these poems were included in the *Obra poética* edition, but the existing poetic corpus is small. It consists of only three complete collections: *Poema en veinte surcos* (1938), *Canción de la verdad sencilla* (1939), and *El mar y tú* (1954). In all, what we have of Burgos's poetry consists of fewer than one hundred and fifty poems.

Poema en veinte surcos, with its echo of Chilean Pablo Neruda's *Veinte poemas de amor y una canción desesperada*, encompasses many themes, but its most salient feature is its poetic voice, that of a rebellious woman who challenges social, political, and cultural injustices in the name of the soul's freedom. Written in a style and language similar to that of the early Neruda—with his neo-Romantic song of the self—the two most disseminated poems of the collection, "Río Grande de Loíza" (Man river of Loíza) and "A Julia de Burgos" (To Julia de Burgos), typify Burgos's thematic choices. They question the place assigned to women in sexist society as well as the colonial enslavement of her people of Puerto Rico.

One has to remember the period in which Burgos was writing, with its ideal of womanhood—passivity, homeboundedness, delicacy, and ignorance—to be able to appreciate the revolutionary nature of her poetic persona in "A Julia de Burgos" and other poems. The speaking voice, the "I" of her most famous feminist poem, "A Julia de Burgos," is a self-confident, politically committed, and assertive woman who questions the socially constructed lie of womanhood while celebrating the authenticity of the female self. The poem is a Whitmanesque song to the self with a difference: it plays with the dichotomy between the social construction "woman" and the inner self which is denied by that construction. The poem is a marvel of split subjectivity, with the desire for freedom playing an important structuring role. Indeed, the entire collection is informed by this search for freedom and unity with the natural world. Contemporary critics agree that the creation of an active female persona may have been her most valuable contribution. Throughout the collection, but especially in this poem, she takes a stand in favor of oppressed groups, including workers, and firmly states that when the masses decided to free themselves from their oppression, she, too, will be there with her torch held high.

The other well-known poem in this collection is "Río Grande de Loíza," a powerfully erotic evocation of the river she played in as a child. The poem is extremely popular in Puerto Rico, where it touches deep chords of national feeling and pride in many Puerto Ricans who can still remember the beauty of the countryside of their childhoods, the landscape they were able to enjoy before the massive urbanization of the 1950s bulldozed it into nonexistence. To fully appreciate the impact of this poem it is important to understand the role which this nostalgia for a lost landscape played in Puerto Rico's collective psyche. Her canto to the powerful man-river, with its unexpectedly political ending, is as much a cry of national identity as it is a song to the forces of nature and Eros.

Lesser known poems in this collection are "Nada" (Nothing) and "Ay ay ay de la grifa negra" (Mulatta's Lament), in which she sings to the beauty of her black heritage and criticizes the whites who engaged in the slave trade. A didactic poem with a beautiful sense of rhythm and phrasing, "Ay ay ay de la grifa negra" celebrates the cosmic race of the new world. In "Nada" Burgos takes cynical males to task for denying the beauty and power of the human body, men who would use women's bodies merely to satisfy their lusts without attending to the other dimensions of womanhood.

Deeply feminist and pro-independence, Julia de Burgos favored the full participation of all human beings in the social and political arena, and many of her most intimate and erotic poems have political content as well. All of her work speaks to this commitment. In fact, even when Burgos was sick and hospitalized in New York, writing intimist poetry concerned mainly with the theme of psychic pain, love, and death, she also wrote numerous political essays and poems and sent them to newspapers. She even expressed a desire to publish a collection of her political essays in book form, a wish that was never fulfilled.

Her third collection of poems, *Canción de la verdad sencilla*, which she wrote while she was in love with Jiménez Grullón, consists mostly of love poetry, with the political and the social message playing more of a background role than in the previous work. Some pieces rework the theme of self and society as it relates to the possibility of actualizing love. This is so, for example, in the poem "Yo fui la más callada" (I was the quiet one) where, as with "A Julia de Burgos," the socially constructed and artificial is contrasted with the simplicity of the authentic and the physical. The tone of this collection is one of hope and, in some pieces, of ecstasy. It is a euphoric celebration of the body, its joy in surrendering itself and the loss of self which accompanies passionate love. This is especially well realized in the poems "Noche de amor en tres cantos" (A night of love in three cantos), "Poema del minuto blanco" (White minute poem), and "Canción para dormirte" (A lullaby for you). In this collection, love is a powerful force, very much like nature in its demands, but also the *sine qua non* of a useful, meaningful existence. In fact, it can be stated without exaggeration that love is presented here as that which will save the poetic persona from being lost in a meaningless void.

El mar y tú, published a year after her death, contains many poems concerned with death, though the tone of the book is not one of hopelessness. Rather, its tone shares with *Poema en veinte surcos* a yearning for a lost connection to the natural world, a sense of alienation and of metaphysical anguish. The erotic is still present, however, though in a different key from her second volume. This collection contains some of her most mature and well-wrought pieces. Her "Poema para mi muerte" (A poem for my death) is a moving affirmation of herself, not as isolated ego, but as a part of the cosmos. She states that she does not want anyone to profane her death with sobs and concludes with the statement that her essence will always be that of a poet.

SURVEY OF CRITICISM

Judging from the prestigious prizes awarded to her, as well as the poetry recitals held in her honor, it is clear that Julia de Burgos's work was recognized as valuable and important during her own lifetime. Until recently, however, critical writing on her work—as opposed to attention paid to her tragic life—was scarce. Moreover, there has been an unfortunate collapsing of her life and her work, with the biography often taking precedence over the writings. A popular notion of Julia de Burgos as the victim of unrequited love has somehow taken hold, for instance, despite much evidence to the contrary. Indeed, Julia de Burgos wrote against and despite the constant odds of poverty, illness, and the indifference of racially discriminatory societies (New York, Cuba). She was anything but a passive victim.

Fortunately, this tendency to distort her work is not generalized. Serious critics recognized her worth early on. Nilita Vientós Gastón, the *grande dame* of the literary and cultural scene in Puerto Rico, acknowledged the importance and value of Burgos's work immediately and wrote laudatory criticism in journals and newspapers. Juan Ramón Jiménez, the Spanish poet who lived in exile in Puerto Rico after the fall of the Republic, is quoted as saying that Burgos was the best poet in Puerto Rico.

Other critics have devoted themselves to analyzing and publishing studies of her work. For example, hardly a year has gone by in which José Emilio González has failed to publish an article on Julia de Burgos. Indeed, his introductory study to the anthology *Obra poética* (1961) is a good starting point for understanding Burgos. His book, *La poesía contemporánea de Puerto Rico: (1930–60)* (1972), contains a useful essay on Burgos as well.

Important, too, is the study by Yvette Jiménez de Báez, *Julia de Burgos: vida y poesía*, which for years was the only available monograph on the poet and which, despite the old-fashioned sound of its title, contains important critical notes on several of her poems.

In recent years, Julia de Burgos has become almost a mythical figure in Puerto Rico, with posters of her face—an icon of Puerto Rican feminism and pro-independence passion—selling widely as cultural artifacts. These are disseminated in *fiestas patronales* (local patron-saint carnivals) as well as in less carnivalesque settings. (For a study of the phenomenon, see Manuel de la Puebla's study "Julia de Burgos como mito" [Julia de Burgos as myth] in the special issue of *Mairena* dedicated to Burgos.)

But her importance for and in popular culture is not the only manifestation of renewed interest in Burgos; there has been an increase in the number of scholarly articles on her work. Several groups have issued publications useful to the researcher. For example, the Center for Puerto Rican Studies, at New York's Hunter College, published a partial bibliography of Burgos, with biographical notes, in 1986. The journal *Mairena* reissued its special number on her life and work, "Homenaje a Julia de Burgos" (Homage to Julia de Burgos), in 1986. This number contains a fairly complete bibliography, a translation into English of "Río Grande de Loíza" by the poet Graciany Miranda Archilla, as well as some of the better critical pieces available on her work. These include an excellent study by Efraín Barradas entitled "Entre la esencia y la forma: sobre el momento neoyorquino en la poesía de Julia de Burgos" (Between form and essence: Julia de Burgos's New York period) and a moving "Invocación a Julia de Burgos" (Invocation to Julia de Burgos) by the poet Francisco Matos Paoli, the opening speech of a special congress held in Puerto Rico in honor of Julia de Burgos in 1961.

María Solá's short anthology, *Julia de Burgos: yo misma fui mi ruta* (1986), collects some of the poet's best pieces and provides a serious and well-researched feminist introduction to Burgos's work, including an excellent analysis of the Romantic elements in the poetry and a sociopolitical analysis that places Burgos in context. She also provides a close reading of several of the better known poems.

Another useful and quite moving piece is Rosario Ferré's* "Carta a Julia de Burgos" and her poem to Julia in Ferré's book of poetry, *Fábulas de la garza desangrada*. This essay and the poem are evidence of how much contemporary Puerto Rican writers value Julia de Burgos. Puerto Rican feminists look to her as a precursor. The titles of Burgos's poems are used in political and educational pamphlets, and Puerto Rico's first shelter for battered women was named after Julia de Burgos.

BIBLIOGRAPHY

Works by Julia de Burgos

Poemas exactos a mí misma (typescript), 1937. (Presumed lost.)
Poema en veinte surcos. San Juan, P.R.: Imprenta Venezuela, 1938.

Canción de la verdad sencilla. San Juan, P.R.: Baldrich, 1939.
El mar y tú, y otros poemas. San Juan, P.R.: Printing and Publishing Co., 1954.
Obra poética. Introd. José Emilio González. San Juan, P.R.: Instituto de Cultura Puer-
   torriqueña, 1961.
Cuadernos de poesía. Ill. José Torres Martinó. San Juan, P.R.: Instituto de Cultura
   Puertorriqueña, 1964. (Porfolio size edition.)
Antología poética. Prol. Ivette Jiménez Báez. San Juan, P.R.: Editorial Coquí, 1967.
Yo misma fui mi ruta. Introd. María M. Solá. San Juan: Ediciones Huracán, 1986.

Works about Julia de Burgos

Barradas, Efraín. "Entre la esencia y la forma: sobre el momento neoyorquino en la
   poesía de Julia de Burgos." *Mairena* 7, 20 (1985, Special reissue 1986):23–48.
Binder, Wolfgang. " 'A Midnight Reality': Puerto Rican Poetry in New York, A Poetry
   of Dreams." *European Perspectives on Hispanic Literature of the United States.*
   Ed. Genevieve Fabre. Houston, Tex: Arte Público, 1988. Pp. 22–32.
Cabrera, Francisco M. *Historia de la literatura puertorriqueña.* Río Piedras, P.R.: Ed-
   itorial Cultural, 1969.
———. "Pensando a Julia." *Guajana* 5 (1974):n.p.
Ferré, Rosario. "A Julia." *Fábulas de la garza desangrada.* Mexico City: Joaquín Mortiz,
   1982. P. 65.
———. "Carta a Julia de Burgos." *Sitio a Eros: Trece ensayos literarios.* Mexico City:
   Joaquín Mortiz, 1980. Pp. 127–32.
———. "De desnuda que está, brilla la estrella." *Third Woman* 3, 1–2 (1986):81–85.
González, José Emilio. *La poesía contemporánea de Puerto Rico.* San Juan, P.R.: Instituto
   de Cultura Puertorriqueña, 1972. Pp. 337–58.
Jiménez de Báez, Yvette. *Julia de Burgos: vida y poesía.* San Juan, P.R.: Editorial Coquí,
   1966.
Laguna Díaz, Elpidio. "Dos instantes de Julia de Burgos: su concepción del tiempo."
   Asomante 25 (1969):38–49.
———. "The Phenomenology of Nothingness in the Poetry of Julia de Burgos." *Latin
   American Women Writers Yesterday and Today.* Eds. Yvette F. Miller and Charles
   M. Tatum. Pittsburgh: *Latin American Literary Review*, Carnegie-Mellon Uni-
   versity, 1977. Pp. 127–33.
López Jiménez, Ivette. "Julia de Burgos: los textos comunicantes." *Sin Nombre* 10, 1
   (Apr.–June 1979):47–68.
Perricone, Catherine R. "A Bibliographic Approach to the Study of Latin American
   Women Poets: Julia de Burgos (Puerto Rico, 1916–1953)." *Hispania* 71, 2 (May
   1988):283.
Puebla, Manuel de la. "Julia de Burgos como mito." *Mairena* 7, 20 (1985):81–91.
Quiroga, Carmen Lucila. "Julia de Burgos: El desarrollo de la conciencia femenina en
   la expresión poética." Ph.D. diss. New York University, 1981. (DAI 41A
   [1981]:5117).
Rivero, Eliana. "Julia de Burgos: su visión poética del ser." *Sin Nombre* 3 (Oct.–Dec.
   1980):51–57.
Santos, Nelly E. "El itinerario temático de Julia de Burgos: el amor y la muerte."
   Cuadernos Americanos 203 (1975):234–46.
———. "Love and Death: The Thematic Journey of Julia de Burgos." *Latin American
   Women Writers Yesterday and Today.* Eds. Yvette F. Miller and Charles W.

Tatum, Pittsburgh: *Latin American Literary Review*, Carnegie-Mellon University, 1977. Pp. 134–47.

Solá, María M., ed. Introd. *Julia de Burgos; Yo misma fui mi ruta*. By Julia de Burgos. San Juan, P.R.: Ediciones Huracán, 1986. Pp. 7–48.

Umpierre, Luz María. "De la protesta a la creación: Una nueva visión de la mujer puertorriqueña en la poesía." *Imagine: International Chicano Poetry Journal* 2, 1 (Summer 1985):134–42.

———. "Metapoetic Code in Julia de Burgos' 'El mar y tú': Towards a Re-Vision." *In Retrospect: Essays on Latin American Literature*. Eds. Elizabeth S. Rogers and Timothy J. Rogers. York, S.C.: Spanish Literature Publishing, 1987. Pp. 85–94.

Vientós Gastón, Nilita. "Al margen de un libro de Julia de Burgos." *Puerto Rico Illustrado*. San Juan, P.R.: n.p., n.d.

MERCEDES CABELLO DE CARBONERA (1845–1909)
Peru

Mercedes Mazquiarán de Rodríguez

BIOGRAPHY

Mercedes Cabello Llosa was born in the town of Moquegua, Peru, on February 7, 1845. She was self-taught; formal education was not prescribed for women at that time. The breadth of her readings and her study of the philosophical ideas that informed the historical period in which she lived are indicative of a high intellectual caliber. She was living in Lima at age twenty; there she married Urbano Carbonera, a noted physician, and took part in the city's social and literary scene until the end of the century. She had no children and was widowed while still young.

In the latter part of the nineteenth century, the Lima bourgeoisie engaged in literary and intellectual pursuits, and their social gatherings often focused on political and philosophical questions, especially Positivism, as well as on current literary issues. Literary reunions fashioned after the European salons, the *veladas literarias*, began to emerge in the 1870s. Cabello frequented these circles, playing the piano and reading papers. She attended the sessions of "El Club Literario" with her husband and the salons of 1876–1877, at the home of Argentine novelist Juana Manuela Gorriti.* Papers and poems Cabello read there were later collected and published by Gorriti as *Veladas Literarias de Lima 1876–1877*. In the years to come, Cabello often attended the get-togethers hosted by her friend and colleague, Clorinda Matto de Turner.* At the same time, she was an habitué of the sessions at the Ateneo under the leadership of Manuel González Prada, whose ideas of social reform and anticolonialism she embraced. It should be remembered, however, that Cabello's works addressed themselves only to urban society and did not echo Matto's concerns about the plight of the Indians.

Cabello's interest in sociopolitical issues followed the ideology of the Positivists, especially Auguste Comte and Herbert Spencer. She expressed her views in various newspapers and journals of Peru, sometimes under the pseudonym of Enriqueta Pradel. In December 1874 she published "Influencia de la mujer en la civilización moderna" (Woman's influence on modern civilization) in a special edition of *El Correo del Perú*. In the name of social progress, she advocated the education of women and their emancipation, as noted by her biographer and critic Augusto Tamayo Vargas (1940, pp. 24–25). The Positivist Eugenio María de Hostos's essay, "La educación científica de la mujer" (Woman's scientific education), published in Chile in the *Revista Sudamericana* in June 1873, preempted hers. Although it is not known whether she had read Hostos, it is likely she had.

Her stance on the role of writers as proselytizers of social reform and her interest in promoting the education of women were well attested in the papers she presented at Gorriti's salons. At the first of those meetings, on July 17, 1876, she read a paper entitled "Importancia de la literatura" (The importance of literature), in which she urged writers to participate in the development of the Peruvian nation (Tamayo, p. 29). In another paper, read in October 1876, "Perfeccionamiento de la educación y de la condición social de la mujer" (On the improvement of woman's schooling and social status), she reiterated her recommendation to educate women in the name of progress and the nation's advancement (Tamayo, p. 30). Although in line with the ideals of Positivism, it was a daring topic for her day.

This preoccupation with the limitations that the lack of schooling imposed on women is also evident in some of her novels. Feminine education was not openly expressed as their main theme, but it did surface in the double-voiced discourse of the narrative in *Las consecuencias* (1889; The consequences) and in *Blanca Sol* (1888). Cabello's women are portrayed either as helpless, suffering creatures or as fallen heroines, doomed victims of the constraints of their female condition. Both situations contrast with the author's own circumstances in society. Cabello had managed to a certain extent to overcome the limitations which her sex and environment had placed on her. Her feminine stereotypes may have represented a veiled protest against the predicament which Peru's patriarchy imposed on women in the late nineteenth century.

Traditional male-dominated Lima society—resentful of Cabello's forthrightness in her criticism of the materialism and vainglory of society, her promotion of education for women, her recognition of Romanticism's false and fanciful embellishment of reality, and, in general, her learned poise—made her, at times, the mark of scorn and ridicule. Such was the case of critic Juan de Arona, who derived from her name the lampoonery "Mierdeces Cabello de Cabrón era" (Tamayo, p. 44).

Although an avowed Positivist, Cabello retained a dosage of idealism mixed with the scientific postulates of the school, not unlike most Spanish Americans of her time. After criticizing Tolstoy for having approached the sciences as a mystic and not as a philosopher, for instance, she then contradicted herself and praised him for preserving spiritual values (see *El Conde León Tolstoy*, 1896; p. 51, Count Tolstoy). Being a Positivist, Cabello presented religion unsympathetically. She argued for the social Positivism of Comte as against Claude Bernard's scientificism. Her sociological approach, based on the harmony of body and spirit, would replace the mesmerizing fanaticism of a society whose anemic morality came from a blood that had been weakened through fasting and other fleshly mortifications (p. 65–66). However, her disapproval of religion focused mainly on representatives of the Church—nuns, priests, and the Pope—and on false religious practices, for example, the mechanical repetition of prayers, charity for the sake of social prestige, simony, and so on.

Cabello went even further in addressing the replacement of religious thought by science in *La religión de la humanidad, carta al Señor D. Juan Enrique Lagarrigue* (The religion of humanity, letter to Mr. Juan Enrique Lagarrigue), published in Lima in 1893. Lucía Guerra Cunningham, in her paper, "Mercedes Cabello de Carbonera: Estética de la moral y los desvíos no-disyuntivos de la virtud," cites Lagarrigue's reply, *Carta sobre la Religión de la Humanidad Dirigida a la Señora doña Mercedes Cabello de Carbonera*, published in Santiago, Chile, by Imprenta Cervantes in 1892 (Cunningham, p. 25). If we assume that the date of Lagarrigue's response is correct, we can conclude that Cabello's essay must have been written earlier than 1893, when it appeared in Lima.

In contrast with the outspokenness of her essays, articles, and commentaries, the style and content of Cabello's early fiction seems timid and hesitant. She had been collaborating in Peruvian periodicals and journals and in those of other Spanish American countries and Madrid for fifteen years by the time her first novel appeared. Despite her diatribes against Romanticism and her declared goal to embrace realism in fiction, her first attempts at the novel belong in the category of the Romantic. These early works were interspersed with Naturalistic comments and *cuadros de costumbres* (sketches of local color), fashionable at the time.

Her first novel, *Los amores de Hortencia, biografía de una mujer superior* (Hortencia's loves, a biography of a superior woman), probably published for the first time in 1886, was not available for this study. Tamayo refers to this novel as her second, perhaps unaware that the author herself, in the prologue to *Sacrificio y recompensa* (1886; Sacrifice and reward), dedicated to Gorriti, referred to it as her first. The confusion is understandable, for Tamayo admits in his essay that he could not find a single copy of *Sacrificio* in the National Library or in the archives of the Ateneo in Lima. He had available to him only a volume belonging to the Cabello family, perhaps without a prologue.

Sacrificio y recompensa, also published in 1886, was her second novel. *Eleodora* followed, appearing first in serial form in Madrid and later printed in 1887 by the Ateneo of Lima, under the auspices of Ricardo Palma. The novel was inspired by one of Palma's own "Tradiciones" (Traditions), "Amor de madre" (A mother's love), and was later reworked and published in 1889 in a longer version, as *Las consecuencias*. This novel, while still imbued with the rhetoric of Romanticism, is a departure from Cabello's preceding novels.

Historical, economic, and sociopolitical issues found more open expression in Cabello's later novels. During her lifetime the War of the Pacific (1879–1883) occurred, the Dreyfus Contract brought foreign investors interested in guano (fertilizer) to Peru, and the Grace Contract gave control of Peruvian railroads to foreign contractors. Finally, there was the conflict between the old colonial aristocracy (in whose ranks were military *caudillos* like Nicolás de Piérola and Manuel Ignacio de Vivanco) and the new moneyed bourgeoisie.

The national climate Cabello observed surfaced particularly in the last two novels, *Blanca Sol* (1888) and *El conspirador* (1892; The conspirator). Tamayo and other critics of Peruvian novels agree in finding allusions to Piérola and Vivanco in *El conspirador*, a narrative that attacks the evils of militarism. *Blanca Sol*, on the other hand, caused great controversy when it appeared as a serial in *La Nación* and in book form, because many people thought it was a *roman à clef* of a well-known fallen woman from Lima's high society. The author took pains to deny the attribution. In the prologue to the second edition, published by Carlos Prince, she reaffirmed her commitment to the realist novel and labeled *Blanca Sol* a social novel. She chided those who identified her heroine with the woman from Lima and stated that if novels were such exact mirrors of reality and persons, it would be necessary to proscribe them. Some critics consider this so-called social novel as the first Naturalistic attempt at a novel to appear in Peru, despite the author's censure of Naturalism. She condemned the French novelist Emile Zola because he portrayed man as a beast. Instead, she adopted Honoré de Balzac's social realism, as she stated in *La novela moderna* (The modern novel), published in 1892 (cf. 1948 ed., p. 36).

In this celebrated essay, Cabello pointed out the shortcomings of Romanticism and Naturalism. She defined her position with respect to the novel as "eclectic" and proposed realism as the best literary mode. She proclaimed that realism should be to art what Romanticism had been to Classicism, an evolution that brought art close to nature and life (p. 51). If Naturalism had chosen to follow the scientific school of Claude Bernard, realism, she said, should uphold the Positivist doctrine of Auguste Comte (p. 51). Let us be "eclectic," she urged, and accept from the Naturalist school only that which is adaptable to the knowledge of humans and society (p. 46). She also rejected the concept of art for art's sake in this essay. Her argument was based on the principle that considered art intimately linked and subordinated to social and political movements, which in turn were enthralled by philosophical ideas of a given moment (p. 51).

Other important essays by Cabello were *Influencia de las Bellas Artes en el progreso moral y material de los pueblos* (n.d.; The influence of the belles-lettres on the moral and material progress of the peoples) and *Independencia de Cuba* (n.d.; Cuba's independence).

Around 1893, mental illness made writing impossible. On January 27, 1900, Mercedes Cabello de Carbonera, then age fifty-four, was admitted as a patient in El Cercado, an asylum for the insane, where she was to spend ten years before her death on October 12, 1909.

MAJOR THEMES

Cabello extracted the themes of her novels from her own readings, her Positivist ideology, and, most importantly, from her own experience. Her fiction depicted the life of Peru's upper classes, particularly Lima's. She criticized the pretense that ruled the lives of the aristocracy's impoverished families, as well as their materialism. She deplored social climbing and political opportunism and the practice of using one's connections to further private ambitions. She also censured *caudillaje*, the attribution of almost messianic qualities to military leaders, and, in a broader sense, she focused attention in her works on the roles society assigned to the sexes.

Unhappy marriage is a recurrent theme in Cabello's novels. Her characters seem to marry for the wrong reasons. Men are guided by lust, vanity, or money, and women aspire to climb the social ladder or to escape from their financial straits. Love is seldom a motive for marriage. In *Los amores de Hortencia* (1886?), the heroine is married to an insensitive man, whose attitude, added to the boredom of provincial life, throws her into the arms of a lover. The irate husband tries to kill the lover, but Hortencia steps in between them and is killed instead. The husband does not go to prison, for patriarchal society sanctions punishment to adulterous wives, leaving the lover to marry another. Only Hortencia loses, for she fails to abide by the social standards for feminine conduct. Mario Castro Arenas's plot summary in his book *La novela peruana* (1967; The Peruvian novel) comments that Hortencia prefigures the protagonist of her later novel, *Blanca Sol* (p. 88). In addition, the essential details of Hortencia's death are basically repeated in *Las consecuencias*.

In *Sacrificio y recompensa*, married couples are mismatched and, therefore, unhappy. The plot follows the saga of two star-crossed young lovers, Alvaro and Catalina. This novel is a Romantic novel in the tradition of the cloak-and-dagger plays of Golden Age drama, although the story line is close to the Duque de Rivas's *Don Alvaro*, whose namesake also figures as Cabello's protagonist. As in Rivas's Romantic drama, fate rules the characters' lives. The heroine, Catalina, sees her affair with Alvaro tragically interrupted when her father, the Spanish governor of Cuba, kills Alvaro's father, a Cuban patriot, in a dispute. The lovers are separated and later reunited in Lima. By then, Alvaro is betrothed to Estela, the daughter of Guzmán, an older Peruvian who had befriended Alvaro in New York, after he had left Cuba. Guzmán marries abroad and returns with his young bride Catalina. The stereotypical complications of Romantic novels are present: secret schemes, duels, death, loss of honor, the convent as refuge for the disgraced heroine, and, finally, retribution and happiness for the main characters. After Guzmán and Estela die, Catalina and Alvaro are married. This is the only case in a Cabello novel in which both spouses marry for love. A secondary character in the story, Elisa Mafey, renounces true love to marry an old man in the hope of attaining a higher social position. His status is counterfeit, however, and Elisa watches her ambitions hindered, and is constrained to live discontentedly.

Sacrificio y recompensa is undeniably Romantic. The author's efforts to introduce scientific references and physiological explanations for certain personality traits sound hollow and trite. Cabello does succeed in drawing animated *cuadros de costumbres*. Her descriptions of life in the village of Chorrillos are filled with anecdotes and stories of local superstitions. Her depiction of Lima's social life is also felicitous: the mansions of the rich, the typical social intercourse at the opera, the ball, the funeral rites, and even the judicial process itself. Cabello's mixture of Romanticism and *costumbrismo* (local color) brings to mind the nineteenth-century Spanish writer Fernán Caballero, a precursor of the realist novel in Spain. In the essay *La novela moderna* (1892), Cabello credited Caballero with having created the *novela de costumbres*, or the mannerist novel (p. 33).

The theme of unhappy marriage also appears in *Las consecuencias*. The protagonist, Eleodora, is the young daughter of a well-meaning but authoritarian father who keeps her out of school and practically isolated at home. Eleodora's mother, on the other hand, is a kind but meek woman, the typical *mujer sufrida* (long-suffering wife), who passively accepts her husband's decisions. Eleodora falls in love with Enrique Guido, the only young man she comes across in her tedious life. She marries him despite her father's opposition. After a brief interlude, which is happy for Eleodora, but not for him (the couple spent two years in the country and had two children), the relationship between the two deteriorates. Their return to Lima marks the downfall of the marriage, since Enrique, a gambler, again takes up with old comrades and goes back to the tawdry atmosphere of gamblers and prostitutes. Once Enrique has used up Eleodora's money, he pawns her jewels. Finally, unable to pay off his remaining debts, Enrique tries to kill his debtor who proposes taking Eleodora as his mistress in lieu of payment. Eleodora unsuccessfully tries to thwart tragedy by interposing herself between the two men. On her deathbed, she falsely declares herself guilty of adultery to save her husband's honor, for the children's sake. She wanted to spare them the shame of their father's crime. (She knew that adultery was considered a lesser offense.) Full of remorse, Enrique clears Eleodora's name and kills himself.

Las consecuencias is a sentimental novel mixed with *cuadros de costumbres*, that is, life on the hacienda of San Eloy, where the couple stays for some time, the evening gatherings at Eleodora's family home, where the guests of her father—all male—played cards, were served hot chocolate, and so on. The narrative exposes the shortcomings of a young girl's sheltered and stultifying life, along with the central theme of the evils of gambling. Eleodora's tragic end is as much a consequence of her upbringing as it is of her husband's vice. Cabello utilizes the figure of Serafina, Eleodora's maid and only companion (later turned go-between), to express a strong indictment against patriarchy and the selfishness of masculine conduct. After Eleodora's death, Serafina visits her parents to express her respects. Upon seeing her, Don Cosme, the father, recriminates her, seeing the tragedy as a consequence of her actions. She in turn asks him why it should not all be the result of her father's imprisonment and the excessive gambling of her husband (p. 245).

Cabello's last two novels represent a departure from the sentimental and Romantic novel. *Blanca Sol* (cf. 1889 ed.), as the subtitle *novela social* (social novel) shows, attempted to make redress for the prevailing mores and social conditions. Cabello forewarns the reader, in the prologue to the second edition, that she considers the mission of the novelist of her time to be the propagation of the postulates of Positivism. She states that, whereas the legislator deals with punishment, and that will never prevent wrong-doing, the novelist, on the other hand, must proclaim that only education and the environment surrounding the individual can act on that mentality which constitutes the backdrop of all human actions (p. v).

Blanca Sol presents the life of a protagonist of that name, referred by some as the Madame Bovary of Spanish America. The novel covers the period from her childhood and adolescence until the height of her social triumphs, and then her continuous descent into prostitution. Blanca Sol's family has lost its fortune, but it maintains its social position under false pretenses. The heroine goes to school, but her education is deficient; she is unprepared to take over her own life. Her mother trains her to use beauty and charm to get a rich husband and to acquire power. She marries an unattractive man she does not love in exchange for a comfortable life and for repayment of the family's debt. Upon dismissing her young sweetheart, she tells him that once she is Rubio's wife, she'll give him all the happiness he now desires (p. 10). Once again, Cabello offers in this novel a pessimistic view of marriage. Blanca Sol cynically avers that marriage without love is nothing but prostitution sanctioned by society (p. 118).

Later, Cabello criticizes Tolstoy's opinion about marriage as expressed in *The Kreutzer Sonata*. In that novel Tolstoy stated that married couples live in a degrading state of sensuality and that marriage should be abolished. Cabello rejects this notion and affirms the virtues of marriage, although she recognizes the need for change. She believes that social evolution is the only possible way to bring change to the condition of women *vis à vis* men. A change in marital relations would come only when women would be "menos hembra y más mujer" (less carnal and more being; see *El Conde Tolstoy*, p. 16).

Blanca Sol is vain, ambitious, and a social climber who arrives at her position of power in high society by means of adulation and coquetry; her charm and astuteness obtain important positions for her mediocre husband. Blanca Sol lives surrounded by admirers and envious friends who, once money and power are lost, turn their back on her. Blanca Sol's narcissistic infatuation with her self and her position ironically results in a special brand of virtue: she remains loyal to her husband, if only out of pride, not for love or for ethical reasons. Conscious of the precariousness of her reputation, Blanca remarks that women like her keep their honor in the iron-safe where their husbands guard their money (p. 62).

Eventually, Rubio faces bankruptcy, no doubt the result of Blanca Sol's life-style. The impact of his financial insolvency and his personal failures ultimately drives him insane. Blanca Sol is then faced with the task of supporting her six children. She pities her two small girls particularly. Alone, Blanca Sol confronts her penury. In an epiphany, she recognizes she has no home, has never done housework, and is uneducated. Her only asset is her body and prostitution her only road to survival. She blames her family and her environment for her down-fall. Yet she is not repentant, but proud and defiant in her distress, a "fallen angel" with traces of Lucifer's bravado. In contrast, Josefina, her former seam-stress, another impoverished aristocrat, dedicated to the cult of domesticity, is rewarded by marrying Blanca's former admirer, Alcides, a wealthy Italian rep-resentative of the new bourgeoisie of foreign origins. Virtuous Josefina then is restored to her former position in society.

Lucía Fox-Lockert, in her study, *Women Novelists in Spain and Spanish America* (1979), sees this novel as an allegory of Peru between 1860 and 1890. The protagonist stands for the traditional child of the Sun, because, in part, her last name makes an allusion to the Inca empire. Fox-Lockert also reminds us that the "sol" is the monetary unit of Peru (p. 153). Indeed, Blanca Sol values money above love and honor and in the end loses all. Cabello's moralizing leads her to present the fall of Blanca Sol, who toasts to the beginning of her new life as a prostitute, highlighted by the rise of noble Josefina to the good life as Alcides's wife.

Cabello's last novel, *El conspirador*, subtitled *Autobiografía de un hombre público* (The conspirator, autobiography of a public figure, cf. 1st ed., 1892), could be considered the anatomy of a career-revolutionary. The novel is narrated in the first person from a masculine point of view. The protagonist, having lost repeated political campaigns, thrives on plotting revolutions against elected can-didates. Cabello sagaciously uses a male perspective to attack militarism and corruption in politics (an area traditionally off-limits to women). Colonel Bello is a professional conspirator. He represents a class of redeeming *caudillos* that has plagued Spanish American republics to this day.

The conspirator (in whom critics have identified aspects of Piérola and of Vivanco, both Peruvian *caudillos* and representatives of the old colonialism), like Blanca Sol before him, blames his times and his environment for his troubles. He claims his faults are not his own, but are those of his generation, a generation whose fatal heritage is the subversive and revolutionary spirit passed on to them by their predecessors, the illustrious men who had defeated Spanish colonial rule in Peru (p. 23).

In *El conspirador*, vibrant *cuadros de costumbres* depict life in the provinces, the celebration of national holidays and popular festivities, as well as the presence and influence of the clergy and the military in the lives of ordinary people. Cabello also portrays the quest for political jobs—bureaucratic positions that paid miserable salaries, but made up for it with "kickbacks" and with the opportunities afforded to government employees. There are always a number of aspiring bureaucrats ready to support a new *conspirador* in the hope of replacing the existing government and of having available these lucrative positions.

Cabello condemns *caudillaje*, authoritarian one-man rule, often by a military man, as well as the supporters of this system. She declares that in Peru, the act of conspiracy is a vice, maybe more prevalent than drinking or gambling (p. 110). *El conspirador* is considered to be the first novel in the true Naturalistic mode written in Peru. Colonel Bello could not escape from his fate any more than his lover, Ofelia, could. His medium dooms him to become a conspirator, and Ofelia's destiny results from her heritage. Bello's friend hints at Ofelia's fate when he says that he believes in the laws of genetics and that children inherit the vices of their parents. The daughter of a whore will be a whore, just as the son of a drunk will inherit that weakness; likewise the children of compulsive gamblers inherit that vice from their parents (pp. 163–64).

Ofelia is beautiful and intelligent, and she is fascinated with politics. Like Blanca Sol before, Ofelia resorts to prostitution after she loses all her money by supporting her lover's conspiracies. She sells herself to finance his campaigns, and, later, to help him escape from prison. He ends his days in poverty in exile. She dies of tuberculosis. Here too, Cabello weaves an allegory of "la patria prostituida," a fatherland prostituted by selfish and unscrupulous men.

SURVEY OF CRITICISM

Cabello wrote articles that appeared regularly in Peruvian newspapers and journals from the early 1870s on. She also collaborated on newspapers in Montevideo, Buenos Aires, Costa Rica, Bogotá, Madrid, and Paris. By the time she published her first novel, she was a noted journalist. Her essays were praiseworthy and brought her recognition. The municipality of Lima awarded her the Gold Medal for her essay *Influencia de las Bellas Letras en el Progreso moral y material de los pueblos* (n.d.). Another essay, *Independencia de Cuba* (n.d.), received the first prize in a literary contest; and *La novela moderna*, her last and most important essay, won the first prize, Rosa de Oro (Golden Rose), in the Concurso Hispanoamericano de la Academia Literaria de Buenos Aires. This prize assured her reputation beyond Peru and made her a continental figure; she traveled to Argentina to accept the honors.

Cabello's second novel, *Sacrificio y recompensa*, received the Gold Medal in an international contest at the Ateneo of Lima in 1886. Her last two novels, though not awarded literary prizes, went through several editions. *Blanca Sol* and *El conspirador* are considered the best of her novels. *Blanca Sol* was first serialized in *La Nación* in 1888. Later the same year, it appeared in book form published by Torres Aguirre. A second edition was published by Carlos Prince, with a prologue by the author, in 1889, and still a third and a fourth edition were printed by Prince in 1894. The novel provoked controversy in Peru, as stated before.

El conspirador was her last and most acclaimed novel. It was printed by E. Sequí and Company in 1892, and also in Lima by Imprenta "La Voce D'Italia," also in 1892. In 1898 it was published in Mexico by Imprenta de Ireneo Paz, with a prologue by Jesús Ceballos Dosamantes.

Cabello's biographer, Augusto Tamayo Vargas, has said Cabello's novelistic approach defends love but shows contempt for men; he considers her perspective provincial (Tamayo, 1940, p. 136). Referring to *El conspirador*, he recognizes as valuable her portrayal of the details and the environment of Peruvian politics (p. 141). In this book on Cabello, Tamayo mentions that the critic Ventura García Calderón in his work, *Del Romanticismo al Modernismo* (Paris, 1910), had enthusiastically stated that some day Cabello would be recognized as the forerunner of the Peruvian novel (p. 134). Alberto Zum Felde points to Cabello and to Matto de Turner* as the initiators of realism in Peru (*Indice crítico de la literatura hispanoamericana*, 1921, Vol. II, 169). About *El conspirador*, Zum Felde writes that its greatest value lies in its powerful documentation of the political reality of Peru in the nineteenth century (p. 170).

Mario Castro Arenas, in *La novela peruana y la evolución social* (1967), states that *El conspirador* is the most aesthetic of the Peruvian novels of the nineteenth century (p. 91). More recently, John S. Brushwood, in his work *Genteel Barbarism, New Readings of Nineteenth-Century Spanish-American Novels* (1981), has given a different opinion. He believes that the novel fails because the narrative voice of the protagonist is too often interrupted by the intrusions of a moralizing voice (p. 17).

BIBLIOGRAPHY

Works by Mercedes Cabello de Carbonera

Los amores de Hortencia. Lima: n.p., n.d. [1886?]

Sacrificio y recompensa. Lima: Imprenta de Torres Aguirre, 1886.

Eleodora. Lima: n.p., 1887.

Blanca Sol. Lima: Ed. Torres Aguirre, 1888; Lima: Ed. Carlos Prince. 2d ed. 1889; 3d ed. 1894; 4th ed. 1894.

Las consecuencias. Lima: Imprenta de Torres Aguirre, 1889.

El conspirador. Lima: E. Sequí and Cía., 1892; Lima: Imprenta "La Voce D'Italia." 2d ed. 1892; Mexico: Imprenta de Ireneo Paz. 3d ed. 1898.

Influencia de las Bellas Letras en el progreso moral y material de los pueblos. Lima: n.p., n.d. [1890s?]

Independencia de Cuba. Lima: n.p., n.d. [1890s?]

La novela moderna. Estudio filosófico. Lima: Tipo-Litografía de Bacigalupi y Cía., 1892; Lima: Ediciones Hora del Hombre, S.A. 2d ed. 1948.

La religión de la humanidad; carta al señor D. Juan Enrique Lagarrigue. Lima: Imprenta de Torres Aguirre, 1893.

El Conde León Tolstoy. Lima: Imprenta de El Diario Judicial, 1896.

Works about Mercedes Cabello de Carbonera

Brushwood, John S. *Genteel Barbarism: New Readings of Nineteenth-Century Spanish American Novels.* Lincoln, Neb.: University of Nebraska, 1981. Pp. 16–17.

Castro Arenas, Mario. "Mercedes Cabello de Carbonera y el Naturalismo." *La novela peruana y la evolución social.* Lima: José Godard, ed., 1967. Pp. 84–104.

Cunningham, Lucía Guerra. "Mercedes Cabello de Carbonera: Estética de la moral y los desvíos no-disyuntivos de la virtud." *Revista de Crítica Literaria Latino-americana* 26 (1987):25–41.

Fox-Lockert, Lucía. "Mercedes Cabello de Carbonera." *Women Novelists in Spain and Spanish America.* Metuchen, N.J.: Scarecrow Press, 1979. Pp. 147–55.

Higgins, James. *A History of Peruvian Literature.* Liverpool: Francis Cairns, 1987. Pp. 77–78.

Jackson, Mary-Garland. "The Roles and Portrayal of Women in Selected Prose Works by Six Female Writers of Peru." Ph.D. diss. University of Kentucky, 1982. Pp. 110–236. (*DAI* 44/01A [1982]:181).

Kaufmann, Adriana. "*El conspirador.* Novela político-social autobiografía de un hombre público (1892) de Mercedes Cabello de Carbonera." Ed. Paul Verdevoye. "*Caudillos,*" "*caciques*" *et dictateurs dans le roman hispano-américain.* Paris: Editions Hispaniques, 1978.

Lewis, Bart L. "Art, Society and Criticism: The Literary Theories of Mercedes Cabello de Carbonera and Clorinda Matto de Turner." *Letras Femeninas* 10, 2 (1984):66–73.

Mari, Bruno. "Mercedes Cabello de Carbonera." *La novela peruana en la narrativa hispanoamericana.* Rome: Editrice Elia, 1977. Pp. 30–31.

Miller, Martin C. "Clorinda Matto de Turner and Mercedes Cabello de Carbonera: Societal Criticism and Morality." Eds. Yvette E. Miller and Charles M. Tatum. *Latin American Women Writers: Yesterday and Today.* Pittsburgh: Latin American Literary Review Press, 1975. Pp. 25–32.

Saver, Laura Judith. "Un análisis de la influencia filosófica de Manuel González Prada en Clorinda Matto y Mercedes Cabello." Ph.D. diss. University of Colorado at Boulder, 1984. (*DAI* 46/02A [1984]:436.)

Tamayo Vargas, Augusto. *Perú en trance de novela; ensayo crítico-biográfico sobre Mercedes Cabello de Carbonera.* Lima: Ediciones Baluarte, 1940.

———. Prol. *La novela moderna. Estudio filosófico.* Lima: Ediciones Hora del Hombre, S.A., 1948. Pp. 9–13.

Zum Felde, Alberto. *Indice crítico de la literatura hispanoamericana.* 2 vols. Mexico: Editorial Guaranía, 1954–1959.

LYDIA CABRERA
(b. 1900)
Cuba

Ada Ortúzar-Young

BIOGRAPHY

Born in Havana on May 20, 1900, Lydia Cabrera was part of a typical well-to-do Cuban family of the turn of the century. The youngest child in a family of eight, she enjoyed the privileges of her social class from an early age. Her father, the patriot Don Raimundo Cabrera Bosch, joined at age sixteen the forces that fought for Cuba's independence from Spain. His best known book, *Cuba y sus jueces* (1887; Cuba and its judges), defended Cuba's values and interests against the injustices he saw in the Spanish colonial government in the island. Cabrera's mother, Elisa Marcaida Casanova, was the typical woman of the times, dedicated to her husband and her children.

The family's prestigious social and economic status had, as one might expect, a profound impact on the young child. First, as was the case in many distinguished households of the time, the family had numerous black servants, *tatas* or nannies, the descendants of slaves. Tata Tula, and the seamstress Teresa (Omí Tomí), among others, would provide a bridge for Cabrera to the magical world of the former slaves. They would fill the young child's imagination with tales and fantasies, fears, and superstitions, and later in life would provide valuable contacts with Afro-Cuban communities. Second, Don Raimundo Cabrera surrounded himself at home with writers, painters and intellectual and political leaders. Often he would allow his daughter to listen to their conversations. There she met the most prominent men of the times: Manuel Sanguily, Enrique José Varona, Juan Gualberto Gómez, and the painter Leopoldo Romañach, whom she considered a childhood friend, among many others. She went with her father to concerts, operas, and the theater, as well as to the meetings of the Sociedad

Económica de Amigos del País. She would accompany her family on their frequent travels to the United States and Europe.

During her childhood Cabrera had little formal schooling. She attended briefly a private school run by the Cuban educator María Luisa Dolz. She received a somewhat heterodox education at her home by private tutors. An attempt to send her to the school of the Sociedad Económica de Amigos del País was unsuccessful. In the family library, guided by her sister Emma, Cabrera read extensively. She went to complete her "Bachillerato" or high school, "por la libre" (on her own), since at the time women could not attend secondary schools. Without her father's knowledge, she also studied for six months at the prestigious Academia de San Alejandro, with the encouragement of her friend the painter Romañach.

In 1923 she organized a retrospective exposition of Cuban art at the old Convento de Santa Clara. Later she established an antique shop in order to have money of her own and to go to Paris to study painting. This trip was to change the course of her life and launch her career as a writer and researcher.

In 1927 Cabrera returned to Paris to study and to paint, and settled in Montmartre. She would remain there, except for some short trips to Cuba, until 1939. She studied at L'Ecole du Louvre, from which she graduated in 1930, and audited courses at L'Ecole des Beaux Arts.

Her stay in Paris coincided with a great aesthetic and ethnographic interest in the so-called primitive civilizations, particularly those from the African continent. The new discoveries and publications of Leo Frobenius awakened an interest among the intellectuals in figurines from Dahomey, masks from the Ivory Coast, and the bronze and wooden figures from other parts of Africa. This influence would have a great impact in the plastic arts through painters such as Pablo Picasso and Georges Braque. In 1917 the French poet Guillerme Apollinaire had published an album of black sculptures. The influence of black music and jazz in particular on Europe goes back to 1914 when Louis Mitchell visited Europe from the United States and from after the end of the war when black rhythms and important performers, such as Josephine Baker, became fashionable. The attraction of Africa and its cultures also had an impact on European literature. Among the most important of such works are Blaise Cendrars's *Antologie nègre* (1921; Negro anthology), Paul Morand's *Magie noire* (1928; Black magic), André Gide's *Retour du Tchad* (1920; Return from Chad) and *Voyages au Congo* (1927; Trips to the Congo), and Philippe Soupault's *Le nègre* (1929; The Negro).

Cabrera participated in this intellectual climate and became familiar with the various European avant-garde movements, such as cubism and surrealism. She also studied Eastern civilizations. She was particularly interested in the cultures of India and Japan, in Buddhism, and in Chinese folklore. These myths and religions would bring to her memory the tales she heard as a small child from the black members of her household. In this way she "discovered" an important part of the heritage of her country while in Paris as did the Guatemalan Nobel prizewinner Miguel Angel Asturias. These events in Europe brought home to

Cabrera the importance of the fact that the slaves imported from Africa formed the center of the national folklore, because of the extinction of Cuba's Indian population.

Cabrera returned to Cuba for two months in 1928 and with the help of Omí Tomí, initiated her first contacts with representatives of black folklore. Cabrera then started writing some "stories" that she sent to Switzerland to entertain her friend, the Venezuelan novelist Teresa de la Parra,* who was ill. The Cuban later showed the stories to Francis de Miomandre, who in turn would take them to Paul Morand, from Gallimard Press. Morand had Miomandre translate them into French, and published *Contes nègres de Cuba* (Negro Stories from Cuba) in 1936. Cabrera returned to Cuba on the eve of the Second World War where she proceeded to make a systematic study of the Afro-Cuban language and traditions. This interest has continued for more than half a century.

In 1940 Cabrera installed herself with her lifelong companion, María Teresa ("Titina") de Rojas, the daughter of her godmother, in "La Quinta San José," a mansion in the Havana suburb of Marianao. Both women wanted to create a house-museum that would trace the evolution of the Cuban home. Eventually, it was to be donated to their country. Their efforts proved fruitful, and they were able to obtain some important pieces of traditional Cuban furniture. They traveled about the island in search of items of historical value: silverware, crystal, porcelain, paintings, embroidery, and the like. By 1960, with the socialist revolution now in control, intellectuals had to decide whether to write for the revolution or leave the country. Cabrera chose to go into exile in June of that year. The museum had by then acquired a substantial collection. It has since been dismantled by the Cuban government.

In the 1980s Lydia Cabrera has resided in Miami, Florida, accompanied by Titina de Rojas until Rojas's death in January 1987. In her apartment Cabrera is surrounded by numerous artifacts she has acquired over the years, particularly those symbolic of the impact that black folklore has had in her life. Cabrera enjoys her independence and continues to write.

MAJOR THEMES

Cabrera's interest in the black goes beyond a frivolous response to a literary fashion. Unlike Nicolás Guillén and Alejo Carpentier whose styles and themes evolved away from these themes, she has devoted more than five decades to the subject. Her contribution to the representation of Afro-Cuban folklore remains unsurpassed by that of any other writer.

Cabrera has devoted her career to researching and writing about a single topic: the residual presence of African folklore in Cuba after centuries of slavery and how the African presence has combined with the local Spanish culture to produce the unique characteristics found in the Afro-Cuban culture of the island. She was attracted to this study by the primitive poetry of oral traditions which was on the verge of disappearing when she discovered them. Cabrera tells us that she is neither an anthropologist nor an ethnographer. She deliberately tried not to read anthropologists in order to avoid any possible influence from specialists that might lead her to see or to find things that were not present in the black communities in Cuba (Hiriart, 1978, p. 74). She was indeed surrounded by an abundance of human material that would become truly accessible only after the aristocratic woman gained the trust of the descendants of the African slaves.

Lydia Cabrera's interest in black folklore does not represent an isolated case in Cuba. The publication of the *Cuentos negros* coincides with the literary movement denominated as *negrista* (dealing with negro subjects) that flourished in Cuba from about 1925 to 1936, with the mulatto poet Nicolás Guillén as one of its best exponents. *Negrista* poetry attempts to reproduce African rhythms through the use of onomatopoeic sounds and African words. In prose, these writers turn to the magical-mythical patterns of black folklore, as seen in Cabrera's work or in Alejo Carpentier's *Ecué-Yamba-O* (1933; Lord, praised be thou). However, the presence of the black in Cuban literature long antedates the *negrista* movement. One can speak of two Afro-Cuban literatures: one, anonymous and transmitted orally by the African descendants; the other, ascribed to an author and written down. The written and the oral traditions that had evolved along parallel lines converge in the *negrista* movement.

Cabrera's writings can be divided into two major groups: her works of fiction and the publications resulting from her ethnographic research. *Cuentos negros de Cuba* (1940), her first collection of short stories to appear in Spanish, is the original version of *Contes nègres de Cuba*, published in Paris in 1936. Dedicated to Teresa de la Parra* and with an introduction by the renowned Cuban anthropologist Fernando Ortiz, her brother-in-law, this collection of twenty-two short stories received immediate acclaim for its author and today is considered a classic of Spanish American literature.

In the tradition of Aesop's fables, most of the characters in this first book are animals. They are not, of course, ordinary animals. They behave like humans, and their actions are in no way limited by the fact that they are animals. The reader encounters characters such as "Jicotea," a type of small freshwater tortoise common in Cuba, bulls, earthworms, toads, hens, deer, horses, rabbits, dogs, cats, mice, and many others. Some of them reappear in later stories as is the case of Jicotea (either as a male or a female), the subject of the collection *Ayapá: Cuentos de Jicotea* (1971; Ayapá: Turtle stories).

Cuentos negros and the two collections that followed are based very loosely on Afro-Cuban legends. Much has been said about the extent to which the author has borrowed or transposed from the stories and myths she heard from blacks and how much is the product of her imagination.

Cuentos negros and its continuation *Por qué . . . Cuentos negros de Cuba* (1948; Why . . . black short stories from Cuba) and *Ayapá: Cuentos de Jicotea* (1971), a total of sixty-nine stories, reproduce and re-create artistically the African legacy, transmitted orally over generations in the form of legends, myths, and religious beliefs, still known by some members of the black population in

Cuba. The universe depicted in these stories reflects a primeval ancestral mentality, always close to nature and prone to recur to the supernatural to explain events and situations. The narratives also show the effects of the modern socioeconomic structures that use the black population, at the same time that they keep them on the outskirts of society. The setting of the stories betrays the dual existence of the former slave; the private world of the blacks dominates in the stories, although one gets a hint of the harsh daily conditions and the blacks' attitudes toward whites.

Religion and the Afro-Cuban's relationship with the gods occupy a prominent place in *Cuentos negros* and *Por qué* . . . This is perhaps the area in which the results of the blacks' centuries of contact with white society are most obvious. The blacks have not fully assimilated the religion of their masters, but rather have combined its practices and beliefs with their own. For every white saint in the Catholic Church, the blacks have their counterpart. These saints are closer to the African pagan gods than to the Christian saints, and they represent figures for whom blacks felt an identification. In this way, the Virgin of the Caridad del Cobre, the patron saint of Cuba, becomes Ochún, Our Lady of Regla is Yemayá, Saint Barbara is Changó, and so on.

The story "Los compadres" (The godparents) in *Cuentos negros* illustrates well the characteristics of these saints, and how they provide a model of behavior here on earth. This is a story about adultery, and possibly incest, since the adulterous couple are godparents. The story begins: "Todos somos hijos de los Santos, y lo de la malicia y el gusto de pecar ya le viene al hombre de los santos" ("We are all offsprings of the saints, and evil intentions and the taste for sin come from the saints," p. 67). It proceeds to describe the less-than-holy behavior of Changó, a quarrelsome god attracted to women, who seduces Ochún by dancing and then lives with her. In the Afro-Cuban pantheon Changó is the god of virility, sensuality, fire, and war. His attributes are lightning and thunder. He presents himself as a warrior, but for the *santeros* (practitioners of Afro-Cuban religion) he is St. Barbara. Cabrera then proceeds to the main plot of the story, as the godfather Capinche tries to seduce his friend's wife, Dolé. The psychological parallels between Changó and Capinche are evident. What would be considered a sin by the Catholic Church is accepted by the African saints.

In "Los compadres," as in other stories, the black woman, particularly the *mulata*, or woman of mixed blood, contrasts sharply with her white counterpart, who is absent from these stories but present in society and in the fiction of the time. Just as in the case of the black woman, the white woman is also made in the image of the virgin. Like Mary she is to be pure and uninterested in sex. The mulatto woman, one of the most vital evidences of mixed racial heritage and one of the most obvious products of the centuries of interrelations between races Cabrera is trying to capture, is very attractive to both black and white men. In Cuban literature in general, and in Cabrera's case in particular, the mulatto woman exploits her sexuality, recognizing perhaps that this may very well be the only avenue open to her to advance socially. Cabrera's stories, then, conform to a traditional literary and social stereotype and help to perpetuate an image that, ultimately, exploits the *mulata* woman. As this case shows, Cabrera is not a very socially conscious writer. She is interested in the folklore of the blacks, not in the sociopolitical situation of her subjects.

The treatment of men in "Los compadres" is also representative of what one finds in numerous stories in *Cuentos negros* and *Por qué*... Departing from the patriarchal conception of the male in African and Cuban traditions, where he is the central figure in the family and the community, quite often the men in these stories tend to be weak and are easily manipulated by their clever and sensuous wives. The black man thus occupies a subservient position, a reflection perhaps of his position in a society dominated by whites, and the debilitating effect on his self-image of centuries of oppression.

The black man, valued in Cuban society for the physical labor he can contribute, is usually portrayed in these stories as lazy. Such is the case in "La vida suave" (The easy life) and "La loma de Mambiala" (Mambiala Hill). In the latter, one of the most successful and representative stories of *Cuentos negros*, the main character, expert at speaking and playing the guitar, refuses to work. On the morning of Palm Sunday, after several days without food for himself and his family, unable to distinguish between reality and illusion, Serapio dreams about a pumpkin. After he prays to God and Mambiala, he returns to a pumpkin field to find that a miracle has occurred. He finds a magic pot, the "Cazuelita Cocina Bueno" (cooking well pot), that will feed him and his black friends. Although white characters are not common in these stories, Serapio's unexpected good fortune attracts the most representative and influential members of the dominant class: the plantation owners, the "very honorable" slave trader, and a millionaire usurer who uses a false document to trick Serapio into selling him the magic pot. Once again poor, Serapio prays for another miracle. This time he receives a magic cane *(el bastón de Manatí)* that will allow him to take revenge against the most prominent members of the society and to get away with it. As the major, the Civil Guard, and the wealthy come expecting a fancy feast at the expense of the poor Serapio, the miracle occurs and they are almost beaten to death by the cane, a satisfaction Serapio could only obtain in the past in dreams.

In 1948 Cabrera published her second collection of short stories entitled *¿Por qué?... Cuentos negros de Cuba*. The title of the book is a question and each story, an answer or an explanation. Twenty-three years were to go by before the publication of her third collection of short stories. In the meantime Cabrera dedicated all these years to the investigation of African folklore in Cuba, research that resulted in the publication of several volumes. In 1971, living in exile, she gathered nineteen stories, some previously published, in a collection entitled *Ayapá: cuentos de Jicotea*, all having a common protagonist, the turtle Jicotea. This character had appeared in her first two collections, either as a male or female, although in *Ayapá* one finds Jicotea's most thorough treatment.

The importance of Jicotea in Cabrera's stories is understandable if one takes into account the popularity and significance of this small animal in the folklore of the African descendants in Cuba. The blacks identified themselves and their situation with that of this small freshwater turtle, so common in Cuba. Like them, this turtle was at the bottom of the social scale in the animal kingdom. It is considered ugly, walks slowly, and has a harsh life, as evidenced by the scars in its back. Like the blacks, it must adjust to its environment in order to survive. In Cabrera's stories, just as in the oral tales narrated by the slaves after a long day in the fields, the apparently helpless Jicotea is shrewd, capable of misleading or swindling the superior adversary. Jicotea has no scruples. The blacks, who identify with it, admire its astuteness and ingenuity. The wise and the elderly think the turtle has supernatural powers and assert that it speaks like the spirits and the *chicherekús* (a wooden figure of black magic). All these are positive qualities.

In Cabrera's first two collections, the gods and their activities occupied a prominent place. The action often went back to "the beginning of things." In *Ayapá*, the reader finds a human-like Jicotea in an identifiable social context corresponding to the Cuba of the late nineteenth and early twentieth centuries, with numerous *costumbrista* (portraying local color) scenes. Her fourth and last collection of short stories, *Cuentos para adultos niños y retrasados mentales* (Stories for the adult child and the mentally retarded), was published in Miami in 1983. Here Cabrera departs from the themes treated in her earlier books. These stories, some merely brief sketches, lack the depth of character and the qualities found in her earlier fiction.

One of the most important characteristics of Cabrera's narrative is the attempt to reproduce verbally African rhythms by using onomatopoeic words or phrases that may remain unintelligible to the reader, but that, in some cases, are the key to understanding the cyclical or repetitive nature of the action. In "¡Sokuando!," Gorrión (Sparrow) tricks Buey (Ox) into believing that he has magical powers and is capable of cutting off the heads of all the members of his species and glueing them back together again. The words "Esékere Uán. ¡Sokuando! Esékere Uán" are repeated as Gorrión performs his ceremony. These words remain a secret for the noninititated. In fact, we are confronted with a ritual of life and death that almost leads to the annihilation of all the oxen. The structural technique of onomatopoeia, as pointed out by Matías Montes Huidobro in *Homenaje a Lydia Cabrera* (In Sánchez, 1977, pp. 41–50) appears frequently in these stories. It helps the reader initiated in Afro-Cuban culture to penetrate the magic world of the blacks. For the reader unable to understand this deeper meaning, they simply form a musical background to the events.

Cabrera approaches her subject with sympathy and respect, almost with devotion. However, references to the socioeconomic oppression of blacks are absent from her work. The protagonist of her stories is not the *cimarrón*, or runaway slave who flees to the woods and forms *palenques* (communities) to avoid slavery and its injustices. Her work is not didactic and, as has been pointed out by some of her critics, she makes little effort to distinguish between good and evil. The behavior of her black characters may seem amoral to the white reader, but Cabrera makes no judgments.

Cabrera's first nonfictional work, a volume of nearly six-hundred pages widely respected by scholars and *santeros* (leaders in Afro-Cuban religious cults) alike, is *El Monte: Igbo-Finda; Ewe Orisha, Vititi Nfinda. (Notas sobre las religiones, la magia, las supersticiones y el folklore de los negros criollos y el pueblo de Cuba)* (1954: The mountain: Igbo-Finda; Ewe Orisha, Vititi Nfinda. Notes on religions, magic, superstitions and folklore of the Creole blacks and the Cuban people). *Monte* in the context of black Cuban lore is a concept that defies translation. It may mean mountain, wild, and woods, simultaneously, and even more. The *monte* is a sacred and magic place, where the human and the divine come together. The importance of the material transcribed in this book for Cuban blacks, and for those interested in this subject, can be compared to that of the Bible for the Judeo-Christian tradition, or the Popol-Vuh for the Mayans.

El Monte is a book difficult to classify. The intention of the author was to transcribe faithfully the materials gathered in her ethnographic "notes." The unscientific method followed by Cabrera was determined by the nature of the explanations and narrations of her black informants. She allows repetitions and contradictions to show the disparity in criteria among the "authorities," the interpreters of a long oral tradition in constant change.

In addition to the apparently intricate structure of the book, Cabrera has provided some organization. The book consists of two essential parts: In the first ten chapters her field notes are organized thematically; the second part is an alphabetical listing of the plants with medicinal value utilized by the *santeros* in their practice of *curanderismo* (native medicine). However, some elements remain obscure, particularly for the noninitiated. Numerous terms employed by the African descendants remain unexplained or untranslated.

El Monte is a landmark in the writer's career and an outstanding contribution to the field of ethnography. It is essential for the understanding of Cabrera's short stories and other publications. Many of the themes one encounters in her fiction appear in this book. *El Monte* relies heavily on narration and storytelling about the gods, their particular characteristics, rites, and miracles. In turn, these stories shed light on the mentality and the private world of black society, their practices and attitudes, which until the publication of *El monte* remained inaccessible to the outsider.

The bulk of Cabrera's publications, which today surpasses twelve volumes, continues to be in the field of ethnography and linguistics. These can be divided into two broad categories. On the one hand, books such as *La sociedad secreta Abakuá: narrada por viejos adeptos* (1959, The Abakuá secret society: narrated by old followers), *Anaforuana: Ritual y símbolos de la iniciación en la Sociedad Secreta Abakuá* (1975; Anaforuana: ritual and symbols of initiation to the Abakuá secret society), *La Regla Kimbisa del Santo Cristo del Buen Viaje* (1977; The Kimbisa cult of the Holy Christ of Good Travels), all deal with the practices of the *reglas* or religious cults of the various sects present on the island. These are copiously illustrated with detailed drawings of figures used in ceremonies. On the other hand, *Yemayá y Ochún: Kariocha, Iyalorichas y Olorichas* (1974; Yemayá and Ochún: Kariocha, Yyalorichas and Olorichas) is a collection of narrations about the two most important goddesses of the Afro-Cuban pantheon and is an example of a second type of work.

In her works of a linguistic nature, Cabrera considers herself a compiler. In *Refranes de negros viejos: recogidos por Lydia Cabrera* (1955; Sayings from old blacks: collected by Lydia Cabrera), one of her most outstanding works of this type, she gathers over six hundred sayings and carefully classifies them according to their meaning (religious, philosophical, those expressing authority, etc.), and according to their origin, such as those imported from Africa or Spain, and those of local origin. In *Francisco y Francisca: Chascarrillos de negros viejos* (1976; Francisco and Francisca: Witty stories from old blacks) one finds Cabrera's humor at its best—something that is not absent from her short stories. These light anecdotes, sometimes with an off-color touch, may offend some readers, but reveal what Jorge Mañach in *Indagación del choteo* (1928; Inquiry into Cuban ways of poking fun) finds inherent in the Cuban character of blacks and whites alike: a tendency to resort to the funny when facing adversity. Other works, such as *Anagó, vocabulario lucumí (El Yoruba que se habla en Cuba)* (1957; Anagó, Lucumí vocabulary. The Yoruba spoken in Cuba) and *Vocabulario Congo (El Bantú que se habla en Cuba)* (1984, Congo vocabulary. The Bantú spoken in Cuba), prove that certain African dialects are still spoken by some sectors of the population. Cabrera's contribution consists of recording this vocabulary transmitted orally, which otherwise would eventually be lost.

SURVEY OF CRITICISM

Cabrera's work was warmly received in Paris, where it first appeared. Some of her stories had been published in such prestigious journals as *Cahiers du Sud*, *Revue de Paris*, and *Les Nouvelles Litteraires*. Her books, *Contes nègres de Cuba* (Gallimard, 1936), and *Pourquoi: nouveaux contes nègres de Cuba* (Gallimard, 1954), a translation of *Por qué . . .*, were highly acclaimed. In Cuba and the United States her work continues to arouse the interest of critics to this day.

Critical response to Cabrera's works has been mostly confined to the first three collections of short stories. Rosa Valdés Cruz, in an article entitled "Los cuentos de Lydia Cabrera: ¿ transposiciones o creaciones?" in *Homenaje a Lydia Cabrera* (Sánchez, p. 93), asks whether we should accept Cabrera's contention that her function is limited to receiving and collecting legends, myths, and rites and translating them onto paper. While this may be the case in her ethnographic works, her short stories reveal a skillful creator of fiction. Her treatment of time and space, the use of the double, as well as the amalgamation of the real and the fantastic, anticipate the techniques later employed by the masters of magical realism, such as the Argentines Jorge Luis Borges and Julio Cortázar, and the Colombian Gabriel García Márquez.

Serious scholars such as Josefina Inclán, Rosario Hiriart, Hilda Perera, Sara Soto, and Rosa Valdés-Cruz have dedicated book-length studies to Cabrera's work. Together they have situated Cabrera's fiction in the context of Cuban literature. Perera, Soto, and Valdés-Cruz, who write on the nature of Cuban society and its cultural mixture (or *idapo*, in the Yoruba dialect), having resulted from centuries of miscegenation and the close coexistence of the races, should be required reading for anyone approaching Cabrera's work for the first time. Perera (1971) focuses on cultural *sincretismo*, the fusion of diverse cultural elements in Cabrera's artistic creations. This critic succinctly traces the number of different places of origin of the African slaves, which accounts for the numerous Afro-Cuban dialects still alive in Cuba. Perera refers to some of the institutions created by the blacks as a means of survival. One example is the *cabildo*, a mutual assistance society that also helped to perpetuate the language, traditions, and religious practices of the African homeland.

Quite helpful for understanding Cabrera's work are several lengthy interviews with the author. The numerous questions posed by Inclán, Levine, Perera, and Valdés-Cruz shed light on Cabrera's childhood and her years in Paris when she became interested in black folklore (and not as an influence of her brother-in-law, the anthropologist Fernando Ortiz, as some have asserted).

Homenaje a Lydia Cabrera (Sánchez, 1977) and *En torno a Lydia Cabrera* (Inclán, 1978) are the most complete collections of studies on Cabrera. They offer a wide selection of essays on the most important aspects of her fiction: magical realism, African folklore, and the originality of her style. Unfortunately, most of these fine essays center, with few exceptions, on the first three collections of stories. There is a need for a thorough analysis that would lead to a deeper understanding of the rest of her work. This apparent omission may be due to the fact that her ethnographic works require arduous and slow reading, in sharp contrast with the short stories, which are easily accessible and thoroughly enjoyable to the casual reader as well as the rigorous scholar. Also lacking is a criticism that would take into account issues of class, gender, and race. A revisionist approach to Cabrera's work would prove extremely revealing.

BIBLIOGRAPHY

Works by Lydia Cabrera

Cuentos negros de Cuba. Havana: Imprenta La Verónica, 1940.
Por qué . . . Cuentos negros de Cuba. Havana: Ediciones C.R., 1948.
El Monte: Igbo-Finda; Ewe Orisha, Vititi Nfinda. (Notas sobre las religiones, la magia, las supersticiones y el folklore de los negros criollos y el pueblo de Cuba). Havana: Ediciones C.R., 1954.
Refranes de negros viejos: recogidos por Lydia Cabrera. Havana: Ediciones C.R., 1955.

Anagó: vocabulario lucumi (El Yoruba que se habla en Cuba). Havana: Ediciones C.R., 1957.
La sociedad secreta Abakuá: narrada por viejos adeptos. Havana: Ediciones C.R., 1959.
Otán Iyebiyé: las piedras preciosas. Miami: Ediciones C.R., 1970.
Ayapá: cuentos de Jicotea. Miami: Ediciones Universal, 1971.
La laguna sagrada de San Joaquín. Madrid: Ediciones R, 1973.
Yemayá y Ochún: Kariocha, Iyalorichas y Olorichas. Madrid: Ediciones C.R., 1974.
Anaforuana: ritual y símbolos de la iniciación en la sociedad secreta Abakuá. Madrid: Ediciones R, 1975.
Francisco y Francisca: chascarrillos de negros viejos. Miami: Ediciones C.R., 1976.
Itinerarios del insomnio: Trinidad de Cuba. Miami: Ediciones C.R., 1977.
La Regla Kimbisa del Santo Cristo del Buen Viaje. Miami: Ediciones C.R., 1977.
Reglas de Congo. Palo Monte—Mayombe. Miami: Ediciones C.R., 1979.
Koeko Iyawó. Aprende Novicia: pequeño tratado de Regla Lucumí. Miami: Ediciones C.R., 1980.
Cuentos para adultos niños y retrasados mentales. Miami: Ediciones C.R., 1983.
La medicina popular en Cuba. Médicos de antaño, curanderos, santeros y paleros de hogaño. Miami: Ediciones C.R., 1984.
Vocabulario Congo: (El Bantú que se habla en Cuba). Miami: Ediciones C.R., 1984.
Supersticiones y buenos consejos. Miami: Ediciones Universal, 1987.
La lengua sagrada de los ñáñigos. Miami: Ediciones C.R., 1988.
Los animales en el folklore y la magia de Cuba. Miami: Ediciones Universal, 1988.

Translations of Lydia Cabrera

"Turtle's Horse." *From the Green Antilles*. Ed. Barbara Howes. New York: MacMillan, 1966. Pp. 275–76.
"Walo-Wila." *From the Green Antilles*. Ed. Barbara Howes. New York: MacMillan Co., 1966. Pp. 277–79.

Works about Lydia Cabrera

Acosta Saignes, Miguel. "*El Monte* de Lydia Cabrera." *Revista Bimestre Cubana* 71 (1956):286–87.
Ben-Ur, Lorraine Elena. "Diálogo con Lydia Cabrera." *Caribe* (Hawaii) 2, 2 (1977):131–37.
Castellanos, Isabel, and Josefina Inclán, eds. *En torno a Lydia Cabrera*. Miami: Ediciones Universal, 1987.
González, Manuel Pedro. "Cuentos y recuentos de Lydia Cabrera." *Nueva Revista Cubana* 2 (1959):153–61.
Gutiérrez, Mariela. *Los cuentos negros de Lydia Cabrera (Un estudio morfológico)*. Miami: Ediciones Universal, 1986.
Hiriart, Rosario. *Cartas a Lydia Cabrera. (Correspondencia inédita de Gabriela Mistral y Teresa de la Parra)*. Madrid: Ediciones Torremozas, 1988.
———. "En torno al mundo negro de Lydia Cabrera." *Cuadernos Hispanoamericanos* (Madrid) 359 (1980):433–40.
———. "La experiencia viva en la ficción: Lydia Cabrera e Hilda Perera." *Círculo* (New Jersey) 8 (1979):121–31.
———. "Lydia Cabrera and the World of Cuba's Blacks." *Américas* (Washington) 3 (1980):40–42.

————. *Lydia Cabrera: Vida Hecha arte*. New York: Eliseo Torres & Sons, 1978.

Inclán, Josefina. *Ayapá y otras Otán Iyebiyé de Lydia Cabrera*. Miami: Ediciones Universal, 1976.

————. *En torno a: "Itinerarios del Insomnio: Trinidad de Cuba" de Lydia Cabrera*. Miami: Peninsular Printing, 1978.

Josephs, Allen. "Lydia and Federico: Towards a Historical Approach to Lorca Studies." *Journal of Spanish Studies: Twentieth Century* 6 (1978):123–30.

Levine, Suzanne Jill. "A Conversation with Lydia Cabrera." *Review* 31 (Jan.-Apr.):13–15.

Mistral, Gabriela. *Siete Cartas de Gabriela Mistral a Lydia Cabrera*. Miami: Peninsular Printing, 1980.

Novás Calvo, Lino. "El Monte." *Papeles de Son Armadans* (Palma de Mallorca) (Sept. 1968):298–304.

Perera, Hilda. *Idapo. El sincretismo en los cuentos negros de Lydia Cabrera*. Miami: Ediciones Universal, 1971.

Sánchez, Reinaldo, et al., eds. *Homenaje a Lydia Cabrera*. Miami: Ediciones Universal, 1977.

Soto, Sara. *Magia e Historia en los "Cuentos Negros," "Por qué" y "Ayapá" de Lydia Cabrera*. Miami: Ediciones Universal, 1988.

Valdés-Cruz, Rosa. "El realismo mágico en los cuentos negros de Lydia Cabrera." *Otros Mundos Otros Fuegos: Fantasía y Realismo Mágico en Iberoamérica*. Ed. Donald A. Yates. East Lansing: Michigan State University Latin American Studies Center, 1975.

————. *Lo ancestral africano en la narrativa de Lydia Cabrera*. Barcelona, Spain: Editorial Vosgos, 1974.

————. "Mitos africanos conservados en Cuba y su tratamiento literario por Lydia Cabrera." *Chasqui* 3, 1 (1973):31–36.

————. "The Short Stories of Lydia Cabrera: Transpositions or Creations." *Latin American Women Writers: Yesterday and Today*. Eds. Yvette E. Miller and Charles Tatum. Pittsburgh: Latin American Literary Review Press, 1975. Pp. 148–54.

Zambrana, María. "Lydia Cabrera, poeta de la metamorfosis." *Orígenes* (Havana) 7 (1950):11–13.

NELLIE CAMPOBELLO
(b. 1900)
Mexico

Catherine Nickel

BIOGRAPHY

Although she has given her date of birth variously as 1909, 1912, and 1913, Nellie Francisca Campobello was actually born in 1900 in the semiarid mountainous state of Durango in northwestern Mexico. Her early life and later writings were strongly influenced by an enduring sense of identity with the proud independent spirit of that region where her family had deep roots. She boasted that her Indian ancestors helped found the town of Villa Ocampo where she was born. As a child she was very active and outgoing, riding horses through the rough terrain and opting for any type of physical outdoor activity over schoolwork. Her family moved from Durango to the neighboring state of Chihuahua, and even to Texas for a short while, and her mother and an aunt provided much of her early education. She spent most of her adult life in Mexico City but always expressed a strong preference for the rural over the urban lifestyle, and maintained a keen interest in the native culture—especially the music and dance—of Mexico.

The violence of the prolonged civil war known as the Mexican Revolution had a profound effect on Campobello. Her father died in the fighting in 1914, and one of her brothers served with the northern army under the command of Francisco (Pancho) Villa. Her mother and other relatives were directly or indirectly involved in the war effort as Villa partisans. Until 1920, Durango and Chihuahua were the sites of almost constant military activities as various political and personal factions struggled to gain ascendency. So until she moved to the nation's capital in 1923, Nellie Campobello's life was filled with stories about executions, ambushes, battles, and the lives and deaths of the soldiers of the north. She witnessed the results of much of this violence herself, helping her mother tend the wounded in a military hospital, watching condemned men being marched off to face firing squads, observing the irregular disposal of the corpses of those who died in combat or in personal disputes. Despite the gruesome nature of much of what occurred (prisoners were sometimes tortured or burned alive, fingers were cut off still-warm corpses to steal their rings), her literary evocations of this period reflect a sense of excitement and wonder at being so close to these extraordinary events. Her works devoted to the Revolution also reveal a profound admiration for the people who suffered or stoically gave their lives for what was ultimately a lost cause. Pancho Villa's impressive military victories occurred during the early period of the Revolution, and he and his forces were largely on the defensive from 1915 until his complete withdrawal from the national military and political struggle in 1920.

Nellie's mother kept the family together until she herself died at the age of thirty-eight, immediately following the death of her youngest son. With five of her brothers and sisters, Nellie moved to Mexico City in 1923. The family had sufficient financial resources to send Nellie and her younger sister Gloria to the English Institute where they devoted themselves to the study of ballet and choreography. The sisters eventually traveled throughout Mexico with a group of young dancers on cultural missions sponsored by the Ministry of Education then headed by José Vasconcelos, and Nellie became particularly proficient at interpreting the native dances of Mexico. She obtained a position as professor of dance at the National University in 1932 and was named director of the National School of Dance in 1937. These interests eventually led her to collaborate with her sister Gloria on a book published in 1940 with the title *Ritmos indígenas de México* (Indigenous rhythms of Mexico). Campobello began writing at an early age, but her reputation as a dancer outweighed her reputation as an author for many years.

Her initial literary effort was an unpublished adolescent romance novel, written at age twelve. In her teens and early twenties she wrote columns on curious or significant current events for periodicals such as *El Universal Gráfico* and *Revista de Revistas*. She published her first book, a collection of fifteen poems entitled simply ¡*Yo! por Francisca* (I, by Francisca) in 1929, but few were aware of the author's identity since the book appeared with only her middle name rather than her first or last name. This highly personalized collection of free verse had little or no discernible impact on the Mexican literary scene.

This was not the case with her second book, *Cartucho. Relatos de la lucha en el norte de México* (1931; *Cartucho. Tales of the Struggle in Northern Mexico,* 1988). There was strong public reaction to this collection of short prose sketches of soldiers, officers, and townspeople of northern Mexico during the Revolution. Some readers praised her brusque, vigorous style, while others were highly critical of the book's unabashed pro-Villa sympathies and its laconic, unadorned prose. Like Martín Luis Guzmán's *El águila y la serpiente* (The Eagle and the Serpent), a literary evocation of the Mexican Revolution published three years earlier and highly regarded by Campobello, *Cartucho* displayed a strong autobiographical flavor and little regard for the elements of a plot line. It also resembled two other novels of the Revolution published in 1931 (*Campamento* [Encampment] by Gregorio López y Fuentes and ¡*Vámonos con Pancho Villa*! [Onward with Pancho Villa] by Rafael Muñoz) in its documentary-style approach to life in a war zone. Campobello's work differed radically from the other two novels, however, in its ability to convey the remarkable candor of a child's perspective on what went on around her, whether it was a general trying unsuccessfully to kidnap her fourteen-year-old cousin Irene from her mother's house or a soldier executed before he had time to say his last words or finish his last cigarette. The second edition of *Cartucho*, somewhat modified, appeared in 1940.

In 1934 Campobello began work on a second novel that was published in 1937 under the title *Las manos de Mamá (My Mother's Hands* 1988). A highly autobiographical work, it consisted primarily of evocations of her dead mother and her own childhood. She again eschewed any interest in linear plot development in favor of impressionistic sketches. These, however, were far more intimate and lyrical than those in *Cartucho*. This collection of bittersweet reminiscences indiscriminately combined observations of the words and acts of "Ella" (She) with pleas and questions directly addressed to the now-departed "Usted" (You). Although the narrative perspective of *Las manos de Mamá* is more complex, it shared with *Cartucho* two salient characteristics: the armed conflict of the Mexican Revolution as its background, and the representation of people and events in a highly personal, partisan way. In 1949 a second edition of *Las manos de Mamá* was published, this one illustrated by the noted Mexican artist, José Clemente Orozco.

In 1940 Campobello published *Apuntes sobre la vida militar de Francisco Villa* (Notes on the military life of Francisco Villa). Although she maintained that it was only an attempt to set the record straight about Villa's activities during the war, he is portrayed as a brilliant military strategist and genuine revolutionary hero rather than a bandit motivated primarily by self-interest. Despite her insistence on its rigorous accuracy, she relied heavily on the personal accounts of Villa supporters for her data. Moreover the straightforward account of his military adventures is embellished with favorable comments on his bravery and idealism, as well as with comparisons to other notable military leaders such as Napoleon.

Although Campobello talked about writing another book based on her experiences in Mexico City, her only significant publication after this point (other than the book on national dances co-authored with her sister in 1940) was a compilation of her writings published under the title *Mis libros* (My books) in 1960. *Mis libros* omitted her study of Mexican dance but included her piece on Villa's military career, the two novels of the Revolution (*Cartucho* and *Las manos de Mamá*), and her poetry. The section devoted to poetry contained the fifteen poems from her first book *Yo*, those published in the slim volume entitled *Tres poemas* (Three poems) in 1957, and fifty-three others. *Mis libros* is introduced by a lengthy prologue expressing her opinions on Mexico's spiritual and political problems, and an account of her own literary career. In this prologue, as well as in subsequent interviews, it is clear that, despite her focus on the vigorous inhabitants of the arid north in her books, her own experiences were considerably more varied and cosmopolitan than one might suppose. She recounts, for example, a brief meeting with Spanish poet and dramatist Federico García Lorca in Cuba, traveling to several parts of Florida, and how she advised Antonin Artaud during his visit to Mexico to experience at first-hand the majestic humility of the Tarahumara Indians of Chihuahua.

Nellie Campobello remained committed to freedom from socially imposed strictures and never married. Her ideas about choreography and literature did not fit contemporary norms, and her dedication to health food and astrology undoubtedly caused some to consider her eccentric. Her pioneering work in dance theory and practice proved influential, but her impact on Mexican literature was less pronounced. While Elena Poniatowska,* for example, cites Campobello as a significant and influential predecessor, Guillermina Bravo admired her more as an avant-garde woman and dancer than as an author (both interviews in *26 Autoras del México Actual* [1978] by Beth Miller and Alfonso González).

MAJOR THEMES

Nellie Campobello's poetry is competent but unexceptional, notable chiefly for its independent tone and vigor. Although the imagery is closely tied to the natural world, relying heavily on mountains, rivers, and the sea, it is always subordinate to an insistent individualism that constantly questions and challenges the world surrounding her. Her poetry tends to be sparse and devoid of elaborate rhetorical flourishes but consistently provides a sense of a lively inquisitive intelligence at the center, struggling with the gap between the way things are and the way they should be. It is doubtful, however, that she would figure in the accounts of the development of Mexican literature if she had restricted herself to poetry.

As one of the novelists of the Revolution, Nellie Campobello was part of an extraordinary literary phenomenon that reached its apogee about a decade after the military stage of the Revolution ended. Although there were a few notable exceptions earlier, such as Mariano Azuela's *Los de abajo* (1918; *The Underdogs*, 1963) and Martín Luis Guzmán's *El águila y la serpiente* (1928), the novel of the Revolution did not really flourish as a significant factor in Mexican literature until 1931. With other novelists of this group, such as Rafael Muñoz, José Mancisidor, and Gregorio López Fuentes, Campobello set out to capture the spirit of that chaotic period when individuals found themselves inexorably drawn into the fighting that raged over all Mexico. These authors were more concerned with providing a vivid impression of life in a violent, confused time than in detailed characterization, balanced structure, or narrative technique, and many of their works blended fiction with a personal account of the action as they experienced it.

Campobello, however, maintained strong interest in the best way to communicate this experience, and developed her own approach to telling the story of the war. Like the other writers of this type of novel, she adopted an essentially episodic structure to present the events narrated. In *Cartucho*, however, she carried this preference for the episodic further than the others and completely abandoned chronological plot development in favor of three topical groupings loosely labeled "Men of the North," "Those who were shot," and "In the fire." The sketches can be read in any order; the three groups are highly unequal in size, with only seven sketches in the first set, twenty-four in the last one, and the majority under the heading "Those who were shot." Campobello's rejection of linear construction and her affinity for a patchwork type of narrative sets her apart from the male writers of the novel of the Revolution.

In each of *Cartucho's* three sections the same topics arise with regularity: Violence, death, loyalty, love, and fatalism recur in some form in almost every piece. Between the episodes of armed conflict, the people boast, tell stories, flirt, sing, and weep. The reader cannot avoid the extraordinary alternation between tenderness and impassive brutality that runs throughout the entire book. Although the themes and their treatment do not vary significantly within the three sections, the reappearance of some individuals in more than one sketch and the ever-present filtering consciousness of the child narrator provide a sense of continuity.

Beyond the recurrent brutality, this collection of short prose pieces is unified by the sensation of wonderment powerfully conveyed by the narrator. She makes us feel the child's keen disappointment at not being allowed to watch a gun battle going on down the street from her window, her astonishment at the crunchy quality of the crystalized blood she finds near a corpse, her sense of loss when, one night while she sleeps, the body of a soldier she saw shot is finally removed after lying several days under her window.

The sketches themselves are so brief (often less than a page in length) and so self-contained that some people consider them short stories rather than components of a novel. They are, for example, listed as individual tales in the *Cuento Mexicano Index* (Mexican story index) by Herbert Hoffman. The stringing together of these semi-independent fragments, however, results in a narrative pastiche whose seemingly random parts come together to form an intelligible and intriguing overall pattern of meaning.

Despite the strong authorial presence throughout *Cartucho*, the reader has the impression that the narrative movement is not subject to the rigorous control of the narrator but rather flows spontaneously by process of association from the imagination of the person who heard and saw it all happen. The skillful piecing together of these various narrative fragments in a nonhierarchic manner is probably the work's most distinctive feature and reflects the random quality of a period in which chance played a more powerful role than human desire or resolve. The lack of a single climactic moment or well-defined end to the action likewise corresponds to the way the Revolution developed in Mexico, and suggests the predominance in the narrative of repeated patterns over specific design.

Another singular feature of *Cartucho* is the blend of detachment and individuality which pervasively informs the work. There is no attempt to interpret events or speculate on what they might mean, but rather a single-minded determination to offer them candidly to the reader devoid of any extraneous detail. Because the narrative line is not interrupted for digressions into analysis, the action seems to develop very rapidly. Typically, an individual soldier rides into town, encounters the narrator, and then rides off to be killed. This pattern of narrative development gives the impression of constant movement and change within an essentially static framework.

This technique also results in numerous ellipses, as in the very first sketch devoted to the young soldier whose nickname is used as the book's title. The first-person narrator informs us laconically that Cartucho did not tell people his real name, that he alluded to becoming a soldier because of a woman, and that he used to take the narrator's little sister Gloria for rides up and down the street on his horse, and got caught up in a gun battle one day while out for a ride with Gloria who was rescued from the scene. Cartucho was never seen again, and there is no indication of exactly how he died—only the remarks of other soldiers to the effect that he had found what he was looking for and would never be back. The piece ends with the observation of another soldier (this one of a philosophical bent) that they were all *Cartuchos* (cartridges), with the implication that he and the others caught up in this sporadic, almost casual violence were as necessary and as expendable as the anonymous dead man. What the reader does not know about the principal figure in this sketch (his origin, his personality, details of his personal history, how and why he dies) almost outweighs what we do know about him. Yet this pared-down anecdote conveys the essence of the soldier's disappearance both convincingly and enchantingly. Like virtually every piece in the book, it combines various levels of past time with direct dialogue, producing the sensation of a past event told with the immediacy of an eternal present, a technique firmly rooted in the ancient art of storytelling.

The entire book is pervaded by the impression of the past being evoked as if memories were being plucked from a dream world. Specific times or dates are almost never mentioned. If any temporal indications are included, they are limited to phrases such as "one day," "at midnight," or "one November morning." In one case when both a day and month are given, the year is deliberately left in doubt. *Cartucho* thus displays many of the qualities of an oral narrative, with a certain artlessness in the construction of the tales and a tendency to treat time as a relative quality.

These short prose pieces also have a great deal in common with the *corrido* (a narrative song accompanied by lively guitar music typical of northern Mexico). There are, in fact, longish fragments of songs embedded in some of the sketches, songs sung by the soldiers or by the women who loved them, filled with action and emotion but completely devoid of sentimentality. One sketch is composed of nothing more than the lyrics of a song. Following the prose version of the death of Martín López, we find a ballad account, attributed to the spontaneous effort of a local poet, retelling the same events in a vigorous assonantal rhyme.

Less concerned with plot, surroundings, or character than with creating the sensation of a truth suddenly revealed, Campobello severely limited descriptive passages to brief but telling observations. She believed that a vocabulary restricted to the plain everyday expressions of the people and a relatively straightforward syntax provided the best way to tell the story of the Revolution. Avoiding the direct use of dialect, she relied instead on a forceful simplicity in expression which was largely neutral in tone but included some of the idiosyncrasies of local speech patterns. In the dialogue especially one finds words and expressions typical of the time and region, with an abundance of diminutives and an occasional sprinkling of contemporary slang: Yankees are referred to as "changos" and rifles are known simply as "the 30–30s." There is a great deal of repetition, and the metaphors and figurative language are effective but not elaborate. The child narrator, for example, occasionally inserts a homey comparison, usually repeating rather than creating these figures of speech. Thus, her mother recalls a night that was "dark as a wolf's mouth," or the narrator remarks that when the soldier fell dead in the river his porous flesh was "stitched with bullet holes."

Her determination to omit all but the most essential elements inspired Campobello's hyperbolic assertion that her works were composed solely of nouns and verbs. Such a pronouncement cannot, of course, be taken literally since her writing clearly contains modifiers, connectives, and other parts of speech. Her adjectives, however, are consistently commonplace, often simple colors or conventional descriptives such as fat, thin, tall, pretty, anxious, brave, nervous, or tired. The adverbs are likewise very ordinary, and the overall effect is one of direct and unpretentious communication, with the accent on action over description.

The various vignettes in *Cartucho* are remarkable for their verve and their ability to make vivid the individuals engaged in the pervasive violence of the Revolution. We gain a sense of how Pancho Villa, his soldiers, and their girlfriends and families spoke and acted. Though they are worth reading for their testimonial value alone, they are even more significant as an evocation of the consciousness of a child with the power to plunge us into a world not ruled by abstractions or irreversible linearity. Beyond their value as vivid pictures of individuals and incidents, they have the capacity to draw the reader into that emotional whirlwind that invariably accompanies such a momentous breakdown in order, and to portray the kaleidoscopic spectacle of a nation at war.

Her second novel, *Las manos de Mamá*, likewise provides an intimate personalized view of the Revolution. In the midst of the reigning chaos, Mamá provides a firm anchor of stability and attains almost mythic proportions in her ability to suffuse everything with her quiet presence. As in the previous book, the chapters are short, and linear plot development is of little importance. The narrator's propensity to switch sometimes to direct address with her departed mother lessens the emotional distance between narrator and reader. The intensity of the author's feelings toward her mother, however, adds a patina of sentimentality not found in *Cartucho*, and the overall result is a less dynamic, less engaging work.

SURVEY OF CRITICISM

Campobello's poetry has evoked little critical commentary over the years. Some of the poems from ¡Yo! por Francisca were translated by Langston Hughes and included in Dudley Fitts's Antología de la poesía latinoamericana contemporánea published in 1942, but examples of her work are not found in the more recent anthologies of Mexican poetry. Not until Doris Meyer's 1986 article on the struggle for self-definition in Campobello's early poetry was there an extended study of any facet of her poetic production. So far Meyer is the only one who has examined how being a woman influenced Campobello's writing.

After 1931, novels devoted to the Mexican Revolution were recognized as forming a distinct literary group, and public and critical interest in them increased. Because of the controversy surrounding Cartucho, Campobello became identified as a significant member of this group of writers. Some authors and critics, like Ermilo Abreu Gómez and Gregorio López y Fuentes, praised Cartucho's honesty and vitality, but others found its underlying ideology or its stylistic innovations distasteful. Her second novel brought her even greater recognition. Immediately after its publication, Las manos de Mamá was reviewed in publications such as Letras de México, El Universal, and Ruta, and she was included in Ernest Moore's 1941 Bibliografía de Novelistas de la Revolución Mexicana.

Even though she was one of the very few female novelists of the Revolution, Campobello did not figure prominently in general studies of Mexican literature. She was not, for example, among the twelve novelists included in Mariano Azuela's 1947 Cien años de novela mexicana, and she was allotted only three lines in José Luis Martínez' 1949 study of twentieth-century Mexican literature (Literatura mexicana siglo XX, 1910–1949). Her work was discussed more extensively in F. Rand Morton's 1949 Los novelistas de la Revolución, but his evaluation of her novels was not entirely favorable. Martín Luis Guzmán was impressed by her devotion to creating a new way to narrate the events of the Revolution, but others found her abrupt style disconcerting.

The most blatantly chauvinistic reaction to her work can be found in Manuel Pedro González' 1951 Trayectoria de la novela en México. He concedes that Cartucho displays an undeniable originality but finds its organization arbitrary, and is repulsed by what he considers its sadistic content. He is astounded by the narrator's insensitivity to death and brutality, especially since he is convinced that such cold indifference is totally unnatural in a woman. He insists that no normal child (especially no girl) would react so impassively to cruelty, and suggests that this anomaly is most likely the result of the direct influence of Isaac Babel's La caballería roja (Red Cavalry) on Campobello's book. Although he admits he may be mistaken, he considers the style and structure of Babel's novel so similar to that of Cartucho that Campobello's debt to a male author is to him most probable. This type of unsubstantiated speculation may be what motivated Campobello in the prologue to Mis libros to deny so vehemently having read any novel of the Revolution prior to writing Cartucho.

In his 1952 study, *Novelistas de Méjico*, J. F. Arias Campoamor designates Campobello's style as surprising and unusual, and argues that the excessive brevity of her sentences robbed her novels of fluidity and clarity. We may assume that, despite her recognition as a member of a significant literary group, her name in 1952 was not yet a household word since, although it was spelled correctly in the body of the text, it was transposed into "Wellie Campo Tello" in the Chronological Table at the end of the Arias Campoamor's book.

The inclusion of both *Cartucho* and *Las manos de Mamá* in the first volume of Antonio Castro Leal's 1960 anthology entitled *La novela de la Revolución* significantly increased Campobello's acceptance as an important author of the Revolution. She is the only woman included in either of the two volumes of this anthology, and Castro Leal's introductory remarks stress the skill with which she presented the war and violence from a child's point of view. Another indication of her status in Mexican literature is her inclusion in Emmanuel Carballo's 1965 *Diecinueve protagonistas de la literatura mexicana del siglo XX*. She and Rosario Castellanos* are the only two women in this collection of interviews with Mexico's outstanding contemporary writers.

Most studies of twentieth-century Mexican literature, especially those concerned with the novel of the Revolution, briefly mention Campobello's two novels, focusing on the directness and brutality of her particular way of writing. From the 1960s on, however, her concision and lack of sentimentality are most often viewed favorably. Few critics in the 1960s, however, studied her books in any detail. Even Max Aub's 1969 *Guía de narradores de la Revolución Mexicana*, in which he identifies her as the most "interesting" female writer of the Mexican Revolution, devotes very little attention to her works.

There is some controversy about whether *Cartucho* really qualifies as a novel or whether it is actually a group of closely related short stories. Some of the "chapters" from *Cartucho* have, in fact, appeared in anthologies of short stories. "Las barajas de Jacinto," from *Las manos de Mamá*, for example, was included in Leal's *Antología del cuento mexicano*, and three pieces from *Cartucho* appear in Aurora M. Ocampo's *Cuentistas mexicanas, Siglo XX* (1976). John Rutherford, in *Mexican Society during the Revolution, A Literary Approach* (1971), flatly declared that neither *Cartucho* nor *Las manos de Mamá* are true novels, but conceded that they are considered as such by "all critics of Mexican literature" (p. 43). If we insist on finding in the novel a sequence of events that results in a transformation of the original set of conditions, then Campobello's works clearly do not qualify. If, however, we recognize that an organic whole may be assembled from bits and pieces, the knitting together of disparate narrative fragments and scenes, then their classification as novels is quite conceivable. They have, in fact, a great deal in common with the modern novel's lack of deep structural unity, its lack of clean beginnings and implacable developments.

In 1970 Gary Keller studied *Cartucho* as one manifestion of the Revolution from a child's perspective, comparing it favorably to two other novels with simlar narratives stances. Extensive studies of Campobello's narrative are found in Gabriella De Beer's 1979 articles on *Cartucho* and *Las manos de Mamá*, and Valeska Strickland Najera's unpublished 1980 dissertation covering all of her works, including the poetry, the biography of Pancho Villa, and the book devoted to dance. Both studies are primarily thematic and stylistic. De Beer emphasizes Campobello's use of stylization and brief impressionistic sketches to make the reader aware of the relative normalcy of the absurd and brutal events, while Najera studies a wider range of narrative techniques. In addition to examining Campobello's language, syntax, and imagery, Najera identifies some techniques associated specifically with the modern novel. Najera also examines Campobello's place in Mexican and Latin American literature.

Dennis Parle's 1985 article concentrates on narrative technique in *Cartucho*, including its multiple points of view and its poetic style and imagery. Doris Meyer's article on *Las manos de Mamá* that same year points out the novel's status as a nontraditional feminist text, tracing the author's textual transformation from dependent to independent being in the portrayal of her relationship with her mother.

To date, critics have focused largely on the child's perspective on violence in *Cartucho* and on specific stylistic elements in Campobello's work, such as her use of short choppy sentences. De Beer acknowledges that Campobello's apparent stylistic simplicity is deceptive, but the nature and evolution of her complex narrative strategies have yet to be explored in any depth. There is also a scarcity of criticism that takes into account the possible impact of her gender on her writing. The fragmentary character of the two novels closely corresponds to the kind of writing often engaged in by women who in their letters, diaries, and other forms of discourse find themselves piecing together small narrative units to create an elaborately intertwined network of meaning. Yet, other than Doris Meyer's studies of her early poetry and of *Las manos de Mamá*, there has been no effort to investigate Campobello's writing from a feminist perspective.

BIBLIOGRAPHY

Works by Nellie Campobello

!Yo! por Francisca. Mexico City: Ediciones LIDN, 1929.
Cartucho. Relatos de la lucha en el norte de Mexico. 1st ed. Jalapa: Ediciones Integrales, 1931. 2d ed. Mexico City: EDIAPSA Iberoamericana de Publicaciones, 1940.
Las manos de Mamá. Mexico City: Editorial Juventudes de Izquierda, 1937, 2d ed. Mexico City: Editorial Villa Ocampo, 1949.
Apuntes sobre la vida militar de Francisco Villa. Mexico City: EDIAPSA, 1940.
Ritmos indígenas de México, with Gloria Campobello. Mexico City:n.p., 1941.
Tres poemas. Mexico City: Compañía General de Ediciones, 1957.
Mis libros. Mexico City: Compañía General de Ediciones, 1960.

Translations of Nellie Campobello

Meyer, Doris, and Irene Matthews, trans. *Cartucho and My Mother's Hands*. Austin: University of Texas Press, 1988.

Works about Nellie Campobello

Carballo, Emmanuel. "Interview with Nellie Campobello." *Diecinueve protagonistas de la literatura mexicana del siglo XX*. Mexico City: Empresas Editoriales, 1965. Pp. 327–38.

De Beer, Gabriella. "Nellie Campobello, Escritora de la Revolución Mexicana." *Cuadernos Americanos* 223 (1979):212–19.

———"Nellie Campobello's Vision of the Mexican Revolution." *The American Hispanist* 4 (Mar.–Apr. 1979):34–35.

Keller, Gary D. "El niño en la Revolución Mexicana: Nellie Campobello, Andrés Iduarte y Cesar Garizurieta." *Cuadernos Americanos* 170 (1970):142–51.

Meyer, Doris. "Divided Against Herself: The Early Poetry of Nellie Campobello." *Revista de Estudios Hispánicos* 20, 2 (May 1986):51–63.

———"Nellie Campobello's *Las manos de Mamá*: A Rereading." *Hispania* 68 (Dec. 1985):747–52.

Miller, Beth, and Alfonso Gonsález, eds. "Guillermina Bravo." "Elena Poniatowska." *26 autoras del México actual*, Mexico City: Costa-Amic, 1978. Pp. 27–42, 301–21.

Najera, Valeska Strickland. "La obra de Nellie Campobello." Ph.D. Diss. Northwestern University, 1980. (DAI 41 [1980]:2626A.)

Parle, Dennis J. "Narrative Style and Technique in Nellie Campobello's *Cartucho*." *Kentucky Romance Quarterly* 32 (1985):201–11.

Poniatowska, Elena. "Introduction." *Cartucho and My Mother's Hands*. By Nellie Campobello. Trans. by Doris Meyer and Irene Matthews. Austin: University of Texas Press, 1988. Pp. vii–xiv.

Verlinger, Dale E. "Nellie Campobello: Romantic Revolutionary and Mexican Realist," *Latin American Women Writers: Yesterday and Today*. Eds. Yvette E. Miller and Charles M. Tatum. Pittsburgh, Pa.: Latin American Literary Review, 1977. Pp. 98–103.

JULIETA CAMPOS
(b. 1932)
Cuba, Mexico

María-Inés Lagos-Pope
Translated by Gabriela Mahn

BIOGRAPHY

Julieta Campos was born in 1932 in Havana, Cuba, where she obtained her doctoral degree in literature. On a scholarship from the Alliance Française she studied at the Sorbonne, earning a certificate in contemporary French literature. In Paris she married the Mexican political scientist Enrique González Pedrero in 1954 and became a Mexican citizen. She has a son, Emiliano, and has resided in Mexico since 1955. Julieta Campos has written works of fiction and criticism, translated about thirty-eight books, and collaborated in journals and cultural supplements, such as *La Cultura en México* and *Plural*, edited by Octavio Paz. In 1965 she published a collection of critical essays on European, American, and Spanish American literature entitled *La imagen en el espejo* (The image in the mirror). *Muerte por agua* (Death by water), her first novel, appeared that same year. In 1967 she obtained a grant from the Sociedad Mexicana de Escritores to work on *Celina o los gatos* (Celina or the cats) which was published in 1968. In 1971 she published *Oficio de leer* (On reading), a collection of forty-six book reviews, and in 1973 *Función de la novela* (The novel's role), a book on literary criticism in which the author reflects on the novel, the nature of fiction, and the relationship between writing and the writer.

In 1974 Campos received the prestigious Xavier Villaurrutia Prize for her novel *Tiene los cabellos rojizos y se llama Sabina* (Her hair is red and her name is Sabina). Since 1977 she has been on the editorial board of *Vuelta*. In 1979 she published a work of fiction—she does not call it a novel—*El miedo de perder a Eurídice* (The fear of losing Eurydice). She has been professor of literature and editor of the *Revista de la Universidad de México*, and in 1978 she was president of the Pen Club of Mexico. She has traveled extensively in Europe and in the Americas, and has attended conferences on women's literature in California and Canada. She considers herself a member of the generation of Mexican writers born between 1930 and 1935. In her opinion what brings them together is not just age, but the shared belief that the text has a logic of its own, independent from the world of historic causality.

In 1982 her husband was elected governor of the state of Tabasco, Mexico, for a six-year term, and since then she has spent time both in Villahermosa, Tabasco, and Mexico City. Her latest book of literary criticism, *La herencia obstinada, Análisis de cuentos nahuas* (Persistent heritage, Analysis of Nahuatl tales), published in 1982, reveals a shift in her intellectual pursuits. The author seems to be moving away from an exclusive European-centered perspective, a change that can also be observed in terms of her creative work. She is planning to write a traditional novel that chronicles the life of a Cuban family from the nineteenth century to the present.

MAJOR THEMES

Julieta Campos's narrative is characterized both by its emphasis on interiority and by the awareness of the fictional nature of the literary text which, as a verbal construct, presents a world image dependent on the vision of the observer and on the choice of narrative method. Her first two works of fiction, *Muerte por agua* (1965) and *Celina o los gatos* (1968), are explorations of the inner world of the characters in enclosed spaces. In her novels *Tiene los cabellos rojizos y se llama Sabina* (1974) and *El miedo de perder a Eurídice* (1979), her main concern is the fictional nature of the story, where the narrator/text/reader relationship is constantly at issue. The defining characteristic of these two novels is the metafictional nature of a self-reflexive narrative that establishes a dialogue with texts from different periods and cultures. In Julieta Campos's work, this intertextual process takes place at two levels. First, as a scholar of contemporary literature and because of her vast knowledge of European, American, and Latin American literatures, Campos writes critical essays that show great sensibility and intelligence in the analysis of texts. Second, her narrative works are simultaneously a theoretical insight into the writing process and a praxis of those theories. Thus, her interest in the theoretical problems that the novel and works of art in general pose are also the themes of her writing.

In reflecting on Campos's fiction we are, by necessity, led to review her critical essays where we find the key to her concerns as a writer. *La imagen en el espejo* (1965), her first book of criticism, is a collection of articles published between 1958 and 1964 in several journals. The book is divided into three sections. The first contains essays on Virginia Woolf, Malcolm Lowry, Nathalie Sarraute, Michael Butor, and Alain Robbe-Grillet, authors for whom Campos shows a special affinity in her fiction. The final essay in this section, "La imagen en el espejo," represents a synthesis of her aesthetic position. This article is very helpful in the study of her work; here she discusses matters that will later appear in her fiction. The second section deals with François Mauriac, Ernest Hemingway, and Simone de Beauvoir, writers who use narrative elements in a traditional way. The third section is devoted to three Latin American authors, Alejo Carpentier, Juan Rulfo, and Agustín Yáñez.

Campos suggests that art is a way of knowing, which helps illuminate human experience. Its role is to discover and name aspects of the world that have not been made explicit by other means. The artist does not carry out this task by representing exactly what he or she observes in reality. Rather, through a process of transfiguration, he or she produces an image of a world that functions on the basis of its own principles and is parallel to historical reality. Campos shows an affinity for the authors she writes about, and particularly for those studied in the first part of her book. She prefers the lyric novel, and, for this reason, she is attracted to the works of Virginia Woolf—whose narrative highlights interiority while avoiding external descriptions—and to those where there is an underground current, such as in the fiction of Joyce, Proust, and Sarraute.

In "La imagen en el espejo" (1964), the essay from which the collection takes its title, Campos elaborates on ideas about the novel that function as a theoretical basis for contemporary fiction and for her own writing. When Campos refers to the main characteristics of twentieth-century narrative, stating that authors place an emphasis on subjectivity and on the creation of new temporal dimensions, disregarding linear time, external descriptions, plot, and intrigue, she is describing her own fiction. She points to the fact that the omniscient narrator of the nineteenth century who saw his characters from the outside has changed, as has the idea of a character conceived as a "well articulated, coherent figure" (p. 78). In the contemporary novel, on the other hand, there are no connecting threads, no stories to tell; there is no progression toward anything. There is only "a world where things happen before they happen, or where nothing happens, where nothing escapes an unavoidable and unsolvable present" (p. 79). The author refers, with admiration, to Claude Mauriac's *L'agrandissement* (1963; The enlargement), a novel in which its creator, just as the Spanish painters Velázquez in *Las Meninas* (1956) or Picasso in *Carnets de La Californie* (1955; Notebooks from "La Californie"), places himself in his work as an additional subject watching himself at the time of creation. In her 1978 novel *Tiene los cabellos rojizos y se llama Sabina*, Campos further develops the theme of the relationship between the artist and his work. This novel synthesizes the aesthetic preoccupations of the author, in that the story that is told is not separate from the narrative process itself. Campos describes this type of novel saying that it is like the x-ray of a novel that allows the reader to glimpse the secrets of its composition by revealing its inner mechanisms. The author becomes "one more object in a world that can be observed from the outside by a spectator capable of observing the world he has created within the world" (p. 90). These remarks aptly describe Campos's last two novels.

In her book *Función de la novela* (1973), Campos further elaborates on her reflections about the nature of fiction. Art plays a significant role in the individual's life, for "once the work of art is finished, it seems as necessary as reality itself and an even more real reality spins off from its totality, from its roundness" (p. 15). For Campos, art is the means by which the writer explains to herself an incoherent and fragmented reality that she confronts daily. By tying loose ends and inscribing in the literary text what has remained untold in the story of life, writing preserves what could have been lost and imposes a unity on the writer's life. These thoughts clarify the role of the narrator's confession in "Celina o los gatos" as he tries to explain to himself, through writing, his married life and the reasons for his failure.

In addition to treating the general problems of the writer and those of the nature of literary discourse, Julieta Campos makes reference to women's issues. On one hand, she shows admiration for the writing of Virginia Woolf and Nathalie Sarraute by preferring inner spaces and fragmented dialogues. She believes in the androgynous nature of writing, and in her narrative discourse she utilizes both male and female points of view. On the other hand, in her essays, and particularly in the one devoted to Simone de Beauvoir in *La imagen en el espejo*, and in interviews, she addresses matters pertaining to women's condition. She believes that, at some point in their development, women writers must confront this problem. According to Campos, one of woman's problems is that "she tends to succumb to the temptation of indifference; to regard the course of life as if it were something that did not affect her personally, something where she could not make a difference. It could be said that a woman must solve two issues, that of her condition as woman and that of her condition as human being" (p. 113). Another factor that influences a woman's life rests on her being directed to express herself through her husband, delegating to him all social responsibilities, while she confines herself to procreating life in a mechanical way, without producing anything that will give her a meaningful existence. Campos agrees with Simone de Beauvoir that, when a woman "does not get involved in life she is not a complete human being" (p. 115). In "Celina o los gatos," Campos deals with the problem of a woman who, as a wife, gets involved in her husband's professional life. Once she distances herself from his world, she realizes that her life as a socialite is also not a solution to enable her to discover her own worth as a human being.

Julieta Campos stated in a 1976 interview with Evelyn Picon Garfield and published in 1985 that her mother's death in Cuba was the decisive factor that led her to express herself as a writer. In her first novel, *Muerte por agua*, she dramatizes the lack of communication between the characters—Eloísa, Laura, and Andrés, mother, daughter, and the daughter's husband, respectively—who live in the old family house in a city by the sea where it always rains. Although they love and respect each other, they keep most of their deep inner thoughts to themselves. Their utterances mostly refer to daily routines or remarks about the weather. But this apparently dull conversation makes them feel safe, since by keeping their true feelings to themselves they cannot hurt each other. As it rains outside, the two women remain in the enclosed and protective house devoted to their domestic duties, while Laura's husband goes out to work. Keeping in line with Campos's preferences as expressed in her critical essays, this novel does not tell a story in the traditional way, but rather portrays the inner world of the characters who, trapped by the rain, take refuge in a private space. The women's world, revolving around the house and repetitive daily routines, is characterized by silence. The text presents two parallel worlds that do not come in contact with each other. One is that of the private thoughts of each character, and the other is that of external gestures, those aspects that the characters decide to reveal about themselves.

The mother/daughter relationship, though affectionate, is not an open one; on the contrary, they do not tell each other what they think for fear of offending. Laura, the daughter, is constantly aware of her own gestures, of what she manifests or externalizes. At times, the household chores they perform together become an exercise in creating façades lacking in spontaneity. Although both the rain and their house-bound existence thrust the women toward each other, enclosing them in the safe world of home, an environment that would facilitate a dialogue, in reality that physical closeness emphasizes their isolation, created in part by the sterility of their verbal exchanges. Nevertheless, there are moments in which the characters come close and enjoy themselves by doing something together. For instance, the women take much pleasure when they decide, without consulting Andrés, to use their elegant china, silverware, and good linen for that evening's dinner; later on, the three of them, at Andrés's suggestion, play a traditional card game.

The emphasis on the insignificance of the dialogue and on the barriers that the characters put up to avoid honest communication underlines the distance that the women create between themselves in order to be able to protect their own private worlds. A moving episode takes place when Laura decides that she is going to go out for a walk. She tells her mother of her intentions, and the mother thinks how wonderful it would be to have the house all to herself, even though she is not going to do anything in particular. She just wants to feel a sense of freedom and relaxation by being all alone in the house. But Laura keeps delaying her departure, until finally the mother's secret hopes are disappointed when her daughter decides not to go out at all. The interaction between mother and daughter, the focus of this narrative, is an infrequent theme in Latin American literature. Female writers in general have avoided this taboo subject matter probably because of self-censorship, since many times the exploration of the mother/daughter relationship produces a negative, or at least critical, image of the mother. By inference from what can be observed in the case of other women writers, there is nothing unusual in the fact that only after her mother's death was Campos able to verbalize the frustration of not having had a more open and intimate relationship with her mother.

Celina o los gatos, Campos's second work of fiction, is a collection of five narratives preceded by an introduction in which the author deals with the history of the cat in Western culture. Campos points out that the way this animal is regarded has changed radically in modern times. From being considered a maleficent and diabolical creature in the Bible, it has come to represent freedom and the depths of being. The first story in the collection is closely related to the introduction. This story focuses on the disintegration of a marriage. In this text, the reader confronts two facts that might seem surprising, considering that we are dealing with a female writer. On one hand, already in the title the female character is identified with cats, mysterious creatures traditionally associated with evil; on the other hand, the narrator is the husband. Thus, although Celina apparently is the central figure in the narrative, it turns out that the main character is the husband, who writes his own version of his relationship with Celina.

The narrator manipulates the narrative, and his confession is characterized by his desire to be precise in his attempt to give coherence to the story of his relationship. The narrator seems to want to discard certain emotions and make it seem that he has been in control of the situation at all times. However, there are signs of ambiguity, vagueness, and lack of control that escape him as he reveals superstitious or irrational reactions. Through his writing, the narrator rationalizes his role in the death of his wife, whom he discovers after she committed suicide. He recognizes his feeling of guilt for having contributed to bringing about her death. He seems to be writing this confession for himself in order to place the events into perspective and explain his own behavior to himself. On one hand, he seeks justification, and on the other, he wants to gain the compassion and understanding of an ideal reader. The narrator fears that his own writing might incriminate him and that his text might become a criminal confession. Although his discourse is characterized by his efforts at being eminently logocentric, as the narrative progresses, we become aware of his inability to maintain that degree of control he had intended as he began his self-analysis. The reader realizes, at the conclusion of the reading, that the narrator has manipulated his information in order to get the reader to trust his discourse. The narrator refuses to accept the split, many-sided, and incongruent self that he has discovered within himself due to his upbringing in a social system that regards the individual as an integrated and unequivocal whole, conditioned by power structures that insure the system's continuity.

In this story the house is again the space where the female character moves. The physician-husband moves within several spaces: the outer space of the world of work, the private space of the houses he has shared with Celina, and his own apartment where he takes refuge when the relationship with his wife begins to deteriorate, while Celina participates only in the private sphere. Since Celina does not have a career, she experiences vicariously her husband's professional life. When she tries to become independent, an action manifested with the purchase of her own house, she directs all her efforts to her social activities. When those activities fail to fulfill her, she abandons them and takes refuge in her private world in the company of her childhood nanny and her oriental cats. Her subsequent suicide suggests two things: First, beneath her apparent happiness lay a profound dissatisfaction; second, seclusion, in the absence of a social projection, leads to death. The image of woman projected by the story corresponds to the view Campos presents in *La imagen en el espejo*, which is that marriage and family life are not enough for a woman to feel fulfilled. Furthermore, as long as woman lives on someone else's terms, she will not be able to be a whole person. The narrator's confession shows that in social relationships the behavior of the man, as well as that of the woman, is greatly influenced by external demands, by social prescriptions that will not allow them to avoid certain patterns of behavior. While for men, the possibility of establishing intimate relationships and expressing irrational ideas seems to be hindered, women are allowed to live like cats. They can lock themselves in the house and forget about the outside world. Although in this text Celina's character represents the traditional woman as seen through the eyes of a man who reads and writes Celina (as has been a practice throughout history), the narrator's confession shows that traditional strategies in the hands of a female writer can produce a subversive text. It also shows that in the relationship between men and women, both play the role of victims and executioners at the same time.

The next three stories, "El bautizo" (Baptism), "Todas las rosas" (All the roses), and "La casa" (The house) are told from the point of view of a female character. In "El bautizo," Natalia, a girl who still plays with dolls, is about to celebrate the baptism of her doll Michel. The narrative tells of her thoughts and ruminations, suggesting that Natalia's childhood is coming to an end. The sense of security she has experienced in the enclosed and protected environment of her family's house is being replaced, in her fantasies, by the instability that characterizes the adult world. Aurelia, the protagonist of "Todas las rosas," has lived in seclusion for many years. Obsessed by the past, especially by a day in which she must have had a shocking experience that, apparently, has left her insane, she is constantly searching for an answer that may allow her to be at peace with herself. In "La casa" the narrator reminisces about family scenes in the old ancestral house in Havana, inscribing in her text the sparkles of life that remain in her memory. The last narrative in the volume, "La ciudad," presents the narrator's impressions of the city of Havana in a sort of collage that brings together her own recollections and descriptions made by other Cuban writers. Campos inserts in the narrative texts by Cirilo Villaverde, Alejo Carpentier, Guillermo Cabrera Infante, and José Lezama Lima that refer to the city of Havana, and also passages from her novel *Muerte por agua*. Thus, she indicates that there are many ways of looking at the city and that the portrait her text offers is but one more. She recognizes that, although language appears to be insufficient to express the experience of life in the city, words are one of the means available. With her text she shows that, in spite of her own efforts and those of her predecessors, many aspects of the human experience inevitably remain silent.

In 1974 Campos published *Tiene los cabellos rojizos y se llama Sabina*. In this novel, a woman gazes at the ocean in Acapulco from a room called *El mirador* (watchtower room), at four o'clock in the afternoon. At that point she is about to leave the resort after her week's vacation has come to an end. The woman is trying to write a novel in which a woman gazes at the ocean in Acapulco at four o'clock in the afternoon of the day she will leave the resort where she has spent a week's vacation. The woman acts simultaneously as the character in her novel and as the person who narrates. She is not the only narrator, however; there is also a male narrator found in another room located directly above hers and called *El laberinto* (labyrinth room). This narrator is also gazing at the ocean but, since he is higher up, he does not have the same field of vision as the woman. In addition to being confronted with the reactions of both the female and male narrators, the reader is confronted with the conversations of other hotel guests. This suggests the presence of an implied narrator who seems to be superimposed over the two narrators mentioned above.

The presence of the two narrators indicates the possibility of two different types of writing. While in "Celina o los gatos" it was the male narrator who wrote the story of his relationship with his wife, in this novel the point of view of the female narrator takes precedence. She dominates the narrative in spite of the existence of a parallel male narrator. From *El laberinto* the male narrator intends to write a traditional story in the style of Truman Capote's *In Cold Blood*. Here, a marginal female character with the characteristics traditionally attributed to women appears. This character is based on the woman from *El mirador*, whom the narrator has seen in the hotel. The male narrator represents the type of logocentric writing that emphasizes the solving of a puzzle, whether it be a crime or a labyrinth, and regards women as passive. The female narrator from *El mirador*, on the other hand, in gazing at the ocean contemplates herself. She sees herself in her double role, as narrator and as character who looks at a knoll in the ocean. The hint of a possible suicide or crime brings the two narrative streams close to each other. Perhaps the female narrator will put an end to her life or will be victim of a crime. Since we are dealing with an open-ended work that might continue *ad infinitum*, the mysterious news of a crime that took place that same afternoon, in that place, and is read in the newspapers later on, remains unsolved.

Although there is a lack of temporal progression in this novel, where the whole so-called action takes place in a matter of a few moments, as the character gazes at the ocean for the last time, the narrative moves with grace and agility. The text reflects on itself, stressing the fact that it is a verbal construct. At the same time, by continually making allusions to other self-reflective works that function as subtexts and counterpoint, such as Claude Mauriac's *L'agrandissement*, Nathalie Sarraute's *Les fruits d'or* (Golden Fruits), Salvador Elizondo's *El hipogeo secreto* (The Secret Catacombs), and Marcel Proust's *A la recherche du temps perdu* (Remembrance of Things Past) among others, Campos reminds the reader that her novel exists in the context of an intertextual dialogue with other literary creations. Just as in the novels mentioned above, and in the painting by Velázquez referred to by Campos in her essay "La imagen en el espejo," we are dealing with a text about the creative process in which the artist sees herself at the moment of creation and allows the reader to be a witness to that process.

In *El miedo de perder a Eurídice*, published in 1979, Julieta Campos develops ideas similar to those she had dealt with in her previous novel. Here we also find a narrator engaged in the writing of a novel, the text we read, and in theorizing about the process. The narrator, Monsieur N., a French teacher at a language institute in a Spanish American country, is sitting in a café called "Minos Palace" where he grades his students' assignments, translations of works by Jules Verne. At the same time, he draws an island on a paper napkin and begins to write a novel in a notebook labeled "Rough Draft." In that novel he tells two parallel stories, that of a couple of lovers who meet in a park to attend a fair at the island on the lake, and that of a pair of castaways who, like Robinson Crusoe, find themselves on a deserted island. The main feature of the text the teacher is writing in his notebook is that it is written on a narrow column, which differentiates it from the rest. Furthermore, the novel Monsieur N. writes carries on a dialogue, with quotations of various literatures of different periods inserted besides the column. The intertextual network thus established suggests that the experience the narrator tries to evoke is nothing new or unique, but rather a universal one.

In his attempt to write his version of a love story on the island, the narrator is giving personal coherence to a story that has been repeated many times throughout the history of humanity. He is an exile who, frustrated by his experience in the tropics, would like to return to France, his native land. Similar to the teacher in Rulfo's "Luvina," Monsieur N. talks to himself, observes the regular customers in the café, and makes up stories that will help him integrate his own experiences with those of others, those he dreams and those he lives, in an attempt to recover paradise, Utopian love, and immortality. The fragmentary nature of the novel produces a multifaceted world. Presented in counterpoint are the texts of the narrator who writes a novel, the possible subtexts, and the text of the implied narrator who may or may not be Monsieur N. himself. The frequent cuts and interruptions emphasize the search for a Utopia that is constantly out of reach.

During the last few years Julieta Campos's preoccupations seem to have taken a new turn, as her latest book of criticism shows. Her interest in the theoretical problems of the contemporary novel has given way to a concern for the preservation and study of the Indian oral narrative tradition of her adopted country. In *La herencia obstinada* (1982), Campos examines a collection of eighteen Nahuatl chronicles from the Mecayapan area of southern Mexico. Her analysis is based on psychoanalysis and on the anthropological theories of Claude Lévi-Strauss. Campos demonstrates that, as in other traditions, there are motifs that become constants, such as the patterns of loss/retrieval, and culture/nature, and the pleasure principle. She also indicates that the Indian vision that these chronicles reveal contains, in its complexity, contradictions common to all human beings. Campos's statement that her next novel will be a traditional one, where she tells the story of a Cuban family from the nineteenth century to the present, suggests her intellectual vitality and her desire for self-renewal.

SURVEY OF CRITICISM

The bibliography on the works by Julieta Campos indicates that, although all of her works have been reviewed in important publications in Mexico, her novel *Tiene los cabellos rojizos y se llama Sabina* has attracted the most critical attention. Hugo Verani's 1976 article in *Texto Crítico* was the first extensive review of her work. Verani points to *Muerte por agua* and *Sabina* in particular as he examines them within the context of the new European novel and the writer's critical thought. Verani states that the originality of these novels does not rest on the subject matter, but rather on their narrative form and literary formulation. The review articles by Martha Paley Francescato and Evelyn Picon Garfield on *Sabina*, as well as the interviews conducted by Picon Garfield and Beth Miller, are important contributions to the study of this writer.

In his perceptive article "Julieta Campos' *Sabina*: In the Labyrinth of Intertextuality" (1984), Juan Bruce-Novoa highlights two significant aspects of this novel. First, Campos introduces the feminine point of view in a type of literary discourse utilized predominantly by men until now. In doing so she rejects logocentric models in order to present a different perspective. This new model corresponds to the point of view of the woman in *El mirador*. Second, in establishing intertextual relationships between Campos's novel and a series of five novels by Anaïs Nin published between 1959 and 1961 (her source of inspiration for the creation of her character Sabina), Bruce-Novoa shows that, with regard to feminine discourse, Julieta Campos's originality rests on her development of the point of view offered by Nin. By using Harold Bloom's concept of *Tessera*, the critic concludes that Campos perfects the work of her forerunners Anaïs Nin, Virginia Woolf, and Nathalie Sarraute.

In an issue of *Revista Iberoamericana* (1985) devoted to female writers, Victorio Agüera examines Campos's novel as feminine discourse from the point of view of the unfolding of Sabina's character, taking as point of departure Lacan's theories. Alicia Rivero Potter (1985) also writes a clear and perceptive essay on this same novel from the point of view of feminine creativity. She establishes the complexity of the relationship between the implied narrator, the narrators, and Campos's desire to explore what is feminine in her fiction and in the world.

In reviewing the critical essays on Julieta Campos's work, we see that, from the beginning, her worth as a writer and as an intellectual has been recognized. However, her creative work has only recently begun to be analyzed seriously. There is much to be done, particularly in regard to her early works.

BIBLIOGRAPHY

Works by Julieta Campos

La imagen en el espejo. Mexico City: Universidad Autónoma de México, 1965.
Muerte por agua. Mexico City: Fondo de Cultura Económica, 1965.
Celina o los gatos. Mexico City: Siglo XXI Editores, 1968.
Oficio de leer. Mexico City: Tezontle, 1971.
Función de la novela. Mexico City: Joaquín Mortiz, 1973.
Tiene los cabellos rojizos y se llama Sabina. Mexico City: Joaquín Mortiz, 1974.
"Historia de un naufragio." *Plural* (May 1976).
"Celina o los gatos." Reprinted in *Cuentistas mexicanas siglo XX.* Ed. Aurora M.
   Ocampo. Mexico City: Universidad Nacional Autónoma de México, 1976.
   Pp. 247–67.
"Literatura y política: ¿relación o incompatibilidad?" *Texto Crítico* 4 (1976):7–9.
"¿Tiene sexo la escritura?" *Vuelta* 21 (Aug. 1978):44–45.
El miedo de perder a Eurídice. Mexico City: Joaquín Mortiz, 1979.
La herencia obstinada. Análisis de cuentos nahuas. Mexico City: Fondo de Cultura
   Económica, 1982.
"Mi vocación literaria." *Revista Iberoamericana* 51, 132–33 (1985):467–70.

Works in Anthologies

"Celina o los gatos." *Cuentistas mexicanas: Siglo XX.* Ed. Aurora M. Ocampo. Mexico
   City: Universidad Nacional Autónoma de México, 1976. Pp. 247–67.
"La casa," from *Celina o los gatos. Puerta Abierta.* Eds. Caridad Silva-Velázquez and
   Nora Erro-Orthmann. Mexico City: Joaquín Mortiz, 1986. Pp. 59–74.

Works about Julieta Campos

Agüera, Victorio G. "El discurso de lo imaginario en *Tiene los cabellos rojizos y se
   llama Sabina.*" *Revista Iberoamericana* 51, 132–33 (1985):531–37.
Avilés Fabila, René. *El escritor y sus problemas.* Mexico City: Fondo de Cultura Econ-
   ómica, 1975. Pp. 78–84.
Bradu, Fabienne. "Julieta Campos: La cartografía del deseo y de la muerte." *Vuelta*
   (Mexico) 11, 128 (July 1987):42–46.
Bruce-Novoa, Juan. "La Sabina' de Julieta Campos, en el laberinto de la intertext-
   ualidad." *La sartén por el mango.* Eds. Patricia González and Eliana Ortega. Río
   Piedras, P.R.: Ediciones Huracán, 1984. Pp. 83–109. This article appeared in
   English as: "Julieta Campos' *Sabina*: In the Labyrinth of Intertextuality." *Third
   Woman* 2, 2 (1984):43–63.
Francescato, Martha Paley. "Un desafío a la crítica literaria: *Tiene los cabellos rojizos
   y se llama Sabina.*" *Revista de Crítica Literaria Latinoamericana* 7, 13
   (1981):121–25.
Garfield, Evelyn Picon. "Review of *Tiene los cabellos rojizos y se llama Sabina.*" *Revista
   Iberoamericana* 112–13 (1980):680–83.
———. "*Tiene los cabellos rojizos y se llama Sabina*, de Julieta Campos. 'Una caída
   interminable en la inmovilidad.' " *ECO* 248 (June 1982):172–91.

————. *Women's Voices from Latin America: Interviews with Six Contemporary Authors.* Detroit: Wayne State University Press, 1985. Pp. 73–96.

Glantz, Margo. "Entre lutos y gatos: José Agustín y Julieta Campos." *Repeticiones: Ensayos sobre literatura mexicana.* Xalapa: Universidad Veracruzana, 1979. Pp. 72–74.

Jitrik, Noé. "La palpitación de un proyecto: Notas sobre textos de Julieta Campos." *La vibración del presente: Trabajos críticos y ensayos sobre textos y escritores latinoamericanos.* Mexico City: Fondo de Cultura Económica, 1987. Pp. 141–55.

Lagos-Pope, Maria-Inés. "Cat/Logos: The Narrator's Confession in Julieta Campos' 'Celina o los gatos' (Celina or the Cats)." *Splintering Darkness: Latin American Women Writers in Search of Themselves.* Eds. Lucía Guerra-Cunningham and Yvette Miller. Pittsburgh: Latin American Literary Review Press, 1990.

Martínez, Martha. "Julieta Campos o la interiorización de lo cubano." *Revista Iberoamericana* 51, 132–33 (1985):793–97.

Miller, Beth and Alfonso González, eds. "Julieta Campos" Interview. *26 autoras del México actual.* Mexico City: Costa-Amic Editor, 1978. Pp. 79–93.

Ocampo de Gómez, Aurora M., and Ernesto Prado Velázquez. *Diccionario de escritores mexicanos.* Mexico City: Universidad Nacional Autónoma de México, 1967. P. 56.

Rivero Potter, Alicia. "La creación literaria en Julieta Campos: *Tiene los cabellos rojizos y se llama Sabina.*" *Revista Iberoamericana* 51, 132–33 (1985):899–907.

Verani, Hugo J. "Julieta Campos y la novela del lenguaje." *Texto Crítico* 2, 5 (1976):132–49.

ROSARIO CASTELLANOS (1925–1974)
Mexico

Maureen Ahern

BIOGRAPHY

Rosario Castellanos was born in Mexico City on May 25, 1925, the first child of Adriana Figueroa and César Castellanos, who returned to their native Chiapas when she was a year old. She grew up on the family ranch on the Jataté River near the Guatemalan border, and later in the town of Comitan, Chiapas. This was a region of centuries-old conflicts between the Chamula Indians and the landholding families, privileged for generations by class, race, and language. Castellanos's earliest years were marked by solitude, death, and parental rejection, themes that dominate her early poetry and prose. The sudden death of her younger brother, who was her parents' favorite, sharpened their rejection of her. In 1941, when the land reform program launched by President Lázaro Cárdenas stripped the provincial elite of their properties, the Castellanos family moved to Mexico City.

In 1944 Castellanos enrolled in the College of Philosophy and Letters at the National University of Mexico, where she joined the group of young Mexican, Guatemalan, and Nicaraguan writers who have become known as the Generation of 1950. They included Emilio Carballido, Luisa Josefina Hernández, Dolores Castro, Jaime Sabines, Ernesto Cardenal, Ernesto Mejía Sánchez, Augusto Monterroso, and others. Most of her earliest writing was published in *América, Revista Antológica*, which was directed by the group's mentor, Efrén Hernández. The death of her parents within a month of each other in 1948 and the experience of reading José Gorostiza's vanguard poem, *Muerte Sin Fin* (Death without end), resulted in the publication of her first long poems, *Trayectoria del polvo* (1948; Trajectory of dust) and *Apuntes para una declaración de re* (1948; Notes for a declaration of faith). It also brought her the freedom she sought to manage her own life and to dedicate herself professionally to literature, she later reflected in an interview (*Confrontaciones: Los Narradores ante el público*, p. 89). Her thesis, *Sobre cultura femenina* (On feminine culture), which she defended in 1950 for the Master of Arts degree in Philosophy, initiated her lifelong inquiry into the question of women's place in culture. That same year, study and travel in Europe brought Castellanos into direct contact with the writings of Simone de Beauvoir, Simone Weil, and Virginia Woolf, the three intellectual mentors who stimulated the development of her thinking in the decade that followed.

At the end of 1951, Castellanos began work as director of cultural programs for the state of Chiapas. In 1953 the Mexican Writers Center awarded her a grant to conduct research on the contribution of women to Mexican culture. The following year another fellowship enabled her to develop her first novel, *Balún-Canán* (1957; *The Nine Guardians*, 1958), which earned her the Mexican Critics' award for the best novel of 1957 and the Chiapas Prize in 1958. In 1956 Castellanos directed the puppet theater, *El Teatro Petul* for the National Indigenist Institute in San Cristóbal de las Casas. For two years the troupe traveled to remote areas of Chiapas, affording the young writer direct contact with the rich Indian cultures of her native region and the chance to write her second novel, *Oficio de tinieblas* (1962; Rites of darkness). When she returned to Mexico City, she continued to work with the Indigenist Institute in the preparation of textbooks for Indian children.

In January 1957 when Castellanos was thirty-two years old, she married Ricardo Guerra, a professor of philosophy at the University of Mexico. It was a difficult marriage which she soon came to perceive as a lonely failure. There were two miscarriages prior to the birth of her son, Gabriel Guerra Castellanos, in 1961, and eventually she obtained a divorce. The poems in *Lívida luz: poemas* (1960; Livid light) and *Materia memorable* (1969; Memorable matter) reflect those experiences of grief, solitude, and rejection.

From 1960 to 1966, Castellanos was press and information director for the National University of Mexico where she also taught courses in comparative literature. In 1963 she began to write short essays for the weekly cultural supplements of several Mexico City newspapers, which were later partly collected in her four volumes of essays. Castellanos held visiting professorships in Latin American literature at the Universities of Wisconsin, Indiana, and Colorado in 1967. This period of her stay in the United States coincided with the commemoration of the fiftieth anniversary of women's suffrage in this country and major demonstrations by the women's liberation movement, events that galvanized Castellanos's thinking. She returned to Mexico to accept a chair of comparative literature at the National University, and also began writing her weekly column for *Excélsior*.

The year 1971 marked the publication of four stories in *Album de familia* (Family album), the essays in *Mujer que sabe latín* . . . (A woman who knows Latin), and the compilation of her collected poems. That same year President Luis Echeverría named her Mexican ambassador to Israel, where she became a very popular and successful diplomat. She also taught seminars on contemporary Mexican literature at the Hebrew University in Jerusalem. In Israel, Rosario Castellanos was free to develop her experimental play, *El eterno femenino* (1975; "The Eternal Feminine") and her best essays about women's cultural issues. Those three years that she and Gabriel lived in Israel were among the happiest and most productive she had ever known. "That's why the accident that killed her was so absurd," Elena Poniatowska* concluded (p. 131).

On August 7, 1974, Rosario Castellanos was electrocuted in her home in Tel Aviv when she turned on a lamp in her living room after stepping out of the shower. A servant found her unconscious, but she died alone in the ambulance before it reached the hospital. She was forty-nine years old. Mexico paid tribute to her at a state funeral in Mexico City, where she is buried at the Rotunda de los Hombres Ilustres (the Tomb of National Heroes). Two collections of essays, *El uso de la palabra* (1974; The right to speak) and *El mar y sus pescaditos* (1975; All the fish in the sea), and the new play were published posthumously in 1974 and 1975.

MAJOR THEMES

Rosario Castellanos used explicit female imagery and domestic experiences to create prose and poetry that speak as a woman, to and about other women. As journalist and professor, she bridged the gap between Mexican culture and her private world. In Rosario Castellanos's prose and poetry, the roles of "woman" and "writer" meet textually and ideologically.

An index to the development of Castellanos's major themes can be found in the hundreds of essays that she wrote for *Novedades, ¡Siempre!, Excélsior*, and other Mexican periodicals during the period 1960–1974. In addition, they are aesthetic creations in their own right. In *Juicios sumarios* (1966; Summary judgments), Castellanos began to develop her ideas about cultural ideology and gender through her readings of her intellectual mentors, Simone de Beauvoir, Simone Weil, and Virginia Woolf. Their role in the development of Castellanos's feminist ideology is evident in her commentary on Beauvoir's arguments that culture determines gender values and roles, and that false myths distort the images of women. Castellanos's analysis of the diaries that the French mystic Simone Weil wrote about her experience as a factory worker helped the Mexican writer to understand the mechanisms of human relationships between the oppressed and the oppressors that she observed in Chiapas. Woolf's presence in Castellanos's work is more subtle, yet substantial, in the mixed modes of biography and literary analysis, the reader in the text, the imagery of the body to explore sexual difference, and her commitment to writing for and about women.

While Castellanos had learned from Beauvoir that the study of a culture's myths was a way of decoding its attitudes toward women, "Otra vez Sor Juana" (1963; "Once Again Sor Juana") presented her own ideas on women as myth and silence in Mexico. She saw three figures in Mexican history who embody the most extreme and diverse possibilities of womanhood. "Each one of them represents a symbol, exercises a vast and profound influence on very wide sectors of the nation, and each arouses passionate reactions. These are the Virgin of Guadalupe, Malinche and Sor Juana"* (*Juicios sumarios*, p. 26). This essay examines the conflicting Mexican attitudes about the Virgin, "a woman who sublimates her condition in motherhood," and the Indian woman Malinche, "who incarnates sexuality in its most irrational aspect" (p. 26). Castellanos rejects the Freudian analysis of Sor Juana, postulated by Ludwig Pfandl, by pointing out the silences in Sor Juana's writing and experiences in a world ruled by masculine logic.

These archetypal figures of Malinche, the Virgin of Guadalupe, and Sor Juana provided Castellanos with a rich cluster of signs that she used to explore gender, sexuality, and inequality through a variety of discourse modes. They became metaphors in her poetry, archetypes in her essays, and actors in her play: three modes of producing meaning in her texts. A major essay, "La Mujer y su Imagen" ("Woman and her Image") in *Mujer que sabe latín . . .* (1973), takes issue with the forces that have kept women outside of history by using the discourse of scientific reporting as caricature and by creating a series of inter-textual mirrors that reflect the destructive stereotypes imposed on them. Castellanos merged the diaries of a nineteenth-century forerunner, Fanny Calderón de la Barca, with her own commentaries to inquire about women's lives within Mexican history. "La mujer mexicana del siglo XIX" ("The Nineteenth-Century Mexican Woman") juxtaposes extended fragments of direct quotations from Calderón's diary entries with Castellanos's own commentary. The resulting colloquium of female voices that span 170 years of Mexican life detected silences that speak louder than words.

In *El uso de la palabra* (1974), "La liberación del amor" ("The Liberation of Love") skillfully reverses male rhetoric to show how women become willing accomplices in their own degradation. "La abnegación es una virtud loca" ("Self-Sacrifice is a Mad Virtue") presents Castellanos's mature ideas about Mexican idealization of maternity and dependency and their noxious effects on an entire culture. But Mexican women have no right to complain, she wrote, because by practicing the code of self-denial and dependency they are in part to blame for their own condition. They must take an active role in their own personal lives. Castellanos's concepts of feminism and culture were never compartmentalized: women's problems are essentially social and economic ones that involve and reflect on her society as a whole. She was aware that freedom based on the dependence and exploitation of other women and classes is a false freedom. In "Herlinda se va" ("Herlinda Leaves"), Castellanos discusses how servitude affects the relationships between women of different social classes in modern Mexico. Using the biography of four women's lives, among them a wrenching confession about her own, the author saw herself as an example of the colonial maternalism on which servitude thrives.

Rosario Castellanos collected the poetry that she had published since 1948, as well as four unpublished collections written between 1968 and 1971, in *Poesía no eres tú* (1972; You are not poetry), herein referred to as *PNET*. (Page numbers correspond to the second edition.) Three central concepts underlie all her verse: the search for her own voice; the reversal of myth imposed on female experience in Mexico; and the exploration of otherness. Through her readings of the Bible and the poetry of Gabriela Mistral* and Jorge Guillén, Castellanos achieved her own style after the rhetorical blind alleys she had met in her early poems. It was in *Al pie de la letra* (1959; Word for word), *Lívida luz* (1960; Livid light), and *Materia memorable* (1969; Memorable matter) that Castellanos developed the cardinal points of her verse: "humor, solemn meditation and contact with my carnal and historical roots. All bathed by that livid light of death that makes all matter memorable" (*Mujer que sabe latín...* p. 207). The reconstruction of female experience in her long poem, "Lamentación de Dido" (Dido's lament), dramatized a woman of antiquity, while the speaking voice of "Malinche" reversed the Mexican ethnic and gender stereotypes that cast this woman as a symbol of betrayal. If male myth has distorted the image of woman, the language that encodes it alienates her in "Monólogo de la extranjera" ("Monologue of a Foreign Woman").

Although many critics have attempted to explain Castellanos's poetry through an obsession with death, it is only one element of a much wider concept that permeates all her writing: the exploration of the other, whether that other be woman, indigenous culture, language, silence, or writing itself. In "Toma de conciencia" ("Consciousness"), the other transcends the self to become the sense of community that enables her to define life in death, self in other, utterance in muteness. "I am a wide patio, a great open house: / a memory" (*PNET*, p. 203). The concept of otherness transcends gender, becoming the passage to creativity itself. "The other. With the other / humanity, dialogue, poetry, begin" ("Poesía no eres tú," *PNET*, p. 302).

In the final four collections of poems, the reading experience is shaped by the poems' female speaking subjects and addressees. Women speak to women, cast in the intimate *tú* form (you), and their voices generate poems from domestic or biographical events that serve as metaphors for an agenda of larger social issues. The monologues of "Autorretrato" ("Self-Portrait") and "Lecciones de cosas" ("Learning about Things") dramatize the way women are socialized to be self-effacing and manipulative, and to play roles that have little to do with their authentic persons. These devastating parodies trace the internalization of subservience in the discourse of its victims. By casting the discourse of her poem, "Kinsey Report," in the format of scientific inquiry, Castellanos enables the responses of the female victims of the double standard to become a way to "say the unsayable" about female sexuality in Mexico.

"Pequeña Crónica" ("Brief Chronicle") uses the metaphor of menstrual flow to consider what blood signifies as a feminine sign: blood as the scribe of our emotional history, and the link between sexuality and textuality. In "Hablando de Gabriel" ("Speaking of Gabriel"), the metaphor of pregnancy provides an example of how the fusion of biography and domesticity became the mainspring for some of Castellanos's most incisive writing. This unconventional poem considers pregnancy in terms of the relationship between body, self, and other, and is an example of how far ahead of her time Castellanos's writing was at that point when it was published in the sixties, nearly a decade before Hélène Cixous called on women to write their bodies and their selves in "Le rire de la Méduse" (*L'Arc* 61 [1975]; "The Laugh of the Medusa," trans. Emily K. Abel and Keith Cohen, in Elizabeth Abel and Emily K. Abel, eds., *The Signs Reader: Women, Gender and Scholarship*, Chicago: University of Chicago Press, 1983, p. 294).

"Ninguneo" (Nobodying) uses a Mexican pun to analyze language and oppression, where the "We" of authoritarian utterance codifies a long tradition of discounting women. Castellanos's view of how language has shut women out of power structures prefigures the ideas that Adrienne Rich and Luce Irigaray published later in the seventies and eighties. "We have to find another language, we have to find another starting point," Castellanos declared in her essay, "El lenguaje como instrumento de la dominación" ("Language as an Instrument of Domination") in *Mujer que sabe latín....* Literature, like women themselves, must find another way of representing female otherness. After contemplating the female characters and writers in "Meditación en el umbral" (Meditation on the brink), whose existence under patriarchal contraints led to suicide, silence, and self-denial, Castellanos searched for "another way" of realizing both living and writing for women that is beyond madness, muteness, or penance. "Another way to be human and free. / Another way to be" (*PNET* p. 316).

Rosario Castellanos's fiction focuses on two themes long overlooked in Mexican letters: the critique of racial and cultural oppression of indigenous peoples in Chiapas and the status of women in provincial and urban Mexico. Her early short stories published in *América: Revista Antológica* became the nucleus for her first novel, *Balún-Canán* (1957), which drew on her childhood memories and the mythic Tzotzil world of Chiapas as narrated through the eyes of a solitary seven-year-old girl. The short stories in *Ciudad Real* (1960; Royal city) consider conflicts between the Indian and the Mexican in terms of the attitude of the conquered toward the conquerors and the treatment of the weak by the powerful, she explained in her interviews with Emmanuel Carballo (p. 420). "El advenimiento del águila" ("The Eagle") explores the conflicts between races through the distortion of linguistic and cultural signs that a corrupt *ladino*, or Spanish-speaker of mixed blood, manipulates to oppress an Indian community.

Oficio de tinieblas (1962) used the historical events of a Chamula Indian uprising in San Cristóbal in 1867 which culminated in the crucifixion of one of the participants. Castellanos recast them into the struggle of Catalina Díaz Puiljá, the Indian woman leader who uses her powers as an *ilol*, or priestess, to lead the rebellion of her people. It is still considered to be one of the best examples of neo-indigenist writing in Latin American letters, signifying a major break with the lurid prose in which regional indigenous cultures were portrayed as exotic worlds populated by poetic victims.

Los convidados de agosto (1964; The guests of August) examined another neglected sector of Mexican society: the life of women in the stifling middle class of provincial Chiapas, whose place—designated by tradition—was "under a man's hand." "Las amistades efímeras" ("Fleeting Friendships") and "El viudo Román" ("The Widower Román") narrate the lives of women whose bodies are used to attest to the honor of their fathers and husbands or as objects of exchange that assure continuity and control in a social community. In these stories Castellanos represents women as signs of conflict. Moreover, their relationships to each other were literary topics that had not been addressed by male writers or critics in Mexico. In this sense her fiction is truly pioneering, for the central questions her work raises about the interdependence of attitudes toward gender and race are the same issues feminists still confront today. The stories in *Album de familia* (1971) shift to the alienation of women in modern urban Mexico and to women's struggles to develop their vocations. "Lección de Cocina" ("Cooking Lesson") demonstrates the author's superb command of feminine metaphors to create discourse that is intrinsically feminist in speech-act situation and in message. The analogies that begin with those between raw beefsteak and the spouses' bodies demonstrate Castellanos's vision of middle-class marriage in Mexico as a social catastrophe.

The author's early one-act satire, *Tablero de Damas* (1952; A chessboard of women), allegedly based on the Nobel Prize-winning writer Gabriela Mistral* and her literary circle, is an acid view of women working against each other according to men's rules. In 1973 Castellanos wrote the three-act farce, *El eterno femenino*, which was published posthumously in 1975. Rafael López Mirnau directed and co-produced it in Mexico City where it opened on April 9, 1976, with Emma Teresa Armendáriz playing the parts of fourteen different female characters. Reviews were mixed, and when financial backing was withdrawn after a few weeks the play was forced to close. The setting is a beauty salon in Mexico City where a hair dryer makes the women who sit under it dream about the past, present, or future. The dream machine generates multiple episodes and characters from Mexican history and myth. "Each character projects her present dimension at the same time that she incarnates the symbol of ancestral lies," wrote Raúl Ortiz in his prologue to the playscript (p. 14). Critique of Mexican culture becomes drama through the performance of stereotypes—and women's collusion with them—that have oppressed women and their lives in Mexico for centuries. One of the most radical theatrical pieces ever staged in Mexico, this play is a showcase for Castellanos's talent for ironic humor and the ways she uses it to demolish the myths inside and outside of women's experiences in Mexico.

In the writing of Rosario Castellanos, women are the textual speakers and hearers, writers and readers, actors and audience. Woman as discursive subject and as sign acquires critical as well as creative value.

SURVEY OF CRITICISM

At the time of Castellanos's death in 1974, her Mexican colleague José Emilio Pacheco wrote in *Excélsior*: "When the commotion passes and people reread her work it will become evident that nobody in her time had as clear a consciousness as she did of the meaning of the two-fold condition of being both a woman and a Mexican. . . . Of course we didn't how how to read her" (Aug. 16, 1974, p. 16). In the decade and a half since these words were published, we are still learning how to read her. Although Castellanos was labeled an indigenist writer early in her career, more recently the pioneering qualities of her thought and writing about gender, poetics, and race are being recognized, as her early essays are re-edited and reread.

Three of Castellanos's essays, "Una tentativa de autocrítica" ("An Attempt at Self-Criticism"), "Si no 'poesía no eres tú', ¿entonces qué?" ("If Not Poetry, Then What?") and "Escrituras tempranas" ("Early Writings"), all recently available in English translation, and three incisive interviews, in Carballo's *Diecinueve protagonistas de la literatura mexicana del Siglo XX* (1965); in the anonymous interview, "Rosario Castellanos," in *Confrontaciones: Los narradores ante el publico* (1966); and Margarita García Flores's *Cartas marcadas* (1979), trace the development of her writing. Four major bibliographies of and about Castellanos's writing have been compiled: The first by Victor Baptiste was included in *La obra poética de Rosario Castellanos* (1972); Germaine Calderón's *El universo poético de Rosario Castellanos* (1979) included a bibliography of Castellanos's writing, a chronological outline, and an appendix of the early poems that were not included in *Poesía no eres tú*. Maureen Ahern compiled "A Critical Bibliography Of and About the Works of Rosario Castellanos" through 1978 (1980) which identified ninety-six uncollected essays, while "A Select Bibliography of Rosario Castellanos Criticism" in *A Rosario Castellanos Reader* (1988) lists major criticism through 1987.

Two major studies of Castellanos's life and its relationship to her writing within the context of contemporary Mexico are the intimate portraits drawn by two fellow writers. José Emilio Pacheco's superb eulogy that became the prologue for *El uso de la palabra*, and Elena Poniatowska's extensive essay, "Rosario Castellanos: ¡Vida nada te debo!" (1985), are the best introductions to Castellanos's writing. A valuable comprehensive study of the author's life and writing in English is Mary Seale Vásquez's essay, "Rosario Castellanos, Image and Idea" (1980). Two more recent accounts by Mexican authors are Perla Schwartz' *Rosario Castellanos: Mujer que supo latin* . . . (1984) and María Estela Franco's *Rosario Castellanos (1925–1974): Semblanza sicoanalítica* (1985).

Although Elena Poniatowska has pointed out that during Castellanos's lifetime the critical reception of her work in traditional Mexican literary circles was the victim of the same kind of literary *ninguneo*, or discounting, that Castellanos noted in the work of other women writers, her prose and poetry won many prestigious literary awards in Mexico: in 1958 the Chiapas Literary Prize for *Balún-Canán*; in 1960 the Xavier Villaurrutia Prize for the poems in *Lívida luz*; in 1962 the Sor Juana Inés de la Cruz Prize for *Oficio de tinieblas*: in 1967 the Carlos Trouyet Prize for Literature; and in 1972 the Elías Souraski Prize for *Poesía no eres tú*. *Balún-Canán* (1957) was immediately translated into English by Irene Nicholson in editions published by Faber and Faber (1958) and Vanguard Press (1959) that were favorably reviewed in both England and the United States. But Castellanos's poetry and essays remained relatively unknown outside of Mexico until the publication in 1971 of *Mujer que sabe latín* . . . (whose title comes from the popular saying, "A woman who knows Latin will never catch a husband or come to any good end"). This work sparked a growing readership among a wider audience of younger writers throughout Mexico and Latin America. Criticism has largely compartmentalized Castellanos's work by genre, which has tended to obscure its rich intratextuality, as well as its central concern with the larger issues of culture, gender, and race in Mexico. A wider perspective of her writing across all the genres can be found in the volume of eight critical studies, *Homenaje a Rosario Castellanos* which Mary Seale Vásquez and Maureen Ahern published in 1980. Recently, Ahern's comprehensive critical study, "Reading Rosario Castellanos: Contexts, Voices and Signs" (1988), reveals how Castellanos's discourse integrates many networks of meaning, creating a plurality of new signs about women in Mexico.

Critical response to the specific genres has focused nearly exclusively on prose and poetry through the categories of indigenism, imagery, and feminism. In 1964 Joseph Sommers was the first critic to categorize Castellanos's novels as part of the "Cycle of Chiapas" and to recognize in them the best examples of a new kind of indigenist writing that attempts to represent the subjects within their own cultural and ideological contexts. His masterful analyses (1978 and 1979) establish the stature of Castellanos's prose in contemporary Latin American letters, while Martin Leinhard (1984) views her fiction in the context of Central American letters. Rómulo Cossé (1982) and Frances R. Dorward (1985) offer substantial analyses of Castellanos's creation of her fictional world; Thomas Washington (1982), Laura Lee Crumley de Pérez (1984), and others discuss the mythic dimensions of her novels. However, the topic of major critical interest is that of gender issues. María Rosa Fiscal examines female imagery in her monograph, *La imagen de la mujer en la narrativa de Rosario Castellanos* (1980), while Beth Miller's *Rosario Castellanos: Una conciencia feminista en México* (1983) addresses major issues of feminism in Castellanos's poetry, prose, and early essays. Many other excellent studies on this topic are listed in the bibliography. A recent essay by Sandra Messinger Cypess (1985), which examines *Balún-Canán* as a model demonstration of discourse as power, points to a new agenda for future Castellanos criticism.

Castellanos's talent as an essayist has begun to attract the attention it so well deserves. Regina Harrison MacDonald's incisive study of "Rosario Castellanos:

On Language'' (1980) demonstrates how Castellanos views language as ''a codifying system for examining false institutions, antiquated prejudices and iron-clad hierarchies that have been erected in the name of Mexican culture'' (p. 41). An important break with the stereotype of Castellanos as an ''indigenist'' writer are the excellent studies by Raquel Scherr (1979) and Naomi Lindstrom (1980) which discuss her early feminist poetics and her feminist criticism. Ahern (1988) analyzes the discursive strategies that Castellanos employed in her essays to inscribe the cultural ideology of women.

Rosario Castellanos's poetry is the genre that has generated the most critical commentary among scholars in Mexico and the United States, including a substantial and growing number of excellent doctoral dissertations. The criticism tends to focus on two categories: female imagery and poetic technique, with special attention to feminine poetic speakers. Baptiste's monograph, *La obra poética de Rosario Castellanos* (1972), was the first study of the syntax, themes, and symbols in her poetry prior to *Materia memorable*; Tey Diana Rebolledo's dissertation ''The Wind and the Tree'' (1979) was the earliest major structural analysis of her poetry. The same year Germaine Calderón's monograph, *El universo poético de Rosario Castellanos*, analyzed the themes, motifs, and influences in all the books of poems that Castellanos published from 1948 to 1972. Eliana Rivero's ''Visión social y feminista en la obra poética de Rosario Castellanos'' (1980) established the feminist parameters of the poet's discourse. They have been followed by many studies of specific feminine imagery and themes, among them the survey by Julian Palley, ''Rosario Castellanos: Eros and Ethos'' (1988). Martha Miller (1982), Marcia Bigelow (1984) and Susan Holm (1986) have applied semiotic and formulist approaches to Castellanos's poetry. A second important essay by Eliana Rivero (1986) argues that Castellanos's poetic development represents a paradigm for the evolution of feminine poetry in Latin America in the twentieth century, as she traces the textual changes that took place as a poetry of lyrical ''interiorism'' became one of radical feminist consciousness. Frank Dauster analyzes the development of Rosario Castellanos's personal vision and place in Mexican letters in his chapter on her search for a voice in *The Double Strand: Five Contemporary Mexican Poets* (1987).

Undoubtedly, the genre most bereft of critical evaluation is Castellanos's drama. Two of the earliest appraisals are still among the best. Kathleen O'Quinn's discussion of the correspondences between the early controversial play, *Tabiero de Damas* (1952) and its later prose counterpart, *Album de familia* (1980), is an example of the kind of intratextual relationships that abound in Castellanos's writing, yet have been relatively unexplored. Kirsten Nigro's analysis (1980) of *El eterno femenino* reveals how the playwright's ''debunking'' of Mexican female figures infuses them with new literary and historical life on the stage and in the minds of the audience. Barbara Bockus Aponte (1987) focuses her study of *El eterno femenino* on the feminist dramatic strategies.

BIBLIOGRAPHY

Works by Rosario Castellanos

Poetry

Trayectoria del polvo. Mexico City: Colección el Cristal Fugitivo, 1948.
Apuntes para una declaracion de fe. Mexico City: Ediciones de *América, Revista Antológica* 1948.
De la vigilia estéril. Mexico City: Ediciones de *América, Revista Antológica*, 1950.
Dos poemas. Mexico City: Icaro, Impresora Económica, 1950.
Presentación al templo: Poemas.(Madrid, 1951). Mexico City: *América, Revista Antológica*, 1952.
El rescate del mundo. Mexico City: Ediciones de *América. Revista Antológica*. 1952. 2d. ed. Tuxtla Gutiérrez, Chiapas: Gobierno del Estado de Chiapas, 1952.
Poemas (1953–1955). Mexico City: Colección Metáfora, 1957.
Salomé y Judith: Poemas dramáticos. Mexico City: Editorial Jus, 1957.
Al pie de la letra: poemas. Xalapa: Universidad Veracruzana, 1959.
Lívida luz: Poemas. Mexico City: Universidad Nacional Autónoma de México, 1960.
Materia memorable. Mexico City: Universidad Nacional Autónoma de México, 1969.
Poesía no eres tú: Obra poética:1948–1971. Mexico City: Fondo de Cultura Económica, 1972. 2d. ed. 1975.
Meditación en el umbral: Antología poética. Comp. Julian Palley. Prol. Elena Poniatowska. Mexico City: Fondo de Cultura Económica, 1985.

Fiction

Balún-Canán. Mexico City: Fondo de Cultura Económica, 1957.
Ciudad real: Cuentos. Xalapa: Universidad Veracruzana, 1960.
Oficio de tinieblas. Mexico City: Joaquín Mortiz, 1962.
Los convidados de agosto. Mexico City: Ediciones Era, 1964.
Album de familia. Mexico City: Joaquín Mortiz, 1971.

Collected Essays

"Sobre cultura femenina". M.A. thesis, Mexico City: Ediciones de *América, Revista Antológica*, 1950. Facultad de Filosofía y Letras, Universidad Autónoma de México, 1950.
Juicios sumarios: Ensayos. Xalapa: Universidad Veracruzana, 1966. 2d ed. *Juicios sumarios: Ensayos sobre literatura*. 2 vols. Mexico City: Fondo de Cultura Económica, Biblioteca Joven, 1984.
Mujer que sabe latín . . . . Sepsetentas 83. Mexico City: Secretaría de Educación Pública, 1973. 2d ed. SepDiana, 1979.
El uso de la palabra. Prol. José Emilio Pacheco. Mexico City: Ediciones de Excélsior-Crónicas, 1974.
El mar y sus pescaditos. Sepsetentas 89. Mexico City: Secretaría de Educación Publica, 1975.

Theater

Tablero de damas: Pieza en un acto. *América: Revista Antológica* 68 (1952):185–224.

"Petul en la escuela abierta." *Teatro Petul*. Mexico City: Instituto Nacional Indigenista, n.d. [1962]. Pp. 42–65.
El eterno femenino: farsa. Mexico City: Fondo de Cultura Económica, 1975.

Translations of Rosario Castellanos

Ahern, Maureen, trans. "Early Writings." *Lives on the Line: The Testimony of Contemporary Latin American Authors*. Ed. Doris Meyer. Berkeley, Los Angeles: University of California Press, 1988. Pp. 86–89.
————, ed. and trans. *Looking at the Mona Lisa*. Rivelin/Ecuatorial Latin American Series. Bradford [England]: Rivelin/Ecuatorial, 1981. Contains seventeen poems.
————, et al., trans. *A Rosario Castellanos Reader*. Ed. and Introd. Maureen Ahern. Texas Pan American Series. Austin: University of Texas Press, 1988. Contains twenty-five poems, five short stories, twelve essays, and the complete text of *The Eternal Feminine*, trans. by Diane Marting and Betty Tyree Osiek.
Bogin, Magda, trans. *The Selected Poems of Rosario Castellanos*. Eds. Cecilia Vicuña and Magda Bogin. St. Paul, Minn.: Greywolf Press, 1988. Contains thirty-four poems.
Bouvier, Virginia Marie, trans. and introd. "Just Like a Woman: A Farce by Rosario Castellanos." Master of Arts Thesis, University of South Carolina, 1984. Act II of the above translation of *El eterno femenino* was published in *Latin American Literary Review* 14, 28 (1986):52–63.
Manguel, Alberto, trans. "Death of the Tiger," *Other Fires: Short Fiction by Latin American Women*. Ed. Alberto Manguel. Canada: Clarkson N. Potter, Publishers, 1986. New York: Crown Publishers, 1986. Pp. 206–17.
Nicholson, Irene, trans. *The Nine Guardians*. London: Faber and Faber, 1958; New York: Vanguard Press, 1959.
Palley, Julian, ed., trans. and introd. *Meditation on the Threshold: A Bilingual Anthology of Poetry*. Tempe, Ariz.: Bilingual Press/Editorial Bilingüe, 1988. Contains forty-three poems.

Works about Rosario Castellanos

Agosín, Majorie. "Rosario Castellanos ante el espejo." *Cuadernos Americanos* 253, 2 (1984):219–26.
Ahern, Maureen. "A Critical Bibliography of and About the Works of Rosario Castellanos." *Homenaje a Rosario Castellanos*. Eds. Ahern and Vásquez. Pp. 121–74.
————. "Reading Rosario Castellanos: Contexts, Voices and Signs." Introd. *A Rosario Castellanos Reader*. Ed. Maureen Ahern. Trans. Maureen Ahern et al. Austin: University of Texas Press, 1988. Pp. 1–70.
————. "A Select Bibliography of Rosario Castellanos Criticism." *A Rosario Castellanos Reader*. Ed. Maureen Ahern. Pp. 70–77.
————, and Mary Seale Vásquez, eds. *Homenaje a Rosario Castellanos*. Valencia, Spain: Albatros-Hispanófila Ediciones, 1980.
Alarcón, Norma. "Rosario Castellanos' Feminist Poetics: Against The Sacrificial Contract." Ph.D. diss. Indiana University, 1983. (*DAI* 44 [1983]:1466a.)
Allgood, Myralyn Frizelle. "Conflict and Counterpoint: A Study of Characters and Characterization in Rosario Castellanos' Indigenist Fiction." Ph. D. diss. University of Alabama, 1986. (*DAI* 46 [1986]:1985a.)
Anderson, Helene M. "Rosario Castellanos and the Structures of Power." *Introductory*

Essays. Vol. 1 of *Contemporary Women Authors of Latin America.* Eds. Doris Meyer and Marguerite Fernández Olmos. 2 vols. Brooklyn, N.Y.: Brooklyn College Press, 1983. 1:22–32.

Aponte, Barbara Bockus. "Estrategias dramáticas del feminismo en *El eterno femenino por Rosario Castellanos.*" *Latin American Theatre Review* 20, 2 (1987):49–58.

Baptiste, Victor N. *La obra poética de Rosario Castellanos.* Santiago de Chile: Ediciones Exégesis, 1972.

Beer, Gabriella de. "El feminismo en la poesía de Rosario Castellanos." *Revista de Crítica Literaria Latinoamericana* 7, 13 (1981):105–12. "Feminism in the Poetry of Rosario Castellanos." *Meditation on the Threshold.* By Rosario Castellanos. Pp. 7–16.

Benedetti, Mario. "Rosario Castellanos y la incomunicación racial." *Letras del continente mestizo.* Montevideo: Arca, 1967. Pp. 130–35.

Bigelow, Marcia Anne. "La evolución de la hablante en la poesía de Rosario Castellanos." Ph.D. diss. University of California, Irvine, 1984. (*DAI* 45 [1984]:533a.)

Bouchony, Claire Tron de. "Women in the Work of Rosario Castellanos: A Struggle for Identity." *Cultures* 8, 3 (1982):66–82.

Bouvier, Virginia M. Introd. "Just Like a Woman." By Rosario Castellanos. *Latin American Literary Review* 14, 28 (1986):47–51.

Calderón, Germaine. *El universo poético de Rosario Castellanos.* Mexico City: Cuadernos del Centro de Estudios Literarios, Universidad Nacional Autónoma de México, 1979.

Carballo, Emmanuel. Interview. "Rosario Castellanos. La historia de sus libros contada por ella misma." *Diecinueve protagonistas de la literatura mexicana del siglo XX.* Mexico City: Empresas Editoriales, 1965. Pp. 411–24.

Castro, Dolores. "El culto a los otros en la obra de Rosario Castellanos." *La Palabra y el Hombre* 11 (1974):13–16.

Cossé, Rómulo. "El mundo creado en *Oficio de tinieblas* de Rosario Castellanos." *Crítica Latinoamericana: Propuestas y Ejercicios.* Xalapa: Universidad Veracruzana, Centro de Investigaciones Lingüístico-Literarios, 1982. Pp. 111–37.

Cypess, Sandra Messinger. "*Balún-Canán*: A Model Demonstration of Discourse As Power." *Revista de Estudios Hispánicos* 19, 3 (1985):1–15.

———. "The Narrator as *niña* in Balún-Canán by Rosario Castellanos." *El niño en las literaturas hispánicas.* Ed. J. Cruz Mendizábal. Indiana, Pa.: Indiana University Press, 1978. Pp. 71–77.

———. "Onomastics and Thematics in *Balún-Canán.*" *Literary Onomastics Studies* 13 (1986):83–96.

Dauster, Frank. "Rosario Castellanos: The Search for a Voice." *The Double Strand: Five Contemporary Mexican Poets.* Lexington, Ky.: University Press of Kentucky, 1987. Pp. 134–62.

Dorward, Frances R. "The Function of Interiorization in *Oficio de Tinieblas.*" *Neophilologus* 69, 3 (1985):374–85.

Fiscal, María Rosa. "Identidad y lenguaje en los personajes femeninos de Rosario Castellanos." *Chasqui* 14, 2–3 (1985):23–35.

———. *La imagen de la mujer en la narrativa de Rosario Castellanos.* Mexico City: Universidad Nacional Autónoma de México, 1980.

Franco, María Estela. *Rosario Castellanos (1925–1974): Semblanza sicoanalítica.* Mexico City: Joaquín Mortiz, 1985.

Frischmann, Donald H. "El sistema patriarchal y las relaciones heterosexuales en *Balún-Canán* de Rosario Castellanos." *Revista Iberoamericana* 51 (1985):665–78.

García Flores, Margarita. "Rosario Castellanos: La lucidez como forma de Vida." Interviews. *Cartas Marcadas*. Mexico City: Difusión Cultural, Depto. de Humanidades, Universidad Nacional Autónoma de México, 1979. Pp. 167–77.

Gómez Parham, Mary. "Intellectual Influences on the Works of Rosario Castellanos." *Foro Literario: Revista de Literatura y Lenguaje* [Montevideo] 7, 12 (1984):34–40.

González, Alfonso. "La soledad y los patrones del dominio en la cuentística de Rosario Castellanos." *Homenaje a Rosario Castellanos*. Eds. Ahern and Vásquez. Pp. 107–13.

Holm, Susan Fleming. " 'But Then Face to Face': Approaches to the Poetry of Rosario Castellanos." Ph.D. diss. University of Kansas, 1986. (*DAI* 47 [1989]:541a.)

——. "Defamiliarization in the Poetry of Rosario Castellanos." *Third Woman* 3, 1–2 (1986):87–97.

Lagos-Pope, María-Inés. "Individuo y sociedad en *Balún-Canán*." *Texto Crítico* 13, 34–35 (1986):82–92.

Leinhard, Martin. "La legitimación indígena en dos novelas centroamericanas." *Cuadernos Hispanoamericanos* 414 (1984):110–20.

Lindstrom, Naomi. "Rosario Castellanos: Pioneer of Feminist Criticism." *Homenaje a Rosario Castellanos*. Eds. Ahern and Vásquez. Pp. 65–73.

——. "Women's Expression and Narrative Technique in Rosario Castellanos' *In Darkness*." *Modern Language Studies* 13, 3 (Summer 1983):71–80.

Lorenz, Gunter W. Interview. "Rosario Castellanos." *Diálogo con Latinoamérica*. Santiago de Chile: Ediciones Universitarias de Valparaiso, Editorial Pomaire, 1972. Pp. 186–211.

Macdonald, Regina Harrison. "Rosario Castellanos: On Language." *Homenaje a Rosario Castellanos*. Eds. Ahern and Vásquez. Pp. 41–64.

Mejías Alonso, Almuñeda. "La narrativa de Rosario Castellanos y el indigenismo." *Cuadernos Americanos* 260, 3 (1985):204–17.

Miller, Beth. "The Poetry of Rosario Castellanos: Tone and Tenor." *Homenaje a Rosario Castellanos*. Eds. Ahern and Vásquez. Pp. 75–83.

——. "Rosario Castellanos' *Guests in August*: Critical Realism and the Provincial Middle Class." *Latin American Literary Review* 7, 14 (1979):5–19.

——. *Rosario Castellanos: Una conciencia feminista en México*. Tuxtia Gutiérrez, Chiapas: Universidad Autónoma de Chiapas, 1983.

Miller, Martha LaFollette. "A Semiotic Analysis of Three Poems by Rosario Castellanos." *Revista/Review Interamericana* 12, 1 (1982):77–86.

Miller, Yvette. "El temario poético de Rosario Castellanos." *Hispamérica* 10, 29 (1981):107–15.

Nelson, Esther W. "Point of View in Selected Poems by Rosario Castellanos." *Revista/Review Interamericana* 12, 1 (1982):56–64.

Nigro, Kirsten F. "Rosario Castellanos's Debunking of the Eternal Feminine." *Journal of Spanish Studies: Twentieth Century* 8 (1980):89–102.

Ocampo, Aurora M. "Debe haber otro modo de ser humano y libre: Rosario Castellanos." *Cuadernos Americanos* 250, 5 (1983):199–212.

——. "Rosario Castellanos y la mujer mexicana." *La Palabra y el Hombre* 53 (1985):101–108.

O'Quinn, Kathleen. "*Tablero de Damas* and *Album de Familia*: Farces on Women Writers." *Homenaje a Rosario Castellanos*. Eds. Ahern and Vásquez. Pp. 99–105.

Ortiz, Raúl. "Presentación" (Prol.). *El eterno femenino*. By Rosario Castellanos. Mexico City: Fondo de Cultura Económica, 1975. Pp. 7–17.

Pacheco, José Emilio. "La Palabra" (Prol.). *El uso de la palabra*. By Rosario Castellanos. Mexico City: Ediciones Excélsior-Crónicas, 1974. Pp. 7–12.

Paley de Francescato, Martha. "Transgresión y aperturas en los cuentos de Rosario Castellanos. *Homenaje a Rosario Castellanos*." Eds. Ahern and Vásquez. Pp. 115–20.

Palley, Julian. "Rosario Castellanos: Eros and Ethos." Introd. *Meditation on the Threshold*. By Rosario Castellanos. Pp. 21–46.

Peña, Margarita. "La 'Lamentación de Dido' de Rosario Castellanos." "*Oficio de tinieblas* o 'la vecindad del cielo'." *Entrelíneas*. Textos de Humanidades 34. Mexico City: Universidad Nacional Autónoma de México, 1983. Pp. 122–38.

Pérez, Laura Lee Crumley de. "*Balún-Canán* y la construcción narrativa de una cosmovisión indígena." *Revista Iberoamericana* 50 (1984):491–503.

———. "La significación del mito indígena en la estructura narrativa de *Balún-Canán*." Ph.D, diss. University of Pittsburgh, 1984, (*DAI* 45 [1984]:853a–854a.)

Ponce, Margarita Cadena. "La ironía en la poesía de Rosario Castellanos." Ph.D, diss. University of Southern California, 1981. (*DAI* 42 [1981]:2697a.)

Poniatowska, Elena. "Rosario Castellanos: ¡vida nada te debo!" *¡Ay Vida, no me mereces!* Mexico City: Editorial Joaquín Mortiz, 1985. Pp. 45–132.

Portal, Marta. "*Oficio de tinieblas*." *Proceso narrativo de la revolución mexicana*. Madrid: Ediciones Cultura Hispánica, 1977. Pp. 212–21.

Rebolledo, Tey Diana. "The Wind and the Tree: A Structural Analysis of the Poetry of Rosario Castellanos." Ph.D. diss. University of Arizona, 1979. (*DAI* 40 [1979]:507a.)

Rivero, Eliana S. "Paradigma de la poética femenina hispanoamericana y su evolución: Rosario Castellanos." *De la crónica a la nueva narrativa mexicana: Coloquio sobre literatura mexicana*. Eds. Merlin H. Forster and Julio Ortega. Mexico City: Editorial Oasis, 1986. Pp. 391–406.

———. "Visión social y feminista en la obra poética de Rosario Castellanos." *Homenaje a Rosario Castellanos*. Eds. Ahern and Vásquez. Pp. 85–97.

Rodríguez-Peralta, Phyllis. "Images of Women in Rosario Castellanos' Prose." *Latin American Literary Review* 6, 11 (1977):68–80.

"Rosario Castellanos." Interview. *Confrontaciones: Los narradores ante el público*. Mexico City: Joaquín Mortiz, 1966. 1:87–98.

Scherr, Raquel Lorraine. "A Voice Against Silence: Feminist Poetics in the Early Works of Rosario Castellanos." Ph.D. diss. University of California, Berkeley, 1979. (*DAI* 41 [1980]:238a.)

Schlau, Stacey. "Conformity and Resistance to Enclosure: Female Voices in Rosario Castellanos' *Oficio de Tinieblas*." *Latin American Literary Review* 12, 24 (1984):45–57.

Schwartz, Perla. *Rosario Castellanos: Mujer que supo latín*. Mexico City: Editorial Katún, 1984.

Sommers, Joseph. "El ciclo de Chiapas: nueva corriente literaria." *Cuadernos Americanos* 133, 2 (1964):246–61.

————. "Forma e ideología en *Oficio de Tinieblas* de Rosario Castellanos." *Revista de Crítica Latinoamericana* 7–8 (1978):73–91.

————. Literatura e historia: "las contradicciones ideológicas de la ficción indigenista." *Revista de Crítica Literaria Latinoamericana* 5, 10 (1979):9–39.

Stoll, Anita K. " 'Arthur Smith Salva Su Alma': Rosario Castellanos and Social Protest." *Revista de Crítica Hispánica* 7, 2 (1985):141–47.

————. "Un análisis de 'Misterios gozosos' por Rosario Castellanos." *Explicación de Textos Literarios* 16, 1 (1988):48–64.

Vásquez, Mary Seale. "Rosario Castellanos, Image and Idea." *Homenaje a Rosario Castellanos*. Eds. Ahern and Vásquez. Pp. 15–40.

Washington, Thomas. "The Narrative Works of Rosario Castellanos: In Search of History—Confrontations with Myth." Ph.D. diss. University of Minnesota, 1982. (*DAI* 43 [1982]:1162a.)

MADRE CASTILLO*
(1671–1742)
Colombia

Stacey Schlau

BIOGRAPHY

Born in the provincial city of Tunja, Colombia, in 1671, Madre Castillo spent her life behind walls—for eighteen years in her family home, and from 1689 to her death in the Franciscan Royal Convent of Saint Clare, where she professed in 1694. Nevertheless, she managed to forge a unique literary and religious identity from her visionary life, which she recounted in both extant major works: *Afectos espirituales* (Spiritual sentiments) and *Su Vida* (Her life). Her spiritual autobiography in particular has become an important source of information about her life.

Francisca Josefa Castillo y Guevara was the daughter of a Spaniard of the lower nobility and a Creole from the same class. The fifth of nine children, she received early training (reading, writing, spiritual lessons) from her mother. As a child, Francisca experienced visions, including conversations with holy figures such as Jesus, and claims to have sought spiritual perfection from an early age. When she was still a young girl, she withdrew as much as possible from family life, finding confirmation for her retirement "from the world" in the popular books of spiritual exercises by Antonio de Molina and by Ignacio de Loyola. Saint Theresa of Avila, whose *Life* her mother read to her throughout her childhood, was another early model; even her early habit of reading ballads and theater pieces imitates the saint's. The identification with Saint Theresa lasted into young adulthood. For several years subsequent to entering the Franciscan convent, in correspondence with the mother superior of the Discalced Carmelite convent in Tunja, she continued to express the desire to become a member of her order. A communication from God, however, assured her that her place was in the convent of Saint Clare, after which her efforts to join the Carmelites ended.

---

*Also Sor Francisca Josefa Castillo y Guevara; Sor Francisca Josefa de la Concepción de Castillo; Francisca Josefa de Castillo Toledo Guevara Niño y Rojas.

When her parents learned that Francisca had decided to become a nun, they tried to dissuade her, but she was determined to make her wish a reality. An aunt who was a member of the religious community in which Francisca eventually professed had been a formative childhood influence, and a confessor supported and helped her to gain entrance into the convent. Like many female saints whose *Lives* frequently aided Madre Castillo at difficult times, she left home without her family's knowledge or consent, and never returned. According to the autobiography, her father died a few months after she carried out the decision, broken-hearted from his daughter's absence; her mother refused to give her the money she required to live as a nun. Nevertheless, several years later, as Sor Francisca de la Concepción, Madre Castillo requested and obtained permission for her mother to enter the convent, so that she might nurse her through a lingering last illness.

Madre Castillo was elected or appointed to many important leadership posts in the convent—mother superior, mistress of the novices, sacristan, archivist, portress—in spite of the difficulties with her sister nuns which she herself emphasizes. Gossip appears on almost every page of the autobiography. She reports, for example, that other nuns call her a ''crazy dog'' and that they find her ''possessed by the devil.'' By recording these insults, and her own reactions of sadness and anger, Madre Castillo communicates an overwhelming sense of isolation and persecution.

Her literacy must have been a factor in assuring the assignments to convent offices, although the tenets propagated by the Council of Trent (1545–1563)— formal enclosure and ''holy ignorance'' for religious women—must have made her ability to read and write a double-edged sword. Madre Castillo never received a formal education, although soon after entering the convent, she, like other women mystics, learned liturgical Latin without ever having taken lessons. Her readings were primarily in religious works: saints' lives, spiritual exercises, the Bible, and other popular religious tracts. The question of how Sor Francisca became a writer as well as a reader, then, may be answered only through an understanding of her socioreligious circumstances.

Writing for her was a means of expressing the mystical experience. At least partly motivated by successive confessors, Madre Castillo recorded her interior and exterior experiences. Her life oscillated between ecstatic sojourns with divine and sacred personages, and the social difficulties of daily life in human community, both of which were at times accompanied by illness and nightmarish visions. In her autobiography she frequently complains about physical ailments, using graphic detail to describe, for example, the loss of all her teeth in a very short period of time. She also frets about the aspersions cast on her honor by the gossip directed against her. Compensatory visions almost always restore her equanimity after these episodes; communications with divine beings replace human speech. Her self-portrait depicts a volatile, ill-at-ease personality who nevertheless achieves a sense of self-worth through her visions.

Madre Castillo continued to enjoy mystical union and to record the details of that knowledge, as well as other, less joyful aspects of her visionary and material life, such as periods of spiritual dryness and illness, until her death at age seventy-one. Because she was considered such a model of piety, confessors ordered her to inscribe her experiences in written texts during her life. After her death, she became an icon of orthodox female spirituality and one of the few early modern women writers of Spain or Spanish America to be anthologized or published, although she is rarely read today.

MAJOR THEMES

In colonial Latin America, even more than in Spain, nuns bore the ideological responsibility of representing ideal womanhood. The Spanish government perceived the New World as a "Western Paradise," abundant in natural resources and inhabited by innocents awaiting conversion. Its conquest and colonization, following on the heels of the "Reconquest," became the ultimate proof of Spain's divine mission as leader of the Catholic world. The image of America as a virgin paradise was reinforced through the concrete representation of Marian chastity and purity that nuns provided (Arenal and Schlau, 1989).

But convents were also educational, economic, and social institutions. They were places of refuge and of education for secular girls and women, as well as monuments to Spain's providential enterprise. Nuns engaged in worldly occupations, such as real estate transactions, even while they continued to dedicate themselves to prayer. Madre Castillo, for instance, saved her convent from financial ruin (with her brother's help) during a term as mother superior.

Most nuns belonged to the creole aristocracy, since a dowry was needed, and the racial hierarchy of the secular world was duplicated in religious institutions. Links between the convent and the upper echelons of the viceregal bureaucracy were necessary for the endowment and continuation of the monastery, and were possible because of family ties. Nevertheless, the relatively peaceful structure of contemplative life, separate from men, although still requiring obedience to male superiors, did give nuns some autonomy. Religious women engaged in inner, sacred adventures rather than the colonizing and administrative activities of their male relatives. The writings of Madre Castillo are the product of this historical context.

As a professed nun was required to follow the rules of her order and the tenets of the Spanish Catholic Church, Madre Castillo faced the necessity of writing without retaining authorship. That is, her works were not written for publication in the conventional sense, but as a pious exercise for herself and a small audience of nuns and clergymen. None was published during her lifetime. Textual revisions primarily involved only such changes or corrections as her confessor deemed necessary for religious reasons. The fear of being considered heterodox is a major theme in Madre Castillo's written documents.

We can read the sexual dynamics of power with which Sor Francisca lived through the gaps not usually visible in more polished writing. Church dogma and custom had codified a power hierarchy in which men were considered superior to women. The cardinal female religious virtues were held to be chastity, obedience, and piety. Writing from within such a social framework, constrained by certain stylistic limitations of religious narrative (especially spiritual auto-biography), and anxious to prove that her unmediated experiences of the divine are not "from the devil," Madre Castillo exemplifies how some early modern Hispanic religious women found the means to express themselves through the discourses of orthodoxy.

Three forms of estrangement play important and interacting roles in Madre Castillo's life and texts: the displacement from dominant literary tradition by virtue of her sex; the difficulties she experienced in social interactions with family, friends, other nuns, confessors, and secular persons; and the exile from the spiritual world (known as *destierro* in Hispanic religious tracts) to which all living beings, imprisoned in physical bodies, are subject, according to Catholic doctrine.

The narrative tone of the *Vida* reveals Madre Castillo's lack of formal literary training. Its structure is episodic but not sequentially linear. The author interrupts herself to recount an incident from an earlier time in her life that she had forgotten, or to render a lyrical description of a vision, or to assert her orthodoxy. She frequently claims to be ambivalent about writing. Although her inferior rela-tionship to male ecclesiastic officials necessitates the use of divine authority in order to validate her writing, the confessor's presence is repeatedly evoked through salutations and comments directed toward him. Rhetorical strategies expressing inadequacy call into question the procedure of textual production itself, and allow the author to evade responsibility for its existence.

In many instances, internal and external suffering are explicitly linked in her works. The theme of illness and anticipated death is paramount in Madre Cas-tillo's *Vida*. Morbidity and mortality offer one possible path toward salvation; the temptations of carnal existence may be fought, and possibly purged; religious fulfillment may be expressed as compensation for earthly pain. In addition, the virtue of imitation of Christ's Passion is essential for salvation.

The realities of ordinary life in early modern Europe and Latin America offer insight into why the theme of exile from the spiritual world might be particularly poignant for early modern women writers: Mortality rates were high, especially in childbirth; girls and women were restricted in actions and denied access to formal education; they were subject to male scrutiny of even their innermost thoughts and feelings; and domestic violence sometimes made their homes unsafe havens. Under these circumstances, women had good reason to be suspicious of material existence, and had a strong need to explain, justify, and even glorify their illnesses (Arenal and Schlau, 1989). Madre Castillo, for instance, prayed to be given some of Christ's suffering and subsequently developed typhoid fever, which she viewed as an answer to her prayer. No greater authority could explain and justify physical and mental suffering, or mitigate the effects of earthly exile.

An examination of Sor Francisca's visionary world reveals several techniques and themes with which she forged a place acceptable to Church officials within the Catholic structures. Typically in Madre Castillo's texts, the physical, psychological, and spiritual realms are presented in a fluctuating reality that ultimately unifies all three. Visions often become a means for getting her out of a difficult spiritual or psychological situation. Access to sacred personages compensates for the misery of daily life (including poverty, illness, and social alienation) and provides a way to gain spiritual and literary acceptance. As abbess, for example, she encounters difficulties with her spiritual daughters. In a vision, Saint Clare (the founder of her order) reprimands the nuns, who have abandoned their abbess. The vision spiritually sustains Madre Castillo, psychologically fuels her sense of self-righteousness, and allows her to continue physically in office. Through the mystic experience, familiar people and things are transformed into participants of another reality, which thereby enables the visionary to accept, at least temporarily, events in the material world.

Although many of Madre Castillo's experiences of mystical union belong to the tradition of divine eroticism exemplified in Fray Luis de León's translation of the Song of Songs, certain visions of mystical love and marriage have permitted Madre Castillo (and other women) to unite God's paternal and husbandly aspects with the erotic implications of attachment to the divine. On one occasion, during a mystic trance, after "hearing" God, she calls him "most true lover" and "delicate husband." While on the one hand this union necessitates a denial of self, it posits a special relationship with divine reality on the other. When a woman mystic becomes the "Bride" of Christ, the balance of power in the earthly gender hierarchy is disturbed. Although she is still required to be obedient to confessors and other ecclesiastic superiors, the ecstatic woman has recourse to an authority higher than theirs. She may even subtly approach equality with Christ through her intimacy with the divinity. Mysticism thereby was an important means toward self-empowerment for women.

Madre Castillo uses another crucial strategy: She consistently appropriates biblical discourse, modifying it to give form and meaning to her spiritual life. She translates freely and paraphrases from the Latin version of the Bible, mixing lines and rearranging quotations from different parts of the Old Testament, especially the Song of Songs and the Psalms. She continually declares her unworthiness and inadequacy, for instance, using formulas from the Bible. By incorporating and restructuring fragments of sacred texts into her writings, Madre Castillo achieves her own glorification as a subject worthy of biblical prose.

Biblical passages, visions, and elements of dogma are most carefully explicated in the *Afectos espirituales*. Here, the inner world takes precedence over the outer. The tone is lyrical and the language is ornate and highly metaphorical. Each episode of the author's spiritual quest—each *afecto*—appears as a discrete unit, varying in length from one to several pages. Madre Castillo is the protagonist, since she either addresses the divinity, cries out her anguish or her unworthiness, or explicates a line from the Bible. The impetus for each varies, but frequently the *afecto* is the result of taking communion. Madre Castillo uses eating the host as a bridge between material and spiritual realities, since she understands the symbolic act in its most literal sense—taking in the body of Christ. Other *afectos* are suggested by reading a passage in a religious tome, or by some negative event in the author's daily life. Many aspects of Catholic tradition and dogma, such as of the dark night of the soul codified by Saint John of the Cross, or the Christian theme of the wandering soul, are transformed into affirmations of the author's singularity through her association with divine figures, who invariably console her, or through visions of devils, who torment her but who only temporarily gain the upper hand. All establish the author's orthodox religiosity through a discourse that recognizes the supremacy of the Church, while subverting its precepts by establishing Madre Castillo's authority.

Through her visionary life, and the act of inscribing it, Madre Castillo solves her problems and is even rewarded in this life for her suffering. By carving out an identity as author through her self-affirming use of the forms of religious authority, including confessors and the Bible, by engaging in a rich and active visionary life that condemns her enemies and offers her consolation for material existence, and by achieving mystical union often enough to mitigate her exile from the divinity, Madre Castillo transforms her alienation, discontent, and suffering into a basis for salvation. Her texts are among the few extant documents that present and discuss the consciousness of early modern Hispanic women.

SURVEY OF CRITICISM

Literary analysis of Madre Castillo's works has been sparse and little has been published, although fragments of her writings appear in Enrique Anderson-Imbert and Eugenio Florit's classic anthology of Spanish American Literature, *Literatura hispanoamericana* (1960). Critical response has generally been written from either an orthodox Catholic perspective, and thus has focused on the religious values transmitted in Madre Castillo's writings, or from a nationalistic slant— especially in occasional pieces in periodicals—and therefore has concentrated on her place as an illustrious example of Colombian letters. In short, much work remains to be done, especially from a feminist literary critical perspective, in order to provide an adequate analysis of Madre Castillo as a female religious writer.

Daniel Samper, in an early (1930) study of Madre Castillo, elaborates at length the dichotomy between the *Vida* and *Afectos espirituales* which most, if not all, critics have maintained to the present. He argues that the spiritual autobiography is stylistically inferior and that the *Afectos* exemplify a more polished, purely lyrical, and adorned prose that more closely conforms to the standards of Baroque excellence.

From the first copies made of Madre Castillo's manuscripts by her nephew and first editor, Antonio María de Castillo y Alarcón, through the first half of this century, scholars had mistakenly attributed three poems found copied in Madre Castillo's breviary. Thought to be the Colombian nun's, they were in fact pieces or adaptations of poems by Sor Juana Inés de la Cruz,* whom Madre

Castillo must have admired. Alfonso Méndez Plancarte, editor of Sor Juana's works, refuted the attribution, affirmed in the 1940 edition of Gómez Restrepo's history of Colombian literature, and proved that the poems were Sor Juana's. Gómez Restrepo reprinted Méndez Plancarte's article in the next edition of his history. From the point of view of feminist literary history, this discovery is important for the proof it offers that women authors did indeed read each other's works and become models for other women writers during the early modern period.

Undoubtedly the most important scholar of Madre Castillo's life and works is Darío Achury Valenzuela. His studies of Madre Castillo provide much-needed background scholarship on her life and writings. This scholar is responsible for the first critical editions of her works (1956), as well as the authoritative *Obras completas* (Complete works) published in 1968, in which he includes a book-length study that situates Madre Castillo in her time and place. His essay lengthily compares her spirituality with Saint Theresa's and Sor Juana Inés de la Cruz's, and offers an orthodox interpretation of her mysticism. Achury Valenzuela also includes such useful appendices as a chart of the specific biblical references used in the *Vida* and the *Afectos espirituales*.

Published earlier in the same year as the *Obras completas*, the study by María Teresa Morales Borrero addresses Madre Castillo's work as religious literature. Morales Borrero discusses Sor Francisca's spirituality by using traditional textual explication to analyze the life and works of her eighteenth-century compatriot. In the first chapter of her study (which originally was a dissertation), Morales Borrero places Sor Francisca in a tradition of Hispanic women mystics, especially the Discalced Carmelites, by providing a list of earlier and later writers. Her purpose is to reiterate what many critics and theologians have said—most Western mystics have been women. By naming the women and giving the titles of some of their works, she not only recognizes their worth, but also makes them more accessible to those scholars who would pursue further study in the field.

In his unpublished doctoral dissertation, Claudio G. Antoni has given a detailed stylistic analysis of Madre Castillo's works, following the methodology of Riffaterre and comparing her linguistic devices to those of two Italian saints: Catherine of Siena (1347?–1380) and Maria Maddalena de' Pazzi (1566–1607). His discussion of Madre Castillo's writings includes an overview of mysticism and a review of the literature about Madre Castillo. Antoni also argues that any similarity critics had previously perceived between her autobiography and Saint Theresa's is purely superficial. His stylistic analysis, at times overly dependent on Riffaterre's complicated morphological system, does offer some insights into certain aspects of Madre Castillo's imagery, and particularly into the similarities and differences between her style and that of the Italian saint. Antoni, however, addresses neither the sexual politics of the three writers nor their gender-based similarities.

The body of criticism about Madre Castillo's life and works, though frequently marred by superficial generalizations about her place in literary and religious history or an emphasis on a single aspect of her writings at the expense of others, has nevertheless laid the factual foundation for more analytical studies in the future.

BIBLIOGRAPHY

Works by Madre Castillo

Vida de la V. M. Francisca Josefa de la Concepción, religiosa del Convento de Sta. Clara de la ciudad de Tunja en el nuebo reyno de Granada, escrita por ella misma dada a luz por don Antonio María de Castillo y Alarcón. Philadelphia: T. H. Palmer, 1817.

Sentimientos espirituales de la venerable Madre Francisca Josefa de la Concepción de Castillo . . . ; dados a luz por su sobrino A. M. de C. y A. Santafé de Bogotá: Imprenta de Bruno Espinosa, 1843.

Mi vida. Biblioteca Popular de Cultura Colombiana, no. 16, Clásicos Colombianos. Bogotá: Imprenta Nacional, 1942.

Afectos espirituales de la V. M. Francisca Josefa del Castillo. Biblioteca Popular de Cultura Colombiana, Part I, no. 24; Part II, no. 36. Bogotá: Ministerio de Educación Nacional, 1956.

Afectos espirituales de la venerable madre y observante religiosa Francisca de la Concepción, en el siglo doña Francisca Josefa de Castillo y Toledo, Guevara, Niño y Roxas, escritos por ella misma, de mandado de sus confesores según primera copia hecha por don Antonio María de Castillo y Alarcón, en Santa Fé de Bogotá, año de 1896 [sic]. 2 vols. Preliminary Study by Darío Achury Valenzuela. Biblioteca de Autores Colombianos nos. 104–105. Bogotá: Ministerio de Educación Nacional, 1956.

Su vida, escrita por ella misma, por mandado de sus confesores. Preliminary Study by Darío Achury Valenzuela. Biblioteca de Autores Colombianos no. 103. Bogotá: Ministerio de Educación Nacional, 1956.

Obras completas de la madre Francisca Josefa de la Concepción de Castillo, según fiel transcripción de los manuscritos originales que se conservan en la Biblioteca Luis-Angel Arango. 2 vols. Introd., notes, and indexes by Darío Achury Valenzuela. Bogotá: Biblioteca Luis-Angel Arango del Banco de la República, 1968.

Translations of Madre Castillo

Jarvis, Kathleen Jeanette. "Madre Castillo's *Afectos espirituales*: Translation and Commentary." M.A. Thesis. University of Texas at Austin, 1985.

Lavrin, Asunción. "Document 10: The Writings of a Mystic (Mother Francisca Josefa de Castillo's Mystical Writings)." *Women and Religion in America. Volume 2: The Colonial and Revolutionary Periods.* Eds. Rosemary Radford Reuther and Rosemary Skinner Keller. San Francisco: Harper and Row, 1983. Pp. 69–71.

Works about Madre Castillo

Achury Valenzuela, Darío. *Análisis crítico de los afectos espirituales de sor Francisca Josefa de la Concepción de Castillo.* Biblioteca de Cultura Colombiana no. 1. Bogotá: Ministerio de Educación Nacional, 1962.

————. *Examen crítico de los afectos espirituales de sor Francisca Josefa del Castillo.* Separata of the *Revista Bolívar*, 59–60.

————. "Introducción." *Obras completas.* Pp. ix–ccxiv.

Antoni, Claudio G. "A Comparative Examination of Style in the Works of Madre Castillo." Ph.D. diss. City University of New York, 1979. (DAI 40 [1979]:5040A.)

Arenal, Electa, and Stacey Schlau. *Untold Sisters: Hispanic Nuns in Their Own Works.* Trans. Amanda Powell. Albuquerque: University of New Mexico Press, 1989.

Garfías, Francisco. "Tres monjas poetisas." *Arbor* 88 (1971):49–63.

Gimbernat de González, Ester. "El discurso sonámbulo de la Madre Castillo." *Letras Femeninas* 13, 1–2 (Spring-Autumn 1987):42–52.

Gómez Restrepo, Antonio. "La Madre Castillo." *Historia de la literatura colombiana.* Vol. 2. 3d ed. Bogotá: Ministerio de Educación Nacional, 1954. 2:50–126.

Gómez Vergara, Max. *La Madre Castillo.* Tunja, Colombia: Publicaciones de la Academia Boyacense de Historia, 1984.

Méndez Plancarte, Alfonso. "Un libro de Gómez Restrepo y una triple restitución de Sor Juana Inés de la Cruz." *Abside* 5 (1941):78–116.

Morales Borrero, María Teresa. *La Madre Castillo: Su espiritualidad y su estilo.* Bogotá: Publicaciones del Instituto Caro y Cuervo, 1968.

Reboledo Palomeque, Angela Inés. "La escritura mística de la Madre Castillo y el amor cortesano: Religiones de amor." *Thesaurus: Boletín del Instituto Caro y Cuervo* (Bogotá) 42,2 (May-Aug. 1987):379–89.

Samper Ortega, Daniel. "La Madre Castillo." *Al galope.* Bogotá: Editorial Minerva, 1930. Pp. 41–75.

Other Works Cited

Anderson Imbert, Enrique, and Eugenio Florit, eds. *Literatura hispanoamericana: Antología e introducción histórica.* N.Y.: Holt, Rinehart, and Winston, 1960.

ROSARIO FERRÉ
(b. 1942)
Puerto Rico

Margarite Fernández Olmos

BIOGRAPHY

Rosario Ferré enjoyed a privileged youth, typical of the upper classes that she would later make the focus of much of her writing. Ferré was born in Ponce, a city on the southern coast of Puerto Rico, to one of the island's most prominent families. (Her father, Luis Ferré, is a former governor of the island.) In the late sixties, she began graduate studies at the University of Puerto Rico. There she came into contact with the Peruvian novelist Mario Vargas Llosa and the Uruguayan critic Angel Rama, and was inspired to pursue her own writing. Ferré has studied English, French, and Latin American literature in universities in Puerto Rico and the United States, and has actively promoted artistic development in Puerto Rico through such endeavors as the literary journal *Zona de carga y descarga*, which she co-founded and directed from 1971 to 1975, and in which her first works of fiction and essay were published. *Zona*'s commitment to artistic and social renovation reflected the literary and political momentum of its era. The literary impact of the enormous growth and development of Latin American literature begun in the sixties coincided with the political debate generated by the movements for social change throughout Latin America.

At the same time in Puerto Rico, important cultural changes were taking place in a society that was rediscovering itself through a revision of the cultural paradigms inherited from the past. One of those changes, the increased female participation in the workforce and in all aspects of Puerto Rican society, and the feminist consciousness that accompanied it (influenced by the international women's movement) resulted in the emergence in the 1970s of a group of women writers whose works would introduce a new vision and another voice into the canon of Puerto Rican literary production. Of the writers to emerge at this juncture, Ferré is among the most talented and versatile. Equally gifted as a poet, essayist, short story writer, and novelist, she is also a literary critic and journalist.

Rosario Ferré's works include her first collection of fourteen short stories and six poems, *Papeles de Pandora* (1976; Pandora's papers), three collections of stories for children, *El medio pollito* (1976; The half a little chicken), *La mona que le pisaron la cola* (1980; The monkey whose tail was stepped on), and *Los cuentos de Juan Bobo* (1981; Tales of Juan Bobo), the short novella *La caja de cristal* (1978; *The Glass Box*, 1986), a collection of poems entitled *Fábulas de la garza desangrada* (1982; Fables of the bleeding hero), and the novel *Maldito Amor* (1986; *Sweet Diamond Dust*, 1988). Her essays and literary criticism include *Sitio a Eros: siete ensayos literarios* (1986; Besieging Eros: seven literary essays), and *"El Acomodador": una lectura fantástica de Felisberto Hernández* (1986; The usher: a fantastic reading of Felisberto Hernández).

In an essay describing her own creative process, "La cocina de la escritura" (1984; "The Writing Kitchen," 1986, 1988), Ferré relates her initial literary attempts which took place in a period of transition following a divorce and a secure life as dutiful wife and mother. Writing represented a new beginning. No longer sheltered and protected, she hoped for adventures that could be experienced, in part, through the imagination. Influenced by her reading of Simone de Beauvoir and Virginia Woolf, Ferré tried to avoid typically "feminine" modes of writing. From Beauvoir she learned to attempt the important "external" subjects such as the great social and historical themes rather than the internal world of emotions and intuition; from Woolf she would learn the necessity of maintaining objectivity and distance, avoiding ire and querulousness, freeing herself from outrage and indignation.

The result was her first short story, "La muñeca menor" (*Papeles*, 1976; "The Youngest Doll," 1986), based on a true incident which Ferré discovered quite by accident on a family visit. The unusual story of a distant cousin who was abused by her husband and forced to live with relatives sparked her creative curiosity. The woman made honey-filled dolls for the young girls of the household, and was shamelessly exploited by a young doctor with whom she had fallen in love and who cheated her out of her remaining money by falsely treating a strange ailment in her leg. Ferré's poetic retelling of the family anecdote grew into "La muñeca menor" with the addition of the female character's retaliation against her abuser, the inclusion of which Ferré later felt went against the standards of her feminist mentors. In the same essay, she confessed: "I had betrayed Simone, writing once again about the interior reality of women; and I had betrayed Virginia letting myself get carried away by my anger, by the fury the story produced in me" ("The Writing Kitchen," p. 233).

The feminist and social concerns Ferré expressed in this first story would be repeated in later works from evolving perspectives and with an increased literary sophistication that place her writing among the best examples of contemporary Latin American literature.

MAJOR THEMES

In her first collection of works, *Papeles de Pandora* (1976), the influence of Julio Cortázar and other Latin American narrators is clearly present. Ferré's unique literary talents and her mastery of language are also visible in the unusual images and distinctive combination of irony, humor, satire, and mystery that distinguish her works. The central theme of the collection is the oppressive nature of the historically assigned roles of women in patriarchal cultures, and woman's rejection of such roles. In *Papeles*, the majority of the protagonists are women of the upper middle classes trapped in confining marriages, often aware of their oppressive situations. For some, the only escape is a retreat into fantasy; others rebel against their "bride-doll" existence. The story mentioned earlier, "La muñeca menor," is typical. In this story, as in others in the collection, Ferré uses the bride-doll image to symbolize the situation of women of a particular class who are little more than adornments, neither left alone nor allowed to participate, excluded from the realms of public power. The reality of Ferré's social criticism is juxtaposed with elements of the fantastic and the grotesque, creating a mysterious, dreamlike atmosphere.

In cases where female characters attempt to rebel against their oppression, the results are often disastrous. In the story "La bella durmiente" (*Papeles;* Sleeping beauty), a "collage" combining letters, wedding invitations and announcements, photo captions, and other documents of a middle-class life, the protagonist attempts to follow her dream of a life in dance. She opposes her family's wishes and must suffer tragic consequences.

Ferré departs from this theme somewhat in other stories in the collection in which the female protagonists' oppression is qualitatively different. In two stories in which the characters are from lower socioeconomic classes—one is a prostitute and the other a maid—the author has sensitively and eloquently described the additional burden of an oppression due not only to sex but also to color and class. One of the more noteworthy examples of contemporary writing in Puerto Rico which deals with the theme of race and class differences among women is "Cuando las mujeres quieren a los hombres" (*Papeles;* "When Women Love Men" 1983). In this story, a white middle-class widow—Isabel Luberza—meets her late husband's black mistress—Isabel la Negra. The theme of the black or mulatto mistress can be found throughout Caribbean literature and is related to the historical difficulty that persons of different races had in legalizing a marital union. The laws and the ideology that created them forced black and mulatto women into the role of mistress and contributed to the myth of the dark-skinned woman as sensual, forbidden fruit.

In contrast to the traditional literary presentation of the black mistress, in Ferré's story Isabel la Negra (based on a legendary madame) thrives economically as she perfects the art of sex with the young white men of the town. After the death of one, she eventually supplants his white widow at charitable and social functions. As a "self-made" woman, she has gained a certain respectability and power. The legal widow, on the other hand, withdraws into an enclosed world of resentment and pain in which she clings to an imagined superiority based on marital status, social-class origins, and color.

Perhaps the most significant aspect of the story is that Ferré presents these very different women as mirror images. She meshes their two voices in an interior monologue that combines their flow of consciousness so as to demonstrate the commonality of their roles as women–both exploited by a man of wealth and power. Ferré does not dismiss the social and economic advantages of the white middle-class wife, but she seeks to give light to the unrecognized affinities between women who share a common victimization.

Critics have commented on Ferré's daring use of sexual language in this story and in others. Her use of language is a challenge to prevailing taboos regarding the propriety of women's expression, particularly in a traditional society such as Puerto Rico where, especially for women of her social class, only a limited reality is encouraged and transmitted. The author goes beyond the internalized restrictions of convention and expresses a "revolutionary eroticism" of the type she ascribes to the Puerto Rican poet Julia de Burgos* in a 1973 editorial in *Zona*, "a revolutionary eroticism, that goes against the very foundation of bourgeois society and points... toward an unmasking of hypocritical morality and a defense of natural values, such as love and equality" (*Zona* [May-June 1973]:3).

In *Sitio a Eros*, Ferré's 1980 collection of essays dealing with the life and work of women writers, she continues her analysis of the obstacles that have traditionally thwarted female artistic productivity. The essays complement her imaginative work and examine the consuming and often forbidden passion of female creativity in such authors as Mary Shelley, George Sand, Flora Tristan, Jean Rhys, Anaïs Nin, Tina Modotti, Alexandra Kollontai, Sylvia Plath, Julia de Burgos, Lilian Hellman, and Virginia Woolf. The first two essays, "La autenticidad de la mujer en el arte" (The authenticity of women in art) and "El diario como forma femenina" (The diary as female mode), form the theoretical basis for the collection. The work is one of the few examples of feminist literary analysis of its type in Latin American letters, and demonstrates Ferré's overwhelming interest in female creativity and the need to achieve artistic and personal authenticity.

Ronald Méndez-Clark (1984) has correctly observed that Ferré's entire corpus—short stories, essays, poems, and even her children's tales—should be considered within the context of the author's unremitting scrutiny of patriarchal culture and woman's *marginality* within the same. Referring specifically to *Papeles de Pandora* and the collection of poetry *Fábulas de la garza desangrada* (1982), he comments about "their conflict with the boundaries that represent, on all levels, male power or with the creative impulses that only materialize in facing—not avoiding—the questions that the condition of women raises" (p. 128).

Whereas in *Papeles* women's marginality is related to specific sociohistoric realities within Puerto Rican society, in *Fábulas* the examination of woman's place in Western culture and tradition is examined from a variety of sources and with a diversity of methods and perspectives. Combining prose and poetry, Ferré conjures her feminine archetypes from the classical period (Antigone, Helen of Troy, Medusa, Andromeda); the New Testament (Salomé, Mary Magdalene); the Western literary tradition (Cervantes's Dorotea, Shakespeare's Desdemona, and Dante's Francesca); and contemporary Puerto Rican literature (Julia de Burgos). Woman as myth and metaphor is one of the obvious themes, but the idea of woman's essential duality is also brought out in the allusions to mirrors and reflections, and in the alternative versions of each woman's reality which Ferré re-creates in order to redefine and reinvent their destinies and the patriarchal reader's expectations.

The subversion of the established order and the reader's complacency toward the status quo is a quality often ascribed to the use of fantasy. It is also a common characteristic of the antiauthoritarian literature for children which emerged in Europe and the United States in the 1960s and continues in Puerto Rico today in such authors as Rosario Ferré. The author has three published collections and a forthcoming volume entitled *Cuentos de hadas* (Fairy tales).

The redefinition of cultural paradigms through literature that takes place throughout Ferré's works for adults can be found in her children's stories as well. A good example is her rereading of the tales of "Juan Bobo" (a folkloric character based on Spanish tradition and therefore common to many Hispanic countries) from an antiauthoritarian and anticolonial perspective, reflecting the author's political commitment. At the same time, the stories maintain an imaginative and poetic simplicity that characterize the best of children's literature.

While many of Ferré's female characters in her earlier works suffer from the type of self-destructive behavior that Jean Franco analyzes in "Self-Destructing Heroines," her children's tales are an interesting departure from this mode. This may be due to the author's personal evolution, but it may also reflect her philosophy regarding the power of such literature for young readers. Several of her children's stories point toward the feminist goal of correcting the androcentric bias of traditional fairy tales and the negative image of women often found there.

Critics have noted the affiliation of Ferré's work with the fairy tale in her 1976 collection of short stories, *Papeles*, not only in the selection of the titles (i.e., "La bella dormiente") but also in the tone and use of fantasy in "La muñeca menor." One of the stories, "Pico Rico Mandorico," based on a children's rhyme, is an interesting example of the author's rereading of traditional texts since, in this case, Ferré's point of departure is the theme of Cristina Rossetti's nineteenth-century poem, *Goblin Market*. In changing *Goblin Market*'s Laura and Lizzie into Alicia and Elisa who now live in a tropical region dominated by a strange and powerful landowner, Ferré has transformed not only the cultural content of the tale but its philosophical dimensions as well, by working from within the female literary tradition. Ferré's story, in which one of the sisters symbolically castrates the abusive patriarchal power of the landowner and enables the collective entity to cast off its masochistic passivity, becomes a parable of female empowerment as well as a sociopolitical critique of the exploitative relationship between landowner and peasants in Latin American society.

Perhaps one of the most distinguishing characteristics of Rosario Ferré as a writer is her ability to fuse the "exterior realities" she aimed for as a novice—the "important" social and historical issues she refers to in "La cocina de la escritura"—with the interior world of emotion, intuition, and passion. A good example of her skill in this regard is the novel *Maldito amor*. The work takes place in Puerto Rico and traces some one hundred years of Puerto Rican history, from the times of the United States invasion of the island in 1898 to an imaginary future in the 1990s in which the United States "threatens" to force the island into becoming independent. It covers several generations of Puerto Rican upper class families and those whose lives are effected by them. We see the changing social and economic relationships that evolve within the original plantation oligarchy, the "sugar barons," who are displaced by large U.S. corporations and eventually become dependent on North American economic interests.

Maldito amor is a composite work that includes a short novella, "Maldito amor," and three additional narratives: "El regalo" (The gift), "Isolda en el espejo" (Isolda in the mirror), and "La extraña muerte del capitancito Candelario" (The unusual death of little Captain Candelario). Although each of the narratives is complete in and of itself, they are all tied together by a common motif: the revision and appropriation of official history by the marginalized sectors of society—women, the poor, and people of color. The work puts into question the relationship between the metahistorical and infrahistorical components of official culture which it scrutinizes and undermines in a subtle and often humorous manner. Less fantastic than earlier works, *Maldito amor* nevertheless manifests several thematic characteristics that can be found throughout Ferré's works: an examination of the role of racial prejudice in the creation of Puerto Rican cultural identity, and an emphasis on the dependent, marginal position of women. With the exception of the last story in which the female character (symbolically referred to as "Barbara") manipulates the male power figure for political ends, the other stories present female characters—wives, students, brides-to-be—who must rely on the powerful and wealthy to realize their goals.

Ferré's first collection of works portrayed many women in unhappy relationships with men; that theme is also found in *Maldito amor*, published exactly ten years later. One is reminded of her words in "La cocina de la escritura" when she relates her feelings after having written "La muñeca menor," a work that she felt initially to be framed in the historical and sociopolitical context she had outlined. Her theme, however, "was still love, complaint, and—oh! I had to admit it—even vengeance. The image of that woman, hovering for years on end at the edge of that cane field with her broken heart, had touched me deeply. It was she who had finally opened the window for me, the window that had been so hermetically sealed, the window to my story" (p. 233). Far from perceiving love as a purely "feminine" concern, Rosario Ferré's writing reveals it in all its aspects and manifestations as a *human* desire and necessity, while the experience of her writing compels her readers to explore the unlocked "windows" of their own.

SURVEY OF CRITICISM

In his selection of twenty Latin American narrators from 1964 to 1980, the distinguished critic Angel Rama (1981) includes a fragment of the novel *Maldito Amor* by Rosario Ferré and refers to her work as being in the forefront of the region's literary production. Ferré has enjoyed equal praise by other noted critics and authors both internationally and from within her own country. Josefina Rivera de Alvarez' history of Puerto Rican literature (1983) recognizes Ferré's important contributions in a variety of genres and gives particular acknowledgment to her poetic achievements in *Fábulas*, considering it "Rosario Ferré's best work and one of exceptional significance within the framework of contemporary Puerto Rican lyric poetry" (p. 731).

In her study of Ferré's short stories in *Papeles de Pandora*, Lisa E. Davis (1979) expresses the opinion that "Rosario Ferré's short stories contribute something original to the genre" (p. 84), and Arcadio Díaz Quiñones (1975) foresaw her literary potential in a perceptive commentary on the story "De tu lado al paraíso" (From your side to Paradise), published in *Sin Nombre* in 1975, prior to the publication of her collection *Papeles*. He notes its "corrosive capability" in drawing "a connection between virginity and prostitution, making use of all manner of biblical reminiscences to underline moral and social corruption, while at the same time analyzing a social class and the female condition" (p. 7).

Ferré's critical essays in *Sitio a Eros* (1986) have received less favorable responses. While many critics find the essays to be a useful complement for understanding Ferré's imaginative work, others consider the biographies of women artists to be impressionistic and biased. María José Chávez, for example, finds them lacking in precision and objectivity.

A recent review of her critical analysis of the Uruguayan short story writer Felisberto Hernández describes Ferré's literary criticism as "clear and cogent," influenced by Tzvetan Todorov and Eric S. Rabkin (Case, 1987). It should be noted that Ferré has written numerous critical essays in journals and periodicals, and introduced to the international reading public the talents of some of Puerto Rico's most noteworthy contemporary artists, whose works she published in the pages of *Zona* during her years as director of the journal.

Ferré's children's stories have also provoked contradictory opinions among critics. All are in agreement as to their literary value: Ferré's poetic retelling of traditional folk and fairy tales are among her best works. The debate has often focused on whether or not they are actually intended for children. In several reviews of her children's collections, Efraín Barradas (1979) expresses the opinion that the tales are really pseudo-fairy tales, intended for adult audiences, with social and political commentary that is inaccessible to children. Despite her use of the fairy tale technique and motifs, Barradas claims that they are an adult's attempt to see through the eyes of a child and view the world outside of accepted rational logic. Luz María Umpierre-Herrera appears to agree with his estimation, stating that the macabre settings and language in such stories as "Pico Rico Mandorico," coupled with its complex erotic and Christian symbolism, demand a more sophisticated reader than is normally found among children.

Margarite Fernández Olmos's analysis of Ferré's children's tales differs from their evaluation. Fernández Olmos maintains that the value of Ferré's stories for young readers should not be dismissed, particularly when one considers that children's literature has traditionally been a cultural projection of adult authors who were well aware of their potential for socialization. According to Fernández Olmos, Ferré's children's stories represent a radical departure from the traditional type of children's tale in Puerto Rico in two repects. First, as opposed to the type of children's tale that relied almost exclusively on folklore or local tradition for its themes, Ferré's stories incorporate a wider variety of influences ranging from the ancient Oriental fable, Spanish picaresque, and European literary fairy tales to Iroquois Indian folklore and Puerto Rican oral literature. Second, Ferré's stories go beyond a simple defense of local culture—the focus of much traditional folklore—to question what is arbitrary and unjust. In a country like Puerto Rico in which the focus of much of the literature is on the experience of cultural and political aggression from without, Ferré achieves the delicate balance required of an artist who, at the same time, is calling for a change in the social relations of power at home, changes that imply more than a simple exchange of authority.

Rosario Ferré's writing began to attract critical attention almost immediately after her first publications. Her social prominence undoubtedly intrigued readers and critics in Puerto Rico whose attitude quickly changed from one of initial curiosity to admiration for her success. Outside of Puerto Rico, Ferré has been the subject of numerous articles, several dissertations, and many conference panels. Her story "La bella durmiente" appears as one of three short novels written by outstanding contemporary Latin American authors in the college text, *Ritos de iniciación*. Rosario Ferré's works are indisputably in the vanguard of Latin American literature today and will continue to be the subject of criticism in years to come.

BIBLIOGRAPHY

Works by Rosario Ferré

Papeles de Pandora. Mexico City: Editorial Joaquín Mortiz, 1976.
El medio pollito. Puerto Rico: Huracán, 1976.
La caja de cristal. Mexico City: La Máquina de Escribir, 1978.
Sitio a Eros: siete ensayos literarios. Mexico City: Editorial Joaquín Mortiz, 1980; expanded 2d ed., 1986.
La mona que le pisaron la cola. Puerto Rico: Huracán, 1980.

"El cuento de hadas." *Sin Nombre* 2 (July-Sept. 1980):36–40.
Los cuentos de Juan Bobo. Puerto Rico: Huracán, 1981.
Fábulas de la garza desangrada. Mexico City: Editorial Joaquín Mortiz, 1982.
"La cocina de la escritura." *La sartén por el mango.* Eds. Patricia Elena González and
      Eliana Ortega. Puerto Rico: Huracán, 1984. Pp. 137–54.
"El Acomodador": una lectura fantástica de Felisberto Hernández. Mexico City: Fondo
      de Cultura Económica, 1986.
Maldito Amor. Mexico City: Editorial Mortiz, 1986.
Sonatinas. Puerto Rico: Huracán, 1989.
El árbol y sus sombras, siete ensayos críticos. Mexico City: Fondo de Cultura Económica
      (forthcoming).

Translations of Rosario Ferré

Ferré, Rosario, trans. "Envoy" (poem). *The Defiant Muse: Hispanic Feminist Poems
      from the Middle Ages to the Present.* Eds. Angel Flores and Kate Flores. New
      York: Feminist Press, 1986. Pp. 112–13.
———. *Sweet Diamond Dust* (novel). New York: Ballantine Press, 1988.
Ferré, Rosario, and Kathy Taylor, trans. "The Glass Box" (novella). *The Massachusetts
      Review* 3 & 4 (Fall-Winter 1986):699–711.
Ferré, Rosario, and Diana Vélez, trans. "The Youngest Doll" (short story). *Feminist
      Studies* 2 (Summer 1986):243–49.
Fischer, Kristen, trans. "Pico Rico Mandorico" (short story). *New England Review and
      Bread Loaf Quarterly* 4 (Summer 1985):498–504.
Rabassa, Gregory, trans. "Four Poems." *Review* 33 (Sept.-Dec. 1984):53–55.
———. "The Youngest Doll" (short story). *The Kenyon Review* 1 (1980):163–67.
Vélez, Diana, trans. "The Writing Kitchen" (essay). *Feminist Studies* 2 (Summer
      1986):227–42.
Ventura, Cynthia, trans. "When Women Love Men" (short story). *Contemporary Women
      Authors of Latin America: New Translations.* Eds. Doris Meyer and Margarite
      Fernández Olmos. New York: Brooklyn College Press, 1983. Pp. 176–85.
"The Writer's Kitchen," *Lives on the Line: The Testimony of Contemporary Latin
      American Authors.* Ed. Doris Meyer. Berkeley, Calif.: University of California
      Press, 1988. Pp. 212–27.

Works about Rosario Ferré

Agosín, Marjorie. "Génesis de 'La bailarina', un poema de Rosario Ferré." *Mairena*
      13 (1983):19–28.
Barradas, Efraín. "De otra manera más de hablar de aquí y el ahora sin así decirlo."
      Claridad (En Rojo) (San Juan) 4–10 (May 1979):5–6.
Case, Thomas E. Review of *El acomodador. World Literature Today* (Spring 1987):253.
Chaves, María José. "La alegoría como método en los cuentos y ensayos de Rosario
      Ferré." *Third Woman* 2 (1984):64–76.
Davis, Lisa, E. "La puertorriqueña dócil y rebelde en los cuentos de Rosario Ferré."
      Sin Nombre 4 (Jan.-Mar. 1979):82–88.
Díaz Quiñones, Arcadio. Prol. *Sin Nombre* 4 (Apr.-June 1975):5–8.
Escalera Ortiz, Juan. "Perspectiva del cuento 'Mercedes Benz 220 SL'." *Revista/Review
      Interamericana* 3 (Fall 1982):407–17.
Fernández Olmos, Margarite. "Constructing Heroines: Rosario Ferré's *cuentos infantiles*

and Feminine Instruments of Change." *The Lion and the Unicorn* 10 (1986):83–94.

———. "From a Woman's Perspective: The Short Stories of Rosario Ferré and Ana Lydia Vega." *Contemporary Women Authors of Latin America: Introductory Essays*. Eds. Doris Meyer and Margarite Fernández Olmos. New York: Brooklyn College Press, 1983. Pp. 78–90.

———. "Luis Rafael Sánchez and Rosario Ferré: Sexual Politics and Contemporary Puerto Rican Narrative." *Hispania* 70, 1(Mar. 1987):40–46.

———. "Sex, Color and Class in Contemporary Puerto Rican Women Authors." *Heresies* 3 (1982):46–47.

———. "Survival, Growth and Change in the Prose Fiction of Contemporary Puerto Rican Women Writers." *Images and Identities: The Puerto Rican in Two World Contexts*. Ed. Asela Rodríguez de Laguna. New Brunswick, N.J.: Transaction Press, 1987. Pp. 76–88.

Franco, Jean. "Self-Destructing Heroines." *The Minnesota Review* 22 (1984):105–15.

Gautier, Marie-Lise Gazarian. "Rosario Ferré" Interview. *Interviews with Latin American Writers*. Elmwood Park, Ill.: Dalkey Archive Press, 1989. 79–92.

Gelpi, Juan. "Especulación, especularidad y remotivación en *Fábulas de la garza desangrada* de Rosario Ferré." *La Chispa '85: Selected Proceedings*. Ed. Gilbert Paolini. New Orleans: Tulane University, 1985. Pp. 125–32.

Guerra Cunningham, Lucía. "Tensiones paradójicas de la femineidad en la narrativa de Rosario Ferré." *Chasqui: Revista de Literatura Latinoamericana* 2–3 (Feb.-May 1984):13–25.

Heinrich, María Elena. "Entrevista a Rosario Ferré." *Prismal/Cabral* 7–8 (Spring 1982): 98–103.

Lagos-Pope, María-Inés. "Sumisión y rebeldía: El doble o la representación de la alienación femenina en narraciones de Marta Brunet y Rosario Ferré." *Revista Iberoamericana* 132–33 (July-Dec. 1985):731–49.

Levine, Linda Gould, Gloria Feiman Waldman, and Rose S. Minc, eds. "No maś máscaras: un diálogo entre tres escritoras del Caribe: Belkis Cuza Malé—Cuba, Matilde Daviú—Venezuela, Rosario Ferré—Puerto Rico." *Literatures in Transition: The Many Voices of the Caribbean Area: A Symposium*. Gaithersburg, Md.; Upper Montclair, N.J.: Hispamérica; Montclair State College, 1982. Pp. 189–97.

López Jiménez, Ivette. "La muñeca menor: ceremonias y transformaciones en un cuento de Rosario Ferré." *Explicación de Textos Literarios* 1 (1982–1983):49–58.

———. "*Papeles de Pandora*: devastación y ruptura." *Sin Nombre* 1(1983):41–52.

Méndez-Clark, Ronald. "La pasión y la marginalidad en (de) la escritura: Rosario Ferré." *La sartén por el mango*. Eds. Patricia Elena González and Eliana Ortega. Puerto Rico: Huracán, 1984. Pp. 119–30.

Rama, Angel. *Novísimos narradores hispanoamericanos en marcha (1964–1980)*. Mexico City: Marcha Editores, 1981. Pp 307–18.

Rivera de Alvarez, Josefina. *Literatura puertorriqueña: su proceso en el tiempo*. Madrid: Ediciones Partenón, 1983. Pp. 720, 721, 729–32, 762–65, 767, 787–90, 838–40, 847, 895.

Rojo, Grínor, and Cynthia Steele. *Ritos de iniciación: tres novelas cortas de Hispanoamérica*. Boston: Houghton Mifflin Co., 1986. Pp. 147–209.

Solá, María. "Habla femenina e ideología feminista en *Papeles de Pandora* de Rosario Ferré." *Alero* 1 (1982):19–26.

Umpierre-Herrera, Luz María. "Los cuentos ¿infantiles? de Rosario Ferré—estrategias subversivas." *Nuevas aproximaciones críticas a la literatura puertorriqueña contemporánea*. Puerto Rico: Editorial Cultural, 1983. Pp. 89–101.

————. "Un manifiesto literario: *Papeles de Pandora* de Rosario Ferré." *The Bilingual Review* 2 (1982):120–26.

Vélez, Diana L. "Power and the Text: Rebellion in Rosario Ferré's *Papeles de Pandora*." *Journal of the Midwest Modern Language Association* 17, 1 (1984):70–80.

SARA GALLARDO
(1931–1988)
Argentina

Norma Beatriz Grasso

BIOGRAPHY

Born in the city of Buenos Aires on December 23, 1931, Sara Gallardo showed a marked interest in literature and an extensive acquaintance with it at an early age. According to the autobiographical sketch included in her delightful story for children, *¡Adelante, la isla!* (Onward, the island!), published in 1982, by the time she was eleven she had devoured countless books that stimulated her imagination and her desire to write. She knew that some day she would be a writer, although she did not yet know what she wanted to write. At about that time, her father decided to buy a house in the country, and she applied herself to exploring the countryside. These childhood experiences would enrich her dreams and, in one form or other, find a place in her works.

Three important events occurred in Sara Gallardo's life in the 1950s: She became a journalist, she married, and in 1958 she published her first novel, *Enero* (January), a small masterpiece about country life. In 1963 she published her second novel, *Pantalones azules* (Blue slacks), which won the Third Municipal Prize, and in 1968, her third novel appeared: *Los galgos, los galgos* (The greyhounds, the greyhounds), the winner of two important prizes—the First Municipal Prize, and the City of Necochea Prize of the Sixth National Festival of Letters. A reduced version of *Los galgos, los galgos* appeared in 1975 under the title *Historia de los galgos* (The story of the greyhounds).

In the 1960s and 1970s, Gallardo traveled extensively in Latin America, Europe, and the Orient, during which time she sent articles on a variety of subjects to the prestigious magazines *Atlántida* and *Confirmado*, both of Buenos Aires; and from 1978 to 1988, to *La Nación* (Buenos Aires), one of the most important newspapers in Argentina. Her trips to northern Argentina in 1968 were the immediate stimulus for her fourth novel, *Eisejuaz*. ("Eisejuaz" is the name of the protagonist, a Chaco Indian.) The work appeared in 1971 and is unquestionably one of her greatest artistic achievements.

Two stories for children, *"Los dos amigos"* (The two friends) and "Teo y la TV" (Theo and TV) appeared in 1974; and a year later, another story for children, *Las siete puertas* (The seven doors); then, in 1977, her collection of short stories, *El país del humo* (The country of the smoke), which contains different types of narratives (fantastic stories, tales, prose poems).

A major change in Sara Gallardo's life took place in 1978 when she settled in Barcelona with her three children thanks to a contract she had with Pomaire Publishing for the publication of her fourth novel, *La rosa en el viento* (The rose in the wind), which appeared in 1979. That same year Gallardo temporarily returned to Buenos Aires on the occasion of the presentation of her latest novel in that city. In an interview with Antonio Requeni for *La Prensa* of Buenos Aires, she says that she decided to settle in Europe because at that time she needed a change. She adds that her European experience has had no influence on her literary works, for she bears her native country within her and projects it everywhere. What has changed, she adds, is her vision of Argentina and its landscape. In *La rosa en el viento* and in some of the stories of *El país del humo*, her vision has reached a mythical dimension. The landscape is no longer the countryside she knew as a girl but Patagonia, where she has never been, and yet which she describes with great enthusiasm. Almost all the protagonists of these two volumes are foreigners who settled in Argentina at the end of the nineteenth century in search of better opportunities or of adventures. This, Gallardo says, illustrates the character of Argentina (or of the American continent) as a territory of wild illusions and lost causes. For Sara Gallardo the real protagonist of *El país del humo* and *La rosa en el viento* is America, the whole continent. The change in her creative process, she adds, may indicate her evolution as a writer or her growing maturity as a person; but it is not a sudden conversion caused by her residence in Europe.

After spending three years in Barcelona, Gallardo moved to Switzerland with her youngest child (from a second marriage), where she lived until 1982. Then she moved to Rome, where she resided for six years. In 1987 Editorial Celtia invited Gallardo to make a selection of her works for publication in a special anthology, *Páginas de Sara Gallardo, seleccionadas por la autora* (Pages of Sara Gallardo, selected by the author), which forms part of an anthology series that includes the names of the most prestigious contemporary Argentine writers.

Sara Gallardo died suddenly on June 14, 1988, during a brief visit to Buenos Aires. She left behind many unfinished projects.

MAJOR THEMES

The theme of alienation in its various aspects (self-estrangement, incommunicability, the separation from God and from nature, and the exploitation of the poor) is at the heart of Gallardo's fiction. But Gallardo does not propound ideas; she presents characters and disappears behind them.

In her first novel, *Enero*, Gallardo combines a study of rural life with certain universal themes, particularly loneliness and lack of communication. Nefer, the protagonist, is an adolescent who has become pregnant as a result of rape at her sister's wedding party. As she cannot confide in her family, her sense of desolation is intensified. Gallardo's juxtaposition of the character's antithetical preoccupations in the first chapter of the novel shows the incompatibility and emotional distance between Nefer and her family. Nefer's interior monologue reveals her critical problem and anguish while her father talks about the harvest, her sister listens to a soap opera on the radio, and her mother grumbles.

This technique, reminiscent of the episode of the fair in Flaubert's *Madame Bovary*, also serves to underscore the dramatic tension between Nefer's inner world and the outside world. The passing of time, expressed through the leitmotif of the harvest, is Nefer's major enemy. She knows that when the harvest comes, she will no longer be able to hide her pregnancy. A sense of powerlessness to change her situation leads to contradictory actions and thoughts, a yearning for a miracle coupled with a death-wish, a rebellious and defiant attitude toward her mother, and an escape through fantasy.

In Nefer's world of make-believe, her ordeal becomes a romantic and impossible dream that further alienates her from herself and from others. She obliterates from memory the painful reality of her rape and transforms it into a love story. Her fantasy becomes so real that she almost succeeds in believing that she is pregnant by the man she "loves," whom she has only seen from a distance, the same way that Don Quixote saw his Dulcinea. But her mother, with her moral righteousness and rigidity, and her empty religious formalism, characteristic of the traditional society of which she is a product, brings her back to a brutal reality and makes her marry the man who raped her in order to save appearances. Although the mother does not know that Nefer is a rape victim, it is unlikely that she would have believed in her innocence, or in the innocence of any rape victim. For her, there are only good women and bad women, and "El que se anda divirtiendo, que la pague." (p. 111, He who is having fun, must pay.)

Nicolás, Nefer's future husband, expresses similar views: "tan mal no lo habrás pasado" (p. 122, you musn't have had such a bad time). Even Nefer herself feels guilty about her condition. For this reason, she does not take Holy Communion, for she fears that God will punish her for her "sin."

In spite of Nefer's vanity and egotism (as seen through her thoughts), it is impossible not to feel compassion for her. The only ones who express sympathy toward her are her father and a youth who works with him, but they cannot change her hopeless situation. In this novel, as well as in the two novels that follow it, Gallardo sees society, with its false traditional *mores* and religious hypocrisy, as a threat to the protagonist's self-realization. In the end, Nefer, who is twice a victim (of rape and of her milieu), is doomed to the frustration of remaining forever lonely, unloved, and unfulfilled.

In *Pantalones azules* and *Los galgos, los galgos*, social and psychological forces combine to make the protagonists, to a considerable extent, victims. Both characters are members of socially elite families, who have lived from their earliest age according to other people's perceptions and expectations of them. Julián in *Los galgos, los galgos* assumes his responsibilities as an attorney in his uncle's office with total disinterest and boredom simply because he is expected to perpetuate family values. Alejandro in *Pantalones azules*, on the other hand, joins an anti-Semitic group and conforms to traditional society blindly, out of a need to "belong." But they are not happy in this condition. A true sense of community and a genuine purpose in life are lacking.

In their personal relations, Julián's only intense ties are with Lisa, an artist separated from her husband. But since their relationship violates the established norms of society, Julián must live in two antithetical worlds. In one, he lives in freedom with Lisa and the greyhounds; in the other he conforms to generally accepted mores and family criteria. Although he resents his family for shunning Lisa, he pays homage to traditional family values at the expense of his deepest ideals and feelings. His infatuation with "tradition" leads him to conceive the wild idea of becoming a rancher; and although he immediately realizes that he has made a major mistake, out of pride and stubbornness (and contrary to Lisa's advice), he carries out his plan. Julián's weakness and lack of courage to break away from the past cost him the loss of the only woman for whom he has ever felt genuine love.

In *Pantalones azules*, Alejandro's relationship with Elisa, in contrast to Julián's in *Los galgos, los galgos*, is based on traditional social and moral standards. She is a Madonna, pure and perfect. But there is no true dialogue between them. Their lack of communication reaches a climax when Alejandro tries to confess to her his infidelity while she was away. Even though he tells her only part of the truth, Elisa's explosion of anger teaches him that true communion between them is impossible. To avoid conflicts in the future, he will always have to withdraw somewhat from her. Alejandro thus gains "emotional" security by giving up his independence and integrity.

Although social pressure is strongly felt, Gallardo does not depict the protagonists as simply victims. As individuals, their personal sense of identity does not depend on family or social criteria but on their freedom to make choices. Both are aware of the dichotomy between their inner and their outside selves, and they are also aware of the duality within themselves. Both are confronted repeatedly with the need to choose and, although there are moments when they approximate the existential view of the need for self-determination, they invariably avoid having to make decisions that will change their lives and deliver them from past conditioning.

Alejandro's major test in life comes through Irma, an art student whose simple love and human warmth are worth far more than his prestigious lineage. His contradictory attitudes toward her stress his dichotomy. On the one hand, he despises her because of her inferior social status as a Polish Jewish immigrant; he hates her for her dignity and mastery over him. On the other hand, he is drawn to her. While despising and hating her, he begins to fall in love with her. But Alejandro is not an existentialist, and he avoids the anxiety connected with emotional conflict. At the end of the novel, Alejandro is "safe" in the burrow of his social world. He pays a high price for security: He loses his self-identity in exchange.

In *Los galgos, los galgos*, the theme of alienation is first encountered in its simplest social form, and then gradually gains in richness and complexity, as Gallardo develops the psychological aspect of Julián's estrangement. His breakup with Lisa leaves him in a state of desolation, although he is reluctant to recognize that he needs her. When his half-hearted attempts to find her fail, he leaves for Paris to take a course at the Sorbonne on the underdeveloped countries, a subject in which he has no interest. He soon gives up his studies, and, like Roquentin in Sartre's novel *Nausea*, he begins to "float." The third part of the novel, apparently a digression completely unrelated to the love story, actually reinforces Julián's escapism and increasing alienation. After three years of shallow affairs and superficial diversions, and only a few meaningful conversations with some soul-mates, he returns to Buenos Aires where he again tries to find Lisa. When he realizes that their relationship is over, he succumbs to the charms of an aristocratic widow Adelina and, adding another link to his chain of errors, he marries her.

Julián's marriage to Adelina plunges him into a spiritual numbness. Life becomes so structured and oppressive that he spends weeks in seclusion, self-absorbed and despondent. Unlike Proust, he does not recapture the past. He is possessed by it and subjects himself to the harshest self-criticism. Gallardo here emphasizes Julián's growing imbalance and morbid excesses, from the neglect of his physical appearance to his irritability and aggressive sexuality. His relationship with Adelina can be best described as sadomasochistic. His hostility toward Adelina and his sexual abuse of her are triggered in part by his desire to see her "porcelain face," as he calls it, express some human emotion, but above all by his perception of her as someone who manipulates people. Julián's view of Adelina is right. Her total composure after each act of sexual violence and her insistence that she needs it; her feeling of despair when she sees him leave and the way she clings to him, begging him to stay, are proof that she will be a masochist as long as she can possess Julián. In turn, Julián allows her domination over him in order to become one with her. The tension between them stems from an interdependence which is a hopeless attempt to escape their aloneness. Julián's passivity and his failure to come to terms with his individual existence are the reasons why, at the end of the novel, he finds himself in spiritual limbo.

Eisejuaz, Gallardo's fourth novel, is a fascinating story, masterfully told, about a man, a seer, who obeys God's "call" to care for his fellow beings. Although this work is unlike anything she had written before, it continues to develop the central theme of alienation of the preceding books. It elevates a primitive man, a Chaco Indian of the extinct tribes in northern Argentina, to the role of protagonist. He makes no claims of divinity, nor does he profess to have the power to heal, but, reminiscent of Jesus, divination and miraculous powers are part of his magico-religious experiences. Eisejuaz, however, is neither a contemplative mystic nor a shaman in the strict sense. He remains a man, torn between contradictory and equal forces. On the one hand lies his deep religious faith (a mixture of Christianity and the animistic religion of the Indians), and on the other, a series of lethal temptations that range from carnal desire to a strong urge to avenge social injustices. It is through this inner struggle that the story of Eisejuaz expresses the universal drama of human existence.

His dream had been to be chief of his people, at the mercy of greedy bosses and landowners, who sold themselves and their daughters for money or sexual gratification. Eisejuaz knows that what they need is a leader who will raise their consciousness and instill in them a sense of self-respect. He knows, too, that their time has come to an end and that the present belongs to the whites. Furthermore, his mission is not to be chief but to fulfill his promise to God and take care of Paqui, a paralyzed white man who is the antithesis of Jesus and Eisejuaz. Paqui is depicted as representing man's lowest possible state, for whom God does not exist and human feelings and relations have no significance. Therefore, when Eisejuaz, despite his wishes, declines the offer to be chief because of his inner mission to save "the carrion of the whites," as everybody calls Paqui, he alienates the very people he wants to help.

Eisejuaz's asceticism and communion with nature in its pristine state cause misunderstandings and his estrangement from the townspeople, who treat him like a parasite. His eclectic religious practices alienate him from the missionary, who fails to understand Eisejuaz's complex spiritual life, which stands nearer to that of a true mystic or a shaman than to the missionary's rigid doctrines and un-Christian attitude. In addition, the chain of lies that Paqui, now transformed into a "holy" man, tells about his benefactor, and that people believe to be true, causes the final break between Eisejuaz and the rest of the community.

Although Sara Gallardo achieves highly sensitive effects, especially in the lyricism of Eisejuaz's and Ayó Vicente Aparicio's chants and rituals, and in the marvelous language that she creates (a fusion of the laconic speech of the Chaco Indians and the rhythms of the New Testament), so similar to poetry, the predominant image of the novel is one of violence. The stories of savage vengeance between rival tribes, the brutal treatment of prostitutes, the mobs that trample people to death, and Paqui's cruelty and greed, all depict human evil. After seeing the misery of the prostitutes (especially of a young Indian girl, sold to a brothel by her own father), Eisejuaz does not ask the Lord any more questions; like Job, for the first time he utters his most heartfelt complaint.

These social realities that reduce men and women to objects and instruments of profit, like prostitution and the exploitation of the workers and of the land, are other aspects of the theme of alienation which Gallardo develops in the novel. However, some characters (besides Eisejuaz) embody affirmation; among them are the Franciscan priest, the young Indian girl, and the future teacher, who complements Eisejuaz. They all have an enormous capacity for love, unselfishness, compassion, and sacrifice. As Eisejuaz prepares the grave where he will be buried next to Paqui, he tells the Indian girl that, because of people like her, the world has not been broken and will not break. Despite the vision of evil and social decay, the novel ends in a note of hope.

Gallardo's fifth novel, *La rosa en el viento* (1979), and some of the stories in *El país del humo* (1977), mark a departure from her previous works in their landscape, protagonists, subject matter, tone, and structure. It is in these two works that Gallardo comes close to the Romantic spirit that appealed to her so much, as she introduces strange characters, adventures, or wild dreamers, and places them in one of the most inhospitable places on earth: windswept Patagonia. However, these works are not entirely Romantic stories. They combine Romantic, surrealist, and mythic elements.

According to Sara Gallardo, *La rosa en el viento* began as a short story she had planned to include in *El país del humo*, but it was too long for a collection of short stories. Later, she went back to it and decided to write a novel. But the novel took a strange form and developed into a spiral movement, like that of a rose that twists and turns (Requeni, 1979). The novel relates the stories of various characters (Russian, Norwegian, Italian, Jewish immigrants) in more or less long short stories focused on present events and the protagonists' family history. What gives unity to the novel is their common background: They are uprooted individuals trying to find their *raison d'être* in a new land.

The novel and many of the stories in *El país del humo* are variations on the theme of estrangement. Because these works encompass so much, it is impossible to do them justice in such a brief space. But in both books the dream of the impossible invariably leads to failure, impotence, disillusionment, and destruction.

In the novel Andrei, a Russian emigré enamored of a woman who does not reciprocate his feelings, gives up his career as a writer and goes to Patagonia in search of gold, convinced that he can conquer her with riches. As he is about to depart, he imagines that he rides thoroughbreds in a distant and prestigious land. Lina, the Jewish immigrant, who follows Andrei to Patagonia a few years later, sees herself in a distant "city" with splendid buildings and surrounded by all the comforts. Orellie Antoine I, a twentieth-century Don Quixote, sees himself as king of Patagonia and Araucanía, restoring the rights of the Indians and putting France back on the map as a great empire. Olaf, a Norwegian who shares a hut and a deaf-mute teenage Indian girl with Andrei, is the only one who has embarked on a long journey without any dreams of conquest. He is there in search of adventures and to forget about his past.

In losing their illusions, the protagonists also lose their ideals and human feelings (with the exception of Orellie Antoine I, who, though defeated, remains a Don Quixote until the end). Their sense of futility and sadness is profoundly linked to sexual frenzy and violence, for they can only express their frustration by sex, or, in Lina's case, by sex and murder. Their spiritual wasteland and isolation from one another correspond to the wilderness of the landscape. Thus, in their quest for the unattainable, the main theme of *La rosa en el viento* and some of the stories of *El país del humo*, the protagonists are doomed to destruction.

SURVEY OF CRITICISM

Sara Gallardo's reputation as a major literary figure in Argentina has long been established, and her works have been acclaimed by well-known literary critics and reviewers, some of whom are also creative writers of note. Yet there are no scholarly publications on Gallardo's complete works or any analytic essays of individual novels or short stories available to this author.

The enthusiastic reviews of her works range from brief notes to longer "studies" of about three pages long. The introduction to *Páginas de Sara Gallardo seleccionadas por la autora* by Ricardo Rey Beckford (himself a poet, short story writer, and essayist) is the longest study of Gallardo's complete works written to date. Because of space limitations, however, it only contains rather brief statements about each novel and collection of short stories, with some perceptive observations about Gallardo's narrative techniques and style. However, from the moment that her first novel (*Enero*) appeared, literary critics and reviewers have widely recognized Gallardo's exceptional talent as a fiction writer. Among the major aspects of her art, they point out the lyrical quality of her rich and articulate prose; the poetic evocation of the milieu; the creation of deeply moving and convincing characters; and her vivid imagination and sense of humor.

In her review of *Enero* for the prestigious literary journal *Sur*, María Elena Walsh (1959), also a poet and short story writer, states that the novel is a masterpiece comparable to the best French novels. Like Juan Carlos Ghiano, a distinguished literary critic and novelist who reviewed *Enero* for *La Prensa* of Buenos Aires, Walsh praises Gallardo's rigorous but spontaneous style, the poetic synthesis of the narration devoid of digressive references to the past or of detailed descriptions, and the cinematic agility of her images. Both critics underline Gallardo's ability to portray simple, authentic characters of the Argentine countryside who, because of their profound human conception, transcend the particular and reach the universal. Walsh adds that, although Gallardo does not sacrifice her art to preach or to expound ideas, the selection of the theme of the novel implies a sincere preoccupation with problems that go beyond the individual.

Since the publication of *La rosa en el viento* in 1979, Gallardo herself has contributed to the evaluation of her works. Through her brief comments on her books which appear in her autobiographical sketch (*¡Adelante, la isla!*, pp. 50–61) and especially in her interview with Antonio Requeni (1979), it is possible to see the development of her artistic creation. As Ricardo Rey Beckford also observes in his preliminary study, Gallardo's literary production can be divided into three distinct periods. The first is the "realistic" period of her first three novels; the second is marked by the unique creation, *Eisejuaz*, considered by Rodolfo Godino and Martín Alberto Noel to be one of the strangest and at the same time most convincing novels ever written by an Argentine novelist; and the third period includes some of the fantastic stories of *El país del humo* and *La rosa en el viento*. As Gallardo herself points out, it represents a change or an "evolution" in her way of conceiving the fictional world. She compares *La rosa en el viento* to a small *concerto* in which certain themes are identified with different instruments and are repeated and played with other rhythms and styles, but as a whole they achieve unity of inspiration and emotion (Requeni, 1979).

Eduardo Gudiño Kieffer (1987), who reviewed *Páginas de Sara Gallardo seleccionadas por la autora* for *La Nación* of Buenos Aires, says that there is an ambiguity in Gallardo's selection that is characteristic of poetry and that leaves the reader "entre este mundo y otros mundos" (p. 5, between this world and other worlds). "This world," he says, because she does not disdain daily events; and "other worlds," because she projects them to a different dimension, at times magical, which leaves the reader fascinated and rejoicing. He concludes his review with a comment about the musical quality of Gallardo's prose and its unity of form and content in a "corpus" that does not admit precise and definitive limits between the physical and the spiritual.

These essays and reviews by some of the better Argentine critics contain a number of perceptive and acute observations on Gallardo's narrative techniques, style, and characterization, and they shed light on individual novels. However, there is need for analytic studies of Gallardo's highly meritorious and challenging works.

BIBLIOGRAPHY

Works by Sara Gallardo

Enero. Buenos Aires: Editorial Sudamericana, 1958.
Pantalones azules. Buenos Aires: Editorial Sudamericana, 1963.
Los galgos, los galgos. Buenos Aires: Editorial Sudamericana, 1968.
Eisejuaz. Buenos Aires: Editorial Sudamericana, 1971.
"Los dos amigos" y "Teo y la TV". Buenos Aires: Editorial Angel Estrada, 1974.
Las siete puertas. Buenos Aires: Editorial Angel Estrada, 1975.
Historia de los galgos. Buenos Aires: Editorial Alfa Argentina, 1975.
El país del humo. Buenos Aires: Editorial Sudamericana, 1977.
La rosa en el viento. Barcelona: Editorial Pomaire, 1979.
¡Adelante, la isla! Buenos Aires: Editorial Abril, 1982.
Páginas de Sara Gallardo seleccionadas por la autora. Preliminary study by Ricardo
    Rey Beckford. Buenos Aires: Editorial Celtia, 1987.

Edition by Sara Gallardo

El secreto claro (diálogos). *H. A. Murena y D. J. Vogelmann*. Buenos Aires: Editorial
  Fraterna, 1978.

Works about Sara Gallardo

Di Paola Levin, Jorge. "Sara Gallardo, una mujer de cuidado." *Confirmado*, June 7,
  1979.
Garasa, Delfín Leocadio. "Un presentido trasmundo." Review of *El país del humo. La
  Nación*, Sept. 11, 1977.
Ghiano, Juan Carlos. "Auténtico realismo." Review of *Enero. La Prensa*, Jan. 4, 1959.
Godino, Rodolfo. "La predilección de Dios." Review of *Eisejuaz. La Nación*, Dec. 19,
  1971.
Gudiño Kieffer, Eduardo. "Este mundo y otros mundos." *La Nación*, June 21, 1987:5.
Noel, Martín Alberto. "Eisejuaz." Review of *Eisejuaz. La Prensa*, Apr. 2, 1972.
———. "El rincón de una memoria." Review of *La rosa en el viento. La Nación*, July
  1, 1979.
Pazos, Luis. "Volver del silencio." *Somos*, May 13, 1977.
Requeni, Antonio. "Diálogo con Sara Gallardo. Vivir en Barcelona." *La Prensa*, May
  6, 1979.
Rey Beckford, Ricardo. "Estudio preliminar." *Páginas de Sara Gallardo seleccionadas
  por la autora*. Buenos Aires: Editorial Celtia, 1987. Pp. 11–27.
Roffé, Reina. "El país de una mujer en soledad." *Siete Días*, Sept. 22, 1977.
Walsh, María Elena. "Enero." Review of *Enero. Sur* 257 (Mar.-Apr. 1959):73–75.
Zaragoza, Celia. "El mundo cotidiano de Sara Gallardo." *La Nación*, Dec. 20, 1970.

GRISELDA GAMBARO
(b. 1928)
Argentina

Sandra Messinger Cypess

BIOGRAPHY

Griselda Gambaro was born in Buenos Aires, Argentina, on July 28, 1928, to first-generation Argentines whose family originated from Italy. (Gambaro's surname is of Italian origin, and, therefore, "Gambaro" is pronounced with the stress on the first syllable.) Her father worked in the post office, and because of her family's limited economic means, after she finished high school in 1943 she went to work in the business office of a publishing company. Through her writing and its successes, including such awards as a Guggenheim in 1982, she has enjoyed greater financial security. Married to the sculptor Juan Carlos Distéfano, Gambaro is the mother of two children: Andrea, born in 1961, and Lucas, born in 1965.

Although Gambaro prefers to live in a small suburb of Buenos Aires, Don Bosco, she has spent some time in Italy and Spain, including a year in Rome in 1970 and almost three years in Barcelona (1977–1980). She has attended many conferences and international drama festivals and been awarded prizes for her fiction as well as her drama. Her first visit to the United States in 1968 was as the guest of the International Exchange Program, and with a Guggenheim award in 1982 she was able to travel to the United States, Mexico, and France, countries in which her work is well known and well received critically. She has returned to the United States frequently as an invited speaker at various conferences and university programs.

Gambaro recalls that from the moment she learned to read she also began to write. She threw away many pieces of work until she was satisfied enough to offer as her first effort worthy of publishing *Madrigal en ciudad* (1963; Madrigal in the city), a collection of three short novellas which won the Prize of the

Argentine Fondo Nacional de las Artes for narrative in 1963. Soon after, she received the Premio Emecé in 1965 for the collection *El desatino* (The blunder), also containing novellas and short stories. At the same time, two prize-winning plays emerged from the prose pieces: *Las paredes* (The walls), earning the Premio de la Asociación de Teatros and the Fondo Nacional de las Artes in 1964, and *El desatino*, the Prize of the *Revista Teatro XX* in 1965. One characteristic of her writing production which emerged from the beginning was her development of some of her fiction into dramatic works almost at the same time as she was writing the prose pieces. She continued this practice until 1972, the year in which she completed work on the novel *Nada que ver con otra historia* (Nothing to do with another story) and the play *Nada que ver* (Out of it). She no longer works in that almost parallel fashion in the two genres; she now writes either a play or a piece of fiction independent of one another. The plays, however, have become more famous than her fiction and have been translated into several languages and staged around the world.

In Argentina, Gambaro was closely associated with the experimental art group located at the Centro de Experimentación Audiovisual del Instituto Torcuato Di Tella, a foundation formed in 1958 to patronize the fine arts and foster socio-logical investigations. The institute, which unfortunately closed in 1971, worked in part as a theatrical laboratory for young writers who were able to experiment with techniques and representations by adapting audiovisual phenomena to the stage. As part of its promotion of vanguardist and creative talents, the institute published as well as produced a number of her plays. Jorge Petraglia, a noted Argentine director and actor, has also been associated with Gambaro's work in both of his talented capacities. Gambaro was once again openly affiliated with a vanguardist theatrical movement in 1981 when she participated in Teatro Abierto (open theater). A group of playwrights, directors, and actors joined together to present twenty-one one-act plays, three plays a day on seven different programs. Like *Decir sí* (Saying yes), presented as part of Teatro Abierto, the majority of the plays were political. The theatrical festival constituted an attack not only on the commercialization of Argentine theater, but also on the military government which was in a weakened enough condition at that time to be unable to prevent the Festival's existence. (In 1983 Girol Press published seven of the plays, including Gambaro's *Decir sí*, in an anthology, *7 dramaturgos argentinos*.)

Gambaro has maintained steady theatrical activity since 1964, when her first produced play, *Las paredes*, also won theatrical prizes. Since then, her productions have continued to be well received in avant-garde Argentine and international theatrical circles. However, despite the fact that Gambaro appears consistently among the names of the top playwrights of her country and of Latin America in general, not all her plays have been produced or published. The explanation has to do with the economics of dramatic productions and, at times in the past, with the political situation. *Información para extranjeros* (Information for foreigners), for example, was written in 1972 at the beginning of the guerrilla movement in Argentina and refers to the "desaparecidos de la guerra sucia" (the people who disappeared during the dirty war) carried on by the military. Gambaro exercised self-censorship when she refused permission for the play to be either performed or published because she was well aware of the dire consequences of such open criticism of the government. It would not be until 1987 that the play would be published by Ediciones de la Flor. Although the army visited her home and confiscated material, she did not fall into official disfavor until 1977; her novel *Ganarse la muerte* (1976; To earn one's death) was critically praised in Spain and in the French translation, yet in Argentina copies were confiscated and its sale prohibited by decree of President Rafael Videla. Because of the very real possibility of political reprisals in that period of the military dictatorship, Gambaro and her family moved to Barcelona where they stayed for three years.

As a woman working in theater, a field that has often been very hostile to women, Gambaro has been asked to comment on the question of discrimination. One of her formal responses can be found in "¿Es posible y deseable una dramaturgia específicamente femenina?" (Is a specifically feminine dramaturgy possible and desirable?), a presentation she gave as part of the Florida International University Symposium on Latin American Theater in 1979, reprinted in the Summer 1980 Supplement of *Latin American Theatre Review*, pp. 17–21. At that time Gambaro stressed her belief that dramatists do not write either as women or as men but as writers who express their particular social experiences, which are naturally tied to their identity within a gender and class. Gambaro emphasized the importance of focusing on the *human* condition and all the elements that influence human relations, of which gender and class are naturally fundamental determining factors. Beginning in the mid-1970s, however, she has become more involved with the particular problems of the female condition in a patriarchal society, and her female characters have increased in number and changed in characterization to reflect the more active stance Gambaro has assumed with regard to women's issues.

MAJOR THEMES

Gambaro's work focuses on the major preoccupations affecting the human condition in the modern world: the alienation of the individual, the difficulties in communicating with others, the individual's subjugation to power, and the abuses of authority.

Gambaro's plays and fictions may be considered tragicomedies based on variations of the grotesque rather than on everyday realistic conventions. Although her presentation of cruelty and violence bespeak a metaphysical anguish, as a Latin American, and particularly as an Argentine writer, she also reacts to a specific sociopolitical milieu, and many of her works can be read as allegories relating to concrete facts and situations in the real world. An allegorical reading is possible even with the early plays where she carefully avoided specific political referents and the use of the Argentine *voseo* in the dialogue (a dialect form of "you" with its own verb conjugations).

Despite anecdotal differences, a recurring pattern of action is found in almost all the plays: An average person finds himself or herself in a not unusual setting which soon becomes transformed into a threatening environment because of the inexplicable menacing actions of adversaries who are often from his or her intimate circle of family and friends. The relationship among the characters is generally that of oppressor to oppressed; the authority figure may be an unsuspected type, as the mother of *El desatino* (1965), who belies her traditional role as a positive nurturing figure, or an obvious dictatorial character named Franco, as in *El campo* (1967, "The Camp"), or the neighborhood barber, as in *Decir sí*. The victim is generally an unassuming individual who does not rise to the challenge of the situation with heroism, but sinks into an abyss of passive cowardice. The Youth of *Las paredes* (1979), Alfonso of *El desatino*, Ignacio of *Los siameses* (1957, The Siamese twins), Martín and Emma of *El campo*, creations of the sixties, are kindred souls to Joe and Valentina of *Dar la vuelta* (1989; Turn around), as well as to the client in *Decir sí*, the aging actress in *El despojamiento* (1981; The striptease); all are physically and spiritually victimized but somehow do not know how to fight back. Gambaro's focus on the victim poignantly stresses the tragedy of life in a controlled society that conjoins the victims themselves to become accomplices of the regime and collaborators in their own victimization. Her plays of the mid-1980s, however, show a marked change in this general pattern so that the victim learns to resist the oppressors. Although in *La malasangre* (1984; Bitter blood), the two rebels Rafael and Dolores suffer like their predecessors, in *Del sol naciente* (1984; From the rising sun) the victims finally join together to express a solidarity of cause that appears to overcome the oppressive system. Instead of an ending in which the oppressor offers the last word, in the final scene Suki, a geisha, and other marginalized figures recognize their common humanity and join forces. The play shows that solidarity on a sociopolitical level can undermine the authoritarian system. In addition, in general humanistic terms, the play reveals that personal relationships no longer need be marked by alienated indifference or moral corruption but should be linked to social responsibility.

Whether the dramatic action is set in faraway Japan, as in *Del sol naciente*, or the temporally distant nineteenth century, as in *La malasangre*, or perhaps in the European period of the Holocaust (*El campo*), Gambaro's plays appear to parallel the trajectory of sociopolitical events of contemporary Argentina as they relate to the individual's response to environment. The initial passivity of her characters, their cruel treatment of one another, and most recently the growing solidarity among the victims reflect a similar inability in her country to counteract the successive military regimes until the debacle occasioned by the Falklands War brought about a group effort to overcome the repression. Her work expresses the duality of contemporary Latin American societies which on the surface appear as controlled, "peaceful" patriarchies, but beneath the surface tranquility, terrible torture, and subjugation await marginalized figures. Gambaro invests the cruel actions and mordant dialogue with macabre humor so that the comic effect heightens the cruelty and sadness of the situations.

An integral aspect of Gambaro's explorations of social relations has to do with the ambiguity and unreliability of our ability to communicate. To express this theme, she creates linguistic games pointing to the multiplicity of meanings inherent in our sign system. The titles she chooses for her works are obvious indications of this play with language, as can be exemplified by reference to *El campo* and *Nada que ver*.

"El campo" signifies "countryside," and carries connotations of peace and tranquility, fresh air, open skies, and physical freedom from constraints. In the play with that title, Martín comes to the "campo" to work, yet the place soon becomes transformed from its traditional reference to assume the particular twentieth-century meaning of a concentration camp. The signs that support the illusion of the first, more harmless meaning of camp—voices of children and farmers singing at work—turn out to exist only as oral signs, tape recordings of a faked reality to confuse Martín and the audience. The menacing treatment of the armed guards, the smell of charred flesh and screams of torture, and Martín's own victimization become the reality of his environment. Martín is transformed into yet another victim in the camp. The trajectory of his experiences, from innocent worker to prisoner, from positive to negative, was first suggested by the ambiguous meaning of the play's title.

Nada que ver is another equivocal title that anticipates a play based on actions of irony and counterpoint. Literally, it means "nothing to see," an irony in a play that is a spectacle meant to be seen. In addition, the phrase is part of a Spanish idiom that conveys the idea that something has nothing to do with another thing, as in "esto no tiene nada que ver con eso" ("this has nothing to do with that"). The title implies that the play has nothing to do with anything else, yet this implication is seen to be patently false once the action begins. Unlike the brief allusion to *Waiting for Godot* at the end of *Los siameses, Nada que ver* clearly wishes to elaborate on its relationship with another well-known text, Mary Shelley's *Frankenstein*. Gambaro offers a mordant parody of the earlier work in order to comment on sociopolitical events relevant to her own time.

The traditional use of rational dialogic exchanges to develop dramatic action, a technique already parodied by the absurdists, undergoes further changes in Gambaro's plays. Whereas in works like Ionesco's *The Bald Soprano*, the characters speak but do not communicate logically, in Gambaro's plays, the victim attempts to communicate, but generally he or she is deliberately deceived by his or her tormentors. When the Youth of *Las paredes* remarks that the walls of his room seem to be growing smaller or that he hears pitiful screams from his invisible neighbors, the spectators, too, notice these real observations. The Custodian ignores or denigrates the observations with the effect that the Youth soon distrusts his own senses and resignedly accedes to whatever the Custodian claims, no matter how "absurd" or out of harmony with the real world. This pattern is found in most of her plays written in the sixties and seventies: The victim's observations of his physical surroundings are verified by the spectators, but the oppressor-figures purposely question and discredit the veracity of the real observations in an attempt to undermine the individual's sense of integrity and well-being. The individual is gradually deprived of the ability to discern for him or herself between real events and the deceptive interpretations offered by the authorities. Attempts to communicate and to make sense of the universe are overwhelmed and the individual is rendered passive, a victim prepared to accept whatever the authorities decide or demand. Gambaro presents this extreme picture of victimization and cowardly compliance in order to shock her spectators out of their own passivity.

In *Puesta en claro* (Made clear), written in 1974, Gambaro begins to change the pattern of victimization for her characters by showing that it is possible for the oppressed to react and rely on their own perception of events. She creates Clara, a blind woman completely dependent on the doctor who says he can restore her sight. The doctor tries to convince Clara that she can see, and as hard as she tries to agree with him, her actions prove to the audience that she cannot see. The doctor further subjugates Clara by marrying her and bringing her to his home to care for his family. There Clara is treated with even greater disdain and cruelty by the supposed children, who are in actuality young men. Clara realizes that she is being mistreated, but appears powerless to defend herself because of both her blindness and her status as a woman. Instead of giving up, however, as did previous characters in Gambaro's dramatic world, Clara uses the elements of her weaknesses to attack the men in control; she cooks a meal for her husband and children which contains a poison that kills them. Despite the title's promise that the events will "make things clear," the audience is not sure whether Clara accidentally or purposely added the poison, whether she has regained her sight or is still blind. What is clear, however, is that she has freed herself from the unjust domination that controlled her by exercising her own free will. Her rejection of passivity anticipates the more active roles created by Gambaro in the eighties.

Although Clara's decisive actions occur at the very end of the play, her spark of power signals a new type of woman character for Gambaro. Previously, relatively few women were dramatized on her stage, and those who appeared fit the stereotypes of the patriarchal woman. Doña Viola and Lily of *El desatino* symbolize aspects of patriarchal images of women: one is the domineering woman corrupted by the patriarchy, while the other is the sex object who serves men's needs. Emma of *El campo* represents the essence of the victim, as does her spiritual sister in *El despojamiento*. The unnamed monologuist of *El despojamiento* offers a vivid dramatic image of the woman who has been physically abused and psychologically dominated to the point that she readily submits to her own subjugation. In contrast, Clara of *Puesta en claro* and Brigita María of *Nada que ver* anticipate Dolores in *La malasangre* and Suki in *Del sol naciente* in that these women are more active and able to attempt their own liberation.

Gambaro's women characters, therefore, reflect the general pattern of behavior of the Argentine people who are able to free themselves from domination only when they achieve political awareness and social solidarity.

Our inability to communicate is a basic human problem that Gambaro explores in a theatrical way by focusing on both its verbal and visual dimensions. The contrast between words and actions typical of Gambaro's dramatic images is graphically demonstrated in *Los siameses*. The play develops as a series of encounters in which Lorenzo, the dominant member of the pair alluded to in the title, is driven by envy to cause the destruction of Ignacio. This relationship re-creates the Cain-and-Abel motif, yet the play never makes explicit that the two are blood-brothers; their fraternal relationship may be a myth exploited by Lorenzo, or if true, a fact not willingly accepted by Ignacio. Lorenzo's attempt at domination is dramatically expressed in the scene where he forces Ignacio to walk with him as if the two were real Siamese twins and attached physically. This theatrical gesture contradicts the verbal messages indicating that the two are physically separate and psychologically different as well. Despite the success of Lorenzo's attempt to dominate Ignacio, Lorenzo discovers the fate Gambaro projects for all her victimizers: The completion of his goal brings about his own destruction.

Gambaro's recurring theme that we exist in a physical environment that is threatening and not to be trusted is well developed in *Información para extranjeros*. Its unconventional structuration of dramatic action as a series of vignettes is also seen in the physical structuring of the stage space. The stage directions state in detail that the theatrical environment should be composed of a series of enclosed spaces, stairways, and halls in which the spectators as well as the actors are expected to move about the alternately darkened and illuminated areas. *Información* becomes more than an interesting theatrical experiment, as it forces the spectators to recognize their general passivity and requires them to question and respond more fully to the nature of events in their environment. In the earlier plays, only the actors were involved with trying to determine the nature of the reality presented to them by the authority figures, but in *Información*, the spectator is made part of the process as well. The boundary between stage and life becomes blurred as the actor/guide asks the spectator to comment on the acting as well as on the reality of the events enacted. Because of its dramatic self-consciousness, the work can be seen as a metatheatrical piece, in which the actors make the spectators aware of their theatricality. The dissolution of the barrier between the events of the stage and the events of the world indicate to the spectator that the kidnappings, acts of cruelty, and torture on stage are also taking place in the real world of the spectator.

The cruel and macabre relationships by which Gambaro expresses the major themes of her dramatic world are also repeated in her narratives. Just as her dramas stand out for their visual images, so, too, does the fiction create striking mental images for the reader. In *Dios no nos quiere contentos* (1979; God does not want us content), the main character, La Ecuyere, is a trapeze artist who is also a contortionist capable of twisting herself into knots. She finds work in a second-rate circus in which the owners constantly exploit her when they do not abandon her by moving away. The Ecuyere pursues the world of the circus despite the exploitation and the problems involved in being part of that world. The narrative is peopled by characters who are grotesque, abandoned by others, sad survivors in a cruel world. One of Ecuyere's companions is a young boy who wants to sing but remains mute until the end when he finally emits a mournful sound. These two sad creatures meet a small child during a bus ride in which the vehicle is so packed with people that the child becomes separated from his mother and somehow winds up, literally, with the Ecuyere. The story of the three orphans who fight for existence is told by means of an omniscient narrator who appears to sympathize with these misfits.

Based on the clues that come from the dramatic pieces, this book can also be considered an allegory, each sign offering a sociopolitical commentary; the Ecuyere can be read as the young woman who must make a way in life by balancing the good with the evil events. Her characteristics as a contortionist and high-wire walker seem to be needed in order to survive in a cruel and unjust society, for she learns to distance herself from painful events as the only way to maintain that equilibrium. The circus is a metaphor for society, and the owners who exploit the woman are not much different from the bosses of a given economic or political structure. While the novel has not achieved the same recognition as Gambaro's plays, it does contain a similar thematic message and graphic images, especially of the Ecuyere as a circus performer.

SURVEY OF CRITICISM

Almost all criticism of Gambaro's work deals with her plays, with the exception of the essay by Helena Araújo, "El tema de la violación en Armonía Somers y Griselda Gambaro," in which *Ganarse la muerte* and *Dios no nos quiere contentos* are studied. Because many of the plays were not published until the eighties, though written earlier, and some have yet to be published ("Viaje de invierno" [Winter voyage], from 1965, and "Nosferatu," 1970), the majority of articles deal with the plays of the sixties. *Los siameses* and *El campo* are the two most often singled out for analysis and are considered the major plays of the early period.

Virginia Ramos Foster, Tamara Holzapfel, and Sandra Cypess were among the first critics in the United States to deal with her work. They initiated the trend to compare the early plays with European currents, especially with the Theater of the Absurd and Artaud's Theater of Cruelty, because of the many surface similarities in tone, techniques, and themes. Most of the comparative studies relate Gambaro to various authors of the Theater of the Absurd of both Europe and Argentina, including Eugene Ionesco, Samuel Beckett, Harold Pinter, and Mario Trejo, Eduardo Pavlovsky, Julio Ardiles Gray, Carlos Traffic. George Woodyard (1969) includes Gambaro's work in his general discussion of the Theater of the Absurd in Latin America. Cypess sees the relationship between Artaud's theories for a Theater of Cruelty and Gambaro's skillful use of physical imagery and scenes of cruelty ("Physical Imagery," 1975). Other areas of similarity include her successful use of nonrhetorical language integrated with gestures and movements and her manipulation of the space of the stage. In the manner Artaud envisioned for his theater, Gambaro makes good use of violent physical images as a potent means to express her own vision of the cruelty of existence.

In response to comments associating her work with international movements, however, Gambaro generally stresses the importance of the Argentine context in the formation of her dramatic vocabulary; she denies having had knowledge of Pinter, for example, at the time she was writing the very plays considered Absurdist in the cruel vein of Pinter (Betsko and Koenig, 1987). Furthermore, David Foster points out that in Gambaro's plays dialogue functions differently both from the traditional presentation and from the innovations of the Theater of the Absurd ("El lenguaje," 1979). Foster suggests that, unlike the language in the Theater of the Absurd, Gambaro does not deny the efficacy of language but is concerned with its use as an instrument of degradation and humiliation. He also contrasts her work with that of Eduardo Pavlovsky, who appears to include more specific details of Argentine reality in his plays, whereas Gambaro makes use of more general metaphors, such as the concentration camp in *El campo*, and as Cypess notes, the Kafkaesque world of *The Trial* in *Las paredes* ("The Plays").

In reaction to the critical attention paid to the universal elements in her work and to her association with the European schools, Gambaro prefers to emphasize her relationship with the Argentine dramatic tradition called the *grotesco-criollo* (native grotesque), as well as the real absurdities of the Argentine political situation as the true inspiration for her tone of black humor and her treatment of that paradox in human nature—the capacity of ordinary human beings to participate in atrocities. With the change in the political situation in Argentina from military dictatorship to democracy, critics have felt at liberty to call attention to the national political allusions inherent in her work. Previously, there was a real concern that references to her sociopolitical message would bring political reprisals against the dramatist. In an interview Gambaro referred to the executive order that was issued in 1977 forbidding the sale of *Ganarse la muerte* (Betsko and Koenig, 1987). Nevertheless, as Cypess and Teresa Méndez-Faith have shown, despite the censorship in Argentina during the military dictatorships, Gambaro criticized the political events of her nation by means of indirection and allegory. Méndez-Faith ("Sobre el uso y abuso de poder") refers to *Las paredes, El campo, Decir sí,* and *El despojamiento* to show their relationship not with the universal absurdist themes with which her works are usually connected, but with the more national Argentine context to which they refer. Cypess also considers this aspect with regard to *Nada que ver* in "Frankenstein's Monsters," and with *La malasangre* and *Del sol naciente* in "La dinámica del monstruo."

Although most critics have focused on thematic studies, Dick Gerdes and Rosalea Postma in their articles were able to show how innovative Gambaro is in regard to physical space on stage in their work on *Información para extranjeros*, a play that they read in its manuscript form of 1973 because its publication was delayed for political reasons until 1987. In "The Texture of Dramatic Action," Foster also broadened the scope of studies by calling attention to the dramatic activity of *Los siameses* and *El campo*, especially the examples of dramatic closure in these two plays. Peter L. Podol's work provides further amplification of Gambaro's technique in his study of props and stage settings as active components of her dramatic world. In addition, he compares her work with the plays of Antonio Buero Vallejo, pointing out the common aspects in dramatic structure and use of stage settings. By juxtaposing the Argentine plays with those of the Spanish playwright, Podol indicates that both authors present a metaphysical and universal dimension at the same time that they explore the contemporary political situations of their respective countries.

Two recent articles point to further new directions in the critical approach to Gambaro's work. In her study of *El despojamiento*, Becky Boling (1987) uses a semiotic approach with a focus on sign systems to illuminate the metatheatrical aspects of the play. She studies the way in which the action of the play deconstructs the actual systems of signs that create meaning within drama and society. For Boling the content and form of *El despojamiento* center on the act of representation so that the action of the play becomes an icon for the victimization of women. Boling clearly analyzes the manner by which Gambaro uses the theatrical event as a way to critique the nature of gender roles as signs within the discourse of society.

Just as there is a need for continued work on the sign systems of Gambaro's plays, Cypess suggests another fruitful area of investigation. Cypess broadens her discussion of Gambaro's work by comparing a play text with the related narrative and then connects both to the more comprehensive literary tradition to which they belong ("Frankenstein's Monster"). Taking the play *Nada que ver* as a point of departure, Cypess points out the intertextual richness of Gambaro's technique. *Nada que ver* recalls not only an international intertext—Mary Shelley's *Frankenstein* and the body of literary and cinematographic clones it has spawned—but also Gambaro's own novel *Nada que ver con otra historia*. In addition, references to contemporary Argentine reality in both texts add to the multiplicity of meanings offered by the sign systems.

As additional plays become more readily available, future considerations of Gambaro should depart from the well-established thematic studies discussing her presentation of both universal metaphysical issues relating to the human condition and the sociopolitical problems of abuses of power and the victimization of human beings in social settings. Aspects still to be explored include the richness of dramatic texture, the multiplicity of meanings of the sign systems, and the interplay of humor and tragedy, the relationship between the narrative and the dramatic pieces. Griselda Gambaro will no doubt continue to produce provocative and significant works that will continue to be read, performed, and studied.

BIBLIOGRAPHY

Works by Griselda Gambaro

Madrigal en ciudad. Buenos Aires: Goyanarte, 1963.

El desatino. Buenos Aires: Emecé, 1965. Novel.

El desatino. Buenos Aires: Torcuato Di Tella, 1965. Play.

Los siameses. Buenos Aires: Insurrexit, 1967. Also *Nueve dramaturgos hispanoamericanos*. Eds. Frank Dauster, Leon Lyday, and George Woodyard. Ottawa: Girol, 1979.

El campo. Buenos Aires: Insurrexit, 1967.

Una felicidad con menos pena. Buenos Aires: Editorial Sudamericana, 1968.

"Teatro de vanguardia en la Argentina de hoy." *Universidad* 81 (1970):301–31.

"La gracia." *El Urogallo* 17 (1972):73–79.

Nada que ver con otra historia. Buenos Aires: Ediciones Noe, 1972.

"Sólo un aspecto." *La Palabra y el Hombre* 8 (1973):52–72.

Ganarse la muerte. Buenos Aires: Ediciones de la Flor, 1976.

La cola mágica. Buenos Aires: Ediciones de la Flor, 1976. (Stories for children).

Conversación con chicos. Buenos Aires: Timerman Editores, 1976.

"Decir sí," *Hispamérica* 7, 21 (1978):75–82. Also *Antología Teatro Abierto*. Ottawa: Girol, 1983. Pp. 59–69.

Teatro: Las paredes. El desatino. Los siameses. Barcelona: Editorial Argonauta, 1979.

Dios no nos quiere contentos. Buenos Aires: Editorial Lumen, 1979.

"¿Es posible y deseable una dramaturgia específicamente femenina?" *Latin American Theatre Review* 13, 2 (Summer supplement 1980):17–22.

"El despojamiento." *Tramoya: Cuaderno de Teatro* 21–22 (1981):119–27.

Teatro. Nada que ver. Sucede lo que pasa. Eds. Miguel Angel Giella, Peter Roster, and Leandro Urbina. Ottawa: Girol, 1983.

Lo impenetrable. Buenos Aires: Torres Aguero Editor, 1984.

Teatro I. Real envido. La malasangre. Del sol naciente. Buenos Aires: Ediciones de la Flor, 1984.

Teatro 2. Dar la vuelta. Información para extranjeros. Puesta en claro. Sucede lo que pasa. Buenos Aires: Ediciones de la Flor, 1987.

Translation of Griselda Gambaro

Oliver, William I., trans. and ed. "The Camp." *Voices of Change in the Spanish American Theater*. Austin: University of Texas Press, 1971. Pp. 47–103.

Works about Griselda Gambaro

Araújo, Helena. "El tema de la violación en Armonía Somers y Griselda Gambaro." *Plural* 15, 179 (1976):21–23. Also *La Scherezada Criolla: Ensayos sobre escritura femenina latinoamericana*. Bogotá: Universidad Nacional de Colombia, 1989. Pp. 85–89.

Betsko, Kathleen, and Rachel Koenig, eds. "Griselda Gambaro. Interview." *Interviews with Contemporary Women Playwrights.* New York: Beech Tree Books, 1987. Pp. 184–89.

Blanco Amores de Pagella, Angela. "Manifestaciones del teatro absurdo en Argentina." *Latin American Theatre Review* 8, 1 (1974):21–24.

Boling, Becky. "From Pin-Ups to Strip-tease in Gambaro's *El despojamiento.*" *Latin American Theatre Review* 20, 2 (1987):59–65.

Boorman, Joan Rea. "Contemporary Latin American Women Dramatists." *Rice University Studies* 64, 1 (1978):69–80.

Carballido, Emilio. "Griselda Gambaro o modos de hacernos pensar en la manzana." *Revista Iberoamericana* 73 (Oct.-Dec. 1970):629–34.

Cypess, Sandra Messinger. "La dinámica del monstruo en las obras dramáticas de Griselda Gambaro." *En busca de una imagen: Ensayos sobre el teatro de Griselda Gambaro y José Triana.* Ed. Diana Taylor. Ottawa: Girol, 1989.

———. "Frankenstein's Monster in Argentina: Gambaro's Two Versions." *Revista Canadiense de Estudios Hispánicos,* in press.

———. "Physical Imagery in the Plays of Griselda Gambaro." *Modern Drama* 18, 4 (1975):357–64.

———. "The Plays of Griselda Gambaro." *Dramatists in Revolt: The New Latin American Theatre.* Eds. George W. Woodyard and Leon F. Lyday. Austin: University of Texas Press, 1976. Pp. 95–109.

———. "Titles as Signs in the Translation of Dramatic Texts" [Garro and Gambaro]. *Translation Perspectives II.* Ed. Marilyn Gaddis Rose. Binghamton, N.Y.: SUNY Binghamton Press, 1985. Pp. 94–104.

Foster, David William. "El lenguaje como vehículo espiritual en *Los siameses* de Griselda Gambaro." *Escritura* 4, 8 (1979):241–57.

———. "The Texture of Dramatic Action in the Plays of Griselda Gambaro." *Hispanic Journal* 1, 2 (1979):57–66.

Foster, Virginia Ramos. "Mario Trejo and Griselda Gambaro: Two Voices of the Argentine Experimental Theatre." *Books Abroad* 42, 4 (1968):534–35.

Garfield, Evelyn Picón. "Una dulce bondad que atempera las crueldades: *El campo* de Griselda Gambaro." *Latin American Theatre Review* 13, 2 (Summer Supplement 1980):95–102.

———. "Griselda Gambaro, Interview." *Women's Voices from Latin America.* Ed. Evelyn Picón Garfield. Detroit: Wayne State University Press, 1985. Pp. 55–71.

Gerdes, Dick. "Recent Argentine Vanguard Theatre: Gambaro's *Información para extranjeros.*" *Latin American Theatre Review* 11, 2 (1978):11–16.

Giella, Miguel A., Peter Roster, and Leandro Urbina. "La ética de la confrontación." "La difícil perfección." Interview. *Teatro: Nada que ver. Sucede lo que pasa.* Ottawa: GIROL, 1983. Pp. 7–20, 21–37.

Holzapfel, Tamara. "Evolutionary Tendencies in Spanish American Absurd Theatre." *Latin American Theatre Review* 13, 2 (1980):11–16.

———. "Griselda Gambaro's Theatre of the Absurd." *Latin American Theatre Review* 4, 1 (1970):5–12.

Laughlin, Karen L. "The Language of Cruelty: Dialogue Strategies and the Spectator in Gambaro's *El desatino* and Pinter's *The Birthday Party.*" *Latin American Theatre Review* 20, 1 (1986):11–20.

McAleer, Janice K. "*El campo* de Griselda Gambaro: Una contradicción de mensajes." *Revista de Estudios Hispánicos* 711 (1982):159–71.

Méndez-Faith, Teresa. "Sobre el uso y abuso de poder en la producción dramática de Griselda Gambaro." *Revista Iberoamericana* 51, 132–33 (1985):831–41.

Monti, Ricardo. "Teatro: 'Sucede lo que pasa.' " *Crisis* 39 (1976):55.

Muxo, David. "La violencia del doble: *Los Siameses* de Griselda Gambaro." *Prismal/Cabral* 2 (1978):24–33.

Podol, Peter L. "Reality Perception and Stage Setting in Griselda Gambaro's *Las paredes* and Antonio Buero Vallejo's *La fundación.*" *Modern Drama* 24, 1 (1981):44–53.

Postma, Rosalea. "Space and the Spectator in the Theatre of Griselda Gambaro: *Información para extranjeros.*" *Latin American Theatre Review* 14, 1 (1980):35–45.

Tschudi, Lilian. "El teatro de Griselda Gambaro." *Teatro argentino actual 1960–1972*. Buenos Aires: Fernando García Cambeiro, 1974. Pp. 88–93.

Waldman, Gloria Feiman. "Three Female Playwrights Explore Contemporary Latin American Reality: Myrna Casas, Griselda Gambaro, Luisa Josefina Hernández." *Latin American Women Writers: Yesterday and Today*. Eds. Yvette E. Miller and Charles M. Tatum. Pittsburgh, Pa.: Latin American Literary Review, 1977. Pp. 75–84.

Woodyard, George W. "The Theatre of the Absurd in Spanish America." *Comparative Drama* 3, 3 (1969):183–92.

Zalacaín, Daniel. "El personaje 'fuera del juego' en el teatro de Griselda Gambaro." *Revista de Estudios Hispánicos* 14, 2 (1979):59–71.

Zayas de Lima, Perla. *Relevamiento del teatro argentino 1943–1975*. Buenos Aires: Editorial Rodolfo Alonso, 1983. Pp. 144–56.

ELENA GARRO
(b. 1920)
Mexico

Anita Stoll

BIOGRAPHY

Elena Garro was born in Puebla, Mexico, on December 15, 1920. Her mother was Mexican and her father Spanish. She spent much of her childhood in Iguala, Guerrero, the setting, she indicates, for her novel *Los recuerdos del porvenir* (1966; *Recollections of Things to Come*, 1969). Her parents spent a great deal of time reading for themselves and to the children. According to Garro, she acquired her love of literature from them and her fascination with the interplay of fantasy and reality from the writers of the Spanish Golden Age such as Cervantes, Lope de Vega, and Calderón de la Barca.

Like her cousin Amalia Hernández of the Ballet Folklórico de México, she also was very interested in dance. At seventeen Garro was choreographer of the University Theater. She attended the National University (UNAM) where she was enrolled in the College of Philosophy and Letters. She married Octavio Paz in 1937 and only then took an interest in writing. She became a reporter and champion of the downtrodden, even to the point of spending time as an inmate in a women's jail in order to expose the poor living conditions. Her daughter Helena Paz was born in 1948.

Because of Paz' studies and diplomatic appointments, the family lived in many places. While in Paris, they knew many writers of the surrealist group such as Benjamin Péret and André Breton. Her first novel and best known work, *Los recuerdos del porvenir*, was written in Switzerland during a long convalescence. Garro had many problems regarding her citizenship and passport since she had failed to choose Mexican citizenship at twenty-one; she had believed it was unnecessary because of her marriage to a Mexican. This later culminated in the definitive loss of her Mexican passport and her acquisition of Spanish citizenship.

Many of Garro's works were written long before their appearance in print. She describes writing *Recuerdos* in the 1950s and then storing the manuscript in a trunk for several years. It was almost destroyed before finally appearing in 1963, winning the prestigious Xavier Villaurrutia Prize for 1964. It was translated into English in 1969. Another early work, the play *Felipe Angeles*, written in 1954, appeared in an obscure journal, *Coatl*, in 1967, but was only performed in Barcelona in 1978 to open the Sitges Festival and then was finally published as a separate volume in 1979. Her excellent short story collection, *La semana de colores* (The week of colors), was also written in the fifties and published in 1964.

The break in the Garro-Paz marriage had become definitive by 1959. She lived in Paris until 1963 and then returned to Mexico, where she continued her work as a writer and reporter, still championing the powerless. When the attack on the gathering in the Plaza de Tlatelolco in 1968 took place, she was named as one of the intellectual instigators of the unrest and was jailed for nine days. When asked about the truth of this assertion, she replied that the seekers of truth should not look to her but rather to those who had signed petitions of protest. This was reported by the press as though she had denounced several prominent intellectuals. She felt so abused by criticism from both sides that she fled to the United States and then to Spain, where she lived in obscurity for several years. Since 1980 she has lived as a near-recluse in Paris with her daughter. She has gradually become reconciled with many Mexican literary figures. With the help of her friend Emilio Carballido she has seen the publication of four new books: *Andamos huyendo Lola* (1980; We are fleeing Lola), a collection of short stories, and three novels, *Testimonios sobre Mariana* (1981; Testimonies about Mariana), *Reencuentro de personajes* (1982; Reencounter of characters), and *La casa junto al río* (1983; The house by the river). A collection of one-act plays published in 1957 with the title *Un hogar sólido y otras piezas en un acto* (A solid home and other one-act plays) was amplified to contain the three-act play *La dama boba* (The lady simpleton) and all of her other one-act plays except *La señora en su balcón* (1960; *The Lady on Her Balcony*, 1976) and republished in 1983 under the title of *Un hogar sólido* (Sources: Carballo, 1986; Muncy, 1986).

MAJOR THEMES

Women and the plight of those on the periphery are constant concerns in Garro's work, and these figures are often the narrators and protagonists. Their persecution and exploitation are related through violent images, language, and atmosphere, creating a world of alienation and loneliness and providing implicitly a criticism of the oppressing forces.

Other recurring themes are time and memory. Garro's conception of time coincides with that of the pre-Columbian culture of Mexico. Chronological or linear time represents the everyday world of strife and struggle, while cyclical or eternal time is a mythic state of happiness and perfection. She understands memory as related to both past and future and emphasizes the repetitive nature of human action. In a letter to Emmanuel Carballo in 1979, she indicated her continuing belief in the validity of ''memories of the future'' as predictors of one's actual future. With this in mind she said that she determined to make later works end happily as a way of influencing her own future (Carballo, 1986, p. 492).

A kind of magical reality, present in many of her works, may be described as the occurrence of events not realistically possible yet presented matter of factly by the author. This expansion of reality to include events that are not within the realm of ordinary reality certainly relates to the Mexican indigenous population's perception of the world in the past and present. Many people have also ascribed this mixture of fantasy and reality to the influence of the surrealists who took seriously the beliefs of the pre-Columbian cultures (Orenstein, 1975). The author herself has denied a surrealist influence, stating that these elements come from the Spanish classical writers (Introduction to *El árbol* [The Tree], 1967). Given the association of Garro and Paz with many of the principal proponents of surrealism in Paris, it is unlikely that she did not absorb some of their ideas, while also taking some of her inspiration from the classics which she read as a child and from her early contacts with the beliefs prevalent in rural Mexico.

Garro wrote *Los recuerdos del porvenir* as an homage to memories of her childhood home, Iguala. This poetic novel is divided into two parts, each centering on a woman. The beautiful Julia is the mistress of General Rosas, the commanding officer of the force occupying the town of Ixtepec during the Cristero Revolt. The tragedy and violence of the situation are described by the town as collective narrator. At the end of the first part, Julia flees with a foreigner, Felipe Hurtado, who has been presented in magical-mythical terms, leaving the reader to decide what happened to them. Isabel becomes Rosas's mistress in the second part, which shows the death and destruction of the town and its people. At the end of the novel, Isabel has turned to stone because of her love for Rosas and abandonment of her family. The reader realizes that the stone of the first sentence of the novel, ''Aquí estoy sentado sobre esta piedra aparente,'' is Isabel, indicating the circular structure of the novel, a reflection of her thesis of the eternal repetition described in the novel's title.

Testimonios sobre Mariana (1981), the first of three novels to be published nearly twenty years after the now classic *Los recuerdos del porvenir*, also deals with the themes of time, memory, and violence found in *Recuerdos*. As in her other novels, much of the violence is manifested as persecution (Muncy, 1985). Many critics have read it as a *roman à clef* presenting an unflattering portrait of her ex-husband. It concerns the memories three different people have of Mariana, the wife of a well-known Latin American archaeologist living in Paris. The first account presented is that of Vicente, Mariana's lover, who believes they have found the perfect love. However, a divorce from his wife is not possible, and Mariana cannot leave her husband Augusto because of their daughter Natalia. The second—and quite different—account, is presented by Mariana's friend,

Gabrielle, who describes her as victimized by Augusto and his circle of friends. However, Gabrielle fails to give her support to Mariana because of the power of Augusto's money. The third point of view is that of André, who befriends Mariana and falls in love with her. He discovers that both Mariana and Natalie have apparently been driven to suicide by Augusto but have nevertheless appeared several times to André, who through his profession of undying love spares them the constant repetition of their suicidal leap from a balcony.

The second of the recently published works was written in the sixties, according to Garro's own recollection in an interview with Michèle Muncy (1986). *Reencuentro de personajes* (1982) is the story of an unhealthy, sadomasochistic relationship between the heroine and her lover, Frank. Muncy and Garro discuss the connection of this novel with *Tender Is the Night* by F. Scott Fitzgerald. Garro recalls that some of the characters in this novel were inspired by the very characters who appeared in Fitzgerald's work whom she met while living in Paris. The themes of time, memory, and violence are again prominent, and, as in *Testimonios*, much of the violence takes the form of persecution of the female protagonist.

La casa junto al río (1983), a short novel in detective style with an underlying mythic structure, recounts the search of the heroine Consuelo for the truth about her vanished relatives. The tale of mystery regarding the past is again the setting for her preoccupation with the same themes already described. The story ends with Consuelo's murder, which is presented again in a magic realist fashion reminiscent of the end of *Testimonios sobre Mariana* and the first half of *Los recuerdos del porvenir*. With her death she passes to another, happier dimension where she is reunited with the sought-after family members.

The same themes are also present in her two collections of short stories. The early *La semana de colores* is a poetic collection of stories illustrating the whole gamut of Garro's concerns. Examples of her interest in the rural population, their folklore, and their oppressed condition are: "Perfecto Luna" (Perfect moon), whose character by this name makes fun of death and is then hounded to death by a "soul in pain"; and "El anillo" (The ring) in which a witch doctor is described as removing from Severina's body animals eating pieces of her heart. The themes of time, memory, and alienated feminine characters are the focus in such stories as "¿Qué hora es?" (What time is it?) and "La culpa es de los Tlaxcaltecas" (It's the Tlaxcaltecans' fault). The later collection, *Andamos huyendo Lola* (1980; We are fleeing Lola) also illustrates her use of the magical as in "La dama y la turquesa" (The lady and the turquoise), the themes of violence and persecutions in "Debo olvidar" (I should forget), and time and memory in "Las cuatro moscas" (The four flies). The "Lola" of the title is a cat through whose eyes we observe the persecution of the mother and daughter, heroines of several of the stories.

"La dama y la turquesa," the last story in *Andamos huyendo Lola*, is exemplary of the themes found in the earlier works and also echoes the endings of earlier works. Time and memory are related to colors as the lady of the turquoise remembers her own lost memory, which was blue. She was forced to leave her home in a turquoise when the owner had it divided into several pieces. She wanders in an alien world of villains who use violent language and who threaten her. At the story's end, a man in a white raincoat who has befriended her gives her a new home in a topaz, and her memory and vision of the world have changed to the golden color of the topaz. The transformational nature of the happy ending of the story repeats the pattern found at the end of the first part of *Los recuerdos del porvenir* in the magical transportation of Julia and Felipe Hurtado, the ending of *Testimonios sobre Mariana* in the reappearance of the apparently dead mother and daughter and their release from the repetitive suicide through love, and Consuelo's violent death which transported her to her sought-after paradise in *La casa junto al río*. These happy endings present magical solutions to otherwise insolubly unhappy circumstances in the lives of these women. They cause one to recall her stated attempt to redirect her own future which she expressed in her communication with Carballo cited earlier. These elements of mystery, threats from a powerful male figure, and the fluidity of the boundary between life and death also describe the feminine gothic, according to Claire Kahane in "The Gothic Mirror" (*The M(o)ther Tongue*, Ithaca, N.Y.: Cornell University Press, 1985, pp. 334–51).

All of Garro's theatrical work dates from the fifties and sixties. The three-act play *Felipe Angeles* was her first theatrical work (Muncy, 1986). It is a tragic drama based on the life of a heroic general of the Mexican Revolution. Using the structure of classical Greek theater, she dramatizes her criticism of the Revolution through this "docudrama" form which has become popular among Spanish American playwrights (Cortés, in Stoll, 1989).

Garro's other three-act work, *La dama boba*, is a clear demonstration of her interest in the Spanish classics and her concern for the downtrodden rural Mexicans. *La dama boba* is the title of a play by Lope de Vega which a Mexico City theatrical troupe touring the provinces is presenting as the play begins. The performance is interrupted abruptly through the disappearance of one of the main actors playing a teacher, kidnapped by a local mayor desperate for a teacher for his town. It is a presentation of the cultural dichotomy between the rural-indigenous and city-European cultures (Mora, 1983). Time and reality are questioned through the clever manipulation of characters and audience, an excellent example of the metatheater of Golden Age drama. An important issue in Lope's play, the conflict between appearance and reality, is also prominent. The leading feminine character, Lupe, represents woman as man's guide to an expanded reality, a belief espoused by the surrealists.

Several of Garro's one-act plays collected in *Un hogar sólido* (1983) manifest most clearly the evidence that leads critics to relate her work to the surrealist current. *Un hogar sólido*, which takes place in a family burial plot, presents dialogue among the various generations of the dead inhabiting the site. In *Encanto, tendajón mixto*, one of the characters vanishes magically with the woman of the shop who has promised him happiness, another example of the woman as conductor to a different level of reality. In *Andarse por las ramas*, the heroine rejects her dull, unimaginative husband, don Fernando de las 7:05, for a search for a more poetic world. *Los pilares de doña Blanca*, a play whose characters are Blanca, Rubí, Cuatro Caballeros, and El Caballero Alazán, is interpreted by Gloria Feman Orenstein as woman's quest for the experience of *l'amour fou* and for ultimate totality in an androgynous union (Orenstein, 1975, p. 111). Also referring to surrealist tenets, she explains the suicide of Clara in *La señora en su balcón* as Clara's choice to merge with the ultimate point at which life and death meet. In *El rey mago*, the jailed Felipe Ramos refuses the invitation of the imaginative child Cándido Morales to escape his mental/physical imprisonment, an illustration of her belief in the special access children have to an expanded reality.

SURVEY OF CRITICISM

Although a few critical studies of Elena Garro appeared before 1980, the bulk of them have been published beginning with this date. Frank Dauster's 1964 study, "El teatro de Elena Garro: Evasión e ilusión," outlined what later was seen as a general movement in her work toward fantasy and illusion. Harry Rosser's study of the interplay between form and content appeared in 1975, as did Gabriela Mora's study of social and feminist issues. Gloria Feman Orenstein's section on Garro in *The Theater of the Marvelous* (1975) outlines her kinship with the surrealists, despite the author's denial of their influence.

Both Mora and Dauster contributed further to the critical corpus in the eighties. Dauster's study (1980) of her novel, *Los recuerdos del porvenir*, underscores the themes of time and memory and the importance of the two central women characters, Julia and Isabel, in a revision of woman's role. Mora added two articles, one giving a feminist reading of two of her one-act plays and the other outlining the metatheatrical nature of *La dama boba*. Robert K. Anderson has contributed several critical pieces on Garro's work, adding to the description of Garro's magic realism and demonstrating her accessibility to archetypal criticism. Richard Callan has also employed this critical approach with his study (1980) of *Los perros*. Carmen Salazar (1987) brings together myth, time, and magic realism in her study of *La semana de colores*. Sandra Cypess employed a semiotic approach in her study "Visual and Verbal Distances in Elena Garro's Theater" (1985), concluding that Garro has succeeded in creating positive feminine images. Michèle Muncy (1986) has outlined the pervasiveness of violence and persecution in Garro's works and has provided essential biographical information through her interview with the author. Delia Galván's essay, "*Felipe Angeles*: sacrificio heroico" (1987), described the connection between this tragic story and the Aztec past of the society. The useful content of Cynthia Duncan's study is obvious from its title: "La culpa es de los Tlaxcaltecas: A Reevaluation of Mexico's Past Through Myth" (1985).

To date three book-length studies have been published on Garro's work. The first, Antonieta Eva Verwey's *Mito y palabra poética en Elena Garro* (1982), is an analysis of the language, structure, and mythic content of *Los recuerdos del porvenir*. In the first chapter the author relates this novel to the new narrative current of Latin America, outlining her preoccupation with time. She then relates it to Juan Rulfo's *Pedro Páramo* and suggests it as a possible influence for Gabriel García Márquez' *Cien años de soledad* (1967; *One Hundred Years of Solitude*, 1970). In the remaining chapters she delves into precisely how language, structure, and myth are central to Garro's first major novel. While Verwey concentrates the body of her work on *Recuerdos*, in an appendix she comments schematically on how these elements figure in Garro's other creations.

The second book, published by the same Querétaro University Press, is Delia Galván's *Las obras recientes de Elena Garro*. The works studied are precisely those that were not available at the time of the Verwey study. Referring to current feminist literary theory, the author analyzes the content and techniques of Garro's works that were published or republished in the late seventies and early eighties while she was living in Europe. She continues Verwey's study of Garro's genial use of narrative techniques such as autoreferentiality, metafiction, cinematography, and the mystery and detective story modes. She finds that the approaches in the various works differ but are unified by an underlying concern with woman's struggle to attain status as a human being.

The third book-length critical appraisal, *A Different Reality: Essays on the Work of Elena Garro*, collected by this author, continues previously indicated areas of investigation and also opens new issues of importance. The section entitled "The Author Speaks" contains "Chronology," Garro's third-person account of the events of her life in chronological order and "Encounter with Elena Garro," the transcription of a taped interview with Michèle Muncy in which Garro responds to queries about the relationship between her life and her literary production. In "The Figure of La Malinche in the Texts of Elena Garro," Sandra Messinger Cypess studies the presence of Cortés's interpreter/mistress Doña Marina in both the novel *Los recuerdos del porvenir* and in the short story from *La semana de colores*, "La culpa es de los Tlaxcaltecas," and shows how this archetypal figure represents a pattern for the female role in past and present Mexico. Delia Galván's study in the anthology, "Feminism in Elena Garro's Recent Works," traces a developing consciousness of the individualized woman in the later published works.

The Stoll collection also includes two studies on Garro's theater and two plays translated by Beth Miller. Vicky Unruh's essay, "(Free)/Plays of Difference: Language and Eccentricity in Elena Garro's Theater," studies her female characters through their use of language. Her relating of Garro's eccentric characters to their "eccentric" language deals with many aspects of her work which have been labeled surrealist. Eladio Cortés's essay "*Felipe Angeles*: Theater of Heroes," outlines the classic nature of the play and also locates it within the subgenre of docudrama, a form often used for social protest and employed here to underscore the falseness of the proceedings against Felipe Angeles.

Several essays deal with Garro's novels, a logical circumstance since, of her eight volumes published to date, five are long narratives. The subject of Michèle Muncy's study, the narrative of cruelty, illustrates its presence in these five novels. Anita Stoll's essay on the short novel, *La casa junto al río*, uses the theories developed by the psychoanalytic studies of Carl Jung and his followers to describe the archetypal nature of the symbols and actions of the story, which may be read as exemplary of the process of growth and maturation in the individual psyche.

Two additional essays in *A Different Reality* provide convincing proof of Garro's kinship with the major writers of this century. In "The Parsifal Motif in Elena Garro's *Testimonios sobre Mariana*: The Development of a Mythological Novel," Joan Marx places Garro in the mainstream of novelistic creation of the twentieth century in her use of mythology as a structuring mechanism for the novel just as James Joyce does in *Ulysses*. Mark Frisch's "Absurdity, Death, and the Search for Meaning in Two of Garro's Novels" cites her use in *Testimonios sobre Mariana* of multiple narrators through whom we meet Mariana and who speak of writing novels about her. Frisch provides a discussion of *La casa junto al río* as an existential study of the human being's confrontation with death.

Magic realism, whose prominence in the stories from *La semana de colores* was noted earlier, is examined by Catherine Larson and Cynthia Duncan. Duncan's "The Theme of the Avenging Dead in Elena Garro's 'Perfecto Luna': A Magical Realist Approach" details the omnipresence of death in Mexican life and redefines the concept of magical realism in the Mexican context. Catherine Larson's "The Dynamics of Conflict in Elena Garro's '¿Qué hora es?' and 'El duende' " outlines the similarities between the two stories in their treatment of the contrasts between life and death, different aspects of time, love and betrayal, contrasting points of view, and reality and illusion.

A Different Reality is also available in a Spanish version under the title of *La otra realidad: asedio a la obra de Elena Garro*. It contains three essays that do not appear in the publication in English. In the first of these additional essays, Robert K. Anderson again takes up the subject of magic realism in the two collections of short stories, *La semana de colores* and *Andamos huyendo Lola* in a study entitled "Una aproximación a la cuentística mágico-realista de Elena Garro." He discusses her preference for narrators and characters who are peripheral to the normal white adult realistic world: the child, the Indian, the neurotic, and the magic being, all contributing perspectives distinctly different from normal expectations. In the second, "Aproximación a los personajes femeninos a partir de *Los recuerdos del porvenir*," Minerva Margarita Villarreal focuses on Garro's women characters as representative of the modern Mexican women who have stepped out of the traditional role. She emphasizes the recurring pair of feminine protagonists found in many of Garro's narratives as evidence of her concern about the feminine condition. The third of these Spanish essays, Patricia Montenegro's "Estructuras narrativas y poder en *Los recuerdos del porvenir"* examines this major novel through a study of the power structures and violence present in it and indicates the repetitive nature of the violence built into the politico-economic structure Garro describes.

BIBLIOGRAPHY

Works by Elena Garro

Un hogar sólido y otras piezas en un acto. Xalapa, Mexico: Universidad Veracruzana, 1958. Republished in 1983 and amplified to contain all of her dramatic work except the one-act *La señora en su balcón* and the three-act *Felipe Angeles.* 1983 ed. contains: "Un hogar sólido," "Los pilares de doña Blanca," "El Rey Mago," "Andarse por las ramas," "Ventura Allende," "El Encanto, Tendajón Mixto," "Los perros," "El árbol," "La Dama Boba," "El rastro," "Benito Fernández," and "La mudanza."
La señora en su balcón. Tercera antología de obras en un acto. Mexico City: Colección Teatro Mexicano, 1960. Pp. 25–40.
Los recuerdos del porvenir. Mexico City: Joaquín Mortiz, 1963. 2d ed. Mortiz, 1977.
"Nuestras vidas son los ríos." *La Palabra y el Hombre* (Xalapa, Veracruz, Mexico) 25 (Jan.-Mar. 1963):123–30.
La semana de colores. Xalapa, Mexico: Universidad Veracruzana, 1964.
"Era Mercurio." *Revista Coatl* (Guadalajara, Jalisco) (n.d.):1–4.
El árbol. Mexico City: Colección Teatro de Bolsillo, 1967.
Felipe Angeles. Mexico City: UNAM, 1979.
Andamos huyendo Lola. Mexico City: Joaquín Mortiz, 1980.
Testimonios sobre Mariana. Mexico City: Grijalbo, 1981.
Reencuentro de personajes. Mexico City: Grijalbo, 1982.
La casa junto al río. Mexico City: Grijalbo, 1983.

Translations of Elena Garro

Simms, Ruth L. C., trans. *Recollections of Things to Come.* Austin: University of Texas Press, 1969. Reprinted 1986.
Colecchia, Francesca, and Julio Matas, trans. "Un hogar sólido (A Solid Home)." *Selected Latin American One-Act Plays.* Pittsburgh: University of Pittsburgh Press, 1973.
Miller, Beth, trans. *The Lady on Her Balcony. Shantih* 3, 3 (Fall-Winter 1976):36–44.
———. *Los Perros [The Dogs]. Latin American Literary Review* 8, 15 (1979):68–85.
Wilson, Tona, trans. "The Day We Were Dogs." *Contemporary Women Authors of Latin America.* Eds. Doris Meyer and Margarite Fernández Olmos. Brooklyn, N.Y.: Brooklyn College Press, 1983. Pp. 186–91.

Works about Elena Garro

Anderson, Robert K. "Myth and Archetype in *Recollections of Things to Come.*" *Studies in Twentieth Century Literature* 9, 2 (Spring 1985):213–27.
———. "The Poetic Mode in Elena Garro's *Los recuerdos del porvenir.*" *Proceedings of the Indiana University of Pennsylvania's Fifth Annual Conference on Hispanic Literatures.* Indiana, Pa.: Indiana University of Pennsylvania, 1979. Pp. 257–66.

208   SPANISH AMERICAN WOMEN WRITERS

————. "La realidad temporal en *Los recuerdos del porvenir*." *Explicación de Textos Literarios* 9, 1 (1981):25–9.
Callan, Richard. "El misterio femenino en *Los perros* de Elena Garro." *Revista Iberoamericana* 46, 100–1 (1980):231–35.
Carballo, Emmanuel. "Elena Garro." *Protagonistas de la literatura mexicana.* Mexico City: Consejo Nacional de Fomento Educativo, 1986. Pp. 490–518.
Cypess, Sandra Messinger. "Visual and Verbal Distances in the Mexican Theater: The Plays of Elena Garro." *Woman as Myth and Metaphor in Latin American Literature.* Eds. Carmelo Virgilio and Naomi Lindstrom. Columbia: University of Missouri, 1985. Pp. 44–62.
Dauster, Frank. "El teatro de Elena Garro: Evasión e ilusión." *Ensayos sobre teatro hispanoamericano.* Mexico City: Sept setentas, 1975. Pp. 66–77. (First appeared as "El teatro de Elena Garro: Evasión e ilusión." *Revista Iberoamericana* 57 (1964):84–89).
————. "Elena Garro y sus *Recuerdos del porvenir*." *Journal of Spanish Studies* 8, 1–2 (1980):57–65.
Duncan, Cynthia. " 'La culpa es de los Tlaxcaltecas': A Reevaluation of Mexico's Past Through Myth." *Crítica Hispánica* 7 (1985):105–20.
Galván, Delia. "*Felipe Angeles de Elena Garro*: sacrificio heroico." *Latin American Theatre Review* 20 (Spring 1987):29–35.
————. *Los obras recientes* de Elena Garro. Querétaro, Mexico: Universidad Autónoma de Querétaro, 1988.
García, Kay Sauer. "Woman and Her Signs in the Novels of Elena Garro: A Feminist and Semiotic Analysis." Ph.D. diss., Rutgers University, 1987. (DAI 48, 3 [Sept. 1987]:660A.)
Larson, Catherine. "Recollections of Plays to Come: Time in the Theatre of Elena Garro." *Latin American Theatre Review* 22, 2 (Spring 1989):5–17.
Marx, Joan Frances. "Aztec Imagery in the Narrative Works of Elena Garro: A Thematic Approach." Ph.D. diss., Rutgers University, 1986. (DAI 47, 1 [July 1986]:193A.)
Miller, Beth, and Alfonso González, eds. "Elena Garro." Interview. *26 autoras del México actual.* Mexico City: Costa-Amic, 1978. Pp. 201–19.
Montenegro, Patricia G. "Structures of Power and their Representations in Three Fictional Works by Elena Garro." Ph.D. diss., Stanford University, 1986. (DAI 47, 9 [Mar. 1987]:3441A.)
Mora, Gabriela. "*La dama boba* de Elena Garro: Verdad y ficción, teatro y metateatro." *Latin American Theater Review* 16, 2 (1983):15–22.
————. "*Los perros* y *La mudanza* de Elena Garro: designio social y virtualidad feminista." *Latin American Theater Review* 8, 2 (1975):5–14.
————. "Rebeldes fracasadas: una lectura feminista de *Andarse por las ramas* y *La señora en su balcón*." *Plaza* (Revista del Departamento de Lenguas Romances de Harvard University) 5–6 (1981–1982):115–31.
————. "A Thematic Exploration of the Works of Elena Garro." *Latin American Women Writers: Yesterday and Today.* Eds. Yvette E. Miller and Charles M. Tatum. Pittsburgh, Pa.: Latin American Literary Review, 1977. Pp. 91–97.
Muncy, Michèle. "Encuentro con Elena Garro." *Hispanic Journal* 7, 2 (Spring 1986):69–76.
————. "Perseguidos y perseguidores: el juego de la violencia en la obra de Elena Garro." *Proceedings of the Indiana University of Pennsylvania's Tenth Annual*

Conference on Hispanic Literatures. Indiana, Pa.: Indiana University of Pennsylvania, 1985. Pp. 308–18.

Orenstein, Gloria Feman. *The Theater of the Marvelous: Surrealism and the Contemporary Stage*. New York: New York University Press, 1975. Pp. 110–17.

Rivera, Margarita Tavera. "Strategies for Dismantling Power Relations: The Dramatic Texts of Elena Garro." Ph.D. diss. Stanford University, 1986. (DAI 47, 6 [Dec. 1986]:2175A.)

Rosser, Harry Enrique. "Form and Content in Elena Garro's *Los recuerdos del porvenir*." *Revista Canadiense de Estudios Hispánicos* 2(1975):282–95.

Salazar, Carmen. "In *illo tempore*: Elena Garro's *La semana de colores*." *In Retrospect: Essays on Latin American Literature*. Eds. Elizabeth S. Rogers and Timothy J. Rogers. York, S.C.: Spanish Literature Publications Co., 1987. Pp. 121–27.

———. "Narrative Technique in the Prose Fiction of Elena Garro." Ph.D. diss. University of Southern California, 1979.

San Pedro, Teresa Anta. "*La héroe de mil caras*: Una caracterización de los personajes femeninos en la narrative de Elena Garro." Ph.D. diss. University of Wisconsin, 1987. (DAI 48, 3 [Sept. 1987]:664A–665A.)

Stoll, Anita, ed. *A Different Reality: Essays on the Works of Elena Garro*. Lewisberg, Pa.: Bucknell University Press, 1990.

Verwey, Antonieta Eva. *Mito y palabra poética en Elena Garro*. Mexico City: Universidad Autónoma de Querétaro, 1982.

Young, Linda Rebeca Stowell. "Six Representative Women Novelists of Mexico 1960–1969." Ph.D diss. University of Illinois at Urbana-Champaign, 1975. (DAI 36,5 [Mar.-April 1976]:6092A–93A.)

GERTRUDIS GÓMEZ DE AVELLANEDA (1814–1873)
Cuba

Hugh A. Harter

BIOGRAPHY

Born in Puerto Príncipe in central Cuba on March 23, 1814, La Avellaneda was baptized María Gertrudis de los Dolores Gómez de Avellaneda y Betancourt. Writers usually refer to her as La Avellaneda, by her first name Gertrudis, or by her nickname Tula. Her father, Manuel Gómez de Avellaneda, sent to Cuba in 1809 as a naval officer and then commander of the Spanish fleet in the area, claimed descent from the royal family of Navarre and from the high aristocracy of Vizcaya. Her mother, Francisca de Arteaga y Betancourt, was of a distinguished family that had been long established on the island. La Avellaneda expressed great pride in her lineage, and of her father in particular, and writes of it in both autobiographical and fictional material. It was a family of conservative provincial respectability, and La Avellaneda, even as a small child, found herself at odds and in conflict with it.

When La Avellaneda was eight, her father died. Don Manuel left a young widow and a second child, a son also named Manuel to whom the sister was to remain attached throughout her life. This death inspired the grieving child to write her first verses and was a loss that La Avellaneda recalled with grief as an adult. Within ten months, the widow took an army lieutenant colonel named Escalada as her second husband. The stepfather was not sympathetic to the growing predilections of his precocious and increasingly rebellious stepdaughter, but as he was frequently away from home on duty, the child was usually able to indulge her reading and writing. The mother tried to channel her daughter's interests into ''more normal'' endeavors, and forbade the reading of plays. La Avellaneda was undaunted: She memorized whole passages of Pierre Corneille and Jean Racine, and she wrote her own plays.

An early portrait shows La Avellaneda as a very attractive young woman, and the time did come, temporarily at least, when she transferred her attentions from literature to the fashions and parties that were the interests of young women of her age and peer group. Her stepfather even arranged a marriage for her, but she refused to go through with the ceremony, which caused bad feelings and recriminations within the family. Later, she broke other engagements and so earned a reputation for capriciousness. She returned to her books, devouring works by Sir Walter Scott, Françoise René de Chateaubriand, Victor Hugo, Lord Byron, Alphonse de Lamartine, and George Sand. As her reading broadened, her literary horizons and the desire to visit the land of her late father became increasingly strong. She now insisted on going to Europe.

Her family, which then consisted of the parents and three younger children as well as Gertrudis and her brother, set sail in April 1836 for Bordeaux, France. This voyage was notable for two things: the writing of the frequently anthologized sonnet, "Al partir" (On leaving) and La Avellaneda's exultation during a hurricane when, to the consternation of the others, she gloried in the violence and savage beauty of the storm. The family went from France to La Coruna, the home of the Escaladas.

The budding author later wrote of the unhappy experience with her stepfather's family who ridiculed her love of literature and dubbed her "doctor" and "atheist." Furthermore, the climate of Galicia with its rain and darkened skies was a sorry contrast to the blue skies and sunshine of Cuba, and the people seemed to the young woman to be as dour as the weather. Undaunted, La Avellaneda was busily working on her first novel, *Sab* (whose title is the name of the main character), which she purportedly had begun in Bordeaux. She also became engaged to a young officer but decided not to marry him. Her fiancé did not approve of his betrothed's dedication to books and writing.

Once Manuel rejoined the family, the two siblings obtained permission to set out for the town in Andalusia in which their father had been brought up. Their disillusionment was swift. The town was small and had dirty and unpaved streets. Soon the spurning of an offer of marriage created a rift with an uncle and other members of the family. After three months, the two "orphans" joined their mother and the other children in a new home in Seville.

The world that La Avellaneda had conjured up in her imaginings had come into sharp and bitter conflict with reality, but the new life in Seville was an exciting one. The author was soon at the center of the most aristocratic circles of the city and was courted and sought out. She spurned another suitor but met her own nemesis in the person of a man two years her junior, Ignacio de Cepeda, who came from a wealthy, conservative, and important family.

Cepeda, described by contemporaries as a "terribly normal man," had an enormous attraction for La Avellaneda. Cold and methodical, he seemed the proverbial opposite of the tempestuous and passionate woman who by turns aggressively pursued him, then feigned disinterested friendship, or railed at him and then abjectly apologized. Their relationship must be viewed as La Avellaneda's deepest emotional involvement, one that endured, with ruptures and reunions, from 1838 to 1854 when Cepeda made the break irreparable by marrying another woman. The reluctant suitor was not unaware of the renown of his *innamorata*, however. In his will, he instructed his widow that the forty letters from La Avellaneda that he had saved over the years were to be published at his expense.

These letters are a valuable source for understanding La Avellaneda's work and life and reveal in varying degrees the tempestuous course of a relationship replete with passion, jealousy, and unrequited love, all themes repeatedly used by the author in her novels, plays, and poems.

One of the ruptures resulted in La Avellaneda's departure for Madrid. It was the summer of 1840. Seville had brought disappointments, conflicts, and heartache, but the time spent there had also been very creative and resulted in the publication of poems and translations. It had also seen the successful production of a first play, *Leoncia* (whose title is the name of the main character). La Avellaneda's literary career was underway.

The aspiring writer arrived in the capital with a letter of introduction from Alberto Lista to the writer Juan Nicasio Gallego. She soon knew, and was admired by, the major literary figures of the epoch. She was welcomed into the famed *Liceo de Madrid* where she impressed her audiences with readings from her works, descriptions of which have come down to us in writings by authors such as José Zorrilla. Her first novel, *Sab*, appeared in 1841. In the same year, a volume of poems entitled *Poesías* was published (Poetry), and in 1842, a second novel, *Dos mujeres* (Two women) came out.

La Avellaneda had entered her most productive period. Poems, novels, and plays issued from her pen in heady profusion. A friendship with the royal family was established. Public honors crowned her successes. By the age of thirty, Gertrudis had published five novels, a volume of poetry, and various articles and separate poems. Three of her plays had been successfully produced. Professional triumphs did not, however, prevent private tragedy.

La Avellaneda had met a talented and handsome poet two years her junior while she was living in Seville. His name was Gabriel García Tassara, and he became the father of the author's only child, a daughter whom she called Brenhilde. The child lived only nine months, completely disavowed by the father who refused the mother's desperate pleas that he come to see the dying infant. La Avellaneda's letters to him are deeply moving.

Shortly afterward, Cepeda came back into the author's life. Extant letters indicate that he knew something of the Tassara affair, and La Avellaneda defends her actions. By this time, however, Cepeda was talking of marriage to someone else, and La Avellaneda, while playing the role of counselor and disinterested friend, declared that she herself would never marry. She did, however, soon become the bride of Pedro Sabater, a poet and writer in his own right who had achieved considerable success in politics despite his youth. The wedding took place in 1846, and soon after, the couple entrained for Paris where the husband underwent an unsuccessful operation for cancer of the larynx. On the return journey to Madrid, Sabater died. His widow entered a convent in Bordeaux, wrote a prayer book while there, and considered becoming a nun. The marriage had lasted four months.

In the following year, the letters to Cepeda and contacts with him resumed. La Avellaneda stated that she had lost the inspiration or desire to write, and again we see the recurrence of the drama of hopeless love terminating in still another rupture, another retreat to a convent to seek expiation through meditation, prayer, and the writing of poetry on religious themes.

By mid-1849, however, the crisis seems to have ended. The author resumed writing, producing a novelette that she would later recast as a drama and more poetry. The biblical drama *Saúl* had seen great critical and box-office success, and another period of prolific creativity had begun. It was to last more than a decade, during which the playwright triumphed again and again. In 1852 alone, five of Tula's plays were produced, four with great success.

Personal tragedies continued to plague her, however. Death struck close members of the family, and Tula's mother became gravely ill. At this difficult time, La Avellaneda had to face her most bitter professional disappointment. Juan Nicasio Gallego's death in 1853 had vacated his chair in the Royal Academy. Gallego purportedly had wanted his friend and protégée to succeed him. La Avellaneda coveted the appointment and became a candidate for the chair. That she possessed the talent, the ability, and the established reputation to merit the post could not be denied. Nevertheless, the decision was not to be made on the basis of merit; it was decided solely on the basis of gender. A final vote was strictly along sexist lines. A woman could not be admitted to the Academy. In the decision's aftermath, La Avellaneda had defenders and attackers, and she herself joined in the acrimonious conflict engendered by it.

In 1855 when she was just over forty years of age, La Avellaneda met her second husband, Domingo Verdugo y Massieu, an aide to the king and associate of the head of the Liberal party. The couple was wed in the Royal Palace. For about two years, the author's pen was silent, but then various poems began to appear, and in 1858 two new dramas, *Baltasar*, a biblical play that received great acclaim, and *Los tres amores* (Three loves), were produced in Madrid. On the opening night of *Los tres amores*, however, a man in the audience caused a highly embarrassing interruption of the action of the play. Five days later, Colonel Verdugo encountered his wife's offender and confronted him about his action. The man attacked the unarmed Verdugo, wounding him so seriously that he was never to recover his health fully. Once the convalescent husband was able to travel, however, the couple went to southern France and then to Barcelona and Valencia where La Avellaneda was fêted at every stop and where special readings of her poems and performances of her plays were given.

In 1859 a close friend of the Verdugos, the Duque de la Torre, whose wife was Cuban-born, was named to the post of governor of Cuba. He asked Verdugo to accompany him. The two couples set sail from Europe in November 1859, and La Avellaneda was once again in the homeland she had not seen for twenty-four years. The receptions given her in Cuba were spectacular and continuous. In 1860 she was crowned in the Teatro Colón in Havana with a gold wreath, and special festivities were prepared to welcome her back to Puerto Príncipe. Her husband was named governor of the province of Cienfuegos and later of Cardenas.

La Avellaneda again was occupied in writing and publishing. She founded and edited a bimonthly magazine entitled the *Album Cubano*, finished a novel set in France in the reign of Louis XV, and wrote two legends based on American themes. Her health was becoming increasingly delicate, however; she suffered attacks of migraines, convulsions, and nerves. The heat of Cuba, to which she was no longer accustomed, began to undermine her health further just as the yellow fever that had severely weakened the already delicate health of her husband brought about his death in 1863. La Avellaneda was a widow again at the age of forty-six.

Only her brother Manuel remained to offer her solace and advice. Through his intervention, the widow gave up renewed plans to enter a convent and decided on a voyage that included a two-month visit to the United States in the spring of 1864. She wrote a poem describing her impressions of Niagara Falls and sailed for England, stopping in London, and then Paris, where Manuel and his wife were living, before returning to Spain and Seville, where she lived for four years. She moved back to Madrid in 1870. By then, she was ill with diabetes. Photographs of her show a corpulent woman much changed from the earlier portraits. Nevertheless, her work went on. She was preparing five volumes of her works for publication. They were incorrectly entitled "complete," as such early works as *Sab* and *Dos mujeres* were excluded, no doubt because by then the conventionally established author found their overtly critical attitudes toward slavery and the education and place of women in Hispanic society too extreme. The five volumes included one of poetry, two of dramas, and two of the novels and other works in prose. They were published over a period of three years, between 1869 and 1871. La Avellaneda was still to write two more plays and to revise the prayerbook that she had completed in Bordeaux after her first husband's death.

Her brother Manuel died suddenly in Paris, and the revolution of 1868 in Spain brought about the abdication and exile of Queen Isabella II, who had repeatedly shown signs of deference for La Avellaneda. These events, combined with continued ill-health, finally brought death in February 1873 at the age of fifty-nine. She was first buried in Madrid, and then her remains were transferred to Seville.

MAJOR THEMES

La Avellaneda's place in the annals of Hispanic literature is owed primarily, at the present time, to her poetry, but this should be considered more a question of literary fashion than of objective evaluation. A study of nineteenth-century drama in Spain, which includes more than reference to the few well-known plays of the beginnings of the Romantic movement in Spain, is long overdue, and La Avellaneda's place in such a study must surely be a prominent one. The same would be true of a new evaluation of the novel in the 1840s and 1850s. Neither appraisal will diminish the importance of La Avellaneda's poetic writings, however. The body of letters to Cepeda and García Tassara must also be considered a major contribution to epistolary literature.

La Avellaneda's gift for poetry became apparent at the age of nine when her father died, if we are to believe autobiographical statements. The first poem we can date with certainty, however, is the sonnet composed at the time of leaving Cuba for Europe in 1836 and entitled "Al partir" (On leaving). Its theme is the poet's love for her native land; a kind of companion piece composed twenty-four years later when the poetess returned to Cuba is entitled "A la vuelta" (On returning). We do not know whether some of the works of the adolescent years were published later. Nevertheless, it was in Seville that writing became more than an avocation for La Avellaneda. Using the pen name of La Peregrina (The Wanderer), she published various poems, some of which were included in her first book, *Poesías*, containing fifty-four pieces and published in Madrid in 1841. Soon the young author's work was being solicited by the best known publications of the day, and by 1850, a second book containing 129 poems came out. Various anthologies of the poetry have appeared since.

La Avellaneda's poetic output constitutes a kind of compendium of the styles in Hispanic poetry from late Neoclassicism through Romanticism. The influences on her work are many and varied, including French as well as Latin American and peninsular Spanish poets. In Madrid, La Avellaneda was in contact with the major figures of her time, including José de Espronceda, José Zorrilla, and Nicomedes Pastor Díaz, poets themselves who ranked their contemporary, appropriately or not, as the greatest woman poet of all Hispanic literature, even over Sor Juana Inés de la Cruz.* The poems represent an impressive technical virtuosity including a number of forms, meters, and rhyme schemes, some of which were in common use at the time but others of which were infrequently utilized or invented by the poet herself.

Like her contemporaries, La Avellaneda wrote poems for all sorts of special public occasions, and while these works may be of interest to the literary historian, they have little appeal today. They include poems written on the death of famous poets such as José María Heredia (Cuba), José de Espronceda (Spain), and Manuel José Quintana (Spain), for the birthdays of prominent people such as Queen Isabella II, or for ceremonies such as the unveiling of a statue to Christopher Columbus. La Avellaneda's translations of lyrical poetry, including poems by Sappho, Petrarch, Hugo, Lamartine, and Byron, to mention only some of them, are sensitive and creative works in their own right.

Much of her lyric poetry has withstood the test of time. It is fundamentally Romantic in feeling and thematic development, and the poet's sentiments and temperament frequently predominate. In such poems as "A la luna" (To the moon), "A las estrellas" (To the stars), and "Al mar" (To the sea), nature is the backdrop against which the poet's own psychic states are projected. The sea's tempestuous waves, for example, are contrasted to the poet's soul in which there are "far more awesome torments/ That your mind may be unable to endure." The moon, witness to the poet's happiness in the past (You who watched my hours of pleasure) continues on its course unperturbed, scattering pearls of light "across the fields and bright flowers," but it does not disperse the shadows and sorrow of the present in the writer's life. The theme of happiness/paradise lost is present in many of the poems of this period that coincides with the tumultuous emotional encounters with Cepeda, to which the love letters provide a parallel expression in prose form. The melancholy of the present finds expression in poems on the theme of death, "Cuartetos escritos en un cemeterio" (Quatrains written in a cemetery), or "El genio de la melancolía" (The spirit of melancholy), a poem sufficiently similar in structure, tone, and language to Gustavo Adolfo Bécquer's better known *Rima V* to suggest that Bécquer (Spain) found his inspiration in the poem of La Avellaneda.

Inevitably, the love affair with Cepeda influenced many of these poems. Romantic love is, of course, a fundamental and omnipresent theme in most of La Avellaneda's works, whatever the genre. This is to be anticipated in a writer primarily associated with the Romantic movement, as we have seen, but biographical facts substantiate the importance of love and its role throughout La Avellaneda's life. The conventions and restraints of society and civilization hamper the freedom of the artist and the person with resulting states of depression, torment, and frustration. Nature's storms are matched or bettered by the poet's turbulent feelings.

In many of the poems that we can identify with the events related to the Cepeda affair, the poet is her own protagonist. Her adversary, the "él" of such poems as the two entitled simply as "A él" (To him), "El porqué de la inconstancia" (The reason for inconstancy), or "Amor y orgullo" (Love and pride), is clearly Ignacio de Cepeda. In the last-named poem, the spurned woman, María, like her poetic creator, is dark-haired, proud, and strong-willed. Like the youthful Gertrudis in her disdain for her early suitors, she has capriciously made of love's pursuits a mere pastime. The lover, however, has reduced her to powerlessness and made of the former temptress an innocent and childlike victim.

A rupture with Cepeda resulted in La Avellaneda's acceptance of her first husband's suit. In a tenderly affectionate poem written during the courtship, the fiancée writes of "the tenderness and warmth I hold in store" for her "idol's altar has been swept away." The passionate tone that dominates the earlier poems has given way to a more modest emotion, but they, like the two elegies written after Sabater's death, "once more darkness, tears, and solitude," bespeak a touching sincerity and depth of feeling.

Poetry itself was another theme developed in such works as "A la poesía" (To poetry), "El poeta" (The poet), or works dedicated to fellow poets whom

La Avellaneda admired. They do not constitute a kind of *ars poetica*, but they do express the poet's attitude toward poetry and its exalted position as art.

If La Avellaneda was highly esteemed as a poet during her lifetime, she was as celebrated, or even more so, as a playwright. She ranks as one of history's most prolific and successful women dramatists. From her first play, *Leoncia*, produced in 1840 in Seville, Cadiz, and Granada with considerable success, she had triumph after triumph, long runs and box-office successes for the period. As a measure of her productivity, we must consider the fact that Gertrudis wrote sixteen full-length dramas, twelve of which were in verse, in addition to three shorter plays, and one translation from the French. Their genres range from the charming comedy *La hija de las flores* (The daughter of the flowers) to such tragic dramas as *Munio Alfonso*, and her biblical tragedies, *Saúl* and *Baltasar* (In *Obras*, Havana, 1914; Madrid, 1974, 1978, 1979.). As a measure of her achievement, in 1852 five of her plays opened in Madrid, four of which were highly successful. In 1855 three new works were produced.

In the tradition of Spanish Golden Age playwrights like Lope de Vega or Tirso de Molina, La Avellaneda relies more on plot than on character development. She is a master at handling complications and sudden turns of plot, and she relies heavily on the proverbial triangle situation for her story lines. She is partial to historical epochs for her tragedies, and claims to utilize elements from the history of her father's family for some of her sources. For the tragedies, she utilizes poetry for her dialogue but prose in her comedies. In some productions elaborate spectacle and music added to the appeal for the audience. Critics' descriptions of *Baltasar*, for example, suggest that, in their use of music and opulent staging, the productions of the biblical plays were similar to opera productions today.

Conflict, the very stuff of drama, abounds in her works. Love, jealousy, suspicion, adultery, and even incest are the themes. There are unhappy or forced marriages, gossip that destroys people's reputations and lives, and mistaken or masked identities. The situations and thematic developments which these represent find recognizable parallels in La Avellaneda's life, as do their counterparts of love and friendship. With the exception of the biblical dramas, the tragedies are set in the Spain of the Middle Ages, *Munio Alfonso, Recaredo*, and *El Príncipe de Viana*, for example (available in many collections of her works); all the comedies, on the other hand, are set in contemporary Spain.

Leoncia, the author's first play, permits the playwright to express frustrations and feelings which she describes in letters and autobiographical writings. Leoncia, the heroine of the title, expresses anguish over her supposed betrayal and abandonment by her lover, Carlos, "always deceived, abandoned . . . , a victim of fate and of perfidy! When I have given my heart, it has been accepted only to be torn into pieces, and thrown aside with contempt, bloody and cut to bits." Despite its melodramatic turns of plot and its hyperbolic language, the play was successfully produced in several provincial cities and reviewed in Madrid.

La Avellaneda's second play, *Munio Alfonso*, a resounding success in Madrid in 1844, is based on a dramatic situation caused (like that of *Leoncia*) by social, and here political restrictions that lie in the path of freedom of choice and individual happiness. Prince don Sancho of Castille is in love with Munio Alfonso's daughter, Fronilde, but for reasons of state the prince is betrothed to the *infanta* of the Kingdom of Navarre. Problems of dynasty and state are circumvented, nevertheless, but not soon enough to avoid the tragic killing of Fronhilde by a father who thinks that his daughter has been seduced and has thereby brought about his dishonor. Munio, returning to the court a hero, is blind to what subsequently happens around him, and Oedipal-like, brings destruction and tragedy to himself and others close to him. La Avellaneda asserted that Munio Alfonso was a historical character and a direct ancestor of her father, but no historical basis for this claim has been found.

The opening of *El príncipe de Viana* (The prince of Viana) in 1844 was accompanied, despite its success, by disturbing reviews. The attacks against the *woman* playwright had begun. They were to continue and to cause La Avellaneda much suffering. This time the protagonist of the title is historically identifiable— Don Carlos, the elder son of Juan II of Aragon and half-brother of Ferdinand, the future husband of Isabella of Castile. The drama centers on the malicious manipulations of the king's second wife which turn the father against the son and finally ends in his murder. La Avellaneda herself did not consider the play worthy of inclusion in her "complete" works.

La Avellaneda's first biblical drama, *Saúl*, was produced in 1849. She saw her subject as eminently suited to a great drama, in which overweening pride was a central theme. She faithfully follows the story of the Bible except for her embroidering of the love between Micol and David. Their scenes contain passages of fine lyrical verse, and she utilizes the theme of David's harp to express her own ideas on poetry and creativity. La Avellaneda's last play to be produced, and an incontestable triumph, *Baltasar* was also a biblical drama. It opened in 1858. The work is based on the story of Belshazzar's feast and the doom of Babylon. The monarch is depicted as corrupt and world-weary, sated with the pleasures of the senses and a victim of what the author writes of in other works as "mi mal" (tedium and paralysis of will). He tells one of his ministers that what he needs is a great passion, whether pleasure or suffering, to take him out of this *ennui*. He is the hollow colossus, briefly ennobled only by his love for the Jewish slave Elda whose nobility of spirit and heroic courage stand in sharp contrast to the decadence of all that Belshazzar and his court represent.

The comedies are in sharp contrast to the melodramatic quality of the historical plays and tragedies. Such plays as *La hija de las flores o todos están locos* (The daughter of the flowers or everybody's crazy) are delightfully light in tone, but have themes that are serious in other treatments: the imposition of a loveless match on a hapless youth through social and material pressures. A young woman, Flora, finds herself in a similar situation, but happily and understandably, in a comedy, the right people marry in the end.

La Avellaneda wrote six full-length novels in a single decade. She also wrote shorter forms of fiction of several types. Only her first novel, *Sab*, published in 1841, has been reprinted or received any critical attention. All of her novels have an intrinsic interest in and of themselves, but they are also documents reflecting La Avellaneda's experiences as a woman, an intellectual, and a writer in a male-dominated world. As in the lyrical poetry and the plays, Gertrudis projects herself and her real-life situations into her fiction. This is particularly true in three of the novels, *Sab, Dos mujeres* (Two women), and *El artista barquero; o, los cuatro cinco de junio* (1890; The boatman artist or four June fifths) in which a kind of spiritual self-portrait is drawn through characters whose duality, like the face of Janus, constitutes an unintegrated whole. On the one side, there is the "good" woman, who is physically beautiful and seemingly fragile. However, she has great strength of will and deep spiritual values; she is tragically vulnerable in matters of the heart, but nevertheless remains devoted and faithful despite wrongs done to her. This is the angelic figure whose counterpart is not the satanic Medusa associated with Romanticism's women protagonists, but only a relatively "bad" woman, one whose talent and cosmopolitanism makes her an object of backbiting and slurs, supposedly corrupted by the world, and criticized as prideful of the accomplishments of her intellect. She is also, however, capable of deep love and of sacrifice for love.

This softening of La Avellaneda's portrayal of the "bad" woman has its explanation. The author herself is often visible behind the fictional guises of her works. The descriptive passages in *Sab*, for example, are clearly reminiscences of places and scenes that La Avellaneda would have known in her native Cuba. The two woman protagonists of Sab, Carlota and Teresa, can be interpreted as two aspects of the author's own character. Both women are sacrificed to love, one to an unhappy marriage, and the other to the refuge and peace of the convent. In *Dos mujeres*, the dual portrait is even clearer. The young and obedient Luisa has had a conventional provincial woman's education in Seville under the strict surveillance of her bigoted mother, Doña Leonor. She has been taught a great deal about sewing, embroidery, and household matters, the rudiments of mathematics and geography, no music or dance, and has had to memorize some sacred history. She has been denied access to all reading except the lives of saints and properly religious works by a mother who laments the ending of the Holy Inquisition. An uncle smuggles her a copy of Bernardin de Saint Pierre's novel of pure love, *Paul et Virginie*, which happened to be one of La Avellaneda's favorite books. This detail links author and protagonist, as does the passionate character of Luisa, "one of those souls of fire, one of those powerful and active imaginations that devour themselves if they do not have other sustenance."

Luisa marries her cousin Carlos who meets the fascinating Countess Catalina, with whom, it is reasonable to suppose, La Avellaneda must have fairly closely identified herself. Catalina is a serious reader: Rousseau's *Julie*, Goethe's *Werther*, Plato's dialogues. At a dinner party in Madrid, she is both praised for her intelligence, her education, and her elegance, and just as quickly damned for her flirtatiousness, and for being a "mannish woman who can talk on any subject, understand everything, and has need of no one." The members of Catalina's own sex are equally quick to criticize her. Carlos's love of his wife is soon replaced by his love for Catalina, but neither he, Luisa, nor Catalina can find happiness. Although Catalina tells her adulterous lover that there is no adultery for the heart, the Church and society see things differently. The strictures of marriage without divorce make any resolution impossible. Catalina dies a suicide; Luisa lives on more or less separated from her husband, who devotes himself to his business affairs.

The theme of frustrated feelings and ambitions is a constant one in La Avellaneda's works, but perhaps no where so strongly related as in the novel *Dolores* (in several major collections, such as *Obras*, Madrid, 1981). It is of particular interest as a kind of psychodrama. The author was insistent that the Dolores of the title and the other characters of the story were historically real persons. She wrote: "Dolores, my dear friend, really existed, as did all of the characters of this story, which appears to be a novel, and whose principal events you can find in the chronicles of that time." She insisted that she was merely faithfully relating "the strange and painful story of that poor creature who really existed, as did all of the persons who gather around her in this brief sketch." Scholars have pointed out, however, that the family names cited do not exist in the detailed historical records extant from the early fifteenth century to which La Avellaneda ascribes them. Dolores is, however, one of La Avellaneda's own baptismal names. The themes developed in the novel recur throughout the author's works: love thwarted by parental interference, and particularly by the mother; exaggerated pride in rank and family position which stifles the individual and makes any reasonable and humane resolution impossible. Doña Beatriz de Avellaneda, the mother/Medea figure, locks Dolores in a remote castle to prevent her from marrying the man she loves. We can reasonably see in this story a fictional projection of the woman who was chained to her family and its conventions despite what she saw, knew, and overtly expressed in the two novels she subsequently eliminated from those so-called complete works she edited before her death, *Dos mujeres* and her first and most powerful novel, *Sab*.

If the mother figure of *Dolores* is a ferocious one, the father figures usually are kind and gentle, protective of the daughters; they try to bring about their children's happiness. The other male figures range from the sensitive, self-sacrificing slave Sab, the heroic and defiant bandit chief Espatolino, or the thoughtful and artistic Hubert Robert, to the doomed Aztec monarchs, both victims of rapacity and both sympathetically portrayed, Montezuma and Cuauhtemoc. There are two notable exceptions in *Sab*: Carlos Otway, who marries the hapless heroine, and his father, both of whom represent a materialism and crassness which La Avellaneda is at pains to portray in a strongly negative light.

The novel that has received well-deserved critical attention recently is La Avellaneda's first book-length work, which we mentioned earlier, *Sab*. It is clearly abolitionist. It was published in 1841, half a century before slavery was to be abolished in Cuba, and was considered sufficiently powerful and subversive to have its entry into Cuba banned. It also had the distinction of preceding its more touted American counterpart, *Uncle Tom's Cabin* (1851–1852), by a decade. The author's voice is loud and clear, speaking with vehemence through the slave Sab of the inhuman conditions on the sugar plantations of Cuba and portraying the injustice of depriving a man of liberty whose nobility of soul and conscience raises him above his masters. Even the priest with whom Sab speaks only reinforces his slavery and tells him that a slave's virtue ''is to obey and keep silent, to serve with humility and resignation his owners, and never to judge them.''

The formal institution of slavery is not the only one that the author attacks. There is an implicit condemnation of the Church in the scene between Sab and the priest, as in the author's views on the implacable rigidity of marriage as an aspect of the enslavement of women: ''Poor and blind victims! Like slaves they patiently drag their chain and lower their heads beneath the yoke of human laws. With no other guide but an innocent and credulous heart, they choose a master for their whole life.'' Even the slave has some possibility of manumission, but woman, ''when she raises her emaciated hands and her abused forehead to ask for freedom, hears the monster with sepulchral voice cry out: 'In the tomb.' ''

The protagonist Carlota is chained to an unhappy life with her husband, Enrique Otway, whom accident of birth has provided with white skin, handsome features, and easy access to the world of business, but with none of the sensitivity and superiority of soul possessed by the black slave who had adored her from afar. The prosaic world in which Carlota ends her life is not that of the Romantic novel. The world of her youthful dreams has been swept away, and she has been reduced to facing the crass reality of her surroundings and her situation.

La Avellaneda's love letters to Cepeda, and the letters to Tassara, must be considered as literature as well as personal documents. In addition to her many letters, La Avellaneda also left numerous prose works that include articles on women, short stories and legends set in Europe and in Latin America, and occasional pieces such as those written for the *Album Cubano* which Tula founded and edited when she returned to Cuba in the 1860s.

SURVEY OF CRITICISM

La Avellaneda was, as we have said, highly regarded by her contemporaries. She was acclaimed by critics and public alike, but her role as woman-playwright brought her particularly unpleasant criticism. For a woman to write poetry was acceptable, but to write plays and novels was another matter. However, even those men who rejected her bid for entry into the Royal Academy as a woman publicly acknowledged Tula's claim to membership on the basis of her literary accomplishments. The eminent Spanish writer Juan Valera has left us a literary portrait of La Avellaneda in her early years in Madrid in his autobiography.

More recently, in 1930, Emilio Cotarelo y Mori published a lengthy study of the author and her works, notable more for the critical material it makes available to the interested reader or scholar than for its judgments on the merits of the works themselves. The book contains various quotations, either direct or indirect, of critics' articles on La Avellaneda's plays and novels, contemporary reports on the poetic and literary events in which the author took part, and detailed information concerning such things as the affair of the Royal Spanish Academy.

Since then, several works have appeared in Spanish, notably the book-length works by Mercedes Ballesteros in 1949 and by Carmen Bravo-Villasante in 1967. In English, the only book to date is the one published in the Twayne series by Hugh A. Harter (1981). Valuable critical information is also included in edited editions of La Avellaneda's works, such as the editions of *Sab* and *Baltasar* by Carmen Bravo-Villasante or anthologies of the poetry by Ramón Gómez de la Serna (1945) and Raimundo Lazo (1972). Two doctoral dissertations have also been recently written on La Avellaneda. The recent interest shown in *Sab* and the questions of slavery and alienation in that novel will, we can hope, attract attention to other novels and to the plays of La Avellaneda where insightful, systematic, and sensitive scholarship is still seriously lacking when we consider the importance of this uniquely talented and perceptive feminist writer.

BIBLIOGRAPHY

Works by Gertrudis Gómez de Avellaneda

Devocionario nuevo y completísimo en prosa y verso. Sevilla: D.A. Izquierdo, 1867.
Obras literarias de la señora doña Gertrudis Gómez de Avellaneda. 5 vols. Madrid: Imprenta M. Rivadenera, 1868–1869.
Obras dramáticas de doña Gertrudis Gómez de Avellaneda. 2 vols. Madrid: n.p., 1877.
Poesías líricas de la señora doña Gertrudis Gómez de Avellaneda. Prol. Juan Nicasio Gallego. Madrid: Leocadio López, 1877.
Cartas inéditas de la Avellaneda. Ed. Domingo Figarola-Caneda. Havana: n.p., 1878–1879.
El artista barquero; o, Los cuatro cinco de junio. 2 vols. Havana: "El Pilar" de Manuel de Armas, 1890.
Cartas inéditas y documentos relativos a su vida en Cuba de 1859 a 1864. Matanzas: Imprenta La Pluma de Oro, 1912.
Autobiografía y cartas de la ilustre poetisa hasta ahora inéditas. Huelva: Imprenta Miguel Mora, 1907; reissued in *Cuba contemporánea*, Havana: Imprenta del Siglo XX, 1914, and Madrid: Imprenta Helénica, 1914.
Memorias inéditas de la Avellaneda. Ed. Domingo Figarola-Caneda. Havana: Impr. de la Biblioteca Nacional, 1914.
Obras de doña Gertrudis Gómez de Avellaneda. 6 vols. Havana: Imprenta A. Miranda, 1914.
Leoncia. Madrid: Rev. de Arch., Bibl. y Museos, 1917.
Diario de amor. Prol., ordering and notes by Alberto Ghiraldo. Madrid: Aguilar, 1928.
Gertrudis Gómez de la Avellaneda, bibliografía e iconografía. Ed. Domingo Figarola-Caneda. Madrid: Sociedad General de Librería, 1929.
Selección poética. Havana: Dirección de Cultura de la Secretaria de Educación, 1936.

Antología, poesías y cartas amorosas. Ed. and Prol. Ramón Gómez de la Serna. Colección Austral. Buenos Aires: Espasa-Calpe Argentina, 1945.
El aura blanca, leyenda. Notes by Isreal M. Moliner. Matanzas, Cuba: n.p., 1959.
Baltasar. Havana: Consejo Nacional de Cultura, 1962.
Sab; Novela. Havana: Consejo Nacional de Cultura, 1965.
Teatro. Introd. José A. Echeverría. Havana: Consejo Nacional de Cultura, 1965.
Poesías selectas. Ed. and Introd. Benito Varela Jacomé. Barcelona: Bruguera, 1968.
Sab. Introd. and ed. Carmen Bravo-Villasante. Salamanca: Anaya, 1970.
Baltasar. Ed. Carmen Bravo-Villasante. Salamanca: Anaya, 1973.
Obras de Gertrudis Gómez de Avellaneda. Biblioteca de Autores Españoles. Ed. José María Castro y Calvo. 5 vols. Madrid: Atlas, 1974, 1978, 1979, 1981.
Antología de la poesía religiosa de la Avellaneda. Eds. Florinda Alzaga and Ana Rosa Núñez. Miami: Universal, 1975.
Cartas inéditas existentes en el Museo del Ejército. Ed. José Priego Fernández del Campo. Madrid: Fundación Universitaria Española, 1975.
Ensayo de diccionario del pensamiento vivo de Avellaneda. Eds. Florinda Alzaga and Ana Rosa Núñez. Miami: Universal, 1975.
Teatro cubano del siglo XIX, Antología. Introd. Natividad González Freire. Havana: Editorial Arte y Literatura, 1975. Pp. 11–362.
Callejas, Bernardo. *Diario de amor*. Ed. Bernardo Callejas. Havana: Editorial Letras Cubanas, 1981.

Translations of Gertrudis Gómez de Avellaneda

Blake, Wilson W., trans. *Cuautemoc, the Last Aztec Emperor*. Mexico City: F. P. Hoeck, 1898.
Burbank, William Freeman, trans. *Belshazzar*. London: B. F. Stevens and Brown, 1914.
Malcolm, Dorrey, trans. *The Love Letters*. Havana: Juan Fernández Burgos, 1956.

Works about Gertrudis Gómez de Avellaneda

Alzaga, Florinda. *Las ansias del infinito en la Avellaneda*. Miami: Ediciones Universal, 1979.
Aramburu Machado, Mariano. *Personalidad literaria de Doña Gertrudis Gómez de Avellaneda*. Madrid: Imprenta Teresiana, 1898.
Arias, Salvador. *Tres poetas en la mirilla: Plácido, Milanés, la Avellaneda*. Havana: Editorial Letras Cubanas, 1981. Pp. 111–46.
Asenjo-Reed, Miriam. "La mujer y su imagen en las novelas de Gómez de Avellaneda." Ph.D. diss. University of North Carolina, 1988. (DAI forthcoming.)
Ballesteros, Mercedes. *Vida de la Avellaneda*. Madrid: Ediciones Cultura Hispánica, 1949.
Bernal, Emilia. "Gertrudis Gómez de Avellaneda. Su vida y su obra." *Cuba Contemporánea* 37 (1925):85–111.
Boyer, Mildred. "Realidad y ficción en *Sab*." *Homenaje a Gertrudis Gómez de Avellaneda*. Eds. Gladys Zaldivar and Rosa Martínez de Cabrera. Pp. 292–300.
Bravo-Villasante, Carmen. *Una vida romántica, La Avellaneda*. Barcelona: Enrique Granados, 1967.
———, ed. *Gertrudis Gómez de Avellaneda: conferencias pronunciadas en la Fundación Universitaria Española con motivo del Centenario de la escritora hispano-cubana*

los días 19, 21, y 23 de noviembre de 1973. Madrid: Fundación Universitaria Española, 1974.

Carlos, Alberto J. "La Avellaneda y la mujer." *Actas del Tercer Congreso Internacional de Hispanistas.* Mexico City: El Colegio de México, 1970.

Chacón y Calvo, José María. *Gertrudis Gómez de Avellaneda. Las influencias castellanas: examen negativo.* Havana: Imprenta Siglo XX, 1914.

Cotarelo y Mori, Emilio. *La Avellaneda y sus obras; ensayo biográfico y crítico.* Madrid: Tipografía de Archivos, 1930.

Deyermond, Alan, and Beth Miller. "On Editing the Poetry of Avellaneda." *Homenaje a Rodolfo Cardona.* Austin, Madrid: Ediciones Cátedra, 1981. Pp. 41–55.

Gallego, Juan Nicasio. *Prólogo a la edición de las poesías de Gertrudis Gómez de Avellaneda.* Madrid: n.p., 1841.

Gil y Carrasco, Enrique. "Adiciones a la bibliografía de la Avellaneda de Nicomedes Pastor Díaz." *Obras literarias.* By Gertrudis Gómez de Avellaneda. Madrid: n.p., 1869. Vol. 1.

Guerra, Lucía, "Estrategias femeninas en la elaboración del sujeto romántico en la obra de Gertrudis Gómez de Avellaneda." *Revista Iberoamericana* 51, 132–133 (July-Dec. 1985):707–22.

Gutiérrez de la Solana, Alberto. "*Sab y Francisco*: Paralelo y contraste." *Homenaje a Gertrudis Gómez de Avellaneda.* Eds. Gladys Zaldivar and Rosa Martínez de Cabrera. Pp. 301–17.

Harter, Hugh A. *Gertrudis Gómez de Avellaneda.* Boston: G. K. Hall, 1981.

Inclán, Josefina. "La mujer en la mujer Avellaneda." *Homenaje a Gertrudis Gómez de Avellaneda.* Eds. Gladys Zaldivar and Rosa Martínez de Cabrera. Pp. 71–92.

Judicini, Joseph V. "The Stylistic Revision of La Avellaneda's *Alfonso Munio*" [*sic*]. *Revista de Estudios Hispánicos* (1977):451–66.

———. "Revision in Characterization and Structure in the Plays of Gertrudis Gómez de Avellaneda." Ph.D. diss. University of California, 1987. (DAI 47,7 [1987]:2607A.)

Lazo, Raimundo. *Gertrudis Gómez de Avellaneda. La mujer y la poetisa lírica.* Mexico City: Editorial Porrúa, 1972.

Marquina, Rafael. *Gertrudis Gómez de Avellaneda. La Peregrina.* Havana: Editorial Tropical, 1939.

Méndez Bejarano, Mario. *Tassara: Nueva biografía crítica.* Madrid: n.p., 1928.

Miller, Beth. "Gertrude the Great: Avellaneda, Nineteenth-Century Feminist." *Icons and Fallen Idols: Women in Hispanic Literatures.* Ed. Beth Miller. Berkeley, Los Angeles, London: University of California Press, 1983. Pp. 201–14.

Netchinsky, Jill Ann. "Engendering a Cuban Literature, Nineteenth-Century Antislavery Narrative (Manzano, Suárez y Romero, Gómez de Avellaneda, A. Zambrana)." Ph.D. diss. Yale University, 1986. (DAI 47,8 [Feb. 1987]:3057A.)

Peña, Margarita. "Tres aspectos de la obra de Gertrudis Gómez de Avellaneda." *Diálogos* 83 (1978):32–35.

Percas Ponseti, Helena. "Sobre la Avellaneda y su novela *Sab.*" *Revista Iberoamericana* 38 (1962):347–57.

Pinera, Estela A. "The Romantic Theater of Gertrudis Gómez de Avellaneda." Ph.D. diss. New York University, 1974. (DAI 35 [1974]:4547.)

Rexach, Rosario. "La Avellaneda como escritora romántica." *Homenaje a Pablo Neruda y Miguel Angel Asturias.* Eds. Francisco Sánchez-Castaner and Luis Sainz de

Medrano. *Anales de literatura hispanoamericana* 2–3. Madrid: Universidad Complutense/Consejo Superior de Investigaciones Científicas, 1973–1974. Pp. 241–54.

————. "Nostalgia de Cuba en la obra de la Avelleneda." *Homenaje a Gertrudis Gómez de Avellaneda.* Eds. Gladys Zaldivar and Rosa Martínez de Cabrera. Pp. 265–280.

Rosello, Aurora J. "La poesía lírica de Gertrudis Gómez de Avellaneda." Ph.D. diss. University of Southern California, 1973. (DAI 33 [1973]:6883.)

Santos, Nelly E. "Las ideas feministas de Gertrudis Gómez de Avellaneda." *Revista/ Review Interamericana* 5 (1975):276–81.

Schlau, Stacey. "Stranger in a Strange Land: The Discourse of Alienation in Gómez de Avellaneda's Abolitionist Novel *Sab.*" *Hispania* 69 (Sept. 1986):495–503.

Schulman, Ivan A. "The Portrait of the Slave: Ideology and Aesthetics in the Cuban Antislavery Novel." *Annals of the New York Academy of Sciences* 292 (1977):356–67.

Sommer, Doris. "Sab c'est moi." *Hispamérica* 16, 48 (Dec. 1987):25–37.

Virgillo, Carmelo. "El amor en la estética de Gertrudis Gómez de Avellaneda. "*Cuadernos Americanos* 219 (1977):244–58.

Williams, Edwin Bucher. "The Life and Dramatic Works of Gertrudis Gómez de Avellaneda." Ph.D. diss. University of Pennsylvania, 1924. (DAI [1924]:6883.)

Zaldivar, Gladys, and Rosa Martínez de Cabrera, eds. *Homenaje a Gertrudis Gómez de Avellaneda.* Miami: Ediciones Universal, Colección Vortex, 1981.

JUANA MANUELA GORRITI (1818–1892)
Argentina

Mary G. Berg

BIOGRAPHY

Juana Manuela Gorriti, novelist, short story writer, and essayist, was born at the Horcones ranch, in the province of Salta, Argentina, on June 15, 1818. Her parents were Feliciana Zuviría and José Ignacio Gorriti, both of families of Spanish descent that had settled in the Salta region, near Tucumán. José Ignacio Gorriti had studied theology and law, but managed the extensive family ranches after 1789; he became active in the revolutionary movement after 1810 and poured the resources of the family fortune into the struggle for independence from Spain. He fought under General Belgrano in the battles of Tucumán (1812) and Salta (1813), was a delegate to the Congress of Tucumán in 1816, and on two occasions was governor of Salta.

Juana Manuela Gorriti was the seventh of eight children. Her early years were spent at the army base in Horcones, where her father was the commanding officer, first as a colonel and later as a general. There she met General Güemes, the famous leader of the gaucho troops of Salta. Juana Manuela Gorriti is described in several accounts as an exceptionally alert and beautiful child, with golden curls and light eyes, fearless and adventurous. When she was six or eight, one of her aunts took her to Salta to study in a convent school, but Gorriti was unhappy there and soon returned home, thus ending her formal education. She became an eager and indiscriminate reader of every book she could find. On November 13, 1831, after several years of civil war, General Gorriti, who fought on the Unitarian side, was defeated by the Federalist Juan Facundo Quiroga, the feared "Tigre de los Llanos" (Tiger of the Plains). General Gorriti fled to Bolivia, establishing himself first in Tarija, near the border, and later in Chuquisaca, where his older brother, the celebrated Independence-movement activist

Canon Juan Ignacio Gorriti, was living in exile. José Ignacio Gorriti was accompanied by his whole family, as well as by Generals Puch and Arenales and some two thousand others who crossed into Bolivia with him. He died in Chuquisaca in 1835.

In 1832 Juana Manuela Gorriti met a Bolivian army officer, Manuel Isidoro Belzú, and she married him in 1833, at age fourteen. Gorriti seems to have had as much difficulty adjusting to married life as she did in becoming a convent pupil. There was considerable gossip in polite Bolivian society about the indecorous behavior of both spouses, but while Belzú continued his wild ways and conspicuous alliances with many women, Gorriti seems to have settled down after the birth of two daughters, Edelmira and Mercedes. In 1842 she may have returned to Horcones for a brief visit but was soon back in La Paz, where she devoted herself to her daughters and to her writing.

When Belzú was exiled for conspiracy against the government, his wife and daughters accompanied him to Peru. Gorriti's first novel, *La quena* (The flute), was serialized in *La Revista de Lima* in 1845 and was the first of many short novels, articles, and stories to be published in rapid succession. Later, Belzú returned to Bolivia alone and served as minister under the president, General Velasco, who assumed office in 1847. Belzú led a successful military coup against Velasco in December 1848 and proclaimed himself dictator of Bolivia. He governed as dictator until 1850 and as constitutional president from 1850 to 1855. Gorriti remained in Lima, where she opened a primary school and a school for young ladies in order to support herself and her two daughters. She began a literary salon that attracted the most prominent writers of the day. Her daughter Edelmira returned to her father, Belzú, in Bolivia and later married General Jorge Córdoba, who became Belzú's successor as president in 1855. Two more children were born to Juana Manuela Gorriti while she lived in Lima: Julio Sandoval and Clorinda Puch. Throughout these years, she continued to write and publish prolifically in such magazines as the Peruvian *El Liberal, Iris*, and *La Revista de Lima*, and the Argentine *Revista del Paraná* and *La Revista de Buenos Aires*. Lima newspapers published her novels in serial supplements that were reproduced widely in newspapers and magazines of Chile, Colombia, Ecuador, Argentina (after the fall of the dictator Rosas), and even in Madrid and Paris.

In 1863 the publication of a two-volume subscription edition of Juana Manuela Gorriti's short novels and essays was announced in Buenos Aires under the title of *Sueños y realidades* (Dreams and realities). On three occasions, manuscripts were lost in transit to Buenos Aires, and Gorriti had to rewrite them from her notes. The volumes were finally published in 1865, very favorably reviewed, and Gorriti was acclaimed as an Argentine writer, despite her prolonged residence abroad.

Bolivia had suffered military coups in 1857 (Linares overthrew Córdoba), 1860 (Achá succeeded Linares), and 1864 (Melgarejo overthrew Achá). Just as Melgarejo was consolidating his power, Belzú returned from Europe, assembled troops, and marched on La Paz, where he was acclaimed by multitudes. His daughter Edelmira led the street fighting against Melgarejo. As he was about to declare his victory on March 28, 1865, Belzú was assassinated by Melgarejo himself. Juana Manuela Gorriti was again living in La Paz in order to be with her daughters; as in Lima, she ran a school for girls and kept writing prolifically. When she was informed of Belzú's death, she demanded that his body be released to her, and she organized a wake that attracted a large crowd. Over eight thousand people, predominantly women, came to Belzú's funeral to hear Gorriti speak, and her oration paid eloquent tribute to her husband's great public popularity. Gorriti became the figurehead of a movement demanding vengeance for Belzú's death, and for this reason she was soon forced to flee from Bolivia. She once again settled in Lima.

When the Spanish besieged Callao, Peru, in 1866, Juana Manuela Gorriti became a heroine of the Peruvian resistance, repeatedly risking her life in order to save the wounded. She was subsequently awarded the Peruvian government's highest decoration for military valor, the "Estrella del 2 de mayo."

Gorriti continued to publish fiction and essays; a series of her short novels appeared in 1874 in the Lima newspaper *El Album*, founded by the Peruvian writer Carolina Freyre de Jaimes. Later in 1874, Gorriti and the poet Numa Pompilio Yona founded the newspaper *La Alborada de Lima*. In February 1875, Gorriti left Lima and traveled through Valparaiso and Montevideo on her way to Argentina; she was in Buenos Aires in 1875 when a special law was passed by the Argentine Senate and Chamber of Deputies providing her with a pension as the daughter of General Juan Ignacio Gorriti. A two-volume collection of her work, entitled *Panoramas de la vida* (Panoramas of life), was planned in Buenos Aires, and Juana Manuela Gorriti hurried to finish her novel *Peregrinaciones de una alma triste* (Peregrinations of a sad soul), so that it could be included. *Peregrinaciones* was dedicated to the women of Buenos Aires, and the volumes of *Panoramas* were published in 1876. A group of Gorriti's admirers put together an album of some sixty compositions written in her honor and presented it to her in a public assembly on September 18, 1875. The ladies of Buenos Aires held their own ceremony of homage on September 24, 1875, at which they presented Gorriti with an engraved gold star. In November 1875, she returned to Lima where she was also met with enthusiastic ceremonies. She reopened her school, and her literary salon again became the most prestigious of its day, gathering such writers as Ricardo Palma, Clorinda Matto,* Mercedes Cabello,* and many others. On Wednesday evenings, a group of thirty or forty men and women would gather for six to eight hours of musical presentations, recitations of verse and fiction, occasional charades, and lectures about current topics of interest. Many of the lectures related to the education of women and the role of women in contemporary society. Paintings and drawings were exhibited. The proceedings of ten of the salon meetings (July 19 to September 21, 1876) were published in 1892 in the first of a projected series of volumes and provide, together with many newspaper accounts of these gatherings, a fascinating glimpse of the intensity of Lima's intellectual life at the time. Juana Manuela Gorriti presented a series of original texts at these occasions, as did her daughter, Mercedes Belzú de Dorado, a much admired poet.

When her visa for Peru expired, Juana Manuela Gorriti returned to Buenos Aires by sea at the end of 1877. She traveled in northern Argentina in January 1878, but she was detained in Tucumán for two months by floods and was not able to reach Salta, which she had particularly wanted to revisit. She spent the next few months of 1878 readying a new collection of fiction, speeches, travel impressions, and other essays which was published late that year under the title *Misceláneas* (Miscellanies). During this time, she began what would become a close friendship with the writer Josefina Pelliza. In July 1878 she received word that her daughter Mercedes was ill in Peru. On July 16, she was accorded a two-year authorization to leave Argentina, and on July 19, she embarked for Peru. Mercedes died in April 1879; Juana Manuela Gorriti wished to return to Argentina but was detained by the war between Chile and the allied Peru and Bolivia. She witnessed the assaults upon Lima in 1881 and wrote of the devastation caused by the war. It was the end of 1882 before she returned to Buenos Aires, after a stay in La Paz, but she soon requested another exit visa which was granted on August 28, 1883.

Gorriti returned to Peru by sea, arriving in Lima in the beginning of 1884 but departing again for Buenos Aires by the end of that year. In August 1886, she visited Salta, traveling as far as possible on the railroad. *La tierra natal* (Birthplace), published in 1889, describes the joys of this trip to the countryside where she grew up. Back in Buenos Aires, she was surrounded by good friends and continued to write fiction and commentaries about contemporary life. She founded a newspaper, *La Alborada Argentina*, in which she published eloquent articles about women's abilities, rights, and education. Josefina Pelliza, Eduarda Mansilla, and many other writers joined her in this advocacy of women's capabilities. In 1886 Juana Manuela Gorriti published *El mundo de los recuerdos* (The world of memories), another collection of stories, legends, articles, and memoirs.

A short novel, *Oasis en la vida* (Oasis in life) was published in 1888, a cookbook in 1890, and a collection of short biographies, *Perfiles* (Profiles), in 1892. She worked on a new set of memoirs that would be published under the title of *Lo íntimo* (1893; The intimate story). She suffered from neuralgia for several years and died of pneumonia on November 6, 1892, at age seventy-five, in Buenos Aires. Her funeral was a major public event that included orations by the poet Carlos Guido y Spano and others. Newspapers of Buenos Aires, Lima, and La Paz dedicated issues to articles about Juana Manuela Gorriti. Clorinda Matto de Turner,* writing in *Los Andes* of Lima on November 19, 1892, summarized her friend's life and included a long list of Juana Manuela Gorriti's best known books, reminding her readers that ''no other woman writer of America or even of Europe can offer the world of letters a richer legacy.''

MAJOR THEMES

Juana Manuela Gorriti's earliest novels and stories are collected in the first volume of *Sueños y realidades* (1865). *La quena*, probably written when she was eighteen, is the first of many novels that tell of the subterranean treasure city of the Incas, all that now remains of the wealth of a defeated and marginalized people. *La quena* is a Romeo-and-Juliet story of the doomed love between the son of an Inca princess and the daughter of a Spanish official. The lovers are betrayed by an African slave who, despite the sympathy she feels for the Indians, ''that proscribed race,'' cannot resist the villain's promise to send her back to her children in Africa. Curiously, passion and not greed is the motive for the many crises of the novel, which ends with an evocation of the bare Andean landscape and the resonance of the eerie harmonies of an Indian flute in the area of the secret underground city.

El guante negro (The black glove), also an early short novel, is the first of Gorriti's tales in which two women, one good and one evil, vie with each other for control of a weak man. It is also the first of a series of civil war stories in which families and lovers are violently divided by their Unitarian or Federalist sympathies. Two strong women, one Unitarian and the other Federalist (Manuela Rosas, the daughter of the Federalist leader), struggle over a young man who is not only incapable of making up his mind between them but who cannot even be decisive about his political allegiance. Worse yet, he writes a letter saying he will defect to the Unitarian side, and this letter falls into Federalist hands. His Federalist father feels obliged to kill him to protect the family honor, and his mother kills her husband in order to save her son, who then dies in the next major battle. The novel is a gory melodrama of death and madness, laden with supernatural omens and symbols that emphasize the horrors of war.

Gubi Amaya; historia de un salteador (Gubi Amaya; A bandit's story) is the first of Gorriti's many episodic travel novels in which a female narrator recounts her adventures as a wanderer. Dressed as a man, the narrator attracts the confidences of both men and women. Men confide in her because they assume she is Emmanuel; women trust her because they see through her disguise and know that she is Emma. The man who is the principal storyteller also has a double identity: He is both ''good Miguel'' and the demoniacally evil bandit-assassin Gubi Amaya. A series of love stories are recounted to the narrator, most of which involve traumatic betrayals; people are not as they seem, and both men and women are shattered when their assumptions about their lovers prove false. Both good and evil are portrayed melodramatically with virtually no moralistic commentary. The strongest emotions are those associated with nostalgia for childhood scenes and events, many of which are Gorriti's own autobiographical memories.

The terrible divisions between Unitarians and Federalists are dramatized in the other major short novels included in the first volume of *Sueños y realidades* such as *La novia del muerto* (The dead man's bride), *La hija del mashorquero*

(The death squad captain's daughter), and *El Lucero del Manantial* (The morning star of the spring) as well as in shorter but no less moving war stories, such as "Una noche de agonía" (A night of agony), which tells of a prisoner's escape after capture in an 1841 battle and the farm woman who hides him from her husband's search party. Women are often portrayed as the mediators between the political divisions that have locked their men into bloodthirsty frenzy. *La novia del muerto* is a story of the doomed love between Horacio, a Unitarian war hero, and Vital, the daughter of Federalists. As in other Gorriti novels, the colors of black and white symbolize the opposition of social forces: his black helmet and her white veil can never be joined without conflict. The lovers meet in church during mass, but even this apparently neutral ground is made impossible for them from within by a corrupt priest and by the chaos of war from without, when crowds burst into the church screaming that the Federalists are coming. When she discovers that, instead of consummating her love with Horacio, she has actually been raped by the priest after Horacio's death, Vital retreats into permanent dementia. It is possible that she believes that it is Horacio's ghost that has appeared to her and that her madness is attributable to grief.

The women protagonists of *La hija del mashorquero* and *El Lucero del Manantial* are no more fortunate in their opposition to the horrors of war and violence. Clemencia in *La hija del mashorquero* succeeds for a time in aiding the victims of her father's death squad butcheries, thus, undoing her father's work insofar as she is able. But she dies in place of the woman she would like to be (the wife of a Unitarian who opposes her father), ironically slaughtered by her own father because he mistakes her for that other woman. *El Lucero del Manantial*, like many of Gorriti's early novels, blends autobiography and history with fiction; it describes a young woman, the daughter of the commander of a frontier fort (like the young Gorriti), who falls in love with the man of her dreams when he rescues her from a runaway horse. She bears his son but marries a man who, years later, opposes Rosas in the legislature. María's husband is assassinated by Rosas's men and her son arrested; she makes a futile try to save her son from execution by appealing to Rosas, whom she recognizes as the boy's father. The story is a romantic melodrama of prescient dreams and uncontrolled passions, and it portrays Rosas as the villain who ironically kills the son he has yearned for and not known he had. False pride and excessive social aspirations are punished in the final novel of the volume, *El lecho nupcial* (The marriage bed).

The topic of retribution is often seen in the works included in the second volume of *Sueños y realidades*. This volume includes such major novels as *El ángel caído* (The fallen angel) of 1862, *El tesoro de los incas* (The treasure of the Incas), some remarkable stories, and two memoirs of events during the wars for Independence: one, a personal series of recollections of the patriotic leader Martín Güemes, and the other, a biography of the war hero General Vidal. In *El ángel caído*, two plots are interwoven—one of interplay between the black slave community and their white masters, and the other of conflict between a weak good girl and a more powerful evil woman, both of whom want the same man. No resolutions are possible: White folly destroys black morality, and vindictiveness overcomes kinder emotions. A review of the period commends Juana Manuela Gorriti's "moral tendencies," but the novel represents the triumph of justice over evil only in the sense that the evil destroyers either repent or are executed.

El tesoro de los incas, one of Juana Manuela Gorriti's most reprinted novels, praises and idealizes Andean scenic beauties, Indian steadfastness, and family solidarity. Although the Indian heroine foolishly reveals the existence of an Inca treasure city to her perfidious Spanish lover, she and her family die under torture rather than collaborate with the greedy white invaders, and the Inca secret remains safe. Other tales included in this second volume of *Sueños y realidades* also portray the callous cupidity of Spaniards and destiny's retribution for selfish behavior, but, in addition, they explore dream worlds, the subconscious, and hypnosis. *Güemes* and *El general Vidal* reflect Gorriti's nostalgia for scenes of her childhood and her wish to write down for posterity the details of the heroic and personal comportment of Independence War heroes. Much of her fiction reveals a less positive side of human nature, but in her accounts of the exploits of Güemes and Vidal, these admirable patriots are seen as infallibly brave, compassionate, ingenious, charismatic, and passionately dedicated.

The two volumes of *Panoramas de la vida* of 1876 collect a series of extraordinarily interesting texts. The opening novel of the first volume, *Peregrinaciones de una alma triste*, recounts a series of adventures experienced by a young lady who runs away from her Lima home and travels. Overprotected and overmedicated for what appears to be terminal tuberculosis, Laura manages to plan and achieve her escape. She frees herself from constraints and social expectations, rejoices in her new independence as a solitary traveler, and throughout the novel, celebrates her newfound ability to survive even extreme adversities: bandits, civil wars, Indian attacks, and abandonment by her lover. In fact, she thrives on danger. Traveling overland through the Amazon jungle, she disguises herself in male dress, "thus avoiding the infinite difficulties that skirts provoke everywhere," but throughout her other escapades, she maintains her public identity as a wealthy young woman. The novel is a balancing act of increasingly extraordinary circumstances coupled with conventional proprieties.

Most of the episodes of the novel involve unhappy romances and injustices done to those who live at the margins of civilized society. Laura travels through countrysides where Indian raids and army incursions are frequent occurrences. She is instrumental in effecting justice or restitution in some situations: she restores a child to his mother, helps to rescue two orphans, allows her grandfather's illegitimate son to walk off with family wealth, buys freedom in Brazil for a slave family, and often tries unsuccessfully to mediate between contradictory social forces. Although the novel begins as a young girl's rebellion against all social restrictions, Laura's behavior throughout her adventures is that of a proper lady traveler: she never catches up with her Hungarian freedom-fighter lover, but her yearning for him keeps her moving along as she describes the scenery, listens to legends and anecdotes in each place she visits, and reacts to horrors with energetic compassion. She does not choose to return home, but she does visit her brother and her aunts and moves on only when her restlessness begins to make her feel ill again.

Juez y verdugo (Judge and executioner) portrays two women, one the embodiment of good and the other of evil, locked in combat. It is a fascinating series of depictions of qualities considered attractive or undesirable in women. The story is told, as is *Peregrinaciones de una alma triste*, within the framework of an enduring friendship between two women: In this case, the good woman's friend wishes to clear her name after she has been unjustly killed, and in *Peregrinaciones*, the narrator is a good friend of Laura's who recounts what Laura has said and written to her. As in *Peregrinaciones*, in *Juez y verdugo* there are extensive descriptions of the countryside and of local customs, but the center of the story is a consideration of power and powerlessness. Virtuous Aura is too innocent to protect herself from manipulative Inés, who tries to control three men simultaneously, with the help of a possibly supernatural ability to hypnotize her prey. Aura follows all the rules, yet she is victimized repeatedly by her father, her husband, and her duplicitous sister-in-law (Inés) who breaks all the rules and almost gets away with it. Virtue is reasserted in the end, but by then Aura has died.

El pozo del Yocci (Yocci's cistern), set in the northern Argentine area of Juana Manuela Gorriti's childhood, juxtaposes two historical periods of armed combat: the 1814 wars for Independence, and the rebellion against Rosas's dictatorship. In both of these disturbed times, women (a mother and her daughter) who fall in love with soldiers suffer through not only military uncertainties and physical dangers, but also the bizarre twists of civil war enmities that pit their lovers against their families. Stable human relationships cannot coexist with the exalted emotions of wartime conditions, and both men and women behave destructively. Isabel's brother dies an acclaimed military hero when he kills her lover (Aura's father); and Isabel's daughter Aura is later slaughtered by her husband (who goes mad and drowns) when she tries to save her brother. The descriptions of the two eras of military clashes are vivid, but the human cost is seen as excessively high. Wartime condones unreasonable behavior on the part of men, often labeling it as patriotism or as a requirement of honor, but the vengeful men die just as certainly as do the victimized women.

The second volume of *Panoramas de la vida* collects a variety of short anecdotes, another Inca treasure story, travel accounts, extensive vignettes of Lima society, commentary on the execution of Camila O'Gorman, a group of lively ghost stories, a tactful and very moving biography of Gorriti's husband, Manuel Isidoro Belzú, and a novel of travel to California during the height of the gold rush, *Un viaje al país del oro* (A journey to the land of gold), which had enjoyed great popularity in 1864 under the title *Un año en California* (A year in California). *Un viaje al país del oro* is an account of the adventures of two young Peruvians, a man and woman who are extremely close friends but not lovers, who make their way through the chaos and violence of the multinational gold field camps, ultimately foil a Navajo villain, and, after many crises, return home exhausted.

Misceláneas (Miscellanies), published in 1878, is a collection of odds and ends, as its title suggest: fragmentary fiction; versions of historical or Indian legends; anecdotes of daily life in Lima and Buenos Aires; book reviews and short public addresses; an account of Gorriti's experiences as a first aid volunteer in the battle of Callao on May 2, 1866; and some fictional sketches based on this adventure. Although there is no single piece of great distinction, the book provides a vivid picture of upper class society, its concerns and its entertainments.

Young people, and especially young women, are described with particular sympathy. Gorriti empathizes with yearnings for adventure and heroic action and often describes conflict with authoritarian parents. Young men sneak off to fight the Spanish in Callao in 1866, and young women smuggle themselves to the battlefront by joining nuns who run a field hospital. Gorriti's descriptions of the limitations of the lives of well-brought-up young ladies are poignant; great imagination and energy are poured into costumes for a fancy dress ball; gossip about eligible young men fascinates but is based on very superficial social encounters; groups of girls giggle and gossip, discuss and share clothing, and support each other in time of difficulty. In "Charlas de salón" (Social chit-chat), bevies of young women yearn to see real *gauchos* (cowboys), wish an overprotective father would allow the reading of Rousseau (the censorship of women's reading is a frequent topic), and try (not very successfully) to set up interesting conversations with men instead of just superficial bantering that offends both modesty and intelligence.

Women in Gorriti's fiction are often seen as compassionate, pious, and victimized, while men are often seen as arrogant, greedy, self-centered, and domineering. These stereotypes are generally absent from the travel accounts and the apparently autobiographical fragments that describe the excitement of being out in the open countryside and having adventures. The public speeches collected in *Misceláneas* are appreciations of other writers, an appeal for Argentine patriotism and unity, and a very moving exhortation to Peruvians (delivered at the Club Literario de Lima, February 4, 1875) to educate their children in Peru rather than sending them to Europe.

El mundo de los recuerdos (1886), unlike the earlier volumes of collected fiction and nonfiction, is unified by a consistent perspective. Although the selections are very diverse, they are fitted together as pieces of the same life experience by an intermittent first-person narrative voice, presumably that of the author herself. There are no clear boundaries between autobiographical reminiscence and fictional re-creation or invention: Gorriti's own memories and her stories about others are interwoven in a complex pattern of spatial and temporal juxtapositions. Childhood and early adult memories are filtered through later disillusionment and nostalgia, but the grief of adult losses and betrayals is mitigated by recall of the emotional clarity of early experiences. Some stories balance earlier and later experiences against each other: a memory of General Güemes's joyful vitality is followed by a more somber description of his death and funeral. A production of Verdi's *Hernani* releases a flood of memories of early experiences in the Argentine countryside in "Romería a la tierra natal" (Pilgrimage to my birthplace); a mismatched couple, who become a Gorriti family joke, reappears in their lives a generation later in "Longevidad de una frase" (Longevity of a saying).

Many of the stories are about pairs of similar or contrasting occurrences. An Indian couple and a well-off white couple suffer equal grief when their children die in "El amartelo" (Obsession), a young man who is devastated by his girlfriend's mercenary fickleness meets her again years later and is again hurt by her in "Epílogo de una tragedia" (Epilogue of a tragedy), and the happiness of peacetime is contrasted with the confusion of war in a number of the stories. Throughout the book, the voice of the reminiscing older narrator constantly qualifies and reflects on the stories of her early adventures. Incidents from childhood are recounted with particular affection in such stories as "La primera decepción" (The first deception) and "Derrotas del heroísmo" (Defeats of heroism). One of the liveliest and most interesting descriptions is of life as a young Bolivian officer's wife in the small town of Oruro in "El banquete de la muerte" (The banquet of death). "Chincha" (Chincha) is a moving account of travel and friendship with Mercedes Cabello de Carbonera.* *El mundo de los recuerdos* is in many ways a personal scrapbook that includes favorite anecdotes, recipes and jokes, tributes to friends and their books, and even two moralistic little texts Gorriti used as dictation exercises in her classes.

Gorriti's last published novel, *Oasis en la vida* (1888; An oasis in life) reads like propaganda for the Buenos Aires Chamber of Commerce, so sunny is its view of life in the big city. As social history of the era, it is full of fascinating detail about where to find the best candied almonds or cold drinks, why a wealthy traveler should stay at the Gran Hotel, medical practices, cab services, the merits of a particular French boarding house, women's clothing and its inconveniences, and La Buenos Aires Insurance Company as a beacon of progress and capitalistic excellence. The novel extolls the merits of Buenos Aires newspapers and provides a veritable *Who's Who in 1888* of outstanding journalists and literary men of public affairs. The plot that provides the continuity is that of the romance and eventual marriage of two deserving orphans, one a writer of serial fiction for a newspaper and the other a piano teacher. The plot is slight, but interest is sustained by the detailed descriptions and lively conversations.

La tierra natal (1889; Birthplace) is the wonderfully vivid account of Juana Manuela Gorriti's 1886 visit to Salta, where she lived as a child. After the end of the railroad line in Rosario, transport is by stagecoach—eight passengers, nine mules, and a driver who is a "pure gaucho right down to his fingernails"— along very bumpy roads. At every turn, Gorriti recognizes places, remembers incidents that took place sixty years before, and is met with great hospitality by the grandchildren of her old friends. Many of the most interesting stories of the civil war days demonstrate the strength and perseverance of strong women who managed to survive during an era of violence, uncertainty, and upheaval. Several generations of Gorriti family anecdotes are recalled as Juana Manuela Gorriti visits the places where they lived; these accounts of the past are woven together with vivid glimpses of the Salta of 1886, its local foods and entertainments.

SURVEY OF CRITICISM

No major studies of Juana Manuela Gorriti's life or writings have yet been published, although aspects of her fiction have been examined recently by Thomas Meehan (1981) and Lucía Guerra Cunningham (1987). The most extensive portrayal of Gorriti's life in recent years is Martha Mercader's fictionalized biography, *Juanamanuela, mucha mujer* (1980; Juanamanuela, quite a woman), which splices together known biographical data, actual texts, and fictional simulated documents and commentaries in an account narrated by the elderly Juana Manuela Gorriti in Buenos Aires. The narrator alternates between description of her immediate circumstances and recollections of her past adventures as she muses over the interconnections between the various eras of her life. I have been told that there are two earlier fictionalizations of Juana Manuela Gorriti's life, by R. E. Alamprese (1935) and María Alicia Domínguez (1937), but they are not easily available.

The major sources of information about Juana Manuela Gorriti's life are biographies by Alfredo O. Conde (1939) and Dionisio Chaca (1940), and the many informative prologues to her books and to the subsequent anthologies of her writings. Among the most informative of these introductory essays are those by José María Torres Caicedo (1865), Pastor S. Obligado (1878 and 1892), Santiago Estrada (1888), and more recently W. G. Weyland (1946) and Antonio Pagés Larraya (1962). There are many blanks in our present knowledge of Juana Manuela Gorriti's life history and it is to be hoped that letters and documents will eventually be published which will illuminate some of the many mysteries.

BIBLIOGRAPHY

Works by Juana Manuela Gorriti

Un año en California. Buenos Aires: El Nacional, 1864. Reprinted in *La Revista de Buenos Aires* 18 (1869). Reprinted as "La leontina" in *Revista del Río de la Plata* (Buenos Aires) 6, 24 (1873):499–580. Revised and reprinted in *Panoramas de la vida* as "Un viaje al país del oro."

Sueños y realidades. Ed. Vicente G. Quesada. Intro. José María Torres Caicedo. Afterword and selection of newspaper reviews, ed. Vicente G. Quesada. 2 vols. Buenos Aires: Casavalle, 1865. 2d ed., with prol. José María Torres Caicedo. 2 vols. Buenos Aires: Biblioteca de "La Nación," 1907. Volume 1 contains: "La quena," "El guante negro," "Gubi Amaya: Historia de un salteador" (concluding with "Un drama en el Adriático"), "Fragmentos del álbum de una peregrina," "La novia del muerto,'' ''La hija del mashorquero: Leyenda histórica,'' ''Una apuesta,'' ''El Lucero del Manantial: Episodio de la dictadura de don Juan Manuel Rosas,'' ''Una noche de agonía: Episodio de la guerra civil argentina en 1841,'' ''El lecho nupcial,'' and ''Tres noches de una historia.'' Volume 2 contains: ''El ángel caído,'' ''El tesoro de los Incas,'' ''Quien escucha su mal oye,'' ''Si haces mal no esperes bien,'' ''Una hora de coquetería,'' ''El ramillete de la velada,'' ''Una redondilla,'' ''El naranjo y el cedro,'' ''La fiebre amarilla,'' ''Güemes: Recuerdos de la infancia'' (concluding with ''Carmen Puch''), and ''El general Vidal.''

''Prólogo.'' *Corona poética ofrecida al pueblo peruano el 28 de julio de 1866.* Ed. Juana Manuela Gorriti. Lima: Imp. dirigida por J. R. Montemayor, 1866. Pp. iii–iv.

Biografía del general Don Dionisio de Puch. Paris: n.p., 1868. *Vida militar y política del general Don Dionisio de Puch.* 2d ed., corrected and augmented. Paris: Imprenta Hispano-Americana de Rouge Hermanos y Comp., 1869.

El pozo del Yocci. Paris: n.p., 1869. Also ed. prol. Arturo Giménez Pastor. Serie 4, Novela, vol. 1, 5. Buenos Aires: Universidad de Buenos Aires, Instituto de Literatura Argentina, Sección de Documentos, 1929.

Panoramas de la vida; colección de novelas, fantasías, leyendas y descripciones americanas. Prol. Mariano Pelliza. 2 vols. Buenos Aires: Casavalle, 1876. Volume 1 contains: ''Peregrinaciones de una [sic] alma triste,'' ''Juez y verdugo,'' and ''El pozo del Yocci.'' Volume 2 contains: ''Un drama en 15 minutos,'' ''El postrer mandato,'' ''Un viaje aciago,'' ''Una querella,'' ''Belzú,'' ''Los mellizos del Illimani,'' ''Una visita al manicomio,'' ''Un viaje al país del oro,'' ''El emparedado,'' ''El fantasma de un rencor,'' ''Una visita infernal,'' ''Yerbas y alfileres,'' ''Veladas de la infancia'' (''Caer de las nubes'' and ''Nuestra Sra. de los Desamparados'') ''Impresiones del 2 de mayo,'' ''Gethsemani,'' ''El día de difuntos,'' ''La ciudad de los contrastes,'' ''Escenas de Lima'' (''Risas y gorgeos,'' ''Una bandada de mariposas,'' ''Crónica de las veredas,'' ''Luz y sombra,'' ''Oásis'' [sic], ''Memento'' and ''Charla femenil''), ''Perfiles divinos: Camila O'Gorman,'' ''Feliza: Felícitas Guerrero de Alzaga'' (''El satélite,'' ''La obsesión,'' ''Un encuentro,'' and ''Mirajes de la última hora'').

Misceláneas; colección de leyendas, juicios, pensamientos, discursos, impresiones de viaje y descripciones americanas. Buenos Aires: Imprenta de M. Biedma, 1878. Intro. and Biog. Pastor S. Obligado. Contains: ''Entre dos cataclismos,'' ''El Machaypuito o el Yaraví de la quena,'' '' Impresiones y paisajes,'' ''Leyendas andinas'' (''La receta del cura de Yana-Rumí,'' ''El chifle del indio''), ''Apreciaciones de una obra,'' '' Veladas de la infancia'' (''La balanza del juicio''), ''Escenas de Lima'' (''El regreso—1875,'' ''El tornar de las hadas,'' ''Con la puerta en las narices,'' ''La túnica de la virgen''), ''En el álbum de H.F.V.—Lima, 1871,'' ''Apuntes de viaje,'' ''La voz del patriotismo,'' ''El tiempo y la eternidad,'' ''Gervasio Méndez,'' ''Recuerdos del 2 de mayo: incidentes y percances,'' ''Coincidencias: La influencia de un mal deseo,'' ''El pan de salud,'' ''Leyendas bíblicas: Un don de precio infinito,'' ''Las dos madres,'' ''Escenas de Buenos Aires'' (''El mes negro,'' ''Memento,'' ''Inocentes,'' ''La noche de San Silvestre,'' ''Espiritismo,'' ''Echar de menos,'' ''El gaucho,'' and ''Charlas de salón'') and ''Club literario de Lima.''

El mundo de los recuerdos. Buenos Aires: Félix Lajouane, editor, 1886. Contains: ''Romería a la tierra natal,'' ''Luz y sombra,'' ''Oásis,'' ''La primera decepción,''

"A dos pasos de la muerte," "Longevidad de una frase," "La Paz," "El amartelo," "Un grupo de caminantes," "Una conversión," "Francesco el mercachifle," "El profesorado," "La vida al pasar," "Derrotas del heroísmo," "Bibliografía," "El banquete de la muerte," "Chincha," " Vaguedades de la mente," "El general Martín Güemes," "Miraflores," and "Epílogo de una tragedia."

Oásis en la vida. Buenos Aires: Félix Lajouane, editor, 1888.

La tierra natal. Prol. Santiago Estrada. Buenos Aires: Félix Lajouane, editor, 1889.

Cocina ecléctica. Buenos Aires: Félix Lajouane, editor, 1890.

"Prólogo." *Días amargos: Páginas del libro de memorias de un pesimista.* By Santiago Vaca-Guzmán. Buenos Aires: Jacobo Peuser, 1891. 3d. ed. Pp. 7–9.

Perfiles (Primera parte). Buenos Aires: Félix Lajouane, editor, 1892.

Veladas literarias de Lima, 1876–1877; tomo primero, veladas I a X. Buenos Aires: Imprenta Europea, 1892.

Lo íntimo de Juana Manuela Gorriti. Prol. Abelardo M. Gamarra. Buenos Aires: Ramón Espasa, 1893.

El tesoro de los incas (leyenda histórica). Intro. José María Monner Sans. Serie 4, Novela, vol. 1, 6. Buenos Aires: Universidad de Buenos Aires, Instituto de Literatura Argentina, Sección de Documentos, 1929.

Páginas literarias: leyendas, cuentos, narraciones. Prol. Antonio Sagarna. Buenos Aires: El Ateneo, 1930. Contains: "El pozo de Yocci," "Una ojeada a la patria," "La novia del muerto," "Una noche de agonía," "Güemes: Recuerdos de la infancia," "El guante negro," "Una apuesta," "Un drama en el Adriático," and "Una redondilla."

Narraciones. Ed. and Prol. W. G. Weyland (Silverio Boj). Buenos Aires: Ediciones Estrada, 1946. Contains: from *Sueños y realidades*—"Gubi Amaya (Una ojeada a la patria, Un drama en el Adriático)," "El tesoro de los incas," "La hija del mashorquero," "El Lucero del Manantial," "La novia del muerto," and "Una noche de agonía;" from *Panoramas de la vida*—"El pozo del Yocci," "Coincidencias (I. El emparedado, II. Un fantasma de un rencor, III. Una visita infernal, IV. Yerbas y alfileres)," "Un drama en 15 minutos," and "El postrer mandato;" from *El mundo de los recuerdos*—"Francesco, el mercachifle" and "El amartelo;" from *Misceláneas*—"El chifle del indio;" and from *Lo íntimo*—"Idilio y tragedia."

Relatos. Ed. and Prol. Antonio Pagés Larraya. Buenos Aires: Editorial Universitaria de Buenos Aires, 1962. Contains: "El pozo del Yocci," "Receta del cura de Yana-Rumi," "El pan de salud," "Un viaje al país de oro" and "Güemes: Recuerdos de la infancia."

Works about Juana Manuela Gorriti

Alamprese, R. E. *Juana Manuela Gorriti.* Buenos Aires: n.p., 1935.

Aliaga Sarmiento, Rosalba. "Juana Manuela Gorriti." *El Monitor de la Educación Común* (Buenos Aires) 57, 784 (Apr. 1938):42–51.

Chaca, Dionisio. *Historia de Juana Manuela Gorriti.* Buenos Aires: Imprenta "El Centenario" de Bruno Laria, 1940.

Conde, Alfredo O. *Ideas de Juana Manuela Gorriti.* Buenos Aires: Instituto Cultural Joaquín V. González, 1945.

————. *Juana Manuela Gorriti*. Buenos Aires: Biblioteca Popular del C. E. XX "Juana Manuela Gorriti," 1939.

Domínguez, María Alicia. *Juana Manuela Gorriti*. Buenos Aires: n.p., 1937.

Estrada, Santiago. "Juana Manuela Gorriti." *Misceláneas*. Barcelona: Henrich y Cia., 1889. Also as prologue to *La tierra natal*. By J. M. Gorriti. First appeared in *El Diario*. (Buenos Aires) Nov. 5, 1888.

Estrella Gutiérrez, Fermín. "Juana Manuela Gorriti." *Diccionario de la literatura latinoamericana. Argentina: Primera Parte*. Ed. Roberto F. Giusti. Washington, D.C.: Unión Panamericana, 1960. Pp. 65–68.

Freyre de Jaimes, Carolina. "Juana Manuela Gorriti. Breve reseña de sus obras literarias. Su vida y sus grandes rasgos." *La Nación* (Buenos Aires), Nov. 7, 1892.

Gamarra, Abelardo M. "Prólogo." *Lo íntimo*. By J. M. Gorriti. Buenos Aires: Ramón Espasa, 1893. Pp. i–viii.

Gatica de Montiveros, María Delia. *Juana Manuela Gorriti; Aspectos de su obra literaria*. Santa Fe (Argentina): Imprenta de la Universidad, 1942.

Giménez Pastor, Arturo. "Noticia." *El pozo del Yocci, novela*. By J. M. Gorriti. Buenos Aires: Universidad de Buenos Aires, 1929. Pp. 171–72.

González Arrili, Bernardo. "Juana Manuela Gorriti." *La Nación* (Buenos Aires), June 14, 1949.

Guerra Cunningham, Lucía. "Visión marginal de la historia en la narrativa de Juana Manuela Gorriti." *Ideologies and Literature* New Series 2, 2 (Fall 1987):59–76.

Gutiérrez, Juan María. "Nota." *Revista del Río de la Plata* (Buenos Aires) 6, 24 (1873):499–501.

Lichtblau, Myron I. *The Argentine Novel in the Nineteenth Century*. New York: Hispanic Institute in the United States, 1959. Pp. 29–30, 86–91.

Meehan, Thomas C. "Una olvidada precursora de la literatura fantástica: Juana Manuela Gorriti." *Chasqui* 10:2–3 (Feb.-May 1981):3–19.

Mercader, Martha. *Juanamanuela, mucha mujer*. Buenos Aires: Editorial Sudamericana, 1980.

Monner Sans, José María. "Noticia." *El tesoro de los incas*. By J. M. Gorriti. Buenos Aires: Universidad de Buenos Aires, 1929. Pp. 239–41.

Monner Sans, Ricardo. "Juana Manuela Gorriti." *La Nación* (Buenos Aires), Apr. 11, 1889.

————. "Juana Manuela Gorriti." *Mensajero del Corazón de Jesús* (Buenos Aires), Nov. 10, 1892.

————. "Juana Manuela Gorriti." *La Ilustración Sud-Americana* (Buenos Aires), Jan. 16, 1893.

Obligado, Pastor S. "Biografía de la romancista argentina Juana Manuela Gorriti." *Misceláneas*. By J. M. Gorriti. Buenos Aires: Imprenta de M. Biedma, 1878. Pp. iii–xxvii.

————. "Rasgos biográficos de la Señora Juana M. Gorriti." *Veladas literarias de Lima*. By J. M. Gorriti. Buenos Aires: Imprenta Europea, 1892. Pp. ix–xli.

Ocampo, Juan Cruz. "Juana Manuela Gorriti." *La Prensa* (Buenos Aires), Sept. 16, 1934.

Pagés Larraya, Antonio. "Juana Manuela Gorriti." *Relatos*. By J. M. Gorriti. Buenos Aires: Editorial Universitaria de Buenos Aires, 1962. Pp. 5–11.

Palma literaria y artística de la escritora argentina Juana M. Gorriti. Buenos Aires: Carlos Casavalle, 1875.

Palma, Ricardo. "Carta a don Julio G. Sandoval." *Veladas literarias de Lima*. By J. M. Gorriti. Buenos Aires: Imprenta Europea, 1892. Pp. v–vii.

Pelliza, Mariano A. "Prólogo." *Panoramas de la vida*. By J. M. Gorriti. Buenos Aires: Casavalle, 1876. I:9–16.

Regazzoni, Susanna. "Juana Manuela Gorriti: Notas sobre la disolución del exotismo." *Romanticismo 2: Atti del III Congreso sul romanticismo spagnolo e ispanoamericano (12–14 Aprile 1974)*. Introd. Ermanno Caldera. Genoa, Italy: Biblioteca di Lett., 1984. Pp. 100–106.

Rohde, Jorge Max. *Las ideas estéticas en la literatura argentina*. Buenos Aires: La Facultad, 1924. III:165–81.

Rojas, Ricardo. *Historia de la literatura argentina*. Buenos Aires: Editorial Guillermo Kraft Limitada, 1960. VIII:490–93.

Sagarna, Antonio. "Un alto valor literario y cívico." *Páginas literarias*. By J. M. Gorriti. Buenos Aires: El Ateneo, 1930. Pp. 12–19.

Sánchez, Luis Alberto. *Historia de la literatura americana (desde los orígenes hasta 1936)*. Santiago: Editorial Ercilla, 1937. Pp. 350–51.

Sosa, Francisco. "Juana Manuela Gorriti." *Escritores y poetas sudamericanos*. Mexico City: Oficina Tip. de la Secretaría de Fomento, 1890. Pp. 53–68.

Torres Caicedo, José Maria. "Juana Manuela Gorriti." *Sueños y realidades*. By J. M. Gorriti. Buenos Aires: Casavalle, 1865. I: i–xv. 1907 ed.:1:5–22.

———. "Señora doña María [*sic*] Manuela Gorriti." *Ensayos biográficos y de crítica literaria sobre los principales publicistas, historiadores, poetas y literatos de la América Latina*. 2d series. Paris: n.p., 1868. III:1–15.

Villarroel, María Zoraida. "Una argentina de antaño: doña Juana Manuela Gorriti." *La Nación* (Buenos Aires), Dec. 13, 1942.

Weyland, W. G. ("Silverio Boj"). Introd. *Narraciones*. By J. M. Gorriti. Buenos Aires: Ediciones Estrada, 1946. Pp. vii–ix.

LUISA JOSEFINA HERNÁNDEZ
(b. 1928)
Mexico

María Elena de Valdés

BIOGRAPHY

Luisa Josefina Hernández was born in Mexico City. Both parents came from Chiapas in the south of Mexico. She credits her father for her education and the care he took of her intellectual development. He had a large library, made up mainly of books dealing with law and history, but he also had some works of literature. He was a supreme court judge. Her mother, who had no formal education, was not interested in acquiring one for herself and did not approve of formal education for Luisa Josefina. Hernández was an avid reader and at age seventeen had read full collections of literary and historical works; she first enrolled at the university in law school, but soon transferred to the Faculty of Philosophy and Letters where she majored in literature and theater. She knows English, French, and German well and has translated into Spanish works by Jean Anouilh, Bertold Brecht, Joseph Campbell, Christopher Fry, Arthur Miller, William Shakespeare, Carl Sternheim, and Dylan Thomas among others.

Hernández began to write and publish when she was twenty-two. In 1950 she wrote her first drama, a one-act play, *El ambiente jurídico* (Judicial surroundings), which focuses with great sensitivity on four law students and the aspirations of two women working to enter into the male-dominated profession.

Luisa Josefina Hernández is one of the few Latin American dramatists who studied to be a playwright. She was a student of Rodolfo Usigli, who has been recognized as one of the foremost dramatists of modern Mexico. She studied theory and dramatic composition with him and received her Master's degree in theater from the National Autonomous University of Mexico (UNAM) in 1955. Her thesis, directed by Usigli, was the play *Los frutos caídos* (The fallen fruit).

When Usigli left UNAM, Hernández was appointed to teach dramatic composition. She has been teaching at UNAM for more than thirty years.

To understand Hernández' swift entry and success in the Mexican theater, the prevailing artistic circumstances of Mexico at the time should be made clear. In 1946 the Mexican government founded the Instituto Nacional de Bellas Artes (INBA) to further the nation's appreciation and development of its arts. This gave the Mexican theater a thrust forward, since at that time productions were staged only if financial success was foreseen in the commercial theater. Only cinema could bring in large audiences. In 1947 Salvador Novo was named director of the Drama Department, ushering in a new era for Mexican arts.

It was in the 1950s that Hernández was launched into an active playwright's life. In 1951, at age twenty-three, she won first prize at the Spring Festival for her play *Aguardiente de caña* (Sugar-cane alcohol). After that beginning, her works were premiered one after the other, most under the auspices of the Drama Department: in 1953, at the Sala Chopin *Los sordomudos* (The deaf-mutes); in 1954, *Botica modelo* (Corner pharmacy), at the Sala del Seguro Social which won a prize from *El Nacional* newspaper; in 1957, *Los frutos caídos*, her Master's thesis, staged at the Granero Theater and also presented by the group "Juan Ruiz de Alarcón" in the city of Campeche. There it was awarded a Regional Festival Prize that won it a presentation at Mexico City's Teatro del Globo from September 27 to October 16 of the same year. In 1958 *Los duendes* (The elves) was premiered at the Sala Villaurrutia, and in 1959 two of her plays were presented: *Arpas blancas, conejos dorados* (White harps, guilded rabbits) at the Orientación, and *Los huéspedes reales* (The real guests). The latter had competed in the National Festival and won the distinction of the best unpublished play of the year. In 1960 Hernández successfully introduced a change in her theater with a historical theme from the Mexican prerevolutionary period, *La paz ficticia* (The fictitious peace), which depicts the genocide of the Yaqui people during the reign of the dictator Porfirio Díaz; it premiered at the Teatro del Bosque.

Hernández has proven to be one of Mexico's leading female writers and a major exponent of woman's reality. She vehemently opposes being considered a feminist; she sees feminism as a fashionable attempt to solve a problem that is inherent to the feminine condition. Women have always had to find ways to assert their rightful place in society without destroying it. She finds herself, at age sixty, without any professional constraints that could in any way be attributed to the fact that she is a woman.

She has published both plays and novels continuously at a pace that makes her one of the most prolific writers of Latin America. Although in a series of interviews (1973, 1976, 1978, 1981, 1984, 1985) she has expressed a preference for the novel, her most important contribution is seen to be in the theater. She has written over thirty plays with a wide range of topics and dramatic forms. Her broad knowledge of classical and modern literature is evident in both her plays and novels. After writing *Los huéspedes reales* in 1958, she decided to write only commissioned plays in the future. But she is always writing—be it commissioned plays, novels, or commentaries for newspapers and journals.

MAJOR THEMES

Hernández has written more than thirty plays and thirteen novels. Not all of this vast production spread over thirty-five years is accessible today, but from the twenty plays and thirteen novels reviewed for this study, specific thematic developments can be discerned and some generalization can be put forward as an introduction. With the notable exceptions of a highly successful incursion into farce with *Los duendes* (1960) and the less developed *Arpas blancas, conejos dorados* (1959), hers is and has been a literature of anger. The fact that Hernández is a woman and there is moral anger at the abuse suffered by her characters, most of whom are women, has led to simplistic generalizations about her literature, yet she is not ideologically tied to any school of thought. Her often brutal unmasking of the feminine abuse of men is an uncomfortable factor that a narrow minded or prescriptive feminism cannot contend with except by omission. The major dialectical axis of her literary production is the activism born out of anger and indignation on the one hand, and anger transcending into contemplation on the other.

Anger as active thinking has developed into two groups of themes in Hernández works: the individual and society. The first group of themes, those of individualization, may be further divided into three groups: the self-realization of women coming to terms with their sexuality; the self-identity of a woman in response to the other; and women's exercise of the will to act or a lack of will. The second group of themes portray social conflicts. There are also three predominant themes in this group: The most basic is social acceptance or marginalization of the individual; second is social justice in the use of authority and privilege; and the most specifically feminine theme is marriage and divorce.

An additional theme to appear in Hernández' writing is the transcendence of anger through mysticism. The themes of anger often interact with each other and develop with complementarity in the dramatic action of the plays or as the central focus of the narration. The mystic theme stands alone in the most recent works, especially the novels, *Apostasía* (1978; Apostasy), *Las fuentes ocultas* (1980; The hidden fountains), and *Apocalipsis cum figuris* (1982; Apocalypse with figures).

Among the plays that deal with the theme of self-realization, *Los frutos caídos* (1957) explores the frustration of a divorced woman in a hypocritical society and her emotional as well as spiritual frustration. The main character is intelligent enough to know that she is doomed to be stifled and yet, like Sisyphus, she must keep trying. Equally grim is *La hija del rey* (1959; The king's daughter) whose protagonist's only sense of identity is in the image others have of her. *Los huéspedes reales* (1958), *El ambiente jurídico* (1950), *Botica modelo* (1953),

Los sordomudos (1954), and *Aguardiente de caña* (1950) all abound in Freudian variations on the crisis of identity and repressed sexuality. The novel *El lugar donde crece la hierba* (1964; The place where the grass grows) develops an identity crisis of a woman who ultimately seeks to retreat from the world by returning to the womb.

The self-other relation (primarily the female-male relationship) is explored in the largest number of plays and always in the breakdown of relationships, usually because of the demand that the woman become the mindless partner of the other. This denial of the other's individuality destroys any possibility of happiness as self-fulfillment. This theme is prevalent in *Agonía* (1951; Agony), *Botica modelo* (1953), the farce *Los duendes* (1960), *Los sordomudos* (1954), and the novels *Los palacios desiertos* (1963; The deserted palaces) and *La cólera secreta* (1964; The secret wrath).

The theme dealing with the exercise of the will to act condemns the weak-willed, spineless characters who lack the courage to grasp what life offers in contrast with those who fight and have the courage to live. This theme of individualization brings out some of Hernández' strongest characterizations; it is featured in plays like *Afuera llueve* (1952; It is raining outside), *Los frutos caídos* (1957), *La hija del rey* (1959), *La corona del ángel* (1951; The angel's crown), and the novel *La memoria de Amadís* (1967; The memory of Amadis), where the weak-willed character is the husband and the strong, but ultimately disillusioned woman is his wife who tries vainly to act for both.

The theme of the individual-community relationship is rich in suggestions of Jung's collective unconscious. This is found in the plays *La pavana de Aranzazú* (1975) and the earlier farce *Los duendes* (1960). Hernández places full emphasis on the biological procreative power in the female as being an endowment of spiritual creativity as well. These two plays show the first signs of what will later turn into a mystical theme of creativity.

The theme of social justice is a particularly rich one. The plays that feature this theme are *Botica modelo* (1953), *La paz ficticia* (1960), *Historia de un anillo* (1961) where a town is massacred because of its belief in basic social justice, *La fiesta del mulato* (written in 1966; *The Mulatto's Orgy*, 1971), which we will study later in this entry as a demonstration of thematic development, and *Escándalo en Puerto Santo* (1962; Scandal in Puerto Santo), which is based on her novel *La Plaza de Puerto Santo* (1961; The square of Puerto Santo). The novel and the play focus on grass-roots social justice in the overthrow of the local social elite. Her novel *La primera batalla* (1965; The first battle) treats the betrayal of the ideals of the Mexican Revolution in contrast with the ideological clarity of the Cuban Revolution.

The last of the societal themes deals with the emptiness that hides behind middle-class social conventions. This theme is intertwined with many of the other themes, especially those of self-realization and the self-other relationship, but in at least one play, one of Hernández' best, *Los frutos caídos* (1957), this theme is central.

The mystical transcendence of anger is the last theme developed thus far in Luisa Josefina Hernández' long and productive career. It was already present as an undercurrent in *Los duendes* of 1960 and began to take on more importance in the novel *Los trovadores* (1973) and the play *La Pavana de Aranzazú* (1975). But it became the dominant theme in *Apostasía* (1978) which was taken from the *auto sacramental* with the same title written in 1974. The mystic theme has continued as the pervasive direction of her writing in *Las fuentes ocultas* (1980) and *Apocalipsis cum figuris* (1982). In these works, the mystical purgation of bodily desires is not presented as a psychological process, but rather as a state of mind already present in the enlightened. The wisdom of the mystical vision is not linked to the Spanish mystical tradition of Saint John of the Cross and Saint Theresa. Rather, it unfolds as a higher plane of existence wherein the character-type transcends anger in the face of rampant injustice through the knowledge that there is a deeper level of human life and consciousness. The enlightened have found a way of living in depth through the realization that the common ground in the spirit of humanity gives life meaning.

Hernández' plays often represent a kind of ideological self-discovery as in *La fiesta del mulato (The Mulatto's Orgy)*, written in 1966; this play depends on rapid changes of scenery, lighting effects, dancing, and above all, music to make its dramatic statement. The reader of the play must therefore compensate for the lack of theatrical devices through a very careful reading and mental enactment of the stage directions. This play has been selected for a more detailed commentary not only because it is one of Hernández' best works, but also because it is her only major work available in English.

The play is set in the mining city of Guanajuato in 1799, that is, about a decade before the Mexican movement for independence from Spain was to begin. The ineffective colonial structure of civil and religious authority serves as a background. There are sixteen characters, only one of whom is given a specific name in the cast of characters, and within the dramatic action. She begins in the play merely as the Mulatto's wife or as the *mestiza* (woman of mixed Indian blood), but as the play progresses she is called by name, María Antonia, and within the play she plays the part of the Marquesa de Cruilles.

The Mulatto and his wife will be the central focus of the play, but the Indian and his newfound friend, the Friar, are the "focalizers." It is through their eyes that we see the dramatic action. The Indian, the Mulatto's servant, is sympathetic; the Friar who represents the viceroy has to be won over.

In total there are twenty separate scenes of dramatic action set in two different time sequences: first, the fiesta and the incidents leading up to it; and, second, the trial of the Mulatto and his wife by the mayor as representative of civil authority and by two priests who represent the Church. There are also twenty separate interventions by the focalizers (the Indian who also takes part in the dramatic action, and the Friar who is both audience to the dramatic action and commentator on it). The play ends when the focalizers merge with the dramatic action.

The dramatic action centers on the sexual fantasy that is played out by the Mulatto and his wife and their trial before the civil and religious authorities as a consequence of their week-long performance. The play opens with the chance encounter of the Friar by the Indian servant of the Mulatto. The lights dim, the voice of the Indian narrates, but the narrative begins to unfold as dramatic action until the characters take over. The Indian takes up his persona within the dramatic action leaving his status as commentator and narrator, but switching back when the Friar wishes to discuss what has been represented in the performance. The dramatic action will also alternate between the Mulatto's fiesta and the preparation for his trial and the trial itself.

The action begins when the Indian seeks out the Mulatto to inform him that the richest vein of gold yet discovered has been found in the Mari Sánchez mine which he owns with two partners in Mexico City. The Mulatto immediately orders a week-long fiesta to be held at the entrance of the mine. Nothing is to be spared; there must be musicians, servants to serve all the food and drink which the workers from the mine and the townspeople can consume. But for himself he asks only to make love to the Marquesa de Cruilles. He knows her only from a painting that hangs in the mayor's palace. The Indian, as *mayordomo* of his master the Mulatto, will see to it that all is done as he has been instructed. He will see to it that the musicians and servants are hired, the food and wine are purchased, the fiesta is organized and begins at once, and most important of all, that the Marquesa goes to the Mulatto. The Indian's solution to this problem is simple; his mistress, the Mulatto's wife, is extraordinarily beautiful and strongly resembles the woman in the painting. Thus, he asks her to dress up like the Marquesa. She willingly obliges without losing sight either of the requirements of acting or the demands of the part she is to play; that is, she becomes an actress. The Indian takes the Mulatto's wife to the Mulatto dressed up like the Marquesa, wearing a dress that is similar to the one in the painting. The resemblance is so remarkable that the painting appears to have come to life.

The Mulatto receives his wife as if she were the Marquesa; he is not surprised, he is overjoyed. The polite conversation between the Mulatto and the Marquesa evokes a beautiful image of the aristocratic lady courted by the Mulatto in Venice. The acting gives way to their sexual desire. He reminds her of their actual situation in Guanajuato and calls her by name: María Antonia.

The scene changes to the city hall; the woman stands on trial accused of imitating the Marquesa, that is, of pretending to be another person; the mayor and the priests are judge and jury. She replies that she is the legitimate wife of the Mulatto and that there is no sin for husband and wife to have sexual intercourse even if it was out in the woods and not in their own bedroom. The priest persists, why did she willingly put on the dress similar to the one in the painting and adopt the personality of another woman? Her reply is direct: She did it so that the Mulatto would want to make love to her. The priests cannot understand sexual fantasy and accuse her of being bewitched into thinking she was another person. She protests vehemently. She has always known who she is—she is the Mulatto's woman. The mayor leaps up and asks her to swear that on the Bible. She replies that she will willingly swear that she has always known that she was herself and not anyone else. The Mulatto is brought into the courtroom. When he sees her he addresses her by name, María Antonia, and then instinctively she begins to play the part of the Marquesa. The mayor triumphantly declares to the Mulatto that this woman who is dressed like the Marquesa de Cruilles, wife of the old viceroy of New Spain, is in fact his wife and that her impersonation has been a masquerade. The Mulatto and his wife look deeply into each other's eyes, and when she is asked to swear she responds that she swears before God that she is the Marquesa de Cruilles and that she belongs body and soul to the Mulatto. Amidst all the shouting and clamor of the priests and the mayor, the Mulatto calmly and firmly tells her: "Thank you, María Antonia."

The scene switches back to the time of the Mulatto's fiesta. The Indian assists his mistress in the daily sojourn from the city house to the site of the fiesta near the mine so that she can once again make love to the Mulatto as the Marquesa. In their conversation María Antonia confesses to the Indian that she has convinced herself that she is the Marquesa; when she is not actually playing the part she thinks of nothing else, and her identification with the Marquesa has become so powerful that she has taken the painting from the mayor's palace.

At the end of each night of celebration outside the mine, María Antonia takes leave and returns to her home in the city escorted by the Indian. There she rests throughout the day in order to resume the fiesta at sunset. During each of these days the sense of one as the necessary complement to the other has been growing until they both begin to feel that they are each other's indispensable other half and that only when they are together are they complete. In other words, their identity is intimately tied up with their physical and spiritual union with the other.

The play ends when the Friar, the commentator of the performance staged for his benefit by the Indian, intervenes with the authority of the viceroy to overrule the mayor and the priests and to free the Mulatto and his wife after months of imprisonment.

The play develops a central issue of feminist thinking: the relationship of woman's identity as an individual and as a social persona. The central question as posed by feminist psychoanalysts like Luce Irigaray (*This Sex Which Is Not One*, Ithaca, N.Y. 1985) is: What reality, independent of her reproductive function, can woman respond to? Woman's two roles of individual and social persona are contradictory in a profound way. Woman as an individual is an equal to man and in some not too distant future may enjoy the same economic, social, and political rights as men. But as a social persona, woman must preserve and maintain her femininity. The value placed on woman as a persona is directly tied to her maternal and to her seductress roles, that is, to her femininity. In other words, in the social order, women are objects, products, that have been produced and packaged through extensive effort and expense to be used and exchanged by men. Women as merchandise, women as commodities, have no place in the social order as subjects.

This aspect of the identity crisis of María Antonia as herself (subject) and María Antonia as the Marquesa (object) is certainly present in the play and is highlighted by such expressions as "I only did it so that he would want me" and "I am his woman body and soul." Clearly, this is the language of woman as sexual commodity.

But *La fiesta del mulato* does not stop here with the feminist unmasking of woman's sexual role, for this self-reduction is transcended with the depiction of the relationship between the Mulatto and María Antonia. Theirs is a tensional relationship which finds that the sexual union is but the threshold to the deeper sense of identity in which the individual discovers that she or he exists to the extent that she or he participates in the experience of the other. Therefore, the conclusion of this very subtle play is that, when either man or woman is isolated and alone, each is indeed separated into the individual (I know I am I) and the social persona (the one they want to be seen as and to be taken as). In the case of María Antonia, the individual is a bored and unhappy individual and the social persona is the Marquesa whose part is inscribed in the sexual fantasy of the Mulatto's own search for identity. María Antonia and the Mulatto discover their identity in each other.

One of the most significant aspects of Hernández' writing for the theater is her ability to make manifest, through dramatic spectacle, the ideological issues of Mexican history. She does not have to revert to direct statements or to philosophical generalizations. The dramatic situation itself speaks eloquently for the psychological implications just below the surface of social convention.

SURVEY OF CRITICISM

Criticism of Hernández' vast body of writings can be divided into three distinct categories: (1) interviews with the author by academics and reporters; (2) doctoral dissertations in U.S. universities and a handful of articles in American journals primarily produced by the authors of the theses; and (3) reviews of first performances of her dramatic works and of her novels. Although the third category is not scholarly, it does reflect Hernández' status in present-day Mexico as a successful dramatist and a largely ignored novelist.

Critical opinion of the performance of her plays has been nurtured through her long career into accepting her particular blend of stagecraft and a unique dramatic development of her themes. In contrast, with each new novel, in spite of radical changes in structure and language, the critical response has been indifferent when not hostile.

I have found seven published interviews with Hernández. The styles of the seven interviews are different, but the scope of questions is similar, of course, since Hernández is being interviewed because of interest in her as a woman writer in today's Mexico. Throughout this decade of interviews, Hernández has been remarkably consistent in her answers. The salient characteristic is her forthrightness and strong convictions. The interview that stands out is the one by Cristina Pacheco (1978) which was directed to a general readership in Mexico itself.

A significant point made in the interviews is her statement that she has never been hampered as a writer by sexist prejudice in a field that is male-dominated. This is clearly an honest assessment by a writer who has published prolifically. She is quick to point out that there are vast social problems that beset Mexicans and that the *machismo* of Mexican males does not create victims and villains but only victims, for both sexes are profoundly affected by the gendered denial of individuality. She has also repeatedly stressed her deep religious convictions and her faith in the power of regeneration of the human being. This theme has become more and more dominant in recent years.

Eleven academic critics have published on the literature of Hernández. Without question, the most valuable contributions to the study of her literature are the three dissertations. The first Ph.D. thesis was written by Sylvia Jean Brann, "El teatro y las novelas de Luisa Josefina Hernández" (1969). This first dissertation broke new ground; it introduced the work of Hernández to North American academic readership. The thesis concentrates primarily on the novels and treats the drama as texts, not as performable plays. Brann argues that, in Hernández' writing (before 1968), character development is kept to a minimum so that the characters will speak as members of the Mexican nation and address the vast social ills of that society. A constant element in this writing, according to Brann, is that these social symbols must at some point take action in their respective worlds. There are in Hernández' repertoire two ways of responding to crisis: Either the character has the courage to live and act, or is paralyzed through a profound fear of self-commitment.

John K. Knowles's thesis (1970) was probably written without knowledge of Brann's work of a year earlier since Knowles does not include it in his bibliography. This thesis, "Luisa Josefina Hernández: A Study of Her Dramatic Theory and Practice" (Rutgers University), was subsequently translated into Spanish and published by UNAM. As the title indicates, Knowles's thesis is a concerted examination of Hernández as a professor and theoretician of theater as well as her work as a dramatist. The dissertation is exceptional because of Knowles's command of dramatic theory and the wide base of comparison used in his discussion of Hernández' plays. He is especially convincing in his study of her early realistic theater. He comments on *Los frutos caídos, Los huéspedes reales, Popol Vuh, La historia de un anillo, La paz ficticia, La fiesta del mulato, Los duendes,* and *Arpas blancas, conejos dorados.* Although I would tend to disagree with his term *didactic art* and would prefer to call it *committed art,* his argument is well presented and supported by ample documentation from dramatic study.

The most recent thesis is by Janis Lynne Krugh, "Solitude and Solidarity:

Major Themes and Techniques in the Theater of Luisa Josefina Hernández''
(1986). The strength of this work is in the direct commentary of six plays:
*Apocrypha, La Pavana de Aranzazú, Los sordomudos, Historia de un anillo,
La fiesta del mulato*, and *Apostasía*. Krugh's understanding of dramatic technique
is excellent in the description of the structure and development of dramatic action.
This strength is especially evident in her study of ritual in *Apocrypha, La Pavana
de Aranzazú*, and *La fiesta del mulato*. The weakness in the thesis is an over-
simplified concept of dramatic theme, for example, the eternal feminine. This
research discrepancy is never more evident than in Krugh's discussion of *La
fiesta del mulato*. The semiotic analysis is again excellent, but her emphasis on
the didactic presentation of the corruption of the last years of Spanish rule misses
the profound revelations of the *mestiza*'s mask.

There is one recent notable exception to theater criticism on Hernández: the
detailed semiotic study of *La paz ficticia* by Fernando de Toro that uses A. J.
Greimas' structuralist model for criticism is adapted with extraordinary ingenuity.

BIBLIOGRAPHY

Works by Luisa Josefina Hernández

Aguardiente de Caña. Play in three acts. 1950. Unpublished.
El ambiente jurídico. One-act play. *América (Revista Antológica)* 64 (Dec. 1950):209–
    24.
Agonía. One-act play. *América (Revista Antológica)* 65 (Apr. 1951):95–110.
La corona del ángel. Play in three acts. 1951. Unpublished.
Afuera llueve. One-act play. *Prometeus* 4 (July 1952):45–68.
Botica modelo. Play in three acts. *El Nacional* (Mexico City) (1953).
La llave del cielo. Play in three acts. Written 1954. Unpublished.
Los sordomudos. Play in three acts. *América (Revista Antológica)* 69 (Mar. 1954):133–
    50.
Los frutos caídos. Play in three acts. Vol. III. *Teatro mexicano del siglo XX*. Ed. Celestino
    Gorostiza. Mexico City: Fondo de Cultura Económica, 1956. Pp. 403–78. 2d ed.
    Teatro mexicano contemporáneo. Ed. Antonio Espina. Madrid: Aguilar, 1962.
    Pp. 439–510.
Los huéspedes reales. Play in three acts and ten scenes. *La Palabra y el Hombre* 2 (Apr.-
    June 1957):91–95. *Ficción* 2. Xalapa: Universidad Veracruzana, 1958. *Teatro
    mexicano del siglo XX*. Vol. 4. Ed. Antonio Magaña Esquivel. Mexico City:
    Fondo de Cultura Económica, 1970. Pp. 84–138.
La hija del rey. Monologue. *México en la Cultura. Novedades* 518 (Feb. 13, 1959):12.
    Cuarta antología de obras en un acto. Ed. Alvaro Arauz. Col. Teatro Mexicano
    24. Mexico City: Col. de Teatro Mexicano, 1965. Pp. 7–15.
El lugar donde crece la hierba. Novel. Col. Ficción 8. Xalapa: Universidad Veracruzana,
    1959.
With Emilio Carballido. "Pastores de la ciudad." *La Palabra y el Hombre* 3, 12 (Oct.-
    Dec. 1959):625–61.
Los duendes. Play in three acts. *La Palabra y el Hombre* 14 (Apr.-June 1960):153–204.

Teatro mexicano 1963. Ed. Antonio Magaña-Esquivel. Mexico City: Aguilar, 1965. Pp. 239–305.

La paz ficticia. Play. *México en la Cultura. Novedades* 598 (28 Aug. 1960):3, 10; 599 (Sept. 4, 1960):5. *Teatro popular mexicano*. Mexico City: Novaro, 1974.

Historia de un anillo. La Palabra y el Hombre 20 (Oct.-Dec. 1961):693–723.

La Plaza de Puerto Santo. Novel. Letras Mexicanas 65. Mexico City: Fondo de Cultura Económica, 1961.

Escándalo en Puerto Santo. Theatrical adaptation of the novel *La plaza de Puerto Santo*. Written 1962, Unpublished.

La calle de la gran ocasión. Dialogues. Ficción 41. Xalapa: Universidad Veracruzana, 1962. 2d ed., 2d series. *Tramoya* 21 (Sept.-Oct. 1981):73–87. Mexico City: Editores Mexicanos Unidos, 1985.

Arpas blancas, conejos dorados. Play in three acts. *La Palabra y el Hombre* 28 (Oct.-Dec. 1963):637–91.

Clemencia. Play in one act and three scenes. *Cuadernos de Bellas Artes* (Mar. 3, 1963):61–80; (Apr. 4, 1963):65–92.

Los palacios desiertos. Novel. Serie del Volador. Mexico City: Joaquín Mortiz, 1963.

La cólera secreta. Novel. Ficción 60. Xalapa: Universidad Veracruzana, 1964.

La noche exquisita. Novel. Ficción 65. Xalapa: Universidad Veracruzana, 1965.

La primera batalla. Novel. Col. Alacena. Mexico City: Era, 1965.

El valle que elegimos. Novel. Novelistas Contemporáneos. Mexico City: Joaquín Mortiz, 1965.

Popol-Vuh. Play in two parts. *La Palabra y el Hombre* 40 (Oct.-Dec. 1966):699–734. *Teatro popular mexicano*. Mexico City: Novaro, 1974.

La memoria de Amadís. Novel. Serie del Volador. Mexico City: Joaquín Mortiz, 1967.

Quetzalcóatl. Play in two parts. Cuadernos de Lectura Popular 172. Mexico City: SEP, 1968. *Revista de Bellas Artes* 20 (Mar.-Apr. 1968):39–58.

Nostalgia de Troya. Novel. Mexico City: Siglo XXI, 1970.

Los trovadores. Novel. Serie del Volador. Mexico City: Joaquín Mortiz, 1973.

Apostasía. Auto sacramental. *Revista de Bellas Artes* 17 (Sept.-Oct. 1974):48–64.

Danza del Urogallo múltiple. One-act play. *Teatro mexicano 1971*. Ed. Antonio Magaña Esquivel. Col. Literaria Dramaturgos. Mexico City: Aguilar, 1974. Pp. 233–63.

La Pavana de Aranzazú, Auto sacramental. *Tramoya* 1 (Oct.-Dec. 1975):14–37.

Auto del Divino Preso. Auto sacramental, 1976. Unpublished.

Hecube. Play. *Tramoya* 5 (Oct.-Dec. 1976):7–30.

Apocrypha. Consenso 2, 3 (May 1978):25–34.

Apostasía. Novel. Col. Cuento y Relato. Mexico City: UNAM, 1978.

Caprichos y disparates de Francisco Goya. Lyrical commentaries. Mexico City: UNAM, Coordinación de Humanidades, 1979.

La fiesta del mulato. Play in two parts. *Tramoya* 17 (Oct.-Dec. 1979):4–29. Written in 1966.

"Ciertas cosas." Monologue. *Tramoya* 18 (Jan.-Mar. 1980):4–10.

Las fuentes ocultas. Novel. Mexico City: Extemporáneos, 1980.

Jerusalén-Damasco. Play. 1980. Unpublished.

Apocalipsis cum figuris. Novel. Serie Ficción. Xalapa: Universidad Veracruzana, 1982.

La cadena. Play. 1983. Unpublished.

El orden de los factores. Play. 1983. Unpublished.

La bicicleta de Quique. Play. n.d. Unpublished.

La mujer sabia. Play. n.d. Unpublished.
La nave mágica. Play. n.d. Unpublished.
Oriflama. Play. n.d. Unpublished.
Carta de navegaciones submarinas. Short novel. Mexico City: Fondo de Cultura Económica, 1987.

Translations of Luisa Josefina Hernández

Colecchia, Francesca, and Julio Matas, eds. and trans. "Dialogues." *Selected Latin American One-Act Plays.* Pittsburgh: University of Pittsburgh, 1973. Pp. 125–39.
Oliver, William I., trans. "The Mulatto's Orgy." *Voices of Change in the Spanish American Theater.* Austin: University of Texas Press, 1971. Pp. 219–55.

Works about Luisa Josefina Hernández

Bearce, Grace M. "Interview with Luisa Josefina Hernández." *Hispania* (May 1981):301–302.
Brann, Silvia Jean. "El teatro y las novelas de Luisa Josefina Hernández." Ph.D. diss. University of Illinois, 1969. (DAI 30/08-A, p. 3450; 70–00801.)
———. "El fracaso de la voluntad en las comedias de Luisa Josefina Hernández." *Latin American Theater Review* 7, 1 (Fall 1983):25–31.
Dauster, Frank N. "La forma ritual en *Los huéspedes reales.*" *Ensayos sobre teatro hispanoamericano.* Mexico City: SepSetentas, 1975. Pp. 60–65.
Espinosa, Tomás. "Dramatis Personae: Luisa Josefina Hernández: 'Afuera llueve.' " Introd. to *La calle de la gran ocasión.* By Luisa Josefina Hernández. Mexico City: Editores Mexicanos Unidos, 1985. Pp. 11–27.
Fox-Lockert, Lucía. "Luisa Josefina Hernández." *Women Novelists in Spain and Spanish America.* Metuchen, N.J.: Scarecrow Press, 1979. Pp. 241–59.
González Cruz, Luis F. "El teatro impreso: el 'eterno femenino': 'Apocrypha' de Luisa Josefina Hernández." *Tramoya* 24–25. (Apr.-Sept. 1982):93–100.
Knowles, John K. "Luisa Josefina Hernández: The Labyrinth of Form." *Dramatists in Revolt. The New Latin American Theater.* Eds. Leon F. Lyday and George W. Woodyard. Austin: University of Texas Press, 1978. Pp. 133–45.
———. "Luisa Josefina Hernández: A Study of her Dramatic Theory and Practice." Ph.D. diss. Rutgers University, 1970. (DAI 30, 12 [1970]: 5448A; 70–10079.)
———. *Luisa Josefina Hernández: Teoría y práctica del drama.* Trans. A. Argudín. Mexico City: UNAM, 1980.
Krugh, Janis Lynne. "Solitude and Solidarity: Major Themes and Techniques in the Theater of Luisa Josefina Hernández." Ph.D. diss. University of Pittsburgh, 1986. (DAI 47/06A, p. 2124; DES 86–20282.)
Miller, Beth, and Alfonso González. "Luisa Josefina Hernández." *Veintiséis autoras del México actual.* Mexico City: Costa-Amic, 1978. Pp. 239–51.
Muncy, Michèle. "Entrevista con Luisa Josefina Hernández." *Latin American Theater Review* 9, 2 (Sept. 1976):69–77.
Nigro, Kirsten. "Entrevista con Luisa Josefina Hernández." *Latin American Theater Review* 18, 2 (Spring 1985):101–104.
———. " 'La fiesta del mulato' de Luisa Josefina Hernández." *Latin American Theater Review* 13, 2 (Supplement Summer 1980):81–86.

Pacheco, Cristina. "Con Luisa Josefina Hernández: La misoginia no existe." *Siempre*
    1321 (Oct. 18, 1978):41–43.
Palls, Terry. "Enajenación brechtiana en cuatro dramas de Luisa Josefina Hernández."
    El Urogallo 7 (Jan.-Feb. 1971):84–87.
Passafari, Clara. "Los secretos senderos de Luisa Josefina Hernández." *Los cambios en
    la concepción y estructura narrativa mexicana desde 1947*. Santa Fé, Argentina:
    Universidad Nacional del Litoral, 1968. Pp. 250–61.
Rodríguez, Teresa B. "Entrevista con Luisa Josefina Hernández." *Hispania* 67 (Sept.
    1984):443–44.
Toro, Fernando de. *"La paz ficticia* de Luisa Josefina Hernández." *Brecht en el teatro
    hispanoamericano contemporáneo: Acercamiento al teatro épico en Hispanoam-
    érica*. Ottawa: Girol Books, 1984. Pp. 122–34.
Waldman, Gloria Feiman. "Three Female Playwrights Explore Contemporary Latin
    American Reality: Myrna Casas, Griselda Gambaro and Luisa Josefina Hernán-
    dez." *Latin American Women Writers: Yesterday and Today*. Eds. Yvette E.
    Miller and Charles M. Tatum. Pittsburgh: Carnegie-Mellon University; Latin
    American Literary Review, 1977. Pp. 75–84.

SARA DE IBÁÑEZ
(1909–1971)
Uruguay

Monique J. Lemaître León

BIOGRAPHY

Born Sara Iglesias Casadei in Chamberlain in the Department of Tacuarembó, on January 11, 1909, Sara de Ibáñez died in Montevideo on April 3, 1971, "at the peak of her poetic power, and even, as it has been written, of her 'delicate beauty' " (Geysse, 1973, p. vii). She spent most of her childhood in the country and eventually moved to Montevideo with her parents. There, she met and married poet Roberto Ibáñez with whom she had three daughters. All of them are distinguished poets in their own right, although Ulalume González de León, a Luis de Camões scholar, short story writer, poet, and frequent contributor to international literary journals, is the best known of the three.

Ibáñez seems to have led a very secluded and private life, which would account for the scarcity of written biographical data to be found in the United States and abroad. Ibáñez was, like many other of her prominent compatriots, namely, Angel Rama and Emir Rodríguez Monegal, a high school teacher of literature, from 1945 until her death. The little that is known outside of Uruguay about her life comes from her husband's "Preface" and the notes to her posthumous volume of poetry. All of her books were awarded prizes in her native country; she received two posthumous awards, one of them consisting in the 1971–1972 Bienal Prize of Literature.

According to her husband, Sara de Ibáñez used to work simultaneously on two or more books, very different in theme, structure, and inspiration. Thus, while two of her most widely acclaimed works, *La batalla* (The battle) and *Apocalipsis XX* (Apocalypse XX) were published, respectively, in 1967 and 1970, several of the poems included in her posthumously published book were also written during those years.

MAJOR THEMES

From her first book, *Canto* (1940), to her last one, *Canto póstumo* (1973; Posthumous canto), the major themes of Sara de Ibáñez's poetry include despair, existential anguish, and pain at the sight of humanity's compulsive drive toward self-annihilation. Death is a constant theme in her poetry. Even life, love, and nature are present only in their relationship to their opposites, which is the void and nothingness. Her poetry owes a great debt to the French Symbolist poets and their heirs, especially to the most hermetic among them.

"Desdén" (Disdain), in *Las estaciones y otros poemas* (1957; The seasons and other poems) is dedicated to Paul Valéry, one of her mentors. (Others were Rubén Darío, Julio Herrera y Reissig, Stéphane Mallarmé, and Arthur Rimbaud.) She herself said that she understood poetry as an exercise in mystery (*Canto póstumo*, p. xxxi). She strives for almost geometrical perfection in the structure of her poems, as if she were striving to exorcise evil through the purity and transparency of the images. This explains the importance of form in her poetry: "...me quema la geometría" ("geometry burns me"), she writes at the end of "Desdén," written in the form of a traditional Spanish *décima*.

In "Desdén," a Platonic composition, the poet plays with the polysemic value of certain words. "Carmen" means "villa/house" in the South of Spain, but it also means "poetic verse." It is phonetically related to *carmín* (crimson), the generic color of the rose, while it also recalls a girl's name: "Carmen" and the "Carmen," the religious order of Carmelite nuns, whose renovator, Saint Theresa of Avila, also wrote poetry. Sara de Ibáñez, fascinated by the Platonic Idea of the rose, struggles to produce her own version of it in "Desdén" and is left with an imprint that only recalls the absent shape of the "ideal" rose (or poem).

Following once more the Platonic concept that all wordly objects are but a copy of an ideal, heavenly, perfect shape, in "La página vacía" (The blank page), Ibáñez plays with Stéphane Mallarmé's notion of "la page blanche" ("the white page"), in true "conceptist" and "culturist" fashion. Conceptism is associated with the seventeenth-century Spanish author Francisco de Quevedo, whose complicated play of ideas was often contrasted to his contemporary and fellow poet Luis de Góngora y Argote's extremely contrived and innovative use of poetic tropes. Góngora's style and that of his followers is known as "culturism." Ibáñez dedicates the poem to her French predecessor, however. Her experiment is an interesting example of what was called, in Mallarmé's time, "pure poetry."

In "La página vacía," polysemism is again put into play: "cerrazón" means "overcast sky," but also "storm clouds," "denseness, slowness," "obstinacy." The same word is also a noun that is derived from the verb "cerrar," "to close," a concept that contrasts with the apparent openness of the white page. The poem is a *tour de force* of ingenuity, which manages to convey to the reader that which, by definition, is still nonexistent, the reality of a poem yet to be written, its potentiality, and the tension that lingers, in this poetic limbo, between the poet and the white page.

Ibáñez' love of symmetry combines with the theme of the duality of human nature in "Caín" from *Hora ciega* (1943, Blind hour, pp. 51–70), in which structure and content are so intimately intertwined, that in a Mallarméan fashion, the poem's description of an absence becomes the poem. Cain, symbolizing humanity before and after the fall, vanishes into nothingness at the end of the poem. *Hora ciega* includes "Soliloquios del soldado" (Soliloquies of the soldier), "Caín," "Los pálidos" (The pale ones), and "Pasión y muerte de la luz" (Passion and death of the light), dedicated to Ibáñez' husband. All the poems reflect on the horrors of war.

Sara de Ibáñez was a virtuoso of poetic meter and rhythm. This accounts for her love of symmetry, which in turn explains her fascination with the duality of human nature. Her poems are difficult to understand because they are predominately abstract in nature and inventive in their imagery. There is little anecdotal content, and the image of the poet is that of a hypersensitive being who can never free himself/herself from the ever-present consciousness of moving toward death; "Escúchate crecer para la muerte . . . " (Listen to yourself moving toward death . . .), she writes in a poem in *Canto* (p. 55). The poetic voice writes that it exists as nothing but a brief parenthesis between nothingness and nothingness, a "paréntesis breve / entre la nada y la nada" ("Hoy" [Today] from *Las estaciones y otros poemas*, p. 39).

Canto is made up of several sections: "Islas" (Islands) consists of sonnets; "Liras" (Lyres) of poems of six five-line stanzas, rhyming ababb; "De los vivos" (Of the living), of sonnets; "De los muertos" (Of the dead), also sonnets; and "Itinerarios" (Itineraries) of a series of love poems dedicated to her husband written in a variety of metrical forms. The images from nature, especially those dealing with the sea, are memorable in spite or because of their hermetic symbolism.

Pastoral (1948) is divided into three sections symbolizing humanity's childhood, youth, and maturity. The poet is symbolized by a shepherd, and the book describes metaphorically the poet's struggles with her craft. The sections "Tiempo I" (Time I) and "Tiempo III" (Time III) are further divided into fifteen sections each, with fifteen hendecasyllable lines per section, arranged in the sequence: two tercets, a quatrain, a tercet, and two lines completing the rhyme. "Tiempo II" (Time II) consists of ten sections of thirty-two lines each, divided into four octets. The poem's early gestation, maturing, and final blossoming is intimately linked to the poet's choice of meter and rhyme. Nothing is left to chance.

The themes of *Pastoral* include Ibáñez' apprenticeship as a poet, while paying homage, through her choice of metaphors, to the poets who influenced her. The image of a "rumor of scars" is important for helping her to show how she grew her own roots. Indeed, the weight of tradition, all poets' inheritance, is constantly thematized, in an original way, in Sara de Ibáñez' poetry.

The ever-present theme of death is most powerfully treated in *Apocalipsis XX* (Apocalypse XX). In this volume, the poet has clearly reached her full maturity as a professional of her craft. She allows herself more freedom of structure, and experiments more with assonance and blank verse to translate an apocalyptic vision of a nuclear holocaust. Her imagination, her sensitivity, and her poetic gifts reach their highest point in this powerful rendering of a reality where flowers are banned forever, and the culprits of the destruction can never again regain their human visage. *Apocalipsis XX* is divided into twenty-one "Visiones" (Visions), three "Letanías" (Litanies) of Truth, Liberty, and Oblivion, four "Apóstrofes" (Apostrophes), and four "Castigos" (Punishments). The central theme of this volume of poetry is the destiny of contemporary man, and it profusely uses biblical references. "Vision I" (p. 7) establishes an interdependence between good and evil, light and darkness, according to a constant in Sara de Ibáñez' work. Repeatedly, a concept contains its opposite, thus establishing a kind of binary dialectic with transmutations of nuance.

In the third part ("Vision XIV" to "Vision XVIII"), *Apocalypsis XX* specifically deals with a nuclear holocaust. In "Vision XIV," we read of a man who alone "poses with grim softness his finger / on the polished nerve of death / which ends in a synchronized button" (p. 49). A nuclear explosion is brought about by a Medusa-like Electra in the narrative. Here the French feminist recovery of Medusa as a symbol of beauty (and not of evil) is far away. Electra's choice of evil and destruction has more to do here with contemporary phonetic associations of her name, like "electricity" or "energy," than with her myth. (One questions, however, why it is that after a man pushes the prophetic button, the forces of destruction are portrayed as female.) The next three Visions of *Apocalypsis XX* describe the atomic mushroom, the destructive aftermath of the explosion, and the resulting human pain, symbolized here by another female image, that of the mothers who have survived the holocaust.

The extraordinary richness and power of Sara de Ibáñez' imagery lies in her images of nature. This is especially true in *Apocalipsis XX*, where the horror of the atomic holocaust is rendered even more vivid by a contrasting of the biblical vision with the melancholy beauty of the nature that was destroyed. In "Letanía del olvido" (Litany of oblivion), a farmer represents the harmony that existed between humanity and nature before the atomic disaster. As if to exorcise the evil of death and destruction, the poem repeatedly begs a demon to leave the peasant alone. Never has Ibáñez' poetry been as powerful and relevant to this century's most urgent problems as in *Apocalipsis XX*. In spite of the obviously metaphysical contents of the text, the question of the survival of the human race is here more than rhetoric; it is a call for total disarmament.

"Diario de la muerte" (Diary of death), included in *Canto póstumo*, is the most personal of Ibáñez' books, because in it she does use her personal experiences and feelings as the poems' themes, and yet it is not anecdotal. Its central theme is the fragility of life, which death destroys, inexorably, after the passage of time. Only art, poetry in this case, can capture this fragility through its symbols. In *Diario de la muerte*, life is seen from the perspective of death, and death from that of life, through an inventiveness that masterfully, through the use of paradox, couples structure and content. The third part, "Gavilla" (Sheaf of grain), includes moving homages to Rubén Darío, and "Trino y uno," contains others to Gabriela Mistral,* José Martí, Delmira Agustini,* and Julio Herrera y Reissig.

Dedicated to Rafael Alberti and María Teresa León who had fled into exile from Spain and were then (1940) living in Argentina, the poem "El muro" (Lamentación por los fusilamientos en España) [The wall (Lament for the firing squad executions in Spain)], is Ibáñez' single most *engagé* work. It refers directly to the war prisoners who were executed by firing squad by the newly victorious fascist government of Francisco Franco. The "wall" thus becomes a symbol of the inhuman polarization that ensues after civil wars, especially those where fascism is victorious, because fascism refuses to pardon those it has defeated. Unlike Ibáñez' earlier poem, "Caín," the evil brother here is not merely the double of his twin, Abel. He also stands alone in his hatred and lust for revenge.

Sara de Ibáñez also wrote patriotic epic poems, such as *Canto a Montevideo* (1941; Song of Montevideo), and *Artigas* (1952). In *Artigas* she exalts the hero of Uruguay's struggle for independence from Spain. Artigas was one of the few major figures of Latin American independence not included in Pablo Neruda's *Canto General* (1950), a lapse some Uruguayans resent, regardless of their admiration for the eminent Chilean bard.

Ibáñez was, without a doubt, a talented and highly imaginative poet. The fact that no translations of her poetry exist in many of the major world languages has condemned her works to be practically unknown outside of Uruguay and a small circle of Latin American intellectuals.

SURVEY OF CRITICISM

During her lifetime Sara de Ibáñez was acclaimed by several famous poets. Latin America's foremost poet, Chilean Nobel prize laureate and a friend of her husband, Pablo Neruda, wrote the prologue to Ibáñez' first published book of poetry, *Canto* (1940). Neruda's prologue is itself a prose poem in which he calls Ibáñez a "grande, excepcional y cruel poeta" (great, exceptional and cruel poet) and compares her to Sor Juana Inés de la Cruz,* the Nobel laureate Gabriela Mistral,* and the Chilean novelist María Luisa Bombal.* He particularly admires Ibáñez' "arrebato sometido al rigor" (p. 8, rage controlled by rigor). Neruda reiterated his admiration for the Uruguayan poet on several occasions, most notably in a 1939 issue of *Taller*, a Mexican literary review directed by Octavio Paz, which published some preview poems from *Canto*.

The great Chilean poet Gabriela Mistral is quoted in Roberto Ibáñez' "Preface" to the 1973 Losada edition of *Canto póstumo* (p. xix) as having written that Ibáñez' poetry was different from that by other Latin American women before her. Mistral* speaks of Ibáñez' mysterious stanzas, and of the heights of meaning in her poetry. No two women poets could be more different than Ibáñez and Mistral, however. On the one hand, we have Ibáñez the aristocratic recluse, the mother, teacher, and wife who labored over poetic tropes in the protected atmosphere of a quasicontemplative world. On the other, we have Mistral, the country teacher born in southern Chile, proud of her Araucanian heritage, single, unprotected, and active in the public sphere. Mistral traveled to every corner of the Americas lecturing on new approaches to education, nutrition, and health care for the beloved children she never had. Her poems were written so the common folk would understand them. As the great reader she was, Mistral recognized Ibáñez talent despite their differences, and she praised the Uruguayan's talent with legendary generosity.

Uruguayan-French poet Jules Supervielle noted Ibáñez' vast knowledge of Western poetry, especially French Symbolist poetry. Another Nobel Prize winner, the Spanish poet Vicente Aleixandre, wrote laudatory reviews of *Canto* and *Canto a Montevideo*. The Brazilian poet Cecilia Meireles (p. xix) joins her compatriots Manuel Bandeira and Carlos Drummond de Andrade in praising Ibáñez' poetry. Ecuadorian poet Jorge Carrera Andrade mentions her poetic sanctity and her angelical vows, while the great Catalan poet, Josep Carner, compares her poetry to that of Garcilaso, given its charm, and to that of Góngora, because of its formal perfection. Ibáñez was translated into French by Emilie Noulet, Carner's wife, who was a scholar specializing in the works of Mallarmé and Paul Valéry.

Spain's Rafael Alberti knew by heart many of Ibáñez' poems and León Felipe counted her among his favorite poets, while the Spanish literary critic Amado Alonso wrote of his awe and admiration when he learned that *Canto a Montevideo* was written in three days to meet a literary competition's deadline. Ibáñez was called the "Great Sara" by Latin American writers such as Pedro Henríquez Ureña, Agustín Yáñez, Octavio Paz, Alí Chumacero, Juan Larrea, Ramón Xirau, and Ricardo Gullón, who finds *Apocalipsis XX* to be her best book (Pp. xxi–xxii). One of today's best literary critics of Latin American literature, Jorge Ruffinelli, a Uruguayan, now professor of Latin American literature at Stanford University, concluded his article, written after Ibáñez' death, by saying that Ibáñez' metaphorical imagination alone would ensure her a place of honor among the best poets of the Spanish language.

Very little has been written about Sara de Ibáñez outside of what can be found in anthologies, reviews, and literary histories where all that can be found are laudatory, impressionistic-type entries. Her extraordinary work is indeed in urgent need of serious, in-depth study of her poetry. No serious analysis of or critical essay on her poetry exists.

BIBLIOGRAPHY

Works by Sara de Ibáñez

Canto. Prol. Pablo Neruda. Buenos Aires: Losada, 1940. 2d ed. Buenos Aires: Losada, 1954.

Canto a Montevideo. Montevideo: Impresora Uruguaya, 1941.
Hora ciega. Buenos Aires: Losada, 1943.
Pastoral. Mexico City: Cuadernos Americanos, 1948.
Artigas. Montevideo: Impresora Uruguaya, 1952.
Las estaciones y otros poemas. Mexico City: Fondo de Cultura Económica, 1957.
La batalla. Buenos Aires: Losada, 1967.
Apocalipsis XX. Caracas: Monte Avila, 1970.
Canto póstumo. Introd. A. Geysse. Buenos Aires: Losada, 1973. (1. *Diario de la muerte*;
      2. *Baladas y canciones*; 3. *Gavilla.*
Poemas escogidos: Sara de Ibáñez. Prol. Pablo Neruda. Mexico City: Siglo Veintiuno,
      1974.

Works about Sara de Ibáñez

Geysse, A. Introd. *Canto póstumo.* By Sara de Ibáñez. Pp. vii–lxvi.
Homenaje a Sara de Ibáñez. Compiled by Roberto Ibáñez. Cuadernos de Literatura, No.
      19; Fundación de Cultura Universitaria, 1971.
Jiménez, José Olivio, *Antología de la poesía hispanoamericana contemporánea (1914–*
      1970). Madrid: Editorial Alianza, 1970. Pp. 404–14.
Neruda, Pablo. Prologue. *Canto.* By Sara de Ibáñez. Pp. i–iii.
Puentes de Oyenard, Sylvia. "Un perfil femenino en la literatura uruguaya: Sara de
      Ibáñez." *Káñina* (Costa Rica) 9,2 (July-Dec. 1985):43–49.
Ruffinelli, Jorge. "Sinópsis sobre Sara de Ibáñez." *Marcha* (Montevideo) (March 16,
      1970).
Suiffet, Norma. "La vida, la muerte y la guerra en la poesía de Sara de Ibáñez." *Tres*
      poetas uruguayos: Juana de Ibarbourou, Sara de Ibáñez, Hugo Petraglia Aguirre.
      Montevideo: Gaceta Comercial, 1955. Pp. 43–69.
Xirau, Ramón. "Sara de Ibáñez," Ch. VII. *Poesía iberoamericana.* Mexico City: Sep-
      Setentas, 1972. Pp. 164–66.
Zapata, Celia de. "Two Poets of America: Juana de Asbaje and Sara de Ibáñez." *Latin*
      American Women Writers: Yesterday and Today. Pittsburgh, Pa.: Latin American
      Literary Review, 1977. Pp. 115–26.

JUANA DE IBARBOUROU
(1892–1979)
Uruguay

Evelyn Uhrhan Irving

BIOGRAPHY

Juana de Ibarbourou was born Juana Fernández Morales in Melo, a town in the eastern Department of Cerro Largo, Uruguay, near the border with Brazil, on March 8, 1892. Almost universally, 1895 is listed as the year of her birth; however, Dora Isella Russell, her recognized biographer, gives no year date, while Jorge Pickenhayn cites Acta no.49 of the Civil Register as his authority for 1892. Juana's mother, Valentina Morales, was a native Uruguayan born in Tacuarí, Cerro Largo; her father, Vicente Fernández, was a native of Galicia, Spain. From one week of age, according to Juana's own words, she had a local black nanny, Feliciana, who spoke a strange mixture of Spanish and Portuguese.

Juana began her education in a religious school but later moved to a coeducational state elementary school. This constituted her formal training. Her mother, a devoutly religious person, strongly influenced that aspect of her life. Juana's almost constant companion, Feliciana, expanded the child's knowledge with stories and songs from her culture; her childhood was nourished with fables. From Feliciana, Juana learned of talking animals, the magic world of ghosts and goblins, lullabies, mime, and the grace of prayer. Juana's so-called atheist father entertained her with the poetry of José de Espronceda, Gaspar Núñez de Arce, and Rosalía de Castro; through their literary works Juana learned to appreciate the musicality of words. This broad introduction to Old and New World ideas was her basic education.

Ibarbourou's writings are from the heart. In "Eternidad" (Eternity) she says that she will continue living in her poems. Not only is this prediction true, but one finds her life laid bare through her own words—both poetry and prose. A one-hour talk given at the Institute of Higher Studies of Montevideo during summer courses in 1956, entitled "Autobiografía lírica" (Lyrical autobiography) describes succinctly her life and style.

A healthy home atmosphere and strong religious faith made her childhood years in Melo happy ones. After a fleeting disappointment in love, she married a career military man, Captain Lucas Ibarbourou, on June 28, 1914. Miguel de Unamuno, the Spanish author and philosopher, identifies the name Ibarbourou as the French-Basque rendering of Ibar-buru, *cabecera del valle* or "county seat/ head of the valley." The *ou* spelling identifies the family as from the French-speaking part of the Basque provinces. Because of Lucas's position, the family— soon to add their one and only child, Julio César—lived in military posts at Canelones, Rocha, Rivera, and Tacuarembó. In 1918 the family moved to Montevideo where Juana spent virtually the remainder of her life until her death in 1979.

Ibarbourou began writing verses at an early age; her first poetry was a sonnet entitled "El cordero" (The lamb). It was not in classic form, for Juana admits that, at the age of thirteen when she wrote it, she was unaware of what sonnet structure was. When the family moved to Montevideo where her mother lived with them in a modest home, she and her mother made artificial flowers. Juana wrote a manual on the art of making artificial flowers at home, but the manuscript was lost at the printers. She had already had some poetry published at Melo in *El Deber Cívico* and elsewhere; when living in Montevideo she courageously took some of her collected poems to the daily paper *La Razón* which she noted published a literary page. Here she used the pseudonym "Jeannette d'Ibar," one she previously had used in *El Deber Cívico* and other publications. By the time she wrote for *Nosotros* in Buenos Aires in February 1919, she asked that her writings be signed "La Poetisa Ibarbourou."

Her first collection of poetry, *Las lenguas de diamante* (Diamond tongues) was published in 1919 with a prologue by the Argentinian novelist Manuel Gálvez. This work was a brilliant success, for its lyrical beauty and lighthearted sincerity brightened a sorrowing world just emerging from the horrors of World War I. This single work would have been sufficient to mark her as an outstanding writer. The following year her prose work *El cántaro fresco* (The cool water jug) appeared. In 1922 her second collection of poetry, *Raíz salvaje* (Wildroot) was published. The year 1930 saw the first edition of another poetic collection, *La rosa de los vientos* (The rose in the storm). Her talent was acknowledged even before the publication of this latest successful work, for on August 10, 1929, in the Legislative Palace of Montevideo, the title of "Juana de América" (Juana of America) was bestowed upon her, before a gathering of some ten thousand people presided over by Juan Zorrilla de San Martín and Alfonso Reyes.

After *La rosa de los vientos*, there was a lull of some twenty years in her poetic output. In the literary arena these were years of various types of experimental writing—ultraism, creationism, surrealism, and so on; Ibarbourou was finding her way, as were many others. However, significant prose works appeared. In 1934 two religious works were published: *Loores de Nuestra Señora* (In praise of the Virgin) and *Estampas de la Biblia* (Portraits from the Bible).

Ibarbourou received new honors, and ten years later *Chico Carlo*, a prose work of childhood memories, was published; in 1945 *Los sueños de Natacha* (Natacha's dreams) heralded a new genre for her: radio dramas written for children. This same year she granted the Uruguayan government the rights to all her published and three unpublished works. These years also held great sadness for her. In 1932 her father died; in 1942 her beloved husband, by then a major in the military; and in 1949 her dear mother. This series of losses would be recorded in her writing.

The year 1950 saw her next published work, *Perdida* (Lost). Lost she was, for now only her son remained. *Perdida* is one of her most desolate poetic works. Still, her recognition and writing continued. In 1953 she traveled to the United States and was proclaimed "Woman of the Americas 1953" by the Union of American Women in New York; this same year Aguilar of Madrid published the first edition of her *Obras completas* (Complete works), edited by Dora Isella Russell.

A complete list of the honors bestowed on her as well as a complete list of published works would be a long one. Suffice it to say that Ibarbourou received further recognition with medals and other honors from Peru, Bolivia, Brazil, Belgium, Mexico, Cuba, Ecuador, Spain, Venezuela, Guatemala, and Chile. She had been made a member of the Uruguayan Academy of Letters in 1947; she was honored at the meeting of the VII General Assembly of Unesco in Montevideo in 1954; in 1959 she was proposed for the Nobel Prize. Schools, streets, sports arenas, parks, and libraries were named after her. Some of her books or portions thereof were translated into French, German, Swedish, Hebrew, and Braille. There were further enlarged editions of her works, and numerous anthologies; no respectable anthology of Latin American literature fails to include at least some of her poetry. In 1968 the third edition of her *Obras completas* appeared, also prepared by Dora Isella Russell and published by Aguilar.

At the time of Ibarbourou's death on July 15 or 16, 1979, she was granted state honors. Her remains rested in the Legislative Palace in Montevideo where fifty years before she had been crowned "Juana de América." They were then borne on a white horse-drawn gun-carriage to the Cementerio del Buceo. Flags were flown at half-mast, and the following December the Ministry of Education and Culture of Uruguay sponsored an international competition on the life and works of Juana de Ibarbourou for the members of the Organization of American States (OAS). Juana de Ibarbourou is a source of pride to her country, and during her lifetime she was respected as such.

MAJOR THEMES

Dora Isella Russell identifies eight themes that characterize Ibarbourou's writings: love, nature, poetry, loneliness and night, time and sadness, death, maternity, peace and war. Jorge Oscar Pickenhayn (1980) confines his number to three: nature, love, and life leading to death. To be sure, the themes are intricately interwoven and rarely separate. They remain fairly constant through Ibarbourou's more than fifty years of writing, although the stress on, and treatment of, each of them vary during her lengthy literary career. Nature and love are at the forefront of her writings; death is approached in various ways. A discussion of her early works, and those that sealed her fame, will serve to point up some of these themes.

Romantic love and nature abound in her first published collection of poetry, *Las lenguas de diamante*. This collection of sixty-five poems divided into three uneven sections, "La luz interior" (Inner light), "Anforas negras" (Black amphoras), and "La clara cisterna" (The limpid cistern), treat love, nature, and death in a youthful, joyous manner. The work exudes happiness and brilliance. Two of her best known poems appear here. In "Rebelde" (Rebel), Juana tells Caron that she will be a scandal in his boat, for while others are praying, groaning, or weeping, she will be singing like a lark on the trip to the opposite shore; here his arms will have to take her from the boat as in a Vandal conquest. In "Vidagarfío" (Life as a pruning hook), she tells her lover that, if she dies, he is not to take her to the cemetery, but is to bury her at ground level so that she can nurture the earth and be part of life. In her verses there are subjective, colorful, aromatic images of nature; the love expressed is pure, natural, and sensitive. The poetic forms are frequently sonnets but free verse abounds, and many irregular verse forms with assonance and internal rhyme appear.

El cántaro fresco (1920), her first collection of prose poems, deals primarily with episodes and incidents in her childhood, showing a close association with nature. In the first selection, a clay jug of cool water fresh from the well exudes beads of water that dampen the tablecloth. This sparks other images, such as Titanio, her Newfoundland dog, pouncing on the spot of sunlight as it dances on the floor, having been filtered through the moving glass curtain of the window. She explains in "Por qué los árboles son altos" (Why trees are tall) that God decreed that their roots be immovable; thus, they can only go upward. Among other titles are "Selva" (The jungle), "Melancolía" (Sadness), "Los grillos" (Crickets), "El cerco azul" (The blue fence or Morning glories), and "El charco" (The puddle). One finds strong allusions to pantheism and animism, with anthropomorphic comparisons, including legends indicative of what she must have learned from Feli, her nanny. Her vocabulary includes neologisms, gallicisms, and Brazilian dialectal forms; similarities to the Spanish poet Juan Ramón Jiménez are evident.

By the time *Raíz salvaje* was completed, Juana was becoming besieged by what she termed "an incurable melancholy beclouding the inner sun." However, her sadness was not unto death. These descriptive poems express awareness and love of nature with its full beauty, vibrant with synesthetic references. Within her at-times expressed sorrow is evident her continued zest for life and the glory of it. She sings of "Olor frutal" (The aroma of fruit), "Noche de lluvia" (A rainy night), "Estío" (Summer), "La luna" (The moon), "Soledad" (Loneliness). Metaphors abound here too and verse forms are varied; she continues the art of repetition, polysyndeton, and onomatopoeia.

In *La rosa de los vientos* her basic themes remain, but her verses have become more reasoned. Her style is moving away from musicality toward a concentration on imagery and more subtle language. Among poems in this collection are "Despertar" (Waking up), "Quietud" (Stillness), "Tiempo" (Time), and "El secreto" (The Secret). These four collections conclude the approximate first decade of the published works that brought Ibarbourou fame.

Loores de Nuestra Señora and *Estampas de la Biblia*, published in 1934, present a distinct change in thematic emphasis. Here Juana devotes herself in prose to purely religious subjects. The *Loores* are a collection of forty (a significant religious number) brief prose poems, each with a Latin title indicative of a virtue or the name of the Virgin. Ibarbourou states in the preface that the image of the Holy Virgin of Perpetual Help was always on the main wall of her mother's bedroom; they prayed to her daily and presented her with floral offerings. In Juana's literary years it was her custom to offer the first copy of each new work to the Virgin in the nearby church she and her son attended in Montevideo.

Ibarbourou continues this religious theme in *Estampas*. In the introduction she explains that one unforgettable night, heroes and heroines of the Old Testament began to speak directly to her in a dream. She says that the forty (note the number again) characters are reproductions of inspired voices, the mysterious work of a superhuman will. She attributes the inspiration to her nightly reading of the Bible before falling asleep, thereby enriching her world of phantoms, alive with beauty and poetry. She hopes that she has not mistaken any concept, word, or color in the first-person autobiographical recountings of each individual as he/she explains his/her purpose or impact on the individual.

In a similar vein of inspiration is the poetic collection *Mensajes del escriba* (Messages from the scribe), never published in book form until *Obras completas*. Ibarbourou describes these poems as having written themselves; she merely records the messages, acting as a scribe. Most of them are in sonnet form. They continue the modernist style with nuances of light, color, jewels, and aroma; they are sometimes happy, sometimes sad.

Much of Ibarbourou's creation involves autobiography. *Romances del destino* (1955; Ballads of destiny) begins with "Autorromance de Juanita Fernández" (Auto-ballad of Juanita Fernández), detailing many aspects of her life. Each of the thirteen poems in this collection, of which ten are in *romance* or ballad form, relates some aspect of her life or feelings. *Chico Carlo* (1944), a collection of seventeen short stories, recounts childhood incidents. Juana appears in the accounts as Susana; Chico Carlo was the son of her mother's friend.

Other biographical prose works are *Angeles pintados* (Painted angels), an early version of *Juan Soldado*, and *Mis amados recuerdos* (My beloved memories) both published in *Obras completas* (1968). The latter collection is especially valuable for its description of visits to the poet in Montevideo by well-known

Spanish and Spanish American literary figures—Alfonso Reyes, Federico García Lorca, José María Vargas Vila, Salvador de Madariaga, Carlos Reyes, Alfonsina Storni,* Gabriela Mistral,* Pablo Neruda, and Juan Ramón Jiménez with his beloved wife Zenobia, among others.

Another topic in Ibarbourou's writings is children. *Juan Soldado* (Soldier John or G.I. Joe) is a series of prose anecdotes involving children, similar to *Chico Carlo*. However, several of these are stories about children, and not actually for them.

In her biographical vein Ibarbourou describes her own profuse childhood experiences. Her love for children is evident in many aspects of her life. She did not, as did Gabriela Mistral, have a teaching career, but she was a devoted daughter and mother. She wrote several lullabies for her own son and for other children. Several school texts of her writings were published beginning in the 1920s.

Two of her works in particular are directed entirely to young people. These are the two collections of radio drama for children: *Los sueños de Natacha* (1945; five plays) and *Puck* (1968; *Obras completas*, nine plays). In many instances she used already familiar children's characters, especially in the first collection— Little Red Riding Hood, Bluebeard, Cinderella; the second included "La campana imposible (Adaptación de una leyenda china)" (The Impossible Bell [An adaptation of a Chinese legend]) and "La opinión general (Adaptación de la fábula de Esopo del mismo nombre)" (Public opinion [Adaptation of Aesop's fable with the same title]).

Ibarbourou also has creations of her own. In her adapted stories, she at times follows the original closely; at others, she takes a new tack so that there is a surprise ending. Generally, she has created less cruel characters, resulting in a happy or less tragic ending. Many of the plays have musical instructions, although the music is not included; they can be dramatized with only slight modifications necessary. Natacha, the heroine of the first play in *Los sueños de Natacha,* was the name of Pedro Henríquez Ureña's older daughter; some of the lullabies included in the play were composed for her. Ibarbourou's basic message, according to Russell, is that daily life is always on the edge of the miraculous, and the marvelous can be obtained if the heart maintains its angelic purity.

Although some thought of death appears in individual early poems, in later years the sorrowful aspects of life were expressed in entire poetic collections. Included among these are *Perdida* (1950), *Elegía* (1967; Elegy), *Diario de una isleña* (1968; *Obras completas*, Diary of an islander), *Destino* (1968; *Obras completas*, Destiny), *Oro y tormenta* (1956; Gold and torment), and *La pasajera* (1967; The traveler) which Russell prefaces with "Angor Dei" (God's anguish— if Christ does not return). *Elegía* is directed primarily at the loss of her husband, whereas *Diario de una isleña* tells of her self-imposed exile from the world into her own life. As noted in the biographical sketch, by 1950 she had lost all of her close family in death except her son; her life became more hermetic. In these works she maintains much of her earlier imagery and attention to the senses. However, her tone is less vibrant, more melancholy, as she looks back on and forward to death.

Ibarbourou's recognition as a great writer will undoubtedly always be based on her earlier works. However, each successive work tends to expand the reader's awareness and appreciation of the themes that dominated her works—a pure simple love for humankind and nature, expressed in the thought of one who could awaken all the senses through the beautiful images she created.

SURVEY OF CRITICISM

Recognized literary figures and critics admired and praised Ibarbourou's work from the outset of her career. In the prologue to her first work, the Argentine novelist Manuel Gálvez first comments on three contemporary women writers of the River Plate area: Delmira Agustini,* Alfonsina Storni, and Juana de Ibarbourou. These three women, together with the Chilean Gabriela Mistral, were early twentieth-century literary contemporaries; all four were outstanding writers. Gálvez describes the River Plate poets as singers almost entirely of love—love of the senses, ardent, almost purely physical love. They depict a kind of love that had never until that time had lyric expression in Hispanic literature—at least it had never been felt and expressed by women.

Gálvez points out differences among this triumvirate. Agustini is romantic, imaginative, and fantastic, while Storni is more human and restless; both expressed sadness in their writings. But Ibarbourou, he remarks, as yet has no sadness or suffering. Her works portray love and nature in wholesome tones; her verses tell of nature, plants, country aromas, bird songs, trees, and flowers. Although Ibarbourou's verse forms are not always perfect, they never lack vigor and exactness. Gálvez concludes that Ibarbourou's first book *Las lenguas de diamante* (1919) is an event in American literature.

Ibarbourou had sent the Spanish philosopher Miguel de Unamuno copies of *Las lenguas de diamante*, and in a letter dated September 18, 1919, he wrote her a glowing approbation of it. He states that his confidence in women as poets disappeared after the poetess Sappho. At best, he said, no Spanish "poetess" would ever write verses as Ibarbourou did, and if she did, she would never publish them after having married the one who inspired them; this reference is to Juana's husband, Lucas. The chaste spiritual nakedness of her fresh and passionate poetry surprised Unamuno. The Uruguayan had sent him copies of her book to be forwarded to the Spanish poets Juan Ramón Jiménez and the Machado brothers; Unamuno said that, in doing so, he would also be recommending her book to them.

Unamuno singles out specific poems for special praise; he notes some unevenness in her work and considers the pessimistic and melancholy tones inappropriate to her. He suggests that she wait until sadness has touched her life before she incorporates this aspect into her poetry. In a letter to Juan Ramón

Jiménez a few days later, Unamuno reiterates his admiration of Ibarbourou's work; he repeats his esteem for it in one of his collaborations for *La Nación*, the well-known and respected daily newspaper of Buenos Aires.

Dora Isella Russell, a poet and Ibarbourou's biographer, knew her personally. Her third edition of Ibarbourou's *Obras completas* (1968) includes previously unpublished collections of poetry and prose. Among them are *Romances del destino, Oro y tormenta, La pasajera, Elegía*—in verse; and in prose, *Diario de una isleña, Mis amados recuerdos*, as well as other uncollected works in verse and prose. The Aguilar editions include an introduction by Ventura García Calderón, comparing Ibarbourou to Walt Whitman and the French Countess Ann de Noailles. Russell prefaces the edition with a long biographical sketch, and photographs of Ibarbourou and her family. The sketch includes literary criticism of Ibarbourou's writing and her place in Latin American literature. Where Ibarbourou has prepared them, the collections are prefaced with a brief introduction by her; Russell has preceded some other collections with a preliminary note. The work thus makes available virtually all of her writings in a single accessible volume.

Probably the most valuable critical study to date is Jorge Oscar Pickenhayn's *Vida y obra de Juana de Ibarbourou* (1980; Life and writings of Juana de Ibarbourou), published one year after Juana's death. The first chapter outlines Juana's life and writings. Chapter 2 analyzes her poetry and Chapter 3, her prose writings, including children's theater. In the final chapter Pickenhayn discusses the fundamental themes which he sees in Ibarbourou's writings: nature, love, and life leading to death.

Other well-known critics have observed the significance of Ibarbourou's writings. Enrique Anderson Imbert and Eugenio Florit (1940) compare her successive lyrical collections with her life cycle: childhood, adolescence, maturity, and old age (p. 581). Ruth Aponte (1983) analyzes this cycle in detail in her dissertation study. Alberto Zum Felde says that Ibarbourou's poetry is created from love for the land and with delicate sensuality. Carmen Conde, a renowned contemporary Spanish poet and the first woman elected to the Spanish Royal Academy of Language, names Ibarbourou "the lyric representative of the language of love, the radiant felicity of one in love, and the glory of the spirit totally in love" (trans., Conde, 1967, p. 233).

In the last decade, and perhaps spurred by a more active feminist movement, several critical studies have appeared. Flor María Blanco (1986) notes that Ibarbourou's poetic works have recurrent themes of "possession" (having) and "privation" (not having something); emphasis is on possession at the beginning of her writings and on privation toward the end. Dolores Koch (1985) senses a new expression of eroticism among the four well-known Latin American poets of this period; she considers Ibarbourou's healthy and natural. Robert Lima (1984) selects works and words of sexual desire among these voices; for him in Ibarbourou these desires are pagan in her songs. Myriam Jehenson (1982) discusses the search for freedom among these women: Ibarbourou has a restlessness, partaking of both eroticism and religious fervor; she internalizes conventional roles. Because of her compliance with the conventions of her world, she loses some freedom.

The poet herself provides critical insight into her manner of writing poetry. In her lecture "Autobiografía lírica" she explains that she created poetry daily, although some was never written down. Her custom was to form oral poetry, beginning with the first line, then adding and repeating until the poem was complete and corrected. Only then, or even later on did she record it on paper. This was the procedure for the poems of *Las lenguas de diamante* (1919) and *Raíz salvaje* (1922). The net result for her was that the poem became part of her, as with a child.

In an article entitled "Páginas olvidadas de Juana de Ibarbourou" (1963; Undiscovered pages of Juana de Ibarbourou), Gastón Figueira includes some prose stories and poetry which did not appear in the *Obras completas* (1968). He remarks on certain similarities both in prose and verse to the ideas and literary genres of Rabindranath Tagore. There are also evident similarities between Ibarbourou and Juan Ramón Jiménez. Dora Isella Russell in an article in *Humboldt*, "El bestiario inocente en la vida y la obra de Juana de America" (1971; The tame bestiary in the life and works of Juana de América), provides an interesting comparison and analysis of the animals she had as a child and in later years, and how they are incorporated into many of her writings.

Modernism with its color, sensualism, and exoticism is fully evident in Ibarbourou's writings. The reader becomes an active participant in virtually every expression in her works. The spikenard as a fragrant flower perfumes her pages; roses and vines color and entwine her expressions. Fire and flame give light and action. Water in all its forms—rain, rivers, falls, lakes, the sea with their concomitant sounds—has a fascination for Ibarbourou; it formulates and punctuates much of her writing. Her prose narration of her visit to Niagara Falls, "Las cataratas del Niágara," is as vivid as if one were at her side as she moved about the area. Violets, which confronted her at every turn in her 1929 crowning as Juana de América, keep blossoming throughout her writings.

It is unfortunate that Ibarbourou's poetry and prose have rarely been translated into English; only isolated poems have been published.

Perhaps if she had been granted the Nobel Prize for Literature when she was nominated for it in 1959, the English-speaking world would now be able to fully appreciate the gratifying technique she had of incorporating a healthy sense of love, nature, and beauty into sensitive poetic and prose masterpieces. Future admirers of her literary talent may help to fill this void.

BIBLIOGRPAHY

Works by Juana de Ibarbourou

Las lenguas de diamante. Prol. Manuel Galvéz. Buenos Aires: Editorial Buenos Aires, 1919. *Las lenguas de diamante.* Prol. José Pereira Rodríguez. Biblioteca Artigas,

Colección de Clásicos Uruguayos, Vol. 42. Montevideo: Ministerio de Instrucción
Pública y Previsión Social, 1963.

El cántaro fresco. Montevideo: Editorial Maximino García, 1920.

Raíz salvaje. Montevideo: Editorial Maximino García, 1922.

Páginas de literatura contemporánea, selection of prose and poetry. Montevideo: Consejo
Nacional de Enseñanza Primaria y Normal, 1924. School text.

La rosa de los vientos. Montevideo-Buenos Aires: Palacio del Libro, 1930.

Estampas de la Biblia. Prol. Gustavo Gallinal. Montevideo: Editorial Barreiro y Ramos,
1934.

Loores de Nuestra Señora. Montevideo: Editorial Barreiro y Ramos, 1934.

Chico Carlo. Montevideo: Editorial Barreiro y Ramos, 1944.

Los sueños de Natacha. Montevideo: Independencia, 1945.

Perdida. Buenos Aires: Editorial Losada, 1950.

Azor. Buenos Aires: Editorial Losada, 1953.

Romances del destino. Madrid: Editorial Cultura Hispánica, 1955.

Los mejores versos de Juana de Ibarbourou. Prol. Julio Garet Mas. Notes by Simón
Latino. Buenos Aires: Poetas de Ayer y Hoy, Cuadernillos de Poesía, 1956.

Oro y tormenta. Santiago de Chile: Zig-Zag, 1956.

Elegía. Río Piedras: Universidad de Puerto Rico, 1967.

La pasajera. Buenos Aires: Editorial Losada, 1967.

Obras completas. Forward by Ventura García Calderón. Compilation, notes, and biographical information by Dora Isella Russell, ed. 3d edition. Madrid: Aguilar,
1968.

Antología poética de Juana de Ibarbourou. Prol. Dora Isella Russell. Madrid: Cultura
Hispánica, 1970.

Translations of Juana de Ibarbourou

No book-length collection of translated poems exists; one or more poems are often included
in anthologies, for example:

Blackwell, Alice Stone, trans. "The Sweet Miracle." *Some Spanish-American Poets*.
Philadelphia: University of Pennsylvania Press, 1937. Pp. 448–49. Bilingual.

Cuesta, Leonel Antonio de la. "Fleeting Restlessness." *Bilingual Anthology of Hispanic
Poetry*. San José: Editorial Alma Mater, 1986. P. 72.

Ibarbourou, Juana de. *Angor Dei* (poem in Spanish and English). Washington, D.C.:
Pan American Union, 1962.

Patterson, Helen Wohl, trans. "Rest"; "The Vine"; "Jasmine of Night and of Noon";
"What I Am for You." *Poetisas de América*. Washington, D.C.: Mitchell Press,
1960. Pp. 178–81. Bilingual.

Torres-Ríoseco, Arturo, trans. "The Bond." *The Epic of Latin American Literature*.
New York: Oxford University Press, 1942. P. 122.

For listings of translated poems, see also:

Corvalán, Graciela N. V. *Latin American Women Writers in English Translation*. Latin
America Bibliography Series no. 9. Los Angeles: California State University,
Latin American Studies Center, 1980. Pp. 62–64.

Hulet, Claude L. *Latin American Poetry in English Translation*. Washington, D.C.: Pan
American Union, 1965. Pp. 162–65.

Works about Juana de Ibarbourou

Anderson Imbert, Enrique, and Eugenio Florit, eds. *Literatura hispanoamericana: antología e introducción histórica*. N.Y.: Holt, Rinehart, and Winston, 1940.

Andrade Coello, A. *Cultura femenina uruguaya: Juana de Ibarbourou*. Quito: n.p.?, 1943.

Aponte, Ruth Idalmi. "El ciclo vital en la poesía de Juana de Ibarbourou." Ph.D. diss. University of Kentucky, 1983. (DAI 45, 4 [Oct. 1984]:1126A.)

———. "La etapa final: Reflexión y búsqueda en la poesía de Juana de Ibarbourou." *Revista/Review Interamericana* 12, 1 (Spring 1982):104–109.

Arbeleche, Jorge. *Juana de Ibarbourou*. Montevideo: Arca, 1978.

Blanco, Flor María. "Possession and Privation in the Poetic Works of Juana de Ibarbourou." Ph.D. diss. University of Connecticut, 1986. (DAI 47, 5 [Nov. 1986]:1738A.)

Bollo, Sarah. *La poesía de Juana de Ibarbourou*. Montevideo: n.p., 1935.

Conde, Carmen. *Once grandes poetisas hispanoamericanas*. Madrid: Cultura Hispánica, 1967. Pp. 229–75.

Figueira, Gastón. "En el cincuentenario de 'Las lenguas de diamante'." *Asomante* 26, 1 (Jan.-Mar. 1970):68–74.

———. "Páginas olvidadas de Juana de Ibarbourou." *Inter-American Review of Bibliography* 13, 3 (July-Sept. 1963):311–24.

Gómez Marín, José Antonio. "La poesía americana de Juana de Ibarbourou." *Cuadernos Hispanoamericanos* 64 (1965):87–93.

Jehenson, Myriam Yvonne. "Four Women in Search of Freedom." *Revista Interamericana* 12 (Spring 1982):87–99.

Koch, Dolores. "Delmira, Alfonsina, Juana y Gabriela." *Revista Iberoamericana* 51 (July-Dec. 1985):723–29.

Lima, Robert. "Cumbres poéticas del erotismo femenino en Hispanoamérica." *Revista de Estudios Hispánicos* (Alabama) 18 (Jan. 1984):41–59.

Penco, Wilfredo, Coord. *Diccionario de literatura uruguaya*. Montevideo: Arca, Credisol, 1987.

Perricone, Catherine R. "A Bibliographical Approach to the Study of Latin American Women Poets: Juana de Ibarbourou (Uruguay, 1895–1979)." *Hispania* 71, 2 (May 1988):280–81.

Pickenhayn, Jorge Oscar. *Vida y obra de Juana de Ibarbourou*. Buenos Aires: Editorial Plus Ultra, 1980.

Queiroz, María José de. *A poesia de Juana de Ibarbourou*. Belo Horizonte, Brazil: Imprensa da Universidade de Minas, 1961.

Russell, Dora Isella. Prologue. *Antología poética de Juana de Ibarbourou*. By Juana de Ibarbourou. Madrid: Cultura Hispánica, 1970.

———. "El bestiario inocente en la vida y la obra de Juana de América." *Humboldt* 12, 45 (1971):74–75.

———. *Juana de Ibarbourou*. Montevideo: Impresora Uruguaya, 1951.

Salcedo Martínez, Pilar. "Psicología del momento creador en la literatura femenina hispanoamericana." Ph.D. diss. Universidad Complutense de Madrid, 1975. (RUCM 24, 100–111 [1975]:148–50.)

SOR JUANA INÉS DE LA CRUZ
(1648?–1695)
Mexico

Julie Greer Johnson

BIOGRAPHY

Juana de Asbaje y Ramírez de Santillana was born in San Miguel de Nepantla, a small town not far from New Spain's impressive capital of Mexico City. The date of her birth, originally stated as November 12, 1651, by Father Diego Calleja, her first biographer, is thought by recent scholars to have occurred several years earlier in 1648. Because she was the illegitimate daughter of Pedro Asbaje and Isabel Ramírez de Santillana, she was brought up by her mother in the home of her maternal grandfather, where his careful guidance and the constant access to his extensive library instilled in her an insatiable desire to learn. Inspired by this experience during her formative years, she became determined to make the acquisition of knowledge her life's goal.

At the age of three, Juana accompanied her sister to school, although she herself was not old enough to attend, and tricked the teacher into instructing her as well. After mastering the ability to read, she urged her mother to let her go to Mexico City to attend the university there. Since this was a privilege accorded only to boys, she even vowed to don masculine attire to permit her to enter the classroom. Forced to remain at home, however, she spent hours pouring over volumes in her grandfather's vast collection of books and became well versed in a number of disciplines.

When Juana was eight, she went to live with her aunt in Mexico City. More determined than ever to gain all the knowledge she could, she devised numerous tricks to make herself learn faster. As she herself admits many years later in correspondence with the bishop of Puebla, she even cut her hair and promised to commit a certain number of lessons to memory before it reached a specific length. This same year, Juana won her first literary prize for a *loa*, or short dramatic poem, composed to celebrate an annual religious festival.

By the time Juana was sixteen years old, her intellectual accomplishments were well known, and she was invited by the viceroy, the Marquis of Mancera, to become a member of the viceregal court. Her wit and beauty contributed a graceful excitement to the royal entourage, and she soon became the favorite lady-in-waiting of the vicereine. In an unprecedented effort to demonstrate the extent of Juana's erudition, the viceroy assembled forty university professors from different fields, who questioned her thoroughly in many areas. Her brilliant performance on this occasion was an important event in the history of scholarship in early Spanish America and a monumental achievement for a colonial woman.

Although Juana wrote numerous works during her years at court, she became disenchanted with the artificial atmosphere it engendered and the constant notoriety it entailed. Hoping to escape this public life, she entered the Convent of the Discalced Carmelites in 1667. Because of the physical demands of the order, she remained there only a few months, returning briefly to the court and the vicereine's care to recuperate her health. The following year, she joined the Hieronymites, where she became a lifelong member of their religious community.

Within the context of seventeenth-century Mexico, Juana's choice to become a nun was probably the only alternative for a single woman with intellectual pursuits. Although the daily routine was demanding and she was often interrupted by inquisitive sisters, the Church offered her the solitude she required to continue her studies and the vast resources she needed to increase her knowledge. While religious themes began to appear in her writings, secular topics persisted in inspiring the majority of her poetic works, a tendency that drew constant criticism from her superiors and made her the center of considerable controversy.

On November 25, 1690, the bishop of Puebla, Don Manuel Fernández de Santa Cruz, wrote the letter to Sor Juana which would pose the greatest challenge she would face with regard to the sincerity of her religious dedication. It may have precipitated a tragic end to Sor Juana's remarkable literary career. The bishop's complaints, encased in great praise of her explication of a sermon written some years earlier by the Portuguese Jesuit, Antonio de Vieira, angered her deeply and provoked her to write a response that was probably regarded as an act of insubordination by ecclesiastical officials. Although the precise reaction of the Church will never be known, both the archbishop, Francisco Aguiar y Seijas, and her Jesuit confessor, Antonio Núñez de Miranda, withdrew their support, and as a result of this abandonment, she began to isolate herself almost totally from life. Sor Juana wrote few works after her letter to the bishop, and those she composed seemed to possess a tone of resignation and a longing for a permanent end to her difficult predicament. She even sold her personal library to help the poor and rededicated herself to the Church through the renewal of her vows. When a number of her sisters became victims of an epidemic that struck Mexico in 1695, she valiantly went to their assistance, and contracting the illness herself, she died at the convent on April 17.

MAJOR THEMES

The works of Sor Juana Inés de la Cruz, the colonial period's most renowned literary figure, exemplify the artistic excellence achieved in Spain's American viceroyalties and reflect the elaborate style of the Baroque era and the influence of its greatest exponents. Amid the creative intricacies of design inspired by such Spanish masters as the poet Luis de Góngora and the dramatist, Pedro Calderón de la Barca, however, there gradually emerges the portrait of a woman who looked to the future for change and who was prepared to support its initiation. Among her many literary compositions, therefore, she reveals the role of a woman as a member of colonial society, as a creator of art, and as a representative of the Catholic Church and suggests the many conflicts they entailed.

Although Sor Juana spent many years behind convent walls, secular themes, especially those of a courtly nature, dominate her literary production. Much of her poetry, for example, was written for or was dedicated to the most eminent figures of her time, from the political leaders of Europe and the New World to New Spain's foremost intellectuals. Among these well-known individuals, she praises the kings of Spain, Philip IV, and Charles II, the viceroys, the Marquis of Mancera and the Marquis of La Laguna, her dear friend and expert mathematician don Carlos de Sigüenza y Góngora, and his worthy adversary, the noted missionary Father Eusebio Francisco Kino.

While the number of encomiums written for colonial men reflects the strict patriarchal society of seventeenth-century New Spain, Sor Juana also included several prominent women among her tributes to the viceroyalty's most influential personages. These ladies were important not only because they were the wives of heads of state, but also because they had played crucial roles in the poet's personal life. The "Laura" and "Lysi" poems, written to the vicereines doña Leonor María de Carreto, the wife of the Marquis of Mancera, and doña María Luisa Gonzaga y Manrique de Lara, the wife of the Marquis of La Laguna, respectively, reflect the deep fondness and gratitude Sor Juana felt for these aristocratic women. Doña Leonor accepted her as a daughter during the time the poetess was at court and nursed her back to health, after she withdrew from the Carmelite Order. The vicereine was saddened by Sor Juana's desire to continue conventual life, and doña Leonor's death in 1673 was a great loss for the poetess to bear. Sor Juana regained her influence at court from 1680 to 1686 when doña María Luisa was her patroness, but the vicereine's departure for Spain at the end of her husband's appointment meant the loss of one of the poet's greatest supporters.

The mode of expression Sor Juana used to describe these women is, to a large extent, formulaic and corresponds to the conventions of courtly love. Feminine portraiture composed in this vein was most commonly used to honor outstanding women, and Sor Juana is quite masterful in comparing aspects of their beauty and virtue to the rare elements found in nature. Although Sor Juana did not experiment to any considerable degree in these poems, she does appear to place more importance on women's less visible qualities than previous poets. In her comic *ovillejos* (a ten-line metrical form), however, she challenges the worn-out imagery of Petrarchan origin traditionally used to describe women and even endeavors to change the way the poet views "his" female subject. Under the guise of painting a portrait of the beautiful maiden Lisarda, Sor Juana, as the artist, emerges as the poem's principal character, and she defines herself as an active woman who has the capability of producing art, not just inspiring it.

In addition to the many tributes Sor Juana wrote for members of the court, she also wrote numerous love poems that have puzzled scholars for years. In these pieces, the poetess purports to love someone who does not return her affection, while being pursued by another. Although much criticism has been written about this aspect of the nun's work, few conclusions can be made regarding their real purpose. The poems may indeed reflect a personal relationship at court, or they may have simply been requested by one of its members to give to a lover. Another possibility for their interpretation lies in Sor Juana's immense popularity within New Spain's social circles, which distracted her from her sincere desire to follow a religious calling.

Other examples of Sor Juana's lyric poetry convey more clearly some of her personal feelings and reflections of her own view of life. Of these, her sonnets are especially notable, and they speak of an attractive but deceptive world, the brevity of human existence, and the indignities of old age. "Este que ves . . ." ("This [portrait] that you see . . .") exemplifies these themes as the poet looks at her own image in a painting intended to capture the perfection of her beauty, and she imagines how the ravages of time will transform her into nothingness.

Sor Juana's longest and most complex poetic work is her *Primero sueño* (First dream) in which she presents a philosophical view of nature and the individual's role within its hierarchical structure. Influenced by Aristotelian-Thomistic thought and scholastic tradition, she describes the effects of nightfall on earth's creatures. Even the poet herself slumbers with the arrival of darkness, and as she sleeps, her soul emerges from her body and aspires to view the world and all the universe. Unable to comprehend such magnificence, her soul withdraws, but determined to gain an all-encompassing knowledge of nature, her spirit begins to examine its various facets one by one. Suspended precariously, then, between the material world and the firmaments, her soul is curiously like humanity itself who seeks to reach great intellectual heights but is forced to content itself with more reasonable goals.

Primero sueño is probably the most elaborate display of Baroque style demonstrated by a New World poet. Nocturnal imagery, mythological allusions, and references to the scientific concepts of Sor Juana's day blend together to create a spectacular poetic vision. According to a statement that she makes in her letter to the bishop of Puebla, the *Primero sueño* had particular significance for her because she had written it for herself alone and not at the request of others.

Apart from her lyrical poetry in which she expounded on the time-honored thematic dualities of love and beauty, life and death, and humanity and nature,

Sor Juana also found considerable irony in colonial living, and she reveals it in several of her satirical poems. Her best known work and one frequently mentioned in connection with her feminism is "Hombres necios que acusáis/a la mujer sin razón" (Stupid men who accuse/ woman without any grounds). Criticizing men in the same manner in which they have assailed women for centuries, Sor Juana blames them for the disharmony that exists between the sexes and defends a woman's position in this controversy. The more women try to please men, she claims, the more difficult it becomes, as women who remain aloof are regarded as cruel and those who are affectionate are considered to be easy. By the close of the poem, the superior attitude that males customarily take in their relationship with the opposite sex has been completely undermined, and men, not coincidentally, appear to have precisely the same faults they find in women.

Although Sor Juana's outspokenness with regard to men's behavior has drawn more attention, she also wrote a series of burlesque sonnets, which are highly critical of some lower class women who failed to meet the standards of responsible conduct. Inés, for example, who is described in the first sonnet, is a loud mouth, and the poet assembles a sequence of auditory images that convey her cacophonous speech. Besides chiding her subject for her actions, she also returns to the theme of feminine portraiture and mocks its focus on a woman's appearance.

Sor Juana's satire is rarely examined and evaluated because of the attractiveness of other aspects of her works; however, it constitutes yet another demonstration of her uniqueness. Because satirical works frequently dealt with distasteful language and subject matter, they were regarded as unladylike, and women, therefore, were not to write in this vein. Sor Juana, however, found this mode of expression challenging and entertaining, and her own critical yet witty compositions compare favorably with other satirists of the colonial period.

In addition to her various secular poems, Sor Juana also wrote theatrical works for presentation at court. Among them is *Los empeños de una casa* (The trials of a noble house), which was performed in 1683 to celebrate the viceroyship of Don Tomás Antonio de la Cerda, the Marquis of La Laguna. The comedy is a fine example of the influence of Spain's Golden Age theater on dramatic works written in the colonies, and its action, therefore, typically revolves around the themes of love, honor, jealousy, and vengeance. Although the events unfold in Spain and the characters ostensibly represent Spanish social types, Sor Juana uses the elaborate edifice of this *comedia de capa y espada* (cloak and dagger play) to comment on her own days at the viceregal court through the character of Doña Leonor and to dramatize how women are perceived as the representation of man's honor. Echoes of her love poetry as well as the theme of the poem "Stupid men," which are heard throughout the play's lively script, also distinguish it, but she predictably concludes the three acts of hilarious mayhem by marrying off most of the comedy's characters. Pedro, however, who sought to compromise Leonor's reputation, is forced to remain a bachelor, and his sister

Ana, who aided in causing detriment to another woman's character, must be content with wedding Juan instead of her true love, Carlos.

Although the bishop of Puebla criticized Sor Juana for not writing on religious subjects, she did write numerous works to celebrate Church holidays. Among them are her *villancicos*, or church carols composed to honor the Virgin and various saints, which were performed in cathedrals throughout New Spain. Incorporated into the sacred ceremony of the occasion, these pieces generally presented the mystery of a particular feast day or the life of a saint; they were sung, interpolated between recited prayers. The portion of the carol known as the *ensalada*, a combination of verses that continues the composition's theme but accords it a lighter treatment, has drawn the attention of scholars. In these lines blacks, Indians, and *mestizos*, often speaking Spanish in a dialect, come forward and comment on their social condition as they express their devotion to the Virgin or their favorite saint.

Inspired by the sacramental plays of Pedro Calderón de la Barca, Sor Juana also wrote religious drama. Her *El divino Narciso* (The divine Narcissus), considered to be a masterpiece, offers a delightful blend of mythology and theology. In this allegory, Echo, who represents the devil, vies for the love of the Christ-like Narcissus with the earthly maiden called Human Nature. Throughout the play, Echo tries to keep the two separated by keeping Narcissus from seeing his own reflection, which is also the image of Human Nature, and falling in love with it. When Echo fails to prevent this, she flies into a rage and is condemned forever to repeating sounds rather than producing them. Narcissus ultimately gives his life because of his love for Human Nature, but a part of him will always remain on earth in the form of a flower or the Eucharistic host. Although the presentation of the fall and the redemption in *El divino Narciso* is ingenious, its humanlike characters, especially those of the females Echo and Human Nature, are also an exceptionally creative feature of the drama and add considerable meaning and depth to its development.

Sor Juana also wrote two notable prose works in epistolary form, which either deal with matters of theology or are related to the place of women in the Church. The first is her *Carta atenagórica* (The Athenagoric Letter) in which she discusses Father Vieira's sermon, and the second, which was promoted by the writing of the first, is her *Respuesta a Sor Filotea de la Cruz* (Reply to Sister Phylotea of the Cross). Responding to the bishop of Puebla, who probably sought to create a degree of sisterly rapport by disguising himself as Phylotea, Sor Juana relates the history of her inclination to learn and defends a woman's right to be educated, to teach, and to write. While following the rhetorical structure of polite correspondence as well as the scholastic methodology of argumentation to rebut the bishop's criticism, she also employs sarcasm throughout her answer to reveal his vulnerability and to punish him for his interference in her personal life. This letter provides the boldest statement of Sor Juana's desire to forge a new image for Spanish American women, and the universality of her intention transcends time and extends across national boundaries.

SURVEY OF CRITICISM

The works of Sor Juana Inés de la Cruz were highly acclaimed during her lifetime and earned for her the distinguished title of the Tenth Muse of Mexico. Apart from presentations and performances of much of her poetry and drama, her carols were printed and distributed among churchgoers for years, and her *Carta atenagórica* and two volumes of her poetry, containing the *Primero sueño* and *Los empeños de una casa*, were published in the 1690s. Five years after her death, *Fama y obras póstumas* ("Fame and posthumous works") appeared, and the *Respuesta a Sor Filotea* and Sor Juana's first biography, written by Father Diego Callejas, were included in its contents. These volumes not only circulated in New Spain but arrived in other viceroyalties of the Spanish empire as well. As a result, the poet Juan del Valle y Caviedes in Peru and the mystic, Mother Francisca Josefa Castillo y Guevara (Madre Castillo*) in New Granada (today's Colombia), may be counted among the Mexican nun's more notable early admirers.

For nearly three hundred years since the death of Sor Juana, the fascination with her life and works has not waned, and this continual enthusiasm has generated volumes of literary criticism. This excitement has been marred by the quality of scholarship they demonstrate, which has been described as superficial and repetitive. Because Sor Juana was the only colonial woman writer to be considered by critics for many years and because so little was known about her, studies focused generally on a comparison of her works to those of the most outstanding male writers of the period or on an examination of her personality. While the former intent clearly revealed her exceptional ability to follow literary tradition, the latter unfortunately led to the publication of several misleading psychoanalyses and biographies of sheer invention.

Over the past twenty years, however, the criticism dealing with Sor Juana has undergone considerable change because of the renewed interest in colonial literature and the growth of the feminist movement. Since Sor Juana is often viewed as America's first feminist, critics have begun reevaluating her works for their uniqueness, especially with regard to precursory statements on women's abilities and their right to individuality and independence. Among the most recent works to examine the innovative features of Sor Juana's literary production with particular attention given to her singular perspective of gender are such general studies as Octavio Paz' *Sor Juana Inés de la Cruz o las trampas de la fe* (1982; *Sor Juana or, The traps of faith*, 1988); the *Proceedings of the Symposium on "Sor Juana Inés de la Cruz y la cultura virreinal"* (1983), edited by Georgina Sabat de Rivers; and Stephanie Merrim's collection of essays entitled *Towards a Feminist Understanding of Sor Juana Inés de la Cruz* (1990). This relatively new approach has also been followed in the analysis of Sor Juana's poetry in Georgina Sabat de Rivers's *El "Sueño" de Sor Juana Inés de la Cruz: tradiciones y originalidad* (1976) and "Sor Juana: Diálogo de retratos" (1982) and in the reviews of her famous letter to the bishop in "La estructura retórica de la *Respuesta a Sor Filotea*'' (1983) by Rosa Perelmuter Pérez, and *Virtue or Vice?: Sor Juana's Use of Thomistic Thought* (1981) by Constance M. Montross.

Although the directions of Sor Juana criticism have changed over the past two decades, the original assessment of her stature as a writer has only been confirmed. As Sor Juana's illustrious contemporary Don Carlos de Sigüenza y Góngora stated in his *Teatro de virtudes políticas* (Theater of political virtues) when he praises the poet for the eminence she had attained and foresees the magnitude of her contribution to history: ''We should applaud the excellent works of the rare talent of Mother Juana Inés de la Cruz, whose fame and name will end only with the world'' (Francisco Pérez Salazar, *Obras de Carlos de Sigüenza y Góngora* [Mexico City, 1929], p.38).

BIBLIOGRAPHY

Works by Sor Juana Inés de la Cruz

Obras completas, Primer tomo, *Inundación Castálida de la Única Poetisa, Musa Dézima, Soror Juana Inés de la Cruz religiosa professa en el Monasterio de San Gerónimo de la Imperial Ciudad de México. Que en varios metros, idiomas y estilos, fertiliza varios assumptos: con elegantes, sutiles, claros, ingeniosos, útiles versos: para enseñanza, recreo, y admiración. Dedícalos a la Excelma. Señor Da. María Luisa Gonzaga Manrique de Lara, Condesa de Paredes, Marquesa de la Laguna, y los saca a luz D. Juan Camacho Gayna, Cavallero del Orden de Santiago, Mayordomo y Cavallerizo que fue de su Excelencia, Gobernador actual de la Ciudad del Puerto de Santa María*. Madrid: Juan García Infanzón, 1689.
Obras completas, Segundo tomo. Sevilla and Barcelona, 1692.
Obras completas, Tercer tomo, *Fama póstuma del Fénix de México*. Madrid, 1700.
Obras escogidas. Buenos Aires: Colección Austral, 1946.
Poesías. Ed., Prol., and Notes by Ermilo Abreu Gómez. Mexico City: Ediciones Botas, 1948.
Obras completas. Ed. Alfonso Méndez Plancarte and Alberto G. Salceda. 3 vols. Mexico City: Fondo de Cultura Económica, 1951–1957.
Los empeños de una casa. Ed. and Prol. Julio Jiménez Rueda. Mexico City: Editorial de la Universidad Nacional Autónoma, 1952.
Primero sueño. Buenos Aires: Universidad de Buenos Aires, 1953.
Antología. Ed. Elias L. Rivers. Salamanca: Ediciones Anaya, 1971.
Obras selectas. Eds. Elias L. Rivers and Georgina Sabat de Rivers. Barcelona: Editorial Noguer, 1976.
Inundación castálida. Ed. Georgina Sabat de Rivers. Madrid: Clásicos Castalia, 1982.

Translations of Sor Juana Inés de la Cruz

Corvalán, Graciela N. V. *Latin American Women Writers in English Translation*, Latin America Bibliography Series No. 9. Los Angeles: California State University, Latin American Studies Center, 1980. Pp. 46–48.
Peden, Margaret Sayers, trans. *A Woman of Genius: The Intellectual Autobiography of Sor Juana Inés de la Cruz*. Salisbury, Conn.: Lime Rock Press, 1982. Bilingual.

Rivers, Elias L., ed. *Renaissance and Baroque Poetry of Spain.* New York: Dell, 1966. Pp. 314–36.

Trueblood, Alan S. ed. *A Sor Juana Anthology.* Cambridge, Mass.: Harvard University Press, 1988.

Warnke, Frank J., trans. *Three Women Poets: Renaissance and Baroque: Louise Labé, Gaspara Stampa, and Sor Juana Inés de la Cruz.* Lewisberg, Pa.: Bucknell Press, 1987. Pp. 81–129.

Works about Sor Juana Inés de la Cruz

Achury Valenzuela, Darío. "Sor Juana Inés de la Cruz y Sor Francisca Josefa de la Concepción: Simpatías y diferencias." *Boletín de la Academia Colombiana* 22, 91 (1972):27–35.

Ackerman, Jane E. "Voice in *El divino Narciso.*" *Bulletin of the Comediantes* 39, 1 (1987):63–74.

Blanco Aguinaga, Carlos. "Dos sonetos del siglo XVII: Amorlocura en Quevedo y Sor Juana." *Modern Language Notes* 77 (1962):145–61.

Chang-Rodríguez, Raquel. "Relectura de *Los empeños de una casa.*" *Revista Iberoamericana* 44, 104–105 (1978):409–19.

Dauster, Frank. "De los recursos cómicos en el teatro de Sor Juana." *Caribe* (University of Hawaii, Department of European Languages and Literatures, Honolulu) 2, 2 (1977):43–54.

Flynn, Gerard. *Sor Juana Inés de la Cruz.* New York: Twayne Publishers, 1971.

Gimbernat de González, Ester. "Los romances filosóficos de Sor Juana Inés de la Cruz." *Explicación de Textos Literarios* (California State University, Department of Spanish and Portuguese, Sacramento) 9, 1 (1980/1981):47–53.

Hiriart, Rosario. "America's First Feminist." *Américas* 25, 5 (1973):2–7.

Johnson, Julie Greer. "A Comical Lesson in Creativity from Sor Juana." *Hispania* 71, 2 (1988):442–44.

———. "The Feminine Perspective." *Women in Colonial Spanish American Literature: Literary Images.* Westport, Conn.: Greenwood Press, 1983. Pp. 157–69.

Leonard, Irving A. *Baroque Times in Old Mexico.* Ann Arbor: University of Michigan Press, 1966. Pp. 172–92.

Luciani, Frederick. "The Burlesque Sonnets of Sor Juana Inés de la Cruz." *Hispanic Journal* 8, 1 (1986):85–95.

———. "Sor Juana Inés de las Cruz: epígrafe, epíteto, epígono." *Revista Iberoamericana* 57, 132–33 (1985):777–83.

Merrim, Stephanie. "Narciso desdoblado: Narcissistic Stratagems in *El divino Narciso* and the *Respuesta a sor Filotea de la Cruz.*" *Bulletin of Hispanic Studies* 64, 2 (1987):111–17.

———, ed. *Towards a Feminist Reading of Sor Juana Inés de la Cruz.* Detroit: Wayne State University Press, 1989.

Montross, Constance M. *Virtue or Vice?: Sor Juana's Use of Thomistic Thought.* Washington, D.C.: University Press of America, 1981.

Parker, A. A. "Calderonian Sources of *El divino Narciso.*" *Romanistisches Jahrbuch* 19 (1968):257–74.

Paz, Octavio. *Sor Juana Inés de la Cruz o las trampas de la fe.* Barcelona: Editorial Seix Barral, 1982.

―――. *Sor Juana, or, The Traps of Faith*. Trans. Margaret Sayers Peden. Cambridge, Mass.: Harvard University Press, 1988.

Perelmuter Pérez, Rosa. "La estructura retórica de la *Respuesta a Sor Filotea*." *Hispanic Review* 51, 2 (1983):147–58.

Puccini, Dario. "Los villancicos de Sor Juana Inés de la Cruz." *Cuadernos Americanos* 142 (1965):223–52.

Roggiano, Alfredo. "Conocer y hacer en Sor Juana Inés de la Cruz." *Caribe* (University of Hawaii, Department of European Languages and Literatures, Honolulu) 1, 2 (1976):29–37.

Sabat de Rivers, Georgina, ed. *Proceedings of the Symposium on "Sor Juana Inés de la Cruz y la cultura virreinal." University of Dayton Review* 16, 2 (1983).

―――. "Sor Juana: Diálogo de retratos." *Revista Iberoamericana* 120–21 (1982):703–13.

―――. *El "Sueño" de Sor Juana Inés de la Cruz: Tradiciones literarias y originalidad*. London: Tamesis, 1976.

Schöns, Dorothy. "Some Obscure Points in the Life of Sor Juana Inés de la Cruz." *Modern Philology* 24, 2 (1926):141–62.

Thurman, Judith. "Sister Juana: The Price of Genius." *Ms. Magazine* 1, 10 (1973):14–21.

Volek, Emil. "Un soneto de Sor Juana Inés de la Cruz 'Detente, Sombra de mi Bien Esquivo'." *Cuadernos Americanos* 223, 2 (1979):196–211.

Williamsen, Vern G. "Forma simétrica en las comedias barrocas de Sor Juana Inés." *Cuadernos Americanos* 224, 3 (1979):183–93.

Other Works Cited

Siguenza y Góngora, Carlos de. *Obras de Carlos de Sigüenza y Góngora*. Ed. Francisco Pérez Salazar. Mexico City: n.p., 1929.

CLAUDIA LARS
(1899–1974)
El Salvador

Amanda Plumlee

BIOGRAPHY

Born in Armenia, in the Department of Sonsonate, El Salvador, on December 29, 1899, Carmen Brannon as an adult adopted the pseudonym Claudia Lars. She was the daughter of an Irish-American father, Peter Patrick Brannon, and a Salvadoran mother, Mela Vega de Brannon. Married to a North American with the surname Beers, Lars had a son Roy Beers who lives in El Salvador. Her second husband was the Guatemalan writer Carlos Samayoa Chinchilla, whom she divorced several years before her death.

As a writer Lars published numerous volumes of poetry and one prose work. While possessing vast knowledge of both Hispanic and North American literature, she never received a university degree. Yet she was actively involved in a number of literary endeavors. In addition to her own writing, she directed a publishing house and the magazine *Cultura* (Culture) for the Salvadoran Ministry of Culture and Education. Her role in this capacity is significant, for normally it is men who control such institutions and decide what should and should not be published according to their own standards. Lars, empowered with the responsibility of being director, could give much badly needed exposure to fellow women writers. She encouraged not only young women writers, but male authors as well. As a result of her encouragement and publishing of these writers, Lars received the affectionate title of Mother Claudia. Along with her involvement in publishing, she collaborated with newspapers and journals in and outside of El Salvador.

Aside from being a prolific writer, Lars traveled extensively. Before her death on July 22, 1974, she had traveled through much of Central America, Mexico, Cuba, and the United States.

MAJOR THEMES

Evident in Claudia Lars's numerous works is a clearly defined thematic development. In creating her own poetic voice, she began with an intimate poetry that addresses personal concerns of the female experience such as motherhood and romantic love. Lars began to produce children's poetry as an extension of her motherhood theme. By referring to her own childhood, she displays a highly autobiographical tone in certain works. Inherent in this autobiographical poetry is the beginning of a transition or shift in focus. In introducing her mixed cultural heritage, the poet goes beyond simple family portraits to presenting Central America as a whole. With a continually expanding focus, the poet's works begin to adopt a certain universality in their philosophical quest for an understanding of human nature, love, and death. Completing her philosophical phase, Lars returns to writing children's poetry and to describing her own childhood. Her late poetry is a combination of personal and social issues. Lars's gradual shift in focus from intimate to social poetry is typical of Hispanic twentieth-century female poets as noted by Mary Crow in the introduction to *Woman Who Has Sprouted Wings: Poems by Contemporary Latin American Women Poets* (1984).

Lars's first volume of poetry was a two-part work entitled *Estrellas en el pozo* (1934; Stars in the well). While the first section of the work presents Lars's views on true poetry (which she equates with nature), the second half is more personal in that it presents an important part of the female experience, motherhood. As a mother herself and as a woman of a traditional culture in which great emphasis is placed on motherhood, Lars treats the institution with much depth and understanding. Her authentic treatment encompasses the various facets of being a mother from a woman's feelings at preconception until the child reaches adulthood. In "¿Qué y de dónde a mí llegaste?" (How and from where did you come to me?), a woman assures her child that she has wanted him or wanted to be a mother since her earliest memories. Moreover, she states "In order for you to arrive / God made me a woman." Thus, Lars reflects traditional religious views about a woman's mothering role. From the time of her dolls to that of caring for a younger brother or sister, a girl receives the message that her primary function in life is biological or emotional mothering and nurturing.

A number of poems in this second section explain the bond that exists between a mother and her child. One such poem is "Madre" (Mother) which describes the experience of being a mother as a mystery. Thus, with the birth of her son Lars could truly appreciate and understand her own mother's love. Moreover, by giving birth she underwent a unique part of the female experience, one denied to men by virtue of their sex. She adds that her child gave a new meaning and purpose to her life. This newfound purpose fulfills an essential component of the female psyche or what psychologist Carol Gilligan believes is the need to nurture or be a caretaker (1982).

In "Romance de los días que vienen" (Romance of the days to come), Lars likens her son's presence in her life to a harvest of hope and a source of security and protection in her old age. Yet as she observes her son, she knows that she must one day share his love with another woman, his future wife. Resigning herself to the inevitability of this future event, she resolves to welcome and to accept her more fully. Hence, Lars breaks with the stereotypical image of the mother-in-law who refuses to relinquish her control or influence on her son's life.

Even though Lars's son will one day leave her home to make one for his own family, their bond will continue. In "Por todos los senderos" (Along every path), the poet assures her son that her presence will accompany him throughout life in the best and worst of times. Thus, her mothering role will extend beyond death and in so doing grant her a sense of immortality.

In 1937 Lars's second collection of poetry, entitled *Canción redonda* (Round), appeared in which she treats another important part of the female experience, romantic love. The realism of her treatment is innovative and challenging for a Latin American woman. Replacing the sweet sentimental verses traditionally associated with women poets is an authentic love poetry with a sensual and erotic quality. "Canción del adiós que se presiente" (Forboding: the song of goodbye) depicts a young woman eagerly awaiting her sexual awakening. She openly admits her sexual desires, an unexpected admission for a Latin American woman whose conservative culture teaches her to deny or repress her sexuality in order to preserve her reputation or honor. Yet despite her readiness to experience the pleasures of love, she feels that they will be brief and fleeting. Their brevity is emphasized by repetition of the phrase "Nos está decretado separarnos" (It is decreed that we will separate).

In "Nada en común tenemos" (We have nothing in common), a mature strong woman is portrayed with the insight and strength to accept the fact that a relationship between two vastly different individuals would only be frustrating and damaging. Her assertive and rational behavior serves as what feminist critic Cheri Register terms a "role model" for other Latin American women who, confronted by a culture that tells them that their self-identity comes from a man, frequently accept less than satisfying relationships (1975).

Lars began to make her most significant contribution to Central American poetry in 1942 when she entered the field of children's literature with the publication of *La casa de vidrio* (Glass house). The work is dedicated to Lars's son, Roy, and contains both poems for and about children. With Lars's characteristic use of nature imagery and clarity of style, the poems describe the world and certain experiences in a way that children can readily understand. In addition, it presents delightful fantasy figures like the Sandman and King Neptune. More important, it denotes a change of focus in her poetry. Her poems about poor children begging for alms reveal a sense of social consciousness.

Further development of this social consciousness appeared four years later in 1946 in *Romances de norte y sur* (Ballads of the north and south). This collection of thirteen ballads reminiscent of the form employed by Federico García Lorca in his *Romancero gitano* (Gypsy Ballad Book), is dedicated to the memory of her father and to El Salvador. The work's dedication speaks of Lars's mixed heritage, the predominant theme. However, these poems present more than autobiographical information about the poet's life. For example, in discussing her grandfather's Indian origin, Lars is touching on a sensitive social issue in Latin America. Although the Indian is a vital part of the cultural identity of Latin America, this group has been relegated to an inferior social position. The poet challenges the highly stratified class system of her culture by openly admitting her Native American ancestry and taking pride in it. She devotes the closing ballads to describing the United States and such Central American countries as Nicaragua and Guatemala. In describing Central America, she reminds present-day readers of its country's beauty, which is too often overshadowed by or forgotten amid current political conflicts and revolution. Thus, with its outward focus and social awareness, this work represents a transition in Lars's poetry to include a broader range of themes beyond the poet's personal experience.

Lars continued her external focus in *Sonetos* (1947; Sonnets). The work's opening section displays a universal note with its emphasis on life's ephemeral nature and death's inevitability. It also pays poetic homage to three famous women poets who have influenced Lars's poetry: Gabriela Mistral* with her themes of children and mothers; Christina Rossetti whose Christian faith colors her melancholy poems on love and death; and Sor Juana Inés de la Cruz* with her religious and feminist poetry. The closing section of the collection entitled "Sonetos de arcángel" (The archangel's sonnets) won Lars the Central American literary contest of 1941. In addition to its highly religious tone, two of Lars's most important symbols appear, the rose and the archangel. According to critic Matilde Elena López (1970), the rose is perfection and beauty, while the archangel represents perfection as well as supreme goodness. Both symbolize humanity's search for these elusive qualities.

Lars's treatment of the philosophical quest progresses in *Donde llegan los pasos* (1953; Where steps lead). In dividing the work into seven distinct sections, each of which represents one of life's fundamental aspects, Lars employs her own quest for understanding to represent that of human beings in general. Hence, this collection is intimate, yet social. Furthermore, it denotes artistic maturity in regard to theme and style. Lars's serious treatment of the abstract concepts of love, death, and religion reflects not only the poet's own intellectual depth, but also the fact that women are capable of addressing issues outside the traditional "sitting room." In addition, while maintaining its essential clarity, Lars's style and use of imagery become slightly complex and a bit more abstract.

Concerning the concept of love, Lars devotes two of the collection's divisions to romantic love. From both the title of the second "Sobre rosas y hombres" (About roses and men) and the opening quotation by Emily Dickinson concerning the fragility of the rose, it is apparent that the rose is an important symbol of this section. As it has through the centuries, the rose symbolizes love which is beautiful and vibrant for a short period before it withers and dies. Furthermore, like the rose's thorns, pain is inherent in love.

Two poems are significant in the second section. The third poem deals with men's fear of emotional intimacy. As her lover sleeps, the female voice in the poem struggles with finding a way to explain her feelings for him. Not only needing to make him understand her feelings, she must also tell him in a manner that will not frighten or threaten him. Upon revealing her emotions or feelings to him, she is embarrassed by his unresponsiveness or avoidance. Thus, the poem realistically reflects love's frustration which is often the result of the effects of socialization on the two sexes. While the female is taught to express her emotions, the male is instructed to deny or repress his.

The sixth poem provides an interesting twist to the love relationship. A woman is recovering from a relationship in which she has been accused of being unfaithful. In the *machista* culture of Latin America, where so many double standards exist for men and women, and where a man is often unfaithful to his partner, men are often insanely jealous and suspicious of women's fidelity. Such transference or projection of behavior frequently results in unfounded accusations, as is the case in this poem. While hurt by her lover's lack of faith in her and abandonment of her, the "I" has remained strong and has refused to be devastated by her lover's unjust rejection. Because of her strength and resolution, she decides to give love a second chance, for the poem ends with her cutting another rose.

The work's fifth section, called "Casa sobre tu pecho" (House upon your chest), begins with a quotation by Christina Rossetti which speaks of finding one's true love after several years of painful searching. Even though she is now in the autumn of her life, and many past loves have faded like summer roses, the poem's protagonist feels a sense of love and security with her present lover. This sense of love and happiness comes from his total understanding and acceptance of her. Unlike her previous lovers, he sincerely wants to know her as a complete person. Therefore, he delves below the surface appearance and looks at her inner being and thoughts. In this way, he discovers and accepts the pain she has suffered in past relationships. Lars suggests that the source of a meaningful relationship rests not on physical attraction or outward signs of wealth and financial security, but on complete mutual understanding and tolerance. The poem further reinforces the theme of conflict as in the previously mentioned poem "Nada en común tenemos."

In the fourth section of the book, entitled "De la calle y el pan" (About the street and bread), Lars expands her concept of love to include the human race. Initially, the symbol of bread represents modern man's greed which prevents his caring for others. The poet writes, "Today bread incites us, from the ovens/ and wins the right to guide the multitudes" (p. 50). Yet Lars refuses to be driven by this materialism and searches for some other meaning or purpose in life. This meaning she discovers in Christianity. To denote her discovery, she transforms the symbol of bread into the body of Christ. The poem closes with the belief that Christ's love offers a means to uniting all human beings.

Not only does Christianity provide hope for eradicating social alienation, but it also promises immortality or life after death. Strongly related to this doctrine is the sixth section of the book, entitled "Los dos reinos" (The two kingdoms). In this section the poetic voice repeatedly expresses the desire to be regenerated upon death into any element of nature like a flower, a blade of grass, a leaf, and the like. In essence she and her poetry will finally achieve complete harmony with nature.

In 1955 Lars returned to writing children's poetry with the publication of *Escuela de pájaros* (School of birds). Written to encourage children to love poetry, this volume actively appeals to a child's imagination with delightful poems about cute animal figures described through the use of amusing and inventive sound and rhythm combinations. Lars is especially playful with sound in "Cucu, cantaba rana" (Cucu, sang the frog), where she skillfully repeats "cucu" along with words that rhyme with it. Any child would be charmed by "Ratita y minero" (The mouse and the little rat), a diminutive couple who dance in the queen's massive palace.

Five years later in 1960, Lars's third work of children's poetry, *Canciones* (Songs), followed. The work is characterized by descriptions of typical objects in nature. There are descriptions, for example, of the moon and the Milky Way, depicted in a manner in which children would portray them. The predominance of both nature imagery and the color green are characteristic of Lars's poetry in general. Mary O'Brien's theory, in her "Feminist Theory and Dialectical Logic," that women are closer to nature because of the age-old association of their fertility to the earth's fecundity may be applied to Lars's poetry which places a great deal of emphasis on motherhood and children (*Feminist Theory: A Critique of Ideology*, 1982).

Lars's last collection of children's poetry, *Girasol* (1962; Sunflower), is actually an anthology containing poems by Lars herself and by many other writers from both Latin America and Spain. Her endeavor is notable for including children's verse by such well-known poets as Federico García Lorca, Antonio Machado, and Juana de Ibarbourou; in this way she proves the importance of children's literature. Unlike most anthologies compiled by men, hers contains an ample representation of women poets. Moreover, this work, along with Lars's own volumes of children's poetry, is an important contribution to children's literature because, as Gastón Figueira (1959) notes, such literature was slow to develop in Latin America.

Also appearing in 1962 was Lars's *Sobre el ángel y el hombre* (Regarding angel and man) for which she won second place in the 1961 Certamen Nacional de Cultura contest. The work is in three parts and is based on the classic conflict of the soul or "angel" versus the flesh or "hombre." Starting with a spiritual quest for finding union with God, the second part interrupts her search to focus on romantic or physical love heavily cloaked in nature imagery. Once again love is a summer rose whose beauty quickly pales. Unable to find lasting satisfaction in love, the lyrical voice returns in Part Three to a spiritual journey reminiscent of that of Spain's sixteenth-century mystics.

Lars returned to writing children's literature in 1969 with the release of her only prose work, *Tierra de infancia* (Childhood land). This collection of short stories is another of Lars's nostalgic journeys into her past. Amidst the splendor of a Salvadoran landscape cloaked in folklore and superstition, one meets the poets' relatives, particularly her grandparents. Once again, Lars not only emphasizes her grandfather's Indian blood, but also shows his concern for and just treatment of the Indians. Lars's grandmother appears as a devout religious woman who fulfills the Latin American mother's obligation to be her family's spiritual teacher and thus the guardian of its moral values for future generations.

In 1973 the first volume of Lars's *Obras escogidas* (Selected works) was published. While this anthology is basically a collection of her earlier published poetry, Volume 2 released a year later contains several of her previously unpublished works as well. Among these are "Nuestro pulsante mundo" (Our pulsating world) and "Cartas escritas cuando crece la noche" (Letters written when it becomes night).

Volume 2 is a mixture of social and intimate poetry. It covers a variety of contemporary issues from drugs in "Muchacho embrujado" (Bewitched boy) to space exploration in "Apollo 8" to nuclear war in "Guardián de Nuestras Llaves" (Keeper of our keys). As for its more personal side, the work displays revealing poems about the male-female relationship. "Simples creadores" (Simple creators) depicts two young lovers in sensual abandonment. Yet despite their ardent and passionate desire, they really do not understand what is about to occur. Their ignorance and naïveté show in this poetic recounting of their first sexual experience. By comparing the sexual act to a man sowing seed, Lars is not only glorifying motherhood, but she is also using reproduction to justify the sexual union. Her justification is typical in a conservative Latin American society where the Catholic Church teaches and its devout followers believe that reproduction is the only acceptable reason for a couple to engage in sex.

Lars addresses another inherent trait or problem of Latin American culture in the poem "Juan Silvestre." In Latin America, *machismo*, or the exaggerated importance that some men have attached to themselves, has produced rigid gender roles and fierce male domination, especially among the working classes. It is this domination and unpleasant social reality that Lars presents in this poem. In describing a poor rural family, she portrays the wife as being submissive and the man as overbearing. Furthermore, he has little respect for women and views them as little more than sexual objects existing for his own pleasure. While Lars disapproves of such a low opinion of women, she does not totally blame the individual male. Instead, she paints him as a frustrated victim of his society, who, feeling debased by his low social position, tries to bolster his self-esteem by manipulating and belittling his wife.

In "Cartas escritas cuando crece la noche," one encounters an intimate or personal note, a letter in the form of a poem to a former lover, who was also a poet. Despite the fact that their relationship ended years ago, Lars still cares for him. There is no bitterness in this poem, just fond and warm memories. More importantly, Lars cherishes him as both a teacher of literature and of love.

SURVEY OF CRITICISM

Even though Claudia Lars was a prolific writer and one of the best poets of El Salvador, there is a dearth of in-depth criticism dealing with her works. The majority of the existing criticism consists of little more than a brief biographical introduction, a few superficial comments about her poetry, and a few of her poems in an anthology or magazine article. Therefore, a new critical analysis of Lars's work is badly needed.

Of the criticism one can readily obtain, the best critical studies of her works have been done by women. One such female critic is Julieta Carrera who included a chapter on Lars in her *La mujer en América escribe . . .* (1956). In this chapter, Carrera makes the important observation that Lars's poetry reflects the experience of a middle-class woman. There is a fallacy but also a foreigner's tendency to view all Latin American women as the same. While sharing a number of cultural similarities, Latin American women of different classes experience life in a slightly different manner because of their social status.

A second important critic of Lars's work is Matilde Elena López (1973–1974) who wrote lengthy introductions to Lars's two-volume collection of selected works. In these introductions she has a particularly good discussion of Lars's major works and themes. She also provides in-depth explanations of Lars's two major symbols, the rose and the angel. In addition, she is very perceptive in describing the significant relationship Lars had with her father. In fact, she feels that a study of the effect this relationship had on Lars's poetry is merited.

In conclusion, Lars's poetry warrants further criticism. Moreover, it would be interesting to apply current existing literary theories to it, including feminist ones. Lars's poetry is a virtually unexplored part of Central American literature.

BIBLIOGRAPHY

Works by Claudia Lars

Estrellas en el pozo. San José, Costa Rica: Convivo, 1934.
Canción redonda. San José, Costa Rica: Convivo, 1937.
La casa de vidrio. Santiago, Chile: Zig-Zag, 1942.
Romances de norte y sur. San Salvador: Funes, 1946.
Sonetos. San Salvador: Estrella, 1947.
Donde llegan los pasos. San Salvador: Ministerio de Cultura, 1953.
Escuela de pájaros. San Salvador: Ministerio de Educación, 1955.
Fábula de una verdad. San Salvador: Ministerio de Cultura, 1959.
Canciones. San Salvador: Ministerio de Cultura, 1960.
Girasol: antologia de poesía infantil. San Salvador: Ministerio de Educación, 1962.

Presencia en el tiempo. San Salvador: Ministerio de Educación, 1962.
Sobre el ángel y el hombre. San Salvador: Ministerio de Educación, 1962.
Del fino amanecer. San Salvador: Ministerio de Educación, 1966.
Nuestro pulsante mundo. San Salvador: Ministerio de Cultura, 1969.
Tierra de infancia. San Salvador: Ministerio de Educación, 1969.
"Apuntes sobre mi amistad con Gabriela Mistral." *Cultura* (San Salvador) 57 (1970):94–
    109.
Obras escogidas. 2 vols. San Salvador: Universitaria, 1973–1974.
Poesía última, 1970–1973. San Salvador: Ministerio de Educación, 1975.
Sus mejores poemas. Sel. and notes by David Escobar Galindo. San Salvador: Ministerio
    de Educación, 1976.

Translations of Claudia Lars

Examples of Lars's poetry are found in the following anthologies:
Fitts, Dudley. *Anthology of Contemporary Latin American Poetry.* New York: New
    Directions, 1942. Pp. 178–81.
Jones, Willis Knapp, ed. *Spanish American Literature in Translation: A Selection of
    Poetry, Fiction, and Drama Since 1888.* New York: Frederick Ungar Publishing
    Co., 1963. Pp. 62–64.
Hulet, Claude. *Latin American Poetry in English.* Washington, D.C.: Pan American
    Union, 1965. P. 158.

Works about Claudia Lars

Alegría, Fernando. "El horizonte mágico de Claudia Lars." *Atenea* 337–338 (1953):64–
    75.
Arce y Valladares, Manuel José. "Panorama de las letras en El Salvador." *Estudios
    Americanos* 11, 54 (1956):271–83.
Argueta, Manlio, ed. *Poesía de El Salvador.* San José, Costa Rica: Editorial Universitaria
    Centroamericana, 1983. Pp. 45–57.
Baeza Flores, Alberto. "La joven poesía centroamericana." *Nuevo Mundo* 45 (Mar.
    1970):66–73.
Canas, Salvador. "La tierra de agua y miel de Claudia Lars." *Cultura* (Jan.-Mar.
    1958):92–95.
Carrera, Julieta. *La mujer en América escribe . . .* Mexico City: Semblanzas, 1956.
    Pp. 225–37.
Cerutti, Franco. "Notas necrológicas: Claudia Lars." *Revista Historio-Crítica de Li-
    teratura Centroamericana* 1, 1 (1974):166–68.
Chavarria López, Mayra. "Notas sobre la poesía de Claudia Lars." *Revista Histórico-
    Crítica de Literatura Centroamericana* 1, 2 (Jan.-June 1975):97–102.
"Claudia Lars en su bella tierra de infancia." *El Imparcial* (Guatemala) (Jan. 1959):24.
Figueira, Gastón. "Wandering Tadpoles and Speckled Roosters." *Américas* 11, 1 (Jan.
    1959):11–14.
Florit, Eugenio, and Enrique Anderson-Imbert, eds. *Literatura hispanoamericana.* New
    York: Holt, Rinehart & Winston, 1960. P. 668.
Gallegos Valdés, Luis. *Panorama de la literatura salvadoreña.* San Salvador: Ministerio
    de Educación, 1962. Pp. 143–48.
Jones, Willis Knapp, ed. *Spanish American Literature.* New York: Frederick Ungar
    Publishing Co., 1963. Pp. 62–63.

Lindo, Hugo. "Presentación de poetas salvadoreños." *Síntesis* 2, 13 (Apr. 1955):46–48.

———. "Tres poetas de El Salvador." *Mundo Hispánico* 2, 20 (1949):19–21.

López, Matilde Elena. Introd. *Obras escogidas*. By Claudia Lars. San Salvador: Universitario, 1973–1974. I:13–111, II:11–20.

———. "Sobre el ángel y el hombre: poesía y estilo de Claudia Lars." *La Universidad* (San Salvador) 95, 1 (Mar.-Apr. 1970):79–106.

Orantes, Alfonso. "*Fábula de una verdad*, nuevo libro de Claudia Lars." *Guión Literario* 5, 49 (Jan. 1960):1, 4.

Perricone, Catherine R. "A Bibliographic Approach to the Study of Latin American Women Poets. Claudia Lars (El Salvador, 1899–1974)." *Hispania* 71, 2 (May 1988):281–82.

Quinteros, Alberto. "Claudia Lars, Alfredo Espino y Arturo Ambrogi." *Síntesis* 1, 12 (Mar. 1955):115–25.

Toruñas, Juan Felipe. *Desarrollo literario de El Salvador, Ensayo*. San Salvador: Ministerio de Cultura, 1952. Pp. 325–28, 413.

Trigueros de León, Ricardo. "Presencia en el tiempo de Claudia Lars." *Guión Literario* 7, 80 (Aug. 1962):1, 4.

Other Works Cited

Crow, Mary. Introduction. *Woman Who Has Sprouted Wings: Poems by Contemporary Latin American Women Poets*. Pittsburgh: Latin American Literary Review Press, 1984.

Gilligan, Carol. *In a Different Voice: Psychological Theory and Women's Development*. Cambridge, Mass.: Harvard University Press, 1982.

O'Brien, Mary. "Feminist Theory and Dialectical Logic." *Feminist Theory: A Critique of Ideology*. Eds. Nannerl O. Keohane, Michelle Z. Rosaldo, and Barbara Gelpi. Chicago: University of Chicago, 1982. Pp. 99–112.

Register, Cheri. "American Feminist Literary Criticism: A Bibliographical Introduction." *Feminist Literary Criticism: Explorations in Theory*. Ed. Josephine Donovan. Lexington: University Press of Kentucky, 1975. 1–28.

MARTA LYNCH
(1925–1985)
Argentina

Birgitta Vance

BIOGRAPHY

Marta Lynch was born Marta Lía Frigerio in Buenos Aires, Argentina. That she was born in 1925 (on March 8), rather than 1929, 1930, or 1934, as she has claimed in various interviews, was not known until after her suicide on October 8, 1985. Her fear of aging, a constant theme in her fiction as in her life, caused her to alter her chronology. For example, when her first book, *La alfombra roja* (1962; The red carpet), appeared, she claimed that she was twenty-nine, when in reality she was thirty-seven. This habit has left the dates of everything, except those of the publication of her books, quite nebulous. She studied liberal arts at the Universidad Nacional de Buenos Aires and married Juan Manuel Lynch, a well-to-do lawyer and businessman some ten years her senior. She had three children early in her marriage: Enrique, Marta Juana, and Ramiro.

Although known internationally for her thirteen novels and collections of short stories which have been translated into Portuguese, French, German, Croatian, Russian, Swedish, Italian, English, and Norwegian, Lynch is equally well known in Argentina for her newspaper articles and television appearances. Her articles, most of which have never been collected in book form, deal with women's themes, travel, politics, social issues, and everyday life. As a result of her enormous popularity, Lynch was often chosen to comment on matters of general popular interest. When the World Cup soccer matches took place in Buenos Aires, for example, it was she who was selected to interview the players, and she was recognized by the man-in-the-street for her political and social activism as much as for her literary endeavors.

Lynch expressed love for her country in everything she said and wrote. Her passionate interest in politics is evidenced in many of her short stories as well as in the novels: *La alfombra roja*, *Al vencedor* (1965; To the victor), *La Señora Ordóñez* (1967; Mrs. Ordóñez), *El cruce del río* (1972; Crossing the river), *Un árbol lleno de manzanas* (1974; A tree laden with apples), *La penúltima versión de la Colorada Villanueva* (1978; Red Villanueva's penultimate version), and *Informe bajo llave* (1983; Report under lock and key). This passion for politics led her first to join the movement of Arturo Frondizi in 1956, but to turn against him, when he became president in 1958. Later, she worked actively for the return of Juan Perón, and was a member of the charter flight that brought him back from Spain. She also supported Raúl Alfonsín, the president until 1989. Lynch has been criticized frequently for her apparent political vacillations, yet they were in keeping with her belief that the intellectual "nunca está de acuerdo con nadie, ni con nada" (never agrees with anyone or anything). (All unattributed quotations are taken from an unpublished interview of Marta Lynch by this author.) At times, when it took a great deal of courage to do so, and everyone else was silent, she spoke out publicly against the government's actions. She denounced the disappearance of the author Haroldo Conti and was one of the few to criticize the military government for waging the Malvinas (Falkland Islands) war against Great Britain.

Lynch was an inveterate traveler. By 1970, when she was invited to be a member of the jury for the Cuban Casa de las Américas prize, she was already familiar with Europe and the United States, but hardly knew Latin America. As a result of the contacts she made in Havana, she received invitations to act as visiting professor at Peruvian, Chilean, and German universities and to lecture in many other Latin American countries. On several occasions, she lived in Lima for months at a time; this city became the *locus* for many of her stories.

By the time *La alfombra roja*, Lynch's first published book, appeared in 1962, she had already written two other novels, and one of them had been a finalist in the prestigious Biblioteca Breve competition organized by the Barcelona publishing house, Seix Barral. Lynch refused to publish either of these works because she judged them "prescindibles" (superfluous). After *La alfombra* won the Fabril Prize, it became an instant popular and critical success and, according to Lynch, completely changed her life: She "became a writer." Her second novel, *Al vencedor* (1965), the story of two young military draftees, she considered prophetic because it foretold the violence that was to invade the country thirteen years later. The two novels have masculine protagonists, a circumstance that is rare in Lynch's fiction. In 1965 Lynch's story, "Justitia parvi hominis" (The justice of the little man), appeared in the collection *Crónicas de la burguesía* (Chronicles of the bourgeoisie). Once again the protagonist was a young male, but the upper middle-class *milieu*, one that was to appear again and again in Lynch's work, was new. The story was published again in her first collection, *Los cuentos tristes* (1967; Sad tales).

These narratives have in common their acute psychological observation, as well as a certain macabre twist to the endings. Although many of them are rather weak, one, "Las señoras que tomaban té" (The ladies having tea), shows remarkable insight into the rivalry felt by two former classmates of a prestigious private school when they meet by chance years later. This book, which won the Primer Premio Muncipal de Prosa (First Municipal Prose Award), also contains a story portraying guerrilla warfare, "El cruce del río," which was expanded in 1972 into the novel of the same name. The other narratives deal with all the themes Lynch was to use throughout her career.

In the same year, 1967, Lynch's most famous novel, *La Señora Ordóñez*, appeared to immediate success. Five editions were published the first year alone, and the novel was made into a film for television in 1984. Lynch was to spend her life denying that the figure of Blanca Ordóñez was autobiographical. Once she was driven to exclaim in exasperation that she more closely resembled a kangaroo than she did Mrs. Ordóñez. Yet this figure, as well as Blanca's reverse side, la Colorada Villanueva, the protagonist of *La penúltima versión de la Colorada Villanueva* (1978), definitely mirrors some of Lynch's attitudes and feelings, as do many of the females in the short stories.

A second sea change in Lynch's life and work occurred following her collaboration on the Casa de las Américas jury when she made contact with leading writers and intellectuals of Latin America. Lynch found her voice in what for many years was to be her favorite book, *Un árbol* (1974), discovering a system of expression that was most faithful to her way of thinking. Stylistically complex, and with an ambiguous ending, this novel that began as a love story quite unwittingly found its theme smothered by the political one, according to Lynch (Paley de Francescato, 1975, p. 41). Against her will, the repression and national disintegration imposed itself on her to such an extent that from this point on the dark side of existence was to be ever present in her work.

Marta Lynch's "new voice" continued in the short story collection, *Los dedos de la mano* (The fingers of a hand), which first appeared in 1976. These are Lynch's first stories to take place outside Argentina, reflecting her travels to Europe and the United States, as well as to other parts of Latin America. The sense of detachment from time and place, of taking part in a dream or a fantasy, occasionally present in *Un árbol*, is found again in "Hotel Taormina," probably the finest piece in the book. Lynch herself had a great affection for this tale and chose to include it in *Páginas de Marta Lynch* (1983; Pages by Marta Lynch), a collection of previously published works selected by the author. "Sentencia" (Sentence) is arguably Lynch's best story to depict the institutionalized violence of Argentina during this period, although otherwise politics are barely represented in the other stories in this book. Love, or more precisely, the memory of love after it has been lost, pervades these fictions, all told from a woman's point of view. In *Los dedos* we become aware of Lynch's extraordinary ear for spoken language, not only the *lunfardo*-tinted *porteño* (inhabitant of Buenos Aires) speech, but also that of other Latin countries.

As the Argentine political situation deteriorated, Marta Lynch's political journalism intensified and in *La penúltima versión de la Colorada Villanueva*, published in 1978, politics once more superimposed itself on a love theme, as they had on *Un árbol*. Even Lynch's most persistent critics approved of this novel, permanently establishing her place in Argentine letters. La Colorada ("Red") Villanueva, Lynch's second great female figure, is the antithesis of Blanca Ordóñez. While Ordóñez, incapable of loving, takes from everyone, la Colorada gives too much of herself: to her own children, to the children in her nursery school, and especially to a deceitful, philandering, improvident husband who has conveniently left the country for political reasons, thereby throwing off his family responsibilities. The novel ends on a vaguely hopeful note, with la Colorada finally giving up hope of a reunion with her husband, Fernando, and resolutely facing life alone.

Lynch's next publication, *Apuntes para un libro de viajes* (1978; Notes for a travel book), is a brief tome collecting travel articles that had appeared in newspapers and magazines. As she crossed Europe, the United States, and Latin America, she attempted to capture the soul or spirit of each place. For example, she viewed North Americans as watching their lives pass by from three boxes: their house, their car, and the television. Following was a collection of short stories entitled *Los años de fuego* (1980; The years of fire) which practically omits politics. She concentrates on a type of love affair consisting of feverish, fleeting meetings in various parts of the globe, over a period of time. For some reason never spelled out, the lovers are unable to stay together, illustrating Lynch's belief that love is made up of *desencuentros* (failed encounters). The year 1982 saw the publication of *Toda la función* (The whole show), a brief book containing two more stories of *desencuentros* and a personal autobiographical note, "Biografía a mi manera" (Biography, my way), focusing on Lynch's books and their critical reception.

In Lynch's next book, *Informe bajo llave* (1983; Report under lock and key), the "negrura interior" (inner blackness, *Toda la función*, p. 73) that had been present in her literature from the very beginning of her career, and had intensified in the early seventies, becomes overwhelming. In the prologue, Lynch informs us that she found the report in question at her psychiatrist's and was given permission to publish it, which seems an obvious literary device, possibly intended by Lynch to protect her privacy. The report, in epistolary form, written by Adela G. at the behest of her psychiatrist, tells of the erotic, sexual obsession of a young woman writer with a *caudillo* or political strongman.

The stories of Lynch's last work, published to great acclaim in the spring of 1985, cover the same spectrum of themes as her previous publications. In *No te duermas, no me dejes* (1985; Don't go to sleep, don't leave me), there are stories of love, of *desencuentros* in which the dark side of existence dominates. The title piece is a love story different from the others in that it celebrates married love and fidelity lasting throughout a long life. Most of the narratives have a simple style; they are chronological rather than written in the "lyrical" mode (see "Survey of Criticism" below) of most of Lynch's former work. There is one political tour de force: the fifty-page long "Entierro de un jefe" (Burial of a leader)—a curiously ironic evocation of the *porteños'* reaction to the death of Juan Perón.

Marta Lynch committed suicide at the height of her success. *No te duermas, no me dejes* had headed the best seller charts since its appearance that year; *La Colorada* was about to be filmed; and Lynch was surrounded by a loving family and friends. If there was any doubt of her fame at the time of her death, it was dispelled by the media's reaction. The notice of her death and then her funeral appeared on the front pages of *La Nación*, Buenos Aires' most influential daily. Spain's *El País* ran an article about her. Her picture appeared on the covers of the periodicals *Somos* and *Fama*, and that of her funeral on *Gente*'s. At first there were rumors of cancer. No one could fathom that a person with "everything" would commit suicide. Lynch had been in analysis for some seventeen years and in the last years under psychiatric care. According to her husband, during the last eight years she had talked frequently about committing suicide before she got old. In Lynch, the fear of aging seemed to be a fear of losing her place as the center of attention; the fear of losing her ability to attract men, rather than a fear of infirmity (as reported in *Gente*, p. 111). This same dread runs throughout her work, beginning as early as *La Señora Ordóñez*. In *La Colorada*, the sex roles are reversed, and it is the male Fernando, "the seducer," who worries about aging and thereby losing his seductive capacity. In her suicide, though not in its form, Lynch followed in the steps of many of the authors she admired: Ernest Hemingway, Virginia Woolf, Cesare Pavese, but especially her beloved Alfonsina Storni,* whose manuscript of the poem, "Hombre pequeñito" (Little man) she kept above her desk.

MAJOR THEMES

Lynch's fiction revolves around two themes ever present in the Argentine life she knew so well: love and politics. Lynch has said of her own works and her life in general: "I admit to four or five obsessions: for example, the obsession of forgetting, of abandonment, of betrayal, of infidelity, sex, lack of love . . . and everything I write has the social and political reality of the country as its backdrop." Both love and politics are a constant in the novels, with the love theme generally outweighing the political. In the short stories, only one of the two is usually present.

Beginning with *La Señora Ordóñez*, love is the prime mover in most of Lynch's fiction. Love can mean romantic love or fornication or the two combined, although basically, for Lynch's protagonists, everything between a man and woman is a only a preliminary for sex. Whatever type of love is present, it is marked by obsession and *desencuentros*. There is no happy love in these stories.

Blanca Ordóñez, the first of Lynch's important female characters, fails in her quest for happiness because she is so other-directed. In *The Lonely Crowd* (1950), David Riesman describes the other-directed person as one who does not respond to internal stimuli at all but who is guided only by his contemporaries. Someone who is other-directed has constantly shifting goals because he is dependent on the signals received from others. Blanca is drawn into politics by her first husband, dabbles in art, but, just as she receives recognition, drops her artistic endeavors again to devote her time to her young lover, Rocky. Blanca Ordóñez has lovers to prove to herself that she is still attractive to men, not because she hopes to find love. She has not loved any of her men, husbands or lovers, not her parents or her children, because she suffers from low responsiveness, as do most other-directed people. Sex provides a defense against total apathy. She feels a certain passion for Rocky, but not enough to stay with him if it means relinquishing her comfortable middle-class existence. It is this dependence on the opinions of others that brings about the ever-present fear of aging in Blanca. The sections of the book narrated by Blanca are full of thoughts of being old, as she catches sight of herself in mirrors, and associates with Rocky (fifteen years her junior) and his friends.

Unlike Blanca Ordóñez, many of Lynch's women are not alienated, in the sense that they are not generally powerless or self-estranged. The only power to which the other female protagonists succumb is the need for a lover. La Colorada, in *La penúltima versión de la Colorada Villanueva*, although intuiting that her marriage with Fernando is over, prefers to pretend that the attachment is still alive. She allows her life to revolve around daydreams of their past and of future reunions, stimulated by Fernando's romantic letters, which are an important stylistic device in the novel. La Colorada needs to believe in the existence of Fernando as her lover, although he is in reality as much of a phantom as Fuentes in the title story of *Los dedos de la mano*. There, the protagonist, a physician and psychologist, invents a phantom lover, complete with photographs, details of his life in another country and of his brief visits to her. The woman is conscious of her lover's nonexistence but needs to invent him to give herself a feeling of completion. La Colorada has managed to ignore all signs of Fernando's desertion until she receives a letter bluntly telling her he wants a permanent separation. At this point, she seeks a temporary lover, Alejandro, to take his place. Only at the very end does la Colorada seem to be willing to stand alone. In a symbolic gesture, she takes a letter from Fernando which hints at a reunion and makes a little boat out of it, letting it sail down the rain-filled gutter.

It has often been observed that Lynch's characters live in a closed, obsessive world. This tendency is carried to its extreme in the case of Adela G., protagonist of *Informe bajo llave* (1983). The book is in the form of a report assigned by Adela's psychiatrist, a type of diary in which she records her encounters and "disencounters" with the object of her obsession, Vargas, a powerful man. Here we have a remarkable study of the erotic attraction of power. From an objective point of view, Vargas is not physically attractive, although Adela is wildly attracted to his physical attributes; he has some repulsive personal habits, their conversations can hardly be considered such, and he treats her abominably. Nevertheless, Adela's life revolves around seeing Vargas and waiting for Vargas to call. Her neurosis takes on physical characteristics: Her hands become cramped and clawlike, preventing her from writing or doing crafts, her previous occupations. We are led to believe that before her encounter with Vargas, she had been a happy, successful woman. Apart from her sexual obsession, she is unable to love, barely seeing her eleven-year-old son, and she is totally disinterested in his phone calls. Adela G.'s total being is wrapped up in her appearance, and she also manifests fear of aging, although she is only twenty-eight at the story's opening. The enormous shifts in her emotional state are evidenced by how she visualizes herself: one day as aging, with thinning hair at the temples, and a few days later describing her hair as splendid.

In her portrayal of Vargas, Lynch returns to the study of *caudillismo* (bossism). According to Lynch, this novel can be seen as an allegory about a country under the boot of an implacable dictator (unpublished interview by Paley de Francescato, May 1983). Our perceptions of Vargas, received only through Adela G., a patently unreliable narrator who constantly loses and then regains an "accurate" view of her situation, are vague and undependable. It is unclear whether Vargas derives his power from politics or from great wealth, unlike the case in the detailed study of a strongman in Lynch's first work, *La alfombra roja*. From this work on, with the exception of one or two short stories, few of Lynch's fictions revolve entirely around politics. Politics seem only to intervene, to give an unexpected twist to the lives depicted. For example, Adela G. becomes one of the *desaparecidos* (disappeared) and, as is typical in such cases, is never heard from again. We can only conjecture whether she was abducted by Vargas himself, by the left because of her association with Vargas, or because of her previous dabbling in left-wing politics.

In *La Colorada*, the political situation impinges to cause la Colorada's already weak family structure to disintegrate completely. Her older daughter follows her father into exile; her younger daughter has been forced to go underground because of her political activity; her brother-in-law, a lieutenant-colonel, has been murdered by a leftist group in which his own son may have been involved. Although always committed politically, Lynch attempts to show a balanced view of the terrible conflicts within Argentina at this time. She does not condemn either the military or their opponents. This is in keeping with her belief in searching always for something other than the position of the left or of the capitalistic and militaristic right: What she calls "esa tercera posición que en realidad es la posición de la justicia y la libertad" (that third position that really is the position of truth and liberty).

SURVEY OF CRITICISM

Critical attention to the work of Marta Lynch has been generally celebratory but fragmentary, largely confined to book reviews and dissertations. Ramón Layera explains the lack of a major study of Lynch's work as being due to the fact that, unless proper value is given to the feminine view of reality (in which respect her work is especially illuminating), Lynch is likely to be overshadowed by such major literary figures as Jorge Luis Borges, Ernesto Sábato, Julio Cortázar, and Manuel Puig, who were all writing in Argentina at the same time.

That Lynch has been considered a feminist by the writers of dissertations written in the United States can be explained by Mary Patricia Mosier's thesis (1979) of an overt and covert ideology in Lynch's early fiction in her Ph.D. dissertation, "An Ideological Study of the Novels of Marta Lynch, 1962–1974." According to Mosier, Lynch's desire to be a critic of Argentine reality leads her to create characters whose failure to realize themselves is apparently due to their social and economic situation. This is the overt intent, the only one discussed in the dissertations by Bradley M. Class (1974); by Amy Kaminsky (1975); and by Lynne Lois Billman (1976). Mosier believes that Lynch's overt leftist and feminist ideology is undermined by a second covert and probably unconscious one that can only be revealed by a close reading of the novels. This reading indicates that the source of the protagonists' problems is their own flawed psyches. Mosier goes further to say that these ideological contradictions are the result of Lynch's individual bias and typical of a reflective liberal in Argentina. The attempt to fit Marta Lynch into preconceived political or feminist ideologies can make of them something of a Procrustean bed, as in Kaminsky's application to Blanca Ordóñez of the findings of the well-known study by Matina Horner which claim that middle-class women have been conditioned to fear professional success. According to this reasoning, Blanca does not pursue her art because she fears succeeding, a claim that Gwendolyn Díaz (1983) rejects in her excellent introduction to *Páginas de Marta Lynch*, finding no evidence in the text to suggest it. In a more fruitful feminist approach, Naomi Lindstrom focuses on Lynch's presentation of women's discourse difficulties in both soliloquies and verbal interactions in *La Señora Ordóñez*, *La Colorada*, and in several short stories. In three articles on the subject, Lindstrom points to how "Lynch's work lays bare some of the mechanisms that put woman at a disadvantage and render her unable to 'state her case' " in a world dominated by male power and fantasy (1978, p. 50).

In the study mentioned above, Díaz takes an in-depth, carefully reasoned look at *La Señora Ordóñez* and *La Colorada*. She perceives the value of Lynch's work to be her innovative treatment of themes traditionally related to the female character and praises her for creating "personajes de vigencia universal" (characters of universal relevance, Introduction to *Páginas de Marta Lynch*, p. 40). Lynch rejects traditional images to create such "existentially authentic" ones as the woman rebel, best exemplified by Blanca Ordóñez, according to Díaz (p. 39). Díaz too seems to accept the "overt ideology" of Marta Lynch and blames society for Blanca's failed and frustrated existence.

Blanca's fear of aging, which Díaz discusses very well, derives from the excessive importance our society gives to women's physical attractiveness (Pp. 27–29). In *La Colorada*, Díaz discovers what for Lynch is a totally new treatment of character: a reversal of sex roles. The masculine characters, Fernando and Alejandro, are assigned traditionally female qualities: beauty, vacuousness, passivity, and the condition of sexual object. Fernando, the husband, is also characterized by his absence, which suggests to Díaz that Fernando, the ideal husband, exists only as a creation of the mind of la Colorada Villanueva, thereby proving the futility of dedicating one's life to an unattainable ideal. La Colorada, on the other hand, takes on "masculine" characteristics by supporting herself and her three children; when she sees that Fernando is unable to support himself in exile, she tries to get an additional job, one that requires the "masculine" quality of courage: supervising a kindergarten that has been attacked several times by guerrillas.

Ernest Lewald (1982), the author of several studies on Lynch, perceives the depiction of male-female relationships in Lynch as a reflection of the Argentine cultural reality described by the sociologist Julio Mafud: the *porteño* cannot approach women on anything but a sexual basis, equating sex with virility or dominance and love with weakness (pp. 176–178). Although this article appeared before *Informe bajo llave*, its findings would suggest that Vargas, too, demonstrates the character and characteristics of the typical male of Buenos Aires, although possibly carried to pathological extremes.

Antonio Cornejo Polar, Eduardo Gudiño Kieffer, Bernice Bennett, and many other critics have referred to Lynch's stylistic modernity, particularly her subtly alternating point of view and her "spatial-temporal games" (Gudiño Kieffer, 1980, p. 48). Gwendolyn Díaz describes Lynch's prose as "lyric," utilizing the definition from an article by Joanna Russ, entitled "What Can a Heroine Do?, or Why Women Can't Write." In "lyric" prose, the author organizes the discrete elements of the novel *"around an unspoken thematic or emotional center*. The lyric mode exists without chronology or causation: Its principle of connections is *associative"* (Russ, emphasis hers, 1973, p. 12). According to Díaz, the "thematic or emotional center" around which *La Señora Ordóñez* and *La Colorada* are organized is the existential frustration of their heroines.

Apart from *La Señora Ordóñez* and *La Colorada*, Lynch's work has received little serious critical attention. Her strengths are seen to be in her innovative treatment of women's themes and her creation of female characters of universal significance against a vividly drawn and accurately observed background of social and political reality, chiefly that of Buenos Aires. It is to be hoped that the unedited novels and rough drafts left behind at her death will be published and that an attempt will be made soon to take a global look at her entire canon.

BIBLIOGRAPHY

Works by Marta Lynch

La alfombra roja. Buenos Aires: Fabril, 1962.
Al vencedor. Buenos Aires: Losada, 1965.
Crónicas de la burguesía. Buenos Aires: J. Alvarez, 1965.

La Señora Ordóñez. Buenos Aires: Jorge Alvarez, 1967.
Los cuentos tristes. Buenos Aires: Centro Editor de América Latina, 1967.
Cuentos de colores. Buenos Aires: Sudamericana, 1970.
El cruce del río. Buenos Aires: Sudamericana, 1972.
Un árbol lleno de manzanas. Buenos Aires: Sudamericana, 1974.
Los dedos de la mano. Buenos Aires: Sudamericana, 1976.
Apuntes para un libro de viajes. Buenos Aires: Cástor y Póllux, 1978.
La penúltima versión de la Colorada Villanueva. Buenos Aires: Sudamericana, 1978.
Los años de fuego. Buenos Aires: Sudamericana, 1980.
Toda la función. Buenos Aires: Editorial Abril, 1982.
Informe bajo llave. Buenos Aires: Sudamericana, 1983.
Páginas de Marta Lynch seleccionadas por la autora. Buenos Aires: Celtia, 1983.
No te duermas, no me dejes. Buenos Aires: Sudamericana, 1985.

Translations of Marta Lynch

Manguel, Alberto, trans. "Latin Lover." *Other Fires: Short Fiction by Latin American Women.* Ed. Alberto Manguel. New York: Clarkson Potter, 1986. Pp. 32–41.
Vance, Birgitta, trans. "Hotel Taormina." *Contemporary Women Authors of Latin America: New Translations.* Eds. Doris Meyer and Margarite Fernández Olmos. Brooklyn N.Y.: Brooklyn College Press, 1983. Pp. 194–204.
———. "Nice Guy." *Shenandoah* 32, 2 (1981):105–11.

Works about Marta Lynch

Bennett, Bernice Lynne. "Narrative Structure in the Novels of Marta Lynch." Ph.D. diss. University of California, 1981. (DAI 42 [1981]:1169A.)
Berenguer Carisomo, Arturo. *Literatura argentina.* Barcelona: Labor, 1970. P. 93.
Billman, Lynne Lois. "The Political Novels of Lucila Palacios and Marta Lynch." Ph.D. diss. Catholic University of America, 1976. (DAI 37 [1976]:1580A.)
Birkemoe, Diane S. "The Virile Voice of Marta Lynch." *Revista de Estudios Hispánicos* 16, 2 (1982):191–211.
Brushwood, John S. *The Spanish American Novel.* Austin: University of Texas Press, 1975. Pp. 230–31.
Capestany, Cecilia Delacre. "*Informe bajo llave.*" *Américas* 36 (1984):59.
Class, Bradley M. "Fictional Treatment of Politics by Argentine Female Novelists." Ph.D. diss. University of New Mexico, 1974. (DAI 35 [1974]:6132A.)
Cociffi, Gabriela. "Las confesiones del marido de Marta Lynch." *Gente* 18, 1056 (1985):4–14.
Cornejo Polar, Antonio. "*Los dedos de la mano.*" *Revista de Crítica Literaria Latinoamericana* 3 (1976):114–15.
Dellepiane, Angela. "La novela argentina desde 1950 a 1965." *Revista Iberoamericana* 34 (1968):237–82.
Díaz, Gwendolyn Josie. "Images of the Heroine: Development of the Female Character in the Novels of Beatriz Guido, Marta Lynch, Syria Poletti." Ph.D. diss. University of Texas, 1981. (DAI 42 [1981]:3174A.)
———. Introduction to *Páginas de Marta Lynch seleccionadas por la autora.* Buenos Aires: Celtia, 1983. Pp. 11–40.
Foster, David William. "Marta Lynch: The Individual and the Argentine Political Process.

La penúltima versión de la Colorada Villanueva.'' Latin American Digest 13, 3 (1979):8–9.

Gudiño Kieffer, Eduardo. ''The Novelist as Historian. *La penúltima versión de la Colorada Villanueva.'' Américas* 32 (1980):47–48.

Kaminsky, Amy Sue Katz. ''Marta Lynch: The Expanding Political Consciousness of an Argentine Woman Writer.'' Ph.D. diss. Pennsylvania State University, 1975. (DAI 36 [1975]:4531A–4532A.)

———. ''The Real Circle of Iron: Mothers and Children, Children and Mothers in Four Argentine Novels.'' *Latin American Literary Review* 9 (1976):77–86.

Layera, Ramón. ''Marta Lynch: *La penúltima versión de la Colorada Villanueva.'' Revista de Crítica Literaria Latinoamericana* 13 (1981):142–46.

Lewald, Ernest. ''Alienation and Eros in Three Stories by Beatriz Guido, Marta Lynch and Amalia Jamilis.'' *Theory and Practice of Feminist Literary Criticism.* Eds. Gabriela Mora and Karen Van Hooft. Ypsilanti: Bilingual Press, 1982. Pp. 175–85.

Lindstrom, Naomi. ''The Literary Feminism of Marta Lynch.'' *Critique: Studies in Modern Fiction* 20 (1978):49–58.

———. ''Woman's Voice in the Short Stories of Marta Lynch.'' *The Contemporary Latin American Short Story.* Ed. Rose Minc. Montclair, N.J.: Senda Nueva de Ediciones, 1979. Pp. 148–53.

———. ''Women's Discourse Difficulties in a Novel by Marta Lynch.'' *Ideologies and Literature: A Journal of Hispanic and Luso-Brazilian Studies* 4, 17 [1983]:339–48.

Mosier, Mary Patricia. ''An Ideological Study of the Novels of Marta Lynch, 1962–1974.'' Ph.D. diss. University of Wisconsin, 1979. (DAI 40 [1979]:3335A.)

Natella, A. Aristides. ''*Un árbol lleno de manzanas.'' Books Abroad* 49–3 (1975):514.

Paley de Francescato, Martha. ''Entrevista a Marta Lynch.'' *Hispamérica* 10 (1975):33–44.

———. Unpublished interview of Marta Lynch. Buenos Aires, 1983.

Russ, Joanna. ''What Can a Heroine Do? or Why Women Can't Write.'' *Images of Women in Fiction. Feminist Perspectives.* Ed. Susan Koppelman Cornillon. Bowling Green, Ohio: Bowling Green University Popular Press, 1973. Pp. 3–20.

Silva-Velázquez, Caridad, and Erro-Orthmann, Nora. *Puerta Abierta. La Nueva Escritora Latinoamericana.* Mexico City: Joaquín Mortiz, 1986. Pp. 173–78.

Stabb, Martin S. ''Argentine Letters and the Peronato: An Overview.'' *Journal of Inter-American Studies and World Affairs* 13 (1971):434–55.

Vance, Birgitta. ''*Los dedos de la mano* by Marta Lynch.'' *Journal of Spanish Studies:20th Century* 5, 3 (1977):250–52.

———. ''Marta Lynch habla de su obra, de la vida y de la política argentina.'' Unpublished interview. Buenos Aires, 1978.

Other Works Cited

Mafud, Julio. *Psicología de la viveza criolla.* Buenos Aires: Americalee, 1965. P. 60.

Riesman, David, with Nathan Glazer and Reuel Denney. *The Lonely Crowd: A Study of the Changing American Character.* New Haven, Ct.: Yale University Press, 1950.

CLORINDA MATTO DE TURNER (1852–1909)
Peru

Mary G. Berg

BIOGRAPHY

Clorinda Matto de Turner is best known for her 1889 novel, *Aves sin nido (Birds Without a Nest*, 1904), which shocked Peruvian readers with its depiction of corruption and exploitation in a small Andean town. In addition to *Aves sin nido* and two other novels, *Indole* (1891; Character) and *Herencia* (1895; Heredity), Matto published a vast number of articles and historical sketches, several collections of biographical essays and travel commentaries, two textbooks for women students, and many translations from Spanish into Quechua.

Grimanesa Martina Mato Usandivaras, who later called herself Clorinda Matto, was born in Cusco, Peru, on November 11, 1852, to Grimanesa Usandivaras and Ramón Mato, owners of a small country estate named Paullo-Chico where Matto and her two brothers, David and Daniel, spent most of their childhood. In her later writing, she often describes the beauties of country life and draws on specific memories of events and people. Her lifelong interest in the well-being of the Indian population and her fluency in the Quechua language are also rooted in early experiences. Her formal schooling took place in Cusco, at a school that would later be renowned as the Colegio Nacional de Educandas. By the age of fourteen, she was editing a student newspaper and writing dramatic skits for private performances. Her mother died in 1862, and in 1868 Matto left school to help run the household and take care of her father and two younger brothers. On July 27, 1871, she married José Turner, an English physician and business entrepreneur, and she moved with him to Tinta, a small town near Cusco. Matto began to write poetry and prose, and was soon publishing articles under various pseudonyms (''Lucrecia,'' '' Betsabé,'' ''Rosario'') in periodicals such as the *Heraldo, El Mercurio, El Ferrocarril*, and *El Eco de los Andes*.

Her particular concerns at first were the emancipation and education of women and the treatment of Indians, but she soon began writing legends and historical sketches, Cusco *tradiciones* (a mixture of history and fiction) in the style of Ricardo Palma's already famous short pieces based on anecdotes of Peruvian history. Matto organized a literary circle, and in February 1876 she began to publish *El Recreo de Cuzco*, a weekly magazine of literature, science, arts, and education, to which she contributed many articles.

When Matto traveled to Lima in 1877, she met with a cordial reception and was included in a number of literary gatherings and festivities, including the prestigious salon of Juana Manuela Gorriti,* a well-known Argentine writer then living in Peru. Gorriti held a literary party in Matto's honor, and among those who read compositions were Gorriti herself, Mercedes Cabello de Carbonera,* and Ricardo Palma, all of whom were to become important friends. Back in Tinta during the first years of the war with Chile, in 1879, Matto actively supported the cause of Andrés Cáceres who, with Indian soldiers, defended the Peruvian Andean region. Matto's home served as a war hospital, and she organized an ambulance system and raised funds for the war effort.

José Turner died in March 1881, during the height of the disorder of the war, and left his widow in desperate financial difficulties. Matto tried to repay his debts and make a success of various business ventures, but in 1883 she moved to Arequipa to become editor of *La Bolsa*, a daily newspaper. She thus became the first woman in America to head an important newspaper. Many of her first articles and editorials in *La Bolsa* are patriotic exhortations to all Peruvians to unite and resolve their problems, but she went on to write about business and agriculture, immigration, Indian problems, and education, particularly women's education. She published a literature textbook for girls in 1884.

Matto's first collection of essays and historical sketches, *Perú—Tradiciones cuzqueñas* (1884; Peru—Cusco Traditions), was published in Arequipa in 1884 with a prologue by Ricardo Palma. Her only play, *Hima-Sumac* (1892; Hima-Sumac), was performed in Arequipa on October 16, 1884, and again in Lima in 1888. It is a moving melodrama of love and betrayal which expresses sympathy for the Indians who are oppressed and tortured by the gold-greedy Spaniards.

Matto moved to Lima in 1886, where she soon became part of the literary gatherings at the Ateneo and the Círculo Literario, a salon attended by Manuel González Prada, an influential speaker and writer whose ideas about progress, national spirit, Indian education, and anticlericalism were to deeply interest and influence Matto. She continued to write articles and fiction. In 1889 she became the director and editor-in-chief of *El Perú Ilustrado*, Lima's most important literary magazine of its time. She published two books in 1889, one a collection of biographical descriptions, *Bocetos al lápiz de americanos célebres* (Pencil Sketches of Renowned Americans), and the other a bombshell novel of scathing criticism of corruption in a small Andean town, *Aves sin nido*, which met with immediate acclaim and notoriety.

Matto published the work of important writers in *El Perú Ilustrado*, often including contributions by such writers as Rubén Darío and Manuel González Prada and members of the literary group who met regularly at her house. On August 23, 1890, *El Perú Ilustrado* printed (without Matto's authorization, she claimed, since she was ill that day) a story about the life of Christ by the Brazilian Henrique Maximiano Coelho Netto which outraged many readers who felt it defamed Christ by portraying him as sexually attracted to Mary Magdalene. The archbishop of Lima prohibited, under penalty of mortal sin, anyone from reading, selling, or discussing the magazine. The magazine and Matto's *Aves sin nido* were both accused of defaming the Church. The controversy raged on. Matto was excommunicated by the archbishop, there were public demonstrations for and against her, she was burned in effigy in Cusco and Arequipa, and *Aves sin nido* was put on the list of Prohibited Books by the Catholic Church. Matto and *El Perú Ilustrado* had many outspoken defenders. Finally, on July 7, 1891, the archbishop's ban on the newspaper was lifted in response to extensive promises on the part of Pedro Bacigalupi, the owner of the paper, that there would be more vigilance over what was published. Four days later, Matto resigned as editor and director of *El Perú Ilustrado*.

The following year, Matto published her second novel, *Indole*, in which a priest is the corrupt and evil villain, and various practices of the Church, army, and government are criticized. With her brother David, Matto founded a feminist press and circulated a prospectus: *Muestrario de la imprenta "La Equitativa" servida por señoras, fundada en febrero de 1892 por Clorinda Matto de Turner* (Sample Book of the Equitable Press, Staffed by Women, Founded in February 1892 by Clorinda Matto de Turner). There she printed her biweekly newspaper, *Los Andes*, and her own next book, *Leyendas y recortes* (1893; Legends and clippings), as well as the work of other women writers. Matto became very involved in politics, defending her longtime friend and admirer, Andrés Avelino Cáceres, and attacking Nicolás de Piérola. Her novel *Herencia*, which criticized the moral degeneracy of Lima society, appeared in early 1895, and in March of that year Piérola took over the government. Matto later described the horrors of those days. Her house was totally destroyed, her press sacked, and her manuscripts were lost. On April 25, 1895, Matto fled to Chile, where she was warmly received. She went on to Argentina and settled in Buenos Aires. She taught courses at two schools for women, translated books of the Bible into Quechua at the request of the American Bible Society, and continued to write articles for various periodicals, including the daily newspapers *La Nación* and *La Prensa* of Buenos Aires. She founded and edited the bimonthly *El Búcaro Americano*, a social and literary magazine particularly interested in publishing the work of women writers. *Aves sin nido* appeared in an English translation by J. H. Hudson in 1904, with its final pessimism about the likelihood of social reform modified into a more optimistic view.

In 1908 Matto traveled extensively in Europe and kept a diary of her impressions of Italy, where she had an audience with the Pope, and of Switzerland, Germany, England, France, and Spain, where she lectured on Argentina and

Peru. She returned to Argentina at the end of the year and, though quite ill, she completed her travel book, *Viaje de recreo* (1909; Pleasure Trip) just before she died of pneumonia on October 25, 1909, in a clinic in Buenos Aires. She left a part of her estate to the Hospital de Mujeres of Cusco, and she gave her library to the Concejo [*sic*] de Educación of Buenos Aires.

At the request of the Peruvian president and Congress, the remains of Clorinda Matto de Turner were returned to Peru in 1924, and she is buried in Lima.

MAJOR THEMES

Throughout her life, Clorinda Matto de Turner was concerned with issues of morality, equality, and justice. She felt that writers had a responsibility to portray the inequities of social reality and to demand reforms. Profoundly patriotic, she encouraged the creation of a specifically Peruvian literature, a literature that would describe the life and customs and heritage of her native country. Her *tradiciones* were based on local folklore and the colonial history of Cusco, most of her essays were about Peruvian events and circumstances, and even the subtitles ("Novela peruana") of her second and third novels indicate they are to be read as depictions of Peruvian reality.

Matto actively supported many political and social causes during her lifetime. From the beginning of her career until her death, she was particularly interested in the implementation of reforms in these areas: the education of women, the improvement of conditions for the Andean Indian population, and the elimination of corruption within the Catholic Church.

These three concerns may be seen clearly in all of Matto's fiction. Several of her *tradiciones* extoll the virtues and beauties of female character and of Indian life, but portray both women and Indians as vulnerable to exploitation, cruelty, and subjugation. Church and civil authorities are sometimes portrayed as corrupt and interested only in their own enrichment. Matto's play, *Hima-Sumac*, (first performed in 1884), based on the legend of the secret treasure of the Incas as told by Matto's mentor Juana Manuela Gorriti in *El tesoro de los Incas* (The treasure of the Incas), published in 1865, is a romantic melodrama in which the heroine, young Hima-Sumac, must decide between the Indian warrior she should love and the duplicitous Spaniard she adores. Like all of Matto's women characters who make the wrong choices, Hima-Sumac lacks a good mother's wise counsel, and, even though she knows rationally that the motives of the Spaniard are suspect, she falls right into his sexual trap. Her father, her Indian fiancé, and his loyal friend are portrayed as strong and noble and do what they can to dissuade and protect Hima-Sumac from her disastrous love. In the end, she dies under torture rather than reveal the Inca secret, but the Indian rebellion led by her fiancé, Tupac Amaru, has been defeated. The vanquished can only hope that in the future, evil and corruption will be overcome by true Peruvian patriots and that then "Peruvian glory, the glory of the Incas, will shine . . . through the centuries" (p. 81).

Indian character and culture are also described very positively in *Aves sin nido*. Again, Indians are seen as vulnerable to corrupt tyranny. Their poetic sensitivity to nature, their peaceableness, the values of compassion and community loyalty which they take for granted, and above all, their gullibility, their assumption that others speak the truth and mean well are again shown to lead them to disaster. They are cruelly exploited by the very agencies that should promote justice: the Church, the government officials and tax collectors, and the legal system. *Aves sin nido* is an eloquent novel of social protest and denunciation, but it is also a story of the women of the town who combat the injustices they perceive.

Aves sin nido is the story of Lucía Marín, a young woman of good family, recently married and now settled with her mining engineer husband in the small Andean town of Killac. As an innocent outsider, Lucía is horrified at the corruption she gradually perceives in Killac. She takes up the cause of a suffering Indian family, sure at first that the priest and town governor cannot possibly mean to allow such exploitation in their town. The institutions that enslave and impoverish Indian inhabitants are explained, and examples of these abuses of power are provided. When the Maríns' house is attacked and Lucía's protegés, the Indian couple, are killed, Lucía and her husband Fernando, together with another progressive-minded city-educated young man, Manuel, dedicate themselves to exposing and reforming this backwoods barbarity. Their efforts only further alienate them from the power structure of the town. Manuel persuades his stepfather to resign as governor, but the man who is sent to replace him is worse. The judge who is charged to investigate just prevaricates. Don Pascual, the priest, cares only for his own physical comforts; his greed, weakness, unrestrained sensuality, and refusal to help the needy are continually criticized. The Church should serve the spiritual needs of its faithful, and priests should be allowed to marry, argues Matto, in order to serve "pure Christianity." Marriage would allow priests a natural outlet for their sexuality and would provide them with the good counsel of a woman.

Women are shown in *Aves sin nido* to be a strong positive moral force. Lucía's charity and compassion cause her husband to become engaged in the struggle of humanitarianism against selfish exploitation. Doña Petronila, wife of the first governor of Killac described in the novel, has managed to raise an exemplary son, Manuel, and her moral excellence tempers the weakness of her husband, although she is unable to change his basic nature. The two Indian mothers, Marcela and Martina, are far more effective at speaking out for Indian rights than are their hardworking, passive husbands. These women do not hold powerful positions in society, so they can only advocate reform by trying to influence the men around them. Lucía does not initially realize how little power she has, but she learns that confrontation is not a successful way to oppose corruption.

The need for education is emphasized. Manuel and the Maríns are able to combat the entrenched evils of the Church, state, and judicial systems because they have been well educated in a more civilized part of the country. When

Lucía and Fernando adopt the two daughters of the Indian couple killed in their struggle to resist injustice, they speak of the need to educate these girls properly in order to reinforce their good instincts. They speak of their intention to enroll Margarita, the eldest girl, in a good school in Lima, far from the stagnant corruptions and medieval tyrannies of small-town life.

Although any positive change in the rural power structure is clearly dependent on the continued presence and energies of enlightened reformers, the Maríns and Manuel all decide to leave Killac to go live in Lima, which is portrayed as the center of civilized and progressive society. In a melodramatic ending, Margarita and Manuel, who have fallen in love, discover they are brother and sister, both offspring of a licentious priest, the predecessor of the lecherous Don Pascual. The book mixes aspects of romantic love and despair, naturalistic and realistic description, travel accounts of the Peruvian countryside, and disquisitions about the roles and capabilities of women.

Human corruptibility and vulnerability are the dominant themes of Clorinda Matto de Turner's second novel, *Indole*, published in 1891. Set in Rosalina, a small Andean town, around 1845, during a time of civil unrest, *Indole* focuses on an upper class young couple, Antonio and Eulalia López, and their struggle to discover their own personal moral values within a social context that often encourages hypocrisy, the importance of appearances, and even outright criminal behavior. Antonio and Eulalia suffer and eventually learn from their experiences, emerging poorer and battered but with their love for each other intact. The villains of the story are the local priest, Isidoro Peñas, who tries repeatedly to seduce and blackmail Eulalia, and a local landowner, Valentín Cienfuegos, who tries to involve Antonio in a get-rich-quick counterfeiting scheme. At the moment when the novel begins, Antonio has lost his family fortune in a business failure but does not tell Eulalia because he does not want her to suffer. This guilty secret is compounded by his shame when he gets involved in the counterfeiting scheme in exchange for cash to keep his business failure from public knowledge. Eulalia turns to the Church for comfort but is nearly raped and blackmailed by an unscrupulous priest. Eulalia and Antonio escape disaster and reestablish some degree of confidence in each other in the end, but they are scarred. As an outward symbol of this, twenty-two-year-old Eulalia's hair has become streaked with white during these few weeks of suffering.

A network of subplots provides more information about the scheming priest, the unhappy marriage of Valentín and Asunción, the idyllic courtship of two country-bred *mestizos*, Foncito and Ziska, and the wartime situation. All of these subplots except the last may be seen as variations on the central theme of the possibility of marital happiness and ethical behavior within a corrupt society. To some extent each subplot offers a mirror image of an option open to Antonio and Eulalia: Antonio might (and does for a time) believe Eulalia guilty of sexual involvement with the priest; Eulalia might become excessively dependent on the Church like Asunción; they might squabble and hide things from each other like Valentín and Asunción; and they might manage to recapture a happy innocence like that of Foncito and Ziska. It is also shown that joining the army offers an escape from immediate difficulties for even the most corrupt (the priest), suggesting that national politics are as corrupt as rural intrigues.

As a married couple, Antonio and Eulalia are compared to and contrasted with the other two couples. Asunción's loneliness has led her to excessive involvement with the priest and Church, and this has embittered Valentín, who like Antonio is a weak man; their weakness allows us to see which way they are blown by the social winds. Asunción and Valentín's mutual rancor and resentment of each other's neglect represent a very real possible future for Antonio and Eulalia if they do not resolve their inability to confide in each other. The happy love and marriage of Foncito and Ziska substantiate the novel's emphasis on the inherent goodness of human nature as well as providing the occasion for many lengthy descriptions of local customs. The gaiety of the wedding party, which takes place at the López house, contrasts with the near dissolution of the López marriage at this very time. One of the novel's themes is the delicate, even precarious balance between good and evil, happiness and suffering, pleasure and pain. People are continuously upsetting this balance, through greed or loneliness or unrealistic preconceptions about sex roles, about personal limits, and about the effectiveness (or ineffectiveness) of social institutions. Eulalia and Antonio are very lucky to be able to make their way through a whole series of unbalanced situations. They emerge at the end wiser about the complexity of life and about the constant effort it takes to maintain a good relationship.

Analysis of the priest's attempt to rape Eulalia makes a strong case for allowing the clergy to marry. As in *Aves sin nido*, the priest is not an inherently evil man but one who chose his profession for the wrong reasons. This is a novel full of people making wrong decisions, but the priest is the most damaged (and in his turn damaging) and most perverted from a natural inclination to love and be loved. The role of the Church in the lives of its faithful believers is examined, particularly the role of the confessional, which creates very intimate bonds between priest and penitent. Ideally, the Church should provide support, comfort, religious guidance, and inspiration, but this presupposes saintlike priests who can love without ever asking anything in return. In both *Aves sin nido* and *Indole*, Matto questions whether men can reasonably be asked to be so self-sacrificing. In both novels, she presents priests who have been unable to resist temptations of sex, power, and money, which have finally made them corrupt and morally bankrupt. In one of the many balances of *Indole*, moral and financial bankruptcy are compared, as well as the poisonous self-loathing that each occasions. Just as the priest is expected to dedicate himself totally to the Church, so, too, does the North American entrepreneur in *Indole* expect unrealistically to be able to dedicate himself to the Calvinist work ethic. He, too, is shown to be unable to sustain this total commitment; he succumbs to alcohol and tobacco.

Each of Matto's novels presents a central social message: *Aves sin nido* dramatizes the gross mistreatment of the Indian citizens of Peru; *Indole* criticizes public (institutional) immorality and hypocrisy, and advocates reform of the clergy; *Herencia* discusses individual morality and the extent to which environment and heredity affect personal values and behavior. In each novel the central social concern is explicit, and reiterative moralizing passages are placed at intervals throughout the novel so that the reader cannot possibly miss the message. In contrast to these series of brief and often simplistic sermons, much of the narrative in each novel involves complex pairings of characters and sets of circumstances that are not easily resolved into black and white moral pronouncements.

Herencia is in many ways the most complicated of the three novels. In *Aves sin nido* and *Indole*, the heroines (Lucía, Eulalia) combat the evil that constitutes the major social theme: exploitation of the Indians, corruption within the Church. *Herencia* is to some extent a sequel to *Aves sin nido*, but its focus is quite different. In *Herencia*, the enemy is within civilized Lima society itself, an inescapable part of the genetic and environmental makeup of the affected individuals. Rather than denouncing a scandalous situation that should be reformed, *Herencia* urges thoughtful consideration of moral values and their implementation through education. There is no single heroine in *Herencia*; instead, the novel presents a series of pairs of women in a panoramic view of Lima society. The good mother, Lucía, is compared to the bad mother, Nieves. The innocent good girl, Margarita, is compared to the innocent corruptible Camila. Margarita and Adelina, one rich and the other poor, compete for the attention of Ernesto Casa-Alta. Camila and Espíritu, one rich and one poor, are both attracted to and callously used by the enterprising Aquilino Merlo. Margarita and Camila marry their men, for better and worse, but Adelina and Espíritu die in poverty although they are as deserving as the girls who have had better fortune. Virtue is no guarantee of reward in Matto's novels, nor is evil often punished.

Herencia exposes and ridicules the pretentious hypocrisy of wealthy Lima society and shows the snobbishness of the rich to be as reprehensible as the deceptions practiced by the poor. Aquilino Merlo makes money in his bar by selling homemade counterfeit liquor, a self-serving fraud that is comparable, later in the book, to the Aguileras's deceit. When their daughter Camila is seduced and impregnated by Aquilino, they whisk him out of town to disguise him as an Italian count so that he can come back and marry Camila in an ostentatious ceremony in the Lima cathedral.

Extensive external descriptions of how the ladies and gentlemen are dressed, of room furnishings, and of apparently inconsequential gossip serve to portray upper class Lima society vividly and simultaneously reveal how little can be discerned beneath this surface. People do not know themselves well, can only guess at the motivations of others, and thus must rely extensively on outer appearance and mannerisms of speech, making quick assumptions about others which are often wrong. *Herencia* is a lively portrait of upper and lower social levels of Lima society, a series of vivid vignettes of social types, and a disquisition about the extent to which a good education and a wholesome environment can improve a young person's chance to be a good adult. Education and positive moral circumstances cannot guarantee happiness, but their lack is seen to be invariably destructive. Matto is fascinated by the ways new scientific discoveries may benefit society, but she emphasizes the need for personal morality: charity, compassion, truthfulness, and a vigorous distinction between good and bad actions. This is especially important, she says in *Herencia*, at a time when government is corrupt and incompetent, when Peru is a nation "held by dirty hands and poisoned hearts" (p. 210).

Matto's essays and speeches throughout her career reiterate many of the concerns emphasized in her novels. She is fascinated by women who have had the energy (and often bizarre eccentricity) to pursue unusual careers. The essays about women included in *Bocetos al lápiz de americanos célebres* (1889), for instance, might be expected to extoll the merits of charitable society matrons, but instead provide brief biographies of such startling women as Francisca Zubiaga de Gamarra, a wild tomboy who led army troops into battle in Bolivia, and María Ana Centeno de Romainville, a fiercely independent defender of Indian rights and a museum founder. Matto's lengthy essay on Latin American women writers in *Boreales, miniaturas y porcelanas* (1902; Northern Lights, miniatures and porcelains) originally a lecture Matto gave in Buenos Aires in 1895, is of particular interest, as well as her views on women's education and women's rights in *Cuatro conferencias sobre América del Sur* (1909; Four lectures about South America). She was deeply committed to improving education and opportunities for women, and in both her fiction and in numerous essays, she encourages better understanding of the abilities and strengths of women and their importance to the well-being of every aspect of society.

SURVEY OF CRITICISM

Clorinda Matto de Turner's early stories and articles were very well received, and she was encouraged by Peru's best known writers. She was crowned with laurel filigree and honored with a golden pen as an outstanding young writer, at Juana Manuela Gorriti's* literary evening party for her in Lima on February 28, 1877. Critics wrote glowing reviews of her various sets of *Tradiciones cuzqueñas* and other writings. The 1884 production in Arequipa of her drama, *Hima-Sumac*, was met with great acclaim, although the reviews of the Lima production in 1888 were less enthusiastic.

As a political activist, Matto was more controversial. She was the editor of a series of influential newspapers and magazines, and a powerful public speaker. Her frontal attacks on corruption in government institutions and in the Catholic Church did not please everyone. Although *Aves sin nido* was commended by President Cáceres, who promised to work for the reforms advocated in the book, it made her many outspoken enemies. The settings of her novels were realistic and in some cases recognizable, though altered. For many years, Matto and her books were a focus of discussion of the roles and limits of the written word.

Excommunicated, reviled, and burned in effigy in Peru in 1895, her house and beloved printing presses destroyed, she was welcomed warmly upon her arrival in Chile and Argentina. She continued to be attacked by critics in Peru even long after her death.

Peruvian critics ignored her writings or tended to dismiss them as political propaganda. In the 1930s and 1940s, a few writers began to discuss her with interest, although essentially all of them viewed her primarily as a social activist, as a South American Harriet Beecher Stowe. *Aves sin nido* is often compared to *Uncle Tom's Cabin.* Concha Meléndez, in a chapter on *Aves sin nido* in a 1934 book about the Indianist novel, praised and analyzed Matto's achievement. In an article commemorating the 90th anniversary of Matto's birth, Alfredo Yépez Miranda spoke of how it was time for Clorinda Matto to be reevaluated as a Peruvian writer of importance and substantial achievement. In more recent years, numerous essays as well as books about Matto by Manuel Cuadros (1949), Francisco Carrillo (1967), and Alberto Tauro (1976) have helped to create awareness of Matto's work. These three books also provide a great deal of biographical and bibliographical information. Much of the research about her writings and detailed critical analysis of her fiction have been done by writers of Ph.D. dissertations in Peru and in the United States, but these manuscripts are unpublished. Among the most interesting are the studies by Clifton McIntosh (1932), Ruth Crouse (1965), George De Mello (1968), and Laura Saver (1984).

Early criticism of Matto emphasizes plot summary and historical relevance, including extensive discussion about whether or not she was the first major Peruvian author to write sympathetically about Indian culture and the plight of the Indian population. More recent critics have been appreciative of Clorinda Matto's dexterous balance between social message on one hand and, on the other, a portrayal of society as a complex pattern of externally discernible characteristics, a set of puzzle pieces to be examined, assembled, and interpreted. Among the many articles that contribute to our understanding of Matto's writings are those by Margaret Campbell (1959), Joye Swain (1974), Martin Miller (1975), Lucía Fox-Lockert (1979, 1981), Bart Lewis (1984), Kenichi Satake (1986), John Brushwood (1981), and especially the many excellent, perceptive analytical essays by Antonio Cornejo Polar, whose prologues to 1974 editions of all three of Matto's novels provide both factual and interpretative information, and whose articles (three in 1977) have continued this elucidation. Efraín Kristal provides excellent discussion of Matto's writing within her political context (1987). But the surface has barely been scratched: Matto's works still await and deserve wider rediscovery and more extensive interpretation.

BIBLIOGRAPHY

Works by Clorinda Matto de Turner

Perú—Tradiciones cuzqueñas. Arequipa: Imp. de '' La Bolsa,'' 1884.
Tradiciones cuzqueñas. Vol. II. Lima: Imp. de Torres Aguirre, 1886. Many subsequent editions containing different selections.

Aves sin nido. Buenos Aires: Félix Lajouane, 1889. Many subsequent editions.
Bocetos al lápiz de americanos célebres. Lima: Peter Bacigalupi y Ca., 1889.
Elementos de Literatura según el Reglamento de Instrucción Pública para uso del bello sexo. Arequipa: Imp. "La Bolsa," 1889.
Indole (Novela peruana). Lima: Tipo-Litografía Bacigalupi, 1891. New edition: Lima, Instituto Nacional de Cultura, 1974.
Hima-Sumac. Drama en tres actos y en prosa. Lima: Imp. "La Equitativa," 1892. New edition: Lima, Servicio de Publicaciones del Teatro Universitario, 1959.
Leyendas y recortes. Lima: Imp. " La Equitativa," 1893.
Herencia (novela peruana). Lima: Imp. Masias, 1895. New edition: Lima, Instituto Nacional de Cultura, 1974.
Analogía. Segundo año de gramática castellana en las escuelas normales, según el programa oficial. Buenos Aires: n.p., 1897.
Apostolcunae ruraskancuna pananchis Clorinda Matto de Turnerpa castellanomanta runa simiman tticrasccan. Traducción al quechua del Evangelio de San Lucas y los Hechos de los Apóstoles. Buenos Aires: n.p., 1901. Subsequent volumes translated into Quechua the Books of St. John, St. Paul, St. Mark, and St. Matthew. Many editions published in Buenos Aires, New York, and Lima.
Boreales, miniaturas y porcelanas. Buenos Aires: Imp. de Juan A. Alsina, 1902.
Cuatro conferencias sobre América del Sur. Buenos Aires: Imp. de Juan A. Alsina, 1909.
Viaje de Recreo. España, Francia, Inglaterra, Italia, Suiza, Alemania. Valencia: F. Sempere y Compañía, 1909.

Translation of Clorinda Matto de Turner

Hudson, J. H., trans. *Birds Without a Nest: A Story of Indian Life and Priestly Oppression in Peru.* London: Charles J. Thynne, 1904.

Works about Clorinda Matto de Turner

Brushwood, John S. "The Popular-Ethnic Sensitivity: Clorinda Matto de Turner's *Aves sin nido.*" *Genteel Barbarism: Experiments in Analysis of Nineteenth-Century Spanish-American Novels.* Lincoln: University of Nebraska Press, 1981. Pp. 139–57.
Campbell, Margaret V. "The *Tradiciones cuzqueñas* of Clorinda Matto de Turner." *Hispania* 42 (1959):492–97.
Carrillo, Francisco. *Clorinda Matto de Turner y su indigenismo literario.* Lima: Biblioteca Nacional, 1967.
Castro Arenas, Mario. "Clorinda Matto de Turner y la novela indigenista." *La novela peruana y la evolución social.* Lima: Cultura y Libertad, 1965. Pp. 105–12.
Cornejo Polar, Antonio. "*Aves sin nido*: indios 'notables' y forasteros." *La novela peruana.* Lima: Horizonte, 1977. Pp. 7–32.
———. "Clorinda Matto de Turner: para una imagen de la novela peruana del siglo XIX." *Escritura* (Lima) 2, 3 (1977):91–107.
———. "Lo social y lo religioso en *Indole* de Clorinda Matto de Turner." *Letras* (Lima) 86–87 (1977–1979):47–60.
———. "Prólogo." *Aves sin nido.* By Clorinda Matto de Turner. Havana: Casa de las Américas, 1974. Pp. vii–xxxv.
———. "Prólogo." *Herencia.* By Clorinda Matto de Turner. Lima: Instituto Nacional de Cultura, 1974. Pp. 7–21.

———. "Prólogo." *Indole*. By Clorinda Matto de Turner. Lima: Instituto Nacional de Cultura, 1974. Pp. 7–32.

Crouse, Ruth Compton. "Clorinda Matto de Turner: An Analysis of Her Role in Peruvian Literature." Ph.D. diss. Florida State University, 1964. (DAI 25 [1965]:5272.)

Cuadros Escobedo, Manuel E. *Paisaje i obra. Mujer e historia: Clorinda Matto de Turner, estudio critico-biográfico.* Cusco: H. G. Rozas Sucesores, 1949.

De Mello, George. "A Literary Life of Clorinda Matto de Turner." M. A. Thesis. University of Colorado, 1959.

———. "The Writings of Clorinda Matto de Turner." Ph.D. diss. University of Colorado, 1968. (DAI 29 [1968]:1225A.)

Fox-Lockert, Lucía. "Clorinda Matto de Turner: *Aves sin nido* (1889)." *Women Novelists of Spain and Spanish America*. Metuchen, N.J.: Scarecrow Press, 1979. Pp. 25–32.

———. "Contexto político, situación del indio y crítica a la iglesia de Clorinda Matto de Turner." *Texto/Contexto en la Literatura Iberoamericana: Memoria del XIX Congreso, Instituto Internacional de Literatura Iberoamericana*. Madrid: XIX Congreso IILI, 1981. Pp. 89–93.

Kristal, Efraín. "The Political Dimension of Clorinda Matto de Turner's *Indigenismo.*" *The Andes Viewed from the City: Literary and Political Discourse on the Indian in Peru 1848–1930*. New York: Peter Lang, 1987. Pp. 127–61.

Lemoine, Joaquín de. "Clorinda Matto de Turner." *Leyendas y recortes*. By Clorinda Matto de Turner. Lima: Imp. "La Equitativa," 1893. Pp. vii–xxxiv.

Lewis, Bart L. "Art, Society and Criticism: The Literary Theories of Mercedes Cabello de Carbonera and Clorinda Matto de Turner." *Letras Femeninas* 10, 2 (1984):66–73.

McIntosh, Clifton Brooke. "*Aves sin nido* and the Beginning of *Indianismo*." Ph.D. diss. University of Virginia, 1932. (DAI S0246 [1932]:9.)

Meléndez, Concha. "*Aves sin nido*, por Clorinda Matto de Turner." *La novela indianista en Hispanoamérica, 1832–1889*. Río Piedras: University of Puerto Rico, 1961. Pp. 177–84. 1st ed. Madrid: Imprenta de la Libreria y Casa Editorial Hernando, 1934.

Miller, Martin C. "Clorinda Matto de Turner and Mercedes Cabello de Carbonera: Societal Criticism and Morality." *Latin American Women Writers: Yesterday and Today*. Eds. Yvette E. Miller and Charles M. Tatum. Pittsburgh: Latin American Literary Review, 1975. Pp. 25–32.

Rodríguez-Luis, Julio. "Clorinda Matto." *Herméneutica y praxis del indigenismo: La novela indigenista de Clorinda Matto a José María Arguedas*. Mexico City: Fondo de Cultura Económica, 1980. Pp. 17–55.

Sandoval, Julio F. "La señora Clorinda Matto de Turner: Apuntes para su biografía." *Perú—Tradiciones cusqueñas*. By Clorinda Matto de Turner. Arequipa: Imp. de "La Bolsa," 1884. Pp. vii–xiv.

Satake, Kenichi. "El mundo privado de Clorinda Matto de Turner en *Herencia*." *Revista de Estudios Hispánicos* 20, 2 (1986):21–37.

Saver, Laura Judith. "Un análisis de la influencia filosófica de Manuel González Prada en Clorinda Matto y Mercedes Cabello." Ph.D. diss. University of Colorado, 1984. (DAI 46 [1985]:436A.)

Swain, Joye R. "An Analysis of *Aves sin nido*." *Neohelicon* (Budapest, Hungary) 2, 1–2 (1974):217–25.

Tamayo Vargas, Augusto. *Guía para un estudio de Clorinda Matto*. Lima: Colección Turismo, 1945.

Tauro, Alberto. *Clorinda Matto de Turner y la novela indigenista*. Lima: Universidad Nacional Mayor de San Marcos, 1976.

Valenzuela, Víctor M. "Clorinda Matto de Turner: *Aves sin nido*." *Grandes escritoras hispanoamericanas: Poetisas y novelistas*. Bethlehem, Pa.: Lehigh University Press, 1974. Pp. 71–82.

Yépez Miranda, Alfredo. "Clorinda Matto de Turner: En el 90° aniversario de su nacimiento." *Revista Universitaria* (Universidad Nacional del Cuzco) 33, 86 (1944):156–74.

MARÍA LUISA MENDOZA
(b. 1938)
Mexico

Magdalena Maiz and Luis H. Peña
Translated by Owen Williams

BIOGRAPHY

María Luisa Mendoza is a novelist, a journalist, a theater critic, and a lecturer. She has written news reports, editorials, articles, and commentaries, skillfully employs the sayings and proverbs of her people, and she has won several prizes for her writings. She has also been elected federal deputy for her state of Guanajuato. Her eagerness to know her people, and to know humanity in all its manifestations, led her to become a journalist and a writer. Widely known and controversial, she dares to speak openly and to write passionately about those subjects which others hush or disguise.

María Luisa Mendoza was born on May 17, 1938, in Guanajuato, "the city of mirrors and evenings," in a house with a balcony that overlooks the Unión gardens and the Juárez Theater. She grew up in the bosom of a traditionally rigid, Catholic, middle-class family where she absorbed the correctness, good manners, and quietness of her mother, María Luisa Romero Ceballos, and the liberal politics of her father, the lawyer Manuel Mendoza Albarrán.

Mendoza was born in a time of historical conflict between two movements: the postrevolutionary movement that longed for the reactionary and dismal restrictions of the past; and the progressive, accusatory, and aggressive movement that demanded fulfillment of the promises of the Mexican Revolution. Mendoza, sickly in childhood, was bedridden for prolonged periods of time. During these periods she read everything that fell into her hands. She then began to experiment with writing and drawing. Having inherited provincial notions of propriety—which intimidated and restricted women—she began to be aware of a sensitivity toward "what people will say" and to develop her own ideas about the notions of honor, modesty, and dignity. She began to react to the gossiping and mean-spiritedness that permeated her provincial universe and that would later be inscribed in her newspaper columns, commentaries, essays, and novels.

During her childhood, Mendoza alternated between Guanajuato and Celaya, where she lived in a house with a façade considered to be an architectural jewel built by the architect Tresguerras. During this period, she attended private schools. Later, as an adolescent, she moved to Mexico City, which at the time was only beginning to awaken to a dizzy and unrestrained modernity. She finished her elementary schooling at the Colegio Francés (de San Cosme) and in the Colegio Anglo Español. During the 1950s she pursued studies in interior design at the Universidad Femenina de México, studied stage design at the Instituto Nacional de Bellas Artes, and Spanish literature at the Universidad Nacional Autónoma de México. When her father died, she found herself without resources and suffered financial difficulties. She found employment in the Department of National Resources, but later she was encouraged to attempt a career in journalism.

Her journalistic career began in 1954 when she began to write for the newspaper, *El Zócalo*, a tabloid with an avid readership. Later she worked for other newspapers such as the *Cine Mundial*, where, for a miserable salary, she did everything from writing headlines to reporting, from doing interviews to writing editorials and crossword puzzles. Although she had begun as most women journalists had, by writing social columns, her tireless search for challenges took her into the field of interviews and drama criticism, to redefine journalistic forms, to create new formats for television, and to the founding of feminist magazines. Mendoza became more daring, more inquisitive, and more accusatory in her writing, and she succeeded to such an extent that she became part of the staffs of such prestigious national newspapers as the *Excélsior, Novedades,* and *El Universal,* and wrote editorials for *El Sol de México.*

Mendoza's experience with *El Sol de México* was her trial by fire, her ritual of initiation. By 1960 she had already co-founded the newspaper *El Día* and was assistant director of the cultural supplement "El Gallo Ilustrado" (The enlightened rooster) and director of the weekly "Fin de Semana" (Weekend) of the same newspaper. She collaborated with *El Día* for ten years and wrote the column that made her famous, "La O por lo redondo" (All around the O), which was published as a book in 1981. A tireless defender of women, "La China" Mendoza contributed to the birth of feminist magazines such as *Mujeres* and *La Mujer de Hoy.*

In addition to these many accomplishments, Mendoza has revealed a capacity for dramatic criticism and a broad knowledge of literature and drama, publishing numerous essays of literary criticism. In addition, her perseverance (after several attempts) culminated in a scholarship from the Centro Mexicano de Escritores in 1968–1969. The scholarship allowed her to devote herself to her writing and resulted in the publication of her novel *Con él, conmigo, con nosotros tres* (1971; In him, in me, in all three of us). Its first edition was sold out in three months, and it won the Magda Donato Prize for the best novel of the year. The novel is a monologue describing the brutal events of the massacre of Tlatelolco on October 2, 1968, and manifesting the painful and bloody burden of an inherited national and personal family history. Belonging to a hybrid literary genre, the novel is a confession/shriek/accusation/lamentation.

In her next project, Mendoza blended the plastic and the literary by collaborating with the painter Carmen Parra to produce a *Libro-Objeto* (1972; Book-object), and she worked with Edmundo Domínguez Aragonés in the making of a chronicle entitled *Dos palabras dos* (Two words two). She published her popular and beloved novel *De Ausencia* (The life of Ausencia Bautista Lumbre) in 1974. This novel is rooted in her childhood and adolescence in Guanajuato. It is a remembrance, an exercise in imagination, and a fantasy of passion, all conveyed through the discourse of a feminine character who feels strongly love, loneliness, life, and the insanity of an immense and perverse appetite for sexual pleasure. After this daring, irreverent, highly erotic, and experimental novel, which may shock the puritanical and certainly challenges the small-minded reader, Mendoza followed with *Las Cosas* (1976; Not just things). This book collects a series of newspaper articles which she began to write in 1954 and which she reworked into a pamphlet format. In them she lovingly recaptures her childhood, life as it was years ago in her home province of Guanajuato, and the details of daily living.

By 1970 Mendoza's versatility was leading her to write prologues for a variety of texts dealing with the indigenous population of Mexico, the media, the Chilean cause, and with "La Pasionaria" (Dolores Ibarruri, the Spanish Communist). Mendoza demanded and gained the right to express herself freely. She brought together her articles and commentaries on political and cultural subjects, publishing them as *Crónica de Chile* (1972; The chronicle of Chile), *Allende el bravo; los días mexicanos* (1973; Allende the courageous: Mexican days), *¡Oiga Usted!* (1973; Listen!), and *Rusia* (1970; Russia). In 1972 she won the Bernal Díaz del Castillo National Journalism Prize for her *Crónica de Chile*. After resigning from *El Día*, she began her work for *El Universal* writing her column "La A por la mañana" (The A in the morning). From 1972 to 1974 she was a commentator on three television shows: the newscast "24 horas" with her segment "¿O sí o no?" (Is it yes or no?); "La Hora 25" with "Entre ceja y ceja" (Between eyebrows), and her own program, "TV Debate." She also worked as a political commentator on radio stations and wrote the column "La O de Dando y Dando" (The O of picking on) for *El Sol de México*, starting in 1976. This active writer traveled constantly as a special journalistic envoy around the world, covering everything from a World's Fair to an interview with Fidel Castro.

Mendoza received further rewards and greater recognition for her article "Notas sobre las notabilísimas notables mujeres" (Notes on very noteworthy notable women), her reports from the Soviet Union, her analyses of Mexican soap operas, and her newspaper essay, "Para hacer notar la notable nota de las nuevas novísimas contemporáneas mexicanas" (1975; To bring to your attention the notable qualities of the brand new contemporary Mexican women). Her profound concern for women, their condition as second-rate citizens, and their enforced silence, moved her to rescue one of them from being forgotten by writing *Tris de sol, Carmen Serdán* (1976; A bit of sun, Carmen Serdán), the biography of a daring woman from a country town. Serdán was a revolutionary who fiercely opposed Porfirio Díaz' political party at the beginning of the century. This biographical essay won for Mendoza the recognition of El Club Primera Plana of professional journalists. From the personal and intimate depths of a feminine voice, sensitive to significant details, Mendoza re-created her province once again by publishing *Teatro Juárez, 75° aniversario* (1978; The Juárez Theater, 75th anniversary), and *Retrato de mi gentedad* (1979; A portrait of my people).

Since 1980, Mendoza has been director of the program "Un Día un escritor" (A writer a day), renamed "Un día un mexicano" (A Mexican a day), in 1987, in which she interviews Mexican writers and intellectuals. From 1981 to the present (1988), she has also kept up her journalistic work through her column, "Trompo a la Uña" (A top on the fingernail), in the newspaper *Excélsior* (Mexico City). Her never-ending restlessness as a writer and storyteller has driven her to write her third novel, *El perro de la escribana o las Piedecasas* (1982; The scribe's dog). This novel is an exercise in confrontation and a self-portrait showing her memory of the stress and struggle of her feminine experience. *El perro de la escribana* challenges literary canons at the same time that it consummates Mendoza's love for language and for feminine sensitivity.

Next, Mendoza became a professor of Mexican literature at the Instituto Politécnico Nacional, received the Golden Medallion "Magdalena Mondragón" bestowed on her by the Asociación de Periodistas Universitarias, A.C. (Association of Women University Journalists), and was awarded the prestigious Premio Nacional de Periodismo e Información in 1984 for her outstanding work over a thirty-year period.

More recently, Mendoza has been made a member of the Academia de Artes y Ciencias Cinematográficas (Academy of Cinematographic Arts and Sciences), a member of the boards of the Asociación de Escritores (Writer's Association) and of PEN Club International, and general secretary of the Asociación Internacional de Escritoras (International Association of Women Writers). As a federal deputy for the Ninth District of Guanajuato, beginning on September 1, 1985, Mendoza has been part of the Interparliamentary Committee of the 53rd Legislature, president of the Committee on Radio, Television, and Cinematography, president of the Editorial Committee, and of the Committees for Libraries, coordinator of the Program for the Advancement of Popular Culture, member of the Committee for Cultural Matters and the Committee for Women's Concerns, to name just a few of her activities.

Her love of children inspired *El día del mar: cuento para niños* (1985; The Sea's Day: A Children's Story). Toward the end of that same year she published the series of short stories entitled *Ojos de papel volando* (1985; Blue flying paper eyes). "La China" Mendoza is a woman who fights falsehood, who struggles against the loss of freedom, against discrimination, against the oppression of women, against illiteracy, against the arms race. Through her writing she has become a fighter for freedom of expression and for freedom of thought.

MAJOR THEMES

In "La China" Mendoza's works, an evidently autobiographical voice and a humorous frame of mind relate joyfully the rites of femininity, its passions and intimacies, its shyness and eroticism. Mendoza explores and describes a hidden feminine universe. She evokes fears, nostalgia, and fantasy; she details the domestic scene and the universe of objects and of generic beliefs and myths. She displays the ordinariness of beings once thought sacred; she confronts ceremonies and dismantles the domestic scene by means of the feminine observation of her characters Delfina Zebadúa, Ausencia Bautista, and Leona Piedecasas. Her language, embracing intimacy, love, hatred, loneliness, melancholy, and sensual pleasure, is woven from an open-ended dialogue between life and death.

Mendoza's works continuously revert to previous times, to her ancestors, to her incomplete genealogies. She violates her own inhibitions to glimpse her provincial childhood, changeable yet static, and a zone of fears, desires, and deceptive appearances. Her impassioned writing searches for the boundaries between that which is remembered and that which is only dreamed, between that which is only imagined and that which is experienced, in order to fuse them into a whole. In order to accomplish this, she employs a feminine sensitivity that takes possession of language and makes it uniquely her own.

Critics have rightly called her "The Empress of Vocabulary," and now that Salvador Novo is gone, she is the only Mexican writer with a reputation for inventing *novocablos*, or neologisms in the style of Novo. Her unique syntax is characterized by a sensual and visceral accumulation, a luxurious use of adjectives in series, and her paragraphs read like litanies. Her feminist writing imitates speech, and her written word becomes sonorous, a symphony of signs composed to the rhythms of a heterogeneous syntax, a meeting place for the popular proverb and the educated conceit, for daring imagery and polite phrasing.

This style begins to make itself known in her first novel *Con él, conmigo, con nosotros tres* (1971), a singular hybrid discourse in which the intimate voice of Delfina Zebadúa Latino, who lives in the Chihuahua Building facing the Plaza of Three Cultures in Tlatelolco, records her suffering behind the suffocating walls of her daily routine, besieged by the discordant echoes of a sinister, bloody night the second of October of 1968. The massacre of student protesters in the Plaza of Three Cultures on that day made evident the demise of the Mexican political system and the inheritance of a failing and aging Revolution.

In the novel, the feminine voice describes physical, personal, social, family, and cultural spaces, making of its statement a topography of existence. Its sextet of chapters are entitled "First War," "Second War," "Third War," "First Culture," "Second Culture," and "Third Culture." Out of Delfina Zebadúa's memory, and an uneven linking of disconnected images, the narrator Delfina articulates a Dantesque vision of the brevity of the moment; she synthesizes the sorrow of death, of abandonment, and of orphanhood which has converged into the "endless dying" that has forced her to be a witness to the Tlatelolco Massacre. Her lucid and agonizing awareness elicits memories of the eroded existence of a family of ancient landowners of Guanajuato who have lost everything through resentment caused by love affairs, unsatisfied sexual anxieties, anger, and loneliness. The record of the Zebadúa Albarrán family goes back to the Wars of Reformation of the nineteenth century and up to the last day in the life of Juan Ruvalcaba Zebadúa, Delfina's cousin, who died in the Plaza of Three Cultures.

Nighttime in Tlatelolco becomes an allegory for the rise and fall of the lineage of the Zebadúa Albarrán in Delfina Zebadúa Latino's interior monologue. Her childish and adolescent memories, permeated with innocence, with sexuality, and with an underground religious tradition, reveal the conventions nourishing provincial traditions, family life, attitudes, and promises for the future. An anguished present, a night of death, of blood and of nightmares, and a past summoned by a gallery of family portraits lend meaning to past and present Mexican history, bring events into relationship with one another, and establish connections within a ceremony of collective sacrifice to the god of power.

The novel's description transcends the limits of a private experience, although it is brought forth by a single female narrator, because she opens all her senses and consciousness to the crime she witnessed in Tlatelolco. Her monologue dissolves the boundaries of a feminine "I" and opens it up to a collective consciousness of "We." Mendoza's novel pleads for the advent of an absent god who seems to have abandoned his children in the midst of that dark night in the Plaza.

Mendoza's next novel, *De Ausencia* (1974), continues her complex effort to appropriate the self. Based on the chronicles of the priest, Marmolejo, *Efémerides Guanajuatenses* (Guanajuato Chronicles), the anecdote is a tale from the last century. It tells the story of Ana Camiña, the daughter of a miner who falls head over heels in love with a millionaire named Mr. Thomas Heller, but later becomes the disillusioned lover of the miner Narciso Muñoz. This novel's protagonist is Ausencia Bautista Lumbre, whose name literally could mean "Horny Absent Baptized." The protagonist is the victim of, and is victimized by love and sexuality. She discovers sex in her adolescence and continually surrenders herself to sexual passion as a celebration. Ausencia acts out and enjoys an erotic passion which the novel, far from disguising, expresses in a pleasingly deliberate manner. Ausencia is a nineteenth-century free woman who consecrates her body and soul to the immediate fulfillment of desire, to the appetites of the moment, and to the delirious surrender to a boundless obsession. She progresses from poverty to the upper middle class, and seduces and bewitches the reader as well as the series of characters who succeed each other in her bed.

Apparently a Romantic novel, *De Ausencia* is divided into seven modern chapters: "Primer Espejo" (First mirror), " Segundo Reverbero" (Second reflection), "Tercer Azogue" (Third quicksilver), "Cuarto Tremol" (Fourth frame of the mirror), "Quinto Foco" (Fifth focus), "Sexto Reflector" (Sixth reflector), and "Séptimo Lago" (Seventh Lake). The first lines of the novel tell how Reynaldo Olavarrieta and Ausencia Bautista give themselves up to their passion in a Zeppelin as it is taking off from Rome. From the mixture of realism and parody, of irony and picaresque narration in the novel, Ausencia Bautista emerges as a Lolita or a Fanny Hill—one of those women who, suffocated by social conventions, allow their desires to show, who express their hunger for love, and who share their loneliness with others.

At the end of a long carnal and loving relationship with Daher Hassid Haller, a fortyish North American of Middle Eastern descent, Ausencia seeks comfort in the company of the good-looking young provincial miner, Macedonio Llamas, with whom she conspires to assassinate her former lover. The *corpus delicti* is never found, but the miner is brought to trial and convicted without confessing or revealing Ausencia's participation. Remorseful, Ausencia travels, observes, and takes part in the splendors of the Belle Epoque in an unconcerned and frivolous Europe. For her crime, destiny (or the devil) rewards her with satiety. Her life is full of amorous adventures in which she takes pleasure without having to search for it. She is rich and beautiful and ageless, being courted at eighty years of age by men who could easily be the grandsons of her first lovers. She flies in a Zeppelin, inaugurates a railroad, voyages in the transatlantic liner *Gigantic* (a vaguely disguised *Titanic*) in an effort to forget, but the memory of her crime of passion invades her dreams and haunts her even at the moment of her tragic death.

A mixture of sensuality, irony, irreverence, and humor, the heroine's adventures are amusing and crazy, but there is an authenticity to her being. In spite of her worldliness and liberated behavior, Ausencia is never able to put behind her the atavistic notions of her provincial upbringing or her sense of guilt for the sadistic murder of her first lover. *De Ausencia* nostalgically denounces the provincial universe and acidly demystifies resignation, prayer, honor, modesty, chastity, and forced fidelity, especially that which is jealously guarded by gossip in a moral world. Mendoza's protagonist contrasts with the prototypical selfsacrificing, chaste, conformist, and traditional feminine character because she is a rebel who is nonconformist in the face of moral and conventional bonds, a type of woman rarely found in modern Mexican literature.

In other works, Mendoza is a chronicler of daily routine and sings to the simple things of life, to the things that we use, to that which surrounds us in everyday living. In *Las cosas* (1976) her ingenious and provocative prose, free and agile, converts ordinary places into original and unique places; she makes us see things with a new vision; she makes the reader feel, smell, and see anew in order to "defamiliarize" things. Having their origin in her newpaper series called "Las Cosas" (1954), these fifty-two literary vignettes are affectionate reminiscences written in a happy and playful manner. They are illustrated with collage-drawings linked by words and inspired by catalogues, weeklies, and nineteenth-century vignettes which European and American department stores used to send to their customers between 1895 and 1927. Here a fresh feminine eye reviews the domestic and social topography of the objects of everyday life: mirrors, cushions, pianos, skillets, and even intangibles, such as swooning or fainting, friendships, envy, forgetfulness, discrimination, and dreams. In the mini-chronicles, Mendoza speaks familiarly and jokes with readers in a sparkling, ingenious, and irreverent voice, drawing them into a close and intimate complicity with the narrator. She Mexicanizes her themes, laughs at consumerism, and denounces the discrimination, oppression, and alienation that objects can produce when they determine the propriety of conduct.

El perro de la escribana (1982), Mendoza's quasi-biographical novel, is a mature work organized in ten sections, each corresponding to a different stage of Leona Piedecasas's life. Leona is the center of the associations and the source of the monologue. Leona's feminine outlook gives meaning to various dwellings in the landscape of her memories. Each of her houses has a different landscape. The objects, utensils, and accessories, together with their owners, symbolize segments of time gone by. Her voice imbues the inhabitants of her world with meaning, and, in turn, these dwellings and inhabitants give her a voice, a point of view, and a significance. Siblings, cousins, real and imagined ancestors, people and homes, become for Piedecasas mysterious symbols of the time periods she is contemplating in her memory.

Leona's memories of her infancy in the faraway house of her ancestors appear in "Primera residencia" (First residence). She evokes the arrival of puberty by means of a terrace, a door with its four leaves, and the furniture in the hallway. "Segunda mansión" (The second mansion) is her memory of her aunt's house in Celaya, its gloomy corridors and silent birds. Within a provincial landscape, her cousins begin to marry, the family expands, and she begins to realize that her female cousins are entering the business of being married women, while her male cousins are entering hopelessness.

In "Tercera morada" (The third dwelling), the houses lose their visual excitement for the narrator, they "contract" under their low roofs, and windows and balconies become fewer. Father and grandfather figures appear while Leona observes her siblings from a greater distance than before. In "Cuarto hogar" (The fourth home), she is transported in her memory to the home of her cousins Pupe and Venevene, while her awareness is flooded by domestic ceremonies birthdays, teas, and evening snacks. "Quinta vivienda" (The fifth house) depicts her childhood confronted by the city, the urban atmosphere, its opacity and its noises, with leaden dawns, and dreams silenced by the hunger that forces one to work. In "Sexto domicilio" (The sixth domicile), the house of her memory becomes smaller as the city grows. In "Séptima estancia" (The seventh sojourn), secret games, the promise of youth, and the whisperings of desire are described as an urban dwelling of rooms and roof terraces in the midst of snatches of light and of memories.

"Octava habitación" (The eighth habitation) is the space that nourishes love and its rituals. It is Leona and her family experiences, and her destiny with them. In "Novena casa" (The ninth house), she faces herself—the cloth of memory at last interweaves with the façade, the chronology of cement and granite of the family home—in order to confront the hunger of being, to face the embrace of emptiness. She discovers that after all is said and done, "Dentro de mí me guardo" (p. 117, I keep myself within myself). The last section, "Décima nada" (The tenth nothing), synthesizes the family past and present from 1694 to 1981. In *El perro de la escribana*, the feminine protagonist discovers herself through a questioning reconstruction of her own and her family's past, through remembering and interpreting memory's meanings. A solitary inhabitant of a world, that is, of a system of personal, family, and social places, the narrator, now in her old age, confronts and unmasks her "places." Her discourse is neither a confession nor a testimony, but a lonely critical monologue of evocation, a merciless settling of accounts between her nostalgia and her present self.

In Mendoza's last published work, *Ojos de papel volando* (1985), nine short stories contain the themes of love and indifference and articulate passionately the feminine experience, interlaced with the words of Sor Juana Inés de la Cruz.* Here Mendoza's colorful, finely tuned, and polished language is permeated by symbols. It represents tradition, identity, and feminine consciousness through a parade of feminine protagonists who lay siege to and question the meaning of personal and family relationships, of passionate, sensual, fraternal, conjugal, and loving relationships.

SURVEY OF CRITICISM

The work of "La China" Mendoza has been accepted warmly by critics of the most varied points of view and of the most differing critical methodologies imaginable. Her literary output requires its own method of reflection and of analysis; perhaps for this reason most critics have limited themselves to dealing with individual works. Certainly, the lack of monographic studies attempting to comprehend her work in a general and thorough manner points out that there is still much criticism to be written about her works.

"La China" Mendoza has had an impact on the Mexican intellectual media from the beginnings of her career as a journalist. She made a way and a name for herself within literary criticism even before her first novel, *Con él, conmigo, con nosotros tres*, was published in 1971. There has been much commentary on her literary work, especially in Mexico, from a great many different points of view: the linguistic, the sociological, the impressionistic, the biographical, the feminist, the cultural, the deconstructivist, in prestigious newspapers in well-known cultural and literary supplements, in university magazines, and in feminist publications. Established writers and well-known Mexican intellectuals, such as Rosario Castellanos,* Emmanuel Carballo, Ricardo Garibay, Juan García Ponce, Sergio Magaña, Elena Poniatowska,* Miguel Donoso Pareja, Gerardo de la Torre, Edmundo Domínguez Aragonés, Miguel Guardia, Rafael Solana, Paco

Ignacio Taibo, and Rubén Salazar Mallén, among others, have written about her, revealing the originality of her use of language as an instrument and as a passion, praising her as an outstanding Mexican and Latin American woman writer. They have examined her sensualism and eroticism, her furious political denunciation of the events of 1968, her obsessive need to describe the feminine experience, and her daring willingness to transgress the canons, myths, and taboos of Mexican literature.

Upon the publication of her first novel *Con él, conmigo, con nosotros tres* (1971), a representative group of Mexican intellectuals embraced with extraordinary enthusiasm her discourse and her ideological position in the face of an event that shook all Mexico. They accepted the author who had witnessed this catastrophic event from her apartment in Tlatelolco and who lived through the sea of blood, grenades, and bullets. The feminist novelist and poet Rosario Castellanos insists that Mendoza symbolizes one of the most important changes in perception and behavior that has taken place in many years because she has acquired "la perspectiva de una nación en cuyo pulso late la historia toda de la humanidad" (the perspective of a nation in whose heartbeat pulses the history of all humanity, *Mujer que sabe latín*, p. 169).

The best evidence of the positive reception and recognition that her work has received is the multitude of articles published in renowned literary supplements and newspapers. *De Ausencia* (1974) burst scandalously upon the Mexican literary scene and was praised for its daring depiction of eroticism, sensuality, and amorous scenes. Her work elicited enthusiastic commentaries about the profane and sexual setting, its elaborate style, and the creation of a feminine character the like of which had never existed before in Mexican literature. *De Ausencia* is an erotic novel which, as David W. Foster accurately points out, places "La China" on a level with authors such as Severo Sarduy, Luis Rafael Sánchez, José Donoso, Manuel Puig, Enrique Medina, Marta Lynch,* Reina Roffé, Silvina Ocampo,* and Luisa Valenzuela,* among others, who defy the taboos and restrictions of Latin American society (1985, pp. 657–58). The criticism accorded to *Las cosas* (1976) highlights Mendoza's combination of labor in cultural newspapers and literary journalism. Her humor, her ironic and nostalgic tone, her love for detail, for recapturing feelings and attitudes, and her ability to write simply with irony and wit attract a wide readership.

Criticism in the United States has centered on the work Mendoza has produced since 1977. This criticism also attributes individuality and originality to her work and judges her to be one of the most daring of Mexican novelists who has "reestablished the poetic dimension to the Mexican novel and who has given an important place in novelistic practice to linguistic elaboration" (Tatum, 1977, p. 38). David W. Foster has recognized her break with formal and thematic conventionalities (1985, p. 659). Dolly and William Young have carried out a comparative analysis of Mendoza and Elena Poniatowska as writers who combine their literary and journalistic work (1983, pp. 72–73).

With the reception given to her novel *El perro de la escribana* (1982), Mendoza definitely became considered one of the most outstanding and experimental novelists within the panorama of Latin American literature. This, her third novel, is considered her most mature work, bringing together her obsessions and her demons, while *Ojos de papel volando* (1985) has been accepted as new territory in which Mendoza is searching for a new style. The many political obligations that Mendoza has assumed recently have aroused an anxious concern in the critics who are waiting for her to complete her *Trenza de seda* (Silk braid), that "great novel which I have already written in my head: three men and one woman, three distinct and different characters in the life of one woman who is aging: an intellectual, a politician, and a peasant" (Maiz and Peña, 1988).

BIBLIOGRAPHY

Works by María Luisa Mendoza

With Francisco Monterde, et al. *Tres conceptos de la crítica teatral*. Mexico City: Universidad Nacional Autónoma de México, 1962.
¿Qué pasa con el teatro en México? Mexico City: Editorial Novaro, 1967.
Con él, conmigo, con nosotros tres: crononovela. Mexico City: Joaquín Mortíz, 1971.
La O por lo redondo. Mexico City: Editorial Grijalbo, 1971.
Crónica de Chile. Mexico City: Editorial Diana, 1972.
With Edmundo Domínguez Aragonés. *Dos palabras dos: crónica de un informe*. Mexico City: Era, 1972.
With Carmen Parra. *Libro-Objeto*. Mexico City: n.p., 1972.
With Edmundo Domínguez Aragonés. *Allende el bravo; los días mexicanos*. Mexico City: Editorial Diana, 1973.
¡Oiga Usted! Mexico City: Samo, 1973.
De Ausencia. Mexico City: Joaquín Mortiz, 1974.
Rusia (URSS). Mexico City: Fondo de Cultura Económica, 1974.
Las cosas. Mexico City: Joaquín Mortiz, 1976.
Tris de sol, Carmen Serdán. Mexico City: Departamento Editorial, Secretaría de la Presidencia, 1976.
Teatro Juárez, 75° Aniversario. Guanajuato, Gto.: Centro de Publicaciones, Gobierno del Estado de Guanajuato, 1978.
Retrato de mi gentedad. Mexico City: Secretaría de Educación Pública, Instituto Nacional de Antropología e Historia, Centro Regional Guanajuato-Querétaro, 1979.
El perro de la escribana o las Piedecasas. Mexico City: Joaquín Mortiz, 1982.
El día del mar: cuento para niños. Mexico City: SEP-CIDCLI, 1985.
Ojos de papel volando. Mexico City: Joaquín Mortiz, 1985.

Works about María Luisa Mendoza

Alcaraz, José Antonio. *"Con él, Conmigo, Con Nosotros tres."* *El Heraldo de México*, Aug. 22, 1971, sec. El Heraldo Cultural, n.p.
Arana, M.D. "Notas de lectura: María Luisa Mendoza." *El Heraldo de México*, June 1, 1971, sec. El Heraldo Cultural, n.p.
Bearse, Grace M. "Entrevista con María Luisa Mendoza." *Hispania* 64. 3 (1981):459.

Carballo, Emmanuel. "Escritoras mexicanas del siglo XX." *El Día* [Mexico City], Nov. 1, 1979, sec. El Gallo Ilustrado, n.p.

Castellanos, Rosario. "María Luisa Mendoza: el lenguaje como instrumento." *Mujer que sabe latín.* Mexico City: SepSetentas, 1979. Pp. 165–70.

Coccioli, Carlo. "La mujer en la literatura y la mediocridad de los hombres." *Siempre* [Mexico City], 1118(1974):n.p.

"*Con El, Conmigo, Con nosotros tres.*" *Recent Books in Mexico; Bulletin of the Centro Mexicano de Escritores* 18, 4 (1971):n.p.

Cordero, Dolores. "¿Por qué me hice escritor?" *Revista de Revistas* (Mexico City) 25 (Nov. 22, 1972):n.p.

"*De Ausencia.*" *Recent Books in Mexico; Bulletin of the Centro Mexicano de Escritores* 21, 6 (1974):n.p.

Domínguez Aragonés, Edmundo. "La China Mendoza agarró y dijo . . ." *Revista de la Universidad de México* 26, 3 (1971):38–39.

Donoso Pareja, Miguel. "*De Ausencia.*" *El Día* (Mexico City), Jan. 2, 1975, sec. Cultura de Hoy, n.p.

Fernández, José de Jesús. "Dos Obras: Dos escritores: Masculino/Femenino." *El Universal* (Mexico City) June 23, 1971, sec. En la Cultura, n.p.

Foster, David W. "Espejismos eróticos: *De Ausencia* de María Luisa Mendoza." *Revista Iberoamericana* 51, 132–33 (1985):657–63.

Galindo, Carmen. "Inminencia misma de la sangre." *Siempre* (Mexico City), Apr. 23, 1971, sec. La Cultura en México, n.p.

García Ponce, Juan. "Las voces de Tlatelolco." *Siempre* (Mexico City), July 21, 1971, sec. La Cultura en México, n.p.

Garibay, Ricardo. "Cómo se pasa la vida." *Excélsior* (Mexico City), Dec. 17, 1972, sec. Diorama de la Cultura, n.p.

Haro, Blanca. "María Luisa Mendoza; novelista recién nacida escritora de ha mucho." *Kena; La Revista de la Mujer Mexicana* 7, 183 (1969):n.p.

———. "La Voz de las escritoras mexicanas: María Luisa Mendoza." *La Mujer de Hoy* (Mexico City) 8, 175 (1969): n.p.

Idalia, María. " 'Voy a cualquier lado, menos a la vejez' ." *Excelsior* (Mexico City) Apr. 14, 1971:1, 14–15, sec. B.

López G., Aralia. "De Ausencia." *Los Universitarios* 38–39 (1974):15.

López Narvaez, Froylán M. "M. L. Mendoza: hacia una topología moral." *Excélsior* (Mexico City), Apr. 18, 1971, Diorama de la Cultura, n.p.

Lozoya, Jorge Alberto. "María Luisa: mitad y mitad." *El Día* (Mexico City), Mar. 28, 1971, sec. El Gallo Ilustrado, n.p.

Magaña, Sergio. "Para circundar el cuadrado." *Excélsior* (Mexico City), Apr. 18, 1971, sec. Diorama de la Cultura, n.p.

Maiz, Magdalena. "La imposibilidad del olvido: crononovela Tlatelolca." *Periodismo y literatura.* Ed. J. Cruz Mendizábal. Indiana, Pa.: Department of Spanish and Classical Languages, Indiana University of Pennsylvania, 1986. Pp. 189–97.

———. "Tres escritoras: Garro, Castellanos, Mendoza." *Plural* 12, 142 (1983):62–65.

———, and Luís H. Peña. "Personal Interview." Jan. 1988.

Marín Martínez, Carlos. "*Con él, conmigo, con nosotros tres.*" *El Día* (Mexico City), Mar. 1971, sec. Gaceta El libro y la Vida:45.

Martí, Ellú. "*De Ausencia.*" *El Heraldo de México*, Dec. 1, 1974, sec. El Heraldo Cultural, n.p.

Martré, Gonzalo. "El 68 en la novela mexicana." *La Palabra y el Hombre* 53–54 (1985):17–22.

Mejía, Eduardo. "¡Qué cosas tiene la China!" *Novedades* (Mexico City) Nov. 7, 1976, sec. La Onda, n.p.

Mejía Prieto, Jorge. "¿Por qué escriben los mexicanos?" *El Heraldo en México*, Sept.15, 1977, sec. El Heraldo Cultural, n.p.

Mendoza, María Luisa. "¿Cómo escribí *De Ausencia?*" *El Correo del Libro,* Sept. 1, 13 (1979):n.p.

Miller, Beth, and Alfonso González, eds. "María Luisa Mendoza." *26 autoras del México actual*. Mexico City: Costa-Amic Editores, 1978. Pp. 254–68.

Moirón, Sara. "María Luisa Mendoza: La literatura como relación amorosa con el mundo." *Excélsior* (Mexico City) Nov. 17, 1974, sec. Diorama de la Cultura, n.p.

Moreno, Hortensia. "Escribir es Feminismo cuando escribe la China." *Ovaciones* (Mexico City) Jan. 16, 1977, n.p.

Peña, Luis H. "María Luisa Mendoza: espacio y escritura." *Plural* 12, 136 (1983):60–62.

Piazza, Guillermo. "Consecuencias del Insomnio." *Novedades* (Mexico City) Dec. 1, 1974, sec. La Onda, n.p.

Pitty, Dimas Lidio. "El lenguaje de la pasión." *El Día* (Mexico City) May 9, 1971, sec. El Gallo Ilustrado, n.p.

Poniatowska, Elena. "Las cosas de la China Mendoza y las 22 piezas de Héctor Azar." *Novedades* (Mexico City) Dec. 21, 1976.n.p.

———. "Por fin surge una escritora mexicana que se atreve a describir escenas amorosas: la China Mendoza." *Novedades* (Mexico City) Apr. 8, 1971, n.p.

Reyes Nevares, Beatriz. "Cosas de la China." *El Nacional* [Mexico City], Dec. 13, 1976, n.p.

———. "Una escritora auténtica: La China Mendoza." *Kena; La Revista de la Mujer Mexicana* 12, 271 (1974): n.p.

Robles, Martha. "María Luisa Mendoza." *La sombra fugitiva; Escritoras en la cultura nacional*. Mexico City: Universidad Nacional Autónoma de México, Instituto de Investigaciones Filológicas, Centro de Estudios Literarios, 1985. Pp. 324–41.

Ruvinskis, Miriam. "Ausencia, la de más ausencia, o la búsqueda sin cuento." *El Heraldo de México*, Jan. 1975, sec. El Heraldo Cultural, n.p.

———. "En busca del libro del año." *Excélsior* (Mexico City) Jan. 2, 1972, sec. Diorama de la Cultura, n.p.

Salazar Mallén, Rubén. "Letras, Más Tlatelolco." *Revista Mañana* (Mexico City) Apr. 10, 1971, n.p.

Sefchovich, Sara. "Mujeres y prosas: el origen de los temblores en México." *FEM* (Mexico City) 3, 10 (Jan.–Oct. 1979):24–30.

Taibo, Paco Ignacio. "La China: un Tianguis de Palabras." *El Universal* (Mexico City) Mar. 29, 1971:1, 4–5, sec. 1.

Tatum, Charles M. "María Luisa Mendoza, atrevida novelista mexicana." *Diálogos/México* 13, 75 (1977):35–37. Also in *Letras Femeninas* 3, 2 (1977):31–39.

———. Review of *De Ausencia. Chasqui* 5, 1 (1975):54–55.

Terán, Luis. "Una China Tlatelolca, periodista por excelencia . . . " *Mujer de Hoy* 222 (May 31, 1971): n.p.

Urrutia, Elena. "¿Qué escribe la mujer en México?" *FEM* (Mexico City) 3, 10 (Jan.–Oct. 1979):9–13.

Villaseñor, Raúl. "*Con él, conmigo, con nosotros tres.*" *Presente, Diario del Sureste* [Villahermosa, Tabasco], May 21, 1971, n.p.

Young, Dolly J., and William D. Young. "The New Journalism in Mexico: Two Women Writers." *Chasqui* 12, 2–3 (1983):72–80.

GABRIELA MISTRAL (1889–1957) Chile

Carmelo Virgillo

BIOGRAPHY

Perhaps as far back as 1913 Lucila Godoy Alcayaga chose for herself the pen name Gabriela Mistral (Guillén de Nicolau, *Desolación-Ternura-Tala-Lagar*, p. xiii) by which she became officially known with the publication of her first book, *Desolación* (Desolation) in 1922. It appears that she greatly admired two European writers who had exercised some influence on modernism: Italy's Gabriele D'Annunzio, whose exquisite prose and verse manifest his fascination with death, and France's Frédéric Mistral, author of the tragic rustic poem "Mireille" (1859) and founder of "Félibrige," a Provençal school dedicated to refining literary language. Born on April 7, 1889, in the small community of Vicuña, in the Elqui Valley of northern Chile, the woman whose works are a hymn to parental affection and family bonds was the product of a broken home.

It is ironic, in fact, that when she was barely three years old, her father, a rural schoolteacher and somewhat of a wandering *payador* or minstrel, abandoned the family, leaving young Lucila in the care of her mother and half-sister Emelina (Gazarian-Gautier, 1975, pp. 3–6). Her half-sister saw to most of Lucila's early studies, while her mother and paternal grandmother attended to her religious education, interspersing it with countless folktales that fired her imagination. Eventually, the shy, sensitive child who liked to spend hours walking in her garden and in the fields surrounding her village of Monte Grande pretending to be carrying on conversations with birds, animals, flowers, streams, and clouds, directed her attention to children and teaching.

Having begun her primary and secondary school career in very remote and primitive rural areas of Chile, Mistral was to practice her profession in some of the most prestigious institutions, rising in the end to national and international prominence. At home her reputation as an accomplished and progressive educator earned her a number of distinctions, among them the principalship of Santiago's renowned Colegio de Señoritas and the Teacher of the Nation Award (1925). In 1922 Mexico called on her to assist celebrated writer and then secretary of education, José Vasconcelos, in reorganizing the school system and in setting up rural libraries. Between 1931 and 1933 she was a visiting lecturer at Barnard College of Columbia, Vassar, Middlebury College, and the University of Puerto Rico. She was also the recipient of doctorates "Honoris Causa" from such distinguished institutions as the University of Florence, the University of California, Columbia University, the University of Puerto Rico, and from her country's own Universidad de Chile.

In assessing the spiritual, intellectual, and artistic growth of this remarkable woman, the first Latin American ever to be awarded the coveted Nobel Prize for Literature (1945) and an individual acclaimed the world over for her humanitarian campaigns, one ought to keep in mind a few important details. They are: her complex ethnic heritage, a number of painful vicissitudes, and her relentless pursuit of love, which she ended up giving freely and abundantly to others, mostly to children, having been herself denied the very thing she wanted the most: motherhood and a family of her own. Of rugged Basque stock on her mother's side, and of Indian and, most likely, Jewish, ancestry on her father's (Arce de Vásquez, 1964, p. 1), trained as a teacher in impoverished regions, Mistral showed from an early age a stubborn determination to embrace the cause of the poor, the weak, and the downtrodden.

As a teenage newspaper columnist writing for local presses, she developed a reputation as a free spirit with antiestablishment, leftist ideas that made her unpopular among her peers and a number of her teachers. Such leanings, although inspired by Christian humanism, were considered dangerous, however, by the bourgeois class and were to work against her as she pursued her education and then as she sought employment. During the years she resided in Mexico (1922–1924), she spearheaded, in the best tradition of an apostolic missionary, an ambitious campaign to bring education to distant and forgotten Indian communities. Believing social and political justice to be rooted in basic Christianity, she was appalled by what she saw as "indifference" to political oppression on the part of the Catholic Church (Taylor, 1975, pp. 109–26). A lay member of the Franciscan Order, she donated the proceeds of the sale of her books to the children of the Spanish Civil War victims.

By and large an admirer of the United States (Johnson, 1951), she nevertheless remained ardently opposed to American foreign policy in Latin America, viewing it as supportive of tyrants who looked after Yankee interests. Yet, rather than directly accusing the American people of willful wrong-doing, she preferred to place the blame on their ignorance of the ways and needs of her people. Thus, she used her various public posts and personal visits to the United States and other foreign countries to bring the rich heritage and plight of her part of the world to the attention of the uniformed. Mistral pursued this cause as her coun-

try's ambassador and, subsequently, as participant in the International Institute
of Intellectual Development, in Paris, and as delegate to the United Nations. In
all of these capacities and also as a lecturer, she propagated Spanish American
literature and culture, enriching her audiences' experience with her towering,
proud, and personable figure—which was quite an accomplishment for someone
who had every reason to grow up self-conscious and introverted as a result of
a less than happy adolescence.

At that time, aside from having been shunned by her peers and disliked by many
adults for her solitary disposition and progressive ideas, she was once again dealt
a most cruel blow: She was accused of robbing the very blind teacher she had
selflessly volunteered to assist. The cowardly theft, perpetrated by jealous classmates, resulted instead in her expulsion from school and in public disgrace (Arce
de Vásquez, 1964, p. 2). This incident severely tested her faith in God and humanity, causing her to turn for a time to Buddhism and the practice of Yoga (Caimano, 1969, p. 138). Her beliefs were further challenged when, barely twenty
years old and teaching in the town of La Cantera, she lost her first love, a very
sensitive, moody, young railroad employee named Romelio Ureta, to suicide. Although by this time the two had parted, the circumstances were particularly painful to Mistral who had not long before endured the stigma of being labeled a
"thief." Ureta's desperate act had in fact been triggered by accusations, in his
case well founded, that he embezzled company funds.

Later in life, suicide continued to deprive Mistral of loved ones: first her close
friends and confidants, German writer Stepan Zweig and his wife, and then Juan
Miguel Godoy, the nephew she had adopted as a son. Her second disappointment
in love occurred when, at age thirty-three, a young Chilean poet she had hoped
to wed—very probably her first and only true passion—suddenly left the simple,
unassuming country woman to marry a wealthy Santiago socialite (Arce de
Vásquez, 1964, pp. 4–5). Perhaps this episode, more than any other occurrence,
contributed to Mistral's resolve to devote the rest of her life to caring for a wider
family—the family of humanity. It was, to be sure, immediately after this sad
turn of events, circa 1920, that her odyssey commences. Her life became a series
of government assignments and unofficial visits that would take her to the re-
motest corners of Chile and then on to Mexico, Brazil—where she lived for six
long years—Argentina, Uruguay, Peru, Central America, the Caribbean, Great
Britain, Portugal, Italy, France, Switzerland, Germany, Denmark, Spain, and,
finally, the United States. Here she died, on January 10, 1957, in Hempstead
General Hospital, on Long Island, after a painful bout with cancer. At her side
was her young companion Doris Dana, with whom she had shared a house in
nearby Roslyn Bay during the previous three years.

Mistral's literary career dates back to 1905, when she first began working as
a columnist for a number of local Chilean papers, most notably *Penumbras, La
Voz de Elqui,* and *Reforma.* Here, in addition to some fine essays, she published
her first poems, the great majority written in the Modernist vein. In 1914, spurred
on by the approval of distinguished writers like Rubén Darío, with whom she

maintained an active correspondence, and encouraged also by the inclusion of her writings in national and foreign anthologies, Mistral entered the "Juegos Florales" (Floral Games) competition sponsored by Santiago's Sociedad de Artistas (Artist Society). She was to win the contest with "Sonetos de la muerte" (Sonnets of death), a composition inspired by Ureta's tragic death. Perhaps the single most important event in the shaping of her career however, occurred, in 1921, when Columbia University professor and critic Federico de Onís devoted an entire lecture to her. A year later, under the auspices of the prestigious Hispanic Institute of New York, he reaffirmed his confidence in the budding poet by publishing *Desolación*. This collection of poems, perhaps her best, was to be the first of a total of four books—a lyric output that includes *Ternura* (1924; Tenderness); *Tala* (1938; Felling), and *Lagar* (1954; Wine press)—published posthumously under one cover, as *Poesías completas* (1958; Complete poetry). In addition, she produced two volumes of prose, *Lecturas para mujeres* (1924; Readings for women) and *Recados: Contando a Chile* (1957; Messages: Telling about Chile), besides countless articles on a variety of topics, scattered throughout foreign and domestic newspapers and periodicals. Many of these have been collected and published posthumously, as were most of her extensive correspondence and *Poema de Chile* (1967; Poem of Chile), Mistral's final tribute to her homeland.

MAJOR THEMES

In all of Mistral's writings one can readily identify a number of themes that disclose the troubled human being, the consummate teacher, the devout Christian, the passionate crusader, and the innovative artist in her. Such themes develop along two basic stages, represented by her lyric output. *Desolación* and *Ternura* constitute the first one, uncharacteristically Romantic. The main preoccupations of this phase, the formative one, are the writer's intimate dilemma and the subsequent search for metaphysical solutions in a life of solitude and service to the less fortunate. *Tala* is a key work in the evolution of Mistral's craft. The very title points to her death and resurrection (Santandreu, p. 23), implicit in her resolve to "chop down" the cross she had built for herself in *Desolación*. The book coincides with the peak of the writer's existential crisis resulting from her exile, the loss of her mother, and her deep religious conflicts. Just as symbolic is the connotation of Mistral's last work, *Lagar*, marking the second and final stage of her artistic development, whose title signifies, in the squeezing of the wine grapes, the writer's ultimate purification (Peña, 1978, p. 13).

Central to the themes of all four books is love, which in turn generates a variety of ancillary motifs. In Mistral's case, this powerful, catalytic force is not the erotic kind that epitomizes the post-modernist feminine poetry of a Delmira Agustini,* an Alfonsina Storni,* or a Juana de Ibarbourou.* It is love in all its width and breadth: the love she feels for a particular man, for any underdog, humanity as a whole, nature, and God. Mistral's personal longings for love—most specifically, for male companionship and children—finds its highest artistic sublimation in her recurring motifs of solitude, glorification of the mother and teacher roles, grief, death, and, ultimately, mysticism.

The uniqueness in the structuring of these themes derives from certain modes of expression and techniques consonant with Mistral's character and personal experiences. One such form is the *recado* or message, which the author herself defines as a type of "poetic newsletter," rustic in tone, like her own spoken words, and addressed to an "ideal" reader under the guise of an often-specific individual (Mistral, "Notas." *Desolación-Ternura-Tala-Lagar*, p. 178). Typical is the "Recado a Victoria Ocampo" (Message to Victoria Ocampo), which Mistral utilizes to articulate her proverbial Pan-American solidarity, as she expresses her affection and gratitude to her friend and fellow-writer for having given so much of herself to her native Argentina and America (*Desolación-Ternura-Tala-Lagar*, pp. 173–74).

Another constant in Mistral's works is the "autobiographical" mode. Here one finds those compositions that show Mistral's consistent reliance on episodes from her troubled life as subjects for thematic treatment. Clear evidence of the deep mark left on her by personal tragedy lies in the numerous poems devoted to the memory of her mother, and her relatives and friends, including her nephew, who took their own lives. Frequently used to express her desolation is the *nocturno* (nocturne), a form that features many of her favorite motifs: nature, solitude, death, motherhood, patriotism, and religious fervor.

Exemplifying this form is "Madre mía" (Mother Dear) from *Lagar*, a tender tribute to the tiny and saintly woman who played a gigantic role in Mistral's life as well as in the lives of anyone she touched. In the composition one notices another of Mistral's recurring features: myth-making. To be sure, the poet's mother is endowed with the transcendence of a larger-than-life figure and is described as the embodiment of nature at its humblest and best—"light as a blade of grass, fragrant as a touch of mint" (Mansini González, 1985, Pp. 439–40). The poet pleads with her mother to materialize in the natural phenomena that make up the cosmos and reflect her being, and to come and rescue her from her loneliness, from the homesickness she feels for her beloved Chile. In another composition, "Nocturno de José Asunción," the suicide of the Colombian poet José Asunción Silva and, secondarily, that of fellow-lyricist Anthero de Quental, serve to transmute Mistral's personal grief into cause for greater, universal mourning: the loss of humanity's faith in Christ and His teachings.

The award-winning "Los sonetos de la muerte," and subsequent compositions like "Interrogaciones" (Questionings), "Volverlo a ver" (To see him again) and "La espera inútil" (The futile wait), conceived presumably to lament the crushing loss of her first love, are paradigmatic of Mistral's penchant for asserting her preeminent role as an artist (Bueno, 1970, p. 386). In the "Sonetos," Ureta's death provides a perfect vehicle for her pessimistic *Weltanschauung* and for manifesting her artistic credo. Mistral also uses this subject masterfully to weave motifs and techniques that were to emblematize nearly all her future works. The "sonetos" feature a poetic persona functioning as lover, mother, and redeemer, who intercedes with God on behalf of the dead young man. The young man, in turn, is made to symbolize all human beings who are tempted, then victimized, by an evil world. Physical love is portrayed as an elusive goal, achievable only in death. Death is now transformed into the desirable shelter where tranquility and rest can at last be attained. Through subtle metaphors, spiritual love, as manifested by the poet's Christian faith, is equated with poetry, which has the power to right all wrongs. Thus, the composition, by its very act of creativity, becomes a promise of redemption, with the artist taking on the role of one whose sacrifice will guarantee the forgiveness of all sins (Martínez-Torentino, 1983, pp. 223–30).

The transcendental nature of this complex role, which transforms the poet into a mediatory force between a confused, suffering humanity and a merciful God, is brought to the fore by virtue of another of Mistral's favorite modes, the "canción de cuna" or cradle song. "Meciendo" (Rocking) offers an ideal example of the masterful melding of Mistral's principal themes. The composition likens the motherly rocking of her child to the strong, vital, and divine impulse that moves the world. Powerful symbolic images of this sublime power are the sea lulling its countless waves, the night-winds restlessly moving the wheatfields to and fro, and, finally, God the Father—the Supreme Creator Himself—silently swaying His infinite domains.

If Mistral envisions teaching as an extension of the mother's creative and nurturing mission, and if the poet sees herself as the natural advocate of both mother and teacher, then her favorite mode in this respect is her *cuento* or story. She uses it in poetry as well as prose to impart her extraordinary knowledge and wisdom, thanks to her myth-making capacities. This can be seen in "La Madre Granada" (Mother Pomegranate). In this *cuento* in verse form, the picture of a pomegranate, supposedly cut in half and showing its scarlet "womb" on an antique and ornate French ceramic plate, becomes the source of a whole fairy tale. Through her tale Mistral translates into childlike, hence intelligible and memorable, terms the timeless beauty and inestimable worth of the creative act implicit in the woman-mother-artist role.

A prophetic iconoclast, Mistral left behind, in *Lecturas para mujeres* (Readings for women), undeniable evidence of her pioneering role in the movement for woman's liberation. In one of the essays, she maximizes her customary metaphorical language to encourage women to take stock of their true worth. To begin, she tells her female readers they should stop fearing men. After all, who gave birth to the male, if not the female? Who nursed him through to adulthood, as a mother-sheep would her flock? Who protected him from the ravishing wolves with her own life when he was but a small lamb? Since myth allows the writer to reconstruct an imperfect world on her own terms, "Cuenta mundo" (World-story), a section of *Ternura*, provides a good example of Mistral's mythification of womanhood. In the short title-poem, "La cuenta mundo" (The world-story teller), the reader learns that the compositions represent an explanation of what the world is all about, as told by an omniscient poetic voice charged with being a mother and a teacher. In effect, each poem is a bit of knowledge and wisdom which the childless poet feels compelled to pass down to the fruit of her creative imagination—the offspring she never had. One such *cuento*, intended to show that there is a strong, feminine impulse in every facet of creation, is "Fruta" (Fruit). The poem underscores woman's dualistic role, the one as elemental as nature itself, and the other as complex and divine as God. By paralleling the fruit of a tree with that of a woman's womb, the poetic voice spells out the traditional message: the priority of the female in the cosmic order, owing to her innate, preordained mission to generate, sustain, and enlighten (Virgillo, 1985, p. 139).

Paradoxically, this position intimates that preeminence presupposes loneliness, for mothers, like teachers, are destined to be forsaken by those they lovingly nurse and guide. Albeit tragic and Sisyphean, such a message is redemptive, and it is brought to bear with even greater force and directness in *Tala*, Mistral's third book of verse. Here the very title alludes to the sacrificial act and regenerative power of trees. Their fate demands that they be separated periodically from their branches and fruits to sustain humankind—an analogy that also calls to mind the lonely and painful act of artistic creation.

Similarly, Mistral saw herself separated from her own birthplace and Latin America by the urgency of her mission. She gives aesthetic form to her feelings through "The Wandering Jew" theme in the poem "Emigrada judía" (Emigrant Jew). Here she states her calling: having to leave the comfort and security of home to make herself available wherever needed. The subject of patriotism, human solidarity, and Christian fervor come together in the verses of "Caída de Europa" (The fall of Europe) where, in addition, familial love is contrasted with the fratricidal tragedy of Second World War Europe. The poetic voice, identified as that of a childless, motherless woman, invites her American brothers and sisters to join her in an evening prayer on behalf of the suffering Old World. Europe is mythified and becomes the needy "Ancient Mother" ("La vieja Madre"), with the New World referred to as "la Gea americana" (loosely translated, "the native American soil"), with which the poet likes to identify herself.

In the final analysis, children remain Mistral's favorite subject, since this theme allows the aging and weary expatriate to escape the present by re-creating the carefree and innocent world of her childhood. To give aesthetic form to her longings, the poet calls on the *ronda*, a popular, musical type of composition, of the kind sung by children in their games. In one such "round," appropriately entitled "Todo es ronda" (Everything is a round), the poet shows this form to be an expression of her joy of living, one of the rare exceptions to her blue moods. She uses it to sing the wonders of Creation, among its manifestations: the beauty of nature, the candor of children, the charm of little animals, the bountiful gifts of Mother Earth. But most of all, along with the "cradle song," Mistral uses the "round" to reconstruct and revitalize an American tradition, lost in time. Through the speech act, and the Baroque language of childhood, she hopes to recover her *mestizaje*—her hybrid native stock (Cuneo, 1985, pp. 19–36).

SURVEY OF CRITICISM

Commentary on Mistral dates back to the early twenties, following the appearance of her first poems in foreign presses. With the endorsement of Columbia University's Hispanic Institute, the publication of *Desolación* (1922), and a year later, with Pedro Prado's eulogistic prologue to the Chilean edition, critical activity around Mistral took a giant step forward. Soon world opinion began to hail the poet's first book as a veritable revelation, a fact attested to by the extensive number of critics and fellow-writers who lauded Mistral's verse. The impressive list included Federico de Onís, Isaac Goldberg and Arturo Torres-Rioseco, the pioneers of Latin American literary studies in the United States; Tristão de Athayde, generally considered the dean of modern Brazilian literary criticism; his Peruvian counterpart, Luis Alberto Sánchez; renowned Chilean authority Raúl Silva Castro; and internationally acclaimed writers and public figures, such as Mexico's José Vasconcelos and Cuba's Jorge Mañach. Theirs and other commentaries, produced in the 1920s and 1930s, found their way into some of the major publishing media of the day: Costa Rica's *Repertorio Americano*; Chile's own *Atenea, Ercilla*, and *Revista Chilena*; Havana's *Revista Cubana*; Mexico's *Revista de Revistas*; and in the United States, *Hispania, Revista Hispánica Moderna, The American Mercury*, and the *Kentucky Herald*.

However, most of what was originally written on Mistral, including Silva Castro's *Estudios sobre Gabriela Mistral* (1935), did more to stifle serious, objective research than promote it. In fact, praises lavished on the poet in these early studies were such that literary interpreters traditionally felt intimidated by the myth built around the writer and tended to approach her works with the reverence reserved to a sacred temple. Mistral's deserved Nobel Prize in 1945 only accentuated her magnitude, and this event, coupled with the dissemination of additional materials the writer herself had failed to publish, caused a veritable flurry of studies. As expected, most of them failed to break new grounds, safely focusing on the writer's life, her religious convictions, her devotion to her country and Latin America, and, consonant with the spirit of the post-Modernist movement, the "feminine" earmarks of her works. This is what one finds in Hernán Díaz Arrieta's (pseud. Alone) *Gabriela Mistral* (1946), perhaps the first comprehensive life-and-works type of study, and in the articles that appeared in the various *Homenajes*, or collections, commemorating the writer's death, in 1957. In the next two decades, a handful of monographic works appeared that utilized new approaches and explored additional facets of her writings. Worthy of mention are Margot Arce de Vásquez's *Gabriela Mistral: persona y poesía* (1958; *Gabriela Mistral: The Poet and Her Work*, 1964), Cora Santandreu's *Aspectos del estilo en la poesía de Gabriela Mistral* (1958), and Sister Mary Preston's "A Study of Significant Variants in the Poetry of Gabriela Mistral" (1964).

Despite the difficulty of gaining access to unpublished materials, the decades of the sixties, seventies, and eighties have produced a worldwide resurgence of Mistral-based criticism. Among the book-length publications exploring new dimensions in Mistral's poetry and prose, one must single out Martin C. Taylor's *Sensibilidad religiosa de Gabriela Mistral* (1975), Roque Esteban Scarpa's *La desterrada en su patria* (1977), Luis Vargas Saavedra's *La prosa religiosa de Gabriela Mistral* (1978), Onilda A. Jiménez's *La crítica literaria en la obra de Gabriela Mistral* (1982), and *Gabriela Mistral* (1980), a collection of critical articles by a select team of international scholars (Humberto Díaz-Casanueva, et al.) Just as significant, but much more numerous and varied, have been notes, articles, and lengthy essays. This renewed critical activity should be attributed to two phenomena: first, the freeing of unpublished manuscripts, heretofore ever zealously guarded by Mistral's designated heirs; and, second, current trends demanding new critical approaches, with a marked emphasis on textual analysis. To date, there appears to be no indication that the trend will end soon, and one can at last look forward to the objective, intrinsic type of criticism Mistral's incomparable craft truly deserves.

BIBLIOGRAPHY

Works by Gabriela Mistral

Desolación. New York: Instituto de las Españas, 1922.

Ternura. Canciones de niños. Madrid: Saturnino Calleja, 1924.

Nubes blancas (poesías) y La oración de la maestra. Barcelona: Bauzá, Colección Apolo, 1925.

Tala. Buenos Aires: Sur, 1938.

Lagar. Santiago de Chile: Editorial del Pacífico, 1954.

Recados: Contando a Chile. Selection, prol. and notes by Alfonso M. Escudero, O.S.A. Santiago de Chile: Editorial del Pacífico, 1957.

Poesías completas. Ed. Margaret Bates. Prol. by Julia Saavedra Molina and Dulce María Loynaz. Biblioteca Premio Nobel. Madrid: Aguilar, 1958.

Cartas de Gabriela Mistral a Juan Ramón Jiménez. Prol. Julio Rodríguez Luis. Publicaciones de la Sala Zenobia-Juan Ramón de la Universidad de Puerto Rico. San Juan, P.R.: Torre, 1961.

Lagar. 2d ed. Santiago de Chile: Editorial del Pacífico, 1961.

Ternura. Colección Austral. 8th ed. Buenos Aires: Espasa Calpe, 1965.

Poema de Chile. Ed. and preface by Doris Dana. Barcelona: Pomaire, 1967.

Lecturas para mujeres. Ed. Palma Guillén de Nicolau. México, Secretaría de Educación, Colección "Sepan Cuantos." 4th ed. Mexico City: Porrúa, 1967.

Poesías completas. Prol. Esther de Cáceres. 4th ed. Madrid: Aguilar, 1968.

Desolación. Colección Austral. 4th ed. Buenos Aires: Espasa-Calpe, 1972.

Tala. Biblioteca Clásica Contemporánea. 5th ed. Buenos Aires: Losada, 1972.

Desolación-Ternura-Tala-Lagar. Introd. Palma Guillén de Nicolau. Colección "Sepan Cuantos." Mexico City: Porrúa, 1973.
Cartas de amor de Gabriela Mistral. Introd., ed. and notes by Sergio Fernández Larrain. Santiago de Chile: Andrés Bello, 1978.
Prosa religiosa de Gabriela Mistral. Introd. and notes by Luis Vargas Saavedra. Santiago de Chile: Editorial Andrés Bello, 1978.

Translations of Gabriela Mistral

Dana, Doris, trans. *Crickets and Frogs, A Fable.* Adapted by Doris Dana. New York: Atheneum, 1972.
———. *Selected Poems of Gabriela Mistral.* Ed. Doris Dana. Baltimore: Published for the Library of Congress by Johns Hopkins University Press, 1971.
Hughes, Langston, trans. *Selected Poems of Gabriela Mistral.* Bloomington: Indiana University Press, 1966 (© 1957).
Roger Martin du Gard. Gabriela Mistral. Boris Pasternak. New York: A. Gregory, 1971.

Works about Gabriela Mistral

Agosin, Marjorie. "Prosas inéditas de Gabriela Mistral." *Los Ensayistas: Boletín Informativo* (Athens, Ga.) 8–9 (1980):149–51.
Arce de Vásquez, Margot. *Gabriela Mistral: The Poet and Her Work.* Trans. Helene M. Anderson. New York: New York University Press, 1964.
———. *Gabriela Mistral: Persona y poesía.* San Juan: Ediciones Asomante, 1958.
Aubrun, Charles V. "Gabriela Mistral, Rubén Darío y la invención poética." *Quaderni Iberoamericani* (Torino, Italy) 42–44 (1973–74):142–46.
Bueno, Salvador. "Aproximaciones a Gabriela Mistral." *Cuadernos Hispanoamericanos* 242 (1970):377–92.
Caimano, Sister Rose Aquin, O. P. *Mysticism in Gabriela Mistral.* New York: Pageant, 1969.
Castelman, William J. *Beauty and the Mission of the Teacher: The Life of Gabriela Mistral of Chile: Teacher, Poetess, Friend of the Helpless, Nobel Prize Laureate.* Smithtown, N.Y.: Exposition, 1982.
Craig, Sister M. Barbara. "Examen de la teoría poética de Carlos Bousoño con una aplicación a la poesía de Gabriela Mistral." Ph.D. diss. Georgetown University, 1969. (DAI 30,4 [1969]:1545A.)
Cuneo, Ana María. "Hacia la determinación del arte poética de Gabriela Mistral." *Revista Chilena de Literatura* 26 (Nov. 1985):19–36.
Daydi Tolson, Santiago. "El yo lírico en *Poema de Chile* de Gabriela Mistral." *Revista Chilena de Literatura* 19 (Apr. 1982):5–20.
Díaz Arrieta, Hernán (Alone). *Gabriela Mistral.* Santiago de Chile: Editorial Nascimiento, 1946.
Díaz-Casanueva, Humberto, et al. *Gabriela Mistral.* Introd. Mirella Servodidio and Marcelo Codduo. Xalapa, Mexico: Centro de Investigaciones Lingüístico-Literarias, Instituto de Investigaciones Humanísticas, Universidad Veracruzana, 1980.
Earle, Peter. "Gabriela Mistral: los contextos críticos." *Gabriela Mistral.* By Díaz-Casanueva et al. Pp. 14–19.
Fraser, Howard M. "Gabriela Mistral's 'Sonnets to Ruth': The Consolation of Passion." *Studies in Twentieth Century Literature* (Lincoln, Nebr.) 3 (1978):5–21.
Gallardo, Andrés. "Planificación lingüística y ejemplaridad literaria: Gabriela Mistral y

la cultura del idioma." *Revista de Lingüística Teórica y Aplicada* 21 (1983):107–15.

Gazarian-Gautier, Marie-Lise. *Gabriela Mistral: The Teacher from the Valley of Elqui.* Chicago: Franciscan Herald Press, 1975.

Jiménez, Onilda Angélica. *La crítica literaria en la obra de Gabriela Mistral.* Miami, Fla.: Ediciones Universal, 1982.

Johnson, Harvey L. "Gabriela Mistral's Affiliation with the United States." *Los Ensayistas: Georgia Series on Hispanic Thought* (Mar. 1951):79–83.

Mandlove, Nancy B. "Gabriela Mistral: The Narrative Sonnet." *Revista/Review Interamericana* 12, 1 (Spring 1982):110–14.

Mansini-González, Shirley. "Mitología y cosmología en Gabriela Mistral y Pablo Neruda." *Discurso Literario: Revista de Temas Hispánicos* 2, 2 (1985):439–55.

Martínez, Torentino. "Alfonsina Storni y Gabriela Mistral: la poesía como condena o salvación." *Escritura: Revista de Teoría y Crítica Literaria* 8, 16 (July-Dec. 1983):223–30.

Peña, Cecilio. *Gabriela Mistral: poemas y estudio.* Montevideo: La Casa del Estudiante, 1978.

Preston, Sister Mary Charles Ann. "A Study of Significant Variants in the Poetry of Gabriela Mistral." Ph.D. diss. Catholic University, 1964. Also: Washington, D.C.: Catholic University Press, 1964.

Santandreu Russo, Cora. *Aspectos del estilo en la poesía de Gabriela Mistral.* Santiago de Chile: Ediciones de los Anales de la Universidad de Chile, 1958.

Scarpa, Roque Esteban. *La desterrada en su patria.* Santiago de Chile: Nascimiento, 1977.

Taylor, Martin C. "Parálisis y progreso en la crítica Mistraliana." *El ensayo y la crítica en Iberoamérica. Memoria del XIV Congreso Internacional de Literatura Iberoamericana* (1969). Eds. Kurt L. Levy and Keith Ellis. Toronto, Canada: Universidad de Toronto, 1970. Pp. 185–90.

———. *Sensibilidad religiosa de Gabriela Mistral.* Madrid: Gredos, 1975.

Silva Castro, Raúl. *Estudios sobre Gabriela Mistral.* Santiago de Chile: Editorial Zig-Zig, 1935.

Vargas Saavedra, Luis. Introd. *La prosa religiosa de Gabriela Mistral.* Santiago de Chile: Editorial Andrés Bello, 1978. Pp. 9–26.

Virgillo, Carmelo. "Woman as Metaphorical System: An Analysis of Gabriela Mistral's Poem 'Fruta'." *Woman as Myth and Metaphor in Latin American Literature.* Eds. Carmelo Virgillo and Naomi Lindstrom. Columbia: University of Missouri Press, 1985. Pp. 137–50.

NANCY MOREJÓN
(b. 1944)
Cuba

Yvonne Captain-Hidalgo

BIOGRAPHY

Nancy Morejón was born in 1944 in Havana. She has published ten volumes of poetry: *Mutismos* (1962; Silences), *Amor, ciudad atribuida* (1964; Love, attributed city), *Richard trajo su flauta* (1967; Richard brought his flute), *Parajes de una época* (1979; Parameters of an epoch), *Poemas* (1980; Poems), *Elogio de la danza* (1982; In praise of dance), *Octubre imprescindible* (1976; Essential October), *Cuaderno de Granada* (*Grenada Notebook*, 1984), *Where the Island Sleeps Like a Wing* (a bilingual anthology, 1985), and *Piedra pulida* (1986; Polished stone). Several anthologies carry a sampling of her poems. Her critical studies include: *Lengua de pájaro* (1971; Bird's tongue) which was written in conjunction with Carmen Gonce and focuses on a mining town in Cuba; *Recopilación de textos sobre Nicolás Guillén* (1974; Critical essays on Nicolás Guillén); and *Nación y mestizaje en Nicolás Guillén* (1980; Nation and racial mixture in Nicolás Guillén). She received a degree in French from the University of Havana and has translated several major Francophone writers from French into Spanish. Morejón has worked as an editor for both *La Gaceta de Cuba* (Cuban Journal, Havana) and UNEAC (National Union of Cuban Writers and Actors). Of her personal life, very little is known outside of Cuba.

MAJOR THEMES

Morejón was fifteen years old at the time of the Cuban Revolution and began publishing her poetry at the age of eighteen. The 1959 change in government serves as a pivotal point for the poet's references to Cuban society—past, present, and future. From the onset, her work acknowledges the significant change occurring in the island nation and holding such political and emotional sway over so much in the Western Hemisphere. The transformation in society was paralleled by changes in all Cuban intellectual and artistic pursuits.

Most of Morejón's poetry is part of a second generation of post-Revolution Cuban poets. Her literature, like that of her peers, treats the Revolution, if not directly, then inferentially. While the literary discourse of the first years following the change generally insisted on an immediate affirmation of the successful conquest of the Batista regime and what the overthrow represented, a few years later that affirmation would be less pronounced and would manifest itself in different ways. Indeed, Morejón's work refers to that moment in history but often elects to do so in a more subdued manner.

Even before the Revolution, there existed in Cuban literature a thematic emphasis on political change. In fact, the national poet of Cuba, Nicolás Guillén, had insisted on such a stance since the 1930s, practically since his first publications. However, the Revolution begins a separate literary period with a poetics of its own. Among the primary attributes of the creativity stemming from the Revolution is the desire to expand notions of cultural centrality—that is, who or what constitutes the norm in society. Thus, literature reconsiders groups that had been marginalized from historiography and general cultural appreciation.

Broadly speaking, as part of the young generation of writers beginning their literary endeavors after the Revolution, Morejón's work is an attempt to redefine Cuban culture and even Cuban history—at least its historiography. As such, her work, like that of many others, would incorporate the black into the mainstream of its literary world as never before. Also evident in her poetry is the centrality afforded women. Ethnicity, rebellion, and the increasing acknowledgment of woman's presence are the three thematic constants that inform her work and are manifested in a number of subthemes like the extended family, love, and the essence of poetry.

Morejón's poetry is truly representative of recent Cuban literature. Within the trend, however, it is possible, indeed necessary, to acknowledge Morejón's uniqueness as an artist. For her, art is not a submissive, derivative literature that emulates other writers or adheres to a prescribed format. Instead, there are specific poetic and cultural qualities that speak to the singularity of her talent.

Moreover, in order for Morejón to achieve the balance found in her largely tripartite focus of revolution, femaleness, and blackness in a poetic form, the writer practices certain tropes that have come to define her poetry as a whole. Understatement that often resides in irony, specific metaphors like birds in flight, and a heightened lyricism aid in determining the intensity of her speaker's thoughts.

In general, we find that emotions are understated rather than embellished with feeling. The speaker, often discernible as a black woman, projects a lyrical vision of self as well as of the world surrounding her. Furthermore, the very fact that Morejón is a Cuban woman of African descent places her within a particular framework that determines her perspective as different both from that of a man and from that of other ethnic groups. Despite, or perhaps in tandem with the Revolution's eagerness to portray a Cuban society now at peace with itself and devoid of any racial differentiation, the poet's ethnicity is one determinant in the development of her work.

Perhaps one key to the ethnic component in Morejón's poetry lies in her association with Nicolás Guillén. Indeed, we see in her work traces of the older poet's concerns: collectivity through the lyrical, blackness, resistance, and literary interests in subject matter beyond Cuba. However, Morejón is not a younger Guillén in female form. The development of her poetry belies such an idea. While many of the broad themes of ethnicity and rebellion are present in her work as they are in Guillén's, her delivery of those themes, her personal approach to poetics, is her own.

One of the primary characteristics of Guillén's verse is humor—humor that can be defined as somewhere between raucous laughter and scathing irony. On the other hand, such humor is largely absent from the younger Cuban. Irony is indeed a defining principle in her poetry, but her ideas are more likely to be expressed in the quiet tone of litotes. For example, in the poem "El sueño de la razón produce monstruos" (The dream of reason produces monsters), a type of *ars poetica*, Morejón's speaker expresses poetic essence through a series of dense, baroque images. Guillén, on the other hand, chooses more direct associations for his poems about the making of art. Such is the case with one of his own metapoetic works "Digo que yo no soy un hombre puro" (I declare myself an impure man).

In Morejón, as in Guillén, the theme of ethnicity extends from one ethnic group such as Afro-Cubans to the entire black race. Her poem "Freedom Now" (original title in English) exemplifies this point. It is a work that achieves its desired effect of contemplating the daily suffering of southern U.S. blacks largely through understatement and imagery of everyday objects and activities. Seemingly disparate images are drawn together and characterize, for the speaker, that region of the United States. Thus, objects of beauty like hairpins and nail polish combine with ice cream cones, Halloween, and schools to depict a society that is made more leisurely through its cheap black labor. Texas itself is a huge white prostitute as different from anything African as can be conceived.

These images of black suffering and white power and immorality are opposed to each other. Reference to monetary worth is not gratuitous here as the poem makes a specific point about commodity and market value. For the dominant white society, black men hold the same worth as roaches and are probably considered as unpleasantly abundant and as expendable. Through the poem's insistence on granting a qualifying adjective to objects, we understand that most animals are worth more than the black human being.

Associations of various images like those cited above become ultimately conjoined into one overall trope of the South as a paradise for whites and a hell for blacks. Perhaps if the poem remained at this level of condemnation, it would be too direct and even trite, for the theme of the lynched, exploited Southern

U.S. black has long existed in Spanish American letters, finding a sympathetic voice in Pablo Neruda and others. What aids in poeticizing the idea of the South as an intolerable place to live is the understatement with which it is conveyed. After all, the opinion is articulated in a reflective and hushed tone, and never as a loud proclamation. Furthermore, that restrained expression achieves litotes through its ironic handling of the theme. Black death and birth are contrasted with more mundane acts like the killing of cockroaches or the drinking of cow's milk. The "great little blond" that is Texas is not so great, nor is she little. Indeed, she is a physically huge and persistent beggar-whore. These are images far from those that Texas holds for itself.

It is a testament to the artist's ability that she is able to pronounce such scathing attacks on racism in the United States without the use of language that confronts the subject in a direct, volatile manner. There is undeniable anger felt in the lines of the poem, but it is achieved as much through the irony of unsuspected contrasts as through nonchalant observance of these contrasts. Morejón proves that one can be scathing and subtle at the same time. For example, "strange cities full of people / who lynch negroes and step on cockroaches," casually suggests the "casualness" with which one lynches blacks. The choice of the indeterminate pronoun "cualquier" in "cualquier vaca sureña exclamaría orgullosa" (any half-assed cow in Dixie would exclaim with pride) further provides the reader with the idea of a quiet, though real, contemplation of the phenomenon of racism. It is a quiet anger that achieves its lasting effect precisely because it does not violently shout its emotion. Emotion here is not equated with a physical "rage" but rather with a more contemplative "anger."

A second context from which we must read her poetry is largely from a female perspective—though not in a combatant opposition to any other group association. Despite its clear persistence in its otherness, the female identification does not necessarily contrast itself to maleness.

The poet's work has proceeded beyond the militant phase of writing and is paving the way for a new stage in the development of discourse by women, not only in Cuba, but in all of Latin America. While not an aggressively female discourse, her work is not obliquely so either, for there exists no denial of woman's importance in all aspects of society. Her poetry strikes a balance, then, and offers a speaker who is truly comfortable with her status as a woman.

One achieves this sense of the poetic figure's self-confidence through an analysis of her poems that include men as subject material. The male image in Morejón's poetry is largely either that of a figure to whom homage is paid or that of a lover to whom emotions are directed. For example, *Piedra pulida* (Polished stone), among other points of focus, unites several love poems. These verses range in subtheme from the joyous harmony of a couple to unrequited love, from the pursuit of a relationship to the rejection felt by the jilted party. The perspective is always that of a woman. Despite the breadth of subthemes, the tone is the same—that of a woman sure of herself. Even when there is lack of harmony such as in "Ardid" (Ruse), it is not the man's maleness that the speaker opposes, but rather her own strength that she affirms.

The poem that most attests to the female speaker as a self-assured being is her "Mujer negra" (Black woman), her signature poem. Although the work confronts the negative realities of slavery and degradation, there is a reigning sense of confidence as the speaker shows the black woman's self-empowerment throughout the ages. It is a work with strong historical overtones for its ability to limn all moments of the black woman's presence in Cuba, from sixteenth-century servitude to mid-twentieth-century revolution. In speaking collectively about black women, physical time is not stressed, as the poetic figure cannot recall the specific night she was taken from her land. What does achieve a lasting hold on her memories is nature's impression on her senses—the smell of the sea or the sight of a seagull in flight, for example. Therefore, even when Africa is no longer a concrete, physical memory, the speaker's resolve to be free is not shaken, partly because of the lingering sense of Africa that girds her attempts to achieve freedom.

Thus, it is possible to view how, from beginning to end, woman's desire for empowerment remains unchanged. Intermittent throughout the poem are images of decisive movement: "I rebelled," "I walked," "I rose up," "I worked on and on," "Here I built my world," "I left for the hills," and "I came down from the Sierra" are verses that are strategically interspersed throughout the poetic figure's recounting of her life since leaving Africa. Combined, the imagery becomes one of constant motion in which rebellion and perseverance, despite the savage history of oppression, define the speaker's attitude.

The poetic figure is ultimately triumphant in her pursuit of freedom because she is forever reacting to the circumstances in which she is placed. "I came down from the Sierra" is the line that emphasizes the end of the struggle, for during the Cuban Revolution the "sierra" was the refuge for those fighting against Batista. Much earlier, it also symbolized the rebellion of the Maroons who escaped from slavery in the past by hiding in the "sierra." Therefore, by descending from the hills, the woman marks the end of her struggle. She affirms: "Now I exist: only today do we own, do we create. / Nothing is foreign to us." In a stance that parallels Nicolás Guillén's speaker in "Tengo" (I have) the woman declares that the revolution that she helped bring about ends her suffering, at least as a black female. (Some critics, however, question the equal treatment of races in Cuban society, as well as the literary translations of these concerns. See, for example, the many works by Carlos Moore on the subject.)

The voice through which the poetic figure projects her bittersweet triumph is not a harsh, accusatory one. Her ruminations are not spoken to the perpetrator, but rather serve as a reflection for articulating her achievements despite severe obstacles. Her tone, then, is factual, and that nonchalant recounting contributes to a sense of a speaker comfortable enough with her historical importance so that there is no sense of urgency about her recounting.

Even in the eerie, ironic truth of "Amo a mi amo" (I love my master) where the speaker appears to experience self-denial, this abnegation is countered by the revelation toward the end of the poem in which the dialectic of love-hate is resolved in a vision of killing the master to the sound of instructive drums. Regardless of the slave bell that calls her back to work and forces her to set her imaginings aside, spiritually she is free.

Just as black people and all women serve as *topos* for the development of Morejón's poetry, so does revolution. Revolution in her works can refer specifically to the Cuban event or to changes in any society. The poems sometimes express what is often referred to as historical "fact" or at other moments speak of desired change as the poetic "I" would have it.

Her poem "Abril" (April) is specific to Cuba in that the victory of the 1959 change in government is its intertext. April serves as a metonymic marker for the two victories that occurred during that month, once the Revolution was firmly established. In April 1961 the Bay of Pigs invasion revealed Cuba's strength against a superpower. Almost two decades later, it is the same month that Fidel Castro lifted restrictions on emigration, prompting the Mariel boatlift that witnessed the exodus of thousands whom he considered to be undesirables.

Beyond the specific events mentioned above, the contemplative voice now views that cycle as an augur of adversity. The island is reflectively surveyed in vigilant serenity. She is pleased with what is before her. However, her pleasure never becomes complacency, for the poetic figure is mindful of likely intrusions into that peaceful world: "And if we fall once again/ our bones will rise up on the sand."

Similar caution is expressed in the poem "En el país de Vietnam" (In the country of Vietnam). The speaker invokes the collective spirit of Cuba and Vietnam in order to combat future threats to their security. Her call to arms and obvious assurance of eventual victory are expressed in hushed approval. Rarely does she articulate her observations through alarm.

In further reference to making a trope of revolution, the month of April in this poem is when leaves begin to stir in anticipation of adversity. The images of incited leaves extend to birds in flight. Bird imagery is present throughout "Abril" and "En el país de Vietnam," as it is throughout the whole of Morejón's work regarding revolution. Its association is largely that of a confident figure in motion, soaring to ever loftier heights. In "Abril," the bird image is also a reassuring one in that the island lying in wait of any possible attacks can sleep like a bird with its wings folded underneath it, ready to spring to attack whenever necessary—hence, the title of her 1985 bilingual collection of poetry.

The protective bird becomes even more specific in the poem " En el país de Vietnam." A seagull surveys the country as a fitting and peaceful replacement for the B–52 bombers that once flew over the country. By the time the speaker identifies herself, the reader already has the impression of a society firmly established in its revolution.

Although her work is adamantly referential in nature, it is not meant to carry the revolution in any direct sense. That is, literary reflection on socioeconomic change in itself does not alter the process of government. It desires to pay homage to the change. At most, her poetry attempts to provide a framework from which we, as readers, can consider a particular revolution or from which we can contemplate changes in the whole of society.

Since there exists a poetic attempt to ponder and even to redefine our perception of certain cultures, particularly the Cuban one in all aspects of its society, it can be argued that Cuban literature, of which Morejón's work is an integral part, as a whole comprises a national mythopoeia. In other words, the literature gives rise to a nucleus of myth-making activities that allow the works to portray a new society, especially within Cuba—one different in many respects from its past portrayal. Furthermore, the content of these works speaks to concerns of present-day Cuba and examines the past as part of a reinterpretation of it.

SURVEY OF CRITICISM

Although an accomplished poet, Morejón has yet to reach the point in her career that would allow her critics to judge definitive stages in her work. The bilingual publications of *Where the Island Sleeps Like a Wing* and *Grenada Notebook* aid in establishing a clearer sense of her trajectory. The texts also help to develop a broader readership for the poet's literature. To date, few studies have assessed the importance of these two works. Until recently, the criticism has mostly introduced her to a readership of Hispanists. The early critiques emphasized the relationship of her poetry to that of the artistic endeavors by other writers as a primary aspect of her work. While that particular focus on her work as representative and the generalizing nature of the articles continues, more is being written about the individual nature of Morejón's talent.

The criticism to date is instructive in its emphasis on the common bonds with other texts and with extratextual stances, while some studies bring attention to the female as an entity in her works. Stephanie Davis-Lett (1980) analyzes the depiction of women of African descent in Morejón's now celebrated "Mujer negra" as well as in two other writers. The critic's "The Image of the Black Woman as a Revolutionary Figure: Three Views" traces the development of the depiction of black women in Spanish American literature and shows how that representation is evolving slowly from that of a mostly sensual figure to a symbol of revolution. Furthermore, in comparing "Mujer negra" to works by two other authors, Davis-Lett concludes that only in Morejón's portrayal is the new image fully drawn. She argues that this is partially due to the poem's sense of a collective self rather than the emphasis on the individual woman found in works by the other two writers.

In "Las nuevas poetas cubanas" (The new Cuban women poets), Eliana Rivero (1978) includes Morejón among three important female talents stemming from post-Revolution Cuba. After summarizing the general trends of the poetry in that nation, she briefly discusses certain key characteristics of Morejón's works.

While not referring to her work as feminist discourse, the critic is nevertheless intent on bringing to light women writers of contemporary Cuba. "El género testimonial: aproximaciones feministas" (The documentary genre: feminist approaches), by Margarite Fernández Olmos (1981) is important for, among other reasons, including Morejón among female writers of the documentary literary tradition and for detailing how her themes are conveyed.

"La negritud hoy: nota sobre la poesía de Nancy Morejón" (Blackness today: notes concerning the poetry of Nancy Morejón), written by Efraín Barradas (1980), establishes interconnections among writers of black literatures throughout the Americas. After the initial historical synopsis that summarizes the changing tenor of the theme of blackness (a translation of Barradas's usage of "negritude" to show his differentiation from the literary movement that gave rise to the term) in several literary moments, the study compares Morejón's poetry with that of one of her U.S. contemporaries, Ntozake Shange. The article concludes that her approach to black femaleness differs significantly in that the Cuban is not at odds with her black man.

Susan Willis (1984–1985) explores the importance of myth and nature as redefining principles of history in Morejón's poetry. By placing the poet's work in a comparative context, Willis asserts that the Cuban's poetry is representative of French and Spanish-speaking Caribbean literature that "demystifies" nature. One of the most recent articles on Morejón's poetry benefits from the previous critiques of the artist's work in that the critic can now assume among her readership a certain familiarity with the poet's literature. She can therefore concentrate on the more detailed aspects of the poetic rendition of themes. "The Poetics of the Quotidian in the Works of Nancy Morejón" by Yvonne Captain-Hidalgo (1987) determines what particular manner of writing characterizes the whole of the poet's work.

While there is not an abundance of criticism on this Cuban poet, the quality of her work and the important translations into other languages assure that Morejón will eventually receive a larger place in the history of Spanish American letters than she now enjoys.

BIBLIOGRAPHY

Works by Nancy Morejón

Mutismos. Havana: El Puente, 1962.
Amor, ciudad atribuida. Havana: El Puente, 1964.
Richard trajo su flauta. Havana: Cuadernos UNEAC, 1967.
Octubre imprescindible. Havana: Unión, 1976.
Parajes de una época. Havana: Letras Cubanas, 1979.
Poemas. Mexico City: Universidad Nacional Autónoma de Mexico, 1980.
Elogio de la danza. Mexico City: Universidad Nacional Autónoma de México, 1982.
Cuaderno de Granada. New York: Círculo Cubano de Nueva York, 1984.

Where the Island Sleeps Like a Wing. San Francisco: Black Scholar Press, 1985.
Piedra pulida. Havana: Letras Cubanas, 1986.

Translations of Nancy Morejón

Grenada Notebook. New York: Círculo Cubano de Nueva York, 1984.
Weaver, Kathleen, trans. *Where the Island Sleeps Like a Wing.* San Francisco: Black
    Scholar Press, 1985.

Works about Nancy Morejón

Araújo, Helena. " 'Mujer Negra'." *La Scherezada Criolla: Ensayos sobre escritura
    femenina latinoamericana.* Bogotá: Universidad Nacional de Colombia, 1989. Pp.
    193–95.
Barnet, Miguel, introd. "The Poetry of Nancy Morejón." Trans. Jane McManus. *Where
    the Island Sleeps Like a Wing.* By Nancy Morejón. Trans. Kathleen Weaver. San
    Francisco: Black Scholar Press, 1985. Pp. ix–xi.
Barradas, Efraín. "La negritud hoy: nota sobre la poesía de Nancy Morejón." *Areíto* 6,
    24 (1980):33–38.
Captain-Hidalgo, Yvonne. "The Poetics of the Quotidian in the Works of Nancy Mo-
    rejón." *Callaloo* 10, 4 (1987):157–62.
Davis-Lett, Stephanie. "The Image of the Black Woman as a Revolutionary Figure: Three
    Views." *Studies in Afro-Hispanic Literature.* New York: Medgar Evers College,
    1980. 2–3:118–31.
Fernández Olmos, Margarite. "El género testimonial: aproximaciones feministas." *Re-
    vista/Review Interamericana* 2, 1 (1981):69–75.
Gilard, Jacques. "La obra poética de Nancy Morejón: un despertar de la negritud."
    Cuba: Les Etapes d'une libération: Hommage à Juan Marinello et Noël Salomon.
    Ed. Robert Jammes. Toulousse: University of Toulousse-Le Mirail, 1979–1980.
    1:319–35.
Grötsch, Kurt, "Sozialistischer Alltag und soziale Poesie bei Nancy Morejón." *Die
    Legitimation der Alltagssprache in der modernen Lyrik: Antworten aus Europa
    und Lateinamerika.* Ed. and Introd. Harald Wentzlaff-Eggebert. Erlangen: Uni-
    versitätsbund Erlangen-Nürnberg, 1984. Pp. 113–34.
Guitart, Jorge, and Kevin Power. "Two Women Poets of Cuba: Belkis Cuza Malé and
    Nancy Morejón." *Latin American Literary Review* 8, 125–26 (1979):130–33.
Moore, Carlos. "Congo or Carabalí?: Race Relations in Socialist Cuba." *Rethinking
    Cuba* [special issue] *Caribbean Review* 15, 2 (1986):12–15, 43.
Rivero, Eliana. "Las nuevas poetas cubanas." *Areíto* 5, 17 (1978):31–35.
Rodríguez, Rafael. "Nancy Morejón en su Habana." [Interview] *Areíto* 8, 32 (1983):23–
    25.
Waldman, Gloria Feiman. "Affirmation and Resistance: Women Poets from the Carib-
    bean." *Contemporary Women Authors of Latin America: Introductory Essays.*
    Eds. Doris Meyer and Margarite Fernández Olmos. Brooklyn, N.Y.: Brooklyn
    College Press, 1983. I:33–57.
Weaver, Kathleen. "The World of Nancy Morejón." Translator's introduction to *Where
    the Island Sleeps Like a Wing.* By Nancy Morejón. Pp. xiii–xvii.
Willis, Susan. "Nancy Morejón: Wresting History from Myth." *Literature and Contem-
    porary Revolutionary Culture: Journal of the Society for the Study of Contem-
    porary Hispanic and Lusophone Revolutionary Literatures* (1984–1985):247–56.

CARMEN NARANJO
(b. 1931)
Costa Rica

Patricia Rubio

Carmen Naranjo, born and educated in Costa Rica, earned a Master's (Licenciatura) in Spanish philology from the University of Costa Rica in 1953. She spent the year 1969 with the International Writing Program at the University of Iowa. She subsequently pursued, with great success, a career in public administration. Naranjo was the first Costa Rican woman to occupy important administrative positions in both national and international organizations, serving as undersecretary of Costa Rica's Social Security System between 1970 and 1972, and as ambassador to India from 1972 to 1974. Between 1974 and 1976 she was minister of culture, youth, and sport, and from 1978 to 1982 she was Costa Rica's UNICEF representative, first, in Guatemala and then in Mexico. In 1982 she returned to Costa Rica to direct the Museum of Costa Rican Art. Since 1984 she has headed the Central American University Publishing House (EDUCA).

Although Carmen Naranjo published poetry first (*América*, 1961) and she has to date produced seven books of poetry, she is better known for her technically innovative prose work. It breaks with the *costumbrista* tradition prevalent until recently in Costa Rican literature, and introduces new modes of narration. In her work, she experiments with fragmentary structures and reduces characters to the level of a mere voice, such as in *Diario de una multitud* (1974; Diary of a multitude); she usually eliminates the narrator's guidance from dialogues or chooses a dialogic structure as in *Los perros no ladraron* (1966; The dogs didn't bark). In most of her work one also finds remarkable poetic prose, and there is in both her poetry and fiction an ever-present concern with the function, meaning, and use of language. ''Now that everyone is screaming / that words become sinister myths'' (*Hacia tu isla*, 1966, "Toward Your Island," p. 29; translations of all quotations are my own).

Both Naranjo's novels and short stories have been recipients of Costa Rica's and Central America's most prestigious awards. *Los perros no ladraron* received the Costa Rican National Prize Aquileo Echeverría in 1966; *Camino al mediodía* (1968; On the way to noon) and *Responso por el niño Juan Manuel* (1971; Requiem for the boy Juan Manuel)—one of her most ambitious novels, along with *Diario de una multitud* and *Sobrepunto* (Overpoint)—won the Central American Floral Games in 1967 and 1968, respectively. *Diario de una multitud*, a "fundamental work in the context of Costa Rican literature" (Chase, 1975, p. 127), received the Premio EDUCA in 1974. Her short stories have not wanted for recognition: her collection *Hoy es un largo día* (1974; Today is a long day) was awarded the Editorial Costa Rica Prize in 1973, and *Ondina* received the EDUCA Prize in 1982 before being published in 1985. Although none of her longer fiction has been translated into English, three of her short stories, "The Flowery Trick," "The Journey of Journeys," and "Inventory of a Recluse" from *Hoy es un largo día* have been included in Victoria Urbano's *Five Women Writers of Costa Rica* (1976).

MAJOR THEMES

Naranjo's literary production has been influenced, as she herself declares, by two seemingly unconnected aspects: her deep knowledge of the inner workings of bureaucracy, and her "intense love for the human being." The themes she explores in both her fiction and poetic works are an expression of these concerns: human frustration, isolation, abandonment, and loneliness; individuals' alienated existences in a materialistic and routine-driven society. Naranjo, however, searches to identify the forces that propel human beings, in spite of immensely unfavorable odds, toward the attainment of a fulfilling life and the realization of their humanness.

Los perros, her first novel, depicts one day in the life of an unnamed, middle-level bureaucrat who, to the point of self-denial, is subservient to the system and the humiliating demands of his boss—a corrupt political appointee. Through the use of a dialogic structure, the novel offers a raw and unmediated vision of the mediocrity permeating the bureaucratic system and the dehumanizing effects the daily routine has on those involved in it. Most characters in the novel are frustrated and selfish individuals whose sole concern is their upward mobility; they do not hesitate to undercut their longtime working companions in order to achieve recognition and personal advancement. Those who escape this characterization and are honestly interested in and dedicated to their work fall victims to the internal power struggles.

The protagonist's progressive awakening to such a state of affairs, and his awareness of being trapped in the system because of his concern for maintaining financial security, his incapability of starting anew, and his family obligations and expectations, underscore this individual's helplessness. Naranjo does not, however, simplistically relieve individuals of their own responsibility vis-à-vis their situation. There is in this novel, as well as in the rest of Naranjo's work dealing with social, economic, and political circumstances influencing human existence, a delicate and meaningful balance between how much of individuals' lots are determined by their circumstances and how much responsibility they have to bear for it.

Naranjo treats inclinations toward fatalism, passivity, pessimism, and conformism as attitudes having a mesmerizing effect on individuals. These inclinations prevent them from taking meaningful action that could, at least in part, improve their lot. *Memorias de un hombre palabra* (1968; Memories of a wordman) is the novel that most clearly focuses on this state of affairs. Naranjo's preoccupation with these attitudes is also the topic of *Cinco temas en busca de un pensador* (1977; Five themes in search of a thinker), a book of essays examining the various expressions and implications of these negative attitudes for human development.

The protagonist of *Memorias*, once again an anonymous individual belonging to the lower middle class, reminisces about his life. It has always been one of deprivation and suffering. As an unwanted child, he grows up with the elusive image of a father who has left him and a mother who denies him the affection he longs for. As a result, he becomes the incarnation of hopelessness, the prototype of the human being devoid of the will to act. He passively and fatalistically accepts a destiny he has not chosen but which he is also incapable or unwilling to change: "I, . . . A coward by birth and in substance. A timorous spectator of life" (*Memorias*, p. 91).

The character experiences a degrading social development. His mother rejects him and forces him out of their dwelling; eventually, he commits fraud and is incarcerated. He regains his freedom but is never able to make it back into the social mainstream. Ironically, however, it is in this marginal existence that he recovers his humanness. He finds other individuals who live, as he does, on the fringes of society. For the first time, he becomes part of a community, developing meaningful bonds and experiencing solidarity. He ceases to be alone.

Marginality is a recurring topic in Naranjo's narrative. Although her poetic *persona* is generally unmistakably female, we have to wait until the publication of *Hoy es un largo día* in order to find women protagonists in Naranjo's narrative. The consequences of woman's exclusion from the spheres of political, social, and economic decision making and her resulting relegation to the private spheres of wife and motherhood have been a constant concern in Naranjo's writings. The general absence of women from important roles in her own fiction underscores their marginality.

Of the longer works only *Sobrepunto* (1985), her latest novel (and in my estimation one of her most solid and interesting ones), has a woman as protagonist. Even she, however, exists only in the memory and the diary of her best male friend. Olga is a victim of abandonment, much like Juan Manuel in *Res-*

ponso and the protagonist of *Memorias*, "Los dos santos medioevales de mi abuela bizantina" (*Ondina*) and "El de las cuatro" (*Hoy*). She is the adopted child of a wealthy couple who bought her from her prostitute mother. Olga, aware of her alien condition, struggles for an identity that eludes her in the bourgeois world to which she has been transplanted.

In *Sobrepunto*, as in previous works, Naranjo explores the roles women are expected to play in Latin American culture and society, roles that are largely determined by male values and concerns. The pattern these characters follow is well known. They are either sexual objects taken advantage of as some of the fragments of *Diario* suggest, or vehicles available to men in their pursuit of expressions of existence which, as revealed in *Sobrepunto*, they cannot attain on their own: "Women carry in them the ambiguity of a dream" (p. 138). In *Diario*, however, some fragments represent the "machista" attitude that men use to keep women under their control and to deprive them of their individual freedom and rights. In all these texts women are ultimately dependent on the roles men assign them. Olga's destiny in *Sobrepunto* is a clear indication of what Latin American women's destiny may be when rebelling and searching for their identity in an ultimately destructive world. Olga's marriage fails, she loses her children, and her ensuing loneliness drives her to a devastating experience with drugs and ultimately to suicide.

In both Naranjo's fiction and poetic work there is a deep concern for the everyday person, for the "Don Nadie" (Mr. Nobody). In spite of the seeming sexism, "Don Nadie" refers to both men and women. Naranjo has taken the term from everyday speech, and with her gift for irony and her acute sense of linguistic nuance, she uses the term to denounce obliquely the sexist gender-marking of many Spanish linguistic constructions.

"Don Nadie" could easily be understood as solely referring to the anonymous individual, a member of the multitude, like the ones in *Diario, Memorias, Los perros*, and so many of her short stories: individuals living in the middle or at the bottom of the social pyramid, mostly powerless, materially deprived, un-educated, and usually ignored by the ruling elites. Although the term clearly refers to such individuals, it also alludes to the human condition in general. As both *Diario* and her book of poems *Homenaje a Don Nadie* (1981; Homage to Mr. Nobody) suggest, all human beings belong to the Don Nadie category. Some individuals recognize it more readily because of their social anonymity and their affective and material deprivation. In some instances, such as in "The Flowery Trick" (*Hoy*), the individual will do anything, even to the point of madness, to achieve recognition. In other cases the Mr. Nobodies-Somebodies (lawyers, medical doctors, politicians, etc.) will make a futile attempt to repress the recognition of their ontological nothingness by means of the material and intellectual opportunities available to them.

It is precisely this notion of the essential equality of all human beings, so often ignored or purposefuly forgotten in Latin America, that leads Naranjo to enunciate a profound criticism of the Costa Rican bourgeoisie in general, and of the way it is directing the country politically in particular. Along with her harsh and often marvelously ironic condemnation of the ruling class, one finds a moving empathy with those who are denied the fulfillment of their basic spiritual and material needs.

Camino al mediodía (1968; perhaps Naranjo's weakest work—partly because of her choice of the dead character's consciousness as the narrator, upsetting the verisimilitude of the fictive world) presents the life of a corrupted, self-righteous, and frivolous executive whose speculative activities lead him to ruin and suicide. His activities, however, are the continuation of the more successful but equally immoral practices of his father and are shared by most of his associates. Everything in *Camino* is at the service of fulfilling the desires and needs of the protagonist: a mannequin-like wife who brought much needed cash and convenient family ties to the marriage, business and political connections that protect his image from embarrassing exposures of his unethical business deals, numerous lovers he "buys" in order to kill his boredom, and a social and economic status that protects him from having to assume his responsibilities.

But *Diario* and *Sobrepunto* (and also *Los perros, Mi guerrilla* [1984], *Hoy, Homenaje*, and *Ondina*) go a step further. In them, one not only finds a profound criticism of the upper middle class, but also a denunciation of the false images Costa Rican ruling elites have created for their country. Naranjo confronts directly what she perceives as the misleading images of Costa Rica as an exemplary democracy, its frequent depiction as the "Switzerland" of Central America, its alleged ethnically homogeneous (white) population, and its development and high standard of living. Naranjo exposes these images as the product of a "history which has been a search for accommodation, for good appearances" (*Diario*, p. 73). According to Naranjo, not recognizing the falsehood of these notions perpetuates a "hybrid system . . . always favoring the privileged ones, the gentlemen of opportunity, in pursuit of the business deal, the easy money" (*Diario*, p. 173). Behind these masks exist grave and complex problems requiring timely and imaginative solutions. Naranjo argues that not recognizing the reality of the underprivileged and the degradation of the upper classes is irresponsible and dangerous for the future of the country as a whole.

Naranjo's condemnation of the Costa Rican elites and of the leadership of the country does not, however, imply her adherence to the policies of the political groups in the opposition. Both *Sobrepunto* and "¿Para qué matar a la condesa?" (Why kill the Countess?, *Hoy*), one of her many excellent short stories, show that she also questions the motives of the opposition. It becomes clear that in Naranjo's view, the elite's final objective is the attainment of power and not solving Costa Rica's problems. The countess in "¿Para qué matar . . . " is sentenced to death because, in giving generously without demanding anything in return, she was setting an undesirable example.

The books *Ondina, Nunca hubo alguna vez* (1984; Once upon never), and *Mi guerrilla* express the need to recognize the ambiguity of reality that cannot be understood in univocal terms or according to specific schemes. Reality, in much of Naranjo's work, as in so much of contemporary Latin American literature, is plural in meaning. Behind the superficial order, the absurd, the unconscious, imagination, chance, and magic exist. Some of her work echoes Julio Cortázar's in which the apparent order in the world is destroyed by the attacks of the unexpected, the bizarre.

Responso highlights the imagination as a means of exploring the extraordinary dimensions of reality, in an attempt made by individuals to overcome their essential isolation. Four friends communicate with each other through Juan Manuel, the fifteen-year-old protagonist of a story one of them has created but to which they all have contributed. Juan Manuel himself has an imaginary friend, and he invents stories in order to overcome his loneliness and sense of abandonment, thus reproducing the situation of his creators. When reality penetrates his dreams, he is no longer able to invent stories. His creators then decide he should die. In losing his imaginative powers all doors—a recurring image in Naranjo's work—have been closed. The four friends also fail. Their interior monologues reveal that they too have remained within their borders, unable to overcome their isolation.

Human loneliness or isolation is Naranjo's underlying theme, the force that brings her whole work together. It is reflected in the human solitude and the anguish deriving from the conviction that in our "difficulty of being" we are alone (*Canción de la ternura*, 1964; Song of tenderness). In Naranjo's work it is impossible to reach the other, the one outside of ourselves, because we are unable to determine our own identity. Everyone suffers the same pain, the anguish of being human; the commonality of the experience, however, does not alleviate the individual's forlornness.

There are no metaphysical or religious solutions in her work. Naranjo centers on our humanness and empathizes with the desperation of those who are conscious of their emptiness and confinement. God, in Naranjo's scheme of things, is an imperfect and mostly insensitive being, one who observes human suffering and does nothing to alleviate it. *Misa a oscuras* (1967; Mass in the dark) is the book that most clearly represents a denial of religion and of God as a means of transcending solitude, injustice, and existential pain. All human beings are orphans walking toward nothingness because "the great creator is asleep" (*Misa*, p. 37). Human beings come from the unknown and ignore what lies at the end. If there are any answers—and there may not be, for, in spite of Naranjo's immense hope and love for human beings, and of her celebration of their heroism, she is still pessimistic—the answers are to be found in human essence as such, in human capability for both degrading and transcending itself, and in the human capacity for love, hate, solidarity, empathy, and imagination. "Let us be children of a real father/ of our father and their father/ Sit down at our table/ eat our soup, live our hunger" (*Misa*, p. 46).

SURVEY OF CRITICISM

Although Carmen Naranjo's work has been widely acclaimed in her country and its importance for the development of Costa Rican and Latin American women's literatures has been well established, it has received little critical attention outside Costa Rican borders. The publication in 1987 of both Luz Martínez's book and Evelyn Picón Garfield's article on her short stories seems to indicate an increasing and well-deserved interest in her fiction. Her poetry, however, is still wanting of thorough consideration. Victoria Urbano's article (1977) on *Canción de la ternura*, Naranjo's second book of poems, is thus far the only serious study of any of her collections of poems. Urbano places *Canción* in the context of Naranjo's later poetic and narrative production. She underscores the fact that Naranjo's poetic interests are not sentimental (typical of the poetry of previous Hispanic women: "Floribela, Juana and Rosalía"), but rather aesthetic and philosophical in nature: human anguish caused by the fluidity of time, an interest in human limitations and ensuing loneliness. She relates Naranjo's poetry to that of César Vallejo, establishing thematic coincidences and poetic differences between the two.

Critical commentary of Naranjo's fiction is mostly celebratory, with the exception of J. Valdeperas's study (1979) which criticizes a "lack of internal tension" in her earlier novels and, probably not totally understanding *Diario*'s objectives, its fragmentary portrayal of Costa Rican society. Studies of her work fall into two main categories: those focusing on its structurally and technically innovative aspects, and those concentrating on its semantic level. Most critical analyses, especially those published in Costa Rica, are superseded by Alicia Miranda Hevia's (1981) and Luz Martínez (1987) book-length studies, both of which were first conceived as doctoral dissertations. Perhaps for this reason, and also because they wrote abroad, both authors feel the need to present Naranjo's work within the broader spectrum of Hispanic and Costa Rican literature, in spite of the fact that they are mostly concerned with structural and semantic issues of Naranjo's *oeuvre*. Miranda traces the influence of Larra's ironic discourse on Naranjo's work, and provides an overview (at times irrelevant to an understanding of her work) of Costa Rican literature. Martínez also follows, at least in part, the historical approach, studying in some detail three other Costa Rican women writers: Carmen Lyra, Yolanda Oreamuno,* and Julieta Pinto. She thus places Naranjo's work in the context of Costa Rican women's literature.

Martínez' book is more general in scope than Miranda's, and although it refers in some detail to Naranjo's poetry, theater, short story, and essay production, it focuses primarily on her longer fiction. The study, though at times repetitive, is valuable for its scope—it is to date the only comprehensive study of Naranjo's work—and for its depth of analysis. It studies the novels both structurally and thematically, tracing human frustration, degradation, anguish, and loneliness in *Los perros, Memorias*, and *Camino*, a trilogy of the middle class, continuing with *Responso*, where "the topic of loneliness and incommunication achieves maximum expression" (p. 317), and culminating in *Diario* and *Sobrepunto*. Miranda suggests that in *Diario* we find the same three social strata represented in the previous novels, except that they are not represented by specific characters, but rather by a "collage of voices" (Chase depicts them as tropisms), which in turn are absorbed by the voices of the crowd.

Martínez defines *Diario* as an antinovel and one that broke new ground for Costa Rican narrative. It does not develop a plot, it has eliminated the narrating voice and substituted it by a plurality of voices, and it has fragmented narrative time and space. As such, *Diario* poses new reading problems because it does not provide sufficient clues for easy understanding. Readers have to engage the text and reconstruct it themselves.

Miranda (1985) disagrees with Martínez about *Diario* in that she identifies a narrating voice who, though not generally represented, nevertheless mediates the discourses and controls the flow of the information. *Diario* for Miranda is, as all of Naranjo's work, a moral text at the semantic level, in the sense that it denounces a particular set of circumstances. The main difference between Miranda's and Martínez' studies of *Diario* is one of focus. Miranda, though interested in the semantic aspect of the novel, concentrates on its discursive and structural levels. She addresses aspects of its prosody, rhythm, irony, the metaphoric and metonymic organization of the text, and she applies the French semiotician Julia Kristeva's categories to the study of its structure.

Sobrepunto, written in the mid-1960s but not published until 1985, will surely attract the attention of future critics, both because it is a solid and interesting novel and because it is Naranjo's only work specifically dealing with woman's condition. Martínez' chapter on the novel is the only critical study of it to date. She carefully analyzes the plot, the characters, and narrative techniques (many of which are pictorial), and places the novel in the context of her previous work. She concludes that *Sobrepunto*, from a woman's perspective, presents a devastating view of Costa Rican society, within which, however, exist individuals—like Olga—who unceasingly pursue authentic modes of existence.

Naranjo's short stories have not received the attention they merit. Apart from Martínez' chapter in her book, which studies them mainly from a thematic perspective, there are only two articles dealing with this portion of her work. The most valuable of the two, both because of its scope and insight, is Picón Garfield's. She focuses on the complexity of human relationships and studies the tensions existing among individuals belonging to the same family and to different economic segments of society, and those existing among individuals who develop relationships of an affectionate kind. Picón Garfield also studies the various narrative recourses Naranjo uses to express the complexity of human interaction.

There are important areas in Naranjo's work that still deserve serious critical consideration. Her poetry is a case in point. Certain aspects of her fiction (as it becomes better known outside of Costa Rica) will also draw critical attention because of the thematic, technical, and artistic interest of her fiction. In due time Naranjo's *oeuvre* will be recognized as important not only for the development of Costa Rican literature, but also for its relevance to Latin American (women's) literature in general.

BIBLIOGRAPHY

Works by Carmen Naranjo

América. 1961; not available in the United States.

Canción de la ternura. San José: Ediciones Elite de Lilia Ramos, 1964.

Hacia tu isla. San José: n.p. 1966.

Los perros no ladraron. San José: Editorial Costa Rica, 1966.

Misa a oscuras. San José: Editorial Costa Rica, 1967.

Camino al mediodía. San José: Editorial Costa Rica, 1968.

Memorias de un hombre palabra. San José: Editorial Costa Rica, 1968.

Responso por el niño Juan Manuel. San José: Editorial Conciencia Nueva, 1971.

Idioma de invierno. San José: Editorial Conciencia Nueva, 1972.

"Oye," "El aire no trae mensajes en este mirar al río," "No sé tampoco de dónde viniste," "No recuerdo tampoco cuándo empecé a quererte," "La vida era simple para ti," "Siempre fuiste el servido." *Poesía contemporánea de Costa Rica: Antología*. Ed. Carlos Rafael Duverrán. San José: Editorial Costa Rica, 1973. Pp. 231–35.

Diario de una multitud. San José: Editorial Universitaria Centroamericana, 1974.

Hoy es un largo día. San José: Editorial Costa Rica, 1974.

Por las páginas de la Biblia y los caminos de Israel. Costa Rica: n.p., 1976. [The book was published by a group of Naranjo's Jewish friends.]

Cinco temas en busca de un pensador. San José: Ministerio de Cultura, Juventud y Deportes, 1977.

"La voz." *Obras breves del teatro costarricense*. Volume I. San José: Editorial Costa Rica, 1977; not available in the United States.

Cultura. San José: Departamento de Publicaciones del Instituto Centroamericano de Administración Pública, 1978.

Homenaje a don Nadie. San José: Editorial Costa Rica, 1981.

Ed., *La mujer y el desarrollo: la mujer y la cultura: antología*. Mexico City: Sep Diana, 1981.

"Manuela siempre." *Escena* 1984; not available in the United States.

Mi guerrilla. San José: Editorial Universitaria Centroamericana, 1984.

Nunca hubo alguna vez. San José: Editorial Universidad Estatal a Distancia, 1984.

With Graciela Moreno. *Estancias y días*. San José: Editorial Costa Rica, 1985.

Ondina. San José: Editorial Universitaria Centroamericana, 1985. Havana: Casa de las Américas, 1988.

Sobrepunto. San José: Editorial Universitaria Centroamericana, 1985.

Translations of Carmen Naranjo

"Listen." *Mundus Artium* 7, 1 (1975):87.

Mathieu, Corina, trans. "The Flowery Trick;" "The Journey of Journeys," trans. Marie J. Panico; "Inventory of a Recluse," trans. Mary Sue Listerman. *Five Women Writers of Costa Rica*. Ed. Victoria Urbano. Beaumont, Tex: Asociación de Literatura Femenina Hispánica, 1976. Pp. 3–18.

Works about Carmen Naranjo

Amoretti, María. "*Camino al mediodía*." *Revista de Filología y Lingüística de la Universidad de Costa Rica* 5 (Feb. 1979):55–59.

————. "Recuento de matices sociales en *Los perros no ladraron.*" *Káñina* (Jan.-June 1979):19–32.

————. "*Responso por el niño Juan Manuel.*" *Káñina* 3–4 (1978):7–13.

Arizpe, Lourdes. "Interview with Carmen Naranjo: Women and Latin American Literature." *Signs* 5, 1 (1979):98–110.

Chase, Alfonso. *Narrativa contemporánea de Costa Rica*. San José: Ministerio de Cultura, Juventud y Deportes, 1975. Pp. 124–25, 127–28.

Coll, Edna. "Naranjo, Carmen." *Indice informativo de la novela hispanoamericana*. Puerto Rico: Editorial Universitaria, 1977. II:54–55.

Coronel Urtecho, José. "Notas para antes o después de la lectura de *Mi guerrilla.*" *Mi guerrilla*. By Carmen Naranjo. San José: Editorial Universitaria Centroamericana, 1984. Pp. 17–26, 85–103.

Cruz Burdiel de López, María. "Estudio de tres cuentos de Carmen Naranjo." *Káñina: Revista de la Universidad de Costa Rica* 41 (1975):101–10.

Lagos, Ramiro. *Mujeres poetas de Hispanoamérica: Movimiento, surgencia e insurgencia*. Bogotá: Ediciones Tercer Mundo, 1986. Pp. 83–84.

Martínez, Luz Ivette. *Carmen Naranjo y la narrativa femenina en Costa Rica*. San José: Editorial Universitaria Costarricense, 1987.

Mathieu, Corina. "Commentary to 'The Flowery Trick' of Carmen Naranjo." *Five Women Writers of Costa Rica*. Ed. Victoria Urbano. Beaumont, Tex.: Asociación de Literatura Femenina Hispánica, 1976. P. 19.

Minc, Rose, and Teresa Méndez-Faith. "Conversando con Carmen Naranjo." *Revista Iberoamericana* 132–33 (June-Dec. 1985):507–10.

Miranda Hevia, Alicia. "Introducción a la obra novelesca de Carmen Naranjo." *Cahiers du Monde Hispanique et Luso-Brésilien* 36 (1981):121–29.

————. "La prosodia de *Diario de una multitud.*" *Káñina* 7, 1 (1983):9–14.

————. *Novela, discurso y sociedad (Diario de una multitud)*. San José: Mesén Editores, 1985.

Picón Garfield, Evelyn. "La luminosa ceguera de sus días: los cuentos 'humanos' de Carmen Naranjo." *Revista Iberoamericana* 138–39 (Jan.-June 1987):287–301.

Rojas de Ayub, María Elena. "Una novela de Carmen Naranjo: *Camino al mediodía.*" *Káñina: Revista de la Universidad de Costa Rica* 34 (Dec. 1972):57–65.

Sandoval de Fonseca, Virginia. *Resumen de la literatura costarricense*. San José: Editorial Costa Rica, 1978. Pp. 39–52.

Schrade, Arlene O. "Naranjo, Carmen." *Women Writers of Spanish America: An Annotated Bio-bibliographical Guide*. Ed. Diane Marting. Westport, Conn.: Greenwood Press, 1987. Pp. 267–68.

Urbano, Victoria. "Carmen Naranjo y su voz plena en *Canción de la ternura.*" *Káñina* 1, 2 (1977):5–31.

————. "The Creation Philosophy of Carmen Naranjo." *Five Women Writers of Costa Rica*. Beaumont, Tex.: Asociación de Literatura Femenina Hispánica, 1976. Pp. 17–18.

Valdeperas, Jorge. *Para una nueva interpretación de la literatura costarricense*. San José: Editorial Costa Rica, 1979. Pp. 119–22.

Vargas, Aura R. "*Los perros no ladraron*: una novedad técnica en la novelística costarricense." *Káñina* 1, 2 (July-Dec. 1977):33–6.

SILVINA OCAMPO
(b. 1903)
Argentina

Melvin S. Arrington, Jr.

BIOGRAPHY

Silvina Ocampo is perhaps better known for her ties to other more illustrious literary figures than for her own work as poet and short story writer. Her sister, Victoria Ocampo* (1890–1979), holds a special place in Spanish American literature for bringing European culture to Argentine letters via her journal and publishing house *Sur*. Silvina's husband, Adolfo Bioy Casares (b. 1914), has achieved international fame as a novelist, and their mutual friend Jorge Luis Borges (1899–1986) has been called the most outstanding Spanish American literary figure in the twentieth century. As a result of her associations with these and other influential writers of the *Sur* generation, she has, to some extent, been ignored and remains the least known member of this group.

Born in a house on Calle Viamonte in Buenos Aires in 1903, Silvina was the youngest of six daughters of Manuel Silvino Ocampo and Ramona Aguirre. The family, whose ancestors included some of Argentina's founding fathers, was prosperous and thus able to provide the children with educational opportunities unavailable to most. Thanks to Silvina's English and French governesses, she acquired fluency in two languages in addition to her native Spanish. At an early age she began to study drawing and painting, an interest she would later share with Borges's sister Norah, who was also an avid painter. In 1927 the journal *Martín Fierro* published some of her sketches—illustrations depicting a moonlit patio and a rose-colored street corner, based on Borges's poems—but she did not actually meet Borges until 1934, the same year she met Bioy Casares.

Ocampo's earliest tastes in literature reveal an interest in French models, a predilection that can be explained by her family's annual trips to Europe and by her exposure to French culture as a young art student in Paris. Some of her initial writings appeared in the newspaper *La Nación* and the journal *Sur*. In fact, it was *Sur* that published her first stories and poems. She was a constant companion of Bioy and Borges, often accompanying them on summer trips and on walks through the city. In 1936 Bioy founded a short-lived literary magazine, *Destiempo*, to which she contributed, but it was not until the following year that she produced her first book, *Viaje olvidado* (1937; Forgotten journey), a short story collection that signaled her interest in vanguard literature.

Ocampo and Bioy were married in 1940 in the small suburb of Las Flores, with Borges serving as best man. On Friday afternoons the couple would hold open house for their literary friends and associates; on such occasions Borges was a regular visitor. Her editorial collaboration with Bioy and Borges resulted in the publication of two influential collections in the early 1940s: *Antología de la literatura fantástica* (1940; Anthology of literature of the fantastic), a work that played a leading role in the development of magical realism in the River Plate region, and *Antología poética argentina* (1941; Anthology of Argentine poetry), a not entirely successful but nevertheless important compendium of early twentieth-century verse. Several key volumes of Ocampo's poetry appeared during this decade. *Enumeración de la patria y otros poemas* (1942; Enumeration of the nation and other poems) was her first book of poetry. It was followed by a work dedicated to Bioy Casares, *Espacios métricos* (1945; Metrical spaces), which won the Premio Municipal de Poesía in 1945, and *Poemas de amor desesperado* (Poems of hopeless love) in 1949. During this period of intense poetic activity, she once again teamed up with Bioy, this time on a detective novel, *Los que aman, odian* (1946; Those who love also hate). Two years later she published an important volume of stories, *Autobiografía de Irene* (1948; Autobiography of Irene).

With the decade of the 1950s came *Los nombres* (1953; The names), for which she won second place in the National Poetry Competition of 1953; a verse drama, *Los traidores* (1956; The traitors), written in collaboration with J. R. Wilcock; and a major collection of stories, *La furia y otros cuentos* (1959; The fury and other stories). In 1954 Ocampo published *Pequeña antología* (1954; Little anthology), a slight volume containing selections from her first three books of poetry.

Ocampo's first publication of the 1960s, *Las invitadas* (1961; The guests), secured her reputation as a short story writer. This work contained forty-four tales and was by far her largest compilation of stories. This was followed the next year by an award-winning volume of poems, *Lo amargo por dulce* (1962; The bitter for the sweet), which garnered the Premio Nacional de Poesía. Her short story collection *El pecado mortal* (1966; The mortal sin) is of little consequence; rather than new stories, it consisted merely of a reprinting of selected works from prior volumes. It does, however, contain José Bianco's brief introductory essay, which was one of the few studies in existence at that time dealing with her work.

Ocampo's last major short story collection, *Los días de la noche* (1970;

Nocturnal days), came out in 1970, a year in which she spent a considerable amount of time in Pau, France. In that same year she also reissued several previously anthologized stories under the title *Informe del cielo y del infierno* (Report on heaven and hell), adding only one that had not been collected earlier. Her other works published during the 1970s, with the exception of a book of poetry, *Amarillo celeste* (1972; Celestial yellow), have been aimed at a youthful audience. These have ranged from brief illustrated volumes, each containing a single story, such as *El caballo alado* (1972; The winged horse) and *El cofre volante* (1974; The flying trunk)—along with its sequel, *El tobogán* (1975; The toboggan)—to a full-length book, *La naranja maravillosa* (1977; The magic orange), composed of juvenile tales, some of which are reworkings of earlier stories written for adults.

In the 1980s, Ocampo has continued to pursue literary activities. In 1984 she gathered a representative sampling of her fiction and poetry, publishing it under the title *Páginas de Silvina Ocampo, seleccionadas por la autora* (1984; Pages from the works of Silvina Ocampo, chosen by the author). This is, without a doubt, the most practical starting point for readers unfamiliar with Ocampo and her writings. Her most recent books, the short story collections *Y así sucesivamente* (And in that way one after another) and *Cornelia frente al espejo* (Cornelia before the mirror) appeared in 1987 and 1988, respectively. Although she has been prominent in Buenos Aires literary circles for many years and has seen her work translated into other tongues, Ocampo has failed to win acclaim beyond the borders of the Southern Cone. This may be explained, in part, by the lack of book-length translations of her work into English, the language that has provided the ticket to overnight international recognition for so many previously obscure Spanish American writers. It is hoped that the recent publication of *Leopoldina's Dream* (1988), a volume containing English versions of a generous sampling of her stories, will fill this void and help secure a wider audience for her writings.

In addition to traveling and writing, Ocampo has maintained an interest in art and has occasionally exhibited her paintings. Owing to her birth into a wealthy family, she has been able to devote herself exclusively to the world of literature and art and has not felt the severe economic pressures or class prejudices experienced by some female authors, particularly those who must work at other occupations for a livelihood. For this reason, Ocampo's themes and literary preoccupations differ considerably from those of other contemporary women writers.

MAJOR THEMES

Ocampo's writings represent a clear departure from the regional themes that dominated the Spanish American literary scene from the 1920s to the 1940s. Instead, her work harks back to an earlier period, that of *modernismo* (''Modernism''), the decadent, turn-of-the-century Spanish American tendency that exalted pure art and established the cult of beauty, a creed best exemplified by the finely sculpted poem often dealing with erotic or exotic subject matter. The abundance of symbolism and classical allusions in her stories and poems indicates the residual effects of this movement. However, Ocampo's experiments with form and with different levels of reality (surrealism and fantasy, for example) reflect the enduring influence of another aesthetic, a literary category contemporaneous with but antithetical to the *criollista* or regional mode, that of vanguardism.

Nevertheless, her work also falls outside the narrowly defined boundaries of vanguardism's contemporary descendant, magical realism. The uniqueness of Ocampo's prose is perhaps best seen in her penchant for juxtaposing fantastic or grotesque elements with everyday situations set in ordinary surroundings, a technique that creates an awareness of irony on the part of the reader. A quick glance at some of her titles will illustrate this inclination toward the paradoxical and the ironic, namely, *Lo amargo por dulce, Amarillo celeste, Los días de la noche*, and *Los que aman, odian*.

While the literary prizes she has received have been for poetry, Ocampo's recognition as a writer is based primarily on her stories. The setting for these short prose pieces, many of which are extremely brief, is the bourgeois reality and social order with which she is familiar. Generally speaking, she avoids themes involving social concerns as well as those dealing with the image of women and other feminist topics. Her best stories are characterized by eccentric child characters, first-person narrators, the ironic interplay between the ordinary and the unusual, a touch of black humor, and a hint of the fantastic. The abnormal, irrational, and sometimes cruel behavior of her protagonists often results in a rite of passage (sexual initiation, psychological maturation, or some other process of growth and development) or in death. The dreamlike nature of these stories, especially the ones in which reality turns into nightmare, argues for interpretations of a psychoanalytical nature.

Mythological allusions and archetypal/religious symbolism are also recurring features of her short fiction. In the story "Las invitadas," for example, young Lucio's birthday party becomes a ritual ceremony in which he, the initiate, plays host to seven ill-mannered girls. The rude, even scandalous behavior of these guests takes on special significance when one realizes that they represent the seven deadly sins. In "La furia," the male narrator considers himself a victim of the object of his affections, a young woman named Winifred, who reminds him of one of the Furies. Winifred, in seeking to atone for an incident in her past, her responsibility in the death of a childhood friend, now commits even greater cruelties with other people. She abandons not only the little boy in her care but also the narrator, an act that provokes the narrator's "fury." Annoyed by the boy's refusal to stop beating on a drum, the narrator, in his growing impatience, silences the child by killing him.

Another selection with mythological overtones is "Ulises" (Ulysses), from Ocampo's recent volume of stories, *Los días de la noche*. This one concerns the close friendship between the narrator, a girl seven years of age, and her schoolmate, Ulises, one year her junior. The boy lives with three elderly women who look much younger than their age and act like children; he, on the other hand, has the face of an old man. Ulises visits a fortuneteller (a modern-day oracle) and obtains a potion that rejuvenates his appearance, but upon returning home he learns that his metamorphosis has also triggered a change in the three women. He finds them looking old and feeble, wearing dark glasses, and weaving (an allusion to the Three Fates). Ironically, the philtre, a device typically used to bring about supernatural transformations, here causes altered phenomena to return to their natural state. When the old women learn what has happened, they visit the fortuneteller and have the process reversed. Another spell and reversal ensue, after which the narrator convinces Ulises to leave his face the way she likes it—old and wrinkled.

Irony serves as the axis around which Ocampo constructs one of her best known works, "Autobiografía de Irene." The protagonist, Irene (whose name forms a sound pair with the word "irony"), is a young woman who knows the future but cannot remember her own past. At the end of the story she begins to relate the events of her life to a stranger, employing the same words with which this selection opens. In her function as narrator Irene performs the same task as a writer, and therefore, she can be viewed as the author's alter ego. This character also appears as the poetic voice in the poem "Autobiografía de Irene" from the collection *Espacios métricos* and as the name of the young protagonist in the children's story *El caballo alado*. The latter Irene lives with her father, a care-taker, in a huge museum filled with paintings and statues. For this little girl, an inhabitant of a marvelous world populated by classical figures, life and art have become indistinguishable. In fact, her favorite museum piece, a statue of the winged horse Pegasus, is also her dearest friend.

Over the years Ocampo's work as a short story writer has been remarkably consistent in terms of themes, style, and overall quality of writing. Her poetry, however, has been somewhat heterogeneous, though no less impressive. Many of her early poems closely adhere to traditional verse patterns and subjects. Length varies considerably, ranging from very brief epitaphs and inscriptions to compositions that fill several pages. Individual selections frequently employ hendecasyllables and alexandrines and usually fall within recognizable categories such as quatrains, *pareados* (rhymed couplets), and sonnets. Later in her career she develops an interest in metrical experimentation; however, this flirtation with freer forms does not lead to an aesthetic conversion.

While praise for her native soil and Argentine nationhood acquire thematic status in Ocampo's initial poetry collection, they are not developed to any significant degree in subsequent works. On the other hand, mythological and historical figures as well as biblical personages figure prominently in the poems written in the 1940s and 1950s. This choice of subject matter clearly demonstrates that her poetic world is a realm dominated by art and the classics rather than the everyday reality of twentieth-century Buenos Aires. Like many Argentine literati, she looked on France as a cultural model and a source of artistic inspiration, a debt she acknowledges in the poem "A Francia" from *Espacios métricos*. This collection is characterized by a preference for traditional forms, universal themes, and poems dealing with historical and legendary subjects. Her use of epigraphs from English and French sources illustrates the influence of these foreign traditions on her formation as a writer and, symbolically, on the development of Argentine national culture. In light of this content, the *espacios* ("spaces") of the title signify distances or gaps that separate the poetic voice temporally and spatially from its subject. This preoccupation with nonnative culture, specifically British and French, continues in *Poemas de amor desesperado*, a work that focuses on jealousy, uncertainty, and other negative aspects of the theme of love.

In *Los nombres*, a pivotal work in terms of form and style, her favorite themes return, but now she expands her technical range to include more free verse. Nevertheless, the vast majority of these selections (over 75 percent), are rhymed, and most follow some readily identifiable metrical or stanzaic form. A good example of the continued presence of elitist subject matter and classical influence is the sonnet "Leda y el cisne" (Leda and the swan), a poem that reveals Ocampo's predilection for relating experience to art. For her, pure art avoids political comment and stands above social concerns—thus, her evocation of the biblical and classical world rather than the contemporary scene. Although she frequently writes poetry in a narrative mode, the lyrical voice dominates here with numerous selections employing a first-person viewpoint. It should be noted, also, that the perspective in these poems is feminine rather than feminist. The theme of creativity arises, appropriately, in the sonnet sequence dedicated to her husband, a section in which her love for him is analogous to her devotion to the creative powers of the imagination.

Her later volumes, *Lo amargo por dulce* and *Amarillo celeste*, contain a mixture of traditional poetic forms and free verse and tend to be more personal in tone, with pessimism coming to the forefront. Classical and historical allusions persist as do many of the themes and techniques developed earlier. These include love and its accompanying emotions—pain and despair, the transitoriness of existence, a growing preoccupation with death, and a fascination with dreams and the imagination. Despite this turn inward, or perhaps because of it, the more recent poetry collections have the greatest appeal.

SURVEY OF CRITICISM

In comparison to the voluminous critical materials on works by male writers of Ocampo's generation, relatively little has been written on her life or works. Those scholars who have examined her literary production in any detail have, for the most part, all but ignored the poetry, which accounts for a large percentage of her total output.

To date, the only extended treatment in English (or any other language) of

Ocampo's writings is Patricia N. Klingenberg's unpublished doctoral dissertation (1981), an important study that provides in-depth coverage of the short stories. Klingenberg, like other critics, comments on the frequent use of sardonic humor, the intertwining of fantastic and grotesque elements, and the preponderance of child protagonists and narrators in these brief, tightly constructed narratives. She also discusses the occurrence of metamorphosis and foretelling the future and the appearance of objects having magical properties, features that link Ocampo's stories to that important body of contemporary fiction in which the line of demarcation between the marvelous and the ordinary, between fantasy and everyday reality, has begun to fade. In a more recent study (1987), Klingenberg offers a feminist reading of Ocampo's short fiction. According to the critic, the depiction of artistic creativity in several stories, especially those activities traditionally associated with women's culture, serves as a means of subverting realism, thereby opening the door to the fantastic and the grotesque.

Other critics have examined specific aspects of Ocampo's work which set it apart from the writings of her contemporaries. Daniel Balderston (1983), for example, focuses on the motif of cruelty, which often turns sadistic in the short stories, most of which are set in the bourgeois world of Buenos Aires, a locale he labels ideal for the narration of fantastic or grotesque events. According to Balderston, Ocampo has not achieved the critical acclaim of some of her compatriots because her texts violate decorum and established ideas concerning literary taste. Unlike Borges and Bioy, who always manage to preserve a sense of propriety no matter how fantastic the tale, Ocampo subscribes to an aesthetic in which pain and pleasure, beauty and horror, are inseparably linked. In some of her stories (e.g., "El pecado mortal" and "Los mastines del templo de Adriano" [The mastiffs of Hadrian's Temple]), there are scenes in which the narrator experiences a form of erotic pleasure by secretly viewing a sexual encounter, thereby becoming an accomplice to the act. Balderston asserts that her stories establish an ironic distance between an innocent, ingenuous narrator (often a child or an adult lacking in discernment, one who does not seem to understand what she is narrating or what is actually happening) and the atrocities or acts of cruelty that are narrated. Irony, which resides in the interval or gap between narrator and events narrated, emerges as a direct result of this technique of distancing.

Sylvia Molloy's articles also examine specific characteristics of Ocampo's work, namely, her tendency toward exaggeration in the depiction of characters, the apparent yet deceptive simplicity of these self-manifesting texts, and her affinity for excessive verbalization in the delineation of a scene or situation, a technique that deliberately undermines the suggestive qualities of language. In opting for statement rather than suggestion, Ocampo achieves a clarity of expression which, at times, produces an unsettling, even disturbing, effect on the reader. Her unusual child characters are often monstrous figures who have cast aside the innocuous traits usually associated with youth and innocence. This penchant for exaggeration and excess also comes into play in her portrayal of adult characters. The titles of individual stories, according to Molloy, convey an impression of simplicity (e.g., "El cuaderno" [The notebook], "Las foto-grafías" [The photographs], "La boda" [The wedding], and so on). However, on closer examination, the reader quickly discovers the true nature of these narratives. The overly simplistic titles provide little more than a façade hiding an inner realm governed by perfect crimes and mortal sins, a zone where mythical elements, allegory, and the fantastic coexist alongside the ordinary. Realistic background details, commonplaces, and an atmosphere of normalcy function as a screen on which the aberrations of her characters are projected. Not surprisingly, the cumulative effect of these excesses produces texts that elicit psychoanalytical readings.

Two studies on "El pecado mortal" offer insight into the archetypal under-pinnings of one of Ocampo's best known stories. Barbara B. Aponte's article (1982) analyzes this selection in terms of the rite of passage from childhood innocence to sexual awareness, a process which, in Western literature, is usually triggered by adult sexual aggression. The story, a work laden with religious/erotic symbolism, concerns the predicament of a young girl, the protagonist, who is lured into the sordid world of a male servant's sexual perversions and afterward makes her first Communion without confessing her sin. The woman who tells the story, otherwise unidentified, narrates in the second person, speak-ing to the protagonist, after the principal incidents have occurred. The identity of the narrator and the mode of narration produce serious ambiguities that leave the text open to multiple interpretations. In Aponte's reading, the consequences of this premature and, therefore, unnatural initiation are harmful to the child.

In a related study, Helena Araújo (1984) provides additional commentary on the principal characters' ritualistic behavior in "El pecado mortal," especially with regard to the awakening of a sexual identity that has been repressed by the solitude of social isolation and other factors. In this case, the seduction, a psychological game of alternating attraction and repulsion, occurs not as a result of violence but rather through enticement. According to Araújo, an implied class conflict arises from the young girl's contact with the servant. Thus, the thematic content of perversion, ritual humiliation, and guilt should be expanded to allow for sociological readings. In contrast to Aponte's conclusion, Araújo views the girl's sexual encounter as an experience that will help her to develop socially and psychologically and, at the same time, to acquire an identity of her own.

As mentioned above, Ocampo's poetry, unlike her short fiction, has not been systematically studied. Given the numerous volumes of poetry among her *oeuvre*, one is surprised to learn that her writings in this genre have failed to capture the attention of critics. Although Enrique Pezzoni and Juan Carlos Ghiano do com-ment briefly on some of Ocampo's poetry collections, their remarks have limited value to the reader seeking in-depth analyses.

By far, the most useful critical essay in this vein is that of Helena Percas (1958), and even this study represents a minimal contribution since it only provides coverage for works published prior to 1950. In her analysis of *Enu-*

meración de la patria, Percas comments on technical aspects (word selection, versification, and rhythm) as well as themes (love and passion for the homeland). Here, Ocampo's random listing of the beauties of small towns and provinces as well as large cities constitutes descriptive verse in the spirit of Walt Whitman, Leopoldo Lugones, Ramón López Velarde, and Pablo Neruda. *Espacios métricos*, a volume composed primarily of traditional verse forms (quatrains, *pareados*, and sonnets, the last named of which, according to Percas, achieve classic perfection) and occasional unrhymed verse, represents a poetic world of fantasy, dreams, and enigmatic symbols. The simple, direct language of these compositions conveys an impression of clarity, but this is quickly darkened by shadows, a condition that, at times, results in hermeticism. Percas calls *Poemas de amor desesperado* the product of a bitterness that has displaced the fantasy of previous works. In this volume her poetry becomes more direct and, at the same time, more personal.

Subsequent volumes have greatly enhanced Ocampo's stock as a poet. However, without significant critical studies on these works, in the eyes of most readers, she will remain a short story writer who, incidentally, also published several books of poetry. What is needed, then, is a comprehensive study of Ocampo's collections of verse, one that will establish her credentials as a poet and complement Klingenberg's thorough treatment of the short stories by illuminating the points of convergence and divergence with respect to the prose and poetry of this important but little-heralded Spanish American woman writer.

BIBLIOGRAPHY

Works by Silvina Ocampo

Viaje olvidado. Buenos Aires: Sur, 1937.

With Jorge Luis Borges and Adolfo Bioy Casares. *Antología de la literatura fantástica*. Buenos Aires: Editorial Sudamericana, 1940.

With Jorge Luis Borges and Adolfo Bioy Casares. *Antología poética argentina*. Buenos Aires: Editorial Sudamericana, 1941.

Enumeración de la patria y otros poemas. Buenos Aires: Sur, 1942.

Espacios métricos. Buenos Aires: Sur, 1945.

With Adolfo Bioy Casares. *Los que aman, odian*. Buenos Aires: Emecé, 1946.

Autobiografía de Irene. Buenos Aires: Sudamericana, 1948.

Sonetos del jardín. Buenos Aires: Colección La Perdiz, 1948.

Poemas de amor desesperado. Buenos Aires: Sudamericana, 1949.

Los nombres. Buenos Aires: Emecé, 1953.

Pequeña antología. Buenos Aires: Ene, 1954.

With J. R. Wilcock. *Los traidores*. Buenos Aires: Losada, 1956.

La furia y otros cuentos. Buenos Aires: Sur, 1959.

Las invitadas. Buenos Aires: Losada, 1961.

Lo amargo por dulce. Buenos Aires: Emecé, 1962.

El pecado mortal. Buenos Aires: Universitaria, 1966.

Informe del cielo y del infierno. Caracas: Monte Avila, 1970.
Los días de la noche. Buenos Aires; Sudamericana, 1970.
Amarillo celeste. Buenos Aires: Losada, 1972.
El caballo alado. Buenos Aires: Flor, 1972.
El cofre volante. Buenos Aires: Estrada, 1974.
El tobogán. Buenos Aires: Estrada, 1975.
La naranja maravillosa. Buenos Aires: Orión, 1977.
Canto escolar. Buenos Aires: Fraterna, 1979.
Páginas de Silvina Ocampo, seleccionadas por la autora. Buenos Aires: Editorial Celtia,
    1984.
Y así sucesivamente. Barcelona: Tusquets Editores, 1987.
Cornelia frente al espejo. Barcelona: Tusquets Editores, 1988.

Translations of Silvina Ocampo

Balderston, Daniel, trans. *Leopoldina's Dream*. By Silvina Ocampo. London and New
    York: Penguin, 1988. Contains thirty-two short stories chosen from *Autobiografía
    de Irene, La furia y otros cuentos, Las invitadas*, and *Los días de la noche*.
Lewald, H. Ernest, ed. and trans. *The Web: Stories by Argentine Women*. Washington,
    D.C.: Three Continents Press, 1983. Pp. 27–34. Contains one story ("The
    Prayer") from *La furia y otros cuentos*.
Manguel, Alberto, ed. *Black Water: The Book of Fantastic Literature*. New York: Clark-
    son N. Potter, 1983. Pp. 612–18. Includes Manguel's translation of "The
    Friends" from *La furia y otros cuentos*.
————, ed. *Other Fires: Short Fiction by Latin American Women*. New York: Clarkson
    N. Potter, 1986. Pp. 147–50. Includes Manguel's translation of two stories from
    La furia y otros cuentos: "Report on Heaven and Hell" and "The Inextinguishable
    Race."
Meyer, Doris, and Margarite Fernández Olmos, eds. *Contemporary Women Authors of
    Latin America: New Translations*. Brooklyn, N.Y.: Brooklyn College Press, 1983.
    Pp. 46–49, 215–16. Contains two poems from *Enumeración de la patria y otros
    poemas* ("San Isidro" and "Buenos Aires"—both translated by Jason Weiss).
    Also includes two Ocampo short stories: One from *Las invitadas* ("The Mastiffs
    of Hadrian's Temple"—Weiss translation) and a selection from *Los días de la
    noche* ("Ana Valerga"—translation by Frances S. Rivers).

Works about Silvina Ocampo

Aponte, Barbara B. "The Initiation Archetype in Arguedas, Roa Bastos and Ocampo."
    Latin American Literary Review 11, 21 (1982):45–55.
Araújo, Helena. "Ejemplos de la 'niña impura' en Silvina Ocampo y Alba Lucía [sic]
    Angel." *Hispamérica* 13 (1984):27–35. Also *La Scherezada criolla: Ensayos
    sobre escritura femenina latinoamericana*. Bogotá: Universidad Nacional de Col-
    ombia, 1989. Pp. 99–106.
Balderston, Daniel. "Los cuentos crueles de Silvina Ocampo y Juan Rodolfo Wilcock."
    Revista Iberoamericana 49 (1983):743–52.
Bianco, José. Introd. *El pecado mortal*. By Silvina Ocampo. Buenos Aires: Editorial
    Universitaria de Buenos Aires, 1966. Pp. 5–8.
Cozarinsky, Edgardo. Introd. *Informe del cielo y del infierno*. By Silvina Ocampo.
    Caracas: Monte Avila, 1970. Pp. 7–13.

Ghiano, Juan Carlos. *Poesía argentina del siglo XX*. Mexico City: Fondo de Cultura Económica, 1957. Pp. 211–14.

Klingenberg, Patricia Nisbet. "El infiel espejo: The Short Stories of Silvina Ocampo." Ph.D. diss. University of Illinois at Urbana-Champaign, 1981. (DAI 42 [1981]:2696-A.)

———. "A Portrait of the Writer as Artist: Silvina Ocampo." *Perspectives on Contemporary Literature* 13 (1987):58–64.

Matamoro, Blas. "La nena terrible." *Oligarquía y literatura*. Buenos Aires: Ediciones del Sol, 1975. Pp. 193–221.

Molloy, Sylvia. "Silvina Ocampo: La exageración como lenguaje." *Sur* 320 (1969):15–24.

———. "Simplicidad inquietante en los relatos de Silvina Ocampo." *Lexis* 2 (1978):241–51.

Percas, Helena. *La poesía femenina argentina (1810–1950)*. Madrid: Ediciones Cultura Hispánica, 1958. Pp. 616–39.

Pezzoni, Enrique. Estudio preliminar. *Páginas de Silvina Ocampo, seleccionadas por la autora*. By Silvina Ocampo. Buenos Aires: Editorial Celtia, 1984. Pp. 13–37.

———. "Ocampo, Silvina." *Enciclopedia de la literatura argentina*. Eds. Pedro Orgambide and Roberto Yahni. Buenos Aires: Editorial Sudamericana, 1970. Pp. 473–77.

VICTORIA OCAMPO
(1890–1979)
Argentina

Doris Meyer

BIOGRAPHY

Victoria Ocampo's role in the world of letters in Latin America is without parallel. Her influence as the founder and publisher of one of the most respected literary journals of this century, *Sur*, as well as her written testimony to a woman's intellectual odyssey, in the form of essays, letters, and a six-volume autobiography, establish her as a unique literary presence in her time. She was not only a trailblazer in the definition of women's right to literary legitimacy in Latin America, but also a pioneer in the effort to internationalize the cultural environment on a continent tending toward political xenophobia and isolationism.

Born in Buenos Aires in 1890, the eldest of six daughters in a wealthy and powerful family, Victoria Ocampo absorbed the traditional Argentina history and culture that her ancestors had helped mold while she simultaneously devoured the French and English poems, plays, and stories taught by her European governesses. In 1896 and again in 1908 the Ocampos traveled to Europe for year-long visits to expand the girls' cultural horizons. (Her youngest sister, Silvina,* also became a writer.) The mature Victoria's love of Paris and London and of the aesthetic and cultural stimulation they represented can be traced back to her childhood. Her limited humanistic studies, stressing the French language in which for many years she wrote more naturally than in Spanish, were considered appropriate for an upper class young woman. Albeit insufficient, this cosmopolitan education was the basis of her later obsession with "building bridges," as she put it, between the two continents that nourished her in flesh and in spirit.

As a child, and later as an adult, Ocampo was headstrong and unrelenting when it came to expressing her preferences, especially for books she read voraciously. Her predilection for the theater turned into a fervent desire to be an actress, but her parents would not hear of it. Rather than hurt them, she turned to writing, at first privately and primarily as therapy for pent-up desires and frustrations. A poignant, revealing testimony to this period in her life can be found in a collection of letters she wrote to her closest friend, Delfina Bunge, between 1906 and 1910, some of which are published in her *Autobiografía* (Autobiography). Here, as a teenager, Ocampo pours out her feelings of being different from other young women in her literary and artistic aspirations, while at the same time feeling drawn to a romantic ideal incarnate in a handsome suitor. Her own exceptional beauty, recorded in numerous photos and paintings, made her a magnet for men who saw her as a muse rather than as the artist she aspired to be; such misunderstandings plagued her all her life.

In 1912 she married an Argentine, Luis Bernardo de Estrada, with a background similar to hers; within a year it became clear that they were totally mismatched. Their marriage was a painful error Ocampo attributed to the repressive social customs of the time. In later life, she would often write about the injustices and indignities experienced by women of her generation. She also became an outspoken activist for women's rights, undoubtedly influenced by her suffering through years of marital estrangement and a clandestine love affair which she dared not make public out of consideration for her tradition-bound family.

Ocampo's first published works in the early 1920s were essays that appeared in *La Nación*, generally dealing with books she had read and found spiritually or intellectually enlightening. It was not customary for women to be admitted to the ranks of this prestigious paper, and Ocampo experienced her share of skeptical reactions by male contemporaries. However, several important friendships—with José Ortega y Gasset, Rabindranath Tagore, Count Hermann Keyserling, and Waldo Frank, all of whom visited Argentina and became admirers of this "Gioconda of the Pampa," as Ortega called her—changed the course of her intellectual life and gave her a seriousness of purpose precipitated as much by their rejected adulations as by their honest encouragement of her talents. Each one was initially a kind of literary hero to her; later, getting to know them individually, she seemed to find her own self-definition in return. With people and with books, Victoria Ocampo was a "reader" who thrived on "spiritual auscultation," but only if the spirit awakened resonances within herself.

After several more trips to Europe and one to the United States (New York would become another favorite city), Ocampo gathered the moral and intellectual support to found a literary journal named *Sur* in 1931. For the next forty-odd years she was its hands-on director and sole financial backer, an enterprise that demanded constant travel and extensive correspondence with distinguished contributors in the arts and letters from all over the world. She also founded a publishing house of the same name in order to publish translations (some done by her, others by colleagues like the then relatively unknown Jorge Luis Borges) of works she passionately admired by authors like Aldous Huxley, André Malraux, C. G. Jung, T. E. Lawrence, Albert Camus, and Virginia Woolf. Woolf, like many of the others, became a personal friend and a major influence on Ocampo's own writing.

At the same time *Sur* was being launched, Ocampo began to publish her own essays in separate volumes, which she called *Testimonios* (1935; Testimonies). Eventually, there were ten volumes, published between 1935 and 1977; together they form a personal collection of her private passions (of the nonsexual sort) and preferences dealing with personalities, books, nature, world events, movies, social customs, and a host of other topics. In a few cases, notably her personal experiences with Virginia Woolf and Count Hermann Keyserling, she published longer monographs in separate editions; the same is true of her studies of Dante (published by Ortega's *Revista de Occidente* Press), T. E. Lawrence, and Bach. Her love of music and her belief in its capacity to express emotions are evident in the organic style of her essays, always highly personal and often lyrical in their rhythmic cadences and *ritornellos*. Her ability to seek out resonances and affinities in other works helped her to identify her own authentic voice.

Ocampo protested frequently that she was incapable of writing fiction because, being an introvert by nature, she could only reach the outside world through her own experience. Writing was a vital necessity, a way to communicate with others and with her inner self. A profoundly shy woman despite her imperious bearing and imposing reputation, she found her greatest pleasure in sharing her enthusiasms in writing, usually waking at dawn and writing in bed for hours before rising. She was an inveterate letter-writer and note-scribbler; her collected (largely unpublished) correspondence in itself constitutes an important part of Latin American cultural history.

Ocampo declared herself and her journal apolitical, yet she took a firm stand against fascism in Italy and Spain, received refugees from Nazi-occupied Europe at her spacious home in San Isidro (a suburb of Buenos Aires), and defied Perón's threats by continuing to publish *Sur*, which had always espoused democratic principles. In 1953 she was summarily arrested and incarcerated for a month in Buen Pastor Prison, an experience that profoundly affected her. It was the first time she had been deprived of all she cared most about (books, friends, family) and the first time she was intimately exposed to women from other social classes. The solidarity and concern these women shared with her touched Ocampo in an almost religious way; she had always been an admirer of Mahatma Gandhi and his doctrine of self-abnegation and nonviolence, but she never had occasion to live his moral teachings in the flesh. This experience also gave new urgency to her writing; it was around this time that she began to write her memoirs, though she refused to publish them during her lifetime. She also wrote a play (unpublished) about the women of Buen Pastor, one of several plays she wrote beginning with the Modernist fable *La laguna de los nenúfares* (1926; The water-lily pond) in the early 1920s.

Victoria Ocampo was actively involved with publishing, writing, translating, and hosting colloquia sponsored by *Sur* until the time of her death in 1979. Two years earlier, she was voted the first woman member of the Argentine Academy of Letters, the most prestigious of many prizes and awards she received during her lifetime. Upon accepting the award in the name of all women who had been denied intellectual equality and opportunity in the past, she said with characteristic directness to her male colleagues in the Academy: "The world is adapting to a new reality, one that can no longer be denied, one that will benefit you as much as it will us women."

MAJOR THEMES

In the tradition of the great Renaissance humanist Michel de Montaigne, Victoria Ocampo believed that understanding and self-development were best achieved by studying the nature of man, understood in the generic sense. In an early essay, "Huxley en Centroamérica," in *Testimonios* I (p. 375), she wrote that she was most moved by how individual human beings accept and endure their destiny, and how they struggle to find their self-expression. The concept of life as a drama—written in its broad outlines by a kind of divine order but interpreted for better or worse by the individual—is central to Ocampo's view of human life and to the spirit of her work. Consequently, she often wrote about the importance of childhood memories as a means of identifying the themes of individual dramas, and her own work was rich in this recollective vein. She would always look beyond the strictly literary and intellectual aspects of a work (or an author), a prime example of this being her 1942 study of T. E. Lawrence in *338171 T. E. (Lawrence de Arabia)*), which was praised by A. W. Lawrence as the most perceptive and well balanced of all the portraits of his famous brother. Ultimately, this approach to reading and writing was profoundly self-referential, that is to say, the biography contained elements of autobiography.

One of Ocampo's earliest themes, expressed in her first published article, "Babel" (1920), reprinted in *Testimonios* I, is that the term *equality* applies to human rights but not to human attributes, and that destiny of birth involves a portion of injustice that cannot be changed by human law. Her European-oriented upbringing led her to look to the Old World as a source of spiritual and artistic education for the New and to focus on culture rather than on socioeconomic questions, thereby conveying the impression of anti-Argentinism and elitism to the populist-oriented public at home. There is no doubt that she was a cultural internationalist before it was acceptable to say so in Latin American literary circles (as it is today), and she was not swayed by left-wing criticism of *Sur*'s editorial policies which tended to reflect her own preferences in the arts and letters. But it would be absurd to deny her deep-seated patriotism, evidenced in many of her works on Argentine history and culture, or her essentially liberal, democratic philosophy.

Building bridges between cultures was an image Victoria Ocampo frequently used to describe the motive behind her testimonial essays. Her intentions were not exclusively to introduce Europe to Latin America; as a Latin American who traveled abroad, she was intimately acquainted with the feeling of "otherness," a recurring theme in her work. She understood and deplored European ignorance and condescension with regard to Latin America; part of her intention in founding *Sur* was to give readers abroad a look at the best of Latin America, from landscapes to authors. Again, Ocampo would find herself in discovering the strengths and beauties of her own continent: "Sólo nos pertenece lo que queremos de verdad. Sólo se poseen las cosas en la medida en que se siente amor por ellas. Toda otra posesión es ilusoria." (Only what we truly love belongs to us. We can only possess things to the extent that we feel love for them. All other possession is illusory, "Nahuel Huapi," *Testimonios* III, p. 209.)

As a woman in a traditional *machista* society, Victoria Ocampo also knew another kind of "otherness" to which she frequently testified in her writing. The demeaning and patronizing attitude of the male literary establishment in Argentina had intimidated but not defeated her as a young woman writer in the 1920s; by the 1930s and 1940s, she had become a knowledgeable and committed feminist, finding inspiration in the writings of Virginia Woolf and doing battle with the Argentine legislature when it tried to rescind certain civil rights accorded to women in the late 1920s. In 1936 she spoke of the need for women's "liberation" in Argentina, in "La mujer, sus derechos y sus responsabilidades" (Woman: her rights and responsibilities). Women's education and free expression, she believed, would not only benefit future generations under their tutelage, but also promote their own self-esteem as independent and responsible human beings. Ocampo knew the pitfalls of stereotyped and idealized images of women; her short book devoted to Keyserling is a classic repudiation of the male tendency to circumscribe women by their own projected fantasies. Once free to express their autonomous selves, she said, women would define a new aesthetic: "Pues entiendo que una mujer no puede aliviarse de sus sentimientos y pensamientos en un estilo masculino, del mismo modo que no puede hablar con voz de hombre" (For I believe that a woman cannot unburden herself of her feelings and thoughts in a masculine style, just as she cannot speak with a man's voice, "Carta a Virginia Woolf," *Testimonios I*, p. 15). Considering this was written in 1934, Victoria Ocampo was clearly a woman ahead of her time.

Everything Ocampo wrote was directly related to her experience, to the point that one could say that her entire work was part of an autobiographical enterprise. Yet the six-volume *Autobiografía*, published posthumously between 1979 and 1984, is more intimate and revealing than the essays in the ten volumes of *Testimonios*. In these memoirs, which she often threatened to destroy before her death, Ocampo traced the contradictions of her emotional and intellectual development as a young woman, focusing on the years before the founding of *Sur*. They are pages she had to write to bear witness to the most agonizing experiences of her female life, which her sense of modesty and privacy did not allow her to articulate in public during her lifetime. As the document of an era in Latin American cultural history, and particularly women's history, it is invaluable; as a work of autobiographical literature, it is a unique example of female discourse and definition. The self that Ocampo portrays is both Latin American and European in formation, both old-fashioned and modern in sensibility, and—most significantly—thoroughly aware of the conflicts that made up her personal drama.

Perhaps the most frequent leitmotif of her work in this regard is a theme symbolized by the title of her first book, *De Francesca a Beatrice* (1924; From Francesca to Beatrice). In Dante's *Divine Comedy*, Francesca represents the earthly passions and Beatrice the divine spirit. Only by striving toward a reconciliation of the two can humanity—individually and collectively—achieve peace. This search for wholeness, or what Ocampo has called her "apetito de unidad" (appetite for unity), informs the best of her writing.

SURVEY OF CRITICISM

Critical reaction to Ocampo's work, beginning in the 1920s with Ortega's epilogue to *De Francesca a Beatrice*, was—as in the case of most talented women of her time—tainted by gender prejudice. Praise of her work was couched in effusive rhetoric that typically praised her as a muse and an exemplary figure of feminine sensitivity. (See my biography, *Victoria Ocampo: Against the Wind and the Tide*, 1979, 1990, for a detailed study of early critical reaction to her work.) As she became more powerful through the publication of *Sur*, both positive and negative criticism followed, such as the 1936 satiric essay *Un coloquio sobre Victoria Ocampo* (A Colloquy About Victoria Ocampo), by Marcos Victoria in which he calls her a "dilettante" and "a society woman" who is most valuable as a "living symbol" of Argentina and thus superfluous as a writer (Victoria, 1934, p. 63). In 1939 Leopoldo Marechal published an essay in *Sur* entitled "Victoria Ocampo y la literatura femenina," in which he praised her flowing, conversational style and noted that literature by women is more attuned to the mutable reality of the senses, whereas men's world is primarily that of the immutable or metaphysical (Marechal, 1939, p. 68); in a later work, *Adán Buenosayres* (Adam Buenosaires, 1948), however, he mocked her intellectualism.

Numerous articles in popular journals of the 1930s and 1940s attest to the status Ocampo had acquired by then as a legendary figure ("the most influential woman in the Argentine," according to a U.S. newspaper; "the intellectual ambassadress of a new people," wrote an Italian journalist). In Argentina, her writing was praised by critics such as Guillermo de Torre and Carlos Alberto Erro, but those who understood her most thoroughly as a writer and a woman were intimate friends such as Gabriela Mistral * and Waldo Frank.

A great deal has been written about Victoria Ocampo but rarely has it been objective. She was sensitive to this and occasionally responded to gross injustices, such as Count Keyserling's portrait of her in his memoirs. Frequent criticism was leveled at her for *Sur*'s supposed elitist attitude toward literature, for being too oriented toward Europe, and for not being supportive of those outside her "inner circle." Ocampo's critics frequently resented what she, as a member of the Argentine oligarchy, stood for as much as what her journal published.

But Ocampo also had many admirers who paid tribute to her; a 1962 volume, *Testimonios sobre Victoria Ocampo* (Testimonies about Victoria Ocampo), is a fascinating resource containing more than one hundred pieces of testimony, including more detailed essays by well-known writers and critics such as Enrique Anderson Imbert, Francisco Ayala, Roger Caillois, Daniel Cosío Villegas, Eduardo Mallea, Ezequiel Martínez Estrada, and Fryda Schultz de Mantovani who, a year later, published the first study of Victoria Ocampo and her work in book format, developed from that essay. Schultz de Mantovani limited her portrait to a biographical sketch and a series of "encounters" based on Ocampo's essays, to which she appended a sampling of the author's work. Neither of these two books, the most important publications about her in the 1960s, falls under the classification of scholarly criticism, yet both do represent the literary world's recognition of her contributions to Argentine literature and culture.

Two volumes devoted to her life and work in greater detail appeared in 1979, the year of her death, although they had been in preparation for some time before that. My own book, *Victoria Ocampo: Against the Wind and the Tide*, is a biography emphasizing the intellectual formation of a woman of intuitive feminist and liberalist principles who defied the strictures of her society in order to satisfy her hunger for knowledge and spiritual fulfillment. *Frente y perfil de Victoria Ocampo* (1980; Face and profile of Victoria Ocampo), by Alba Omil, is an impressionistic study of the woman and her work, with greater emphasis given to thematic preferences and her use of language and style.

In 1980 *Sur* published a special issue dedicated to its founder which includes twenty-one essays from the 1962 volume of homages, a handful of recent tributes, and a biobibliography built on quotations from her writings. Recognition of the woman and her accomplishments still seems to overshadow an appreciation of her literary contributions. A fiftieth anniversary issue of *Sur* in 1981 contains two essays, one by María Luisa Bastos and another by Enrique Pezzoni (both of whom were close to Ocampo for many years), that shed more light on the unique qualities of her writing. Bastos points out the didactic impulse behind the *Testimonios*, and Pezzoni singles out the dialectic of "acercamiento y distanciamiento" (approaching and distancing) that informs Ocampo's search for first-person authenticity. Another approach similar to these can be found in Marta Gallo's article (1985) comparing the *Testimonios* to the genre practiced by the medieval chronicle writer as well as the contemporary journalist. None of these critical studies represents a feminist perspective. My articles on Ocampo, published after the 1979 biography, endeavor to take that point of view and to focus on the expression of female experience found in her writing. In one study ("Victoria Ocampo: A Thirst for the Ultimate"), I point out the connection between Victoria's admiration of Gandhi and T. E. Lawrence (based on her belief in the ethic of nonviolence and an urge toward spiritual transcendence) and the impact of being imprisoned under Perón in 1953 alongside women of the most diverse social and political backgrounds.

Blas Matamoro's 1986 book, *Genio y figura de Victoria Ocampo* (1986;

Character and portrait of Victoria Ocampo), is derived mainly from Ocampo's writings and contains only occasional interpretations of her work as a female writer. His view of Ocampo as an androgynous writer who looked mainly to men for the approval she never received from her father does not take into significant account her extensive writings about women writers and women's unique literary perspective. This work is more useful for its retrospective analysis of the contributions of *Sur*.

Ironically, it may well be the medium of the cinema, which she so passionately responded to, that brings Ocampo to the attention of a larger public. A movie made for Argentine television by the Argentine director Oscar Barney Finn, entitled *Los cuatro rostros de Victoria Ocampo* (The four faces of Victoria Ocampo) was scheduled to be aired in the spring of 1989 and will also be presented at a European film festival.

Finally, it should be noted that David William Foster's 1980 bibliography of works by and about Victoria Ocampo is the most complete to date and should be used as a starting point for further studies, which are sorely needed to do justice to the significance of her literary achievements.

BIBLIOGRAPHY

Works by Victoria Ocampo

De Francesca a Beatrice. Madrid: Revista de Occidente, 1924.
La laguna de los nenúfares. Madrid: Revista de Occidente, 1926.
Testimonios. Madrid: Revista de Occidente, 1935.
Domingos en Hyde Park. Buenos Aires: Sur, 1936.
San Isidro. Buenos Aires: Sur, 1941.
Testimonios; segunda serie. Buenos Aires: Sur, 1941.
338171 T. E. (Lawrence of Arabia). Buenos Aires: Sur, 1942.
Testimonios; tercera serie. Buenos Aires: Sur, 1946.
Soledad sonora (Testimonios; cuarta serie). Buenos Aires: Sudamericana, 1950.
El viajero y una de sus sombras: Keyserling en mis memorias. Buenos Aires: Sudamer-
    icana, 1951.
Virginia Woolf en su diario. Buenos Aires: Sur, 1954.
Testimonios; quinta serie (1950–1957). Buenos Aires: Sur, 1957.
Habla el algarrobo. Buenos Aires: Sur, 1959.
Tagore en las barrancas de San Isidro. Buenos Aires: Sur, 1961.
Testimonios; sexta serie (1957–1962). Buenos Aires: Sur, 1963.
Juan Sebastián Bach, el hombre. Buenos Aires: Sur, 1967.
Testimonios; séptima serie (1962–1967). Buenos Aires: Sur, 1967.
Diálogo con Borges. Buenos Aires: Sur, 1969.
Diálogo con Mallea. Buenos Aires: Sur, 1969.
Testimonios; octava serie (1968–1970). Buenos Aires: Sur, 1971.
Testimonios; novena serie (1971–1974). Buenos Aires: Sur, 1975.
Testimonios; décima serie (1975–77). Buenos Aires: Sur, 1977.

Published posthumously:
Autobiografía I: El archipiélago. Buenos Aires: Sur, 1979.
Autobiografía II: El imperio insular. Buenos Aires: Sur, 1980.
Autobiografía III: La rama de Salzburgo. Buenos Aires: Sur, 1981.
Autobiografía IV: Viraje. Buenos Aires: Sur, 1982.
Autobiografía V: Figuras simbólicas; Medida de Francia. Buenos Aires: Sur, 1983.
Autobiografía VI: Sur y Cía. Buenos Aires: Sur, 1984.
Páginas dispersas de Victoria Ocampo. Buenos Aires: Sur, 1987.

Translations of Victoria Ocampo

Garnett, David, trans. *338171 T. E. (Lawrence of Arabia)*. Intro. A. W. Lawrence. New
    York: E. P. Dutton, 1963.
Kellerman, Owen, trans. "Aries and Capricorn." *Testimonies: Alberdi and Sarmiento
    in Modern Argentine Life*. By Nicolás Repetto and Victoria Ocampo. Tempe:
    Arizona State University Center for Latin American Studies, 1974. Pp. 25–36.
Meyer, Doris, trans. "Misfortunes of an Autodidact," "The Water Lily Pond." *Con-
    temporary Women Authors of Latin America: New Translations*. Eds. Doris Meyer
    and Margarite Fernández Olmos. Brooklyn N.Y.: Brooklyn College Press, 1983.
    Pp. 77–106, 217–25.
————. "A Selection of Essays (15) by Victoria Ocampo." *Victoria Ocampo: Against
    the Wind and the Tide*. By Doris Meyer. New York: Braziller, 1979. Pp. 195–
    284. Reprinted University of Texas, 1990.
————. "Woman's Past and Present." *Lives on the Line: The Testimony of Contemporary
    Latin American Authors*. Ed. Doris Meyer. Berkeley: University of California,
    1988. Pp. 49–58.
Ocampo, Victoria, trans. "Letter to Waldo Frank." *Review* (Spring 1974):51–52.
————. *Tagore on the Banks of the River Plate. Rabindranath Tagore: A Centenary
    Volume*. New Delhi: Sahitya Akademi, 1961.
Onís, Harriet de, trans. "The Lakes of the South." *The Green Continent*. Ed. Germán
    Arciniegas. New York: Alfred A. Knopf, 1944. Pp. 116–22.
Treitel, Renata, with Maralee Waidner, trans. "Yesterday, Today and Tomorrow."
    Nimrod (Spring-Summer 1976):151–56.

Works about Victoria Ocampo

Adam, Carlos. "Bio-bibliografía de Victoria Ocampo." *Boletín Capilla Alfonsina* 29
    (1974):38–67.
Basaldúa, Hector, ed. *Testimonios sobre Victoria Ocampo*. Buenos Aires: n.p., 1962.
Bastos, María Luisa. "Escrituras ajenas, expresión propia: *Sur* y los *Testimonios* de
    Victoria Ocampo." *Revista Iberoamericana* 110–11 (Jan.–June 1980):123–37.
Bianco, José. "Victoria." *Vuelta* 53 (Apr. 1981):4–6.
Christ, Ronald. "Figuring Literarily: An Interview with Victoria Ocampo." *Review*
    (Winter 1972):5–13.
————. "To Build Bridges: Victoria Ocampo, Grand Lady of *Sur*." *Nimrod* (Spring-
    Summer 1976):135–41.
Cincuentenario (1931–1981). Special issue of *Sur* 348 (Jan.-June 1981). (Contains essays
    about *Sur* and Ocampo by María Luisa Bastos, Enrique Anderson Imbert, Eduardo
    González Lanuza, Alicia Jurado, and Enrique Pezzoni.)
Correas de Zapata, Celia. "Victoria Ocampo y Virginia Woolf: La rebeldía en el ensayo."

Ensayos hispanoamericanos. By Celia Correas de Zapata. Buenos Aires: Corregidor, 1978. Pp. 165–81.

Estiú, Emilio. "El problema estético en la obra de Victoria Ocampo." *Cuadernos del Idioma* 8 (1967):27–49.

Foster, David William. "Bibliography of Writings by and about Victoria Ocampo (1890–1979)." *Inter-American Review of Bibliography* 30 (1980):51–58.

Gallo, Marta. "Las crónicas de Victoria Ocampo: Versatilidad y fidelidad de un género." *Revista Iberoamericana* (July-Dec. 1985):679–86.

Greenberg, Janet Beth. "The Divided Self: Forms of Autobiography in the Writings of Victoria Ocampo " Ph.D. diss. University of California, Berkeley, 1986. (DAI 47, 7 [Jan. 1987]:2603A.)

Jurado, Alicia. "Victoria Ocampo: mi predecesora." *Boletín de la Academia Argentina de Letras* 46 (Jan.-Dec. 1981):81–95.

Keyserling, Hermann A. von. "Victoria Ocampo." *Viajes a través del tiempo*. Buenos Aires: Sudamericana, 1949–1951. II:447–91.

King, John. *SUR: A Study of the Argentine Journal and Its Role in the Development of a Culture (1931–1970)*. Cambridge, England: Cambridge University Press, 1986.

Kripalani, Krishna. "Victoria Ocampo: A Cultural Bridge Between Three Continents." *The Visvabharati Quarterly* 43 (1979):277–86.

"Letras en homenaje al cincuentenario de la revista *SUR* 1951–1981." *Letras de Buenos Aires* 2 (Jan.-Mar. 1981):133–63. (Contains essays by Alicia Jurado, Enrique Pezzoni, and Enrique J. G. Cobo Borda on Ocampo's literary journal and her writings.)

Marechal, Leopoldo. "Victoria Ocampo y la literatura femenina. " *Sur* (Jan. 1939):66–70.

Matamoro, Blas. *Genio y figura de Victoria Ocampo*. Buenos Aires: Editorial Universitaria de Buenos Aires, 1986.

Meyer, Doris. " 'Feminine' Testimony in the Works of Teresa de la Parra, María Luisa Bombal and Victoria Ocampo." *Contemporary Women Authors of Latin America: Introductory Essays*. Eds. Doris Meyer and Margarite Fernández Olmos. Brooklyn, N.Y.: Brooklyn College Press, 1983. Pp. 3–13.

———. "The Multiple Myths of Victoria Ocampo." *Revista/Review Interamericana* (Fall 1982):385–92.

———. *Victoria Ocampo: Against the Wind and the Tide*. New York: Braziller, 1979. (To be reprinted in Spring 1990 by the University of Texas Press.)

———. "Victoria Ocampo: A Thirst for the Ultimate." *The Visvabharati Quarterly* 44 (1979–1980):113–29.

Mistral, Gabriela. "Victoria Ocampo." *Gabriela piensa en . . . .* Ed. and prol. Roque Esteban Scarpa. Santiago de Chile: Editorial Andrés Bello, 1978. Pp. 49–56.

Omil, Alba. *Frente y perfil de Victoria Ocampo*. Buenos Aires: Sur, 1980.

Ortega, Julio. "Victoria Ocampo y *Sur*." *Lexis* 5 (July 1981):187–92.

Rodríguez Monegal, Emir. "Victoria Ocampo." *Vuelta* (Mexico) 30 (May 1979):44–47.

Schultz de Mantovani, Fryda. *Victoria Ocampo*. Buenos Aires: Ediciones Culturales Argentinas, 1963.

Torre, Guillermo de. "Victoria Ocampo, memorialista." *Tres conceptos de la literatura hispanoamericana*. Buenos Aires: Losada, 1963. Pp. 96–114.

Torres Fierro, Danubio. "Entrevista a Victoria Ocampo." *Plural* 5 (1975):18–25.

Victoria, Marcos. *Un coloquio sobre Victoria Ocampo*. Buenos Aires: "Futura," 1934.

"Victoria Ocampo, 10 años después." *Cultura de la Argentina Contemporánea* (Edición Aniversario) 5, 30 (1989):8–43. (Contains essays and testimonies about Ocampo by a variety of Argentine writers, as well as her Academy speech of acceptance and photos.)

Victoria Ocampo (1890–1979): Un homenaje. Special issue of *Sur* 346 (Jan.-June 1980). (Contains numerous essays by friends and colleagues of Ocampo.)

EUNICE ODIO
(1922–1974)
Costa Rica

Rima de Vallbona
Translated by Bertie Acker

BIOGRAPHY

Born in San José, Costa Rica, and descended from Basque, Navarrian, and Catalonian ancestors, Eunice Odio Boix was a woman of restless and rebellious temperament. Her independence could be seen from an early age when she used to run away from home to wander about the streets of her native city. In fact, Odio's mother did not dare to enroll her daughter in school until she had reached eight years of age, for she feared that the child's innate rebelliousness might cause her to be expelled. According to what Odio relates in her letters, she learned to read in only two days at school, and from that moment on abandoned her meanderings through the town to take refuge in the world of books. As she was very gifted, she grew bored in class and surreptitiously would read Jules Verne, Emilio Salgari, and others, paying no attention to the teacher. Nonetheless, when she finished elementary school she received the gold pen that was given to the most distinguished student.

Years later, in Mexico, her aggressive and rebellious spirit led her to quarrel with the intelligentsia of the left with whom she was associated in her youth. This alienated sectors that controlled a large part of the cultural and artistic activity in Mexico where the myth of the Revolution still prevailed, explains Juan Liscano (1975, Pp. 32–33). Nor did she know how to get along in the literary world where mutual interests and influence count for so much. Because of her attitude, her name was anathema in Costa Rica, even after her death: Only recently was one of her books, *Los elementos terrestres* (1948; The elements of earth) published there for the first time, as was its second edition (San José: Editorial Costa Rica, 1984). Her works were at last included on the reading list for Costa Rican students.

At the age of nine, chicken pox and measles left Eunice so weak that her parents sent her to relatives to recuperate on their ranch deep in the jungle. This was her first contact with the fierce, savage nature of the country. To her the countryside represented her "paradise visited," and it left an enduring impression on her sensitive soul. From this contact was born her mythic concept of nature and of the great river which, together with the mythic image of the father figure, are projected throughout her poems as a theme and as an integral part of her lyric discourse.

During the first period of her poetic production, Odio, an impassioned individualist, distinguished herself from her peers in the ranks of the extreme left by her belligerence. Later she adopted a completely opposite attitude that led her to react against communism. When the ex-Communist leader Carlos Pellecer changed his ideological position, she wrote to him: "quisiera ser no una enemiga de la política soviética, sino tres, doblemente encarnizada" (I would like not to be an enemy of Soviet politics, but rather three enemies, doubly obstinate). She justified her hatred by saying that in the Soviet system, the state serves the few in order to better oppress and exploit the many. In the same letter, she called the socialist experience a true "suicidal impulse" (*Eunice Odio en Guatemala*, 1983, pp. 132–35). Her own political position thus evolved, in later life, into a constant defense of democracy. In the final years of her life, and perhaps because of her friendship with Elena Garro,* her passionate feelings brought her to a fanatical religious devotion for the Archangel Saint Michael.

Eunice Odio's literary career began in 1945 with the publication of her first poems in the pages of *Repertorio Americano*, founded and directed by Joaquín García Monge. Two years later she was awarded the prestigious Central American prize for poetry, "15th of September," for her poetic volume *Los elementos terrestres*, which was published in Guatemala in 1948. Because of the welcome she was given in that country and the indifference she faced in her own country, Odio became a Guatemalan citizen.

Many of the poems she wrote during this epoch only became known the year she died (1974), in an anthology prepared by the author herself for Editorial de Universidades Centroamericanas (EDUCA), which was given the title *Territorio del alba y otros poemas* (1974; Territory of dawn and other poems). These poems were probably the ones that had formed a part of three books that she mentioned and that have never been found: *Filo de luna nueva, Pobre calle pobre*, and *Agua, camina, clara*. Her second book, *Zona en territorio del alba* (1953; Zone in the territory of dawn), was written between 1946 and 1948, but it was not published until 1953 in Argentina, as an example of the best contemporary Central American poetry. A year afterward, she finished *El tránsito de fuego* (1957; Path of fire), a work she had begun in 1948 and published in San Salvador in 1957. In this extensive poem of over four hundred pages, Eunice Odio left her lyrical voice indelibly etched on Latin American geography.

In February 1955 she took up residence in Mexico, where she remained until her death, translating foreign books into Spanish for different publishing houses.

She also served as a reporter for *El Diario de Hoy* and published articles in literary journals in Mexico and throughout the world, among them *Zona Franca, Revista Mexicana de Literatura, Pájaro Cascabel, Cuadernos de Bellas Artes, Cultura, El Cuento, El Libro y el Pueblo*, and *Cuadernos*. Her residence in Mexico was interrupted by two and a half years spent in the United States. The painful life of a writer without national roots takes on a tragic dimension in Eunice Odio's poetry as it is distilled in the word *apátrida* (exile or person without a native land). In several instances she refers to the creator (or poet) as an *apátrida* who would thus share her own condition as an exile.

Odio lived in the most deplorable poverty and isolation in the final days of her life in Mexico. She was so alone that her body was not found until several days after her death in 1974. However, as early as 1973 the critic Carlos Duverrán lamented that Eunice Odio's work was unknown in Costa Rica. The following year Juan Liscano wrote in Venezuelan newspapers that it was incredible that in Latin America the works of Eunice Odio were unknown, although she was in his opinion an exceptional and overwhelming poet.

In effect, Eunice Odio's poetry is composed with intense connotative depth, a wealth of primordial intuition, a mastery of lyric resources, artistic perfection, thematic universality, the graceful management of the rhythmic elements that constitute the texture of her poems, and the mythic cosmovision that broadens the spatial-temporal outlines of her texts. For these reasons, Humberto Díaz-Casanueva considers society's ignorance of her work arbitrary and deems it equivalent to the proscription of one of the most exceptional lyric poets in America.

Odio's life was a continual irony. Fascinated and drawn by the light that was made the flesh of poetry in her verse, she died the most obscure death. A worshipper of life and of the highest ideals in art and beauty, she spent her last years destroying herself with alcohol and filled with an insolent and vile fury that drove her friends to distance themselves from her. Devoted to Mexico, she declared it her true country, and she confessed that a love of Mexico and a desire to be Mexican had besieged her since she was a child. Nonetheless, none of her major works was published in that country; not even the negotiations that have been conducted in an effort to publish her complete works have crystallized up to the present. Upon examining anthologies of contemporary Mexican poets, one observes that her name does not appear in them.

Only a very small circle of Hispanic intellectuals knows her poetry. However, her talent has also been manifested with equal artistic vocation in prose.

MAJOR THEMES

Around the mid-twentieth century, Costa Rican poetry began to join the new universal vanguardist movements led by the voices of Eunice Odio, Alfredo Cardona Peña, Isaac Felipe Azofeifa, and Arturo Echeverría. Although dedicated to an ontological search, and although some are still possessed by a nostalgia for eternity, these are the poets who initiated the break with traditional lyric poetry in this Central American country.

Eunice Odio's poetry stems from the Romanticism of poets she herself calls the *románticos exasperados* (exasperated Romantics), because they assume such a passionate and vigilant attitude. They hunger for space, thus breeding feelings of unbounded terror and anguish in themselves. With *El tránsito de fuego*, there is no doubt that she joins the ranks of what she called "the family of the metaphysical poets" who do not seek external reality in their poetry, but rather the mystery of the internal and the depths of being.

The poetics of Eunice Odio are gradually defined throughout her production as an aesthetic-ascetic initiation: a "path of fire" in which the poet is transfigured into a demiurge whose written word has powers to invoke whatever is named. A poem, as a result of this intense process, is not merely a hobby nor even a means of leaving a name for posterity. Rather, it is a sustained asceticism and a longing for perfection. Yearning to enjoy that "Great Ballad," Odio rejects the solitude in which she is mired, because every poet's duty is to mingle with humanity and to be *pluránimo* (or plural in spirit). Odio's neologism attains a transcendent significance in her poetry; it expresses the creator's tragic condition of being the aggregate of all souls, and it constitutes one of the essential themes in her lyrical creation. In Odio's texts creator and poet are equivalent terms. Poetic creation and divine creation operate by means of words, another of the recurrent and transcendental themes in her writings.

There is in Odio's poetry an evolutionary process that has its roots in traditional attitudes obvious in the first poems she published or wrote between 1945 and 1947. This loyalty to tradition does not imply a rejection of the new lyric processes of that time. On the contrary, it embraces them and assimilates them, fusing new and old harmoniously. A reconciliation of traditional elements with the latest poetic innovations represents an essential characteristic of all her literature. The poems from this initial stage, in spite of being only the first fruits of her literary efforts, already reveal a poet with a mastery over the lyrical resources she manipulates. In particular, circumstantial themes predominate. She relates the death of a poet friend, or a visit from other friends; other poems are of a political nature showing a leftist tendency, a certain rebellious attitude, and a conscientious stand on world problems, specifically on the Spanish Civil War.

A second evolutionary stage is represented by *Los elementos terrestres* (1948), a collection of eight relatively lengthy poems in free verse. The unity of the text is sustained by the mystic-erotic theme and by a cosmic concept of reality. The connotative power of the polyvalent lyric images suggests the cyclical processes of nature, love, and poetic creation: Nature, Beloved, and Poet give life to the "terrestrial elements" that are respectively, fruit, son, and poem. The erotic-mystic lyricism of this text is composed of themes of supreme pleasures of the body, flesh, and sex, which, molded in daring images full of sensuality, capture the utmost ecstasy and a cosmic fusion with nature. The female lyric voice declares: "my sex like the world / floods and has birds" (p. 21). In turn, the masculine speaker says to his beloved: "yo haré que de tus muslos / bajen manojos de agua / y entrecortada espuma, / y extraños secretos" (p. 28, I will cause from your thighs / water abundantly to flow / and confused foam / and strange secrets). This is Odio's first text in which one can see traces of the Bible: themes, tone, metaphors, key words, and rhythmic devices (i.e., mystic eroticism, sensual images, parallel versification, alliteration, anaphora, accents). They refer especially to The Song of Songs, Job, Genesis, and Psalms; at the same time, the biblical traces recall the "Cántico espiritual" (Spiritual Canticles) of St. John of the Cross. In accordance with these models, the feminine voice prevails over the masculine.

Zona en territorio del alba (1953) represents Odio's definitive entrance into the vanguardism then in vogue. Odio adheres to creationism and to some techniques that belong to superrealism. The book contains a series of unconnected poems written between 1946 and 1948, rather short and in free verse. They have extremely varied themes such as infancy (a theme that will become obsessive in her last years as evidenced in her letters, which also constitute a rich literary corpus), friendship, and art expressed through the medium of dance. In general, these pieces have no unifying thread save their vanguardist tendency. However, it must be recognized that the lyrical resources used in them can be considered an effective trial effort that will reach fulfillment in later poems.

El tránsito de fuego (1957), the culmination of Odio's creative genius, is a lengthy poem, allegorical in nature, in the form of a dialogue. It is divided into four parts: " Integración de los padres" (Integration of the parents); "Proyecto de mí mismo" (Projection of self); "Proyecto de los frutos" (Projection of the fruits); and "La alegría de los creadores" (Joy of the creators). These four parts have a solid, organic unity. Nevertheless, they maintain such independence that, separated from the whole to which they belong, they still preserve their poetic identity and integrity. The lyricism of this text, always of the highest quality, is expressed with a restrained vehemence that transfigures the images into areas endowed with cosmic divinity. Aesthetic rigor and a hermetic quality characterize this book, making the poems at times completely impenetrable. Most of all, the expressive resources and the theme have been fused together so artistically that they become the most authentic poetry.

Because of the dialogue and the participation of the choruses, this metaphysical poetry is also dramatic. This drama, which does not conspire against the lyrical essence of the text, becomes notable following *Los elementos terrestres*, though not in such a conspicuous and mature form. In *El tránsito de fuego*, the voices of mythological and symbolic creatures stand out. Some come from the classical world, whereas others are invented by the author. Both attempt to unravel the mystery of Ion, the creator. These myths transmit to the poem a marked polyvalence giving it diverse superimposed levels and making it complex and difficult to analyze.

Furthermore, throughout these pages autobiographical traces lie hidden. One of these touches on the escapades of Odio when she was a child; the author confesses that she re-created those flights from home, as well as the mythified image of her own father, in "El Ido" *(Antología*, p. 48). This mythic father is the literary embodiment of Ion, he who has powers, like Apollo and Quetzalcoatl, to teach men propitiatory services and rituals, Liscano explains *(Antología,* pp. 61–62). This critic concludes by saying that Odio's creation of myths culminates, a decade before her death, in the cult which she professed to the Archangel Saint Michael and which crystallized in one of her most perfect poems, "Archangel Michael." Frustrated motherhood is present as an autobiographical reference as well as a basic theme. Other themes, besides those already mentioned, run the gamut from the disquieting birth of man, his painful human reality, solitude, life, death, love, and even biblical and ontological-metaphysical themes.

According to Juan Liscano *(Antología,* p. 42) in reality two themes predominate in *El tránsito de fuego*—that of the creator and his works, on the one hand and that of the grievous condition of creators who are exiles and "pluránimos" on the other. The tragic condition of Ion, the creator, is greatly intensified when he recognizes that he is "la suma de todas las ánimas" (the sum of all souls), and he postulates the horror of knowing that he is scattered in others: "I am their name and I contain them all. / / But they, Lord, are each one" (p. 196). Standing before a woman who has made love with a young man, Ion complains because he does not know which one of the three he is, since the night before his body was filled with the amorous sounds from her body (p. 199).

In his exile, as a dispersed spirit, Ion discovers that no one knows him and then he finds himself forced to accept solitude (p. 45). In contrast, and giving a more tragic dimension to Ion the creator, is the fact that men and women, despite being his own children and living transitory lives (p. 324), have the immense power of creating their creator in their dreams (p. 204).

In her work as in her personal life, light is a lyric-ontological obsession for Odio. Light in *El tránsito de fuego* represents the supreme and total achievement of the creator, a beginning from the origins or birth until the closing of total night in the cycles of day and night, as in those of creation. Light, clarity, brilliancy, splendor, dawn, aurora, day, fire, illumination, and morning are key words that signal a longing for total "light-realization." Thus, *El tránsito de fuego* is an allegory of the ascent of the creator toward the morning of creation. The first part of the text develops in an antithetical climate in which emptiness and expansion, sleep and waking, night and day, silence and the word, shadow and light, dying (dust, "downward") and living (undying, going "to the heights," "upward") struggle against each other.

In the evolution of Odio's literary creation, the final stage emerges in 1954, the year she finished writing *El tránsito de fuego*, when she began to produce prose in a constant and intense way. Actually, the author published only two booklets in prose: *El rastro de la mariposa* (1968; *The Trace of the Butterfly*, 1978, a story), and *En defensa del castellano* (1972; In defense of Spanish, a polemic essay). The rest of her prose is found in the following collections: the

Antología (1975; Anthology) compiled by Juan Liscano; *La obra en prosa de
Eunice Odio* (1980; Eunice Odio's prose works) gathered by Rima de Vallbona;
and *Eunice Odio en Guatemala* (1983; Eunice Odio in Guatemala) compiled by
Mario A. Esquivel.

In about 1959 Odio declared that she had achieved the supreme ambition of
her life: to write stories. She confessed that her difficulty in dealing with that
genre was rooted in language, since until then she had been trained in poetic
discourse, which is essentially synthetical, while narrative writers must concentrate on analysis (Odio, *En defensa del castellano*, 1972, p. 24). As she implies
in her letters, she wrote only three stories. Two of them, "Había una vez un
hombre" (1965; "Once there was a man," 1978), and *El rastro de la mariposa*
(1968), were published. However, the third, "Omar 7" (whose title is a name),
has thus far not been found. Her works in prose, whether essays or stories, have
the merit of being written with a generous dose of restraint, although they do
not achieve the creative luminosity of her poetry.

The creationism that Eunice Odio follows has the mark of moderation, for it
is nourished by traditional, Romantic, and biblical elements. Perhaps because
of this presence of the traditional, her poetry never reaches the exaggerated
revolutionary ruptures that characterize many twentieth-century poets, neither in
the initial stage of *Los elementos terrestres* nor in the stages that follow. She
does not experiment by eliminating punctuation from her poetry, as many have
done; nor does she venture into antipoetry. She does not even attempt Concrete
poetry, although her lyric texts are characteristically composed with a rigid
structural exactness in which signified and signifier blend harmoniously.

SURVEY OF CRITICISM

Eunice Odio en Guatemala (1983), edited by Mario A. Esquivel, contains a
series of Eunice Odio's works that were published in Guatemalan magazines
and newspapers. In addition, it offers copies of the criticism that greeted the
appearance of *Los elementos terrestres*. In the aforementioned criticism, all of
an impressionistic nature, the following tendencies are observed: First, critics
utilized a reasoning that belonged more to the newspaper social columns written
for women at that time; second, they evaluated her as a budding poet within the
linguistic paradigms of what was then considered feminine poetic discourse. The
latter tendency consisted of discounting her merit as a poet to view her, above
all, in the light of her political leanings.

Within these parameters, Augusto Monterroso insists particularly on Odio's
ideological aggressiveness during the first stage of her literary career. He comments that, although in Costa Rica she is judged an excellent poet, she is even
more esteemed because of her advanced leftist ideas (*Eunice Odio en Guatemala*,
p. 165). Later, after pointing out in a very superficial way certain points of
convergence between her poetry and that of Rafael Alberti, Federico García
Lorca, Juan Ramón Jiménez, and other Spanish poets, Monterroso affirms that

some of Odio's poems also have a great bellicose power, born in particular of the passion that the Spanish civil war awakened in her. Inspired by Spain's tragic history, an unsuspected virility emerges in her verses and she becomes a bold social poet. It is necessary to clarify that she later abandoned the social poetry of her early period, so that Costa Rica had to await Jorge Debravo who later cultivated social themes.

In the mediocre criticism of a time that tended to exalt her, not as the most exceptional poet of that period, but rather as a very beautiful woman free of the prejudices of society, a tasteless, sexually biased discussion, "Eunice Odio" by Héctor Benigno del Cordón stands out (Esquivel, 1983, pp. 169–91). In addition, inane references to her poetry abound, references more appropriate to the social pages of a newspaper than to literary criticism (pp. 175, 177).

An article published in the *New York Times* in 1969 stands apart from other criticism of that period. It refers to the interesting literary phenomenon of the excellent, rich, and valuable contribution of novels, short stories, plays, and poetry written by women. The writer of the article points out that these women writers, displaying great sincerity, deviate from the sociopolitical literature that was the accepted style of that time (p. 179). Moreover, the article singles out Eunice Odio for her professionalism, the lofty metaphysical character of *El tránsito de fuego*, and the exceptional value of her lyric creation. Finally, the article notes that Odio's works were becoming known in the Hispanic world alongside those of Pedro Salinas (Spain) and César Vallejo (Peru).

One must give Alberto Baeza Flores credit for having been a pioneer in rescuing the work of Eunice Odio. He included one of her poems in his *Antología de la poesía hispanoamericana* (1959: Anthology of Hispanic American poetry) at a time when her poetry had not yet received any great acclaim in the world of letters.

The Venezuelan poet and critic, Juan Liscano, has also played an effective role in rescuing Odio's works. His first contribution saved for posterity a collection of thirty-one letters (from 1965 to 1974), which reveal much about her life and her writings. Second, his essay "Eunice hacia la mañana" (1975) may be considered the first complete and objective treatment of her work. His essay stresses the biblical vein in her poetry and offers valuable information about the myths created by Odio and about some passages of an autobiographical character in *El tránsito de fuego*. Stefán Baciu affirms that Liscano's book is a necessary and fundamental work for knowing Eunice Odio. However, he indicates that it was a mistake to eliminate her vehemently expressed political opinions from her letters. In a chapter of his book, *Costa Rica en seis espejos*, the Rumanian critic provides a list of Eunice Odio's political essays as well as a listing of the journals in which they were published, a very valuable bibliographic contribution.

María Cruz Burdiel de las Heras analyzes in detail the traces of the Bible first pointed out by Liscano. In her "La poesía bíblica y Eunice Odio" (1987), she makes it clear that not only The Song of Songs, but also Job, Genesis, and Psalms left their mark on *Los elementos terrestres*.

"Tránsito de Eunice Odio" by Humberto Díaz-Casanueva describes the dramatic character of Eunice Odio's poetry and her "tendency toward the geometric" (*Antología*, 1975, p. 11) and contrasts *Residencia en la tierra* by Chilean Pablo Neruda with *El tránsito de fuego*. One of the most important studies is the one Alfonso Chase did on images in Odio's poetry (1975). Not only does the author undertake a minute and accurate review of the symbol of the angel from her first to her last poetic compositions, but he also analyzes, scrutinizes, and unravels a whole world of symbols that tend to fuse the biblical world with Greek myths. In these symbols, according to Chase, there is a marked narcissism (p. 6).

Conscious of the necessity of divulging Odio's literary production in the land of her origin, Rima de Vallbona has dedicated several studies to that purpose. *La obra en prosa de Eunice Odio* (1980) rescues some prose pieces that were published in magazines and newspapers from around the world between 1957 and 1974. This material covers essays about literature and painting, reviews, letters, and short stories. Furthermore, it offers the investigator the most complete bibliography by and about Eunice Odio. "Eunice Odio, gota de carne huracanada y sola" (1980), the essay that serves as an introduction to the book, undertakes an examination of Odio's poetry and comprises a synchronic analysis of two stories contained in the book. Vallbona's "La palabra ilimitada de Eunice Odio: *Los elementos terrestres*" (1984) introduces the second edition of that text printed after a lapse of more than thirty-five years. Her study concentrates on the lyrical polyvalence of the three levels that are superimposed and harmoniously fused into a cyclic poetic structure.

Recently, in "Eunice Odio: una mujer contra las máscaras" (1987), Laureano Albán compares *Los elementos terrestres* with the stereotyped concepts of Latin American machismo interpreted by Mexican poet and essayist Octavio Paz in "Mexican Masks," a chapter in his book *The Labyrinth of Solitude*. Throughout Albán's analysis he observes that in Odio's *Elementos* she breaks with the established norms of her patriarchal and bourgeois society. In this poetry, woman assumes an egalitarian and active stance relative to men. The critic then concludes that Odio lived contrary to the existential and social paradigms that her epoch assigned to her as a "respectable woman" (p. 327).

These new scholars by fomenting a systematic and methodical criticism of Odio's writings, as well as new editions and anthologies, are at last giving her the recognition and the place that are her due in contemporary Latin American poetry.

BIBLIOGRAPHY

Works by Eunice Odio

Los elementos terrestres. Guatemala: Editorial El Libro de Guatemala, 1948.
Zona en territorio del alba. Mendoza, Argentina: Brigadas Líricas, 1953.

El tránsito de fuego. San Salvador: Editorial del Ministerio de Cultura, 1957.

El rastro de la mariposa. Mexico City: Alejandro Finisterre, ed., n.d. First published in the magazine *Zona Franca* 58 (June 1968):7–13.

En defensa del castellano. Mexico City: Gráficas de Menhir, 1972

Los trabajos de la catedral. Mexico City: Editorial Espacio, [1971]. This small book, a very limited edition, is the last part of ''Proyecto de los Frutos'' from *El tránsito de fuego.*

Territorio del alba y otros poemas. Ed. Italo Vallecillos. San José: Editorial de Universidades Centroamericanas (EDUCA), 1974.

Antología. Rescate de un gran poeta. Ed. Juan Liscano. Caracas: Monte Avila Editores, C.A., 1975.

La obra en prosa de Eunice Odio. Ed. Rima de Vallbona. San José: Editorial Costa Rica, 1980.

Eunice Odio en Guatemala. Ed. Mario A. Esquivel. San José: Instituto del Libro, Ministerio de Cultura, 1983.

Translations of Eunice Odio

Bellver, Catherine G. trans. ''The Trace of the Butterfly'' (*El rastro de la mariposa*). *Five Women Writers of Costa Rica.* Ed. Victoria Urbano. Beaumont, Tex.: Asociación de Literatura Femenina Hispánica, 1978. 33–43.

Espadas, Elizabeth, trans. ''Once There Was a Man'' (''Había una vez un hombre''). *Five Women Writers of Costa Rica.* Pp. 22–32.

Works about Eunice Odio

Aguilar de la Torre. ''Resurrección de Eunice Odio.'' *Excélsior* (Mexico) Mar. 19, 1978:1–9.

Albán, Laureano. ''Eunice Odio: una mujer contra las máscaras (*Los elementos terrestres* ante ''Máscaras mexicanas'').'' *Revista Iberoamericana* 138–39 (Jan.-June 1987):325–30.

Baciu, Stefán. ''Admirable, querida Eunice.'' *El Imparcial* (Guatemala) July 10, 1974.

———. ''Eunice Odio Boix y Grave Peralta o el 'destino implacable' de la poesía (Esbozo para un retrato).'' *Costa Rica en seis espejos.* San José: Departmento de Publicaciones, Ministerio de Cultura, 1976. Pp. 123–39.

Baeza Flores, Alberto. ''Carta sin sobre a Eunice Odio.'' *Ancora* (Costa Rica) Nov. 11, 1984:1 and 3.

———. ''Eunice Odio: sueño y raíz, misterio y poesía.'' Prologue to *Zona en territorio del alba.* By Eunice Odio. Mendoza, Argentina: Brigadas Líricas, 1953. n.p. [–5.]

———. ''Tras un ángel que bajó a la mañana.'' *Evolución de la poesía costarricense (1974–1977).* San José: Editorial Costa Rica, 1978. Pp. 201–10.

———. ''Un retrato de Eunice Odio con sus caídas y grandezas.'' *La Nación* (Costa Rica) June 3, 1974:3–B.

Barrios Galindo, Ricardo, alias El Duque Floris. ''Notas bibliográficas—Las obras últimas de El Libro de Guatemala.'' *Diario de Centro América*, Sept. 25, 1948:3. Reproduced in *Eunice Odio en Guatemala*:172–74.

Burdiel de las Heras, María Cruz. ''La poesía bíblica y Eunice Odio.'' *Foro Literario* (Uruguay) 17 (First Semester 1987):42–50.

Cardona Peña, Alfredo, Augusto Monterroso, et al. ''Corona fúnebre para Eunice Odio.''

Territorio del alba y otros poemas. By Eunice Odio. San José: EDUCA, 1974. Pp. 239–44.

Chase, Alfonso. "Imágenes en la poesía de Eunice Odio: los ángeles." *Repertorio Americano* 2 (Jan.-Feb.-Mar. 1975):3–9.

———. "Nuestra Eunice." *Territorio del alba y otros poemas.* Pp. 245–47.

Díaz-Casanueva, Humberto. "Tránsito de Eunice Odio." *Antología.* By Eunice Odio. Ed. Juan Liscano. Pp. 9–14.

Duverrán, Carlos Rafael. "Eunice Odio: su mundo transfigurado." *Andromeda* 3 (Oct.-Dec. 1987):2–5.

———. Introducción. *Poesía contemporánea de Costa Rica (Antología).* San José: Editorial Costa Rica, 1973. Pp. 9–18.

Esquivel, Mario A. "Presentación." *Eunice Odio en Guatemala.* Pp. 15–40.

"Eunice Odio en la Revista *Brecha.*" Selection of paragraphs and translations to Spanish by Cristián Rodríguez from the article published in the *New York Times*, Sept. 18, 1960. Reproduced in *Eunice Odio en Guatemala.* Pp. 178–80.

Fernández de Ulibarri, Rocío. "La voz de Eunice Odio se hace presente." *La Nación,* Oct. 31, 1984:8.

Huerta, Efraín. "Deslindades costarricenses." *Ancora* July 31, 1977:3–10.

Liscano, Juan. "Crítica a la crítica literaria." *El Nacional* (Caracas) Nov. 19, 1974: A4. With very slight modifications, it was published in the Cultural Supplement *La Nación* (Argentina) Sept. 21, 1975.

———. "Eunice hacia la mañana." *Antología.* By Eunice Odio. Caracas: Monte Avila Editores, 1975. Pp. 27–70.

Miranda Hevia, Alicia. "Eunice Odio, siempre y todavía." *La República,* Sept. 23, 1984.

Peña, Margarita. "El epistolario de Eunice Odio." *Uno a Uno* (Mexico) 70 (Jan. 25, 1978):18.

Porras, José A. "Nuestra Eunice Odio en Guatemala." *La República* (Costa Rica), Mar. 29, 1984:10.

Sandoval de Fonseca, Virginia. "Eunice Odio (1922–1974)." *Resumen de literatura costarricense.* San José: Editorial Costa Rica, 1978. Pp. 167–68.

Vallbona, Rima de. "Estudio valorativo de la obra de Eunice Odio." *Atenea* (Universidad de Puerto Rico) 1–2, (Jan.-Dec. 1985):91–101.

———. "Eunice Odio." *Women Writers of Spanish America—An Annotated Bio-Bibliographical Guide.* Ed. Diane E. Marting. Westport, Conn.: Greenwood Press, 1987. Pp. 281–83.

———. "Eunice Odio, a Homeless Writer." *Five Women Writers of Costa Rica.* Ed. Victoria Urbano. Beaumont, Tex.: Lamar University Printing Department, 1978. Pp. 44–50.

———. "Eunice Odio, 'gota de carne, huracanada y sola' (Introducción)." *La obra en prosa de Eunice Odio.* By Eunice Odio. San José: Editorial Costa Rica, 1980. Pp. 13–76.

———. "Eunice Odio: rescate de un poeta." *Revista Interamericana de Bibliografía/Inter-American Review of Bibliography* 2 (1981):199–214.

———. "La palabra ilimitada de Eunice Odio: *Los elementos terrestres.*" *Los elementos terrestres.* By Eunice Odio. 2d ed. San José: Editorial Costa Rica, 1984. Pp. 11–36.

————. ''Trayectoria actual de la poesía femenina en Costa Rica.'' *Káñina: Revista de Artes y Letras de la Universidad de Costa Rica* 3 and 4 (July-Dec. 1978):15–29.

Other Works Cited

Baeza Flores, Alberto. *Antología de la poesía hispanoamericana*. Buenos Aires: Ed. Tirso, 1959. Pp. 255–56.

YOLANDA OREAMUNO
(1916–1956)
Costa Rica

Arlene Schrade

BIOGRAPHY

Born on April 8, 1916, in San José, Costa Rica, Oreamuno was the only child of Carlos Oreamuno Pacheco and Margarita Unger Salazar. Because her father died when she was approximately nine months old, she was left in the care of her mother, but spent most of her youth and adolescence in the company of her maternal grandmother. There were also summers with her family on her father's side in Cartago and in Siquirres. As a child she loved the country and the water; even at an early age, she found them a source of peace and tranquility. Her forty years of life seem evenly divided into two twenty-year periods. The first twenty saw a personable, talented, beautiful, and popular society girl whose literary interests developed early. Her second twenty years were fraught with tragedy, loneliness, serious illnesses, and severe psychological pain.

Oreamuno studied at the Colegio Superior de Señoritas where, at sixteen, she won honorable mention for "¿Qué hora es?" (What time is it?), an essay on the role of women in secondary school life in Costa Rica. Later, she took up secretarial studies, hoping to use this skill to support her writing. In 1936, at the age of twenty, she published her first known story, "La Lagartija de la Panza Blanca" (The little lizard with the white tummy), a children's story for adults (Chase, *Relatos escojidos*, 1977) and "Para 'Revenar' No para Max Jiménez" (For "Revenar" not for Max Jiménez); she was at this time not only one of the most beautiful women in the country, but also one of the most controversial because of her life and beliefs. She worked at the Chilean legation where she met diplomat Jorge Molina Wood, married him, and moved to Chile. It is widely believed that she truly loved him, and he, in turn, encouraged her reading and writing. While in Chile she wrote two gems of fantasy that shaped her powers of observation, a characteristic of her later work: "Las Mareas Vuelven de Noche" (The tide comes at night) and "Don Juvencio" (Sir Juvencio). These remained in the hands of Herman Max and were finally published in 1971. She returned to Costa Rica in late 1936 after her husband, the victim of an incurable malady, committed suicide.

In July 1937 she married the economist and distinguished member of the then legal Costa Rican Communist party, Oscar Barahona Streber, and became involved with Marxist ideas, Communist groups, the public defense of Spanish Republicanism, and anti-Franco activities. This was one of her most prolific years as a writer. She was twenty-one. Her work appeared in *Repertorio Americano*, edited by Joaquín García Monge, who became her mentor, publisher, and friend. In that year she wrote and published many short stories: "40° sobre Cero" (40° (C) above zero), "18 de Setiembre" (The 18th of September), "Misa de Ocho" (8 O'Clock Mass), "Vela Urbana" (Urban vigil), "El Espíritu de mi Tierra" (The spirit of my land), "Insomnio" (Insomnia), and "El Negro, Sentido de la Alegría" (The Negro, feeling happiness).

In 1938 she began writing her novel *Por tierra firme* (For native land) in addition to several critical articles that were misunderstood by critics and the Costa Rican power elite as attacks on institutions and people in that country. At this time she formed lifelong friendships with the poet Eunice Odio* and the painter Margarita Bertheau. She published "Medios que usted sugiere al Colegio para librar a la mujer costarricense de la frivolidad ambiente" (Suggested means for schools to liberate the Costa Rican woman from the atmosphere of frivolity). In 1939 the essay "El ambiente tico y los Mitos Tropicales" (The Costa Rican ambience and tropical myths) and "El último Max Jiménez ante la indiferencia nacional" (The latest Max Jiménez in the face of national indifference) appeared.

In 1940 Oreamuno sent *Por tierra firme* to the novel section of the Congress of Spanish American writers sponsored by Farrar and Rinehart. The jury awarded first prize to Oreamuno, Fabián Dobles, and José Marín Cañas—a three-way Costa Rican tie. Because of this decision, Oreamuno refused to send her manuscript to New York. It was subsequently lost. She published "La vuelta a los lugares comunes" (Return to familiar places), and "Panorama poético colombiano construído solo en recuerdo" (Poetic Colombian panorama formed only on remembrance) also in 1940.

On September 21, 1942, her only child, her son Sergio Siméon Barahona Oreamuno, was born. This year was also marked by gradually deteriorating marital relations. Although she wrote many texts, owing to her tormented life she never published them. In 1943 she decided to leave Costa Rica for Mexico traveling through Guatemala, where she tried to write piecemeal the last chapters of a novel she called *Casta sombría* (Dark race), also known as *Dos tormentas y una aurora* (Two tempests and a dawn). It is not known if she actually wrote this work, but she spoke of it in 1944 in her letters, where she said that, when finished, it would be published by Editorial Leyenda with a prologue by Alfonso Reyes. She published "Protesta contra el folklore" (A protest against folklore) in 1943 and "Apología del limón dulce y del paisaje" (A defense of the sweet lime and the countryside), "Pasajeros al Norte" (Passengers to the north), and "Juan Ferrero" (Juan Ferrero), a fragment of *Dos tormentas y una aurora*, in 1944.

In 1945 Oreamuno announced that Alfonso Reyes had failed completely as a friend and the novel would not be published. She divorced her second husband and a great dispute followed over the custody of their son. He was taken away from her, and she could not see him. It was at about this time that her illnesses and severe psychological problems began; she suffered a lack of visual focus and had an operation for a bad kidney. Many other operations followed. Her health was broken, and she went through profound terrors of which she spoke eloquently in her letters. She wrote and published one of her most beautiful texts, "México es mío" (1945; Mexico is mine) and, according to Eunice Odio, began a new novel which she converted into a long story called "Valle Alto" (1946; High valley).

In 1946 "Valle Alto" was published. In 1947 she spoke again in a letter of another novel, *De ahora en adelante* (From now on), also known as *Nuestro silencio* (Our silence). She sent it and another novel, *La ruta de su evasión* (The path of their evasion) to a literary contest in Guatemala. For several months she lived in Guatemala under great economic and personal hardships and formed a deep personal relationship with Antonio Morales Nadjler, a relationship that never stabilized and only added more fuel to her mental anguish. She reread Marcel Proust, her great literary hero, and worked on other texts half-written or dreamed in the wake of her tragic experiences. She also published "Max Jiménez y los que Están" (1947; Max Jiménez and those who are here). In 1948 she won the "15 de Setiembre" prize for the novel in Guatemala for *La ruta de su evasión*. The other novel sent to the contest, *De ahora en adelante*, was never recovered, and possibly was burned, as it was the law for works not selected. She became a Guatemalan citizen and spoke highly of that country for recognizing and appreciating her as Costa Rica had not, a state of affairs that was to wound her deeply all her life. She published "Un regalo" (A gift) and "La llave" (The key), and in a letter to Joaquín García Monge, she stated she was no longer Costa Rican and wanted nothing more to do with the country. She was much changed by her problems, her illnesses, and the absence of her son.

In 1949 she had established herself in Guatemala and lived with Eunice Odio* in a rooming house. There she worked and imagined projects, though suffering from a great spiritual imbalance. She fought with friends and was consumed with amorous dissatisfactions. With the help of friends and her prize money she traveled to the United States for surgery, but became gravely ill in a charity hospital in Washington, D.C. A coffin was purchased, last rites were administered, and she was expected to die imminently. But she survived. She spoke of her novel, *José de la Cruz recoge su muerte* (José de la Cruz suspends his death), but no one knew if she actually wrote it or merely dreamed it. In 1950 *La ruta de su evasión* was published in Guatemala, and in *Diario* in Costa Rica, Lilia

Ramos published the first serious analysis of her work. Ramos was a friend, correspondent, and defender of Oreamuno's work before the ignorance and frequent attacks in Costa Rica. Oreamuno continued to suffer serious economic difficulties and decided, after another of her frequent amorous breaks, to return to Mexico. From then on she struggled against an incurable heart-valve lesion that exhausted her.

In 1951, again established in Mexico, she formed friendships with Juan Rulfo and Vicente Sáenz among others. At this time she was considered for a film contract which she did not receive, and she published her last known and most mature story, "De su obscura familia" (1951; Of his obscure family). In 1954 she traveled to Costa Rica for the last time where she was received by her old friends Lilia Ramos and Margarita Bertheau. She discussed her previous work with them and announced the completion of *José de la Cruz recoge su muerte*. According to Eunice Odio,* Oreamuno spoke of two more books, "Un lobo en la Majada (el aprisco)" (A wolf in the sheep-fold [The corral]) and "Las bodas de Canaán" (Wedding at Canaan), supposedly long stories that were never published. She returned to Mexico, and in 1955, her health much worse, she went to live in the home of Mexican friends, painter Reyes Maza and his wife, the writer María Luisa Algarra, who took care of her in her illnesses. Finally, in 1956 she went to live again with her friend Eunice Odio* and died on July 8, 1956, early on a Sunday morning. She was buried with only a stone, no. 7–363, to mark her grave.

In 1961 Editorial Costa Rica under the direction of Lilia Ramos published *A lo largo del corto camino* (Along the short road), No. 2 in a series of Costa Rican authors. It contained most of Oreamuno's published work, including four chapters of *La ruta de su evasión*, some letters, an outline of her life, and some commentaries. Her friends had her remains brought back to Costa Rica and buried. At this time a reevaluation of her work began. In 1977 Editorial Costa Rica published *Relatos escojidos: Yolanda Oreamuno* (Selected stories: Yolanda Oreamuno), edited by Alfonso Chase, a collection of her fiction with a critical commentary by the editor.

MAJOR THEMES

Oreamuno began writing at the end of one era and the beginning of another. In Costa Rica *costumbrismo*, a literary style emphasizing regional customs, predominated, but Oreamuno's intent was to avoid local accents and to strive for universality by penetrating the passionate, human soul. As such, she was experimental, psychological, and suprarealistic. Also as such, she was to incur the wrath of her contemporaries.

The overall characteristics of her work include themes like solitude, incommunication, indifferences to the needs of others, the restless search for eternal youth, obsessive ideas that destroy the humanity of individuals, the return to a primitive instinct in contact with the forces of nature, the frivolity of the social world including male-female relationships, death (especially in her letters), a spiritual atmosphere, and the use of the imagination.

Throughout almost all her narrative, Oreamuno wrote of the agony of existence. Her characters, climates, and themes are infused with her "yo": "I." It is difficult to classify her work because it fits into no school and because of its experimental nature. The writings resemble mood pieces, fragments, sketches, or tone poems. In her fiction Oreamuno explicated the creative act, depicted the sociological in spiritual and physical exploitation, and seemed to reach a maturity in her later Mexican cycle in which a unique sense of realism predominated. Although these stories occur against a Mexican backdrop, the characters are anonymous and the narrative focuses on human encounters without deliberate intent.

Oreamuno's work forms part of Spanish American expressionism, in the realm of the "fantastic," and ranges from the metaphysical to the marvelous. Some of these stories present the supernatural by means of rational explications that are highly intelligent. They paint the exoticism of unknown and inexplicable worlds that are poetic and chaotic, making the unreal seem real. The most intense of these is "Las mareas vuelven de noche," which Oreamuno wrote in Chile at the age of twenty-one. Here is "an intriguing fantasy, a disturbing dream, and an ambivalent world in which exterior reality is transposed with the aid of the author's sensitive imagination into poetic experience" (Asociación de Literatura Femenina, *Five Women Writers of Costa Rica*, 1978). "Las mareas" epitomizes the theme of universality and the sensual male-female relationship that is quintessentially Oreamuno.

Oreamuno's only extant novel, *La ruta de su evasión*, deals with the necessity that all human beings have of evading the reality that imprisons them. The author resides within her characters; her terms are introspective and psychological. In *La ruta*, the influence of the great European and North American masters–Marcel Proust, Thomas Mann, James Joyce, Virginia Woolf, and William Faulkner— is evident. The author's use of modern techniques of the avant-garde expresses itself primarily by means of the interior monologue and of the revelation of conscious thought through narration. The Vasco family, father, mother, and three sons with their wives and lovers, is explored through the feminine characters and their motives, the external descriptions, the social scene, and above all the sexual and amorous behaviors and thoughts of the characters. The characteristics of Oreamuno herself may be seen reflected in the searching character of Teresa, the mother, in Elena, the torturer, and in Aurora, the character of hope. There are also secondary themes of life and death, love, the problem of human relationships, solitude, honor, and pain as the essence of life. *La ruta* is an urban novel, written on two levels, one in the present and one in the mental sphere of thought and remembrance. Latent ideas generate conscious thought and the interpretation of dreams where time passes on a psychic plane. In many of her sketches, Oreamuno is obsessed with time.

In addition to her fiction, Oreamuno wrote essays that show a search and a desire for authenticity in art. They are personal, passionate protests and attacks against what the author considered a mediocre Costa Rican citizenry that exhibited negative criticism toward positive values in art. Oreamuno believed they constantly attacked the person and not the art, perpetuated myths, and failed in the education of women. She wrote both subjective and objective essays according to Vallbona (1972). The objective group is clear, direct, precise, without lyricism or unnecessary words. These pieces are orderly with a measured style and a sense of equilibrium. Most, however, are subjective; in these, the writer's tone is apologetic, admiring, hyperbolic, recriminating, passionate, or protesting. As original, personal impressions, the "I" is omnipresent.

According to Victoria Urbano (1968), Oreamuno exhibits two major themes in her essays: the objectivity of her criticism, and subjectivity where the central theme is she/herself. The objective criticism was written to laud or condemn artists and styles. Here Oreamuno attacked Costa Ricans for their indifference, mediocrity, and cowardice in judging their national artistic work, their indulgence toward bad poets and prose writers, their ultrapatriotism, antiaggressive spirit, and lack of responsibility, and their vices and jokes. On the other hand, she praised what she considered was good.

Alfonso Chase defines an important theme in Oreamuno's work: the depiction of characters who voluntarily live away from the logical archetypes of universal reason, beings who put themselves into experiences defined by their own social pathology. These are characters who are immersed in a collective world where their function consists of discovering that which for all others remains hidden (Chase, *Relatos escojidos*, 1977).

In all of Yolanda Oreamuno's writing she is searching: searching for self, searching for a Latin American identity, searching for form. She sought her own consciousness through her literary creations and, for the first time, an authentic Latin American voice. If at times she failed, at other times she succeeded brilliantly. In the vanguard of twentieth-century literary efforts in Spanish America, she was one of the first, and certainly one of the first women, to bridge the gap between the traditional writers of the nineteenth and early twentieth centuries and the brilliant new generations that most say began with the Argentine short-story writer and poet, Jorge Luis Borges.

SURVEY OF CRITICISM

Throughout most of her tragic, tormented life, Oreamuno was ignored by the Costa Rican and Latin American public, though harshly criticized privately. With the exception of Lilia Ramos, a friend and defender who began to give serious attention to Oreamuno's work around 1950, there was virtually no criticism until 1961, five years after Oreamuno's death. Editorial Costa Rica issued *A lo largo del corto camino* as No. 2 in its series of Costa Rican authors. In addition to much of her published work, this volume contains a brief biography, and some letters and commentaries, most of which were printed earlier in *Re-*

pertorio Americano. They should be considered commentaries and not true critical analyses in that they are intensely personal and often defensively pro-Oreamuno or anti-Oreamuno. The only other available criticism of the author's canon is a thesis by Manuel Picado (1973) done at the University of Costa Rica, critical essays by Victoria Urbano (1968) and Rima de Vallbona (1972), and an introductory analysis by Alfonso Chase in *Relatos escojidos: Yolanda Oreamuno* (1977). All of these critics are or were Costa Rican academics—the two women at universities in Texas and Chase at the Universidad Nacional in Heredia, Costa Rica. What has been written in English are brief explanations of "Valle alto" and "Las mareas vuelven de noche" in *Five Women Writers of Costa Rica* (1978). In the *A lo largo del corto camino* collection, those commentaries that do not deal with Oreamuno's work directly, and that includes most of them, are testimonials to "La ilustrísima" (or the illustrious one), as they called her. Those pieces that do consider her work are either celebratory or negative, and sometimes both.

The most positive and objective analyses are those written by Ermilo Abreu Gómez, José Marín Cañas, and Guido Fernández. Abreu (Mexico) describes Oreamuno's work as personal, almost intimate, poetic, rhythmic, and displaying the plasticity of the three-dimensional sense present in all modern Latin American novels. He views her work as having authentic value, though not belonging to any school.

José Marín Cañas, a family friend and contemporary author, states that Oreamuno had a restless talent, an avid curiosity, and a bitter and penetrating sensibility. Of the books with which he was familiar, one remained lost in the dissipations of her own doubts, never acquiring a name, and was the most human, tender, and brilliant. He knew her to have a great temperament, and stated that her advice, criticisms, and attitudes showed an extraordinary artistic sensitivity. Guido Fernández maintains that Oreamuno did not live up to her promise, but even so she was imaginative, vigorous, and full of color. He says she opened a new perspective for Costa Rican literature, giving it a wider and more ambitious horizon, and that she was part of a great vanguard of contemporary masters without a school.

Lilia Ramos, who was the first to seriously consider Oreamuno's work, recognizes that the author rejected what she considered dead and foolish ideas. Attacking Oreamuno's critics, Ramos writes that they were jealous because they could not accomplish what Oreamuno did. These critics, says Ramos, considered Oreamuno's educational background poor and her vocabulary awkward. They said she lacked a system, imitated Proust and Joyce, and so on. Ramos understood that Oreamuno was controversial, that she promoted restlessness, awakened consciences, and bared hidden things; these, however, were not weaknesses according to Ramos, but simply a reason for the public's attitude toward Oreamuno. Ramos considers Oreamuno's work outstanding, and speaks of her personal accent and singularity. Ramos believes "De su obscura familia" to be

Oreamuno's best story. She calls Oreamuno's heroes characters of flesh and blood (Ramos, *A lo largo del corto camino*, p. 335).

The most denigrating comments are those of Fabián Dobles (1945) and Abelardo Bonilla (1961), two other contemporary Costa Rican writers. Instead of directly attacking Oreamuno, Dobles reproves a Mexican journalist who reported that Oreamuno had said Costa Rica had no tradition of folklore. Her "Contra el folklore" was a well-known criticism of the provincialism of the Costa Rican literary tradition. Here she had touched naked nerves. Those who had written and were writing within Costa Rican regional realism felt insulted. Dobles argued that, although Costa Rica did not have a great tradition of folklore, it did not mean that work based on Costa Rican peasants and workers had no worth; fiction, he said, was either good or not good; and the innocent man in the street could not be blamed for writers' problems. Dobles argued that Oreamuno's words would discourage contemporary Costa Rican writers who looked for true grist for their narrative mills in the reality of Costa Rican life. He believed that writers needed to look to their own reality rather than far away. Oreamuno's defenders say he misunderstood her point. She was, they maintain, not saying there was no human worth in the Costa Rican people, but that to concentrate on the specific was to trivialize the universal.

In the most direct attack of all, Abelardo Bonilla (1961) writes that of all the Costa Rican writers who remain in the shadows of popular indifference, Oreamuno is at the bottom of the group. He maintains that it is the wider public and not the critical minority who appreciates the artistic values of a nation. He calls her a writer of authentic value, but believes the woman eclipsed the writer, a writer who did not mature. She had, he says, an extraordinary personality, a strong individuality, and too many dreams. She wanted to surpass in literature what her life did not afford her, but it was beyond her capabilities. He states that in her first novel of strength, *Por tierra firme*, she showed both her strongest and her weakest characteristics. Part I, the memories of childhood, was vivid and sure, original, elegant, and poetic like some of her stories, especially those written in Mexico with Mexican settings. The second part, where she deserted her personal themes and created an imaginative adventure, was much inferior, as was *La ruta de su evasión*. The author, he asserts, attempted an enterprise that was astonishing in its proportions. Her strong and audacious novel revealed the vitality and artistic ambition of the writer battling with her limitations— limitations, in a special sense, that began when she was very young, at sixteen, when she was interested in the masters, particularly Proust. Bonilla believes Joyce prevailed and influenced *La Ruta*, especially in the interior monologues.

Three Costa Rican academics, Alfonso Chase, Victoria Urbano, and Rima de Vallbona, present detailed analyses of most of Oreamuno's writings. Chase discusses Oreamuno's narratives one by one in addition to her themes, life, characteristics, and the "myth" of Yolanda Oreamuno. He maintains that not only did no one value or understand her, but also that they misrepresented and denied her, both personally and professionally. In discussing *La ruta*, Chase describes it as a literary achievement with regard to the most notable observation of the feminine character, the techniques of introspection, and the admirable quality of the external descriptions. Chase continues to say that the novel was the most ambitious of Oreamuno's work in its formal structure and its use of sociological and psychological elements. This time, he maintains, not Oreamuno's own anguished experiences but rather the collective ones of her generation, predominate. With regard to one of her own letters, Chase says that she was influenced by Proust, perhaps more because of the similarity of their corepresentation in the creative cult of genius. Finally, Chase describes Oreamuno's place in the setting of her times and the special themes and techniques of her creations. They are introspection, the monologue, and the beginnings of psychoanalytical portrayal, the search for her own conscience through literature, the pain of humanity, Marxist sympathies, experimental narration, and the union of life and work.

In her critical analysis, Victoria Urbano also discusses Oreamuno's life, themes, and her mature work: "Valle alto," "De su obscura familia," and *La ruta de su evasión*. Only Urbano has dealt extensively with Oreamuno's language, her idioms, words, thought, and poetry. Urbano analyzes *La ruta* extensively and sees it as a beacon pointing in the new direction from which the "Boom" in Latin American literature was to come. She deals with Oreamuno's themes of night, loneliness, nature, and climate, and the sexual in her work. Urbano points out the lack of local vocabulary as a result of Oreamuno's concern with universality.

Rima de Vallbona's criticism concentrates on the literary characteristics of Oreamuno's work. Her treatment points out the rich imagination and subjective sensuality particularly regarding nature. She also admires Oreamuno's marked use of introspection and psychoanalysis in her work. Vallbona describes Oreamuno's style as agile, passionate, lyrical, and rich in images, indicating that there is an intense poetic quality in her work as well as a baroque reality.

Oreamuno has been considered the first great Costa Rican literary figure, and we can be grateful that the small circle of her intimate friends salvaged much of her work and her letters. Those valuable letters have yet to be considered seriously. Many called her talent "God given" and *La ruta* brilliant. José Luis Cifuentes (1966) called the novel extraordinary and a great Latin American novel.

In reviewing the criticism of Yolanda Oreamuno's literary output, it is safe to say that, as yet, she has not been recognized and awarded her place in Latin American letters. There have been too many critics unable to separate the writer and her work, and too much concern over the myth of Yolanda. A second problem has been that she was ignored and misrepresented, possibly because she was female, beautiful, talented, rebellious, and intelligent, inclined toward Marxism, the avant-garde, and the experimental, and unafraid to attack the power base. Those who have analyzed her work with any depth and objectivity, however, agree that she was courageous and an important universal figure in twentieth-century Latin American literature.

BIBLIOGRAPHY

Works by Yolanda Oreamuno

"La lagartija de la panza blanca." *Repertorio Americano* 32, 24 (1936):373. *Bueha* 1 (1956). *Páginas ticas.* Ed. by Carlos Luis Sáenz Elizondo (Anthology for secondary schools). San José, Costa Rica: Empresa Editoral Las Américas, 1958. *El cuento en Costa Rica.* Ed. Elizabeth Portuguez de Bolaños. San José, Costa Rica: Antonio Lehmann, 1964.

"Para 'Revenar' No para Max Jiménez." *Repertorio Americano* 32, 24 (1936):339.

"40 sobre cero" (en Panamá). *Repertorio Americano* 33, 1 (1937):5. *Brecha* 2 (Oct. 1959):11–12. *Escritores de Costa Rica.* Ed. Rogelio Sotela. San José, Costa Rica: Imprenta Lehmann, 1942.

"18 de septiembre." *Repertorio Americano* 33, 8 (1937):118.

"Misa de ocho." *Repertorio Americano* 33, 5 (1937):66.

"Vela urbana." *Repertorio Americano* 33, 8, 9 (1937):136.

"Insomnio." *Repertorio Americano* 33, 12 (1937):187. *Bueha* 8 (Apr. 1961):24–5.

"El negro, sentido de la alegría." *Repertorio Americano* 33, 18 (1937):282. *Bueha* 1, 1 (1956):3.

"El espíritu de mi tierra." *Repertorio Americano* 34, 9 (1937):137. *La Nación* (Saturday, Dec. 9, 1967):49. *Historia y antología de la literatura costarricense.* Ed. Abelardo Bonilla. San José, Costa Rica: Imprenta Trejos Hermanos, 1961. Pp. 116–121. *La Prensa Libre* (July 6, 1963).

"Medios que usted sugiere al colegio para librar a la mujer costarricense de la frivolidad ambiente." *Repertorio Americano* 36, 2 (1938):21–22, 30.

"El ambiente tico y los mitos tropicales." *Repertorio Americano* 36, 11 (1939):169–70.

"El último Max Jiménez ante la indiferencia nacional." *Repertorio Americano* 36, 18 (1939):281, 283.

"La vuelta a los lugares comunes." *Repertorio Americano* 37, 1 (1940):8, 12.

"Panorama poético colombiano construído solo en recuerdo." *Repertorio Americano* 37, 5 (1940):73–75.

"Protesta contra el folklore." *Repertorio Americano* 40, 6 (1943):84.

"Apología del limón dulce y del paisaje." *Repertorio Americano* 41, 5 (1944):73.

"Pasajeros al norte." *Repertorio Americano* 41, 12 (1944):182–83.

"México es mío." *Repertorio Americano* 41, 15 (1945):236.

"Valle Alto." *Repertorio Americano* 42, 14 (1946):216–21. *Brecha* (Dec. 4, 1958):10–13, 16. *El cuento costarricense.* Ed. Seymour Menton. Mexico City: Ediciones De Andrea, 1964. Pp. 126–36.

"Max Jiménez y los que están." *Repertorio Americano* 43, 4 (1947):53–55.

"Un regalo." *Repertorio Americano* 44, 2:20–23. Supplement to *El Nacional* (Mexico) (May 25, 1948). *Revista de Maestro* (Guatemala) 12–14, 55 (Apr.-Sept. 1947):198–207.

La ruta de su evasión. Guatemala: Editorial del Ministerio de Educación Pública, 1949. San José, Costa Rica: Editorial EDUCA, 1971.

"De su obscura familia." *Revista Mexicana de Cultura* 201 (Jan. 28, 1951):9.

A lo largo del corto camino. San José: Editorial Costa Rica, 1961. (This anthology contains all that the author published in *Repertorio Americano*, except "18 de setiembre.")

"Don Juvencio." *Tertulia* 1 (Nov.-Dec. 1971):10–14.

"Las mareas vuelven de noche." *Tertulia* 2 (Nov.-Dec. 1971):5–9.

Relatos escojidos: Yolanda Oreamuno. Ed. Alfonso Chase. San José: Editorial Costa Rica, 1977.

Translations of Yolanda Oreamuno

Bellver, Catherine G., trans. "The Tide Returns at Night." *Five Women Writers of Costa Rica: Naranjo, Odio, Urbano, Valbona, Oreamuno*. Beaumont, Tex.: Asociación de Literatura Femenina Hispánica, 1978.

O'Nan, Martha, trans. "High Valley." *Five Women Writers of Costa Rica: Naranjo, Odio, Urbano, Vallbona, Oreamuno*. Beaumont, Tex.: Asociación de Literatura Femenina Hispánica, 1978.

Works about Yolanda Oreamuno

Abreu Gómez, Ermilo. "Yolanda Oreamuno." *El Nacional* (Mexico) (Oct. 3, 1944). *Repertorio Americano* 41, 12 (1961):183.

Acuña, José Basileo. "Yolanda Oreamuno, en mesa redonda." *La Nación* (July 11, 1971).

Bellver, Catherine G. "The Tide Returns at Night." *Five Women Writers of Costa Rica*. 1978.

Bonilla, Abelardo. "Yolanda Oreamuno." *A lo largo del corto camino*. Ed. Alfonso Chase. San José, Costa Rica: Ed. EDUCA, 1961. Pp. 253–55.

Castegnaro, Ernest. "Valores de Costa Rica." *La Nación* (July 13, 1969):15.

———. "Yolanda Oreamuno." *La Nación* (Sept. 17, 1973):15.

Certad, Aquiles. "Diálogo con Yolanda Oreamuno." *La Prensa Libre* (Nov. 27, 1961):2 B.

Chase, Alfonso. "La firme evasión de Yolanda Oreamuno." *La República* (June 7, 1964):23.

———. "Yolanda Oreamuno y Marcel Proust." *La República* (Aug. 13, 1970):9, 14.

Cifuentes, José Luis. "La sombra de Yolanda." *La Nación* (Nov. 5, 1966):42.

Dobles, Fabián. "Defensa y realidad de una literatura." *Repertorio Americano* 41, 13 (Mar. 20, 1945):277. *A lo largo del corto camino*. Ed. Alfonso Chase. San José, Costa Rica: Ed. EDUCA, 1961. P. 321.

Dueñas, Guadalupe. "Un grito de liberación." *La Nación* (Jan. 1, 1972).

Echandi, Mario. "Yolanda Oreamuno está sepultada en Costa Rica." *La República* (Aug. 25, 1970):22.

Echeverría Loria, Arturo. "Yolanda Oreamuno o la ruta de su evasión." *A lo largo del corto camino*. Ed. Alfonso Chase. San José, Costa Rica: Ed. EDUCA, 1961. Pp. 369–71.

Fernández, Guido. "Frente a un astigmatismo aldeano." *A lo largo del corto camino*. Ed. Alfonso Chase. San José, Costa Rica: Ed. EDUCA, 1961. Pp. 365–67. *Diario de Costa Rica* (July 22, 1956):12.

Fernández, Rocío. "En busca de Yolanda Oreamuno." *Revista de Excélsior* (Mar. 7, 1976):7.

Fernández Leys, Alberto. "Yolanda Costa Rica." *Brecha* (Feb. 6, 1962):23.

García Carillo, Eugenio. "Cartas íntimas de una dama de la literatura." *La República* (Apr. 30, 1970):9.

———. "Combinación de criolla y francesa es peligrosa." *La República* (June 13, 1970):9.

———. "Marcel Proust en Costa Rica." *La República* (July 12, 1971):9.

———. "Por la ruta de sus novelas." *Universidad* (July 12, 1971):5.

———. "Un embajador, 'buen burgués'." *La República* (Feb. 4, 1971):9.

Gruber, Vivian. "Reality in the Fiction of 'High Valley'." *Five Women Writers of Costa Rica*. 1978. Pp. 75–6.

Hurtado, Gerardo César. "Presencia de Yolanda Oreamuno." *La Nación* (July 8, 1970):15.

Loaiza, Norma. "Yolanda vista por Victoria." *La Nación* (Dec. 30, 1968):40.

Marín Cañas, José. "La inevitabilidad de su presencia." *Diario de Costa Rica* (July 22, 1956):12.

Marsicovetere y Durán, Miguel. "Yolanda Oreamuno." *Revista del Maestro* (Guatemala), 13–14, 55 (Apr.-Sept. 1949):198.

Miranda Arellano, Gladis. "El mito de Yolanda Oreamuno." *Posdata*. Supplement to *Excélsior* (Mar. 20, 1976):6.

———. "La novela en Costa Rica." *La República* (Feb. 17, 1975):13.

Padilla, Guillermo. "Comienza su existencia." *Diario de Costa Rica* (July 22, 1956):12.

———. "Yolanda Oreamuno en la vida y en la muerte." *A lo largo del corto camino*. Ed. Alfonso Chase. San José, Costa Rica: Ed. EDUCA, 1961. Pp. 357–59.

Picado, Manuel. "*La Ruta de su Evasión* de Yolanda Oreamuno." Thesis, Departmento de Filología, Linguística y Literatura, Universidad de Costa Rica, 1973.

Portuguéz de Bolaños, Elizabeth. "Yolanda Oreamuno." *El cuento en Costa Rica*. San José, Costa Rica: Editorial Antonio Lehmann, 1964. San José, Costa Rica: Librería e Imprenta Atenea, 1964. Pp. 214–17.

Ramos, Lilia. "Sin noviciado, Yolanda Oreamuno escribe libros psicoanalíticos." *Repertorio Americano* 44, 12 (1950):185–88. *El Imparcial de Guatemala* (May 6, 1950):3.

———. "Yolanda Oreamuno en mi recuerdo eviterno." *A lo largo del corto camino*. Ed. Alfonso Chase. San José, Costa Rica: Ed. EDUCA, 1961. Pp. 331–42.

———. "Yolanda Oreamuno en recado a María de los Angeles Vargas de López." *La Nación* (Apr. 28, 1962):30.

Sandoval de Fonseca, Virginia. *Resumen de literatura costarricense*. San José: Editorial Costa Rica, 1978. Pp. 37–39.

Soto de Avila, Victor. "Yolanda Oreamuno." *A lo largo del corto camino*. Ed. Alfonso Chase. San José, Costa Rica: Ed. EDUCA, 1961. Pp. 317–320.

Succar Guzman, Habib. "A los 20 años de la muerte de Yolanda Oreamuno." *La Hora* (July 9, 1976):8.

Trejos, Inés. "Yolanda Oreamuno: Una figura siempre vigente en las letras nacionales." *La Prensa Libre* (Feb. 17, 1971):24.

Ulloa Zamora, Alfonso. "La mujer en la literatura costarricense." *Brecha* (Jan. 5, 1962):7–9.

Urbano, Victoria. *Una escritora costarricense: Yolanda Oreamuno* (critical essay). Madrid: Ediciones Castilla de Oro, 1968.

Vallbona, Rima de. "*La ruta de su evasión* de Yolanda Oreamuno: Escritura proustiana suplementada." *Revista Iberoamericana* 53, 138–139 (Jan.-June 1987):193–217.

———. *Yolanda Oreamuno presentada por Rima de Vallbona.* Series: ¿Quién fue y que hizo? No. 5. San José, Costa Rica: Departmento de Publicaciones, Ministerio de Cultura, Juventud y Deportes, 1972.

Zendejas, Adelina. "Escritora psicoanalista." *Tiempo* (Mexico) (Dec. 15, 1944):33.

OLGA OROZCO
(b. 1920)
Argentina

Elba Torres de Peralta
Translated by Gustavo V. Segade

BIOGRAPHY

Olga Orozco was born in Toay, a small town in the province of La Pampa, Argentina, where she spent the first seven years of her life. When she was eight her family moved to Bahía Blanca, and the location of her formative years then alternated between that city and Buenos Aires. Nevertheless, it is Toay that the poet has evoked as her refuge, her safe retreat, throughout her life.

She lives her childhood in fear, in wonder, bedazzled by "the house" that acts as a protective garden that even now, the poet declares, "receives me miraculously from the depths of each fall, of each nightmare, of each hell. In the face of every disaster I always say to myself, 'At the bottom there is always a garden.' In that garden I am a strange, timid little girl who plays at being invisible or at becoming someone else" (*La Opinión Cultural* [Buenos Aires], Jan. 22, 1978:2).

In countless interviews with the author, an attempt has been made to elucidate certain biographical details that would complement a comprehensive study of her texts. Her answers always allude to the fundamental motivation that constitutes the *numen* of her own vision of reality and of that space that contains the other. That *numen*, by its very nature, engenders a language that, without avoiding the questions, invariably represents the artistic efforts of the poet to reconstitute the "neofantastic" world that she evokes through the word.

In the narrative text, *La oscuridad es otro sol* (1967; Darkness is another sun), which the poet herself categorizes as autobiographical, there is an intimate relationship between the subjectivity of the narrator and the physical environment. This relationship results in a persona appropriated and transformed by the narrative subjectivity while it narrates the events of *La oscuridad es otro sol*.

That same appropriation and transformation of reality is attested to in "Anotaciones para una autobiografía" (Notes for an autobiography), in which the author describes her neofantastic vision of the world. She combines fictional and realistic elements so that the lines between reality and fiction are rendered indistinct. For instance, she asserts in a serious tone that in her childhood she was a dwarf and was blinded by the dark, that she wanted to be a sleepwalker, that she was weak-willed, and that she was terrified of speaking about herself. When she does speak of her inner life, she refers to an invading force that does not allow her to be herself. Out of this neofantastic discourse comes the dwarf girl, the girl blinded by the dark, and the would-be sleepwalker, all from a literary space also inhabited by the narrator, who is conscious of the existential duality in which matter and spirit are conjoined.

Orozco also mentions in "Anotaciones" the effects that the sea had on her early years in Bahía Blanca, fusing realistic natural elements with fantastic creative powers, such as her desire to become invisible, to develop multiple personalities, to travel on magnetic waves, and to speed-read other people's minds (*Páginas de Olga Orozco*, pp. 217–19). These linguistic signifiers, as framed by her semantic memory, constitute a genuine contribution to the biography of the poet.

The persona of *La oscuridad es otro sol* unfolds in the figures of Lía (fiction) and Olga (nonfiction). In their alternating and simultaneous permutations, they constitute one person whose biographical time conforms to particular geographic, political, and social circumstances that, although not mentioned explicitly in linguistic signifiers in her texts, are implicit in the reference code of her entire poetic production of forty years.

Olga Orozco's discourse about her childhood is a debate between the anxiety provoked in her by the happenings, encounters, surprises, games, and characters who populate her physical environment on the one hand, and her desire for an identity on the other. It is to this process that the poet alludes in "Anotaciones para una autobiografía."

It is important to point out some relevant aspects of the culture and history of the *pampas*. There exist, for example, myths and legends that range from the notion that the human race had its origins in La Pampa to the belief that the "City of the Caesars" was built in that region (Alberto Grassi, *La Pampa y sus derechos*, Buenos Aires, 1929). This explains, in part, the fabulous dimension that La Pampa acquires in "Anotaciones para una autobiografía," in which the houses tear themselves from their foundations and walk among the errant dunes and thistles.

Orozco's childhood was spent among the mentally ill and bedraggled characters who escaped from abandoned jails and hospitals and for whom the child's grandmother used to provide food and shelter. Her Sicilian immigrant father, Carmelo Gugliotta, played an important role in the development of La Pampa. He was the *intendente*, or appointed mayor, of Toay for many years. He brought electricity to the town, and, according to the author, it was he who, at the opening ceremonies, "threw the switch, an event that has probably marked me forever" (Orozco, Letter to Peralta, Oct. 1986). Her father also served on the Board of Education, owned agricultural and lumber interests, and displayed extraordinary generosity toward the needy. He had brought with him from Sicily the classical cultural heritage that enriched Argentine intellectual life in general, and in particular served to familiarize Olga with Dante, Petrarch, Alfieri, and many other poets whom he read to the little girl in Italian and then translated for her. Although she does not refer directly to her parents in her narrative texts, in her poetry she recaptures her memory and connects the particular to the universal and the artistic.

MAJOR THEMES

The most important artistic avant-garde movements of the twentieth century occurred in the 1920s, the decade of Olga Orozco's birth. Her *ars poetica* is framed by a particular aesthetic and world-view which she inherited: Pablo Neruda and the Romantic-surrealist-existentialist current; André Breton and surrealism; Rainer Maria Rilke and symbolism; Marcel Proust and the meaning of the repetition of time; Lubics Milosz and his *Song of Knowledge*; Antonio Machado and the elegiac tone of his poetry; Stefan George and the search for the secret of God; Jean-Paul Sartre and his theory of the absurdity of the rational system; Albert Camus and Martin Heidegger and the angst of Being on this earth. To these intellectual influences one must add the historical-political events of the epoch: the bellicose European atmosphere from 1935 to 1945 and the consequences of two world wars for culture, the change of values, the failure of utopian optimism, and the resultant darkest despair.

Olga Orozco feels and knows herself to be a citizen of a world in convulsions. Her first publications coincide with the advent of Peronismo in Argentina (1946), which shook the foundations of the sociopolitical and cultural structure of the country. Her poetry is the incantation with which she exorcises herself in order to gain access to the uncommunicative zones within her being. This magic supplants the necessity for referring to the events of the century explicitly, and, although poetry does not replace the world, Orozco feels that in itself it constitutes a symbolic transference of spaces and intellectual foci. This transference occurs in the folds of the unconscious and, far from eliminating it after it has been lived, the poet instead projects the transference as a significant synthesis of her thematic system.

The vision of her poetry is projected toward transcendence and simultaneously completes a circle that signifies a return to the essential human necessity, that which the Romantics called the need for "grasping the Center." Her system of transferences and conversions, her vertical vision, and her need to "grasp the Center" prompt us to define Orozco's poetry in the manner of the Symbolists, as a self-sufficient unit that does not merely describe the world, but rather exists as a unique timespace within it.

As a self-sufficient unit, Olga Orozco's poetry is elaborated within a system of codified signs that can be deciphered only intratextually. Through intertextuality we arrive at the *etymon* of her texts, the nucleus of her poetry, its essence. This nucleus contains a succession of ideas, a chain that is linked to a fundamentally gnostic attitude operating as an internal law within Orozco's texts. Her poetry identifies with the permanent divine-human duality, and accentuates the "adventure of intelligence." The language structuring that "adventure" accepts no limits. In her texts the words create a magical, meaningful space, constituting motifs such as prophets, broken mirrors, pennants, dice, talismans, wolves, moats, traps, empty footsteps, torn tablecloths, windows, herbs, rumors, leaves, doors, sands, flowers, things forgotten, eternity, maps, skins and furs, winds, skies, abysses, faces, absences, witches, and stamps.

The dynamics of Orozco's poetry transform and transpose reality's tangible elements and generate a metamorphosis that produces worlds and signs that, within their own poetic code, act in the realm of the possible. The multiple associations derived from the symbols elaborated in the texts lead us toward myth, mysticism, cartomancy, the essence of *homo ludens*, religions, and in other unsuspected directions.

Yet in spite of the many connotations of the author's texts, her poetry is not generated from heterogeneous fragments. The multiplicity of motifs listed above is not a fragmentation of Orozco's themes, but rather the author's way of defining the world through the fragmentation of a unique whole, the timespace when we were one in God. The essence of Orozco's poetry is contained in its macrotheme, the theme that unifies her literary production: "God unfolding in the mask of the Many." This vision of original sin and her desire to return to original unity before the Fall are reiterated in her subthemes, or microthemes. These smaller elements give us the religious experience, the act of love, and creation itself. In her microtheme of creation, the self becomes a plural subject, a metaphor with a cosmic equivalent.

Communication of the plural subject and its cosmic equivalent is established between God and the poetic self, whose salvation depends on emulating God through the word; it is precisely through the act of creation that the artist attains her own identity which will allow her to communicate with the All. "I think I am speaking to God," the poet affirms. "I believe that all that is imponderable can be summed up in God. When I criticize, I am criticizing reality as an imperfect emanation of the invisible or the immanent, but when I inquire, I am querying much less immediate entities, those who guard the keys to the enigmas" (Orozco, Interview with Peralta, Buenos Aires, Oct. 1984). Orozco's concept of the ontological essence of the human being is related to her own poetry through the quest as an activity of consciousness, which her poetic language, as a most personal system, translates into a God diluted into the Many.

In Orozco's poetry, mimesis is produced by her efforts to harmonize the place she inhabits, which the poet feels only as a flash of reality, with that other dimension which she intuits and which extends beyond the palpable, the place of origin, the beginning of everything. In the poem, "La realidad y el deseo" (Reality and desire, from *Mutaciones de la realidad*, 1979), the meaning of reality is intensified in her conception of an incomplete, lonely God, who, through His unfolding into humanity, through making a mere particle of Himself a part of each of us, has relegated Himself to the solitude that our absence makes Him feel.

"La realidad y el deseo" is the fleeting vision of God, of Paradise lost, of all that has been denied the human race since the Fall. The "territory adorned by death's bubbles" refers to both the Fall and its consequences and the negativity in the finite nature of matter. The "derelict table" reinforces the previous system of symbols and refers to the imponderability of destiny, our ignorance of fate's designs. The remaining verses allude to the impossibility of communicating with the All. There is always the same lone persona in this poem: the incomplete and mutilated being always searching for her totality, the mature Olga Orozco who uses childhood experiences as the source of her imagery. Her vision of reality, childhood, the erotic, the transcendence of love, emissaries, dangerous games, the past, the present, the future, life on earth, and death, all become one time-space. Each is an element forming part of her macrocorpus, her macrotheme: the unfolding of God in mask of the Many.

It is impossible to classify the poetic work of Orozco or to limit the possibilities for interpreting her texts. It still behooves the critic, however, to study the poet's own, stated premises in regard to her work, which she calls a "bridge to knowl-edge," a place where the immediate is transformed into an intimate dialogue between language and the universe. To do without this notion is to ignore Orozco's explicit need to go beyond the night of the Fall, that is, to transcend the human limitations imposed by humanity's original separation from God.

SURVEY OF CRITICISM

The Works about Olga Orozco section in the Bibliography that accompanies this entry offers evidence of critical interest in the Argentine poet's works and of the place her writings occupy in twentieth-century poetry. The numerous literary prizes and honors which the author has received on international, national, and regional levels further attest to the fact that her works have indeed been noticed by the informed reader. Her most recent national award was the Fortavat Foundation Prize in 1987. Spain, the United States, Canada, France, Italy, and Mexico head the list of countries that have recognized the value of her artistic creation.

Juan Liscano (1975), the noted Argentine poet and critic, was the first to point out that the keys to Orozco's poetry "are to be found in a prose narrative of hers entitled *La oscuridad es otro sol*." Cristina Piña has written numerous articles that are an important contribution to structuralist criticism, and describe the framework of Orozco's poetic constructs. Piña's prologue to *Páginas de Olga Orozco* (1984) is essential for an understanding of the style and themes of Orozco's work. The first book-length study of the evolution of Orozco's central theme within the context of her entire body of work is Elba Peralta's *La poética de Olga Orozco* (1988).

A lack of comprehensive studies of a given author's works is often due to problems of her hermeneutic complexity, as occurred with much of the poetry of Pablo Neruda before Dámaso Alonso. Critical readers have too often believed that Orozco's writing is cryptic and impossible to reach. A recent example can be found in Silvia Molloy's "Nota Preliminar" to a special issue of *Revista Iberoamericana* (1983), dedicated to Argentine literature, in which she writes of Orozco's absence as an "injustice." Another, more recent case of exclusion of critical works on Orozco's poetry occurred in New York at the 1987 Convention of the Instituto Internacional de Literatura Iberoamericana. Raquel Chang Rodríguez, the first woman to preside over the prestigious event, and a critic of recognized talent, apologized for not including a study of Orozco's work by claiming that the topic was too complex to be treated.

BIBLIOGRAPHY

Works by Olga Orozco

Desde lejos. Buenos Aires: Editorial Losada, 1946.
Las muertes. Buenos Aires: Editorial Losada, 1951.
Los juegos peligrosos. Buenos Aires: Editorial Losada, 1962.
La oscuridad es otro sol. Buenos Aires: Editorial Losada, 1967.
Las muertes. Los juegos peligrosos. Buenos Aires: Editorial Losada, 1972.
Museo salvaje. Buenos Aires: Editorial Losada, 1974.
Veintinueve poemas. Prol. by Juan Liscano. Caracas: Monte Avila Editores, 1975.
Cantos a Berenice. Buenos Aires: Editorial Sudamericana, 1977.
Mutaciones de la Realidad. Buenos Aires: Editorial Sudamericana, 1979.
Obra poética. Buenos Aires: Ediciones Corregidor, 1979.
Antología. Buenos Aires: Centro Editor de América Latina, 1982.
La noche a la deriva. Mexico City: Fondo de Cultura Económica, 1984.
Páginas de Olga Orozco. Selections by the author with Prol. by Cristina Piña. Buenos
    Aires: Editorial Celta, 1984.
Antología poética. Madrid: Instituto de Cooperación Iberoamericana, 1985.
En el revés del cielo. Buenos Aires: Editorial Sudamericana, 1987.

Works about Olga Orozco

Alifano, Roberto. "Olga Orozco: Reflexiones para un Ars Poetica." *Proa* (Buenos Aires)
    2 (Dec.-Jan. 1988–1989):77–81.
Ara, Guillermo. *Suma de la poesía argentina*. Buenos Aires: Guadalupe, 1970. I:140–
    42. 2:130.
Campanella, Hebe M. "La voz de la mujer en la joven poesía argentina." *Cuadernos
    Hispanoamericanos* 300 (June 1975):543–64.
Cobo Borda, J. C. "Poesía argentina: Notas de lectura." *Usos de la imaginación*. Buenos
    Aires: Ediciones de El Imaginario, 1984.

Colombo, Stella Maris. "Metáfora y cosmovisión en la poesía de Olga Orozco." (Rosario) *Cuadernos Aletheia* (1983).

Gómez Paz, Julieta. *Cuatro actitudes poéticas.* Buenos Aires: Conjunta Editores, 1977.

———. *Dos textos sobre la poesía de Olga Orozco.* Buenos Aires, Ediciones Tekné, 1980.

Guiano, Juan Carlos. *Poesía argentina del siglo XX.* Mexico City-Buenos Aires: Fondo de Cultura Económica, 1957.

Lindstrom, Naomi. "Olga Orozco: La voz poética que llama entre mundos." *Revista Iberoamericana* 51, 132–133 (July-Dec. 1985):765–75.

Liscano, Juan. "Olga Orozco y su trascendente juego poético." Prol. to *Veintinueve poemas.* By Olga Orozco. Caracas: Monte Avila, 1975.

———. "Olga Orozco y sus juegos peligrosos." *Descripciones.* Prol. by Alberto Girri. Buenos Aires: Ediciones de la Flor, Monte Avila, 1983. Pp. 73–101.

Loubet, Jorgelina. "Lo cotidiano, el fulgor y el signo en la obra de actuales escritoras argentinas." *Zona Franca* 20 (Sept.-Oct. 1980):6–23.

Luzzani Bystrowicz, Telma. "Olga Orozco: Poesía de la totalidad." *Capítulo* 112 Centro Editor de América Latina, 1981.

———. "Prólogo." *Olga Orozco, Poesía.* By Olga Orozco. Buenos Aires: Centro Editor de América Latina, 1982.

Omil, Alba. *Ensayo de literatura argentina.* San Miguel de Tucumán: Ediciones de la Universidad, 1984.

Orphée, Elvira. "La poética en la obra de Olga Orozco." *América en Letras* 2 (Mar. 1984).

Peralta, Elba Torres de. "Motivos claves en la poética de Olga Orozco." *La Crítica Literaria en Latinoamérica: Actas del XXIV Congreso del Instituto Internacional de Literatura Iberoamericana.* Palo Alto, Calif.: Stanford University Press, 1987. Pp. 259–65.

———. "*La oscuridad es otro sol* de Olga Orozco." *El Universitario* (Mexico) 187 (Oct. 1981).

———. *La poética de Olga Orozco: Desdoblamiento de Dios en máscara de todos.* Madrid: Editorial Playor, 1988.

———. "Un proceso de individuación existencial." *Proceedings of the Pacific Coast Council on Latin American Studies Literary Journal* 10 (1982–1983):91–97.

———. "Trayectoria estética de la mujer en la poesía hispanoamericana." *Evaluación de la literatura femenina de Latinoamérica, Siglo XX.* San José: Educa, Universidad de Costa Rica, 1985. Pp. 59–84.

Pichon Riviere, Marcelo. "Múltiples formas de la transparencia." *Plural* 4 (Jan. 1975).

Piña, Cristina. " 'Carina' de Olga Orozco: Un análisis estilístico." *Explicación de Textos Literarios* 12, 2 (1983–1984):59–78.

———. "Prólogo." *Páginas de Olga Orozco seleccionadas por la autora.* Buenos Aires: Editorial Celta, 1984.

Rebok, María Gabriela. "Finitud, creación poética y sacralidad en la obra de Olga Orozco." *Revista de la Sociedad Argentina de Filosofía* (Córdoba) 5, 3 (1985):51–64.

———. "Olga Orozco y el anhelo de la unidad perdida." *Pliego de Poesía* (Buenos Aires) (Spring 1985).

Running, Thorpe. "Imagen y creación en la poesía de Olga Orozco." *Letras Femeninas* 13 (Spring-Autumn 1987):12–20.

Ruschi Crespo, María Julia de. "La misma sustancia del abismo." *La Opinión Cultural* (Jan. 25 1981).

Tacconi, María del Carmen. "Para una lectura simbólica de Olga Orozco." *Sur* 348 (Jan.-June 1981):115–23.

Zolezzi, Emilio. "Olga Orozco o la creación incesante." *Clarín* (May 22, 1975).

Other Works Cited

Molloy, Silvia. "Nota Preliminar." *Revista Iberoamericana* (1983):125.

TERESA DE LA PARRA*
(1889–1936)
Venezuela

Gabriella Ibieta

BIOGRAPHY

To assume that Teresa de la Parra's character in *Ifigenia* (1924; Iphigenia), María Eugenia Alonso, is the writer's alter ego is to presuppose the absence of distance between the author and her creation, to impose the writer's life onto her character, and, ultimately, to ignore de la Parra's own peripatetic life. Although she used, or rather transformed, some of her early experiences into fiction, the point of view through which these materials are presented reveals the author's analytical and ironic gifts. In fact, the author's life was very different from her character's, whose provincial existence largely contributed to her downfall: a marriage to a man she despised. Teresa de la Parra never married, and her life was devoted to writing, traveling, and cultivating family relationships and friendships. Unlike her character, she did not suffocate in old traditions: She surpassed them.

Teresa de la Parra belonged to a well-to-do family; her father, Rafael Parra Hernáiz, was consul of Venezuela in Berlin, and her mother, Isabel Sanojo Ezpelosín, came from an aristocratic family. Teresa was born in Paris, on October 5, 1889, but her citizenship was Venezuelan. Her early years were spent in Venezuela, at the family hacienda, "Tazón," which she would later re-create in *Las Memorias de Mamá Blanca* (1929; *Mamá Blanca's Souvenirs*, 1959). After her father's death at the turn of the century, her family moved to Spain, where Teresa attended the School of the Sacred Heart in Valencia. She had already tried her hand at writing during this period and received a prize for her poetry, which was published in the school newspaper.

Between 1909 and 1923, Teresa de la Parra lived in Caracas, where her main activity was writing. During this period, she developed a close friendship with

*Ana Teresa Parra Sanojo.

Emilia Ibarra, on whom the character of Mercedes Galindo in *Ifigenia* is loosely based. In 1915, under the pseudonym "Frufrú," de la Parra published two short stories in the newspaper *El Universal*: "Un evangelio indio: Buda y la leprosa" (An Indian gospel: Buda and the woman leper), and "Flor de loto: una leyenda japonesa" (Lotus flower: a Japanese legend). Possibly from this period are three other stories, not published until 1982: "El ermitaño del reloj" (The mechanical clock's hermit); "El genio del pesacartas" (The paperweight's genie); and "Historia de la señorita grano de polvo, bailarina del sol" (Story of Miss Dustball, the sun's ballerina). In 1920 she published a travel diary in the magazine *Actualidades*, edited by Rómulo Gallegos. Entitled *Diario de una caraqueña por el Lejano Oriente* (Diary of a Caracas woman in the Far East in *Obras completas*), the text recounts the experiences of Teresa's sister, María, who wrote many letters home describing her trip. That same year, de la Parra submitted an entry to a national short story contest sponsored by the newspaper *El luchador*, "Mamá X," which won a special prize. Encouraged by the author's success, Rafael Pocaterra, editor of the literary magazine *La Lectura Semanal*, invited her to submit another text for his publication. Sure of the writer's talent and popularity, Pocaterra issued six thousand copies of the magazine (a considerable quantity for Caracas at the time), which sold out in a few days. With this publication, *Diario de una señorita que se fastidia* (Diary of a young lady who gets bored), Teresa de la Parra established herself as a serious writer in her country's literary circles. She would transcend these boundaries, becoming well known in Latin America and France for what was at this time a work-in-progress, *Ifigenia*.

In 1923 de la Parra left for Paris, initiating a pattern that would continue throughout her life: prolonged stays in France, Spain, and Switzerland, with intermittent trips to Colombia, Cuba, and Venezuela. In Paris, she was part of the literary salons that assembled the many Latin American intellectuals then living there, among whom were Simón Barceló, Ventura García Calderón, and Gonzalo Zaldumbide. (A series of letters, as well as testimony from friends and acquaintances, point to a mysterious and complicated romance between de la Parra and Zaldumbide.) The year 1924 proved to be a turning point for the writer in several ways. Her novel *Ifigenia* was published to great acclaim, winning a ten thousand franc prize, but it was also during that year that her dear friend, Emilia Ibarra, died. The writer's intellectual and spiritual involvement with this woman had sustained her through her years of literary apprenticeship in Caracas, and she felt her loss even more acutely in the midst of her success. The author's correspondence with Zaldumbide is most intense during this period. Her letters reveal the complexity and anguish of their relationship. She shares with him her pain and establishes differences between "tenderness" and "love," adding that, since Emilia's death, she is in dire need of understanding and tenderness. Her fear of intimacy with the male is expressed in her confession to Zaldumbide: "I am afraid of you and horrified by all other men." She then appeals to him, asking him to love her "with a woman's soul." According to several sources, de la Parra and Zaldumbide had considered marriage, but by 1927 he had already married someone else. The end of their romantic involvement is insinuated in a letter she wrote to him during that year, in which she told him that one of her friends would return to him a ring that he had given her as a token of his love. They remained friends, however, and their correspondence continued until 1933.

Between 1925 and 1930, de la Parra reached the height of her writing career. *Ifigenia* was translated into French by Francis de Miomandre (a well-known writer and mediator between France and Spanish America), who also wrote an enthusiastic prologue. Polemics for and against *Ifigenia*'s feminism arose: Teresa de la Parra had become famous. She was invited to speak about Simón Bolívar at a congress in Havana, Cuba, in 1927, where she would meet someone who would play an important role in her life during her last years—writer Lydia Cabrera,* whose *Cuentos negros* (1936; Black stories) was dedicated to her. It was also during this period that de la Parra published her second novel, *Las memorias de Mamá Blanca* (1929), which appeared in both Spanish and French. After a trip to Italy with Cabrera, the Venezuelan went to Colombia in 1930 to give lectures on the role of women in Spanish American culture and history, from colonial times to the present, which were published by Arturo Uslar Pietri in 1961 under the title *Tres conferencias inéditas* (Three unpublished lectures).

Upon her return to Europe in 1931, de la Parra began to experience even more acute symptoms of the illness that would take her life at the age of forty-seven: tuberculosis. Between 1932 and 1936, the writer struggled in vain against the ravaging disease, an experience recorded in her diary, *Bellevue-Fuenfría-Madrid* (published in 1982), and wrote to relatives and friends. Cabrera's devoted friendship sustained her throughout her agony. In January 1936 they both left Fuenfría for Madrid, where they shared an apartment. On April 23, Teresa de la Parra died in the company of women: her mother, her sister María and her friend Lydia Cabrera.

MAJOR THEMES

The series of short stories that Teresa de la Parra wrote around 1915 shows a particular ease with language and an elegance of expression that would characterize her later work. These stories, however, do not exhibit any of the themes that de la Parra would explore in her major works. Instead, they reveal a fashionable affiliation with *Modernismo*, particularly with Darío's gemlike texts in *Azul* (1888). It is very much to her credit that she was able to "escape" the shadow of Spanish America's major literary movement and develop her own voice. Without totally dismissing these early manifestations of her literary gifts, it should be said that these texts can be considered primarily as exercises toward the later originality and authenticity of her craft.

Based on one of her sister María's trips, the *Diario de una caraqueña por el Lejano Oriente* is an interesting experiment in the use of first-person narration, de la Parra's preferred mode. As she would later do in *Ifigenia*, the author constructs a character whose writing clearly imitates her speech. The similarities end here, however, since the *Diario*, a short, descriptive text without any complexities, merely records the narrator's travel impressions. One of its most interesting aspects, however, is the appreciation of external reality as an aesthetic object. The narrator likens some of what she sees to a film, which, although a cliché for the modern reader, was in 1920 a rather sophisticated perception.

In *Ifigenia*, Teresa de la Parra explored the theme of female identity through the psychological and emotional development of its main character and narrator, María Eugenia Alonso. Divided into four parts, this long novel traces the protagonist's attempts to come to terms with her own self, often through mirroring techniques. The first part functions as a frame; it is an unusually long letter to the narrator's childhood friend, Cristina de Iturbe (whose last name recalls Emilia's "Ibarra"). In it, María Eugenia recounts her experiences in Paris and presents herself as a sophisticated and daring modern woman. In reality, however, she is trapped by the provincial atmosphere of her native Caracas. What is established here is the distance between what the narrator believes herself to be and what she really is, a theme that will be developed throughout the novel.

In Part II, the interlocutor has changed: María Eugenia is now writing a diary and thus talking to herself. Her frustrations with her old-fashioned grandmother and spinster aunt are told in delightful detail, as she continues to define herself and to flaunt her advanced, and therefore scandalous, ideas. The character of Mercedes Galindo is introduced in this part and indeed plays an important role in María Eugenia's life and development. A sophisticated married woman in her thirties, Mercedes symbolizes everything that María Eugenia would like to become. Exotic, modern, charming, and beautiful, Mercedes leads the kind of life that is denied to María Eugenia, not merely because of her age, but most importantly because of her status (or lack of it, by society's standards) as an unmarried woman. In her friend's "salons," María Eugenia flourishes, liberated from the suffocating atmosphere of her exclusively female household. It is there that she meets Gabriel Olmedo, with whom she falls madly in love. Also in this part, the influence of literature on the young woman's consciousness and forming identity comes into play. She is accused by her aunt of reading pernicious and immoral novels, and advised by her grandmother to discontinue this practice. As her flirtation with Gabriel develops, her literary imagination becomes more fanciful. She writes him a letter (which she does not send) in which she identifies herself with the Beloved of the "Song of Songs," expressing her love for him in passionate, lyrical terms. With the pretext of returning some books, she also sends him a poem she has written, "Juliet's Balcony," and indeed waits for him metaphorically, expecting that he will take her away from her humdrum existence.

Also in this second part the plot is the richest and most interesting, full of insightful perceptions of the young woman's fertile imagination. In a long section in which María Eugenia recalls her childhood friendship with Cristina, the theme of reflexivity becomes more fully developed. In her letter, María Eugenia had narrated an incident in which, alone in a hotel lobby in Paris, she had looked at herself in the mirror, assessing her appearance and at the same time projecting a newer, more sophisticated self onto her own reflected image. As she records her memories of Cristina, this theme of reflexivity becomes apparent. A "perfect" child, pale, pretty, impeccably groomed, and intelligent, Cristina had been María Eugenia's model, her "other" self. By imitating Cristina, not only in dress and hairstyle, but also in mannerisms, María Eugenia began to form her identity in terms of "other." That this other was female and her own age shows María Eugenia's desire to see herself in another, to forge her image of her self, in her own search of self, through the mirror. (This metaphor can also be applied to her obsessive diary-writing, a way of "seeing" herself on the blank page.) The mirroring also plays an important role in her friendship with Mercedes Galindo. The narrator's disappointment in her childhood friend, her sense of loss, will repeat itself later in the book, through Mercedes's inexplicable absence. María Eugenia's disillusionment at the end of Part II, however is caused almost exclusively by the fact that Gabriel Olmedo is engaged to someone else, a rich, vulgar woman.

An orphan, María Eugenia comes from a distinguished but impoverished family, and her only options in life, within the context of the book, are rather limited. When she "sees herself" in her spinster aunt, she is horrified by what she sees. Her sensuous and romantic nature had caused her to pine away for the impossible love of Gabriel Olmedo. In Part III, however, the reader finds "another" María Eugenia. Two years have gone by since Gabriel's wedding, and the narrator finds herself ready to be pressured, subtly but firmly, by her Aunt Clara and her grandmother, to accept the courtship of a man she despises. César Leal, a distinguished member of the establishment, a senator, and a rigid pedant, seems to have only one virtue, his faithfulness to María Eugenia (as is suggested by his last name, meaning "loyal"). Interestingly, her kind Uncle Pancho denounces the relationship as inane and urges her to break it. (Here, the patriarchal authority has been usurped by the older women—aunt and grandmother—who represent the traditional values María Eugenia has tried to escape.) The narrator's transformation into a submissive and somewhat trivial creature is reinforced by her relatives' perceptions of her as "otra persona" (someone else). The "otherness" that had been explored through her friendship with women in Part II has now become alien, for by defining herself in terms of her fiancé, María Eugenia is betraying her still shapeless self. This betrayal leads her even to deny her love of literature and her devotion to writing during a conversation with her Uncle Pancho at which César Leal is also present. This self-denial marks María Eugenia's failed efforts at establishing a strong identity in which a private and a public self could coexist harmoniously. Her inner self tells her: "There is no love," while her public self enthusiastically prepares the wedding "trousseau." The identification with Cristina has now become complete: María Eugenia will also marry and gain a new identity. However, when she talks to Leal about her vision of herself as a married woman, modeled after Mercedes Galindo, she is shocked to find out how different his vision is, how traditional and repressive.

If Mercedes had provided an attractive version of the young matron, the rumors of her impending divorce quickly dispel that notion for María Eugenia. All she has to look forward to is a loveless, lifeless marriage to César Leal.

María Eugenia's descent into self-denial and sacrifice becomes more accentuated in Part IV. Even though self-analysis and introspection characterize the entire novel, María Eugenia's isolated sense of self becomes more sharply delineated in this last part. Whereas Part II showed several of her interactions with her relatives and friends, the last section of the novel portrays her living more and more inside her head, obsessed about the impossibility of reestablishing a relationship with Gabriel Olmedo. The plot is extremely contrived here, since what brings the two lovers together is Uncle Pancho's grave illness: Alarmed by his friend's condition, Olmedo reappears, willing and able to care for the sick man night and day as a sort of practical nurse. The other person at the bedside is, of course, María Eugenia. The ill-fated lovers' conversations, then, take place in this morbid (and almost absurd) setting. The trappings of conventional society become apparent when, in typical "macho" fashion, Gabriel denounces his wife as vulgar, stupid, and unbearable, yet declares the impossibility of divorcing her. His situation does not affect his feelings for María Eugenia: He is finally responding to her poem of years before, "Juliet's Balcony" and is ready to take her away, albeit not as his wife. With César Leal temporarily out of the picture (away on business), the ground is fertile for María Eugenia's reassessment of herself through an "other," this time a male love object. She decides to abandon everything and run away with Gabriel. She is stopped, symbolically, by her Aunt Clara, who, having heard some noises coming from her room late one night, had gone up to find out what was wrong. The scene that ensues is representative of the complexity of the problem of female identity in this novel. As she tries to hide her suitcase and her true intentions, something happens inside María Eugenia, as she "loses consciousness of [her] own personality." She drops the suitcase and, in a voice that "does not resemble [her] own," implores her aunt to stay with her, adding that she wanted to stay there, with her grandmother, just like her aunt. The identification with Aunt Clara is important, here, since the spinster aunt had represented everything that María Eugenia had wanted to avoid. Again, the fruitless search for a viable self has forced her to latch on to yet another possible image of the self. In the face of her imminent marriage to César Leal after the return of Gabriel Olmedo, spinsterhood seems preferable.

But Iphigenia cannot escape her destiny, and María Eugenia must marry César Leal. In the novel's last pages, the narrator chooses yet another identity. Here again her infatuation with literature (as in Gustave Flaubert's *Madame Bovary*) leads her to mythify her situation. Although the rhetoric of this section is difficult to accept, *Ifigenia's* conclusion is extremely interesting. María Eugenia Alonso is not a feminist. Teresa de la Parra has created a complex and tortured character whose genuine search for a female identity has been thwarted not only by her environment, but also by her own grandiose fantasies about herself. The author has portrayed her character ironically. María Eugenia's identification with the classical Iphigenia (sacrificed to the gods by her father for the sake of the community) is inappropriate. It is important to remember that it is the aunt and the grandmother who represent patriarchal authority: They have identified with the oppressor. María Eugenia's identification with the victim, then, stems from faulty vision, from not seeing the vulnerability of the oppressor. Yet María Eugenia has had no successful female models: She does not want to be Aunt Clara; she no longer believes that Mercedes Galindo had a truly happy life; she cannot have everything that Cristina has (love and money). It is not so much the idea of ''sacrifice'' that is unconvincing to the modern reader, but María Eugenia's willingness to embrace it, in pseudomystical, almost erotic terms. If this is considered a weakness in the novel, it should be noted that Teresa de la Parra is not offering here a ''feminist'' alternative. Rather, *Ifigenia* shows the reality of many of the author's contemporaries. For this reason, and for its genuine portrayal of a woman in search of her own self, the novel is an important and commendable achievement.

In *Las memorias de Mamá Blanca*, Teresa de la Parra also explores, though to a lesser degree, questions of gender and female identity. In the novel's opening pages, the narrator declares that she is merely editing a manuscript left to her by her dear friend, Mamá Blanca. She establishes her identification with Mamá Blanca, who was already in her seventies when the narrator, a child at the time, met her. The ''spiritual affinity'' between the old woman and the girl is expressed through their playful conversations, love of music, tenderness, and devotion. Mamá Blanca is described as a free spirit, without any particular craft, but with the soul of an artist. What the manuscript reveals, however, is her art and craft as a writer. That the author uses the framing device is an important detail, since the narrator and ''editor'' of the memoirs is identifying herself with Mamá Blanca, her role model.

The narrator of the memoirs, Mamá Blanca, looks back on her idyllic existence at the family hacienda, ''Piedra Azul,'' where she lived with her parents, her five sisters, a Jamaican governess called Evelyn, and several servants and peons. The incidents narrated take place over the course of two years, beginning when Blanca Nieve (Mamá Blanca) was only five. The point of view, however, is not that of the child, but of the older woman reflecting on the ''perfect'' world of childhood. ''Piedra Azul'' is likened to Eden, and its inhabitants, like Adam and Eve, live out a peaceful, innocent existence. Their expulsion from paradise is symbolized by the family's move to Caracas when the ruler of Eden, the father, sells the hacienda. In a household of women, the father is viewed as ''the supreme authority'' and as an ''equestrian deity,'' who is always either ensconced in his study or going off on horseback. The reader also learns that, even before marrying, this father had wanted a son whose name would be the same as his, Juan Manuel. He cannot forgive his six daughters, and one of them, Blanca Nieve, cannot forgive him. This negative image of the father is contrasted with other sympathetic male figures: Cousin Juancho, whose warmth and storytelling are appreciated by the little girls, and Vicente Cachocho (his last name is a colloquialism for "lice"), a humble peon who opens up the wonderful world of nature by answering the girls' inquiries. The theme of social injustice is introduced through the depiction of this character, who, more insignificant than "lice," is kind, dignified, and brave. In defiance of the feudal system represented by the patriarch and his hacienda, Vicente Cachocho joins one of the many revolutions against the rich and the powerful. Opposite the stern, "masculine" father is the mother, the epitome of femininity: She is soft, childish, and pretty, and does not seem to have any responsibilities in the children's upbringing, except when it comes to play.

At least in the eyes of Mamá Blanca, the childhood self, Blanca Nieve, is very much her own person. With a delightful sense of irony, the narrator begins her memoirs by describing herself as a dark-haired, dark-eyed, dark-skinned child, whose name ("Snow White") denied all these qualities and made her feel a little bit like a joke. The dissociation between a given name (a form of identity) and one's own person points to the conflicts involved in developing an identity, and in this case, a female identity. To add insult to injury, Blanca Nieve is the only sister with straight hair; but the daily ritual of putting her hair in curlers, while at first detested, forms a special bond between mother and daughter. At first reluctant to endure the tediousness of the procedure, the child is lured by her mother's storytelling, which lulls her into a kind of peaceful stupor, leaving her, in her own words, "openmouthed." The presence of the mirror in this ritual accentuates the search for self that is central to Teresa de la Parra's fiction. While Blanca Nieve loses her individuality by becoming like her sisters and having her hair curled, she is aware of the artificiality of this new self. The description of Mamá Blanca which frames the memoirs gives credence to the theory that Blanca Nieve was able, despite the conflictive aspects of her childhood, to form a genuine identity.

The book's conclusion also points in that direction. After the move to Caracas, the daughters convince the mother to make a visit to "Piedra Azul." But nothing is the same: The new owners have completely transformed the place; Vicente Cachocho is gone and so is Candelaria, the old cook; and so is Blanca Nieve. The book ends with a disappointing return to Caracas. If the reader is left wondering what happened to Blanca Nieve, she or he must go back to the beginning: That Blanca Nieve forged herself an authentic identity is attested by Mamá Blanca's strong and loving presence.

In 1930 Teresa de la Parra was invited to offer a series of lectures in Bogotá. Published in 1961, these texts deal with the influence of women on Spanish American culture and history. The opening paragraphs are revealing of de la Parra's ideas on feminism: Women must be strong and healthy, must work and be financially independent, and should consider men as their friends and companions, not as their owners or enemies. She declares herself a moderate feminist, and argues that a radical and abrupt change would not bring about the sort of stability she envisions between the two sexes. Her argument is difficult to follow:

She proceeds to show, through a survey of some of the most important female figures in the history of Spanish America, from the conquest to independence, that steady progress had been made and that these women (for example, Queen Isabella, Doña Marina, Sor Juana,* Manuela Sáenz) had left a deep imprint on the culture and destiny of Spanish America. Although the text has some validity for its awareness of women and their impact on society, its major flaw is its mild, rosy tone and its avoidance of some crucial points. For instance, in her discussion of Doña Marina ("la Malinche"), de la Parra does not offer any analysis of Doña Marina's inferior position in reference to the Spanish conquistador Hernán Cortés, or the symbolic dimensions of their union, the institutionalization of *mestizaje* (miscegenation).

Like her character María Eugenia Alonso in *Ifigenia*, Teresa de la Parra kept a diary; entitled *Bellevue-Fuenfría-Madrid*, it does not record any of her feelings or ideas about her craft, her personal life, or her illness (details of which are nonetheless documented in an almost obsessive fashion). A partial explanation for this phenomenon might be the fact that the diary has not been published in its entirety. It is indeed in her fiction that Teresa de la Parra comes most alive as an engaging (and *engagé*) writer. If her feminism seems tame when compared to today's standards, it should be noted that it was deemed as rather advanced and polemical for its time. Her strengths lie in her delightful, ironic style and in her authentic portrayal of a woman's search for a viable identity. For these reasons, aesthetic as well as thematic, her work remains provocative, relevant, and appealing to the modern reader.

SURVEY OF CRITICISM

In 1926, a letter to literary critic Lisandro Alvarado appeared in one of Caracas' major newspapers. It was signed by María Eugenia Alonso, the narrator/protagonist of *Ifigenia*, and it had been written by Teresa de la Parra. In it, the author reminds the critic that the points of view expressed in the novel belong to *her*, and not to Teresa de la Parra. A fine example of irony, and somewhat reminiscent of Sor Juana's* *Respuesta a Sor Filotea (Response to Sor Filotea)*, the document points to the two major issues that marked the reception of *Ifigenia*: shock at the outrageous views of the protagonist, and the inability to separate her from the author. Even though an excerpt from *Ifigenia* had been published to great acclaim by *La Lectura Semanal*, the work in its entirety presented problems that the reading public could not accept at that time. For instance, de la Parra's acute and often negative observations about the suffocating atmosphere of Caracas' upper class society did not go unnoticed: As is often the case, people did not appreciate being reminded of their provincialism and narrowmindedness. In a letter to her friend Rafael Carías, de la Parra complains about the readers' poor perception of *Ifigenia's* irony, a defect that led to their identification of the character with the author. Interestingly, however, the Venezuelans and other Latin Americans then living in Paris were generally enthusiastic about the novel.

A much tamer work, *Las memorias de Mamá Blanca* was popular upon its publication both in Paris and in Caracas.

After the initial controversy regarding *Ifigenia*, Teresa de la Parra was relatively ignored. In 1954 Ramón Díaz Sánchez published *Teresa de la Parra: claves para una interpretación* (1954), an interesting book that offers some general analysis of the writer's works and many anecdotes about her life (taken mostly from her letters, to which the author had access). Although it is neither a biography nor an interpretive study, the book provides some relevant material, which in conjunction with some other sources, could be useful. Also from this period is Marco Antonio Martínez' article on the religious aspects of *Las memorias de Mamá Blanca*.

Only within the past few years Teresa de la Parra's work has received the kind of attention it deserves. The excellent edition of her complete works, including a series of unpublished stories, letters, and a diary, prepared by Velia Bosch and Julieta Fombona, and published by Biblioteca Ayacucho in 1982, has no doubt sparked a new interest in her. The accompanying essays by the editors provide a clear and useful introduction to the thematic and stylistic aspects of de la Parra's fiction. Fombona, for instance, calls *Ifigenia* "a misunderstanding," that becomes fully realized at the end. By pointing out the particular structure of a first-person narrative framed by a long letter to which the answer, in its superficiality and paucity, constitutes a nonanswer, and by acutely observing that the identity of the speaker is defined not only by what is said, but also by *how* what is said is received, the critic reaches, not a conclusion, but a crucial question: Who is the speaker in the novel? She suggests that María Eugenia's false sense of herself (though constructed by herself) gradually disappears in the novel, as César Leal's presence and influence become stronger. The speaker, then, is molded by the words of others. María Eugenia's search for an identity is frustrated by her acquiescence in assuming an identity assigned to her by others (Cristina, Mercedes, Aunt Clara, Leal). In her essay, Bosch offers a general biographical and critical survey, briefly sketching de la Parra's works and providing a cultural and historical context. The edition is complemented by a detailed chronology and a bibliography.

The most recent articles on de la Parra attempt to "rescue" her work in terms of its importance for feminist critics. Edna Aizenberg (1985) applies the concept of the *Bildungsroman* to *Ifigenia*, arguing that the protagonist's efforts to successfully complete the processes of apprenticeship are doomed by the patriarchal structures that rule her life. She also observes the double role of literature as a liberating and a constricting force, since María Eugenia's identification with fictional heroines, especially Iphigenia, ultimately stops her from forging an identity of her own. Doris Meyer (1983) touches on a similar aspect when she acutely observes María Eugenia's conflict in trying to be both a self and an other. Meyer also establishes an analogy between the protagonist's experience as she looks in the mirror, feeling in the presence of a very familiar and beloved person who was not herself, and the female reader's experience, "seeing her own self in the mirror of the book.'' The same critic also cites Elaine Showalter's term, ''*ad feminam* criticism,'' in pointing out the condescending attitude of some male critics, who were more interested in de la Parra's ''feminine'' charms than in her ''female'' fiction (for instance, Francis de Miomandre). Francine Masiello (1985) applies several concepts of feminist criticism to de la Parra's work. She defines *Ifigenia* as an avant-garde novel that transgresses the limits of conventional narrative through its upheaval of traditional frames of reference. She also points out the text's ''abandonment of faith'' in genealogy, through the dead father in *Ifigenia* and the emotionally absent father in *Las memorias de Mamá Blanca*, which in turn generates a different kind of conspiracy between women. María Eugenia's ''mirror'' relationships with both Cristina Iturbe and Mercedes Galindo in *Ifigenia*, and the narrator's affinities with Mamá Blanca in the *Memorias* confirm this theory.

As demonstrated by the three essays discussed above, Teresa de la Parra's work remains rich in possibilities for the contemporary feminist critic, since it raises the kinds of problems that women (in and out of literature) are still concerned with: the constrictions of gender and the formation of a truly female identity.

BIBLIOGRAPHY

Works by Teresa de la Parra

Diario de una señorita que se fastidia. Caracas: La Lectura Semanal, 1922.
La Mamá X. Caracas: Tipografía Moderna, 1923.
Ifigenia; diario de una señorita que escribió porque se fastidiaba. Prol. and Afterword, by Francis de Miomandre. Paris: Editorial Franco-Ibero-Americana, 1924.
Las memorias de Mamá Blanca. Paris: Editorial ''Le Livre Libre,'' 1929.
Cartas. Prol. Mariano Picón Salas. Caracas: Librería Cruz del Sur, 1951.
Tres conferencias inéditas. Prol. Arturo Uslar Pietri. Caracas: Ediciones Garrido, 1961.
Obras completas. Prol. Francis de Miomandre. Introd. Carlos García Prada. Caracas: Editorial Arte, 1965.
Obra (Narrativa, ensayos, cartas). Edition, chronology, and critical studies by Velia Bosch and Julieta Fombona. Caracas: Biblioteca Ayacucho, 1982.

Translation of Teresa de la Parra

Onís, Harriet de, trans. *Mamá Blanca's Souvenirs*. Introd. Dillwyn F. Ratcliff. Washington, D.C.: Pan American Union, 1959.

Works about Teresa de la Parra

Acker, Bertie. ''Ifigenia: Teresa de la Parra's Social Protest.'' *Letras Femeninas* 14, 1–2 (Spring-Fall 1988):73–79.
Aizenberg, Edna. ''El bildungsroman fracasado en Latinoamérica: el caso de *Ifigenia*, de Teresa de la Parra.'' *Revista Iberoamericana* 51 (July-Dec. 1985):539–46.
Bosch, Velia. *Esta pobre lengua viva. Relectura de la obra de Teresa de la Parra: A*

medio siglo de "Las memorias de Mamá Blanca." Caracas: Ediciones de la Presidencia de la República, 1979.

———. "Estudio crítico." *Obra (Narrativa, ensavos, cartas).* By Teresa de la Parra. Ed. Velia Bosch and Julieta Fombona. Caracas: Biblioteca Ayacucho, 1982. Pp. xxvii–xxxvii.

———, ed. *Teresa de la Parra ante la crítica.* Caracas: Monte Avila, 1980.

Daireaux, Max. "Le roman de Teresa de la Parra: *Ifigenia." Revue de l'Amerique Latine* 4 (Aug. 1925).

Díaz Sánchez, Ramón. *Teresa de la Parra: claves para una interpretación.* Caracas: Ediciones Garrido, 1954.

Fombona, Julieta. "Teresa de la Parra: Las voces de la palabra." *Obra (Narrativa, ensayos, cartas).* By Teresa de la Parra. Ed. Velia Bosch and Julieta Fombona. Caracas: Biblioteca Ayacucho, 1982. Pp. ix–xxvi.

Fox-Lockert, Lucía. "Teresa de la Parra (Ana Teresa Parra Sanojo): *Ifigenia* (1924)." *Women Novelists in Spain and Spanish America.* Metuchen, N.J.: Scarecrow Press, 1979. Pp. 156–65.

Fuenmayor Ruíz, Víctor. *El inmenso llamado: las voces en la escritura de Teresa de la Parra.* Caracas: Universidad Central de Venezuela, 1974.

Garrels, Elizabeth. *Las grietas de la ternura: Nueva lectura de Teresa de la Parra.* Caracas: Monte Avila, 1985.

Llebot, Amaya. *'Ifigenia': Caso único en la literatura nacional.* Caracas: Universidad Central de Venezuela, 1974.

Martínez, Marco Antonio. "El tema religioso en *Las memorias de Mamá Blanca." Revista Nacional de Literatura* (Caracas) 109 (Mar.-Apr. 1955).

Masiello, Francine. "Texto, ley, transgresión: especulación sobre la novela (feminista) de vanguardia." *Revista Iberoamericana* 51 (July-Dec. 1985):807–22.

Meyer, Doris. " 'Feminine' Testimony in the Works of Teresa de la Parra, María Luisa Bombal, and Victoria Ocampo." *Contemporary Women Authors of Latin America: Introductory Essays.* Eds. Doris Meyer and Margarite Fernández Olmos. Brooklyn, N.Y.: Brooklyn College Press, 1983. I:3–15.

Miró, Clemencia. "Teresa de la Parra (a Lydia Cabrera)." *Revista Hispánica Moderna* (New York) 3 (Oct. 1936):35–38.

Mistral, Gabriela. "Dos recados sobre Teresa de la Parra." *Sur* (Buenos Aires) 25 (Oct. 1936).

Moon, Marion D. "Feminism in the Works of Teresa de la Parra." Master's Thesis. University of Georgia, 1972.

Mora, Gabriela. "La otra cara de *Ifigenia*: una revaluación del personaje de Teresa de la Parra." *Sin Nombre* (Puerto Rico) 7, 3 (1976):130–44.

Piedrahita, Carmen. "Literatura sobre la problemática femenina en Latinoamérica." *Cuadernos Americanos* (Mexico) 236 (1981):22–38.

Stillman, Ronnie Gordon. "Teresa de la Parra, Venezuelan Novelist and Feminist." *Latin American Women Writers: Yesterday and Today.* Eds. Yvette E. Miller and Charles M. Tatum. Pittsburgh: Latin American Literary Review, 1977. Pp. 42–48.

VIOLETA PARRA
(1917–1967)
Chile

Marjorie Agosín
Translated by Janice Molloy

BIOGRAPHY

Violeta Parra's birthplace holds a special significance in the life of this important Chilean artist. Parra was born in the south of Chile close to the city of Chillán, a region known for its pottery. She was born in the village of San Carlos Nuble on October 4, 1917. Violeta was born into a family of musicians: Her father played the violin and her mother sang. From a young age, Violeta sang and traveled with her brothers and sisters. In this environment, Violeta learned folk songs from the elderly residents of her town and from her own family.

Following in the footsteps of her older siblings and because of the enormous financial difficulties faced by the Parra family, the adolescent Violeta moved from the rural town of her childhood to Santiago in 1930. In the capital, Violeta began to sing with her sister Hilda as the now famous Parra Duo. Violeta became involved in a series of activities related to folklore, involving not only Latin American music, but also the music of Spain, especially the *flamenco*. She did not sing in social clubs; on the contrary, she perfomed in working-class areas, realizing her own marginality and that of her people. This was a difficult but fruitful period for Violeta, because she became aware of the ignorance of Chileans with respect to local folk music.

In the twenty years that followed, Parra married Luis Cereceda, gave birth to and raised two children, and survived various illnesses. She also dedicated time and effort to collecting the folklore and the innumerable cultural legacies that she would later return to the people.

In the 1950s Parra began to have great artistic influence, above all with the programs she did on Radio Chile called "Chile Laughs and Sings." Here, Parra began the most interesting stage of her career, where she presented a treasury of artistic activity from throughout the country by means of the mass media. On her program, Parra sang folk songs, spoke about local customs, and introduced singers from various regions.

In those years, Parra also dedicated herself fervently to the task of collecting folklore by traveling throughout the country. In 1950 and 1951 Parra was the director of the Museum of Popular Art in Concepción. In 1953 she was invited to attend the International Conference of Communist Youth in Poland. Violeta Parra was no longer unknown, and after fighting to be allowed access to the public, she not only became known herself, but also introduced the voices of other working-class individuals. Parra continued collecting folklore until the 1960s. Her collection included music, as well as a wide range of material including folk sayings and regional costumes.

Between 1962 and 1964, Parra traveled through Europe. She sang in L'Escale in Paris and in Geneva. She traveled between Europe and Chile, working ceaselessly. She extended her work to the interpretation of folk themes throughout Latin America. She also began her own period as a creator, a stage that would last the rest of her life, and composed songs such as "Volver a los diecisiete" (Return to 1917) and "El guillatún" (The request), a type of Araucan ballet for an orchestra.

In 1963 Parra achieved rare success for a Latin American artist when she exhibited her famous tapestries in the Museum of Mankind in Paris. These tapestries exhibited the vibrant colors that were typical of her work. Nevertheless, always wanting to be close to her family and her children, Angel and Isabel, who also sang, Violeta returned to Chile the same year. There, she opened an alternative music center called "La Carpa de la Reina," the Queen's Tent. Parra gave many folk groups their start at this center.

Despite Parra's many successes, the tireless artist's spirit deteriorated; she felt alone and misunderstood. At times the public did not attend performances at "La Carpa de la Reina" because of the distance or the winter mud. Her personal life also suffered. Her companion in those last years, the Swiss Gilvert Favre, abandoned her. Parra wanted to compose, to toast, to share with others, but she found herself abandoned. She composed her last songs, among them "Gracias a la vida" (Thanks to life), and committed suicide in the Queen's Tent on February 5, 1967.

MAJOR THEMES

Within the rich and complex lyrical production of Violeta Parra, her compositions can be divided into three main categories: autobiography, love, and politics. Violeta definitively began to create her own compositions after 1960. It is surprising that there are no published chronologies of her poetic production, even of the posthumously published *Décimas* (Poems).

Décimas (1970) is Parra's autobiography in verse where she emphasizes the rural world in which she grew up. Little known by critics and the reading public,

Décimas brings together a complex and varied group of poems dominated by the theme of life's experience. The autobiographical character of the book permits Parra to delve deeply not only into certain key aspects of her individual existence—woman, mother, and worker—but also into the evolution of her social consciousness within her country's historical framework.

In *Décimas*, Parra also begins to assume the role of a witness to the problems of women, as is demonstrated in her compositions treating rape and marriage as a shackle. Parra presents marriage as captivity comprised of emotional and physical bonds. At the same time, she examines the fate of women who because of their marginal existence, do not have other options besides the maintenance of a family. One of the more notable aspects of *Décimas* is the image of the rural woman in all of her splendor but in her infancy, a period still not invaded by the social struggles of the future. The structure of *Décimas* resembles the movements of a musical symphony, beginning with the *allegro* of a happy and almost magical childhood, and passing through the second movement that reflects uncertainty and change. The third movement, which musically is *adagio*, reflects woman and her society, and the fourth and final movement exalts a new life and the discovery of one's own strength and worth.

Parra's *Décimas* covers almost forty years of Chile's turbulent political history, from the prosperous times when rural landowners like Violeta Parra's grandparents lived, down to the economic and social ruin of the present. The poems do not represent a learned approach to this history; within their framework, Parra profiles herself spontaneously and dedicates herself to creating and sketching creations formed from her lyric and imaginative impulses.

In the area of love poetry, the well-known compositions "Volver a los diecisiete" and "Gracias a la vida" stand out. Parra's love lyrics usually possess religious elements where Parra questions God about the pains of the soul. One of the most typical songs is "¿Qué será Dios del cielo?" (What will God of the sky be?). Most of these melodies possess a soft and delicate rhythm, through which the poet presents her hopes for a cure from the pains of the spirit and the turbulence produced by love. Another essential characteristic of Parra's love poetry is the possibility of restoring order in the world through reciprocal affection, as exemplified in the poem, "¿Qué será Dios del cielo?," emphasizing that it is the spirit that heals humanity's afflictions.

An abundance of metaphors is clearly observed in Parra's love poetry, in which she invokes God, the soul, and nature to calm the spirit's pains. Words are often repeated to give them an essential meaning. The images of light, clarity, and the idea of the reemergence of a state of innocence are profiled in "Volver a los diecisiete" and its unforgettable verse "Sólo el amor con su ciencia nos vuelve tan inocentes" (Only love with its science returns us to our innocent state).

Within Parra's lyrical poetry, some poems emphasize the denial of love and take on the traditional form of the Spanish *romancero* (collection of lyrical ballads). Nevertheless, this type of poem is more rare than the poems where reflection about love predominates. Understanding, compassion, and reflection are key elements in Parra's lyrics.

Parra's political songs are her most famous compositions: for example, "La carta" (The letter) and "Que viven los estudiantes" (Let the students live). These songs possess a rapid rhythm, as well as a certain directness. Accusatory and inquisitive, the poems accompany the daily, political actions and the history of her country. Through her songs, Parra has become one of the most recognized figures in Chile's political battles for justice for the dispossessed and the marginal. Parra composed many songs attacking false leaders who make promises they will never fulfill. Within her political lyrics, she at times reflects on her own pain, the constant feeling of abandonment that goes with being a member of a marginal social class. Through her voice, she attempts to recuperate her identity and power at all costs.

In most of Parra's political songs, a pattern reiterates the conditions of the oppressed, repeating a phrase several times in the same verse. In her later political poems, a religious element appears, in which the poor look toward heaven and God. "Yo canto a la diferencia" (I sing about difference), "La carta," and "Que viven los estudiantes" belong to a group of political songs where the basic ideology is the idea of the voice as a transforming, political force. Women appear in political battles as equal to men, especially in the moving song, "Ayúdame, Valentina" (Help me, Valentina), where the speaker asks Valentina Telescova for social vindication. The *machista* ideology so common in Latin American songbooks gives way to a vision of class struggle where women play an integral role.

Two fundamental books edited by Parra, *Poésie Populaire des Andes* (1964) and *Canciones folklóricas chilenas* (1977), represent her first attempts to collect the folk songs of Chile. In these books, one can see the methods she utilized to collect traditional songs, and the subject matter she liked to collect in the form of sayings and songs.

SURVEY OF CRITICISM

The marked absence of serious critical texts on Violeta Parra's art is surprising, an art that includes paintings, poetry, pottery, the creation of *arpilleras* (tapestries), and cooking, as well as her immense collection of folklore. Most of the criticism about Parra focuses on her tormented existence and aborted love affairs. In this sense, she provides a good example of the female artist's marginalization. Despite the fact that Parra revolutionized Latin American music, initiated a counterculture, and introduced a new way of integrating indigenous culture and popular song, her work remains dispersed in unimportant publications. Even Parra's important paintings are only mentioned in long-lost catalogues from her expositions in Switzerland, France, and Chile.

Parra introduced the testimonial genre in Chile, the so-called life histories that began to have an impact in Latin American in the early 1970s. *Violeta Parra,*

Gracias a la vida (Subercaseux and Londoño, 1976) is one of the pioneering works on the life and work of this unique artist. Through interviews with her closest family members such as her mother and her brothers Nicanor and Roberto, Subercaseux and Londoño attempt to create an image of Violeta Parra and her childhood in the countryside and, more than anything, to show the forces that formed her. It is interesting that the people interviewed are the same ones Parra herself interviewed in her career as a collector of folklore, for example, Doña Rosita Lorca. The image of an individual who reports and is in turn reported on provides us with an opportunity to observe how Violeta formed relationships with the people around her.

Toda Violeta Parra (1985), an anthology edited by Alfonso Alcalde, resembles *Gracias a la vida*. Nevertheless, this book is useful to round out the figure of Violeta Parra, because it includes interviews with different people who speak about her, as well as a number of new songs that do not appear in other collections.

To the present, the most complete biography has been that of Parra's daughter, Isabel, *El libro mayor de Violeta Parra* (1985). Isabel speaks about her experiences as the daughter of this complex woman, as well as about her relationship with Violeta as a teacher and guide to folklore. She also discusses the many art festivals in which Violeta exhibited her pottery and paintings, and sang.

The most important aspect of *El libro mayor de Violeta Parra* is the collection of fifty-six unedited letters sent to different people. The book includes letters written to, for example, Margot Loyola, the Chilean folklorist, who was Parra's companion during many Parisian adventures, and Gilvert Favre, a friend and the central figure in her life for more than ten years. In these letters, the image of a tireless woman appears, one who created from a vision and who experienced many artistic periods. The annotated bibliography in this book is an excellent introduction to approaching Violeta Parra's texts.

La guitarra indócil (1986) by Patricio Manns is a difficult book to classify because it combines perfectly the biographical and musical-literary aspects of Parra's life. Manns's text is principally an introspective monologue about his personal relationship with Parra and his musical apprenticeship with her. This work discusses certain fundamental and little-examined topics, including her rough and raw voice, and the revitalization and incorporation of rural customs in her performances. The book also includes an interesting chapter on the period in which the Parra family formed "La peña de los Parra," an alternative center for popular music, introducing this type of music to Chile and to the rest of Latin America.

Juan Andrés Piña's prologue to Parra's *21 son los dolores* (1977) and Javier Martínez Reverte's essay in *Violeta Parra: Violeta del pueblo* (1976) are basic introductions to the comprehensive works of Violeta Parra. Piña's excellent essay examines Parra's revitalization of various ancient instruments, including the large *guitarrón* that she incorporated into her songs. He also introduces Parra's theories about music, and discusses many aspects of her personality that were previously unexplored. Osvaldo Rodríguez' work, *Cantores que reflexionan* (1984), is a fascinating study of the development of the New Song in Chile. Rodríguez dedicates a serious chapter to the role of Violeta Parra as precursor to the New Song movement, and examines her relationship with the musicians who made this type of music popular.

As noted above, there are many journalistic articles that add little to an understanding of Violeta Parra as an individual or an artist. The few serious articles that focus on Parra indicate how much remains to be researched. In the article, "Décimas de Violeta Parra o la separación de la conciencia de lo individual," Adriana Castillo de Berchenko (1981) analyzes the collective spirit of Violeta's autobiography as a profound solidarity with female experiences, including pregnancy, marriage (where the woman is usually mistreated), and rape. Castillo de Berchenko also studies the lyrical composition of Parra's *Décimas*, which she compares to the seven parts of a symphony.

Up to now, only one full-length study has been dedicated to Parra's fundamental book, *Décimas*. The first critical book on the poetry of Violeta Parra with special attention to her autobiographical work, *Décimas* (1970), has just been published by this author and Inés Dölz-Blackburn: *Violeta Parra: Santa de pura greda. Un estudio sobre su obra poética*.

Detailed studies dedicated to textual analysis of Parra's works include only Naomi Lindstrom's excellent study (1985) of *21 son los dolores*. In her article, Lindstrom analyzes with profundity and rigor the origins and traditional elements of the song, "21 son los dolores," and demonstrates how Parra deconstructs the folk symbology both to incorporate this tradition and to combine it with her own innovative imagination. Lindstrom also examines how Parra created alternate systems for sharing her music with others, including the establishment of "La peña de los Parra" and her preference for singing in informal settings.

Gina Cánepa-Hurtado's essay, "La canción de lucha de Violeta Parra y su ubicación en el complejo cultural chileno entre los años 1960 a 1973," is a model of the type of study that should be written about Parra's work. Cánepa takes an historical and cultural approach to Parra's work and demonstrates the relationship of her music and writings to the Chilean cultural legacy. In this article, she describes with singular intensity the popular struggles in which Parra played an essential role, such as her role in protesting unemployment under the dictatorship of General Carlos Ibáñez del Campo.

BIBLIOGRAPHY

Works by Violeta Parra

Canciones folklóricas chilenas. Santiago de Chile: Nascimento, 1977.
Cantos folklóricos chilenos. Musical transcriptions by Luis Gastón Soublette. Photographs by Sergio Larraín and Sergio Bravo. Santiago de Chile: Nascimento, 1979.

"Cuentos folklóricos." *Atenea* 423 (July-Sept. 1970):34–39.
Décimas: autobiografía en versos. Havana: Casa de las Américas, 1971.
Décimas: autobiografía en versos. Mexico City: Ediciones de Cultura Popular, 1974.
Décimas: autobiografía en versos. Barcelona: Pomaire, 1976.
Décimas: autobiografía en versos chilenos. Santiago de Chile: Pomaire, 1970.
Décimas: autobiografía en versos chilenos. Santiago de Chile: Nueva Universidad, 1972.
Poésie populaire des Andes. Ed. Panchita González-Battle. Bilingual ed. Paris: Maspero, 1964.
Toda Violeta Parra. Anthology. Ed. Alfonso Alcalde. Buenos Aires: Ediciones de la Flor, 1974.
21 son los dolores. Prol. Juan Andrés Piña. Santiago de Chile: Aconcagua, 1977.
Violeta del pueblo. Prol. and notes by Javier Martínez Reverte. Madrid: Visor, 1976.

Recordings (Singles)

Cuecas. Isabel and Violeta Parra. Santiago de Chile: Demon, 1965.
Las Hermanas Parra. A series of recordings made between 1949 and 1952 by Hilda and Violeta Parra. Santiago de Chile: R.C.A. Victor.
Qué pena siente el alma and *Casamiento de negros*. Santiago de Chile: Odeón, 1953.
El tocador afuerino. Violeta Parra and Gilvert Favre. Santiago de Chile: Odeón, 1965.

Recordings (Full-length)

Canciones de Violeta Parra. Serie Música de esta América. Havana: Casa de las Américas, 1971.
Canciones reencontradas en Paris. Santiago de Chile: Dicap, 1971.
Canto para una semilla. Autobiographical poems by Violeta Parra with music by Luis Advis. Performed by Isabel Parra and Inti-Illimani. Santiago de Chile: Dicap, 1972.
La Carpa de la Reina. By Violeta Parra and others. Santiago de Chile: Odeón, 1966.
La cueca presentada por Violeta Parra. El folklore de Chile, Vol. III. Santiago de Chile: Odeón, 1957.
Los Parra de Chile. Violeta Parra and her children. Berlin: Amiga, 1962.
Recordando a Chile: canciones de Violeta Parra. Santiago de Chile: Odeón, 1965.
Un río de Sangre: Le Chili de Violeta Parra. Paris: Arion, 1974.
Toda Violeta Parra. El folklore de Chile, Vol. V. Santiago de Chile: Odeón, 1960.
La tonada presentada por Violeta Parra. El folklore de Chile, Vol. IV. Santiago de Chile: Odeón, 1957.
Las últimas composiciones de Violeta Parra. Acompañamientos instrumentales de Isabel y Angel Parra. Santiago de Chile: R.C.A. Victor, 1966.
Violeta Parra acompañada de guitarra. El folklore de Chile, Vol. I, II. Santiago de Chile: Odeón, 1956.
Violeta Parra ausente presente . . . Paris: Le Chant du Monde, 1975.
Violeta Parra: Cantos de Chile. Paris: Le Chant du Monde, 1956.
Violeta Parra—Décimas. Santiago de Chile: Alerce, 1976.

Works about Violeta Parra

Agosín, Marjorie. Introduction to "Bibliografía de Violeta Parra." *Revista Inter-Americana de Bibliografía* (Washington, D.C.) 32, 2 (1982):179–190.

————, and Inés Dölz-Blackburn. *Violeta Parra: Santa de pura greda. Un estudio sobre su obra poética*. Santiago de Chile: Planeta, 1988.

Alcalde, Alfonso, ed. *Toda Violeta Parra*. 6th ed. Buenos Aires: Ediciones de la Flor, 1985.

————. "Violeta Parra." *Gente de carne y hueso*. Santiago de Chile: Universitaria, 1971. Pp. 15–17.

Alegría, Fernando. "Violeta Parra." *Retratos contemporáneos*. New York: Harcourt, Brace and Jovanovich, 1979. Pp. 165–68.

Arguedas, José María. "Análisis de un genio popular hacen artistas y escritores." *Revista de Educación* (Santiago de Chile) 13 (1968):66–76.

————. "Der Fall Violeta Parra." *Guitarre des dammernden Morgens das neue chilenische Lied*. Ed. Carlos Rincón et al. Berlin: Aufbau-Verlag, 1975. Pp. 136–38.

Barraza, Fernando. "Del arroyito a Violeta Parra." *La nueva canción chilena*. Santiago de Chile: Quimantú, 1972. Pp. 17–27.

Bello, Enrique. "Homenaje a Violeta Parra." *Boletín de la Universidad de Chile* 74 (May 1967):60–61.

Bessière, Bernard. "Violeta Parra. La permanence du thème folklorique." *La nouvelle chanson chilienne en exil*. 2 vols. Place de la Tour, Va.: Ed. d'Aujourd'hui, 1980. I:228–41.

Brown, Alison M. "The New Song Movement: A History of Popular Politics and Cultural Change, 1964–1973." Unpublished B.A. Honors Thesis. Harvard College, 1979.

Brunhammer, Yvonne. *Violeta Parra*. Paris: Musée des Arts Décortifs, Palai du Louvre-Pavillon de Marsan, 1964.

Cánepa-Hurtado, Gina. "La canción de lucha de Violeta Parra y su ubicación en el complejo cultural chileno entre los años 1960 a 1973. Esbozo de sus antecedentes sociohistóricos y categorización de los fenómenos atingentes." *Revista de Crítica Literaria Latinoamericana* 9, 17 (1983):147–70.

————. "Violeta Parra y sus relaciones con la canción de lucha latinoamericana." Ph.D. diss. West Berlin, 1981.

————. "Zum Leben und Zur Arbeit Violeta Parra's." 40 Kunstlerinnen Zum Thema Zensur und Exil. Unpublished document presented for the exposition, "Chilenas, dentro y afuera." Berlin, 1983.

Castillo de Berchenko, Adriana. "Décimas de Violeta Parra o la separación de la conciencia de lo individual." *Ventanal* 2 (1981):21–31.

Clouzet, Jean. *La nouvella chanson chilienne*. Paris: Seghers, 1975. I:21–32.

Engelbert, Manfred, ed. "Eifunhrung." *Violeta Parra, Lieder aus Chile*. Frankfurt: Verlag Klaus Dieter Vervuert, 1987. Pp. 9–47.

Epple, Juan Armando. "Notas sobre la cueca larga de Violeta Parra." *Cuadernos Americanos* 124, 3 (1979):232–48.

————. "Violeta Parra: The Founding Voice of the New Latin American Song Movements." *University of Oregon Newsletter* (Mar. 4, 1984):11–12.

————. "Violeta Parra y la cultura popular chilena." *Literatura Chilena en el Exilio* 1, 2 (Apr. 1977):4–11.

Huasi, Julio. "Violeta de América." *Casa de las Américas* 65–66 (1971):91–104.

Jara Turner, Joan y Gustavo Becerra. *La nueva canción chilena: Ieri, oggi, domani*. Rome: ONAE-DICAP, 1976. 10–16.

Lasko, Susan. "Songs of Struggle, Songs of Hope: The Chilean New Songs." Unpublished Senior Essay. University of California, Santa Cruz, 1977.

Letelier, Alfonso. "In Memorium Violeta Parra." *Revista Musical Chilena* 21, 100 (Apr.-June 1967):109–11.

Lindstrom, Naomi. "Construcción folklórica y desconstrucción individual en el texto de Violeta Parra." *Nueva canción y canto nuevo.* Madrid: Ediciones la Frontera, 1985. 9, 3 + 4. *Literatura Chilena: Creación y Crítica* (Los Angeles) 9 (Summer-Fall 1985):33–34.

Lipthay, Isabel. "Canto nuevo, un movimiento." *Hoy* (Jan. 30-Feb. 5, 1980):41–42.

Manns, Patricio. *La guitarra indócil.* Concepción, Chile: Latinoamericana Reunida, 1986.

———. *Violeta Parra.* Madrid: Júcar, 1978.

Martí Fuentes, Adolfo. "La poesía popular de Violeta Parra." *Casa de las Américas* 69 (1971):203–206.

Martínez Reverte, Javier. *Violeta del pueblo.* Madrid: Visor, 1976.

Müller-Bergh, Klaus. "Fulgor y muerte de Violeta Parra." *Revista Interamericana de Bibliografía* 23, 1 (Jan.-Mar. 1978):47–53.

Orrego-Salas, Juan. "La nueva canción chilena: tradición, espíritu y contenido de su música." *Literatura Chilena en el Exilio* 4, 2 (Apr. 1980):2–7.

Parra, Angel. "Porträt der Violeta Parra." *Guitarre des dammernden Morgens das neue chilenische Lied.* Ed. Carlos Rincón et al. Berlin: Aufbau-Verlag, 1975. Pp. 129–31.

Parra, Isabel. *El libro mayor de Violeta Parra.* Madrid: Michay, 1985.

———. "Porträt der Violeta Parra," *Guitarre des dammernden Morgens das neue chilenische Lied.* Ed. Carlos Rincón et al. Berlin: Aufbau-Verlag, 1975. Pp. 134–35.

"La Parra madre y los otros Parra." *Revista del Domingo, El Mercurio* (Santiago de Chile) 614 (1978).

Perfil de la creación musical en la nueva canción chilena desde sus orígenes hasta 1973. Santiago de Chile: CENECA Working Paper, 1980.

Piña, Juan Andrés. "Prados y flores y portentos." *Hoy* (Mar. 5 to 11, 1980):39–41.

———. Prologue to *21 son los dolores.* By Violeta Parra. Santiago de Chile: Aconcagua, 1977. Pp. 13–25.

———. "Violeta Parra, la flor y el futuro." *Hoy* (Dec. 7, 1977):32–36.

Rodríguez, Osvaldo. *Cantores que reflexionan. Notas para una historia personal de la nueva canción chilena.* Madrid: LAR, 1984.

Subercaseaux, Bernardo, and Jaime Londoño. *Gracias a la vida, Violeta Parra.* Buenos Aires: Galerna, 1976.

———. "Merci, a la vie, Violeta Parra." *Europe* (Paris) 570 (1976):233–39.

———. "Notas en Violeta Parra." *Papers in Romance* 2, 1 (Autumn 1979):76–78.

Villalobos C., Max. "Violeta Parra, hermana mayor de los cantores populares." *Revista Musical Chilena* 12, 60 (July-Aug. 1958):71–77.

CRISTINA PERI ROSSI
(b. 1941)
Uruguay

Gabriela Mora

BIOGRAPHY

Cristina Peri Rossi was born in Montevideo, Uruguay, in 1941. Her father was a textile worker and her mother a teacher who gave Cristina a love of reading. The grandparents immigrated to Uruguay from Italy. She remembers an unhappy childhood brightened by an uncle—a confirmed bachelor and a Communist—with an enticing library. In search of her identity, Peri began writing at an early age but kept it a secret from her family whom she knew would disapprove of her doing anything that was not in conformity with the traditional female role. Having studied letters at the University in Montevideo, she earned her living as a journalist and teacher of literature. Her outspoken support of the left's resistance to the increasing oppression by the Uruguayan government made her a target of persecution. She fled to Spain in 1972 and now makes her home in Barcelona.

While in Uruguay, Peri published *Viviendo* (Living) in 1963. The book's three realistic stories offer a dark vision of the enclosed world inhabited by women. In the title story, a thirty-four-year-old woman sees herself condemned to spinsterhood. "El Baile" (The dance) and "No sé qué" (I don't know what) discreetly suggest lesbian relations. Lonely and caught in the boring routine of everyday life, the women in these stories are unable to change their destinies.

In 1968 Peri won the Prize Arca for young Uruguayan authors with *Los museos abandonados* (1969; The abandoned museums), four short stories portraying a decaying, meaningless culture. In three of the stories, a man and a woman enact sad, erotic games. Cut off from the outside world, they are unable to see the destruction around them or to communicate with each other. An unusual touch of the fantastic enhances the interest of "Los extraños objectos voladores" (The strange flying objects), the realistic first story about peasant poverty and powerlessness.

The novel *El libro de mis primos* (1969; The book of my cousins) won the first prize offered in 1968 by *Marcha*, a prestigious magazine published in Montevideo. Peri uses the main narrator, a child with a keen, critical eye for the faults of his upper class family, to develop a devastating satire of capitalism, patriarchal institutions, and militarism. Revolutionary and feminist in its themes, *El libro* is also radical in its form. Peri mixes prose and verse, shifts perspectives and voices, and makes unexpected use of rhetorical and typographical devices.

In 1970 Peri published *Indicios pánicos* (1970; Signs of panic), a book composed of forty-six difficult to classify fragments. Many of the pieces are short stories, poems, essays, and aphorisms. A powerful indictment against fascism, it has been considered a prediction of the repression to come under dictatorship. The book was banned in Uruguay when the military took power in 1973.

Although Peri had been publishing poetry in different journals for some years, her first book of poems, *Evohé* (the traditional cry of the Greek Bacchae to invoke Bacchus), did not appear until 1971. An open celebration of the female body, the volume shook Montevideo's intellectual world. Using a subversive language of passion and desire, the poet makes "word" and "woman" synonymous, playing sensual and erotic games with both.

Established in Barcelona and writing on literature and art for several newspapers and magazines, in 1975 Peri published *Descripción de un naufragio* (Description of a shipwreck). The political strain in this book of poetry about love and exile is more evident than in previous collections of poems. Mixing verse with a quasi-narrative mode, *Descripción* sometimes echoes the social poetry of Pablo Neruda and Ernesto Cardenal. Similar themes and motifs are seen in *Diáspora*, a book of poems in manuscript, which won the 1973 Inventarios Provisionales Prize and was published in 1976. Again, Peri uses free types of verse to speak about social revolution, aesthetic creations, and lesbian love—recurrent themes in her work. In another book of poetry, *Lingüística general* (General linguistics), published in Valencia (Spain) in 1979, Peri continues her exploration of art, language, and lesbian relationships with her inventive and playful free verse.

Children play a significant part in many of Peri's short stories. Several of the eight stories in *La tarde del dinosaurio* (The afternoon of the dinosaur), a collection published in 1976, have child protagonists who are wiser than adults. As in all of her fiction, the lives of these characters—children and adults—are revealed in a poetry-like prose that reflects Peri's humor and lyric sensitivity. These aspects of her writing enrich *La rebelión de los niños* (The children's rebellion), a collection of eight stories published in 1980 with a preface by Julio Cortázar, the Argentinean writer. Children and adolescents are the protagonists of situations in which they and the adults witness and experience different kinds of repression.

In 1983 the prestigious Barcelona publishing house Seix Barral issued *El museo de los esfuerzos inútiles* (The museum of the useless efforts), a collection of thirty prose pieces, some of which defy generic classification. Several are short stories, while others are journalistic-like chronicles or vignettes. Loneliness and absurdity dominate Peri's black-humored portrayal of different aspects of contemporary life. Some outrageously funny narratives are satires against psychoanalysis, artificial beauty, war, and political oppression.

In 1984 Seix Barral published *La nave de los locos* (The ship of fools), perhaps Peri's most important novel so far. The old medieval metaphor popularized by Sebastian Brant (*Narrenschiff)* in the fifteenth century and used by, among others, philosopher Michel Foucault in the twentieth to begin his well-known *Histoire de la folie* (1961; *Madness and Civilization*, 1965) offers a fundamental thematic key to *La nave*. It was originally entitled "El tapiz de la creación" (The tapestry of creation), after the eleventh-century weaving in the Cathedral of Gerona, Spain, and the narrative fragments that comprise the main "story" are interrupted by faithful descriptions of the tapestry. In contrast to the tapestry's immutable message of harmony in the world created by God, the episodes of Peri's book show the injustice and oppression in contemporary life. A beaten prostitute, a man "disappeared" for political reasons, and a poor woman seeking an abortion, reflect the loss of paradise as depicted by the medieval artisan. This and other intertextual biblical references in the novel are not to be interpreted as a call for religion, a subject often satirized by the author. On the contrary, there is a clear understanding among the characters that the harmony they all admire and pursue is mythical.

In *La nave* Peri provides a new view of the erotic through the tender love of men for young boys or old ladies, a woman's respect for an impotent man, and a theater scene depicting lesbian affection. Like other contemporary fiction, her novel omits or distorts information, requiring the reader to search for clues and explanations in the episodes, news reports, footnotes, fictitious surveys, and the descriptions of the tapestry. *La nave* condemns the aggressive exercise of power and celebrates the victims who resist by transgressing social conventions.

Una pasión prohibida (A forbidden passion) was published in 1986. Its twenty prose pieces have a parabolic, aphoristic quality that give them an unusual texture. The author's characteristic bent toward satire appears in stories like "La revelación" (The revelation) and "El juicio final" (The last judgment), which mock the cliché-like ideas ordinary citizens have of the phenomena alluded to in the titles. The book also makes fun of misguided patriotism ("Patriotismo"), futile promises and self-righteousness ("La gratitud es insaciable"—Gratitude is insatiable), and sacred commandments such as forgiving our enemies ("Una lección moral"—A moral lesson). Echoes of the mysterious, like those in Julio Cortázar's stories, are found in "La condena" (The sentence) and "El umbral" (The threshold).

MAJOR THEMES

In her prose and poetry, Peri Rossi uses the themes of love, politics, and art to speak against all forms of oppression. Her celebration of homosexual love, for example, serves as an erotic motif as well as a political one through which she speaks for the rights of the individual. For Peri, however, freedom does not mean what in *La nave de los locos* she calls "ombliguismo" (navel-ism), the act of those who only look at their navels without concern for the rest of the world. From her earliest work, Peri has written militantly in favor of solidarity and collectivity. She expresses her views not in a pamphleteering mode but through the depiction of love that bridges sex, age, race, and nationality. Thus, the loving admiration that a man has for an old, fat woman in *La nave* saves their sexual encounter from any hint of mockery or debasement. The same can be said of the homosexual relationships that appear in several of Peri's works.

Peri's political sophistication infuses her stories with a clear understanding of the causes and effects of social ills. The reader can perceive those causes in spite of the elliptic and indirect fashion with which the stories refer to them. For example, the lives of the poor street children of her later prose are connected in subtle ways to those of the selfishly uncaring rich and powerful. But if capitalism is one of Peri's targets, she also indicts the pseudorevolutionaries living comfortable lives and compromising or betraying their ideals.

Without direct reference to the history or geography of her native country, Peri's allusions to the "disappeared" and her biting satires against militarism and dictatorships point clearly to the recent experience of Uruguay and the other countries of the Southern Cone. But the author is not only concerned with Latin American problems. In fact, together with the Argentineans Jorge Luis Borges and Julio Cortázar, she is one of Latin America's most internationalist writers vis-à-vis themes and forms. Many of the short stories in *La tarde del dinosaurio* and *La rebelión de los niños* offer an apocalyptic vision of wars, famines, atomic devastation, and surrealistic landscapes. The disintegrating world is saved by the likes of Federico, the guerrilla fighter in *El libro de mis primos*, or the wise, mature children of *La rebelión de los niños*. Peri explains her extensive use of children as characters by saying they have eyes not yet weakened by the conformity and frustration of adulthood. Children are the best witnesses of a corrupt world, she says in John F. Deredita's interview (1978, p. 142).

Exile, another of Peri's recurrent motifs, is narratively developed to reveal a wide variety of connotations: from the brutal treatment of citizens by a fascist regime to a metaphysical longing for the Lost Paradise. One of the main characters of *La nave de los locos* thinks that "exile is the true condition of mankind" (p. 106), the situation facing the "expatriates" populating that novel. Even Peri's descriptions of city streets, government offices, and public places evoke a sense of strangeness and alienation. For a good illustration see her portrayal of a European airport—it could be any airport of today—in "Una pasión prohibida," a short story in the book of the same name. The enormity of the spaces, the bright colors of the plastic furniture, and the mechanical devices, among other well-observed details, are used by Peri as a powerful means to evoke feelings of being lost and alone.

In her attack on social ills, the bourgeois family is one of Peri's favorite targets for parodies and satires in which the status of women occupies a prominent place. For example, in *El libro de mis primos*, she hilariously depicts the empty lives of rich ladies whose chief occupation is the pursuit of the smallest speck of dust in the house. Not humorous, however, are the reflections on the "special" destiny of married women:

Desde el momento que esa inversión de semen se realizaba, la *extraña* portadora de él, la *extranjera* que había abierto sus piernas ante uno de los nuestros, . . . se volvía un *objeto* venerable . . . pasaba a integrar la familia . . . . Desde ese momento . . . sus contactos con el exterior se disolvían, pasaba a estar bajo nuestra protección, ya nadie ni nada podía restituirla al tránsito, a las calles . . . como bajo la protección de un ejército de alabarderos, sus días se deslizarían ya prendidos para siempre a los nuestros. (*El libro*, p. 15. Mis subrayados.)

(From the moment that the investment of semen was made, the *strange woman* who carried it, the *foreign woman* who had opened her legs in front of one of us, . . . became a sacred *object* . . . she would become part of the family. From that moment . . . her contacts with the outside world ceased, she was under our protection, nobody or nothing could return her circulation, to the streets . . . as if under the protection of an army of halberdiers, her days would be fastened forever to ours.) [My emphasis and translation.]

As is obvious in the above passage, Peri castigates the making of woman into an object whose only value is her ability to prolong the family name. The closed world to which she is condemned after marriage accentuates her lifelong alienation.

Among other themes related to the oppression of women in *El libro*, virginity, rape, and female passivity are motifs worked out in unusual, polysemous ways in the chapter "El velorio de la muñeca de mi prima Alicia" (The wake of my cousin Alice's doll). Here as in other chapters of the book, Peri portrays women as victims of the socioeconomic system but chastises them—the grandmother Clara, for example—for allowing themselves to be made into custodians of the patriarchal family tradition. Private ownership is the basis of cultural attitudes that encourage men to consider women as property. Men are raised to think of females as beautiful things, that, together with the oriental rugs, crystal, and objects d'art, enhance family wealth. These same men weaken the economies of their Latin American countries as they push "to acquire commodities . . . bonds of foreign companies, investing dollars in private banks and building summer houses" (*El libro*, 1969, p. 14). The epitome of this greedy human type is the cousin's grandfather whose Pantagruelian appetite symbolizes the voracity of his class. In a long, funny list of the food he consumes, Peri Rossi parodies the land and money he has seized and the poor he has annihilated (*El libro*, 1969, p. 83).

An admirer of the contemporary forms popularized by Julio Cortázar, Peri has distinguished herself with daring experiments in textual constructions. Her narratives are characterized by changes in the points of view of multiple narrators, temporal breaks, and sheer a-chronologies. She also puts into her fictions historical names, events, and words. Peri Rossi breaks generic narrative conventions by mixing prose and verse and interpolating songs, jokes, footnotes, and news items. In her prose and poetry Peri uses typography as an imaginative and expressive vehicle. Unconventional uses of such features of punctuation as capital letters, quotation marks, blank spaces, and parentheses are among the signs she frequently employs. In her poems, the introduction of narrative modes and plays on words contribute to the novelty she has brought into her verses. The author delights in choosing terms for their unusual sounds and multiple connotations that add sensuality and ambiguity to the lyrical quality of her style. For example, one of the poems of *Descripción de un naufragio* (Description of a shipwreck), untitled (as are the book's other poems) and without punctuation, speaks of the pilgrimage of the exile at the same time that the words of the page are arranged in the outline of a sailboat. Yet, the typographical and intertextual games used in the poems do not diminish the intensity or the emotion of loss the verses project.

SURVEY OF CRITICISM

The recently ended period of repression in Uruguay, Peri's exile to Spain, and the fact she is a woman who writes razor-sharp criticism of capitalist society may explain why her work has not been better known in the Spanish-speaking world. Some brief reviews appeared in Uruguayan periodicals, but Peri's work did not receive serious attention until 1969 when the internationally known Uruguayan writer Mario Benedetti published "Cristina Peri Rossi: Vino nuevo en odres nuevos" (Cristina Peri Rossi: new wine in new bottles) in Montevideo's then prestigious magazine *Marcha*. In this essay which Benedetti included in his *Literatura uruguaya del siglo XX* (1969, pp. 321–27), he reviews *Viviendo* and *Los museos abandonados*, noting linkages between the short stories and commenting on their political message. Of the political content he wrote: "We could say that the stories of *Viviendo* are the museums before being abandoned, that is, both represent a rotten order, without a valid answer for contemporary man" (p. 324). In this article Benedetti refers to two of Peri's uncollected pieces: the story "Los amores" (The loves), and the poem "Homenaje a los trabajadores uruguayos del primero de mayo, aplastados por soldados y policías" (Homage to the Uruguayan workers crushed by soldiers and police on the first of May). In the story, Benedetti suggests, Peri shows her characters' resistance to change as being near the edge of insanity. Benedetti says that, in spite of its pamphlet-like title, the poem is not a pamphlet, but a good example of political poetry. With its "devastating irony" and "controlled energy," the poem reminds him of Ernesto Cardenal's work (p. 324). The lack of an obvious, strident political tone in *Los museos abandonados* is praised by Benedetti, who considers the book an allegory of the terror that gripped Uruguay in the 1970s.

John F. Deredita's "Desde la diáspora: entrevista con Cristina Peri Rossi" (1978; From the diaspora: an interview with Cristina Peri Rossi) has contributed greatly to our knowledge about the life and thinking of this Uruguayan author. After Deredita's opening biobibliographical paragraph, he allows her to speak at length about important subjects. Deredita elicits from Peri autobiographical details as well as her literary preferences: Felisberto Hernández, Julio Cortázar, J. D. Salinger, Jonathan Swift, and a few others. Peri also gives her views on politics and sexual revolution, which she sees as necessarily linked. She accepts Deredita's claim that her writing shows her penchant for digression and explains: "The fertility of digression is its ambiguity. . . . Literature is poetry and poetry is ambiguity" (p. 140).

Tomás G. Brena's essay on *Evohé*, Peri's first book of poetry, appears in his *Exploración estética: estudio de doce poetas de Uruguay y uno de Argentina* (1974). In spite of its length, this essay adds little to our understanding of the poems. The inflated style of the critic, his statement of the obvious, and the lack of bibliographical data flaw the study. More to the point but too inclined to easy labels is Rosa María Pereda's short review of *Los museos abandonados* (1974). For example, she insists on the *barroquismo* (baroque style) of the book but does not support her claim. Enrique Molina Campos follows this pattern of generalization in "El naufragio de Cristina Peri Rossi," a review of *Descripción de un naufragio* (1974). Although the critic says little about *Descripción*, he at least summarizes some of the features of Peri's writings, points out important facts of recent Uruguayan history, and provides biobibliographical information.

Marta Morello-Frosch's "Entre primos y dinosaurios con Cristina Peri Rossi" (Among cousins and dinosaurs with Cristina Peri Rossi) in Lucía Guerra Cunningham's *Mujer y sociedad en América Latina* (1980) considers *Los museos abandonados, El libro de mis primos*, and *La tarde del dinosario*. In her general overview of these texts, Morello-Frosch stresses Peri's political message and her audacious formal experiments.

Gabriela Mora in "El mito degradado de la familia en *El libro de mis primos* de Cristina Peri Rossi" (The degraded myth of the family in *The Book of My Cousins* by Cristina Peri Rossi), one of the essays in *The Analysis of Literary Texts* (1980), studies some aspects of Peri's first novel. As the title of the article suggests, Mora uses the book's portrait of the family to examine sexual roles and politics. Aspects of the novel's structure and language are also discussed.

The Uruguayan critic Hugo Verani has written two substantial articles about Peri Rossi. In his "Una experiencia de límites: la narrativa de Cristina Peri Rossi" (An experience of limits: the narrative of Cristina Peri Rossi) (1982), he reviews major features of Peri's fiction. Emphasizing the author's breaking of generic conventions, he claims her work is united by its lyric vision of the world. He says: "The lyric attitude, the playful exploration of reality, her lavishness with metaphors, the digressive and accumulative forms, are signs of a poetic reality and of a total experience that tolerate no limits" (p. 305). Verani links Peri's preference for fragmentariness, humor, and eroticism to the writings of Felisberto Hernández, her Uruguayan forerunner. The hyperbolic language of Peri's *El libro de mis primos*, Verani states, reminds him of Colombian Gabriel

García Márquez' style (p. 310). Verani also asserts that *El libro* "ensambla episodios en una disposicón arbitraria y sin orden fijo, sin ser suscitados unos por otros" (joins episodes in an arbitrary manner without fixed order, without one leading to the other, p. 312). As a result, the book is "una libre fusión de textos relativamente independientes en un esquema digresivo" (a free fusion of relatively independent texts within a digressive pattern). To our mind, however, the order of sequences is not arbitrary and the episodes do relate to each other. This type of structure—not new in contemporary fiction—is one more device to emphasize the novel's call for freedom.

Hugo Verani refers to Peri Rossi's poetry in "La rebelión del cuerpo y el lenguaje: A propósito de Cristina Peri Rossi" (The rebellion of body and language: apropos of Cristina Peri Rossi; 1982). The critic sees love as the major theme of Peri's poems: "From *Evohé* to *Lingüística general*, Peri Rossi's poetry seeks to find itself in Love. . . . All her books are marked by the sign of love and desire. Desire that reads like liberation" (p. 200). Verani sees the eroticism of *Evohé* as "individualistic self-affirmation and liberation of repressed sexual desire, without hiding the homosexual character of its passion" (p. 20). For Verani, Peri's books of poetry after *Evhoé* are more immersed in social history and contemporary circumstances but continue her preoccupation with questions of Eros and art.

Amy Kaminsky's "Gender and Exile in Cristina Peri Rossi" (1987) focuses on the motif of exile. Kaminsky astutely reads some stories from *El museo de los esfuerzos inútiles* and *La tarde del dinosaurio* and some poems from *Descripción de un naufragio* and *Lingüística general*. According to Kaminsky, the male exile, chosen by Peri as protagonist of her stories, is "feminized" by his displacement into a foreign culture. Women, on the other hand, having learned "alienation" at home, can find in exile "possibilities of growth and transcendence." For this critic, the poems of *Descripción* "offer testimony to political repression," but their language still "reinscribes male dominance and female subordination." In contrast, *Lingüística general* is freed of the male voice, and its speaker "fully embraces her status as outsider not only as political exile but as a lesbian as well."

Gabriela Mora's essay, "*La nave de los locos* y la búsqueda de la armonía" (1988; *The Ship of Fools* and the quest for harmony), attempts to decipher the novel's message and find the theme that unites its heterogeneous structure. Mora's thesis is that the longing for harmony is the unifying theme, with harmony understood as acts or words accepted as *natural*, as phenomena integrated in a balanced way in a more just world. Peri uses human situations such as homosexual love, male impotence, or love in old age, situations that break with "normal" forms of social conduct, to question accepted behaviors. The novel's subtext keeps asking, why do we tolerate the disappearance of a political opponent, the beating of a woman, or obstacles to a needed abortion while we do not accept love affairs based on tenderness and respect? Which is "natural" and which is against nature?

BIBLIOGRAPHY

Works by Cristina Peri Rossi

*Viviendo.*Montevideo: Alfa, 1963.
Los museos abandonados. Montevideo: Arca, 1969.
El libro de mis primos. Montevideo: Biblioteca de Marcha, 1969.
Indicios pánicos. Montevideo: Nuestra América, 1970.
Evohé. Montevideo: Editorial Giron, 1971.
Descripción de un naufragio. Barcelona: Lumen, 1975.
Diáspora. Barcelona: Lumen, 1976.
La tarde del dinosaurio. Barcelona: Planeta, 1976.
Lingüística general. Valencia (Spain): Prometeo, 1979.
La rebelión de los niños. Caracas: Monte Avila, 1980.
El museo de los esfuerzos inútiles. Barcelona: Seix Barral, 1983.
La nave de los locos. Barcelona: Seix Barral, 1984.
Una pasión prohibida. Barcelona: Seix Barral, 1986.

Works about Cristina Peri Rossi

Araújo, Helena. *La Scherezada criolla: Ensayos sobre escritura femenina.* Bogotá: Universidad Nacional de Colombia, 1989. Pp. 64–70, 161–66.
Benedetti, Mario. "Cristina Peri Rossi: Vino nuevo en odres nuevos." *Literature uruguaya siglo XX.* 2d ed. Montevideo: Alfa, 1969. Pp. 321–27.
Brena, Tomás G. "Cristina Peri Rossi." *Exploración estética: Estudio de doce poetas de Uruguay y uno de Argentina.* Montevideo: Impresora Record, 1974. Pp. 463–84.
Deredita, John F. "Desde la diáspora: entrevista con Cristina Peri Rossi." *Texto Crítico* (Veracruz, Mexico: Universidad Veracruzana) 9 (1978):131–42.
Kaminsky, Amy. "Gender and Exile in Cristina Peri Rossi." *Continental, Latin American and Francophone Writers.* Eds. Eunice Myers and Ginette Adamson. New York: University Press of America, 1987. Pp. 149–59.
Molina Campos, Enrique, "El naufragio de Cristina Peri Rossi." *Camp de l'Arp* 22 (July 1975):26–27.
Mora, Gabriela. "El mito degradado de la familia en *El libro de mis primos* de Cristina Peri Rossi." *The Analysis of Literary Texts: Current Trends in Methodology.* Ed. Randolph D. Pope. Ypsilanti, Mich.: Bilingual Press, 1980. Pp. 66–77.
———. "*La nave de los locos* y la búsqueda de la armonía." *Nuevo Texto Crítico* (Stanford, Calif.) 1, 2 (1988):343–52.
Morello-Frosch, Marta. "Entre primos y dinosaurios con Cristina Peri Rossi." *Mujer y sociedad en América Latina.* Ed. Lucía Guerra Cunningham. Santiago de Chile: Editorial del Pacífico, 1980. Pp. 193–201.
Narváez, Carlos Raúl. "Critical Approaches to Cristina Peri Rossi's *El libro de mis primos.*" Ph.D. diss. Columbia University, 1984. (DAI 44, 12 [1984]:3703A).
Ordoñez, Montserrat. "Cristina Peri Rossi: Asociaciones." *Eco* 248 (June 1982):196–205.
Pereda, Rosa María. "Cristina Peri Rossi: la parábola de un naufragio." *Camp de l'Arp* 13 (Oct. 1974):27.

Pittarello, Elide. "Cristina Peri Rossi: Los extraños objetos voladores o la disfatta del soggetto." *Studi di Letteratura Ispano-Americana* 13–14 (1983):63–78.

Sosnowski, Saúl. "*Los museos abandonados* de Cristina Peri Rossi: Reordenación de museos y refugios." *Actualidades* 6 (1980–1982):67–74.

Verani, Hugo. "Una experiencia de límites: la narrativa de Cristina Peri Rossi." *Revista Iberoamericana* 118–19 (Jan.-June 1982):303–16.

———. "La rebelión del cuerpo y del lenguaje: A propósito de Cristina Peri Rossi." *Revista de la Universidad de México* 37 (Mar. 1982):19–22.

Other Works Cited

Foucault, Michel. *Histoire de la folie*. Paris: Librairie Plon, 1961.

———. *Madness and Civilization*. Trans. Richard Howard. New York: Pantheon Books, 1965.

ALEJANDRA PIZARNIK
(1936–1972)
Argentina

Ana María Fagundo

BIOGRAPHY

Alejandra Pizarnik (also known as Flora Alejandra Pizarnik) was born in Avellaneda, in the province of Buenos Aires on April 16, 1936, into a family of Eastern European immigrants to Argentina. She studied philosophy and letters at the University of Buenos Aires, and painting under the tutelage of Juan Battle Planas. From 1964 to 1968, she lived in Paris where she worked for the journal *Cuadernos* and for various French publishers. She also took courses in contemporary French literature and the history of religion at the Sorbonne. Pizarnik translated into Spanish various French authors such as Antonin Artaud, Henry Michaux, Ives Bonnefoy, and Leopold Senghor. In 1969 she was awarded a Guggenheim Fellowship and in 1971 a Fulbright. On September 26, 1972, while away for a weekend from the clinic where she was hospitalized in Buenos Aires, she died from an overdose of senocal.

MAJOR THEMES

Whether Alejandra Pizarnik committed suicide or whether she took too many tranquilizers by error, we will never know for sure, but what we can easily ascertain is that her poetry is "death-driven" from the very start. Her poetry is an obsessive search for a realm where the human soul will find its total peace and its infinite expression. Pizarnik constantly tries to go beyond the limits of human perception. She would like to find a state of mind that would be as absolute as the Absolute itself, and she searched for it through painting, music, and poetry. The Argentine poet belongs to the tradition of poets who write with death constantly knocking at their doors. The awareness of death and the obsessive desire to flee from human limitations make her work as urgent as it makes it disquieting.

Love and poetry ("the word" as she calls it) are her other two major themes. Love appears in the poems as the real force capable of engaging the poet in the here-and-now, but the love that the poems refer to is ultimately turned into disenchantment. Poetry is also, for a time, a distraction from her ever-present preoccupation with death. Pizarnik's predicament as a poet appears in her writings as rather desolate and dramatic. Her poetry reads as though the poet had been snatched from a paradise of harmony and thrown into the wandering and pointless realm of destructive self-awareness.

Alejandra Pizarnik's work is influenced by the avant-garde. Her paintings are surrealistic, and her criticism and translations are of avant-garde authors. In her literary works she uses some avant-garde techniques such as disjointed expression, illogical connections, and hermetic allusions. Her poems have a marked oneiric quality. Stylistically, her poetry ranges from the short and concentrated verses of the first five books to the open suggestive prose poems of her last two books.

In Alejandra Pizarnik's first book of poems, *La tierra más ajena* (1955; The more foreign earth), there is a dilemma and a struggle between the zest for life and the overpowering presence of death. The theme of love is also present but not as a celebration.

In her second book, *La última inocencia* (1956; The last innocence), Pizarnik expresses her desperation at not finding a reason for living. She confesses her exhaustion with anything alive, anything human. Tired even of seeing death acting around her, she wishes for her "older sister" (as she calls death) to take her to her "sweet home." The poet does not find meaning in anything, not even in death. In "Poema a Emily Dickinson" (Poem to Emily Dickinson), Pizarnik commends the Amherst poetess for her love of eternity, although her own view of life and death is quite different from Dickinson's. The journey into her self becomes all the more consuming as the Argentinian poet continues probing into the mystery of existence. Many of the poems depict a feeling of strangeness as if the poet were doubting her own identity: "alejandra, alejandra / underneath I am / alejandra" (p. 27).

The search for the meaning of human existence becomes excruciating and almost unbearable in Pizarnik's third book of poems, *Las aventuras perdidas* (1958; The lost adventures). Fear and loneliness are the emotions that pervade the entire book. There is also a sense of a great loss, of having been expelled from the paradise of childhood where innocence and happiness were once possible. The death-wish becomes her only alternative. The slightest ray of hope has disappeared; the light is no longer possible. In the poem entitled "Cenizas" (Ashes), Pizarnik depicts a delirious miser on top of a mountain of gold, casting words toward the sky but unable to tell of her love, and in "El despertar" (The awakening), the poet asks to be relieved from the feeling of self-destruction:

"Señor / arroja los féretros de mi sangre" (p. 53, Lord / expel the coffins from my blood).

In her desire to attain a sort of revelation that will render all expression unnecessary as part of her search of the Absolute, Pizarnik reduces her verse to a minimal expression, as though words were superfluous once a vision has been attained. The preoccupation with craft is constant in Pizarnik and can be seen through her various books. She also refers to it in her diaries. Her fourth book of poems, *Arbol de Diana* (1962; Tree of Diana), is a good example of her concern with poetic expression. The poems in this book are terse, brief, and concentrated. At times a poem has but two lines: "explain with words of this world / that a ship parted from me taking me" (p. 23). Through the concentrated and plain language of this book Pizarnik has arrived at a kind of certainty in her poetry. She accepts her perpetual dissatisfaction with reality and the human condition. There is a kind of self-assurance, a feeling that her poetic quest has taken her beyond human reality to a vision of the life beyond. The desire to break from the limitations of life is now totally assumed.

A poetry that depends for its existence on apprehending and expressing the dimension of the infinite is necessarily a poetry preoccupied with the abstract rather than the concrete, with the life of the intellect rather than with the life of the emotions or the senses. Yet, there is a moment, however brief, in Alejandra Pizarnik's poetic trajectory when the work of the senses is celebrated in the poems. This occurs in the first part of her fifth book of poems, *Los trabajos y las noches* (1965; Works and nights). The presence of love lightens Pizarnik's poetic world and inspires her most lyrical poems. But the joyous celebration of love is the lesser part of this book. For the most part, it deals with the theme of death through the familiar symbols of Pizarnik's "season in hell," namely, the wind, the night, the forest, and ashes.

Of the last three books that Pizarnik published while still alive, two are poetic prose. *Extracción de la piedra de locura* (1968; Extraction from the stone of madness) is a collection of prose poems in which the poet, painfully lucid, reviews her past, delves into the present, and foresees, in an oneiric way, her future. The artist is now in full command of her expression. She can confess with pain and yet with secret pride: "Palabra por palabra yo escribo la noche" (p. 13, Word upon word I write the night). The poetic gift she fully possesses sustains her search for meaning. The death-wish so prevalent in Alejandra Pizarnik's poetry—her desire to attain the Absolute—appears now as joyful and yet painful liberation from human confinement. Death has now acquired a new meaning. Despite the bareness of the desolate soul, there is a vision of a future resting place where the anguish of self-awareness will no longer exist. In the last section of the poem "Noche compartida con el recuerdo de una huida" (Night shared with the memory of a flight), the poet envisions herself dead, wrapped in a lavender shroud, and cradled by the tender music of a song that says nothing of life or of death, a song that becomes a drawing of a small house under a sun. Inside this house she can stand up and walk. Music, painting, and poetry—three lifelong pursuits of Pizarnik come together in an image of the Absolute.

In *El infierno musical* (1971; Musical hell), Pizarnik alludes to the fragmentary nature of her writing and feels torn between her desire to achieve the perfect expression of her vision and the awareness that what she has been able to capture are but disjointed fragments. Poetry becomes "A desperate projection of verbal matter / liberated from itself / sinking into itself" (p. 21). The question of self-identity, the lost world of childhood, and the ultimate impossibility of poetic expression are recurrent themes in this book. Pizarnik's concerns as an artist are now reenacted as if in a concerted final effort at finding the meaning of human existence.

La condesa sangrienta (1971; The bloody countess) is a story based on the historical figure of the perverse Erszébet Báthory who lived in sixteenth-century Hungary. Pizarnik describes with a mixture of sarcasm and irony the life of this aristocrat. Lust, lesbianism, torture, sadism, and violent death are presented in a graphic way as though Pizarnik were trying to capture the horrifying obsession that lured the countess into committing hundreds of crimes on young girls. The countess' absolute lack of restraint poses a special fascination for Alejandra Pizarnik who, in her own way, wanted to transcend the limitations of the human condition and to reach the Absolute in an experience of total liberty.

The posthumously published work *Textos de sombra y últimos poemas* (1982; Texts of shadows and last poems) is a collection of prose and verse that has the urgency of something written from a point of no return. Pizarnik has passed the limitation of the written word. Some of the remarks and poems have an un-bearably painful lucidity, while others are totally chaotic. Profanity, biting hu-mor, puns, senseless alliterations, and verbal violence take over the discourse as though the poet were negating the possibility of the written text, or as though she were plunged in a whirlpool of madness. This text reveals the woman and the poet through diary notations, narrative, short pieces of dialogue, and poems. Some of the writings carry the dates of composition, thus providing an insight into Pizarnik's final days. In the poems that precede her death by a short time, there is a feeling that the final end is approaching and that there is no ultimate meaning in life.

SURVEY OF CRITICISM

The Argentinian critic and poet Cristina Piña has published several articles and a book on Pizarnik. In the monograph *La palabra como destino de acercamiento a la poesía de Alejandra Pizarnik* (1981), Piña states that the thrust of all of Pizarnik's poetry is self-destruction. The end of her poetry is to achieve death. Even if she did not commit suicide, her poetic self was obsessed with death. Piña states that she does not believe in criticism that incorporates biographical aspects of the writer in any way. Thus, she intends to write a perfectly objective work about the poetry of Pizarnik. Piña alludes to the preoccupation that Alejandra Pizarnik had with poetic language and sees as fundamental in her poetry the theme of the fall from the paradise of childhood. She also studies the problem of the self and the various poetic symbols such as the wind, the bird, the garden, and the light.

In contrast to the detached criticism of Piña, one could mention the essay by Julieta Gómez Paz in *Cuatro actitudes poéticas* (1977; Four poetic attitudes). This critic studies four prominent Argentinian women poets of the twentieth century. In her study of Pizarnik, Gómez Paz blends the person and the poet in an effort to explore the core of Pizarnik's works. She compares the poet with the French Symbolist Arthur Rimbaud, establishing certain similarities between them. Both writers discover the horror of the human condition and decide not to become accomplices to a trivial existence, an existence that ignores the Absolute. Ultimately, both withdraw from life: Pizarnik by committing suicide and Rimbaud by exiling himself to a desert life in Africa. Gómez Paz dwells on the final meaning of Pizarnik's quest and states that what Alejandra ultimately wished for was to be restored to wholeness, because in the human dimension of reality people are incomplete. According to this critic, Pizarnik's poetry is a testimony to her immolation in an attempt to reach the Absolute.

In his introduction to *Alejandra Pizarnik: A Profile Anthology* (1987), the American critic Frank Graziano states that poetry has had its history of suicides. He names several poets who have committed suicide, among them Sylvia Plath whom Pizarnik somewhat resembles as a poet dissatified with the human condition. According to Graziano, Pizarnik lived in a constant dualism of creation and self-destruction; he feels, as Cristina Piña does, that even if Alejandra Pizarnik had not committed suicide, her poetry nonetheless aims at self-annihilation. He states that Pizarnik's predicament lies in the difference between reality and fiction. The fiction—the poetic work—was what maintained her, but when she lost interest in writing, she precipitated into self-destruction.

Inés Malinow, in her introduction to *Poemas* (1986), traces the development of Pizarnik's poetry, taking into account the personal life of the poet whom she knew well. She explains how, at an early age, Pizarnik felt like a stranger in this world, like someone different from the rest, and how difficult it was for the poet to accept completely either her own homosexuality or the lack of appreciation of poets in contemporary society. Malinow quotes from Pizarnik's letters and diaries to document her ideas and, in this way, traces a clear and moving picture of the woman behind the poet.

Alejandro Fontela's introduction to *Antología* (1982) points at the singularity and the strangeness of Pizarnik's poetic world and language. He emphasizes three aspects of Pizarnik's poetry: affection, intelligence, and an aesthetic sense. Fontela says that this poetry represents both a celebration and a pain. He points out that the first book was an experiment: Pizarnik's search for her own poetic voice. The rest of her poetic production he divides into two categories: The first category comprises her first four books and the second, the last two. All of her works develop the same themes and attitudes. The only difference between his two categories is that in the last two books the aesthetic and human experiences are much more profound. Fontela also points out the relation between the poetic text and painting in Pizarnik. The poet would have liked to write the poem with the same clarity and precision that lines can have on a canvas.

In summary, it could be said that all of the critics of Pizarnik's poetry coincide in their interpretation of her poetic world. However, what still remains to be written is a psychological analysis of her poetry in the light of mental disorder and even madness. The notations in her diaries, particularly toward the end of her life, indicate a severe deterioration in her capacity to function in an orderly way. Her posthumous poems and notations (*Textos de sombras y últimos poemas*) are revealing of this state of mind. One cannot help thinking that had Pizarnik been born centuries earlier, she might have been a mystic writer—a Saint John of the Cross or a Saint Theresa—but in our anguished twentieth century, a writer like Alejandra Pizarnik could not find her place.

Her poetry seems detached from the world of the senses as though the physical world with its beckoning sensual possibilites was never to enter through eyes, nostrils, ears, or skin. Pizarnik consumes herself in her own quest for infinity, in her own anguish and fear, in her own loneliness, and, in a way, in her own limitations. There is a conspicuous lack of sensuality in her poetry, although the desire to love and be loved appears in the poems and in the diary notations. She who wanted to transcend her human confinement ended up being more confined because of her inability to accept and to work with the limits of the human condition.

BIBLIOGRAPHY

Works by Alejandra Pizarnik

La tierra más ajena. Buenos Aires: Ediciones Botella al Mar, 1955.
La última inocencia. Buenos Aires: Ediciones Poesía Buenos Aires, 1956.
Las aventuras perdidas. Buenos Aires: Ediciones Botella al Mar, 1958.
Arbol de Diana. Introd. Octavio Paz. Buenos Aires: Sur, 1962. Buenos Aires: Editorial Sudamericana, 1965.
Los trabajos y las noches. Buenos Aires: Editorial Sudamericana, 1965.
Extracción de la piedra de locura. Buenos Aires: Editorial Sudamericana, 1968.
Nombres y figuras. Barcelona(?): La Esquina, 1969.
La condesa sangrienta. Buenos Aires: Editorial Aquarius, 1971. Prose.
El infierno musical. Buenos Aires: Editorial Siglo XXI, 1971.
El deseo de la palabra. "Palabras Iniciales" by Octavio Paz. Colección OCNOS. Barcelona: Barral Editores, 1975.
Textos de sombras y últimos poemas. Buenos Aires: Editorial Sudamericana, 1982. Poems and prose notations published posthumously by Olga Orozco* and Ana Becciú.
Poems. Alejandra Pizarnik. Introd. Inés Malinow. Buenos Aires: Endymion, 1986.

Translation of Alejandra Pizarnik

Fort, María Rosa; Frank Graziano, and Suzanne Jill Levine, trans. *Alejandra Pizarnik: A Profile Anthology*. Ed. and Introd. Frank Graziano. Durango, Colo.: Logbridge-Rhodes, 1987.

Works about Alejandra Pizarnik

Aronne-Amestoy, Lida. "La palabra en Pizarnik o el miedo de Narciso." *Inti: Revista de Literatura Hispánica* 18–19 (Fall-Spring 1983–1984):229–44.
Beneyto, Antonio. "Alejandra Pizarnik: Ocultándose en el lenguaje." *Quimera: Revista de Literatura* 34 (Dec. 1983):23–27.
Borinsky, Alicia. "Muñecas reemplazables." *Río de la Plata: Culturas* (Paris) 7 (1988):41–48.
Camara, Isabel. "Literatura o la política del juego en Alejandra Pizarnik." *Revista Iberoamericana* 51, 132–133 (July-Dec. 1985):581–89.
DiAntonio, Robert E. "On Seeing Things Darkly in the Poetry of Alejandra Pizarnik: Confessional Poetics or Aesthetic Metaphor?" *Confluencia: Revista Hispánica de Cultura y Literatura* 2, 2 (Spring 1987):47–52.
Fontela, Alejandro. Introduction. *Alejandra Pizarnik: Poemas, Antología*. Buenos Aires: Centro Editor de América Latina, 1982.
Friedman Goldberg, Florinda. "Alejandra Pizarnik: Palabra y sombra." *Noah: Revista Literaria* 1, 1 (Aug. 1987):58–62.
Gómez Paz, Julieta. *Cuatro actitudes poéticas*. Buenos Aires: Conjunta Editorial, 1977. Pp. 11–47.
Graziano, Frank. "Introduction." *Alejandra Pizarnik: A Profile Anthology*. Durango, Colo.: Logbridge-Rhodes, 1987. Pp. 9–17.
Lagunas, Alberto. "Alejandra Pizarnik: Textos inéditos y un reportaje desconocido." *Proa* (Buenos Aires) 2 (Dec.-Jan. 1988–1989):43–48.
Lasarte, Francisco. "Más allá del surrealismo: La poesía de Alejandra Pizarnik." *Revista Iberoamericana* 49, 125 (Oct.-Dec. 1983):867–77.
Malinow, Inés. "Introduction." *Poemas. Alejandra Pizarnik*. Buenos Aires: Endymion, 1986. Pp. 7–11.
Piña, Cristina. "Alejandra Pizarnik o el yo transformado en lenguaje." *El Ornitorrinco* (Buenos Aires) (Oct.-Nov. 1977):21–24.
———. *La palabra como destino de acercamiento a la poesía de Alejandra Pizarnik*. Buenos Aires: Ediciones Botella al Mar, 1981.
Running, Thorpe. "The Poetry of Alejandra Pizarnik." *Chasqui: Revista de Literatura Latinoamericana* 14, 2–3 (Feb.-May 1985):45–55.

JOSEFINA PLÁ
(b. 1909)
Paraguay

Linda Britt

BIOGRAPHY

Josefina Plá is one of the most influential Spaniards to settle in Latin America in recent literary history. Born in November 1909 in Fuerteventura in the Canary Islands, she then spent her childhood and adolescence on the mainland, in San Sebastián. Her father's abundant library, though not heavily endowed with collections of poetry, introduced her to the octosyllable through the Spanish *romancero* (ballads) and fostered her early literary development. She confides that she wrote her first verses when she was six years old and that she published poems for the first time, under a pseudonym, when she was fourteen. Because of the favorable reception of those poems, shortly thereafter she submitted others under her own name to the journal *Donostia* of San Sebastián.

It was also in San Sebastián, while still a teenager, that she met the love of her life, a Paraguayan artist named Andrés Campos Cervera, who was later better known by a pseudonym indicative of his artistic calling, Julián de la Herrería (a name that means blacksmithing). He was in Spain studying the art of ceramics. Six days after they met, however, he left to return to Paraguay. Twenty months later, from Paraguay, her parents received a request for their consent to the marriage of Plá to Campos Cervera. The couple was married by proxy, and Plá traveled alone to Paraguay in 1927, when she was barely eighteen years old.

In Asunción, Plá became involved in her husband's ceramics studio and developed an interest in ceramics herself, later exhibiting works of her own. She also continued to develop her writing, as she worked for several Paraguayan and Argentine journals and newspapers. This interest in journalism was not only artistic; it was also a financial necessity for the struggling artists. Her interests expanded; Plá's was the first female voice heard on the radio in Paraguay, as she was hired in 1928 by the first radio station established in that country.

From 1930 to 1932, Plá and her husband were again in Spain, working in ceramics in Valencia and then exhibiting their works in Madrid.

Returning to Paraguay in 1932, Plá dedicated herself to literary activities. She was an editor of *El Liberal*, and in 1934, she published her first collection of poems, *El precio de los sueños* (The price of dreams), which included primarily romantic love poetry. All activities during the period from 1932 to 1935, however, were deeply influenced by historical events in Paraguay. The Chaco War lasted three years, completely absorbing the people of Paraguay, and was to have a direct impact on Josefina Plá's writing, although this impact was not to become visible for many years.

Following the war, Plá and Campos Cervera returned to Spain, to Valencia. They were then trapped when another conflict broke out, the Spanish civil war, and were unable to leave the country. In July 1937, Campos Cervera became ill and died. Plá then chose to return to her adopted country the next year. In Paraguay she eventually became a mentor to a generation of poets (including Augusto Roa Bastos and Hérib Campos Cervera), and was a leading figure in the revival of arts and letters in postwar Paraguay, especially of lyric poetry. She spoke of poetry as transcending political limits, in an age when censorship was common. Plá's poetry became an end rather than just a means to espouse political themes.

Plá's own written output is prolific. Drawing deeply on personal experience as well as on her active study of Paraguay's culture and literature, she has produced an impressive quantity as well as an amazing variety of works. Her work is uneven; some of her verses are stiff and predictable; some of her prose is repetitive. Yet there are flashes of brilliance. She explored all avenues of literary creativity. In her first experiments with some genres, including drama and the novel, she collaborated with other authors. Alone she continued writing verses, producing many books of poetry, most of which were published in the 1960s and 1970s, though containing poems written much earlier. She has written, alone and in collaboration with others, numerous plays, some of which remain unpublished and most of which have never been presented on stage. Among her most famous works in print are *Historia de un número* (History of a number), written in 1949 but not published until 1967, and performed in Mexico in 1968, and *Fiesta en el río* (Celebration in the river), which won a prize as the best new Paraguayan play in 1977 but had been written some twenty years earlier. She has published several collections of short stories, including *La mano en la tierra* (1963; The hand in the earth) and *La pierna de Severina* (1983; Severina's leg).

In collaboration with Angel Pérez Pardella, she also wrote a novel, *Alguien muere en San Onofre de Cuarumí* (1984; Someone's dying in San Onofre de Cuarumí). This novel is representative of the maturity of style and the depth of reflection that Plá has achieved in the last decade in prose as well as in verse, a maturity absent from her earlier production.

In addition to her creative output, Plá has published historical, biographical, and critical studies of several other subjects, including lacemaking, ceramics, the Guaraní language, and Paraguayan theater, and has taught the history of the theater in universities in Asunción.

Together with her nephew, Hérib Campos Cervera, and Augusto Roa Bastos, both of whom might be considered her disciples, she is thought to be most influential in the direction of Paraguayan letters beginning in the 1940s. Josefina Plá was at the forefront of what Hugo Rodríguez-Alcalá termed "the literary vanguard" in Paraguay (1982, p. 255).

MAJOR THEMES

There is an evolution in Josefina Plá's literary production that roughly corresponds to her chronological development. Her first efforts, though showing signs of promise, are weak and draw their themes from well-known peninsular authors. *Fiesta en el río*, a play about the custom in a medieval town of punishing unwed mothers by immersing them up to their necks in the cold river, won first prize in a drama contest in 1977 when submitted by Plá under a pseudonym. (Under different pseudonyms, two other plays by Plá won second and third prizes in the same contest.) This play is a rather strange blend of Calderonian honor tragedy with Federico García Lorca's *La casa de Bernarda Alba* and Alejandro Casona's *La dama del alba*, all presented in very lyrical language from a perspective that tends toward heavyhandedness. A young woman in a rural medieval setting has a brief affair with a mysterious traveler, who leaves the next day, only to return in time to save her from being tortured in the river because "she expected nothing from him." She refuses to marry him, preferring to remain independent, causing her spurned fiancé (not the father of her child) to declare that "women are free to marry or not" (*Fiesta*, III, xviii).

Aquí no ha pasado nada (1945; Nothing has happened here), a play written in collaboration with R. Centurión Miranda, is a drawing-room comedy with a rather absurd plot that contains none-too-subtle hints of Plá's feminist concerns. The protagonist in the play, Muriel, has an extramarital affair in order to conceive a child. Her husband, Efraín, understands her motives and defends her rights as a woman, while declaring man to be merely a slave of his sexual egotism.

In later works, Plá's women become stronger and better developed as her rhetoric tones down to allow the characters to speak quietly for themselves. Her short stories are filled with primarily humble, disadvantaged women, most of them widows or single mothers. "Rooted in reality," as Plá herself noted, her literary creations, especially in her fiction, paint a difficult reality. The two bloody wars in Paraguayan history, the war with Brazil, Argentina, and Uruguay in 1870, and the Chaco War against Bolivia in the early 1930s, decimated

Paraguay, especially the male population of the country. Plá wrote an elegy to the dead men of the Chaco War, *Los treinta mil ausentes* (1985; The thirty thousand absent ones), but her most memorable works of fiction contain powerful portrayals of the women left behind, women without husbands, all who tell of their children, brothers, lovers, and fathers who had died on the battlefield. *Alguien muere en San Onofre de Cuarumí*, her novel written in collaboration with Angel Pérez Pardella, is a masterful story, told in dialogue and flashbacks, of the survival of four women who suffered seemingly insurmountable hardships because of the 1870 war.

Plá's interest in history and in the history of women extends back to the time of the conquest as well. She wrote a nonfiction work entitled *Algunas mujeres de la conquista* (1985; Some women of the conquest), which includes a chapter on Isabel de Guevara, a woman Plá admires for her frankly written letter to the queen of Spain in which Guevara described the hardships of the lives of the women in colonial Paraguay. Isabel de Guevara is also the subject of one of Plá's *Romances femeninos en Tierra del Paraguay* (1977; Ballads of women in the land of Paraguay, *Antología poética*).

Plá's lyrical output is not predominantly feminist, however. Hugo Rodríguez-Alcalá has called her the "poet of death" (1968, p. 100) and the theme of death does figure prominently in her poetry. Except for *Los treinta mil ausentes*, death is treated intimately in her verses, as she draws on her personal experience with the subject. Her reactions to the death of her husband become the focus for the majority of her poetry written after 1937. Her initial pain can be seen in previously unpublished poems that appeared in 1977 in her *Antología poética* (Poetic anthology), some from as early as 1937. A constant theme is her inability to forget her beloved, together with her refusal to accept the finality of his absence. That she believes her love can transcend death and thus conquer it is evident in a wonderful short collection of poems entitled *El polvo enamorado* (1968; Enamored dust), which draws both title and theme from Francisco de Quevedo's sonnet. Love, death, and resurrection form an eternal triangle in Josefina Plá's lyric poetry. The pain of love lost and the power of love to overcome death continue as themes in later books, as in *Follaje del tiempo* (1981; Foliage of time) and *Tiempo y tiniebla* (1982; Time and darkness).

While timeless themes such as love and death predominate in some of her works, one of her most famous plays, an expressionist farce entitled *Historia de un número*, treats a more specifically modern dilemma: the struggle to survive in an overpopulated, mechanized society that identifies its citizens by number. In the play, Plá tells the story of a fatherless boy who has no "number"—meaning no identity and thus none of the privileges society has to offer—who, when he finally turns to a life of crime, is caught and forced to wear a uniform with the ill-auguring number 131313.

The existential struggle is also a concern in Plá's verses. Plá herself sees poetry as the expression of the solitary confrontation of man with himself (or woman with herself). Thus, she writes of death as she knows it, of love as she has experienced it, and of "the other," that is, she, seeing herself as everything she names in her verses, which, in effect, makes her immortal. Her concern for the downtrodden, her depiction of everyday tragedies, and the humanity so evident in Plá's prose are supplanted in her verse by rather hermetic poetic themes that are in part autobiographical and almost entirely self-reflective. In the introduction to *Cambiar sueños por sombras* (1984; Exchange dreams for shadows), she even includes an "Autodedicatoria" (Dedication to myself). But the themes she struggles with are eternal; thus, her poems have perhaps a more universal appeal than does her more regional prose.

Plá's regionalism is nevertheless an important aspect of her work that should be highlighted. In her narrative poems, her short stories, her novel, and her studies of Paraguayan culture, Josefina Plá is indeed a writer of her adopted country. She embraces its culture, immersing herself in its study and its emanation. Her love for her adopted country is in evidence everywhere in her writings, from her tender depictions of its peoples in her fiction, to her critical examination of the history of its literature and its people, to her study of its language, Guaraní, to her presentation of its plastic arts, ceramics, and lace-making.

This regional awareness and depiction, while perhaps not universally appealing, characterizes all of her most vibrant, powerful writings. Reminiscent of Uruguayan Horacio Quiroga's stories of violence and death, Plá's short stories also often tell tragic tales, as in "Mala idea" (Bad idea) from *La mano en la tierra*, in which Benicia tries to kill her common-law husband with an ax because he uncovered skeletons instead of buried treasure when he plowed their poor farmland, but instead she herself dies, and her final convulsion throws her face to face with a recently overturned skull. This story and others from the same collection and from *El espejo y el canasto* (1981; The mirror and the basket), are written largely in the dialect of rural Paraguay, which is at times difficult to understand, especially when combined, as in *Alguien muere en San Onofre de Cuarumí*, with the absence of punctuation marks. This experimental style, however, is highly effective in creating the authenticity and sincerity that characterize Plá's narrative.

SURVEY OF CRITICISM

Perhaps the fact that many of Josefina Plá's works languished for decades before being published explains the dearth of criticism on her writing. Many of the books that appeared in the 1960s and 1970s, including *La raíz y la aurora* (1960; The root and the dawn), *Rostros en el agua* (1962; Faces in the water), *El espejo y el canasto* (1981), and *Fiesta en el río* (1977), contain poems and stories that were written in the 1930s and 1940s. According to the author, there are plays, poems, and stories that still remain unavailable to the reading and viewing public. There is ample material within reach, however. Plá's *Antología poética* (1977) presents some of her previously unedited writings in more or less chronological order and provides a framework for studying her poetic trajectory.

Among the critics who have studied Plá's poetry are two of her Paraguayan disciples, eminent writers in their own right. Hugo Rodríguez-Alcalá is, at the moment, the critic who has written and published most on Plá's poetry, although he was not the first. That honor goes to Augusto Roa Bastos, who in 1966 wrote "La poesía de Josefina Plá" (The poetry of Josefina Plá), lauding her verses as absorbing, intelligent, and burning, but structurally and formally monotonous (p. 58). He was right. At that point, the poetry Plá had published was structurally rigid. In her early poetry, and even continuing into her later verses, the sonnet is her preferred poetic form. In the 1970s Plá began to experiment successfully with language and verse forms in her poetry. The techniques that she was using in the narrative, such as experimentation with dialect, absence of punctuation, and loose structure, began to spill over into her verse as well.

Both Roa Bastos and Rodríguez-Alcalá insist that Plá is a major figure in Paraguay, Roa Bastas calling her the founder of the renaissance of Paraguayan poetry (1966, p. 61), and Rodríguez-Alcalá noting that the resurgence of the lyric during the 1950s and 1960s was due especially to Josefina Plá (1968, p. 81.) Largely because of the Chaco War, literary movements did not follow the same course in Paraguay as in its neighboring countries, Argentina and Uruguay. While the avant-garde shook Argentina in the 1920s, it did not reach Paraguay until twenty years later, its principal leaders being Plá and her nephew, Hérib Campos Cervera, joined later by Roa Bastos.

These two writers, Roa Bastos and Rodríguez-Alcalá, offer little concrete criticism of Plá's poetry. Rodríguez-Alcalá does survey the poetry published before 1968, noting the sincerity and sobriety of the poems from her early collections. He also emphasizes the themes that predominate in her poems: love, pain, death, and the desire for the impossible (1968, p. 89).

Beyond published articles, some criticism can be found in the introductions to several of her books; Roberto Juarroz, for example, notes the penetrating images in *Invención de la muerte* (p. ii, Invention of death). The poems from *El polvo enamorado* are introduced by José Ramón Heredia, who remarks on the naturalness and simplicity of her poetic expression (p. iii), as well as on her treatment of the existential problem of humanity (p. i). Others who have performed similar functions for Plá's book are Francisco Pérez-Maricevich (for her *Antología Poética* and *El espejo y el canasto*) and José-Luis Appleyard (*La Pierna de Severina*).

Plá's one-act farce, *Historia de un número*, has attracted the attention of more than one literary critic. This play about an anonymous being who fails at everything in life, including career and love, has been treated as a drama written to criticize society. Lorraine Roses, in an article from 1981, writes that the play is a symbolic drama that represents the life cycle of forsaken man. As this symbolic man suffers one setback after another, we are witness to the cruelty of the society that rejects him (our society), never allowing him to find his place within it. She notes further that the drama emphasizes women's disadvantaged status in society by presenting a woman suffering because of her status (1981, p. 109). Certainly in the play the woman is blamed by her lover for opening the door to allow their numberless son to enter the world. Lydia Hazera recognizes the same social symbolism in the play, noting that the child, born into an overpopulated world, is completely denied access to the socioeconomic system because he does not possess the necessary identification number (1986–1987, p. 61). It is curious that this brief play, among all of Plá's work, should attract the attention of international critics, but its message of society trampling on the underdog perhaps explains its universal appeal.

Another writer has commented extensively on Josefina Plá, and that is the poet/playwright/novelist herself. In prologues, epilogues, and interviews, Plá has shared many thoughts on her writings. She has defined poetry as a creation that should serve humanity (in *Tiempo y tiniebla*, 1982, p. 8), an aim that is not overtly visible in all her poetry, at least not in a social sense. She seeks poetry that challenges the reader to "alzarse hasta la poesía" (to rise to the level of the poetry, *Tiempo*, p. 14). She has also said that "toda poesía arraiga . . . en una realidad más verdadera que la cotidiana" (all poetry is rooted . . . in a reality more real than daily reality), and has expanded that artistic reality into her prose and drama as well.

There is much need for further analysis of Plá's work. The feminist aspect of her writing has scarcely been mentioned among those critics who have studied her works, and certainly merits consideration. No area of her production has been overstudied; thus, linguistic, thematic, and synthetic examinations of her art are needed.

BIBLIOGRAPHY

Works by Josefina Plá

El precio de los sueños. Asunción: El Liberal, 1934.
With R. Centurion Miranda. *Aquí no ha pasado nada*. Asunción: Imprenta Nacional, 1945.
Rapsodia de Eurídice y Orfeo. Asunción: Imprenta Nacional, 1949.
La raíz y la aurora. Asunción: Ediciones Diálogo, 1960.
La mano en la tierra. Asunción: Alcor, 1963.
Rostros en el agua. Asunción: Ediciones Diálogo, 1963.
Invención de la muerte. Asunción: Ediciones Diálogo, 1965.
Satélites oscuros. Asunción: Ediciones Diálogo, 1966.
El polvo enamorado. Asunción: Ediciones Diálogo, 1968.
Desnudo día. Asunción: Ediciones Diálogo, 1969.
Historia de un número. Asunción: Ediciones Diálogo, 1969.
Antología poética. Asunción: Ediciones Cabildo, 1977.
Fiesta en el río. Asunción: Siglo Veintiuno, 1977.
El espejo y el canasto. 2d ed. Asunción: Napa, 1981.

Follaje del tiempo. Asunción: Editora Litocolor, 1981.
Tiempo y tiniebla. Asunción: Alcándara, 1982.
La pierna de Severina. Asunción: El Lector, 1983.
Cambiar sueños por sombras. Asunción: Alcándara, 1984.
With Angel Pérez Pardella. *Alguien muere en San Onofre de Cuaramí.* Asunción: Zenda, 1984.
Algunas mujeres de la conquista. Asunción: NewPrint, 1985.
Los treinta mil ausentes. Asunción: Arte Nuevo, 1985.

Works about Josefina Plá

Hazera, Lydia D. "Signos y mensaje de 'Historia de un número' de Josefina Plá." *Explicación de Textos Literarios* 15, 1 (1986–1987):59–64.
Roa Bastos, Augusto. "La poesía de Josefina Plá." *Revista Hispánica Moderna* 32 (Jan.-July 1966):56–61.
Rodríguez-Alcalá, Hugo. "Josefina Plá, española de América, y la poesía." *Cuadernos Americanos* 159 (1968):73–101.
———. "Josefina Plá y la poesía." *Papeles de San Armadans* (Mallorca) 58 (1970):19–64.
———. "El vanguardismo en el Paraguay." *Revista Iberoamericana* 48 (1982):241–55.
Roses, Lorraine. "La expresión dramática de la inconformidad social en cuatro dramaturgas hispanoamericanas." *Plaza: Literatura y Crítica* 5–6 (1981–1982):97–114.
Zapata, Celia Correas de. "Escritoras latinoamericanas: Sus publicaciones en el contexto de las estructuras de poder." *Revista Iberoamericana* 51, 132–33 (July-Dec. 1985):591–603.

SYRIA POLETTI
(b. 1921)
Argentina

Susana Hernández-Araico

BIOGRAPHY

Born and raised in northern Italy, this short-story writer, novelist, and author of children's literature emigrated to Argentina when she was twenty-two. Her childhood and adolescence spent between the Dolomites and Venice have proved a forceful inspiration for her writing. Of particular influence were the years she lived with her maternal grandmother after her immediate family left her behind and emigrated to Argentina.

Poletti's own initial experience in the Argentinian cities of Gualeguay, Rosario, and Córdoba afforded her a strong feeling for the rural landscape and for the difficulties of Italian immigrants in adapting there as well as in the capital. Since the late 1940s, Poletti has lived in Buenos Aires where she started earning a living through radio and newspaper journalism. By this time, her artistic mastery of Spanish explains the appearance of several of her short stories in well-known newspapers and magazines. In 1953 two of her short stories won the children's literature contest sponsored by the publisher Guillermo Kraft, who included them the following year in the anthology, *Veinte cuentos infantiles* (Twenty children's stories). This was to be the first of Poletti's numerous appearances in anthologies.

In 1964 Poletti's story "Rojo en la salina" (Red in the salt mine)—later to form part of her own collection, *Historias en rojo* (1967; Sensational mysteries; 1969 Municipal First Prize)—was published in the anthology *Cuentos de crimen y misterio* (Tales of crime and mystery), which included other Argentine writers like Jorge Luis Borges and Adolfo Bioy Casares. In 1965 the Donzel Prize in Spain assured the publication of one of Poletti's children's stories in the world anthology *Botella al mar* (Bottle in the ocean). In 1971 two of her short stories from her own acclaimed collection *Línea de fuego* (1964; No man's

462 SPANISH AMERICAN WOMEN WRITERS

land), were included in the anthology *Narradores argentinos de hoy* (Contemporary Argentinian fiction writers), edited by Eduardo Romano: "En el principio era la cal" (In the beginning was the lime) and "Un carro en la esquina" (A cart on the corner). In 1973 another story from *Línea de fuego*, "Tren de medianoche" (The midnight train), appeared in the anthology *Mi mejor cuento* (My best short story), together with contributions by Silvina Ocampo* and Borges, among others. The following year, her story "Rojo en la salina" was included in *Cuentos policiales argentinos* (Argentinian mystery tales), which also featured Borges. In 1975 "Alas mojadas" (Wet wings), a chapter from her novel *Extraño oficio* and a tightly constructed story in its own right, appeared in the anthology *Así escriben las mujeres* (Women write this way)—along with works by Silvina Bullrich,* Luisa Mercedes Levinson, Marta Lynch,* Olga Orozco,* and eight other outstanding Argentinian women writers. More recently, the 1986 anthology of Latin American women writers, *Puerta abierta* (Open door) included "Tren de medianoche."

Poletti has published two novels. In 1962 *Gente conmigo* (People with me) won the Losada International Prize and the Municipal Second Prize. It was later (1964) made into a movie, directed by J. Darnell, which competed in the Venice Film Festival and received an honorable mention at the Swiss festival in Locarno. *Gente conmigo* was also adapted for both radio and television. Her second novel, *Extraño oficio*, appeared in 1971, earning a nomination for the Argentinian National Prize in Literature. Since Poletti's fiction has been acclaimed as the saga of Italian immigrants whose hardships in Europe—exacerbated by World War II—continue in Argentina, the Italo-Argentinian community considers Poletti one of its major cultural figures, together with Ernesto Sábato. In the late 1960s, the Italian government invited her to participate in a conference in Milan on "The Crisis of Today's Novel," where she joined some of Italy's most prestigious writers (Umberto Eco, Alberto Moravia, Italo Calvino, etc.). In 1974 she was again honored by the Italian government with the distinguished title of Grand Knight of the Star of Solidarity for her outstanding contribution to the cultural bond between Italy and Argentina. The following year, the National Office of Immigration in Buenos Aires honored her with special acknowledgment of her life and works as part of the centenary commemoration of the enactment of Immigration Law No. 817.

Poletti's fiction repeatedly focuses on the experiences of Italian immigrants from a child's point of view. Her aesthetic preoccupation with childhood and adolescence has resulted in numerous works written for those age groups. In 1966 the author published two illustrated children's books, *Inambú busca novio* (Husband-hunting by a partridge) and *El rey que prohibió los globos (The King Who Forbade Balloons*, 1987). In 1972 the author published her book of children's stories, *Reportajes supersónicos* (Gardenless Ninín, the supersonic reporter), singled out by Unesco's Research Institute for Children's and Young Readers' Books in Munich with a recommendation for translation into all languages.

In 1977 Poletti published *Taller de imaginería* (Imagination's workshop), a collection comprising three new stories ("La pala" [The shovel], "Agua en la boca" [Water-filled mouth], and "Taller de imaginería"), five stories from *Línea de fuego*, four sections (short stories in their own right) from *Extraño Oficio*, a summary of Poletti's newspaper interviews, and the author's biobibliography. Intended mainly for high school courses, this book demonstrates Poletti's particular interest in adolescent readers. The following year, her story for young readers, *El juguete misterioso* (1977; The mysterious toy), appeared in book form.

Since then, Poletti has published several books for children and/or young readers: *El misterio de las valijas verdes* (1978; The mystery of the green suitcases), *Marionetas de aserrín* (1980; Sawdust marionettes), and *El monito Bam-Bín* (1985; The little monkey Bam-Bin). In 1981 Gaglianone Art Books published her allegorical story, *Amor de alas* (Winged love), illustrated by Raúl Soldi. In 1985 Unesco placed *Alelí y el payaso Bumbum* (Alelí and Bumbum the Clown) on its International Library for Children and Young Adults' honor list.

Among her activities in the Buenos Aires literary scene, Poletti has conducted writers' workshops and has supported the publication of aspiring younger authors. Her introduction to her students' *Cuentos desde el taller* (1983; Tales from the workshop) and her prologues to Haidé Daibán's and Susana Raffo's books of poetry attest to her supportive role for other writers, particularly women. Thus, in 1975, the International Year of Women, the Buenos Aires Women's Press Club justifiably paid tribute to Poletti for her contribution to Argentinian letters.

MAJOR THEMES

The inspirational force of an old woman stands out among Syria Poletti's major themes. For example, this character plays a prominent role in *Gente conmigo* as the narrator's loving grandmother who exemplifies and instills in the young girl a missionary sense of service through her writing skills. She is a nurturing, selfless woman who compensates for her poverty (caused by her predatory son and daughter in *Extraño oficio*) with her spiritual wealth which she transmits to the child. Her aristocratic origin, useless per se in the face of socioeconomic progress, indicates a sensitive soul's alienation in the midst of materialistic values. As the owner of a treasure chest of books, she holds the key to the best of Poletti's cultural tradition. The old woman possesses special insights into people and lets them be themselves as long as they do not squelch the child's bold inquisitiveness.

The old woman represents the hearth that warms the girl abandoned by her mother who leaves on a mysterious train. The grandmother figure is also associated with a winding river and a gently persuasive summons to life, away from a suicidal plunge into the cold current. The character of the old woman is linked to the angels on her mantelpiece who impress the child narrator and spur her imagination. In fact, angels recur throughout Poletti's fiction. Eventually, the old woman herself becomes a guardian angel for the narrator, a fairy-godmother, a veritable muse—though always actively involved in the narrator's aesthetic search for authenticity and her frustrated longing for a male companion.

Besides the elderly woman in the two novels, the character also appears prominently in "Tren de medianoche," "Apenas una planta" (Barely a plant), and "Línea de fuego," the title story of the collection. She plays an important part in "El hombre de las vasijas de barro" (The madman with clay bowls) and "Estampa antigua" (Old image) in the mystery collection *Historias en rojo*, in a way that likens her to Agatha Christie's elderly female detective. Furthermore, the old woman reappears in "Agua en la boca" in *Taller de imaginería, Marionetas de aserrín*, and *Amor de alas*. In each of Poletti's works, the old woman evolves into a symbol of the wisdom, imagination, and creativity that can lead inexperienced youth toward self-realization. She represents the unobtrusive, magical sorceress, the weaver of tales pointing the way toward truth. This motif also suggests the narrator-author's ideal for herself as an inspirational force, particularly in a milieu afflicted with a potentially violent "generation gap." All in all, the old woman signifies the struggle to remain faithful to one's origin and destiny, the battle to retain one's roots—dug in with hard claws, if need be—against the winds of change. This context thus highlights the image of a goat—associated with the old woman—whose hoofs maintain a delicate footing in its instinctive uphill journey (cf. *Gente conmigo, Extraño Oficio*, and *Amor de alas*).

Another major theme of Poletti's, complementing that of the old woman, is childhood or adolescence, particularly as experienced by a young girl. In both of Poletti's novels, the female narrator engages the reader in a retrospective vision of her childhood which predetermined her "strange craft" as a mature woman. An early fascination with words, writing letters, and reading books stems from the girl's inquisitive imagination. Though keenly aware of how her parents abandoned her, she capitalizes on her freedom from the traditionally debilitating protection under which most girls grow up. Her exuberant individualism easily bypasses the societal expectations for a young female. With a blithe lack of inhibition, she plays with boys like an equal and enjoys close friendships with older nontraditional women, especially her grandmother who encourages her freedom-loving ways, joy of learning, and appreciation for the mystery of beauty. The technique of retrospective self-analysis of childhood and adolescence helps the mature narrator who has become a writer (of legal documents in *Gente conmigo*, of fiction in *Extraño oficio*) bear the burden of her loneliness and frustrated desire for an authentic male companion. The narrative search into the past in both novels concludes in the present realization that her unique destiny as a thinker and writer precludes a reliable relationship with a conventional male. Only a heroic one—like Miko in *Extraño oficio*—can commune with her both physically and spiritually. But his obsession with a political cause eliminates the possibility of companionship.

The theme of betrayal by the weak yet presumptuous man is interwoven with that of the precocious-girl-mature-woman-writer. This theme is presented from a child's point of view in the person of her uncle who turns his back on his elderly mother for social prestige, as represented by either a superficial wife (*Extraño oficio* and "Estampa antigua") or professional success as a classical musician ("Tren de medianoche"). The outcome of *Gente conmigo* hinges precisely on the deceptive lover's abuse of the female narrator's emotional vulnerability, out of his desire to climb socially through a profitable marriage and professional opportunities. In *Oficio*, one of the final scenes presents the male lover's cynical attempt to part amicably with the narrator by introducing her to his future wife. A final allegorical section in the same novel depicts men as children who derive their apparent strength from a strong maternal figure, herself destined to loneliness since they must abandon her to flaunt their acquired vigor before other weaker females.

Poletti does transcend the sexual barrier, however, to portray female betrayal (cf. "Cosquín de noche" [Cosquín at night], "Altavoces" [Loudspeakers], and "Estampa antigua") and the loneliness of an abandoned, misunderstood boy ("Un muchacho con suerte" [A lucky boy]) as well as that of a mature male artist/writer whose aesthetic vocation is deeply rooted in the joys and hardships of his unconventional upbringing ("Taller de imaginería"). Poletti evidently realizes that these are human experiences common to both sexes; but she emphasizes the female experience. The young-girl narrator appears as a traitor, admirable for disregarding her contemptible father's needs ("Los caballos" [The horses] in *Línea* and "Pisadas de caballo" [Horses' tracks] in *Historias*). The despicable, mature female traitor, blind to her own children's or companion's needs, is nevertheless worthy of respect because of her boundless passion or sexuality. Such a woman is genuine, completely true to herself in opposition to artificial norms. This is the case of the child-narrator's own mother in *Gente conmigo, Oficio*, and "Tren," the two mothers in "Cosquín," and the male protagonist's fiancée in "Altavoces." Yet the narrator—whether an adult or adolescent female—seeks to transcend the enslavement of her sexual passion ("Tren"), which facilitates a male's abuse or betrayal—as in "Las vírgenes prudentes" (Prudent virgins), "Mala suerte" (Bad luck), "Pisadas" in *Historias*, and "Caballos" in *Línea*. In these last three stories, a repulsive father figure appears to the perceptive female adolescent as totally devoid of any moral worth. In "Rojo en la salina" and "Cosquín," the father figure's weakness impels the wife to assume almost total responsibility for the household. The children's perceptive presence in these stories highlights a woman's dilemma within such marriages based on betrayal or unequal distribution of responsibility.

Syria Poletti is so intent on portraying the richness of childhood and adolescence that she always includes youngsters in her fiction, even in her superbly crafted mysteries, *Historias*. Her affinity for children and her appreciation for their demanding taste for good stories has inspired her extensive production for children and young (or youthful) adults, from her first published story, "Fantoches de nieve" ("Snow Puppets," in *La Nación*, 1950) to her more recent

Alelí. Even the children's book, *Inambú*, illustrates through the character of a female bird the theme of a girl's destiny to become a storyteller and her apparently conflicting need for a mate. In *Amor de alas*, a hunchbacked mountain girl proves to be a wonder-worker, a magical sorceress with the power to discover water. Her ugly hump turns out to be an embryonic wing complemented by the angelical protagonist's single wing, which had also set her apart from her kindred. Thus, Poletti emphasizes for her young or youthful readers the positive value of that sense of personal difference afflicting the perceptive child, adolescent or adult. The author points to creative transcendence as the fruition of such distinctiveness, while reassuring her readers of all ages that each person is not really alone in her or his uniqueness.

Poletti's allegorical tale elaborates the symbolism of physical deformity in her two novels. In *Gente conmigo*, and *Oficio*, the female narrator is afflicted with a physical problem that sets her apart from desirable women. In *Gente*, this handicap precludes an immigration visa for Argentina and sharpens the narrator-protagonist's sense of physical unattractiveness which, in turn, intensifies her admiration of beauty in men and other women. In *Oficio*, the deformity is not as serious; it does not deter the adolescent narrator from any activity or movement. In this novel, the self-assured girl realizes that her physical difference is an excuse for others to attempt to stifle her aspirations. The deformity then functions as an outward sign of her unconventionality as a female which, according to others, cripples a woman if she is to attain security within the social establishment. This meaning becomes quite clear in *Amor de alas*, where the angelical male figure afflicted with a single wing is undeterred in his search for a similar companion with whom he can fly. He finds such a mate in the little mountain girl, ostracized because of her hunchback, which turns out to be a single wing also. Poletti thus conveys allegorically the theme of physical deformity as symbolic of the alienation that being different produces. If Poletti's two novels focus this theme on the female experience, *Amor* transcends sexual barriers and illustrates the theme for both man and woman. Each one's sense of distinctiveness need not result in loneliness if they find each other, if the male ceases to consider a female's unconventional power a repulsive deformity and appreciates it as a necessary complement to his limited abilities.

Another important theme of Poletti's related to the alienation caused by deformity is the tragic madness that war produces. A World War I asylum for veterans appears in the chapter "Pajaros de barro" (Clay birds) in *Oficio*, in "Línea de fuego" in *Línea*, and in "El hombre de las vasijas de barro" in *Historias*. One madman in particular makes an impact on the child narrator in these three stories. For the implied more mature narrator, the madman represents the plight of war that has historically mutilated her people's psyche in northern Italy. In "Línea," the tragic madman provides the only link between the narrator and her idyllic childhood. After emigrating to Argentina, she returns to her town in Italy and regrets to find everything changed. Only the madman recognizes her as the child she once was. A connection thus emerges between the alienation of madness caused by World War I and the alienating effect of the massive emigration that resulted from World War II. Moreover, the narrator herself identifies closely with the lucid madman as a symbol of her own personal separateness both from her land and from "normal" people.

The theme of Italian immigration into Argentina is the most noticeable one in Poletti's novels and short stories. In many cases, it provides the narrative framework for all the other themes. Most of her characters are portrayed as Italians either in their own Alpine villages, in Buenos Aires, or in the Argentinian countryside. In their own native environment, protagonists lament the departure of emigrants and prepare to emigrate themselves. Once in Argentina, the immigrants exemplify the difficulties and disenchantments of acculturation compounded by the struggle for economic survival. These immigrants look back longingly on their homeland knowing fully well that there is no return. They therefore seek to re-create sentimentally the old country in the new one, either in their memory, social relationships, or work activities.

The author's own experience as an Italian immigrant successfully writing in Spanish lends authenticity to her narrative voice in *Gente conmigo* and *Oficio*, both of which attest to Poletti's artistic commitment to her cultural heritage. *Gente conmigo* brings out the sense of service to her own people in Argentina that saves the immigrant writer-narrator from despondency and despair in her struggle for survival with dignity. In *Oficio*, the protagonist reminisces in elaborate detail on her own past in northern Italy as she attempts to trace her aesthetic destiny that culminates in Argentina. Although the narrator bypasses altogether the process of emigration out of Italy and into Buenos Aires, her retrospective view of her life in her native country is a necessary sentimental journey back in time which enables her to continue facing loneliness and displacement in the Argentinian capital. Poletti's focus on immigration thus goes beyond a topical discussion of its causes and effects to a symbolic treatment of its ramifications, namely, uprootedness and all its psychological implications.

SURVEY OF CRITICISM

Most criticism of Poletti's works exists in the form of reviews in newspapers and journals shortly after the publication of each of her books. So few monographs have been written on Poletti that one can justifiably say her works have suffered critical neglect, particularly within the academic establishment. Only two doctoral dissertations have chosen Poletti for concentrated analysis: Diane Solomon Birkemoe, "La obra de Syria Poletti," University of Illinois, 1968; and Dany Magarotto, "La inmigracion italiana en la Argentina a través de la obra de Syria Poletti," Bordeaux, 1976.

As Magarotto's title indicates, the tendency has been to bring out the reflection of reality or "real life" in the author's novels and short stories, that is, the portrayal of Italian immigrants or autobiographical experience. This reductive method, downplaying the author's creative artistry, is due to her frequent recourse

to a first-person narrator, her own status as an Italian immigrant, and her imaginative reworking of events and people from her past. In general, reviews of
Gente conmigo comment favorably on its authenticity of style and characters.
They praise the author for avoiding literary fads and for not playing games with
her readers. Poletti is thus deprived of recognition for her technical accomplishment in writing a love story of social implications within the framework of a
mystery novel.

Her short stories in *Línea* likewise are praised as the "moving testimony" of
personal experience in northern Italy, as an actual reminiscence of Poletti's
childhood, overflowing with sensibility. No one has observed the new dimension
of humor the author successfully achieves in some stories in this collection.
Historias is also seen as a very similar transcription of Poletti's own life, without
any "twistings of expression." Nevertheless, reviews do point to her emphasis
on the complexity of motivations. Still, they make no attempt to evaluate the
stylistic accomplishment of such psychological depth. Presumably, Poletti writes
not to display her talent but to document human experience poetically.

The author finally receives critical attention for her accomplished narrative
construction in *Oficio*, where she noticeably experiments with the traditional
subdivisions of a novel. She is praised for "dismembering" experience, for
sharing it with her readers in "overlapping fragments." Yet the critical focus
on Poletti's "realism" persists.

As for her exceptional female protagonists, Rogelio Barufaldi's extensive
review (1963) highlights Nora's sexual frustration in *Gente*, adding that she
compensates for it through her altruistic service to her people. Only one of all
the reviewers of Poletti's works suggests her feminist stance. L.A. Cousillas
(1962) notes her "courage" to write "in woman," implying that Poletti's choice
of a female narrator generates a female discourse, a different language. No critic
has followed up on this tantalizing suggestion in an extended fashion. Comments
on Poletti's language have merely expressed amazement at the Italian immigrant's
artistic mastery of Spanish. Castelli analyzes Poletti's effective use of dialogue
and grammatical details involved in the narrator's shift from her memory to her
present experience. No connection is made, however, between these techniques
and the narrator's constant challenging of established tenets about womanhood.

Celia Correas de Zapata, in her paper "Crónica de una rebeldía" (1978)—at
one of the first Latin American Women Writers' Symposiums (San José State
University, 1976) which Poletti attended—has commented on Poletti's portrayal
of heroically unconventional women. It still remains to be stated that Poletti
demythifies womanhood. Nora's imprisonment in *Gente conmigo* is a symbol
of the solitary confinement within her own conscience, the terribly constricting
remorse she herself suffers, for having gone through an abortion. This novel,
written by a woman in 1961, asserting Argentina's Italian heritage, has yet to
be read as a defiance to the cultural principle that women were made to be
mothers. It should be noted that the female protagonist is reborn to her life of
social commitment only after a dream finally frees her from the terrible guilt of

abortion. Criticism of Poletti's works has altogether bypassed this revolutionary destruction of the myth of motherhood.

Castelli's critical survey focuses on the myth of Sisyphus in *Gente conmigo*, as suggested by the repeated image of a woman struggling uphill with the heavy load of menial chores. However, the narrator-protagonist continually rejects this image and finally manages to replace it with that of a goat—an instinctive climber in close contact with the ground it treads, endowed with a lightfooted sense of balance for stony, steep ascents. Instead of the menial chores necessary for survival, the burden the narrator-protagonist accepts to bear is her vocation to write. In this sense, too, Poletti breaks with the myth of woman's role in society. But serious studies of her novels and short stories have yet to treat such issues. Poletti's children's books, which also offer new images of female youth, likewise remain virtually in critical oblivion, except for very brief reviews.

BIBLIOGRAPHY

Works by Syria Poletti

Gente conmigo. Buenos Aires: Losada, 1962.
Línea de fuego. Buenos Aires: Losada, 1964.
El rey que prohibió los globos. Rosario, Argentina: Constancio C. Vigil, 1966.
Inambú busca novio. Rosario: Constancio C. Vigil, 1966.
Historias en rojo. Buenos Aires: Calatayud, 1967.
Extraño oficio (Crónicas de una obsesión). Buenos Aires: Losada, 1971.
Reportajes supersónicos. Buenos Aires: Sigmar, 1972.
El juguete misterioso. Buenos Aires: Sigmar, 1977.
La gente. Ed. Catalina Paravati. Buenos Aires: Kapelusz, 1977. Anthology of previous works.
Taller de imaginería. Buenos Aires: Losada, 1977.
El misterio de las valijas verdes. Buenos Aires: Plus Ultra, 1978.
Marionetas de aserrín. Buenos Aires: Crea, 1980.
Amor de alas. Buenos Aires: Arte Gaglianone, 1981.
Cuentos desde el Taller "Leonor Alonso": dirigido por Syria Poletti. Buenos Aires: Plus Ultra, 1983.
Alelí y el payaso Bumbum. Buenos Aires: Arte Gaglianone, 1985.
El monito Bam-Bin. Buenos Aires: El Ateneo, 1985.

Translations of Syria Poletti

Ashe, Susan, trans. "Bride by Proxy." *Translation. The Journal of Literary Translation* 17 (1987):72–82.
Lewald, Ernst H., trans. "The Final Sin." *The Web: Stories by Argentine Women*. Ed. Ernest H. Lewald. Washington, D.C.: Three Continents Press, 1983. Pp. 61–65.
Thomas de Giovanni, Norman, and Susan Ashe, trans. *The King Who Forbade Balloons*. Buenos Aires: Arte Gaglianone, 1987.

Works about Syria Poletti

Avilés Fabila, René. "Para niños y adultos (*Taller de imaginería*)." *Visión, La Revista Interamericana* 49, 10 (Nov. 4, 1977):56

Barufaldi, Rogelio. "*Gente conmigo* de Syria Poletti." *Señales* 140 (Jan.-Mar. 1963):37–41.

"Biobibliografía de Syria Poletti." *Taller de imaginería*. By Syria Poletti. Buenos Aires: Losada, 1977. Pp. 175–79.

Birkemoe, Diane Solomon. "Contemporary Women Novelists of Argentina (1945–67)." Ph.D diss. University of Illinois, 1968. (DAI 29 [1968]:2249A.)

Blasi Brambilla, Alberto. "Vuelo vivencial (*Amor de alas*)." *Clarín* (Buenos Aires) Jan. 14, 1982.

Briozzo, Olga Teresa. "Una fuente inagotable (*Marionetas de aserrín*)." *La Capital* (Mar del Plata), June 8, 1980.

Carrega, Hemilce. "Original aporte a nuestra novelística." *La Prensa* (Buenos Aires), Nov. 4, 1962.

Castellanos, Luis Arturo. *El cuento en la Argentina*. Sante Fe, Argentina: Colmegna, 1967. Pp. 55, 58, 62–63.

Castelli, Eugenio. "La palabra-mito en Syria Poletti." *Sur* 348 (1981):101–107.

———. "Para una evaluación crítica de la novelística de Syria Poletti." *Káñina, Revista de Artes y Letras, Univ. de Costa Rica* 9,2 (1985):51–56; *Evaluación de la literatura femenina de Latinoamérica, siglo XX*. 2 vols. II. Simposio Internacional de Literatura, July 9–13 1984, Vol. 1. San José, Costa Rica: EDUCA, 1985. Pp. 243–51.

Correas de Zapata, Celia. "Syria Poletti: Crónica de una rebeldía." *Ensayos hispanoamericanos*. Buenos Aires: Corregidor, 1978. Pp. 203–22.

Cousillas, L. A. "*Gente conmigo*—Syria Poletti: una mujer en la esperanza." *Noticias* (Buenos Aires) Oct. 7, 1962.

"Los cuentos y textos de *Taller de imaginería*." *La Opinión* (Los Angeles), Mar. 30, 1977.

Denevi, Marco. "Para leer a Syria Poletti." *Historias en rojo*. By Syria Poletti. Buenos Aires: Losada, 1973. Pp. 9–10.

Díaz, Gwendolyn Josie. "Images of the Heroine: Development of the Female Character in the Novels of Beatriz Guido, Marta Lynch, and Syria Poletti." Ph.D. diss. University of Texas, 1981. (DAI 42, 7 [Jan. 1982]:3174A.)

Fornaciari, Dora. "Reportajes periodísticos a Syria Poletti." *Taller de imaginería*. By Syria Poletti. Buenos Aires: Losada 1977. Pp. 143–71.

Giusti, Roberto F. "Ingenio y humanidad en el cuento (*Línea de fuego*)." *La Prensa*, Mar. 28, 1965.

González, Nora. "*Línea de fuego* de Syria Poletti." *Señales* 150 (3d quarter 1965):11–12.

Granata, María. "Introducción." *Taller de imaginería*. By Syria Poletti. Buenos Aires: Losada, 1977. Pp. 9–10.

———. "Syria Poletti y su valioso aporte a la literatura infantil (*Reportajes supersónicos*)." *Clarín* Mar. 3, 1973.

Hernández-Araico, Susana. "*Amor de alas* de Syria Poletti y la evolución de su arte narrativo." *Proceedings of the 1982 Meeting of the Pacific Coast Council of Latin American Studies* 12 (1985–1986):131–36; *Evaluación de la literatura femenina de Latinoamérica, Siglo XX.* 2 vols. II° Simposio Internacional de Literatura, July 9–13, 1984, Vol 1. San Jose, Costa Rica: EDUCA, 1985. Pp. 235–40.

———. "Poletti, Syria." *Women Writers of Spanish America: An Annotated Bio-Bibliographical Guide.* Ed. D. E. Marting. Westport, Conn: Greenwood Press, 1987. Pp. 310–13.

"*Historias en rojo.*" *La Nación,* Mar. 17, 1968.

J.N. "Una desgarrada novela en la que se vive el drama de los emigrantes." *La Razón* (Buenos Aires), Nov. 3, 1962.

Lacau, María Hortensia. "*Amor de alas.*" *La Prensa,* Sept. 19, 1982.

"Libros para chicos (*Reportajes supersónicos*)." *La Nación,* Feb. 24, 1973.

"Literatura infantil: *El rey que prohibió los globos.*" *Convicción,* Sept. 5, 1982.

Magarotto, Dany. "La inmigración italiana en la obra de Syria Poletti." These de doctorat. Université de Bordeaux, 1976.

Malinow, Inés. "El testimonio apasionado de *Gente conmigo.*" *La Nación,* Nov. 25, 1962.

Martínez, Adolfo C. "El camino del recuerdo (*Taller de imaginería* por Syria Poletti)." *La Nación,* May 22, 1977.

Mathieu, Corina S. "Syria Poletti: Intérprete de la realidad argentina." *Sin Nombre* 13. 3 (1983):87–93.

M. A. v. P. "Substancia y verismo en Syria Poletti (*Línea de fuego*)." *La Nación,* Dec. 19, 1965.

Mazzei, Angel. "*Extraño oficio.*" *La Nación,* Oct. 24, 1971.

"Una novelista ante su obra." *La Nación,* May 2, 1965.

"Nuevos libros para los chicos (*El juguete misterioso*)." *La Nación,* Aug. 5, 1977.

Omil, Alba. "Syria Poletti y la estructuración novelesca (*Extraño oficio*)." *El Día* (La Plata), Jan. 11, 1981.

Paravati, Catalina. "Estudio preliminar." *La gente.* By Syria Poletti. Ed. Catalina Paravati. Buenos Aires: Kapelusz, 1977. Pp. 9–34.

Poletti, Syria. "Aproximaciones a una nueva literatura infantil." *Evaluación de la literatura femenina de Latinoamérica, siglo XX.* 2 vols. II° Simposio Internacional de Literatura. July 9–13, 1984, vol. 2. San José, Costa Rica: EDUCA, 1987. Pp. 179–94.

———. "Complejidad del escritor argentino." *La gente.* Ed. Catalina Paravati. Buenos Aires: Kapelusz, 1977. Pp. 161–65.

———. "La fuente mágica o de cómo nació este cuento." *Marionetas de aserrín.* By Syria Poletti. Buenos Aires: Crea, 1980. Pp. 41–60.

"Relatos policiales con énfasis en las motivaciones." *Clarín,* Jan. 18, 1968.

"Resumen cronológico de la vida y obra de Syria Poletti." *La gente.* By Syria Poletti. Ed. Catalina Paravati. Buenos Aires: Kapelusz, 1977. Pp. 7–8.

"Será presentado un libro de Syria Poletti en Bariloche (*Amor de alas*)." *Río Negro* (General Roca, Argentina) Feb. 3, 1982:15.

S.F. "Cinco relatos (*Historias en rojo*)." *La Razón* (Buenos Aires), Feb. 17, 1968.

"Syria Poletti" *Quien es quien en la Argentina.* 9th ed. 2d printing. Buenos Aires: Quien Es Quien, 1969. Pp. 589–90.

"El texto iluminado (*Amor de alas*)." *La Nación* (Buenos Aires) Dec. 20, 1981.

ELENA PONIATOWSKA
(b. 1933)
Mexico

Beth E. Jörgensen

BIOGRAPHY

Elena Poniatowska Amor was born in Paris, France, on May 19, 1933. Her father is French of Polish ancestry, and her mother, Paula Amor, a Mexican who was raised in France. In 1942 Poniatowska moved with her mother and her younger sister to Mexico City, where her father joined them several years later. Poniatowska's first language is, therefore, French, and in Mexico she was sent to a private British-run school where she learned English. She spent two years in the United States, attending a Catholic boarding school at the Sacred Heart Convent outside of Philadelphia. Speaking French and English with her family and their friends, Poniatowska learned Spanish from the young women who worked as servants in her parents' home. At the age of twenty Poniatowska still felt herself to be a foreigner in her adopted country. Her upper class family background with its cosmopolitan orientation had denied her a knowledge of Mexican history and culture, and her limited education provided little preparation for a career. Nevertheless, the Spanish language itself and her friendship with Mexican domestic workers provided a linguistic and emotional link to people of other social classes, which is one basis for her orientation as a writer.

Poniatowska's long experience as a journalist is another decisive factor in the formation of her career as a writer. In 1954 she started to work for the Mexico City newspaper *Excélsior* and was assigned to do daily interviews with writers, artists, and musicians. That same year she published *Lilus Kikus*, a short work of fiction whose title is the protagonist's name. Journalism and imaginative literature have always been simultaneous and intertwined activities in Poniatowska's professional life. As a result, she combines a journalist's habits of observation and attentive listening with a writer's preoccupation with language and textual strategies. After a year at *Excélsior* she moved to *Novedades*, for which she continues to write. The interview is her principal genre; in 1978 she won the Mexican National Journalism Prize for her work as an interviewer. Journalism has provided Poniatowska with essential tools for her literary career: economic independence, access to the Mexican social, political, and cultural milieu, and opportunities to listen to the voices and stories of others, a practice that has become the hallmark of her writing.

After *Lilus Kikus*, Poniatowska's early publications include *Palabras cruzadas* (1961; Crossed words), a selection of interviews; and *Todo empezó el domingo* (1963; It all began on Sunday), a volume of brief sketches of daily life and Sunday pastimes of Mexico City's working classes. The twenty years from 1969 to 1988 represent her period of greatest literary production. Beginning with *Hasta no verte, Jesús mío* (1969; *Until We Meet Again*, 1987), and including such important titles as *La noche de Tlatelolco* (1971; *Massacre in Mexico*, 1975), *Querido Diego, te abraza Quiela* (1976; *Dear Diego*, 1986), *De noche vienes* (1979, You come by night), *Fuerte es el silencio* (1980; Silence is strong), *La "Flor de Lis"* (1988), and *Nada, nadie* (1988; Nothing, nobody), Poniatowska has firmly established herself as one of Spanish America's foremost writers.

MAJOR THEMES

A quick review of Elena Poniatowska's published works reveals the variety of themes and literary forms which her writing embraces. A common thread, however, connects her political and social chronicles, her novels and short stories, her interviews and her testimonial works. That common thread is the profound commitment to interpreting contemporary Mexican society, with special attention to the silenced voices and the marginalized lives that constitute the majority experience in the vast human landscape of her country. Her books record such events as the 1968 Mexican student movement, a hunger strike by mothers of the "disappeared," and the 1985 earthquake in Mexico City; they offer as protagonists street vendors, a quadriplegic woman of the middle class, student dissidents, and political prisoners. For this reason most readers concur in considering Poniatowska to be a literary champion of the oppressed. In the process of allowing the other to speak for him or herself, Poniatowska often effaces her own participation in the dialogue, an aspect of her written work that will merit further attention in this entry.

In addition, an important group of fictional texts represents a more introspective mode as the author raises issues of social class, construction of male and female identity, female sexuality, language, and power relations in ways that intimately explore her own experience as a female member of Mexico's privileged minority. The following analysis of Poniatowska's work will be organized on the basis of this broad division, rather than offering a strictly chronological overview.

The dynamics of reciprocity and mutual influence inherent in the journalistic interview conceived as an open-ended dialogue make it an ideal form for the discovery of self and of the other which is central to Poniatowska's writing. Two books offer a selection of her interviews. *Palabras cruzadas* includes fourteen articles based on interviews conducted between 1954 and 1961. Alfonso Reyes, Diego Rivera, Lázaro Cárdenas, and Luis Buñuel are among those represented. *Domingo siete* (1982; Sunday seven) publishes the interviews that Poniatowska carried out in the summer of 1982 with the seven candidates entered in that year's presidential election.

Palabras cruzadas is an interesting text both for the view it provides of Poniatowska's early procedures as a journalist and for the light it sheds on some of the foremost figures of Mexican society of the 1950s. Naive and even frankly ignorant of Mexican politics and culture, Poniatowska admits that she initially relied on her youth and spontaneity and the trick of the trivial question to disarm her subjects and start the conversation. The interview then took its momentum from her ability to create further questions out of previous responses. The tone is personal and often impertinent, but the results fly in the face of the prevailing solemnity and formality of much Mexican journalism. With experience, Poniatowska left behind these techniques (born of necessity), without ever abandoning the idea of the interview as a conversation which, no matter how carefully prepared, must leave room for the unexpected. The articles of *Palabras cruzadas* provide fascinating insights into important questions of relations of authority and the power of language and silence to manipulate the other. They are the practical manifestations of an ideology that conceives of human existence not as a closed experience of separation and alienation, but as an open, active engagement with the other. This stance on the part of Elena Poniatowska has had far-reaching implications for her own development as a writer and for Mexican literature as a whole.

The consideration of the interview helps one to understand Poniatowska's body of nonfiction books. Within this broad category are included *Gaby Brimmer* (1979; a testimonial piece co-authored with its protagonist), *La noche de Tlatelolco* and *Nada, nadie* (works of oral history), and *Fuerte es el silencio* (chronicles of contemporary Mexico). In all of them, the interview has served not only as a source of information, but, more significantly, also as an informing device that determines the structure and the language of the text. Characteristics of the works are the evidence of a collaborative process, the prevalence of colloquial language, and an emphasis on recording little heard or actively suppressed stories of marginalized people. *Gaby Brimmer*, for example, is the story of a young woman paralyzed since birth by cerebral palsy. With the one toe that she is able to control, Gaby types her communication with the world and writes original poetry. Poniatowska based the book on her correspondence with Gaby and on interviews with the protagonist's mother and her nanny, which Poniatowska then edited into a rich tapestry of interwoven voices. The resulting text portrays the joys, frustrations, tensions, and hope that constitute a human life radically dependent on and rebellious against others.

La noche de Tlatelolco, an account of the 1968 student movement in Mexico City, and Nada, nadie, which treats the earthquake which the capital suffered in 1985, are oral histories. In both books Poniatowska edits hundreds of individual testimonies into a coherent yet fragmented and polysemic narrative. The Mexican student movement is one of the most dramatic political and social phenomena of recent Mexican history. The title La noche de Tlatelolco commemorates the massacre by government troops of hundreds of unarmed civilians at a rally in the Plaza de Tlatelolco on October 2, 1968. The killings and the subsequent arrests of student dissidents effectively silenced the movement, which had been active since July of that year. In the immediate aftermath, the Mexican press was silent and the Mexican public ignorant of the extent of the violence. However, in the years that followed a whole body of Tlatelolco literature has been written.

Elena Poniatowska's La noche de Tlatelolco, one of the first published accounts of the massacre, is the most widely read of these works. It recuperates a broad view of the student movement in the form of a montage of oral testimonies, graffiti, police records, newspaper articles, rally songs and chants, speeches by government officials, and other literary and historical texts. The juxtaposition of heterogeneous elements successfully conveys the difficulty of arriving at a single, definitive interpretation of any event. The book's intertextual aspect gives an important historical dimension to a series of actions which, in effect, lasted only a few months. Poniatowska's inclusion of sixteenth-century indigenous chronicles of the conquest of Mexico, for example, suggests that the abuses perpetrated by the Spaniards during the conquest are repeated in the present-day clash between the established authorities and an opposition movement.

One of the most intriguing features of La noche de Tlatelolco is the apparent absence of a single unifying narrative voice. Instead, there is an elusive editorial figure who appears and disappears in a gesture of constant self-effacement. The narrator as editor limits her direct intervention in the text in favor of seeming to allow the many voices to speak for themselves in a collective version of the events. However, she skillfully and consciously uses the editorial functions of selection, ordering, repetition, and juxtaposition of the fragmentary languages to create a perspective that favors the students and at the same time reveals the internal problems that plagued the movement. Among her nonfiction titles, La noche de Tlatelolco is without doubt Poniatowska's finest achievement.

The third type of nonfiction text written by Elena Poniatowska occurs in the form of chronicles or reportage. In Todo empezó el domingo, her first attempt to portray lower class life, the masses who frequent Chapultepec Park, a flea market, public spas, and boxing matches are observed directly but from a distance by the narrator, who supplies an abundance of picturesque detail. El último guajolote (1982; The last turkey) is a nostalgic evocation via text and photographs of street vendors and artisans, a disappearing subculture in the rapidly changing capital city. The best of these collections of chronicles is Fuerte es el silencio, which brings together five articles on separate topics including the student movement, a hunger strike by mothers of the "disappeared," and a communal squatters' village that was destroyed by the authorities. The silence paradoxically affirmed by the title and overcome by the chronicles themselves is the silence of women, the poor, political prisoners, and those who suffer injustice and injury in Mexican society. Poniatowska's own intervention in these texts is greatly highlighted in comparison to her previous works. Her presence points up certain contradictions between her sympathetic view of her subjects and her occasional incomprehension of their motives and goals. As a writer she is torn between a deep sense of responsibility and solidarity, and a desire to retreat to the comfort and security of her home and family. Nevertheless, in spite of the evident contradictions and ambivalence, the articles are another valuable product of Poniatowska's commitment to telling Mexico's "other history."

Poniatowska's first novel serves as a bridge between the study of her works of nonfiction and fiction. *Hasta no verte, Jesús mío* gives a first-person account of the life of a poor, illiterate woman born in 1900, who narrates her own story retrospectively in the late 1960s. The book is a novel and must be read as fiction, although it is based on Poniatowska's interviews with a real-life resident of Mexico City's slums. Jesusa Palancares, the novel's protagonist, suffered the early death of her mother and a hard childhood under the care of her father and several "stepmothers." As an adolescent she was caught up in the Mexican Revolution, and she lived most of her adult years in Mexico City working as a poorly paid maid, waitress, beauty shop operator, factory worker, and washerwoman. Jesusa's outstanding characteristics include her fierce independence, her refusal to remarry after the death of her brutal first husband, her aggressiveness, generosity, pride, spirituality, resourcefulness, and physical indomitability.

Jesusa has been variously viewed by readers of the novel as a new, liberated heroine, or as a failure, a victim of society. A careful analysis of her language and of the dynamics of narrative perspective reveals, however, that the book powerfully documents one woman's struggle, with its share of successes and defeats, to overcome the constraints placed on her self-realization by a prevailing ideology that is patriarchal, racist, and based on class divisions. Violence, economic exploitation, material need, incarceration, lack of access to education, and continual migrations in search of work and shelter are the constants of her existence. Jesusa is alternately rebellious and resigned in the face of this reality, but her behavior and personality always challenge the conventional traits of the typical Mexican literary heroine—passivity, piety, submissiveness, patience. In its portrayal of a lower class female protagonist *Hasta no verte, Jesús mío*, then, offers a striking critique of twentieth-century Mexican literature, social history and politics, the Catholic Church, class conflict, and sexual inequality.

In her works of fiction, Poniatowska has employed a variety of forms to speak critically and self-critically of female experience vis-à-vis the privileged signs of Mexican patriarchy. In the short stories collected in *De noche vienes*, the epistolary novel *Querido Diego, te abraza Quiela*, and the novel of development

La *"Flor de Lis,"* she incorporates autobiographical elements and a limited use of documentary materials to create urban female protagonists of the privileged and oppressed classes. In her fiction Poniatowska demonstrates a preference for present-tense narration and for eyewitness or I-protagonist narrative perspectives.

Los cuentos de Lilus Kikus (1967; The Lilus Kikus stories) and *De noche vienes* are two collections of short stories. *Los cuentos de Lilus Kikus* brings together the twelve connected narratives of the 1954 *Lilus Kikus* with twelve additional stories. As Poniatowska's earliest work of fiction, the original *Lilus Kikus* is a fascinating study in the problematical process of maturation which the main character undergoes. Indeed, Juan Bruce-Novoa describes the book as a "schematic *Bildungsroman*" that depicts adolescence as a time of increasing limits for the female child who must be socialized to conform to her role in a male social order (1983, p. 511). There is a pessimistic tone in these stories, which usually end in deception and feelings of guilt and fear, but Poniatowska's incipient feminism is at work in her ironic treatment of the confrontation between female desire and patriarchal social structures.

De noche vienes reissues several of the stories contained in *Los cuentos de Lilus Kikus* and adds eight new pieces. Almost all the stories feature female protagonists, many of whom are younger women caught in love relationships characterized by incommunication, rejection, inertia, and loneliness. Issues of social class are also raised in several stories that pay tribute to the durability of the existing class divisions. "Love Story" explores a wealthy woman's emotional dependence on her servant. Her dependence grows to obsessive proportions and betrays the sterility and frivolity of the protagonist's life. In "El limbo" (Limbo), the daughter of a wealthy family is shown to be hopelessly naive and ultimately egocentric in her clumsy attempts to "help" a servant who has recently given birth to a child. One of the best pieces is the title story, "De noche vienes," which parodies the sexual double standard in its humorous portrayal of a nurse who manages a career and five simultaneous marriages, all the while dutifully caring for her ailing father on weekends. At her trial for bigamy "in the fifth degree," the male judge is particularly incensed at the protagonist's air of innocence and utter candor, while a group of women rally to her defense by organizing a demonstration. The stories of *De noche vienes*, while not often offering a positive alternative, do effectively expose and critique many manifestations of female subordination and class conflict in Mexican society.

Querido Diego, te abraza Quiela is an epistolary novel comprised of twelve letters written by a woman to her absent lover. The Quiela of the title is based on Angelina Beloff, a Russian-born painter, and Diego on Diego Rivera (1886–1957), the Mexican muralist. The historical figures were lovers in Paris for ten years, until 1921, when Rivera returned to Mexico and ceased to communicate with Beloff. The letters, fictional and not historical, express Quiela's love for Diego, her extreme dependence on him, her hopes for a future reunion in Mexico, her memories of their life together and of the death of their infant son, and her anguish at Diego's silence. Quiela arouses both sympathy and impatience in the reader as she fluctuates between attempts at self-affirmation through her own painting and her self-destructive obsession with Diego, a godlike figure of power and creativity. In the language that describes Rivera and Quiela, the conventional masculine-feminine dichotomies of activity-passivity, strength-weakness, independence-dependence, and dominance-submission are exaggerated to extreme proportions. The reader's perception of this exaggeration and its destructive effect on Quiela creates a distance between reader and protagonist that permits us to see the novel as a critique of feminine socialization and not as an affirmation of the traditional values Quiela has internalized.

La *"Flor de Lis"* significantly expands on Poniatowska's earlier depictions of characters and circumstances that mirror her own experience. The novel is a woman-centered *Bildungsroman* narrated by the protagonist. Strongly autobiographical, it portrays the quest for self-knowledge and social and cultural identity of its young protagonist, Mariana. Mariana's family relationships, her education and religious training, her understanding of sex roles and social position, her awareness of her own sexuality, and her particular sense of uprootedness as a French native brought to Mexico at the age of nine unfold in the novel in consonance with the young girl's limited but developing awareness. The sense of a gradually unfolding consciousness is achieved through the remarkably consistent restriction of narrative perspective to Mariana and the predominant use of the present tense, which conveys the immediacy of relived experience. These textual strategies reflect Mariana's inability to analyze her situation or to achieve the degree of maturity that is the typical conclusion of the *Bildungsroman*.

Her stymied development is also evident in the portrayal of her ambivalent, highly charged relationship with her mother. The mother is a beautiful but distracted and elusive figure whom the narrator futilely seeks to make whole and present with her words. The child's sense of loss and her need for her mother threaten to thwart the young woman's chances for growth. However, the novel also shows other factors in Mariana's life which permit her to distance herself from her fear of abandonment and from the model of female vulnerability and wasted potential which is her mother's legacy. Her exposure to people and places outside of the family circle, her growing class consciousness, and her genuine interest in Mexico as a source of cultural roots offer Mariana needed alternatives. The book ends with a rambling meditation on her family and a bold rejection of dependency on her female forebears, which are Mariana's first steps toward freeing herself from them.

One of the outstanding features of Poniatowska's writing is her tendency to blur the boundaries between fictional and nonfictional modes of discourse. The close connection between her practice of journalism and her writing of imaginative literature challenges our notions of the document, fiction, and the role of the writer in the production of any text. Several other common threads also run through her works: the author's commitment to depicting contemporary Mexican society, the colloquial dimensions of her literary language, and her desire to broaden her own ideological horizons by recording other voices and other lives.

Whether in an interview with a figure of the cultural elite or in a chronicle about the children of Mexico City's slums, Poniatowska demonstrates her tremendous capacity for listening to what is spoken, what is silenced, and what is masked in the speech of her interlocutor. The result of her work is a literature that recuperates, criticizes, and reinvents many dimensions of Mexican life.

SURVEY OF CRITICISM

Critical studies of Elena Poniatowska's work lag behind her well-established reputation and her broad readership. The existing criticism consists primarily of journal articles and interviews with the author. Two of the interviews are particularly useful as sources of biographical information and observations by the author on her own writing: Margarita García Flores's "Entrevista a Elena Poniatowska" (1976) and Magdalena García Pinto's 1983 interview in *Historias íntimas: Conversaciones con diez escritoras hispanoamericanas* (1988). Two articles that offer a broad view of Poniatowska's work from a similar perspective are Carlos Monsiváis's "Mira, para que no comas olvido" (1981) and Bell Gale Chevigny's "The Transformation of Privilege in the Work of Elena Poniatowska" (1985). Both critics emphasize Poniatowska's role as a socially committed writer, and Monsiváis attributes her political awakening to the 1968 student movement. Chevigny traces Poniatowska's transformation from a woman of privilege into a champion of the oppressed through the evolution of her portrayals of women and of social and political struggle.

Juan Bruce-Novoa's analysis of *Lilus Kikus* in the aforementioned article disputes the idea of 1968 as a moment of sudden politicization for the writer. He sees the origins of her commitment in her earliest published work of fiction and what he calls "the indomitable feminist spirit of the child Lilus" (1983, p. 516). Another analysis of the female experience in Poniatowska's fiction appears in Cynthia Steele's 1985 article "La creatividad y el deseo en *Querido Diego, te abraza Quiela*, de Elena Poniatowska." Steele examines Quiela's psychological state (depression, loneliness) in the light of work in psychoanalytic theory by John Bowlby, Jessica Benjamin, and Nancy Chodorow.

Of Poniatowska's nonfiction titles, *La noche de Tlatelolco* has attracted some critical attention, although it is still little, relative to the importance of the work. Ronald Christ's early review (1975) of the English translation of the book and Zunilda Gertel's 1984 essay highlight Poniatowska's role as editor of the oral history. In "The Essential Extra: The Editor as a Parergonal Figure in Elena Poniatowska's *La noche de Tlatelolco*" (1989), Beth Jörgensen pursues this feature of the work by deconstructing the play of presence and absence of the narrator as editor. The narrator as "frame" is shown to have an intimate and essential connnection to the testimonies, rather than existing apart from them as a neutral agent of transmission.

Hasta no verte, Jesús mío has been the main object of critical essays dealing with Poniatowska's writing. At least a dozen articles and chapters in two books examine the novel, mostly from a thematic point of view. Charles Tatum (1977) interprets the novel within the picaresque tradition. He asserts that it ultimately portrays the defeat of the protagonist in her "submission" to a spiritualist sect. Tatum's reading ignores Jesusa's eventual separation from the "Spiritual Work" and the complexity of her response to her historical and social circumstance. Joel Hancock (1983) uses an "images of women" approach to defend Jesusa Palancares as a "liberated female hero" in her opposition to traditional stereotypes. Finally, Edward Friedman devotes a chapter of his book *The Anti-heroine's Voice: Narrative Discourse and Transformations of the Picaresque* (1987) to the study of the tension between "document" and "fiction" and to the use of irony in the novel. However, the essay suffers from a mistaken identification of Poniatowska as editor of the work, and of the text as, in large part, "unmediated" testimonial narration.

On the whole, the existing criticism on Poniatowska's works establishes some important groundwork, but it leaves open a myriad of possibilities for future study. Some texts have been completely neglected, and in general there is a need for more indepth, theoretically rigorous analyses from a variety of critical stances. There is no doubt that Poniatowska's literary *corpus*, which continues to grow, merits such increased attention.

BIBLIOGRAPHY

Works by Elena Poniatowska

Lilus Kikus. Mexico City: Colección Los Presentes, 1954.
"Melés y Teleo." *Revista Panoramas* 2 (1956):135–299.
Palabras cruzadas; crónicas. Mexico City: Era, 1961.
Todo empezó el domingo. Mexico City: Fondo de Cultura Económica, 1963.
Los cuentos de Lilus Kikus. Mexico City: Universidad Veracruzana, 1967.
Hasta no verte, Jesús mío. Mexico City: Era, 1969.
La noche de Tlatelolco: testimonios de historia oral. Mexico City: Era, 1971.
El Primer Primero de Mayo. Mexico City: Centro de Estudios Históricos del Movimiento Obrero Mexicano, 1976.
Querido Diego, te abraza Quiela. Mexico City: Era, 1976.
De noche vienes. Mexico City: Grijalbo, 1979. Mexico City: Era, 1985.
Gaby Brimmer and Elena Poniatowska. *Gaby Brimmer*. Mexico City: Grijalbo, 1979.
Fuerte es el silencio. Mexico City: Era, 1980.
La casa en la tierra. Photos by Mariana Yampolsky. Mexico City: INA-Fonapas, 1980.
Domingo siete. Mexico City: Ediciones Océano, 1982.
El último guajolote. Mexico City: Martín Casillas, 1982.
¡Ay vida, no me mereces! Mexico City: Joaquín Mortiz, 1986.
Hector García: México sin retoque. Mexico City: Universidad Nacional Autónoma de México, 1987.
La "Flor de Lis". Mexico City: Era, 1988.
Nada, nadie. Mexico City: Era, 1988.

Translations of Elena Poniatowska

Bogin, Magda, trans. *Until We Meet Again*. New York: Pantheon, 1987.
Kolovakos, Gregory, and Ronald Christ, trans. "And Here's To You, Jesusa." *Lives on the Line: The Testimony of Contemporary Latin American Authors*. Ed. and Introd. Doris Meyer. Berkeley, Calif.: University of California, 1988. Pp. 137–55.
Lane, Helen R., trans. *Massacre in Mexico*. New York: Viking Press, 1975.
Silver, Katherine, trans. *Dear Diego*. New York: Pantheon Books, 1986.

Works about Elena Poniatowska

Bruce-Novoa, Juan. "Elena Poniatowska: The Feminist Origins of Commitment." *Women's Studies International Forum* 6, 5 (1983):509–16.
Capistrán, Miguel. "La transmutación literaria." *Vida Literaria* (Mexico) 3 (1970):12–14.
Chevigny, Bell Gale. "The Transformation of Privilege in the Work of Elena Poniatowska." *Latin American Literary Review* 8, 26 (1985):49–62.
Christ, Ronald. "The Author as Editor." *Review* 15 (1975):78–79.
——. "*Los cuentos de Lilus Kikus*." *Recent Books in Mexico* 14, 5 (1967):5.
Flori, Mónica. "Visions of Women: Symbolic Physical Portrayal as Social Commentary in the Short Fiction of Elena Poniatowska." *Third Woman* 11, 2 (1984):77–83.
Foster, David William. "Latin American Documentary Narrative." *Publication of the Modern Language Association* 99, 1 (1984):41–55.
Fox-Lockert, Lucía. *Women Novelists in Spain and Spanish America*. Metuchen, N.J.: Scarecrow Press, 1979. Pp. 260–77.
Friedman, Edward. "The Marginated Narrator: *Hasta no verte, Jesús mío* and the Eloquence of Repression." *The Antiheroine's Voice: Narrative Discourse and Transformations of the Picaresque*. Columbia: University of Missouri Press, 1987. Pp. 170–87
Galindo, Carmen. "Vivir del milagro." *Vida Literaria* (Mexico) 3 (1970):8–9.
García Flores, Margarita. "Entrevista a Elena Poniatowska." *Revista de la Universidad de México* 30, 7 (1976):25–30.
García Pinto, Magdalena. "Entrevista con Elena Poniatowska." *Historias íntimas: Conversaciones con diez escritoras latinoamericanas*. Hanover, N.H.: Ediciones del Norte, 1988. 175–98.
Gauzarian Gautier, Marie-Lise. "Elena Poniatowska" Interview. *Interviews with Latin American Writers*. Elmwood Park, Ill.: Dalkey Archive Press, 1969. Pp. 199–216.
Gertel, Zunilda. "La mujer y su discurso: conciencia y máscara." *Cambio social en México visto por autores contemporáneos*. Ed. José Anadón. Notre Dame, Ind.: University of Notre Dame, 1984. Pp. 45–60.
Hancock, Joel. "Elena Poniatowska's *Hasta no verte, Jesús mío*: The Remaking of the Image of Woman." *Hispania* 66, 3 (1983):353–59.
Jörgensen, Beth E. "The Essential Extra: The Editor as a Parergonal Figure in Elena Poniatowska's *La noche de Tlatelolco*." *Latin American Perspectives* (forthcoming 1989).
——. "La intertextualidad en *La noche de Tlatelolco* de Elena Poniatowska." *Hispanic Journal* 10, 2 (Spring 1989):81–93.

———. "Texto e ideología en la obra de Elena Poniatowska." Ph.D. diss. University of Wisconsin-Madison, 1986. (DAI 47, 4 [1986]:1344A.)

Lemaître, Monique J. "Jesusa Palancares y la dialéctica de la emancipación femenina." *Hispamérica* 10, 30 (1981):131–35.

López Negrete, Cecilia. "Con Elena Poniatowska." *Vida Literaria* (Mexico) 3 (1970):16–19.

Loustanau, Martha O. "Mexico's Contemporary Women Novelists." Ph.D. diss. University of New Mexico, 1973. Pp. 187–201. (DAI 34, 5 [1973]:2637A.)

Méndez-Faith, Teresa. "Entrevista con Elena Poniatowska." *Inti* (Providence, R.I.) 15 (1982):54–60.

Miller, Beth. "Elena Poniatowska." *Veinte y seis autoras del México actual*. Mexico City: Costa-Amic, 1978. Pp. 299–321.

———"Personas y personajes: Castellanos, Fuentes, Poniatowska y Sáinz." *Mujeres en la literatura*. Mexico City: Fleischer, 1978. Pp. 65–75.

Monsiváis, Carlos. " 'Mira para que no comas olvido . . . ', las precisiones de Elena Poniatowska." *La Cultura en México*, July 15, 1981:2–4.

Monterde, Francisco. "Cuadro vivo del pueblo." *Vida Literaria* (Mexico) 3 (1970):5–7.

Pérez-Robles, Xiúhnel. "*La noche de Tlatelolco*." *Cuadernos Americanos* 177 (1971): 79–82.

Poniatowska, Elena. "*Hasta no verte, Jesús mío*." *Vuelta* (Mexico) 2, 24 (1978):5–11.

Portal, Marta. *Proceso narrativo de la revolución mexicana*. Madrid: Espasa-Calpe, 1980. Pp. 285–92.

Starčević, Elizabeth D. "Breaking the Silence: Elena Poniatowska, a Writer in Transition." *Literatures in Transition: The Many Voices of the Caribbean Area: A Symposium*. Ed. Rose S. Minc. Gaithersburg, Md.: Hispamérica, 1982. Pp. 63–68.

———. "Elena Poniatowska: Witness for the People." *Contemporary Women Authors of Latin America*. Eds. Doris Meyer and Margarite Fernández Olmos. Brooklyn N.Y.: Brooklyn College Press, 1983. Pp. 72–77.

Steele, Cynthia. "La creatividad y el deseo en *Querido Diego, te abraza Quiela* de Elena Poniatowska." *Hispamérica* 41 (1985):17–28.

Tatum, Charles. "Elena Poniatowska's *Hasta no verte, Jesús mío*." *Latin American Women Writers: Yesterday and Today*. Eds. Yvette E. Miller and Charles M. Tatum. Pittsburgh: The Review, 1977. Pp. 49–58.

Young, Rinda Rebeca Stowell. "Six Representative Women Novelists of Mexico, 1960–1969." Ph.D. diss. University of Illinois-Urbana Champaign, 1975. Pp. 85–139. (DAI 36, 9 [1975]:6092A.)

MAGDA PORTAL
(1903–1989)
Peru

Daniel R. Reedy

BIOGRAPHY

Poet, essayist, novelist, political activist, María Magdalena Julia Portal was born in Barranco, a coastal suburb of Lima, Peru, on May 27, 1903, to working-class parents. She changed her legal name to Magda later in life. The theme of social injustice which is dominant in her literary works had its origin in part in economic problems her family experienced after the death of her father, when she was five, and then of her stepfather, some ten years later. Although her mother sold family possessions to pay bills, creditors forced them from their home. Portal was later to state that her first-hand experience with social injustice as a child led her to accept more readily the radical views of many of her contemporaries.

Portal began to write works of fiction—poems, short stories, and a novel—as a teenager, but most of her early writings were lost or destroyed. Owing to her family's financial problems, she found employment but attended classes in the evenings at the University of San Marcos where she was exposed to philosophical concepts and political ideas that had been unknown to her.

She met and later married a fellow student, Federico Bolaños, but the marriage was unsuccessful. Her personal circumstances were further complicated when she subsequently fell in love with another of the Bolaños brothers, Reynaldo, a poet known by the pen name, Serafín Delmar. Magda and Serafín's often tumultuous relationship continued intermittently through more than twenty years of political persecutions, exile, and imprisonments.

By 1923 Magda Portal was directly involved in student political activities, and she participated in demonstrations against the government of President Augusto B. Leguía. Her first literary triumph occurred in August (1923) when she was awarded First Prize in a Poetry Contest sponsored by the University of San Marcos. Two years later in 1925, following the birth of her daughter Gloria, Magda and Delmar abandoned Peru for Bolivia where they spent a year lecturing on literature and the socialization of the arts, as well as publishing *Bandera Roja* (Red banner), a worker's newspaper. They wrote and published jointly in 1926 a volume titled *El derecho de matar* (Right to kill) containing fifteen brief, doctrinaire short stories. Their journalistic activities and involvement in Bolivian political intrigues forced their return to Lima in early 1926.

In Lima, Portal became increasingly involved in Peruvian literary and political life. She founded and published several numbers of an avant-garde literary journal which she referred to as a "review of supra-cosmopolitan art" and whose title changed sporadically from *Trampolín* to *Hangar*, to *Rascacielos*, and finally to *Timonel* before its demise in 1927. She also taught in the Universidades Manuel González Prada, which provided free classes for working-class students, and collaborated regularly in the journal *Amauta*, which was edited by José Carlos Mariátegui, one of Peru's leading socialists and intellectuals, at whose encouragement she published her first volume of poetry, *Una esperanza i el mar* (One hope and the sea), in 1927. Her affiliation with Mariátegui and other leftist writers ultimately led to her arrest in June 1927 as part of a group of supposed Communists. Her deportation to Cuba by the Leguía government followed shortly thereafter. The following year she was reunited in Mexico with Serafín Delmar and other Peruvian exiles. Among them was Victor Raúl Haya de la Torre, the founder of the Popular Revolutionary Alliance for America (APRA), an international political party with strong ties to Peru.

After three years of political activity with the APRA in Mexico and various countries of the Caribbean, Portal and other Peruvian exiles returned to Peru via Chile in late 1930. She immediately assumed responsibilities as a founding leader of the Peruvian Aprista party (PAP) whose leadership, programs, and political objectives were essentially those of the international APRA organization in which she had participated in Mexico.

In the PAP, Portal was the leader of the Feminine Sector of the National Executive Committee, through which she worked for the emancipation of women through programs of education and their increased involvement in the political life of the country. Two of her essays on these topics are found in a short volume entitled *Hacia la mujer nueva y El Aprismo y la mujer* (1933; Toward the new woman and Aprismo and women).

The government's persecution of APRA leaders led to Portal's going underground for some sixteen months while continuing to work as the head of the Women's Branch of the APRA. Her companion, Serafín Delmar, was sentenced to twenty years in prison for complicity in an assassination attempt against President Sánchez Cerro. Portal herself was arrested in November 1934 and was subsequently sentenced to five hundred days in the women's prison of Santo Tomás in Lima. Historical events and personal experiences from this period serve as the basis for many of her poems in *Costa sur* (1945; South Coast) and her novel *La trampa* (1956; The trap).

Released from prison in 1936, Magda Portal continued her political labors for APRA until early 1939 when she left Peru with her daughter, Gloria. Six years of exile followed in Argentina, Uruguay, and Chile. In Chile, she worked in the Ministry of Education and became affiliated with the Association of Socialist Women, earning her the attention of such well-known figures as Venezuela's Rómulo Betancourt and Chile's socialist leader, Salvador Allende.

In advance of Peru's presidential elections in 1945, Portal returned to her native country with Gloria to renew her activities in APRA which had recently made major election gains. She was the organizer and president of the First National Congress of Aprista Women in 1946, but personal tragedy marred Portal's future shortly thereafter when her daughter Gloria committed suicide in early 1947, the result in part of a frustrated infatuation with a young man involved in politics.

APRA's support for women's rights and their involvement in the political process reached its culmination in late 1948 when the military government took Portal and other Aprista leaders into custody after an armed revolt. When she faced a military tribunal in 1950, Portal declared that she felt deceived and defrauded by APRA. Although she was acquitted of the conspiracy charges, all vestiges of affiliation between her and APRA were erased by the publication of her accusatory essay, ¿Quiénes traicionaron al pueblo? (Who betrayed the people?), in late 1950.

During a trip to Buenos Aires in mid-1950, many of Portal's unpublished writings from over some twenty years were lost in transit or confiscated by authorities, never to be recovered. After her return to Lima that same year, she renewed her ties to social, political, and literary activities in Peru, writing for newspapers and journals. In 1956 she published her only novel, La trampa, a work of obvious political implications, and in 1966 Constancia del Ser (Constancy of being) appeared, containing selections from her earlier volumes of poetry together with previously unpublished poems. For twelve years (1958–1971) she was the director of Mexico's Fondo de Cultura Económica publishing house in Lima.

Portal became an active affiliate of the Lima-based feminist group ALIMUPER (Alliance for the Liberation of Peruvian Women) and in 1978 was an unsuccessful candidate for election to the Constitutional Assembly representing the Revolutionary Action Socialist party in Peru. In recent years her activities have involved writing for numbers of periodicals, and she continues to serve as an officer of Peru's National Association of Writers and Artists (ANEA), having been president from 1982 to 1986. In June 1981 she was honored as a writer and activist by the Fourth Inter-American Congress of Women Writers at its meeting in Mexico City.

MAJOR THEMES

Magda Portal's first published poems are typified by a preoccupation with the theme of solitude and the symbolic image of the sea to which she personally compares herself. These poems are pensive and somber in tone, yet more refined and less sentimental than the works of many of her contemporaries. Other themes that most come to the fore are anguish and love, as well as an occasional note of restlessness. Although she planned a first volume of poetry around 1924 to be titled "Anima absorta" (Soul entranced), it never appeared. Her first published collection of poetry, *Una esperanza i el mar* (1927), was well received in Lima where it was awarded the Municipal Prize as the best book of poetry that year. Of the forty-two poems in the volume, only "Canto proletario" (Proletarian song) and "Grito" (Shout) are clearly indicative of the strong sociopolitical notes that were to have a more dominant presence in the themes of her later volumes.

The dates of composition for the poems in *Costa sur*, published in Chile in 1945, are not known, but casual evidence suggests they were composed from the late 1920s to shortly before their publication as a volume. Divided into three sections, the first two divisions, "Realidad del Ser" (Reality of being) and "Las palabras perdidas" (Lost words), reveal few thematic changes from many of the poems published more than two decades earlier. The lyric voice of some of these poems still finds a correspondence with the eternal ebb and flow of the sea. A sense of solitude surrounds the narrator, leaving her in a state of loneliness and abandonment; yet there is always a sense of expectation that someone will come and the situation will change. These themes are the basis for such poems as "Pescadora de sueños" (Fisherwomen of dreams), "Retorno a la soledad" (Return to solitude), "Abandonada" (Abandoned), and "Canción Amarga" (Bitter song), among others.

The final section of the book, "Destino del hombre" (Man's destiny), is clearly linked to many of Portal's political experiences during the period from 1930 to 1945. She remembers the cadavers of young men shot during the uprisings of 1932; her praise of the APRA party is marked with six thousand crosses of those who have already died; "Celda N° 2" (Cell No. 2) recalls her own imprisonment in the Santo Tomás Prison, as does "Madrugada en la cárcel" (Daybreak in jail) in which she reflects on the five hundred days of her prison sentence.

Constancia del Ser (1965), contains the author's selection of poems from her earlier collections, together with some twenty-five previously unpublished works. In a prefatory "message," Portal mentions that these poems represent a revisiting of times past, roads traveled, and voices heard. They are her attempt to leave a statement of having existed, a Constancy of Being. The penultimate section of the book ("Constancia del ser"), contains several poems whose sentiments convey more profound depth of meaning than do many of her earlier compositions. Particularly noteworthy are the anguished poems evoking the death of Portal's daughter Gloria: "Balada triste" (Sad ballad), "El largo soñar" (The long sleep), and "Las palabras oscuras" (Dreaded words). Anguished images accentuate the separation and absence of the beloved, the wounds that cannot heal, the happiness that can never return, and the desire to communicate across the abyss that separates life from death. For the poet, solitude surrounds her now with an impenetrable shield, and she awaits the inexorable approach of death which becomes something more desired than feared.

A strong note of social protest dominates the final section of this book called "Destino del hombre" (Man's destiny). Some of the poems originally appeared in *Amauta* and other journals during the late 1920s. Others appear in *Constancia del ser* for the first time. Among the best of these poems is "Digo . . ." (I declare . . .) which stresses the theme of liberty while condemning all who would stifle freedom. The poem also attacks war, nuclear arms, political hypocrisy, and social injustice in its various manifestations. Also included in *Constancia del ser* is a short section of prose poems. In "Coloquio de las madres" (Mothers' colloquies), a mother converses with her heart, the earth, her conscience, and destiny. Themes of maternal love are obvious in each of these pieces.

Portal's first work of prose fiction was a volume of short stories or vignettes entitled *El derecho de matar* (1926) which she and Serafín Delmar co-authored, each having contributed half of the pieces. The basic themes of these brief narratives relate to the misery of poverty. In "Círculos violetas" (Violet circles), Portal tells of a woman who destroys her newborn child rather than subject it to an environment of poverty and disease. Other works mention the Russian Revolution. In one, Christ is seen as the child of a bourgeois family; He is in reality Lenin, the man of peace and justice. The battlefields of Europe during World War I and the Russian Revolution are the common backdrop of most of these stories which are affirmations of why a mistreated, hungry peasant or laborer is justified when he revolts and kills his oppressor. Only one story by Portal, "Noche" (Night), is set in an environment that could be construed as Peruvian or Latin American. It deals with the story of an Indian, a peon, who is unjustly charged with a crime. The thesis of the work asserts that prison will convert this honest man into a hardened criminal.

La trampa (1956), Magda Portal's only novel, is loosely structured and gives evidence that it was hastily written. In fact, Portal has acknowledged that it was the product of nine months of intensive writing with the intention of using the work to sway public opinion and gain the release from prison of a young man, Carlos Steer Lafón, who was responsible for the double assassination of newspaper magnate Antonio Miró Quesada and his wife on May 16, 1935, in Lima.

The novel combines two story lines. One is the real-life story of Charles Stool (Carlos Steer) which details how he was trained by APRA leaders to assassinate the newspaper editor. The other plot centers on the story of María de la Luz, who is a thinly veiled characterization of Magda Portal herself. Thus, the episodic format of the novel revolves around Charles Stool's years in prison while also describing María de la Luz' life as a political activist and leader in the Unionista (APRA) party.

The portrayal of María de la Luz as a political prisoner clearly calls to mind Magda Portal's imprisonment during 1935–1936. The female protagonist is seen both as a strong political figure and as a person who shows intense human compassion. In prison, for example, she conducts classes to teach her fellow prisoners to read. And she defends women and their role in the Unionista party despite the male-dominated leadership of the party's inner circle.

La Trampa is clearly a work of little aesthetic import. Nonetheless, it has some value as a work that is inextricably linked to the sociohistorical context on which it is based. Were the assassination of the Miró Quesadas not so well known an event in Peru and elsewhere in Latin America, the story of Charles Stool and María de la Luz would not be sufficient attraction to make the novel worthwhile.

Had Magda Portal never written a poem or piece of fictional prose, there is some likelihood that she would have won recognition for her essays which deal with the APRA party, international political topics, and matters related to the rights of women. Her first volume of essays, *América Latina frente al Imperialismo y Defensa de la Revolución Mexicana* (1931; Latin America against imperialism and A defense of the Mexican Revolution), was the product of presentations Portal made during travels to Puerto Rico, the Dominican Republic, and Colombia during 1929. Her purpose in these public conferences was twofold: to address the issues of U.S. military and economic imperialism and to explore the possibility of establishing APRA cells in each of the places visited.

There is little that is original in Portal's volume. The role of the United States as an economic imperialist power after World War I is underscored, and issues such as the Panama Canal and Monroe Doctrine are addressed. The thesis or refrain that recurs throughout the book is that the ideological unity of the people will someday lead to a victorious struggle in which the conditions of the working masses will be improved and a society with equal justice will be established. In order to achieve the social emancipation of the peoples of Latin America, the battle must be waged against foreign imperialism.

In the Mexican Revolution, Portal sees as praiseworthy the nationalization of lands, the division of landholdings into small plots for the indigenous communities, and the formation of agricultural and economic cooperatives. Mexico's Revolution transcends its own environment and serves as an example that other peoples of Latin America should follow. If other Latin American countries join together to do battle against the foreign imperialists, they can be unified to such an extent that the formation of a Confederation of Latin American Republics, as envisioned by Simón Bolívar, may yet be possible. This hemispheric unification plan was initially a central aim of the international Aprista movement.

Magda Portal authored a number of essays on women in Latin American society. Two were published in a single volume, *Hacia la mujer nueva y El aprismo y la mujer* (1933). Her emphasis is strongly political as she points out the historical exclusion of women from major political roles, but she maintains that APRA will prepare women for more meaningful duties in the political process through a program of educational, political, and philosophical orientation. In particular, she argues that the party will: (1) work for the recognition of political rights for women with the assurance that they will be able to hold office, either elected or appointed; (2) establish the independence of women in terms of their civil rights within a marriage; and (3) provide for equality before the law of all classes of children, illegitimate and legitimate.

La mujer en el partido del Pueblo (1948; Women in the party of the people) is based on Portal's inaugural address to the First Convention of Aprista Women, in Trujillo in 1946. Her remarks provide an overview of the active, militant role of women in APRA and their struggle in Peru for recognition and equality during a period of social and political upheaval over some two decades. Portal argues that women must find ways to ensure their rights of personhood so that they can develop freely in society without unjust limitations being imposed on them. No longer will their influence be limited to "bedroom politics"; they will assume their legitimate rights as equals of men.

In some respects the subject of Portal's essay entitled *Flora Tristán, precursora* (1945; Flora Tristán, Precursor), is of fundamental importance to her views on the rights and roles of women and on her own view of self. The figure of Flora Tristán (1803–1844), a French-born daughter of a Peruvian father and a French mother, provides many parallels with Magda Portal's personal travails and political struggles. Portal also sees Flora Tristán as a precursor of feminism, the symbol of the struggle of women to support exploited classes in their battles against social prejudice, and one of the formative voices in the international workers' movement, before Marx and Engels. Much of Portal's knowledge of Tristán is based on Tristán's *Pérégrinations d'une paria, 1833–1834* (1838; Pereginations of a Pariah), which contains her autobiography and her journal notes of a trip to Peru to reclaim a family inheritance.

Portal's separation from the APRA political organization after the military revolt of 1948 and her own trial by a military tribunal in 1950 are detailed in her accusatory essay, *¿Quiénes traicionaron al pueblo?*, in which she sets forth her reasons for feeling deceived and defrauded by APRA. Although she condemns many party leaders, including its founder Víctor Raúl Haya de la Torre, her remarks show that most of her original convictions and idealism remained unchanged: "I continue to believe that the tremendous impact of these crucial times gives the masses a sense of history and social conscience . . . so that . . . their strength and unity will increase, and they will at last arrive at their future destiny of being a civilized people with liberty, with democracy, and with Justice" (p. 30).

SURVEY OF CRITICISM

Because of her involvement as an activist and revolutionary leader, it comes as no surprise that Portal's political activities have often eclipsed her contributions as a writer of substance. Differences of political orientation undoubtedly led some Peruvian critics to show little regard for her works or at best to treat them with indifference. In his *Literatura peruana del siglo XX* (1965; Twentieth century Peruvian literature), Peruvian literary critic Estuardo Núñez notes accurately that a sense of social commitment overshadows a sense of pure artistry in some of her poetic works. He makes a similar observation about her novel *La trampa*, underscoring that its political intent obscures the artistic effects and purpose of the novel. About her first work of poetry, *Una esperanza i el mar* (1927), Núñez observes that it marks a movement away from the excessive sentimentality and dry, prosaic verse of the time and toward a modern sensibility.

At the time she won the poetry prize in 1923, Ladislao F. Meza, writing in Lima's *Mundial* (August 1923), found important parallels to draw between Magda Portal and other Spanish American poets such as Delmira Agustini* (Argentina), Juana de Ibarbourou* (Uruguay), and Gabriela Mistral* (Chile). Meza called Portal's short, lyric poems brilliant, finding significant changes in them from her earlier timid verses written under the pseudonym of Tula Sovaina. The jury of three male judges who selected her "Nocturnos" (Nocturnes) for the prize observed in her poetry a "tortured and feminine soul" in which "throbbed profoundly the mysteries and anguish of everyday tragedy" (*El Tiempo*, Lima, Aug. 22, 1923).

José Carlos Mariátegui, Magda Portal's political ally and artistic mentor during the 1920s, points to her as Peru's first "poetess," a term which he defines as "someone who creates a feminine poetry" (*Siete ensayos de interpretación de la realidad peruana* [1927; *Seven Interpretive Essays on Peruvian Reality*, 1971]). He finds at the core of her poetry a contrast between her eagerness to create and live even though her soul seems in agony—a dramatic conflict that gives psychological depth to her poetry. He notes that Portal's lyricism is found in "the voice of a woman who lives passionately and intensely, glowing with love and longing, tormented by truth and hope" (p. 263).

By the time of her imprisonment in 1935–1936, Magda Portal was better known as a political figure than she was as a writer. An October 1935 issue of *Claridad*, a leftist journal in Buenos Aires, was devoted entirely to Portal's life, political activities, and her imprisonment in Santo Tomás. Articles praise her tenacity, intelligence, and tirelessness which, in the words of one observer, make of her life "a lesson for men and women throughout the Continent" ("Apuntes biográficos sobre Magda Portal," p. 13). Her fellow Peruvian and Aprista colleague Luis Alberto Sánchez calls her an authentic revolutionary and observes that her literary orientation has developed from pure art to social art and finally to the doctrinaire ("Odisea y calvario de Magda Portal," p. 16).

Although her first book of poetry won only the attention of a small audience, Portal's second volume *Costa sur* was seen as having a greater depth of concerns and verbal dexterity in expression of ideas, and demonstrated artistic ability. Yet in the view of Chilean critic Ricardo A. Latcham (as reprinted from *La Nación*, Dec. 24, 1944), *Costa sur* combined the characteristic lyricism of her earlier poetry with an orientation toward social and political concerns in which there was less artistic rigor and purity of expression.

In four separate, yet interrelated articles, Daniel Reedy examines the evolution of Portal's poetry with particular attention to its emphasis on sociopolitical content ("Magda Portal: Peru's Voice of Social Protests," 1970); the historical context and literary genesis of *La trampa* ("*La trampa*: Génesis de una novela política," 1980); Portal's role in the struggle for women's rights in Peru ("Aspects of the Feminist Movement in Peruvian Letters and Politics," 1975); and a capsule view of her life, and literary and political activities as part of the homage to her at the Fourth Inter-American Congress of Women Writers ("Magda Portal," 1981). In each of these articles, Reedy deals with the salient characteristics of Portal's writings, especially the inseparability of the aesthetics of her works from her political commitment, which is identifiable less with a particular ideology than with a sense of personal mission.

In some respects Magda Portal is only now being discovered within and outside of her own country. Esther Andradi and Ana María Portugal, writing in their admirable study of Peruvian women (*Ser mujer en el Perú*, 1978), have pointed out that Portal is the only woman in Peru to have been actively involved in Peruvian political life for more than fifty years. They also note quite accurately that she is one of Peru's important writers who, being a woman, has been the object of discrimination by a patriarchal society which has largely seen the literary vocation as being more appropriate for men than for women.

BIBLIOGRAPHY

Works by Magda Portal

With Serafín Delmar. *El derecho de matar*. La Paz: n.p., 1926.
Una esperanza i el mar. Lima: Minerva, 1927.
América latina frente al imperialismo y *Defensa de la Revolucíon Mexicana*. Lima: Cahuide, 1931.
Hacia la mujer nueva. El aprismo y la mujer. Lima: Cooperativa Aprista "Atahualpa," 1933.
Flora Tristán, precursora. Lima: Páginas Libres, 1945; 2d ed. revised, Lima: La Equidad, 1983.
Costa sur. Santiago: Nueva, 1945.
La mujer en el partido del pueblo. Lima: El Condor, 1948.
¿Quiénes traicionaron al pueblo? Lima: Salas e Hijos, 1950.
La trampa. Lima: Raíz, 1956; 2d ed. revised, Lima: Poma, 1982.
Constancia del ser. Lima: P. L. Villanueva, 1965.

Works about Magda Portal

Andradi, Esther, and Ana María Portugal. "Magda Portal, escritora y política." *Ser mujer en el Perú*. Lima: Mujer y Autonomía, 1978. Pp. 209–32.
"Apuntes biográficos sobre Magda Portal." *Claridad* (Buenos Aires) 294 (Oct. 1935):13–14.
Carrillo, Enrique A. "Juegos florales de 1923." *El Tiempo* (Aug 22, 1923):n.p.
Haya de la Torre, Víctor Raúl. "La misión admirable de Magda Portal en las Antillas." *Claridad* (Buenos Aires) 294 (Oct. 1935):23–24.
Herrera, Oscar. "Magda Portal." *Claridad* (Buenos Aires) 294 (Oct. 1935):22.

Latcham, Richard. "Crónica literaria" (from *La Nación*, Dec. 24, 1944). *Constancia del ser*. By Magda Portal. Pp. 217–20.

Mariátegui, José Carlos. "Literature on Trial." *Seven Interpretive Essays on Peruvian Reality*. Trans. Marjory Urquidi. Austin: University of Texas Press, 1971. Pp. 182–287.

Meza, Ladislao. "Magda Portal, laureada." *Mundial* (Lima) 170 (Aug. 1923):n.p.

Núñez, Estuardo. *Literatura peruana del siglo XX*. Mexico: Editorial Pormaca, 1965.

Portugal, Enrique S. "Una mujer indoamericana debe ser libertada." *Claridad* (Buenos Aires) 294 (Oct. 1935):17–18.

Reedy, Daniel R. "Aspects of the Feminist Movement in Peruvian Letters and Politics." *The Place of Literature in Interdisciplinary Approaches*. Ed. Eugene R. Huck. Carrollton, Ga.: Thomasson Printing Co., 1975. Pp. 53–64.

——. "Magda Portal." *Los Universitarios* (Mexico) 187 (July 1981):3–6.

——. "Magda Portal: Peru's Voice of Social Protest." *Revista de Estudios Hispánicos* 4, 1 (Apr. 1970):85–97.

——. "*La trampa*: Génesis de una novela política." *Texto/contexto en la literatura iberoamericana* (Memoria del XIX° Congreso del Instituto Internacional de Literatura Iberoamericana). Eds. Keith McDuffie and Alfredo Roggiano. Madrid: Artes Gráficas Benzal, 1980. Pp. 299–306.

Sánchez, Luis Alberto. "Odisea y calvario de Magda Portal." *Claridad* (Buenos Aires) 294 (Oct. 1935):16.

Seoane, Manuel. "Escorzo de Magda Portal." *Claridad* (Buenos Aires) 294 (Oct. 1935):19–21.

Velarde, Hernán. "Magda Portal." *Estampa, Revista de Expreso* (Mar. 19, 1967):4–5.

ARMONÍA SOMERS
(b. 1920)
Uruguay

Nora Erro-Orthmann

BIOGRAPHY

Armonía Somers, the pseudonym of the distinguished writer Armonía Etchepare de Henestrosa, was born in Uruguay around 1920. There is no agreement among the critics about the author's date of birth; some contend she was born in 1914 while others date it at 1917 and even 1930. Although she is generally considered to belong to the so-called Generation of 1945, composed of such well-known writers and critics as Carlos Martínez Moreno, Mario Benedetti, Angel Rama, and Emir Rodríguez Monegal, she does not share the group's common concerns and themes.

Before publishing her first novel in 1950, Somers had a long and outstanding career in education. She taught in Montevideo and was director of the National Museum of Education. Her profound involvement in education led her to participate in many international organizations such as the United Nations Educational, Scientific and Cultural Organization (Unesco), and the Organization of American States (OAS). She published widely in the field of education and was editor of *Boletín Informativo de la Biblioteca y Museo Pedagógicos*, founder and editor of the journal of the Center for Educational Documentation and Dissemination, *Documentum, 1961*, and editor of *Anales* and *Enciclopedia de Educación, 1967–71*. Her book, *Educación de la adolescencia*, received prizes from the Municipality of Montevideo and the University of the Republic. In 1972 she left her career in education to dedicate herself to writing fiction.

Somers's first novella, *La mujer desnuda* (1950; The naked woman), caused a sensation in literary circles when it was published by the magazine *Clima*. Its overt sexual overtones were considered scandalous in the provincial Uruguayan society of the time. This allegoric tale tells the story of Rebeca Linke's rebellion upon reaching her thirtieth birthday. Presented in a symbolic and nebulous atmosphere with lyrical overtones, the story emphasizes the protagonist's anguished search for freedom.

The novella became the focus of much discussion, to the point that *Clima*, bowing to public demand, published the complete text of the novella almost immediately. Copies of the book were snapped up as quickly as the magazine. Critics speculated that it had been written by a man, and the names of Carlos Brandy and Taco Larreta were put forth as putative authors.

Following *La mujer desnuda*, Somers continued to address the topics of sexuality, eroticism, and death in her work. In 1953 *El derrumbamiento* (The cave-in) was published, her first collection of short stories: "El derrumbamiento," "Réquiem por Goyo Ribera" (Requiem for Goyo Ribera), "El despojo" (Plunder), "La puerta violentada" (Forced door), and "Saliva del paraíso" (Saliva from Paradise). In all of these stories the Uruguayan author presents despairing people, both men and women, seeking redemption from a useless, hopeless existence. These stories all treat common themes: violence, lack of communication, despair, death, desperation, and loneliness. The title story attracted critical attention particularly for its portrayal of unusual characters and for its theme. It was much criticized for its portrayal of an erotic relationship between the Virgin Mary and the Negro, presented through a dialogue revealing the sensual responses of the man to the seductive behavior of the Virgin, here transformed from a statue into a woman. This collection was awarded a prize by the Uruguayan Ministry of Public Education and Social Planning in 1953.

After ten years of silence, Somers published a second collection of short stories entitled *La calle del viento norte* (1963; The street of the North Wind), again with five stories: "La calle del viento norte," "El ángel planeador" (The angel who landed), "Muerte por alacrán" (Death by a scorpion), "La subasta" ("The auction"), and "El hombre del túnel" (The man in the tunnel).

Two years later, in 1965, the Uruguayan author published her second novel, *De miedo en miedo* (From one fear to the next). This novel deals with a man seaching for some meaning in his life who, in a vain effort to understand himself as an adult, analyzes his childhood and his adolescence. The protagonist reports his feelings and emotions, interpreting his experiences through a series of notes which he throws into a river after they are written.

Basically, *De miedo en miedo* consists of a monologue by a nameless man in his forties. The narrator relates the story of his life to the reader in the first person, in several nonchronological segments. While working in a bookstore, he meets a woman, and they begin a very intense relationship. Since the narrator is married, they meet frequently in the bookstore, cafés, and parks. During these encounters, he relates to the woman many of his previous experiences and feelings. These anecdotes, as well as the conversations of the couple, are dispersed among the protagonist's daily activities. His intense communication with this woman comes to an abrupt end when she decides not to see him anymore. The novel concludes with the protagonist alone, confused, and anguished as he confronts nothingness. His last experience the narrator describes as that of giving birth to fear because he realizes that life has no meaning and only leads to death.

Eighteen of Somers's short stories that had appeared in books, anthologies, and magazines between 1953 and 1967 were collected by Editorial Arca in 1967 in two volumes and published under the title *Todos los cuentos* (All the short stories). This collection is comprised of Somers's best known and most representative stories dealing with sex, frustration, failure to communicate, anguish, fear, and death.

A third novel, *Un retrato para Dickens* (1969; A portrait for Dickens), gives further evidence of the author's creative power and technical innovations. The novel tells the story of an orphaned adolescent girl rescued from the river by the chief of police, to whom she relates her miserable life in a tenement. The picture that emerges is one of misery, poverty, and abuse. The influence of Charles Dickens's *Oliver Twist* is clear from the title, characters, and themes. In this work Somers combines several narratives: the story of the young girl (recounted in the first person), the biblical book of Tobias, excerpts from a pastry cookbook by F. Figueredo (published in Argentina in 1914), and recollections of a parrot named Asmodeo, in a clear reference to the devil Asmodeo as related in the Bible. This complex narrative structure is used to elucidate and develop two of the main themes of the novel: the struggle between Good and Evil, and the suffering of the innocent. *Un retrato para Dickens* has been awarded prizes by both the Uruguayan Ministry of Education and Culture and the city of Montevideo.

In 1978 *Muerte por alacrán* was published in Buenos Aires. This book consisted of eleven short stories published previously as well as a new text entitled "Esperando a Polidoro" (Waiting for Polidoro). Among the titles printed in this volume were: "La calle del viento norte," "El entierro" (The burial), "La inmigrante" (The immigrant), and "El hombre del túnel."

Armonía Somers's fiction presents a strange, imaginative, fantastic—yet fascinating—view of human nature. In her narrative she introduces a series of animalistic characters, which in many ways do not differ much from human beings. In 1982 *Tríptico darwiniano* (Darwinian Triptych) appeared. Designed and published by Somers's late husband, Rodolfo A. Henestrosa, the book included a prologue by Jean Andrew, a well-known critic, and three short stories: "Mi hombre peludo" (My hairy man), "El eslabón perdido" (The lost link), and "El pensador de Rodin" (The thinker of Rodin). All three narratives were heavily influenced by Edgar Allan Poe, Horacio Quiroga (Uruguay), Leopoldo Lugones (Argentina), and Gustave Flaubert, and depict a woman reporter, a poet, and a dyslexic child, respectively, in relationships with apes. In these writings the author tries to elucidate the barrier between the human and the animal.

Sólo los elefantes encuentran mandrágora (1983; Only elephants find mandrake roots), is by far Somers's most ambitious, voluminous (it contains 349 pages), and complex work to date. The book was ostensibly discovered and edited by Victoria von Scherrer, but it is never clear whether this is a real or fictitious person. The title of the novel alludes to mandrake roots, a plant associated with magic and witchcraft. The work relates in poetic and subjective language the intense, personal experience of a woman searching for meaning in her life.

The protagonist, Sembrando Flores de Médicis, is sick in a hospital, where she is being treated for shortness of breath and palpitations. She writes her memoirs while at the hospital, relating her present situation, with all its physical discomforts, to the story of her life and to her family's history, while at the same time meditating on literary, linguistic, philosophical, social, and religious topics. Inserted into the main thread of the narrative is the 1872 novel written by Enrique Pérez Escrich, entitled *El manuscrito de la madre* (The mother's manuscript), and read by Sembrando's mother to Abigail de la Torre, one of the characters in the novel, whose life story is also woven into the work. This amalgamation of different narratives creates a complex work distinguished by an air of unreality, fantasy, and phantasmagoric illusions. The novel concludes with an epilogue by the same Victoria von Scherrer, explaining that she found these notebooks written by her friend, Sembrando Flores de Médicis, following Médicis's death in an automobile accident; she felt it was her duty to publish these notebooks, without comments, as homage to the woman she knew.

Viaje al corazón del día (1986; Voyage to the heart of the day), subtitled *Elegía por un secreto amor* (Elegy for a secret love), is Somers's last novel to date (1988). The story is told by Laura, who writes the novel, as she states in a prologue, to record a strange and unusual tale, one that leads the reader to experience a frightful nightmare in the name of Allah, the Moslem prophet. The narrative is dedicated to Laurent, Laura's lover, and is preceded by a quotation from the Koran (Chapter XCI), which deals with the idea that purity of the soul brings happiness. The novel, divided into two parts and an epilogue, ostensibly tells the story of Encarnación de Cienfuegos and her family. However, the main story-within-a-story is the protagonist Laura Kadisja Hassan's tragic love for Laurent (the name given to him by Laura but whose real name is Macario), the grandson of Encarnación.

Laura, the child of Encarnación's sister and an Arab, is raised by her aunt following the death of her parents in a shipwreck. She narrates the story to Father Artemio, a priest, after Laurent's death. Interspersed throughout this first-person narrative are letters written by Encarnación, the aunt, to Refugios, Encarnación's administrator and confidant, who supplies the rest of the family history, including that of Laura. Incorporated into Part One is a letter from Laura to Refugio, narrating the events that took place after her aunt's death; Part One ends with Laura's account of the death of Laurent at the seaside. Part Two consists of a letter from Fraulein Hildegard, Laura's music tutor. A short epilogue written by Laura many years later, after her receipt of Fraulein Hildegard's letter, concludes this story of unhappy love.

Armonía Somers's production has increased in quantity and quality in recent years. Since 1972 she has written a book of short stories and two novels. The novels contain diverse experiments in fictional technique and a more complex use of language. The Uruguayan writer continues to write fiction and will publish other works in the near future.

MAJOR THEMES

The writings of Armonía Somers present her vision of a nightmarish, chaotic, senseless, and cruel world in which God does not exist. Her characters are anguished and lonely, attempting to survive in a world that offers no resolution or redemption of their desperate plights. Considering Somers's concern for human existence, it is not surprising that her major themes include loneliness, anguish, love, sex, lack of communication, and death.

From *La mujer desnuda* to *Viaje al corazón del día*, Somers focuses on the absurd and solitary nature of men and women. She describes the human condition as a pressing search for meaning and purpose. Rebeca Linke, the main character of *La mujer desnuda*, is only the first of many protagonists who rebel against the barrenness of life. Disillusioned with her humdrum existence, the protagonist takes off her clothes and, covered only by a coat, takes the train to her house in the country. There she abandons the coat and initiates a series of adventures in which she seduces various men, disrupting the life of everyone, including that of a priest. This search for freedom, honesty, and candor in a society bound by prejudice and taboo, both moral and religious, ends in death. This unorthodox, daring, and erotic story creates the pattern and establishes the themes of the works to come. Sexuality, eroticism, and death become essential components of Somers's writings.

Love, as in most of Somers's works, does not resolve human suffering, and her characters, in spite of their need to communicate, in the end always fail to develop a lasting relationship capable of providing hope for the future. Rarely does Somers present a happy relationship between man and woman in her writings, and, if she does, it is usually destined to end disastrously. This is true of her portrayal of Laura and Laurent's tragic love affair in *Viaje al corazón del día*, for example.

Somers's prose defies convention and explores themes considered taboo in her society. The outstanding example of her unorthodox treatment of subject and character took place early in her career. In "El derrumbamiento," a Negro, Tristán, takes refuge in a broken-down hut, during a rainstorm, while being pursued by the police for having killed a white man. Delirious, feverish, and confused, he lies down on the floor naked because his clothes are soaking wet. He finds a small statue of the Virgin Mary surrounded by light and prays to her for help. In a purposely ambiguous scene the character sees the Virgin come to life. She comes down from her pedestal and begs him to hold and caress her, to melt away the imprisoning wax that surrounds her, so that she can avenge her son. At first, he refuses out of respect and reverence to the Virgin. Finally, he agrees to her urging. Grateful for his help, she saves him from his pursuers by destroying the house.

In "La inmigrante," Somers deals openly with a lesbian relationship, and, in "El despojo" and "El hombre del túnel," she explores the themes of sexual aggression by misogynists and of female eroticism, respectively. In her treatment of these erotic episodes and experiences, there is a good deal of sex-role reversal: for example, men experience the feelings and happenings normally associated with women, such as rape and giving birth. Somers challenges the myths created by society and proposes a different version. She questions the hypocrisy of social and religious morality and conventions and suggests a more realistic and honest interpretation of life.

Death permeates most of Somers's writing, as she examines the role which the fear of death plays in the lives of her characters. In "El hombre del túnel," the protagonist, in the last moments of her life, recalls and analyzes her most important experiences. In both "El ángel planeador" and "Réquiem por Goyo Ribera," the main characters confront the death of another, someone who has influence over his or her current existence, and who causes grief and anguish. "El entierro" presents a grotesque, comic, and irreverent treatment of death as a group of friends lose their friend's corpse on the way to the cemetery. Somers's novels present a view of the relationship between life and death that is both subtle and complex. Death can give meaning to an otherwise meaningless, anguished, and hopeless existence; it can also provide freedom, as it does for the protagonist of *La mujer desnuda*.

Somers's fiction raises both existential and metaphysical concerns. In *Un retrato para Dickens*, the plight of the young girl is compared to that of Tobias in the Bible, and the author questions the validity of her suffering. At the end of the novel, the taste of the piece of cake that the little girl dreamed about before, and now enjoys as a reward, offers but a brief reprieve in a desolate and anguished life. In *Sólo los elefantes encuentran mandrágora*, different elements are brought together: the universal and the regional, the social and the personal, the historical and the fictitious, in an effort to portray and define the nature of human life.

Somers's characters come from all walks of life, but, more often than not, they are murderers, rapists, psychopaths, drifters, lesbians, drunkards, orphans— maladjusted or marginalized individuals trying to survive in a hostile universe. To these, one must add the numerous examples of animals, real or fictitious (spiders, mules, apes, scorpions), which play important roles in her narratives. These characters, both human and animal, provide a sordid, nightmarish view of the world. Many of the short stories and novels are based on her own dreams, nightmares and experiences, as well as those of her friends (Garfield, 1985, p. 32). By expressing her repressed instincts or irrational phobias, these narratives also served to exorcise demons.

Somers's style and structure gain power as her vision becomes richer and more complex. In her last three novels, she juxtaposes several narratives together in order to provide multiple foci for her world of existential distress. The various texts, including excerpts from the Bible, cookbooks, and the Koran, suggest alternate points of view in the exploration of human condition. The structural complexity of these works reflects the complexity of themes in the various threads of the story. Thus, the author challenges the reader to make sense of the pieces of the puzzle.

Somers's originality clearly rests in her unusual presentation of themes—a blend of realism, fantasy, and absurdity—written in lyrical, symbolic, and poetic language. She is a rebellious writer. Her work is polemical, her style vigorous, with touches of humor and keen sarcasm. Her fiction, a chaotic quest for a radical new meaning for humankind, has won her a place among the most accomplished writers in Latin American letters.

SURVEY OF CRITICISM

Armonía Somers is a novelist and short story writer whose critical reputation is still gathering momentum. Although her works have received attention from well-known literary critics in her own country, such as Mario Benedetti, Walter Rela, Angel Rama, Jorge Rufinelli, Alberto Zum Felde, and Arturo Sergio Visca, there is still a lack of studies about her and her works, a lack that needs to be filled by perceptive, well-informed critical essays. With the exception of Evelyn Picón Garfield, in her book entitled *Women's Voices from Latin America* (1985), most of the articles written about Somers deal almost exclusively with the author's initial works.

Angel Rama, Armonía Somers's earliest and most perceptive critic, alluded in one of his first essays to the strange, lyrical, and unusual quality of the Uruguayan writer's prose (1963, p. 30). Alberto Cousté (1967), in "Armonía Somers, al este del paraíso," examines and discusses the theme and style of Somers's earlier works: *La mujer desnuda*, *De miedo en miedo*, and *Todos los cuentos*. In her article "Yo soplo desde el páramo," Garfield analyzes the theme of death in Somer's short stories, emphasizing the relevance of this topic in her narrative. Later, in Garfield's book *Women's Voices from Latin America*, she traces the development of various themes (death, love, relationships, and so on) through an analysis of all Somers's writings published until 1985. This is the most complete evaluation of Armonía Somers's work to date.

BIBLIOGRAPHY

Works by Armonía Somers

La mujer desnuda. Montevideo: Clima, 1950.
El derrumbamiento. Montevideo: Ediciones Salamanca, 1953.
La calle del viento norte y otros cuentos. Montevideo: Arca, 1963.
De miedo en miedo (Los manuscritos del río). Montevideo: Arca, 1965.

Todos los cuentos, 1953–67. 2 vols. Montevideo: Arca, 1967.
Un retrato para Dickens. Montevideo: Arca, 1969.
Muerte por alacrán. Buenos Aires: Editorial Calicanto, 1979.
Tríptico Darwiniano. Montevideo: Ediciones de la Torre, 1982.
Sólo los elefantes encuentran mandrágora. Buenos Aires: Editorial Legasa, 1983.
Viaje al corazón del día. Elegía por un secreto amor. Montevideo: Arca, 1986.

Translations of Armonía Somers

Hertelendy, Susana, trans. "Madness." *The Eye of the Heart: Short Stories from Latin America.* Ed. Barbara Howes. New York and Indianapolis: Avon Books, 1973. Pp. 419–21.
Hohenstein, Anne, trans. "The Immigrant." *Diana's Second Almanac.* Ed. T. Ahern. Providence, R.I.: Diana's Bimonthly Press, 1980. Pp. 4–35.
Manguel, Alberto, trans. "The Fall." *Other Fires: Short Fiction by Latin American Women.* Ed. Alberto Manguel. Toronto: Lester & Orpen Dennys, 1986. Pp. 9–23.

Works about Armonía Somers

Araújo, Helena. "Armonía Somers: *El derrumbamiento,*" "Armonía y su Tríptico Darwiniano." *La Scherezada Criolla: Ensayos sobre escritura femenina latino-americana.* Bogotá: Universidad Nacional de Colombia, 1989. Pp. 75–81; 171–73.
———. "Escritura femenina: sobre un cuento de Armonía Somers." *Cuéntame tu vida* (Cali, Colombia) 5 (1981):19–24.
"Armonía Somers: los lobos esteparios." *Capítulo Oriental* (Montevideo) 33 (1968):563.
Benedetti, Mario. "*El derrumbamiento.*" *Número* (Montevideo) 5, 22 (Jan.-Mar. 1953):102–103.
———. *Literatura uruguaya siglo XX.* 2d ed. Montevideo: Alfa, 1969. Pp. 205–09.
Cotelo, Rubén. *Narradores uruguayos.* Caracas: Monte Avila, 1969. Pp. 149–70.
Cousté, Alberto. "Armonía Somers, al este del paraíso." *Primera Plana* (Buenos Aires) 242 (1967):52–53.
Espada, Roberto de. "Armonía Somers o el dolor de la literatura." *Maldoror* (Montevideo) (1st trimester 1972):62–66.
Garfield, Evelyn Picón. "Armonía Somers." *Women's Voices from Latin America.* Detroit: Wayne State University Press, 1985. Pp. 31–51.
Rama, Angel. *La generación crítica 1939–1969.* Montevideo: Arca, 1972. Pp. 29, 96, 97.
———. "La insólita literatura de Somers: la fascinación del horror." *Marcha* (Montevideo) 1188 (1963):27–30.
———. "Raros y malditos en la literatura uruguaya." *Marcha* (Montevideo) 1319 (1966):30–31.
Rela, Walter. *Diccionario de escritores uruguayos.* Montevideo: Edición de la Plaza, 1986. Pp. 124–27.
"Testimonio: Una gran escritora uruguaya (A.S.) habla para *Rumbos.*" *Rumbos* (Montevideo) 1 (Oct. 3, 1969):8–9.
Visca, Arturo Sergio. *Antología del cuento uruguayo: los nuevos.* Montevideo: Ediciones de la Banda Oriental, 1968. Pp. 11–12.
———. "El mundo narrativo de Armonía Somers." *Nueva antología del cuento uruguayo.* Montevideo: Ediciones de la Banda Oriental, 1976. Pp. 260–63.
Zum Felde, Alberto. *Indice crítico de la literatura hispanoamericana.* 2d ed. Madrid: Aguilar, 1964. P. 501.

ALFONSINA STORNI
(1892–1938)
Argentina

María A. Salgado

BIOGRAPHY

Alfonsina Storni's works are a reflection of her eventful, dramatic, and often painful life. Her birth, on May 29, 1892, in Sala Caprisca (Switzerland), was the first unlikely event of her erratic fate. She was born away from Argentina simply because her Italian-Swiss parents, Alfonso and Paulina, were in Europe visiting family and friends. Alfonsina would be four years old before her family returned to the town of San Juan, Argentina, where her father and his older brothers owned a beer factory. Soon after their return their business began to fail, and the family's social position and emotional stability rapidly deteriorated. Alfonso began to drink heavily and to disappear on mysterious hunting trips. Despite her family's problems, not all was sadness in Alfonsina's childhood. On the contrary, she started attending school and spent many happy hours roaming the countryside with her older brother and sister.

By 1900 the family's economic situation became untenable, and the Stornis moved to Rosario, Argentina. At first, her mother Paulina supported the family by sewing. Later, Alfonso opened a café which he ran with the help of his wife and four children. When in 1904 this new venture also failed, Paulina and her two girls went back to sewing. Family responsibilities became almost unbearable for the thirteen-year-old girl when, in 1906, she was forced to support her family by taking a job at a hat factory.

A more promising future opened up for Alfonsina the following year, when she had the occasion to act in a play performed by a company on tour in Rosario. Her performance was good enough for another company, that of José Tallaví, to offer her a permanent position. She toured the country for one year before quitting when she found herself unable to tolerate the stress of acting and the upheavals of life on the road. Upon returning to Rosario, Alfonsina found that her mother had remarried and moved away. Aware of the need to further her education, she entered the Normal School at Coronda. Storni supported herself by working at the school and secretly singing in a bar on weekends. She graduated two years later with the title of "Rural Teacher."

By 1911 all seemed to be going her way. She began to teach at an elementary school in Rosario, and her first poems were published in the local newspapers. Unfortunately, fate intervened again: She fell in love with a married man and found herself pregnant at the age of nineteen. Not wanting to create problems for her lover and trying to avoid personal rejection, Alfonsina resigned her teaching job and moved into the anonymous world of Buenos Aires. There, she worked at a succession of low-paying jobs before finding a more secure position in 1914.

In the meantime, her son Alejandro Alfonso had been born in April 1912. That same year the journal *Fray Mocho* published her first short story, "De la vida" (About life), a bitter attack on the hypocrisy of the middle class. From this time on, slowly but firmly, Storni began to infiltrate her country's male-dominated literary scene. By 1916, the year she published her overly melodramatic and sentimental first book of verse, *La inquietud del rosal* (Uneasiness of the rosebush), she became a member of the prestigious literary group *Nosotros* and a regular contributor to the journal *La Nota* (The note). In this journal, and later in *Nosotros* and *La Nación*, she published most of her feminist writings. In 1917 she was able to secure a teaching position and was awarded the Yearly Prize of the National Council of Women.

Storni's next three books appeared in rapid succession, *El dulce daño* (1918; Sweet sorrow), *Irremediablemente* (1919; Irremediably), and *Languidez* (1920; Languor). The last one received two prestigious prizes: first place for the Buenos Aires Municipal Prize and second for the National Prize for Literature. Storni's fame was growing in 1920, and at the young age of twenty-eight, she became a regular contributor to the prestigious newspaper *La Nación*, for which she wrote under her own name and the pseudonym Tao-Lao. She also joined the literary group "Anaconda," headed by the well-known Uruguayan short-story writer Horacio Quiroga.

The year 1921 marked a new direction for Storni. She began a long association with the Teatro Infantil Labardén (Labardén Children's Theater), for which she taught classes and wrote many of the plays performed by the students. With this new position Storni found the means to express her affinity for the dramatic arts and to apply the knowledge she had acquired during her acting stint with the theater company. Her dedication to this job was rewarded with other appointments, first at the Drama and Declamation School (1923) and later at the Conservatory of Music and Declamation (1926), all in Buenos Aires.

In 1925 Storni published *Ocre* (Ochre), a book that marks a departure from her earlier romantic, self-centered themes. A collection of prose poems, *Poemas de amor* (Love poems), appeared in 1926. The year 1927 saw the performance of her full-length play *El amo del mundo* (The master of the world). The play closed almost immediately because of the negative reception of public and critics alike. Undaunted, Storni began to write a second play, *La técnica de Mister Dougall* (Mister Dougall's technique), a work she completed but never saw performed or published.

Storni made the first of her two trips to Europe in 1930. While in Spain she was impressed by that country's literary scene, dominated at that time by Federico García Lorca, Rafael Alberti, Luis Cernuda, and the other members of the Generation of 1927. Her writings after this date began to evidence the effects of her literary discoveries. Her new approach to writing theater is obvious in her two full-length plays, *Dos farsas pirotécnicas* (1932; Two pyrotechnical farces). After her second trip to Spain in 1934, a similar experimentation became evident in her last books of verse, *Mundo de siete pozos* (1934; World of seven wells) and *Mascarilla y trébol* (1938; Mask and clover).

In 1935 Storni underwent a radical mastectomy. When the cancer spread in 1938, she no longer had the will to fight. Instead, she followed the path already taken by two of her friends, the writers Leopoldo Lugones (Argentina) and Horacio Quiroga (Uruguay), committing suicide by drowning in the Mar del Plata on October 25, 1938.

MAJOR THEMES

Being poor, a woman, the mother of an illegitimate son, and lacking in formal education were drawbacks that forced Alfonsina Storni to face almost insurmountable challenges merely to survive. The fact that she succeeded and became a respected teacher and a much admired poet is to her credit. Inevitably, however, her disappointments, the prejudices she faced, and the accompanying spiritual solitude she had to combat most of her life, affected her literary themes. This is particularly true in her earlier books, the ones that established her reputation as a sensitive and rebellious ''poetess,'' whose verses were seen as characterized, paradoxically, by erotic passion and a strong note of feminist protest. It is true that these two themes—love and feminism—predominate in her works, but they are not the only ones. She also wrote of art, of her concerns for humankind, of her intense feelings for nature—represented particularly by the images of the moon and of the changing sea—and she wrote of the alienation of city life, and of the pervasive presence of death.

Storni's first volume, *La inquietud del rosal* (1916), though containing poems of apprenticeship, also announces her major themes and her intense, conscious dedication to the craft of poetry. Above all, in poems like ''La loba'' (The she-wolf) it reveals a spirit unafraid of social prejudices and willing to give free expression to her feminine yearnings and feelings. Because of Storni's youth and her unawareness of literary trends, it is not surprising that *La inquietud* is marred by her outmoded adherence to the fast-declining influence of what was then mistakenly defined as early Modernist tenets and of the even more distant echoes of Romanticism. Her book had resonance, but it was mostly due to what was then considered Storni's audaciously feminine tone. In fact, the book is of uneven merit. Its relative lack of worth was recognized by Storni, who never reprinted it and who did not choose any of its verses for her *Antología poética* (1938; Poetic anthology) which appeared posthumously. Yet the main difference between this book and the three that quickly followed is a matter of form rather than theme, since all four speak of the inner self.

El dulce daño was written when love (sweet sorrow) was paramount in her life. At the time she was criticized for the erotic nature of some of her texts. The book, divided in two parts, is arranged to tell a story. In the first part the poetic voice speaks to her lover. The poem "Viaje finido" (Completed trip) marks the end of the love affair, and it serves as a transition to the second part, which begins with "Tú me quieres blanca" (You want me pure). This poem is an angry battle-cry introducing a series of texts in which Storni speaks of her emotional displacement in a world ruled by social prejudices. "Tú me quieres blanca" itself is one of the strongest poetic indictments against the *macho* attitude of the Spanish American male, who being a libertine wants the object of his affection to be "pure." Not since Sor Juana,* in colonial times, had a woman written so artfully about this topic.

Storni's next volume, *Irremediablemente* (1919), received good reviews. It retells, with improved technical command, the story of her deeply felt love experience. Again, the poems are arranged to tell a story. As in a novel, they are structured into two sections, a prologue, and an epilogue. The first part recaptures "humble, amorous, and passionate" moments of her life, and the second deals with the contrasting "bitter, sylvan, and tempestuous" times. This book contains well-known feminist poems like "Hombre pequeñito" (Little man) and a few, such as "Peso ancestral" (Ancestral weight), "Bien pudiera ser" (It could well be), and "Veinte siglos" (Twenty centuries), which show Storni's growing preoccupation with voicing the collective concerns of women.

The year 1919 was a very prolific one for Storni. She continued to write on the relations between the sexes not only in her poetry, but also in six short stories, two short novels, and a series of essays, all of them published by well-known journals. The last book of poetry of Storni's first phase, *Languidez* (1920), speaks of her need to move in another direction by announcing in the opening remarks that this volume "closes a modality." She dedicated this book to those who like herself "have never fulfilled a single one of their dreams." As these words indicate, the overall tone of the book is one of despair. According to Rachel Phillips (1975), in it Storni suggests that poetry and love are "the sacrificial acts humanity ignores or, worse yet, misjudges" (p. 39).

Ocre (1925) heralds the literary phase which Storni admitted she preferred. Yet, at first glance, the changes are not obvious. She does abandon her reliance on similes in favor of metaphors, but there are no drastic changes in form, or even in content. In fact, three-fourths of the book consists of traditional sonnets dealing with male-female relations, or with praises of women in which she empathizes with their plight (such as "Palabras a Delmira Agustini" [Words to Delmira Agustini*]). The tone, however, is different, for in *Ocre*, she introduces a highly ironic mode, characteristic of her mature works. She writes of her bitter, though somewhat more accepting, attitude toward the growing "poverty of her spiritual and amorous life" (Rosenbaum, 1945, p. 213). According to Rachel Phillips (1975), *Ocre* is a book of transition in which Storni continues to maintain the imagery of male-female tensions, while dismissing the male partner as superficial and incapable of passion, and endowing the female with a very complex personality. Phillips concludes that the struggle "exhausts and defeats the 'yo' ['I'] of these poems" (pp. 45–46). One year later Storni published *Poemas de amor*; although translated into French and published that same year, this book never attained the acclaim of her previous works. After *Poemas*, nine long years elapsed before Storni published another book of poetry. Instead, she concentrated on writing for the theater.

The first play Storni wrote for adults, *El amo del mundo*, opened March 10, 1927. It closed three days later. The reasons for its failure paralleled, in a sense, the failure of her first book of poems. Both had the technical defects of a typical beginner's work, and, in addition, both incorporated her immediate, "raw," autobiographical experiences. This play, originally titled "Dos mujeres" (Two women), reflects Storni's profound cynicism. The plot deals with a love triangle involving a superficial middle-aged man, an independent, mature woman, and a flirtatious coquette. "The crux of the play is the inability of a mature man to accept as his wife a woman of equal maturity and independence who is an unmarried mother" (Phillips, p. 62).

According to Sonia Jones, the failure of *El amo* prevented the performance of Storni's second play, *La técnica de Mister Dougall*. First, the actress for whom she wrote it showed no interest, and, to make matters worse, Storni claimed that the play "had hit a stone wall" as two different producers refused to read it (quoted by Jones, 1979, p. 91). In Jones's opinion, the fears of another failure were unfounded. The play did present the same thesis as the earlier one, but Storni had been able to distance herself from her feelings. As a result, "the technical improvements far outweigh the defects in this second play" (Jones, p. 93).

Following Storni's 1930 trip to Spain, she published two dramas that contrasted sharply with the traditional repertoire of the Argentine stage of her time. The two plays, entitled *Cimbelina en 1900 y pico* and *Polixena y la cocinerita*, are based, respectively, on Shakespeare's *Cymbeline* and Euripides's *Hecuba*. Her plays often involve grotesque distortions, and she describes her *Dos farsas pirotécnicas*, using the model of Spaniard Ramón del Valle-Inclán's *esperpento*, as life seen in a concave mirror. The original texts were political plays in which the women appeared only as minor characters. However, the deforming technique of the *esperpento* allows Storni to "mirror" the models inaccurately in the farces. Thus, she re-creates modern plays in which strong women become the main protagonists. These highly experimental farces show her concern for avant-garde techniques, a concern that would also become prominent in the poetry she wrote after her second trip to Spain in 1934.

The only other dramatic text for adults written by Storni was an entr'acte, entitled *Intermedio poético* (Poetic interlude). She wrote it for Carlos Cucullu's two-act drama *Judith*. Her text describes how the Old Testament heroine of his play saves her city. It was performed on August 18, 1938, and later published in libretto form (Jones, 1979, p. 107).

The many plays Storni wrote for the Children's Theater were written to be performed *for* and *by* children. As such, they are less technically and thematically complex than regular plays. Instead, they emphasize simplicity of form, clarity of exposition, fantasy, and obvious humor. A selection of these plays was published in 1950 by R. J. Roggero under the title *Teatro infantil* (Children's theater). Of these, the most elaborate and interesting is "Blanco . . . Negro . . . Blanco" (white . . . black . . . white), a "poetic fantasy" written in the *commedia dell'arte* tradition with Pierrot and Colombine as the main characters. Storni patterned it after a play by Argentine Leopoldo Lugones, *El payaso negro* (The black clown). Some other plays included in this volume are: "El dios de los pájaros" (The god of birds), "Los degolladores de estatuas" (The executioners of statues), "Pedro y Pedrito" (Pedro and Pedrito), and "Un sueño en el camino" (A dream in the path). Phillips believes that Storni's plays prove her talent as a dramatist and as a poet. She explains that Storni's "dramatic talent is what is best about her poetry," but by the same token, "her poetic intuition" is what brings to life her children's plays. Phillips also asserts that Storni's single theatrical failure was more than amply compensated by the "ironic profundity of her farces" and the "lively charm" of her children's plays (p. 80).

Storni's return to poetry in 1934 signals a totally new modality within her works, a modality that she considered her best and most important contribution, although it was never favored by her reading public or by the critical circles that determined the "merit" of literary creations in her world. For critics and readers alike, by 1934 Storni had lost her ability to move the heart and was making a vain and anachronistic effort to create a cerebral, avant-garde poetry of abstract images. In *Mundo de siete pozos* (1934; an abstract metaphor that refers to the human head, literally a "world of seven wells"), and for the first time in her poetic career, form-conscious Storni abandoned regularity of line and strophic composition to adopt the irregular structure of rhythm. She also experimented with surrealistic imagery achieved through the fragmentation of reality.

The two most powerful themes of this book are those of urban alienation and death—now associated persistently with the sea. The thought of finding peace in its icy depths becomes an obsession. In the first half of *Mundo*, Storni describes objects and scenes from new and unexpected angles. Her emphasis on detail, used to understand better the whole, is evident in poems like "Mundo de siete pozos" and "Retrato de García Lorca" (Portrait of García Lorca). At times the poems create the disjointed impression of a world about to disintegrate. This is the case in "Ojo" (Eye), where she focuses on a world of details and grotesque distortions. The emphasis is on seemingly dismembered beings or truncated, distorted buildings. In the section "Motivos de ciudad" (Motifs of the city), Storni connects urban alienation to the emptiness of the poetic I. This association is evident in "Calle" (Street), "Plaza de invierno" (Winter Plaza), and "Selvas de mi ciudad" (Jungles of my city). In the last section of the book, Storni returns to the sonnet form to write of her subjective feelings, feelings close to those she expressed in her earlier poems.

For Phillips, this book shows the first sign of what in *Mascarilla* will become Storni's assimilation of an aesthetic of the grotesque: "The poetry which results here, and to a greater degree in *Mascarilla y trébol*, is far more *esperpéntico* in the true meaning of the word than were the 'farsas pirotécnicas' of 1931" (p. 84). Not surprisingly, the feeling the book leaves with the reader is one of extreme pessimism and despair.

Mascarilla y trébol (1938), her last book, contains fifty-two unrhymed sonnets, called "anti-sonnets" by Storni. In them, she intensifies her use of nightmarish sea imagery to portray the depths of her grief. Formally, this book is marked by her control of technique and her command of style and language. The subtitle, *Círculos imantados* (Magnetic circles), points to her poetic elaboration of scientific and pseudoscientific spiritualist theories dealing particularly with the magical and metaphysical significance of the circle. In *Mascarilla*, the abstract nature of Storni's poetic inspiration does not make for easy comprehension. She foresaw this problem and commented in her introductory "Brief Explanation" on the obscurity of her poems. They were, she said, "the individual results of moments of near loss of consciousness," written in moments of trance-like, intense inspiration. In *Mascarilla*, Storni abandoned her earlier intimate preoccupation with love and passion (demythified in "A Eros" [To Eros], the first poem of this collection), to give herself wholly to her poetic craft. Poetry justifies her existence and has the potential to free her of emotional burdens, allowing for a more transcendent vision. She sings to this liberating force in the last poem of the book, "A Madona Poesía" (To Madonna poetry). *Mascarilla* gives shape to a vision that combines the sights of the physical world with the private world of dreams.

Cancer crossed Storni's path at this moment of her development as a writer. She had attained poetic maturity and was prepared to offer her best works, but it was not to be. The day after her suicide, her poem "Voy a dormir" (I am going to sleep) appeared in the newspaper.

SURVEY OF CRITICISM

During her lifetime Storni's poetry was the object of both flattering adulation and bitter attacks. Without a doubt, the fact that she was a woman had a great deal to do with the critics' attitudes. She was much praised as Argentina's foremost woman poet, indeed, as one of the best three living Spanish American women poets; together with Gabriela Mistral* of Chile, and Juana de Ibarbourou* of Uruguay, Storni was honored, early in 1938, by the University of Montevideo. But she was also chastised for her ardent feminism and her erotic poems. The view that has prevailed is that of the rebellious feminist poet of her early years, of the writer who fought back with aggressive insolence against the attacks aimed at her personal life. These early poems are indeed the most striking—though not necessarily the most poetic—and Storni criticism has never recovered from their sensationalism. The fact is, however, that as time passed she did temper her voice, learning to develop an ironic sense of humor, but most critics never noticed the change. To this day, some still continue to assert her failure as a poet, basing themselves on what they consider her inability to transcend her personal problems—a defect only found in her early writings.

Conflicting opinions as to the value of Storni's works were openly aired in reviews and articles written during her lifetime. *La inquietud del rosal* did not fare badly. It was, after all, a first book. But the general laudatory tone with which it was received soon changed. Critics began to disapprove of her tendency to delve into openly sexual themes. Reviews of her poetry through the 1920s leveled strong attacks against her works. Some accused her of "undressing herself" in public and advised her that, as a woman, she ought not to write poetry but to inspire it; others insisted that Storni, like all women poets, had been unable to overcome her sexual instincts, thus causing her poetry to remain in an erotic sphere (opinions quoted by Phillips, pp. 29–30 and pp. 40–41). Writing in 1975, Phillips notes that it is particularly ironic that, while during Storni's early career critics attacked her for writing feminine, erotic poetry, in later years they offered "equally adverse criticism . . . for having 'lost her lyricism'," when, according to Phillips, what had occurred was that Storni "did in fact emerge from the 'woman poet' stereotype" (p. 41).

Another attack frequently leveled at Storni during her lifetime had less to do with the merit of her poetry than with the fact that she was writing in an age of transition. Most critics classify her works within the ill-defined area of post-Modernism. She started writing in the wane of Modernism, a movement she clearly admired and followed in her early books, and she did not belong to the Vanguardia (avant-garde) until it too had began to wane. As a result, her works stand outside the poetic fashions of her day. But critics have insisted on placing her within the narrow confines of established literary movements, ignoring that her strength lies in her originality. Thus, some attack her works for not being in the Modernist vein of "art-for-art's-sake," while others attack them for not being sufficiently *engagé* ("committed politically"). She answered this last objection in an interview quoted by Sonia Jones: "From the spiritual point of view . . . I see no reason why fruit should be more useful than flowers. A flower is useful because it is beautiful. And there have been times when the contemplation of a rose has been of greater benefit to me than a book of moral and philosophical maxims" (p. 53).

Criticism of Storni's poetry maintains much this same tenor until the publication of her radically different last two books. Then the attacks concentrated on her new poetic style. Storni had expected a negative reaction. She had already published selected poems in the local press and had read others to some of her literary friends. She had found little private support and expected even less sympathy from public reviews. She was right. Most critics complained that her musicality had changed "into a severe, harsh, and obscure poetry [which lacked] the grace and voluptuousness that used to be characteristic [of her previous volumes]" (quoted by Jones, p. 83). Years later, evaluating her writings from a more modern viewpoint, Julieta Gómez Paz considered her last book not to be, as most critics had claimed, a series of abstract, cerebral poems but, rather, Storni's moving final look at the physical world she so strongly loved (1966, p. 87).

Understandably, with the passage of time, critics have become more objective. Two of the first to herald this change were María Teresa Orosco and Arturo Capdevilla. They published their thorough overviews of her life, works, and critical reception in 1940 and 1948, respectively. One of the earliest and most valuable studies written in English appeared between those two dates in Sidonia Carmen Rosenbaum's, *Modern Women Poets of Spanish America* (1945). Another valuable early study was done by Helena Percas in *La poesía femenina argentina (1810–1950)* (Argentine feminine poetry [1810–1950]), published in 1958.

During the last twenty years, new perspectives on women's writing and on traditional sexual roles have changed the way critics view Storni's place in Hispanic letters. Of particular value have been the critical studies written by women. One of the earliest to undertake a reevaluation was Julieta Gómez Paz (1966). More thorough and modern in her approach was Rachel Phillips (1975). She examines Storni's work with the additional purpose of appealing for a single standard of literary criticism, not a sexist one. Phillips studies Storni's works, concentrating on her transformation from "poetess to poet." Her conclusion points out that at "the end of her life she was in touch with a poetic intuition that is truly inspired and inspiring" (p. 122).

Sonia Jones (1979) took a more traditional approach. Her book researches in detail Storni's life and evaluates all the genres the poet employed. For Jones, Storni could be characterized as a fighter. She sees her principal value in her function as a role model for other women artists: " . . . her ultimate significance as a writer rests not so much with how she expressed herself, as it does with what she stood for and what she was as a human being" (p. 132).

The many studies dedicated to Storni's work have begun to establish her rightful place in modern Hispanic letters. There is no doubt that as one of Argentina's early feminists she worked hard to secure sexual equality, and her life and her accomplishments have served as living examples to other women. As a writer, and within Spanish literary canons, she wrote works of great value and originality. Thus, it may be asserted that her life and her works have been fundamental in establishing the foundations of contemporary feminist discourse in Hispanic letters.

BIBLIOGRAPHY

Works by Alfonsina Storni

"De la vida" (short story). *Fray Mocho* (Buenos Aires) 1, 23 (Oct. 4, 1912):n.p.
La inquietud del rosal. Buenos Aires: La Facultad, 1916.
El dulce daño. Buenos Aires: Sociedad Cooperativa Editorial Limitada, 1918.
Irremediablemente. . . . Buenos Aires: Sociedad Cooperativa Editorial Limitada, 1919.
Una golondrina (novel). *Hebe* (Buenos Aires) 7 (1919):3–26. Reprinted in *Cinco cartas y Una golondrina*.
Un alma elegante (novel). *La novela elegante* (Buenos Aires) 1, 3 (Dec. 15, 1919).
Languidez. Buenos Aires: Sociedad Cooperativa Editorial Limitada, 1920.
Las mejores poesías de los mejores poetas: Alfonsina Storni. Barcelona: Cervantes, 1923.
Ocre. Buenos Aires: Babel, 1925.
Poemas de amor (prose poems). Buenos Aires: Nosotros, 1926.
"Poemas." *Poemas de Gabriela Mistral, Juana de Ibarbourou, Delmira Agustini, Alfonsina Storni*. Bogotá: Ediciones Colombia, 1926.
El amo del mundo (play). *Bambalinas* (Buenos Aires) 9, 470 (Apr. 16, 1927):1–39.
"Entretelones de un estreno." *Nosotros* (Buenos Aires) 21, 215 (Apr. 1927):48–55.
"Autodemolición." *Repertorio Americano* (San José, Costa Rica) 11, 21 (June 7, 1930):329, 331.
Dos farsas pirotécnicas (theater). Buenos Aires: Cooperativa Editorial "Buenos Aires," 1932. Contains "Cimbelina en 1900 y pico" and "Polixena y la cocinerita."
"Respuesta a una encuesta: 'Una generación se juzga a sí misma'." *Nosotros* (Buenos Aires) 26, 279–280 (Aug.-Sept. 1932):158–59.
Mundo de siete pozos. Buenos Aires: Tor, 1934.
Antología poética. Compiled by Alfonsina Storni. Buenos Aires: Espasa-Calpe Argentina, 1938. Reprinted: Buenos Aires: Losada, 1956.
"Entre un par de maletas a medio abrir y la manecilla del reloj." *Revista Nacional* (Montevideo) (Feb. 1938):214–22. Reprinted: Ed. José Forgione. Buenos Aires: Talleres Gráficos de Ediciones Católicas Argentinas, 1939.
Mascarilla y trébol. Círculos imantados. Buenos Aires: El Ateneo, 1938.
"Alrededor de la muerte de Lugones." *Nosotros* (Buenos Aires) 2d series. 3, 26–28 (May-July 1939):218–21.
Antología poética. Prol. Alfonsina Storni. Buenos Aires, Mexico City: Espasa-Calpe Argentina, 1940.
Obra poética. Buenos Aires: Roggero-Ronal, 1946.
Teatro infantil. Buenos Aires: Ramón J. Roggero y Cía., 1950. Contains: "Negro . . . Blanco . . . Negro," "Pedro y Pedrito," "Jorge y su conciencia," "Un sueño en el camino," "Los degolladores de estatuas," "El dios de los pájaros."
Los mejores versos. Buenos Aires: Nuestra América, 1958.
Cinco cartas y Una golondrina. Buenos Aires: Instituto Amigos del Libro Argentino, 1959.
Alfonsina Storni. Antología. Ed. María de Villarino. Buenos Aires: Ministerio de Educación y Justicia, Dirección General de Cultura, 1961.
Poesías de Alfonsina Storni. Prol. Alejandro Alfonso Storni. Buenos Aires: Universitaria de Buenos Aires, 1961.

Alfonsina Storni. Commemorative ed. Ed. Carlos A. Andreola. Buenos Aires: Nobis, 1963.
Obra poética completa. 2d ed. Buenos Aires: Sociedad Editora Latino Americana, 1964.
Poesías sueltas. Buenos Aires: Sociedad Editora Latino Americana, 1964.
Obras completas. Buenos Aires: Sociedad Editora Latino Americana, 1976.

Translations of Alfonsina Storni

Alfonsina Storni: Argentina's Feminist Poet. The Poetry in Spanish with English Translations. Ed. Florence Williams Talamantes. Los Cerrillos, N.M.: San Marcos Press, 1975.
Benson, Rachel, ed. and trans. *Nine Latin American Poets*. New York: Las Américas, 1968. Pp. 252–81.
Freeman, Marion. *Alfonsina Storni: Selected Poems*. Franconia, N.Y.: White Wine Press, 1988.
Humphries, Rolfe, Muna Lee, Richard O'Connell, and Donald Dwenish Walsh, trans. *Anthology of Contemporary Latin American Poetry*. Bilingual ed. Ed. Dudley Fitts. Norfolk, Conn.: New Directions, 1947. Pp. 514–21.
Johnson, Mildred E., ed. and trans. *Swans, Cygnets, and Owl. An Anthology of Modern Poetry in Spanish America*. Introd. John S. Brushwood. Columbia: University of Missouri Press, 1956. Pp. 150–55.
Loos, Dorothy Scott, trans. *Alfonsina Storni—Selected Poems*. Brattleboro, Vt.: Amana Books, 1988.

Works about Alfonsina Storni

Andreola, Carlos Alberto. *Alfonsina Storni, inédita: revelación y eglogario de documentos estrictamente desconocidos, de su vida y de su obra*. Buenos Aires: Cabant & Cía., 1974.
―――. *Alfonsina Storni. Vida-Talento-Soledad. Primera biografía integral y documentada*. Buenos Aires: Plus Ultra, 1976.
Baralis, Marta. *Contribución a la bibliografía de Alfonsina Storni*. Buenos Aires: Fondo Nacional de las Artes, 1964.
Capdevilla, Arturo. *Alfonsina. Epoca, dolor y obra de la poetisa Alfonsina Storni*. Buenos Aires: Centurión, 1948.
Etchenique, Nira. *Alfonsina Storni*. Buenos Aires: La Mandrágora, 1958.
Gironella, María de las Mercedes. *Alfonsina Storni y Teresa de Jesús*. Buenos Aires: Anaconda, 1940.
Fernández Moreno, César. "Dos épocas en la poesía de Alfonsina Storni." *Revista Hispánica Moderna* 24 (1958):27–35.
―――. *Situación de Alfonsina Storni*. Santa Fé, Argentina: Castelleví, 1959.
Figueras, Miriam, and María Teresa Martínez. *Alfonsina Storni. Análisis de poemas y antología*. [Montevideo]: Librería Editorial Ciencias. [1979].
Gómez Paz, Julieta. *Leyendo a Alfonsina Storni*. Buenos Aires: Losada, 1966.
Jones, Sonia. *Alfonsina Storni*. TWAS 519. Boston: G. K. Hall, 1979.
Kirkpatrick, Gwen. "Alfonsina Storni: 'Aquel micromundo poético'." *Modern Language Notes* 99, 2 (1984):386–92.
Koch, Dolores. "Delmira, Alfonsina, Juana y Gabriela." *Revista Iberoamericana* 132–33 (July-Dec. 1985):723–29.

Mañach, Jorge. "Liberación de Alfonsina Storni." *Revista Iberoamericana* (Mexico) 1, 1 (May 1939):73–76.

Nalé Roxlo, Conrado, and Mabel Mármol. *Genio y figura de Alfonsina Storni.* 2d ed. Buenos Aires: Universitaria de Buenos Aires, 1964.

Orosco, María Teresa. *Alfonsina Storni.* Buenos Aires: Imprenta de la Universidad, 1940. Pp. 75–237.

Percas, Helena. "Alfonsina Storni y la Generación del 16." *La poesía femenina argentina (1810–1950).* Madrid: Ediciones Cultura Hispánica, 1958. Pp. 77–249.

Pérez Blanco, Lucrecio. *La poesía de Alfonsina Storni.* Madrid: [n.p.], 1975.

Phillips, Rachel. *Alfonsina Storni. From Poetess to Poet.* London: Tamesis Books, 1975.

Rosenbaum, Sidonia Carmen. "Alfonsina Storni." *Modern Women Poets of Spanish America.* New York: Hispanic Institute, 1945. Pp. 205–227.

Titiev, Janice Geasler. "Alfonsina Storni's *Mundo de siete pozos*: Form, Freedom, and Fantasy." *Kentucky Romance Quarterly* 23 (1976):185–97.

———. "Alfonsina Storni's *Poemas de amor*: Submissive Woman, Liberated Poet." *Journal of Spanish Studies: Twentieth Century* 8, 3 (1980):279–92.

———. "The Poetry of Dying in Alfonsina Storni's Last Book." *Hispania* 68 (Sept. 1985):467–73.

Zardoya, Concha. "La muerte en la poesía femenina latinoamericana." *Cuadernos Americanos* (Mexico) 71, 5 (Sept.-Oct. 1953):233–70.

MARTA TRABA
(1930–1983)
Argentina, Colombia

Celia Correas de Zapata
Translated by John Benson

BIOGRAPHY

The life of Marta Traba cannot be considered separately from her literary legacy. An observer of her times, she entitled one of her novels *Homérica latina* (1979; Latin Homerica), to highlight both her feeling of personal odyssey and the common destiny of the nations of Latin America. Someone once defined Traba as a ''cultural agitator,'' though she was much more than that. She raised her impassioned, volcanic, Amazonian voice throughout the hemisphere in the vanguard of literary and artistic criticism, writing essays, founding art magazines, teaching art and literature in the universities, and denouncing the abuse of the oppressed in her criticism as well as in her novels.

Traba's essays on contemporary Latin American, U.S., and European art combine her sensitivity as an artist, her introspection as a thinker, and her feeling as a poet. Traba began her literary career with a collection of poems, *Historia natural de la alegría* (1951; A natural history of happiness). From the beginning, from the schooldays in which her independent streak became evident, she recognized the essential loneliness of the writer. Believing in the inescapable social responsibility of the writer, Traba gave evidence of her rebellious nature throughout her career.

Often by personal choice—in her role of visiting professor—though sometimes obliged by governmental fiat, Traba traveled frequently throughout Europe and then Latin America, pausing here and there for varying lengths of time. Although she was born in Argentina, she died a Colombian citizen. She lived in Caracas for a long while and visited Mexico, Puerto Rico, Uruguay, Central America, and, finally, the United States. Her travels showed her how little Latin Americans understand each other and how often the same patterns of corruption and oppression recur from country to country.

In response to her travels and experiences, Traba developed a profound inter-American consciousness, developing into the combative critic and cultural agitator that provoked her expulsion from Colombia by President Carlos Lleras Restrepo. "Marta Traba Forced to Leave Country," reported *El Tiempo* on June 23, 1967, after Traba protested the military's presence at the University of Bogotá. After public opinion condemned the government's action, President Lleras reconsidered and withdrew the demand for her exile on the condition that she not teach. Earlier, she had received the coveted Casa de las Américas Prize in 1966 for her first novel, *Las ceremonias del verano* (The ceremonies of summer). The confrontation with President Lleras occurred the following year, and Angel Rama was surprised by the controversy that this art critic and novelist could stir up in official circles. In 1983, the year of her death, Traba became a Colombian citizen at the invitation of President Belisario Betancourt.

Marta Traba was born to Spanish immigrants in Buenos Aires, Argentina, on January 25, 1930. Her father, Francisco Traba, was a journalist and worked for the magazine *Caras y Caretas*. From 1934 to 1946, Marta received public schooling. After completing high school two years ahead of schedule, she resided in the Belgrano suburb, the background to the first part of *Las ceremonias del verano*. She was only twenty when she graduated in philosophy and letters from the University of Buenos Aires, and for her outstanding performance, she was awarded a scholarship from critic Jorge Romero Brest to spend a summer studying in Chile. Later she would work as both disciple and assistant for Romero Brest in his courses on art history and aesthetics. Her first articles appear in 1949 in Brest's magazine *Ver y Estimar* (Buenos Aires).

Toward the end of 1949 she went to Europe on what turned out to be one of the most important trips of her life. In addition to studying the history of art and aesthetics at the Sorbonne and the Louvre, she met the Colombian journalist Alberto Zalamea whom she married in 1950. The year after her marriage she returned briefly to Buenos Aires and then traveled to Rome, during which time her first son Gustavo was born and her book of poems *Historia natural de la alegría* was published in Buenos Aires. During the two-year stay in Rome's Castelgandolfo, she did research in art history and had experiences that later became a part of *Las ceremonias del verano*, while Zalamea worked as an international correspondent for *El Tiempo* (Bogotá).

On her arrival in Colombia in 1954, Traba was appointed professor of art history at the Universidad de América in Bogotá where she took up residence with her family. By then, established as an art critic, poet, journalist, teacher, wife, mother, and agitator for social change, she launched the magazine *Prisma* and was instrumental in helping the government establish the first Museum of Modern Art in Bogotá on July 27, 1965. She also published her first book on painting in Bogotá, *El museo vacío* (1958; The empty museum), soon to be followed by a stream of notes, articles, and twenty-two books on art culminating in *Siglo XX en las artes plásticas latinamericanas: una guía* (1982–1983; The twentieth century in Latin American plastic arts: a guide), a work supported by a grant from the National Endowment for the Arts and the Organization of American States' Museum of Modern Art.

Traba's knowledge of European and U.S. art is impressive, as seen in her fundamentally lyrical essays on Pablo Picasso and American painters such as Frederick Edwin Church, Edward Hopper, and Milton Avery. Traba distinguishes herself not simply by the breadth of her learning—solidly based on the classics and the Renaissance—and her innate lucidity, capacity for work, and decided opposition to ignorance and government corruption in Latin America; her courage also stands out. She takes on an entire continent with the impassioned conviction of a Joan of Arc as she herself put it in her "Entrevista Atemporal" (*Marta Traba*, 1984, p. 344, Atemporal interview). She initially gave cautious approval to the Cuban Revolution, especially with respect to its literacy campaign, as chronicled in a collection of speeches and articles entitled *El son se quedó en Cuba* (1966; The Music Stayed in Cuba). However, the seventies brought her disillusionment as she denounced the imprisonment of poet Herberto Padilla. Fidel Castro then blacklisted her.

After divorcing Alberto Zalamea, Traba traveled to Chile in 1969 for a conference of Latin American writers and later married Uruguayan critic Angel Rama. In the ensuing ten years she was invited to various Latin American as well as American universities (Middlebury, Vermont, Harvard, MIT, Stanford, San José State University) before finally settling in Washington, D.C., and teaching at the University of Maryland with Angel Rama. When the Department of State denied them resident visas in 1982, Colombian President Betancourt offered both Traba and Rama Colombian citizenship and took up the matter with President Ronald Reagan (*Marta Traba*, 1984, p. 374). By then she had already undergone her first operation for cancer.

In 1983 Traba and Angel Rama went to live in Paris and were invited by Betancourt that same year to attend the First Spanish American Culture Conference in Bogotá. Accompanied by other Latin American literary figures, they boarded a plane in Madrid's Barajas Airport. The plane exploded on takeoff; Traba and Rama and 170 other passengers died in the Spanish aviation accident on November 27, 1983.

After the author's death in 1983, three books were published posthumously: *En cualquier lugar* (novel, 1984), *Mothers and Shadows* (a 1986 translation of *Conversación al sur*) *De la mañana a la noche* (stories, 1986). *Conversación al sur* (1981) and *En cualquier lugar* (1984) were to form a trilogy with the novel *Veinte años no es nada* which was interrupted by her death. Her last posthumous novel, *Casa sin fin*, appeared in 1988.

MAJOR THEMES

Traba's main works fall into three categories: the novel; art criticism; and literary criticism and the essay. As a critic, Traba was basically an essayist capable of penetrating analysis informed by broad learning. Always essentially a critic, she witnesses, testifies, documents, judges, defines, denounces, teaches, and struggles against social injustice and proposes solutions, always with passion and rage, but with increasing anger toward the end of her life. In her "Atemporal Interview," she describes her profession: "Criticism is a matter of constraining, throwing into relief, precisely defining ideas and concepts . . . . South America is a land of apologists, not critics. The spectacle of people kneeling solemnly and pinning medals on one another, calls for, clamors for criticism. I believe that the lack of critical acumen is at the root of all our problems: until we succeed in developing it we are doomed to second-rate nationhood. That's why I try to teach how to discern and to judge—if not justly (who could be right all the time?) then at least in an informed fashion" (*Marta Traba*, 1984, p. 374).

Traba's essays on art are a constant fusion of art and the critical essay. Her theory on the close relationship between critical style and literary style bears close examination. She received the Guggenheim Award in 1968 to write a book later published in Mexico entitled *Dos décadas vulnerables de las artes plásticas latinoamericanas, 1950–1970* (1973; Two vulnerable decades of Latin American plastic arts, 1950–1970), and then continued publishing on Colombian art. It is at this time that she became aware of the interrelatedness of literature and art criticism. Passages from "Angulo Eluard-Picasso" (Eluard-Picasso Angle) and an article on Juan Rulfo would be sufficient to show that both pieces of criticism—one on art and one on literature—are really literary texts written by an essayist (*Marta Traba*, 1984, pp. 225–35). Her literary essay "La literatura se llenó de adioses" (Literature filled with goodbyes) describes a passage in *Pedro Páramo*, the 1955 novel by Rulfo (Mexico).

Damián Bayón singles out three critical voices in her works: (1) the critic-as-judge; (2) the militant critic; and (3) the theoretical critic. Traba's political and social commitment lent militance to her criticism. Although theoreticians are not normally inclined to be as vehement as Marta Traba was, she could analyze reflectively when she desired. As a great social critic, she used fiction to draw attention to the most ominous events of our time, for instance. A woman, she adopted a lucid feminism, urging women to realize their exclusion from society, to "speak" instead of "being spoken for."

Although Traba's greatest talents lie in criticism and the essay, her greatest success and influence is due to her novels. She herself once pointed out the creative role of the critic: "The critic succeeds as a creator insofar as he [or she—editor] succeeds as an essayist: someone who examines and recombines material in a new way" (*Marta Traba*, 1984, p. 38). As a novelist and short story writer, Traba treats the following fundamental themes: the journey, oppression, exile, loss and internalization of that which is lost, and poverty. All her fiction deals with one or more of these themes in one way or another and is colored by her concern about love, love of life, love of humanity, lack of communication, and human rights.

Traba's career in fiction begins with *Las ceremonias del verano* (1966) which

Mario Benedetti called "four demonstrations of love, four explosions of light," and which establishes the themes of pilgrimage and personal odyssey that reappear thirteen years later—though in different form—in *Homérica latina* (1979). This chronicle of travels is motivated not by personal choice, as in *Las ceremonias*, but by the terror and menace of repressive Latin American governments. The heroine-narrator of *Las ceremonias del verano* moves from Buenos Aires to Paris, Rome, Castelgandolfo and to Colombia in search of herself and guided by the intangible mentor, love.

What are the principal themes in her work from *Las ceremonias del verano* to the publication of *Homérica latina* in 1979 when she began to denounce oppression openly? We must look at *Los laberintos insolados* (1967; The labyrinths in the sun, novel), *Pasó así* (1968; It happened like this, stories), and *La jugada del sexto día* (1969; The sixth day's play, novel). Beginning with *Las ceremonias*, Traba skillfully employs cutting and flashbacks, interior monologue, stream-of-consciousness, multiple points of view within the narrator, ambiguity, and lyricism characteristic of a contemplative artist—all hallmarks of the modern Latin American novel.

Los laberintos (1967) shares the journey leitmotiv with *Las ceremonias* and Traba's later works of protest. The importance of the journey is clear from the hero's name—Ulises Blanco—and from the fact that some chapters explicitly make reference to Homer ("Penelope," "Circe," "Ithaca"). The journey of the hero from Colombia to New York and the family tragedy in which he abandons wife and daughter for Trizzie/Circe both serve to illustrate the contrast between hidebound Latin American tradition and the frivolity of life in the labyrinths of New York. (Thersites of *Homérica latina* calls to mind yet another Homeric figure.)

In *Pasó así* (1968), however, Traba uses a direct, linear style notable for its strange tone. The unique quality of these stories resides in this equivocal tone. The unifying theme is the poverty and mediocrity of the Latin American *barrio*. Mystery arises when the author poses ambiguous situations that never achieve a satisfying, rational denouement—confirming Jorge Luis Borges's postulate that "the resolution of a mystery is never superior to the mystery." Among the most notable stories are "La historia de los almohadones de terciopelo" (The velvet pillows), "La identificación" (The identification) and "El matrimonio" (The marriage), ranging in tone from indifference to pathos. The themes are the invisible quality of the poor, the people condemned to mediocrity by chronic problems, and the large and small problems of everyday life that affect the members of the *barrio* in their carbon-copy dwellings. Throughout the book the themes of slum life common to Argentina, Chile, and Brazil are explored.

In summary, Marta Traba the critic-judge stands behind Marta Traba the novelist, judging society; the art critic is also there, embroidering the tapestry of the human comedy, along with the untiring social activist denouncing the sordid conditions of the oppressed in Latin America. Elena Poniatowska* justifiably called her work the "novel of oppression." Even in her posthumous collection of American short stories *De la mañana a la noche* (1986; From Morning to Night) Traba studies the lack of communication in the United States, though with a difference: Progress, and not poverty, is the culprit.

SURVEY OF CRITICISM

Traba claimed on numerous occasions that art criticism and literature go together, and, as she put it when she decided to devote herself exclusively to literature: "a critic is first of all a writer; but it seems that my work in painting is at an end" (*Marta Traba*, p. 349). She was considered an art critic from the very beginning of her career, perhaps because so few Latin American women worked in that field at the time. In addition, her opinions on art were spread by magazines, books, speeches, university classes, and television programs, bringing her recognition first in Colombia and then throughout the continent.

Criticism has pointed out Traba's Pan-Americanism, her lifelong search for a common Latin American identity. Some have also likened her to Bolívar for her revolutionary fervor in attacking the political problems of the continent. The origins of Marta Traba the social reformer and brilliant essayist are to be found in her early correspondence from Paris and Rome, where artist, poet and philosopher came together in judgement of man's destiny in society.

Traba was one of the first Latin American woman writers to broach the subject of political kidnappings and torture of political prisoners in her novel *Homérica latina* (1979). Later her personal reaction to the reality of torture and kidnapping of political activists took the form of the twin novels *Conversación al sur* (1981) and *En cualquier lugar* (1986).

Conversación al sur was translated by Jo Labanji and published as *Mothers and Shadows* in 1986; it is without a doubt Marta Traba's most well-received book. Traba was pleased with its success and proud to be counted among the writers of the "literature of the oppressed." Irene, one of the main characters of *Conversación al sur*, reflects on the atmosphere of death and terror that characterized Argentina during the seventies: "I keep asking myself, when did it happen? When did two deaths no longer mean too many deaths, or that one hundred dead was a massacre? That's just what bothers me, because once you get to that point, there is no longer any gulf between life and death" (*Conversación al sur*, p. 33).

Mexican writer Elena Poniatowska* believes that one cannot read *En cualquier lugar* without being changed by it and that Traba understands how the little people begin to count for us (*En cualquier lugar*, p. 16). In this novel of exile, Traba holds the hope—personified by Alicia—that women can aid in the restructuring of a strife-torn society. Mariana, at times, represents the futility of human struggle. The voluntary and obligatory exile that Traba suffered in the United States had given her a kind of clairvoyance by the time she left it for the last time.

Conversación al sur (1981) and *En cualquier lugar* (1986) are witnesses to our time. *Conversación al sur* achieves a distinct feeling of space and emotion in spite of the constant travels of the characters. In *En cualquier lugar*, however, we float in a kind of fog with no definite point of reference, no answers, incapable of communicating with others. Once the reader identifies Mariana with Traba, he or she begins to understand that the long pilgrimage that began in *Homérica latina* is coming to an end with the careworn indifference of Mariana in the last part of the novel. Evelyn Picón Garfield (1985) has pointed out the similarity of structural techniques in *Conversación al sur* and in Argentinian novelist Manuel Puig's *El beso de la mujer araña* (1976).

After *Las ceremonias del verano* (1966) Traba had no solid critical successes until the publication of *Conversación al sur* in 1981: *Los laberintos insolados* (1967) and *La jugada del sexto día* (1969) were practically ignored. From 1966 to 1969 we find only four brief critical studies of her work.

Pasó así (1971)—an admirable collection of short stories—attracted attention in two papers, one by Marta Morello Frosch ("Sobre *Pasó así*," Conference of Inter-American Women Writers, San José State University, 1976) and another by Celia Correas de Zapata ("El equívoco en Marta Traba," Philological Association of the Pacific Coast, University of Southern California, 1977, which appeared later in *Ensayos hispanoamericanos*). Writing on Traba began in earnest in 1981 with the publication of *Conversación al sur*, and was spurred on further by her death in 1983.

After Traba's death, two major efforts were made to collect her essays on Latin American art and to compile a comprehensive series of articles on her last novels. The Museum of Modern Art in Bogotá, which she founded in 1965—aided by dozens of writers, critics, artists and her collaborators—published a four hundred page volume illustrated with pictures of Traba, her family and friends, spanning many years. The Puerto Rican literary journal *Sin Nombre* has dedicated an entire issue to her. As interest in her work continues to grow, her essays on artistic and social expression in Latin America will undoubtedly be the object of further research.

BIBLIOGRAPHY

Works by Marta Traba

Historia natural de la alegría. Buenos Aires: Editorial Losada, 1951.
El museo vacío. Bogotá: Ediciones MITO, 1958.
Los cuatro monstruos cardinales. Mexico City: Ediciones Era, 1965.
Las ceremonias del verano. Premios de Casa. Havana: Casa de las Américas, 1966. Also: Buenos Aires: Editorial Jorge Alvarez, 1966. Also: Barcelona: Montesinos Editor, 1981.
El son se quedó en Cuba. Bogotá: Ediciones Reflexión, 1966.
Los laberintos insolados. Barcelona: Editorial Seix Barral, 1967.
Pasó así. Montevideo: Editorial Arca, 1968.
La jugada del sexto día. Santiago de Chile: Editorial Universitaria, 1969.

Dos décadas vulnerables en las artes plásticas latinoamericanas, 1950–1970. Mexico
City: Siglo XXI Editores, 1973.
Homérica latina. Bogotá: Carlos Valencia Editores, 1979.
Conversación al sur. Mexico City: Siglo XXI, 1981.
Siglo XX en las artes plásticas latinoamericanas: una guía. Washington, D.C.: National
Endowment for the Arts and Humanities in conjunction with the OAS. Museum
of Latin American Art, 1982–1983.
En cualquier lugar. Bogotá: Siglo XXI de Colombia, 1984.
Marta Traba: selección de textos. Ed. Emma Araújo de Vallejo. Bogotá: Planeta Col-
ombiana, Museo de Arte Moderno, 1984.
"Hipotesis sobre una escritura diferente." *La sartén por el mango.* Eds. Eliana Ortega
and Patricia Elena González. Río Piedras, P.R.: Huracán, 1984. Pp. 21–26.
De la mañana a la noche. Montevideo: Monte Sexto, 1986.
Casa sin fin. Montevideo: Monte Sexto, 1988.

Translation of Marta Traba

Labanji, Jo, trans. *Mothers and Shadows.* London: Reader's International, 1986.

Works about Marta Traba

Agosín, Marjorie. "Entrevista con Marta Traba." *Punto de Vista* (Kent, Ohio) 2, 1
(1979):38–41.
———. "Marta Traba." *Sin Nombre* 14, 3 (Apr.-June 1984):97–100.
Bayón, Damián. "El espléndido no conformismo de Marta Traba." *Sin Nombre* 14, 3
(Apr.-June 1984):92–96. Also in *Marta Traba: selección de textos.* Ed. Emma
Araújo de Vallejo. Bogotá: Planeta Colombiana, Museo de Arte Moderno, 1984.
Benited, Marimar. "Apuntes sobre los escritos de Marta Traba en Puerto Rico." *Sin
Nombre* 14, 3 (Apr.-June 1984):123–26.
Calderón, Alfonso. "Laberintos de verano." *Ercilla* 32, 1.645 (Dec. 14, 1966):35.
———. "La gente por dentro." *Ercilla* 34, 1.732 (Aug. 28, 1968):51.
Chevigny, Bell. "Ambushing the Will to Ignorance: Elvira Orphée's *La última conquista
del Angel* and Marta Traba's *Conversación al sur.*" *El cono sur: Dinámica y
dimensiones de su literatura.* Ed. Rose S. Minc. Upper Montclair, N.J.: Montclair
State College, 1985. Pp. 98–104.
———. "Angel Rama and Marta Traba: A Latin American Odyssey Ends." *Nation*
(Feb. 4, 1984):126–28.
Cobo Borda, Juan Gustavo. "Marta Traba, novelista." *Cuadernos Hispanoamericanos:
Revista Mensual de Cultura Hispánica* (Madrid) 414 (Dec. 1984):121–30. Prol.
to *En cualquier lugar.* By Marta Traba. Bogotá: Siglo XXI Editores de Colombia,
1984.
———. "Spanish American Fiction, 1981." *Center for Inter-American Relations Review*
31 (Apr. 1982):83–87.
Correas de Zapata, Celia. "Constantes ideológicas en la vida y obra de Marta Traba."
38th Annual Conference, Pacific Northwest Council on Foreign Languages, Seattle, Wash., 1987.
———. "El equívoco en *Pasó así* de Marta Traba." *Ensayos hispanoamericanos.* Argentina: Ediciones Corregidor, 1978. Pp. 279–91.
———. "Marta Traba's *Homérica latina*: Social Protest in Latin America." Pacific

Coast Council on Latin American Studies (PCCLAS) meeting, Chico State University, Chico, California, 1979.

————. "Panamericanismo en la obra de Marta Traba." Congreso de Escritores, Universidad de Costa Rica, Costa Rica, 1983.

————. "La represión social en dos novelas de Marta Traba: *Conversación al sur* y *En cualquier lugar*." 25th Congress on Iberoamerican Literature, Instituto Internacional Iberoamericano, CUNY, 1987.

García Pinto, Magdalena. "Entrevista: Marta Traba." *Hispamérica* 38 (Aug. 13, 1984):37–46.

García Ponce, Juan. "Una narración lírica." *Quimera: Revista de Literatura* 17 (Mar. 1982):50–52.

García Ramos, Reinaldo. "La novelista y sus veranos." *Casa de las Américas* 6, 36–37 (May-Aug. 1966):190–94.

Garfield, Evelyn Picón. *Women's Voices from Latin America: Interviews with Six Contemporary Authors*. Detroit: Wayne State University Press, 1985. Pp. 11–16, 117–23.

Grossman, Edith. "In Memoriam." *Center for Inter-American Relations Review* 32 (1984):8.

Mejía Duque, Jaime. "*Las ceremonias del verano*." *Boletín Cultural y Bibliográfico* (Bogotá) 10, 4 (1967):867–70.

Montero, Oscar. "La enunciación infatigable de *Los laberintos insolados* de Marta Traba." *Prismal/Cabral: Revista de Literatura Hispánica/Caderno Afro-Brasileiro* (College Park, Md.) (Autumn 1984):12–13, 93–102.

Moreira, Victor. "Marta Traba, una muñeca de trapo que dice cosas terribles." *La Nación* (Aug. 25, 1969):16–17.

Morello Frosch, Marta. "Sobre *Pasó así*." Conference of Inter-American Women Writers. San Jose State University, 1976.

Museo de Arte Moderno de Bogotá. *Marta Traba*. 1st ed. Bogotá: Planeta Colombiana Editorial, S.A., 1984.

Poniatowska, Elena. "Marta Traba o el salto al vacío." *Revista Iberoamericana* 51, 132–33 (June-Dec. 1985):883–97. Also in Prol. to *En cualquier lugar*. By Marta Traba. Bogotá: Siglo XXI Editores de Colombia, 1984.

Rama, Angel. "La persecución de Marta Traba." *Punto Final* 1, 18 (Dec. 1966):20–21.

Sola, María. "*Conversación al sur*, novela para no olvidar." *Sin Nombre* 12, 4 (July-Sept. 1982):64–71.

————. "Escribo como mujer: Trayectoria de la narrativa de Marta Traba." *Sin Nombre* 14, 3 (Apr.-June 1984):101–14.

Torres Martino, J.A. "Marta Traba: La vigilia por Puerto Rico." *Sin Nombre* 14, 3 (Apr.-June 1984):117–22.

SALOMÉ UREÑA DE HENRÍQUEZ (1850–1897)
Dominican Republic

Lizabeth Paravisini-Gebert

BIOGRAPHY

Salomé Ureña de Henríquez, the Dominican Republic's "Muse of Civilization," was born in Santo Domingo on October 21, 1850. She was a member of two old but impoverished Dominican families. Her father, Nicolás Ureña de Mendoza, was a well-known lawyer, senator, magistrate, educator, essayist, and poet whose work was frequently published in the Dominican press. Her mother, Gregoria Díaz y León, belonged to an old landowning family.

Ureña de Henríquez received her early education from her mother and showed a keen interest in reading from a young age. She later attended two small elementary schools in Santo Domingo, elementary schools being the only ones then open to women. Her father, however, insisted that Salomé have the best education available at the time and took charge of her secondary education himself. The educational program he designed for her focused on mathematics, botany, and literature, with an emphasis on the Spanish classics, and included French and English literature studied in the original. Her readings included the works of Spanish poets like Juan Nicasio Gallego, Fray Luis de León, and Manuel José Quintana, whose influence will be found in her work. She was known for her talent for memorizing poetry.

Ureña's family provided a lively intellectual environment. Although she never traveled outside the country, her home was often visited by well-known Dominican and foreign intellectuals, among them Josefa Antonia Perdomo and Josefa Antonia del Monte, two local women poets—and possible role models— who were friends of the family and visited frequently.

Salomé Ureña grew up during a period of great political agitation in the Dominican Republic, and the historical events of her childhood and adolescence had a significant impact on the patriotic themes and tone of her poetry. She was born six years after the end of the Haitian domination of the country (which lasted from 1822 to 1846) and grew up during the period of unrest that followed, marked by sporadic wars with Haiti and the threat of a new Haitian takeover. In 1861, when Ureña was eleven, the Dominican Republic was re-annexed by Spain, an event followed by the war of Restoration, the Dominican nationalist struggle against Spain. Independence was restored in 1865, but Ureña was to see twenty-three different governments come and go between 1865 and her death in 1897. As a result, her poetry voiced her desire to see her country liberated from foreign powers and free from the chaos of dictatorship.

Ureña began writing poetry at the age of fifteen and published her work for the first time at seventeen, under the pen name "Herminia." The pseudonym was abandoned in 1874 when another "Herminia" published a somewhat frivolous article on French fashions in a local newspaper. From then on she published her work under her own name.

Her poetry appeared generally in newspapers in Santo Domingo and was occasionally reprinted in foreign newspapers. It was enthusiastically received by contemporary Dominican youth, who often memorized it and copied it graffiti-style on walls. The first anthology of Dominican poetry, *Lira de Quisqueya* (1874; Quisqueyan lyre), included ten of her poems and a brief biographical note. By 1878 her fame was such that a celebration was organized in her honor at which she was presented with a medal offered by public subscription.

Ureña dedicated the years 1878 and 1879 to a broadening of her scientific and literary scholarship under the guidance of Francisco Henríquez y Carvajal, a noted Dominican intellectual who became her husband in 1880. Henríquez y Carvajal would become president of the Republic in 1916, nineteen years after Ureña's death. The couple was to have four children, three of whom survived. All three of them, Pedro, Camila, and Maximiliano, would in time become leading Dominican authors and intellectuals in their own right.

The year 1879 also marked the arrival in the Dominican Republic of Puerto Rican intellectual and educator Eugenio María de Hostos, a friend and collaborator of Henríquez y Carvajal. Hostos was to be in charge of organizing the Escuela Normal de Santo Domingo, a teacher-training institute, and would play a vital role in the development of higher education in the country. He became Ureña's close friend and mentor in her own illustrious career as educator.

Ureña's marriage in 1880 coincided with the publication of her first volume of poetry, sponsored by the Sociedad Amigos del País (the Friends of the Country Society). The volume, simply entitled *Poesías* (Poems), included thirty-three short poems and her long narrative poem "Anacaona." It appeared with a prologue by Monsignor Fernando Arturo de Meriño and a biographical sketch by José Lamarche. A second edition appeared in 1920 with a prologue by her son Pedro Henríquez Ureña.

In 1881, deeply disappointed by political events in Santo Domingo, Ureña wrote "Sombras" (Shadows), a poem considered by many to be her best work, but unfortunately a text that was followed by prolonged periods of literary silence. The literary silence may well have been the result of marriage, childrearing, and the demands of the educational career she started in the same year; but it has been most often interpreted by critics and biographers as her patriotic protest against the moral failure of the Meriño government. The government, for which expectations were high, had resorted to tyrannical measures, passing the Decree of San Fernando, which sentenced to death anyone caught in possession of arms. In "Sombras," Ureña writes about her loss of faith in the possibilities of realizing her dreams of progress and intellectual glory for the Dominican Republic. The poem, however, ends with a note of hope, looking forward to an end to the "raging hurricane" and "black disappointment" engulfing the country.

"Sombras" is evidence of a political disappointment that served as the stimulus for the creation of an educational institute that would contribute to the improvement of conditions in her country: the Instituto de Señoritas (the Institute for Young Women). Founded on November 3, 1881, it was the first institution of higher education for women in the country, and is considered to be the most important women's institution in the history of the Dominican Republic. Ureña's goal was to provide women with the opportunity to acquire the education and skills necessary to make a valid contribution to the development of Dominican society and citizenry. Hostos, her mentor and collaborator, was later to praise her for having reacted so admirably against the traditionally poor education of Latin American women, helping to form a group of intelligent, well-educated, and self-assured women, able to have a say in determining the direction of Dominican society.

The institute opened with fourteen students and had its first graduation on April 17, 1887, with six young women receiving their teaching diplomas. Ureña wrote "Mi ofrenda a la patria" (My offering to the nation), a poem celebrating the advantages of female education, for the occasion. She ran the Institute from 1881 to 1893, working tirelessly despite having sole responsibility for her home and family during her husband's four-year absence from the country while studying medicine in France. The Institute closed on December 1893 because of Ureña's worsening health problems. It was to reopen in January 1896. On September 1897, six months after Ureña's death, it was rechristened Instituto Salomé Ureña.

Following the birth of her daughter Camila in 1892, Ureña became seriously ill with pneumonia. She never fully recovered from her illness, which was the occasion for her poem "Umbra-Ressurexit," a brief meditation on her recovery. Her worsening state of health prompted a move to the northern city of Puerto Plata in June 1896, where she finished her poem "Mi Pedro" (My Pedro), a moving tribute to her son Pedro's intellectual promise. It is believed to be her last completed poem.

She died on March 6, 1897, a few months after returning to Santo Domingo, possibly of consumption. Her death was widely grieved and her funeral, a moving outburst of popular emotion, marked the first occasion on which Dominican women marched in a civic act.

MAJOR THEMES

Ureña's position as one of the Dominican Republic's national poets remains unchallenged almost a century after her death. Her literary production was not extensive, comprising only one volume of poetry published at the age of thirty, followed by a handful of poems added to the volume after her death. However, she lived during the crucial period of national consolidation for the Dominican Republic—a period of armed struggle and political definition—and belonged to a generation of writers who, conscious of their historical role, tried to give shape in their works to a national sense of selfhood.

Ureña was the first Dominican woman to write poetry that moved away from domestic concerns. Contrary to the stereotypes of the nineteenth-century female poet, she was the embodiment of the civic poet, believing that poetry could play an important role in the struggle against war and tyranny and in the promotion of peace, education, and progress. Thus, she used her poetry to promote her civic interests, especially the implantation and development of a rationalist form of education that would make possible the kind of intellectual achievement that in her view constituted the true glory of a nation. As such, her poetry voiced the hopes and dreams of the newly consolidated Republic.

She is best known for her patriotic poetry, in which she exalts the glories of the nation and encourages the pursuit of civilization and progress in a neoclassical style. Her intimate poetry, Romantic in tone and domestic in theme, is less known and admired.

Ureña's civic poetry shows the decisive influence of the philosophical and sociological tenets of Positivist Rationalism. Under the influence of Eugenio María de Hostos, who is credited with introducing these intellectual currents to Santo Domingo, Ureña developed a social and educational philosophy based on the concept of progress, which stemmed from the theories of social evolution associated with Auguste Comte, the founder of Positivism, and Herbert Spencer, the founder of evolutionist philosophy. In her opinion, three essential aspects of civic life had to be stimulated if Dominicans were to build a great nation: the value of work, the love for science and the arts, and the preservation of peace as the means of assuring the country's cultural development.

As a follower of Positivist thought, Ureña believed in the intimate relationship between art and science, a belief central to the theme of her poetic and educational work. Her adoption of Positivist thought contributed to her maturing as a poet and an educator at a time when romantic idealism and colonial education were giving way to the fervor for progress and intellectual achievement, thus giving her a role as spokesperson for the aspirations of the men and women of her country.

Progress is one of the main themes in Ureña's work from 1873 to 1880, as titles such as "La gloria del progreso" (1873; The glory of progress), "La fe en el porvenir" (1878; Faith in the future), and "Luz" (1880; Light) indicate. Focusing on the need to develop the arts, crafts, and sciences as the basis for a new Dominican society, the poems proclaim her faith in a grand future for her country.

The compositions inspired by her country's educational institution, such as "Mi ofrenda a la patria" and "Para la distribución de premios del Colegio San Luis Gonzaga" (1876; On the distribution of prizes at the San Luis Gonzaga School) add to this theme Ureña's faith in the power of youth and education to overcome backwardness and tyranny. This second theme permeates patriotic poems such as "A mi Patria" (1878; To my country), which develop Ureña's belief in the link between education and the attainment of democracy and peace in the Dominican Republic.

Behind this concern with progress, education, and peace lies Ureña's deeply felt patriotism. Indeed, her patriotic poetry was influential in the development of the concept of the Dominican Republic as a nation. The definition of "nation" that emerges from her poems conforms to the ideal of a sacred entity to be venerated by Dominicans, as in "El cantar de mis cantares" (1879; Song of my songs).

This concept of nation was firmly based on the heroic deeds that led to independence, as expressed in "Diez y seis de agosto" (1874; Sixteenth of August) and "Hecatombe" (1878; Hecatomb), her poems on the subject of the Spanish annexation of Santo Domingo. They express her defense of the restoration of Dominican sovereignty, celebrate the courage of the Dominicans who fought in the War of Restoration, and give expression to her democratic ideals and her joy at the defeat of despotism.

The aspirations for her country that she voiced in these and similar poems coincided perfectly with the aspirations of the emerging Dominican bourgeoisie, which, having consolidated its power through the War of Restoration and the elimination of the Haitian threat, needed powerful symbols to solidify the emerging concept of nationhood. Ureña's poetry was instrumental in elaborating the idea of a proud nation with a promising future required by Dominican aspirations; and since war, dictatorship, and obscurantism were a threat to these aspirations, she used her poetry as a weapon against the combative spirit of the times, counseling against the indiscriminate and generalized use of brute force, and deploring the abandonment of reason in the wielding of power. In poems such as "A mi Patria" (1878; To my country), she calls for peace as the first step toward the glorious future of an enlightened nation that awaited the Dominican Republic.

Ureña had already developed the idea of a glorious future for the Dominican Republic—an ideal central to her concept of nation—in "Ruinas" (1876; Ruins), a poem about the ruins of the Spanish colonial period, when Santo Domingo boasted of being the Athens of the new world. It is a poem full of admiration for the lost colonial splendors, in which she describes the nation's high destiny as symbolized by the impressive architectural ruins. In "Ruinas," Ureña attempts to strengthen the Dominicans' faith in their destiny by awakening them to a re-creation of their past glory. Recent critics have pointed out the apparent contra-diction between her admiration of the Dominican Republic's Spanish past (as found in "Ruinas" and "Colón," 1879) and her opposition to Spanish re-annexation of the country, claiming she was oblivious to the evils of colonialism. But her nostalgia for the Spanish colonial past may have responded to the threat from non-Spanish governments, and the need to reestablish the Spanish heritage after the Haitian domination, and as such fits perfectly well with her aspirations for the country.

The poems included in the volume of her complete works are divided into three groups: "A la Patria," which includes her patriotic poetry; "Poesías ín-timas," which includes her domestic and sentimental poetry; and "Varia," which includes patriotic and sentimental poetry, as well as elegies to friends and poems dedicated to friends in exile. This last section also includes her long narrative poem "Anacaona."

Ureña's intimate poetry, grouped under "Páginas íntimas" (Intimate pages) in the volume of her complete works, comprises some fourteen poems on do-mestic themes. Unlike her civic poetry, her intimate poems are full of melancholy and sadness and have been vilified by critics as containing nothing but "perpetual complaints." The subject matter may account for the critics' disparaging view of this group of poems, since the themes—the near-fatal illness of her son, the death of her father, the birth of her first child, the pressures brought on her by her husband's prolonged absences—are those determined by male critics to be "female" subjects, lacking the "powerful virile accent" they have chosen to admire in Ureña's poetry.

It is in her intimate poetry, however, that Ureña escapes the limitations of her training in the Spanish classics and finds an avenue for self-expression. They give voice to her fears and her need for support and companionship. It is in poems such as "Quejas" (1879; Laments) and "Amor y Anhelo" (1879; Love and longing) that we glimpse the woman behind the "goddess of civilization" that she embodied in her civic poetry. "Quejas," in which she expresses her passion for her absent lover, offers verses of surprising candor and sensuality, especially given the times, the constraints of her culture, and the fact that Ureña was unmarried at the time of publication. "Angustias" (1888; Anguish), written during her husband's four-year absence in France, is also interesting in this context as an expression both of her longing for him and of her impatience at the burden that his absence places on her.

It is not surprising, given the critics' lack of appreciation of Ureña's domestic poetry, that the poems set aside as the best of the group are those on the subject of motherhood, such as "En horas de angustia" (1884; At times of anguish), written during the serious illness of her second son (she had already lost her first), and "En el nacimiento de mi primogénito" (1882; On the birth of my firstborn), poems that validate Ureña's domestic role. The poems are remarkable for the simplicity of the style, which is never allowed to overshadow the depth of the emotions. However, a reevaluation of Ureña's domestic poetry should include a fresh look at equally excellent poems like "Quejas," "Amor y Anhelo," and "¡Adelante!" (1889; Forward), a poem of encouragement to her husband.

Ureña's domestic poetry is stylistically different from her civic poetry. A loyal follower of Spanish Neoclassicism in her civic poetry, where she preferred the *silva*, she showed a marked preference for Romantic alexandrine verses in her domestic poetry. Her ability to move effortlessly from Neoclassical to Romantic tendencies to suit her theme and mood attests to the solid grounding in her craft that she received from her early education.

Thorough knowledge of her craft also accounts for the technical excellence of her poems, a characteristic noted by all of her critics. Ureña's work has been praised for the fluidity and spontaneity of a style where there are no noticeable defects. Her poems are marked by the absence of complex rhetorical devices, the avoidance of oratorical or bombastic elements, and the classical serenity of the tone. It is not a poetry that surprises with unexpected originality or brilliant images; its excellence lies in its harmonious construction, the regularity of the rhyme patterns, and its conformity to classical principles. It is a poetry that values the development of the idea more highly than aesthetic elements. Throughout her work, she favored simple combinations of rhyme and meter and avoided structurally complex poetic forms such as the sonnet.

Ureña departed from these classical principles in her domestic poetry, and in her work on the subject of the legendary Dominican Indian Princess Anacaona.

"Anacaona" was Ureña's most ambitious work, a long narrative poem belonging to the Latin American *indianista* (having Indian themes) tradition. In Santo Domingo, as elsewhere in Latin America, *indianismo* responded to the need to recover the nation's historical origins through the use of the heroic pre-Columbian Indian past as the symbol of the emerging sense of nationhood. *Indianista* works were popular with Ureña's contemporaries in the Dominican Republic and the rest of Latin America.

"Anacaona," included in Ureña's 1880 volume of poetry, is an ambitious work because of its length (thirty-nine cantos) and its intensity. In it, Ureña attempted to capture a crucial moment in Dominican history—the Taíno Indian uprising against the Spanish conquistadors in Hispaniola, the first such confrontation on the American continent and one that resulted in the destruction of the Taíno world at the hand of the Spaniards. In "Anacaona," as is characteristic in Romantic literature, Ureña experimented with a wide variety of meter and rhyme patterns. Despite this variety, the poem has great internal coherence and offers a fairly accurate, though romanticized, version of the fierce struggle leading to the destruction of Taíno society in Hispaniola. The poem emphasizes the heroic struggle as a symbol of national identification and as a vehicle for structuring a valid concept of nationality.

"Anacaona," however, is an uneven work, often harshly criticized by Dominican critics and compared unfavorably with the highly respected work of Dominican *indianistas* José Joaquín Pérez and Manuel de Jesús Galván (whose *Enriquillo* is considered to be one of Latin America's *indianista* masterpieces). Indeed, Ureña's poetic talents were not suited to the type of work she attempted in "Anacaona." The metric variety is admirable, but she lacks the versatility needed for the wide range of description, epic narration, lyricism, and pathos of a poem that attempts to encompass the tragic destiny of a doomed people. The poem does not consistently reach the level of excellence of her civic and domestic poetry.

Yet, despite the uneven quality of the work, it contains sections worthy of Ureña's best work. "Canto XIX," for example, is often praised for the masterful examples of heptasyllabic verses, which give sections of the poem a remarkable melodious flow. There are numerous examples of passages of extraordinary descriptive beauty in the poem. The poem has the added interest of offering a unique heroine in Anacaona, the widowed Indian princess who assumed the leadership of her people in the struggle against the Spanish conquistadors, and died a heroic martyr to her cause. Ureña's determined heroine offers a refreshing contrast to the predominantly passive Indian beauties of the *indigenista* tradition.

Apart from the volume that includes her poetry (and "Anacaona"), very little else of Ureña's writing has been preserved. A volume of her letters and other prose writings, announced as forthcoming by her son Pedro Henríquez Ureña in his introduction to the 1920 edition of his mother's work, has never appeared. Only one of her letters is available—addressed to the president of the committee in charge of the erection of a commemorative statue to Juan Pablo Duarte, the leader of the Dominican War of Independence, enclosing the funds collected as a contribution by the students in the institute. Her remaining published prose is limited to two short speeches written for the institute's graduation ceremonies. The later of the two, read at the closing of the school in 1893, when her health was already failing, offers interesting insights into Ureña's goals when founding the institute thirteen years earlier. Her objective, as expressed in the text, was to offer women the same opportunity open to male students to gain the skills needed to work toward social progress in the Dominican Republic.

Ureña's entire body of work—her educational efforts, her civic and domestic poetry, and "Anacaona"—reflects her desire to achieve the "social reform that begins with the development of conscience" of which she spoke in her final address to her students. The unity of that body of work lies precisely in its didactic intention, in the goal of serving the social needs of her country as she saw them, from her efforts on behalf of progress and educational reform, culminating in the foundation of the institute, to her attempt to create a body of poetic work that would contribute to the task of national definition. The transcendence of her poetic and social work assures her a continuing prominent position in Dominican literary and cultural history.

SURVEY OF CRITICISM

The critical literature on the work of Salomé Ureña is not extensive; apart from Joaquín Balaguer's 1950 introduction to her complete works—a study on which most subsequent critical appraisals have been based—there are no in-depth studies of her poetry.

The initial critical response to the publication of her poems was extremely enthusiastic, so much so, that by her late teens she had already become a nationally known figure. Early praise for her work can be found in the articles published by the Dominican publication *El Estudio* on the occasion of the presentation of a medal to Salomé Ureña in 1878. An article published in 1880 by the Puerto Rican poet Lola Rodríguez de Tío, whose poetic styles and themes are similar to Ureña's, underscores the patriotic function of Ureña's poetry. Similarly, Hostos, one of her early critics, considered her "patriotic fiber" the greatest attribute of her poetry. Marcelino Menéndez y Pelayo, in the introduction to his *Antología de poetas hispanoamericanos* (Madrid, 1893–1895), compared her work to that of Spanish poets Juan Nicasio Gallego and Manuel José Quintana, both ardent patriots.

No extensive biography of Ureña has appeared to date. A biographical sketch published as part of the introduction to her *Poesías escogidas* (1920) by her son Pedro Henríquez Ureña has been the basis of the biographical notes accompanying subsequent critical studies. A short biographical pamphlet by Silveria Rodríguez Demorizi (first published in 1931) focuses on Ureña's education, social and pedagogical contributions, and her role as wife and mother.

The most extensive analysis of Ureña's poetry is that of Joaquín Balaguer, published as an introduction to her *Poesías completas* (1950). Balaguer attempts a general evaluation of Ureña's poetic work, calling her "a great poet who embodied the hope and aspirations of the newly consolidated Republic." His essay contains the most systematic analysis of Ureña's poetic style, praising the "negative perfection" of her technique—his phrase for describing the absence of technical flaws in Ureña's poetry.

Carlos Federico Pérez' essay on Salomé Ureña in his book *Evolución poética dominicana*, and Nestor Contín Aybar's "Salomé Ureña de Henríquez," in his *Historia de la literatura dominicana* II, are primarily reference texts based on Balaguer's work.

José Alcántara Almanzar, in *Estudios de poesía dominicana* and *Narrativa y sociedad en Hispanoamérica*, has focused on the ideological implications of Ureña's Positivist philosophy, presenting a Marxist analysis of Ureña's ideological connections to bourgeois thought and aspirations in the Dominican Republic. Dominican woman poet Chiqui Vicioso, in a 1984 newspaper article, challenges the critical devaluation of Ureña's domestic poetry, paving the way for reassessment of her entire body of work following feminist critical theory. Both Vicioso and Daisy Cocco de Filippis, the latter in a 1987 article on Dominican women poets, point to the possible impact of Ureña's marriage on her literary production after 1880, indicating the need to reevaluate the connection between her life and works. The lack of comprehensive critical works on Ureña points to the need for more consistent and systematic analysis of the work of a poet whose prominent place in the history of Dominican literature merits serious critical attention.

BIBLIOGRAPHY

Works by Salomé Ureña

Poesías. Santo Domingo: Sociedad Amigos del País, 1880.
Poesías escogidas. Prol. Pedro Henríquez Ureña. Madrid: n.p., 1920.
Poesías completas: Edición conmemorativa del centenario de su nacimiento, 1850–1950. Prol. Joaquín Balaguer. Ciudad Trujillo: Impresora Dominicana, 1950.
Poesías escogidas. Prol. Pedro Henríquez Ureña. Ciudad Trujillo: Librería Dominicana, 1960.
Poesías completas. Prol. Joaquín Balaguer. Santo Domingo: Publicaciones ONAP, 1985.

Works about Salomé Ureña

Alcántara Almanzar, José. *Estudios de poesía dominicana*. Santo Domingo: Alfa y Omega, 1979. Pp. 51–71.
———. *Narrativa y sociedad en Hispanoamérica*. Santo Domingo: Instituto Tecnologico de Santo Domingo, 1984. Pp. 12–16, 21–24.
Balaguer, Joaquín. Prol. to *Poesías completas*. By Salomé Ureña de Henríquez. Ciudad Trujillo: Impresora Dominicana, 1950. Also: Santo Domingo: Publicaciones ONAP, 1985.
Cocco de Filippis, Daisy. "La mujer dominicana y el quehacer literario." *Diario la Prensa* Mar. 1, 1987:B8–B9.
Contín Aybar, Nestor. "Salomé Ureña de Henríquez." *Historia de la literatura dominicana II*. San Pedro de Macorís: Universidad Central del Este, 1983. Pp. 82–87.
Lamb, Ruth S. "La poesía de Salomé Ureña de Henríquez." *Revista Iberoamericana* 44 (1957):346–58.
Nolasco, Flérida de. "Estudio de la obra poética de Salomé Ureña de Henriquez." *Revista Lyceum* 25 (1951):12–13.
Pérez, Carlos Federico. "Salomé Ureña y la culminación de la influencia neoclásica." *Evolución poética dominicana*. Buenos Aires: Editorial Poblet, 1956. Pp. 129–44.
Rodríguez Demorizi, Emilio. *Salomé Ureña y el Instituto de Señoritas: Para la historia de la espiritualidad dominicana*. Ciudad Trujillo: Impresora Dominicana, 1960.
Rodríguez Demorizi, Silveria. *Salomé Ureña de Henríquez*. Santo Domingo: Taller, 1984.
Valledeperes, Manuel. "Salomé Ureña, poetisa y maestra." *Revista Interamericana de Bibliografía* 19 (1969):23–38.
Vicioso, Chiqui. "Salomé Ureña a 134 octubres: una desmitificación necesaria." *El Nuevo Diario*, Oct. 10, 1984:9.

LUISA VALENZUELA
(b. 1938)
Argentina

Sharon Magnarelli

BIOGRAPHY

Born in 1938 in Buenos Aires, Argentine writer Luisa Valenzuela began working as a journalist at age seventeen. Her mother, Luisa Mercedes Levinson, was also a writer, and Valenzuela mentions that during her childhood, Argentine literary notables made frequent visits to her home: Jorge Luis Borges and Ernesto Sábato, to mention just two examples. In spite of her early literary surroundings, Valenzuela has unquestionably earned her reputation, as both a journalist and a writer, on her own merits. She has worked for *El Mundo* (Buenos Aires) and *La Nación* (Buenos Aires), where she rose to assistant director of the Sunday supplement; she also edited *Crisis* (Buenos Aires), a magazine of literature, sociology, and politics. In 1963 she won honorable mention in the Premio Kraft for her work in journalism. She continues in that field, publishing in various prestigious newspapers and magazines in the United States, including the *New York Times*, the *Village Voice*, and the *New York Review of Books*. At the same time, Valenzuela has gained international acclaim for her prose fiction. Her short stories have been published as collections in Spanish and in English as well as individually in many of the major literary magazines of the United States. With the exception of *El gato eficaz* (literally "The Effective/Efficacious Cat" but sometimes translated "Cat-O-Nine Deaths"), all of her novels have been translated and published in English as well as Spanish.

Valenzuela's first short story, "Ciudad ajena" ("City of the Unknown"), which forms part of *Los heréticos* (1967; *The Heretics*, 1976), was written at age eighteen and immediately published. A few years later, while living in France and homesick for Buenos Aires, she wrote *Hay que sonreír* (1966; *Clara*, 1976), her first novel, which she has described as written in the style of a Buenos Aires tango. From 1959 to 1961 she lived and worked in Paris. In 1969 she participated in the University of Iowa's International Writers Program while she wrote her second novel, *El gato eficaz* (1972). More recently, she has been director of the New York Institute for the Humanities and writer in residence at both New York University and Columbia University, where she also has taught creative writing. A resident of the United States and a voluntary exile of her native Argentina since 1979, Valenzuela has traveled extensively throughout the United States, Latin America, and Europe. In 1983 she held a Guggenheim Fellowship. At present she divides her time among New York City, Buenos Aires, and Tepoztlán, Mexico.

But perhaps most importantly, Valenzuela lives what she writes. Like her prose production, she is actively involved in combatting repression and censorship, on the political, sexual, and literary levels. She has worked with Amnesty International, is currently a member of the Freedom to Write Committee of PEN International, and serves on the Board of Directors of the Fund for Free Expression, a branch of America Watch.

MAJOR THEMES

To date, Valenzuela has published four novels and five collections of short stories. Throughout the trajectory of her work she has focused on three principal and interrelated themes: politics, language, and women. Her deadly serious games with language are designed to demonstrate how the dominant group has used discourse to oppress and repress, on both the personal and the political level. To her mind, language is ever fluid, ever changing, but always dangerous, for it necessarily falsifies the reality it pretends to portray. As a result, discourse can be and is used to distract from the important issues and to superimpose a new perception of that reality, one that benefits those who wield the power and the word. Valenzuela repeatedly attempts to employ discourse against itself to expose the prestidigitation that underlies the peremptory manipulation of language.

In the course of her literary production, Valenzuela has moved from the thematics of the personal and a naturalistic style, as evidenced in *Hay que sonreír*, into the thematics of the political and a more lyrical, metaphoric, or oneiric style as evidenced in *Cola de lagartija* (1983; *The Lizard's Tail*, 1983). Nevertheless, she has demonstrated in her recent *Cambio de armas* (1983; *Other Weapons*, 1985), a collection of five often metaphoric tales of political terror and oppression, that the personal is political and that the metaphoric or the oneiric is often all too real; nightmares are our reality. There seems to be a recognition (conscious or not) within Valenzuela's work that political tyranny and the abuse of power are macrocosmic manifestations of the oppression and hierarchism that mark many of our interpersonal relationships, especially the male-female. With the passage of time, Valenzuela's works have become more intricate, perhaps even baroque in style, and her plots less linear. In this respect her works have become less readable by Cervantes's *desocupado lector* (lazy, uninvolved reader), for she demands more and more of her readers and refuses to leave them resting passively and complacently in their armchairs, on either a literary or a political level.

Her preoccupation with the three interrelated themes of politics, language, and women is already apparent in her first major work, *Hay que sonreír*, published in 1966. This novel narrates the story of the young, innocent prostitute, Clara, as she passes through the hands of a series of men, each exploiting her and molding her into a reflection of himself until she is victim of the final linguistic and physical violence on her being. Her throat is cut, severing her head from her body, while she repeats the masculinist adage, one must keep smiling. Although the novel has often been viewed as a Romantic novel, it might better be labeled a debunking of the myths of Romanticism, for Clara wanders ever in search of love, never fully giving up on her hope (formulated no doubt by the rhetoric of popular culture and the tango) to find a man to love and protect her, but she encounters only disappointment and exploitation.

In this sense the novel might perhaps be interpreted as a *Bildungsroman* (novel of apprenticeship) of failure, for there can be little doubt that Clara never really learns, never escapes from the romantic mythology and from the *hay que* (one must) with which the patriarchal institutions, home, Church, state, and school, have showered her during her entire life. Clara's essential problem, one we all share to a greater or lesser degree, is her incapacity to see beyond the discourse of the androcentric society. She accepts the words of the various institutions as Truth and never fully comprehends that the sociopolitical discourse is not employed as an instrument to reveal truth and reality, but rather as an instrument to hide or disguise and in turn repress her and keep her in her proper place, subservient. Indeed, she dies repeating the words of her husband, the magician, who must finally kill her because she has been oblivious to his other means of control, thus rendering them invalid. Only by eliminating her completely can he finally and irrevocably master her and thereby confirm and guarantee his own prepotency, a power that he himself holds in doubt. The patriarchy's continual linguistic victimization of Clara has still been insufficient to validate incontrovertibly the masculinist power, a "power" which in the works of Valenzuela is shown to need constant and repeated authentication via the medium of the woman. Therefore, rather than merely inundating her body in and with supplemental discourse that distorts reality or debauching that body by prostituting it, Alejandro (an ironic allusion to Alexander the Great perhaps), as representative of the patriarchal society, must enact the final transgression and eliminate that body, and along with it her voice, in order to sustain and fortify his own self-image.

Thus, on some level Clara becomes a symbol of all who are degraded and metaphorically prostituted as they are denied access to a world in which both mind and body can be used without contradiction. Although *Hay que sonreír* depicts the private journey of Clara, there can be little doubt that her personal life is the product of her confrontation with social and religious mores, both of which are perpetuated and inculcated via the vehicle of discourse. Her relationship with the various representatives of the patriarchy mirrors that of us all, male and female.

The relationship between women and patriarchal, institutionalized religion which, in Western culture at least, provides us with most of our preconceptions and beliefs about the female, only hinted at in *Hay que sonreír*, is developed more fully in Valenzuela's next published volume, *Los heréticos*. Here religion, specifically Catholicism, occupies the role that politics will later assume. As the title suggests, the collection is heretical, for it amusingly and subtly debunks our Christian perception of women as well as many of our Catholic rituals. At the same time, it undermines the power of language and the myths created by that language, beliefs often purported to be religious dogma, wrapped in an aura of religion, but ultimately sexual in origin and founded on a male fear of female power, real or imagined. Again, Valenzuela demonstrates how discourse is used to distort our perception of reality. In the first story, "Nihil obstat," and in a direct reflection of Christian teachings, the narrator learns that women and the female body are evil and sinful, and, ever in pursuit of self-gain, he hopes to be rewarded in heaven for his rejection of them. But the paradigm of the process of his acquisition of that knowledge undermines the canon-myth, for this "truth" is inculcated by a homosexual who plays at being a priest and who desires the boy's body for himself. Like Clara, our narrator here, though male, is apparently too young or naive to perceive the inherent contradictions in the discourse proffered him.

In "Proceso a la Virgen" ("Trial of the Virgin"), the statue of the Virgin is blamed for her failure to produce the desired miracles: either allow the husbands to possess María physically or transfer the object of that desire from María to their wives. Curiously, the statue, a sign not recognized as such (the people perceive it *as* the Virgin, not as a representation, a supplement), mirrors the virginal character named María in that both are the brunt of the hatred of the townspeople, both male and female, a hatred occasioned by the men's desire for María. Yet, the story leaves no doubt that the men desire the guileless María because she is unattainable and for the purity and innocence that would be destroyed were they to possess her. They desire her for precisely what they would destroy in her. At the same time both female figures (statue and girl), as objects of desire, are blamed for the desire that emanates from the townspeople themselves, just as the evil within humankind has long been imputed to witches.

Similarly, in "Una familia para Clotilde" ("A Family for Clotilde"), the female is again the locus of desire as father and son compete for sexual primacy with Clotilde. The respective and reflexive resolve of each to prove himself superior to his adversary leads each to use his wife-mother as an instrument to defeat and frustrate the desires of the other. Their plans fail with a poignant feminist poetic justice when the mother's relationship with Clotilde effectively excludes both males from any physical or emotive relationship with either woman. Thus, in his zeal for ascendancy each male has vanquished not only his "enemy," but also its mirror reflection, himself. But then, Clotilde recognized earlier that she was the real man there. Again, Valenzuela posits that it is precisely the object of desire that the male destroys or changes in his path to self-validation, thereby rendering that object undesirable.

The remaining stories of the collection continue in the vein established by the first two stories as women are shown to be products and victims of the patriarchy and its discourse. Frequently, the female characters are inculpated (in an ironic mode, by the male characters, not by Valenzuela) when they fail to live up to the masculinist ideals as in "El pecado de la manzana" ("The Sin of the Apple") and "La profesora" ("The Teacher"). In "El pecado de la manzana," the ever-repeated tale of the "original" sin is told from the perspective of the apple, which literally and metaphorically falls "naturally," according to the men eying her greedily. Valenzuela's point, of course, is that the sin, the metaphoric fall, is neither "natural" nor does it originate in the apple but rather in those who made it/her fall and then used discourse metonymically to twist cause and effect. Similarly, in "La profesora," Mendizábal never comprehends that his former teacher's "failure" to meet his ideal is not due to an inherent weakness on her part but rather to his own fanciful, mythic mind-set. The final words of the story highlight her "fall," a metaphoric descent in his esteem, mediated by him, but nonetheless metonymically inverted so that she is viewed as the agent.

Although the collection continually reminds us of the pernicious dangers of language—the protagonist of "El abecedario" ("The Alphabet") decides to follow the alphabet letter by letter and logically on the thirteenth week "murió de meningitis" ("died of meningitis")—and its potentially inhibiting effects on women, we nevertheless find a number of female characters who exhibit their own brand of power, a power that is difficult to articulate since it is not recognized or admitted by androcentric society and thus lacks a designating name. It might be the power of witchcraft or the supernatural, but it is unquestionably a power over life and death as dramatized in "Alirka, la de los caballos" ("Irka of the Horses"), "Cuidad ajena," and "Julia J," where females seem to have the power both to create and to destroy. In "La desolada" ("Forsaken Woman") and "Los Menestrales" ("The Minstrels"), the female protagonists temporarily escape the oppression of patriarchal society by weaving their stories, a metaphoric form of control, just as the women in "Alirka" weave/knit their alternative world. In this respect the collection offers its own model for reading, for Valenzuela, too, uses storytelling to weave nets that simultaneously, if indeed paradoxically, captivate us and free us as they unmask the mythicizing power of language.

El gato eficaz, published in 1972, presents a new Pandora's box on both a literary and a mythic level. The female narrator has allowed all the evils of the world, in the form of "black cats of death," to escape while she articulates a subtle protest against the waste and corruption of the androcentric world. Once again the text plays with our myths and our discourse, ever deconstructing both. Although generally labeled a novel, *El gato eficaz* in fact defies genre definition.

Playful and serious at the same time, this innovative work undermines traditional concepts of literature and literary devices. The first-person narrator, by means of its continual fluctuation and metamorphosis, becomes an overtly fictional entity that paradoxically includes and excludes any and all "persons" outside of the novel. The repeated use of linguistic games and twists along with the incorporation of several types of discourse (journalistic, instructional, automatic, diary, legal), a technique found frequently in Valenzuela, demythologizes writing in the conventional sense, for it overtly illustrates how the word creates a new reality as it divorces itself from its previous referent. The work toys with and repudiates the dialectical structure of language by means of its play on antonyms such as dog and cat, life and death, woman and man, love and hatred. The suggestion is that the imposition of this antithetical language makes the world appear dichotomous and thus perhaps it is language itself that creates and then reinforces the polar oppositions we believe we perceive.

It is here more than in any of her previous works that Valenzuela evokes the erotic and vivaciously and humorously says what supposedly cannot, ought not to be said. Through her levity Valenzuela lifts the veil of censorship, particularly self-censorship, and speaks of topics historically deemed inappropriate for women. In one section entitled "Juguemos al fornicón" ("Let's Play Fornication"), she provides the rules for playing at the game of lovemaking; in another, the act of "telecoito," long-distance coitus, is described. Already on the first page, the narrator assures us, tongue in cheek and with double meaning, that a bed is not a place to die. And throughout, the discourse, the narrative, is motivated by male absence. As in "Cuarta versión" ("Fourth Version"), the female here writes while she awaits the return of the lover, says the unsayable, and creates her own world which paradoxically sometimes even excludes the one who motivated that discourse.

Aquí pasan cosas raras (1975; *Strange Things Happen Here*, 1979) is surely one of Valenzuela's most overtly political works to date. Written in Argentina near the height of the political terrorism of the 1970s, the collection focuses on the oppression of human beings by other human beings and our apparently limitless capacity for double thinking and double speaking as once again Valenzuela suggests that the political is defined by its misuse of discourse. Although the collection centers on specific events in an identifiable locale, its universality rests on the fact that the situations depicted have occurred or could occur almost anywhere at any time, in kind if not in detail.

In the first story, which provides the collection's title, two men are torn between conflicting desires: that of alleviating their poverty by appropriating the briefcase and sport jacket inexplicably left in their path, and the diametrically opposed desire to avoid confrontation or problems with the police whom they imagine to be watching them at every turn. "Los mejor calzados" ("The Best Shod") is an ironic and tragic glimpse of a city proud of its reputation for having the best shod beggars in the world. Unfortunately, the surplus of shoes available to the beggars is the product of an endless surplus of dead bodies from which the shoes are confiscated: those disappeared and tortured by the secret police and then cast aside. In yet another story, "Camino al ministerio" ("On the Way to the Ministry"), Valenzuela plays with the words of the title so that the preparation for the political position becomes almost mystical and resembles that of a religious leader. The would-be politician prepares his feet by burning the soles to develop calluses and be better able to step on anything (and implicitly anybody) as he undergoes various forms of almost ritualistic deprivation. This portrayal would be most telling in and of itself, but Valenzuela adds another twist: The neighbors support him in his endeavors, be they political or religious, in the hopes of profiting from his position. Ironically, their "affection" for their hero allows him to starve to death in his zeal. People do receive the government they deserve, Valenzuela proposes.

Like *El gato*, this collection too evinces its thematics of the erotic. In "Amor por los animales" ("Love of Animals"), the occupants of a blue car chase a white car in pursuit of an imagined and delectable "mina" (woman). Unfortunately, their imagination is belied by reality, for the white car carries only two male terrorists and illegal arms. In the typical Valenzuela metonymic inversion, the occupants of the blue car, initially motivated not by politics but simply by erotic desire, are taken into custody, questioned, and probably tortured after the two cars crash. In a parallel inversion of cause and effect, reality and fantasy, life and art, the two cars are fashioned into a work of art. Thus, the police state, eroticism, and commercial art come to overlap as each affects the other. Similarly, in "Cine porno" ("Porno Flick"), Valenzuela anticipates Susan Griffin's 1981 study, *Pornography and Silence*, which convincingly demonstrates that violence, pornography, and oppressive police states such as that of Nazi Germany are all products of the same mind-set. In each case the human being is mentally converted into an object, a nonbeing to be disposed of at will by those who may well assume the role of oppressor to compensate for and disguise their own sense of impotence.

"Unlimited Rapes United, Argentina" brings the attention back to the personal, but the personal is again shown to be a microcosm of national politics, where violation and violence are institutionalized and sanctioned, and language is used to distort reality. The irony of one of the final sentences says it all as the husband asserts that it is for his wife's sake that he pays the high dues to support the Frontal Rapists. The agency will be pleased to fulfill its duties— presumably raping the wife—even though they acknowledge it is difficult to do their job when criticized by the ladies because they are only men and cannot function under criticism. Meanwhile, the wife is paradoxically ever grateful to her husband for the sacrifices he makes for her and for defending her (rhetoric also employed by the military regime). Thus, the morpheme "defend" (not unlike countless others) is stripped of its normal significance (it is metaphorically raped) and inverted so that on both a personal and a political level what is labeled "defending" becomes a question of codified rape.

One of the most salient features of Valenzuela's novel, *Como en la guerra*

(1977; *He Who Searches*, n.d.), is its resilience and capacity to withstand a variety of readings on any number of levels. On one level it can be read in its classical mythic structure as a journey (via Barcelona, Mexico, and Buenos Aires) in search of the self or origins, but significantly the self the male narrator seeks via his journey, both real and imagined, linguistic and spatial, is a female self, she, a "she" that ultimately exists perhaps only as an idealistic figment of his imagination. On another level it might be read as a search for truth (nonetheless still female, she), as the psychoanalyst, after probing the mind of the female patient (who apparently proves to be a terrorist), tries to find her in reality, in time and space. In this respect it might be said that he seeks truth at the borderline between science, the scientific method, and humanism, while the text seems to suggest that the scientific method is inadequate to discover truth if it pretends to divorce itself from its subject matter: humanity, the human mind, and human emotions. Thus, Valenzuela again highlights the subjective nature of truth, especially the truth "produced" by words.

Nevertheless, the novel takes on quite a different aura if we focus on the textual frame, for, contrary to appearances, the search may take place in the mind, but it does not take place in a void. Rather, the mythic search itself is framed by two frighteningly real political situations: the final one in which the narrator, the searcher, finds himself in tyrannized Argentina, performing terrorist activities, and the initial one in which he is being interrogated and tortured, presumably also in Argentina in the 1970s. Unlike canonical novels, *Como en la guerra* begins not with chapter one but with "Página cero," which postdates the remainder of the novel and its search and whose political horrors provide quite a different framework for comprehending the novel. Thus, the mythic journey, the search, the tale is equally a form of escape, and we are led to surmise that the remainder of the text actually takes place in the narrator's mind just before he is killed as he seeks in his own words to reshape and recompose himself. Valenzuela posits the relativity and interrelationship of all times, but more importantly she highlights the brutality of the reality that cannot be erased by our mythic impulses. The metaphoric suggestion is that we continually begin at page one, but that we need to go back to zero to seek the hidden source, that which has been silenced. The work ends in circularity, psychological at least, for as a terrorist he has just blown up a building that falls apart to reveal its secret contents, "her" in her glass coffin. Presumably, at the same moment we also return to page zero where he is being raped with a gun barrel and the trigger is pulled, producing its own less elegant explosion.

Four of the stories from *Los heréticos* and fourteen stories from *Aquí pasan cosas raras* (1975) comprise the first part of Valenzuela's next published work, *Libro que no muerde* (1980; Book which does not bite), while the remainder of the text is the collection of short prose pieces which shares the book's title. Many of these pieces are amusing and insightful nuggets of wisdom or observations on language, politics, and life in general, although some are as short as one sentence. The collection evinces a definitive affinity to the rest of Valenzuela's literary production in many ways. The theme of the search, so central to *Como en la guerra*, continues as Valenzuela posits that both the search and an attitude of continual questioning are valid modes of life. She reminds us that the answers sought may well already exist within us, making the search one of interiority and self, if we will just ask the right questions. The theme of politics is still present in this volume but not to the degree of some of her other works, even though "Pequeño manual de vampirología teórica" ("Small Manual of Theoretic Vampirology") does proffer a thinly veiled, if indeed amusing, metaphor of the Argentine political situation of the 1970s. Still, the caustic nature of Valenzuela's presentation of the political is attenuated here by its alternation with clever and frequently amusing observations about various aspects of our everyday life, as she subtly admonishes that however abstract, ostensibly distant, or unpleasant the political may often be, it is an ineluctable part of everyday life whether or not we like it.

Much of *Libro que no muerde* is composed of self-conscious vignettes that question the act of writing itself as well as the nontransparence of language, often employing the metaphor of the sea/lagoon and its miasmas of which Valenzuela will avail herself in *Cola de lagartija*. At the same time, there is a recognition throughout this text that discourse, words, cannot be isolated or disassociated from the speaking and writing subject, however monstrous those words may sometimes prove to be. Once again in this collection we are offered an amusing, often poignant, depiction of eroticism and the relationship between the sexes.

Donde viven las águilas (1983; Where the eagles dwell), as the title suggests, takes us in many of its stories to the high plateau of Mexico, with its hazy, magical ambience, and offers us a glimpse of vestiges of an ancient civilization and a view of life different from that of contemporary society. In this world they speak a language of silences and time stands still. In fact, the first part of the text is full of moments that recall the magical transformation, in Mexico, which the narrator of *Como en la guerra* underwent in that novel. Although not all the stories take place in this magical world, many of the ones that do not still often focus on the inexplicable. In one story male and female characters interchange sex-related characteristics. In another, "El custodio Blancanieves" ("The Snow White Guard"), even the ostensibly law-abiding, morally upright, if indeed tedious, security guard enigmatically steals money and disappears from the face of the earth.

The stories of the second half of the collection, however, return more overtly to the question of politics. In the final story, "Los censores" (The censors), Juan seeks a job as a censor in order to intercept his own letter and thus protect himself and his addressee from persecution by the censors. Perversely, he becomes so well trained, so adept and zealous in his job, that when his letter does finally reach his desk, he condemns it and by association himself. He is shot at dawn, for the potential victim has been converted to victimizer, and, in turn, he has become his own victim, illustrating how ubiquitous and polymorphous are the ills of the society evoked.

In *Cambio de armas* (1983; *Other Weapons*, 1985) the personal and the political are most directly intermingled, and contemporary woman's plight is most directly attacked. Here each story focuses on a female protagonist, and each is narrated by a female. Significantly, too, each of the tales evokes the tension between political and erotic relationships while centering on the latter, no doubt because the erotic is what can be narrated; the political must be censored to a greater or lesser degree. Still, it is the erotic that functions throughout the text as a metaphor or synecdoche and thus a shield behind which the subtext, the political, rests. One merely reflects and/or disguises, distracts from the other, Valenzuela purports.

In the first tale, "Cuarta versión," the female narrator attempts to rewrite Bella's love story from the sea of papers she has found. Bella's love story, however, proves to be the tale of her death, for she is shot in the process of gaining political asylum for others. The narrative technique which piles layer upon layer of truth, fiction, reality, fantasy, language, fact, reminds us of the impossibility of expressing truth via language and highlights the inevitable identification between narrator and protagonist, reader and narrative.

The question of linguistic identification is dealt with once more in "La palabra asesino" ("The Word Killer") as the female protagonist is alternately attracted to and repelled by the killer until she exorcises her desire by articulating the word. Once said, the word becomes "other" and the emotional enslavement is broken. Similarly, in "Ceremonias de rechazo" ("Rituals of Rejection"), Amanda is psychologically able to distance herself from her lover and to recuperate her independence and sense of self by creating for herself a new mask, both linguistic and physical.

The culmination of the volume, which shares the collection's title, again highlights the questions of women, language, and politics as it depicts a former terrorist physically and erotically enslaved by the army colonel she attempted to assassinate. He has managed to erase her past and even her language while imposing his own on her and forcing her to be completely dependent on him. The strategy has worked only partially, however, for in the final gesture of the text, she points the thing he calls a revolver at him, and the reader is left to wonder whether or not she will actually pull the trigger. The point Valenzuela seems to be making is that the language of dominance is ever fragile, always threatening to break down and betray its speaker. Our linguistic weapons can be used against us.

Finally, Valenzuela's most recent novel, *Cola de lagartija* (*The Lizard's Tail*, 1983) is no doubt her most imaginative endeavor to date, but let us note that its metaphoricity in no way detracts from the trenchant and scathing criticism of the Argentine political situation and the use of language and rhetoric to distort and pervert. The two central characters of the novel are the Brujo, based on the factual figure of Isabel Perón's Minister of Social Well-Being, and the character-narrator, Luisa Valenzuela. The Brujo's principal activities include writing his autobiography, the Bible as he labels it, and, like any politician, conquering the world, annexing everything to his kingdom, by means of rhetoric or force as the case may be. At the same time, unlike other mere mortals, he is blessed with three testicles, the quintessence of masculinity. Paradoxically, however, his third testicle is a female, a pure egg, which he will inseminate and from which he will give birth to himself. From his mythic and myopic perspective he is complete in himself and thus a worthy god figure. Fortunately for the reader, the Brujo's mythomania is attenuated and balanced by the discourse of the character, Luisa Valenzuela, who is writing a novel about the Brujo and trying to deconstruct and make sense of the absurdities and atrocities that surround and inundate her world. The novel concludes as the Brujo explodes in a bloody overabundance of self-generated arrogance and exaggeration, and the long-promised river of blood proves to be only a thread of blood, but a thread that, like discourse and the metaphoric lagoon, traps us all even as we attempt to deconstruct and disarm it.

SURVEY OF CRITICISM

Valenzuela's works have received significant attention and acclaim in the United States. Ironically, she is probably better known in the United States than in her native Argentina, although she is certainly well respected by other Hispanic literary notables: "Courageous—with neither self-censorship or prejudice—careful of her language—which is excessive when necessary but magnificently refined and modest as well, whenever reality is" (Julio Cortázar, 1979, p. 44); "she is Latin American literature's heiress" (Carlos Fuentes). In the United States, her stories are frequently included in anthologies of women writers and Latin American writers, and she has been mentioned or had her books reviewed in *MS Magazine, Time Magazine, Saturday Review, Village Voice, El Espectador* (Bogotá), and *Los Universitarios* (Mexico), among others. *The Review of Contemporary Fiction* dedicated a special issue to her work, and in-depth studies on her works have appeared in most major Hispanic literary journals in the United States.

Studies of her works have tended to focus on her use of language as both a tool and content, form and message, for as already noted, she plays with language in her texts, but she also comments on the use and abuse of discourse, particularly the rhetoric employed by representatives of patriarchal sociopolitical institutions. The article by Marta Morello-Frosch (1986) focuses specifically on this aspect. Taking a somewhat different approach, Martha Paley Francescato (1985) studies *Cola de lagartija* in terms of Lacanian gender differentiation and nondifferentiation and the phallocentric manipulation of discourse that is eventually undermined by the female. Also focusing on discourse and rhetoric, Diane Marting (1986) examines nonreferentiality in *Aquí pasan cosas raras*. The first book-length study of Valenzuela's work, Sharon Magnarelli's *Reflections/Refractions: Reading Luisa Valenzuela*, appeared in 1988. In this volume each of Valenzuela's published works is analyzed in regard to women, politics, and discourse as Magnarelli posits that Valenzuela's books reflect and refract the three while it subsumes them all. In earlier publications Magnarelli studied *El gato eficaz* in a number of articles (1979, 1983), by analyzing the underlying relationship among women, cats, and language and demonstrating that women and cats are products of the myth-making properties of discourse. Z. Nelly Martínez has taken a post-structuralist approach to *El gato eficaz* in her study of that novel (1979) and sees *Donde viven las águilas* in terms of holism in another article (1986). At least one anthology of critical essays is planned for the near future. Ediciones del Norte has included Valenzuela in their series of interviews on videotape.

BIBLIOGRAPHY

Works by Luisa Valenzuela

Hay que sonreír. Buenos Aires: Américalee, 1966.
Los heréticos. Buenos Aires: Paidós, 1967.
El gato eficaz. Mexico City: Joaquín Mortiz, 1972.
Aquí pasan cosas raras. Buenos Aires: Ediciones de la Flor, 1975.
Como en la guerra. Buenos Aires: Sudamericana, 1977.
Libro que no muerde. Mexico City: UNAM, 1980.
Cambio de armas. Hanover, N.H.: Ediciones del Norte, 1982.
Cambio de armas. Mexico City: Martín Casillas, 1983.
Cola de lagartija. Buenos Aires: Bruguera, 1983.
Donde viven las águilas. Buenos Aires: Celtia, 1983.

Translations of Luisa Valenzuela

Bonner, Deborah, trans. *Other Weapons*. Hanover, N.H.: Ediciones del Norte, 1985.
Carpentier, Hortense, and J. Jorge Castello, trans. *Clara: Thirteen Short Stories and a Novel*. New York: Harcourt Brace Jovanovich, 1976. Translation of *Hay que sonreír* and *Los heréticos*.
Lane, Helen, trans. *He Who Searches*. Elmwood Park, Ill.: Dalkey Archive Press, n.d. Translation of *Como en la guerra*.
————. *Strange Things Happen Here: Twenty-six Short Stories and a Novel*. New York: Harcourt Brace Jovanovich, 1979. Translation of *Aquí pasan cosas raras* and *Como en la guerra*.
"A Legacy of Poets and Cannibals: Literature Revives in Argentina." *Lives on the Line: The Testimony of Contemporary Latin American Authors*. Ed. Doris Meyer. Berkeley: University of California, 1988. Pp. 290–97.
Magnarelli, Sharon, trans. "The Snow White Guard." *Landscapes of a New Land*. Ed. Marjorie Agosín. Buffalo, N.Y.: White Pine Press, 1989. Pp. 122–27.
Rabassa, Gregory, trans. *The Lizard's Tail*. New York: Farrar, Straus and Giroux, 1983.

Works about Luisa Valenzuela

Araújo, Helena. "Valenzuela's *Other Weapons*." *The Review of Contemporary Fiction* 6, 3 (1986):78–81.

Callejo, Alfonso. "Literatura e irregularidad en *Cambio de armas* de Luisa Valenzuela." *Revista Iberoamericana* 51, 132–33 (1985):575–80.

Case, Barbara. "On Writing, Magic, and Eva Perón: An Interview with Argentina's Luisa Valenzuela." *Ms. Magazine* 12, 4 (Oct. 1983):18–20.

Cortázar, Julio. "Luisa Valenzuela." *Review* 24 (1979):44.

Fores, Ana M. "Valenzuela's *Cat-O-Nine Deaths*." *The Review of Contemporary Fiction* 6, 3 (1986):39–47.

Garfield, Evelyn Picón. "Interview with Luisa Valenzuela." *The Review of Contemporary Fiction* 6, 3 (1986):25–30.

———. "Muerte—metamorfosis—modernidad: *El gato eficaz* de Luisa Valenzuela." *Insula* 400–401 (1980):17.

Gazarian Gautier, Marie-Lise. "Luisa Valenzuela." *Interviews with Latin American Writers*. Elmwood, Ill.: Dalkey Archive Press, 1989. Pp. 293–322.

———. "The Sorcerer and Luisa Valenzuela: Double Narrators of the Novel/Biography, Myth/History." *The Review of Contemporary Fiction* 6, 3 (1986):105–108.

Glantz, Margo. "Luisa Valenzuela's *He Who Searches*." *The Review of Contemporary Fiction* 6, 3 (1986):62–66.

———. "Para un modelo crítico." *Bellas Artes* (Mexico) 21 (1981):2.

Gómez Engler, Raquel. "Borrón y cuenta nueva: Reflexión sobre el uso de las máscaras de belleza en un cuento de Luisa Valenzuela." *Alba de América* 3, 4–5 (1985):123–28.

Hicks, Emily. "That Which Resists: The Code of the Real in Luisa Valenzuela's *He Who Searches*." *The Review of Contemporary Fiction* 6, 3 (1986):55–61.

Maci, Guillermo. "The Symbolic, the Imaginary and the Real in Luisa Valenzuela's *He Who Searches*." *The Review of Contemporary Fiction* 6, 3 (1986):67–77.

Magnarelli, Sharon. "Censorship and the Female Writer: An Interview/Dialog with Luisa Valenzuela." *Letras Femeninas* 10, 1 (1984):55–64.

———. "*El gato eficaz* de Luisa Valenzuela." *Universitario* (Mexico) 187 (1981):21.

———. "Entrevista con Luisa Valenzuela." *Espejo de Escritores*. Videocassette. Hanover, N.H.: Ediciones del Norte, 1985.

———. "Gatos, lenguaje y mujeres en *El gato eficaz* de Luisa Valenzuela." *Revista Iberoamericana* 45, 108–109 (1979):603–11.

———. "Humor and Games in Luisa Valenzuela's *El gato eficaz*: The Looking-Glass World Re-visited." *Modern Language Studies* 13, 3 (1983):81–89.

———. "Juego/fuego de la esperanza: En torno a *El gato eficaz* de Luisa Valenzuela." *Cuadernos Americanos* 247 (1983):199–208.

———. "*The Lizard's Tail* by Luisa Valenzuela: Discourse Denatured." *The Review of Contemporary Fiction* 6, 3 (1986):97–104.

———. "Luisa Valenzuela: From *Hay que sonreír* to *Cambio de armas*." *World Literature Today* 58, 1 (1984):9–13.

———. "Luisa Valenzuela's *Cambio de armas*: Subversion and Narrative Weaponry." *Romance Quarterly* 34, 1 (1987):85–94.

———. *Reflections/Refractions: Reading Luisa Valenzuela*. New York: Peter Lang, 1988.

———. "Women, Language, and Cats in Luisa Valenzuela's *El gato eficaz*: Looking-

Glass Games of Fire.'' *The Lost Rib*. Lewisburg, Pa.: Bucknell University Press, 1985. Pp. 169–85.

Marcos, Juan Manuel. ''Luisa Valenzuela, más allá de la araña de la esquina rosada.'' *Prismal/Cabral* 11 (1983):57–65.

Martínez, Z. Nelly. ''*El gato eficaz* de Luisa Valenzuela: La productividad del texto.'' *Revista Canadiense de Estudios Hispánicos* 4 (1979):73–80.

———. ''Luisa Valenzuela's *The Lizard's Tail*: Deconstruction of the Peronist Mythology.'' *El Cono Sur: Dinámica y dimensiones de su literatura: A Symposium*. Rose S. Minc, ed. Montclair, N.J.: Montclair State College, 1985.

———. ''Luisa Valenzuela's 'Where the Eagles Dwell': From Fragmentation to Holism.'' *The Review of Contemporary Fiction* 6, 3 (1986):109–15.

Marting, Diane. ''Female Sexuality in Selected Short Stories by Luisa Valenzuela: Toward an Ontology of her Work.'' *The Review of Contemporary Fiction* 6, 3 (1986):48–54.

Morello-Frosch, Marta. ''*Other Weapons*: When Metaphors Become Real.'' *The Review of Contemporary Fiction* 6, 3 (1986):82–87.

Mull, Dorothy S. ''Ritual Transformation in Luisa Valenzuela's 'Rituals of Rejection'.'' *The Review of Contemporary Fiction* 6, 3 (1986):88–96.

———, and Elsa B. de Angulo. ''An Afternoon with Luisa Valenzuela.'' *Hispania* 69, 2 (1986):350–52.

Ordóñez, Montserrat. ''Máscaras de espejos, un juego especular: Entrevista—asociaciones con la escritora argentina Luisa Valenzuela.'' *Revista Iberoamericana* 51, 132–33 (1985):511–19.

———. ''Memoria y poder en tres escritoras del Cono Sur.'' *El Espectador: Magazín Dominical* (Bogotá) 94 (Jan. 13, l985): 14–16.

Paley Francescato, Martha. ''*Cola de lagartija*: látigo de la palabra y la triple P.'' *Revista Iberoamericana* 51, 132–33 (l985):875–82.

Sabino, Osvaldo R. ''Los nombres y los gatos: Luisa Valenzuela y sus siete libros.'' *Alba de América* 1, 1 (l983):155–66.

Sheppard, R. Z. ''Where the Fiction Is 'Fantástica'.'' *Time* Mar. 7, 1983:78–82.

Umpierre, Luz María. ''Luisa Valenzuela: *Cola de lagartija*.'' *Revista Iberoamericana* 51, 130–31 (l985):430–32.

INDIAN WOMEN WRITERS OF SPANISH AMERICA

Nancy Gray Díaz

INTRODUCTION

The works of Domitila Barrios, Rigoberta Menchú, and some other Latin American Indian women writers have special significance as social statements, as models of *literatura testimonial* (testimonial literature), and as deeply felt and eloquent accounts of authentic human experience. Both Barrios and Menchú have taken active roles as leaders in the political struggles of their peoples and have gained considerable moral authority for what they have to say about feminism and the class struggle in their respective countries. Their works deserve inclusion in the study of Latin American literature both because they are central to the genre of testimonial literature and because they illuminate areas of the Latin American experience which the literate classes—who write and publish books—have little understood.

Both Barrios's and Menchú's accounts, like most works of testimonial literature, were told orally, recorded, and then written down by others. Barrios's story is *"Si me permiten hablar . . ."* (1976; the English translation is *Let Me Speak*, 1978) with Moema Viezzer. Menchú's narrative is written and organized by Elizabeth Burgos: *Me llamo Rigoberta Menchú y así me nació la conciencia* (1983; English version: *I, Rigoberta Menchu, An Indian Woman of Guatemala*, trans. Ann Wright, 1984). Also to be considered in this chapter are two other autobiographical accounts given in *Dos mujeres indígenas* (1976; Two Indian women), one by Basilia, a Quechua woman of Bolivia, and the other by Facundina, a Chiriguano woman of northern Argentina. Basilia's narration is translated into Spanish from Quechua by her daughter and transcribed and interpreted by the anthropologist June Nash. Facundina's story is rendered by another anthropologist, Manuel María Rocca. Also recommended to the reader is the story of Elvia Alvarado, *Don't Be Afraid, Gringo: A Honduran Woman Speaks from the Heart* (1987), which is translated and edited by Medea Benjamin and published by the Institute for Food and Development Policy for the purpose of educating the English-speaking public about the critical problems of poverty and oppression in Honduras.

BIOGRAPHY

Domitila Barrios was born on May 7, 1937, in Siglo XX, a major tin mining community in the highlands of Bolivia. Although she is Spanish-speaking, her father, who was Indian, was fluent in both Quechua and Aymara. At the age of three, her family moved to Pulacayo, an industrial town in the Department of Potosí. Her father, a tailor by trade, was politically militant and a union leader; he had been persecuted for his political activities from before the time his children were born. When Domitila was still a child, her father taught her about the political struggles of the working class in Bolivia; he instilled in her the belief that women must learn to understand and involve themselves in public affairs just as men must. Her mother died sometime after Domitilia reached her tenth birthday, and she took charge of her four younger sisters. She attended school through the sixth grade but paid a terrible price: since there was no one to care for her sisters, one little one, left unattended, ate carbide ashes out of a garbage can, became ill, and died. Her father's eventual remarriage did not help the situation since Domitila and her sisters were rejected by their stepmother, and Domitila eventually ran away with a young miner whom she married and with whom she has had seven children. It was with him that she returned to Siglo XX, which has been her home when not in exile.

During the early years of her stay in Siglo XX, Domitila felt a conflict between her religion (she was a Jehovah's Witness) and her growing commitment to political activities, but with time she determined that working for improved living conditions through the Housewives' Committee was her true vocation. The development of her political and social consciousness has been fostered not only by the cruelty of her own oppression, but also by her determined sense of solidarity with the miners and the Bolivian people.

Barrios's relationship with the union leaders began when, after two years in Siglo XX, the authorities came to evict her from her house. Her husband was away, and she was pregnant. The union leader Federico Escobar intervened and forced the authorities to reverse the eviction. In 1963 the miners of Siglo XX took four North Americans hostage in response to the arrest and imprisonment of union leaders who had attended a workers' congress. The Housewives' Committee supported the miners' action by guarding the prisoners, and it was at this time that Barrios became a full participating member of the committee and came to work with Norberta de Aguilar, the well-known leader of the committee. Barrios gives an eyewitness account of the September Massacre (at Siglo XX, September 1965) and the San Juan Massacre (June 24, 1967). In both cases heavily armed soldiers ambushed the miners, the women, and children. In Domitila's words: "There were scenes I'll never forget, that are still vivid and that were really ghastly. Entire families died. Rivers of blood flowed. There were people who died in bed, because the soldiers were shooting wild, really wild, at everything" (*Let Me Speak*, p. 116). She recounts many details to convey the savagery of the army against the people.

In the aftermath of the San Juan massacre, Barrios was arrested on false charges of killing a lieutenant and of being a Communist. Secretly transported to La Paz with her two-year-old daughter, she suffered the torture of being told that her other children had also been sequestered and were being held in an underground tunnel without food. Then the authorities tried to force her to give up her right to her children, but she refused and was eventually released. It turned out that her children had been at home in the care of her father all the time. Shortly afterward she was arrested again, and this time, seven months pregnant, she was beaten mercilessly. As she was forced to give birth in her cell alone, her baby died, and she became seriously ill. The passages describing the agony of her loss are among the most moving of this wrenching account.

Released once more, she and her family were exiled to Los Yungas, a tropical region, which they found uncongenial because of the heat and the food. There she made a long, slow recovery from her ordeal. In 1974, having returned to Siglo XX, Barrios was approached by Helena Solberg-Ladd, the Brazilian filmmaker, who asked permission to feature her in the film *La doble jornada (The Double Day*, 1975). Barrios agreed and also accepted Solberg-Ladd's invitation to attend the International Women's Year Conference in Mexico City. At the conference she found that she had little in common with the concerns of North American feminists. Instead of identifying men as adversaries, she spoke against North American imperialism, which results in an economic system of abject misery in Bolivia. Furthermore, she argued that women's main task is not to fight against their *compañeros* (mates, companions, or fellow-workers), but to work with them to create a "system in which men and women will have the right to live, to work, to organize" (p. 199).

In her second book, *Aquí también, Domitila* (1985; Here, too, Domitila), Barrios relates her experiences from 1976 to 1983: her participation in a hunger strike in La Paz to achieve amnesty for political prisoners; her travels in Europe and Latin America to denounce violations of human rights in Bolivia and to promote understanding and solidarity among workers; her participation as a member of the jury at the Russell Tribunal; and her years of exile in Sweden (after the Bolivian government sentenced her to death in absentia).

Rigoberta Menchú was born in San Miguel Uspantán, El Quiché, Guatemala, in 1959. Until she was twenty years old, she spoke only Quiché; she decided to learn Spanish for political reasons, and her account is rendered in her own words with very little correction, for the purpose of preserving the authenticity of her manner of expression. Like Barrios, Menchú had a father and also a mother who were active in community affairs and who became political activists as a reaction to the oppression to which they and their community were subjected. Unlike Barrios, Menchú belongs to a very traditional Indian community, one that preserves the ceremonies, diet, clothing, language, and values of its ancestors. Much of Menchú's account is devoted to the loving description of her people's customs and ways of life and to the moving record of the loss of her family members, one by one.

Menchú's family were farmers on a small plot in the western highlands of Guatemala. Since the farm did not produce enough to sustain the family, they would have to travel back and forth to the tropical coastal areas to cut sugar cane or pick coffee during eight months of the year. Menchú describes the hardships of the journey to the coast: Forced to ride crowded together with children and their farm animals in a covered truck for two nights and a day without stop, the people would become ill from the smell and the rapid change in climate. Menchú never attended school because of the deep distrust which the Indians have for the schools (the schools foster *ladino*—that is, Hispanicized Indian or dominant— culture and require the children to adapt to the alien ways), and at the age of eight, she began to work for a salary on the plantation. Meals were served only to those who worked, and in order to feed their small children, the parents would have to deprive themselves. Two of her young siblings died on the plantations, one from malnutrition and one from exposure to chemical spraying, which was routinely carried out without concern for the people working in the fields.

At age thirteen, Menchú went to the capital to work as a servant. Unable to speak Spanish, unfamiliar with the city, she was a virtual prisoner to the harsh and contemptuous treatment of her employer. Furthermore, she was cheated of her wages and given less nourishment than the family dog. It was at that time that she learned that her father had been imprisoned for leading community resistance against *ladino* landowners who had seized the community lands. Vicente Menchú was released, and, together with many supporters formed the CUC, the Committee for Peasant Unity, which was to foment political opposition to those who were defrauding the peasants of their lands. Menchú's father and the other leaders of the CUC went underground to protect their families. Nevertheless, her mother, her brothers, and Rigoberta herself began to work actively to organize the people of other villages. She decided at this time to learn other languages—Mam, Cakchiquel, Tzutuhil, and Spanish—so as to be able to communicate with people in as many villages as possible. She decided that Spanish was the language of the authorities, and the Indians' inability to use it was one of the key reasons why the system could be subverted to cheat them.

As a result of her family's involvement in nonviolent political protest of their abject living conditions, Rigoberta's brother, mother, and father were killed. Her brother was tortured, then burned alive. Her mother was kidnapped, tortured almost to death, revived, then tortured again until she died. Many Indian women were raped, and many others suffered the same fate as Menchú's family members.

The circumstances surrounding Menchú's father's death eventually resulted in her exile. In 1981 Vicente Menchú led a march on the capital in order to protest and to bring to the attention of the outside world the problems of the Guatemalan Indians. They took over the Spanish embassy but were caught, and the leaders were burned to death. The next year, after having had to go underground to avoid capture by the army, Rigoberta Menchú decided to go abroad to try to publicize the plight of her people. In speaking of her decision to dedicate her life to her people, to forego marriage and children; in affirming her religious faith and her love of her people; and in remembering the horror and pain of her losses, she quotes her sister: ''I am happy; don't feel sorry for me. Even though I have to suffer hunger, pain, long journeys on foot in the mountains, I am doing it with so much love, and I am doing it for you'' (p. 268). In 1982, at the age of twenty-three, Rigoberta Menchú told her story to Elizabeth Burgos in Paris, and it was published in 1983.

Both Basilia and Facundina form a sharp contrast to Barrios and Menchú because they are not political activists. Both tell their stories at the behest of the anthropologists, and their accounts lack the spirit, passion, and energy that inform the narratives of Barrios and Menchú. In 1976, when June Nash interviewed her, Basilia was retired and ill after a lifetime of great diligence and hard work. She had a total of $150.00 to sustain her for the rest of her life, for she was not permitted to work any longer. Embittered and fiercely resentful against the government of Bolivia, her dead parents, and her children, she tells a life story filled with struggle, misery, and a sense of betrayal by both the authorities and her family. Yet her story so totally lacks any concern for others and is so vindictive that it tends to alienate. Facundina, a sixty-five-year-old woman, who has lived in both Argentina and Bolivia because of the migrations of her husband, represents the case of a woman without a sense of community, having neither the ties of a traditional Indian village nor the sense of belonging to a town or region. Both her story and that of Basilia contribute much to our understanding of the lives, feelings, and experiences of contemporary Latin American Indian women, and in many ways they may be more typical of the lives of millions of women than those of the activists. Nevertheless, the literary quality of their narratives does not match that of Barrios or Menchú.

MAJOR THEMES

Typical of these women's writings is the preoccupation with women's traditional roles and spheres—marriage and family, domestic life, the community, women's work; with hardship, oppression, and the proper response to these; with race relations; with religion; and with the vision of their children's and the society's future. Marriage and children are major concerns in all of these women's narratives, as would be expected especially in societies that have little consciousness of, or access to, birth control. Throughout Domitila Barrios's narrative, concern for her children's safety, welfare, and future is a central motive in her actions, although she does not often refer to them as individuals, nor does she give them more importance than the children of the other miners. For Menchú, the decision not to marry is an extraordinary sacrifice, but one that she feels she must make in order to continue her political work. Basilia resents her grown children for neglecting her in her old age and says that children come from God, for if it were up to women, there would be no children.

Menchú treasures the domestic life of her people. She devotes much time to the description of the daily routines of preparation of food, care of children and animals, and religious ceremonies, which are an integral part of the domestic life of family and community. For Barrios, on the other hand, domestic responsibilities are a political issue. Since her husband's miner's wage will not sustain the family, she must get up at four in the morning, bake a hundred *salteñas* (meat pies), and go to the market to sell them. When she comes home, there is the hard work of washing, cooking, and caring for her children. The work at home is unpaid work for the boss, she states. Basilia's discussion of work is exceptional for several reasons. Her family owned land, and, as she says, she worked day and night "like a burro" for her parents. Later, she went to work in the mine and earned enough to set her parents up in a store. Nevertheless, they forced her to separate from her husband so as to have control of her earnings, and, when they died, they left her nothing. Proud of having worked in the mine "like a man," Basilia describes with satisfaction her aptitude for the work and her ambition. As a result of this role, however, she suffered the contempt of her bosses and the male workers. Women who do this kind of work are the objects of derision in the society in general. When she worked as a seamstress in a factory, she experienced the antagonism of the other women because she consistently exceeded the quotas. Because of her marriage to a landowner and of belonging at least for a time to the privileged class, Basilia looks back with nostalgia to the days before the 1952 revolution. The fact that as a result of that revolution the Indian population and the peasants made such gains as land reform, the nationalization of the mines, universal suffrage, and educational reform has no importance for her.

Both Barrios and Menchú have come to accept a major role in their communities, and, in taking on this role, they have built on the roles of model women who came before them. The analysis of their reasons for, and feelings about, these roles is a crucial motive for telling their stories. As was already stated, Domitila Barrios grew to a leadership position after her apprenticeship in the Housewives' Committee. Rigoberta Menchú describes in loving terms the example set by her mother, who, though limited by the control and jealousy of her husband during the early years of their marriage, grew to a position of great respect and influence in the community as a healer, a midwife, and finally as a political organizer. Like Barrios's father, Menchú's mother taught her that she had just as much responsibility to participate in the struggle for justice as did a man.

Another major, common theme in the narratives of Barrios and Menchú is the description of abuses and the analysis of oppression. Both are aware from an early age of the harshness of their existence, and both define their coming of age in terms of their developing understanding of injustice and oppression. Barrios states from the beginning that Bolivia is a country rich in natural resources but whose economy is controlled by multinational corporations. Although it is clear that both have been exposed to sophisticated political analyses of under-development, the origins of their arguments are autochthonous, coming strongly and consistently from their own direct experience. Menchú's discourse especially is so pervasively subjective that the political is integral to the personal.

Although both women give consideration to feminist ideas, for them the class struggle precedes opposition to male dominance. They separate themselves from the feminist movements of the industrialized countries, seeing those as permeated by bourgeois values. Even though Barrios occasionally mentions her husband's disapproval of her political activities, she and the other women work to defend and protect him and the other miners. Menchú describes the differences between men's and women's lives and duties, analyzes the reasons and consequences for them, and assents to them. For example, her mother gave larger portions of food to her father because, according to her, he had to expend more energy in his work. Both women express full commitment to the struggles of their *compañeros*. Nevertheless, both women also give special attention to women's issues. Barrios and her women allies fight for the rights of the "rock pile women," widows for whom the only form of employment is to collect rocks with some ore in them from rock piles, grind them, and turn in the minute amount of ore to the company. Menchú lends support and counsel to young women raped by soldiers.

The view of race relations in these narratives is very much influenced by class considerations. In Bolivia the *campesino* (peasant farmer) class is made up almost entirely of Indians who continue to speak Quechua and Aymara and retain their traditional dress and customs. The mine workers, although Indian by blood, have left many of the traditional ways and do not usually retain ties to the *campesino* communities. (However, as June Nash demonstrates in *We Eat the Mines and the Mines Eat Us*, the mine workers retain a world-view that belongs to the pre-Columbian past.) In *Let Me Speak*, Barrios mentions the Bolivian Indian peasants, who are much worse off even than the miners, but she shows little interest in, or sense of solidarity with, them. However, later, in her work for the Assembly for Human Rights of Bolivia, she had the opportunity to review at first hand the conditions and demands of these fellow-countrymen and women and became militant on their behalf, as well as that of the mine workers. Rigoberta Menchú, on the other hand, affords us a view of life from inside a traditional community, and it reveals a visceral distrust of those who have abandoned the Indian ways to become part of the larger society. Basilia demonstrates outright her contempt for the Indian peasants, and Facundina reflects graphically the poignant condition of people who are caught in between, who belong neither to the traditional communities nor to the society at large.

Religion and folkloric beliefs are important concerns in the accounts of Barrios, Menchú, and Basilia. As previously mentioned, Barrios struggled for several years between the demands of her religious community, which opposed her political activities, and the commitment she felt toward those activities. In her view, "religion in Bolivia put itself at the service of the powerful" (p. 64); she does not belong to an organized religion but maintains her faith in God. Both Barrios and Menchú denounce the disruptive role of organized religion, whether Catholic or the Jehovah's Witnesses, in the struggle for racial and economic justice, although they praise the efforts of individual priests.

Rigoberta Menchú's faith is expressed vehemently and analyzed as part of her developing consciousness, as a justification for her activism and as a reason for being. She rejects the notion that there is a contradiction in believing in both the Christian Bible and the traditional religious practices of her people. For her, the Christian God corresponds to the one god of her people, the Sun. Citing the stories of Judith and Moses from the Bible, she finds justification for civil disobedience. On the other hand, her beliefs in nagualism (the idea that one has an animal alter ego) and in the sacredness of the earth and the corn, for example, clearly enrich her sense of identity and give her added joy and fulfillment in the meaning of her life.

Basilia's beliefs are also syncretic but of a sort that cause her to fear evil spirits and alter her routines in order to placate them. The system of beliefs in supernatural forces and beings to which she makes constant reference is described by June Nash (*We Eat the Mines and the Mines Eat Us*) as revolving around forces that determine one's fate in the mines and rituals that involve agriculture and the earth. Thus, for all of these women, religious beliefs inform their view of the world and influence their moral judgments and actions.

Both Domitila Barrios and Rigoberta Menchú focus determinedly on the future society which they hope to see created; the commitment to their peoples expresses itself in a vision of hope and promise for the future. Barrios envisions a Bolivia governed by the working class, a people proud of their own heritage and not so impressed as they tend presently to be by things and ideas from abroad. She believes that Bolivia is a country rich in natural resources, and she opposes the presence of multinational corporations and the drain of Bolivian economic resources in profits and foreign investment. She believes that "socialism will be the tool which will create the conditions for women to reach their level" (p. 234), and this will happen through women's own struggle alongside the men. Rigoberta Menchú refers to herself as a revolutionary Christian and sees her own mission as that of condemning and denouncing the injustices practiced against the people. She believes that the transformation of society will come through the people's revolutionary movements and not through existing governmental structures. The society she envisions, then, would put an end to the routine and systematic violence practiced against the poor; it would be a more equitable society without malnutrition and the other evils of poverty; it would allow a fair distribution of land and protect the property rights of the small landowner; furthermore it would defend the rights to work and earn a fair wage, to buy necessities at fair prices, to organize and to live according to one's own cultural heritage without fear of discrimination; and it would develop an economy that would move away from the dependence that fosters exploitation. Menchú opposes Marxism on religious grounds; presumably the society she envisions for the future is one in which the individual and community would have the maximum opportunity for spiritual and cultural growth.

SURVEY OF CRITICISM

With the exception of a few pieces on Domitila Barrios, no important commentary has as yet emerged on the Latin American Indian women writers discussed in this chapter. Three essays discuss Barrios from psychological, sociological, and political perspectives, respectively, and one discusses her narrative in a literary context. *We Eat the Mines and the Mines Eat Us* is a very important discussion of the history, politics, and anthropology of the Bolivian mine workers which uses Domitila Barrios as a source.

Lawrence R. Alschuler (1980) discusses the development of Barrios's consciousness of oppression and her thinking about liberation. He analyzes step by step how she has attained "critical consciousness," in Paulo Freire's terms, without having benefited from higher education or having experienced living in a technological society. In a review article, Ricardo A. Godoy (1985) compares *Let Me Speak* to *The Devil and Commodity Fetishism in South America* by Michael T. Taussig, the latter being an anthropological work that studies the concept of the devil among Bolivian tin miners. Referring to *Let Me Speak*, Godoy states that "throughout the book, one is impressed by Barrios' sincerity, commitment, penetrating intelligence, and courage" (p. 276). Nevertheless, he finds fault with her examination of Bolivian society for her almost total exclusion of the agrarian sector. As noted above, her second book amply demonstrates her widening consciousness of, and solidarity with, the *campesinos* of Bolivia and other Latin American countries. In an essay on women's involvement in recent Bolivian political movements, Gloria Ardaya Salinas (1986) discusses both the *Barzolas*, a female branch of the MNR, the Revolutionary Nationalist Movement, and the Housewives' Committee. This essay does not so much examine Barrios's work as use it as a primary source for the study of the Housewives' Committee as an important organization in recent Bolivian political history.

Finally, in her article "El género testimonial: aproximaciones feministas," Margarite Fernández Olmos incorporates several testimonial narratives by women, Domitila Barrrios's prominent among them, into the testimonial genre as originally defined by Miguel Barnet. Focusing on Elena Poniatowska's* *Hasta no verte, Jesús mío* (1969; *Until We Meet Again*, 1987), Margaret Randall's *El pueblo no sólo es testigo* (The people are not only witnesses), Miguel Barnet's *La canción de Rachel* (1969; Rachel's song), Barrios's *Let Me Speak*, and *Quarto de despejo: Diario de uma favelada* (1960; *Child of the Dark: Diary of a Woman of the Brazilian Slums*, 1962) by Carolina Maria de Jesús, Fernández Olmos points to the importance to the women's movement of these testimonial narratives for their honest and complex analyses of the conditions of women's lives, for their artistry in the selection and ordering of their material, and for the richness of expression of their emotional experience. In addition, she signals the importance of their manner of expression, the fact that these women, who are not well educated, have nevertheless mastered powerful and eloquent means of communication. She shows that thereby they contribute significantly to the democratization of Latin American literature.

BIBLIOGRAPHY

Works of Oral Testimony by Spanish American Indian Women Writers

Barrios de Chungara, Domitila. *Aquí también, Domitila*. Ed. David Acebey. Mexico City: Siglo Veintiuno Editores, 1985.

―――. *"Si me permiten hablar . . ."*: *Testimonio de Domitila una mujer de las minas de Bolivia*. Ed. Moema Viezzer. Mexico City: Siglo Veintiuno Editores, 1976.

Dos mujeres indígenas: Basilia por June Nash, Facundina por Manuel María Rocca. Mexico City: Instituto Indigenista Interamericano, 1976.

Menchú, Rigoberta. *Me llamo Rigoberta Menchú y así me nació la conciencia*. Ed. Elizabeth Burgos. Mexico City: Siglo Veintiuno Editores, 1983.

Méscue, Evangelino. "Entrevista con Rigoberta Menchú." *Los agentes de Xibalbá*. Bogotá: Editorial Memoria, 1986.

Translations

Benjamin, Medea, ed. and trans. *Don't Be Afraid, Gringo: A Honduran Woman Speaks from the Heart. The Story of Elvia Alvarado*. San Francisco: Institute for Food and Development Policy, 1987.

Kreger, Regina Ann, trans. "Things Happened to Me as in a Movie." By Rigoberta Menchú. *You Can't Drown the Fire: Latin American Women Writing in Exile*. Ed. Alicia Portnoy. Pittsburgh: Cleis Press, 1988. Pp. 18–23.

Ortiz, Victoria, trans. *Let Me Speak! Testimony of Domitila, A Woman of the Bolivian Mines*. By Domitila Barrios de Chungara with Moema Viezzer. New York: Monthly Review Press, 1978.

Randall, Elinor, trans. "Two Deaths," "The Russell Tribunal," and "Then Who Died?" By Domitila Barrios de Chungara as interviewed by Moema Viezzer. *You Can't Drown the Fire: Latin American Women Writing in Exile*. Ed. Alicia Portnoy. Pittsburgh: Cleis Press, 1988. Pp. 38–49.

Wright, Ann, trans. *I, Rigoberta Menchú, An Indian Woman of Guatemala*. By Rigoberta Menchú. Ed. Elizabeth Burgos Debray. London: Verso Editions, 1984.

Works about Spanish American Indian Women Writers

Alschuler, Lawrence R. "The Conscientization of Domitila: A Case Study in the Political Psychology of Liberation." *Contemporary Crises* 4 (1980):27–41.

Ardaya Salinas, Gloria. "The Barzolas and the Housewives Committee." *Women and Change in Latin America*. Eds. June Nash and Helen Safa. South Hadley, Mass.: Bergin and Garvey, 1986. Pp. 326–43.

Fernández Olmos, Margarite. "El género testimonial: Aproximaciones feministas." *Re-vista/Review Interamericana* 21, 1 (Spring 1981):69–75.
Godoy, Ricardo A. "Bolivian Mining." *Latin American Research Review* 20, 1 (1985):272–77.
Randall, Margaret. "Escritura y testimonio femeninos." *Plural* 10, 2d época, 120 (Sept. 1981):26–8.

Other Works Cited

Barnet, Miguel. "La canción de Rachel," "La novel testimonio: socio-literatura." *La canción de Rachel*. Barcelona: Editorial Estela, 1969.
Jesus, Carolina Maria de. *Quarto de despejo: Diario de uma favelada*. Rio de Janeiro: Livraria Francisco Alves, 1960.
———. *Child of the Dark: Diary of a Woman of the Brazilian Slums*. Trans. David St. Clair. N.Y.: New American Library, 1962.
Nash, June. *We Eat the Mines and the Mines Eat Us: Dependency and Exploitation in Bolivian Tin Mines*. New York: Columbia University Press, 1979.
Poniatowska, Elena. *Hasta no verte, Jesús mío*. Mexico City: Era, 1969.
———. *Until We Meet Again*. Trans. Magda Bogin. N.Y.: Pantheon, 1987.

LATINA WRITERS IN THE UNITED STATES

Norma Alarcón

INTRODUCTION

Although archival research will eventually make clear that women of Spanish American descent have been writing and publishing in the United States since the nineteenth century, their numbers have grown considerably over the past few decades. Moreover, among some a dramatic change in consciousness has taken place which is very much in step with such Anglo-American political events as the civil rights movements (which included Afro-Americans, Native Americans, Asian Americans, Chicanos and Puerto Ricans), the movement against the war in Vietnam and the Anglo-American feminist movement. On a global scale one can point to the "invention" of the Third World with attendant anticolonialist and independence struggles that have included the Cuban and Nicaraguan revolutions. The convergence of national and international politics has contributed in a large way to the change in consciousness that is best exemplified in the work of Chicana and Puerto Rican writers among those of Spanish American descent in the United States.

I can best exemplify this idea by noting that the terms *Chicana* and *Neorican* (or *Nuyorican*) were recuperated and coined, respectively, in order to create a critical space and to articulate similarities and differences between such spheres as United States/Mexico and United States/Puerto Rican Island. The slash functions as a conscious cultural and political intervention in which the territories on either side of the slash play a role of transformation for the subject posed on the slash itself. In addition, the umbrella term *United States Latinas* has been coined with the express purpose of broadening our U.S. political and literary movement but only a few outside of Chicanas and Puerto Ricans take advantage of it.

However, the claim may be made that among those who would see themselves as U.S. Latina Writers, the dominant language of expression is English. Yet no sooner claimed than it is belied. The Chicana writer Lucha Corpi, for example, writes poetry in Spanish and prose in English, others code-switch, often within the same text. For the U.S. Latina writer linguistic use and preference is a "free or wild zone" within which she feels comfortable—purisms have no purchase there. In a sense, one becomes a Latina writer in the United States and part of a literary canon formation within its borders, not only because one practices writing in the United States, but also because in the contemporary period the major thematics of Latina writers in the United States emerge from the interstices of previously established literary canons. Thus, what one chooses to call "home," even in linguistic terms, becomes a vital political decision that affects the thematic directions of the literary work.

Paradoxically, if Spanish for some no longer functions to bind to Spanish America, neither does English bind to Anglo-America, as older literary grouping by language would have it, however, culturally and politically race, gender and class elements do. In other words language alone can no longer serve as the only criterion for the grouping and discussion of literature. For example, to further complicate matters, in the 1980's, many of those who view themselves as U.S. Latina writers, have come to claim an affinity with other non-Anglo-European women in the United States, such as American Indians, Asian Americans, and Afro-Americans. They claim to belong as well under the umbrella term *women (writers) of color*. In this way race and gender with implied ethnic and social class differentials also make a bid as criteria for the discussion of writing. Many traditional modes of literary approaches have been profoundly destabilized.

HISTORICAL BACKGROUND

With the exception of first-generation Cuban immigrants to the United States, the Latina writers discussed in this chapter were born either in the 1940's or the 1950s. Although individual biographies are impossible given the focus here on groups, a quick overview of the sociopolitical events which many have experienced is in order.

In the post-World War II period, the Puerto Rican Independence Movement was dramatized at gunpoint in 1954 in the U.S. Congress by Lolita Lebrón and her cohorts. The Bracero Program with Mexico initiated by the United States during World War II began to be increasingly scrutinized for its exploitation of workers. This scrutiny, carried out in the 1950s and 1960s, contributed in no small way to the unionization of farmworkers, which subsequently spearheaded the strike led by César Chávez and Dolores Huerta in 1965. In 1968 the Poor People's Campaign in Washington, D.C., included Latinas, as did the marches against Vietnam sponsored by the Puerto Rican Socialist party. The powerful Third World student strikes of 1968–1969 in Berkeley and elsewhere, such as the walkouts by Chicano high school students in Los Angeles, left few untouched in the coastal urban areas. Moreover, political awareness was often transmitted to the rural areas of the Midwest and the Southwest, and contributed to a national consciousness of Latinos as a people and community.

The post-World War II period gave rise, then, to great political unrest among the two groups—Chicanos and Puerto Ricans—who had accumulated an overwhelming negative experience within U.S. borders, starting in 1848 with the Anglo-American takeover from what is now the American Southwest and in 1898 with the takeover of Puerto Rico from Spain. The political unrest was accompanied not only by a transvaluation of history and ethnicity, but also by the rapid growth of the Small Press Movement which gained momentum in the late 1960s in all sectors of society. If the political movements spurred a transvaluation of negated experience, the mushrooming of Latino newspapers, journals, and presses left no community untouched through the 1960s and 1970s but also provided the forums for the articulation of the newer and different emerging consciousness.

MAJOR THEMES

Chicana and Puerto Rican Writers

The major interrelated and simultaneous themes in the formation of the emerging identity articulated by Chicana and Puerto Rican writers in the United States are language, gender, and racial ethnicity. The newer identity emerges from a dialectical experience of fundamental differences not only from herself, but also from multiple social others. In the linguistic frame, the chicana poet Alma Villanueva phrases it thus: "and I am / back a stranger, / English/Spanish / making knots of / my tongue" (*Bloodroot*, p. 67). Chicana writer Lorna D. Cervantes observes: "They give me a name / that fights me" (*Emplumada*, p. 44). The Puerto Rican Sandra Maria Esteves, rephrases it: "I speak the alien tongue / in sweet boriqueño thoughts" (*Yerba Buena*, p. 20), and Luz María Umpierre tells us: "ANGLICISMO / COCHE NOT CARRO / PUERTORRI-QUEÑISMO / CENA NOT COMIDA . . . FAMILIARIZE YOURSELF WITH THE CASTILLIAN WORD" (*En el país de las maravillas*, p. 8). The disquisition on language rejects all purisms not only thematically, but also in practice as many either switch back and forth between English and Spanish or write whole poems in either language that often defy hegemonic lexical and syntactic conventions.

These poets take aesthetic risks. The Chicana writer Margarita Cota-Cárdenas takes innovative poetic risks one step further and pens a novel, *Puppet* (1985), integrating all possible Latina speaking modes in the heart of the community. Although a thematized reflection on language as a medium that fights the articulation of self is not new, especially in the twentieth century, what is new is the resurfacing of multiple languages and sociolects as objects of reflection and practice which hegemonic literary canons attempt to suppress as "bad" literature. For the U.S. Latina writer then, as for Latinos, the initial strategy for actualizing her work has entailed a justification of multiple linguistic media as a fact of experience and a denunciation of aesthetic conventions that would frustrate self-expression.

When English predominates, loss (of Spanish) is highlighted; when a text is fully bilingual, constrastive spheres surface. In either case, a racial and/or gendered thematics is effected in the relationship to the "mother" tongue (Spanish) and the tongue of the oppressor (English). Latinas, for whom both race and gender have intersected forcefully in their individual lives, such as the Chicanas Gloria Anzaldúa, Ana Castillo, and Lorna D. Cervantes and the Puerto Ricans Sandra María Esteves, Luz María Umpierre, and Nicolasa Mohr, thematize a doubled racial marginalization, in the United States and within the pan-Hispanic sphere where it has not received as much attention from literature scholars, as it merits. The specific force of the intersection of race and gender in personal experience produces thematic figurations that often differ in no small degree from those Latina writers who have been more protected from daily racial strife by social status or physical appearance.

Thus in the gendered genealogical quest, for example, the writer selects and revises figures from the pre-Columbian or African heritage or selects them from a more recent historical past which may include the "biographical" mother and her role in the construction of the family and kinship ties. The work of writers who have been relatively protected from continuous racial strife often results in an abstracted and distanced voice with respect to racial difference and places the affective accent on gender. At times, of course, these are subtle differences but even they are of grave importance to the ways in which experience shapes self-consciousness. The internalized racism between Latinas is extensively treated, for example, in Ana Castillo's *The Mixquiahuala Letters*. Yet it is not emphasized in Lucha Corpi's and Sandra Cisneros' work. On the other hand, the racial theme vis-à-vis Anglo-American society is addressed by virtually everyone. Thus, while external pressure unites them, internal pressure divides them. The internal pressure may be traced to the Spanish colonial experience, whereas the external may be traced to the Anglo-American neocolonial one.

Although the work of some, such as Cervantes, Castillo, Umpierre, and Esteves, refuses to let us disentangle the thematic intersection of race and gender, the work of others such as Alma Villanueva lends itself easily to an analysis strictly by gender. In either case, however, the thematics of gender originates in the kinship group and moves outward by spreading to women's employment positions outside the home as servants, field, factory and clerical workers, welfare recipients, and objects of rape and sexual violence. The educational process within the family and through external institutions is also a site of cultural struggle.

Romantic love and erotic desire constitute a major crucible for the exploration of heterosexual (Mora, Cisneros, Curiel), bisexual (Castillo), and lesbian (Um-pierre, Anzaldúa, Moraga) relations and practices. These two themes deepen the exploration of the complex ways in which sexuality is constructed within the family and at times harbor an explicit or implicit differential comparison to the construction of sexualities in Anglo-America. For some, religion (especially Catholicism) enters here as a sexually repressive force that is at times liberated through attack on the Church/priest/family or through the use of non-Christian figures who free sexuality through a differently conceived spiritual force. Desire may be represented as union or misalliance with *him*, or redirected from *him to her*. She, however, may represent alternately the fulfillment of lesbian sexual desire and love or the recuperation of the female self as object of female desire and love.

Other Latina Writers in the United States

Lourdes Casal, like most of the Cuban immigrants born in the 1930s or early 1940s, came to the United States as an adult and writes all of her work in Spanish. Yet, the language used does not completely prevent her from pursuing an identity in analogous ways to that of Chicanas and U.S. Puerto Ricans. If language shapes us, in some sense, we do not have to remain passive recipients of its *a priori* significations. In many ways, the bicultural and multicultural writers of our time are displacing ethnocentric cosmopolitanism and are laying bare its ultraconservative bias. This literature, like that of the avant-garde of the early twentieth century, exceeds its "borders."

Thus, for example, Casal situates herself firmly within the historical events of her time. She states, "So I had left Cuba, where a revolution was taking place, and had come to suffer a process of radicalization inside the United States. . . . I didn't fit anywhere in the United States. Because I'm black, a woman and latin. . . . I participated in the struggles against racial discrimination or against the war in Vietnam" (Randall, 1982, p. 124). For Casal, Havana and New York represent the political and cultural axes with which and against which the self is recreated: "Recrearlo todo en la palabra / . . . esta batalla incesante y dolo-rosa" (Casal, 1981, p. 58, Recreate everything in the word / . . . this ceaseless and painful battle). Her Cuba was never "the easy island" but "the one that raised its head . . . in passages and conspiracies . . . the Cuba whose heroic people lived through the sixties . . . making history / and remaking herself" (Randall, 1982, p. 131). For Casal, the truth of her time is wrested from the streets.

The major differentiation one can make between Chicanas and Puerto Ricans and almost all others writing in the United States—Cubans, Chileans, Argentines and more recently Central Americans—is that the more recently arrived group has yet to understand fully the multicultural and political struggles of the earlier group. Often the more recently arrived groups situate themselves in the "exile" modality as Eliana Rivero has observed. Often they see their work as aligned within the literary canon of the country of origin, or, as in the case of the Chilean

Majorie Agosín, they straddle the fence by publishing their work in bilingual editions. Nostalgia for the homeland pervades many of their works and the writer frequently suggests a desire to return there as soon as political conditions permit. The Dominican Julia Alvarez and the second-generation Cuban Achy Obejas thematize the ironies and conflicts inherent in such longings. Currently, however, for those who claim a place in the nation of origin's canon a whole category has emerged—*Literatura del Exilio* (Exile Literature), a literature that often does not thematize the author's Anglo-American experience, although it is not monolithic, and the thematic strands can vary drastically. The tone and thematics of Exile Literature varies according to the writer's (political) position with respect to the conditions that caused her exile.

One of the most astounding aspects of some first-generation Cuban poets who came to the United States after 1959 as a result of the Cuban Revolution is the suppression of that historical experience. In this they differ, for example, from Chileans who came to the United States after the fall of Allende in 1973. In the case of certain Cubans the privatization of alienation may lead to idealized figurations for the expression of mental and spiritual anguish or as modes of flight from the world. For example, Rita Geada's work exhibits one of the paths taken by women of Spanish American descent when the experience of the body, even as "neutered" flesh, is denied as a legitimate point of departure for the expression of self and experience or, if noted, is viewed as a burden one must transcend in quest of a " higher" truth. Geada's "flight" from the world, history, and experience denies value to existential engagement. Geada writes "Nuestro tiempo no ha llegado aun" (*Mascarada*, p. 15, Our time has not yet arrived). Because "our time has not yet arrived," the poem goes on to devalue the time of others calling it a "sucia farsa," an absurd noise and fury. The exile is double—from "home" and from the world. Here the "ser o parecer" (to be or to seem) thematics of traditional Hispanic literature is treated once more. The response to the question "Who am I?" in Geada's work is foreclosed by the *a priori* answers of the traditional metaphysical quest for being in Hispanic literature. Thus the answer to her question " ¿hemos de aprender a callar, / a soportar / el silencio?" (*Mascarada*, p. 16, Must we learn to be quiet / to put up with / silence?), is yes, of course. Themes such as truth, love, existence are not constructed intersubjectively, but emerge as *a priori* metaphysical givens that silence us.

The quest for a "higher" truth in the work of Geada is opposed by a "baser" worldly ground by the Afro-Cuban American writer Lourdes Casal. Since Casal like Geada was born in the 1930s and both write in Spanish, the extreme contrast cannot be accounted for by pointing to linguistic or "generational" differences. In fact, if one places Geada's texts in dialogue with Casal's, Geada in effect questions the merits of Casal's historical and existential engagement, and would "silence" Casal's work as so much noise. In other words, Casal's text, like that of Chicanas and U.S. Puerto Ricans, emerges as one of those suppressed by the

Hispanic idealistic hegemony where contestative difference is erased in the name of a "higher" truth.

Second-generation Cuban writers such as Achy Obejas put into question the value of nostalgia. The time of the home of the past does not stop, nor can all of the past be put to work in the new one. Similarly, the second-generation Dominican Julia Alvarez explores her ambivalence toward a "lost" Caribbean, especially as the former home imposes gendered bourgeois ways of being in women's work and education (*Homecoming*). The Chilean Marjorie Agosin, who is a first-generation immigrant, unlike Alvarez, writes all of her work in Spanish. Like Alvarez, however, she is ambivalent toward the Chilean "home" with respect to the traditional expectations of bourgeois women's existence. However, Agosin tries to disrupt women's upper-class claustrophobia by projecting herself into the existence of the socially and economically oppressed woman—the servants to women of her own social sphere. Writers like Agosin interrogate their own experience with that of other women, a technique of multiple dimensions, as already noted. However, there are subtle differences of linguistic figurations and tone when writers interrogate themselves by projecting onto women who are socially and racially different. It is difficult to avoid falling prey to maternalism, sentimentalism, or the view that the oppressed are more "heroic," and experience a "better" type of suffering.

In general, poetry dominates the literary production of these writers. Novelists like the Argentine Luisa Valenzuela* and the Chilean Isabel Allende* covet fame in the United States, but aspire to a place in the literary canon of "home."

SURVEY OF CRITICISM

The most ambitious critical project to date is the collection of essays *Breaking Boundaries: Latina Writings and Critical Readings* (1989), edited by Asunción Horno-Delgado et al. Divided into four sections, the collection aims to encompass "all" Latinas writing in the United States—Chicanas, Puertorriqueñas, Cubanas, and Latinoamericanas from other countries. Many of the thematics discussed above are deepened, clarified, and explored through a look at individual writers, though not all writers listed in the bibliography are covered. Salient omissions, for example, are the important works of the Chicanas Alma Villanueva and Gloria Anzaldúa, and the Dominican Julia Alvarez. Yet, this excellent critical collection has the distinction of being the first published by a university press. (The only other exception is Marta Sánchez' work on Chicana poets.) Latina writers and critics are "invisible" because their work has been available mostly through small presses and journals which are often unrecognized in the academy or by the general public. Thus, the major role of *Breaking Boundaries* is necessarily to focus attention on a literary process that has been ongoing for three decades. Overall, the book represents a good start for anyone interested in further work in this literary area. The special issue collection from *The Americas Re-*

view, edited by María Herrera-Sobek and Helena Maria Viramontes, is an excellent complement to the Chicana section of *Breaking Boundaries*. The collection brings into play the question of the relationship of dominant literary and feminist theories to the work of minority women, and the role of the ethnopolitical community in the formation of Chicana feminism.

The journal *Third Woman* is also a good source of information. It was launched in 1981 with the express purpose of identifying Latina writers throughout the United States. As a result, a series of regional issues were compiled, i.e. Midwest, East Coast, Southwest; more recently, the theme of Latina sexuality was explored. In a sense, *Third Woman* helped inaugurate and define the 1980s as the decade in which U.S. Latinas would begin to receive recognition in writing, research, and criticism. Many of the writers mentioned were published or discussed in *Third Woman*, some for the first time.

La sartén por el mango (1984), edited by Patricia Elena González and Eliana Ortega, is of interest to all of us, not only because it has an avowedly feminist focus on Latin American women writers, but also because it represents the first documented *encuentro* (1983) where the proceedings were disrupted owing to the salient omission and lack of recognition of U.S. Latinas. It appears to have fueled the following fighting words in the prologue to *Cuentos: Stories by Latinas* (1983), edited by Alma Gómez et al.:

> True, the woman writer in Latin America, as in the U.S., is constrained by her sex in terms of subject matter and recognition. Class, race, and education, however, as it combines with sex, are much more critical in silencing the would-be Latina writer than discrimination on sex alone. As long as the Latin American woman writer tows the line of her brothers, there will be a place for her in their literary milieu. . . . We are Latina writers and activists who identify as U.S. Third World women (pp. viii, x).

Most of the works discussed and listed in the critical bibliography provided contain extensive bibliographies of articles written over the past three decades. Thus the listing has been kept brief, noting resources that can be used as a start.

BIBLIOGRAPHY

Translated, English and mixed-language works are included under the author's works rather than in a separate section.

Works by Chicanas

Anzaldúa, Gloria. *Borderlands/La Frontera: The New Mestiza*. San Francisco: Spinsters/ Aunt Lute, 1987.

Castillo, Ana. *The Invitation*. n.p., 1979.

———. *Women Are Not Roses*. Houston: Arte Público Press, 1984.

———. *My Father Was A Toltec*. Novato, Calif.: West End Press, 1984.

———. *The Mixquiahuala Letters*. Binghamton, N.Y.: Bilingual Press, 1986.

Cervantes, Lorna Dee. *Emplumada*. Pittsburgh: University of Pittsburgh Press, 1981.

Cisneros, Sandra. *The House On Mango Street*. Houston: Arte Público Press, 1985. 2d rev. ed., 1988.

———. *My Wicked Wicked Ways*. Bloomington, Ind.: Third Woman Press, 1987.

Corpi, Lucha. *Palabras de mediodía/Noon Words*. Trans. Catherine Rodríguez-Nieto. Berkeley, Calif.: El Fuego de Aztlán Publications, 1980.

———. *Delia's Song*. Houston: Arte Público Press, 1989.

Cota-Cárdenas, Margarita. *Puppet*. Austin, Tex.: Relámpago Books, 1985.

Curiel, Barbara Brinson. *Speak To Me From Dreams*. Berkeley, Calif.: Third Woman Press, 1989.

Mora, Pat. *Chants*. Houston: Arte Público Press, 1984.

———. *Borders*. Houston: Arte Público Press, 1986.

Moraga, Cherríe. *Loving In The War Years: Lo que nunca pasó por sus labios*. Boston: South End Press, 1983.

———. *Giving Up The Ghost*. Los Angeles: West End Press, 1986.

Tafolla, Carmen. *Get Your Tortillas Together*. San Antonio, Tex.: M&A Publications, 1976.

Vigil, Evangelina. *Thirty An' Seen A Lot*. Houston: Arte Público Press, 1982.

Vigil-Piñon, Evangelina. *The Computer Is Down*. Houston: Arte Público Press, 1987.

Villanueva, Alma. *Bloodroot*. Austin, Tex.: Place of Herons Press, 1977.

———. *Mother May I?* n.p.: Motheroot Publications, 1978.

———. *Life Span*. Austin, Tex.: Place of Herons Press, 1985.

———. *The Ultraviolet Sky*. Tempe, Ariz.: Bilingual Press, 1988.

Viramontes, Helena Maria. *The Moths And Other Stories*. Houston: Arte Público Press, 1985.

Works by Puerto Ricans in the United States

Barradas, Efraín, and Rafael Rodríguez, eds. *Herejes y mitificadores: Muestra de poesía puertorriqueña en los Estados Unidos*. Río Piedras, P.R.: Ediciones Huracán, 1980.

Cofer, Judith Ortiz. *Peregrina*. Golden, Colo.: Riverstone Press of the Foothills Art Center, 1986.

———. *Terms Of Survival*. Houston: Arte Público Press, 1988.

———. *In The Line Of The Sun*. Athens, Ga.: University of Georgia Press, 1989.

Esteves, Sandra Maria. *Yerba Buena*. New York: Greenfield Review Press, 1980.

———. *Tropical Rains: A Bilingual Downpour*. Bronx, N.Y.: African Caribbean Poetry Theater, 1984.

Mohr, Nicholasa. *Nilda*. New York: Harper and Row, 1973. 2d. ed. Houston: Arte Público Press, 1983.

———. *El Bronx Remembered: A Novella and Stories*. New York: Harper and Row, 1976.

———. *In Nueva York*. New York: Dial Press, 1977.

———. *Felita*. New York: Dial Press, 1979.

———. *Rituals of Survival: A Woman's Portfolio*. Houston: Arte Público Press, 1985.

Morales, Aurora Levins, and Rosario Morales. *Getting Home Alive*. Ithaca, N.Y.: Firebrand Books, 1986.

Umpierre, Luz María. *Una puertorriqueña en penna*. San Juan, P.R.: Masters, 1979.

———. *En el país de las maravillas*. Bloomington, Ind.: Third Woman Press, 1985.

———. *Y otras desgracias/And Other Misfortunes*. Bloomington, Ind.: Third Woman Press, 1985.

———. *The Margarita Poems*. Bloomington, Ind.: Third Woman Press, 1987.

Valle, Carmen. *Un poco de lo no dicho*. New York: Editorial La Ceiba, 1980.

———. *Diarios robados*. Buenos Aires: Ediciones de la Flor, 1982.

———. *Glenn Miller y varias vidas después*. Puebla: Premià Editora, 1983.

Zavala, Iris. *Chiliagony*. Trans. Susan Pensak. Bloomington, Ind.: Third Woman Press, 1984.

Works by Cubans in the United States

Burunat, Silvia, and Ofelia García, eds. *Veinte años de literatura cubanoamericana*. Tempe, Ariz.: Bilingual Press, 1988.

Casal, Lourdes. *Los fundadores: Alfonso y otros cuentos*. Miami: Ediciones Universal, 1973.

———. *Palabras juntan revolución*. Havana: Casa de las Américas, 1981.

Castillo, Amelia del. *Cauce del tiempo*. Miami, Fla.: Hispanova de Ediciones, 1981.

Escandell, Noemi. *Cuadros*. Somerville, N.J.: Slusa, 1982.

———. *Palabras/Words*. Somerville, N.J.: Slusa, 1986.

Geada, Rita. *Pulsar del alba*. Lisbon, Portugal: Panorámica Luso-Hispánica, 1963.

———. *Cuando cantan las pisadas*. Buenos Aires: Americalée, 1967.

———. *Mascarda*. Barcelona: Nudo al Alba-Carabela, 1970.

———. *Vertizonte*. Madrid-Miami: Hispanova, 1977.

Islas, Maya. *Sola . . . desnuda . . . sin nombre*. New York: Editorial Mensaje, 1974.

———. *Sombras papel*. Barcelona: Editorial Rondas, 1978.

Prida, Dolores. *Beautiful Señoritas and Other Plays*. Houston: Arte Público Press, 1989.

Randall, Margaret, ed. *Breaking The Silences: 20th Century Poetry by Cuban Women*. Vancouver, Canada: Pulp Press Book Publishers, 1982.

Rivero, Eliana. *De cal y arena*. Sevilla: Aldebaran, 1975.

———. *Cuerpos breves*. Tucson, Ariz.: Scorpion Press, 1977.

Robles, Mireya. *Tiempo artesano*. Barcelona: Editorial Campos, 1973.

———. *Time, The Artisan*. Trans. Angela de Hoyos. Austin, Tex.: Dissemination Center for Bilingual Bicultural Education, 1975.

———. *En esta aurora*. San Antonio, Tex.: M&A Editions, 1976.

———. *Hagiografía de Narcisa la bella*. Hanover, N.H.: Ediciones del Norte, 1985.

Works by Other Latinas in the United States

Agosin, Marjorie. *Chile: Gemidos y cantares*. Quillota, Chile: Editorial el Observador, 1977.

———. *Conchalí*. Montclair, N.J.: Senda Nueva de Ediciones, 1980.

———. *Brujas y algo más / Witches and Other Things*. Trans. Cola Franzen. Pittsburgh: Latin American Review Press, 1986.

———. *Hogueras*. Santiago de Chile: Editorial Universitaria, 1986.

———. *Mujeres de humo*. Madrid: Ediciones Torremozas, 1987.

———. *Women Of Smoke*. Trans. Naomi Lindstrom. Pittsburgh: Latin American Literary Review Press, 1988.

Alvarez, Julia. *Homecoming*. New York: Grove Press, 1984.

Fox, Lucía. *Ayer es nunca jamás*. Lima: Editorial Colegio Salesiano, 1980.

Gómez, Alma, Cherríe Moraga, and Mariana Romo-Carmona, eds. *Cuentos: Stories by Latinas*. New York: Kitchen Table Press, 1983.

Gómez-Lance, Betty. *Vivencias*. Costa Rica-Kalamazoo: n.p., 1981.

Guerra, Lucía. *Más allá de las máscaras*. Puebla: Premià Editora, 1984.

Vallbona, Rima de. *Noche en vela*. San José: Editorial Costa Rica, 1968.

———. *Polvo del camino*. San José: Editorial Costa Rica, 1968.

———. *Cosecha de pescadores*. San José: Editorial Costa Rica, 1981.

———. *Mujeres y agonías*. Houston: Arte Público Press, 1982.

———. *Las sombras que perseguimos*. San José: Editorial Costa Rica, 1983.

Vicioso, Sherezada. *Viaje desde el agua*. Santo Domingo, Dom. Rep.: Visuarete, 1981.

———. *Un extraño ulular traía el viento*. Santo Domingo: Alfa y Omega, 1985.

Vigil, Evangelina, ed. "Woman Of Her Word: Hispanic Women Write." Special issue of *Revista Chicano-Riqueña* 11 (1983).

Works about Latina Writers in the United States

Alarcón, Norma. "Chicana Writers and Critics in a Social Context: Towards a Contemporary Bibliogaphy." *Third Woman: The Sexuality of Latinas* 5 (1989); 169–78.

———. "Traddutora, Traditora: A Paradigmatic Figure of Chicana Feminism." *Cultural Critique* 13 (Fall 1989).

———. "What Kind of Lover Have You Made Me Mother?" *Women of Color: Perspectives on Feminism and Identity*. Ed. Audrey T. McCluskey. Occasional Papers Series, Vol. 1, No. 1. Bloomington, Ind.: Women's Studies Program, 1985. Pp. 85–110.

Azize, Yamila. "Poetas puertorriqueñas en Nueva York." *Cupey* 4, 1 (Jan.-June 1987):17–24.

González, Patricia E., and Eliana Ortega, eds. *La sartén por el mango*. Río Piedras: Editorial Huracán, 1985.

Herrera-Sobek, María, ed. *Beyond Stereotypes: Critical Analysis of Chicana Literature*. Binghamton, N.Y.: Bilingual Press, 1985.

Herrera-Sobek, María, and Helena Maria Viramontes, eds. "Chicana Creativity and Criticism: Charting New Frontiers in American Literature." Special issue of *The Americas Review* 15, 3–4 (1987).

Horno-Delgado, Asunción, Eliana Ortega, Nina M. Scott and Nancy Saporta Sternbach, eds. *Breaking Boundaries: Latina Writings and Critical Readings*. Amherst: University of Massachusetts Press, 1989.

Rebolledo, Tey Diana. "The Maturing of Chicana Poetry: The Quiet Revolution of the 1980s." *For Alma Mater: Theory and Practice in Feminist Scholarship*. Eds. Paula Treichler, Cheris Kamarae, and Beth Stafford. Urbana: University of Illinois, Press, 1985, Pp. 143–58.

Rodríguez de Laguna, Asela. *Imágenes e identidades: El puertorriqueño en la literatura*. Río Piedras, P.R.: Ediciones Huracán, 1985.

Sánchez, Marta Ester. *Contemporary Chicana Poetry: A Critical Approach to an Emerging Literature*. Los Angeles: University of California Press, 1985.

Turner, Faythe Elaine. *Puerto Rican Writers on the Mainland: The Neoricans*. Ph.D. diss., University of Massachusetts, 1978.

Umpierre, Luz María. *Nuevas aproximaciones críticas a la literatura puertorriqueña*. Río Piedras: Editorial Cultural, 1983.

Yarbro-Berjarano, Yvonne. "The Female Subject in Chicano Theatre: Sexuality, 'Race' and Class." *Theatre Journal* (Dec. 1986):389–407.

THE LATIN AMERICAN WOMAN WRITER: A BIBLIOGRAPHY OF BIBLIOGRAPHIES AND GENERAL CRITICISM

BOOKS

Agosín, Marjorie. *Silencio e imaginación: metáforas de la escritura femenina*. Mexico City: Katún, 1986.

Alarcón, Norma, and Sylvia Kossnar. *Bibliography of Hispanic Women Writers*. Chicano-Riqueño Studies Bibliography Series, No. 1. Bloomington, Ind.: Chicano-Riqueño Studies, 1980.

Araújo, Helena. *La Scherezada criolla: Ensayos sobre la escritura femenina latinoamericana*. Bogotá: Universidad Nacional de Colombia, 1989.

Bradu, Fabienne. *Señas particulares: escritora*. Mexico City: Fondo de Cultura Económica, 1987.

Carrera, Julieta. *La mujer de América: semblanzas*. Mexico City: Ed. Alonso, 1956.

Castellanos, Rosario. *Sobre cultura femenina*. Mexico City: Ed. de América, 1950.

Cicchitti, Vicente, et al. *La mujer: símbolo del mundo nuevo*. Buenos Aires: Fernando García Cambeiro, 1976.

Cortina, Lynn Rice. *Spanish American Women Writers: A Bibliographical Guide to Research*. New York: Garland Publishing, 1983.

Corvalán, Graciela N. V. *Latin American Women Writers in English Translation: A Bibliography*. Los Angeles: California State University, 1980.

Cunningham, Lucía Guerra. *Mujer y sociedad en América Latina*. Santiago de Chile: Editorial del Pacífico, 1980.

Delgado, J. B., and V. Salado Alvarez. *Nuevas orientaciones de la poesía femenina*. Mexico City: Imprenta Victoria, 1924.

Fox-Lockert, Lucía. *Women Novelists in Spain and Spanish America*. Metuchen, N.J.: Scarecrow Press, 1979.

Franco, Rosa. *Origen de lo erótico en la poesía femenina americana*. Buenos Aires: Ed. Stilcograf, 1960.

González, Patricia Elena, and Eliana Ortega, eds. *La sartén por el mango*. Río Piedras, P.R.: Huracán, 1984.

González-Ruano, C. *Literatura americana: ensayos de madrigal y de crítica*. Vol. 1: *Poetisas modernas*. Madrid: Imprenta Artística, 1924.

Handelsman, Michael H. *Amazonas y artistas. Un estudio de la prosa de la mujer ecuatoriana*. 2 vols. Guayaquil: Casa de la Cultura Ecuatoriana, 1978.

Horno-Delgado, Asunción, et al. *Breaking Boundaries: Latina Writings and Critical Readings*. Amherst: University of Massachusetts, 1989.

Loustaunau, Martha Oehmke. "Mexico's Contemporary Women Novelists." Ph.D. diss. University of New Mexico, 1973. (DAI 34, 3 [Nov.-Dec. 1973]:2637A.)

Marting, Diane. *Spanish American Women Writers: A Bio-Bibliographical Guide*. Westport, Conn.: Greenwood Press, 1987.

Medina, J. T. *La literatura femenina en Chile*. Santiago de Chile: Imprenta Universitaria, 1923.

Meyer, Doris, and Margarite Fernández Olmos, eds. *Contemporary Women Authors of Latin America*. Vol. 1: *Introductory Essays*. Brooklyn, N.Y.: Brooklyn College Press, 1983.

Miller, Beth. *Mujeres en la literatura*. Mexico City: Fleischer Editora, 1978.

———, ed. *Women in Hispanic Literature. Icons and Fallen Idols*. Berkeley: University of California Press, 1983.

Miller, Beth, and Alfonso González. *26 autoras del México actual*. Mexico City: Costa-Amic, 1978.

Miller, Yvette, and Charles Tatum, eds. *Latin American Women Writers—Yesterday and Today*. Pittsburgh: Latin American Literary Review Press, 1977.

Miranda, S., Estrela. *Algunas poetisas de Chile y Uruguay: Su sentido de la vida y su interpretación del paisaje*. Prol. Worberto Pinilla. Santiago de Chile: Nascimento, 1937.

Muriel, Josefina. *Cultura femenina novohispana*. Mexico City: UNAM, 1982.

Percas, Helena. "Women Poets of Argentina (1810–1950)." Ph.D. diss. Columbia University, 1951. (DAI 12 [1952]:70A.)

Robles, Martha. *La sombra fugitiva: escritoras en la cultura nacional*. Mexico City: UNAM, Instituto de Investigaciones Filológicas, Centro de Estudios Literarios, 1985.

Rodríguez, María Cristina. "The Role of Women in Caribbean Prose Fiction." Ph.D. diss. City University of New York, 1979. (DAI 39 [1979]:6115A.)

Rosenbaum, Sidonia. *Modern Women Poets of Spanish America*. Westport, Conn.: Greenwood Press, 1978. (Reprint)

Salcedo Martínez, Pilar. "Psicología del momento creador en la literatura femenina hispanoamericana." Ph.D. diss. Universidad Complutense de Madrid, 1975. (RUCM 24, 100–111 [1975]:148–50.)

Sánchez, Marta Ester. *Contemporary Chicana Poetry: A Critical Approach to an Emerging Literature*. Berkeley and Los Angeles: University of California, 1985.

Schlau, Stacey, and Electa Arenal. *Untold Stories: Hispanic Nuns in Their Own Works*. Albuquerque: University of New Mexico Press, 1988.

Valenzuela, Víctor. *Grandes escritoras hispanoamericanas, poetisas y novelistas*. Bethlehem, Pa.: Lehigh University Press, 1974.

Valis, Noël, and Carol Maier, eds. *In the Feminine Mode: Essays on Hispanic Women Writers*. Lewisburg, Pa.: Bucknell University Press, 1988.

Young, Linda Rebeca Stowell. "Six Representative Women Novelists of Mexico, 1960–

1969.'' Ph.D. diss. University of Illinois at Urbana-Champaign, 1975. (DAI 36, 9 [1975]:6092A–93A.)

Zanelli López, I. *Mujeres chilenas de letras*. Santiago de Chile: Imprenta Universitaria, 1917.

ARTICLES IN JOURNALS AND CHAPTERS OF BOOKS

Aguirre, Mirta. ''Cultura.'' *Influencia de la mujer en Iberoamérica*. Havana: Imp. P. Fernández, 1947.

Alegría, Fernando. ''Aporte de la mujer al nuevo lenguaje poético de Latinoamérica.'' *Plural* 10, 2d Series, 120 (Sept. 1981):63–69. Also *Revista/Review Interamericana* 12, 1 (Spring 1982):27–35.

Araújo, Helena. ''¿Crítica literaria feminista?'' *Actas, Coloquio Internacional, Los escritores hispanoamericanos frente a sus críticos*. Toulouse: Université de Toulouse-Le Mirail, 1983.

———. ''Escritoras latinoamericanas: ¿Por fuera del 'Boom'?'' *Quimera* (Barcelona) 30 (Apr. 1983):8–11.

———. ''¿Escritura femenina?'' *Escandalar* (New York) 15 (1981):32–36.

———. ''Narrativa femenina latinoamericana.'' *Hispamérica* 2, 32 (Aug. 1982):23–34.

Arenal, Electa. ''Two Poets of the Sandinista Struggle.'' *Feminist Studies* 7, 1 (Spring 1981):19–37.

Baeza Flores, Alberto. ''La poesía femenina costarricense: Breve balance y perspectivas.'' *Káñina* (Costa Rica) 9, 2 (1985):91–96.

Benvenuto, Ofelia Machado Bonat de. ''La poesía femenina.'' *Circunstanciales* (Montevideo) (1941):35–43.

Billick, David J. ''Women in Hispanic Literature: A Checklist of Doctoral Dissertations and Master's Theses, 1905–1975.'' *Women's Studies Abstracts* (1978):1–11.

Boorman, Joan. ''Contemporary Latin American Women Dramatists.'' *Rice University Studies* 64, 1 (1978):69–80.

Bula Piriz, R. ''Sobre poetisas uruguayas.'' *Hiperión* 92 (1943):2–12; no. 93:8–16.

Bullrich, Silvina. ''La mujer, eterna postergada, ¿por qué?'' *Páginas de Silvina Bullrich, seleccionadas por la autora*. Preliminary Study by Nicolás Cócaro. Buenos Aires: Celtia, 1983. Pp. 124–28.

Carrera, Julieta, ''La novela femenina mexicana.'' *Cuadernos* 3 (Sept.-Dec. 1953):101–104.

Castedo-Ellerman, Elena. ''Feminism or Feminity? Six Women Writers Answer.'' *Américas* 30, 10 (Oct. 1978):19–24.

Castillo Ledón, A.G.C. ''Poetisas modernas de México.'' *Boletín de la Unión Panamericana* 74 (1940):645–56.

Chase, Kathleen. ''Latin American Women Writers: Their Present Position.'' *Books Abroad* 33 (1969):150–51.

Coelho, Nelly Novaes. ''A presença de 'Nova Mulher' na ficção brasileira actual.'' *Revista Iberoamericana* 126 (Jan.-Mar. 1984):141–54. (About Brazil)

Consolé, Alfredo. ''Nuestras poetisas de hoy.'' *Dos conferencias literarias: Poetas a los veinte años; Nuestras poetisas de hoy*. Buenos Aires: Ferrari Hermanos, 1935.

Cuenca, H. ''Apuntes sobre poesía femenina venezolana.'' *El Universal* (Caracas) Mar. 3, 1940.

Cunningham, Lucía Guerra. "El personaje literario femenino y otras mutilaciones."
    Hispamérica 43 (1986):3–19.
———. "La mujer latinoamericana y la tradición literaria femenina." *Fem* 3, 10 (Jan.-
    Oct. 1979):14–18.
Cypess, Sandra Messinger. "Women Dramatists of Puerto Rico." *Revista/Review In-
    teramericana* 9, 1 (Spring 1979):24–41.
———. "Visual and Verbal Distances: The Woman Poet in a Patriarchal Culture."
    Revista/Review Interamericana 12, 1 (Spring 1982):150–57.
Dölz-Blackburn, Inés. "Recent Critical Bibliography on Women in Hispanic Literature."
    Discurso Literario 3, 2 (Spring 1986):331–34.
Dorn, Georgette M. "Four Twentieth-Century Latin American Women Authors." *SE-
    COLAS Annals (Southeastern Council on Latin American Studies)* (Marietta, Ga.)
    10 (1979):125–33.
Esteves, Sandra Maria. "The Feminist Viewpoint in Poetry of the Puerto Rican Woman
    in the United States." Puerto Rican Women Writers and the Image of Women in
    Literature: Images and Identities, The Puerto Rican in Literature. National Public
    Conference. Newark, N.J. Apr. 7, 1983.
Fernández Olmos, Margarite. "El género testimonial: Aproximaciones feministas." *Re-
    vista/Review Interamericana* 1 (Spring 1981):69–75.
Francescato, Martha Paley. "Women in Latin America: Their Role as Writers and Their
    Image in Fiction." *Women in Latin American Literature: A Symposium.* Program
    in Latin American Studies Occasional Papers Series, No. 10. Amherst: University
    of Massachusetts, International Area Studies Programs, 1979.
Franco, Jean. "Apuntes sobre la crítica feminista y la literatura hispanoamericana."
    Hispamérica 45 (1986):31–43.
———. "Opportunities for Women's Studies Research in the Hispanic Field." *Women
    in Print.* Vol. 1: *Opportunities for Women's Studies Research in Language and
    Literature.* Eds. Joan Hartman and Ellen Messer-Davidow. New York: Modern
    Language Association of America, 1982. Pp. 159–71.
———. "Self-Destructing Heroines." *Minnesota Review,* ns 22 (Spring 1984):105–15.
Franulic, L. "Panorama de la literatura femenina actual." *Hoy* 8, 316 (1937):63–66.
Gatell, Angelina. "La poesía femenina en el romanticismo cubano." *Cuadernos His-
    panoamericanos* 55 (1963):541–44.
Goes, Marta. "As mulheres toman a palavra." *Leia* (Feb. 1985):20–21. (About Brazil)
Goldberg, Isaac. "Literary Ladies of the South." *American Mercury* 7 (1976):488–542.
González Freire, Nati. "La mujer en la literatura de América Latina." *Cuadernos His-
    panoamericanos* 414 (Dec. 1984):84–92.
González y Contreras, G. "Interpretación de la poesía femenina." *Revista Nacional de
    Cultura* 2, 25 (1941):84–104.
Guerrero, Arturo. "En Colombia: Cosecha de escritoras." *El Tiempo, Lecturas Dom-
    inicales* (Bogotá) Nov. 29, 1987:4–7.
Guiteras, J. P. "Poetisas cubanas." *Revista Cubana* 2 (1877):481–501.
Harrison, Polly F. "Images and Exile: The Cuban Woman and Her Poetry." *Revista/
    Review Interamericana* 4 (1974):184–219.
Hernández-Araico, Susana. "Tres voces femeninas en la poesía hispanoamericana de
    hoy. (Sonia Luz Carrillo, Isabel Velasco, Magdalena Harriague.)" *Alba de Amér-
    ica* 1 (July-Dec. 1982):167–80.
Ilack, L. "Tres escritoras mexicanas." *El Libro y el Pueblo* (1934):165–74.

Jiménez, Ivette López. "Entrada en la escritura: Mujeres en la tradición hispánica." *Cupey, Revista de la Universidad Metropolitana* (Río Piedras, P.R.) 4, 2 (Aug.-Dec. 1987):47–59.

———. "Puerto Rico: Las nuevas narradoras y la identidad cultural." *Perspectives on Contemporary Literature* 8 (1982):77–84.

Jiménez, Reynaldo L. "Cuban Women Writers and the Revolution: Toward an Assessment of Their Literary Contributions." *Folio* 11 (1978):75–95.

Jordan, Dawn M. "Building a History of Women's Literature in Brazil." *Plaza: Literatura y Crítica* (Cambridge, Mass.) 5–6 (Autumn-Spring 1981–1982):75–96. (About Brazil)

Junior, Peregrino. "Contribución de la mujer a la poesía brasileña." *Revista de Cultura Brasileña* 37 (June 1974):35–69. (About Brazil)

Knaster, Meri. "Literature." *Women in Spanish America: An Annotated Bibliography from Pre-Conquest to Contemporary Times*. Boston: G. K. Hall, 1977. Pp. 42–94.

Labarca, E. "Mujeres de letras argentinas." *Atenea* 1, 3 (1924):248–50.

———. "Poetisas uruguayas." *Atenea* 1, 1 (1924):60–62.

Latcham, R. A. "Aspectos de la literatura femenina en Chile." *La Revista Católica de Santiago de Chile* 14 (1923):738–92.

Lee, Muna. "Puerto Rican Women Writers: The Record of One Hundred Years." *Books Abroad* 8, 1 (1934):7–10.

Lemistre Pujol, Annie. "Los orígenes de la literatura femenina en Latinoamérica y Costa Rica." *Káñina* (Costa Rica) 9, 2 (1985):85–90.

Leonardos, Stella. "Acima do tumulto de hoje, Belas vozes femeninas." *Jornal de Letras* (Copacabana) 342, 1 (1979):3. (About Brazil)

Lima, Robert. "Cumbres poéticas del erotismo femenino en Hispanoamérica." *Revista de Estudios Hispánicos* 18, 1 (1984):41–59.

Lindstrom, Naomi. "Feminist Criticism of Latin American Literature: Bibliographic Notes." *Latin American Research Review* 15, 1 (1980):151–59.

"Literatura. II° Encuentro Feminista Latinoamericano y del Caribe." *Revista Isis de las Mujeres* (Rome) 1 (June 1984):68–69.

Lobo, Luiza. "Women Writers in Brazil Today." *World Literature Today* 61, 1 (Winter 1987):49–54. (About Brazil)

Maiz, Magdalena. "Una aproximación al paisaje cotidiano: Narrativa femenina mexicana." *Cuadernos de Aldeeu* 1, 2–3 (May-Oct. 1983):347–354.

Mandolini, H. "Genio y lirismo femeninos." *Nosotros* 77 (1932):326–40.

March, Susana. "El tema religioso en las poetisas mejores posmodernistas." *Cuadernos Hispanoamericanos* 67, 198 (June 1966):506–28.

Marting, Diane. "La crítica feminista literaria y la novela no-realista: María Luisa Bombal y Luisa Valenzuela." *Evaluación de Literatura Femenina de Latinoamérica, Siglo XX. II° Simposio Internacional de Literatura*. Ed. Juana Alcira Arancibia. San José de Costa Rica: Instituto Literario y Cultural Hispánico, 1985. I:49–57.

———. "Spanish America." *Women Writers in Translation: An Annotated Bibliography 1945–1982*. Eds. Margery Resnick and Isabelle de Courtivron. New York: Garland Publishing, 1984. Pp. 227–46.

Masiello, Francine. "Texto, ley, transgresión: Especulación sobre la novela (feminista) de vanguardia." *Revista Iberoamericana* 51, 132–33 (July-Dec. 1985):807–22.

Miguel, María Esther de. "La circunstancia femenina en el texto literario." *Fem* 6, 21 (Feb.–Mar. 1982):53–55.

Miller, Beth. "A Random Survey of the Ratio of Female Poets to Male in Anthologies: Less-Than-Tokenism as a Mexican Tradition." *Latin American Women Writers: Yesterday and Today*. Eds. Yvette Miller and Charles Tatum. Pittsburgh: Latin American Literary Review, 1977. Pp. 11–17.

Mora, Gabriela. "Crítica feminista. Apuntes sobre definiciones y problemas." *Theory and Practice of Feminist Literary Criticism*. Eds. Gabriela Mora and Karen S. Van Hooft. Ypsilanti, Mich.: Bilingual Press, 1982. Pp. 2–13.

———. "Crítica literaria feminista: Aproximaciones a su teoría y práctica." *Fem* 6, 21 (Feb.–Mar. 1982):53–55.

———. "Narradoras hispanoamericanas: Vieja y nueva problemática en renovadas elaboraciones." *Theory and Practice of Feminist Literary Criticism*. Eds. Gabriela Mora and Karen S. Van Hooft. Ypsilanti, Mich.: Bilingual Press, 1982. Pp. 156–71.

Mora Escalante, Sonia Marta; Flora Ovares Ramírez, and Margarita Rojas González. "El segundo sexo: la segunda literatura." *Káñina* (Costa Rica) 9, 2 (1985):19–24.

Núñez y Domínguez, J. de J. "La producción literaria femenina hispanoamericana." *Revista de la Raza* 14, 151–52 (1928):28–30.

Ocampo, Victoria. "La mujer y su expresión." *Testimonios*. 2d Series. Buenos Aires: Sur, 1941. (Also: *Revista de la Universidad de México* 31, 12 [Aug. 1977]:29–32.)

Ordóñez, Montserrat. "Escritoras latinoamericanas: encuentros tras desencuentros." *Boletín Americanista* (Barcelona) 36 (Jan. 1987):135–55.

Osorio, Lilia. "Ser, tradición, escritura." *Fem* 6, 21 (Feb.-Mar. 1982):23–27.

Oviedo de la Vega, Adela. "Influencia y conocimiento de la literatura femenina en las Américas." *Káñina* (Costa Rica) 9, 2 (1985):31–38.

Oyarzún, Mila. "La poesía femenina en Chile." *Atenea* 20, 218 (July 1943):168–94.

Pacífico, Patricia. "A Feminist Approach to Three Latin American Women Writers." *Una historia de servicio/A History of Service. 66° Aniversario de la Universidad Interameriana / 66th Anniversary of Inter-American University*. Puerto Rico: Inter-American University Press, 1979. Pp. 136–42.

Pasamanik, Luisa. "Poetisas de América—El canto inconcluso de un cisne." *Nivel* 53 (1967):7.

Percas de Ponseti, Helena. "Reflexiones sobre la poesía femenina hispanoamericana." *Revista/Review Interamericana* 12, 1 (Spring 1982):49–55.

Pereira de Padilla, Joaquín, and Asela B. Tejada. "Contribución de la mujer en la poesía y en la narrativa infantil panameña." *Káñina* (Costa Rica) 9, 2 (1985):77–84.

Perricone, Catherine. "A Bibliographic Approach to the Study of Latin American Women Poets." *Hispania* 71, 2 (May 1988):262–87.

Petit de Murat, U. "Avance arrollador de la literatura femenina." *Cúspide* 2, 6 (1938).

Piedrahita, Carmen. "Literatura sobre la problemática femenina en Latinoamérica." *Cuadernos Americanos* 236, 3 (May-June 1981):222–38.

Pimentel-Anduiza, Luz Aurora. "Conciencia ficcional femenina/escritura." *Plural* 189 (June 1987):43–48.

Pinto, Mercedes. "Cuatro poetisas uruguayas." *Revista de Cuba* 4, 10–12 (1935):46–81.

————. *Las poetisas, primer grupo: Ofelia Machado; Sara Bollo; Luisa Luisi; María Eugenia Vaz Ferreira.* Montevideo: Comisión Nacional de Centenario, 1931.

Poniatowska, Elena. "La literatura de las mujeres es parte de la literatura de los oprimidos." *Fem* 6, 21 (Feb.-Mar. 1982):23–27.

Randall, Margaret. "Escritura y testimonio femeninos." *Plural* 10, 2d series, 120 (Sept. 1981):26–28.

Redondo, Susana. "Proceso de la literatura femenina hispanoamericana." *Cuadernos del Congreso por la Libertad de la Cultura* (Paris) 6 (May-June 1954):34–38.

Reedy, Daniel R. "Aspects of the Feminist Movement in Peruvian Letters and Politics." *SECOLAS Annals* 6 (Mar. 1975):53–64.

Rivero, Eliana. "Las nuevas poetas cubanas." *Areito* (New York):5, 17 (Nov. 1978):31–37.

Roggiano, Alfredo. "Una importante historia de la poesía femenina argentina." *La Nueva Democracia* (New York) 41, 3 (1961):52–61.

Rosman-Askot, Adriana. "La [des] colonización de la escritora (y de la instrucción literaria)." *Revista Hispánica Moderna* 42, 1 (June 1989):77–82.

Russotto, Margara. "No basta un cuarto propio." *Fem* 6, 21 (Feb.-Mar. 1982):13–15.

Sánchez, Luis Alberto. "Mujeres hispanoamericanas en la poesía posmodernista." *Historia comparada de las literaturas americanas.* Vol. 3. *Del naturalismo al posmodernismo.* Buenos Aires: Losada, 1974. Pp. 321–48.

Sefchovich, Sara. "Primera parte: la salamandra." "Segunda parte: el espejo" (Introduction). *Mujeres en el espejo, I: Narradoras latinoamericanas, siglo XX.* Mexico City: Folios Ediciones, 1983.

Shea, Maureen. "A Growing Awareness of Sexual Oppression among Contemporary Latin American Women Writers." *Confluencia: Revista Hispánica de Cultura y Literatura* 4, 1 (Fall 1988):53–59.

————. "Latin American Women Writers and the Growing Potential of Political Consciousness." Ph.D. diss. University of Arizona, 1987. (DAI 49, 3 [Sept. 1988]:515A.)

Silva Castro, Raúl. "Mujeres en las letras chilenas." *Cuadernos del Congreso por la Libertad de la Cultura* (Paris) 94 (1965):75–80.

Silveira, Alcântara. "De Saturno a São Paulo." *Estado de São Paulo, Suplemento Literário*, Aug. 30, 1969:3. (About Brazil)

————. "Presença femenina na literatura nacional—1." *Estado de São Paulo, Suplemento Literário*, Jan. 6, 1968:4. (About Brazil)

Sotomayor de Concha, G. "La labor literaria de las mujeres chilenas." *Actividades femeninas en Chile.* Santiago de Chile: n.p., 1928.

Steele, Cynthia. "Toward a Socialist Feminist Criticism of Latin American Literature." *Ideologies and Literature* 4, 16 (May-June 1983):323–29.

Suárez Calimano, E. "El narcisismo en la poesía femenina de Hispanoamérica." *Nosotros* 72 (1931):27–55.

Sullivan, Constance. A. "Re-Reading the Hispanic Literary Canon: The Question of Gender." *Ideologies and Literature* 4, 2d cycle, 16 (May-June 1983):93–101.

Temple, Ella Dunbar. "Curso de la literatura femenina a través del período colonial en el Perú." *Tres* 1, 1 (July 1939):25–56.

Traba, Marta. "Hipótesis sobre una escritura diferente." *Quimera* (Barcelona) 13 (1981):9–11. (Also: *Fem* 6, 21 [1982]:9–12)

Ugalde, Sharon Keefe. "Process, Identity, and Learning to Read: Female Writing and

Feminist Criticism in Latin America Today." *Latin American Research Review* 24, 1 (1989):222–32.

Ugarte, Manuel. "Women Writers of South America." *Books Abroad* 5 (1931):27–55.

Umpierre, Luz María. "De la protesta a la creación: Una nueva visión de la mujer puertorriqueña en la poesía." *Imagine: International Chicano Poetry Journal* 2, 1 (Summer 1985):134–42.

Urrutia, Elena. "¿Qué escribe la mujer en México?" *Fem* 3, 10 (Jan.-Oct. 1979):9–12.

Valdivieso, Mercedes. "Literatura femenina: literatura de vanguardia y de ruptura." *Fem* 4, 16 (Sept. 1980–Jan. 1981):102–104.

Vallbona, Rima de. "Trayectoria actual de la poesía femenina en Costa Rica." *Káñina* (Costa Rica) 5, 2 (1981):18–27.

Vela, Arqueles. "Quinta Parte." *El modernismo.* Sepan Cuantos, Núm. 217. Mexico City: Porrúa, 1972. Pp. 117–53.

Venture Young, Ann. "Introduction." *The Image of Black Women in Twentieth Century South American Poetry: A Bilingual Anthology.* Ed. and trans. Ann Venture Young. Washington, D.C.: Three Continents Press, 1987. Pp. 3–40.

Welker, G. "Las poetisas (segundo grupo)." *Historia sintética de la literatura uruguaya.* 2 vols. Montevideo: n.p., 1931.

Wilson-Serfaty, Sheilah R. "Art by Gender: The Latin American Woman Writer." *Revista Canadiense de Estudios Hispánicos* 6, 1 (Fall 1981):135–37.

Zapata, Celia Correas de. "Breve historia de la mujer en la narrativa hispanoamericana." *Actas del Sexto Congreso Internacional de Hispanistas.* Asociación Internacional de Hispanistas. Toronto: University of Toronto, 1980.

———. "Escritoras latinoamericanas: Sus publicaciones en el contexto de las estructuras del poder." *Revista Iberoamericana* 51, 132–33 (July-Dec. 1985):591–603.

———. "La mujer en las letras de América." *Ensayos hispanoamericanos.* Buenos Aires: Corregidor, 1978. Pp. 45–75.

———. "One Hundred Years of Women Writers in Latin America." *Latin American Literary Review* 3, 6 (Spring-Summer 1975):7–16.

Zardoya, Concha. "La muerte en la poesía femenina latinoamericana." *Cuadernos Americanos* 12, 5 (Sept.-Oct. 1953):233–70.

APPENDIX A:
LIST OF AUTHORS BY BIRTH DATE

See the chapters "Indian Women Writers of Spanish America" and "Latina Writers in the United States" for additional authors.

1648?–1695	Sor Juana Inés de la Cruz
1671–1742	Madre Castillo
1814–1873	Gertrudis Gómez de Avellancda
1818–1982	Juana Manuela Gorriti
1845–1909	Mercedes Cabello de Carbonera
1850–1897	Salomé Ureña de Henríquez
1852–1909	Clorinda Matto de Turner
1886–1914	Delmira Agustini
1889–1936	Teresa de la Parra
1889–1957	Gabriela Mistral
1890–1979	Victoria Ocampo
1892–1938	Alfonsina Storni
1892–1979	Juana de Ibarbourou
1897–1967	Marta Brunet
1899–1974	Claudia Lars
b. 1900	Lydia Cabrera

b. 1900	Nellie Campobello
1903–1989	Magda Portal
b. 1903–6?	Silvina Ocampo
1909–1971	Sara de Ibáñez
b. 1909	Josefina Plá
1910–1980	María Luisa Bombal
1914–1953	Julia de Burgos
b. 1915	Silvina Bullrich
1916–1956	Yolanda Oreamuno
1917–1967	Violeta Parra
b. 1920	Elena Garro
b. 1920	Olga Orozco
b. 1920	Armonía Somers
b. 1921	Syria Poletti
1922–1974	Eunice Odio
b. 1924	Claribel Alegría
1925–1974	Rosario Castellanos
1925–1985	Marta Lynch
b. 1928	Griselda Gambaro
b. 1928	Luisa Josefina Hernández
1930–1983	Marta Traba
1931–1988	Sara Gallardo
b. 1931	Carmen Naranjo
b. 1932	Julieta Campos
b. 1933	Elena Poniatowska
1936–1972	Alejandra Pizarnik
b. 1938	María Luisa Mendoza
b. 1938	Luisa Valenzuela
b. 1939	Albalucía Angel
b. 1940	Fanny Buitrago

b. 1941   Cristina Peri Rossi

b. 1942   Isabel Allende

b. 1942   Rosario Ferré

b. 1944   Nancy Morejón

APPENDIX B:
LIST OF AUTHORS BY COUNTRY

See ''Latina Writers in the United States'' for additional authors.

ARGENTINA

Silvina Bullrich

Facundina (Indian Writers)

Sara Gallardo

Griselda Gambaro

Juana Manuela Gorriti

Marta Lynch

Silvina Ocampo

Victoria Ocampo

Olga Orozco

Alejandra Pizarnik

Syria Poletti

Alfonsina Storni

Marta Traba

Luisa Valenzuela

BOLIVIA

Domitila Barrios (Indian Writers)

Basilia (Indian Writers)

Facundina (Indian Writers)

CHILE

Isabel Allende
María Luisa Bombal
Marta Brunet
Gabriela Mistral
Violeta Parra

COLOMBIA

Albalucía Angel
Fanny Buitrago
Madre Castillo
Marta Traba

COSTA RICA

Carmen Naranjo
Eunice Odio
Yolanda Oreamuno

CUBA

Lydia Cabrera
Julieta Campos
Gertrudis Gómez de Avellaneda
Nancy Morejón

DOMINICAN REPUBLIC

Salomé Ureña de Henríquez

EL SALVADOR

Claribel Alegría
Claudia Lars

GUATEMALA

Rigoberta Menchú (Indian Writers)

MEXICO

Nellie Campobello
Julieta Campos
Rosario Castellanos

Elena Garro
Luisa Josefina Hernández
Sor Juana Inés de la Cruz
María Luisa Mendoza
Elena Poniatowska

NICARAGUA

Claribel Alegría

PARAGUAY

Josefina Plá

PERU

Mercedes Cabello de Carbonera
Juana Manuela Gorriti
Clorinda Matto de Turner
Magda Portal

PUERTO RICO

Julia de Burgos
Rosario Ferré

URUGUAY

Delmira Agustini
Sara de Ibáñez
Juana de Ibarbourou
Cristina Peri Rossi
Armonía Somers

VENEZUELA

Teresa de la Parra

APPENDIX C: LIST OF AUTHORS BY GENRE

See the chapters "Indian Women Writers of Spanish America" and "Latina Writers in the United States" for additional authors.

AUTOBIOGRAPHIES AND AUTOBIOGRAPHICAL STATEMENTS IN PROSE AND VERSE

Silvina Bullrich

Madre Castillo

Gertrudis Gómez de Avellaneda

Sor Juana Inés de la Cruz

Victoria Ocampo

CHILDREN'S AND JUVENILE LITERATURE

Marta Brunet

Fanny Buitrago

Lydia Cabrera

Rosario Ferré

Claudia Lars

María Luisa Mendoza

Gabriela Mistral

Silvina Ocampo

Syria Poletti

Alfonsina Storni

DRAMA, PLAYS, DRAMATIC PROSE, AND VERSE

Fanny Buitrago

Rosario Castellanos

Griselda Gambaro

Elena Garro

Gertrudis Gómez de Avellaneda

Luisa Josefina Hernández

Sor Juana Inés de la Cruz

Clorinda Matto de Turner

Silvina Ocampo

Victoria Ocampo

Eunice Odio

Josefina Plá

Alfonsina Storni

POETRY, PROSE POEMS

Delmira Agustini

Claribel Alegría

Marta Brunet

Silvina Bullrich

Julia de Burgos

Nellie Campobello

Rosario Castellanos

Madre Castillo

Rosario Ferré

Gertrudis Gómez de Avellaneda

Juana Manuela Gorriti

Sara de Ibáñez

Juana de Ibarbourou

Sor Juana Inés de la Cruz

Claudia Lars

Gabriela Mistral

Nancy Morejón

Carmen Naranjo

Silvina Ocampo

Eunice Odio

Olga Orozco

Violeta Parra

Cristina Peri Rossi

Alejandra Pizarnik

Josefina Plá

Magda Portal

Alfonsina Storni

Marta Traba

Salomé Ureña de Henríquez

PROSE (INCLUDING POETIC PROSE)

Short Fiction (stories, microtexts, *estampas*, etc.)

Claribel Alegría

Albalucía Angel

María Luisa Bombal

Marta Brunet

Fanny Buitrago

Silvina Bullrich

Lydia Cabrera

Nellie Campobello

Julieta Campos

Rosario Castellanos

Madre Castillo

Rosario Ferré

Sara Gallardo

Griselda Gambaro

Elena Garro

Gertrudis Gómez de Avellaneda

Juana Manuela Gorriti

Juana de Ibarbourou

Marta Lynch

Clorinda Matto de Turner

María Luisa Mendoza

Gabriela Mistral

Carmen Naranjo

Silvina Ocampo

Eunice Odio

Yolanda Oreamuno

Teresa de la Parra
Cristina Peri Rossi
Alejandra Pizarnik
Syria Poletti
Elena Poniatowska
Armonía Somers
Marta Traba
Luisa Valenzuela

Long Fiction (novels, etc.)

Claribel Alegría
Isabel Allende
Albalucía Angel
María Luisa Bombal
Marta Brunet
Fanny Buitrago
Silvina Bullrich
Mercedes Cabello de Carbonera
Nellie Campobello
Julieta Campos
Rosario Castellanos
Rosario Ferré
Sara Gallardo
Griselda Gambaro
Elena Garro
Gertrudis Gómez de Avellaneda
Juana Manuela Gorriti
Luisa Josefina Hernández
Marta Lynch
Clorinda Matto de Turner
María Luisa Mendoza
Carmen Naranjo
Silvina Ocampo
Yolanda Oreamuno
Teresa de la Parra
Cristina Peri Rossi
Syria Poletti
Elena Poniatowska

Magda Portal
Armonía Somers
Marta Traba
Luisa Valenzuela

Nonfiction Prose (essays, letters, journalism, criticism, lectures, etc.)

Delmira Agustini
Claribel Alegría
Silvina Bullrich
Julia de Burgos
Lydia Cabrera
Nellie Campobello
Julieta Campos
Rosario Castellanos
Rosario Ferré
Gertrudis Gómez de Avellaneda
Juana Manuela Gorriti
Juana de Ibarbourou
Sor Juana Inés de la Cruz
Marta Lynch
Clorinda Matto de Turner
María Luisa Mendoza
Gabriela Mistral
Nancy Morejón
Carmen Naranjo
Victoria Ocampo
Eunice Odio
Yolanda Oreamuno
Teresa de la Parra
Alejandra Pizarnik
Josefina Plá
Syria Poletti
Elena Poniatowska
Magda Portal
Alfonsina Storni
Marta Traba
Salomé Ureña de Henríquez
Luisa Valenzuela

TITLE INDEX

Note: For purposes of alphabetization, non-English letters are treated as English, e.g., "ñ" as an "n," "ç" as a "c."

"Abandonada" (Magda Portal), 486

"El abecedario" (Luisa Valenzuela), 536

"Absurdity, Death and the Search for Meaning in Two of Garro's Novels" (Mark Frisch), 206

"El Acomodador": una lectura fantástica de Felisberto Hernández (Rosario Ferré), 166

Adán Buenosayres (Leopoldo Marechal), 376

"¡Adelante!" (Salomé Ureña de Henríquez), 528

¡Adelante, la isla! (Sara Gallardo), 176, 183

"El advenimiento del águila" (Rosario Castellanos), 145

"A él" (Gertrudis Gómez de Avellaneda y Arteaga), 216

"A Eros" (Alfonsina Storni), 507

Afectos espirituales de la V. M. Francisca Josefa del Castillo (Madre Castillo), 156, 160–61, 162

"Afuera lleuve" (Luisa Josefina Hernández), 244

"Agonía" (Luisa Josefina Hernández), 244

"Agua en la boca" (Syria Poletti), 463, 464

"El agua, motivo primordial de *La última niebla*" (Saúl Sosnowski), 50

"Aguardiente de caña" (Luisa Josefina Hernández), 242, 244

Aguas abajo (Marta Brunet), 54, 57

"A Julia de Burgos" (Julia de Burgos), 88–89

"A la luna" (Gertrudis Gómez de Avellaneda y Arteaga), 216

"A la patria" (Salomé Ureña de Henríquez), 527

"A la poesía" (Gertrudis Gómez de Avellaneda y Arteaga), 216–17

"A las estrellas" (Gertrudis Gómez de Avellaneda y Arteaga), 216

"Alas mojadas" (Syria Poletti), 462

"A la vuelta" (Gertrudis Gómez de Avellaneda y Arteaga), 215

Album de familia (Rosario Castellanos), 141, 146, 149

Album familiar (Claribel Alegría), 11,
    12–13
Alejandra Pizarnik: A Profile Anthology
    (Introduction by Frank Graziano), 450
Alejandra Pizarnik: poemas, antología
    (Introduction by Alejandro Fontela),
    450–51
Alelí y el payaso Bumbum (Syria Poletti),
    463, 466
Aleluyas para los más chiquitos (Marta
    Brunet), 55, 59
La alfombra roja (Marta Lynch), 292,
    293, 298
*Alfonsina. Epoca, dolor y obra de la
    poetisa Alfonsina Storni* (Arturo
    Capdevilla), 509
Alfonsina Storni (María Teresa Orosco),
    509
"Alfonsina Storni" (Sidonia Carmen
    Rosenbaum), 505, 509
Alfonsina Storni (Sonia Jones), 505, 508,
    509
Alfonsina Storni: From Poetess to Poet
    (Rachel Phillips), 504, 505, 506, 507,
    508, 509
"Alfonsina Storni y la Generación del
    16" (Helena Percas), 509
*Alguien muere en San Onofre de
    Cuarumí* (Josefina Plá and Angel Pérez
    Pardella), 454, 456, 457
Algunas mujeres de la conquista (Josefina
    Plá), 456
"Alienation and Eros in Three Stories by
    Beatriz Guido, Marta Lynch and
    Amalia Jamilis" (Ernest Lewald), 300
"Alirka, la de los caballos" (Luisa
    Valenzuela), 536
"Al mar" (Gertrudis Gómez de
    Avellaneda y Arteaga), 216
A lo largo del corto camino (Yolanda
    Oreamuno), 397, 399–400, 401
"Al partir" (Gertrudis Gómez de
    Avellaneda y Arteaga), 211, 215
Al pie de la letra: poemas (Rosario
    Castellanos), 144
"Altavoces" (Syria Poletti), 465
Al vencedor (Marta Lynch), 293

"A madona poesía" (Alfonsina Storni),
    507
Amarillo celeste (Silvina Ocampo), 362,
    363, 365
"El Amartelo" (Juana Manuela Gorriti),
    235
Amasijo (Marta Brunet), 55–56, 59
"El ambiente jurídico" (Luisa Josefina
    Hernández), 241, 243–44
"El ambiente tico y los mitos tropicales"
    (Yolanda Oreamuno), 395
América (Carmen Naranjo), 350
*América latina frente al imperialismo y
    defensa de la Revolución Mexicana*
    (Magda Portal), 488
"American Feminist Literary Criticism:
    A Bibliographical Introduction" (Cheri
    Register), 284
"A mi patria" (Salomé Ureña de
    Henríquez), 526
"Las amistades efímeras" (Rosario
    Castellanos), 146
El amo del mundo (Alfonsina Storni),
    503, 505
Amor, ciudad atribuída (Nancy
    Morejón), 341
Amor de alas (Syria Poletti), 463, 464,
    466
"Los amores" (Cristina Peri Rossi), 441
Los amores de Afrodita (Fanny Buitrago),
    66, 68–69
Los amores de Hortencia (Mercedes
    Cabello de Carbonera), 96, 98
"Amor por los animales" (Luisa
    Valenzuela), 538
La amortajada (María Luisa Bombal),
    44–46
"Amor y anhelo" (Salomé Ureña de
    Henríquez), 527, 528
"Amor y orgullo" (Gertrudis Gómez de
    Avellaneda y Arteaga), 216
"Anacaona" (Salomé Ureña de
    Henríquez), 523, 527, 528, 529
*Anaforuana: ritual y símbolos de la
    iniciación en la sociedad secreta
    Abakuá* (Lydia Cabrera), 112–13
Anagó: vocabulario lucumí (El Yoruba

que se habla en Cuba) (Lydia
Cabrera), 113
*Análisis crítico de los afectos espirituales
de sor Francisca Josefa de la
Concepción de Castillo* (Darío Achury
Valenzuela), 162
"Un análisis de la influencia filosófica de
Manuel González Prada en Clorinda
Matto y Mercedes Cabello" (Laura
Judith Saver), 312
"An Analysis of *Aves sin nido*" (Joye R.
Swain), 312
Andamos huyendo Lola (Elena Garro),
200, 202, 206
Las andariegas (Albalucía Angel), 31–
32, 36, 37–38
"Andarse por las ramas" (Elena Garro),
204
"Anforas negras" (Juana de Ibarbourou),
264
"El ángel caído" (Juana Manuela
Gorriti), 231–32
"Angeles pintados" (Juana de
Ibarbourou), 265
"El ángel planeador" (Armonía Somers),
494, 498
"Angulo Eluard-Picasso" (Marta Traba),
516
"Angustias" (Salomé Ureña de
Henríquez), 527
"Un año en California" (Juana Manuela
Gorriti), 233
"La anomalía del ensueño: los niños en
Marta Brunet y Ana María Matute"
(Marjorie Agosín), 61
Los años de fuego (Marta Lynch), 295
"Años de miel" (Fanny Buitrago), 67
"Anotaciones para una autobiografía"
(Olga Orozco), 408
"Antigua sin sombra" (Albalucía Angel),
36
Antología: rescate de un gran poeta
(Eunice Odio), 382, 386–87, 388, 390
Antología de la literatura fantástica
(Silvina Ocampo), 361
Antología de poetas hispanoamericanos
(Introduction by Marcelino Menéndez
y Pelayo), 530

Antología poética (Alfonsina Storni), 504
Antología poética (Josefina Plá), 456,
457–58; (Introduction by Francisco
Pérez-Maricevich), 458
Antología poética argentina (Silvina
Ocampo), 361
"Aparición de una novelista" (Amado
Alonso), 49–50
"Apenas una planta" (Syria Poletti), 464
Apocalipsis cum figuris (Luisa Josefina
Hernández), 243, 245
Apocalipsis XX (Sara de Ibáñez), 254,
257, 259
"Apocrypha" (Luisa Josefina
Hernández), 250
"Apollo 8" (Claudia Lars), 288
"Apología del limón dulce y del paisaje"
(Yolanda Oreamuno), 396
Apostasía (Luisa Josefina Hernández),
243, 245, 250
"Apóstrofes" (Sara de Ibáñez), 257
"Una aproximación a la cuentística
mágico-realista de Elena Garro"
(Robert K. Anderson), 206
"Aproximación a los personajes
femeninos a partir de *Los recuerdos
del porvenir*" (Minerva Margarita
Villarreal), 206
"Apuntes biográficos sobre Magda
Portal" *Claridad*, 490
Apuntes para una declaración de fe
(Rosario Castellanos), 140
Apuntes para un libro de viajes (Marta
Lynch), 295
*Apuntes sobre la vida militar de
Francisco Villa* (Nellie Campobello),
119
Aquí no ha pasado nada (Josefina Plá
and R. Centurión Miranda), 455
Aquí pasan cosas raras (Luisa
Valenzuela), 537–38, 539, 542
Aquí también, Domitila (Domitila Barrios
de Chungara), 548
El árbol (Elena Garro), 201
"El árbol" (María Luisa Bombal), 46–47
Arbol de Diana (Alejandra Pizarnik), 448
Un árbol lleno de manzanas (Marta
Lynch), 293, 294, 295

"Armonía Somers" (Evelyn Picón
    Garfield), 498, 499
"Armonía Somers, al este del paraíso"
    (Alberto Cousté), 499
"Arpas blancas, conejos dorados" (Luisa
    Josefina Hernández), 242, 243, 249
Artigas (Sara de Ibáñez), 258
El artista barquero; o, los cuatro cinco
    de junio (Gertrudis Gómez de
    Avellaneda y Arteaga), 219
"Art, Society and Criticism: The Literary
    Theories of Mercedes Cabello de
    Carbonera and Clorinda Matto de
    Turner" (Bart L. Lewis), 312
Ashes of Izalco (Claribel Alegría and
    Darwin Flakoll), 10
"Aspectos de conflicto y enajenamiento
    de la mujer en las novelas de Silvina
    Bullrich, Beatriz Guido y Clarice
    Lispector" (Anna C. Tavenner), 80
Aspectos del estilo en la poesía de
    Gabriela Mistral (Cora Santander
    Russo), 337–38
"Aspects of the Feminist Movement in
    Peruvian Letters and Politics" (Daniel
    R. Reedy), 491
Los astros del abismo (Delmira
    Agustini), 5
"La autenticidad de la mujer en el arte"
    (Rosario Ferré), 168
"Auténtico realismo" (Juan Carlos
    Ghiano), 183
"The Author as Editor" (about Elena
    Poniatowska; Ronald Christ), 479
Autobiografía de Irene (Silvina Ocampo),
    361, 364
Autobiografía I: el archipiélago (Victoria
    Ocampo), 375
Autobiografía II: el imperio insular
    (Victoria Ocampo), 375
Autobiografía III: la rama de Salzburgo
    (Victoria Ocampo), 375
Autobiografía IV: viraje (Victoria
    Ocampo), 375
Autobiografía V: figuras simbólicas;
    Medida de Francia (Victoria Ocampo),
    375

Autobiografía VI: sur y Cía (Victoria
    Ocampo), 375
"Autodedicatoria" (Josefina Plá), 457
"Autorromance de Juanita Fernández"
    (Juana de Ibarbourou), 265
La Avellaneda y sus obras; ensayo
    biográfico y crítico (Emilio Cotarelo y
    Mori), 221–22
Las aventuras perdidas (Alejandra
    Pizarnik), 447
Aves sin nido (Clorinda Matto de
    Turner), 303, 304, 305, 307–8, 309,
    310, 311, 312; Prologue by Antonio
    Cornejo Polar, 312
"Aves sin nido: indios 'notables' y
    forasteros" (Antonio Cornejo Polar),
    312
"Ay ay ay de la grifa negra" (Julia de
    Burgos), 89
Ayapá: cuentos de Jicotea (Lydia
    Cabrera), 108–9, 111
"Ayúdame, Valentina" (Violeta Parra),
    430

"Babel" (Victoria Ocampo), 374
Bahía Sonora, relatos de la isla (Fanny
    Buitrago), 65, 67
"El baile" (Cristina Peri Rossi), 436
"Un baile en Punta de Oro" (Fanny
    Buitrago), 67
"Balada triste" (Magda Portal), 486
Baltasar (Gertrudis Gómez de Avellaneda
    y Arteaga), 213, 217, 218, 222
Balún-Canán (Rosario Castellanos), 141,
    145, 148
"Balún-Canán: A Model Demonstration
    of Discourse as Power" (Sandra
    Messinger Cypess), 148
"El banquete de la muerte" (Juana
    Manuela Gorriti), 235
"The Barzolas and the Housewives
    Committee" (Gloria Ardaya Salinas),
    554
La batalla (Sara de Ibáñez), 254
"El Bautizo" (Julieta Campos), 134
"Because I Want Peace" (Claribel
    Alegría and Darwin Flakoll), 14

"La bella durmiente" (Rosario Ferré), 167, 169, 172

Bestia dañina (Marta Brunet), 54, 56, 59

"El bestiario inocente en la vida y en la obra de Juana de Ibarbourou" (Dora Isella Russell), 269

"Between 'in longer' and 'not yet': Woman's Space in *Misiá Señora*" (Sharon Keefe Ugalde), 38

"Bibliography of Writings by and about Victoria Ocampo (1890–1979)" (David William Foster), 378

La bicicleta (Silvina Bullrich), 78–79

"Bien pudiera ser" (Alfonsina Storni), 504

Bienvenido (Marta Brunet), 54, 56–57, 58

"El bildungsroman fracasado en Latinoamérica: el caso de *Ifigenia*, de Teresa de la Parra" (Edna Aizenberg), 424

"Biografía a mi manera" (Marta Lynch), 295

"Biografía de la romancista argentina Juana Manuela Gorriti" (Pastor S. Obligado), 236

Blanca Sol (Mercedes Cabello de Carbonera), 95, 97, 98, 100, 101, 102

"Blanco ... Negro ... Blanco" (Alfonsina Storni), 506

Bloodroot (Alma Villaneuva), 559

Bocetos al lápiz de americanos célebres (Clorinda Matto de Turner), 304, 311

Bodas de cristal (Silvina Bullrich), 74, 76–77

"Bolivian Mining" (Ricardo A. Godoy), 554

Boreales, miniaturas y porcelanas (Clorinda Matto de Turner), 311

"Botica modelo" (Luisa Josefina Hernández), 242, 243–44

Breaking Boundaries: Latina Writings and Critical Readings (Asunción Horno-Delgado et al.), 563, 564

Breaking the Silences: 20th Century Poetry by Cuban Women (Margaret Randall), 561

Los burgueses (Silvina Bullrich), 75, 77, 79

El caballo alado (Silvina Ocampo), 362, 364

"Los caballos" (Syria Poletti), 465

"Caín" (Sara de Ibáñez), 256, 258

La caja de cristal (Rosario Ferré), 166

Los cálices vacíos (Delmira Agustini), 1, 2, 3–5

"Calle" (Alfonsina Storni), 507

La calle del viento norte y otros cuentos (Armonía Somers), 494, 495

Calles de Buenos Aires: Barrio Norte (Silvina Bullrich), 76

Cambiar sueños por sombras (Josefina Plá), 457

Cambio de armas (Luisa Valenzuela), 533, 541

Camino al mediodía (Carmen Naranjo), 351, 354, 356

"Camino al ministerio" (Luisa Valenzuela), 538

"Camino de los búhos" (Fanny Buitrago), 66

"La campana imposible (Adaptación de una leyenda china)" (Juana de Ibarbourou), 266

"Campirana" (Albalucía Angel), 35

El campo (Griselda Gambaro), 189, 190, 191, 193, 194, 195

"Canción amarga" (Magda Portal), 486

"Canción del adiós que presiente" (Claudia Lars), 284

Canción de la ternura (Carmen Naranjo), 355, 356

Canción de la verdad sencilla (Julia de Burgos), 86, 88, 89–90

"La canción de lucha de Violeta Parra y su ubicación en el complejo cultural chileno entre los años 1960 a 1973. Esbozo de sus antecedentes sociohistóricos y categorización de los fenómenos atingentes" (Gina Cánepa-Hurtado), 432

Canciones (Claudia Lars), 287

Canciones folklóricas chilenas (Violeta Parra), 430

"Canción para dormirte" (Julia de Burgos), 90

Canción redonda (Claudia Lars), 284

"El cantar de mis cantares" (Salomé Ureña de Henríquez), 526

El cántaro fresco (Juana de Ibarbourou), 262, 264

Canto (Sara de Ibáñez), 255, 256, 258, 259; Prologue by Pablo Neruda, 258

Canto a Montevideo (Sara de Ibáñez), 258, 259

"Canto XIX" (Salomé Ureña de Henríquez), 529

Canto póstumo (Sara de Ibáñez), 255, 257–58; Preface by Roberto Ibáñez, 254, 258

"Canto proletario" (Magda Portal), 486

Cantores que reflexionan: notas para una historia personal de la nueva canción chilena (Osvaldo Rodríguez), 432

Cantos de la mañana (Delmira Agustini), 1, 3–4

"Un carro en la esquina" (Syria Poletti), 462

"La carta" (Violeta Parra), 430

"Carta a Julia de Burgos" (Rosario Ferré), 91

Carta atenagórica (Sor Juana Inés de la Cruz), 277, 278

"Carta a Virginia Woolf" (Victoria Ocampo), 375

"Cartas escritas cuando crece la noche" (Claudia Lars), 288–89

"Carta sobre la religión de la humanidad dirigida a la señora doña Mercedes Cabello de Carbonera" (Juan Enrique Lagarrigue), 96

"The Cartography of Memory" (Claribel Alegría and Darwin Flakoll), 14

Cartucho: relatos de la lucha en el norte de México (Nellie Campobello), 118–19, 121–22, 123, 124, 125

"La Casa" (Julieta Campos), 134

La casa del abuelo (Fanny Buitrago), 65, 66, 68

La casa del arco iris (Fanny Buitrago), 66, 68

La casa de los espíritus (Isabel Allende), 20, 21, 24, 26

"*La casa de los espíritus*: mirada, espacio, discurso de la otra historia" (René Campos), 26

"*La casa de los espíritus*: una aproximación sociolingüística" (Mario Rojas), 26, 28

"*La casa de los espíritus* de Isabel Allende: un caleidoscopio de espejos desordenados" (Mario Rojas), 26, 27

La casa de vidrio (Claudia Lars), 284

La casa junto al río (Elena Garro), 200, 202, 203, 206

Casa sin fin (Marta Traba), 515

"Casa sobre tu pecho" (Claudia Lars), 286

"Castigos" (Sara de Ibáñez), 257

"Las cataratas de Niágara" (Juana de Ibarbourou), 269

"Celda N⁰ 2" (Magda Portal), 486

Celina o los gatos (Julieta Campos), 128, 129, 131, 132–34, 135

"Cenizas" (Alejandra Pizarnik), 447

Cenizas de Izalco (Claribel Alegría and Darwin Flakoll), 9, 10, 11, 12, 13, 15–16

"Cenizas de Izalco" (Rachel Schwartz), 16

"Los censores" (Luisa Valenzuela), 540–41

"El cerco azul" (Juana de Ibarbourou), 264

Las ceremonias del verano (Marta Traba), 514, 516–17, 519

"Ceremonias de rechazo" (Luisa Valenzuela), 541

"El charco" (Juana de Ibarbourou), 264

"Charlas de salón" (Juana Manuela Gorriti), 234

Chico Carlo (Juana de Ibarbourou), 263, 265, 266

"Chincha" (Juana Manuela Gorriti), 235

"El ciclo vital en la poesía de Juana de Ibarbourou" (Ruth Idalmi Aponte), 268

"Cimbelina en 1900 y pico" (Carmen Naranjo), 352

Cincuentenario (1931–1981), special
  issue of *Sur*, 377
"Cine porno" (Luisa Valenzuela), 538
"Círculos violetas" (Magda Portal), 487
"La ciudad" (Julieta Campos), 134
"Ciudad ajena" (Luisa Valenzuela), 532,
  536
Ciudad Real: Cuentos (Rosario
  Castellanos), 145
Clara: Thirteen Short Stories and a Novel
  (Luisa Valenzuela), 532
"La clara cisterna" (Juana de
  Ibarbourou), 264
"Clorinda Matto de Turner: An Analysis
  of Her Role in Peruvian Literature"
  (Ruth Compton Crouse), 312
"Clorinda Matto de Turner: *Aves sin nido*
  (1889)" (Lucía Fox-Lockert), 312
"Clorinda Matto de Turner: para una
  imagen de la novela peruana del siglo
  XIX" (Antonio Cornejo Polar), 312
"Clorinda Matto de Turner and Mercedes
  Cabello de Carbonera: Societal
  Criticism and Morality" (Martin C.
  Miller), 312
*Clorinda Matto de Turner y la novela
  indigenista* (Alberto Tauro), 312
*Clorinda Matto de Turner y su
  indigenismo literario* (Francisco
  Carrillo), 312
"La cocina de la escritura" (Rosario
  Ferré), 166, 170–71
El cofre volante (Silvina Ocampo), 362
Cola de lagartija (Luisa Valenzuela),
  533, 540, 541–42
"*Cola de lagartija*: látigo de la palabra y
  la triple P" (Martha Paley
  Francescato), 542
Cola de zorro (Fanny Buitrago), 65, 67
La cólera secreta (Luisa Josefina
  Hernández), 244
"The Colombian Novel of the Atlantic
  Coast" (Nancy McCarty), 70
"Colón" (Salomé Ureña de Henríquez),
  527
"Coloquio de las madres" (Magda
  Portal), 487

Un coloquio sobre Victoria Ocampo
  (Marcos Victoria), 376
Como en la guerra (Luisa Valenzuela),
  538–39, 540
"Los compadres" (Lydia Cabrera), 109
"A Comparative Examination of Style in
  the Works of Madre Castillo" (Claudio
  G. Antoni), 162
El Conde León Tolstoy (Mercedes
  Cabello de Carbonera), 96
"La condena" (Cristina Peri Rossi), 438
La condesa sangrienta (Alejandra
  Pizarnik), 449
"La condición humana de la mujer"
  (Angel Rama), 60
*Con él, conmigo, con nosotros tres:
  cronovela* (María Luisa Mendoza),
  317–18, 320–21, 324, 325
"Con Luisa Josefina Hernández: La
  misoginia no existe" (Cristina
  Pacheco), 249
"The Conscientization of Domitila: A
  Case Study in the Political Psychology
  of Liberation" (Lawrence R.
  Alschuler), 554
Las consecuencias (Mercedes Cabello de
  Carbonera), 95, 96, 98, 99
El conspirador (Mercedes Cabello de
  Carbonera), 97, 101, 102–3
Constancia del ser (Magda Portal), 485,
  486, 487
"Construcción folklórica y
  desconstrucción individual en el texto
  de Violeta Parra" (Naomi Lindstrom),
  432
"Contemporary Women Novelists of
  Argentina (1945–67)" (Diane Solomon
  Birkemoe), 79, 467
Contes nègres de Cuba (Lydia Cabrera),
  107, 108
"Contexto político, situación del indio y
  crítica a la iglesia de Clorinda Matto
  de Turner" (Lucía Fox-Lockert), 312
Conversación al sur (Marta Traba), 515,
  518–19
"A Conversation with Lydia Cabrera"
  (Suzanne Jill Levine), 114

Los convidados de agosto (Rosario Castellanos), 146

"El cordero" (Juana de Ibarbourou), 262

Cornelia frente al espejo (Silvina Ocampo), 362

"La corona del ángel" (Luisa Josefina Hernández), 244

Correspondencia íntima (Delmira Agustini), 1, 6, 7

Las cosas (María Luisa Mendoza), 318, 322–23, 325

"Cosquín de noche" (Syria Poletti), 465

Costa sur (Magda Portal), 484, 486, 490

"La creación literaria en Julieta Campos: *Tiene los cabellos rojizos y se llama Sabina*" (Alicia Rivero Potter), 137

"La creatividad y el deseo en *Querido Diego, te abraza Quiela* de Elena Poniatowska" (Cynthia Steele), 479

La creciente (Silvina Bullrich), 79

Crickets and Frogs, A Fable (Gabriela Mistral), 339

"El criollismo de Marta Brunet" (Luis Merino Reyes), 60

"Cristina Peri Rossi" (Tomás G. Brena), 442

"Cristina Peri Rossi: la parábola de un naufragio" (Rosa María Pereda), 442

"Cristina Peri Rossi: vino nuevo en odres nuevos" (Mario Benedetti), 441

"A Critical Bibliography of and About the Works of Rosario Castellanos" (Maureen Ahern), 147

La crítica literaria en la obra de Gabriela Mistral (Onilda A. Jiménez), 338

"Crónica literaria" (Ricardo Latcham), 490

Crónicas de Chile (María Luisa Mendoza), 318

Crónicas de la burguesía (Marta Lynch), 293

"Las crónicas de Victoria Ocampo: versatilidad y fidelidad de un género" (Marta Gallo), 377

El cruce del río (Marta Lynch), 293, 294

Cuaderno de Granada (Nancy Morejón), 341

"Cuando las mujeres quieren a los hombres" (Rosario Ferré), 167–68

"40° [Cuarenta] sobre cero" (Yolanda Oreamuno), 395

"Cuarta versión" (Luisa Valenzuela), 537, 541

"Cuartetos escritos en un cementerio" (Gertrudis Gómez de Avellaneda y Arteaga), 216

"Cuarto hogar" (María Luisa Mendoza), 323

Cuatro actitudes poéticas (Julieta Gómez Paz), 450

Cuatro conferencias sobre América del Sur (Clorinda Matto de Turner), 311

"Las cuatro moscas" (Elena Garro), 202

"Cucu, cantaba rana" (Claudia Lars), 287

Cuentos: Stories by Latinas (Alma Gómez et al.), 564

Cuentos para Mari-Sol (Marta Brunet), 54, 59

Cuentos de hadas (Rosario Ferré), 169

Los cuentos de Juan Bobo (Rosario Ferré), 166, 169

Los cuentos de Lilus Kikus (Elena Poniatowska), 477

"Los cuentos de Lydia Cabrera: ¿transposiciones o creaciones?" (Rosa Valdés Cruz), 113

Cuentos desde el Taller "Leonor Alonso": dirigido por Syria Poletti (Syria Poletti), 463

"Los cuentos ¿infantiles? de Rosario Ferré—estrategias subversivas" (Luz María Umpierre-Herrera), 172

Cuentos negros de Cuba (Lydia Cabrera), 108, 109

Cuentos para adultos niños y retrasados mentales (Lydia Cabrera), 111

Cuentos para Mari-Sol (Marta Brunet), 54, 59

Los cuentos tristes (Marta Lynch), 293

"La culpa es de los Tlaxcaltecas" (Elena Garro), 202, 205

" 'La culpa es de los Tlaxcaltecas': A Reevaluation of Mexico's Past Through Myth" (Cynthia Duncan), 204

"Cumbres poéticas del erotismo femenino en Hispanoamérica" (Robert Lima), 268

"El custodio Blancanieves" (Luisa Valenzuela), 540

"Dadme mi número" (Julia de Burgos), 88

"La dama boba" (Elena Garro), 200, 203

" 'La dama boba' de Elena Garro: verdad y ficción, teatro y metateatro" (Gabriela Mora), 203, 204

"La dama y la turquesa" (Elena Garro), 202–3

De amor y de sombra (Isabel Allende), 21, 22, 24–25, 26

Dear Diego (Elena Poniatowska), 473

De Ausencia (María Luisa Mendoza), 318, 321–22, 325

"Debo olvidar" (Elena Garro), 202

Una década de la novela colombiana: la experiencia de los setenta (Raymond Leslie Williams), 38

"Décima nada" (María Luisa Mendoza), 324

Décimas: autobiografía en versos (Violeta Parra), 428

Décimas: autobiografía en versos chilenos (Violeta Parra), 428–29, 432

"Décimas de Violeta Parra o la separación de la conciencia de lo individual" (Adriana Castillo de Berchenko), 432

"Decir sí" (Griselda Gambaro), 187, 189, 194

"*Los dedos de la mano*" (Antonio Cornejo Polar), 300

Los dedos de la mano (Marta Lynch), 294, 297

"Defensa y realidad de una literatura" (Fabián Dobles), 401

De Francesca a Beatrice (Victoria Ocampo), 376

"Los degolladores de estatuas" (Alfonsina Storni), 506

"De la calle y el pan" (Claudia Lars), 286

De la mañana a la noche (Marta Traba), 515, 518

"De la vida" (Alfonsina Storni), 502

"Delmira, Alfonsina, Juana y Gabriela" (Dolores Koch), 268

Delmira Agustini (Ofelia Machado), 6

Delmira Agustini: espíritu de su obra y su significación (Sarah Bollo), 6

Delmira Agustini and the Quest for Transcendence (Doris Stephens), 6

Delmira y otras rupturas (Milton Schinca), 7

"De los muertos" (Sara de Ibáñez), 256

"De los vivos" (Sara de Ibáñez), 256

Del Romanticismo al Modernismo (Ventura García Calderón), 103

De miedo en miedo (Los manuscritos del río) (Armonía Somers), 494–95, 499

De noche vienes (Elena Poniatowska), 473, 476–77

"De otra manera más de hablar de aquí y el ahora sin así decirlo" (Efraín Barradas), 171

El derecho de matar (Magda Portal and Serafín Delmar), 484, 487

"Derrotas del heroismo" (Juana Manuela Gorriti), 235

El derrumbamiento (Armonía Somers), 494, 497–98

"Un desafío a la crítica literaria: *Tiene los cabellos rojizos y se llama Sabina*" (Martha Paley Francescato), 137

"El desarrollo de la novela de Marta Brunet" (John F. Tull), 60

El desatino (Griselda Gambaro), 187, 189, 191

Descripción de un naufragio (Cristina Peri Rossi), 437, 441, 442, 443

"Desde la diáspora: entrevista con Cristina Peri Rossi" (John F. Deredita), 439, 441–42

"Desdén" (Sara de Ibáñez), 255

Desolación (Gabriela Mistral), 330, 333, 337

Desolación-Ternura-Tala-Lagar (Gabriela Mistral), 334

"La desolada" (Luisa Valenzuela), 536

"El despertar" (Alejandra Pizarnik),
447–48

"Despertar" (Juana de Ibarbourou), 265

Despierta, mi bien, despierta (Claribel
Alegría), 11, 12, 15

"El despojamiento" (Griselda Gambaro),
189, 191, 194, 195

"El despojo" (Armonía Somers), 494,
498

Después del escándalo (Silvina Bullrich),
80

La desterrada en su patria (Rogue
Esteban Scarpa), 338

*Las desterradas del paraíso,
protagonistas en la narrativa de María
Luisa Bombal* (Marjorie Agosín), 50

"Destino del hombre" (Magda Portal),
486, 487

"De su obscura familia" (Yolanda
Oreamuno), 397, 400–401, 402

El detén (Claribel Alegría), 16

"De tu lado al paraíso" (Rosario Ferré),
171; Prologue by Arcadio Díaz
Quiñones, 171

El día del mar: cuento para niños (María
Luisa Mendoza), 319

"Diálogo con Sara Gallardo: Vivir en
Barcelona" (Antonio Requeni), 182,
183, 184

"El diario como forma femenina"
(Rosario Ferré), 168

"Diario de la muerte" (Sara de Ibáñez),
257–58

"Diario de una caraqueña por el lejano
Oriente" (Teresa de la Parra), 416,
417–18

"Diario de una isleña" (Juana de
Ibarbourou), 266, 268

Diario de una multitud (Carmen
Naranjo), 350, 351, 353, 354, 356,
357

Diario de una señorita que se fastidia
(Teresa de la Parra), 416

Los días de la noche (Silvina Ocampo),
361–62, 363–64

Diáspora (Cristina Peri Rossi), 437

"18 [Diez y ocho] de septiembre"
(Yolanda Oreamuno), 395

"Diez y seis de agosto" (Salomé Ureña
de Henríquez), 526

*A Different Reality: Essays on the Works
of Elena Garro* (Anita Stoll), 205, 206

"Digo . . ." (Magda Portal), 487

"La dinámica del monstruo en las obras
dramáticas de Griselda Gambaro"
(Sandra Messinger Cypess), 194

"El dios de los pájaros" (Alfonsina
Storni), 506

Dios no nos quiere contentos (Griselda
Gambaro), 192–93

"The Dirty Scarecrow" (Fanny
Buitrago), 64

"El discurso de lo imaginario en *Tiene
los cabellos rojizos y se llama Sabina*"
(Victorio G. Agüera), 137

"Divided Against Herself: The Early
Poetry of Nellie Campobello" (Doris
Meyer), 126

El divino Narciso (Sor Juana Inés de la
Cruz), 277

"La Doctora Lyuba" (Albalucía Angel),
35

"Dolores" (Gertrudis Gómez de
Avellaneda y Arteaga), 220

Domingo siete (Elena Poniatowska), 474

Don Alvaro (Duque de Rivas), 98

Donde viven las águilas (Luisa
Valenzuela), 540, 543

Don Florisondo (Marta Brunet), 54

"Don Juvencio" (Yolanda Oreamuno),
394–95

*Don't Be Afraid, Gringo: A Honduran
Woman Speaks from the Heart. The
Story of Elvia Alvarado* (Medea
Benjamin), 546–47

"Los dos amigos" y "Teo y la TV"
(Sara Gallardo), 177

*Dos décadas vulnerables en las artes
plásticas latinoamericanas, 1950–1970*
(Marta Traba), 516

"Dos estilos de novela: Marta Brunet y
María Luisa Bombal" (Martha E.
Allen), 61

Dos farsas pirotécnicas (Alfonsina
Storni), 503, 505

"Dos lecturas del cisne: Rubén Darío y Delmira Agustini'' (Silvia Molloy), 7

Dos mujeres (Gertrudis Gómez de Avellaneda y Arteaga), 212, 214, 219–20

Dos mujeres indígenas: Basilia por June Nash, Facundina por Manuel María Rocca 546, 550

Dos palabras dos: crónica de un informe (María Luisa Mendoza), 318

"Los dos reinos'' (Claudia Lars), 287

"Dos veces Albalucía Angel'' (Isaías Peña Gutiérrez), 38

Dos veces Alicia (Albalucía Angel), 31, 32–33

"Los duendes'' (Luisa Josefina Hernández), 242, 243, 244, 245, 249

El dulce daño (Alfonsina Storni), 502, 504

"The Dynamics of Conflict in Elena Garro's '¿Qué hora es?' and 'El duende' '' (Catherine Larson), 206

"Ecolalia e intertextualidad en *La última niebla*'' (Kemy Oyarzún), 50

"La educación científica de la mujer'' (Eugenio María de Hostos), 95

Eisejuaz (Sara Gallardo), 177, 180–82, 184

Elegía (Juana de Ibarbourou), 266, 268

Los elementos terrestres (Eunice Odio), 382, 383, 385–86, 388, 389, 390

"Elena Garro'' (Emmanuel Carballo), 201

"Elena Garro y sus *Recuerdos del porvenir*'' (Frank Dauster), 204

"Elena Poniatowska: The Feminist Origins of Commitment'' (Juan Bruce-Novoa), 477, 479

"Elena Poniatowska's *Hasta no verte, Jesús mío*'' (Charles Tatum), 480

"Elena Poniatowska's *Hasta no verte, Jesús mío*: The Remaking of the Image of Women'' (Joel Hancock), 480

Eleodora (Mercedes Cabello de Carbonera), 96

Elogio de la danza (Nancy Morejón), 341

Los empeños de una casa (Sor Juana Inés de la Cruz), 276–77, 278

Emplumada (Lorna Dee Cervantes), 559

"Encanto, tendajón mixto'' (Elena Garro), 203–4

En cualquier lugar (Marta Traba), 515, 518–19

"Encuentro con Elena Garro'' (Michèle Muncy), 202, 204, 205

En defensa del castellano (Eunice Odio), 387, 388

"En el nacimiento de mi primogénito'' (Salomé Ureña de Henríquez), 527–28

En el país de las maravillas (Luz María Umpierre), 559

"En el principio era la cal'' (Syria Poletti), 462

Enero (Sara Gallardo), 176, 178–79, 183

"Enero'' (Review of *Enero*; María Elena Walsh), 183

"En horas de angustia'' (Salomé Ureña de Henríquez), 527–28

"En la playa'' (Fanny Buitrago), 68

"El entierro'' (Armonía Somers), 495, 498

"Entierro de un jefe'' (Marta Lynch), 296

En torno a: "Itinerarios del Insomnio: Trinidad de Cuba'' de Lydia Cabrera (Josefina Inclán), 114

"Entre la esencia y la forma: sobre el momento neoyorquino en la poesía de Julia de Burgos'' (Efraín Barradas), 91

"Entre primos y dinosaurios con Cristina Peri Rossi'' (Marta Morello-Frosch), 442

"Entrevista a Elena Poniatowska'' (Margarita García Flores), 479

"Entrevista a Isabel Allende/Interview with Isabel Allende'' (Marjorie Agosín), 21, 22

"Entrevista a Marta Lynch'' (Martha Paley de Francescato), 294, 298

"Entrevista atemporal'' (Marta Traba), 515, 516

"Entrevista con Elena Poniatowska'' (Magdalena García Pinto), 479

Enumeración de la patria y otros poemas (Silvina Ocampo), 361, 367–68

"Epílogo de una tragedia" (Juana Manuela Gorriti), 235

"El equívoco en *Pasó así* de Marta Traba" (Celia Correas de Zapata), 519

"Eramos tres" (Claribel Alegría), 13, 14

"El ermitaño del reloj" (Teresa de la Parra), 416

"Erosion" (Claribel Alegría), 13

"Escándalo en Puerto Santo" (Luisa Josefina Hernández), 244

Una escritora costarricense: Yolanda Oreamuno (Victoria Urbano), 399, 400, 402

"La escritora Marta Brunet en las letras chilenas" (Nicómedes Guzmán), 60

"Escrituras ajenas, expresión propia: *Sur* y los *Testimonios* de Victoria Ocampo" (María Luisa Bastos), 377

"Escrituras tempranas" (Rosario Castellanos), 147

Escuela de pájaros (Claudia Lars), 287

"El eslabón perdido" (Armonía Somers), 495

Espacios métricos (Silvina Ocampo), 361, 364, 365, 368

"Los espectros de la Calle de Cantarana" (Fanny Buitrago), 67

"Espejismos eróticos: *De Ausencia* de María Luisa Mendoza" (David W. Foster), 325

El espejo y el canasto (Josefina Plá), 457, 458

"Esperando a Polidoro" (Armonía Somers), 495

Una esperanza i el mar (Magda Portal), 484, 486, 490

"El espíritu de mi tierra" (Yolanda Oreamuno), 395

"El espléndido no conformismo de Marta Traba" (Damián Bayón), 516

"¿Es posible y deseable una dramaturgia específicamente femenina?" (Griselda Gambaro), 188

"The Essential Extra: The Editor as a Parergonal Figure in Elena

Poniatowska's *La noche de Tlatelolco*" (Beth E. Jörgensen), 479

Estaba la pájara pinta sentada en el verde limón (Albalucía Angel), 31, 33–35

"*Estaba la pájara pinta sentada en el verde limón*: novela testimonial/documental de 'la violencia' en Colombia" (Dick Gerdes), 38–39

Las estaciones y otros poemas (Sara de Ibáñez), 255, 256

"Estampa antigua" (Syria Poletti), 464, 465

Estampas de la Biblia (Juana de Ibarbourou), 262, 265

"Estampas de la guerrilla" (Albalucía Angel), 35

"Este mundo y otros mundos" (Eduardo Gudiño Kieffer), 184

"Este que ves . . ." (Sor Juana Inés de la Cruz), 275

"Estío" (Juana de Ibarbourou), 264

"Estrategias dramáticas del feminismo en *El eterno femenino* por Rosario Castellanos" (Barbara Bookus Aponte), 149

Estrellas en el pozo (Claudia Lars), 283

"La estructura retórica de la *Respuesta a Sor Filotea*" (Rosa Perelmuter Pérez), 278–79

"Estructuras narrativas y poder en *Los recuerdos del porvenir*" (Patricia Montenegro), 206

Estudios de poesía dominicana (José Alcántara Almanzar), 530

"Estudios sobre Gabriela Mistral" (Raúl Silva Castro), 337

"Eternidad" (Juana de Ibarbourou), 261

El eterno femenino: farsa (Rosario Castellanos), 142, 146, 149; Introduction by Raúl Ortiz, 146

"Eunice hacia la mañana" (Juan Liscano), 389

"Eunice Odio, 'gota de carne, huracanada y sola' (Introducción)" (Rima Vallbona), 390

"Eunice Odio: una mujer contra las máscaras (*Los elementos terrestres* ante

'Máscaras mexicanas')'' (Laureano
Albán), 390
Eunice Odio en Guatemala (Eunice
Odio), 383, 388–90; Introduction by
Mario A. Esquivel, 389
Eva Luna (Isabel Allende), 22, 25–26
''Un evangelio indio: Buda y la leprosa''
(Teresa de la Parra), 416
Evohé (Cristina Peri Rossi), 437, 442,
443
''Una experiencia de límites: la narrativa
de Cristina Peri Rossi'' (Hugo Verani),
442–43
''La expresión dramática de la
inconformidad social en cuatro
dramaturgas hispanoamericanas''
(Lorraine Roses), 458–59
Extracción de la piedra de locura
(Alejandra Pizarnik), 448
''La extraña muerte del capitancito
Candelario'' (Rosario Ferré), 170
*Extraño oficio (Crónicas de una
obsesión)* (Syria Poletti), 462, 463,
464, 465, 466, 467, 468
''Los extraños objetos voladores''
(Cristina Peri Rossi), 436–37

Fábulas de la garza desangrada (Rosario
Ferré), 166, 168, 169
Fama y obras póstumas (Sor Juana Inés
de la Cruz), 278
''Una familia para Clotilde'' (Luisa
Valenzuela), 535–36
Family Album (Claribel Alegría), 11
''Fantoches de nieve'' (Syria Poletti),
465
''El fatalismo en la obra de Marta
Brunet'' (Víctor M. Valenzuela), 60
''La fe en el porvenir'' (Salomé Ureña de
Henríquez), 526
Felipe Angeles (Elena Garro), 200, 203
''*Felipe Angeles*: Theater of Heroes''
(Eladio Cortés), 205
''*Felipe Angeles* de Elena Garro:
sacrificio heroico'' (Delia Galván), 204
''Female Roles in the Fiction of Silvina
Bullrich'' (Erica Frouman-Smith), 80
''Female Sexuality in Selected Short

Stories by Luisa Valenzuela: Toward
an Ontology of Her Work'' (Diane
Marting), 542
'' 'Feminine' Testimony in the Works of
Teresa de la Parra, María Luisa
Bombal, and Victoria Ocampo'' (Doris
Meyer), 424–25
''Feminist Theory: A Critique of
Ideology'' (Mary O'Brien), 287
''Las ficciones de Isabel Allende''
(Marcelo Coddou), 26
''Fictional Treatment of Politics by
Argentine Female Novelists'' (Bradley
M. Class), 299
''La fiesta del mulato'' (Luisa Josefina
Hernández), 244, 245–48, 249, 250
Fiesta en el río (Josefina Plá), 454, 455,
457
''The Figure of La Malinche in the Texts
of Elena Garro'' (Sandra Messinger
Cypess), 205
''Five Women Writers of Costa Rica''
(Victoria Urbano), 351
Flora Tristán, precursora (Magda
Portal), 489
La ''Flor de Lis'' (Elena Poniatowska),
473, 477, 478
''Flor de loto: una leyenda japonesa''
(Teresa de la Parra), 416
*Flowers from the Volcano/Flores del
volcán* (Claribel Alegría), 10, 11, 12,
13, 15, 17
Follaje del tiempo (Josefina Plá), 456
''Form and Content in Elena Garro's *Los
recuerdos del porvenir*'' (Harry
Enrique Rosser), 204
''Four Women in Search of Freedom''
(Myriam Yvonne Jehenson), 268
''Frankenstein's Monster in Argentina:
Gambaro's Two Versions'' (Sandra
Messinger Cypess), 195
''(Free)/Plays of Difference: Language
and Eccentricity in Elena Garro's
Theater'' (Vicky Unruh), 205
''Frente a un astigmatismo aldeano''
(Guido Fernández), 400
Frente y perfil de Victoria Ocampo (Alba
Omil), 377

"From Pin-Ups to Strip-tease in Gambaro's *El despojamiento*" (Becky Boling), 195

"Los frutos caídos" (Luisa Josefina Hernández), 241, 242, 243, 244, 245, 249

Las fuentes ocultas (Luisa Josefina Hernández), 243, 245

Fuerte es el silencio (Elena Poniatowska), 473, 474, 475–76

Función de la novela (Julieta Campos), 128, 130–31

La furia y otros cuentos (Silvina Ocampo), 361

"Gabriela Mistral" (Hernán Díaz Arrieta), 337

Gabriela Mistral (Humberto Díaz-Casanueva), 338

Gabriela Mistral: The Poet and Her Work (Margot Arce de Vásquez), 337

Gaby Brimmer (Gaby Brimmer and Elena Poniatowska), 474

Los galgos, los galgos (Sara Gallardo), 176, 179, 180

Ganarse la muerte (Griselda Gambaro), 188, 193, 194

La garza sucia (Fanny Buitrago), 64

El gato eficaz (Luisa Valenzuela), 532, 533, 536–37, 538, 543

"*El gato eficaz* de Luisa Valenzuela: la productividad del texto" (Z. Nelly Martínez), 543

"Gatos, lenguaje y mujeres en *El gato eficaz* de Luisa Valenzuela" (Sharon Magnarelli), 543

"Gavilla" (Sara de Ibáñez), 258

"Gender and Exile in Cristina Peri Rossi" (Amy Kaminsky), 443

"El General Vidal" (Juana Manuela Gorriti), 232

"El género testimonial: aproximaciones feministas" (Margarite Fernández Olmos), 554–55

"El genio de la melancolía" (Gertrudis Gómez de Avellaneda y Arteaga), 216

"El genio del pesacartas" (Teresa de la Parra), 416

Genio y figura de Delmira Agustini (Clara Silva), 6

Genio y figura de Victoria Ocampo (Blas Matamoro), 377–78

Gente conmigo (Syria Poletti), 462, 463, 464, 465, 466, 467, 468–69

"*Gente conmigo* de Syria Poletti" (Rogelio Barufaldi), 468

"*Gente conmigo*—Syria Poletti: una mujer en la esperanza" (L. A. Cousillas), 468

Genteel Barbarism, New Readings of Nineteenth-Century Spanish-American Novels (John S. Brushwood), 103

Gertrudis Gómez de Avellaneda (Hugh A. Harter), 222

Gertrudis Gómez de Avellaneda: la mujer y la poetisa lírica (Raimundo Lazo), 222

Girasol: antología de poesía infantil (Claudia Lars), 287

Los girasoles en invierno (Albalucía Angel), 31, 32

"The Glass Box" (Rosario Ferré), 166

"La gloria del progreso" (Salomé Ureña de Henríquez), 526

"Gracias a la vida" (Violeta Parra), 429

Gracias a la vida, Violeta Parra (Bernardo Subercaseaux and Jaime Londoño), 430–31

"La gratitud es insaciable" (Cristina Peri Rossi), 438

Grenada Notebook (Nancy Morejón), 341, 347

"Los grillos" (Juana de Ibarbourou), 264

"Griselda Gambaro: Interview" (Kathleen Betsko and Rachel Koenig), 194

"Grito" (Magda Portal), 486

"El guante negro" (Juana Manuela Gorriti), 230

"Guardián de nuestras llaves" (Claudia Lars), 288

"Gubi Amaya: historia de un salteador" (Juana Manuela Gorriti), 230

"Güemes: recuerdos de la infancia" (Juana Manuela Gorriti), 232

*Guía de narradores de la revolución
mexicana* (Max Aub), 125
"El guillatún" (Violeta Parra), 428
La guitarra indócil (Patricio Manns), 431

"Había una vez un hombre" (Eunice
Odio), 388
"Hablando de Gabriel" (Rosario
Castellanos), 144–45
*Hacia la mujer nueva y El aprismo y la
mujer* (Magda Portal), 484, 488
Hacia tu isla (Carmen Naranjo), 350–51
Hasta no verte, Jesús mío (Elena
Poniatowska), 473, 476, 479–80
Hay que sonreír (Luisa Valenzuela), 532,
533, 534–35
"Hecatombe" (Salomé Ureña de
Henríquez), 526
Herencia (novela peruana) (Clorinda
Matto de Turner), 303, 305, 310–11;
Prologue by Antonio Cornejo Polar,
312
*La herencia obstinada. Análisis de
cuentos nahuas* (Julieta Campos), 129,
136–37
Los heréticos (Luisa Valenzuela), 532,
535, 539
"Herlinda se va" (Rosario Castellanos),
143
He Who Searches (Luisa Valenzuela),
539
"La hija de las flores" (Gertrudis Gómez
de Avellaneda y Arteaga), 217, 218
"La hija del mashorquero" (Juana
Manuela Gorriti), 230–31
"La hija del rey" (Luisa Josefina
Hernández), 243
*Hima-Sumac. Drama en tres actos y en
prosa* (Clorinda Matto de Turner), 304,
306, 311
Historia de Juana Manuela Gorriti
(Dionisio Chaca), 236
"Historia de la señorita grano de polvo,
bailarina del sol" (Teresa de la Parra),
416
"La historia de los almohadones de
terciopelo" (Marta Traba), 517

Historia de los galgos (Sara Gallardo),
176
"La historia de María Griselda" (María
Luisa Bombal), 47, 49
"Historia de un anillo" (Luisa Josefina
Hernández), 244, 249, 250
Historia de un número (Josefina Plá),
454, 456, 458–59
Historia natural de la alegría (Marta
Traba), 513, 514
"Las historias de Mamá Tolita" (Marta
Brunet), 59
Historias en rojo (Syria Poletti), 461,
464, 465, 466, 468
*Un hogar sólido y otras piezas en un
acto* (Elena Garro), 200, 203–4
"El hombre de las vasijas de barro"
(Syria Poletti), 464, 466
"El hombre del túnel" (Armonía
Somers), 494, 495, 498
*El hombre de paja y las distancias
doradas* (Fanny Buitrago), 64–65, 67
"Hombre pequeñito" (Alfonsina Storni),
504
"Hombres necios que acusáis a la mujer
sin razón" (Sor Juana Inés de la Cruz),
276
Homecoming (Julia Alvarez), 563
Homenaje a don Nadie (Carmen
Naranjo), 353, 354
"Homenaje a los trabajadores uruguayos
del primero de mayo, aplastados por
soldados y policías" (Cristina Peri
Rossi), 441
Homenaje a Lydia Cabrera (Reinaldo
Sánchez), 111, 113, 114
Homenaje a Rosario Castellanos
(Maureen Ahern and Mary Seale
Vásquez), 148
Homérica latina (Marta Traba), 513,
517, 518, 519
Hora ciega (Sara de Ibáñez), 256
El hostigante verano de los dioses (Fanny
Buitrago), 64, 67, 69
"Hotel Taormina" (Marta Lynch), 294
The House of the Spirits (Isabel Allende),
20, 23–24
"Hoy" (Sara de Ibáñez), 256

Hoy es un largo día (Carmen Naranjo), 351, 352, 353, 354

"Los huéspedes reales" (Luisa Josefina Hernández), 242, 243–44, 249

Humo hacia el sur (Marta Brunet), 54, 55–56, 57, 58, 59

"Humor and Games in Luisa Valenzuela's *El gato eficaz*: The Looking-Glass World Re-visited" (Sharon Magnarelli), 543

"Huxley en Centroamérica" (Victoria Ocampo), 374

Idapo: el sincretismo en los cuentos negros de Lydia Cabrera (Hilda Perera), 114

"La identificación" (Marta Traba), 517

"An Ideological Study of the Novels of Marta Lynch, 1962–1974" (Mary Patricia Mosier), 299

"El Ido" (Eunice Odio), 386–87

Ifigenia; diario de una señorita que escribió porque se fastidiaba (Teresa de la Parra), 415, 416, 417, 418–21, 423, 424, 425

La imagen de la mujer en la narrativa de Rosario Castellanos (María Rosa Fiscal), 148

La imagen en el espejo (Julieta Campos), 128, 129–30, 131, 134, 135–36

"Imágenes en la poesía de Eunice Odio: los ángeles" (Alfonso Chase), 390

"The Image of the Black Woman as a Revolutionary Figure: Three Views" (Stephanie Davis-Lett), 347

"Importancia de la literatura" (Mercedes Cabello de Carbonera), 95

In a Different Voice: Psychological Theory and Women's Development (Carol Gilligan), 283

Inambú busca novio (Syria Poletti), 462, 466

Independencia de Cuba (Mercedes Cabello de Carbonera), 97, 102

Indicios pánicos (Cristina Peri Rossi), 437

Indole (Novela Peruana) (Clorinda Matto de Turner), 303, 305, 308–310;

Prologue by Antonio Cornejo Polar, 312

"La inevitabilidad de su presencia" (José Marín Cañas), 400

El infierno musical (Alejandra Pizarnik), 449

"Influencia de la mujer en la civilización moderna" (Mercedes Cabello de Carbonera), 95

Influencia de las Bellas Letras en el progreso moral y material de los pueblos (Mercedes Cabello de Carbonera), 97, 102

Informe bajo llave (Marta Lynch), 293, 295, 297–98, 300

Informe del cielo y del infierno (Silvina Ocampo), 362

"In *illo tempore*: Elena Garro's *La semana de colores*" (Carmen Salazar), 204

"La inmigración italiana en la Argentina a través de la obra de Syria Poletti" (Dany Magarotto), 467

"La inmigrante" (Armonía Somers), 495, 498

La inquietud del rosal (Alfonsina Storni), 502, 503–4, 508

"La insólita literatura de Somers: la fascinación del horror" (Angel Rama), 499

"Insomnio" (Yolanda Oreamuno), 395

"Intermedio poético" (Alfonsina Storni), 506

"Interview with Julieta Campos" (Beth Miller and Alfonso González), 137

"An Interview with Women Writers in Colombia" (Raymond Leslie Williams), 38

"Introducción, *La casa de los espíritus*: de la historia a la Historia" (Marcelo Coddou), 26, 28

Invención de la muerte (Josefina Plá; Introduction by Roberto Juarroz), 458

Las invitadas (Silvina Ocampo), 361

I, Rigoberta Menchú, An Indian Woman of Guatemala (Rigoberta Menchú), 546

Irremediablemente . . . (Alfonsina Storni), 502, 504

"Isabel Allende and the Testimonial
Novel" (Michael Moody), 24, 26
"Isabel Allende: *La casa de los
espíritus*" (Marjorie Agosín), 26
"Isabel viendo llover en Barataria" (Juan
Manuel Marcos), 26, 27
"Islas" (Sara de Ibáñez), 256
"Las islas nuevas" (María Luisa
Bombal), 47–48
"Isolda en el espejo" (Rosario Ferré),
170
"Itinerarios" (Sara de Ibáñez), 256

"Josefina Plá, española de América, y la
poesía" (Hugo Rodríguez-Alcalá),
456, 458
Juana de Ibarbourou (Dora Isella
Russell), 263
Juana Manuela Gorriti (Alfredo O.
Conde), 236
"Juana Manuela Gorriti" (Antonio Pagés
Larraya), 236
"Juana Manuela Gorriti" (José María
Torres Caicedo), 236
"Juana Manuela Gorriti" (Santiago
Estrada), 236
Juanamanuela, mucha mujer (Martha
Mercader), 236
"Juan Ferrero" (Yolanda Oreamuno),
396
"Juan Silvestre" (Claudia Lars), 288
"Juan Soldado" (Juana de Ibarbourou),
265, 266
"Juego/fuego de la esperanza: en torno a
El gato eficaz de Luisa Valenzuela"
(Sharon Magnarelli), 543
"Juez y verdugo" (Juana Manuela
Gorriti), 233
La jugada del sexto día (Marta Traba),
517, 519
El juguete misterioso (Syria Poletti), 463
"El juicio final" (Cristina Peri Rossi),
438
Juicios sumarios: ensayos (Rosario
Castellanos), 142, 143
Julia de Burgos: vida y poesía (Yvette
Jiménez de Báez), 90–91
Julia de Burgos: Yo misma fui mi ruta

(Julia de Burgos; Introduction by María
M. Sola), 91
"Julia J." (Luisa Valenzuela), 536
"Julieta Campos y la novela del
lenguaje" (Hugo J. Verani), 137
"Justicia parvi hominis" (Marta Lynch),
293

The Kreutzer Sonata (León Tolstoy), 100

Los laberintos insolados (Marta Traba),
517, 519
The Lady on Her Balcony (Elena Garro),
200
Lagar (Gabriela Mistral), 333, 334
"La lagartija de la panza blanca"
(Yolanda Oreamuno), 394
La laguna de los nenúfares (Victoria
Ocampo), 373
"Lamentación de Dido" (Rosario
Castellanos), 144
Languidez (Alfonsina Storni), 502, 504
"El largo soñar" (Magda Portal), 486
"Laura" (Sor Juana Inés de la Cruz),
274
"Lección de cocina" (Rosario
Castellanos), 146
"Una lección moral" (Cristina Peri
Rossi), 438
"El lecho nupcial" (Juana Manuela
Gorriti), 231
"Una lectura de 'Soledad de la sangre'
de Marta Brunet" (Gabriela Mora), 61
"Lectura interpretativa de 'Las trenzas'
de María Luisa Bombal" (Julia S.
Hermosilla), 50
Lecturas para mujeres (Gabriela Mistral),
333, 335
"Lengua de pájaro" (Nancy Morejón and
Carmen Gonce), 341
"El lenguaje como instrumento de la
dominación" (Rosario Castellanos),
145
"El lenguaje como vehículo espiritual en
Los siameses de Griselda Gambaro"
(David William Foster), 194
Las lenguas de diamante (Juana de
Ibarbourou), 262, 264, 267, 269

Leoncia (Gertrudis Gómez de Avellaneda y Arteaga), 212, 217, 218

Leopoldina's Dream (Silvina Ocampo), 362

"Letanía del olvido" (Sara de Ibáñez), 257

"Letanías" (Sara de Ibáñez), 257

Let me Speak! Testimony of Domitila, A Woman of the Bolivian Mines (Domitila Barrios de Chungara), 546, 548, 552, 553

"Letras de emergencia: Claribel Alegría" (George Yúdice), 10

Leyendas y recortes (Clorinda Matto de Turner), 305

Leyendo a Alfonsina Storni (Julieta Gómez Paz), 509

"La liberación del amor" (Rosario Castellanos), 143

El libro blanco (Delmira Agustini), 6

El libro de mis primos (Cristina Peri Rossi), 437, 439, 440, 442–43

El libro mayor de Violeta Parra (Isabel Parra), 431

Libro-objeto (María Luisa Mendoza), 318

Libro que no muerde (Luisa Valenzuela), 539, 540

Lilus Kikus (Elena Poniatowska), 472, 477

"El limbo" (Elena Poniatowska), 477

Línea de fuego (Syria Poletti), 461–62, 463, 464, 465, 466–67, 468

Lingüística general (Cristina Peri Rossi), 437, 443

"Liras" (Sara de Ibáñez), 256

"Literary Convention and Sex-Role Analysis: Silvina Bullrich's 'Abnegation' " (Naomi Lindstrom), 81

"The Literary Feminism of Marta Lynch" (Naomi Lindstrom), 299

Literatura hispanoamericana: antología e introducción histórica (Enrique Imbert Anderson and Eugenio Florit), 268

Literatura peruana del siglo XX (Estuardo Núñez), 489–90

Literatura puertorriqueña: su proceso en el tiempo (Josefina Rivera de Alvarez), 171

"La literatura se llenó de adioses" (Marta Traba), 516

La literatura uruguaya del 900 (S. Cabrera), 7

"Literature on Trial" (José Carlos Mariátegui), 490

Lívida luz: Poemas (Rosario Castellanos), 141, 144, 148

The Lizard's Tail (Luisa Valenzuela), 533

"La llave" (Yolanda Oreamuno), 396

Lo amargo por dulce (Silvina Ocampo), 361, 363, 365

Lo ancestral africano en la narrativa de Lydia Cabrera (Rosa Valdés-Cruz), 114

"La loba" (Alfonsina Storni), 503

Lo íntimo de Juana Manuela Gorriti (Juana Manuela Gorriti), 229

"The Lonely Crowd: A Study of the Changing American Character" (David Riesman), 296

"Longevidad de una frase" (Juana Manuela Gorriti), 235

Loores de Nuestra Señora (Juana de Ibarbourou), 262, 265

"Lo secreto" (María Luisa Bombal), 42

"Lo social y lo religioso en *Indole* de Clorinda Matto de Turner" (Antonio Cornejo Polar), 312

Los que aman, odian (Silvina Ocampo), 361, 363

"Love Story" (Elena Poniatowska), 477

"El lucero del manantial" (Juana Manuela Gorriti), 231

El lugar donde crece la hierba (Luisa Josefina Hernández), 244

Luisa en el país de la realidad (Claribel Alegría), 9

Luisa in Realityland (Claribel Alegría and Darwin Flakoll), 9, 10, 12, 13

"Luisa Josefina Hernández: A Study of Her Dramatic Theory and Practice" (John K. Knowles), 249

Luisa Josefina Hernández: teoría y práctica del drama (John K. Knowles), 249

"Luisa Valenzuela" (Julio Cortázar), 542

"Luisa Valenzuela's 'Where the Eagles

Dwell': From Fragmentation to
Holism'' (Z. Nelly Martínez), 543
"La Luna" (Juana de Ibarbourou), 264
"Luz" (Salomé Ureña de Henríquez),
526
Lydia Cabrera: Vida hecha arte (Rosario
Hiriart), 114
"Lysi" (Sor Juana Inés de la Cruz), 274

"Madre" (Claudia Lars), 283
"La Madre Castillo" (Daniel Samper
Ortega), 161
*La Madre Castillo: su espiritualidad y su
estilo* (María Teresa Morales Borrero),
162
Madrigal en ciudad (Griselda Gambaro),
186
"Madrugada en la cárcel" (Magda
Portal), 486
"Magda Portal" (Daniel R. Reedy), 491
"Magda Portal, escritora y política"
(Esther Andradi and Ana María
Portugal), 491
"Magda Portal, laureada" (Ladislao
Meza), 490
"Magda Portal: Peru's Voice of Social
Protest" (Daniel R. Ready), 491
*Magia e historia en los "Cuentos
Negros," "Por qué" y "Ayapá" de
Lydia Cabrera* (Sara Soto), 114
"La maja y el ruiseñor" (María Luisa
Bombal), 42
"Mala idea" (Josefina Plá), 457
"Mala suerte" (Syria Poletti), 465
Maldito amor (Rosario Ferré), 166, 170,
179
Mamá Blanca's Souvenirs (Teresa de la
Parra), 415
La Mamá X (Teresa de la Parra), 416
"Mammy deja el oficio" (Fanny
Buitrago), 69
La mampara (Marta Brunet), 54, 55, 56,
58
Mañana digo basta (Silvina Bullrich), 78
La mano en la tierra (Josefina Plá), 454,
457
Las manos de Mamá (Nellie
Campobello), 119, 123, 124, 125

"Mar, cielo, y tierra" (María Luisa
Bombal), 47
"Las mareas vuelven de noche"
(Yolanda Oreamuno), 394–95, 398,
400
"The Marginated Narrator: *Hasta no
verte, Jesús mío* and the Eloquence of
Repression" (Edward Friedman), 480
*María Luisa Bombal: la femineidad
enajenada* (Hernán Vidal), 50
"María Luisa Mendoza, atrevida
novelista mexicana" (Charles M.
Tatum), 325
"María Luisa Mendoza: el lenguaje como
instrumento" *Mujer que sabe latín*
(Rosario Castellanos), 325
María Nadie (Marta Brunet), 55, 56, 58–
59
"María Rosa, Flor del Quillén" (Marta
Brunet), 54, 56
Marionetas de aserrín (Syria Poletti),
463, 464
"Marta Brunet" (Dora Isella Russell), 60
"Marta Brunet" (Hernán Díaz Arrieta),
60
"Marta Brunet" (Hugo Montes Brunet),
60
"Marta Brunet: *Humo hacia el sur*"
(César Rosales), 60
"Marta Brunet" (Julia García Games),
60
"Marta Brunet" (Julieta Carrera), 60
"Marta Brunet" (María Carolina Geel),
60
"Marta Brunet, *María Nadie*" (Homero
Castillo), 60
"Marta Brunet: *María Nadie*" (Lucía
Fox-Lockert), 61
"Marta Brunet: *María Nadie*" (Víctor
M. Valenzuela), 60
"Marta Brunet" (Milton Rossel), 60
"Marta Brunet: *Montaña adentro*"
(Emilio Vaisse), 60
"Marta Brunet, puente de plata hacia el
sur" (Julio Durán Cerda), 60
"Marta Brunet: *Raíz del sueño*"
(Guillermo de Torre), 60

"Marta Brunet" (Víctor M. Valenzuela), 60

"Marta Brunet en su ficción y en la realidad" (Emir Rodríguez Monegal), 60

"Marta Brunet y su narrativa chilena" (Guillermo de Torre), 60

"Marta Lynch: *La penúltima versión de la Colorada Villanueva*" (Ramón Layera), 298–99

"Marta Lynch: The Expanding Political Consciousness of an Argentine Woman Writer" (Amy Sue Katz Kaminsky), 299

"Marta Lynch habla de su obra, de la vida y de la política argentina" (Birgitta Vance), 293, 296

Marta Traba (Museo de Arte Moderno de Bogotá), 519

Marta Traba: selección de textos (Marta Traba), 515, 516, 518

El mar y sus pescaditos (Rosario Castellanos), 142

El mar y tú, y otros poemas (Julia de Burgos), 86, 87, 88, 90

Mascarada (Rita Geada), 562

Mascarilla y trébol: Círculos imantados (Alfonsina Storni), 503, 507

Massacre in Mexico (Elena Poniatowska), 473

Materia memorable (Rosario Castellanos), 141, 144, 149

"El matrimonio" (Marta Traba), 517

"Max Jiménez y los que están" (Yolanda Oreamuno), 369

El medio pollito (Rosario Ferré), 166

"Medios que usted sugiere al colegio para librar a la mujer costarricense de la frivolidad ambiente" (Yolanda Oreamuno), 395

"Meditación en el umbral" (Rosario Castellanos), 145

"Los mejor calzados" (Luisa Valenzuela), 537–38

"Melancolía" (Juana de Ibarbourou), 264

Me llamo Rigoberta Menchú y así me nació la conciencia (Rigoberta Menchú), 546, 550

La memoria de Amadís (Luisa Josefina Hernández), 244

Las memorias de Mamá Blanca (Teresa de la Parra), 415, 417, 421–22, 424, 425

Memorias de un hombre palabra (Carmen Naranjo), 352, 353, 356

"Los menestrales" (Luisa Valenzuela), 536

"Mensajes del escriba" (Juana de Ibarbourou), 265

"Mercedes Cabello de Carbonera" (Lucía Fox-Lockert), 101

"Mercedes Cabello de Carbonera: estética de la moral y los desvíos no-disyuntivos de la virtud" (Lucía Guerra Cunningham), 96

"México es mío" (Yolanda Oreamuno), 396

El miedo de perder a Eurídice (Julieta Campos), 128, 129, 136

Mientras los demás viven (Silvina Bullrich), 75

Mi guerrilla (Carmen Naranjo), 354

"Mi hombre peludo" (Armonía Somers), 495

"La mimesis de la interioridad: 'Soledad de la sangre' de Marta Brunet y 'El árbol' de María Luisa Bombal." (Marjorie Agosín), 61

"Mi ofrenda a la patria" (Salomé Ureña de Henríquez), 524, 526

"Mi Pedro" (Salomé Ureña de Henríquez), 524

" 'Mira para que no comas olvido . . . ', las precisiones de Elena Poniatowska" (Carlos Monsiváis), 479

"Mireille" (Frédéric Mistral), 330

Misa a oscuras (Carmen Naranjo), 355

"Misa de ocho" (Yolanda Oreamuno), 395

"Mis amados recuerdos" (Juana de Ibarbourou), 265, 268

Misceláneas; colección de leyendas, juicios, pensamientos, discursos, impresiones de viaje y descripciones americanas (Juana Manuela Gorriti), 229, 234

Misiá Señora (Albalucía Angel), 31–32, 36–37

Mis libros (Nellie Campobello), 119–20, 124

Mis memorias (Silvina Bullrich), 76

El misterio de las valijas verdes (Syria Poletti), 463

"El misterio femenino en *Los perros* de Elena Garro" (Richard Callan), 204

"El mito degradado de la familia en *El libro de mis primos* de Cristina Peri Rossi" (Gabriela Mora), 442

Mito y palabra poética en Elena Garro (Antonieta Eva Verwey), 205

The Mixquiahuala Letters (Ana Castillo), 560

El Modernismo en el Uruguay (Sarah Bollo), 7

Un momento muy largo (Silvina Bullrich), 75

La mona que le pisaron la cola (Rosario Ferré), 166

El monito Bam-Bin (Syria Poletti), 463

Los monstruos sagrados (Silvina Bullrich), 77

"*Montaña adentro*" (Fernando García Oldini), 60

Montaña adentro (Marta Brunet), 53, 56, 58, 60

El monte: Igbo-Finda; Ewe Orisha, Vititi Nfinda: (notas sobre las religiones, la magia, las supersticiones y el folklore de los negros criollos y el pueblo de Cuba) (Lydia Cabrera), 112

Mothers and Shadows (Marta Traba), 515, 518

"Motivos de ciudad" (Alfonsina Storni), 507

"Un muchacho con suerte" (Syria Poletti), 465

"Muchacho embrujado" (Claudia Lars), 288

Muerte por agua (Julieta Campos), 128, 129, 131–32, 134, 137

Muerte por alacrán (Armonía Somers), 494, 495

La mujer desnuda (Armonía Somers), 493–94, 497, 498, 499

"La mujer dominicana y el quehacer literario" (Daisy Cocco de Filippis), 530–31

La mujer en América escribe . . . (Julieta Carrera), 289

La mujer en el partido del pueblo (Magda Portal), 489

Mujer que sabe latín . . . (Rosario Castellanos), 141, 143, 144, 145, 148

"La mujer y su discurso: conciencia y máscara" (Zunilda Gertel), 479

"La mujer y su imagen" (Rosario Castellanos), 143

"The Mulatto's Orgy" (Luisa Josefina Hernández), 245–48

"Multiplicidad, dialéctica y reconciliación del discurso en *La casa de los espíritus*" (Juan Manuel Marcos and Teresa Méndez-Faith), 26, 27

El mundo de los recuerdos (Juana Manuela Gorriti), 229, 234–35

Mundo de siete pozos (Alfonsina Storni), 503, 506–7

"El mundo literario de María Luisa Bombal" (Arthur A. Natella), 50

"El mundo privado de Clorinda Matto de Turner en *Herencia*" (Kenichi Satake), 312

El mundo que yo vi (Silvina Bullrich), 75

"La muñeca menor" (Rosario Ferré), 166, 169, 170

"Munio Alfonso" (Gertrudis Gómez de Avellaneda y Arteaga), 217–18

"El muro (Lamentación por los fusilamientos en España)" (Sara de Ibáñez), 258

El museo de los esfuerzos inútiles (Cristina Peri Rossi), 437–38, 443

Los museos abandonados (Cristina Peri Rossi), 436–37, 441, 442

El museo vacío (Marta Traba), 514

Mutaciones de la Realidad (Olga Orozco), 411

Mutismos (Nancy Morejón), 341

"Myth and Archetype in *Recollections of Things to Come*" (Robert K. Anderson), 204

"Nación y mestizaje en Nicolás Guillén" (Nancy Morejón), 341

"Nada" (Julia de Burgos), 89

Nada, nadie (Elena Poniatowska), 473, 474, 475

"Nada en común tenemos" (Claudia Lars), 284, 286

Nada que ver con otra historia (Griselda Gambaro), 187, 190, 191, 194, 195

"Nahuel Huapi" (Victoria Ocampo), 375

La naranja maravillosa (Silvina Ocampo), 362

Narraciones (Juana Manuela Gorriti; Introduction by W. G. Weyland ["Silverio Boj"]), 236

La narrativa de María Luisa Bombal: una visión de la existencia femenina (Lucía Guerra Cunningham), 42

La narrativa de Marta Brunet (Esther Melón de Díaz), 60

Narrativa y sociedad en Hispanoamérica (José Alcántara Almanzar), 530

"The Narrative Prose of Marta Brunet" (Roger Martin Peel), 60

"Narrative Structure in the Novels of Marta Lynch" (Bernice Lynne Bennett), 300

"Narrative Style and Technique in Nellie Campobello's *Cartucho*" (Dennis J. Parle), 126

"El naufragio de Cristina Peri Rossi" (Enrique Molina Campos), 442

La nave de los locos (Cristina Peri Rossi), 438, 439, 443

"*La nave de los locos* y la búsqueda de la armonía" (Gabriela Mora), 443

"La negritud hoy: nota sobre la poesía de Nancy Morejón" (Efraín Barradas), 348

"El negro, sentido de la alegría" (Yolanda Oreamuno), 395

"Nellie Campobello's *Las manos de Mamá*: A Rereading" (Doris Meyer), 124, 126

New Islands (María Luisa Bombal), 47

"The New Journalism in Mexico: Two Women Writers" (Dolly J. Young and William P. Young), 325

"Noche" (Magda Portal), 487

"Noche compartida con el recuerdo de una huida" (Alejandra Pizarnik), 447–49

"Una noche de agonía" (Juana Manuela Gorriti), 231

"Noche de amor en tres cantos" (Julia de Burgos), 90

"Noche de lluvia" (Juana de Ibarbourou), 264

La noche de Tlatelolco: testimonios de historia oral (Elena Poniatowska), 473, 474, 475, 479

"Nocturnos" (Magda Portal), 490

Los nombres (Silvina Ocampo), 361, 365

No me agarran viva: la mujer salvadoreña en lucha (Claribel Alegría and Darwin Flakoll), 9, 15

"No sé qué" (Cristina Peri Rossi), 436

"Notas sobre el criollismo chileno y el personaje femenino en la narrativa de Marta Brunet" (Sonia Riquelme), 60

No te duermas, no me dejes (Marta Lynch), 295, 296

La novela de la Revolución (Antonio Castro Leal), 125

La novela moderna: estudio filosófico (Mercedes Cabello de Carbonera), 97, 99, 102

La novela peruana y la evolución social (Mario Castro Arenas), 98, 103

"Las novelas de Isabel Allende y el papel de la mujer como ciudadana" (Gabriela Mora), 27–28

Novelistas de Méjico (J. F. Arias Campoamor), 125

"The Novelist as Historian: *La penúltima versión de la Colorada Villanueva*" (Eduardo Gudiño Kieffer), 300

"Novena casa" (María Luisa Mendoza), 324

"La novia del muerto" (Juana Manuela Gorriti), 230, 231

Novísimos narradores hispanoamericanos en marcha (1964–1980) (Angel Rama), 171

"Nuestro pulsante mundo" (Claudia Lars), 288

"Las nuevas poetas cubanas" (Eliana Rivero), 347

Nunca hubo alguna vez (Carmen Naranjo), 354

"La obra de Nellie Campobello" (Valeska Strickland Najera), 126

La obra en prosa de Eunice Odio (Eunice Odio), 388, 390

Obra (Narrativa, ensayos, cartas) (Teresa de la Parra), 424; "Estudio Crítico" by Velia Bosch, 424

Obra poética (Julia de Burgos), 88, 90

La obra poética de Rosario Castellanos (Victor N. Baptiste), 147, 149

Obras completas (Juana de Ibarbourou), 263, 265, 266, 269

Obras completas de Delmira Agustini (Delmira Agustini), 4, 5

Obras completas de la madre Francisca Josefa de la Concepción de Castillo, según fiel transcripción de los manuscritos originales que se conservan en la Biblioteca Luis-Angel Arango (Madre Castillo), 162

Obras completas de Marta Brunet (Marta Brunet), 55

Obras de doña Gertrudis Gómez de Avellaneda (Gertrudis Gómez de Avellaneda y Arteaga), 217, 220

Obras escogidas (Claudia Lars), 288; Introduction by Matilde Elena López, 289

Las obras recientes de Elena Garro (Delia Galván), 205

Ocre (Alfonsina Storni), 502, 504–5

"Octava habitación" (María Luisa Mendoza), 323–24

Octubre imprescindible (Nancy Morejón), 341

"Odisea y calvario de Magda Portal" (Luis Alberto Sánchez), 490

Oficio de leer (Julieta Campos), 128

Oficio de tinieblas (Rosario Castellanos), 141, 145–46, 148

Of Love and Shadows (Isabel Allende), 21

¡Oh Gloria inmarcesible! (Albalucía Angel), 31, 33, 35–36

"Ojo" (Alfonsina Storni), 506–7

Ojos de papel volando (María Luisa Mendoza), 319, 324, 326

"Olga Orozco y su trascendente juego poético" (Juan Liscano), 411

"Olor frutal" (Juana de Ibarbourou), 264

"Una olvidada precursora de la literatura fantástica: Juana Manuela Gorriti" (Thomas C. Meehan), 236

Once grandes poetisas hispanoamericanas (Carmen Conde), 268

"Once There Was a Man" (Eunice Odio), 388

Ondina (Carmen Naranjo), 351, 352, 354

"La opinión general (Adaptación de la fábula de Esopo del mismo nombre)" (Juana de Ibarbourou), 266

Oro y tormenta (Juana de Ibarbourou), 266, 268

La oscuridad es otro sol (Olga Orozco), 407, 408, 411

Other Weapons (Luisa Valenzuela), 533

"*Other Weapons*: When Metaphors Become Real" (Marta Morello-Frosch), 542

La otra gente: cuentos (Fanny Buitrago), 65, 67, 69

La otra realidad: asedio a la obra de Elena Garro (Anita Stoll), 206

"Otra vez Sor Juana" (Rosario Castellanos), 142–43

Páginas de Marta Lynch, seleccionadas por la autora (Marta Lynch), 294, 299; Introduction by Gwendolyn Josie Díaz, 299–300

Páginas de Olga Orozco (Olga Orozco), 408, 411; Prologue by Cristina Piña, 411

Páginas de Sara Gallardo, seleccionadas por la autora (Sara Gallardo), 177, 183; "Estudio preliminar" by Ricardo Rey Beckford, 183, 184

Páginas de Silvina Bullrich, seleccionadas por la autora (Silvina

Bullrich), 80; "Estudio preliminar" by
  Nicolás Cócaro, 80–81
*Páginas de Silvina Ocampo,
  seleccionadas por la autora* (Silvina
  Ocampo), 362
"Páginas olvidadas de Juana de
  Ibarbourou" (Gastón Figueira), 269
"La página vacía" (Sara de Ibáñez),
  255–56
*Paisaje i obra. Mujer e historia:
  Clorinda Matto de Turner, estudio
  crítico-biográfico* (Manuel E. Cuadros
  Escobedo), 312
"Paisajes del Otún" (Albalucía Angel),
  35
El país del humo (Sara Gallardo), 177,
  182, 183, 184
"Pájaros de barro" (Syria Poletti), 466
"La pala" (Syria Poletti), 463
"La palabra" (about Rosario Castellanos;
  José Emilio Pacheco), 147
"La palabra asesino" (Luisa Valenzuela),
  541
*La palabra como destino de acercamiento
  a la poesía de Alejandra Pizarnik*
  (Cristina Piña), 449–50
"La palabra ilimitada de Eunice Odio:
  Los elementos terrestres" (Rima
  Vallbona), 390
"La palabra-mito en Syria Poletti"
  (Eugenio Castelli), 469
"Palabras a Delmira Agustini"
  (Alfonsina Storni), 505
Palabras cruzadas; crónicas (Elena
  Poniatowska), 473, 474
Palabras juntan revolución (Lourdes
  Casal), 561
"Las palabras oscuras" (Magda Portal),
  486
"Las palabras perdidas" (Magda Portal),
  486
Los palacios desiertos (Luisa Josefina
  Hernández), 244
"Los pálidos" (Sara de Ibáñez), 256
Los pañamanes (Fanny Buitrago), 65, 68
Panorama literario de Chile (Raúl Silva
  Castro), 60
"Panorama poético colombiano

construído solo en recuerdo" (Yolanda
  Oreamuno), 395
*Panoramas de la vida: colección de
  novelas, fantasías, leyendas y
  descripciones americanas* (Juana
  Manuela Gorriti), 228, 232–33
Pantalones azules (Sara Gallardo), 176,
  179–80
Papeles de Pandora (Rosario Ferré), 166,
  167, 168, 169, 171
"Paradigma de la poética femenina
  hispanoamericana y su evolución:
  Rosario Castellanos" (Eliana S.
  Rivero), 149
"The Paradoxes of Silvina Bullrich"
  (Erica Frouman-Smith), 81
Parajes de una época (Nancy Morejón),
  341
"Para la distribuición de premios del
  Colegio San Luis Gonzaga" (Salomé
  Ureña de Henríquez), 526
"Para leer a Isabel Allende: su vida en su
  obra" (Marcelo Coddou), 20
"Para 'Revenar' No para Max Jiménez"
  (Yolanda Oreamuno), 394
*Para romper el silencio: resistencia y
  lucha en las cárceles salvadoreñas*
  (Claribel Alegría and Darwin Flakoll),
  9
"The Parsifal Motif in Elena Garro's
  Testimonios sobre Mariana: The
  Development of a Mythological
  Novel" (Joan Frances Marx), 206
La pasajera (Juana de Ibarbourou), 266,
  268
"Pasajeros al norte" (Yolanda
  Oreamuno), 396
"Pasajeros de la noche" (Fanny
  Buitrago), 65
Los pasajeros del jardín (Silvina
  Bullrich), 75
Una pasión prohibida (Cristina Peri
  Rossi), 438, 439
"La pasión y la marginalidad en la
  escritura: Rosario Ferré" (Ronald
  Méndez-Clark), 168
"Pasión y muerte de la luz" (Sara de
  Ibáñez), 256

Pasó así (Marta Traba), 517, 519
"A Passage to Androgyny: Isabel
   Allende's *La casa de los espíritus*"
   (Linda Gould Levine), 26–27
Pastoral (Sara de Ibáñez), 256
"Paternidad" (Fanny Buitrago), 68
"Patriotismo" (Cristina Peri Rossi), 438
"Pavana de Aranzazú" (Luisa Josefina
   Hernández), 244, 245, 250
"La paz ficticia" (Luisa Josefina
   Hernández), 242, 244, 249, 250
" 'La paz ficticia' de Luisa Josefina
   Hernández" (Fernando de Toro), 250
"El pecado de la manzana" (Luisa
   Valenzuela), 536
El pecado mortal (Silvina Ocampo), 361,
   367
"Pedro y Pedrito" (Alfonsina Storni),
   506
"El pensador de Rodin" (Armonía
   Somers), 495
*La penúltima versión de la Colorada
   Villanueva* (Marta Lynch), 293, 294–
   95, 296, 297, 298, 299–300
Pequeña antología (Silvina Ocampo),
   361
"La pequeña comedia humana en la obra
   de Silvina Bullrich" (Nicolás Cócaro),
   80
"Pequeña crónica" (Rosario
   Castellanos), 144
"Pequeño manual de vampirología
   teórica" (Luisa Valenzuela), 540
"Perdida (Juana de Ibarbourou), 263,
   266
"Peregrinaciones de una alma triste"
   (Juana Manuela Gorriti), 228, 232–33
"Perfeccionamiento de la educación y de
   la condición social de la mujer"
   (Mercedes Cabello de Carbonera), 95
Perfiles (Primera parte) (Juana Manuela
   Gorriti), 229
El perro de la escribana o las piedecasas
   (María Luisa Mendoza), 319, 323,
   324, 325–26
Los perros no ladraron (Carmen
   Naranjo), 350, 351, 353, 354, 356
"Los perros y *La mudanza* de Elena

Garro: designio social y virtualidad
   feminista" (Gabriela Mora), 204
"Perseguidos y perseguidores: el juego
   de la violencia en la obra de Elena
   Garro" (Michèle Muncy), 204, 206
Perú—Tradiciones cuzqueñas (Clorinda
   Matto de Turner), 304
"Pescadora de sueños" (Magda Portal),
   486
"Peso ancestral" (Alfonsina Storni), 504
"Pico Rico Mandorico" (Rosario Ferré),
   169, 172
Piedra pulida (Nancy Morejón), 341, 344
La pierna de Severina (Josefina Plá),
   454, 458; Introduction by José Luís
   Appleyard, 458
"Los pilares de doña Blanca" (Elena
   Garro), 204
"Pisadas de caballo" (Syria Poletti), 465
"Un plano americano" (Albalucía
   Angel), 35
"Plaza de invierno" (Alfonsina Storni),
   507
La Plaza de Puerto Santo (Luisa Josefina
   Hernández), 244
"Poema a Emily Dickinson" (Alejandra
   Pizarnik), 447
Poema de Chile (Gabriela Mistral), 333
"Poema del minuto blanco" (Julia de
   Burgos), 90
Poema en veinte surcos (Julia de
   Burgos), 86, 88, 90
"Poema para mi muerte" (Julia de
   Burgos), 88, 90
Poemas (Nancy Morejón), 341
Poemas (Salomé Ureña de Henríquez),
   523
Poemas. Alejandra Pizarnik (Alejandra
   Pizarnik; Introduction by Inés
   Malinow), 450
Poemas de amor (Alfonsina Storni), 502,
   505
Poemas de amor desesperado (Silvina
   Ocampo), 361, 365, 368
Poemas exactos a mí misma (Julia de
   Burgos), 86
"La poesía bíblica y Eunice Odio"
   (María Cruz Burdiel de las Heras), 389

La poesía contemporánea de Puerto Rico
    (José Emilio González), 90
La poesía de Delmira Agustini (Manuel
    Alvar), 6
"La poesía de Josefina Plá" (Augusto
    Roa Bastos), 458
"Poesía de Marta Brunet" (Hugo Montes
    Brunet), 60
Poesía no eres tú: obra poética: 1948–
    1971 (Rosario Castellanos), 143–44,
    145, 147, 148
Poesías completas (Delmira Agustini), 6
Poesías completas (Gabriela Mistral), 333
Poesías completas (Salomé Ureña de
    Henríquez; Prologue by Joaquín
    Balanguer), 530
Poesías escogidas (Salomé Ureña de
    Henríquez; Prologue by Pedro
    Henríquez Ureña), 530
"Poesías íntimas" (Salomé Ureña de
    Henríquez), 527
Poesías selectas (Gertrudis Gómez de
    Avellaneda y Arteaga), 212, 215
Poésie populaire des Andes (Violeta
    Parra), 430
"El Poeta" (Gertrudis Gómez de
    Avellaneda y Arteaga), 216–17
La poética de Olga Orozco:
    desdoblamiento de Dios en máscara de
    todos (Elba Torres de Peralta), 411–12
" ' Las Poetisas' ante la crítica: el caso
    de Delmira Agustini" (Dwight García),
    7
"El Polaris" (Albalucía Angel), 35
"The Political Dimension of Clorinda
    Matto de Turner's *Indigenismo*"
    (Efraín Kristal), 312
"The Political Novels of Lucila Palacios
    and Marta Lynch" (Lynne Lois
    Billman), 299
"Polixena y la cocinerita" (Alfonsina
    Storni), 505
El polvo enamorado (Josefina Plá, 456,
    458; Introduction by José Ramón
    Heredia), 458
"Popol-Vuh" (Luisa Josefina
    Hernández), 249
"The Popular-Ethnic Sensitivity: Clorinda

Matto de Turner's *Aves sin nido*"
    (John Brushwood), 312
"Por la vereda tropical" (Albalucía
    Angel), 35
Por qué . . . Cuentos negros de Cuba
    (Lydia Cabrera), 108, 109
"Por qué los árboles son altos" (Juana
    de Ibarbourou), 264
"El porqué de la inconstancia"
    (Gertrudis Gómez de Avellaneda y
    Arteaga), 216
"Por tierra firme" (Yolanda Oreamuno),
    401
"Por todos los senderos" (Claudia Lars),
    284
"Possession and Privation in the Poetic
    Works of Juana de Ibarbourou" (Flor
    María Blanco), 268
"Postales de Boyacá y una fotico en
    Sante Fe" (Albalucía Angel), 35
El pozo del Yocci (Juana Manuela
    Gorriti), 233
El precio de los sueños (Josefina Plá),
    454
La primera batalla (Luisa Josefina
    Hernández), 244
"La primera decepción" (Juana Manuela
    Gorriti), 235
"Primera residencia" (María Luisa
    Mendoza), 323
Primero sueño (Sor Juana Inés de la
    Cruz), 275, 278
"La princesa chibcha" (Fanny Buitrago),
    65
"El Príncipe de Viana" (Gertrudis
    Gómez de Avellaneda y Arteaga), 217,
    218
*Proceedings of the Symposium on "Sor
    Juana Inés de la Cruz y la cultura
    virreinal"* (Georgina Sabat de Rivers),
    278
"Proceso a la Virgen" (Luisa
    Valenzuela), 535
*Proceso intelectual del Uruguay y crítica
    de su literatura* (Alberto Zum Felde), 6
"La profesora" (Luisa Valenzuela), 536
La prosa religiosa de Gabriela Mistral

(Introduction by Luis Vargas Saavedra), 338

"Protesta contra el folklore" (Yolanda Oreamuno), 395–96, 401

"Puck" (Juana de Ibarbourou), 266

"La puerta violentada" (Armonía Somers), 494

"La puertorriqueña dócil y rebelde en los cuentos de Rosario Ferré" (Lisa Davis), 171

Puppet (Margarita Cota-Cárdenas), 559

"¿Qué hora es?" (Elena Garro), 202

"Quejas" (Salomé Ureña de Henríquez), 527, 528

"La Quena" (Juana Manuela Gorriti), 227, 230

Querido Diego, te abraza Quiela (Elena Poniatowska), 473, 476–78

"¿Qué será Dios del cielo?" (Violeta Parra), 429

"Qué vivan los estudiantes" (Violeta Parra), 430

"¿Qué y de dónde a mí llegaste?" (Claudia Lars), 283

¿Quiénes traicionaron al pueblo? (Magda Portal), 485, 489

"Quietud" (Juana de Ibarbourou), 265

Raíz del sueño (Marta Brunet), 54, 58, 59

Raíz salvaje (Juana de Ibarbourou), 262, 264, 269

La raíz y la aurora (Josefina Plá), 457

"Rasgos biográficos de la Señora Juana Manuela Gorriti" (Pastor S. Obligado), 236

El rastro de la mariposa (Eunice Odio), 387, 388

"Ratita y minero"(Claudia Lars), 287

"Reading Rosario Castellanos: Contexts, Voices and Signs" (Maureen Ahern), 148

"Realidad del Ser" (Magda Portal), 486

"La realidad y el deseo" (Olga Orozco), 411

"Rebelde" (Juana de Ibarbourou), 264

"Rebeldes fracasadas: una lectura feminista de *Andarse por las ramas* y *La señora en su balcón*" (Gabriela Mora), 204

"La rebelión del cuerpo y del lenguaje: a propósito de Cristina Peri Rossi" (Hugo Verani), 442, 443

La rebelión de los niños (Cristina Peri Rossi), 437, 439

"Recopilacilón de textos sobre Nicolás Guillén" (Nancy Morejón), 341

"Recaredo" (Gertrudis Gómez de Avellaneda y Arteaga), 217

Los recuerdos del porvenir (Elena Garro), 199, 200, 201, 202, 203, 204, 205, 206–7

La redoma del primer ángel (Silvina Bullrich), 74

"Reencuentro con Marta Brunet" (Milton Rossel), 60

Reencuentro de personajes (Elena Garro), 200

Reflections/Refractions: Reading Luisa Valenzuela (Sharon Magnarelli), 542–43

Refranes de negros viejos: recogidos por Lydia Cabrera (Lydia Cabrera), 113

"El regalo" (Rosario Ferré), 170

"Un regalo" (Yolanda Oreamuno), 396

La Regla Kimbisa del Santo Cristo del Buen Viaje (Lydia Cabrera), 112–13

Relatos Escojidos: Yolanda Oreamuno (Yolanda Oreamuno), 394, 397, 399, 400

La religión de la humanidad; carta al señor D. Juan Enrique Lagarrique (Mercedes Cabello de Carbonera), 96

Reloj de sol (Marta Brunet), 54, 56–57, 59

Reportajes supersónicos (Syria Poletti), 462

"Réquiem por Goyo Ribera" (Armonía Somers), 494, 498

Responso por el niño Juan Manuel (Carmen Naranjo), 351, 355, 356

Respuesta a Sor Filotea de la Cruz (Sor Juana Inés de la Cruz), 277, 278

"Retorno a la soledad" (Magda Portal), 486

"Retrato de García Lorca" (Alfonsina Storni), 506

Retrato de mi gentedad (María Luisa Mendoza), 319

Un retrato para Dickens (Armonía Somers), 495, 498

Reunión de directorio (Silvina Bullrich), 78, 80

"La revelación" (Cristina Peri Rossi), 438

"El rey mago" (Elena Garro), 204

El rey que prohibió los globos (Syria Poletti), 462

Richard trajo su flauta (Nancy Morejón), 341

"Río Grande de Loíza" (Julia de Burgos), 88, 89, 91

Ritmos indígenas de México (Nellie Campobello), 118

Ritos de iniciación: tres novelas cortas de Hispanoamérica (Grínor Rojo and Cynthia Steele), 172

"Rojo en la salina" (Syria Poletti), 461, 462, 465

"Romance de los días que vienen" (Claudia Lars), 283–84

Romances del destino (Juana de Ibarbourou), 265, 268

Romances de norte y sur (Claudia Lars) 284–85

"Romances femeninos en tierra del Paraguay" (Josefina Plá), 456

"Romería a la tierra natal" (Juana Manuela Gorriti), 235

La rosa de los vientos (Juana de Ibarbourou), 262, 265

La rosa en el viento (Sara Gallardo), 177, 182–83, 184

"Rosario Castellanos: Eros and Ethos" (Julian Palley), 149

"Rosario Castellanos, Image and Idea" (Mary Seale Vásquez), 147

"Rosario Castellanos" (Interview in *Confrontaciones: los narradores ante el público*), 141, 147

"Rosario Castellanos, la historia de sus libros contada por ella misma" (Emmanuel Carballo), 147

"Rosario Castellanos: la lucidez como forma de vida" (Margarita García Flores), 147

Rosario Castellanos: mujer que supo latín (Perla Schwartz), 147

Rosario Castellanos (1925–1974): Semblanza sicoanalítica (María Estela Franco), 147

"Rosario Castellanos: On Language" (Regina Harrison Macdonald), 148–49

"Rosario Castellanos's Debunking of the Eternal Feminine" (Kirsten F. Nigro), 149

"Rosario Castellanos: The Search for a Voice" (Frank Dauster), 149

Rosario Castellanos: una conciencia feminista en México (Beth Miller), 148

"Rosario Castellanos: ¡Vida nada te debo!" (Elena Poniatowska), 147

El Rosario de Eros (Delmira Agustini), 4, 5

"Rosas de Saron" (Fanny Buitrago), 69

Rostros en el agua (Josefina Plá), 457

"Ruinas" (Salomé Ureña de Henríquez), 526–27

"Ruptura y perseverancia de estereotipos en *La casa de los espíritus*" (Gabriela Mora), 27

"Rural Life in Chile Finds a New Portrayer" (Januario Espinosa), 60

La ruta de su evasión (Yolanda Oreamuno), 396, 297, 398, 401, 402

"*La ruta de su evasión* de Yolanda Oreamuno" (Manuel Picado), 400

Sab (Gertrudis Gómez de Avellaneda y Arteaga), 211, 212, 214, 219, 220–21, 222

"La 'Sabina' de Julieta Campos, en el laberinto de la intertextualidad" (Juan Bruce-Novoa), 137

Sacrificio y recompensa (Mercedes Cabello de Carbonera), 96, 98, 99, 102

"Saliva del paraíso" (Armonía Somers), 494

"Salomé Ureña a 134 octubres: una

desmitificación necesaria'' (Chiqui Vicioso), 530–31

"Salomé Ureña de Henríquez" (Nestor Contín Abybar), 530

Salomé Ureña de Henríquez (Silveria Rodríguez Demorizi), 530

"Salomé Ureña y la culminación de la influencia neoclásica" (Carlos Federico Pérez), 530

Los salvadores de la patria (Silvina Bullrich), 77, 79, 80

La sartén por el mango (Patricia E. González and Eliana Ortega), 564

"Saúl" (Gertrudis Gómez de Avellaneda y Arteaga), 213, 217, 218

"El secreto" (Juana de Ibarbourou), 265

"A Select Bibliography of Rosario Castellanos Criticism" (Maureen Ahern), 147

Selected Poems of Gabriela Mistral (Gabriela Mistral), 339

"Self-Destructing Heroines" (Jean Franco), 170

"Selva" (Juana de Ibarbourou), 264

"Selvas de mi ciudad"(Alfonsina Storni), 507

La semana de colores (Elena Garro), 200, 202, 205, 206

La señora en su balcón (Elena Garro), 200, 204

La Señora Ordóñez (Marta Lynch), 293, 294, 296–97, 299, 300

"Las señoras que tomaban té" (Marta Lynch), 293–94

Sensibilidad religiosa de Gabriela Mistral (Martin C. Taylor), 338

"Sentencia" (Marta Lynch), 294

"Séptima estancia" (María Luisa Mendoza), 323

"Ser o no ser es la divisa" (Julia de Burgos), 87

Sexo y poesía en el 900 uruguayo (Emir Rodríguez Monegal), 7

"Sexto domicilio" (María Luisa Mendoza), 323

Los siameses (Griselda Gambaro), 189, 190, 192, 193, 195

Las siete puertas (Sara Gallardo), 177

Siglo XX en las artes plásticas latinoamericanas: una guía (Marta Traba), 515

"Signos y mensaje de 'Historia de un número' de Josefina Plá" (Lydia D. Hazera), 459

Silvina Bullrich (Silvina Bullrich), 80

"Si me permiten hablar . . .": *Testimonios de Domitila una mujer de las minas de Bolivia* (Domitila Barrios de Chungara), 546

"Simples creadores" (Claudia Lars), 288

"Sin noviaciado, Yolanda Oreamuno escribe libros psicoanalíticos" (Lilia Ramos), 397

"Si no 'poesía no eres tú' ¿entonces qué?" (Rosario Castellanos), 147

Sitio a Eros: siete ensayos literarios (Rosario Ferré), 166, 168, 171

"Sobre cultura femenina" (Rosario Castellanos), 141

Sobre el ángel y el hombre (Claudia Lars), 287

"Sobre el ángel y el hombre: poesía y estilo de Claudia Lars" (Matilde Elena López), 285

"Sobre el uso y abuso de poder en la producción dramática de Griselda Gambaro" (Teresa Méndez-Faith), 194

"Sobre *Pasó así*" (Marta Morello Frosch), 519

Sobrepunto (Carmen Naranjo), 351, 352, 353, 354, 356, 357

"Sobre rosas y hombres" (Claudia Lars), 285

"La sobrevida poética de Claribel Alegría" (Basilia Papastamatiu), 16

Sobrevivo (Claribel Alegría), 10, 13

"Social Denunciation in the Language of 'The Tree' by María Luisa Bombal" (Mercedes Valdivieso), 50

La sociedad secreta Abakuá: narrada por viejos adeptos (Lydia Cabrera), 112–13

"¡Sokuando!" (Lydia Cabrera), 111

"Soledad" (Juana de Ibarbourou), 264

"Soledad de la sangre" (Marta Brunet), 57

" 'Soledad de la sangre': A Study in Symmetry" (Charles Param), 61

"Soliloquios del soldado" (Sara de Ibáñez), 256

"Solita sola" (Marta Brunet), 56, 59

"Solitude and Solidarity: Major Themes and Techniques in the Theater of Luisa Josefina Hernández" (Janis Lynne Krugh), 249

Sólo los elefantes encuentran mandrágora (Armonía Somers), 495–96, 498

"Sombras" (Salomé Ureña de Henríquez), 523, 524

"Sonetos del arcángel" (Claudia Lars), 285

Sonetos (Claudia Lars), 284

El son se quedó en Cuba (Marta Traba), 515

"Los sordomudos" (Luisa Josefina Hernández), 242, 244, 250

Sor Juana Inés de la Cruz o las trampas de la fe (Octavio Paz), 278

"Sorrow" (Claribel Alegría), 10, 11, 13, 14

"Souvenir de San Andrés" (Albalucía Angel), 35

"Structure, Imagery and Experience in María Luisa Bombal's 'The Tree' " (Andrew P. Debicki), 50

"A Study of Significant Variants in the Poetry of Gabriela Mistral" (Sister Mary Preston), 338, 340

"La subasta" (Armonía Somers), 494

El "Sueño" de Sor Juana Inés de la Cruz: tradiciones literarias y originalidad (Georgina Sabat de Rivers), 278

"Un sueño en el camino" (Alfonsina Storni), 506

"Los sueños del silencio" (Albalucía Angel), 36

Los sueños de Natacha (Juana de Ibarbourou), 263, 266

Sueños y realidades (Juana Manuela Gorriti), 227, 230–31, 232

"Sumisión y rebeldía: el doble o la representación de la alienación femenina en narraciones de Marta Brunet y Rosario Ferré" (María-Inés Lagos-Pope), 61

Su vida, escrita por ella misma, por mandado de sus confesores (Madre Castillo), 156, 159, 161, 162

Su vida y yo (Silvina Bullrich), 79

Sweet Diamond Dust (Rosario Ferré), 166

"Syria Poletti: crónica de una rebeldía" (Celia Correas de Zapata), 468

Tablero de damas: pieza en un acto (Rosario Castellanos), 146, 149

"*Tablero de damas* and *Album de familia*: Farces on Women Writers" (Kathleen O'Quinn), 149

Tala (Gabriela Mistral), 333, 336

Taller de imaginería (Syria Poletti), 463, 464, 465

"Tamalitos de Cambray" (Claribel Alegría), 10

La tarde del dinosaurio (Cristina Peri Rossi), 437, 439, 442, 443

Teatro: Las paredes. El desatino. Los siameses (Griselda Gambaro), 187, 189, 190, 192, 193, 194, 195

"El teatro de Elena Garro: evasión e ilusión" (Frank Dauster), 204

"Teatro de virtudes políticas" (Carlos de Sigüenza y Góngora), 279

Teatro infantil (Alfonsina Storni), 506

Teatro Juárez, 75° aniversario (María Luisa Mendoza), 319

Teatro, Nada que ver. Sucede lo que pasa (Griselda Gambaro), 187

Teatro 1 Real envido. La malasangre. Del sol naciente (Griselda Gambaro), 189, 191, 194

Teatro 2 Dar la vuelta. Información para extranjeros. Puesta en claro. Sucede lo que pasa (Griselda Gambaro), 187–88, 189, 191, 192, 195

"El teatro y las novelas de Luisa Josefina Hernández" (Silvia Jean Brann), 249

Teléfono ocupado (Silvina Bullrich), 75

"El tema de la violación en Armonía Somers y Griselda Gambaro" (Helena Araújo), 193

"El tema religioso en *Las memorias de*

Mamá Blanca'' (Marco Antonio Martínez), 424

''Temas y técnicas en 'Los amores de Afrodita' por Fanny Buitrago'' (María Salgado), 70

''Tengo'' (Nicolás Guillén), 345

''Tengo una muñeca vestida de azul'' (Albalucía Angel), 36

''Una tentativa de autocrítica'' (Rosario Castellanos), 147

''Tercera morada'' (María Luisa Mendoza), 323

Teresa de la Parra: claves para una interpretación (Ramón Díaz Sánchez), 424

''Teresa de la Parra: las voces de la palabra'' (Julieta Fombona), in *Obra (Narrativa, ensayos, cartas)* (Teresa de la Parra), 424

''Teresa de la Parra, Marta Brunet y Magdalena Mondragón: abresurcos en la novelística hispanoamericana'' (Edna Coll), 61

Ternura (Gabriela Mistral), 333, 335

Ternura: canciones de niños (Gabriela Mistral), 333

Territorio del alba y otros poemas (Eunice Odio), 383

El tesoro de los incas (Juana Manuela Gorriti), 231, 232

Testimonios (Victoria Ocampo), 373, 374, 375, 377

Testimonios: tercera serie (Victoria Ocampo), 375

Testimonios sobre Mariana (Elena Garro), 200, 201–2, 203, 206

Testimonios sobre Victoria Ocampo (Héctor Basaldúa), 377

''Texto, ley, transgresión: especulación sobre la novela (feminista) de vanguardia'' (Francine Masiello), 425

Textos de sombras y últimos poemas (Alejandra Pizarnik), 449, 451

''The Texture of Dramatic Action in the Plays of Griselda Gambaro'' (David William Foster), 195

The Theater of the Marvelous: Surrealism and the Contemporary Stage (Gloria Feman Orenstein), 204

''The Theme of the Avenging Dead in Elena Garro's 'Perfecto Luna': A Magic Realist Approach'' (Cynthia Duncan), 206

They Won't Take Me Alive (Claribel Alegría), 9, 10, 14

''Tiempo'' (Juana de Ibarbourou), 265

Tiempo y tiniebla (Josefina Plá), 456, 459

Tiene los cabellos rojizos y se llama Sabina (Julieta Campos), 128, 129, 130, 134–35, 137

''*Tiene los cabellos rojizos y se llama Sabina*, de Julieta Campos: 'Una caída interminable en la inmovilidad' '' (Evelyn Picón Garfield), 137

''Tierra Brava'' (Marta Brunet), 54

Tierra de infancia (Claudia Lars), 288

La tierra más ajena (Alejandra Pizarnik), 447

La tierra natal (Juana Manuela Gorriti), 229, 235–36

''Tiquete a la pasión'' (Fanny Buitrago), 66

El tobogán (Silvina Ocampo), 362

Toda la función (Marta Lynch), 295

''Todas las rosas'' (Julieta Campos), 134

Toda Violeta Parra (Violeta Parra), 431

Todo empezó el domingo (Elena Poniatowska), 473, 475

Todos los cuentos, 1953–67 (Armonía Somers), 495, 499

''Toma de conciencia'' (Rosario Castellanos), 144

Towards a Feminist Reading of Sor Juana Inés de la Cruz (Stephanie Merrim), 278

Los trabajos y las noches (Alejandra Pizarnick), 448

Tradiciones cuzqueñas (Clorinda Matto de Turner), 311

''The *Tradiciones cuzqueñas* of Clorinda Matto de Turner'' (Margaret V. Campbell), 312

Los traidores (Silvina Ocampo), 361

La trampa (Magda Portal), 484, 485, 487–88, 490

"*La Trampa*: génesis de una novela política" (Daniel R. Reedy), 491

"The Transformation of Privilege in the Work of Elena Poniatowska" (Bell Gale Chevigny), 479

"Tránsito de Eunice Odio" (Humberto Díaz-Casanueva), 390

El tránsito de fuego (Eunice Odio), 383, 385, 386, 387, 389, 390

"Un trapo de piso" (Marta Brunet), 58

Trayectoria de la novela en México (Manuel Pedro Gonzales), 124

Trayectoria del polvo (Rosario Castellanos), 140

"Treatment of Politics by Argentine Female Novelists" (Bradley M. Class), 79

Los treinta mil ausentes (Josefina Plá), 456

"Tren de medianoche" (Syria Poletti), 462, 464, 465

"Trenzas" (María Luisa Bombal), 47, 48–49

"Los tres amores" (Gertrudis Gómez de Avellaneda y Arteaga), 213

338171 T. E. (Lawrence of Arabia) (Victoria Ocampo), 374

Tres conferencias inéditas (Teresa de la Parra), 417

Tres poemas (Nellie Campobello), 119

"Trino y uno" (Sara de Ibáñez), 258

Tríptico darwiniano (Armonía Somers), 495

Tris de sol, Carmen Serdán (María Luisa Mendoza), 319

Los trovadores (Luisa Josefina Hernández), 245

"Tú me quieres blanca" (Alfonsina Storni), 504

"Turistiando en el valle" (Albalucía Angel), 35

La última inocencia (Alejandra Pizarnik), 447

"La última niebla" (Cedomil Goič), 50

La última niebla (María Luisa Bombal), 42, 43–44, 45, 46

El último guajolote (Elena Poniatowska), 475

"El último Max Jiménez ante la indiferencia nacional" (Yolanda Oreamuno), 395

"El umbral" (Cristina Peri Rossi), 438

"Umbra-Ressurexit" (Salomé Ureña de Henríquez), 524

El universo poético de Rosario Castellanos (Germaine Calderón), 147, 149

"Unlimited Rapes United, Argentina" (Luisa Valenzuela), 538

Until We Meet Again (Elena Poniatowska), 473

"Untimeliness" (Claribel Alegría and Darwin Flakoll), 13

El uso de la palabra (Rosario Castellanos), 142, 143, 147

"Valle Alto" (Yolanda Oreamuno), 396, 400, 402

"El vanguardismo en el Paraguay" (Hugo Rodríguez-Alcalá), 455

"The Vaporous World of María Luisa Bombal" (Margaret V. Campbell), 50

"Varia" (Salomé Ureña de Henríquez), 527

"Veinte siglos" (Alfonsina Storni), 504

26 [Veinte y seis] autoras del México actual (Beth Miller and Alfonso González), 120

21 [Veinte y uno] son los dolores (Violeta Parra; Prologue by Juan Andrés Piña), 431–32

Veladas literarias de Lima 1876–1877 (Juana Manuela Gorriti), 94

"Vela urbana" (Yolanda Oreamuno), 395

"El velorio de la muñeca de mi prima Alicia" (Cristina Peri Rossi), 440

Viaje al corazón del día: elegía por un secreto amor (Armonía Somers), 496, 497

"Un viaje al país del oro"(Juana Manuela Gorriti), 233–34

Viaje de Recreo: España, Francia,

Inglaterra, Italia, Suiza, Alemania
(Clorinda Matto de Turner), 306
"Viaje finito" (Alfonsina Storni), 504
Viaje olvidado (Silvina Ocampo), 361
Vibraciones (Silvina Bullrich), 73
Victoria Ocampo (Fryda Schultz de
Mantovani), 377
*Victoria Ocampo: Against the Wind and
the Tide* (Doris Meyer), 376, 377
"Victoria Ocampo: A Thirst for the
Ultimate" (Doris Meyer), 377
*Victoria Ocampo (1890–1979): un
homenaje*, special issue of *Sur*, 377
"Victoria Ocampo y la literatura
femenina" (Leopoldo Marechal), 376
Vida de la Avellaneda (Mercedes
Ballesteros), 222
"Vida-garfío" (Juana de Ibarbourou),
264
Una vida romántica, La Avellaneda
(Carmen Bravo-Villasante), 222
Vida y obra de Juana de Ibarbourou
(Jorge Oscar Pickenhayn), 263, 268
Violeta del pueblo (Javier Martínez
Reverte), 431
*Violeta Parra: santa de pura greda. Un
estudio sobre su obra poética* (Marjorie
Agosín and Inés Dölz-Blackburn), 432
"Las vírgenes prudentes" (Syria Poletti),
465
*Virtue or Vice?: Sor Juana's Use of
Thomistic Thought* (Constance M.
Montross), 279
"Visiones" (Sara de Ibáñez), 257
"Visión marginal de la historia en la
narrativa de Juana Manuela Gorriti"
(Lucía Guerra Cunningham), 236
"Visión social y feminista en la obra
poética de Rosario Castellanos"
(Eliana S. Rivero), 149
"Víspera de boda" (Fanny Buitrago), 67
"Visual and Verbal Distances in the
Mexican Theater: The Plays of Elena
Garro" (Sandra Messinger Cypess),
204
"El Viudo Román" (Rosario
Castellanos), 146
Viviendo (Cristina Peri Rossi), 436, 441

*Vocabulario Congo: (El Bantú que se
habla en Cuba)* (Lydia Cabrera), 113
"Volver a los diecisiete" (Violeta Parra),
428, 429
"Voy a dormir" (Alfonsina Storni), 507
"La vuelta a los lugares comunes"
(Yolanda Oreamuno), 395

"Wandering Tadpoles and Speckled
Roosters" (about Claudia Lars; Gastón
Figueira), 287
"Washington, ciudad de las ardillas"
(María Luisa Bombal), 48
*We Eat the Mines and the Mines Eat Us:
Dependency and Exploitation in
Bolivian Tin Mines* (June Nash), 552,
553, 554
"What Can a Heroine Do? or Why
Women Can't Write" (Joanna Russ),
300
"When Women Love Men" (Rosario
Ferré), 167–68
Where the Island Sleeps Like a Wing
(Nancy Morejón), 341, 347
"Where Was Your Childhood Lost"
(Claribel Alegría and Darwin Flakoll),
13
"The Wind and the Tree: A Structural
Analysis of the Poetry of Rosario
Castellanos" (Tey Diana Rebolledo),
149
*Woman Who Has Sprouted Wings: Poems
by Contemporary Latin American
Women Poets* (Introduction by Mary
Crow), 283
*Women's Voices from Latin America:
Interviews with Six Contemporary
Authors* (Evelyn Picón Garfield), 137,
519
"The Works of Silvina Bullrich" (Bobs
M. Tusa), 79
"The World is Full of Stories/Interview
with Isabel Allende" (Jo Anne
Engelbert and Linda Gould Levine),
23, 25
"The Writing Kitchen" (Rosario Ferré),
166

"The Writings of Clorinda Matto de Turner" (George De Mello), 312

Y así sucesivamente (Silvina Ocampo), 362

Yemayá y Ochún: Kariocha, Iyalorichas y Olorichas (Lydia Cabrera), 113

Yerba Buena (Sandra María Esteves), 559

"Yo canto a la diferencia" (Violeta Parra), 430

"Yo fui la más callada" (Julia de Burgos), 89

"Yolanda Oreamuno" (Abelardo Bonilla), 401

"Yolanda Oreamuno" (Ermilo Abreu Gómez), 400

Yolanda Oreamuno presentada por Rima de Vallbona (Rima de Vallbona), 399, 400, 402

"Yolanda Oreamuno y Marcel Proust" (Alfonso Chase), 402

Yo misma fui mi ruta (Julia de Burgos), 91

¡Yo! por Francisca (Nellie Campobello), 118, 119

"The Youngest Doll" (Rosario Ferré), 166

Zona en territorio del alba (Eunice Odio), 383, 386

SUBJECT INDEX

Note: Page numbers in italics indicate an entry devoted entirely to the author or group of authors.

Abandonment. *See* Loneliness

Adolescence. *See* Childhood; Children

Adultery, theme of, and Cabrera, 109

Africa, theme of: and Cabrera, 106, 107–8, 113, 114; and Morejón, 345. *See also* Black themes

African-American culture. *See* Africa, theme of; Black themes; Race

Agosín, Marjorie, in "Latina Writers," 561–62, 563

Agrarian reform. *See* Land reform

Agustini, Delmira, *1–8*; and Ibáñez, 258; and Ibarbourou, 267; and Portal, 490; and Storni, 505

Alegría, Claribel, *9–19*

Alienation, theme of: and Bombal, 50; and Gallardo, 177–78, 180, 181; and Gambaro, 188, 190, 192; and Ocampo, Victoria, 456; and Plá, 456; and Poletti, 466–67; and Storni, 506–7. *See also* Marginality; Otherness

Allende, Isabel, *20–30*; and Latina writers, 563

Alvarado, Elvia, in "Indian Women Writers," 547

Alvarez, Julia, in "Latina Writers," 562, 563

Angel, Albalucía, *31–40*

Anger, theme of, and Hernández, 243, 245

Animals, theme of: and Brunet, 59; and Cabrera, 108, 110–11; and Campos, 132–34; and Lars, 287; and Somers, 495, 498; and Valenzuela, 536–37, 543; and Indian women writers, 553

Antinovel, the, and Naranjo, 357

Anzaldúa, Gloria, in "Latina Writers," 560, 561, 563

Argentina: Bullrich and, 74, 76, 77, 78–79, 80; Gallardo and, 177; Gorriti and, 226, 230–31, 232, 233, 236; Latina writers and, 561; Lynch and, 292–93, 294–95, 295–96, 298; Ocampo, Silvina, and, 364–65; Ocampo, Victoria, and, 373, 374, 375; Orozco and, 408; Traba and, 518; Valenzuela and, 537, 539, 540, 541–42

Art: Agustini and, 1; Angel and, 31, 32; Sor Juana Inés de la Cruz and, 274, 275; Traba and, 513, 514–15, 517

Authority, abuse of, and Gambaro, 188, 189, 190, 191. *See also* Military; Oppression

Autobiography: Ibarbourou and, 265, 269; Lars and, 283, 285; Lynch and, 294, 295; Mendoza and, 318, 320; Mistral and, 334; Ocampo, Victoria, and, 374, 375, 377; Odio and, 386–87; Orozco and, 407; Parra, Violeta, and, 428–29, 432; Plá and, 457; Poletti and, 467–68; Poniatowska and, 477; Storni and, 505

Avant-garde techniques: Bombal and, 41, 42–43, 45, 50; Pizarnik and, 447; Portal and, 484; Storni and, 503, 505–6; Traba and, 513; Latina writers and, 561. *See also Vanguardismo*

Avellaneda, Gertrudis Gómez de. *See* Gómez de Avellaneda, Gertrudis

Baroque style, Sor Juana Inés de la Cruz and, 274, 275

Barrios, Domitilia, in "Indian Women Writers," 546, 547–48, 550, 551–53, 554

Basilia, in "Indian Women Writers," 546, 550, 551, 552, 553

Beauvoir, Simone de: and Bullrich, 76; and Campos, 131; and Castellanos, 141, 142; and Ferré, 166

Betrayal, and Buitrago, 65, 66, 68–69

Biblical themes: Bombal and, 46; Gómez de Avellaneda and, 218; Ibáñez and, 255, 256, 257; Odio and, 386, 388, 389, 390; Peri Rossi and, 438; Somers and, 495, 498, 499; Storni and, 506; Indian women writers and, 553

Black themes: Angel and, 36; Burgos and, 89; Cabrera and, 106–14; Ferré and, 167, 169–70; Gómez de Avellaneda and, 214, 220, 222; Gorriti and, 230, 231, 232; Morejón and, 342–44, 345–46, 348; Somers and, 494, 495. *See also* Africa, theme of; Race; Slavery

Bolivia, Indian women writers and, 547–48, 550, 552, 553, 554

Bombal, María Luisa, *41–52*; Ibáñez and, 258

Brunet, Marta, *53–63*

Buitrago, Fanny, *64–71*

Bullrich, Silvina, *72–84*; Poletti and, 462

Bureaucracy, theme of, and Naranjo, 351

Burgos, Julia de, *85–93*

Cabello de Carbonera, Mercedes, *94–104*; and Gorriti, 228, 235; and Matto de Turner, 304

Cabrera, Lydia, *105–16*; and Teresa de la Parra, 417

Campobello, Nellie, *117–27*

Campos, Julieta, *128–39*

Capitalism, Peri Rossi, and, 439, 440

Carbonera, Mercedes Cabello de. *See* Cabello de Carbonera, Mercedes

Casal, Lourdes, in "Latina Writers," 562

Castellanos, Rosario, *140–55*

Castillo, Ana, in "Latina Writers," 560, 561

Castillo, Madre, *156–64*; and Sor Juana Inés de la Cruz, 278

Catholic Church: Alegría and, 16; Angel and, 36; Cabello de Carbonera and, 96; Castillo and, 158–62; Hernández and, 243, 245; Sor Juana Inés de la Cruz and, 274; Latina writers and, 561; Matto de Turner and, 305–12 passim; Mistral and, 331; Poniatowska and, 476; Somers and, 494; Valenzuela and, 535, 536. *See also* Religion

Cats. *See* Animals

Censorship: Angel and, 34; Valenzuela and, 533, 540–41

Central America: Alegría and, 9–10, 14, 16; Lars and, 285. *See also* Costa Rica; El Salvador; Guatemala

Cervantes, Lorna D., in "Latina Writers," 559, 560

Chaco War, the, and Plá, 454, 455–56. *See also* Violence; War

Chicana writers, 557, 558, 559–61, 563–64

Childhood, theme of: and Angel, 34, 36, 37; and Bombal, 45; Gorriti, 234; and Ibarbourou, 264, 265, 266; and Lars,

283, 284, 287, 288; and Naranjo, 352, 353, 355; and Ocampo, Silvina, 363–64, 366, 367; and Ocampo, Victoria, 374; and Oreamuno, 401; and Orozco, 408; and Pizarnik, 447, 450; and Poletti, 462, 464, 465–66; and Poniatowska, 477, 479; and Somers, 494. *See also* Children

Children: Alegría and, 12, 13, 16; Brunet and, 56, 59; Campobello and, 121, 123, 124, 125, 126; Indian women writers and, 550, 551; Mistral and, 331, 335, 336; Peri Rossi and, 437, 439; Plá and, 459; Portal and, 489; Storni and, 506. *See also* Childhood

Children's literature, and Ferré, 166, 168, 169, 171–72

Chile, theme of: and Allende, 21, 22–25; and Brunet, 56, 58–59; and Latina writers, 561–62, 563; and Mistral, 333; and Parra, Violeta, 429, 432

Cisneros, Sandra, in "Latina Writers," 560, 561

Class struggle, the: and Alegría, 10, 15; and Angel, 31, 32, 35, 36; and Ferré, 169; and Indian women writers, 546–50, 551–52, 553; and Parra, Violeta, 430; and Poniatowska, 473

Colombia: Angel and, 32, 33–36; Buitrago and, 66, 70

Color, people of. *See* Black themes; Indian themes/characters

Colors, theme of, and Garro, 202–3

Communication, lack of, and Gambaro, 190, 192. *See also* Alienation

Communism, theme, of: and Indian women writers, 548, 554; and Portal, 487

Convents: Castillo, Madre, and, 157; Sor Juana Inés de la Cruz and, 273

Corpi, Lucha, in "Latina Writers," 558, 560

Corruption: Cabello de Carbonera and, 101, 102; Naranjo and, 354

Costa Rica, Oreamuno and, 394, 395, 399

Cota-Cárdenas, Margarita, in "Latina Writers," 559

Creationism. *See Vanguardismo*

Creativity, theme of, and Silvina Ocampo, 365

Cristero Revolt, the, and Garro, 201. *See also* Violence; War

Cruelty, theme of, and Silvina Ocampo, 366. *See also* Torture; Violence

Cruz, sor Juana Inés de la. *See* Juana Inés de la Cruz, sor

Cuba: Burgos and, 86; Latina writers and, 558, 561, 562; Morejón and, 341–42, 345, 346–47; Traba and, 515

Cuban Revolution, the: and Latina writers, 562; and Morejón, 341–42, 346–47; and Traba, 515. *See also* Cuba

Curiel, Barbara Brinson, in "Latina Writers," 561

Dance, theme of, and Campobello, 118, 120

Darío, Rubén: Agustini and, 1, 2, 3, 4, 5; Matto de Turner and, 305

Death, theme of: and Agustini, 3, 4, 5; and Alegría, 9, 13–15, 16; and Bombal, 44–45, 46; and Buitrago, 65, 66; and Burgos, 88, 90; and Ibáñez, 255, 257–58; and Ibarbourou, 264, 266–67, 268; and Mistral, 334–35; and Pizarnik, 446–49; and Plá, 456, 457, 458; and Portal, 486; and Somers, 495, 497, 498, 499; and Storni, 506

Deformity, theme of, and Poletti, 466

Desire. *See* Eroticism; Lesbianism; Love; Sexuality

Diary form: Alegría and, 12, 15–16; Ferré and, 168; Lynch and, 297; Matto de Turner and, 305; Parra, Teresa de la, and, 416, 417–18; Pizarnik and, 449, 451

"Disappeared," the: and Alegría, 11, 13, 17; and Allende, 21, 22, 24; and Peri Rossi, 438, 439, 443; and Poniatowska, 473, 476; and Valenzuela, 537–38

Discrimination. *See* Oppression; Prejudice

Dominican Republic, the: and Ureña de

Henríquez, 523, 524, 525, 526–27, 530; and Latina writers, 562

Education of women: Agustini and, 6; Alegría and, 16; Brunet and, 53; Bullrich and, 73, 76, 80; Cabello de Carbonera and, 95; Cabrera and, 106; Castillo and, 157; Gómez de Avellaneda and, 214; Gorriti and, 229, 234; Hernández and, 241; Ibarbourou and, 261; Sor Juana Inés de la Cruz and, 272, 277; Latina writers and, 560, 564; Matto de Turner and, 304, 306, 307–8, 310, 311; Ocampo, Victoria, and, 375; Oreamuno and, 394, 395, 399; Poniatowska and, 478; Portal and, 484, 488; Storni and, 502; Ureña de Henríquez and, 522, 524, 525, 529
El Salvador, Alegría and, 9–10, 14, 16
Environment, theme of, and Gambaro, 189, 190, 192
Eroticism: Agustini and, 1, 2, 3–6, 7; Bombal and, 44, 45; Madre Castillo and, 160; Ferré and, 168; Ibarbourou and, 268, 269; Latina writers and, 560–61; Peri Rossi and, 436, 437, 438, 439, 442; Storni and, 503, 507, 508; Valenzuela and, 538, 540, 541. See also Homosexuality; Lesbianism; Love; Sexuality
Esteves, Sandra Maria, in "Latina Writers," 559, 560
Ethnography. See Folklore
Europe, theme of, and Angel, 31, 32
Exile, theme of: and Alegría, 11, 16; and Indian women writers, 548, 549–50; and Latina writers, 561–62; and Madre Castillo, 159; and Odio, 384; and Peri Rossi, 439, 441, 443; and Poletti, 462, 467; and Traba, 516, 518. See also Travel literature
Existential themes, Plá, and, 456. See also Alienation; Otherness

Facundina, in "Indian Women Writers," 546, 550, 552
Fairy tales: Bombal and, 42, 47, 49;

Ferré and, 169–70, 172. See also Folklore; Legends; Myth
Fantastic, the: and Bombal, 42, 47; and Ocampo, Silvina, 361, 363, 366; and Oreamuno, 398; and Orozco, 407, 408; and Peri Rossi, 436–37
Fantasy: Brunet and, 58, 59; Ferré and, 169; Garro and, 204
Feminism: Alegría and, 11–12, 15, 17; Allende and, 23, 26–27; Angel and, 31–32, 36, 37, 38; Bombal and, 50; Bullrich and, 81; Burgos and, 88, 89, 91; Campobello and, 126; Castellanos and, 144, 145, 146, 148, 149; Ferré and, 166, 169; Garro and, 205; Hernández and, 242, 247–48, 249; Indian women writers, 546, 548, 552, 554; Sor Juana Inés de la Cruz and, 276; Latina writers and, 557, 564; Lynch and, 299; Matto de Turner and, 305, 311; Mendoza and, 319–20, 324; Mistral and, 335; Ocampo, Silvina, and, 364, 366; Ocampo, Victoria, and, 372, 373, 375, 377; Teresa de la Parra and, 417, 420–21, 422–23, 424–25; Parra, Violeta, and, 429; Peri Rossi and, 437, 440, 442, 443; Plá and, 455, 456, 459; Poletti and, 468; Poniatowska and, 477, 478, 479; Portal and, 484, 485, 488–89, 491; Storni and, 502, 503, 504, 508, 509; Traba and, 516; Ureña de Henríquez and, 530; Valenzuela and, 535
Ferré, Rosario, 165–75; and Brunet, 61; and Burgos, 91
Folklore: Brunet and, 53, 59; Cabrera and, 107–14; Ferré and, 169–70, 172; Garro and, 202; Oreamuno and, 395–96, 401; Parra, Violeta, and, 427–28, 430, 431, 432. See also Fairy tales; Legends; Myth
Folk music. See Folklore
Frankenstein, and Gambaro, 190, 194, 195
Freedom, theme of: and Burgos, 88, 89; and Portal, 487; and Somers, 493–94, 497. See also Human rights
French literature: Bombal and, 41;

Bullrich and, 72, 73, 80; Ocampo, Silvina, and, 360, 365; Ocampo, Victoria, and, 371

Gallardo, Sara, *176–85*
Gambaro, Griselda, *186–98*
Games, Bullrich and, 78
Garro, Elena, *199–209*; and Odio, 383
Geada, Rita, in "Latina Writers," 562
Gender: Agustini and, 7; Alegría and, 11, 12, 15; Allende and, 23; Angel and, 35, 36; Bombal and, 45; Bullrich and, 81; Campos and, 131; Castellanos and, 141, 142–46, 147, 148, 149; Gómez de Avellaneda and, 213, 218, 221; Indian women writers and, 552; Sor Juana Inés de la Cruz and, 276; Latina writers and, 557, 560, 564; Lars and, 286, 288; Naranjo and, 353; Parra, Teresa de la, and, 421; Storni and, 504–5; Valenzuela and, 533, 535–36, 540. *See also* Feminism; Prejudice
Godoy Alcayaga, Lucila. *See* Mistral, Gabriela
Gómez de Avellaneda, Gertrudis, *210–25*
Gorriti, Juana Manuela, *226–40*; and Cabello de Carbonera, 94, 95; and Matto de Turner, 304, 306
Gothic, female, and Garro, 203
Grotesque, the: and Gambaro, 188, 194; and Storni, 505, 507
Guatemala, Indian women writers and, 548–49

Henríquez, Salomé Ureña de. *See* Ureña de Henríquez, Salomé
Hermeticism, Ibáñez and, 255–56
Hernández, Luisa Josefina, *241–53*
History: Allende and, 23–25, 27–28; Castellanos and, 143; Gómez de Avellaneda and, 217; Ibáñez and, 258; Plá and, 456. *See also* Chaco War, the; Cuban Revolution, the; Cristero Revolt, the; Independence from Spain; Mexican Revolution; Spanish Civil War; Tlatelolco, Massacre at the Plaza de; *names of specific countries*
Homosexuality, theme of: and Brunet,

60; and Peri Rossi, 438–43. *See also* Eroticism; Lesbianism; Love; Sexuality
Human rights: and Alegría, 9–10; and Indian women writers, 548, 552; and Latina writers, 557; and Ocampo, Victoria, 374

Ibáñez, Sara de, *254–60*
Ibarbourou, Juana de, *261–71*; and Portal, 490; and Storni, 507–8
Illness, theme of: and Castillo, Madre, 159, 160; and Ferré, 166
Immigrants, theme of, and Gallardo, 182. *See also* Exile, theme of
Imperialism: Alegría and, 11, 16; Indian women writers and, 548
Independence from Spain: and Gorriti, 226, 228, 231, 232, 233, 244; and Hernández, 245, 250; and Ureña de Henríquez, 523, 525, 526–27
Indian themes/characters: Allende and, 25; Angel and, 35, 37; Buitrago and, 65; Campos and, 136; Castellanos and, 140, 141, 145–46, 148; Gallardo and, 180–81, 182; Garro and, 204, 205, 206; Gorriti and, 230–35 passim; Indian women writers and, 546–55; Lars and, 285, 288; Matto de Turner and, 303, 304, 306–8, 312; Ureña de Henríquez and, 528–29
Indian women writers, *546–56*
Interiority, Campos and, 129, 131
Intertextuality, Campos and, 129, 136, 137. *See also* Metaliterature

Jail. *See* Prison
Juana Inés de la Cruz, sor, *272–81*; and Castellanos, 143; and Castillo, Madre, 162; and Lars, 285; and Parra, Teresa de la, 423; and Storni, 504
Justice, social, Hernández and, 244. *See also* Class struggle; Feminism; Freedom; Human rights

Land reform: Indian women writers and, 553, 554; Portal and, 488
Language: choice of English or Spanish, by "Latina Writers," 558, 559–60;

manipulation of, and Valenzuela, 533, 534, 536, 537, 539, 540, 541, 542–43; use of Spanish vs. Indian, by Indian women writers, 546, 547, 548, 549, 552

Lars, Claudia, *282–91*

Latina writers, *557–68*; Agosín, Marjorie, 561–62, 563; Allende, Isabel, 563; Alvarez, Julia, 562, 563; Anzaldúa, Gloria, 560, 561, 563; Casal, Lourdes, 562; Castillo, Ana, 560, 561; Cervantes, Lorna D., 559, 560; Chicana writers, 557, 558, 559–61, 563–64; Cisneros, Sandra, 560, 561; Corpi, Lucha, 558, 560; Cota-Cárdenas, Margarita, 559; Esteves, Sandra Maria, 559, 560, 561; Geada, Rita, 562; Mohr, Nicolasa, 560; Mora, Pat, 561; Moraga, Cherríe, 561; Neorican writers, 557, 559–61; Obejas, Achy, 562, 563; Umpierre, Luz María, 559, 560, 561; use of term, 557–58; Valenzuela, Luisa, 563; Villanueva, Alma, 559, 560, 563

Legends, and Orozco, 408. *See also* Fairy tales; Myths

Lesbianism, theme of: and Latina writers, 561; and Peri Rossi, 436, 437, 438, 443; and Pizarnik, 449, 450; and Somers, 498. *See also* Eroticism; Homosexuality; Love; Sexuality

Liberation: female (*see* Feminism); political (*see* Class struggle; Human rights; Oppression; Revolution)

Loneliness, theme of: and Bombal, 48; and Brunet, 56, 57, 58, 59, 60; and Bullrich, 76, 78; and Gallardo, 178–79, 180; and Naranjo, 355, 356; and Pizarnik, 447, 451; and Poletti, 464, 465. *See also* Solitude

Love, theme of: and Agustini, 2, 3–6; and Alegría, 12, 15; and Allende, 23, 24, 25–26; and Bombal, 43–44, 45–46, 48; and Brunet, 56; and Buitrago, 66, 68, 69, 70; and Bullrich, 78; and Burgos, 90; and Gallardo, 179; and Gómez de Avellaneda, 216, 217, 218, 220; and Gorriti, 230, 231; and

Hernández, 247, 248; and Ibáñez, 256; and Ibarbourou, 264, 268; and Sor Juana Inés de la Cruz, 274, 275, 276; and Lars, 283, 285, 286, 288–89; and Latina writers, 560–61, 562; and Lynch, 294, 295, 296–97, 300; and Matto de Turner, 308, 309; and Mendoza, 318, 321–22, 324; and Mistral, 333–34; and Morejón, 344; and Ocampo, Silvina, 365, 368; Parra, Teresa de la, and, 419–20; and Parra, Violeta, 429–30; and Peri Rossi, 443; and Pizarnik, 447, 448, 451; and Plá, 454, 455, 456, 458; and Poniatowska, 477; and Somers, 497; and Storni, 504, 505, 507; and Traba, 516, 517; and Ureña de Henríquez, 527; and Valenzuela, 534, 538. *See also* Eroticism; Homosexuality; Lesbianism; Sexuality

Lynch, Marta, *292–302*; and Poletti, 462

Magic, theme of: and Garro, 203; and Poletti, 464, 466; and Somers, 495–96; and Valenzuela, 540. *See also* Fairy tales; Legends; Myth

Magic realism: Allende and, 21, 23, 26, 27; Garro and, 202, 204, 206

Male-female relations. *See* Feminism; Gender; Love; Oppression; Prejudice

Marginality, theme of: and Ferré, 170; and Naranjo, 352, 353; Parra, Violeta, and, 429, 430; and Poniatowska, 474, 476; and Somers, 498

Marriage, theme of: and Bombal, 44, 45, 46, 47; and Buitrago, 69; and Bullrich, 76–77; and Cabello de Carbonera, 98, 100; and Castellanos, 146; and Gómez de Avellaneda, 221; and Indian women writers, 550–51; Parra, Violeta, and, 429, 432; and Poniatowska, 477

Marxism. *See* Communism

Maternity. *See* Motherhood

Matto de Turner, Clorinda, *303–15*; and Cabello de Carbonera, 94, 103; and Gorriti, 228, 229

Memory, theme of: and Alegría, 16; and Garro, 200–201, 202–3, 204

Men, theme of, and Cabrera, 110
Menchú, Rigoberta, in "Indian Women
Writers," 546, 548–49, 550–51, 552,
553, 554
Mendoza, María Luisa, *316–29*
Metaliterature: Agustini and, 2; Angel
and, 33; and Campos, 129, 135, 136;
Gambaro and, 192, 195; Garro and,
203, 204, 205; Hernández and, 245–47
Metaphysical themes: Odio and, 385–86,
387, 389; Latina writers and, 562. *See
also* Catholic Church; Religion
Metapoetry. *See* Metaliterature
Metatheatre. *See* Metaliterature
Mexican Revolution, the: and
Campobello, 117–26; and Garro, 203;
and Mendoza, 319, 320; and
Poniatowska, 476; and Portal, 488. *See
also* Mexico
Mexico: Campobello and, 117–26;
Castellanos and, 143; Garro and, 200,
203; Latina writers and, 557; Mendoza
and, 318, 319, 320–21, 325;
Poniatowska and, 473, 475, 476, 478,
479; Portal and, 488
Military, the: and Alegría, 17; and
Allende, 21, 22; and Cabello de
Carbonera, 97, 101; and Peri Rossi,
437, 439
Mistral, Gabriel, *330–41*; and
Castellanos, 144, 146; and Ibáñez,
258–59; and Ibarbourou, 267; and
Lars, 285; and Ocampo, Victoria, 376;
and Portal, 490; and Storni, 507
Modernismo: Agustini and, 1, 2, 5, 6–7;
Mistral and, 332; Ocampo, Silvina,
and, 362–63; Parra, Teresa de la, and,
417; Storni and, 503, 508
Mohr, Nicolasa, in "Latina Writers,"
560
Mora, Pat, in "Latina Writers," 561
Moraga, Cherríe, in "Latina Writers,"
561
Morejón, Nancy, *341–50*
Motherhood, theme of: and Alegría, 12,
14–15; and Angel, 36; and Brunet, 58,
59; and Buitrago, 65, 66–68, 69; and
Campobello, 119, 123; and Campos,

131, 132; and Castellanos, 143; and
Gómez de Avellaneda, 220; and Lars,
283–84, 288; and Mistral, 334, 335,
336; and Poletti, 468–69; and
Poniatowska, 478; and Portal, 487; and
Ureña de Henríquez, 527–28. *See also*
Childhood; Children
Mysticism, theme of: and Madre Castillo,
160, 162; and Hernández, 243, 245.
See also Catholic Church; Religion
Myth: Angel and, 37; Bombal and, 46,
47, 48, 49; Buitrago and, 65, 66; Ferré
and, 169–70, 172; Garro and, 200,
204, 205, 206; Sor Juana Inés de la
Cruz and, 277; Mistral and, 334, 335,
336; Ocampo, Silvina, and, 363–64,
365; Odio and, 383, 386–87, 389, 390;
Orozco and, 408, 410

Naranjo, Carmen, *350–59*
Naturalism, Cabello de Carbonera and,
97, 102
Nature, theme of: and Burgos, 89, 90;
and Gómez de Avellaneda, 216; and
Ibáñez, 256; and Ibarbourou, 264, 268,
269; and Lars, 287; and Odio, 385
Neo-fantastic, the. *See* Fantastic, the
Neorican writers, 557, 559–61

Obejas, Achy, in "Latina Writers," 562,
563
Ocampo, Silvina, *360–70*; and Ocampo,
Victoria, 371; and Poletti, 462
Ocampo, Victoria, *371–81*; and Bombal,
41; and Mistral, 334; and Ocampo,
Silvina, 360
Odio, Eunice, *382–93*; and Oreamuno,
395, 396, 397
Old age, theme of: and Bombal, 43; and
Poletti, 463–64
Oppression: Ferré and, 167, 170;
Gambaro and, 189, 190; Indian women
writers and, 551–52
Oreamuno, Yolanda, *394–406*; and
Naranjo, 356
Orozco, Olga, *407–14*; and Pizarnik,
451; and Poletti, 462

Otherness: Morejón and, 344; Ocampo,
     Victoria, and, 374–75

Paraguay, Plá and, 454, 457
Parent-child relationship, Buitrago and,
     65, 66–68, 69. *See also* Children;
     Childhood; Motherhood
Parra, Teresa de la, *415–26*; and Brunet,
     61
Parra, Violeta, *427–35*
Passivity, theme of, and Naranjo, 352
Patriotic themes. *See names of specific
     countries*
Peace, theme of. *See* War
Peri Rossi, Christina, *436–45*
Peru: Matto de Turner and, 306, 309,
     310; Portal and, 484
Philosophical poetry, Lars and, 285
Pizarnik, Alejandra, *446–52*
Plá, Josefina, *453–60*
Poetry, theme of: and Gómez de
     Avellaneda, 216–17, 218; and
     Pizarnik, 447, 448, 449. *See also*
     Metaliterature
Poletti, Syria, *461–71*
Political themes: Alegría and, 9–10, 11–
     12, 13–17; Allende and, 21, 22–23,
     27, 28; Angel and, 31, 33–36; Cabello
     de Carbonera and, 97, 101; Gambaro
     and, 188, 190, 192; Indian women
     writers and, 546–50, 551; Latina
     writers and, 558–64 passim; Odio and,
     383, 385, 388, 389; Parra, Violeta,
     and, 430; Peri Rossi and, 437, 438,
     439, 440, 441, 442; Plá and, 454; and
     Poniatowska, 473, 475–76, 479; Portal
     and, 484, 485, 486, 487, 490; Traba
     and, 514, 515, 516, 517, 518; Ureña
     de Henríquez and, 523, 524, 525,
     526–27, 530; Valenzuela and, 533,
     537, 538, 539, 540, 541. *See also*
     Feminism; Human rights; War; *names
     of specific countries and wars*
Poniatowska, Elena, *472–82*; and
     Castellanos, 142, 147; and Traba, 517,
     518
Pornography, theme of, and Valenzuela,
     538

Portal, Magda, *483–92*
Positivism: Bombal and, 43, 48, 49;
     Cabello de Carbonera and, 95–96, 100;
     Ureña de Henríquez and, 525, 530
Poverty: Angel and, 35; Brunet and, 58;
     Castillo, Madre, and, 160; Ferré and,
     170; Indian women writers and, 546–
     50, 551, 552, 553; Mistral and, 331;
     Peri Rossi and, 437, 438, 439, 440;
     Poletti and, 463; Poniatowska and,
     476; Portal and, 487; Traba and, 516–
     517. *See also* Class struggle
Power's abuse, theme of, and
     Valenzuela, 533, 534, 535
Prejudice: Bullrich and, 78, 81; Burgos
     and, 87, 88
Pride, theme of, and Gómez de
     Avellaneda, 218
Prison: Alegría and, 9; Allende and, 23;
     Angel and, 34; Brunet and, 57; Indian
     women writers and, 548; Portal and,
     484, 486, 487–88
Progress, theme of, and Ureña de
     Henríquez, 526
Prostitution: Buitrago and, 69; Cabello de
     Carbonera and, 101, 102; Ferré and,
     167–68, 171; Gallardo and, 181–82;
     Valenzuela and, 534–35
Puerto Rico: Burgos and, 85, 87, 89, 91;
     Latina writers and, 557, 558, 559
Pure poetry, theme of, and Ibáñez, 255–
     56. *See also* Poetry theme of

Race: Ferré and, 167–68, 170; Indian
     women writers and, 552; Latina writers
     and, 558, 560, 561, 564. *See also*
     Black themes; Indian themes; Indian
     women writers
Rape, theme of: and Allende, 23; and
     Buitrago, 65, 68, 69; and Valenzuela,
     538, 539; and Indian women writers,
     549, 552; and Latina writers, 560. *See
     also* Violence, theme of
Realism, Cabello de Carbonera and, 97
Religion: Agustini and, 3–4; Bombal and,
     42, 45; Cabello de Carbonera and, 96;
     Cabrera and, 109, 111, 112; Gallardo
     and, 181; Ibarbourou and, 265; Indian

women writers and, 547, 550, 552–53;
Latina writers and, 561; Lars and, 285,
286–87, 288; Mistral and, 331, 332,
333, 335; Naranjo and, 355; Odio and,
383, 386; Orozco and, 410–11; Peri
Rossi and, 438; Somers and, 497, 498;
Valenzuela and, 535, 536, 538. *See
also* Catholic Church; Metaphysical
themes

Repression, theme of, and Allende, 21–
22, 23–25. *See also* Freedom; Human
rights; Military, the; Oppression;
Political themes; Torture

Revolution, theme of: and Alegría, 10,
12, 14, 15, 16; and Cabello de
Carbonera, 101; Indian women writers
and, 553; Peri Rossi and, 437, 442.
See also Cuban Revolution, the;
Mexican Revolution, the

Romanticism: and Cabello de Carbonera,
99; and Odio, 385, 388

Rossi, Cristina Peri. *See* Peri Rossi,
Cristina

Rural themes, Brunet and, 53, 54, 55,
57, 58

Salons, literary: and Cabello de
Carbonera, 94; and Gorriti, 94; and
Matto de Turner, 94

Satire: Sor Juana Inés de la Cruz and,
276; Peri Rossi and, 438, 439–40

Schools. *See* Education of women

Science: Bombal and, 46, 47, 48;
Cabello de Carbonera and, 96

Seclusion, Campos and, 131–32, 133–34

Sexism, Gómez de Avellaneda and, 213,
218, 221. *See also* Feminism; Gender;
Oppression; Prejudice

Sex roles, Lynch and, 300–301. *See also*
Feminism; Gender

Sexuality: Agustini and, 2, 3–6, 7;
Alegría and, 16; Angel and, 34, 36;
Brunet and, 56, 57, 59–60; Buitrago
and, 64; Bullrich and, 78; Cabrera and,
109–10; Castellanos and, 144; Gallardo
and, 183; Hernández and, 246–47,
248; Lars and, 284, 288; Latina writers
and, 561, 564; Lynch and, 295, 297–

98; Matto de Turner and, 307;
Mendoza and, 318, 321–22, 325;
Ocampo, Silvina, and, 366, 367; Odio
and, 385–86, 387; Peri Rossi and, 43–
46; Pizarnik and, 449; 450;
Poniatowska and, 473, 477, 478;
Somers and, 493, 494, 495, 497, 498;
Storni and, 508; Valenzuela and, 533,
534, 535, 536. *See also* Eroticism;
Love

Shelley, Mary, and Gambaro, 190, 194,
195

Slavery, theme of, and Gómez de
Avellaneda, 214, 220, 222. *See also*
Africa, theme of; Black themes; Race

Solidarity, theme of, and Gambaro, 189.
See also Class struggle

Solitude, theme of: and Bullrich, 78; and
Plá, 456; and Portal, 485–86. *See also*
Loneliness

Somers, Armonía, *493–500*

Sor Juana Inés de la Cruz. *See* Juana
Inés de la Cruz, sor

Spain: Buitrago and, 65; Burgos and, 86;
Ibáñez and, 258; Odio and, 385, 389.
See also Exile, theme of; Independence
from Spain

Spanish Civil War: Ibáñez and, 258;
Odio and, 385, 389

Stereotypes, female, and Bullrich, 81.
See also Feminism; Gender

Storni, Alfonsina, *501–12*; and
Ibarbourou, 267

Storytelling: Alegría and, 10–11; Allende
and, 22, 25; Parra, Teresa de la, and,
422; Poletti and, 466; Valenzuela and,
536

Struggle. *See* Class struggle; Human
rights; Revolution

Student movement, the, and
Poniatowska, 475–76, 479. *See also*
Tlatelolco, massacre at the Plaza de

Suicide, Campos and, 133–34

Surrealism, Garro and, 201, 203–4, 205

Testimonial literature: Alegría and, 9, 10,
14; Allende and, 24, 25; Angel and,
34–35, 38; Indian women writers and,

546, 554–55; Parra, Violeta, and, 430–31; Poniatowska and, 474–75, 479–80

Theatre: Gambaro and, 186–95 passim; Hernández and, 241–42, 248, 249, 250; Sor Juana Inés de la Cruz and, 276, 277; Storni and, 501–2, 503, 505–6

Time, theme of: and Garro, 200–206 passim; and Oreamuno, 398

Tlatelolco, massacre at the Plaza de: and Garro, 200; and Mendoza, 318, 320–21, 325; and Poniatowska, 473, 475, 479. *See also* Mexico

Torture, theme of: and Allende, 23; and Gambaro, 189, 190, 192; and Indian women writers, 548, 549; and Pizarnik, 449; and Traba, 518; and Valenzuela, 537–38, 539

Traba, Marta, *513–21*

Travel literature: Angel and, 32, 37; Lynch and, 295; Matto de Turner and, 305–6, 308; Parra, Teresa de la, and, 416, 417–18; Traba and, 516–17; Valenzuela and, 539. *See also* Exile, theme of

Umpierre, Luz María, in "Latina Writers," 559, 560, 561

United States, the: and Alegría, 16; and Bombal, 48; and Burgos, 86, 87; and Castellanos, 141; and Lars, 285; and Indian women writers, 547, 548; and Latina writers, 557–64; and Lynch, 295; and Mistral, 331; and Morejón, 343–44; and Portal, 488; and Traba, 518

Urban themes, and Storni, 506–7

Ureña de Henríquez, Salomé, *522–31*

Uruguay: Ibáñez and, 258; Peri Rossi and, 439

Valenzuela, Luisa, *532–45*; in "Latina Writers," 563

Vanguardismo: Gambaro and, 187; Ocampo, Silvina, and, 363; Odio and, 384–85, 386, 388; Oreamuno and,

398, 400; Orozco and, 409; Plá and, 455; Storni and, 508. *See also* Avant-garde techniques

Venezuela, theme of, and Teresa de la Parra, 423

Victim, theme of, and Gambaro, 189, 190–91, 192, 195

Villanueva, Alma, in "Latina Writers," 559, 560, 563

Violence, theme of: and Alegría, 14; and Allende, 22, 24; and Angel, 31, 33–34; and Brunet, 56; and Buitrago, 65, 68, 69; and Campobello, 117–26; and Gallardo, 181; and Garro, 201, 202, 204, 206–7; and Lynch, 294; and Somers, 494; and Valenzuela, 534, 538, 541. *See also* Political themes; Rape; Torture; War

War, theme of: and Angel, 35, 37; and Gorriti, 230–31, 233, 235, 236; and Ibáñez, 256, 257, 258; and Lars, 288; and Lynch, 294; and Matto de Turner, 304; and Mendoza, 320; and Peri Rossi, 439; and Plá, 454, 455–56; and Poletti, 466; and Ureña de Henríquez, 523, 525, 526–27. *See also* Cuban Revolution, the; Mexican Revolution, the; Military, the; *names of specific countries and wars*

Women: Campos and, 131; Castellanos and, 141–49 passim. *See also* Feminism; Gender; Human rights; Lesbianism; Oppression

Women's rights. *See* Feminism; Gender; Human rights; Prejudice

Women writers: Bullrich and, 75–76; Ferré and, 169; Matto de Turner and, 305; Poletti and, 464–65, 469

Woolf, Virginia: and Allende, 27; and Campos, 130, 131, 137; and Castellanos, 141, 142; and Ferré, 166, 168; and Victoria Ocampo, 372–73, 375; and Oreamuno, 398

Work, theme of, and Indian women writers, 551, 552

ABOUT THE EDITOR, CONTRIBUTORS, AND TRANSLATORS

DIANE E. MARTING is Assistant Professor of Spanish American literature at Columbia University. She received a Fulbright dissertation grant to Brazil and was a Fulbright Senior Lecturer to Colombia in 1988 and 1989. She has edited *Women Writers of Spanish America: An Annotated Bio-Bibliographical Guide* (Greenwood Press, 1987) and has published translations, reviews, bibliographies, critical articles, and original poetry. She is currently finishing a book of comparative feminist criticism: *The Sexual Woman in Twentieth-Century Latin American Novels*.

BERTIE ACKER received her doctorate from the University of Texas in 1971. She has been on the faculty at the University of Texas at Arlington since 1965, and is the author of *El cuento mexicano contemporáneo: Rulfo, Arreola y Fuentes* (1984), and of articles on contemporary Latin American novels and short stories that have appeared in various literary journals and books.

MARJORIE AGOSÍN is Associate Professor of Spanish and author of several books of criticism: *Silencio e imaginación: metáforas de la escritura femenina* (1986); *Scraps of Life: The Chilean Arpillera*; and the poetry collection, *Women of Smoke*. She is also the author of many essays on contemporary Latin American women writers.

MAUREEN AHERN is Professor of Spanish at Arizona State University where she teaches Latin American literature and literary translation. She is the author of a number of critical articles on Peruvian and Mexican poets, and is the co-editor and co-translator of several anthologies of contemporary Peruvian poetry. With Mary Seale-Vásquez, she edited *Homenaje a Rosario Castellanos*

(1980). She is the editor and translator of *A Rosario Castellanos Reader* (1988), an anthology of the Mexican writer's poetry, essays, fiction, and drama in English translation, which also includes her critical essay, "Reading Rosario Castellanos: Contexts, Voices and Signs."

NORMA ALARCÓN is Assistant Professor of Chicano and Ethnic Studies at the University of California, Berkeley. She has published numerous articles on Chicana writers, translated into Spanish with Ana Castillo the popular book *This Bridge Called My Back* (*Esta Puente Mi Espalda*, 1988); and is publisher and editor of *Third Woman* journal and Third Woman Press.

MELVIN S. ARRINGTON, JR., who holds the Ph.D. degree from the University of Kentucky, is Associate Professor of Modern Languages at the University of Mississippi, where he teaches Spanish American literature. He has contributed articles and reviews to *Hispania, Latin American Literary Review, South Eastern Latin Americanist*, and other journals.

TERESA R. ARRINGTON is Assistant Professor of Spanish at the University of Mississippi. She received her Ph.D. in Spanish linguistics in 1977 from the University of Kentucky. She has published previously on Spanish linguistics, foreign language teaching methodology, and transformational grammar, and has presented papers on various aspects of Spanish American language and literature. In addition, she has held several professional offices in state and national language organizations and is currently secretary-treasurer of the Mississippi Foreign Language Association.

JOHN BENSON is a graduate student in the Spanish program at San Jose State University. He has read papers on the philosophies of Severo Sarduy and Marshall MacLuhan and on the prospects for contemporary Latin American literature in translation.

MARY G. BERG is a fellow at the Harvard University Center for Literary and Cultural Studies. She has taught Spanish and Latin American literature for many years and has published articles on Lugones, Borges, García Márquez, Cortázar, Ciro Alegría, Bombal, Rulfo, and other Latin American writers.

LINDA BRITT is Assistant Professor of Spanish at Bates College. She earned her Ph.D. at the University of Virginia with a dissertation on Federico García Lorca. In addition to her works on García Lorca, she has published on Cervantes and is currently (1988) translating fiction by Carmen Naranjo.

YVONNE CAPTAIN-HIDALGO is Assistant Professor of Spanish at George Washington University. She received a postdoctoral fellowship for the 1987–1988 academic year from the William Monroe Trotter Institute at the University of Massachusetts, Boston. During that year she completed a book-length study: "Parallel Dimensions in Literary History: Manuel Zapata Olivella and the Spanish American Narrative Tradition." Professor Captain-Hidalgo has published in the *Afro-Hispanic Review, Callaloo, Cuadernos Americanos*, and *Discurso Literario*. Her areas of specialization are the Caribbean, Afro-Hispania, and Hispanic film.

LUCÍA GUERRA CUNNINGHAM is Professor at the University of California in Irvine. Her main field of specialization is Latin American literature with an emphasis on critical theory. She is the author of *La narrativa de María Luisa Bombal* (1980); *Texto e ideología en la narrativa chilena* (1987); and the novel *Más allá de las máscaras* (1984). In 1979 her translation (*New Islands*, 1982) of María Luisa Bombal's work received the Annual Award from the Translation Center of Columbia University. She is the editor of *Mujer y sociedad en América Latina* (1980) and *Tradición y marginalidad en la literatura chilena* (1983).

SANDRA MESSINGER CYPESS, who holds the Ph.D. degree from the University of Illinois, is Associate Professor of Spanish and Comparative Literature at the State University of New York-Binghamton, where she was also director of the Latin American and Caribbean Area Studies Program. She has published numerous articles on Latin American women writers with a particular focus on their contributions to Latin American drama. Her articles on narrative and theater have appeared in scholarly journals in English and Spanish, including *Latin American Theatre Review, Modern Drama, Texto Crítico*, and *Revista Canadiense de Estudios Hispánicos*.

NANCY GRAY DÍAZ is Assistant Professor of Spanish at Rutgers University at Newark. She is the author of *The Radical Self: Metamorphosis to Animal Form in Modern Latin American Narrative* (1988) and papers, articles, reviews, and other pieces in the fields of Latin American and comparative literature.

NORA ERRO-ORTHMANN, a native of Salto, Uruguay, holds a Ph.D. from the University of Toronto. She is currently teaching Latin American literature at Florida Atlantic University in Boca Raton, Florida. She is the co-author of *Puerta abierta: La nueva narradora latinoamericana* (1986). Her published works include articles on Carlos Martínez Moreno and Puerto Rican literature.

ANA MARÍA FAGUNDO was born in Tenerife, Spain, in 1938. She received her Ph.D. in comparative literature from the University of Washington, Seattle, and has been Professor of Twentieth Century Spanish literature and Creative Writing at the University of California, Riverside, since 1967. Ana María Fagundo is a poet, having published to date seven books of poems and she is the founder and editor of the poetry and short story journal *Alaluz* (1969 to the present). She is the author of *Vida y obra de Emily Dickinson* (1973) and numerous articles on contemporary Spanish poetry. At present, she has in press *Antología bilingüe de poesía norteamericana:1950–1980*.

ERICA FROUMAN-SMITH, Assistant Professor of Spanish at Long Island University, wrote her Ph.D. dissertation on Silvina Bullrich. She has published work in *Chasqui, Discurso Literario, Latin American Literary Review*, and *Review: Latin American Literature and Arts* on contemporary Latin American writers. She has translated many Latin American women writers and has also interviewed both Silvina Bullrich and Amparo Dávila.

DWIGHT GARCÍA is Associate Professor of Spanish at the University of Puerto Rico, Bayamón. He has published poems, translations, and articles in *Sin Nombre, International Poetry Review, Revista Interamericana, Plural, Hispamérica*, and others. In 1978 he was awarded the Luis Palés Matos Poetry Award by *Sin Nombre*.

NORMA BEATRIZ GRASSO, born in Buenos Aires, Argentina, earned a Ph.D. at Indiana University with a dissertation on the theory of the novel in Argentina. She has been a National Endowment for the Humanities fellow in comparative literature at Princeton University and is currently Associate Professor of Literature and Language at Stockton State College (New Jersey).

HUGH A. HARTER is the author or co-author of various books, articles, and reviews in Spanish, French, and other Western languages and cultures. He has been Professor at Wesleyan University, Elmira College, the University of Pittsburgh, Chatham College, Loyola University in Chicago, Ohio Wesleyan University, and the Universidad Católica de Arequipa, Peru. Most recently, he was director of the International Institute, Miguel Angel, 8, Madrid. He is at present working with overseas programs in Spain and France through Horizons for Learning, of which he is president, and Cursos Americanos e Internacionales en Segovia, of which he is administrator. His most recent book is a bilingual edition of Nobel Laureate Vicente Aleixandre's *Shadow of Paradise*. He was a postdoctoral Mellon fellow in Pittsburgh and a recipient of a Joint-Committee grant for Spain.

SUSANA HERNÁNDEZ-ARAICO, Professor of Spanish at California State Polytechnic University, Pomona, has concentrated her research and publications on Spanish Golden Age Drama, particularly on Calderón de la Barca. As a Mexican female scholar, she considers it a moral obligation to disseminate information about Latin American women writers and to contribute to the recognition of their talents and accomplishments. In 1981 she undertook a series of interviews of female authors in Argentina, Chile, and Peru, whose impact has proved to be a major motivating force for her.

GABRIELLA IBIETA is Assistant Professor of Spanish and Comparative Literature at Drexel University in Philadelphia and has been a National Endowment for the Humanities fellow in Comparative Literature at Princeton University. She is the author of *Tradition and Renewal in "La gloria de don Ramiro"* (1986) and has contributed articles to *Chasqui, Revista de Estudios Hispánicos*, and *Revista Iberomericana*, among others.

EVELYN UHRHAN IRVING is Professor Emerita of Tennessee Technological University, and earned her Ph.D in Spanish and linguistics from the University of Illinois, Urbana-Champaign. In addition to teaching Spanish language and literature, ESL and FL teaching methods, she has researched and written extensively on Rubén Darío; her articles and book reviews have appeared in U.S. and international journals. She collected and edited *Short Stories by Rafaela Contreras de Darío* (1965).

IVETTE LÓPEZ JIMÉNEZ is Professor of Spanish at the University of Puerto Rico, Bayamón. She has published articles on Julia de Burgos, Francisco Matos Paoli, Rosario Ferré, Angelamaría Dávila, and other Latin American writers.

JULIE GREER JOHNSON is Associate Professor of Spanish in the Department of Romance Languages at the University of Georgia. She is the author of *Women in Colonial Spanish American Literature: Literary Images* (Greenwood Press, 1983) and *The Book in the Americas: The Role of Books and Printing in the Development of Culture and Society in Colonial Latin America* (1988) and has contributed articles to *Celestinesca, Hispania, Hispanic Journal, Hispanófila, Kentucky Romance Quarterly, Latin American Literary Review, Latin American Theatre Review, North Dakota Quarterly*, and *South Atlantic Bulletin*.

BETH E. JÖRGENSEN, Assistant Professor of Spanish at the University of Rochester, earned her Ph.D. at the University of Wisconsin-Madison. She has published articles on the work of Elena Poniatowska.

MARÍA-INÉS LAGOS-POPE is Associate Professor of Spanish at Washington University in St. Louis. She has taught at SUNY-Binghamton, where she was director of the Center for the Study of United States Hispanics, and at the Spanish School of Middlebury College. She has published articles on Latin American women writers in *Revista Iberoamericana, Hispamérica, Latin American Literary Review, Texto Crítico*, and in other publications. She has edited *Exile in Literature* (1988), and is the author of *H. A. Murena en sus ensayos y narraciones: De líder revisionista a marginado* (forthcoming) and is completing a book on the narrative of Spanish American women writers to be published by Bilingual Press.

MONIQUE J. LEMAÎTRE LEÓN is Associate Professor of Spanish at Northern Illinois University. She is a Mexican citizen, born and raised in Mexico City. She holds an M.A. degree in French literature and a Ph.D. in Latin American literature from the University of Pittsburgh. She is the author of *Octavio Paz: Teoría y práctica* (1976) and *Texturas* (1986). Her articles on Carlos Fuentes, Jorge Luis Borges, Julio Cortázar, César Vallejo, Juan Goytisolo, Elena Poniatowska, Isabel Allende, Roque Dalton, Gabriel García Márquez, and Antonio Skármeta have appeared in *Revista Iberoamericana, Idealogies & Literature, Hispámerica, Espiral/Revista*, and *Plural*. She has been a Mellon and a Woodrow Wilson fellowship recipient.

LINDA GOULD LEVINE is Professor of Spanish literature at Montclair State College (New Jersey) where she also teaches Women's Studies. She received her Ph.D. from Harvard University, is the author of a book on Juan Goytisolo and an edition of his works, and is co-author with Gloria Waldman of *Feminismo ante el franquismo: entrevistas con feministas de España* (1980). Her articles have appeared in *Cuadernos Americanos, Revista Iberoamericana, Anales de la Literatura Española Contemporánea, Society of Spanish and Spanish-American Studies*, and other publications.

SHARON MAGNARELLI is Professor in the Department of Foreign Languages at Albertus Magnus College, New Haven, Connecticut. She is the author of *The Lost Rib: Female Characters in the Spanish American Novel* and *Reflections/ Refractions: Reading Luisa Valenzuela*. She has published on Spanish American narrative and theater in numerous scholarly journals.

GABRIELA MAHN is Translation Testing Coordinator at the Translation, Research, and Instruction Program at SUNY-Binghamton, and an ATA accredited translator from English to Spanish. She is the translator of Pablo Neruda's *Una casa en la arena* and of articles in various publications.

MAGDALENA MAÍZ is completing her Ph.D. in Spanish at Arizona State University and is instructor of Spanish at Davidson College, North Carolina. She has published in *Cuadernos de Aldeuu, El Excélsior, Hispania, La Palabra y el Hombre*, and *Plural*. Her M.A. thesis was a project entitled "Elena Garro's Dramatic Discourse." Her dissertation topic is "Writing and the Rhetoric of Memory: Mexican Modern Autobiography."

DORIS MEYER, Professor of Hispanic Studies at Connecticut College, is the author of a biography of Victoria Ocampo and numerous articles on Latin American women writers. She is the co-editor of *Contemporary Women Authors of Latin America: Introductory Essays and New Translations* (1983, 2 vols.), and editor of *Lives on the Line: The Testimony of Contemporary Latin American*

Authors (1988). She has also translated works by women authors, including Nellie Campobello's *Cartucho* (1988).

JANICE MOLLOY is a freelance translator who lives in Boston. She has a B.A. in Anthropology and Spanish from Wellesley College, and a M.S. in Spanish from Georgetown University. She is the translator of numerous articles by Marjorie Agosin and of her book entitled *Women of Smoke* (1988).

GABRIELA MORA teaches contemporary Hispanic American literature at Rutgers University (New Brunswick, N.J.). She is the author of *Hostos intimista: introducción a su Diario* (1976); *En torno al cuento: De la teoría general y de su práctica en Hispanoamérica* (1985). She edited with Karen Van Hooft *Theory and Practice of Feminist Literary Criticism* (1982). Her articles have appeared in *Escritura, Inti, Revista Iberoamericana, Discurso Literario, Hispamérica*, and other scholarly magazines.

CATHERINE NICKEL is Assistant Professor of Spanish at the University of Nebraska-Lincoln. She has worked in various editorial capacities on several journals including *Anales de la Literatura Española Contemporánea, Cuadernos de Poética, Studies in Twentieth Century Literature, Letras Femeninas*, and the *Journal of Interdisciplinary Literary Studies*. She has published articles on Federico García Lorca, Ramón del Valle-Inclán, and Ernesto Sábato in journals such as *Hispania, Hispanic Journal, Studies in Short Fiction, Siglo XX*, and *Rocky Mountain Review*, and co-edited the Proceedings of the Mid-America Conference on Hispanic Literature.

MARGARITE FERNÁNDEZ OLMOS, Associate Professor of Spanish at Brooklyn College, CUNY, is co-editor of *Contemporary Women Authors of Latin America: Introductory Essays and New Translations* (1983), and author of *La cuentística de Juan Bosch: un análisis crítico-cultural* (1982). In addition, she has published on contemporary Latin American literature in such journals as *Hispania, Revista Canadiense de Estudios Hispánicos, Revista Iberoamericana*, and *Heresies*.

ADA ORTÚZAR-YOUNG is Associate Professor of Spanish and Chair of the Spanish Department at Drew University (New Jersey). She received her undergraduate degree from the University of Wisconsin and her Ph.D. from New York University. She is the author of *Tres representaciones literarias de la vida política cubana* (1980) and is working on a book-length study of the Hispanic cultural presence in the United States, with special emphasis on the three largest groups: Mexicans, Puerto Ricans, and Cubans. She has been an NEH fellow at Yale University and has presented numerous papers at professional conferences, some dealing with feminist criticism.

LIZABETH PARAVISINI-GEBERT is Associate Professor of Caribbean literature at Lehman College/CUNY. She is the editor of a forthcoming anthology of essays on Puerto Rican women writers. Her publications include essays on Caribbean literature, feminist criticism, literary parody, and detective fiction, as well as translations of works by Caribbean women writers. She is the recipient of a 1987 Social Science Research Council Fellowship for completion of a book on the novel and Caribbean historiography.

LUIS H. PEÑA is Assistant Professor of Spanish at Davidson College and earned his Ph.D. at Arizona State University. He has published in several renowned journals such as *Cuadernos Americanos, Centro para la Investigación de la Literatura Hispanoamericana, La Palabra y el Hombre, Plural*, and *Revista de Crítica Latinoamericana*. His book, *The Metamorphosis of Desire: Contemporary Narrative Production in Mexico, 1958–1970*, is soon to be published.

ELBA TORRES DE PERALTA was born in Córdoba, Argentina, and now resides in California, where she is Professor of Hispanic literature at the California State University, Los Angeles. She is the author of many critical studies, which include *La temática de Malvina Rosa Quiroga* (1970), and *La poética de Olga Orozco: Desdoblamiento de Dios en máscara de todos* (1988). As a poet, she has published *Preludios* (1978) and *Ausencias* (1985).

AMANDA PLUMLEE is Assistant Professor of Spanish and Italian at Davis and Elkins College, Elkins, W.V. She was a Fulbright Scholar in 1983 and did research on Ecuadorian women poets. She has published and given lectures within Ecuador on this topic. She received the Ph.D. from the University of Tennessee in December 1988 with a doctoral dissertation entitled "Twentieth-Century Ecuadorian Women Poets."

DANIEL R. REEDY is Professor of Spanish American literature and Dean of the Graduate School at the University of Kentucky and holds the Ph.D. from the University of Illinois. His publications include books and articles on Peruvian and Latin American literature from the colonial era to the contemporary period.

MERCEDES MAZQUIARÁN DE RODRÍGUEZ is Associate Professor of Spanish at Hofstra University. She holds a doctoral degree from the University of Havana and a Ph.D. from New York University. She has edited an anthology of twentieth-century Spanish American essays and has published articles on Unamuno, Martínez-Menchén, and Esther Tusquets.

PATRICIA RUBIO is Assistant Professor of Spanish at Skidmore College and has published (in co-authorship) *Claves de la narrativa contemporánea* (1972), *Diccionario de términos e 'ismos' literarios* (1977), and *Carpentier ante la crítica: bibliografía comentada* (1985). She has also published articles on Cuban and Mexican literatures in *Revista Canadiense de Estudios Hispánicos, Semiosis, Revista de Crítica Literaria Latinoamericana, Salmagundi* and *Garabato*. She is presently co-authoring a critical annotated bibliography of Gabriela Mistral.

MARÍA A. SALGADO was born in Tenerife, Spain, and is Professor of Contemporary Spanish American literature at the University of North Carolina at Chapel Hill. In addition to books on Juan Ramón Jiménez and Rafael Arévalo Martínez, she has published numerous articles in *Revista Iberoamericana, Hispania, Cuadernos Hispanoamericanos, La Torre, Thesaurus*, and several other journals.

STACEY SCHLAU directs the Women's Studies Program and teaches Women's Studies, Spanish, and Spanish American literature at West Chester University (Pennsylvania). She has published several articles on Spanish American women narratists, and with Electa Arenal has co-authored *Untold Sisters: Hispanic Nuns in Their Own Works* (1989).

ARLENE SCHRADE is Professor of Education specializing in foreign languages at the University of Mississippi. Her degrees include a Ph.D. from the Ohio State University where her specialization was in Latin American and Golden Age literatures, and *diplomas de estudio* from the University of Costa Rica, the University of Madrid, and Sonoma State (CA) University at Morelia, Michocán, Mexico. Her publications include Spanish texts for elementary, secondary, and university levels; "Sex Shock: The Humanistic Woman in the Super-Industrial Society," in *Monster or Messiah? The Computer Impact on Society* (Ed. Walter Mathews, 1980); and contributions to *Women Writers of Spanish America* (Ed. Diane Marting, Greenwood Press, 1987).

GUSTAVO V. SEGADE was born in New York City and now resides in California, where he is Professor of Hispanic literature and directs the English/Spanish Translation Certificate Program at San Diego State University. His publications include *Critical Issues in Contemporary Latin American Poetic Theory* (1978), and the translation of Sergio Elizondo's *Perros y antiperros/Dogs and Antidogs*. He is currently translating Olga Orozco's *Cantos a Berenice* (Songs to Berenice) and Elba Peralta's *La poética de Olga Orozco* (The poetry of Olga Orozco). As a poet, his long poem, "State of the Art," received the First Prize in Poetry at the Chicano Literary Contest, University of California, Irvine, 1986.

NANCY SAPORTA STERNBACH teaches Latina/o and Latina American literature at Smith College. She is the co-editor of *Breaking Boundaries: Latina Writing and Critical Readings* (1989) and the author of several articles on Latin American women's literature and feminist movements. Currently, she is working on women's essays.

ANITA STOLL, Professor of Spanish at Cleveland State University, has published various articles on twentieth-century Mexican authors, pedagogy, and Golden Age drama, has edited a play by Lope de Vega, *La noche de San Juan* (1988), a volume on Elena Garro's work, *A Different Reality: Essays on the Work of Elena Garro* (1989), and a volume on the presence of women in Golden Age drama (with Dawn L. Smith, in Press).

MARÍA ELENA DE VALDÉS is Admissions and Programs Officer of the School of Graduate Studies at the University of Toronto. She also teaches contemporary Spanish American literature. She publishes feminist literary criticism and feminist discourse analysis.

RIMA DE VALLBONA is Professor of Spanish at the University of St. Thomas (Houston). She has published the following books: *Noche en vela* (novel, 1968), *Yolanda Oreamuno* (literary study, 1971), *Polvo del camino* (short stories, 1973), *La salamandra rosada* (short stories, 1979), *La obra en prosa de Eunice Odio* (literary study, 1981), *Mujeres y agonías* (short stories, 1982), *Las sombras que perseguimos* (novel, 1983), *Baraja de soledades* (short stories, 1983) and *Cosecha de pecadores* (short stories, 1988). Among the literary prizes she has received are the National Novel Prize (1968, Costa Rica), the Jorge Luis Borges Short Story Prize (1977, Argentina), the Agripina Montes del Valle Latin American Novel Prize (1978, Colombia), and the Ancora Award for the 1983–1984 Best Book in Costa Rica.

BIRGITTA VANCE has published a study of the Spanish civil war novel. She is Associate Professor of Spanish at the University of Michigan-Flint and a translator for Spanish and German.

DIANA VÉLEZ is Associate Professor of Spanish at the University of Iowa, where she teaches Latin American literature, Spanish-English translation, and the literature of U.S. Latinos. Her book, *Reclaiming Medusa: Short Stories by Contemporary Puerto Rican Women* was published in 1988.

CARMELO VIRGILLO is Professor of Romance Languages at Arizona State University, specializing in eighteenth-, nineteenth-, and twentieth-century literature. He teaches Italian, Portuguese, and Spanish and is the author or co-author of *Correspondência de Machado de Assis com Magalhaes de Azeredo* (1969), *Aproximaciones al estudio de la literatura hispánica* (1985), *Woman as Myth and Metaphor in Latin American Literature* (1985), *Bibliografia analítico-descritiva de Henriqueta Lisboa* (1988), and articles on Hispanic and Brazilian literature.

OWEN WILLIAMS has spent several years in Guatemala and El Salvador. He has taught high school Spanish in Kansas and Arizona and received his M.A.

from Northern Arizona University, Flagstaff. At present he is working toward a Ph.D. at the University of Nebraska-Lincoln. He is especially interested in contemporary Central American writers.

RAYMOND LESLIE WILLIAMS is Professor of Spanish and teaches Spanish American literature at the University of Colorado-Boulder. He has published essays and three books on contemporary Spanish American fiction, most recently, *Mario Vargas Llosa* (1986).

CELIA CORREAS DE ZAPATA was born in Mendoza, Argentina, and is Professor of Spanish and Latin American literature at San José State University. She earned her Ph.D. at the University of California at Irvine and is the author of books and articles on Latin American contemporary fiction. She has also published collections of her poetry and edited anthologies in both Spanish and English of work by Latin American women writers. Among the most recent are *Detrás de la reja* (1980) and *Latin American Women Writers: The Magic and the Real* (forthcoming).